PETERSON'S
COMPETITIVE
COLLEGES®

2004–2005

THOMSON

PETERSON'S

Australia • Canada • Mexico • Singapore • Spain • United Kingdom • United States

About The Thomson Corporation and Peterson's

The Thomson Corporation, with 2002 revenues of US$7.8 billion, is a global leader in providing integrated information solutions to business and professional customers. The Corporation's common shares are listed on the Toronto and New York stock exchanges (TSX: TOC; NYSE: TOC). Its learning businesses and brands serve the needs of individuals, learning institutions, corporations, and government agencies with products and services for both traditional and distributed learning. Peterson's (www.petersons.com) is a leading provider of education information and advice, with books and online resources focusing on education search, test preparation, and financial aid. Its Web site offers searchable databases and interactive tools for contacting educational institutions, online practice tests and instruction, and planning tools for securing financial aid. Peterson's serves 110 million education consumers annually.

ISSN 0887-0152
ISBN 0-7689-1646-1 (sponsor version)
       0-7689-1389-6 (trade version)

Printed in the United States of America

10 9 8 7 6 5 4 3 2 1   06 05 04

Twenty-fourth Edition

CONTENTS

Why Should You Consider a
Competitive College? 1

Understanding the College Admission
Process 3

Applying to Professional Colleges for
Art and Music 7

Paying for College. 8

Sponsor List. 15

Competitive Colleges and Universities . . . 17

Appendixes. 453
    Ten Largest Colleges 454
    Ten Smallest Colleges. 454
    Colleges Accepting Fewer than Half of
        Their Applicants 454
    Single-Sex Colleges 455
    Predominantly African-American Colleges. 455
    Colleges with Religious Affiliation 455
    Public Colleges 457

Indexes 459
    Majors by College 460
    Geographic Index of Colleges 521

WHY SHOULD YOU CONSIDER A COMPETITIVE COLLEGE?

Excellent colleges typically take great care in admitting students. For them, selecting the entering class is, as Bill Fitzsimmons, Dean of Admissions and Financial Aid at Harvard University, describes it: a process of "sculpting" the best possible class from the pool of qualified applicants. The goal of an admission committee is to bring together a community of students who can learn from one another, each one bringing their own particular talents, skills, and experiences that will contribute to the development of all the others.

Students who have excelled in high school want to go on excelling. They need an educational environment that will push them, test them, help them go beyond their past accomplishments. They require a college that "fits," one that will help them develop into what they can uniquely become.

At the start, you'll likely find that everyone's list of "best" colleges is very much alike. Except for adding the most popular regional schools or schools serving an unusual interest or a family's traditional alma mater, your initial list and your classmates' basic lists probably will include the Ivy League schools and one or more of up to a dozen other similarly prestigious colleges and universities. The one quality shared by

these schools is prestige. It certainly can be argued that it helps to graduate from a prestigious college. But prestige is a limited and very expensive factor upon which to base one's college choice. You and we know that there are truly excellent college choices beyond the eight Ivy League schools and a newsstand magazine's designated top schools. One of these "other" college choices could very well be the best fit for your particular requirements and goals.

We make only one assumption in *Competitive Colleges*. This is that the most influential factor in determining your experience on campus is the other students you will find there. In selecting colleges for inclusion in this book, we measure the competitiveness of the admission environment at colleges. This is measured over a meaningful period of time by entering-class statistics, such as GPA, class rank, and test scores. The 433 colleges selected for inclusion in this book routinely attract and admit an above-average share of the nation's high-achieving students.

Selecting a college is a great adventure, and Peterson's wants to guide you in this quest. For additional information on the colleges listed in this guide, be sure to check out Peterson's Web sites: *www.petersons.com* and *www.collegeswantyou.com*.

UNDERSTANDING THE COLLEGE ADMISSION PROCESS

BY TED SPENCER, Director of Undergraduate Admissions at the University of Michigan

The process you are about to begin, that of choosing a college, can be very challenging, sometimes frustrating, but most often rewarding. As Director of Undergraduate Admissions at a large, selective university, I would like to provide some basic information about the admission process that should help you get into the college of your choice. Although each competitive college or university has its own distinctive qualities and goals, the process of applying to them is strikingly similar. The following will give you the basic information you need to know to help you plan and apply to college.

GATHERING INFORMATION

How do you get the information you need to choose a college? Although colleges publish volumes of information about themselves that they are willing to mail or give out in person, another way to find out about them is through a guide such as *Competitive Colleges.*

The major difference between the college-published materials and this book is that the colleges present only the most appealing picture of themselves and are perhaps, then, somewhat less objective. As a student seeking information about college, you should review both the information provided in books like this one and the information sent by the colleges. Your goal should be to use all of the available literature to assist you in developing your list of the top five or ten colleges in which you are interested.

Chances are that if you are a top student and you have taken the PSAT, SAT I, SAT II, ACT, or AP (Advanced Placement) tests, you will receive a great deal of material directly from many colleges and universities. Colleges purchase lists of names of students taking these exams and then screen the list for students they think will be most successful at their institutions. Some colleges will also automatically mail course catalogs, posters, departmental brochures, and pamphlets, as well as videocassettes. If you do not

receive this information but would like a sample, write or call that particular college.

My advice is to take a look at the materials you receive and then use them to help you decide (if you don't already know) about the type of college you would like to attend. Allow the materials to help you narrow your list of top schools by comparing key facts and characteristics.

OTHER HELPFUL SOURCES

Published information about colleges, printed by the colleges, is certainly an important way to narrow your choices. But there are at least five other means of learning more about colleges and universities:

- *High School Counselors.* Most high school counselors have established positive relationships with the college representatives in your state as well as with out-of-state universities where large numbers of their students apply. As you attempt to gain more information while narrowing your choice of colleges, the high school counselor can give you a fairly accurate assessment of colleges to which you will have the best chance of gaining admission.

- *Parents.* Because most prospective students and their parents are at that stage in life in which they view issues in different ways, students tend to be reluctant to ask parents' opinions about college choices. However, you may find that parents are very helpful because they often are actively gathering information about the colleges that they feel are best suited for you. And not only do they gather information—you can be sure that they have thoroughly read the piles of literature that colleges have mailed to you. Ask your parents questions about what they have read and also about the colleges from which they graduated. As alumni of schools on your list, parents can be a very valuable resource.

- *College Day/Night/Fairs Visitation.* One of the best ways to help narrow your college choices is to meet with a person representing a college while they are visiting your area or high school. In fact, most admission staff members spend a good portion of the late spring and fall visiting high schools and attending college fairs. In some cases, college fairs feature students, faculty members, and alumni. Before attending one of these sessions, you should prepare a list of questions you would like to ask the representatives. Most students want to know about five major areas: academic preparation, the admission process, financial aid, social life, and job preparation. Most college representatives can be extremely helpful in addressing these questions as well as the many others that you may have. It is then up to you to decide if their answers fit your criteria of the college you are seeking.

- *Alumni.* For many schools, alumni are a very important part of the admission process. In some cases, alumni conduct interviews and even serve as surrogate admission officers, particularly when admission office staff cannot travel. As recent graduates, alumni can talk about their own experience and can give balance to the materials you have received from the college or university.

- *Campus Visits.* Finally, try to schedule a campus visit as part of your information-gathering process in an effort to make sure that the reality lives up to the printed viewbook. Most colleges and universities provide daily campus tours to both prospective and admitted students. The tours for prospective students are generally set up to help you answer questions about the following: class size and student-to-teacher ratio; size of the library, residence halls, and computer centers; registration and faculty advising; and retention, graduation rates, and career placement planning. Since the tours may not cover everything you came prepared to ask about, be sure to ask questions of as many staff, students, and faculty members as possible before leaving the campus.

THE ADMISSION PROCESS

ADMISSION CRITERIA

After you go through the process of selecting a college or narrowing your choices to a few schools, the admission process now focuses on you—your academic record and skills—and judgment will be passed on these pieces of information for admission to a particular school. The first things you should find out about each college on your priority list are the admission criteria—what it takes to get in:

1. Does the college or university require standardized tests—the ACT or SAT I? Do they prefer one or the other, or will they accept either?
2. Do they require SAT II Subject Tests and, if so, which ones?
3. Are Advanced Placement scores accepted and, if so, what are the minimums needed?
4. In terms of grades and class rank, what is the profile of a typical entering student?

It is also important to find out which type of admission notification system the college uses—rolling or deferred admission. On a rolling system, you find out your status within several weeks of applying; with the deferred system, notification is generally made in the spring. For the most part, public universities and colleges use rolling admission and private colleges generally use deferred admission.

THE APPLICATION

The application is the primary vehicle used to introduce yourself to the admission office. As with any introduction, you should try to make a good first impression. The first thing you should do in presenting your application is to find out what the college or university wants from you. This means you should read the application carefully to learn the following:

1. Must the application be typed, or can you print it?
2. Is there an application fee and, if so, how much is it?
3. Is there a deadline and, if so, when is it?
4. What standardized tests are required?
5. Is an essay required?
6. Is an interview required?

7. Should you send letters of recommendation?

8. How long will it take to find out the admission decision?

9. What other things can you do to improve your chances of admission?

My advice is to submit your application early. It does not guarantee admission, but it is much better than submitting it late or near the deadline. Also, don't assume that colleges using rolling admission will always have openings close to their deadlines. Regardless of when you submit it, make sure that the application is legible and that all the information that is requested is provided.

TRANSCRIPTS

While all of the components of the application are extremely important in the admission process, perhaps the single most important item is your transcript because it tells: (1) what courses you took; (2) which courses were college-preparatory and challenging; (3) class rank; and (4) grades and test scores.

- *Required Course Work.* Generally speaking, most colleges look at the high school transcript to see if the applicant followed a college-preparatory track while in high school. So, if you have taken four years of English, math, natural science, social sciences, and foreign language, you are on the right track. Many selective colleges require four years of English; three years each of math, natural science, and social science; and two years of a foreign language. It is also true that some selective colleges believe students who are interested in majoring in math and science need more than the minimum requirements in those areas.

- *Challenging Courses.* As college admission staff members continue to evaluate your transcript, they also look to see how demanding your course load has been during high school. If the high school offered Advanced Placement or Honors courses, the expectation of most selective colleges is that students will have taken seven or more honors classes or four or more AP courses during their four years in high school. However, if you do elect to take challenging courses, it is also important that you make good grades in those courses. Quite often, students ask, "If I take

honors and AP courses and get a 'C,' does that count more than getting a 'B' or higher in a strictly college-prep course?" It's a difficult question to answer, because too many C's and B's can outweigh mostly A's. On the other hand, students who take the more challenging courses will be better prepared to take the more rigorous courses in college. Consequently, many colleges will give extra consideration when making their selections to the students who take the more demanding courses.

- *Transcript Trends.* Because the courses you take in high school are such a critical part of the college decision-making process, your performance in those courses indicates to colleges whether you are following an upward or downward trend. Beginning with the ninth grade, admission staff look at your transcript to see if you have started to develop good academic habits. In general, when colleges review your performance in the ninth grade, they are looking to see if you are in the college-preparatory track.

By sophomore year, students should begin choosing more demanding courses and become more involved in extracurricular activities. This will show that you are beginning to learn how to balance your academic and extracurricular commitments. Many admission officers consider the sophomore year to be the most critical and telling year for a student's future success.

The junior year is perhaps the second-most-important year in high school. The grades you earn and the courses you take will help to reinforce the trend you began in your sophomore year. At the end of your junior year, many colleges will know enough about the type of student you are to make their admission decision.

The upward and positive trend must continue, however, during your senior year. Many selective schools do not use senior grades in making their admission decisions. However, almost all review the final transcript, so your last year needs to show a strong performance to the end. The research shows that students who finish their senior year with strong grades will start their freshman year in college with strong grades.

THE APPLICATION REVIEW PROCESS

WHAT'S NEXT?

At this point, you have done all you can do. So you might as well sit back and relax, if that's possible, and wait for the letters to come in the mail. Hopefully, if you've evaluated all the college materials you were sent earlier and you prepared your application carefully and sent it to several colleges, you will be admitted to either your first, second, or third choice. It may help your peace of mind, however, to know what happens to your application after the materials have been submitted.

Once your application is received by the admission office, it is reviewed, in most cases by noncounseling staff, to determine if you have completed the application properly. If items are missing, you will receive a letter of notification identifying additional information that must be provided. Be sure to send any additional or missing information the college requests back to them as soon as possible. Once your application is complete, it is then ready for the decision process.

READER REVIEW

The process by which the decision is finalized varies from school to school. Most of the private colleges and universities use a system in which each application is read by 2 or more admission staff members. In some cases, faculty members are also readers. If all of the readers agree on the decision, a letter is sent. Under this system, if the readers do not agree, the application will be reviewed by a committee or may be forwarded to an associate dean, dean, or director of admission for the final decision. One advantage to this process is that each applicant is reviewed by several people, thereby eliminating bias.

COMMITTEE REVIEW

At some universities, a committee reviews every application. Under that system, a committee member is assigned a number of applications to present. It is that member's responsibility to prepare background information on each applicant and then present the file to the committee for discussion and a vote. In this process, every applicant is voted on.

COUNSELOR REVIEW

The review process that many selective public institutions use is one in which the counselor responsible for a particular school or geographical territory makes the final decision. In this case, the counselor who makes the admission decision is also the one who identified and recruited the student, thereby lending a more personal tone to the process.

COMPUTER-GENERATED REVIEW

Many large state universities that process nearly 20,000 applications a year have developed computer-generated guidelines to admit their applicants. If applicants meet the required GPA and test scores, they are immediately notified of the decision.

Once the decisions are made using one of these methods, colleges use a variety of ways to notify students. The common methods used are early action or early decision, rolling admission, and deferred admission.

A WORD OF ADVICE

When you start the admission process, do so with the idea of exploring as many college opportunities as you can. From the very beginning, avoid focusing on just one college or, for that matter, one type of college. Look at private, public, large, small, highly selective, selective—in short, a variety of colleges and universities. Take advantage of every available resource, including students, parents, counselors, and college materials, in order to help identify the colleges that will be a great fit for you.

Finally, the most important thing you can do is to build a checklist of what you want out of the college experience and then match your list with one of the many wonderful colleges and universities just waiting for you to enroll.

APPLYING TO PROFESSIONAL COLLEGES FOR ART AND MUSIC

BY THERESA BEDOYA, Dean of Admissions, Maryland Institute, College of Art

The term "competitive" will have a different meaning if you are applying to a professional college specializing in art or music. The goal of selective art and music colleges is to admit students of extraordinary talent. Since you are using this resource as part of your college search, you most likely have distinguished yourself academically. But to gain admission to the music and art colleges listed in this book, you will also need to be competitive in your achievements in the arts.

ADMISSION CRITERIA

In order to choose the most talented students from those who apply, most professional art and music colleges require evidence of talent, skill, ability, experience, and desire as demonstrated in an audition or by a portfolio of artwork. Each art and music college has expectations and academic requirements particular to the program of study you choose.

Admission will be based upon the review of traditional criteria such as your grade point average, level of course work, test scores, essays, and interviews. However, for most professional colleges, the evaluation of your portfolio or your audition will supersede the review of all other criteria for admission. (Many visual arts colleges even prescreen potential applicants through review of the portfolio prior to application in order to determine eligibility for admission. This process, which occurs early in the senior year, allows students the opportunity to gain valuable guidance early in the admission process. It also creates a more "acceptable" pool of applicants and is the reason that acceptance rates at many visual arts colleges appear to be higher than other selective

institutions.) In some cases, the evaluation of your talent and academic achievement will be given equal weight.

In contrast, most comprehensive colleges and universities offering majors in art and music will rely on academic criteria to make an admission decision. The portfolio or audition, if required, will play a secondary role. You should take these factors into account when deciding whether to apply to art and music schools or to colleges and universities that offer art and music programs.

PREPARING FOR YOUR PORTFOLIO REVIEW OR AUDITION

If you are interested in the visual arts, you should gain as much studio experience as possible in order to develop a strong portfolio. Take full advantage of your high school art program and enroll in extra Saturday or summer classes or seek private tutoring. Exhibit your artwork when the opportunity is provided. Become better informed as an artist by studying art history and the works of contemporary artists.

If you plan to study music, remember that experience and confidence need to be clearly evident in your audition. Therefore, become involved as much as possible in your own high school music activities as well as local, district, and state youth orchestras, choirs, and performance ensembles. The more you perform and study, the more confident you will be on stage.

Contact the schools to which you are applying early in the process to learn how and when they will receive your portfolio or conduct your audition.

PAYING FOR COLLEGE

BY DON BETTERTON, Director of Financial Aid at Princeton University

Regardless of which college a student chooses, higher education requires a major investment of time, energy, and money. By taking advantage of a variety of available resources, most students can bring the education that is right for them within reach.

A NOTE OF ENCOURAGEMENT
While there is no denying that the cost of an education at some competitive colleges can be high, it is important to recognize that, although the rate of increase in costs during the last ten years has outpaced gains in family income, there are more options available to pay for college than ever before.

Many families find it is economically wise to spread costs out over a number of years by borrowing money for college. A significant amount of government money, both federal and state, is available to students. Moreover, colleges themselves have expanded their own student aid efforts considerably. In spite of rapidly increasing costs, most competitive colleges are still able to provide financial aid to all admitted students with demonstrated need.

In addition, many colleges have developed ways to assist families who are not eligible for need-based assistance. These include an increasing number of merit scholarships as well as various forms of parental loans. There also are a number of organizations that give merit awards based on a student's academic record, talent, or special characteristics. Thus, regardless of your family's income, if you are academically qualified and knowledgeable about the many different sources of aid, you should be able to attend the college of your choice.

ESTIMATING COSTS
If you have not yet settled on specific colleges and you would like to begin early financial planning, estimate a budget. By calculating a 5 percent increase on 2003–04 charges, we can estimate 2004–05 expenses at a typical competitive college as follows: tuition and fees, about $22,900; room and board, about $7900;

and an allowance for books and miscellaneous expenses, about $2375. Thus a rough budget (excluding travel expenses) for the year is $33,175.

IDENTIFYING RESOURCES
There are essentially four sources of funds you can use to pay for college:
- money from your parents,
- need-based scholarships or grants from a college or outside organization,
- your own contribution from savings, loans, and jobs, and
- assistance unrelated to demonstrated financial need.

All of these are considered by the financial aid office, and the aid "package" given to a student after the parental contribution has been determined usually consists of a combination of scholarships, loans, and campus work.

THE PARENTAL CONTRIBUTION
The financial aid policies of most colleges are based on the assumption that parents should contribute as much as they reasonably can to the educational expenses of their children. The amount of this contribution varies greatly, but almost every family is expected to pay something.

Because there is no limit on aid eligibility based solely on income, the best rule of thumb is *apply for financial aid if there is any reasonable doubt about your ability to meet college costs*. Since it is generally true that applying for financial aid does not affect a student's chances of being admitted, any candidate for admission should apply for aid if his or her family feels they will be unable to pay the entire cost of attendance. (In spite of considerable publicity on the subject, there are still only a handful of competitive colleges that practice need-sensitive admissions.)

Application for aid is made by completing the Free Application for Federal Student Aid (FAFSA). In addition, many competitive colleges will require you to also file a separate application called PROFILE, since they need more detailed information to award their own funds. The financial aid section of a college's admission information booklet will tell you which financial aid application is required, when it should be filed, and whether a separate aid form of the college's own design is also necessary.

Colleges use the same government formula (the Federal Methodology) to determine eligibility for federal and state student aid. This process of coming up with an expected contribution from you (the student) and your parents is called "need analysis." The information on the FAFSA—parental and student income and assets, the number of family members, and the number attending college as well as other variables—is analyzed to derive the Expected Family Contribution (EFC).

You can estimate how much your parents might be asked to contribute for college by consulting the "Approximate Expected Family Contribution Chart." Keep in mind that the actual parental contribution is determined on campus by a financial aid officer, using the government formula as a guideline.

Competitive colleges that also require the PROFILE will have at their disposal information they will analyze in addition to what is reported on the FAFSA. The net result of this further examination (for example, adding the value of the family home to the equation) will usually increase the expected parental contribution compared to the Federal Methodology.

Parental Borrowing

Some families who are judged to have sufficient resources to be able to finance their children's college costs find that lack of cash at any moment prevents them from paying college bills without difficulty. Other families prefer to use less current income by extending their payments over more than four years. In both instances, these families rely on borrowing to assist with college payments. Each year parental loans become a more important form of college financing.

The PLUS program, part of the Federal Family Education Loan Program, is designed to help both aid and non-aid families. It allows parents to pay their share of educational costs by borrowing at a reasonable interest rate, with the backing of the federal government. These loans are available through both the Direct Loan (DL) program, administered at the college or university, and the Federal Family Education Loan (FFEL), administered through banks and financial institutions. These loans have a variable interest rate, capped at a maximum 9 percent. For 2003–04, the interest rate for PLUS loans is 4.22 percent. Parents are notified of interest rate changes throughout the life of the loan. Interest is charged on the loan from the date of the first disbursement until the loan is paid. Many competitive colleges, state governments, and commercial lenders also have their own parental loan programs patterned along the lines of PLUS. For more information about parental loans, contact a college financial aid office or your state higher education department.

NEED-BASED SCHOLARSHIP OR GRANT ASSISTANCE

Need-based aid is primarily available from federal and state governments and from colleges themselves. It is not necessary for a student to apply directly for a particular scholarship at a college; the financial aid office will match an eligible applicant with the appropriate fund.

The Federal Pell Grant is by far the largest single form of federal student assistance; an estimated 4 million students receive awards annually. Families with incomes of up to $35,000 (higher when other family members are in college or family assets are relatively low) may be eligible for grants up to $4050 per year.

By filing the FAFSA, you automatically apply for the Federal Pell Grant and most state administered financial aid programs. Most state aid programs are not portable, meaning that they cannot be used out-of-state. Check with your state department of higher education for additional information on application procedures and restrictions.

THE STUDENT'S OWN CONTRIBUTION

All undergraduates, not only those who apply for financial aid, can assume responsibility for meeting a portion of their college expenses by borrowing, working during the academic year and the summer, and contributing a portion of their savings. Colleges require aid recipients to provide a "self-help" contribution before awarding scholarship money because they believe students should pay a reasonable share of their own educational costs.

Student Loans

Many students will be able to borrow to help pay for college. Colleges administer three loans (all backed by the federal government): the Direct Stafford Loan, FFEL Stafford Loan, and the Federal Perkins Loan. Students must demonstrate financial need to be eligible for the Perkins loan. While every student is eligible for the Stafford Loan Program, financial need must be demonstrated to have the interest on the loan subsidized by the federal government.

Note: Rather than providing FFEL Stafford Loans, many colleges have made arrangements to participate in the Direct Stafford Loan Program. Under the Direct Loan Program, the college serves as the lender, while under the FFEL, students and parents deal with a private lender, usually a bank or credit union. As far as the student is concerned, the loan terms are essentially the same.

Summer Employment

All students, whether or not they are receiving financial aid, should plan to work during the summer months. Students can be expected to save from $800 to $1850 before their freshman year and $1500 to $2550 each summer while enrolled in college. It is worthwhile for a student to begin working while in high school to increase the chance of finding summer employment during college vacations.

Term-Time Employment

Colleges have student employment offices that find jobs for students during the school year. Aid recipients on work-study receive priority in placement, but once they have been assisted, non-aid students are helped as well. Some jobs relate closely to academic interests; others should be viewed as a source of income rather than intellectual stimulation. A standard 8- to 15-hour-per-___ job does not normally interfere with aca-___ ___ork or extracurricular activities and results ___ ___ately $1500 to $2500 in earnings dur-___ ___mic year.

___ ___ulated prior to starting college ___ college bills. The need

analysis system expects 35 percent of each year's student savings to go toward college expenses. This source can often be quite substantial, particularly when families have accumulated large sums in the student's name (or in a trust fund with the student as the beneficiary). If you have a choice whether to keep college savings in the parents' name or the student's name, you should realize that the contribution rate on parental assets is 5.6 percent, compared to 35 percent for the student's savings.

AID NOT REQUIRING NEED AS AN ELIGIBILITY CRITERION

There are scholarships available to students whether or not they are eligible for need-based financial aid. Awards based on merit are given by certain state scholarship programs, and National Merit Scholarship winners usually receive a $2500 stipend regardless of family financial circumstances. Scholarships and prizes are also awarded by community organizations and other local groups. In addition, some parents receive tuition payments for their children as employment benefits. Most colleges offer merit scholarships to a limited group of highly qualified applicants. The selection of recipients for such awards depends on unusual talent in a specific area or on overall academic excellence.

The Reserve Officers' Training Corps sponsors an extensive scholarship program that pays for tuition and books and provides an expense allowance of $1500 per school year. The Army, Air Force, and Navy/Marine Corps have ROTC units at many colleges. High school guidance offices have brochures describing ROTC application procedures.

Students are encouraged to aggressively seek out private sources of financial aid. Many books are available, including *Peterson's Scholarships, Grants & Prizes*. Peterson's Web site, www.petersons.com, has scholarship search features and links to other financial aid related topics. Additionally, on the Web, Peterson's offers BestCollegeDeals (for U.S. citizens looking for information on U.S. colleges) where you'll get personalized financial aid guidance. BestCollegeDeals allows you to compare costs—including tuition, fees, room, and board—and financial aid offerings from colleges in the U.S., estimate how much your family may be expected to contribute toward your education, determine your out-of-pocket cost of attendance, find need-based and merit-based offerings, and uncover unique Best College Deals—and lucrative offerings from institutions you might never have even considered.

Aid recipients are required to notify the college financial aid office about outside awards, as colleges take into consideration grants from all sources in developing the financial aid package for their students.

A SIMPLE METHOD FOR ESTIMATING EXPECTED FAMILY CONTRIBUTION

The chart that follows will enable parents to make an approximation of the yearly amount the national financial aid need analysis system will expect them to pay for college.

To use the chart, you need to work with your income, assets, and size of your family. Read the instructions below and enter the proper amounts in the spaces provided.

1. Parents' total income before taxes

   A. Adjusted gross income (equivalent to tax return entry; use actual or estimated) _____A

   B. Nontaxable income (Social Security benefits, child support, welfare, etc.) _____B

      Total Income: A + B _____ ①

2. Parents' total assets

   C. Total of cash, savings, and checking accounts _____C

   D. Total value of investments (stocks, bonds, real estate other than home, etc.) _____D

      Total Assets: C + D _____ ②

3. Family size (include student, parents, other dependent children, and other dependents) _____③

Now find the figures on the "Approximate Expected Family Contribution Chart" that correspond to your entries in ①, ②, and ③ to determine your approximate expected parental contribution, interpolating as necessary.

4. Estimated parental contribution from chart _____④

If there will be more than one family member in college half-time or more, divide the figure above by the number in college.

5. Estimated parental contribution for each person in college _____⑤

6. Student's savings _____ × .35 =_____ ⑥

7. Finally, add the estimated parental contribution in ⑤ and the estimated student contribution in ⑥ to arrive at the total Expected Family Contribution _____⑦

This number can be compared to college costs to determine an approximate level of need.

APPROXIMATE EXPECTED PARENTAL CONTRIBUTION CHART

Assets		$20,000	30,000	40,000	50,000	60,000	70,000	80,000	90,000	100,000
						Income Before Taxes				
$20,000										
Family Size	3	$0	870	2,450	4,350	7,000	9,800	12,600	15,500	18,000
	4	0	80	1,670	3,350	5,600	8,300	11,000	14,000	17,100
	5	0	0	930	2,500	4,500	7,000	9,700	12,600	15,600
	6	0	0	100	1,700	3,350	5,500	8,100	11,000	14,000
$30,000										
Family Size	3	$0	870	2,450	4,350	7,000	9,800	12,600	15,500	18,000
	4	0	80	1,670	3,350	5,600	8,300	11,000	14,000	17,100
	5	0	0	930	2,500	4,500	7,000	9,700	12,600	15,600
	6	0	0	100	1,700	3,350	5,500	8,100	11,000	14,000
$40,000										
Family Size	3	$0	870	2,450	4,350	7,000	9,800	12,600	15,500	18,000
	4	0	80	1,670	3,350	5,600	8,300	11,000	14,000	17,100
	5	0	0	930	2,500	4,500	7,000	9,700	12,600	15,600
	6	0	0	100	1,700	3,350	5,500	8,100	11,000	14,000
$50,000										
Family Size	3	$0	870	2,450	4,350	7,500	10,300	13,000	16,000	19,000
	4	0	80	1,670	3,350	6,000	8,800	11,500	14,400	17,500
	5	0	0	930	2,500	4,700	7,400	10,100	13,000	16,100
	6	0	0	100	1,700	3,600	5,900	8,500	11,400	14,500
$60,000										
Family Size	3	$0	870	2,450	5,100	8,050	10,800	13,600	16,500	19,600
	4	0	80	1,670	3,950	6,550	9,300	12,200	15,000	18,100
	5	0	0	930	3,000	5,300	7,900	10,800	13,600	16,700
	6	0	0	100	2,150	4,000	6,300	9,100	12,000	15,000

		Income Before Taxes								
	Assets	$20,000	30,000	40,000	50,000	60,000	70,000	80,000	90,000	100,000
	$80,000									
FAMILY SIZE	3	$0	870	2,450	6,000	9,200	12,000	14,800	17,600	20,700
	4	0	80	1,670	4,700	7,600	10,500	13,200	16,100	19,200
	5	0	0	930	3,700	6,100	9,000	11,800	14,700	17,800
	6	0	0	100	2,700	4,700	7,400	10,200	13,100	16,200
	$100,000									
FAMILY SIZE	3	$0	870	2,450	7,000	10,300	13,000	15,900	18,800	21,850
	4	0	80	1,670	5,600	8,700	11,500	14,300	17,200	20,300
	5	0	0	930	4,400	7,100	10,200	12,900	15,800	18,900
	6	0	0	100	3,300	5,500	8,500	11,300	14,200	17,300
	$120,000									
FAMILY SIZE	3	$0	870	2,450	8,100	11,400	14,200	17,000	19,900	23,000
	4	0	80	1,670	6,600	9,800	12,600	15,500	18,400	21,500
	5	0	0	930	5,300	8,200	11,300	14,100	17,000	20,000
	6	0	0	100	4,000	6,500	9,700	12,500	15,300	18,400
	$140,000									
FAMILY SIZE	3	$0	870	2,450	9,300	12,600	15,400	18,200	21,000	24,100
	4	0	80	1,670	7,600	11,000	13,900	16,700	19,500	22,600
	5	0	0	930	6,100	9,500	12,500	15,200	18,100	21,200
	6	0	0	100	4,700	7,600	10,800	13,600	16,500	19,600

This chart makes the following assumptions:
• two parent family where age of older parent is 45
• lower income families will file the 1040A or 1040EZ tax form
• student income is less than $2300
• there are no student assets
• there is only one family member in college

All figures are estimates and may vary when the complete FAFSA or PROFILE application is submitted.

SPONSOR LIST

These sponsors arranged for copies of *Competitive Colleges* to reach outstanding students—students eager to learn more about top schools. This icon appears in each sponsor's profile:

Agnes Scott College
Albright College
Alfred University
Alma College
American University
Amherst College
Augustana College (IL)
Barnard College
Baylor University
Belmont University
Beloit College
Bennington College
Berry College
Bethel College (MN)
Birmingham-Southern College
Boston College
Boston University
Brandeis University
Brown University
Bryn Mawr College
Bucknell University
Butler University
Calvin College
Canisius College
Carnegie Mellon University
Carroll College (MT)
Chapman University
Christian Brothers University
Claremont McKenna College
Clarkson University
Clemson University
College of Charleston
College of New Jersey
College of Saint Benedict
College of the Atlantic
College of the Holy Cross
The College of Wooster
Converse College

Cooper Union for the Advancement
    of Science and Art
Cornell College
Cornell University
Dartmouth College
Davidson College
Denison University
DePauw University
Drake University
Earlham College
Elizabethtown College
Embry-Riddle Aeronautical
    University
Emerson College
Emory University
Eugene Lang College, New School
    University
Florida Institute of Technology
Fordham University
Franciscan University of
    Steubenville
Georgia State University
Gettysburg College
Gordon College
Goucher College
Grove City College
Hamilton College
Hampshire College
Harding University
Haverford College
Hendrix College
Hillsdale College
Hiram College
Hobart and William Smith Colleges
Illinois College
Illinois Institute of Technology
Iowa State University of Science and
    Technology
Ithaca College

John Carroll University
Juniata College
Lafayette College
Lawrence Technological University
Lebanon Valley College
Lipscomb University
List College, Jewish Theological
    Seminary of America
Loyola College in Maryland
Loyola University Chicago
Loyola University New Orleans
Lycoming College
Marietta College
Marquette University
Maryville College
McDaniel College
Mercer University
Messiah College
Michigan State University
Middlebury College
Mills College
Morehouse College
Mount Holyoke College
Muhlenberg College
New College of Florida
New Jersey Institute of Technology
New York School of Interior Design
North Central College
Oberlin College
Oglethorpe University
Ohio Northern University
Ohio Wesleyan University
Oklahoma State University
Pitzer College
Pomona College
Presbyterian College
Princeton University
Providence College
Quincy University

Quinnipiac University
Randolph-Macon Woman's College
Reed College
Regis University
Rensselaer Polytechnic Institute
Rice University
Ripon College
Rochester Institute of Technology
Saint Francis University
St. John's College (MD)
St. John's College (NM)
Saint John's University (MN)
Saint Joseph's University
St. Lawrence University
Saint Louis University
Saint Mary's College
Saint Mary's College of California
St. Mary's College of Maryland
St. Norbert College
Samford University
Sarah Lawrence College
Seattle University
Siena College
Simon's Rock College of Bard
Simpson College
Skidmore College
Smith College
Southern Methodist University
Southwestern University
Southwest Missouri State University

State University of New York
  at Binghamton
Stevens Institute of Technology
Susquehanna University
Swarthmore College
Sweet Briar College
Syracuse University
Texas Christian University
Texas Tech University
Transylvania University
Trinity College (CT)
Trinity University
Tulane University
Union College (NY)
Union University
United States Air Force Academy
United States Merchant Marine
  Academy
United States Military Academy
University at Buffalo, the State
  University of New York
The University of Alabama in
  Huntsville
University of Dayton
University of Georgia
University of Illinois at
  Urbana-Champaign
University of Michigan
University of Minnesota,
  Twin Cities Campus

University of Nebraska–Lincoln
Univesity of Oklahoma
University of Redlands
University of Rhode Island
University of Rochester
University of St. Thomas
University of San Diego
University of Scranton
University of South Carolina
University of Southern California
University of the Sciences in
  Philadelphia
University of the South
Valparaiso University
Villanova University
Virginia Military Institute
Virginia Polytechnic Institute and
  State University
Wabash College
Washington College
Washington University in St. Louis
Wellesley College
Wells College
Wesleyan College
Wesleyan University
Westminster College
Westmont College
Williams College

COMPETITIVE COLLEGES AND UNIVERSITIES

17

COLLEGE OR UNIVERSITY NAME

SETTING ■ PUBLIC/PRIVATE ■ INSTITUTIONAL CONTROL ■ COED?
CITY, STATE

Web site: www.website.com
Contact: Contact name and mailing address
Telephone: Telephone number **Fax:** Fax number
E-mail: E-mail address

Academics

• Degrees awarded
• Most frequently chosen fields
• Faculty, including student-faculty ratio

The Student Body

• How many students on campus and number who are undergrads
• Percent of women and men
• Where students come from
• Percent of students from in-state
• Who they are (international students and ethnic makeup)
• How many students come back for the sophomore year

Facilities and Resources

• Computer resources
• Network, e-mail, and online services
• Library facilities

Campus Life

• Organizations, activities, and student participation
• Fraternities and sororities
• Sports ("m" for men, "w" for women; neither "m" nor "w" means both)

Campus Safety

• Late-night transport/escort service
• Emergency telephone alarm devices
• 24-hour patrols
• Electronically operated residence hall entrances

Applying

• Required documentation and standardized tests
• GPA minimum
• Interviews
• Deadlines

Getting in Last Year
• Number who applied
• Percent accepted
• Number enrolled (percent)
• Percent h.s. achievers
• Average GPA
• SAT I/ACT performance
• Number of National Merit Scholars
• Number of class presidents
• Number of valedictorians

Graduation and After
• Percent graduating in 4, 5, or 6 years
• Percent pursuing further study, with most popular fields, if provided
• Percent with job offers within 6 months
• How many organizations recruit on campus
• Major academic awards won by students

Financial Matters
• Tuition and fees
• Room and board
• Percent of need met
• Average financial aid received per undergraduate

ABILENE CHRISTIAN UNIVERSITY

URBAN SETTING ■ PRIVATE ■ INDEPENDENT RELIGIOUS ■ COED
ABILENE, TEXAS

Web site: www.acu.edu
Contact: Mr. Robert Heil, Director of Admissions and Enrollment, Zellner
  Hall Room 2006A, ACU Box 29000, Abilene, TX 79699-9000
Telephone: 325-674-2765 or toll-free 800-460-6228 **Fax:** 915-674-2130
E-mail: info@admissions.acu.edu

Getting in Last Year
4,011 applied
53% were accepted
949 enrolled (45%)
21% from top tenth of their h.s. class
3.60 average high school GPA
27% had SAT verbal scores over 600
30% had SAT math scores over 600
48% had ACT scores over 24
5% had SAT verbal scores over 700
5% had SAT math scores over 700
8% had ACT scores over 30
7 National Merit Scholars
24 valedictorians

Graduation and After
26% graduated in 4 years
24% graduated in 5 years
4% graduated in 6 years
30% pursued further study
85% had job offers within 6 months
140 organizations recruited on campus

Financial Matters
$13,290 tuition and fees (2003–04)
$5080 room and board
77% average percent of need met
$10,210 average financial aid amount received
  per undergraduate (2002–03)

Academics

ACU awards associate, bachelor's, master's, doctoral, and first-professional **degrees** and
post-bachelor's certificates. Challenging opportunities include advanced placement
credit, student-designed majors, an honors program, double majors, independent study,
and a senior project. Special programs include internships, summer session for credit,
off-campus study, and study-abroad.

The most frequently chosen **baccalaureate** fields are business/marketing, education,
and interdisciplinary studies. A complete listing of majors at ACU appears in the Majors
Index beginning on page 460.

The **faculty** at ACU has 227 full-time members, 74% with terminal degrees. The
student-faculty ratio is 16:1.

Students of ACU

The student body totals 4,648, of whom 4,111 are undergraduates. 55.7% are women
and 44.3% are men. Students come from 47 states and territories and 40 other countries.
82% are from Texas. 74% returned for their sophomore year.

Facilities and Resources

Student rooms are linked to a campus network. 700 **computers** are available on campus
that provide access to the Internet. The **library** has 481,689 books and 2,439 subscriptions.

Campus Life

There are 104 active organizations on campus, including a drama/theater group,
newspaper, radio station, television station, choral group, and marching band. 14% of
eligible men and 15% of eligible women are members of local **fraternities** and local
sororities.

ACU is a member of the NCAA (Division II). **Intercollegiate sports** (some offering
scholarships) include baseball (m), basketball, cross-country running, football (m), golf
(m), softball (w), tennis, track and field, volleyball (w).

Campus Safety

Student safety services include late-night transport/escort service, 24-hour emergency
telephone alarm devices, and 24-hour patrols by trained security personnel.

Applying

ACU requires SAT I or ACT, a high school transcript, and 2 recommendations. It
recommends an interview and a minimum high school GPA of 2.0. Application deadline:
8/1; 3/1 priority date for financial aid.

AGNES SCOTT COLLEGE

URBAN SETTING ■ PRIVATE ■ INDEPENDENT RELIGIOUS ■ WOMEN ONLY
DECATUR, GEORGIA

Web site: www.agnesscott.edu
Contact: Ms. Stephanie Balmer, Dean of Admission, 141 East College Avenue,
    Decatur, GA 30030-3797
Telephone: 404-471-6285 or toll-free 800-868-8602 **Fax:** 404-471-6414
E-mail: admission@agnesscott.edu

Academics

Agnes Scott awards bachelor's and master's **degrees** and post-bachelor's certificates.
Challenging opportunities include advanced placement credit, accelerated degree
programs, student-designed majors, double majors, independent study, and a senior
project. Special programs include internships, summer session for credit, off-campus
study, study-abroad, and Navy and Air Force ROTC.

The most frequently chosen **baccalaureate** fields are social sciences and history,
English, and psychology. A complete listing of majors at Agnes Scott appears in the
Majors Index beginning on page 460.

The **faculty** at Agnes Scott has 77 full-time members, 96% with terminal degrees.
The student-faculty ratio is 10:1.

Students of Agnes Scott

The student body totals 923, of whom 898 are undergraduates. Students come from 41
states and territories and 29 other countries. 50% are from Georgia. 8.4% are international students. 19.3% are African American, 4.3% Asian American, and 3.4%
Hispanic American. 84% returned for their sophomore year.

Facilities and Resources

Student rooms are linked to a campus network. 372 **computers** are available on campus
that provide access to the Internet. The **library** has 171,891 books and 1,118 subscriptions.

Campus Life

There are 77 active organizations on campus, including a drama/theater group,
newspaper, choral group, and marching band. No national or local **sororities**.

Agnes Scott is a member of the NCAA (Division III). **Intercollegiate sports** include
basketball, cross-country running, soccer, softball, swimming, tennis, volleyball.

Campus Safety

Student safety services include security systems in apartments, public safety facility,
surveillance equipment, late-night transport/escort service, 24-hour emergency
telephone alarm devices, and 24-hour patrols by trained security personnel.

Applying

Agnes Scott requires an essay, SAT I or ACT, a high school transcript, and 2 recommendations, and in some cases SAT II Subject Tests. It recommends an interview and a
minimum high school GPA of 3.0. Application deadline: 3/1; 5/1 for financial aid, with a
2/15 priority date. Early and deferred admission are possible.

Agnes Scott College is committed to a 21st-century curriculum that emphasizes
academic excellence through the
liberal arts and sciences and is
enhanced by experience-based learning, including internships, collaborative research, independent study, and
study abroad. Programs such as the
First-Year Seminars, Atlanta
Semester, Global Awareness and
Global Connections, and Language
Across the Curriculum enrich the
Agnes Scott experience. In the last
10 years, Agnes Scott has had 5
Fulbright scholars, 4 Goldwater
scholars, and an NCAA semifinalist; it
ranks 7th nationally in the percentage
of graduates who earn PhD's in
education and 15th in the area of
humanities. Atlanta, the South's most
dynamic and international city,
provides opportunities for fun as well
as for internships, community service,
and cultural events. Agnes Scott is an
excellent value in terms of academic
quality, personalized attention, and a
residential community with a student-
governed honor system.

Getting in Last Year
782 applied
66% were accepted
213 enrolled (41%)
47% from top tenth of their h.s. class
3.64 average high school GPA
62% had SAT verbal scores over 600
43% had SAT math scores over 600
76% had ACT scores over 24
16% had SAT verbal scores over 700
4% had SAT math scores over 700
25% had ACT scores over 30
10 National Merit Scholars

Graduation and After
58% graduated in 4 years
4% graduated in 5 years
2% graduated in 6 years
25% pursued further study (9% arts and sci-
    ences, 5% law, 3% medicine)
48% had job offers within 6 months
42 organizations recruited on campus

Financial Matters
$20,470 tuition and fees (2003–04)
$7760 room and board
97% average percent of need met
$21,263 average financial aid amount received
    per undergraduate

ALBANY COLLEGE OF PHARMACY OF UNION UNIVERSITY

URBAN SETTING ■ PRIVATE ■ INDEPENDENT ■ COED
ALBANY, NEW YORK

Web site: www.acp.edu
Contact: Mr. Robert Gould, Director of Admissions, 106 New Scotland Avenue, Albany, NY 12208-3425
Telephone: 518-445-7221 or toll-free 888-203-8010 **Fax:** 518-445-7202
E-mail: admissions@acp.edu

Getting in Last Year
741 applied
64% were accepted
206 enrolled (43%)
48% from top tenth of their h.s. class
3.40 average high school GPA
34% had SAT verbal scores over 600
49% had SAT math scores over 600
3% had SAT verbal scores over 700
6% had SAT math scores over 700
5 valedictorians

Graduation and After
63% graduated in 5 years
10% graduated in 6 years
10% pursued further study
100% had job offers within 6 months
45 organizations recruited on campus

Financial Matters
$16,662 tuition and fees (2003–04)
$5500 room and board
78% average percent of need met
$12,320 average financial aid amount received per undergraduate (2002–03 estimated)

Academics
Albany College of Pharmacy awards bachelor's and first-professional **degrees**. Challenging opportunities include advanced placement credit and accelerated degree programs. Special programs include internships, summer session for credit, off-campus study, and Army and Air Force ROTC.

The most frequently chosen **baccalaureate** field is health professions and related sciences. A complete listing of majors at Albany College of Pharmacy appears in the Majors Index beginning on page 460.

The **faculty** at Albany College of Pharmacy has 63 full-time members, 75% with terminal degrees. The student-faculty ratio is 14:1.

Students of Albany College of Pharmacy
The student body totals 886, of whom 701 are undergraduates. 61.3% are women and 38.7% are men. Students come from 10 states and territories and 7 other countries. 88% are from New York. 3.6% are international students. 2.1% are African American, 0.4% American Indian, 8.3% Asian American, and 1% Hispanic American. 93% returned for their sophomore year.

Facilities and Resources
Student rooms are linked to a campus network. 47 **computers** are available on campus that provide access to the Internet. The **library** has 16,124 books and 3,576 subscriptions.

Campus Life
There are 14 active organizations on campus, including a newspaper and choral group. 15% of eligible men and 15% of eligible women are members of national **fraternities** and national **sororities**.

Intercollegiate **sports** include basketball, soccer.

Campus Safety
Student safety services include 24-hour emergency telephone alarm devices, 24-hour patrols by trained security personnel, and electronically operated dormitory entrances.

Applying
Albany College of Pharmacy requires an essay, SAT I or ACT, a high school transcript, and 2 recommendations, and in some cases an interview. It recommends a minimum high school GPA of 2.0. Application deadline: 2/1; 2/1 priority date for financial aid.

ALBERTSON COLLEGE OF IDAHO

SMALL-TOWN SETTING ■ PRIVATE ■ INDEPENDENT ■ COED
CALDWELL, IDAHO

Web site: www.albertson.edu
Contact: Brandie Allemand, Associate Dean of Admission, 2112 Cleveland Boulevard, Caldwell, ID 83605-4494
Telephone: 208-459-5305 or toll-free 800-224-3246 **Fax:** 208-459-5757
E-mail: admission@albertson.edu

Academics

Albertson awards bachelor's and master's **degrees**. Challenging opportunities include advanced placement credit, student-designed majors, an honors program, double majors, independent study, and a senior project. Special programs include internships, off-campus study, and study-abroad.

The most frequently chosen **baccalaureate** fields are social sciences and history, biological/life sciences, and business/marketing. A complete listing of majors at Albertson appears in the Majors Index beginning on page 460.

The **faculty** at Albertson has 71 full-time members, 93% with terminal degrees. The student-faculty ratio is 10:1.

Students of Albertson

The student body totals 853, of whom 841 are undergraduates. 55.2% are women and 44.8% are men. Students come from 21 states and territories. 75% are from Idaho. 1.9% are international students. 0.4% are African American, 0.8% American Indian, 3.5% Asian American, and 4.5% Hispanic American. 73% returned for their sophomore year.

Facilities and Resources

Student rooms are linked to a campus network. 240 **computers** are available on campus that provide access to online course syllabi, course assignments, course discussion and the Internet. The **library** has 183,308 books and 703 subscriptions.

Campus Life

There are 55 active organizations on campus, including a drama/theater group, newspaper, and choral group. 19% of eligible men and 19% of eligible women are members of national **fraternities**, national **sororities**, local fraternities, and local sororities.

Albertson is a member of the NAIA. **Intercollegiate sports** (some offering scholarships) include baseball (m), basketball, golf, skiing (cross-country), skiing (downhill), soccer, softball (w), tennis, volleyball (w).

Campus Safety

Student safety services include late-night transport/escort service, 24-hour emergency telephone alarm devices, 24-hour patrols by trained security personnel, student patrols, and electronically operated dormitory entrances.

Applying

Albertson requires an essay, SAT I or ACT, a high school transcript, and 1 recommendation. It recommends an interview. Application deadline: 6/1; 2/15 priority date for financial aid. Early and deferred admission are possible.

Getting in Last Year
950 applied
77% were accepted
252 enrolled (35%)
33% from top tenth of their h.s. class
3.60 average high school GPA
33% had SAT verbal scores over 600
39% had SAT math scores over 600
60% had ACT scores over 24
6% had SAT verbal scores over 700
4% had SAT math scores over 700
7% had ACT scores over 30
1 National Merit Scholar

Graduation and After
22% pursued further study
20 organizations recruited on campus

Financial Matters
$14,400 tuition and fees (2003–04)
$5015 room and board
83% average percent of need met
$14,738 average financial aid amount received per undergraduate

ALBION COLLEGE

SMALL-TOWN SETTING ■ PRIVATE ■ INDEPENDENT RELIGIOUS ■ COED
ALBION, MICHIGAN

Web site: www.albion.edu
Contact: Mr. Doug Kellar, Associate Vice President for Enrollment, 611 East
Porter Street, Albion, MI 49224
Telephone: 517-629-0600 or toll-free 800-858-6770
E-mail: admissions@albion.edu

Getting in Last Year
1,534 applied
87% were accepted
487 enrolled (37%)
32% from top tenth of their h.s. class
3.54 average high school GPA
46% had SAT verbal scores over 600
44% had SAT math scores over 600
66% had ACT scores over 24
7% had SAT verbal scores over 700
9% had SAT math scores over 700
12% had ACT scores over 30
1 National Merit Scholar
19 class presidents
23 valedictorians

Graduation and After
64% graduated in 4 years
4% graduated in 5 years
1% graduated in 6 years
83% had job offers within 6 months
186 organizations recruited on campus

Financial Matters
$21,948 tuition and fees (2003–04)
$6262 room and board
95% average percent of need met
$18,706 average financial aid amount received
per undergraduate

Academics

Albion awards bachelor's **degrees**. Challenging opportunities include advanced placement credit, student-designed majors, an honors program, double majors, independent study, and a senior project. Special programs include internships, summer session for credit, off-campus study, and study-abroad.

The most frequently chosen **baccalaureate** fields are social sciences and history, English, and psychology. A complete listing of majors at Albion appears in the Majors Index beginning on page 460.

The **faculty** at Albion has 123 full-time members, 93% with terminal degrees. The student-faculty ratio is 13:1.

Students of Albion

The student body is made up of 1,732 undergraduates. 56.5% are women and 43.5% are men. Students come from 32 states and territories and 19 other countries. 94% are from Michigan. 1.3% are international students. 2.4% are African American, 0.3% American Indian, 2.1% Asian American, and 0.8% Hispanic American. 86% returned for their sophomore year.

Facilities and Resources

Student rooms are linked to a campus network. 411 **computers** are available on campus that provide access to the Internet. The **library** has 363,000 books and 2,016 subscriptions.

Campus Life

There are 122 active organizations on campus, including a drama/theater group, newspaper, radio station, television station, choral group, and marching band. 40% of eligible men and 40% of eligible women are members of national **fraternities** and national **sororities**.

Albion is a member of the NCAA (Division III). **Intercollegiate sports** include baseball (m), basketball, cheerleading, cross-country running, football (m), golf, soccer, softball (w), swimming, tennis, track and field, volleyball (w).

Campus Safety

Student safety services include late-night transport/escort service, 24-hour emergency telephone alarm devices, 24-hour patrols by trained security personnel, student patrols, and electronically operated dormitory entrances.

Applying

Albion requires an essay, SAT I or ACT, a high school transcript, and 1 recommendation, and in some cases SAT II Subject Tests, SAT II: Writing Test, and an interview. It recommends a minimum high school GPA of 3.0. Application deadline: 7/1; 2/15 priority date for financial aid. Early and deferred admission are possible.

ALBRIGHT COLLEGE

SUBURBAN SETTING ■ PRIVATE ■ INDEPENDENT RELIGIOUS ■ COED
READING, PENNSYLVANIA

Web site: www.albright.edu
Contact: Mr. Gregory E. Eichhorn, Vice President for Enrollment
Management, PO Box 15234, 13th and Bern Streets, Reading, PA
19612-5234
Telephone: 610-921-7260 or toll-free 800-252-1856 **Fax:** 610-921-7294
E-mail: admission@albright.edu

Academics

Albright awards bachelor's and master's **degrees.** Challenging opportunities include
advanced placement credit, accelerated degree programs, student-designed majors, an
honors program, double majors, independent study, and a senior project. Special
programs include internships, summer session for credit, off-campus study, and study-
abroad.

The most frequently chosen **baccalaureate** fields are business/marketing, social sciences and history, and psychology. A complete listing of majors at Albright appears in the
Majors Index beginning on page 460.

The **faculty** at Albright has 103 full-time members, 82% with terminal degrees. The
student-faculty ratio is 13:1.

Students of Albright

The student body totals 2,127, of whom 2,046 are undergraduates. 55.8% are women
and 44.2% are men. Students come from 20 states and territories and 26 other countries.
69% are from Pennsylvania. 3.5% are international students. 8.7% are African
American, 0.3% American Indian, 1.8% Asian American, and 4.2% Hispanic American.
81% returned for their sophomore year.

Facilities and Resources

Student rooms are linked to a campus network. 326 **computers** are available on campus
that provide access to the Internet. The 2 **libraries** have 218,232 books and 8,190
subscriptions.

Campus Life

There are 70 active organizations on campus, including a drama/theater group,
newspaper, radio station, television station, and choral group. 29% of eligible men and
32% of eligible women are members of national **fraternities** and national **sororities.**

Albright is a member of the NCAA (Division III). **Intercollegiate sports** include
badminton (w), baseball (m), basketball, cheerleading (w), cross-country running, field
hockey (w), football (m), golf (m), soccer, softball (w), swimming, tennis, track and field,
volleyball (w), wrestling (m).

Campus Safety

Student safety services include late-night transport/escort service, 24-hour emergency
telephone alarm devices, 24-hour patrols by trained security personnel, student patrols,
and electronically operated dormitory entrances.

Applying

Albright requires an essay, SAT I or ACT, a high school transcript, 1 recommendation,
and secondary school report (guidance department). It recommends an interview. Application deadline: 3/1; 3/1 priority date for financial aid. Early and deferred admission
are possible.

> **I**t used to be acceptable to
> enter college undecided about a
> major; in fact, it was expected.
> But things have changed, and today
> there is more pressure on students
> to choose a major as soon as they
> walk on campus. Pressure doesn't
> lead to wise decisions, so Albright
> has developed a program, the Alpha
> Program, specially designed for the
> undecided student. Through a
> structured package of academic
> guidance, peer support, special
> events, and career counseling, the
> Alpha Program helps students to
> choose not only the right major, but
> also the right career and the right
> future.

Getting in Last Year
2,967 applied
72% were accepted
456 enrolled (21%)
19% from top tenth of their h.s. class
3.27 average high school GPA
16% had SAT verbal scores over 600
18% had SAT math scores over 600
1% had SAT verbal scores over 700
2% had SAT math scores over 700
4 class presidents
4 valedictorians

Graduation and After
60% graduated in 4 years
7% graduated in 5 years
32% pursued further study (12% arts and
   sciences, 9% law, 5% business)
98% had job offers within 6 months
70 organizations recruited on campus

Financial Matters
$23,430 tuition and fees (2003–04)
$7149 room and board
76% average percent of need met
$16,536 average financial aid amount received
   per undergraduate

ALFRED UNIVERSITY
RURAL SETTING ■ PRIVATE ■ INDEPENDENT ■ COED
ALFRED, NEW YORK

Web site: www.alfred.edu
Contact: Mr. Scott Hooker, Director of Admissions, Alumni Hall, Alfred, NY 14802-1205
Telephone: 607-871-2115 or toll-free 800-541-9229 **Fax:** 607-871-2198
E-mail: admwww@alfred.edu

Through the Colleges of Business and Liberal Arts & Sciences and the Schools of Art & Design and Engineering, Alfred University offers more than 60 majors and programs of study, high-technology opportunities, and top-notch facilities, and provides its students an outstanding academic experience in an up-close-and-personal learning environment. Through research, co-op and internship opportunities, active learning, and study abroad, students gain extensive knowledge that makes them more marketable for graduate or professional school placement or securing employment within the workforce. All students are encouraged to value diversity, tolerance, and interdisciplinary work.

Getting in Last Year
2,169 applied
69% were accepted
474 enrolled (32%)
23% from top tenth of their h.s. class
32% had SAT verbal scores over 600
30% had SAT math scores over 600
6% had SAT verbal scores over 700
5% had SAT math scores over 700
7 National Merit Scholars
4 valedictorians

Graduation and After
44% graduated in 4 years
18% graduated in 5 years
2% graduated in 6 years
24% pursued further study
61% had job offers within 6 months
96 organizations recruited on campus

Financial Matters
$19,278 tuition and fees (2003–04)
$9012 room and board
92% average percent of need met
$19,352 average financial aid amount received per undergraduate

Academics
Alfred awards bachelor's, master's, and doctoral **degrees** and post-master's certificates. Challenging opportunities include advanced placement credit, accelerated degree programs, student-designed majors, an honors program, double majors, independent study, and a senior project. Special programs include cooperative education, internships, summer session for credit, off-campus study, study-abroad, and Army ROTC.

The most frequently chosen **baccalaureate** fields are visual/performing arts, engineering/engineering technologies, and business/marketing. A complete listing of majors at Alfred appears in the Majors Index beginning on page 460.

The **faculty** at Alfred has 186 full-time members. The student-faculty ratio is 12:1.

Students of Alfred
The student body totals 2,367, of whom 2,055 are undergraduates. 52.4% are women and 47.6% are men. Students come from 38 states and territories and 32 other countries. 70% are from New York. 1.8% are international students. 5.2% are African American, 0.7% American Indian, 2% Asian American, and 3.8% Hispanic American. 82% returned for their sophomore year.

Facilities and Resources
Student rooms are linked to a campus network. The 2 **libraries** have 288,137 books and 1,478 subscriptions.

Campus Life
There are 90 active organizations on campus, including a drama/theater group, newspaper, radio station, television station, and choral group. No national or local **fraternities** or **sororities**.

Alfred is a member of the NCAA (Division III). **Intercollegiate sports** include basketball, cross-country running, equestrian sports, football (m), lacrosse, skiing (downhill), soccer, softball (w), swimming, tennis, track and field, volleyball (w).

Campus Safety
Student safety services include late-night transport/escort service, 24-hour emergency telephone alarm devices, and student patrols.

Applying
Alfred requires SAT I or ACT, a high school transcript, and 1 recommendation, and in some cases an essay, an interview, and portfolio. It recommends SAT II: Writing Test and an interview. Application deadline: 2/1. Early and deferred admission are possible.

ALLEGHENY COLLEGE

SMALL-TOWN SETTING ■ PRIVATE ■ INDEPENDENT ■ COED
MEADVILLE, PENNSYLVANIA

Web site: www.allegheny.edu
Contact: Dr. W. Scott Friedhoff, Vice President for Enrollment, 520 North Main Street, Box 5, Meadville, PA 16335
Telephone: 814-332-4351 or toll-free 800-521-5293 **Fax:** 814-337-0431
E-mail: admissions@allegheny.edu

Academics

Allegheny awards bachelor's **degrees**. Challenging opportunities include advanced placement credit, student-designed majors, double majors, independent study, and a senior project. Special programs include internships, off-campus study, and study-abroad.

The most frequently chosen **baccalaureate** fields are social sciences and history, English, and psychology. A complete listing of majors at Allegheny appears in the Majors Index beginning on page 460.

The **faculty** at Allegheny has 134 full-time members, 90% with terminal degrees. The student-faculty ratio is 13:1.

Students of Allegheny

The student body is made up of 1,849 undergraduates. 51.5% are women and 48.5% are men. Students come from 33 states and territories. 67% are from Pennsylvania. 0.8% are international students. 1.9% are African American, 0.3% American Indian, 2.1% Asian American, and 1.4% Hispanic American. 85% returned for their sophomore year.

Facilities and Resources

Student rooms are linked to a campus network. 336 **computers** are available on campus that provide access to the Internet. The **library** has 279,648 books and 3,500 subscriptions.

Campus Life

There are 87 active organizations on campus, including a drama/theater group, newspaper, radio station, television station, and choral group. 26% of eligible men and 29% of eligible women are members of national **fraternities** and national **sororities**.

Allegheny is a member of the NCAA (Division III). **Intercollegiate sports** include baseball (m), basketball, cross-country running, football (m), golf (m), lacrosse (w), soccer, softball (w), swimming, tennis, track and field, volleyball (w).

Campus Safety

Student safety services include local police patrol, late-night transport/escort service, 24-hour emergency telephone alarm devices, 24-hour patrols by trained security personnel, student patrols, and electronically operated dormitory entrances.

Applying

Allegheny requires an essay, SAT I or ACT, a high school transcript, and 2 recommendations. It recommends SAT II Subject Tests, SAT II: Writing Test, and an interview. Application deadline: 2/15; 2/15 priority date for financial aid. Early and deferred admission are possible.

Getting in Last Year

2,438 applied
82% were accepted
481 enrolled (24%)
41% from top tenth of their h.s. class
3.68 average high school GPA
53% had SAT verbal scores over 600
52% had SAT math scores over 600
73% had ACT scores over 24
9% had SAT verbal scores over 700
9% had SAT math scores over 700
10% had ACT scores over 30
18 National Merit Scholars
20 valedictorians

Graduation and After

60% graduated in 4 years
6% graduated in 5 years
1% graduated in 6 years
31% pursued further study (12% arts and sciences, 6% medicine, 5% education)
92% had job offers within 6 months
45 organizations recruited on campus

Financial Matters

$24,400 tuition and fees (2003–04)
$5880 room and board
94% average percent of need met
$19,624 average financial aid amount received per undergraduate

ALMA COLLEGE

SMALL-TOWN SETTING ■ PRIVATE ■ INDEPENDENT RELIGIOUS ■ COED
ALMA, MICHIGAN

Web site: www.alma.edu
Contact: Mr. Paul Pollatz, Director of Admissions, Admissions Office, Alma, MI 48801-1599
Telephone: 989-463-7139 or toll-free 800-321-ALMA **Fax:** 989-463-7057
E-mail: admissions@alma.edu

Alma's undergraduates thrive on challenging academic programs in a supportive, small-college atmosphere. The College is committed to a liberal arts and sciences curriculum with opportunities for one-on-one research and publication with faculty members whose first priority is teaching. Students enjoy small classes in modern facilities, including the new Alan J. Stone Center for Recreation. Alma College offers excellent preparation for professional careers in business, law, medicine, the arts, and a wide range of other fields.

Getting in Last Year
1,497 applied
77% were accepted
322 enrolled (28%)
32% from top tenth of their h.s. class
3.43 average high school GPA
60% had ACT scores over 24
10% had ACT scores over 30
7 National Merit Scholars
25 valedictorians

Graduation and After
54% graduated in 4 years
15% graduated in 5 years
2% graduated in 6 years
30% pursued further study (6% theology, 5% arts and sciences, 4% law)
96% had job offers within 6 months
38 organizations recruited on campus

Financial Matters
$18,854 tuition and fees (2003–04)
$6712 room and board
86% average percent of need met
$16,461 average financial aid amount received per undergraduate

Academics
Alma awards bachelor's **degrees**. Challenging opportunities include advanced placement credit, student-designed majors, double majors, independent study, and a senior project. Special programs include internships, summer session for credit, off-campus study, study-abroad, and Army ROTC.

The most frequently chosen **baccalaureate** fields are business/marketing, social sciences and history, and education. A complete listing of majors at Alma appears in the Majors Index beginning on page 460.

The **faculty** at Alma has 84 full-time members, 88% with terminal degrees. The student-faculty ratio is 12:1.

Students of Alma
The student body is made up of 1,291 undergraduates. 58.5% are women and 41.5% are men. Students come from 20 states and territories. 96% are from Michigan. 0.1% are international students. 2.2% are African American, 0.8% American Indian, 1.2% Asian American, and 1.5% Hispanic American. 85% returned for their sophomore year.

Facilities and Resources
Student rooms are linked to a campus network. 684 **computers** are available on campus that provide access to the Internet. The **library** has 246,649 books and 1,157 subscriptions.

Campus Life
There are 96 active organizations on campus, including a drama/theater group, newspaper, radio station, choral group, and marching band. 17% of eligible men and 22% of eligible women are members of national **fraternities**, national **sororities**, local fraternities, and local sororities.

Alma is a member of the NCAA (Division III). **Intercollegiate sports** include baseball (m), basketball, cross-country running, football (m), golf, soccer, softball (w), swimming, tennis, track and field, volleyball (w).

Campus Safety
Student safety services include 24-hour emergency telephone alarm devices and 24-hour patrols by trained security personnel.

Applying
Alma requires SAT I or ACT, a high school transcript, minimum SAT score of 1030 or ACT score of 22, and a minimum high school GPA of 3.0. It recommends an essay and an interview. Application deadline: rolling admissions; 3/1 priority date for financial aid. Early and deferred admission are possible.

AMERICAN UNIVERSITY

SUBURBAN SETTING ■ PRIVATE ■ INDEPENDENT RELIGIOUS ■ COED
WASHINGTON, DISTRICT OF COLUMBIA

Web site: www.american.edu
Contact: Dr. Sharon Alston, Director of Admissions, 4400 Massachusetts
    Avenue, NW, Washington, DC 20016-8001
Telephone: 202-885-6000 **Fax:** 202-885-1025
E-mail: afa@american.edu

Academics

AU awards associate, bachelor's, master's, doctoral, and first-professional **degrees** and post-bachelor's certificates. Challenging opportunities include advanced placement credit, accelerated degree programs, student-designed majors, an honors program, double majors, independent study, and a senior project. Special programs include cooperative education, internships, summer session for credit, off-campus study, study-abroad, and Army and Air Force ROTC.

The most frequently chosen **baccalaureate** fields are social sciences and history, business/marketing, and communications/communication technologies. A complete listing of majors at AU appears in the Majors Index beginning on page 460.

The **faculty** at AU has 492 full-time members, 95% with terminal degrees. The student-faculty ratio is 14:1.

Students of AU

The student body totals 10,977, of whom 5,752 are undergraduates. 61.9% are women and 38.1% are men. Students come from 54 states and territories and 118 other countries. 5% are from District of Columbia. 7.4% are international students. 5.5% are African American, 0.3% American Indian, 4.7% Asian American, and 4.5% Hispanic American. 86% returned for their sophomore year.

Facilities and Resources

Student rooms are linked to a campus network. 600 **computers** are available on campus that provide access to online course support, wireless campus and the Internet. The 2 **libraries** have 763,000 books and 3,100 subscriptions.

Campus Life

There are 128 active organizations on campus, including a drama/theater group, newspaper, radio station, television station, and choral group. 14% of eligible men and 16% of eligible women are members of national **fraternities** and national **sororities**.

AU is a member of the NCAA (Division I). **Intercollegiate sports** (some offering scholarships) include basketball, cross-country running, field hockey (w), golf (m), lacrosse (w), soccer, swimming, tennis, track and field, volleyball (w), wrestling (m).

Campus Safety

Student safety services include late-night transport/escort service, 24-hour emergency telephone alarm devices, 24-hour patrols by trained security personnel, and electronically operated dormitory entrances.

Applying

AU requires an essay, SAT I or ACT, a high school transcript, 2 recommendations, and a minimum high school GPA of 2.0, and in some cases TOEFL for all whose first language is not English, regardless of citizenship.. It recommends SAT II Subject Tests, SAT II: Writing Test, an interview, and a minimum high school GPA of 3.0. Application deadline: 2/1; 3/1 for financial aid. Early and deferred admission are possible.

American University attracts academically distinctive and intensely engaged students who want to understand how the world works. American's diverse campus community; location in Washington, D.C.; Honors Program study-abroad options; and emphasis on turning ideas into action and action into service prepare students to be major contributors in their fields.

Getting in Last Year
10,282 applied
59% were accepted
1,238 enrolled (20%)
36% from top tenth of their h.s. class
3.42 average high school GPA
64% had SAT verbal scores over 600
54% had SAT math scores over 600
85% had ACT scores over 24
17% had SAT verbal scores over 700
10% had SAT math scores over 700
23% had ACT scores over 30
13 National Merit Scholars
13 valedictorians

Graduation and After
65% graduated in 4 years
6% graduated in 5 years
1% graduated in 6 years
85% had job offers within 6 months
200 organizations recruited on campus

Financial Matters
$24,839 tuition and fees (2003–04)
$9746 room and board
79% average percent of need met
$24,370 average financial aid amount received
  per undergraduate

AMHERST COLLEGE
SMALL-TOWN SETTING ■ PRIVATE ■ INDEPENDENT ■ COED
AMHERST, MASSACHUSETTS

Web site: www.amherst.edu
Contact: Mr. Thomas Parker, Dean of Admission and Financial Aid, PO Box 5000, Amherst, MA 01002
Telephone: 413-542-2328 **Fax:** 413-542-2040
E-mail: admission@amherst.edu

Amherst seeks talented students who have demonstrated their passion for learning along with a willingness to be involved in the world around them. With its dynamic, dedicated faculty, Amherst is a lively intellectual and cultural community in which students are active members; small classes and a wide variety of extracurricular offerings provide many opportunities for exploration. An open curriculum, with majors ranging from neuroscience to law, jurisprudence, and social thought, allows students substantial freedom to pursue their goals.

Getting in Last Year
5,631 applied
18% were accepted
413 enrolled (41%)
86% from top tenth of their h.s. class
93% had SAT verbal scores over 600
93% had SAT math scores over 600
99% had ACT scores over 24
64% had SAT verbal scores over 700
65% had SAT math scores over 700
71% had ACT scores over 30
84 National Merit Scholars
34 valedictorians

Graduation and After
89% graduated in 4 years
6% graduated in 5 years
1% graduated in 6 years
30% pursued further study
60% had job offers within 6 months
54 organizations recruited on campus

Financial Matters
$29,730 tuition and fees (2003–04)
$7740 room and board
100% average percent of need met
$26,080 average financial aid amount received per undergraduate (2002–03 estimated)

Academics
Amherst College awards bachelor's **degrees**. Challenging opportunities include student-designed majors, an honors program, double majors, independent study, and a senior project. Special programs include off-campus study and study-abroad.

The most frequently chosen **baccalaureate** fields are social sciences and history, English, and foreign language/literature. A complete listing of majors at Amherst College appears in the Majors Index beginning on page 460.

The **faculty** at Amherst College has 182 full-time members, 93% with terminal degrees. The student-faculty ratio is 8:1.

Students of Amherst College
The student body is made up of 1,623 undergraduates. 48.6% are women and 51.4% are men. Students come from 50 states and territories and 31 other countries. 15% are from Massachusetts. 5.9% are international students. 10.3% are African American, 0.2% American Indian, 12.4% Asian American, and 7.5% Hispanic American. 96% returned for their sophomore year.

Facilities and Resources
Student rooms are linked to a campus network. 182 **computers** are available on campus that provide access to the Internet. The 6 **libraries** have 977,379 books and 5,348 subscriptions.

Campus Life
There are 100 active organizations on campus, including a drama/theater group, newspaper, radio station, and choral group. No national or local **fraternities** or **sororities**.

Amherst College is a member of the NCAA (Division III). **Intercollegiate sports** include baseball (m), basketball, cross-country running, field hockey (w), football (m), golf, ice hockey, lacrosse, soccer, softball (w), squash, swimming, tennis, track and field, volleyball (w).

Campus Safety
Student safety services include late-night transport/escort service, 24-hour emergency telephone alarm devices, 24-hour patrols by trained security personnel, student patrols, and electronically operated dormitory entrances.

Applying
Amherst College requires an essay, SAT I and SAT II or ACT, a high school transcript, and 3 recommendations. Application deadline: 12/31; 2/15 priority date for financial aid. Early and deferred admission are possible.

ASBURY COLLEGE

SMALL-TOWN SETTING ■ PRIVATE ■ INDEPENDENT RELIGIOUS ■ COED
WILMORE, KENTUCKY

Web site: www.asbury.edu

Contact: Mr. Stan F. Wiggam, Dean of Admissions, 1 Macklem Drive,
   Wilmore, KY 40390

Telephone: 859-858-3511 ext. 2142 or toll-free 800-888-1818 **Fax:**
   859-858-3921

E-mail: admissions@asbury.edu

Academics

Asbury College awards bachelor's and master's **degrees**. Challenging opportunities
include advanced placement credit, double majors, independent study, and a senior
project. Special programs include internships, summer session for credit, study-abroad,
and Army and Air Force ROTC.

The most frequently chosen **baccalaureate** fields are communications/communica-
tion technologies, education, and English. A complete listing of majors at Asbury College appears in the Majors Index beginning on page 460.

The **faculty** at Asbury College has 90 full-time members, 78% with terminal
degrees. The student-faculty ratio is 11:1.

Students of Asbury College

The student body totals 1,258, of whom 1,191 are undergraduates. 58.2% are women
and 41.8% are men. Students come from 43 states and territories and 10 other countries.
30% are from Kentucky. 1% are international students. 0.9% are African American,
0.3% American Indian, 0.9% Asian American, and 1% Hispanic American. 83%
returned for their sophomore year.

Facilities and Resources

Student rooms are linked to a campus network. 183 **computers** are available on campus
that provide access to the Internet. The **library** has 155,320 books and 14,550 subscriptions.

Campus Life

There are 35 active organizations on campus, including a drama/theater group,
newspaper, radio station, television station, and choral group. No national or local
fraternities or **sororities**.

Asbury College is a member of the NAIA and NCCAA. **Intercollegiate sports**
include basketball, cross-country running, soccer, softball (w), swimming, tennis, track
and field, volleyball (w).

Campus Safety

Student safety services include late night security personnel, late-night transport/escort
service, 24-hour emergency telephone alarm devices, and electronically operated dormitory entrances.

Applying

Asbury College requires an essay, SAT I or ACT, a high school transcript, 3 recom-
mendations, and a minimum high school GPA of 2.5, and in some cases an interview.
Application deadline: rolling admissions; 7/30 for financial aid, with a 3/1 priority date.
Early and deferred admission are possible.

Getting in Last Year

820 applied
73% were accepted
258 enrolled (43%)
30% from top tenth of their h.s. class
3.55 average high school GPA
44% had SAT verbal scores over 600
34% had SAT math scores over 600
13% had SAT verbal scores over 700
6% had SAT math scores over 700
4 National Merit Scholars

Graduation and After

49% graduated in 4 years
13% graduated in 5 years
1% graduated in 6 years
57 organizations recruited on campus

Financial Matters

$16,500 tuition and fees (2003–04)
$4204 room and board
78% average percent of need met
$12,170 average financial aid amount received
   per undergraduate

AUBURN UNIVERSITY

SMALL-TOWN SETTING ■ PUBLIC ■ STATE-SUPPORTED ■ COED
AUBURN UNIVERSITY, ALABAMA

Web site: www.auburn.edu
Contact: Doyle Bickers, Director, Admissions and Records, 202 Mary Martin Hall, Auburn University, AL 36849-5145
Telephone: 334-844-6444 or toll-free 800-AUBURN9 (in-state)
E-mail: admissions@auburn.edu

Getting in Last Year
12,439 applied
78% were accepted
3,706 enrolled (38%)
31% from top tenth of their h.s. class
3.51 average high school GPA
27% had SAT verbal scores over 600
37% had SAT math scores over 600
56% had ACT scores over 24
5% had SAT verbal scores over 700
7% had SAT math scores over 700
10% had ACT scores over 30
31 National Merit Scholars

Graduation and After
37% graduated in 4 years
24% graduated in 5 years
6% graduated in 6 years
35% pursued further study (9% business, 6% medicine, 5% arts and sciences)
75% had job offers within 6 months
75 organizations recruited on campus

Financial Matters
$4426 resident tuition and fees (2003–04)
$12,886 nonresident tuition and fees (2003–04)
$5970 room and board
53% average percent of need met
$6551 average financial aid amount received per undergraduate (2002–03)

Academics
Auburn awards bachelor's, master's, doctoral, and first-professional **degrees** and post-master's certificates. Challenging opportunities include advanced placement credit, accelerated degree programs, an honors program, double majors, independent study, and a senior project. Special programs include cooperative education, internships, summer session for credit, study-abroad, and Army, Navy and Air Force ROTC.

The most frequently chosen **baccalaureate** fields are business/marketing, engineering/engineering technologies, and education. A complete listing of majors at Auburn appears in the Majors Index beginning on page 460.

The **faculty** at Auburn has 1,171 full-time members, 93% with terminal degrees. The student-faculty ratio is 16:1.

Students of Auburn
The student body totals 23,152, of whom 19,251 are undergraduates. 48.3% are women and 51.7% are men. Students come from 54 states and territories and 65 other countries. 52% are from Alabama. 0.8% are international students. 7.1% are African American, 0.5% American Indian, 1.5% Asian American, and 1.2% Hispanic American. 84% returned for their sophomore year.

Facilities and Resources
Student rooms are linked to a campus network. 600 **computers** are available on campus for student use. The 3 **libraries** have 2,591,255 books and 23,121 subscriptions.

Campus Life
There are 300 active organizations on campus, including a drama/theater group, newspaper, radio station, television station, choral group, and marching band. 18% of eligible men and 34% of eligible women are members of national **fraternities** and national **sororities**.

Auburn is a member of the NCAA (Division I). **Intercollegiate sports** (some offering scholarships) include baseball (m), basketball, cross-country running, equestrian sports (w), football (m), golf, gymnastics (w), soccer (w), softball (w), swimming, tennis, track and field, volleyball (w).

Campus Safety
Student safety services include late-night transport/escort service, 24-hour emergency telephone alarm devices, 24-hour patrols by trained security personnel, and electronically operated dormitory entrances.

Applying
Auburn requires SAT I or ACT, a high school transcript, and a minimum high school GPA of 2.0, and in some cases a minimum high school GPA of 3.0. Application deadline: 8/1; 3/1 priority date for financial aid. Early and deferred admission are possible.

AUGUSTANA COLLEGE

SUBURBAN SETTING ■ PRIVATE ■ INDEPENDENT RELIGIOUS ■ COED
ROCK ISLAND, ILLINOIS

Web site: www.augustana.edu
Contact: Mr. Martin Sauer, Director of Admissions, 639 38th Street, Rock Island, IL 61201-2296
Telephone: 309-794-7341 or toll-free 800-798-8100 **Fax:** 309-794-7422
E-mail: admissions@augustana.edu

Academics

Augie awards bachelor's **degrees**. Challenging opportunities include advanced placement credit, accelerated degree programs, an honors program, double majors, independent study, and a senior project. Special programs include internships, summer session for credit, and study-abroad.

The most frequently chosen **baccalaureate** fields are business/marketing, biological/life sciences, and social sciences and history. A complete listing of majors at Augie appears in the Majors Index beginning on page 460.

The **faculty** at Augie has 145 full-time members, 93% with terminal degrees. The student-faculty ratio is 12:1.

Students of Augie

The student body is made up of 2,309 undergraduates. 57.9% are women and 42.1% are men. Students come from 26 states and territories and 19 other countries. 87% are from Illinois. 0.9% are international students. 2.1% are African American, 0.3% American Indian, 1.9% Asian American, and 2.6% Hispanic American. 85% returned for their sophomore year.

Facilities and Resources

Student rooms are linked to a campus network. 600 **computers** are available on campus that provide access to the Internet. The 4 **libraries** have 190,641 books and 1,705 subscriptions.

Campus Life

There are 109 active organizations on campus, including a drama/theater group, newspaper, radio station, and choral group. 36% of eligible men and 40% of eligible women are members of local **fraternities** and local **sororities**.

Augie is a member of the NCAA (Division III). **Intercollegiate sports** include baseball (m), basketball, cross-country running, football (m), golf, soccer, softball (w), swimming, tennis, track and field, volleyball (w), wrestling (m).

Campus Safety

Student safety services include late-night transport/escort service, 24-hour emergency telephone alarm devices, 24-hour patrols by trained security personnel, and electronically operated dormitory entrances.

Applying

Augie requires SAT I or ACT and a high school transcript, and in some cases an essay, an interview, and 2 recommendations. Application deadline: rolling admissions; 4/1 priority date for financial aid. Deferred admission is possible.

Augustana College seeks to develop in students the characteristics of liberally educated persons: clarity of thought and expression, curiosity, fair-mindedness, appreciation for the arts and cultural diversity, intellectual honesty, and a considered set of personal values and commitments. Students combine exploration of the arts, sciences, and humanities with in-depth study in their major field(s), guided by an excellent, committed faculty; they grow personally and socially through participation in wide extracurricular and cocurricular opportunities on one of the most beautiful campuses in the country. Special features include innovative interdisciplinary first-year honors programs, foreign study, and internships—both domestic and international.

Getting in Last Year
3,021 applied
90% were accepted
614 enrolled (23%)
35% from top tenth of their h.s. class
3.53 average high school GPA
72% had ACT scores over 24
17% had ACT scores over 30

Graduation and After
71% graduated in 4 years
5% graduated in 5 years
1% graduated in 6 years
42% pursued further study (22% arts and sciences, 7% business, 4% medicine)
67% had job offers within 6 months
189 organizations recruited on campus

Financial Matters
$20,829 tuition and fees (2003–04)
$5781 room and board
86% average percent of need met
$15,207 average financial aid amount received per undergraduate

Augustana College

URBAN SETTING ■ PRIVATE ■ INDEPENDENT RELIGIOUS ■ COED
SIOUX FALLS, SOUTH DAKOTA

Web site: www.augie.edu
Contact: Mr. Robert Preloger, Vice President for Enrollment, 2001 South
    Summit Avenue, Sioux Falls, SD 57197
Telephone: 605-274-5516 ext. 5504 or toll-free 800-727-2844 ext. 5516
    (in-state), 800-727-2844 (out-of-state) **Fax:** 605-274-5518
E-mail: info@augie.edu

Getting in Last Year
1,692 applied
79% were accepted
438 enrolled (33%)
33% from top tenth of their h.s. class
3.60 average high school GPA
57% had SAT verbal scores over 600
46% had SAT math scores over 600
70% had ACT scores over 24
19% had SAT verbal scores over 700
15% had SAT math scores over 700
18% had ACT scores over 30
1 National Merit Scholar
32 valedictorians

Graduation and After
51% graduated in 4 years
18% graduated in 5 years
2% graduated in 6 years
23% pursued further study (12% arts and
    sciences, 3% law, 3% medicine)
94% had job offers within 6 months
60 organizations recruited on campus

Financial Matters
$16,972 tuition and fees (2003–04)
$5026 room and board
91% average percent of need met
$13,811 average financial aid amount received
    per undergraduate (2002–03 estimated)

Academics

Augustana awards bachelor's and master's **degrees**. Challenging opportunities include advanced placement credit, accelerated degree programs, student-designed majors, an honors program, double majors, independent study, and a senior project. Special programs include cooperative education, internships, summer session for credit, off-campus study, and study-abroad.

The most frequently chosen **baccalaureate** fields are business/marketing, education, and health professions and related sciences. A complete listing of majors at Augustana appears in the Majors Index beginning on page 460.

The **faculty** at Augustana has 106 full-time members, 82% with terminal degrees. The student-faculty ratio is 13:1.

Students of Augustana

The student body totals 1,848, of whom 1,810 are undergraduates. 63.5% are women and 36.5% are men. Students come from 35 states and territories and 12 other countries. 45% are from South Dakota. 2.1% are international students. 0.8% are African American, 0.3% American Indian, 0.7% Asian American, and 0.5% Hispanic American. 76% returned for their sophomore year.

Facilities and Resources

Student rooms are linked to a campus network. 360 **computers** are available on campus that provide access to the Internet. The 2 **libraries** have 268,645 books and 1,418 subscriptions.

Campus Life

There are 54 active organizations on campus, including a drama/theater group, newspaper, radio station, and choral group. No national or local **fraternities** or **sororities**.

Augustana is a member of the NCAA (Division II). **Intercollegiate sports** (some offering scholarships) include baseball (m), basketball, cheerleading (w), cross-country running, football (m), golf, soccer (w), softball (w), tennis, track and field, volleyball (w), wrestling (m).

Campus Safety

Student safety services include late-night transport/escort service, 24-hour emergency telephone alarm devices, 24-hour patrols by trained security personnel, and electronically operated dormitory entrances.

Applying

Augustana requires SAT I or ACT, a high school transcript, 1 recommendation, minimum ACT score of 20, and a minimum high school GPA of 2.5, and in some cases an essay. It recommends an interview. Application deadline: 8/1; 3/1 priority date for financial aid. Deferred admission is possible.

AUSTIN COLLEGE

SUBURBAN SETTING ■ PRIVATE ■ INDEPENDENT RELIGIOUS ■ COED
SHERMAN, TEXAS

Web site: www.austincollege.edu
Contact: Ms. Nan Davis, Vice President for Institutional Enrollment, 900
North Grand Avenue, Suite 6N, Sherman, TX 75090-4400
Telephone: 903-813-3000 or toll-free 800-442-5363 **Fax:** 903-813-3198
E-mail: admission@austincollege.edu

Academics

AC awards bachelor's and master's **degrees**. Challenging opportunities include advanced placement credit, student-designed majors, an honors program, double majors, independent study, and a senior project. Special programs include internships, summer session for credit, off-campus study, and study-abroad.

The most frequently chosen **baccalaureate** fields are social sciences and history, business/marketing, and biological/life sciences. A complete listing of majors at AC appears in the Majors Index beginning on page 460.

The **faculty** at AC has 92 full-time members, 99% with terminal degrees. The student-faculty ratio is 13:1.

Students of AC

The student body totals 1,332, of whom 1,294 are undergraduates. 56.2% are women and 43.8% are men. Students come from 30 states and territories and 25 other countries. 90% are from Texas. 2% are international students. 3.8% are African American, 1.1% American Indian, 10% Asian American, and 7% Hispanic American. 86% returned for their sophomore year.

Facilities and Resources

Student rooms are linked to a campus network. 165 **computers** are available on campus that provide access to the Internet. The **library** has 195,328 books and 1,008 subscriptions.

Campus Life

There are 50 active organizations on campus, including a drama/theater group, newspaper, and choral group. 21% of eligible men and 19% of eligible women are members of local **fraternities** and local **sororities**.

AC is a member of the NCAA (Division III). **Intercollegiate sports** include baseball (m), basketball, cheerleading, cross-country running, football (m), golf (m), soccer, swimming, tennis, volleyball (w).

Campus Safety

Student safety services include late-night transport/escort service, 24-hour emergency telephone alarm devices, 24-hour patrols by trained security personnel, and electronically operated dormitory entrances.

Applying

AC requires an essay, SAT I or ACT, a high school transcript, and 2 recommendations, and in some cases an interview. It recommends an interview and a minimum high school GPA of 3.0. Application deadline: 8/15; 4/1 priority date for financial aid. Early and deferred admission are possible.

Getting in Last Year

1,328 applied
72% were accepted
338 enrolled (35%)
45% from top tenth of their h.s. class
3.39 average high school GPA
62% had SAT verbal scores over 600
63% had SAT math scores over 600
69% had ACT scores over 24
15% had SAT verbal scores over 700
10% had SAT math scores over 700
14% had ACT scores over 30
4 National Merit Scholars
11 valedictorians

Graduation and After

68% graduated in 4 years
6% graduated in 5 years
1% graduated in 6 years
32% pursued further study (10% education, 6% arts and sciences, 6% medicine)
45% had job offers within 6 months
18 organizations recruited on campus

Financial Matters

$17,925 tuition and fees (2003–04)
$6822 room and board
96% average percent of need met
$17,454 average financial aid amount received per undergraduate

AZUSA PACIFIC UNIVERSITY

SMALL-TOWN SETTING ■ PRIVATE ■ INDEPENDENT RELIGIOUS ■ COED
AZUSA, CALIFORNIA

Web site: online.apu.edu
Contact: Mrs. Deana Porterfield, Dean of Enrollment, 901 East Alosta
Avenue, PO Box 7000, Azusa, CA 91702-7000
Telephone: 626-812-3016 or toll-free 800-TALK-APU
E-mail: admissions@apu.edu

Getting in Last Year

2,472 applied
83% were accepted
912 enrolled (45%)
29% from top tenth of their h.s. class
3.62 average high school GPA
24% had SAT verbal scores over 600
28% had SAT math scores over 600
44% had ACT scores over 24
3% had SAT verbal scores over 700
3% had SAT math scores over 700
8% had ACT scores over 30

Graduation and After

42% graduated in 4 years
11% graduated in 5 years
2% graduated in 6 years
23 organizations recruited on campus

Financial Matters

$19,024 tuition and fees (2003–04)
$5696 room and board
74% average percent of need met
$8008 average financial aid amount received
per undergraduate (2001–02)

Academics

APU awards bachelor's, master's, doctoral, and first-professional **degrees**. Challenging opportunities include advanced placement credit, accelerated degree programs, freshman honors college, an honors program, double majors, and a senior project. Special programs include cooperative education, internships, summer session for credit, off-campus study, study-abroad, and Army ROTC.

The most frequently chosen **baccalaureate** fields are business/marketing, health professions and related sciences, and liberal arts/general studies. A complete listing of majors at APU appears in the Majors Index beginning on page 460.

The **faculty** at APU has 268 full-time members, 73% with terminal degrees. The student-faculty ratio is 12:1.

Students of APU

The student body totals 8,191, of whom 4,373 are undergraduates. 64.5% are women and 35.5% are men. Students come from 44 states and territories and 52 other countries. 81% are from California. 1.9% are international students. 3.5% are African American, 0.3% American Indian, 5.7% Asian American, and 12.2% Hispanic American. 83% returned for their sophomore year.

Facilities and Resources

300 **computers** are available on campus that provide access to the Internet. The 3 **libraries** have 176,679 books and 14,000 subscriptions.

Campus Life

There are 32 active organizations on campus, including a drama/theater group, newspaper, choral group, and marching band. No national or local **fraternities** or **sororities**.

APU is a member of the NAIA. **Intercollegiate sports** (some offering scholarships) include baseball (m), basketball, cross-country running, football (m), golf (m), soccer, softball (w), tennis (m), track and field, volleyball.

Campus Safety

Student safety services include late-night transport/escort service, 24-hour emergency telephone alarm devices, 24-hour patrols by trained security personnel, student patrols, and electronically operated dormitory entrances.

Applying

APU requires an essay, SAT I or ACT, a high school transcript, 2 recommendations, and a minimum high school GPA of 2.5, and in some cases an interview. Application deadline: 6/1; 7/1 for financial aid, with a 3/2 priority date. Early and deferred admission are possible.

BAKER UNIVERSITY

SMALL-TOWN SETTING ■ PRIVATE ■ INDEPENDENT RELIGIOUS ■ COED
BALDWIN CITY, KANSAS

Web site: www.bakeru.edu
Contact: Ms. Annette Galluzzi, Vice President for Marketing, PO Box 65,
Baldwin City, KS 66006-0065
Telephone: 785-594-6451 ext. 344 or toll-free 800-873-4282 **Fax:**
785-594-8372
E-mail: admission@bakeru.edu

Academics

Baker awards bachelor's and master's **degrees**. Challenging opportunities include
advanced placement credit, student-designed majors, an honors program, double majors,
independent study, and a senior project. Special programs include internships, summer
session for credit, study-abroad, and Army and Air Force ROTC.

The most frequently chosen **baccalaureate** fields are business/marketing, health
professions and related sciences, and education. A complete listing of majors at Baker
appears in the Majors Index beginning on page 460.

The **faculty** at Baker has 63 full-time members, 76% with terminal degrees. The
student-faculty ratio is 12:1.

Students of Baker

The student body is made up of 1,015 undergraduates. 56.9% are women and 43.1% are
men. Students come from 21 states and territories and 7 other countries. 73% are from
Kansas. 0.7% are international students. 4.8% are African American, 1% American
Indian, 0.7% Asian American, and 2% Hispanic American. 74% returned for their
sophomore year.

Facilities and Resources

Student rooms are linked to a campus network. 129 **computers** are available on campus
that provide access to the Internet. The **library** has 84,114 books and 507 subscriptions.

Campus Life

There are 75 active organizations on campus, including a drama/theater group,
newspaper, radio station, and choral group. 50% of eligible men and 52% of eligible
women are members of national **fraternities**, national **sororities**, and local fraternities.

Baker is a member of the NAIA. **Intercollegiate sports** (some offering scholarships)
include baseball (m), basketball, cheerleading, cross-country running, football (m), golf,
soccer, softball (w), tennis, track and field, volleyball (w).

Campus Safety

Student safety services include 24-hour emergency telephone alarm devices, 24-hour
patrols by trained security personnel, student patrols, and electronically operated dormitory entrances.

Applying

Baker requires SAT I or ACT, a high school transcript, and 1 recommendation, and in
some cases an essay and an interview. It recommends minimum ACT score of 21 and a
minimum high school GPA of 3.0. Application deadline: rolling admissions; 3/1 priority
date for financial aid. Deferred admission is possible.

Getting in Last Year

945 applied
82% were accepted
226 enrolled (29%)
3.45 average high school GPA
19% had SAT verbal scores over 600
20% had SAT math scores over 600
48% had ACT scores over 24
2% had SAT verbal scores over 700
8% had ACT scores over 30

Graduation and After

40% graduated in 4 years
15% graduated in 5 years
2% graduated in 6 years
68% had job offers within 6 months
63 organizations recruited on campus

Financial Matters

$14,560 tuition and fees (2003–04)
$5300 room and board
$10,900 average financial aid amount received
per undergraduate (2002–03 estimated)

BALDWIN-WALLACE COLLEGE

SUBURBAN SETTING ■ PRIVATE ■ INDEPENDENT RELIGIOUS ■ COED
BEREA, OHIO

Web site: www.bw.edu
Contact: Ms. Grace B. Chalker, Interim Associate Director of Admissions, 275 Eastland Road, Berea, OH 44017-2088
Telephone: 440-826-2222 or toll-free 877-BWAPPLY (in-state) **Fax:** 440-826-3830
E-mail: admission@bw.edu

Getting in Last Year
2,211 applied
82% were accepted
702 enrolled (39%)
27% from top tenth of their h.s. class
3.52 average high school GPA
33% had SAT verbal scores over 600
31% had SAT math scores over 600
47% had ACT scores over 24
5% had SAT verbal scores over 700
6% had SAT math scores over 700
8% had ACT scores over 30
23 valedictorians

Graduation and After
48% graduated in 4 years
18% graduated in 5 years
33% pursued further study (26% arts and sciences, 5% law, 2% medicine)
85% had job offers within 6 months
65 organizations recruited on campus

Financial Matters
$18,478 tuition and fees (2003–04)
$5402 room and board
85% average percent of need met
$14,893 average financial aid amount received per undergraduate (2002–03 estimated)

Academics

B-W awards bachelor's and master's **degrees**. Challenging opportunities include advanced placement credit, accelerated degree programs, student-designed majors, an honors program, double majors, independent study, and a senior project. Special programs include internships, summer session for credit, off-campus study, study-abroad, and Army and Air Force ROTC.

The most frequently chosen **baccalaureate** fields are business/marketing, education, and social sciences and history. A complete listing of majors at B-W appears in the Majors Index beginning on page 460.

The **faculty** at B-W has 165 full-time members, 76% with terminal degrees. The student-faculty ratio is 14:1.

Students of B-W

The student body totals 4,692, of whom 3,862 are undergraduates. 60.7% are women and 39.3% are men. Students come from 30 states and territories and 14 other countries. 91% are from Ohio. 1.4% are international students. 4.4% are African American, 0.3% American Indian, 1.3% Asian American, and 1.4% Hispanic American. 85% returned for their sophomore year.

Facilities and Resources

Student rooms are linked to a campus network. 450 **computers** are available on campus that provide access to the Internet. The 3 **libraries** have 200,000 books and 883 subscriptions.

Campus Life

There are 100 active organizations on campus, including a drama/theater group, newspaper, radio station, and choral group. 18% of eligible men and 22% of eligible women are members of national **fraternities** and national **sororities**.

B-W is a member of the NCAA (Division III). **Intercollegiate sports** include baseball (m), basketball, cross-country running, football (m), golf, soccer, softball (w), swimming, tennis, track and field, volleyball (w), wrestling (m).

Campus Safety

Student safety services include late-night transport/escort service, 24-hour emergency telephone alarm devices, 24-hour patrols by trained security personnel, student patrols, and electronically operated dormitory entrances.

Applying

B-W requires an essay, SAT I or ACT, a high school transcript, 1 recommendation, and a minimum high school GPA of 2.6. It recommends an interview and a minimum high school GPA of 3.2. Application deadline: rolling admissions; 9/1 for financial aid, with a 5/1 priority date. Deferred admission is possible.

BARD COLLEGE
RURAL SETTING ■ PRIVATE ■ INDEPENDENT ■ COED
ANNANDALE-ON-HUDSON, NEW YORK

Web site: www.bard.edu
Contact: Ms. Mary Inga Backlund, Director of Admissions, PO Box 5000, 51 Ravine Road, Annandale-on-Hudson, NY 12504-5000
Telephone: 845-758-7472 **Fax:** 845-758-5208
E-mail: admission@bard.edu

Academics
Bard awards associate, bachelor's, master's, and doctoral **degrees**. Challenging opportunities include advanced placement credit, accelerated degree programs, student-designed majors, double majors, independent study, and a senior project. Special programs include internships, off-campus study, and study-abroad.

The most frequently chosen **baccalaureate** fields are visual/performing arts, social sciences and history, and English. A complete listing of majors at Bard appears in the Majors Index beginning on page 460.

The **faculty** at Bard has 123 full-time members, 100% with terminal degrees. The student-faculty ratio is 9:1.

Students of Bard
The student body totals 1,605, of whom 1,382 are undergraduates. 57.8% are women and 42.2% are men. Students come from 50 states and territories and 43 other countries. 30% are from New York. 6.3% are international students. 3% are African American, 0.5% American Indian, 4.8% Asian American, and 5% Hispanic American. 86% returned for their sophomore year.

Facilities and Resources
Student rooms are linked to a campus network. 400 **computers** are available on campus that provide access to the Internet. The 4 **libraries** have 275,000 books and 1,400 subscriptions.

Campus Life
There are 70 active organizations on campus, including a drama/theater group, newspaper, radio station, and choral group. No national or local **fraternities** or **sororities**.

Bard is a member of the NCAA (Division III) and NAIA. **Intercollegiate sports** include basketball, cross-country running, rugby (m), soccer, squash, tennis, volleyball.

Campus Safety
Student safety services include late-night transport/escort service, 24-hour emergency telephone alarm devices, 24-hour patrols by trained security personnel, student patrols, and electronically operated dormitory entrances.

Applying
Bard requires an essay, a high school transcript, and 3 recommendations, and in some cases an interview. It recommends SAT II Subject Tests, SAT I or ACT, an interview, and a minimum high school GPA of 3.0. Application deadline: 1/15; 3/15 for financial aid, with a 2/15 priority date. Early and deferred admission are possible.

Getting in Last Year
3,367 applied
39% were accepted
382 enrolled (29%)
61% from top tenth of their h.s. class
3.5 average high school GPA
88% had SAT verbal scores over 600
68% had SAT math scores over 600
31% had SAT verbal scores over 700
15% had SAT math scores over 700

Graduation and After
55% graduated in 4 years
11% graduated in 5 years
2% graduated in 6 years
55% pursued further study (43% arts and sciences, 5% law, 3% business)
60% had job offers within 6 months

Financial Matters
$29,038 tuition and fees (2003–04)
$8544 room and board
87% average percent of need met
$21,466 average financial aid amount received per undergraduate (2002–03 estimated)

Barnard College

URBAN SETTING ■ PRIVATE ■ INDEPENDENT ■ WOMEN ONLY
NEW YORK, NEW YORK

Web site: www.barnard.edu
Contact: Ms. Jennifer Gill Fondiller, Dean of Admissions, 3009 Broadway, New York, NY 10027
Telephone: 212-854-2014 **Fax:** 212-854-6220
E-mail: admissions@barnard.edu

Barnard is a small, selective liberal arts college for women, located in New York City. Its superb faculty, more than 60% of whom are women, is made up of leading scholars who serve as dedicated, accessible teachers. Barnard's unique affiliation with Columbia University, situated just across the street, gives students a vast selection of additional course offerings and extracurricular activities, NCAA Division I Ivy League athletic competition, and a fully coeducational social life. Its metropolitan location means that students have access to thousands of internships and excellent cultural, intellectual, and social resources.

Getting in Last Year
4,034 applied
31% were accepted
554 enrolled (44%)
82% from top tenth of their h.s. class
3.86 average high school GPA
91% had SAT verbal scores over 600
89% had SAT math scores over 600
95% had ACT scores over 24
47% had SAT verbal scores over 700
29% had SAT math scores over 700
47% had ACT scores over 30
21 National Merit Scholars

Graduation and After
75% graduated in 4 years
9% graduated in 5 years
24% pursued further study (6% arts and sciences, 6% law, 4% education)
68% had job offers within 6 months
41 organizations recruited on campus

Financial Matters
$26,528 tuition and fees (2003–04)
$10,462 room and board
100% average percent of need met
$24,416 average financial aid amount received per undergraduate (2002–03 estimated)

Academics
Barnard awards bachelor's **degrees**. Challenging opportunities include advanced placement credit, accelerated degree programs, student-designed majors, an honors program, double majors, independent study, and a senior project. Special programs include internships, off-campus study, and study-abroad.

The most frequently chosen **baccalaureate** fields are social sciences and history, psychology, and English. A complete listing of majors at Barnard appears in the Majors Index beginning on page 460.

The **faculty** at Barnard has 186 full-time members, 94% with terminal degrees. The student-faculty ratio is 10:1.

Students of Barnard
The student body is made up of 2,281 undergraduates. Students come from 50 states and territories and 35 other countries. 36% are from New York. 3% are international students. 5% are African American, 0.7% American Indian, 18.7% Asian American, and 6.4% Hispanic American. 93% returned for their sophomore year.

Facilities and Resources
Student rooms are linked to a campus network. 150 **computers** are available on campus that provide access to the Internet. The **library** has 201,566 books and 544 subscriptions.

Campus Life
There are 100 active organizations on campus, including a drama/theater group, newspaper, radio station, television station, choral group, and marching band. No national or local **sororities**.

Barnard is a member of the NCAA (Division I). **Intercollegiate sports** include archery, basketball, crew, cross-country running, fencing, field hockey, golf, lacrosse, soccer, softball, swimming, tennis, track and field, volleyball.

Campus Safety
Student safety services include 4 permanent security posts, late-night transport/escort service, 24-hour emergency telephone alarm devices, and 24-hour patrols by trained security personnel.

Applying
Barnard requires an essay, SAT I and SAT II or ACT, a high school transcript, and 3 recommendations. It recommends an interview. Application deadline: 1/1; 2/1 for financial aid. Early and deferred admission are possible.

BATES COLLEGE

SMALL-TOWN SETTING ■ PRIVATE ■ INDEPENDENT ■ COED
LEWISTON, MAINE

Web site: www.bates.edu
Contact: Mr. Wylie L. Mitchell, Dean of Admissions, 23 Campus Avenue,
Lewiston, ME 04240-6028
Telephone: 207-786-6000 **Fax:** 207-786-6025
E-mail: admissions@bates.edu

Academics

Bates awards bachelor's **degrees**. Challenging opportunities include advanced placement credit, accelerated degree programs, student-designed majors, an honors program, double majors, independent study, and a senior project. Special programs include internships, off-campus study, and study-abroad.

The most frequently chosen **baccalaureate** fields are social sciences and history, biological/life sciences, and English. A complete listing of majors at Bates appears in the Majors Index beginning on page 460.

The **faculty** at Bates has 163 full-time members, 96% with terminal degrees. The student-faculty ratio is 10:1.

Students of Bates

The student body is made up of 1,746 undergraduates. 52.1% are women and 47.9% are men. Students come from 44 states and territories and 68 other countries. 12% are from Maine. 5.8% are international students. 2.2% are African American, 0.3% American Indian, 3.4% Asian American, and 1.9% Hispanic American. 93% returned for their sophomore year.

Facilities and Resources

Student rooms are linked to a campus network. 1,150 **computers** are available on campus that provide access to course web pages, course evaluation, financial records and the Internet. The **library** has 568,750 books and 2,311 subscriptions.

Campus Life

There are 91 active organizations on campus, including a drama/theater group, newspaper, radio station, television station, and choral group. No national or local **fraternities** or **sororities**.

Bates is a member of the NCAA (Division III). **Intercollegiate sports** include baseball (m), basketball, crew, cross-country running, field hockey (w), football (m), golf, lacrosse, skiing (cross-country), skiing (downhill), soccer, softball (w), squash, swimming, tennis, track and field, volleyball (w).

Campus Safety

Student safety services include late-night transport/escort service, 24-hour emergency telephone alarm devices, 24-hour patrols by trained security personnel, student patrols, and electronically operated dormitory entrances.

Applying

Bates requires an essay, a high school transcript, and 3 recommendations. It recommends an interview. Application deadline: 1/15; 2/1 for financial aid. Early and deferred admission are possible.

Getting in Last Year

4,089 applied
31% were accepted
487 enrolled (39%)
65% from top tenth of their h.s. class
92% had SAT verbal scores over 600
93% had SAT math scores over 600
29% had SAT verbal scores over 700
34% had SAT math scores over 700

Graduation and After

84% graduated in 4 years
5% graduated in 5 years

Financial Matters

$37,500 comprehensive fee (2003–04)
100% average percent of need met
$24,457 average financial aid amount received
    per undergraduate

As a selective Baptist university, Baylor is committed to educating the whole student—mind, body, and spirit. Each student enjoys the individual attention of a dedicated faculty, the options afforded by a comprehensive range of challenging academic programs, and a supportive environment that fosters intellectual, social, and spiritual growth. Baylor's strong core curriculum, based on the liberal arts, crosses all majors and emphasizes analytical skills and ethical practices. With competitive financial assistance packages, Baylor strives to help families from all financial backgrounds achieve their dreams of the best education possible. Students should visit Baylor and discover why it is frequently cited as a best value.

Getting in Last Year
8,931 applied
82% were accepted
2,678 enrolled (36%)
38% from top tenth of their h.s. class
43% had SAT verbal scores over 600
51% had SAT math scores over 600
56% had ACT scores over 24
9% had SAT verbal scores over 700
10% had SAT math scores over 700
6% had ACT scores over 30
37 National Merit Scholars

Graduation and After
40% graduated in 4 years
26% graduated in 5 years
4% graduated in 6 years
329 organizations recruited on campus

Financial Matters
$18,430 tuition and fees (2003–04)
$5434 room and board
69% average percent of need met
$11,518 average financial aid amount received per undergraduate (2002–03 estimated)

BAYLOR UNIVERSITY
URBAN SETTING ■ PRIVATE ■ INDEPENDENT RELIGIOUS ■ COED
WACO, TEXAS

Web site: www.baylor.edu
Contact: Mr. James Steen, Director of Admission Services, PO Box 97056, Waco, TX 76798-7056
Telephone: 254-710-3435 or toll-free 800-BAYLOR U **Fax:** 254-710-3436
E-mail: admissions_office@baylor.edu

Academics
Baylor awards bachelor's, master's, doctoral, and first-professional **degrees** and post-master's certificates. Challenging opportunities include advanced placement credit, accelerated degree programs, student-designed majors, an honors program, double majors, and a senior project. Special programs include internships, summer session for credit, study-abroad, and Air Force ROTC.

The most frequently chosen **baccalaureate** fields are business/marketing, education, and social sciences and history. A complete listing of majors at Baylor appears in the Majors Index beginning on page 460.

The **faculty** at Baylor has 777 full-time members, 75% with terminal degrees. The student-faculty ratio is 16:1.

Students of Baylor
The student body totals 13,937, of whom 11,712 are undergraduates. 58.3% are women and 41.7% are men. Students come from 50 states and territories and 90 other countries. 85% are from Texas. 1.4% are international students. 6.4% are African American, 0.6% American Indian, 5.2% Asian American, and 7.9% Hispanic American. 84% returned for their sophomore year.

Facilities and Resources
Student rooms are linked to a campus network. 1,500 **computers** are available on campus that provide access to the Internet. The 9 **libraries** have 2,252,780 books and 8,429 subscriptions.

Campus Life
There are 289 active organizations on campus, including a drama/theater group, newspaper, radio station, television station, choral group, and marching band. 15% of eligible men and 17% of eligible women are members of national **fraternities**, national **sororities**, local fraternities, and local sororities.

Baylor is a member of the NCAA (Division I). **Intercollegiate sports** (some offering scholarships) include baseball (m), basketball, cross-country running, football (m), golf, soccer (w), softball (w), tennis, track and field, volleyball (w).

Campus Safety
Student safety services include bicycle patrols, late-night transport/escort service, 24-hour emergency telephone alarm devices, 24-hour patrols by trained security personnel, and electronically operated dormitory entrances.

Applying
Baylor requires an essay, SAT I or ACT, and a high school transcript. It recommends an interview. Application deadline: rolling admissions; 3/1 priority date for financial aid. Early admission is possible.

BELLARMINE UNIVERSITY

SUBURBAN SETTING ■ PRIVATE ■ INDEPENDENT RELIGIOUS ■ COED
LOUISVILLE, KENTUCKY

Web site: www.bellarmine.edu
Contact: Mr. Timothy A. Sturgeon, Dean of Admission, 2001 Newburg Road,
    Louisville, KY 40205-0671
Telephone: 502-452-8131 or toll-free 800-274-4723 ext. 8131 **Fax:**
    502-452-8002
E-mail: admissions@bellarmine.edu

Academics

Bellarmine awards bachelor's, master's, and doctoral **degrees** and post-bachelor's and
post-master's certificates. Challenging opportunities include advanced placement credit,
accelerated degree programs, student-designed majors, an honors program, double
majors, independent study, and a senior project. Special programs include internships,
summer session for credit, off-campus study, study-abroad, and Army and Air Force
ROTC.

The most frequently chosen **baccalaureate** fields are business/marketing, health
professions and related sciences, and social sciences and history. A complete listing of
majors at Bellarmine appears in the Majors Index beginning on page 460.

The **faculty** at Bellarmine has 115 full-time members, 72% with terminal degrees.
The student-faculty ratio is 13:1.

Students of Bellarmine

The student body totals 3,134, of whom 2,561 are undergraduates. 60.1% are women
and 39.9% are men. Students come from 39 states and territories. 69% are from
Kentucky. 0.3% are international students. 3.6% are African American, 0.3% American
Indian, 1.5% Asian American, and 0.8% Hispanic American. 78% returned for their
sophomore year.

Facilities and Resources

Student rooms are linked to a campus network. 160 **computers** are available on campus
that provide access to the Internet. The **library** has 97,737 books and 401 subscriptions.

Campus Life

There are 61 active organizations on campus, including a drama/theater group,
newspaper, and choral group. 2% of eligible men and 2% of eligible women are
members of national **fraternities** and national **sororities**.

Bellarmine is a member of the NCAA (Division II). **Intercollegiate sports** (some
offering scholarships) include baseball (m), basketball, cross-country running, field
hockey (w), golf, lacrosse (m), soccer, softball (w), tennis, track and field, volleyball (w).

Campus Safety

Student safety services include 24-hour locked residence hall entrances, security cameras,
late-night transport/escort service, 24-hour emergency telephone alarm devices, 24-hour
patrols by trained security personnel, student patrols, and electronically operated dormitory entrances.

Applying

Bellarmine requires an essay, SAT I or ACT, a high school transcript, recommendations,
and a minimum high school GPA of 2.0. It recommends an interview. Application
deadline: 2/1; 3/1 priority date for financial aid. Early and deferred admission are possible.

Getting in Last Year
1,485 applied
82% were accepted
453 enrolled (37%)
18% from top tenth of their h.s. class
3.53 average high school GPA
33% had SAT verbal scores over 600
28% had SAT math scores over 600
53% had ACT scores over 24
2% had SAT verbal scores over 700
4% had SAT math scores over 700
6% had ACT scores over 30
1 National Merit Scholar
3 class presidents

Graduation and After
54% graduated in 4 years
7% graduated in 5 years
2% graduated in 6 years
Graduates pursuing further study: 5% arts and
    sciences, 2% business, 2% law
75% had job offers within 6 months
42 organizations recruited on campus

Financial Matters
$18,490 tuition and fees (2003–04)
$5620 room and board
89% average percent of need met
$13,762 average financial aid amount received
    per undergraduate (2002–03 estimated)

BELMONT UNIVERSITY

URBAN SETTING ■ PRIVATE ■ INDEPENDENT RELIGIOUS ■ COED
NASHVILLE, TENNESSEE

Web site: www.belmont.edu
Contact: Dr. Kathryn Baugher, Dean of Enrollment Services, 1900 Belmont
Boulevard, Nashville, TN 37212-3757
Telephone: 615-460-6785 or toll-free 800-56E-NROL **Fax:** 615-460-5434
E-mail: buadmission@mail.belmont.edu

Belmont University brings together the best of liberal arts and professional education in a Christian community of learning and service. Located in Nashville on the former Belle Monte estate, Belmont offers a campus rich in heritage with the conveniences and advantages of one of the fastest-growing cities in the nation. Belmont students benefit from an education marked by personal attention from professors; special academic opportunities, such as the Belmont Undergraduate Research Symposium, studies abroad, and the honors program; and outstanding internship opportunities in many areas, including business, health care, education, communication arts, and the music industry.

Getting in Last Year
1,607 applied
75% were accepted
603 enrolled (50%)
34% from top tenth of their h.s. class
3.43 average high school GPA
34% had SAT verbal scores over 600
37% had SAT math scores over 600
63% had ACT scores over 24
2% had SAT verbal scores over 700
6% had SAT math scores over 700
10% had ACT scores over 30
22 valedictorians

Graduation and After
37% graduated in 4 years
16% graduated in 5 years
1% graduated in 6 years
23% pursued further study (10% arts and sciences, 10% business, 8% education)
80% had job offers within 6 months
180 organizations recruited on campus

Financial Matters
$15,954 tuition and fees (2003–04)
$6032 room and board
34% average percent of need met
$2796 average financial aid amount received per undergraduate (2002–03)

Academics
Belmont awards bachelor's, master's, and doctoral **degrees** and post-bachelor's certificates. Challenging opportunities include advanced placement credit, accelerated degree programs, student-designed majors, an honors program, double majors, independent study, and a senior project. Special programs include cooperative education, internships, summer session for credit, study-abroad, and Army ROTC.

The most frequently chosen **baccalaureate** fields are visual/performing arts, business/marketing, and liberal arts/general studies. A complete listing of majors at Belmont appears in the Majors Index beginning on page 460.

The **faculty** at Belmont has 199 full-time members, 67% with terminal degrees. The student-faculty ratio is 11:1.

Students of Belmont
The student body totals 3,629, of whom 2,989 are undergraduates. 60.6% are women and 39.4% are men. Students come from 49 states and territories and 23 other countries. 49% are from Tennessee. 1.6% are international students. 3.7% are African American, 0.5% American Indian, 1.3% Asian American, and 1.7% Hispanic American. 77% returned for their sophomore year.

Facilities and Resources
Student rooms are linked to a campus network. 350 **computers** are available on campus that provide access to individual student information via BANNER web and the Internet. The **library** has 184,835 books and 1,311 subscriptions.

Campus Life
There are 54 active organizations on campus, including a drama/theater group, newspaper, radio station, television station, choral group, and marching band. 6% of eligible men and 8% of eligible women are members of national **fraternities**, national **sororities**, local fraternities, and local sororities.

Belmont is a member of the NCAA (Division I). **Intercollegiate sports** (some offering scholarships) include baseball (m), basketball, cheerleading, cross-country running, golf, soccer, softball (w), tennis, track and field, volleyball (w).

Campus Safety
Student safety services include bicycle patrol, late-night transport/escort service, 24-hour emergency telephone alarm devices, 24-hour patrols by trained security personnel, and electronically operated dormitory entrances.

Applying
Belmont requires an essay, SAT I or ACT, a high school transcript, recommendations, resume of activities, and a minimum high school GPA of 3.0, and in some cases an interview. Application deadline: 5/1; 3/1 priority date for financial aid. Early and deferred admission are possible.

BELOIT COLLEGE

SMALL-TOWN SETTING ■ PRIVATE ■ INDEPENDENT ■ COED
BELOIT, WISCONSIN

Web site: www.beloit.edu
Contact: Mr. James S. Zielinski, Director of Admissions, 700 College Street,
   Beloit, WI 53511-5596
Telephone: 608-363-2500 or toll-free 800-9-BELOIT **Fax:** 608-363-2075
E-mail: admiss@beloit.edu

Academics

Beloit awards bachelor's **degrees**. Challenging opportunities include advanced placement credit, student-designed majors, double majors, independent study, and a senior project. Special programs include internships, summer session for credit, off-campus study, and study-abroad.

   The most frequently chosen **baccalaureate** fields are social sciences and history, biological/life sciences, and English. A complete listing of majors at Beloit appears in the Majors Index beginning on page 460.

   The **faculty** at Beloit has 103 full-time members, 94% with terminal degrees. The student-faculty ratio is 11:1.

Students of Beloit

The student body is made up of 1,332 undergraduates. 61.4% are women and 38.6% are men. Students come from 47 states and territories and 40 other countries. 18% are from Wisconsin. 5.5% are international students. 2.7% are African American, 0.3% American Indian, 3.3% Asian American, and 2.7% Hispanic American. 91% returned for their sophomore year.

Facilities and Resources

Student rooms are linked to a campus network. 152 **computers** are available on campus that provide access to the Internet. The **library** has 183,736 books and 946 subscriptions.

Campus Life

There are 85 active organizations on campus, including a drama/theater group, newspaper, radio station, television station, and choral group. 15% of eligible men and 5% of eligible women are members of national **fraternities**, local fraternities, and local **sororities**.

   Beloit is a member of the NCAA (Division III). **Intercollegiate sports** include baseball (m), basketball, cross-country running, football (m), golf, soccer, softball (w), swimming, tennis, track and field, volleyball (w).

Campus Safety

Student safety services include late-night transport/escort service, 24-hour emergency telephone alarm devices, 24-hour patrols by trained security personnel, and electronically operated dormitory entrances.

Applying

Beloit requires an essay, SAT I or ACT, a high school transcript, and 1 recommendation, and in some cases an interview. It recommends an interview. Application deadline: 1/15; 3/1 priority date for financial aid. Early and deferred admission are possible.

Experiential learning, interdisciplinary thought, and global understanding are the hallmarks of a Beloit education. Since its founding more than 150 years ago, Beloit prepares students to be at home in the world of ideas and to be active participants in changing contemporary times. It is on this 40-acre campus—reminiscent of its New England heritage—that students combine rigorous academics with internships, research opportunities, community service, and global engagement in order to become responsible leaders in the 21st century.

Getting in Last Year
1,901 applied
69% were accepted
346 enrolled (26%)
34% from top tenth of their h.s. class
3.51 average high school GPA
70% had SAT verbal scores over 600
53% had SAT math scores over 600
87% had ACT scores over 24
22% had SAT verbal scores over 700
11% had SAT math scores over 700
27% had ACT scores over 30
14 National Merit Scholars
12 valedictorians

Graduation and After
60% graduated in 4 years
9% graduated in 5 years
3% graduated in 6 years
29% pursued further study (22% arts and sciences, 3% medicine, 2% business)
64% had job offers within 6 months

Financial Matters
$24,386 tuition and fees (2003–04)
$5478 room and board
100% average percent of need met
$17,839 average financial aid amount received per undergraduate (2001–02)

BENEDICTINE UNIVERSITY
SUBURBAN SETTING ■ PRIVATE ■ INDEPENDENT RELIGIOUS ■ COED
LISLE, ILLINOIS

Getting in Last Year
303 enrolled
20% from top tenth of their h.s. class
3.40 average high school GPA
47% had ACT scores over 24
6% had ACT scores over 30
18 valedictorians

Graduation and After
39% graduated in 4 years
11% graduated in 5 years
2% graduated in 6 years
25 organizations recruited on campus

Financial Matters
$17,470 tuition and fees (2003–04)
$6370 room and board
100% average percent of need met
$10,984 average financial aid amount received per undergraduate (2001–02)

Web site: www.ben.edu
Contact: Ms. Kari Gibbons, Dean of Undergraduate Admissions, 5700 College Road, Lisle, IL 60532-0900
Telephone: 630-829-6306 or toll-free 888-829-6363 (out-of-state) **Fax:** 630-960-1126
E-mail: admissions@ben.edu

Academics
Benedictine University awards associate, bachelor's, master's, and doctoral **degrees**. Challenging opportunities include advanced placement credit, accelerated degree programs, an honors program, double majors, independent study, and a senior project. Special programs include internships, summer session for credit, off-campus study, study-abroad, and Army ROTC.

The most frequently chosen **baccalaureate** fields are business/marketing, biological/life sciences, and psychology. A complete listing of majors at Benedictine University appears in the Majors Index beginning on page 460.

The **faculty** at Benedictine University has 94 full-time members. The student-faculty ratio is 13:1.

Students of Benedictine University
The student body totals 2,968, of whom 2,114 are undergraduates. 62.6% are women and 37.4% are men. Students come from 25 states and territories and 8 other countries. 96% are from Illinois. 1.9% are international students. 10.4% are African American, 13.1% Asian American, and 7.5% Hispanic American. 77% returned for their sophomore year.

Facilities and Resources
Student rooms are linked to a campus network. 102 **computers** are available on campus for student use. The **library** has 166,341 books and 8,900 subscriptions.

Campus Life
There are 38 active organizations on campus, including a drama/theater group, newspaper, television station, and choral group. No national or local **fraternities** or **sororities**.

Benedictine University is a member of the NCAA (Division III). **Intercollegiate sports** include baseball (m), basketball, cross-country running, football (m), golf (m), soccer, softball (w), swimming, tennis (w), track and field, volleyball (w).

Campus Safety
Student safety services include late-night transport/escort service, 24-hour emergency telephone alarm devices, 24-hour patrols by trained security personnel, and electronically operated dormitory entrances.

Applying
Benedictine University requires an essay, ACT, a high school transcript, and recommendations, and in some cases an interview. It recommends rank in top 50% of high school class, ACT score of 21. Application deadline: rolling admissions; 6/30 for financial aid, with a 4/15 priority date. Deferred admission is possible.

BENNINGTON COLLEGE

SMALL-TOWN SETTING ■ PRIVATE ■ INDEPENDENT ■ COED
BENNINGTON, VERMONT

Web site: www.bennington.edu
Contact: Mr. Ben Jones, Dean of Admissions and Financial Aid, One College Drive, Bennington, VT 05201
Telephone: 802-440-4312 or toll-free 800-833-6845 **Fax:** 802-440-4320
E-mail: admissions@bennington.edu

Academics

Bennington awards bachelor's and master's **degrees** and post-bachelor's certificates. Challenging opportunities include accelerated degree programs, student-designed majors, double majors, independent study, and a senior project. Special programs include cooperative education, internships, off-campus study, and study-abroad.

The most frequently chosen **baccalaureate** fields are visual/performing arts, English, and social sciences and history. A complete listing of majors at Bennington appears in the Majors Index beginning on page 460.

The **faculty** at Bennington has 64 full-time members, 69% with terminal degrees. The student-faculty ratio is 9:1.

Students of Bennington

The student body totals 795, of whom 642 are undergraduates. 67.3% are women and 32.7% are men. Students come from 45 states and territories and 18 other countries. 5% are from Vermont. 5.6% are international students. 1.4% are African American, 0.3% American Indian, 1.4% Asian American, and 2.7% Hispanic American. 80% returned for their sophomore year.

Facilities and Resources

Student rooms are linked to a campus network. 61 **computers** are available on campus that provide access to the Internet. The 3 **libraries** have 128,413 books and 250 subscriptions.

Campus Life

There are 26 active organizations on campus, including a drama/theater group, newspaper, radio station, and choral group. No national or local **fraternities** or **sororities**.

Intercollegiate sports include baseball, basketball.

Campus Safety

Student safety services include late-night transport/escort service, 24-hour emergency telephone alarm devices, and 24-hour patrols by trained security personnel.

Applying

Bennington requires an essay, SAT I or ACT, a high school transcript, an interview, and 2 recommendations. Application deadline: 1/1; 3/1 priority date for financial aid. Early and deferred admission are possible.

A Bennington education imparts more than a body of knowledge or an excellent liberal arts education. It imparts an approach to life—the belief that the way to get things done is to do them. The College was founded 7 decades ago on the premise that people learn best by pursuing that which most interests them and by working closely with teachers who are themselves actively engaged in their fields. Self-direction is central; the power of the Bennington experience has everything to do with the role students have in shaping their education, and the result is lifelong confidence, adaptability, and independence of mind.

Getting in Last Year
773 applied
68% were accepted
172 enrolled (33%)
23% from top tenth of their h.s. class
3.48 average high school GPA
76% had SAT verbal scores over 600
45% had SAT math scores over 600
80% had ACT scores over 24
29% had SAT verbal scores over 700
6% had SAT math scores over 700
30% had ACT scores over 30

Financial Matters
$28,770 tuition and fees (2003–04)
$7140 room and board
75% average percent of need met
$20,119 average financial aid amount received per undergraduate (2002–03 estimated)

BENTLEY COLLEGE

SUBURBAN SETTING ■ PRIVATE ■ INDEPENDENT ■ COED
WALTHAM, MASSACHUSETTS

Web site: www.bentley.edu
Contact: Director of Admission, 175 Forest Street, Waltham, MA 02452-4705
Telephone: 781-891-2244 or toll-free 800-523-2354 (out-of-state) **Fax:** 781-891-3414
E-mail: ugadmission@bentley.edu

Getting in Last Year

5,474 applied
46% were accepted
955 enrolled (38%)
37% from top tenth of their h.s. class
35% had SAT verbal scores over 600
63% had SAT math scores over 600
62% had ACT scores over 24
3% had SAT verbal scores over 700
11% had SAT math scores over 700
10% had ACT scores over 30

Graduation and After

66% graduated in 4 years
10% graduated in 5 years
2% graduated in 6 years
81% had job offers within 6 months
294 organizations recruited on campus

Financial Matters

$24,324 tuition and fees (2003–04)
$9580 room and board
96% average percent of need met
$21,514 average financial aid amount received per undergraduate (2002–03 estimated)

Academics

Bentley awards associate, bachelor's, and master's **degrees** and post-bachelor's and post-master's certificates. Challenging opportunities include advanced placement credit, accelerated degree programs, student-designed majors, an honors program, and a senior project. Special programs include internships, summer session for credit, off-campus study, study-abroad, and Army ROTC.

The most frequently chosen **baccalaureate** fields are business/marketing, computer/information sciences, and interdisciplinary studies. A complete listing of majors at Bentley appears in the Majors Index beginning on page 460.

The **faculty** at Bentley has 260 full-time members, 83% with terminal degrees. The student-faculty ratio is 13:1.

Students of Bentley

The student body totals 5,673, of whom 4,344 are undergraduates. 42.5% are women and 57.5% are men. Students come from 40 states and territories and 62 other countries. 57% are from Massachusetts. 7.7% are international students. 3.3% are African American, 0.1% American Indian, 7.2% Asian American, and 3.9% Hispanic American. 93% returned for their sophomore year.

Facilities and Resources

Student rooms are linked to a campus network. The **library** has 212,573 books and 1,993 subscriptions.

Campus Life

There are 90 active organizations on campus, including a drama/theater group, newspaper, radio station, and choral group. Bentley has national **fraternities**, national **sororities**, and local fraternities.

Bentley is a member of the NCAA (Division II). **Intercollegiate sports** (some offering scholarships) include baseball (m), basketball, cross-country running, field hockey (w), football (m), ice hockey (m), lacrosse (m), soccer, softball (w), swimming, tennis, track and field, volleyball (w).

Campus Safety

Student safety services include security cameras, late-night transport/escort service, 24-hour emergency telephone alarm devices, 24-hour patrols by trained security personnel, and electronically operated dormitory entrances.

Applying

Bentley requires an essay, SAT I or ACT, a high school transcript, and 2 recommendations. It recommends an interview. Application deadline: 2/1; 2/1 for financial aid. Early and deferred admission are possible.

BEREA COLLEGE

SMALL-TOWN SETTING ■ PRIVATE ■ INDEPENDENT ■ COED
BEREA, KENTUCKY

Web site: www.berea.edu
Contact: Mr. Jamie Ealy, Director of Admissions, CPO 2220, Berea, KY
40404
Telephone: 859-985-3500 or toll-free 800-326-5948 **Fax:** 859-985-3512
E-mail: admissions@berea.edu

Academics

Berea awards bachelor's **degrees**. Challenging opportunities include advanced placement credit, student-designed majors, an honors program, double majors, independent study, and a senior project. Special programs include internships, summer session for credit, off-campus study, and study-abroad.

The most frequently chosen **baccalaureate** fields are business/marketing, home economics/vocational home economics, and engineering/engineering technologies. A complete listing of majors at Berea appears in the Majors Index beginning on page 460.

The **faculty** at Berea has 130 full-time members, 91% with terminal degrees. The student-faculty ratio is 11:1.

Students of Berea

The student body is made up of 1,560 undergraduates. 60.1% are women and 39.9% are men. Students come from 44 states and territories and 65 other countries. 41% are from Kentucky. 7.5% are international students. 17.2% are African American, 0.7% American Indian, 1.4% Asian American, and 1.1% Hispanic American. 80% returned for their sophomore year.

Facilities and Resources

Student rooms are linked to a campus network. 260 **computers** are available on campus that provide access to the Internet. The 3 **libraries** have 330,401 books and 1,069 subscriptions.

Campus Life

There are 77 active organizations on campus, including a drama/theater group, newspaper, and choral group. No national or local **fraternities** or **sororities**.

Berea is a member of the NAIA. **Intercollegiate sports** include baseball (m), basketball, cross-country running, golf (m), soccer, softball (w), swimming, tennis, track and field, volleyball (w).

Campus Safety

Student safety services include crime prevention programs, late-night transport/escort service, 24-hour emergency telephone alarm devices, 24-hour patrols by trained security personnel, and electronically operated dormitory entrances.

Applying

Berea requires an essay, SAT I or ACT, a high school transcript, an interview, and financial aid application. It recommends 2 recommendations. Application deadline: rolling admissions; 8/1 for financial aid, with a 4/15 priority date.

Getting in Last Year

2,119 applied
25% were accepted
396 enrolled (75%)
29% from top tenth of their h.s. class
3.37 average high school GPA
30% had SAT verbal scores over 600
25% had SAT math scores over 600
40% had ACT scores over 24
6% had SAT verbal scores over 700
1% had SAT math scores over 700
4% had ACT scores over 30

Graduation and After

29% graduated in 4 years
18% graduated in 5 years
2% graduated in 6 years
125 organizations recruited on campus

Financial Matters

$507 tuition and fees (2003–04)
$4523 room and board
82% average percent of need met
$24,668 average financial aid amount received
per undergraduate

BERRY COLLEGE

SUBURBAN SETTING ■ PRIVATE ■ INDEPENDENT RELIGIOUS ■ COED
MOUNT BERRY, GEORGIA

Web site: www.berry.edu
Contact: Mr. Garreth M. Johnson, Dean of Admissions, PO Box 490159,
2277 Martha Berry Highway, NW, Mount Berry, GA 30149-0159
Telephone: 706-236-2215 or toll-free 800-237-7942 **Fax:** 706-290-2178
E-mail: admissions@berry.edu

Berry College is an independent, coeducational college with fully accredited arts, sciences, and professional programs as well as specialized graduate programs in education and business administration. The College serves humanity by inspiring and educating students regardless of their economic status and emphasizes a comprehensive educational program committed to high academic standards, Christian values, and practical work experiences. The campus is an unusually beautiful environment with approximately 28,000 acres of land. Fields, forests, lakes, and mountains provide scenic beauty in a protected natural setting. The College is located in Rome, Georgia, 65 miles northwest of Atlanta and 65 miles south of Chattanooga.

Getting in Last Year
1,846 applied
83% were accepted
505 enrolled (33%)
40% from top tenth of their h.s. class
3.64 average high school GPA
49% had SAT verbal scores over 600
39% had SAT math scores over 600
64% had ACT scores over 24
8% had SAT verbal scores over 700
6% had SAT math scores over 700
12% had ACT scores over 30
10 valedictorians

Graduation and After
50% graduated in 4 years
11% graduated in 5 years
1% graduated in 6 years
25% pursued further study (11% arts and sciences, 5% medicine, 2% theology)
97.4% had job offers within 6 months
138 organizations recruited on campus

Financial Matters
$15,220 tuition and fees (2003–04)
$6190 room and board
86% average percent of need met
$13,396 average financial aid amount received per undergraduate

Academics
Berry awards bachelor's and master's **degrees** and post-master's certificates. Challenging opportunities include advanced placement credit, accelerated degree programs, student-designed majors, an honors program, double majors, independent study, and a senior project. Special programs include cooperative education, internships, summer session for credit, and study-abroad.

The most frequently chosen **baccalaureate** fields are education, business/marketing, and social sciences and history. A complete listing of majors at Berry appears in the Majors Index beginning on page 460.

The **faculty** at Berry has 148 full-time members, 87% with terminal degrees. The student-faculty ratio is 12:1.

Students of Berry
The student body totals 2,045, of whom 1,895 are undergraduates. 63.3% are women and 36.7% are men. Students come from 34 states and territories and 22 other countries. 80% are from Georgia. 2% are international students. 2.6% are African American, 0.1% American Indian, 1% Asian American, and 0.8% Hispanic American. 76% returned for their sophomore year.

Facilities and Resources
Student rooms are linked to a campus network. 100 **computers** are available on campus that provide access to the Internet. The 2 **libraries** have 291,337 books and 1,400 subscriptions.

Campus Life
There are 75 active organizations on campus, including a drama/theater group, newspaper, television station, and choral group. No national or local **fraternities** or **sororities**.

Berry is a member of the NAIA. **Intercollegiate sports** (some offering scholarships) include baseball (m), basketball, cheerleading, cross-country running, golf, soccer, tennis, track and field, volleyball (w).

Campus Safety
Student safety services include lighted pathways, 24-hour emergency telephone alarm devices, 24-hour patrols by trained security personnel, and electronically operated dormitory entrances.

Applying
Berry requires SAT I or ACT and a high school transcript. Application deadline: 7/23; 4/1 priority date for financial aid. Early and deferred admission are possible.

BETHEL UNIVERSITY

SUBURBAN SETTING ■ PRIVATE ■ INDEPENDENT RELIGIOUS ■ COED
ST. PAUL, MINNESOTA

Web site: www.bethel.edu
Contact: Mr. Jay Fedje, Director of Admissions, 3900 Bethel Drive, St. Paul, MN 55112
Telephone: 651-638-6242 or toll-free 800-255-8706 ext. 6242 **Fax:** 651-635-1490
E-mail: bcoll-admit@bethel.edu

Academics

Bethel awards associate, bachelor's, and master's **degrees**. Challenging opportunities include advanced placement credit, accelerated degree programs, student-designed majors, freshman honors college, an honors program, double majors, independent study, and a senior project. Special programs include internships, summer session for credit, off-campus study, study-abroad, and Army and Air Force ROTC.

The most frequently chosen **baccalaureate** fields are business/marketing, education, and health professions and related sciences. A complete listing of majors at Bethel appears in the Majors Index beginning on page 460.

The **faculty** at Bethel has 165 full-time members, 72% with terminal degrees. The student-faculty ratio is 15:1.

Students of Bethel

The student body totals 3,303, of whom 2,911 are undergraduates. 61.1% are women and 38.9% are men. Students come from 41 states and territories. 73% are from Minnesota. 0.1% are international students. 1.6% are African American, 0.4% American Indian, 2.9% Asian American, and 1% Hispanic American. 87% returned for their sophomore year.

Facilities and Resources

Student rooms are linked to a campus network. 110 **computers** are available on campus for student use. The 2 **libraries** have 173,000 books and 14,678 subscriptions.

Campus Life

There are 37 active organizations on campus, including a drama/theater group, newspaper, radio station, television station, and choral group. No national or local **fraternities** or **sororities**.

Bethel is a member of the NCAA (Division III). **Intercollegiate sports** include baseball (m), basketball, cross-country running, football (m), golf (m), ice hockey, soccer, softball (w), tennis, track and field, volleyball (w).

Campus Safety

Student safety services include late-night transport/escort service, 24-hour emergency telephone alarm devices, 24-hour patrols by trained security personnel, student patrols, and electronically operated dormitory entrances.

Applying

Bethel requires an essay, a high school transcript, and 2 recommendations, and in some cases an interview. It recommends an interview. Application deadline: 3/1; 4/15 priority date for financial aid. Early admission is possible.

Bethel College provides academic excellence in a dynamic Christian environment. *U.S. News & World Report* has recognized Bethel as one of the top Midwestern Universities in the nation. The beautiful lakeside, 231-acre campus provides the ideal background for the integration of faith and learning. An outstanding faculty, numerous extracurricular activities, and off-campus study opportunities make Bethel a great place to be. Students are actively involved in their education, which prepares them both for life and a living. Bethel is committed to providing a high-quality liberal arts education to prepare tomorrow's leaders to make a difference in their community, the church, and the world.

Getting in Last Year
1,512 applied
91% were accepted
658 enrolled (48%)
35% from top tenth of their h.s. class
3.24 average high school GPA
46% had SAT verbal scores over 600
48% had SAT math scores over 600
48% had ACT scores over 24
17% had SAT verbal scores over 700
10% had SAT math scores over 700
9% had ACT scores over 30
9 National Merit Scholars

Graduation and After
62% graduated in 4 years
7% graduated in 5 years
1% graduated in 6 years
75% had job offers within 6 months
100 organizations recruited on campus

Financial Matters
$18,800 tuition and fees (2003–04)
$6380 room and board
83% average percent of need met
$14,810 average financial aid amount received per undergraduate

BIOLA UNIVERSITY

SUBURBAN SETTING ■ PRIVATE ■ INDEPENDENT RELIGIOUS ■ COED
LA MIRADA, CALIFORNIA

Web site: www.biola.edu
Contact: Mr. Greg Vaughan, Director of Enrollment Management, 13800
 Biola Avenue, La Mirada, CA 90639
Telephone: 562-903-4752 or toll-free 800-652-4652 **Fax:** 562-903-4709
E-mail: admissions@biola.edu

Getting in Last Year
1,901 applied
78% were accepted
814 enrolled (55%)
50% from top tenth of their h.s. class
3.55 average high school GPA
37% had SAT verbal scores over 600
32% had SAT math scores over 600
53% had ACT scores over 24
7% had SAT verbal scores over 700
6% had SAT math scores over 700
7% had ACT scores over 30
11 class presidents
5 valedictorians

Graduation and After
39% graduated in 4 years
10% graduated in 5 years
2% graduated in 6 years
70% had job offers within 6 months
130 organizations recruited on campus

Financial Matters
$19,564 tuition and fees (2003–04)
$5967 room and board
77% average percent of need met
$13,701 average financial aid amount received
 per undergraduate (2002–03 estimated)

Academics
Biola awards bachelor's, master's, doctoral, and first-professional **degrees**. Challenging opportunities include advanced placement credit, accelerated degree programs, freshman honors college, an honors program, double majors, independent study, and a senior project. Special programs include cooperative education, internships, summer session for credit, off-campus study, study-abroad, and Army and Air Force ROTC. A complete listing of majors at Biola appears in the Majors Index beginning on page 460.
 The **faculty** at Biola has 183 full-time members. The student-faculty ratio is 18:1.

Students of Biola
The student body totals 4,666, of whom 3,232 are undergraduates. 62.8% are women and 37.2% are men. Students come from 47 states and territories and 40 other countries. 71% are from California. 3.5% are international students. 3.6% are African American, 0.3% American Indian, 7.4% Asian American, and 9.4% Hispanic American. 84% returned for their sophomore year.

Facilities and Resources
Student rooms are linked to a campus network. 150 **computers** are available on campus that provide access to the Internet. The **library** has 270,456 books and 13,123 subscriptions.

Campus Life
There are 33 active organizations on campus, including a drama/theater group, newspaper, radio station, television station, and choral group. No national or local **fraternities** or **sororities**.
 Biola is a member of the NAIA. **Intercollegiate sports** (some offering scholarships) include baseball (m), basketball, cross-country running, soccer, softball (w), swimming, tennis (w), track and field, volleyball (w).

Campus Safety
Student safety services include access gates to roads through the middle of campus, late-night transport/escort service, 24-hour emergency telephone alarm devices, 24-hour patrols by trained security personnel, student patrols, and electronically operated dormitory entrances.

Applying
Biola requires an essay, SAT I or ACT, a high school transcript, an interview, and 2 recommendations. It recommends a minimum high school GPA of 3.0. Application deadline: 3/1; 3/2 priority date for financial aid. Early and deferred admission are possible.

BIRMINGHAM-SOUTHERN COLLEGE

URBAN SETTING ■ PRIVATE ■ INDEPENDENT RELIGIOUS ■ COED
BIRMINGHAM, ALABAMA

Web site: www.bsc.edu
Contact: Ms. Sheryl E. Salmon, Associate Vice President for Admission, Box 549008, Birmingham, AL 35254
Telephone: 205-226-4696 or toll-free 800-523-5793 **Fax:** 205-226-3074
E-mail: admissions@bsc.edu

Academics

Birmingham-Southern awards bachelor's and master's **degrees**. Challenging opportunities include advanced placement credit, student-designed majors, an honors program, double majors, independent study, and a senior project. Special programs include internships, summer session for credit, off-campus study, study-abroad, and Army and Air Force ROTC.

The most frequently chosen **baccalaureate** fields are business/marketing, social sciences and history, and visual/performing arts. A complete listing of majors at Birmingham-Southern appears in the Majors Index beginning on page 460.

The **faculty** at Birmingham-Southern has 96 full-time members, 95% with terminal degrees. The student-faculty ratio is 12:1.

Students of Birmingham-Southern

The student body totals 1,388, of whom 1,303 are undergraduates. 58% are women and 42% are men. Students come from 28 states and territories. 75% are from Alabama. 0.5% are international students. 5.8% are African American, 0.3% American Indian, 2.1% Asian American, and 0.9% Hispanic American. 82% returned for their sophomore year.

Facilities and Resources

Student rooms are linked to a campus network. 156 **computers** are available on campus for student use. The **library** has 232,330 books and 949 subscriptions.

Campus Life

There are 70 active organizations on campus, including a drama/theater group, newspaper, radio station, and choral group. 47% of eligible men and 58% of eligible women are members of national **fraternities** and national **sororities**.

Birmingham-Southern is a member of the NCAA (Division I). **Intercollegiate sports** (some offering scholarships) include baseball (m), basketball, cross-country running, golf, riflery (w), soccer, softball (w), tennis, volleyball (w).

Campus Safety

Student safety services include vehicle safety inspection, late-night transport/escort service, 24-hour emergency telephone alarm devices, 24-hour patrols by trained security personnel, and electronically operated dormitory entrances.

Applying

Birmingham-Southern requires an essay, SAT I or ACT, a high school transcript, 1 recommendation, and a minimum high school GPA of 2.0, and in some cases an interview. It recommends an interview. Application deadline: rolling admissions; 3/1 priority date for financial aid. Early and deferred admission are possible.

> The College continues to be recognized as one of the nation's leading liberal arts colleges by *National Review, U.S. News & World Report,* and *Money* magazine. Special features of the curriculum are the Interim Term and the Honors Program, as well as undergraduate research, the Hess Center for Leadership and Service, and international study programs. The Interim Term (January) provides an opportunity for independent study, foreign and domestic trips, and internships with government and private organizations. The College has been recognized for its outstanding track record of graduate admission to medical, law, and graduate schools and job placement.

Getting in Last Year
1,080 applied
89% were accepted
356 enrolled (37%)
53% from top tenth of their h.s. class
3.35 average high school GPA
59% had SAT verbal scores over 600
52% had SAT math scores over 600
78% had ACT scores over 24
15% had SAT verbal scores over 700
13% had SAT math scores over 700
28% had ACT scores over 30
17 National Merit Scholars
28 valedictorians

Graduation and After
66% graduated in 4 years
8% graduated in 5 years
39% pursued further study (13% arts and sciences, 8% business, 7% medicine)
34 organizations recruited on campus

Financial Matters
$18,930 tuition and fees (2003–04)
$6104 room and board
82% average percent of need met
$15,639 average financial aid amount received per undergraduate (2002–03 estimated)

BOSTON COLLEGE
SUBURBAN SETTING ■ PRIVATE ■ INDEPENDENT RELIGIOUS ■ COED
CHESTNUT HILL, MASSACHUSETTS

Web site: www.bc.edu
Contact: Mr. John L. Mahoney Jr., Director of Undergraduate Admission, 140 Commonwealth Avenue, Devlin Hall 208, Chestnut Hill, MA 02467-3809
Telephone: 617-552-3100 or toll-free 800-360-2522 **Fax:** 617-552-0798
E-mail: ugadmis@bc.edu

Boston College is a university with international stature strengthened by the more than 450-year tradition of Jesuit education, which emphasizes rigorous academic development grounded in the arts and sciences and a commitment to the development of the whole person. Through opportunities to participate in honors programs, research with faculty members, independent study, study abroad, and service learning, students are challenged to fulfill their potential as scholars. With artistic, cultural, service, social, religious, and athletic opportunities that abound on campus and throughout the city of Boston, students are challenged to fulfill their potential as caring, thoughtful individuals and future leaders in society.

Getting in Last Year
22,424 applied
31% were accepted
1,839 enrolled (27%)
73% from top tenth of their h.s. class
79% had SAT verbal scores over 600
87% had SAT math scores over 600
23% had SAT verbal scores over 700
36% had SAT math scores over 700
7 National Merit Scholars

Graduation and After
17% pursued further study (5% arts and sciences, 5% law, 3% business)

Financial Matters
$27,542 tuition and fees (2003–04)
$9300 room and board
100% average percent of need met
$18,830 average financial aid amount received per undergraduate (2000–01)

Academics
BC awards bachelor's, master's, doctoral, and first-professional **degrees** and post-master's certificates (also offers continuing education program with significant enrollment not reflected in profile). Challenging opportunities include advanced placement credit, accelerated degree programs, student-designed majors, freshman honors college, an honors program, double majors, and independent study. Special programs include internships, summer session for credit, off-campus study, study-abroad, and Army and Air Force ROTC.

The most frequently chosen **baccalaureate** fields are business/marketing, social sciences and history, and communications/communication technologies. A complete listing of majors at BC appears in the Majors Index beginning on page 460.

The **faculty** at BC has 639 full-time members, 98% with terminal degrees. The student-faculty ratio is 14:1.

Students of BC
The student body totals 13,611, of whom 8,851 are undergraduates. 52.3% are women and 47.7% are men. Students come from 50 states and territories and 100 other countries. 28% are from Massachusetts. 1.6% are international students. 5.4% are African American, 0.3% American Indian, 8.8% Asian American, and 6.4% Hispanic American. 95% returned for their sophomore year.

Facilities and Resources
Student rooms are linked to a campus network. 200 **computers** are available on campus for student use. The 7 **libraries** have 1,976,743 books and 21,121 subscriptions.

Campus Life
There are 171 active organizations on campus, including a drama/theater group, newspaper, radio station, television station, choral group, and marching band. No national or local **fraternities** or **sororities**.

BC is a member of the NCAA (Division I). **Intercollegiate sports** (some offering scholarships) include baseball (m), basketball, cross-country running, fencing, field hockey (w), football (m), golf, ice hockey, lacrosse, sailing, skiing (downhill), soccer, softball (w), swimming, tennis, track and field, volleyball (w), water polo (m), wrestling (m).

Campus Safety
Student safety services include late-night transport/escort service, 24-hour emergency telephone alarm devices, 24-hour patrols by trained security personnel, and electronically operated dormitory entrances.

Applying
BC requires an essay, SAT II: Writing Test, SAT I and SAT II or ACT, a high school transcript, and 2 recommendations. Application deadline: 1/2; 2/1 priority date for financial aid. Early and deferred admission are possible.

Boston University

URBAN SETTING ■ PRIVATE ■ INDEPENDENT ■ COED
BOSTON, MASSACHUSETTS

Web site: www.bu.edu
Contact: Ms. Kelly A. Walter, Director of Undergraduate Admissions, 121
  Bay State Road, Boston, MA 02215
Telephone: 617-353-2300 **Fax:** 617-353-9695
E-mail: admissions@bu.edu

Academics
Boston University awards bachelor's, master's, doctoral, and first-professional **degrees** and post-master's certificates. Challenging opportunities include advanced placement credit, accelerated degree programs, student-designed majors, an honors program, double majors, independent study, and a senior project. Special programs include cooperative education, internships, summer session for credit, off-campus study, study-abroad, and Army, Navy and Air Force ROTC.

The most frequently chosen **baccalaureate** fields are social sciences and history, communications/communication technologies, and business/marketing. A complete listing of majors at Boston University appears in the Majors Index beginning on page 460.

The **faculty** at Boston University has 2,500 full-time members. The student-faculty ratio is 14:1.

Students of Boston University
The student body totals 29,048, of whom 17,681 are undergraduates. 58.9% are women and 41.1% are men. Students come from 54 states and territories and 103 other countries. 22% are from Massachusetts. 6.9% are international students. 2.2% are African American, 0.4% American Indian, 12.5% Asian American, and 4.9% Hispanic American. 85% returned for their sophomore year.

Facilities and Resources
Student rooms are linked to a campus network. 750 **computers** are available on campus that provide access to research and educational networks and the Internet. The 19 **libraries** have 2,244,486 books and 29,389 subscriptions.

Campus Life
There are 380 active organizations on campus, including a drama/theater group, newspaper, radio station, television station, choral group, and marching band. 4% of eligible men and 6% of eligible women are members of national **fraternities** and national **sororities**.

Boston University is a member of the NCAA (Division I). **Intercollegiate sports** (some offering scholarships) include basketball, crew, cross-country running, field hockey (w), golf, ice hockey (m), lacrosse (w), soccer, softball (w), swimming, tennis, track and field, wrestling (m).

Campus Safety
Student safety services include security personnel at residence hall entrances, self-defense education, well-lit sidewalks, late-night transport/escort service, 24-hour emergency telephone alarm devices, 24-hour patrols by trained security personnel, and electronically operated dormitory entrances.

Applying
Boston University requires an essay, SAT I or ACT, a high school transcript, and 2 recommendations, and in some cases SAT II Subject Tests, SAT II: Writing Test, an interview, and audition, portfolio. It recommends SAT II: Writing Test and a minimum high school GPA of 3.0. Application deadline: 1/1; 2/15 priority date for financial aid. Early and deferred admission are possible.

Boston University (BU) has 11 undergraduate schools and colleges with more than 250 programs of study in areas as diverse as biochemistry, theatre arts, physical therapy, elementary education, and broadcast journalism. Students can customize their own major, either through the Boston University Collaborative Degree Program or the University Professors Program. BU has an international student body, with students from every state and more than 100 countries. In addition, opportunities to excel exist in all areas of study through research, internships, directed study, and honors programs.

Getting in Last Year
29,356 applied
52% were accepted
3,961 enrolled (26%)
60% from top tenth of their h.s. class
3.5 average high school GPA
78% had SAT verbal scores over 600
85% had SAT math scores over 600
96% had ACT scores over 24
21% had SAT verbal scores over 700
25% had SAT math scores over 700
34% had ACT scores over 30
117 valedictorians

Graduation and After
62% graduated in 4 years
12% graduated in 5 years
2% graduated in 6 years
25% pursued further study
325 organizations recruited on campus

Financial Matters
$28,906 tuition and fees (2003–04)
$9288 room and board
90% average percent of need met
$25,338 average financial aid amount received per undergraduate

BOWDOIN COLLEGE

SMALL-TOWN SETTING ■ PRIVATE ■ INDEPENDENT ■ COED
BRUNSWICK, MAINE

Web site: www.bowdoin.edu
Contact: Mr. Scott Steinberg, Director of Admissions Operations, 5000 College Station, Brunswick, ME 04011-8441
Telephone: 207-725-3197 **Fax:** 207-725-3101
E-mail: admissions@bowdoin.edu

Getting in Last Year
4,719 applied
24% were accepted
465 enrolled (40%)
72% from top tenth of their h.s. class
92% had SAT verbal scores over 600
91% had SAT math scores over 600
47% had SAT verbal scores over 700
40% had SAT math scores over 700
20 National Merit Scholars
31 valedictorians

Graduation and After
81% graduated in 4 years
7% graduated in 5 years
1% graduated in 6 years
15% pursued further study (5% arts and sciences, 4% medicine, 3% law)
85% had job offers within 6 months
50 organizations recruited on campus

Financial Matters
$30,120 tuition and fees (2003–04)
$7670 room and board
100% average percent of need met
$26,003 average financial aid amount received per undergraduate

Academics

Bowdoin awards bachelor's **degrees**. Challenging opportunities include advanced placement credit, accelerated degree programs, student-designed majors, double majors, and independent study. Special programs include off-campus study and study-abroad.

The most frequently chosen **baccalaureate** fields are social sciences and history, biological/life sciences, and foreign language/literature. A complete listing of majors at Bowdoin appears in the Majors Index beginning on page 460.

The **faculty** at Bowdoin has 154 full-time members, 97% with terminal degrees. The student-faculty ratio is 10:1.

Students of Bowdoin

The student body is made up of 1,647 undergraduates. 49.5% are women and 50.5% are men. Students come from 50 states and territories and 29 other countries. 13% are from Maine. 3.2% are international students. 4.8% are African American, 0.8% American Indian, 10.2% Asian American, and 5.1% Hispanic American. 93% returned for their sophomore year.

Facilities and Resources

Student rooms are linked to a campus network. 310 **computers** are available on campus that provide access to the Internet. The 7 **libraries** have 948,879 books and 1,983 subscriptions.

Campus Life

There are 109 active organizations on campus, including a drama/theater group, newspaper, radio station, television station, and choral group. No national or local **fraternities** or **sororities**.

Bowdoin is a member of the NCAA (Division III). **Intercollegiate sports** include baseball (m), basketball, cross-country running, field hockey (w), football (m), golf, ice hockey, lacrosse, sailing, skiing (cross-country), soccer, softball (w), squash, swimming, tennis, track and field, volleyball (w).

Campus Safety

Student safety services include self-defense education, whistle program, late-night transport/escort service, 24-hour emergency telephone alarm devices, 24-hour patrols by trained security personnel, student patrols, and electronically operated dormitory entrances.

Applying

Bowdoin requires an essay, a high school transcript, and 3 recommendations. It recommends an interview. Application deadline: 1/1; 2/15 for financial aid. Deferred admission is possible.

BRADLEY UNIVERSITY
URBAN SETTING ■ PRIVATE ■ INDEPENDENT ■ COED
PEORIA, ILLINOIS

Web site: www.bradley.edu
Contact: Mr. Thomas Richmond, Director of Admissions, 1501 West Bradley Avenue, 100 Swords Hall, Peoria, IL 61625-0002
Telephone: 309-677-1000 or toll-free 800-447-6460
E-mail: admissions@bradley.edu

Academics
Bradley awards bachelor's and master's **degrees**. Challenging opportunities include advanced placement credit, accelerated degree programs, student-designed majors, an honors program, double majors, independent study, and a senior project. Special programs include cooperative education, internships, summer session for credit, off-campus study, study-abroad, and Army ROTC.

The most frequently chosen **baccalaureate** fields are business/marketing, engineering/engineering technologies, and communications/communication technologies. A complete listing of majors at Bradley appears in the Majors Index beginning on page 460.

The **faculty** at Bradley has 332 full-time members, 83% with terminal degrees. The student-faculty ratio is 15:1.

Students of Bradley
The student body totals 6,137, of whom 5,305 are undergraduates. 54.1% are women and 45.9% are men. Students come from 42 states and territories and 55 other countries. 86% are from Illinois. 1.3% are international students. 5.6% are African American, 0.4% American Indian, 2.6% Asian American, and 1.8% Hispanic American. 89% returned for their sophomore year.

Facilities and Resources
Student rooms are linked to a campus network. 2,000 **computers** are available on campus that provide access to the Internet. The **library** has 424,753 books and 1,996 subscriptions.

Campus Life
There are 220 active organizations on campus, including a drama/theater group, newspaper, radio station, television station, and choral group. 34% of eligible men and 37% of eligible women are members of national **fraternities** and national **sororities**.

Bradley is a member of the NCAA (Division I). **Intercollegiate sports** (some offering scholarships) include baseball (m), basketball, cheerleading, cross-country running, golf, soccer (m), softball (w), tennis, track and field (w), volleyball (w).

Campus Safety
Student safety services include bicycle patrol, late-night transport/escort service, 24-hour emergency telephone alarm devices, 24-hour patrols by trained security personnel, and electronically operated dormitory entrances.

Applying
Bradley requires an essay, SAT I or ACT, and a high school transcript. It recommends an interview, recommendations, and a minimum high school GPA of 3.0. Application deadline: rolling admissions; 3/1 priority date for financial aid. Early and deferred admission are possible.

Getting in Last Year
5,207 applied
69% were accepted
1,105 enrolled (31%)
25% from top tenth of their h.s. class
40% had SAT verbal scores over 600
46% had SAT math scores over 600
68% had ACT scores over 24
4% had SAT verbal scores over 700
8% had SAT math scores over 700
12% had ACT scores over 30
2 National Merit Scholars

Graduation and After
49% graduated in 4 years
18% graduated in 5 years
1% graduated in 6 years
18% pursued further study (10% arts and sciences, 4% engineering, 2% law)
294 organizations recruited on campus

Financial Matters
$16,930 tuition and fees (2003–04)
$5980 room and board
83% average percent of need met
$11,997 average financial aid amount received per undergraduate (2001–02)

BRANDEIS UNIVERSITY

SUBURBAN SETTING ■ PRIVATE ■ INDEPENDENT ■ COED
WALTHAM, MASSACHUSETTS

Web site: www.brandeis.edu
Contact: Ms. Deena Whitfield, Director of Enrollment, 415 South Street,
    Waltham, MA 02254-9110
Telephone: 781-736-3500 or toll-free 800-622-0622 (out-of-state) **Fax:**
    781-736-3536
E-mail: sendinfo@brandeis.edu

Brandeis's top-ranked faculty members focus on teaching undergraduates and are accessible to students during classes, during office hours, and even at home. Students become involved in cutting-edge faculty research at the Volen Center for Complex Systems—studying the brain's cognitive processes—and throughout the University. Brandeis has an ideal location on the commuter rail 9 miles west of Boston, state-of-the-art sports facilities, and internships that complement interests in law, medicine, government, finance, the media, public service, and the arts. Brandeis offers broad, renewable financial aid for domestic and international students, including both need-based aid and scholarships that cover up to 100% of tuition.

Getting in Last Year
5,770 applied
44% were accepted
824 enrolled (33%)
69% from top tenth of their h.s. class
86% had SAT verbal scores over 600
83% had SAT math scores over 600
98% had ACT scores over 24
33% had SAT verbal scores over 700
31% had SAT math scores over 700
50% had ACT scores over 30
21 National Merit Scholars

Graduation and After
80% graduated in 4 years
4% graduated in 5 years
1% graduated in 6 years
23% pursued further study (11% arts and
    sciences, 6% law, 3% medicine)
126 organizations recruited on campus

Financial Matters
$29,875 tuition and fees (2003–04)
$8323 room and board
84% average percent of need met
$21,053 average financial aid amount received
    per undergraduate (2002–03 estimated)

Academics
Brandeis awards bachelor's, master's, and doctoral **degrees** and post-bachelor's certificates. Challenging opportunities include advanced placement credit, student-designed majors, an honors program, double majors, independent study, and a senior project. Special programs include internships, summer session for credit, off-campus study, study-abroad, and Army and Air Force ROTC.

The most frequently chosen **baccalaureate** fields are social sciences and history, biological/life sciences, and area/ethnic studies. A complete listing of majors at Brandeis appears in the Majors Index beginning on page 460.

The **faculty** at Brandeis has 335 full-time members, 98% with terminal degrees. The student-faculty ratio is 9:1.

Students of Brandeis
The student body totals 4,985, of whom 3,175 are undergraduates. 56.2% are women and 43.8% are men. Students come from 46 states and territories and 57 other countries. 24% are from Massachusetts. 6.9% are international students. 2.5% are African American, 0.2% American Indian, 8.2% Asian American, and 2.5% Hispanic American. 94% returned for their sophomore year.

Facilities and Resources
Student rooms are linked to a campus network. 104 **computers** are available on campus that provide access to educational software and the Internet. The 3 **libraries** have 938,835 books and 15,835 subscriptions.

Campus Life
There are 184 active organizations on campus, including a drama/theater group, newspaper, radio station, television station, and choral group. No national or local **fraternities** or **sororities**.

Brandeis is a member of the NCAA (Division III). **Intercollegiate sports** include baseball (m), basketball, cross-country running, fencing, golf (m), sailing, soccer (w), softball (w), swimming, tennis, track and field, volleyball (w).

Campus Safety
Student safety services include late-night transport/escort service, 24-hour emergency telephone alarm devices, 24-hour patrols by trained security personnel, and electronically operated dormitory entrances.

Applying
Brandeis requires an essay, SAT I and SAT II or ACT, a high school transcript, and 2 recommendations. It recommends an interview and a minimum high school GPA of 3.0. Application deadline: 1/15; 1/31 priority date for financial aid. Deferred admission is possible.

BRIGHAM YOUNG UNIVERSITY

SUBURBAN SETTING ■ PRIVATE ■ INDEPENDENT RELIGIOUS ■ COED
PROVO, UTAH

Web site: www.byu.edu
Contact: Mr. Tom Gourley, Dean of Admissions and Records, A-153 Abraham
 Smoot Building, Provo, UT 84602
Telephone: 801-422-2507 **Fax:** 801-422-0005
E-mail: admissions@byu.edu

Academics

BYU awards bachelor's, master's, doctoral, and first-professional **degrees**. Challenging
opportunities include advanced placement credit, accelerated degree programs, freshman
honors college, an honors program, double majors, independent study, and a senior
project. Special programs include cooperative education, internships, summer session for
credit, off-campus study, study-abroad, and Army and Air Force ROTC.

The most frequently chosen **baccalaureate** fields are business/marketing, social sciences and history, and education. A complete listing of majors at BYU appears in the
Majors Index beginning on page 460.

The **faculty** at BYU has 1,269 full-time members. The student-faculty ratio is 21:1.

Students of BYU

The student body totals 33,008, of whom 29,932 are undergraduates. 49.3% are women
and 50.7% are men. Students come from 54 states and territories and 119 other
countries. 28% are from Utah. 3.3% are international students. 0.4% are African
American, 0.7% American Indian, 3.1% Asian American, and 3.2% Hispanic American.
93% returned for their sophomore year.

Facilities and Resources

Student rooms are linked to a campus network. 2,000 **computers** are available on
campus that provide access to intranet and the Internet. The 3 **libraries** have 2,511,155
books and 619,493 subscriptions.

Campus Life

There are 390 active organizations on campus, including a drama/theater group,
newspaper, radio station, television station, choral group, and marching band. No
national or local **fraternities** or **sororities**.

BYU is a member of the NCAA (Division I). **Intercollegiate sports** (some offering
scholarships) include baseball (m), basketball, cheerleading, cross-country running,
football (m), golf, gymnastics (w), soccer (w), softball (w), swimming, tennis, track and
field, volleyball.

Campus Safety

Student safety services include late-night transport/escort service, 24-hour emergency
telephone alarm devices, 24-hour patrols by trained security personnel, and electronically operated dormitory entrances.

Applying

BYU requires an essay, ACT, a high school transcript, an interview, and 1 recommendation. Application deadline: 2/15; 4/2 priority date for financial aid. Early and
deferred admission are possible.

Getting in Last Year
9,300 applied
78% were accepted
5,331 enrolled (74%)
3.71 average high school GPA
54% had SAT verbal scores over 600
60% had SAT math scores over 600
83% had ACT scores over 24
14% had SAT verbal scores over 700
17% had SAT math scores over 700
22% had ACT scores over 30
140 National Merit Scholars

Graduation and After
75% had job offers within 6 months
600 organizations recruited on campus

Financial Matters
$3150 tuition and fees (2003–04)
$5354 room and board
40% average percent of need met
$3853 average financial aid amount received
 per undergraduate (2001–02)

BROWN UNIVERSITY

URBAN SETTING ■ PRIVATE ■ INDEPENDENT ■ COED
PROVIDENCE, RHODE ISLAND

Web site: www.brown.edu
Contact: Mr. Michael Goldberger, Director of Admission, Box 1876,
Providence, RI 02912
Telephone: 401-863-2378 **Fax:** 401-863-9300
E-mail: admission_undergraduate@brown.edu

Brown is a university/college with a renowned faculty that teaches students in the undergraduate college, the graduate school, and the medical school. The unique, nonrestrictive curriculum allows students freedom in selecting their courses, and they may choose their concentration from 83 areas, complete a double major, or pursue an independent concentration. The 140-acre campus is set in a residential neighborhood (National Historic District) and features state-of-the-art computing facilities and an athletics complex. A real sense of community exists on campus, as every student has an academic adviser, and there are several peer counselors in the residence halls.

Getting in Last Year
15,157 applied
16% were accepted
1,393 enrolled (57%)
87% from top tenth of their h.s. class
87% had SAT verbal scores over 600
91% had SAT math scores over 600
91% had ACT scores over 24
51% had SAT verbal scores over 700
55% had SAT math scores over 700
50% had ACT scores over 30
152 valedictorians

Graduation and After
83% graduated in 4 years
11% graduated in 5 years
2% graduated in 6 years
35% pursued further study (10% arts and sciences, 10% law, 9% medicine)
60% had job offers within 6 months
400 organizations recruited on campus

Financial Matters
$29,846 tuition and fees (2003–04)
$8096 room and board
100% average percent of need met
$23,249 average financial aid amount received per undergraduate (2002–03 estimated)

Academics

Brown awards bachelor's, master's, doctoral, and first-professional **degrees**. Challenging opportunities include advanced placement credit, accelerated degree programs, student-designed majors, an honors program, double majors, independent study, and a senior project. Special programs include internships, summer session for credit, off-campus study, study-abroad, and Army ROTC.

The most frequently chosen **baccalaureate** fields are social sciences and history, liberal arts/general studies, and biological/life sciences. A complete listing of majors at Brown appears in the Majors Index beginning on page 460.

The **faculty** at Brown has 776 full-time members, 98% with terminal degrees. The student-faculty ratio is 8:1.

Students of Brown

The student body totals 7,882, of whom 5,906 are undergraduates. 55% are women and 45% are men. Students come from 52 states and territories and 72 other countries. 4% are from Rhode Island. 6.3% are international students. 6.3% are African American, 0.5% American Indian, 13.4% Asian American, and 6.6% Hispanic American. 97% returned for their sophomore year.

Facilities and Resources

Student rooms are linked to a campus network. 400 **computers** are available on campus that provide access to the Internet. The 6 **libraries** have 3,000,000 books and 17,000 subscriptions.

Campus Life

There are 240 active organizations on campus, including a drama/theater group, newspaper, radio station, television station, choral group, and marching band. 12% of eligible men and 2% of eligible women are members of national **fraternities**, national **sororities**, and coed fraternity.

Brown is a member of the NCAA (Division I). **Intercollegiate sports** include baseball (m), basketball, crew, cross-country running, equestrian sports (w), fencing, field hockey (w), football (m), golf, gymnastics (w), ice hockey, lacrosse, skiing (downhill) (w), soccer, softball (w), squash, swimming, tennis, track and field, volleyball (w), water polo, wrestling (m).

Campus Safety

Student safety services include late-night transport/escort service, 24-hour emergency telephone alarm devices, 24-hour patrols by trained security personnel, and electronically operated dormitory entrances.

Applying

Brown requires an essay, SAT I and SAT II or ACT, a high school transcript, and 2 recommendations, and in some cases 3 recommendations. Application deadline: 1/1; 2/1 for financial aid. Early and deferred admission are possible.

BRYAN COLLEGE

SMALL-TOWN SETTING ■ PRIVATE ■ INDEPENDENT RELIGIOUS ■ COED
DAYTON, TENNESSEE

Web site: www.bryan.edu
Contact: Mr. Mark A. Cruver, Director of Admissions and Enrollment
Management, PO Box 7000, Dayton, TN 37321-7000
Telephone: 423-775-2041 ext. 207 or toll-free 800-277-9522 **Fax:**
423-775-7199
E-mail: admiss@bryan.edu

Academics

Bryan awards associate and bachelor's **degrees**. Challenging opportunities include
advanced placement credit, an honors program, double majors, independent study, and a
senior project. Special programs include internships, summer session for credit, and
study-abroad.

The most frequently chosen **baccalaureate** fields are business/marketing, psychology, and education. A complete listing of majors at Bryan appears in the Majors Index
beginning on page 460.

The **faculty** at Bryan has 35 full-time members, 80% with terminal degrees. The
student-faculty ratio is 14:1.

Students of Bryan

The student body totals 615, of whom 557 are undergraduates. Students come from 33
states and territories and 7 other countries. 77% returned for their sophomore year.

Facilities and Resources

Student rooms are linked to a campus network. 74 **computers** are available on campus
that provide access to the Internet. The **library** has 98,413 books and 4,212 subscriptions.

Campus Life

There are 7 active organizations on campus, including a drama/theater group,
newspaper, and choral group. No national or local **fraternities** or **sororities**.

Bryan is a member of the NAIA and NCCAA. **Intercollegiate sports** (some offering
scholarships) include baseball (m), basketball, soccer, tennis, volleyball (w).

Campus Safety

Student safety services include police patrols, late-night transport/escort service, student
patrols, and electronically operated dormitory entrances.

Applying

Bryan requires an essay, ACT, a high school transcript, 3 recommendations, and a
minimum high school GPA of 2.0, and in some cases an interview. Application deadline:
rolling admissions; 5/1 priority date for financial aid. Early and deferred admission are
possible.

Getting in Last Year

539 applied
35% were accepted
55% from top tenth of their h.s. class
3.48 average high school GPA
31% had SAT verbal scores over 600
23% had SAT math scores over 600
49% had ACT scores over 24
11% had SAT verbal scores over 700
6% had SAT math scores over 700
7% had ACT scores over 30

Graduation and After

37% graduated in 4 years
8% graduated in 5 years
2% graduated in 6 years
75% had job offers within 6 months
18 organizations recruited on campus

Financial Matters

$13,500 tuition and fees (2003–04)
$4400 room and board
69% average percent of need met
$10,035 average financial aid amount received
per undergraduate

BRYN MAWR COLLEGE
SUBURBAN SETTING ■ PRIVATE ■ INDEPENDENT ■ WOMEN ONLY
BRYN MAWR, PENNSYLVANIA

Web site: www.brynmawr.edu
Contact: Ms. Jennifer Rickard, Dean of Admissions and Financial Aid, 101 North Merion Avenue, Bryn Mawr, PA 19010
Telephone: 610-526-5152 or toll-free 800-BMC-1885 (out-of-state)
E-mail: admissions@brynmawr.edu

Bryn Mawr, a liberal arts college located in suburban Philadelphia, is a diverse community of individuals who share a profound intellectual committment, a willingness to take risks, and the purposeful vision required to press ideas into action. Bryn Mawr offers the benefits of proximity to Philadelphia with its rich cultural and social resources, as well as an active academic and social consortium with neighboring Haverford College, nearby Swarthmore College, and the University of Pennsylvania.

Getting in Last Year
1,748 applied
51% were accepted
352 enrolled (39%)
56% from top tenth of their h.s. class
82% had SAT verbal scores over 600
68% had SAT math scores over 600
38% had SAT verbal scores over 700
15% had SAT math scores over 700
5 National Merit Scholars
20 valedictorians

Graduation and After
78% graduated in 4 years
6% graduated in 5 years
1% graduated in 6 years
20% pursued further study
52% had job offers within 6 months
65 organizations recruited on campus

Financial Matters
$27,520 tuition and fees (2003–04)
$9370 room and board
99% average percent of need met
$25,139 average financial aid amount received per undergraduate

Academics
Bryn Mawr awards bachelor's, master's, and doctoral **degrees**. Challenging opportunities include advanced placement credit, accelerated degree programs, student-designed majors, an honors program, double majors, independent study, and a senior project. Special programs include summer session for credit, off-campus study, study-abroad, and Air Force ROTC.

The most frequently chosen **baccalaureate** fields are social sciences and history, mathematics, and English. A complete listing of majors at Bryn Mawr appears in the Majors Index beginning on page 460.

The **faculty** at Bryn Mawr has 146 full-time members, 97% with terminal degrees. The student-faculty ratio is 8:1.

Students of Bryn Mawr
The student body totals 1,781, of whom 1,334 are undergraduates. Students come from 48 states and territories and 44 other countries. 20% are from Pennsylvania. 7.6% are international students. 3.5% are African American, 12% Asian American, and 3.1% Hispanic American. 95% returned for their sophomore year.

Facilities and Resources
Student rooms are linked to a campus network. 200 **computers** are available on campus that provide access to the Internet.

Campus Life
There are 100 active organizations on campus, including a drama/theater group, newspaper, and choral group. No national or local **sororities**.

Bryn Mawr is a member of the NCAA (Division III). **Intercollegiate sports** include badminton, basketball, crew, cross-country running, field hockey, lacrosse, soccer, swimming, tennis, track and field, volleyball.

Campus Safety
Student safety services include shuttle bus service, awareness programs, bicycle registration, security Website, late-night transport/escort service, 24-hour emergency telephone alarm devices, 24-hour patrols by trained security personnel, and electronically operated dormitory entrances.

Applying
Bryn Mawr requires an essay, SAT I and SAT II or ACT, a high school transcript, and 3 recommendations. It recommends an interview. Application deadline: 1/15; 2/2 for financial aid. Early and deferred admission are possible.

Bucknell University

SMALL-TOWN SETTING ■ PRIVATE ■ INDEPENDENT ■ COED
LEWISBURG, PENNSYLVANIA

Web site: www.bucknell.edu
Contact: Mr. Mark D. Davies, Dean of Admissions, Lewisburg, PA 17837
Telephone: 570-577-1101 **Fax:** 570-577-3538
E-mail: admissions@bucknell.edu

Academics

Bucknell awards bachelor's and master's **degrees**. Challenging opportunities include advanced placement credit, student-designed majors, an honors program, double majors, independent study, and a senior project. Special programs include internships, summer session for credit, off-campus study, study-abroad, and Army ROTC.

The most frequently chosen **baccalaureate** fields are social sciences and history, business/marketing, and engineering/engineering technologies. A complete listing of majors at Bucknell appears in the Majors Index beginning on page 460.

The **faculty** at Bucknell has 291 full-time members, 96% with terminal degrees. The student-faculty ratio is 12:1.

Students of Bucknell

The student body totals 3,678, of whom 3,486 are undergraduates. 50.3% are women and 49.7% are men. Students come from 48 states and territories and 46 other countries. 32% are from Pennsylvania. 2.1% are international students. 2.7% are African American, 0.4% American Indian, 6% Asian American, and 2.1% Hispanic American. 94% returned for their sophomore year.

Facilities and Resources

Student rooms are linked to a campus network. 610 **computers** are available on campus that provide access to the Internet. The **library** has 710,985 books and 5,853 subscriptions.

Campus Life

There are 135 active organizations on campus, including a drama/theater group, newspaper, radio station, and choral group. 51% of eligible men and 51% of eligible women are members of national **fraternities** and national **sororities**.

Bucknell is a member of the NCAA (Division I). **Intercollegiate sports** (some offering scholarships) include baseball (m), basketball, crew (w), cross-country running, field hockey (w), football (m), golf, lacrosse, soccer, softball (w), swimming, tennis, track and field, volleyball (w), water polo.

Campus Safety

Student safety services include well-lit pathways, self-defense education, safety/security orientation, late-night transport/escort service, 24-hour emergency telephone alarm devices, 24-hour patrols by trained security personnel, and student patrols.

Applying

Bucknell requires an essay, SAT I or ACT, a high school transcript, and 2 recommendations. It recommends an interview. Application deadline: 1/1; 1/1 for financial aid.

With 3,350 undergraduates and 150 graduate students, Bucknell is the largest of the top 40 "national liberal arts colleges" and one of just 5 among the group that is a university. Its combination of an intimate college experience and the extensive choices offered by a distinguished university gives students opportunities they won't find elsewhere. With the help of committed professors who provide sound advice, students find many ways to add breadth, depth, and imagination to their program of study.

Getting in Last Year
7,706 applied
38% were accepted
906 enrolled (31%)
69% from top tenth of their h.s. class
77% had SAT verbal scores over 600
88% had SAT math scores over 600
15% had SAT verbal scores over 700
29% had SAT math scores over 700

Graduation and After
83% graduated in 4 years
6% graduated in 5 years
22% pursued further study (7% arts and sciences, 3% engineering, 3% law)
97% had job offers within 6 months
267 organizations recruited on campus

Financial Matters
$28,960 tuition and fees (2003–04)
$6302 room and board
100% average percent of need met
$19,000 average financial aid amount received per undergraduate

---

BUTLER UNIVERSITY

URBAN SETTING ■ PRIVATE ■ INDEPENDENT ■ COED
INDIANAPOLIS, INDIANA

Web site: www.butler.edu
Contact: Mr. William Preble, Dean of Admissions, 4600 Sunset Avenue,
    Indianapolis, IN 46208-3485
Telephone: 317-940-8100 ext. 8124 or toll-free 888-940-8100 **Fax:**
    317-940-8150
E-mail: admission@butler.edu

A t Butler University, students are actively engaged in the learning experience from the minute they step on campus. With small class sizes, students receive direct access to faculty members, personalized attention, and hands-on learning opportunities. Participation in research is an opportunity rarely offered to undergraduates; at Butler, students not only have the chance to participate in research with faculty members, they also originate research projects and develop them into professional presentations and publications. Butler students receive research grants through the Butler Summer Institute and present their projects at the Undergraduate Research Conference, hosted by Butler every April.

Getting in Last Year
4,329 applied
77% were accepted
976 enrolled (29%)
45% from top tenth of their h.s. class
3.60 average high school GPA
45% had SAT verbal scores over 600
52% had SAT math scores over 600
79% had ACT scores over 24
8% had SAT verbal scores over 700
9% had SAT math scores over 700
18% had ACT scores over 30
11 National Merit Scholars
59 valedictorians

Graduation and After
53% graduated in 4 years
9% graduated in 5 years
7% graduated in 6 years
19% pursued further study (7% arts and sciences, 4% medicine, 2% law)
92% had job offers within 6 months
213 organizations recruited on campus

Financial Matters
$21,210 tuition and fees (2003–04)
$7040 room and board
$16,400 average financial aid amount received per undergraduate

Academics
Butler awards associate, bachelor's, master's, and first-professional **degrees** and post-bachelor's certificates. Challenging opportunities include advanced placement credit, student-designed majors, an honors program, double majors, independent study, and a senior project. Special programs include cooperative education, internships, summer session for credit, off-campus study, study-abroad, and Army and Air Force ROTC.

The most frequently chosen **baccalaureate** fields are business/marketing, health professions and related sciences, and education. A complete listing of majors at Butler appears in the Majors Index beginning on page 460.

The **faculty** at Butler has 269 full-time members, 84% with terminal degrees. The student-faculty ratio is 13:1.

Students of Butler
The student body totals 4,424, of whom 3,657 are undergraduates. 63.1% are women and 36.9% are men. Students come from 42 states and territories and 51 other countries. 60% are from Indiana. 2% are international students. 3.8% are African American, 0.2% American Indian, 2.1% Asian American, and 1.5% Hispanic American. 88% returned for their sophomore year.

Facilities and Resources
Student rooms are linked to a campus network. 250 **computers** are available on campus that provide access to e-mail and the Internet. The 2 **libraries** have 308,689 books and 2,000 subscriptions.

Campus Life
There are 100 active organizations on campus, including a drama/theater group, newspaper, radio station, television station, choral group, and marching band. 24% of eligible men and 24% of eligible women are members of national **fraternities** and national **sororities**.

Butler is a member of the NCAA (Division I). **Intercollegiate sports** (some offering scholarships) include baseball (m), basketball, cross-country running, football (m), golf, lacrosse (m), soccer, softball (w), swimming, tennis, track and field, volleyball (w).

Campus Safety
Student safety services include late-night transport/escort service, 24-hour emergency telephone alarm devices, 24-hour patrols by trained security personnel, and electronically operated dormitory entrances.

Applying
Butler requires an essay, SAT I or ACT, and a high school transcript, and in some cases an interview and audition. It recommends SAT II Subject Tests. Application deadline: 8/15; 3/1 priority date for financial aid. Deferred admission is possible.

CALIFORNIA INSTITUTE OF TECHNOLOGY

SUBURBAN SETTING ■ PRIVATE ■ INDEPENDENT ■ COED
PASADENA, CALIFORNIA

Web site: www.caltech.edu
Contact: Mr. Daniel T. Langdale, Director of Admissions, 1200 East
    California Boulevard, Pasadena, CA 91125-0001
Telephone: 626-395-6341 **Fax:** 626-683-3026
E-mail: ugadmissions@caltech.edu

Academics

Caltech awards bachelor's, master's, and doctoral **degrees**. Challenging opportunities
include student-designed majors, double majors, and independent study. Special
programs include internships, off-campus study, study-abroad, and Army and Air Force
ROTC.

The most frequently chosen **baccalaureate** fields are engineering/engineering
technologies, physical sciences, and mathematics. A complete listing of majors at Caltech
appears in the Majors Index beginning on page 460.

The **faculty** at Caltech has 292 full-time members, 97% with terminal degrees. The
student-faculty ratio is 3:1.

Students of Caltech

The student body totals 2,172, of whom 891 are undergraduates. 33.3% are women and
66.7% are men. Students come from 46 states and territories and 28 other countries.
41% are from California. 7.5% are international students. 1.3% are African American,
0.6% American Indian, 31.1% Asian American, and 7.3% Hispanic American. 95%
returned for their sophomore year.

Facilities and Resources

Student rooms are linked to a campus network. 600 **computers** are available on campus
that provide access to the Internet. The 11 **libraries** have 3,165,000 books and 3,500
subscriptions.

Campus Life

There are 85 active organizations on campus, including a drama/theater group,
newspaper, and choral group. No national or local **fraternities** or **sororities**.

Caltech is a member of the NCAA (Division III). **Intercollegiate sports** include
baseball (m), basketball, cross-country running, fencing, golf (m), soccer (m), swimming,
tennis, track and field, volleyball (w), water polo.

Campus Safety

Student safety services include late-night transport/escort service, 24-hour emergency
telephone alarm devices, and 24-hour patrols by trained security personnel.

Applying

Caltech requires an essay, SAT II: Writing Test, SAT I or ACT, SAT II Subject Test in
Math Level II C and either physics, chemistry, or biology, a high school transcript, and 2
recommendations. Application deadline: 1/1; 1/15 priority date for financial aid. Early
and deferred admission are possible.

Getting in Last Year
3,071 applied
17% were accepted
191 enrolled (37%)
94% from top tenth of their h.s. class
94% had SAT verbal scores over 600
100% had SAT math scores over 600
77% had SAT verbal scores over 700
96% had SAT math scores over 700
56 National Merit Scholars
76 valedictorians

Graduation and After
79% graduated in 4 years
8% graduated in 5 years
2% graduated in 6 years
Graduates pursuing further study: 26% arts
    and sciences, 20% engineering, 3% medicine
109 organizations recruited on campus

Financial Matters
$24,117 tuition and fees (2003–04)
$7560 room and board
100% average percent of need met
$23,427 average financial aid amount received
    per undergraduate (2002–03 estimated)

CALIFORNIA POLYTECHNIC STATE UNIVERSITY, SAN LUIS OBISPO

SMALL-TOWN SETTING ■ PUBLIC ■ STATE-SUPPORTED ■ COED
SAN LUIS OBISPO, CALIFORNIA

Web site: www.calpoly.edu
Contact: Mr. James Maraviglia, Director of Admissions and Evaluations, San Luis Obispo, CA 93407
Telephone: 805-756-2311 **Fax:** 805-756-5400
E-mail: admprosp@calpoly.edu

Getting in Last Year
20,827 applied
38% were accepted
2,828 enrolled (35%)
42% from top tenth of their h.s. class
3.71 average high school GPA
36% had SAT verbal scores over 600
62% had SAT math scores over 600
69% had ACT scores over 24
4% had SAT verbal scores over 700
14% had SAT math scores over 700
9% had ACT scores over 30

Graduation and After
15% pursued further study
90% had job offers within 6 months
630 organizations recruited on campus

Financial Matters
$3281 resident tuition and fees (2003–04)
$10,049 nonresident tuition and fees (2003–04)
$7619 room and board
76% average percent of need met
$6847 average financial aid amount received per undergraduate (2001–02)

Academics
Cal Poly State University awards bachelor's and master's **degrees**. Challenging opportunities include advanced placement credit, an honors program, double majors, independent study, and a senior project. Special programs include cooperative education, internships, summer session for credit, off-campus study, study-abroad, and Army ROTC.

The most frequently chosen **baccalaureate** fields are engineering/engineering technologies, agriculture, and business/marketing. A complete listing of majors at Cal Poly State University appears in the Majors Index beginning on page 460.

The **faculty** at Cal Poly State University has 791 full-time members, 67% with terminal degrees. The student-faculty ratio is 19:1.

Students of Cal Poly State University
The student body totals 18,303, of whom 17,257 are undergraduates. 44.2% are women and 55.8% are men. Students come from 48 states and territories and 41 other countries. 94% are from California. 0.9% are international students. 1% are African American, 0.8% American Indian, 11.3% Asian American, and 9.6% Hispanic American. 89% returned for their sophomore year.

Facilities and Resources
Student rooms are linked to a campus network. 1,880 **computers** are available on campus for student use. The **library** has 763,651 books and 5,529 subscriptions.

Campus Life
There are 360 active organizations on campus, including a drama/theater group, newspaper, radio station, choral group, and marching band. 8% of eligible men and 9% of eligible women are members of national **fraternities**, national **sororities**, local fraternities, and local sororities.

Cal Poly State University is a member of the NCAA (Division I). **Intercollegiate sports** (some offering scholarships) include baseball (m), basketball, cross-country running, equestrian sports, football (m), golf (m), gymnastics (w), soccer, softball (w), swimming, tennis, track and field, volleyball (w), wrestling (m).

Campus Safety
Student safety services include late-night transport/escort service, 24-hour emergency telephone alarm devices, 24-hour patrols by trained security personnel, student patrols, and electronically operated dormitory entrances.

Applying
Cal Poly State University requires SAT I or ACT and a high school transcript. Application deadline: 11/30; 3/2 priority date for financial aid. Early admission is possible.

CALVIN COLLEGE

SUBURBAN SETTING ■ PRIVATE ■ INDEPENDENT RELIGIOUS ■ COED
GRAND RAPIDS, MICHIGAN

Web site: www.calvin.edu
Contact: Mr. Dale D. Kuiper, Director of Admissions, 3201 Burton Street, SE, Grand Rapids, MI 49546-4388
Telephone: 616-526-6106 or toll-free 800-688-0122 **Fax:** 616-526-6777
E-mail: admissions@calvin.edu

Academics

Calvin awards bachelor's and master's **degrees** and post-bachelor's certificates. Challenging opportunities include advanced placement credit, accelerated degree programs, student-designed majors, an honors program, double majors, independent study, and a senior project. Special programs include internships, summer session for credit, off-campus study, study-abroad, and Army ROTC.

The most frequently chosen **baccalaureate** fields are business/marketing, social sciences and history, and education. A complete listing of majors at Calvin appears in the Majors Index beginning on page 460.

The **faculty** at Calvin has 305 full-time members, 83% with terminal degrees. The student-faculty ratio is 13:1.

Students of Calvin

The student body totals 4,323, of whom 4,289 are undergraduates. 55.7% are women and 44.3% are men. Students come from 48 states and territories and 44 other countries. 61% are from Michigan. 8% are international students. 0.8% are African American, 0.5% American Indian, 2.5% Asian American, and 0.9% Hispanic American. 87% returned for their sophomore year.

Facilities and Resources

Student rooms are linked to a campus network. 700 **computers** are available on campus that provide access to the Internet. The 2 **libraries** have 801,802 books and 2,658 subscriptions.

Campus Life

There are 52 active organizations on campus, including a drama/theater group, newspaper, radio station, and choral group. No national or local **fraternities** or **sororities**.

Calvin is a member of the NCAA (Division III). **Intercollegiate sports** include baseball (m), basketball, cross-country running, golf, soccer, softball (w), swimming, tennis, track and field, volleyball (w).

Campus Safety

Student safety services include crime prevention programs, crime alert bulletins, late-night transport/escort service, 24-hour emergency telephone alarm devices, 24-hour patrols by trained security personnel, student patrols, and electronically operated dormitory entrances.

Applying

Calvin requires an essay, SAT I or ACT, a high school transcript, 1 recommendation, and a minimum high school GPA of 2.5. It recommends an interview. Application deadline: 8/15; 2/15 priority date for financial aid. Deferred admission is possible.

> **C**alvin brings together some remarkable minds—4,300 students and 290 professors who chose this institution because it values both intellect and faith. Through intellectual curiosity, spirited interaction, and conscientious work, Calvin people tackle some big questions—always questioning, always analyzing—exploring what it means to work for renewal in God's world.

Getting in Last Year

1,933 applied
99% were accepted
1,042 enrolled (55%)
25% from top tenth of their h.s. class
3.54 average high school GPA
53% had SAT verbal scores over 600
52% had SAT math scores over 600
69% had ACT scores over 24
16% had SAT verbal scores over 700
14% had SAT math scores over 700
16% had ACT scores over 30
19 National Merit Scholars
34 valedictorians

Graduation and After

56% graduated in 4 years
16% graduated in 5 years
1% graduated in 6 years
20% pursued further study (5% arts and sciences, 2% education, 2% medicine)
73% had job offers within 6 months
295 organizations recruited on campus

Financial Matters

$16,775 tuition and fees (2003–04)
$5840 room and board
91% average percent of need met
$12,252 average financial aid amount received per undergraduate (2002–03 estimated)

CANISIUS COLLEGE

URBAN SETTING ■ PRIVATE ■ INDEPENDENT RELIGIOUS ■ COED
BUFFALO, NEW YORK

Web site: www.canisius.edu
Contact: Miss Penelope H. Lips, Director of Admissions, 2001 Main Street,
Buffalo, NY 14208-1098
Telephone: 716-888-2200 or toll-free 800-843-1517 **Fax:** 716-888-3230
E-mail: admissions@canisius.edu

<table>
<tr><td>

Canisius College believes
they are a place where
leaders are made.
Thousands of Canisius graduates are
leaders in their professions, including
doctors, lawyers, scientists, business
executives, and teachers. Canisius
has everything students want in a
college experience, including more
than 70 majors and special
programs, small classes taught by
caring faculty members,
state-of-the-art living and learning
environments, and an unlimited
range of learning options outside the
classroom. It's a great start to a
career and future. It's how leaders
are made.

</td></tr>
</table>

Getting in Last Year
3,437 applied
83% were accepted
836 enrolled (29%)
23% from top tenth of their h.s. class
3.45 average high school GPA
27% had SAT verbal scores over 600
32% had SAT math scores over 600
50% had ACT scores over 24
4% had SAT verbal scores over 700
4% had SAT math scores over 700
8% had ACT scores over 30
12 valedictorians

Graduation and After
53% graduated in 4 years
12% graduated in 5 years
2% graduated in 6 years
28% pursued further study (8% education,
   6% arts and sciences, 3% medicine)
68.6% had job offers within 6 months
30 organizations recruited on campus

Financial Matters
$20,193 tuition and fees (2003–04)
$7970 room and board
80% average percent of need met
$16,917 average financial aid amount received
   per undergraduate

Academics

Canisius awards bachelor's and master's **degrees** and post-master's certificates. Challenging opportunities include advanced placement credit, student-designed majors, an honors program, independent study, and a senior project. Special programs include internships, summer session for credit, off-campus study, study-abroad, and Army ROTC.

The most frequently chosen **baccalaureate** fields are business/marketing, education, and communications/communication technologies. A complete listing of majors at Canisius appears in the Majors Index beginning on page 460.

The **faculty** at Canisius has 212 full-time members, 97% with terminal degrees. The student-faculty ratio is 14:1.

Students of Canisius

The student body totals 5,095, of whom 3,535 are undergraduates. 55.3% are women and 44.7% are men. Students come from 23 states and territories and 38 other countries. 94% are from New York. 2.4% are international students. 7.1% are African American, 0.5% American Indian, 1.3% Asian American, and 2.6% Hispanic American. 83% returned for their sophomore year.

Facilities and Resources

Student rooms are linked to a campus network. 325 **computers** are available on campus that provide access to online accounts and the Internet. The 2 **libraries** have 328,278 books and 1,637 subscriptions.

Campus Life

There are 100 active organizations on campus, including a drama/theater group, newspaper, radio station, and choral group. 2% of eligible men and 2% of eligible women are members of national **fraternities** and national **sororities**.

Canisius is a member of the NCAA (Division I). **Intercollegiate sports** (some offering scholarships) include baseball (m), basketball, cross-country running, golf (m), ice hockey (m), lacrosse, soccer, softball (w), swimming (w), volleyball (w).

Campus Safety

Student safety services include crime prevention programs, closed-circuit television monitors, late-night transport/escort service, 24-hour emergency telephone alarm devices, 24-hour patrols by trained security personnel, and electronically operated dormitory entrances.

Applying

Canisius requires SAT I or ACT and a high school transcript, and in some cases an interview. It recommends an interview and recommendations. Application deadline: rolling admissions; 2/15 priority date for financial aid. Early and deferred admission are possible.

CARLETON COLLEGE

SMALL-TOWN SETTING ■ PRIVATE ■ INDEPENDENT ■ COED
NORTHFIELD, MINNESOTA

Web site: www.carleton.edu
Contact: Mr. Paul Thiboutot, Dean of Admissions, 100 South College Street, Northfield, MN 55057
Telephone: 507-646-4190 or toll-free 800-995-2275 **Fax:** 507-646-4526
E-mail: admissions@acs.carleton.edu

Academics

Carleton awards bachelor's **degrees**. Challenging opportunities include advanced placement credit, accelerated degree programs, student-designed majors, double majors, independent study, and a senior project. Special programs include internships, off-campus study, and study-abroad.

The most frequently chosen **baccalaureate** fields are social sciences and history, biological/life sciences, and physical sciences. A complete listing of majors at Carleton appears in the Majors Index beginning on page 460.

The **faculty** at Carleton has 196 full-time members, 95% with terminal degrees. The student-faculty ratio is 9:1.

Students of Carleton

The student body is made up of 1,943 undergraduates. 51.9% are women and 48.1% are men. Students come from 49 states and territories and 30 other countries. 24% are from Minnesota. 4.7% are international students. 5% are African American, 0.6% American Indian, 8.9% Asian American, and 4% Hispanic American. 97% returned for their sophomore year.

Facilities and Resources

Student rooms are linked to a campus network. 221 **computers** are available on campus that provide access to the Internet. The 2 **libraries** have 662,871 books and 10,964 subscriptions.

Campus Life

There are 132 active organizations on campus, including a drama/theater group, newspaper, radio station, and choral group. No national or local **fraternities** or **sororities**.

Carleton is a member of the NCAA (Division III). **Intercollegiate sports** include baseball (m), basketball, cross-country running, football (m), golf, soccer, softball (w), swimming, tennis, track and field, volleyball (w).

Campus Safety

Student safety services include late-night transport/escort service, 24-hour emergency telephone alarm devices, 24-hour patrols by trained security personnel, student patrols, and electronically operated dormitory entrances.

Applying

Carleton requires an essay, SAT I or ACT, a high school transcript, and 2 recommendations. It recommends SAT II Subject Tests, SAT II: Writing Test, and an interview. Application deadline: 1/15; 2/15 priority date for financial aid. Early and deferred admission are possible.

Getting in Last Year
4,737 applied
30% were accepted
488 enrolled (35%)
71% from top tenth of their h.s. class
91% had SAT verbal scores over 600
92% had SAT math scores over 600
94% had ACT scores over 24
52% had SAT verbal scores over 700
44% had SAT math scores over 700
58% had ACT scores over 30
83 National Merit Scholars
68 valedictorians

Graduation and After
85% graduated in 4 years
4% graduated in 5 years
1% graduated in 6 years
20% pursued further study (11% arts and sciences, 1% medicine, 1% law)
47% had job offers within 6 months
43 organizations recruited on campus

Financial Matters
$28,527 tuition and fees (2003–04)
$5868 room and board
100% average percent of need met
$18,832 average financial aid amount received per undergraduate (2001–02)

CARNEGIE MELLON UNIVERSITY

URBAN SETTING ■ PRIVATE ■ INDEPENDENT ■ COED
PITTSBURGH, PENNSYLVANIA

Web site: www.cmu.edu
Contact: Mr. Michael Steidel, Director of Admissions, 5000 Forbes Avenue,
    Warner Hall, Room 101, Pittsburgh, PA 15213
Telephone: 412-268-2082 **Fax:** 412-268-7838
E-mail: undergraduate-admissions@andrew.cmu.edu

First envisioned by steel magnate and philanthropist Andrew Carnegie, Carnegie Mellon University has steadily built upon its foundations of excellence and innovation to become one of America's leading universities. Carnegie Mellon's unique approach to education—giving students opportunities to become experts in their chosen fields while studying a broad range of course work across disciplines—helps students become leaders and problem solvers today and tomorrow. The University offers more than 90 majors and minors across 6 undergraduate colleges. Whether students are interested in creating the technology of tomorrow or getting their break on Broadway, a Carnegie Mellon education can take them there.

Getting in Last Year
14,467 applied
38% were accepted
1,341 enrolled (24%)
72% from top tenth of their h.s. class
3.60 average high school GPA
78% had SAT verbal scores over 600
97% had SAT math scores over 600
96% had ACT scores over 24
30% had SAT verbal scores over 700
66% had SAT math scores over 700
52% had ACT scores over 30

Graduation and After
66% graduated in 4 years
12% graduated in 5 years
3% graduated in 6 years
20% pursued further study (9% arts and sciences, 7% engineering, 2% medicine)
60% had job offers within 6 months
945 organizations recruited on campus

Financial Matters
$29,410 tuition and fees (2003–04)
$8155 room and board
83% average percent of need met
$19,732 average financial aid amount received per undergraduate (2002–03 estimated)

Academics
CMU awards bachelor's, master's, and doctoral **degrees** and post-master's certificates. Challenging opportunities include advanced placement credit, accelerated degree programs, student-designed majors, freshman honors college, an honors program, double majors, independent study, and a senior project. Special programs include cooperative education, internships, summer session for credit, off-campus study, study-abroad, and Army, Navy and Air Force ROTC.

The most frequently chosen **baccalaureate** fields are engineering/engineering technologies, computer/information sciences, and visual/performing arts. A complete listing of majors at CMU appears in the Majors Index beginning on page 460.

The **faculty** at CMU has 773 full-time members, 98% with terminal degrees. The student-faculty ratio is 11:1.

Students of CMU
The student body totals 9,756, of whom 5,484 are undergraduates. 39.8% are women and 60.2% are men. Students come from 52 states and territories and 61 other countries. 24% are from Pennsylvania. 11.5% are international students. 4.9% are African American, 0.4% American Indian, 23.2% Asian American, and 5.2% Hispanic American. 93% returned for their sophomore year.

Facilities and Resources
Student rooms are linked to a campus network. 450 **computers** are available on campus that provide access to the Internet. The 3 **libraries** have 961,507 books and 5,714 subscriptions.

Campus Life
There are 100 active organizations on campus, including a drama/theater group, newspaper, radio station, choral group, and marching band. 15% of eligible men and 11% of eligible women are members of national **fraternities**, national **sororities**, and local sororities.

CMU is a member of the NCAA (Division III). **Intercollegiate sports** include basketball, cross-country running, football (m), golf (m), soccer, swimming, tennis, track and field, volleyball (w).

Campus Safety
Student safety services include late-night transport/escort service, 24-hour emergency telephone alarm devices, 24-hour patrols by trained security personnel, and electronically operated dormitory entrances.

Applying
CMU requires an essay, SAT II Subject Tests, SAT I or ACT, a high school transcript, and 1 recommendation, and in some cases SAT II: Writing Test and portfolio, audition. It recommends an interview. Application deadline: 1/1; 2/15 priority date for financial aid. Early and deferred admission are possible.

CARROLL COLLEGE

SMALL-TOWN SETTING ▪ PRIVATE ▪ INDEPENDENT RELIGIOUS ▪ COED
HELENA, MONTANA

Web site: www.carroll.edu
Contact: Ms. Candace A. Cain, Director of Admission, 1601 North Benton
Avenue, Helena, MT 59625-0002
Telephone: 406-447-4384 or toll-free 800-992-3648 **Fax:** 406-447-4533
E-mail: enroll@carroll.edu

Academics

Carroll awards associate and bachelor's **degrees**. Challenging opportunities include
advanced placement credit, accelerated degree programs, student-designed majors, freshman honors college, an honors program, double majors, independent study, and a senior
project. Special programs include cooperative education, internships, summer session for
credit, study-abroad, and Army ROTC.

The most frequently chosen **baccalaureate** fields are social sciences and history,
education, and biological/life sciences. A complete listing of majors at Carroll appears in
the Majors Index beginning on page 460.

The **faculty** at Carroll has 79 full-time members, 67% with terminal degrees. The
student-faculty ratio is 13:1.

Students of Carroll

The student body is made up of 1,411 undergraduates. 58.3% are women and 41.7% are
men. Students come from 27 states and territories and 8 other countries. 65% are from
Montana. 0.9% are international students. 0.3% are African American, 0.9% American
Indian, 0.8% Asian American, and 1.4% Hispanic American. 80% returned for their
sophomore year.

Facilities and Resources

Student rooms are linked to a campus network. 91 **computers** are available on campus
that provide access to online book order and the Internet. The 2 **libraries** have 89,003
books and 2,721 subscriptions.

Campus Life

There are 35 active organizations on campus, including a drama/theater group,
newspaper, radio station, and choral group. No national or local **fraternities** or **sororities**.

Carroll is a member of the NAIA. **Intercollegiate sports** (some offering scholarships) include basketball, cheerleading, football (m), golf (w), soccer (w), swimming, volleyball (w).

Campus Safety

Student safety services include late-night transport/escort service and electronically operated dormitory entrances.

Applying

Carroll requires an essay, SAT I or ACT, a high school transcript, 1 recommendation,
and a minimum high school GPA of 2.0, and in some cases SAT II Subject Tests, SAT II:
Writing Test, and an interview. It recommends an interview and a minimum high school
GPA of 3.0. Application deadline: 6/1. Deferred admission is possible.

Carroll College, located in
Helena, Montana,
maintains an excellent
reputation for academics,
preprofessional programs, and career
and graduate school placement. A
Catholic institution, Carroll's intimate
class sizes provide a personalized
undergraduate experience for men
and women. With scholarships and
individualized attention to each
student's financial needs, Carroll is
an affordable value.

Getting in Last Year
899 applied
83% were accepted
310 enrolled (42%)
25% from top tenth of their h.s. class
3.40 average high school GPA
27% had SAT verbal scores over 600
23% had SAT math scores over 600
50% had ACT scores over 24
7% had SAT verbal scores over 700
4% had SAT math scores over 700
5% had ACT scores over 30
25 valedictorians

Graduation and After
47% graduated in 4 years
13% graduated in 5 years
22% pursued further study (4% arts and sciences, 3% medicine, 2% business)
55% had job offers within 6 months
100 organizations recruited on campus

Financial Matters
$14,666 tuition and fees (2003–04)
$5810 room and board
85% average percent of need met
$13,799 average financial aid amount received
per undergraduate

CASE WESTERN RESERVE UNIVERSITY

URBAN SETTING ■ PRIVATE ■ INDEPENDENT ■ COED
CLEVELAND, OHIO

Web site: www.case.edu
Contact: Ms. Elizabeth H. Woyczynski, Director of Undergraduate
    Admission, 10900 Euclid Avenue, Cleveland, OH 44106
Telephone: 216-368-4450 **Fax:** 216-368-5111
E-mail: admission@case.edu

Getting in Last Year
4,680 applied
75% were accepted
878 enrolled (25%)
63% from top tenth of their h.s. class
73% had SAT verbal scores over 600
84% had SAT math scores over 600
90% had ACT scores over 24
29% had SAT verbal scores over 700
44% had SAT math scores over 700
43% had ACT scores over 30
59 National Merit Scholars
72 valedictorians

Graduation and After
52% graduated in 4 years
22% graduated in 5 years
2% graduated in 6 years
**41% pursued further study (14% engineering,
    10% arts and sciences, 9% medicine)**
96% had job offers within 6 months
191 organizations recruited on campus

Financial Matters
$24,342 tuition and fees (2003–04)
$7660 room and board
94% average percent of need met
**$23,571 average financial aid amount received
    per undergraduate**

Academics
CWRU awards bachelor's, master's, doctoral, and first-professional **degrees** and post-bachelor's certificates. Challenging opportunities include advanced placement credit, accelerated degree programs, student-designed majors, an honors program, double majors, independent study, and a senior project. Special programs include cooperative education, internships, summer session for credit, off-campus study, study-abroad, and Army and Air Force ROTC.

The most frequently chosen **baccalaureate** fields are engineering/engineering technologies, biological/life sciences, and social sciences and history. A complete listing of majors at CWRU appears in the Majors Index beginning on page 460.

The **faculty** at CWRU has 600 full-time members, 96% with terminal degrees. The student-faculty ratio is 8:1.

Students of CWRU
The student body totals 9,186, of whom 3,587 are undergraduates. 39.4% are women and 60.6% are men. Students come from 50 states and territories and 24 other countries. 55% are from Ohio. 4.5% are international students. 4.6% are African American, 0.4% American Indian, 15.2% Asian American, and 2.1% Hispanic American. 93% returned for their sophomore year.

Facilities and Resources
Student rooms are linked to a campus network. 100 **computers** are available on campus that provide access to software library, CD-ROM databases and the Internet. The 7 **libraries** have 2,236,337 books and 17,506 subscriptions.

Campus Life
There are 100 active organizations on campus, including a drama/theater group, newspaper, radio station, choral group, and marching band. 34% of eligible men and 17% of eligible women are members of national **fraternities**, national **sororities**, and local sororities.

CWRU is a member of the NCAA (Division III). **Intercollegiate sports** include baseball (m), basketball, cross-country running, football (m), soccer, softball (w), swimming, tennis, track and field, volleyball (w), wrestling (m).

Campus Safety
Student safety services include crime prevention programs, late-night transport/escort service, 24-hour emergency telephone alarm devices, 24-hour patrols by trained security personnel, student patrols, and electronically operated dormitory entrances.

Applying
CWRU requires an essay, SAT I or ACT, a high school transcript, and 1 recommendation. It recommends SAT II Subject Tests and an interview. Application deadline: 1/15; 2/15 priority date for financial aid. Early and deferred admission are possible.

CEDARVILLE UNIVERSITY

RURAL SETTING ■ PRIVATE ■ INDEPENDENT RELIGIOUS ■ COED
CEDARVILLE, OHIO

Web site: www.cedarville.edu
Contact: Mr. Roscoe Smith, Director of Admissions, 251 North Main Street,
   Cedarville, OH 45314-0601
Telephone: 937-766-7700 or toll-free 800-CEDARVILLE **Fax:** 937-766-7575
E-mail: admiss@cedarville.edu

Academics

Cedarville awards bachelor's and master's **degrees**. Challenging opportunities include advanced placement credit, accelerated degree programs, an honors program, double majors, independent study, and a senior project. Special programs include internships, summer session for credit, off-campus study, study-abroad, and Army and Air Force ROTC.

The most frequently chosen **baccalaureate** fields are education, business/marketing, and communications/communication technologies. A complete listing of majors at Cedarville appears in the Majors Index beginning on page 460.

The **faculty** at Cedarville has 200 full-time members, 63% with terminal degrees. The student-faculty ratio is 14:1.

Students of Cedarville

The student body totals 2,997, of whom 2,996 are undergraduates. 54% are women and 46% are men. Students come from 49 states and territories and 16 other countries. 33% are from Ohio. 0.5% are international students. 1.3% are African American, 1.2% Asian American, and 1.3% Hispanic American. 81% returned for their sophomore year.

Facilities and Resources

Student rooms are linked to a campus network. 1,600 **computers** are available on campus that provide access to software packages and the Internet. The **library** has 149,164 books and 4,932 subscriptions.

Campus Life

There are 52 active organizations on campus, including a drama/theater group, newspaper, radio station, and choral group. No national or local **fraternities** or **sororities**.

Cedarville is a member of the NAIA and NCCAA. **Intercollegiate sports** (some offering scholarships) include baseball (m), basketball, cheerleading, cross-country running, golf (m), soccer, softball (w), tennis, track and field, volleyball (w).

Campus Safety

Student safety services include late-night transport/escort service, 24-hour emergency telephone alarm devices, 24-hour patrols by trained security personnel, student patrols, and electronically operated dormitory entrances.

Applying

Cedarville requires an essay, SAT I or ACT, a high school transcript, 2 recommendations, and a minimum high school GPA of 3.0, and in some cases an interview. Application deadline: rolling admissions; 3/1 priority date for financial aid. Early and deferred admission are possible.

Getting in Last Year
2,174 applied
81% were accepted
787 enrolled (45%)
33% from top tenth of their h.s. class
3.60 average high school GPA
49% had SAT verbal scores over 600
45% had SAT math scores over 600
67% had ACT scores over 24
12% had SAT verbal scores over 700
9% had SAT math scores over 700
14% had ACT scores over 30
13 National Merit Scholars
82 valedictorians

Graduation and After
56% graduated in 4 years
16% graduated in 5 years
2% graduated in 6 years
Graduates pursuing further study: 1% business, 1% engineering, 1% arts and sciences
99% had job offers within 6 months
328 organizations recruited on campus

Financial Matters
$14,944 tuition and fees (2003–04)
$5010 room and board
41% average percent of need met
$10,749 average financial aid amount received per undergraduate (2001–02)

CENTENARY COLLEGE OF LOUISIANA

SUBURBAN SETTING ■ PRIVATE ■ INDEPENDENT RELIGIOUS ■ COED
SHREVEPORT, LOUISIANA

Web site: www.centenary.edu
Contact: Mr. Tim Crowley, Director of Admissions, Office of Admissions, Centenary College of Louisiana, 2911 Centenary Boulevard, PO box 41188, Shreveport, LA 71134-1188
Telephone: 318-869-5134 or toll-free 800-234-4448 **Fax:** 318-869-5005
E-mail: egregory@centenary.edu

Getting in Last Year
802 applied
74% were accepted
197 enrolled (33%)
38% from top tenth of their h.s. class
3.24 average high school GPA
46% had SAT verbal scores over 600
41% had SAT math scores over 600
71% had ACT scores over 24
6% had SAT verbal scores over 700
5% had SAT math scores over 700
14% had ACT scores over 30

Graduation and After
39% graduated in 4 years
15% graduated in 5 years
300 organizations recruited on campus

Financial Matters
$17,250 tuition and fees (2003–04)
$5850 room and board
79% average percent of need met
$12,815 average financial aid amount received per undergraduate (2002–03 estimated)

Academics
Centenary awards bachelor's and master's **degrees.** Challenging opportunities include advanced placement credit, student-designed majors, an honors program, double majors, independent study, and a senior project. Special programs include internships, summer session for credit, off-campus study, study-abroad, and Army ROTC.

The most frequently chosen **baccalaureate** fields are business/marketing, biological/life sciences, and social sciences and history. A complete listing of majors at Centenary appears in the Majors Index beginning on page 460.

The **faculty** at Centenary has 74 full-time members, 93% with terminal degrees. The student-faculty ratio is 12:1.

Students of Centenary
The student body totals 997, of whom 845 are undergraduates. 58.9% are women and 41.1% are men. Students come from 36 states and territories and 14 other countries. 61% are from Louisiana. 3.2% are international students. 7% are African American, 1.2% American Indian, 2.4% Asian American, and 2.2% Hispanic American. 80% returned for their sophomore year.

Facilities and Resources
Student rooms are linked to a campus network. 250 **computers** are available on campus that provide access to the Internet. The 2 **libraries** have 325,671 books and 59,899 subscriptions.

Campus Life
There are 34 active organizations on campus, including a drama/theater group, newspaper, radio station, and choral group. 25% of eligible men and 20% of eligible women are members of national **fraternities** and national **sororities.**

Centenary is a member of the NCAA (Division I). **Intercollegiate sports** (some offering scholarships) include baseball (m), basketball, cross-country running, golf, gymnastics (w), riflery, soccer, softball (w), tennis, volleyball (w).

Campus Safety
Student safety services include late-night transport/escort service, 24-hour emergency telephone alarm devices, 24-hour patrols by trained security personnel, and electronically operated dormitory entrances.

Applying
Centenary requires an essay, SAT I or ACT, a high school transcript, 1 recommendation, and a minimum high school GPA of 2.0, and in some cases SAT II Subject Tests. It recommends an interview and class rank. Application deadline: 2/15; 2/15 priority date for financial aid. Early and deferred admission are possible.

CENTRAL COLLEGE
SMALL-TOWN SETTING ■ PRIVATE ■ INDEPENDENT RELIGIOUS ■ COED
PELLA, IOWA

Web site: www.central.edu
Contact: Mr. John Olsen, Vice President for Admission and Student
  Enrollment Services, 812 University Street, Pella, IA 50219-1999
Telephone: 641-628-7600 or toll-free 800-458-5503 **Fax:** 641-628-5316
E-mail: admissions@central.edu

Academics
Central awards bachelor's **degrees**. Challenging opportunities include student-designed majors, an honors program, double majors, independent study, and a senior project. Special programs include internships, summer session for credit, off-campus study, and study-abroad.

The most frequently chosen **baccalaureate** fields are business/marketing, education, and social sciences and history. A complete listing of majors at Central appears in the Majors Index beginning on page 460.

The **faculty** at Central has 96 full-time members, 88% with terminal degrees. The student-faculty ratio is 14:1.

Students of Central
The student body is made up of 1,698 undergraduates. 57.1% are women and 42.9% are men. Students come from 33 states and territories and 13 other countries. 81% are from Iowa. 1% are international students. 0.9% are African American, 0.3% American Indian, 1.1% Asian American, and 1.6% Hispanic American. 84% returned for their sophomore year.

Facilities and Resources
Student rooms are linked to a campus network. 256 **computers** are available on campus that provide access to student academic records and data and the Internet. The 4 **libraries** have 220,526 books and 1,161 subscriptions.

Campus Life
There are 72 active organizations on campus, including a drama/theater group, newspaper, radio station, and choral group. 15% of eligible men and 7% of eligible women are members of national **fraternities**, national **sororities**, local fraternities, and local sororities.

Central is a member of the NCAA (Division III). **Intercollegiate sports** include baseball (m), basketball, cross-country running, football (m), golf, soccer, softball (w), tennis, track and field, volleyball (w), wrestling (m).

Campus Safety
Student safety services include late-night transport/escort service, 24-hour emergency telephone alarm devices, student patrols, and electronically operated dormitory entrances.

Applying
Central requires SAT I or ACT and a high school transcript, and in some cases an essay, an interview, and 3 recommendations. It recommends an interview and a minimum high school GPA of 2.0. Application deadline: rolling admissions; 3/1 priority date for financial aid. Deferred admission is possible.

Getting in Last Year
1,865 applied
83% were accepted
417 enrolled (27%)
27% from top tenth of their h.s. class
3.43 average high school GPA
49% had ACT scores over 24
5% had ACT scores over 30
27 valedictorians

Graduation and After
59% graduated in 4 years
6% graduated in 5 years
2% graduated in 6 years
15% pursued further study (9% arts and sciences, 4% medicine, 1% business)
95% had job offers within 6 months
70 organizations recruited on campus

Financial Matters
$17,753 tuition and fees (2003–04)
$6145 room and board
82% average percent of need met
$15,658 average financial aid amount received per undergraduate (2002–03 estimated)

CENTRE COLLEGE

SMALL-TOWN SETTING ■ PRIVATE ■ INDEPENDENT RELIGIOUS ■ COED
DANVILLE, KENTUCKY

Web site: www.centre.edu
Contact: Mr. J. Carey Thompson, Dean of Admission and Financial Aid, 600 West Walnut Street, Danville, KY 40422-1394
Telephone: 859-238-5350 or toll-free 800-423-6236 **Fax:** 859-238-5373
E-mail: admission@centre.edu

Getting in Last Year

1,409 applied
75% were accepted
272 enrolled (26%)
50% from top tenth of their h.s. class
3.70 average high school GPA
62% had SAT verbal scores over 600
56% had SAT math scores over 600
85% had ACT scores over 24
20% had SAT verbal scores over 700
12% had SAT math scores over 700
24% had ACT scores over 30
1 National Merit Scholar
37 valedictorians

Graduation and After

78% graduated in 4 years
3% graduated in 5 years
40% pursued further study (34% arts and sciences, 21% law, 13% medicine)
70% had job offers within 6 months
25 organizations recruited on campus

Financial Matters

$20,400 tuition and fees (2003–04)
$6900 room and board
100% average percent of need met
$19,585 average financial aid amount received per undergraduate (2002–03 estimated)

Academics

Centre awards bachelor's **degrees**. Challenging opportunities include advanced placement credit, student-designed majors, double majors, independent study, and a senior project. Special programs include internships, off-campus study, study-abroad, and Army and Air Force ROTC.

The most frequently chosen **baccalaureate** fields are social sciences and history, English, and psychology. A complete listing of majors at Centre appears in the Majors Index beginning on page 460.

The **faculty** at Centre has 90 full-time members, 97% with terminal degrees. The student-faculty ratio is 11:1.

Students of Centre

The student body is made up of 1,062 undergraduates. 52.1% are women and 47.9% are men. Students come from 33 states and territories and 10 other countries. 70% are from Kentucky. 1.1% are international students. 2.3% are African American, 0.2% American Indian, 2.6% Asian American, and 0.3% Hispanic American. 90% returned for their sophomore year.

Facilities and Resources

Student rooms are linked to a campus network. 150 **computers** are available on campus that provide access to the Internet. The 2 **libraries** have 217,751 books and 750 subscriptions.

Campus Life

There are 76 active organizations on campus, including a drama/theater group, newspaper, and choral group. 60% of eligible men and 65% of eligible women are members of national **fraternities** and national **sororities**.

Centre is a member of the NCAA (Division III). **Intercollegiate sports** include baseball (m), basketball, cheerleading (w), cross-country running, field hockey (w), football (m), golf, soccer, softball (w), swimming, tennis, track and field, volleyball (w).

Campus Safety

Student safety services include late-night transport/escort service, 24-hour emergency telephone alarm devices, 24-hour patrols by trained security personnel, and electronically operated dormitory entrances.

Applying

Centre requires an essay, SAT I or ACT, a high school transcript, and 1 recommendation. It recommends an interview. Application deadline: 2/1; 3/1 for financial aid. Early and deferred admission are possible.

Chapman University

Suburban setting ■ Private ■ Independent Religious ■ Coed
Orange, California

Web site: www.chapman.edu
Contact: Mr. Michael O. Drummy, Associate Dean for Enrollment Services and Chief Admission Officer, One University Drive, Orange, CA 92866
Telephone: 714-997-6711 or toll-free 888-CUAPPLY **Fax:** 714-997-6713
E-mail: admit@chapman.edu

Academics

Chapman awards bachelor's, master's, and first-professional **degrees** and post-bachelor's certificates. Challenging opportunities include advanced placement credit, accelerated degree programs, an honors program, double majors, independent study, and a senior project. Special programs include cooperative education, internships, summer session for credit, study-abroad, and Army and Air Force ROTC.

The most frequently chosen **baccalaureate** fields are visual/performing arts, business/marketing, and communications/communication technologies. A complete listing of majors at Chapman appears in the Majors Index beginning on page 460.

The **faculty** at Chapman has 233 full-time members, 88% with terminal degrees. The student-faculty ratio is 16:1.

Students of Chapman

The student body totals 5,138, of whom 3,443 are undergraduates. 57.1% are women and 42.9% are men. Students come from 40 states and territories and 45 other countries. 74% are from California. 2.8% are international students. 2.4% are African American, 0.4% American Indian, 7.4% Asian American, and 9.5% Hispanic American. 84% returned for their sophomore year.

Facilities and Resources

278 **computers** are available on campus that provide access to the Internet. The 2 **libraries** have 188,682 books and 1,777 subscriptions.

Campus Life

There are 60 active organizations on campus, including a drama/theater group, newspaper, radio station, and choral group. 14% of eligible men and 17% of eligible women are members of national **fraternities** and national **sororities**.

Chapman is a member of the NCAA (Division III). **Intercollegiate sports** include baseball (m), basketball, cheerleading, crew (w), cross-country running, football (m), golf, soccer, softball (w), swimming (w), tennis, track and field (w), volleyball (w), water polo.

Campus Safety

Student safety services include full safety education program, late-night transport/escort service, 24-hour emergency telephone alarm devices, 24-hour patrols by trained security personnel, and electronically operated dormitory entrances.

Applying

Chapman requires an essay, SAT I or ACT, a high school transcript, 1 recommendation, and a minimum high school GPA of 2.75. It recommends SAT II Subject Tests, SAT II: Writing Test, an interview, and a minimum high school GPA of 3.5. Application deadline: 1/31; 3/2 priority date for financial aid. Early admission is possible.

Determining the cost of a Chapman education at the beginning of the application process is now possible through Chapman's Early Aid Estimator program. In the early fall, all high school seniors and prospective transfer students in Chapman's inquiry database are furnished with an estimator form that can be completed and returned to Chapman for analysis at no charge. Using in-house needs analysis software and merit eligibility formulas, Chapman responds with an estimate of the student's aid and scholarship eligibility. Under the previous system, students were unable to receive this information until admission had been determined and aid notification had been sent, usually in late spring.

Getting in Last Year
3,084 applied
62% were accepted
850 enrolled (45%)
41% from top tenth of their h.s. class
3.56 average high school GPA
43% had SAT verbal scores over 600
45% had SAT math scores over 600
61% had ACT scores over 24
7% had SAT verbal scores over 700
5% had SAT math scores over 700
5% had ACT scores over 30
27 National Merit Scholars
27 class presidents
24 valedictorians

Graduation and After
70 organizations recruited on campus

Financial Matters
$24,590 tuition and fees (2003–04)
$8528 room and board
100% average percent of need met
$18,066 average financial aid amount received per undergraduate (2002–03)

CHRISTENDOM COLLEGE

RURAL SETTING ■ PRIVATE ■ INDEPENDENT RELIGIOUS ■ COED
FRONT ROYAL, VIRGINIA

Web site: www.christendom.edu

Contact: Mr. Paul Heisler, Director of Admissions, 134 Christendom Drive, Front Royal, VA 22630-5103

Telephone: 540-636-2900 ext. 290 or toll-free 800-877-5456 ext. 290 **Fax:** 540-636-1655

E-mail: admissions@christendom.edu

Getting in Last Year

227 applied
80% were accepted
98 enrolled (54%)
59% from top tenth of their h.s. class
3.54 average high school GPA
80% had SAT verbal scores over 600
41% had SAT math scores over 600
33% had SAT verbal scores over 700
12% had SAT math scores over 700
2 National Merit Scholars
2 class presidents
2 valedictorians

Graduation and After

53% graduated in 4 years
2% graduated in 5 years
18% pursued further study (6% law, 4% arts and sciences, 4% education)
76% had job offers within 6 months
6 organizations recruited on campus

Financial Matters

$13,420 tuition and fees (2003–04)
$4990 room and board
90% average percent of need met
$9730 average financial aid amount received per undergraduate

Academics

Christendom awards associate, bachelor's, and master's **degrees**. Challenging opportunities include advanced placement credit, accelerated degree programs, double majors, independent study, and a senior project. Special programs include cooperative education, internships, summer session for credit, and study-abroad.

The most frequently chosen **baccalaureate** fields are social sciences and history, English, and foreign language/literature. A complete listing of majors at Christendom appears in the Majors Index beginning on page 460.

The **faculty** at Christendom has 23 full-time members, 78% with terminal degrees. The student-faculty ratio is 12:1.

Students of Christendom

The student body totals 433, of whom 366 are undergraduates. 57.4% are women and 42.6% are men. Students come from 41 states and territories and 2 other countries. 22% are from Virginia. 2.7% are international students. 0.3% are African American, 1.9% Asian American, and 4.1% Hispanic American. 84% returned for their sophomore year.

Facilities and Resources

24 **computers** are available on campus that provide access to the Internet. The **library** has 64,265 books and 249 subscriptions.

Campus Life

There are 15 active organizations on campus, including a drama/theater group, newspaper, and choral group. No national or local **fraternities** or **sororities**.

Christendom is a member of the NCCAA.

Campus Safety

Student safety services include night patrols by trained security personnel, late-night transport/escort service, and 24-hour emergency telephone alarm devices.

Applying

Christendom requires an essay, SAT I or ACT, a high school transcript, and 2 recommendations. It recommends an interview and a minimum high school GPA of 3.0. Application deadline: 3/1; 4/1 priority date for financial aid. Early admission is possible.

CHRISTIAN BROTHERS UNIVERSITY

URBAN SETTING ■ PRIVATE ■ INDEPENDENT RELIGIOUS ■ COED
MEMPHIS, TENNESSEE

Web site: www.cbu.edu
Contact: Ms. Tracey Dysart, Dean of Admissions, 650 East Parkway South, Memphis, TN 38104
Telephone: 901-321-3205 or toll-free 800-288-7576 **Fax:** 901-321-3202
E-mail: admissions@cbu.edu

Academics

CBU awards bachelor's and master's **degrees**. Challenging opportunities include advanced placement credit, accelerated degree programs, an honors program, double majors, and a senior project. Special programs include internships, summer session for credit, off-campus study, study-abroad, and Army, Navy and Air Force ROTC.

The most frequently chosen **baccalaureate** fields are business/marketing, psychology, and engineering/engineering technologies. A complete listing of majors at CBU appears in the Majors Index beginning on page 460.

The **faculty** at CBU has 105 full-time members, 85% with terminal degrees. The student-faculty ratio is 12:1.

Students of CBU

The student body totals 1,929, of whom 1,582 are undergraduates. 56.6% are women and 43.4% are men. Students come from 33 states and territories and 26 other countries. 85% are from Tennessee. 2.4% are international students. 34.8% are African American, 0.1% American Indian, 5.1% Asian American, and 1.7% Hispanic American. 84% returned for their sophomore year.

Facilities and Resources

Student rooms are linked to a campus network. 300 **computers** are available on campus that provide access to online class listings, e-mail, course assignments and the Internet. The **library** has 92,000 books and 520 subscriptions.

Campus Life

There are 23 active organizations on campus, including a drama/theater group, newspaper, and choral group. 24% of eligible men and 20% of eligible women are members of national **fraternities**, national **sororities**, and local sororities.

CBU is a member of the NCAA (Division II). **Intercollegiate sports** (some offering scholarships) include baseball (m), basketball, cheerleading, cross-country running, golf (m), soccer, softball (w), tennis, volleyball (w).

Campus Safety

Student safety services include late-night transport/escort service, 24-hour emergency telephone alarm devices, 24-hour patrols by trained security personnel, student patrols, and electronically operated dormitory entrances.

Applying

CBU requires an essay, SAT I or ACT, a high school transcript, and a minimum high school GPA of 2.5, and in some cases recommendations. It recommends an interview. Application deadline: 3/1; 2/15 priority date for financial aid. Early and deferred admission are possible.

Students from all over the country and the world come to Christian Brothers University (CBU) for a vibrant and involved education that is academically rigorous, exciting, and diverse. Students are passionate about this extraordinary environment that prepares them for the real world by pushing them to step up, ask questions, and get involved. This Catholic university was founded in 1871 by the Brothers of the Christian Schools and is part of the Lasallian Community active in 81 countries of the world and in more than 1,000 educational institutions. Excellence in teaching and individualized attention are hallmarks of the University. Students learn in a value-oriented, interfaith educational community, preparing them for professional careers and lives of moral responsibility and community involvement. CBU is known for providing students of all backgrounds and faiths a well-rounded education built on individualized attention, hands-on learning, encouragment of ethical development, and a passion for achievement above and beyond one's potential. CBU offers degrees in engineering, business, science, liberal arts, and education to nearly 2,000 students.

Getting in Last Year

879 applied
85% were accepted
281 enrolled (38%)
27% from top tenth of their h.s. class
3.38 average high school GPA
24% had SAT verbal scores over 600
30% had SAT math scores over 600
41% had ACT scores over 24
3% had SAT verbal scores over 700
4% had SAT math scores over 700
6% had ACT scores over 30

Graduation and After

12% pursued further study
85.7% had job offers within 6 months
211 organizations recruited on campus

Financial Matters

$17,190 tuition and fees (2003–04)
$5100 room and board
75% average percent of need met
$12,522 average financial aid amount received per undergraduate (2002–03 estimated)

CLAREMONT MCKENNA COLLEGE

SMALL-TOWN SETTING ■ PRIVATE ■ INDEPENDENT ■ COED
CLAREMONT, CALIFORNIA

Web site: www.claremontmckenna.edu
Contact: Mr. Richard C. Vos, Vice President/Dean of Admission and
Financial Aid, 890 Columbia Avenue, Claremont, CA 91711
Telephone: 909-621-8088 or toll-free 909-621-8088 **Fax:** 909-621-8516
E-mail: admission@mckenna.edu

Claremont McKenna College (CMC) infuses a traditional liberal arts education with its own pragmatic sensibilities. CMC's focus on economics, government, and international relations allow it to fully prepare students for leadership in business, government, and other professions. CMC's enrollment of approximately 1,000 students ensures a personalized educational experience. However, with 4 other colleges—Harvey Mudd, Pitzer, Pomona, and Scripps—and 2 graduate schools right next door, CMC students also have access to the academic, intellectual, social, and athletic resources typical of a medium-sized university.

Getting in Last Year
2,892 applied
29% were accepted
284 enrolled (34%)
83% from top tenth of their h.s. class
3.91 average high school GPA
93% had SAT verbal scores over 600
95% had SAT math scores over 600
98% had ACT scores over 24
46% had SAT verbal scores over 700
51% had SAT math scores over 700
53% had ACT scores over 30
14 National Merit Scholars
7 class presidents
20 valedictorians

Graduation and After
80% graduated in 4 years
4% graduated in 5 years
2% graduated in 6 years
25% pursued further study (7% law, 5% medicine, 4% arts and sciences)
64% had job offers within 6 months
200 organizations recruited on campus

Financial Matters
$27,700 tuition and fees (2003–04)
$9180 room and board
100% average percent of need met
$23,920 average financial aid amount received per undergraduate

Academics
CMC awards bachelor's **degrees**. Challenging opportunities include advanced placement credit, accelerated degree programs, student-designed majors, an honors program, double majors, independent study, and a senior project. Special programs include internships, off-campus study, study-abroad, and Army and Air Force ROTC.

The most frequently chosen **baccalaureate** fields are social sciences and history, interdisciplinary studies, and psychology. A complete listing of majors at CMC appears in the Majors Index beginning on page 460.

The **faculty** at CMC has 142 full-time members, 91% with terminal degrees. The student-faculty ratio is 7:1.

Students of CMC
The student body is made up of 1,050 undergraduates. 44.8% are women and 55.2% are men. Students come from 45 states and territories and 21 other countries. 49% are from California. 97% returned for their sophomore year.

Facilities and Resources
Student rooms are linked to a campus network. 120 **computers** are available on campus that provide access to the Internet. The 4 **libraries** have 2,028,793 books and 6,028 subscriptions.

Campus Life
There are 280 active organizations on campus, including a drama/theater group, newspaper, radio station, and choral group. No national or local **fraternities** or **sororities**.

CMC is a member of the NCAA (Division III). **Intercollegiate sports** include baseball (m), basketball, cross-country running, football (m), golf (m), lacrosse (w), soccer, softball (w), swimming, tennis, track and field, volleyball (w), water polo.

Campus Safety
Student safety services include late-night transport/escort service, 24-hour emergency telephone alarm devices, 24-hour patrols by trained security personnel, student patrols, and electronically operated dormitory entrances.

Applying
CMC requires an essay, SAT I or ACT, a high school transcript, 3 recommendations, and a minimum high school GPA of 3.0. It recommends SAT II Subject Tests and an interview. Application deadline: 1/2; 2/1 for financial aid. Early and deferred admission are possible.

CLARKSON UNIVERSITY

SMALL-TOWN SETTING ■ PRIVATE ■ INDEPENDENT ■ COED
POTSDAM, NEW YORK

Web site: www.clarkson.edu
Contact: Mr. Brian T. Grant, Director of Admission, Holcroft House, Potsdam, NY 13699-5605
Telephone: 315-268-6479 or toll-free 800-527-6577 **Fax:** 315-268-7647
E-mail: admission@clarkson.edu

Academics

Clarkson awards bachelor's, master's, and doctoral **degrees**. Challenging opportunities include advanced placement credit, accelerated degree programs, student-designed majors, an honors program, double majors, independent study, and a senior project. Special programs include cooperative education, internships, summer session for credit, off-campus study, study-abroad, and Army and Air Force ROTC.

The most frequently chosen **baccalaureate** fields are engineering/engineering technologies, business/marketing, and interdisciplinary studies. A complete listing of majors at Clarkson appears in the Majors Index beginning on page 460.

The **faculty** at Clarkson has 179 full-time members, 91% with terminal degrees. The student-faculty ratio is 17:1.

Students of Clarkson

The student body totals 3,105, of whom 2,723 are undergraduates. 24.1% are women and 75.9% are men. Students come from 39 states and territories and 33 other countries. 77% are from New York. 2.6% are international students. 2.6% are African American, 0.5% American Indian, 2% Asian American, and 1.6% Hispanic American. 86% returned for their sophomore year.

Facilities and Resources

Student rooms are linked to a campus network. 400 **computers** are available on campus that provide access to the Internet. The 2 **libraries** have 272,204 books and 1,656 subscriptions.

Campus Life

There are 62 active organizations on campus, including a drama/theater group, newspaper, radio station, television station, and choral group. 20% of eligible men and 16% of eligible women are members of national **fraternities**, national **sororities**, and local fraternities.

Clarkson is a member of the NCAA (Division III). **Intercollegiate sports** (some offering scholarships) include baseball (m), basketball, cross-country running, golf (m), ice hockey, lacrosse, skiing (cross-country), skiing (downhill), soccer, swimming, tennis, volleyball (w).

Campus Safety

Student safety services include late-night transport/escort service, 24-hour emergency telephone alarm devices, 24-hour patrols by trained security personnel, and electronically operated dormitory entrances.

Applying

Clarkson requires SAT I or ACT, a high school transcript, and 1 recommendation. It recommends SAT II Subject Tests and an interview. Application deadline: 3/15; 3/1 priority date for financial aid. Early and deferred admission are possible.

Clarkson is an independent technological university with majors in engineering, business, science, health sciences, and liberal arts. Set in upstate New York's Adirondack foothills near the St. Lawrence River Valley, the 3000-student campus combines high-powered academics with a friendly, personal atmosphere. Students enjoy easy access, not only to Clarkson's faculty and technology-rich facilities, but also to outstanding outdoor recreational opportunities. Rigorous academic programs emphasize hands-on learning and a collaborative approach in project-based problem solving. Students develop technical expertise, skills in communication and teamwork, and versatility vital in today's knowledge-based economy. Graduates succeed as innovative leaders in technology-based fields.

Getting in Last Year
2,698 applied
81% were accepted
721 enrolled (33%)
34% from top tenth of their h.s. class
3.49 average high school GPA
34% had SAT verbal scores over 600
61% had SAT math scores over 600
67% had ACT scores over 24
5% had SAT verbal scores over 700
13% had SAT math scores over 700
11% had ACT scores over 30
21 valedictorians

Graduation and After
55% graduated in 4 years
14% graduated in 5 years
1% graduated in 6 years
29% pursued further study (5% arts and sciences, 5% engineering, 4% business)
72% had job offers within 6 months
105 organizations recruited on campus

Financial Matters
$23,500 tuition and fees (2003–04)
$8726 room and board
88% average percent of need met
$15,500 average financial aid amount received per undergraduate (2002–03 estimated)

CLARK UNIVERSITY

URBAN SETTING ■ PRIVATE ■ INDEPENDENT ■ COED
WORCESTER, MASSACHUSETTS

Web site: www.clarku.edu
Contact: Mr. Harold M. Wingood, Dean of Admissions, Admissions House, 950 Main Street, Worcester, MA 01610
Telephone: 508-793-7431 or toll-free 800-GO-CLARK **Fax:** 508-793-8821
E-mail: admissions@clarku.edu

Getting in Last Year

3,950 applied
63% were accepted
541 enrolled (22%)
30% from top tenth of their h.s. class
3.41 average high school GPA
49% had SAT verbal scores over 600
54% had SAT math scores over 600
63% had ACT scores over 24
8% had SAT verbal scores over 700
10% had SAT math scores over 700
14% had ACT scores over 30
7 valedictorians

Graduation and After

60% graduated in 4 years
6% graduated in 5 years
1% graduated in 6 years
30% pursued further study (16% arts and sciences, 4% business, 3% education)
313 organizations recruited on campus

Financial Matters

$26,965 tuition and fees (2003–04)
$5150 room and board
97% average percent of need met
$23,136 average financial aid amount received per undergraduate

Academics

Clark awards bachelor's, master's, and doctoral **degrees** and post-bachelor's and post-master's certificates. Challenging opportunities include advanced placement credit, accelerated degree programs, student-designed majors, an honors program, double majors, independent study, and a senior project. Special programs include internships, summer session for credit, off-campus study, study-abroad, and Army, Navy and Air Force ROTC.

The most frequently chosen **baccalaureate** fields are social sciences and history, psychology, and business/marketing. A complete listing of majors at Clark appears in the Majors Index beginning on page 460.

The **faculty** at Clark has 167 full-time members, 98% with terminal degrees. The student-faculty ratio is 10:1.

Students of Clark

The student body totals 3,084, of whom 2,190 are undergraduates. 60.6% are women and 39.4% are men. Students come from 47 states and territories and 56 other countries. 37% are from Massachusetts. 6.7% are international students. 2.8% are African American, 0.2% American Indian, 3.7% Asian American, and 3% Hispanic American. 85% returned for their sophomore year.

Facilities and Resources

Student rooms are linked to a campus network. 200 **computers** are available on campus that provide access to on-line course support and the Internet. The 5 **libraries** have 289,658 books and 1,383 subscriptions.

Campus Life

There are 74 active organizations on campus, including a drama/theater group, newspaper, radio station, television station, and choral group. No national or local **fraternities** or **sororities**.

Clark is a member of the NCAA (Division III). **Intercollegiate sports** include baseball (m), basketball, cheerleading, crew, cross-country running, field hockey (w), lacrosse (m), soccer, softball (w), swimming, tennis, volleyball (w).

Campus Safety

Student safety services include late-night transport/escort service, 24-hour emergency telephone alarm devices, 24-hour patrols by trained security personnel, student patrols, and electronically operated dormitory entrances.

Applying

Clark requires an essay, SAT I or ACT, a high school transcript, and 2 recommendations. It recommends an interview. Application deadline: 2/1; 2/1 priority date for financial aid. Early and deferred admission are possible.

CLEMSON UNIVERSITY
SMALL-TOWN SETTING ■ PUBLIC ■ STATE-SUPPORTED ■ COED
CLEMSON, SOUTH CAROLINA

Web site: www.clemson.edu
Contact: Mr. Timothy R. Galbreath, Assistant Director of Admissions, 105 Sikes Hall, PO Box 345124, Clemson, SC 29634
Telephone: 864-656-2287 **Fax:** 864-656-2464
E-mail: cuadmissions@clemson.edu

Academics
Clemson awards bachelor's, master's, and doctoral **degrees**. Challenging opportunities include advanced placement credit, accelerated degree programs, an honors program, double majors, and a senior project. Special programs include cooperative education, internships, summer session for credit, study-abroad, and Army and Air Force ROTC.

The most frequently chosen **baccalaureate** fields are business/marketing, engineering/engineering technologies, and education. A complete listing of majors at Clemson appears in the Majors Index beginning on page 460.

The **faculty** at Clemson has 952 full-time members, 88% with terminal degrees. The student-faculty ratio is 15:1.

Students of Clemson
The student body totals 17,016, of whom 13,813 are undergraduates. 45.1% are women and 54.9% are men. Students come from 52 states and territories and 58 other countries. 71% are from South Carolina. 0.5% are international students. 7.4% are African American, 0.2% American Indian, 1.6% Asian American, and 0.9% Hispanic American. 89% returned for their sophomore year.

Facilities and Resources
Student rooms are linked to a campus network. 1,000 **computers** are available on campus that provide access to wireless network and the Internet. The 2 **libraries** have 1,648,741 books and 5,978 subscriptions.

Campus Life
There are 250 active organizations on campus, including a drama/theater group, newspaper, radio station, television station, choral group, and marching band. 15% of eligible men and 22% of eligible women are members of national **fraternities** and national **sororities**.

Clemson is a member of the NCAA (Division I). **Intercollegiate sports** (some offering scholarships) include baseball (m), basketball, cheerleading, crew (w), cross-country running, football (m), golf (m), soccer, swimming, tennis, track and field, volleyball (w).

Campus Safety
Student safety services include late-night transport/escort service, 24-hour emergency telephone alarm devices, 24-hour patrols by trained security personnel, and electronically operated dormitory entrances.

Applying
Clemson requires SAT I or ACT and a high school transcript. It recommends an essay and recommendations. Application deadline: 5/1; 4/1 priority date for financial aid.

Clemson's honors program, known as Calhoun College, promotes continued intellectual growth, cultivates a lifelong love of learning, and prepares students to be leaders. Calhoun scholars develop a broad range of academic interests through General Honors, and they pursue independent study and research through Departmental Honors. The honors college's highly selective Dixon Fellows Program prepares students to compete for prestigious postgraduate scholarships, such as Rhodes, Marshall, Truman, and Fulbright. Clemson's honors program includes more than 1,000 students. Membership benefits include priority registration, research grants, and heart-of-campus housing for 300 scholars.

Getting in Last Year
11,315 applied
52% were accepted
2,753 enrolled (47%)
42% from top tenth of their h.s. class
3.88 average high school GPA
47% had SAT verbal scores over 600
63% had SAT math scores over 600
79% had ACT scores over 24
7% had SAT verbal scores over 700
13% had SAT math scores over 700
20% had ACT scores over 30
23 National Merit Scholars
88 valedictorians

Graduation and After
39% graduated in 4 years
29% graduated in 5 years
5% graduated in 6 years
85% had job offers within 6 months
392 organizations recruited on campus

Financial Matters
$6934 resident tuition and fees (2003–04)
$14,532 nonresident tuition and fees (2003–04)
$5038 room and board
75% average percent of need met
$8518 average financial aid amount received per undergraduate (2002–03 estimated)

CLEVELAND INSTITUTE OF MUSIC

URBAN SETTING ■ PRIVATE ■ INDEPENDENT ■ COED
CLEVELAND, OHIO

Web site: www.cim.edu
Contact: Mr. William Fay, Director of Admission, 11021 East Boulevard,
    Cleveland, OH 44106-1776
Telephone: 216-795-3107 Fax: 216-791-1530
E-mail: cimadmission@po.cwru.edu

Getting in Last Year
349 applied
40% were accepted
67 enrolled (48%)

Graduation and After
90% pursued further study (90% arts and
    sciences)

Financial Matters
$22,768 tuition and fees (2003–04)
$7260 room and board
80% average percent of need met
$15,299 average financial aid amount received
    per undergraduate (2002–03)

Academics

Cleveland Institute of Music awards bachelor's, master's, and doctoral **degrees** and post-bachelor's certificates. Challenging opportunities include advanced placement credit, accelerated degree programs, and a senior project. Special programs include internships, summer session for credit, off-campus study, and Army and Air Force ROTC.

The most frequently chosen **baccalaureate** field is visual/performing arts. A complete listing of majors at Cleveland Institute of Music appears in the Majors Index beginning on page 460.

The **faculty** at Cleveland Institute of Music has 32 full-time members, 6% with terminal degrees. The student-faculty ratio is 7:1.

Students of Cleveland Institute of Music

The student body totals 413, of whom 245 are undergraduates. 59.2% are women and 40.8% are men. Students come from 38 states and territories and 15 other countries. 18% are from Ohio. 11.8% are international students. 0.4% are African American, 0.4% American Indian, 8.6% Asian American, and 4.1% Hispanic American. 96% returned for their sophomore year.

Facilities and Resources

Student rooms are linked to a campus network. 25 **computers** are available on campus that provide access to the Internet. The **library** has 48,128 books and 115 subscriptions.

Campus Life

Active organizations on campus include a choral group. No national or local **fraternities** or **sororities**.

This institution has no intercollegiate sports.

Campus Safety

Student safety services include late-night transport/escort service, 24-hour emergency telephone alarm devices, 24-hour patrols by trained security personnel, and electronically operated dormitory entrances.

Applying

Cleveland Institute of Music requires an essay, SAT I or ACT, a high school transcript, 2 recommendations, and audition. It recommends an interview. Application deadline: 12/1; 2/15 for financial aid. Early and deferred admission are possible.

Coe College

Urban setting ■ Private ■ Independent Religious ■ Coed
Cedar Rapids, Iowa

Web site: www.coe.edu
Contact: Mr. John Sullivan, Executive Director of Admission and Financial Aid, 1220 1st Avenue, NE, Cedar Rapids, IA 52402-5070
Telephone: 319-399-8500 or toll-free 877-225-5263 **Fax:** 319-399-8816
E-mail: admission@coe.edu

Academics

Coe awards bachelor's and master's **degrees**. Challenging opportunities include advanced placement credit, accelerated degree programs, student-designed majors, an honors program, double majors, independent study, and a senior project. Special programs include internships, summer session for credit, off-campus study, study-abroad, and Army and Air Force ROTC.

The most frequently chosen **baccalaureate** fields are business/marketing, social sciences and history, and psychology. A complete listing of majors at Coe appears in the Majors Index beginning on page 460.

The **faculty** at Coe has 74 full-time members, 95% with terminal degrees. The student-faculty ratio is 12:1.

Students of Coe

The student body totals 1,317, of whom 1,290 are undergraduates. 56.4% are women and 43.6% are men. Students come from 34 states and territories and 16 other countries. 70% are from Iowa. 3.4% are international students. 1.9% are African American, 0.2% American Indian, and 0.8% Asian American. 81% returned for their sophomore year.

Facilities and Resources

Student rooms are linked to a campus network. 260 **computers** are available on campus that provide access to the Internet. The 2 **libraries** have 213,270 books and 750 subscriptions.

Campus Life

There are 60 active organizations on campus, including a drama/theater group, newspaper, radio station, and choral group. 26% of eligible men and 19% of eligible women are members of national **fraternities** and national **sororities**.

Coe is a member of the NCAA (Division III). **Intercollegiate sports** include baseball (m), basketball, cheerleading (w), cross-country running, football (m), golf, soccer, softball (w), swimming, tennis, track and field, volleyball (w), wrestling (m).

Campus Safety

Student safety services include late-night transport/escort service, 24-hour emergency telephone alarm devices, 24-hour patrols by trained security personnel, and electronically operated dormitory entrances.

Applying

Coe requires an essay, SAT I or ACT, a high school transcript, and 1 recommendation. It recommends an interview and a minimum high school GPA of 3.0. Application deadline: 3/1; 4/30 for financial aid, with a 3/1 priority date. Early and deferred admission are possible.

Getting in Last Year

1,336 applied
71% were accepted
322 enrolled (34%)
28% from top tenth of their h.s. class
3.58 average high school GPA
42% had SAT verbal scores over 600
42% had SAT math scores over 600
51% had ACT scores over 24
3% had SAT verbal scores over 700
9% had SAT math scores over 700
8% had ACT scores over 30
15 valedictorians

Graduation and After

63% graduated in 4 years
6% graduated in 5 years
1% graduated in 6 years
26% pursued further study (17% arts and sciences, 2% business, 2% law)
98% had job offers within 6 months
90 organizations recruited on campus

Financial Matters

$21,605 tuition and fees (2003–04)
$5780 room and board
94% average percent of need met
$18,365 average financial aid amount received per undergraduate (2002–03 estimated)

COLBY COLLEGE
SMALL-TOWN SETTING ■ PRIVATE ■ INDEPENDENT ■ COED
WATERVILLE, MAINE

Web site: www.colby.edu
Contact: Mr. Steve Thomas, Director of Admissions, Office of Admissions and Financial Aid, 4800 Mayflower Hill, Waterville, ME 04901-8848
Telephone: 207-872-3471 or toll-free 800-723-3032 **Fax:** 207-872-3474
E-mail: admissions@colby.edu

Getting in Last Year
4,126 applied
34% were accepted
474 enrolled (34%)
62% from top tenth of their h.s. class
88% had SAT verbal scores over 600
89% had SAT math scores over 600
96% had ACT scores over 24
34% had SAT verbal scores over 700
37% had SAT math scores over 700
36% had ACT scores over 30
21 valedictorians

Graduation and After
84% graduated in 4 years
2% graduated in 5 years
18% pursued further study (7% arts and sciences, 4% law, 3% medicine)
75% had job offers within 6 months
47 organizations recruited on campus

Financial Matters
$37,570 comprehensive fee (2003–04)
100% average percent of need met
$24,111 average financial aid amount received per undergraduate

Academics
Colby awards bachelor's **degrees**. Challenging opportunities include advanced placement credit, student-designed majors, an honors program, double majors, independent study, and a senior project. Special programs include internships, off-campus study, study-abroad, and Army ROTC.

The most frequently chosen **baccalaureate** fields are social sciences and history, area/ethnic studies, and English. A complete listing of majors at Colby appears in the Majors Index beginning on page 460.

The **faculty** at Colby has 157 full-time members, 97% with terminal degrees. The student-faculty ratio is 10:1.

Students of Colby
The student body is made up of 1,768 undergraduates. 53.8% are women and 46.2% are men. Students come from 48 states and territories and 69 other countries. 13% are from Maine. 6.8% are international students. 1.9% are African American, 0.3% American Indian, 4.7% Asian American, and 2.9% Hispanic American. 93% returned for their sophomore year.

Facilities and Resources
Student rooms are linked to a campus network. 300 **computers** are available on campus that provide access to the Internet. The 3 **libraries** have 350,000 books and 1,850 subscriptions.

Campus Life
There are 114 active organizations on campus, including a drama/theater group, newspaper, radio station, and choral group. No national or local **fraternities** or **sororities**.

Colby is a member of the NCAA (Division III). **Intercollegiate sports** include baseball (m), basketball, cheerleading, crew, cross-country running, field hockey (w), football (m), golf, ice hockey, lacrosse, skiing (cross-country), skiing (downhill), soccer, softball (w), squash, swimming, tennis, track and field, volleyball (w).

Campus Safety
Student safety services include campus lighting, student emergency response team, self-defense class, property id program, party monitors, late-night transport/escort service, 24-hour emergency telephone alarm devices, 24-hour patrols by trained security personnel, and electronically operated dormitory entrances.

Applying
Colby requires an essay, SAT I or ACT, a high school transcript, and 2 recommendations. It recommends an interview. Application deadline: 1/1; 2/1 for financial aid. Early and deferred admission are possible.

COLGATE UNIVERSITY

RURAL SETTING ■ PRIVATE ■ INDEPENDENT ■ COED
HAMILTON, NEW YORK

Web site: www.colgate.edu
Contact: Mr. Gary L. Ross, Dean of Admission, 13 Oak Drive, Hamilton, NY 13346-1383
Telephone: 315-228-7401 **Fax:** 315-228-7544
E-mail: admission@mail.colgate.edu

Academics

Colgate awards bachelor's and master's **degrees**. Challenging opportunities include advanced placement credit, student-designed majors, an honors program, double majors, independent study, and a senior project. Special programs include internships, off-campus study, and study-abroad.

The most frequently chosen **baccalaureate** fields are social sciences and history, English, and psychology. A complete listing of majors at Colgate appears in the Majors Index beginning on page 460.

The **faculty** at Colgate has 241 full-time members, 97% with terminal degrees. The student-faculty ratio is 10:1.

Students of Colgate

The student body totals 2,800, of whom 2,796 are undergraduates. 50.4% are women and 49.6% are men. Students come from 50 states and territories and 35 other countries. 31% are from New York. 96% returned for their sophomore year.

Facilities and Resources

Student rooms are linked to a campus network. 181 **computers** are available on campus that provide access to software applications and the Internet. The 2 **libraries** have 1,110,309 books and 2,315 subscriptions.

Campus Life

There are 125 active organizations on campus, including a drama/theater group, newspaper, radio station, television station, and choral group. 35% of eligible men and 32% of eligible women are members of national **fraternities**, national **sororities**, and local fraternities.

Colgate is a member of the NCAA (Division I). **Intercollegiate sports** (some offering scholarships) include basketball, crew, cross-country running, field hockey (w), football (m), golf (m), ice hockey, lacrosse, soccer, softball (w), swimming, tennis, track and field, volleyball (w).

Campus Safety

Student safety services include late-night transport/escort service, 24-hour emergency telephone alarm devices, 24-hour patrols by trained security personnel, student patrols, and electronically operated dormitory entrances.

Applying

Colgate requires an essay, SAT I and SAT II or ACT, a high school transcript, and 3 recommendations. Application deadline: 1/15; 2/1 for financial aid. Deferred admission is possible.

Getting in Last Year

6,789 applied
31% were accepted
725 enrolled (34%)
64% from top tenth of their h.s. class
3.54 average high school GPA
82% had SAT verbal scores over 600
90% had SAT math scores over 600
94% had ACT scores over 24
33% had SAT verbal scores over 700
40% had SAT math scores over 700
62% had ACT scores over 30
29 valedictorians

Graduation and After

83% graduated in 4 years
4% graduated in 5 years
1% graduated in 6 years
17% pursued further study (5% law, 3% arts and sciences, 3% medicine)
78% had job offers within 6 months
128 organizations recruited on campus

Financial Matters

$29,940 tuition and fees (2003–04)
$7155 room and board
100% average percent of need met
$25,421 average financial aid amount received per undergraduate

COLLEGE OF CHARLESTON

URBAN SETTING ■ PUBLIC ■ STATE-SUPPORTED ■ COED
CHARLESTON, SOUTH CAROLINA

Web site: www.cofc.edu

Contact: Mr. Donald Burkard, Dean of Admissions, 66 George Street, Charleston, SC 29424-0001

Telephone: 843-953-5670 or toll-free 843-953-5670 (in-state) **Fax:** 843-953-6322

E-mail: admissions@cofc.edu

The Honors Program at the College of Charleston challenges intellectually talented students to make the most of their opportunities and to become actively involved in their own education. In Honors classes, students take responsibility for their own learning through class discussions, interaction with with faculty members and fellow students, and independent research. Honors students are advised by specially chosen faculty advisers, receive priority registration, and have the opportunity to room with other Honors students in Honors residence halls. Classes, seminars, and student gatherings are held in the Honors Center, the historic William Aiken House built in 1839, and located in the center of campus.

Getting in Last Year
7,606 applied
60% were accepted
1,874 enrolled (41%)
28% from top tenth of their h.s. class
3.67 average high school GPA
56% had SAT verbal scores over 600
53% had SAT math scores over 600
52% had ACT scores over 24
8% had SAT verbal scores over 700
6% had SAT math scores over 700
2% had ACT scores over 30
24 valedictorians

Graduation and After
36% graduated in 4 years
17% graduated in 5 years
3% graduated in 6 years
92% had job offers within 6 months
287 organizations recruited on campus

Financial Matters
$5770 resident tuition and fees (2003–04)
$13,032 nonresident tuition and fees (2003–04)
$6117 room and board
67% average percent of need met
$8324 average financial aid amount received per undergraduate (2002–03 estimated)

Academics
C of C awards bachelor's and master's **degrees** (also offers graduate degree programs through University of Charleston, South Carolina). Challenging opportunities include advanced placement credit, accelerated degree programs, an honors program, double majors, independent study, and a senior project. Special programs include cooperative education, internships, summer session for credit, off-campus study, study-abroad, and Air Force ROTC.

The most frequently chosen **baccalaureate** fields are business/marketing, social sciences and history, and communications/communication technologies. A complete listing of majors at C of C appears in the Majors Index beginning on page 460.

The **faculty** at C of C has 487 full-time members, 86% with terminal degrees. The student-faculty ratio is 14:1.

Students of C of C
The student body totals 11,536, of whom 9,824 are undergraduates. 63.1% are women and 36.9% are men. Students come from 52 states and territories and 76 other countries. 67% are from South Carolina. 2.3% are international students. 8.4% are African American, 0.3% American Indian, 1.5% Asian American, and 1.4% Hispanic American. 84% returned for their sophomore year.

Facilities and Resources
Student rooms are linked to a campus network. 300 **computers** are available on campus that provide access to the Internet. The 2 **libraries** have 476,108 books and 3,723 subscriptions.

Campus Life
There are 144 active organizations on campus, including a drama/theater group, newspaper, radio station, and choral group. 15% of eligible men and 20% of eligible women are members of national **fraternities** and national **sororities**.

C of C is a member of the NCAA (Division I). **Intercollegiate sports** (some offering scholarships) include baseball (m), basketball, cross-country running, equestrian sports (w), golf, sailing, soccer, softball (w), swimming, tennis, volleyball (w).

Campus Safety
Student safety services include late-night transport/escort service, 24-hour emergency telephone alarm devices, 24-hour patrols by trained security personnel, and student patrols.

Applying
C of C requires an essay, SAT I or ACT, a high school transcript, and recommendations. It recommends an interview. Application deadline: 4/1, 4/1 for nonresidents; 3/15 priority date for financial aid. Early and deferred admission are possible.

THE COLLEGE OF NEW JERSEY

SUBURBAN SETTING ■ PUBLIC ■ STATE-SUPPORTED ■ COED
EWING, NEW JERSEY

Web site: www.tcnj.edu
Contact: Ms. Lisa Angeloni, Dean of Admissions, PO Box 7718, Ewing, NJ 08628
Telephone: 609-771-2131 or toll-free 800-624-0967 **Fax:** 609-637-5174
E-mail: admiss@tcnj.edu

Academics

TCNJ awards bachelor's and master's **degrees** and post-bachelor's and post-master's certificates. Challenging opportunities include advanced placement credit, an honors program, double majors, independent study, and a senior project. Special programs include internships, summer session for credit, off-campus study, study-abroad, and Army and Air Force ROTC.

The most frequently chosen **baccalaureate** fields are education, business/marketing, and English. A complete listing of majors at TCNJ appears in the Majors Index beginning on page 460.

The **faculty** at TCNJ has 326 full-time members, 90% with terminal degrees. The student-faculty ratio is 12:1.

Students of TCNJ

The student body totals 6,912, of whom 5,938 are undergraduates. 59.8% are women and 40.2% are men. Students come from 14 states and territories and 10 other countries. 95% are from New Jersey. 0.1% are international students. 5.9% are African American, 0.1% American Indian, 4.9% Asian American, and 5.8% Hispanic American. 95% returned for their sophomore year.

Facilities and Resources

Student rooms are linked to a campus network. 800 **computers** are available on campus that provide access to the Internet. The **library** has 550,000 books and 7,900 subscriptions.

Campus Life

There are 185 active organizations on campus, including a drama/theater group, newspaper, radio station, and choral group. 20% of eligible men and 20% of eligible women are members of national **fraternities**, national **sororities**, local fraternities, and local sororities.

TCNJ is a member of the NCAA (Division III). **Intercollegiate sports** include baseball (m), basketball, cheerleading, cross-country running, field hockey (w), football (m), golf (m), lacrosse (w), soccer, softball (w), swimming, tennis, track and field, wrestling (m).

Campus Safety

Student safety services include late-night transport/escort service, 24-hour emergency telephone alarm devices, 24-hour patrols by trained security personnel, student patrols, and electronically operated dormitory entrances.

Applying

TCNJ requires an essay, SAT I or ACT, and a high school transcript, and in some cases an interview and art portfolio or music audition. Application deadline: 2/15; 3/1 priority date for financial aid. Early and deferred admission are possible.

The College of New Jersey (TCNJ) attracts New Jersey's highest achieving students and students from other states who meet its admissions requirements. With high expectations for both its students and itself, the College has created a culture of constant questioning. On an elegant campus, in small classes, students and faculty members collaborate in a transformative educational process. From undergraduate research to internships and study abroad, TCNJ students have opportunities to shape their education in exciting ways. From the first year on, students blur the boundaries between living and learning, and between "student" and "life."

Getting in Last Year

6,373 applied
48% were accepted
1,178 enrolled (38%)
66% from top tenth of their h.s. class
67% had SAT verbal scores over 600
78% had SAT math scores over 600
16% had SAT verbal scores over 700
25% had SAT math scores over 700
17 National Merit Scholars

Graduation and After

62% graduated in 4 years
16% graduated in 5 years
3% graduated in 6 years
16% pursued further study (6% education, 3% arts and sciences, 2% business)
84% had job offers within 6 months
350 organizations recruited on campus

Financial Matters

$8206 resident tuition and fees (2003–04)
$12,781 nonresident tuition and fees (2003–04)
$7744 room and board
76% average percent of need met
$2449 average financial aid amount received per undergraduate (2001–02)

COLLEGE OF SAINT BENEDICT
COORDINATE WITH SAINT JOHN'S UNIVERSITY (MN)

SMALL-TOWN SETTING ■ PRIVATE ■ INDEPENDENT RELIGIOUS ■ COED, PRIMARILY WOMEN

SAINT JOSEPH, MINNESOTA

Web site: www.csbsju.edu
Contact: Ms. Karen Backes, Associate Dean of Admissions, PO Box 7155, Collegeville, MN 56321
Telephone: 320-363-2196 or toll-free 800-544-1489 **Fax:** 320-363-2750
E-mail: admissions@csbsju.edu

Through a partnership of 2 national liberal arts colleges, the College of Saint Benedict (for women) and Saint John's University (for men) come together to offer one exceptional education. Enriched by a Catholic and Benedictine tradition, the colleges promote an integrated learning experience that combines a challenging academic program with extensive opportunities for international study, leadership, service, spiritual growth, and cultural and athletic involvement. The colleges' residential campuses, set amid the woods and lakes of central Minnesota, are excellent places for active students to become fully immersed in their college education.

Getting in Last Year
1,174 applied
90% were accepted
502 enrolled (47%)
41% from top tenth of their h.s. class
3.7 average high school GPA
39% had SAT verbal scores over 600
40% had SAT math scores over 600
63% had ACT scores over 24
8% had SAT verbal scores over 700
6% had SAT math scores over 700
10% had ACT scores over 30
5 National Merit Scholars

Graduation and After
72% graduated in 4 years
6% graduated in 5 years
13% pursued further study (5% arts and sciences, 3% education, 2% law)

Financial Matters
$20,685 tuition and fees (2003–04)
$5987 room and board
92% average percent of need met
$16,190 average financial aid amount received per undergraduate (2002–03 estimated)

Academics
St. Ben's awards bachelor's **degrees** (coordinate with Saint John's University for men). Challenging opportunities include advanced placement credit, accelerated degree programs, student-designed majors, an honors program, double majors, independent study, and a senior project. Special programs include internships, off-campus study, study-abroad, and Army ROTC.

The most frequently chosen **baccalaureate** fields are English, business/marketing, and social sciences and history. A complete listing of majors at St. Ben's appears in the Majors Index beginning on page 460.

The **faculty** at St. Ben's has 148 full-time members, 74% with terminal degrees. The student-faculty ratio is 13:1.

Students of St. Ben's
The student body is made up of 2,054 undergraduates. 100% are women. Students come from 31 states and territories and 24 other countries. 86% are from Minnesota. 3.5% are international students. 0.6% are African American, 0.1% American Indian, 2.1% Asian American, and 1% Hispanic American. 88% returned for their sophomore year.

Facilities and Resources
Student rooms are linked to a campus network. 541 **computers** are available on campus that provide access to the Internet. The 3 **libraries** have 805,376 books and 5,735 subscriptions.

Campus Life
There are 90 active organizations on campus, including a drama/theater group, newspaper, radio station, and choral group. No national or local **fraternities** or **sororities**.

St. Ben's is a member of the NCAA (Division III). **Intercollegiate sports** include basketball (w), cheerleading, cross-country running (w), golf (w), ice hockey (w), skiing (cross-country) (w), soccer (w), softball (w), swimming (w), tennis (w), track and field (w), volleyball (w).

Campus Safety
Student safety services include well-lit pathways, late-night transport/escort service, 24-hour emergency telephone alarm devices, 24-hour patrols by trained security personnel, student patrols, and electronically operated dormitory entrances.

Applying
St. Ben's requires an essay, SAT I or ACT, a high school transcript, and 1 recommendation. It recommends an interview and a minimum high school GPA of 3.0. Application deadline: 1/15; 3/15 priority date for financial aid. Early and deferred admission are possible.

THE COLLEGE OF ST. SCHOLASTICA

SUBURBAN SETTING ■ PRIVATE ■ INDEPENDENT RELIGIOUS ■ COED
DULUTH, MINNESOTA

Web site: www.css.edu
Contact: Mr. Brian Dalton, Vice President for Enrollment Management, 1200 Kenwood Avenue, Duluth, MN 55811-4199
Telephone: 218-723-6053 or toll-free 800-249-6412 **Fax:** 218-723-5991
E-mail: admissions@css.edu

Academics

St. Scholastica awards bachelor's and master's **degrees** and post-bachelor's and post-master's certificates. Challenging opportunities include advanced placement credit, accelerated degree programs, student-designed majors, an honors program, double majors, independent study, and a senior project. Special programs include internships, summer session for credit, off-campus study, study-abroad, and Air Force ROTC.

The most frequently chosen **baccalaureate** fields are health professions and related sciences, business/marketing, and computer/information sciences. A complete listing of majors at St. Scholastica appears in the Majors Index beginning on page 460.

The **faculty** at St. Scholastica has 123 full-time members, 61% with terminal degrees. The student-faculty ratio is 13:1.

Students of St. Scholastica

The student body totals 2,838, of whom 2,308 are undergraduates. 70.5% are women and 29.5% are men. Students come from 19 states and territories and 10 other countries. 89% are from Minnesota. 1.5% are international students. 2.7% are African American, 1.9% American Indian, 1.1% Asian American, and 0.5% Hispanic American. 82% returned for their sophomore year.

Facilities and Resources

Student rooms are linked to a campus network. 145 **computers** are available on campus that provide access to the Internet. The 2 **libraries** have 125,091 books and 1,135 subscriptions.

Campus Life

There are 45 active organizations on campus, including a drama/theater group, newspaper, and choral group. No national or local **fraternities** or **sororities**.

St. Scholastica is a member of the NCAA (Division III) and NAIA. **Intercollegiate sports** include baseball (m), basketball, cross-country running, ice hockey (m), soccer, softball (w), tennis, volleyball (w).

Campus Safety

Student safety services include student door monitor at night, late-night transport/escort service, 24-hour emergency telephone alarm devices, 24-hour patrols by trained security personnel, and electronically operated dormitory entrances.

Applying

St. Scholastica requires SAT I or ACT and a high school transcript, and in some cases an interview and a minimum high school GPA of 2.0. It recommends an essay, PSAT, an interview, and recommendations. Application deadline: rolling admissions; 3/15 priority date for financial aid. Early and deferred admission are possible.

Getting in Last Year

1,206 applied
88% were accepted
437 enrolled (41%)
27% from top tenth of their h.s. class
3.50 average high school GPA
33% had SAT verbal scores over 600
29% had SAT math scores over 600
50% had ACT scores over 24
4% had SAT verbal scores over 700
4% had SAT math scores over 700
5% had ACT scores over 30

Graduation and After

58% graduated in 4 years
6% graduated in 5 years
1% graduated in 6 years
30% pursued further study (18% arts and sciences, 5% medicine, 1% education)
4 organizations recruited on campus

Financial Matters

$19,302 tuition and fees (2003–04)
$5668 room and board
82% average percent of need met
$15,908 average financial aid amount received per undergraduate (2002–03 estimated)

COLLEGE OF THE ATLANTIC
SMALL-TOWN SETTING ■ PRIVATE ■ INDEPENDENT ■ COED
BAR HARBOR, MAINE

Web site: www.coa.edu
Contact: Ms. Sarah G. Baker, Director of Admission, 105 Eden Street, Bar Harbor, ME 04609-1198
Telephone: 207-288-5015 ext. 233 or toll-free 800-528-0025 **Fax:** 207-288-4126
E-mail: inquiry@ecology.coa.edu

College of the Atlantic integrates student qualities of intellectual rigor, self-motivation, independence, and passion for the environment with institutional characteristics of self-designed concentrations of study, small seminar-style classes, and an abundance of supplementary fieldwork, allowing students the opportunity to combine areas of academic interest with the interdisciplinary liberal arts exploration of human ecology. At a college where questioning ideas and seeking relationships are encouraged, faculty members work along with students as they develop individualized programs of study that enable them to address ecological problems from multiple perspectives. This personalized approach to education, combined with practical experience in problem solving, allows students to develop the important skills necessary to make meaningful contributions to society.

Academics
COA awards bachelor's and master's **degrees**. Challenging opportunities include advanced placement credit, accelerated degree programs, student-designed majors, independent study, and a senior project. Special programs include cooperative education, internships, off-campus study, and study-abroad. A complete listing of majors at COA appears in the Majors Index beginning on page 460.

The **faculty** at COA has 18 full-time members. The student-faculty ratio is 10:1.

Students of COA
The student body totals 262, of whom 250 are undergraduates. 53.6% are women and 46.4% are men. Students come from 37 states and territories and 32 other countries. 37% are from Maine. 16.9% are international students. 0.8% are African American, 0.8% Asian American, and 0.8% Hispanic American. 91% returned for their sophomore year.

Facilities and Resources
Student rooms are linked to a campus network. 48 **computers** are available on campus that provide access to the Internet. The **library** has 37,049 books and 469 subscriptions.

Campus Life
There are 12 active organizations on campus, including a drama/theater group, newspaper, and choral group. No national or local **fraternities** or **sororities**.

This institution has no intercollegiate sports.

Campus Safety
Student safety services include late-night transport/escort service, 24-hour emergency telephone alarm devices, and 24-hour patrols by trained security personnel.

Applying
COA requires an essay, a high school transcript, and 3 recommendations, and in some cases an interview. It recommends SAT I and SAT II or ACT, an interview, and a minimum high school GPA of 3.0. Application deadline: 2/15; 2/15 priority date for financial aid. Early and deferred admission are possible.

Getting in Last Year
270 applied
69% were accepted
67 enrolled (36%)
23% from top tenth of their h.s. class
3.4 average high school GPA
64% had SAT verbal scores over 600
48% had SAT math scores over 600
100% had ACT scores over 24
13% had SAT verbal scores over 700
25% had ACT scores over 30
6 National Merit Scholars
3 class presidents
2 valedictorians

Graduation and After
49% graduated in 4 years
4% graduated in 5 years
3% pursued further study (2% arts and sciences)
80% had job offers within 6 months

Financial Matters
$23,961 tuition and fees (2003–04)
$6543 room and board
85% average percent of need met
$21,823 average financial aid amount received per undergraduate

COLLEGE OF THE HOLY CROSS

SUBURBAN SETTING ■ PRIVATE ■ INDEPENDENT RELIGIOUS ■ COED
WORCESTER, MASSACHUSETTS

Web site: www.holycross.edu
Contact: Ms. Ann Bowe McDermott, Director of Admissions, 105 Fenwick
Hall, 1 College Street, Worcester, MA 01610-2395
Telephone: 508-793-2443 or toll-free 800-442-2421 **Fax:** 508-793-3888
E-mail: admissions@holycross.edu

Academics

Holy Cross awards bachelor's **degrees**. Challenging opportunities include advanced
placement credit, accelerated degree programs, student-designed majors, an honors
program, double majors, independent study, and a senior project. Special programs
include internships, off-campus study, study-abroad, and Army, Navy and Air Force
ROTC.

The most frequently chosen **baccalaureate** fields are social sciences and history,
psychology, and English. A complete listing of majors at Holy Cross appears in the
Majors Index beginning on page 460.

The **faculty** at Holy Cross has 228 full-time members, 95% with terminal degrees.
The student-faculty ratio is 11:1.

Students of Holy Cross

The student body is made up of 2,773 undergraduates. 53.7% are women and 46.3% are
men. Students come from 48 states and territories and 18 other countries. 34% are from
Massachusetts. 1% are international students. 3% are African American, 0.3% American
Indian, 4% Asian American, and 5% Hispanic American. 98% returned for their
sophomore year.

Facilities and Resources

Student rooms are linked to a campus network. 426 **computers** are available on campus
that provide access to the Internet. The 3 **libraries** have 584,883 books and 1,921
subscriptions.

Campus Life

There are 94 active organizations on campus, including a drama/theater group,
newspaper, radio station, choral group, and marching band. No national or local
fraternities or **sororities**.

Holy Cross is a member of the NCAA (Division I). **Intercollegiate sports** (some
offering scholarships) include baseball (m), basketball, crew, cross-country running, field
hockey (w), football (m), golf, ice hockey, lacrosse, soccer, softball (w), swimming, tennis,
track and field, volleyball (w).

Campus Safety

Student safety services include late-night transport/escort service, 24-hour emergency
telephone alarm devices, 24-hour patrols by trained security personnel, and electronically operated dormitory entrances.

Applying

Holy Cross requires an essay, SAT II: Writing Test, SAT I and SAT II or ACT, a high
school transcript, and 2 recommendations. It recommends an interview. Application
deadline: 1/15; 2/1 for financial aid. Early and deferred admission are possible.

Getting in Last Year
5,035 applied
42% were accepted
698 enrolled (33%)
68% from top tenth of their h.s. class
71% had SAT verbal scores over 600
79% had SAT math scores over 600
19% had SAT verbal scores over 700
14% had SAT math scores over 700
2 National Merit Scholars
19 valedictorians

Graduation and After
87% graduated in 4 years
2% graduated in 5 years
1% graduated in 6 years
23% pursued further study (9% arts and sciences, 7% law, 2% education)
69% had job offers within 6 months
47 organizations recruited on campus

Financial Matters
$28,011 tuition and fees (2003–04)
$8440 room and board
100% average percent of need met
$21,917 average financial aid amount received
per undergraduate

THE COLLEGE OF WILLIAM AND MARY

SMALL-TOWN SETTING ■ PUBLIC ■ STATE-SUPPORTED ■ COED
WILLIAMSBURG, VIRGINIA

Web site: www.wm.edu
Contact: Ms. Karen R. Cottrell, Associate Provost for Enrollment, PO Box 8795, Williamsburg, VA 23187-8795
Telephone: 757-221-4223 **Fax:** 757-221-1242
E-mail: admiss@wm.edu

Getting in Last Year

10,161 applied
34% were accepted
1,326 enrolled (38%)
85% from top tenth of their h.s. class
4.0 average high school GPA
88% had SAT verbal scores over 600
86% had SAT math scores over 600
89% had ACT scores over 24
43% had SAT verbal scores over 700
35% had SAT math scores over 700
78% had ACT scores over 30
15 National Merit Scholars
29 class presidents
121 valedictorians

Graduation and After

79% graduated in 4 years
7% graduated in 5 years
31% pursued further study
47% had job offers within 6 months
111 organizations recruited on campus

Financial Matters

$6430 resident tuition and fees (2003–04)
$21,130 nonresident tuition and fees (2003–04)
$5794 room and board
80% average percent of need met
$8664 average financial aid amount received per undergraduate

Academics

William and Mary awards bachelor's, master's, doctoral, and first-professional **degrees** and post-master's certificates. Challenging opportunities include advanced placement credit, accelerated degree programs, student-designed majors, an honors program, double majors, independent study, and a senior project. Special programs include summer session for credit, study-abroad, and Army ROTC.

The most frequently chosen **baccalaureate** fields are social sciences and history, business/marketing, and biological/life sciences. A complete listing of majors at William and Mary appears in the Majors Index beginning on page 460.

The **faculty** at William and Mary has 563 full-time members, 91% with terminal degrees. The student-faculty ratio is 12:1.

Students of William and Mary

The student body totals 7,749, of whom 5,748 are undergraduates. 56.2% are women and 43.8% are men. Students come from 50 states and territories and 52 other countries. 65% are from Virginia. 2% are international students. 5.6% are African American, 0.5% American Indian, 6.7% Asian American, and 3.4% Hispanic American. 94% returned for their sophomore year.

Facilities and Resources

Student rooms are linked to a campus network. 225 **computers** are available on campus that provide access to the Internet. The 10 **libraries** have 2,043,345 books and 11,688 subscriptions.

Campus Life

There are 300 active organizations on campus, including a drama/theater group, newspaper, radio station, television station, and choral group. William and Mary has national **fraternities** and national **sororities**.

William and Mary is a member of the NCAA (Division I). **Intercollegiate sports** (some offering scholarships) include baseball (m), basketball, cross-country running, field hockey (w), football (m), golf, gymnastics, lacrosse (w), soccer, swimming, tennis, track and field, volleyball (w).

Campus Safety

Student safety services include late-night transport/escort service, 24-hour emergency telephone alarm devices, 24-hour patrols by trained security personnel, student patrols, and electronically operated dormitory entrances.

Applying

William and Mary requires an essay, SAT I or ACT, and a high school transcript. It recommends SAT II Subject Tests, SAT II: Writing Test, and 1 recommendation. Application deadline: 1/5; 3/15 for financial aid, with a 2/15 priority date. Early and deferred admission are possible.

THE COLLEGE OF WOOSTER

SMALL-TOWN SETTING ■ PRIVATE ■ INDEPENDENT RELIGIOUS ■ COED
WOOSTER, OHIO

Web site: www.wooster.edu
Contact: Mr. Paul Deutsch, Dean of Admissions, 847 College Avenue, Wooster, OH 44691
Telephone: 330-263-2270 ext. 2118 or toll-free 800-877-9905 **Fax:** 330-263-2621
E-mail: admissions@wooster.edu

Academics

Wooster awards bachelor's **degrees**. Challenging opportunities include advanced placement credit, student-designed majors, double majors, independent study, and a senior project. Special programs include internships, summer session for credit, off-campus study, and study-abroad.

The most frequently chosen **baccalaureate** fields are social sciences and history, English, and visual/performing arts. A complete listing of majors at Wooster appears in the Majors Index beginning on page 460.

The **faculty** at Wooster has 134 full-time members, 97% with terminal degrees. The student-faculty ratio is 12:1.

Students of Wooster

The student body is made up of 1,871 undergraduates. 53.2% are women and 46.8% are men. Students come from 39 states and territories and 21 other countries. 58% are from Ohio. 6.7% are international students. 4.9% are African American, 0.3% American Indian, 1.5% Asian American, and 1% Hispanic American. 87% returned for their sophomore year.

Facilities and Resources

Student rooms are linked to a campus network. 275 **computers** are available on campus that provide access to the Internet. The 4 **libraries** have 581,518 books.

Campus Life

There are 102 active organizations on campus, including a drama/theater group, newspaper, radio station, choral group, and marching band. 9% of eligible men and 10% of eligible women are members of local **fraternities**, local **sororities**, and coed fraternity.

Wooster is a member of the NCAA (Division III). **Intercollegiate sports** include baseball (m), basketball, cross-country running, field hockey (w), football (m), golf (m), lacrosse, soccer, softball (w), swimming, tennis, track and field, volleyball (w).

Campus Safety

Student safety services include late-night transport/escort service, 24-hour emergency telephone alarm devices, 24-hour patrols by trained security personnel, student patrols, and electronically operated dormitory entrances.

Applying

Wooster requires an essay, SAT I or ACT, a high school transcript, and 2 recommendations. It recommends an interview. Application deadline: 2/15; 2/15 priority date for financial aid. Early and deferred admission are possible.

Wooster's curriculum provides students the breadth that is to be found in hundreds of course offerings and the depth that comes from 37 majors and programs of study. Small classes and an accessible faculty committed to teaching undergraduates ensure individual attention for every student. A First-Year Seminar in Critical Inquiry links advising with teaching in a small seminar setting, while senior-year students work one-on-one with a faculty member on an Independent Study Project, a concept that was introduced into Wooster's curriculum more than 50 years ago. Wooster is one of the very few colleges that requires independent research of every student.

Getting in Last Year
2,560 applied
70% were accepted
552 enrolled (31%)
36% from top tenth of their h.s. class
3.58 average high school GPA
53% had SAT verbal scores over 600
53% had SAT math scores over 600
73% had ACT scores over 24
15% had SAT verbal scores over 700
9% had SAT math scores over 700
16% had ACT scores over 30

Graduation and After
61% graduated in 4 years
5% graduated in 5 years
2% graduated in 6 years
71% had job offers within 6 months
30 organizations recruited on campus

Financial Matters
$25,040 tuition and fees (2003–04)
$6260 room and board
95% average percent of need met
$21,812 average financial aid amount received per undergraduate

---

COLORADO CHRISTIAN UNIVERSITY

SUBURBAN SETTING ■ PRIVATE ■ INDEPENDENT RELIGIOUS ■ COED
LAKEWOOD, COLORADO

Web site: www.ccu.edu
Contact: Mr. Rodney Stanford, Director of Undergraduate Admission, 180 South Garrison Street, Lakewood, CO 80226
Telephone: 303-963-3203 or toll-free 800-44-FAITH **Fax:** 303-963-3201
E-mail: admission@ccu.edu

Getting in Last Year
920 applied
76% were accepted
265 enrolled (38%)
24% from top tenth of their h.s. class
3.52 average high school GPA
35% had SAT verbal scores over 600
29% had SAT math scores over 600
53% had ACT scores over 24
10% had SAT verbal scores over 700
4% had SAT math scores over 700
5% had ACT scores over 30

Graduation and After
31% graduated in 4 years
6% graduated in 5 years
1% graduated in 6 years

Financial Matters
$15,040 tuition and fees (2003–04)
$5320 room and board
58% average percent of need met
$8771 average financial aid amount received per undergraduate

Academics
CCU awards associate, bachelor's, and master's **degrees**. Challenging opportunities include advanced placement credit, accelerated degree programs, student-designed majors, an honors program, double majors, independent study, and a senior project. Special programs include cooperative education, internships, summer session for credit, off-campus study, study-abroad, and Army ROTC.

The most frequently chosen **baccalaureate** fields are business/marketing, liberal arts/general studies, and psychology. A complete listing of majors at CCU appears in the Majors Index beginning on page 460.

The **faculty** at CCU has 40 full-time members, 85% with terminal degrees. The student-faculty ratio is 21:1.

Students of CCU
The student body totals 1,583, of whom 1,462 are undergraduates. 59.9% are women and 40.1% are men. Students come from 45 states and territories and 9 other countries. 59% are from Colorado. 0.6% are international students. 4% are African American, 1% American Indian, 1.2% Asian American, and 5.5% Hispanic American. 58% returned for their sophomore year.

Facilities and Resources
Student rooms are linked to a campus network. 141 **computers** are available on campus that provide access to the Internet. The 2 **libraries** have 71,565 books and 1,192 subscriptions.

Campus Life
There are 26 active organizations on campus, including a drama/theater group, newspaper, and choral group. No national or local **fraternities** or **sororities**.

CCU is a member of the NCAA (Division II). **Intercollegiate sports** (some offering scholarships) include basketball, cross-country running, golf (m), soccer, tennis, volleyball (w).

Campus Safety
Student safety services include 24-hour emergency telephone alarm devices, 24-hour patrols by trained security personnel, and student patrols.

Applying
CCU requires an essay, SAT I or ACT, a high school transcript, and 2 recommendations, and in some cases an interview, 3 recommendations, and a minimum high school GPA of 2.8. Application deadline: 8/1; 3/15 priority date for financial aid. Deferred admission is possible.

The Colorado College

URBAN SETTING ■ PRIVATE ■ INDEPENDENT ■ COED
COLORADO SPRINGS, COLORADO

Web site: www.coloradocollege.edu
Contact: Mr. Mark Hatch, Dean of Admission and Financial Aid, 900 Block
  North Cascade, West, Colorado Springs, CO 80903-3294
Telephone: 719-389-6344 or toll-free 800-542-7214 **Fax:** 719-389-6816
E-mail: admission@coloradocollege.edu

Academics

CC awards bachelor's and master's **degrees** (master's degree in education only). Challenging opportunities include advanced placement credit, student-designed majors, double majors, independent study, and a senior project. Special programs include internships, summer session for credit, off-campus study, study-abroad, and Army ROTC.

The most frequently chosen **baccalaureate** fields are social sciences and history, biological/life sciences, and English. A complete listing of majors at CC appears in the Majors Index beginning on page 460.

The **faculty** at CC has 166 full-time members, 96% with terminal degrees. The student-faculty ratio is 9:1.

Students of CC

The student body totals 1,968, of whom 1,941 are undergraduates. 54.4% are women and 45.6% are men. Students come from 52 states and territories and 26 other countries. 30% are from Colorado. 1.9% are international students. 1.8% are African American, 1.6% American Indian, 4.4% Asian American, and 7% Hispanic American. 92% returned for their sophomore year.

Facilities and Resources

Student rooms are linked to a campus network. 235 **computers** are available on campus that provide access to the Internet. The 3 **libraries** have 535,657 books and 1,313 subscriptions.

Campus Life

There are 80 active organizations on campus, including a drama/theater group, newspaper, radio station, and choral group. 16% of eligible men and 18% of eligible women are members of national **fraternities** and national **sororities**.

CC is a member of the NCAA (Division III). **Intercollegiate sports** (some offering scholarships) include basketball, cross-country running, football (m), ice hockey (m), lacrosse, soccer, softball (w), swimming, tennis, track and field, volleyball (w).

Campus Safety

Student safety services include whistle program, student escort service, late-night transport/escort service, 24-hour emergency telephone alarm devices, 24-hour patrols by trained security personnel, and electronically operated dormitory entrances.

Applying

CC requires an essay, SAT I or ACT, a high school transcript, and 3 recommendations. It recommends an interview. Application deadline: 1/15; 2/15 for financial aid. Deferred admission is possible.

Getting in Last Year

3,533 applied
56% were accepted
524 enrolled (27%)
44% from top tenth of their h.s. class
70% had SAT verbal scores over 600
70% had SAT math scores over 600
82% had ACT scores over 24
22% had SAT verbal scores over 700
16% had SAT math scores over 700
23% had ACT scores over 30
8 National Merit Scholars
28 valedictorians

Graduation and After

70% graduated in 4 years
7% graduated in 5 years
7% pursued further study (5% arts and sciences, 1% business, 1% law)
89 organizations recruited on campus

Financial Matters

$27,635 tuition and fees (2003–04)
$6840 room and board
95% average percent of need met
$21,385 average financial aid amount received per undergraduate (2002–03 estimated)

COLORADO SCHOOL OF MINES

SMALL-TOWN SETTING ■ PUBLIC ■ STATE-SUPPORTED ■ COED
GOLDEN, COLORADO

Web site: www.mines.edu
Contact: Ms. Tricia Douthit, Associate Director of Admissions, Student
Center, 1600 Maple Street, Golden, CO 80401
Telephone: 303-273-3224 or toll-free 800-446-9488 ext. 3220 (out-of-state)
Fax: 303-273-3509
E-mail: admit@mines.edu

Getting in Last Year

3,049 applied
79% were accepted
668 enrolled (28%)
50% from top tenth of their h.s. class
3.70 average high school GPA
52% had SAT verbal scores over 600
79% had SAT math scores over 600
88% had ACT scores over 24
11% had SAT verbal scores over 700
25% had SAT math scores over 700
26% had ACT scores over 30
72 class presidents
80 valedictorians

Graduation and After

27% graduated in 4 years
33% graduated in 5 years
4% graduated in 6 years
15% pursued further study (11% engineering,
1% arts and sciences, 1% business)
68% had job offers within 6 months
107 organizations recruited on campus

Financial Matters

$6380 resident tuition and fees (2003–04)
$19,570 nonresident tuition and fees (2003–
04)
$6100 room and board
90% average percent of need met
$13,100 average financial aid amount received
per undergraduate

Academics

CSM awards bachelor's, master's, and doctoral **degrees**. Challenging opportunities
include advanced placement credit, accelerated degree programs, an honors program,
double majors, independent study, and a senior project. Special programs include
cooperative education, internships, summer session for credit, study-abroad, and Army
ROTC.

The most frequently chosen **baccalaureate** fields are engineering/engineering
technologies, mathematics, and physical sciences. A complete listing of majors at CSM
appears in the Majors Index beginning on page 460.

The **faculty** at CSM has 188 full-time members, 92% with terminal degrees. The
student-faculty ratio is 15:1.

Students of CSM

The student body totals 3,398, of whom 2,664 are undergraduates. 23.4% are women
and 76.6% are men. Students come from 51 states and territories and 62 other countries.
79% are from Colorado. 3.6% are international students. 1.2% are African American,
0.9% American Indian, 5.3% Asian American, and 6.7% Hispanic American. 88%
returned for their sophomore year.

Facilities and Resources

Student rooms are linked to a campus network. 400 **computers** are available on campus
that provide access to the Internet. The **library** has 150,000 books and 4,883 subscriptions.

Campus Life

There are 95 active organizations on campus, including a drama/theater group,
newspaper, choral group, and marching band. 19% of eligible men and 19% of eligible
women are members of national **fraternities** and national **sororities**.

CSM is a member of the NCAA (Division II). **Intercollegiate sports** (some offering
scholarships) include baseball (m), basketball, cross-country running, football (m), golf
(m), skiing (downhill) (m), soccer (m), softball (w), swimming, tennis, track and field, volleyball (w), wrestling (m).

Campus Safety

Student safety services include late-night transport/escort service, 24-hour emergency
telephone alarm devices, and 24-hour patrols by trained security personnel.

Applying

CSM requires SAT I or ACT and a high school transcript, and in some cases an essay, an
interview, and recommendations. It recommends rank in upper one-third of high school
class. Application deadline: 6/1; 3/1 priority date for financial aid. Deferred admission is
possible.

COLORADO STATE UNIVERSITY

URBAN SETTING ■ PUBLIC ■ STATE-SUPPORTED ■ COED
FORT COLLINS, COLORADO

Web site: www.colostate.edu
Contact: Ms. Mary Ontiveros, Director of Admissions, Spruce Hall, Fort
    Collins, CO 80523-0015
Telephone: 970-491-6909 **Fax:** 970-491-7799
E-mail: admissions@vines.colostate.edu

Academics

Colorado State awards bachelor's, master's, doctoral, and first-professional **degrees**.
Challenging opportunities include advanced placement credit, accelerated degree
programs, student-designed majors, an honors program, double majors, independent
study, and a senior project. Special programs include cooperative education, internships,
summer session for credit, off-campus study, study-abroad, and Army and Air Force
ROTC.

The most frequently chosen **baccalaureate** fields are business/marketing, engineer-
ing/engineering technologies, and social sciences and history. A complete listing of
majors at Colorado State appears in the Majors Index beginning on page 460.

The **faculty** at Colorado State has 865 full-time members, 99% with terminal
degrees. The student-faculty ratio is 17:1.

Students of Colorado State

The student body totals 26,870, of whom 21,689 are undergraduates. 50.9% are women
and 49.1% are men. 81% are from Colorado. 1.2% are international students. 2% are
African American, 1.2% American Indian, 2.7% Asian American, and 6.1% Hispanic
American. 82% returned for their sophomore year.

Facilities and Resources

Student rooms are linked to a campus network. 2,530 **computers** are available on
campus that provide access to the Internet. The 4 **libraries** have 1,882,297 books and
20,712 subscriptions.

Campus Life

There are 300 active organizations on campus, including a drama/theater group,
newspaper, radio station, television station, choral group, and marching band. 8% of
eligible men and 8% of eligible women are members of national **fraternities**, national
sororities, local fraternities, and local sororities.

Colorado State is a member of the NCAA (Division I). **Intercollegiate sports** (some
offering scholarships) include basketball, cross-country running, football (m), golf,
softball (w), swimming (w), tennis (w), track and field, volleyball (w), water polo (w).

Campus Safety

Student safety services include late-night transport/escort service, 24-hour emergency
telephone alarm devices, 24-hour patrols by trained security personnel, student patrols,
and electronically operated dormitory entrances.

Applying

Colorado State requires SAT I or ACT and a high school transcript. It recommends an
essay and recommendations. Application deadline: 7/1; 3/1 priority date for financial aid.
Deferred admission is possible.

Getting in Last Year

12,027 applied
79% were accepted
3,802 enrolled (40%)
21% from top tenth of their h.s. class
3.50 average high school GPA
27% had SAT verbal scores over 600
33% had SAT math scores over 600
54% had ACT scores over 24
3% had SAT verbal scores over 700
3% had SAT math scores over 700
7% had ACT scores over 30
14 National Merit Scholars

Graduation and After

33% graduated in 4 years
25% graduated in 5 years
4% graduated in 6 years
501 organizations recruited on campus

Financial Matters

$3744 resident tuition and fees (2003–04)
$14,216 nonresident tuition and fees (2003–
    04)
$6045 room and board
82% average percent of need met
$7948 average financial aid amount received
    per undergraduate (2002–03)

COLUMBIA COLLEGE

URBAN SETTING ■ PRIVATE ■ INDEPENDENT ■ COED
NEW YORK, NEW YORK

Web site: www.college.columbia.edu
Contact: Mr. Eric Furda, Director of Undergraduate Admissions, 212
   Hamilton Hall MC 2807, 1130 Amsterdam Avenue, New York, NY 10027
Telephone: 212-854-2522 **Fax:** 212-854-1209

Getting in Last Year
14,648 applied
11% were accepted
1,010 enrolled (61%)
81% from top tenth of their h.s. class
3.80 average high school GPA
89% had SAT verbal scores over 600
93% had SAT math scores over 600
96% had ACT scores over 24
60% had SAT verbal scores over 700
59% had SAT math scores over 700
47% had ACT scores over 30
284 National Merit Scholars

Graduation and After
84% graduated in 4 years
6% graduated in 5 years
2% graduated in 6 years
80% pursued further study
300 organizations recruited on campus

Financial Matters
$29,788 tuition and fees (2003–04)
$8802 room and board
100% average percent of need met
$27,079 average financial aid amount received
  per undergraduate

Academics

Columbia awards bachelor's **degrees**. Challenging opportunities include advanced placement credit, accelerated degree programs, student-designed majors, double majors, and a senior project. Special programs include internships, summer session for credit, off-campus study, study-abroad, and Army, Navy and Air Force ROTC.

The most frequently chosen **baccalaureate** fields are social sciences and history, English, and visual/performing arts. A complete listing of majors at Columbia appears in the Majors Index beginning on page 460.

The **faculty** at Columbia has 689 full-time members. The student-faculty ratio is 7:1.

Students of Columbia

The student body is made up of 4,181 undergraduates. 50.8% are women and 49.2% are men. Students come from 54 states and territories and 72 other countries. 25% are from New York. 5.5% are international students. 8.4% are African American, 0.3% American Indian, 12.2% Asian American, and 7.7% Hispanic American. 97% returned for their sophomore year.

Facilities and Resources

Student rooms are linked to a campus network. 400 **computers** are available on campus that provide access to the Internet. The 21 **libraries** have 7,200,000 books and 66,000 subscriptions.

Campus Life

There are 300 active organizations on campus, including a drama/theater group, newspaper, radio station, television station, choral group, and marching band. 19% of eligible men and 25% of eligible women are members of national **fraternities**, national **sororities**, and coed fraternities.

Columbia is a member of the NCAA (Division I). **Intercollegiate sports** include archery (w), baseball (m), basketball, crew, cross-country running, fencing, field hockey (w), football (m), golf (m), lacrosse (w), softball (w), swimming, track and field, wrestling (m).

Campus Safety

Student safety services include 24-hour ID check at door, late-night transport/escort service, 24-hour emergency telephone alarm devices, 24-hour patrols by trained security personnel, and student patrols.

Applying

Columbia requires an essay, SAT II Subject Tests, SAT II: Writing Test, SAT I or ACT, a high school transcript, and 3 recommendations. Application deadline: 1/2; 2/10 for financial aid. Early and deferred admission are possible.

COLUMBIA UNIVERSITY, THE FU FOUNDATION SCHOOL OF ENGINEERING AND APPLIED SCIENCE

URBAN SETTING ■ PRIVATE ■ INDEPENDENT ■ COED
NEW YORK, NEW YORK

Web site: www.engineering.columbia.edu
Contact: Mr. Eric J. Furda, Director of Undergraduate Admissions, 212
   Hamilton Hall MC 2807, 1130 Amsterdam Avenue, New York, NY 10027
Telephone: 212-854-2522 **Fax:** 212-854-1209

Academics

Columbia SEAS awards bachelor's, master's, and doctoral **degrees**. Advanced placement credit is a challenging opportunity. Special programs include internships, summer session for credit, study-abroad, and Army, Navy and Air Force ROTC.

The most frequently chosen **baccalaureate** fields are engineering/engineering technologies, social sciences and history, and computer/information sciences. A complete listing of majors at Columbia SEAS appears in the Majors Index beginning on page 460.

The **faculty** at Columbia SEAS has 130 full-time members. The student-faculty ratio is 8:1.

Students of Columbia SEAS

The student body totals 2,782, of whom 1,360 are undergraduates. 26% are women and 74% are men. Students come from 44 states and territories and 59 other countries. 30% are from New York. 12.1% are international students. 2.9% are African American, 33.5% Asian American, and 5.6% Hispanic American. 96% returned for their sophomore year.

Facilities and Resources

Student rooms are linked to a campus network. 400 **computers** are available on campus that provide access to the Internet. The 21 **libraries** have 7,200,000 books and 66,000 subscriptions.

Campus Life

There are 300 active organizations on campus, including a drama/theater group, newspaper, radio station, television station, choral group, and marching band. 19% of eligible men and 25% of eligible women are members of national **fraternities**, national **sororities**, and coed fraternities.

Columbia SEAS is a member of the NCAA (Division I). **Intercollegiate sports** include archery (w), baseball (m), basketball, crew, cross-country running, fencing, field hockey (w), football (m), golf (m), lacrosse (w), softball (w), swimming, track and field, wrestling (m).

Campus Safety

Student safety services include 24-hour ID check at door, late-night transport/escort service, 24-hour emergency telephone alarm devices, and 24-hour patrols by trained security personnel.

Applying

Columbia SEAS requires an essay, SAT II Subject Tests, SAT II: Writing Test, SAT I or ACT, a high school transcript, and 3 recommendations. It recommends an interview. Application deadline: 1/2; 2/10 for financial aid. Early and deferred admission are possible.

Getting in Last Year

2,219 applied
29% were accepted
314 enrolled (48%)
89% from top tenth of their h.s. class
3.80 average high school GPA
91% had SAT verbal scores over 600
89% had SAT math scores over 600
96% had ACT scores over 24
52% had SAT verbal scores over 700
60% had SAT math scores over 700
89% had ACT scores over 30
91 National Merit Scholars

Graduation and After

81% graduated in 4 years
6% graduated in 5 years
2% graduated in 6 years
300 organizations recruited on campus

Financial Matters

$29,788 tuition and fees (2003–04)
$8802 room and board
100% average percent of need met
$26,470 average financial aid amount received per undergraduate

CONCORDIA COLLEGE

SUBURBAN SETTING ■ PRIVATE ■ INDEPENDENT RELIGIOUS ■ COED
MOORHEAD, MINNESOTA

Web site: www.concordiacollege.edu
Contact: Mr. Scott E. Ellingson, Director of Admissions, 901 8th Street
    South, Moorhead, MN 56562
Telephone: 218-299-3004 or toll-free 800-699-9897 **Fax:** 218-299-3947
E-mail: admissions@cord.edu

Getting in Last Year

2,444 applied
86% were accepted
783 enrolled (37%)
29% from top tenth of their h.s. class
42% had SAT verbal scores over 600
36% had SAT math scores over 600
54% had ACT scores over 24
5% had SAT verbal scores over 700
4% had SAT math scores over 700
7% had ACT scores over 30

Graduation and After

57% graduated in 4 years
6% graduated in 5 years
2% graduated in 6 years
23% pursued further study (12% arts and
    sciences, 3% law, 2% medicine)
75% had job offers within 6 months
75 organizations recruited on campus

Financial Matters

$16,560 tuition and fees (2003–04)
$4540 room and board
32% average percent of need met
$12,375 average financial aid amount received
    per undergraduate (2001–02)

Academics

Concordia awards bachelor's **degrees**. Challenging opportunities include advanced placement credit, an honors program, double majors, independent study, and a senior project. Special programs include cooperative education, internships, summer session for credit, off-campus study, study-abroad, and Army and Air Force ROTC.

The most frequently chosen **baccalaureate** fields are education, biological/life sciences, and business/marketing. A complete listing of majors at Concordia appears in the Majors Index beginning on page 460.

The **faculty** at Concordia has 175 full-time members, 78% with terminal degrees. The student-faculty ratio is 14:1.

Students of Concordia

The student body is made up of 2,856 undergraduates. 63.2% are women and 36.8% are men. Students come from 39 states and territories and 42 other countries. 63% are from Minnesota. 6% are international students. 0.6% are African American, 0.3% American Indian, 1.5% Asian American, and 0.9% Hispanic American. 80% returned for their sophomore year.

Facilities and Resources

Student rooms are linked to a campus network. 303 **computers** are available on campus that provide access to the Internet. The **library** has 299,808 books and 1,433 subscriptions.

Campus Life

There are 80 active organizations on campus, including a drama/theater group, newspaper, radio station, television station, and choral group. 4% of eligible men and 4% of eligible women are members of local **fraternities**, local **sororities**, and local coed fraternity.

Concordia is a member of the NCAA (Division III). **Intercollegiate sports** include baseball (m), basketball, cross-country running, football (m), golf, ice hockey, soccer, softball (w), swimming (w), tennis, track and field, volleyball (w), wrestling (m).

Campus Safety

Student safety services include well-lit campus, 24-hour locked wing doors, late-night transport/escort service, 24-hour emergency telephone alarm devices, 24-hour patrols by trained security personnel, and student patrols.

Applying

Concordia requires SAT I or ACT, a high school transcript, and 2 recommendations. It recommends ACT. Application deadline: rolling admissions. Early and deferred admission are possible.

CONNECTICUT COLLEGE

SUBURBAN SETTING ■ PRIVATE ■ INDEPENDENT ■ COED
NEW LONDON, CONNECTICUT

Web site: www.connecticutcollege.edu
Contact: Ms. Martha Merrill, Dean of Admissions and Financial Aid, 270
 Mohegan Avenue, New London, CT 06320-4196
Telephone: 860-439-2200 **Fax:** 860-439-4301
E-mail: admission@conncoll.edu

Academics

Connecticut awards bachelor's and master's **degrees**. Challenging opportunities include advanced placement credit, accelerated degree programs, student-designed majors, an honors program, double majors, independent study, and a senior project. Special programs include internships, summer session for credit, off-campus study, and study-abroad.

The most frequently chosen **baccalaureate** fields are social sciences and history, biological/life sciences, and English. A complete listing of majors at Connecticut appears in the Majors Index beginning on page 460.

The **faculty** at Connecticut has 151 full-time members, 89% with terminal degrees. The student-faculty ratio is 10:1.

Students of Connecticut

The student body totals 1,849, of whom 1,837 are undergraduates. 59.4% are women and 40.6% are men. Students come from 45 states and territories and 57 other countries. 16% are from Connecticut. 8.6% are international students. 3.6% are African American, 0.5% American Indian, 3.5% Asian American, and 3.9% Hispanic American. 92% returned for their sophomore year.

Facilities and Resources

Student rooms are linked to a campus network. 461 **computers** are available on campus that provide access to the Internet. The 2 **libraries** have 496,817 books and 2,279 subscriptions.

Campus Life

There are 60 active organizations on campus, including a drama/theater group, newspaper, radio station, and choral group. No national or local **fraternities** or **sororities**.

Connecticut is a member of the NCAA (Division III). **Intercollegiate sports** include basketball, crew, cross-country running, field hockey (w), ice hockey, lacrosse, sailing, soccer, squash, swimming, tennis, track and field, volleyball, water polo.

Campus Safety

Student safety services include late-night transport/escort service, 24-hour emergency telephone alarm devices, 24-hour patrols by trained security personnel, and electronically operated dormitory entrances.

Applying

Connecticut requires an essay, ACT or 3 SAT II Subject Tests (any 3), a high school transcript, 2 recommendations, and a minimum high school GPA of 2.0. It recommends SAT I and an interview. Application deadline: 1/1; 1/15 for financial aid. Deferred admission is possible.

Getting in Last Year

4,396 applied
35% were accepted
511 enrolled (33%)
46% from top tenth of their h.s. class
83% had SAT verbal scores over 600
84% had SAT math scores over 600
20% had SAT verbal scores over 700
17% had SAT math scores over 700

Graduation and After

83% graduated in 4 years
4% graduated in 5 years
17% pursued further study (11% arts and
 sciences, 2% education, 2% law)
88% had job offers within 6 months
74 organizations recruited on campus

Financial Matters

$35,625 comprehensive fee (2003–04)
100% average percent of need met
$24,120 average financial aid amount received
 per undergraduate

CONVERSE COLLEGE

URBAN SETTING ■ PRIVATE ■ INDEPENDENT ■ WOMEN ONLY
SPARTANBURG, SOUTH CAROLINA

Web site: www.converse.edu
Contact: Director of Undergraduate Admissions, 580 East Main Street, Spartanburg, SC 29302
Telephone: 864-596-9040 ext. 9746 or toll-free 800-766-1125 **Fax:** 864-596-9225
E-mail: admissions@converse.edu

Founded in 1889 and located in Spartanburg, South Carolina, Converse College is a private, residential, liberal arts college for women that *U.S. News & World Report* consistently ranks as a top Southern college. Converse's Nisbet Honors Program offers the academically gifted student the challenge and community in which she may grow to her full potential. The Honors Program includes opportunities to do independent research with faculty mentors, to take interdisciplinary honors courses that are team-taught by faculty members from different academic areas, to interact with nationally known visiting scholars, and to meet socially to discuss intellectually challenging topics. Honors Program students are eligible for the College's top scholarships, which range up to full comprehensive fee.

Getting in Last Year
508 applied
69% were accepted
179 enrolled (51%)
30% from top tenth of their h.s. class
3.60 average high school GPA
33% had SAT verbal scores over 600
27% had SAT math scores over 600
48% had ACT scores over 24
6% had SAT verbal scores over 700
4% had SAT math scores over 700
7% had ACT scores over 30

Graduation and After
49% graduated in 4 years
27% pursued further study (10% education, 5% arts and sciences, 5% business)
60% had job offers within 6 months

Financial Matters
$18,915 tuition and fees (2003–04)
$5795 room and board
88% average percent of need met
$15,053 average financial aid amount received per undergraduate (2002–03 estimated)

Academics

Converse awards bachelor's and master's **degrees** and post-master's certificates. Challenging opportunities include advanced placement credit, accelerated degree programs, an honors program, double majors, independent study, and a senior project. Special programs include internships, summer session for credit, off-campus study, study-abroad, and Army ROTC.

The most frequently chosen **baccalaureate** fields are visual/performing arts, business/marketing, and education. A complete listing of majors at Converse appears in the Majors Index beginning on page 460.

The **faculty** at Converse has 72 full-time members, 93% with terminal degrees. The student-faculty ratio is 14:1.

Students of Converse

The student body totals 1,124, of whom 701 are undergraduates. Students come from 25 states and territories and 6 other countries. 75% are from South Carolina. 2.1% are international students. 9.8% are African American, 0.6% American Indian, 0.3% Asian American, and 1% Hispanic American. 69% returned for their sophomore year.

Facilities and Resources

Student rooms are linked to a campus network. 65 **computers** are available on campus that provide access to the Internet. The **library** has 129,411 books and 1,467 subscriptions.

Campus Life

There are 30 active organizations on campus, including a drama/theater group, newspaper, and choral group. No national or local **sororities**.

Converse is a member of the NCAA (Division II). **Intercollegiate sports** (some offering scholarships) include basketball, cheerleading, cross-country running, soccer, tennis, volleyball.

Campus Safety

Student safety services include late-night transport/escort service, 24-hour emergency telephone alarm devices, 24-hour patrols by trained security personnel, and electronically operated dormitory entrances.

Applying

Converse requires an essay, SAT I or ACT, a high school transcript, and a minimum high school GPA of 2.00, and in some cases 1 recommendation. It recommends an interview and a minimum high school GPA of 2.50. Application deadline: 8/1; 3/1 priority date for financial aid. Early and deferred admission are possible.

COOPER UNION FOR THE ADVANCEMENT OF SCIENCE AND ART

URBAN SETTING ■ PRIVATE ■ INDEPENDENT ■ COED
NEW YORK, NEW YORK

Web site: www.cooper.edu
Contact: Mr. Richard Bory, Dean of Admissions and Records and Registrar, 30 Cooper Square, New York, NY 10003
Telephone: 212-353-4120 **Fax:** 212-353-4342
E-mail: admission@cooper.edu

> **E**ach of Cooper Union's schools—Art, Architecture, Engineering—adheres strongly to preparation for its profession within a design-centered, problem-solving philosophy of education in a full tuition scholarship environment. A rigorous curriculum and group projects reinforce this unique atmosphere in higher education and are factors in *Money* magazine's decision to name Cooper Union "In a Class by Itself."

Academics

Cooper Union awards bachelor's **degrees** (also offers master's program with enrollment generally made up of currently-enrolled students). Challenging opportunities include advanced placement credit, student-designed majors, an honors program, independent study, and a senior project. Special programs include internships, summer session for credit, off-campus study, and study-abroad.

The most frequently chosen **baccalaureate** fields are engineering/engineering technologies, visual/performing arts, and architecture. A complete listing of majors at Cooper Union appears in the Majors Index beginning on page 460.

The **faculty** at Cooper Union has 56 full-time members, 75% with terminal degrees. The student-faculty ratio is 7:1.

Students of Cooper Union

The student body totals 955, of whom 918 are undergraduates. 35.2% are women and 64.8% are men. Students come from 41 states and territories. 59% are from New York. 8.8% are international students. 5% are African American, 0.7% American Indian, 24.9% Asian American, and 7.5% Hispanic American. 94% returned for their sophomore year.

Facilities and Resources

Student rooms are linked to a campus network. 400 **computers** are available on campus that provide access to the Internet. The **library** has 97,000 books and 370 subscriptions.

Campus Life

There are 65 active organizations on campus, including a drama/theater group and newspaper. 20% of eligible men and 10% of eligible women are members of national **fraternities** and national **sororities**.

Intercollegiate sports include basketball (m), soccer (m), table tennis, tennis, volleyball.

Campus Safety

Student safety services include security guards, 24-hour emergency telephone alarm devices, 24-hour patrols by trained security personnel, and electronically operated dormitory entrances.

Applying

Cooper Union requires SAT I or ACT, a high school transcript, and a minimum high school GPA of 2.0, and in some cases an essay, SAT II Subject Tests, 3 recommendations, and portfolio, home examination. It recommends a minimum high school GPA of 3.0. Application deadline: 1/1; 4/15 priority date for financial aid. Early and deferred admission are possible.

Getting in Last Year
2,414 applied
12% were accepted
207 enrolled (70%)
80% from top tenth of their h.s. class
3.20 average high school GPA
85% had SAT verbal scores over 600
86% had SAT math scores over 600
30% had SAT verbal scores over 700
54% had SAT math scores over 700

Graduation and After
63% graduated in 4 years
10% graduated in 5 years
48% pursued further study
98% had job offers within 6 months
80 organizations recruited on campus

Financial Matters
$1400 tuition and fees (2004–05)
$13,000 room and board
92% average percent of need met
$5578 average financial aid amount received per undergraduate (2001–02)

CORNELL COLLEGE

SMALL-TOWN SETTING ■ PRIVATE ■ INDEPENDENT RELIGIOUS ■ COED
MOUNT VERNON, IOWA

Web site: www.cornellcollege.edu
Contact: Mr. Jonathan Stroud, Dean of Admissions and Financial Assistance, 600 First Street West, Mount Vernon, IA 52314-1098
Telephone: 319-895-4477 or toll-free 800-747-1112 **Fax:** 319-895-4451
E-mail: admissions@cornellcollege.edu

Few colleges are truly distinctive like Cornell, recognized as one of the nation's finest colleges. At Cornell, students immerse themselves in a single subject through the College's One-Course-At-A-Time (OCAAT) academic calendar. Additionally, the flexibility of OCAAT provides numerous off-campus study opportunities. A standardized schedule enables students to pursue extracurricular interests with the same passion as they do their coursework. This attractively diverse college community typically receives applicants from all 50 states and more than 40 countries. The College's beautiful hilltop campus is listed in its entirety on the National Register of Historic Places.

Getting in Last Year
1,555 applied
69% were accepted
367 enrolled (34%)
29% from top tenth of their h.s. class
3.54 average high school GPA
59% had SAT verbal scores over 600
54% had SAT math scores over 600
68% had ACT scores over 24
17% had SAT verbal scores over 700
16% had SAT math scores over 700
25% had ACT scores over 30
3 National Merit Scholars
31 valedictorians

Graduation and After
63% graduated in 4 years
5% graduated in 5 years
33% pursued further study
10 organizations recruited on campus

Financial Matters
$21,790 tuition and fees (2003–04)
$6035 room and board
98% average percent of need met
$19,455 average financial aid amount received per undergraduate

Academics

Cornell awards bachelor's **degrees**. Challenging opportunities include advanced placement credit, student-designed majors, double majors, independent study, and a senior project. Special programs include internships, off-campus study, and study-abroad.

The most frequently chosen **baccalaureate** fields are social sciences and history, education, and psychology. A complete listing of majors at Cornell appears in the Majors Index beginning on page 460.

The **faculty** at Cornell has 85 full-time members, 85% with terminal degrees. The student-faculty ratio is 12:1.

Students of Cornell

The student body is made up of 1,117 undergraduates. 59.2% are women and 40.8% are men. Students come from 42 states and territories and 14 other countries. 31% are from Iowa. 1.5% are international students. 2.5% are African American, 0.6% American Indian, 0.8% Asian American, and 2.6% Hispanic American. 81% returned for their sophomore year.

Facilities and Resources

Student rooms are linked to a campus network. 100 **computers** are available on campus that provide access to the Internet. The **library** has 197,780 books and 1,236 subscriptions.

Campus Life

There are 76 active organizations on campus, including a drama/theater group, newspaper, radio station, and choral group. 30% of eligible men and 32% of eligible women are members of local **fraternities** and local **sororities**.

Cornell is a member of the NCAA (Division III). **Intercollegiate sports** include baseball (m), basketball, cross-country running, football (m), golf, soccer, softball (w), tennis, track and field, volleyball (w), wrestling (m).

Campus Safety

Student safety services include 24-hour emergency telephone alarm devices and 24-hour patrols by trained security personnel.

Applying

Cornell requires an essay, SAT I or ACT, a high school transcript, and 1 recommendation. It recommends an interview and a minimum high school GPA of 2.80. Application deadline: 2/1; 3/1 for financial aid, with a 3/1 priority date. Deferred admission is possible.

CORNELL UNIVERSITY

SMALL-TOWN SETTING ■ PRIVATE ■ INDEPENDENT ■ COED
ITHACA, NEW YORK

Web site: www.cornell.edu
Contact: Mr. Jason Locke, Director of Undergraduate Admissions, 410
  Thurston Avenue, Ithaca, NY 14850
Telephone: 607-255-5241 **Fax:** 607-255-0659
E-mail: admissions@cornell.edu

Academics

Cornell awards bachelor's, master's, doctoral, and first-professional **degrees**. Challenging opportunities include advanced placement credit, accelerated degree programs, student-designed majors, an honors program, double majors, independent study, and a senior project. Special programs include cooperative education, internships, summer session for credit, off-campus study, study-abroad, and Army, Navy and Air Force ROTC.

The most frequently chosen **baccalaureate** fields are engineering/engineering technologies, business/marketing, and social sciences and history. A complete listing of majors at Cornell appears in the Majors Index beginning on page 460.

The **faculty** at Cornell has 1,643 full-time members, 91% with terminal degrees. The student-faculty ratio is 9:1.

Students of Cornell

The student body totals 19,620, of whom 13,655 are undergraduates. 49.5% are women and 50.5% are men. Students come from 56 states and territories and 107 other countries. 38% are from New York. 7.1% are international students. 4.7% are African American, 0.5% American Indian, 16.4% Asian American, and 5.2% Hispanic American. 96% returned for their sophomore year.

Facilities and Resources

Student rooms are linked to a campus network. 2,500 **computers** are available on campus that provide access to the Internet. The 18 **libraries** have 7,200,000 books and 64,760 subscriptions.

Campus Life

There are 754 active organizations on campus, including a drama/theater group, newspaper, radio station, choral group, and marching band. 27% of eligible men and 24% of eligible women are members of national **fraternities**, national **sororities**, and local fraternities.

Cornell is a member of the NCAA (Division I). **Intercollegiate sports** include baseball (m), basketball, crew, cross-country running, equestrian sports (w), fencing (w), field hockey (w), football (m), golf (m), gymnastics (w), ice hockey (m), lacrosse, soccer, squash, swimming, tennis, track and field, volleyball (w), wrestling (m).

Campus Safety

Student safety services include escort service, late-night transport/escort service, 24-hour emergency telephone alarm devices, 24-hour patrols by trained security personnel, and electronically operated dormitory entrances.

Applying

Cornell requires an essay, SAT I or ACT, a high school transcript, and 1 recommendation, and in some cases SAT II Subject Tests and an interview. It recommends SAT II Subject Tests. Application deadline: 1/1; 2/10 for financial aid. Early and deferred admission are possible.

C ornell University, an Ivy League land-grant school located in central New York, is home to 13,800 undergraduates pursuing studies in more than 70 majors found in the University's 7 small to midsized undergraduate colleges: Agriculture & Life Sciences; Architecture, Art, & Planning; Arts & Sciences; Engineering; Hotel Administration; Human Ecology; and Industrial & Labor Relations. Students come from all 50 states and more than 100 countries. Cornell's special features include a world-renowned faculty; an outstanding undergraduate research program; 17 libraries; superb research and teaching facilities; a large, diverse study-abroad program; more than 500 student organizations; 36 varsity sports; and a graduation rate close to 90%.

Getting in Last Year
20,441 applied
31% were accepted
3,135 enrolled (49%)
87% from top tenth of their h.s. class
85% had SAT verbal scores over 600
91% had SAT math scores over 600
95% had ACT scores over 24
37% had SAT verbal scores over 700
58% had SAT math scores over 700
51% had ACT scores over 30
178 National Merit Scholars

Graduation and After
85% graduated in 4 years
6% graduated in 5 years
1% graduated in 6 years
32% pursued further study
53% had job offers within 6 months
740 organizations recruited on campus

Financial Matters
$28,754 tuition and fees (2003–04)
$9580 room and board
100% average percent of need met
$24,500 average financial aid amount received
  per undergraduate

COVENANT COLLEGE

SUBURBAN SETTING ■ PRIVATE ■ INDEPENDENT RELIGIOUS ■ COED
LOOKOUT MOUNTAIN, GEORGIA

Web site: www.covenant.edu

Contact: Mrs. Elysa Lochstampfor, Admissions Administrative Assistant,
14049 Scenic Highway, Lookout Mountain, GA 30750

Telephone: 706-419-1149 or toll-free 888-451-2683 (in-state) **Fax:**
706-419-2255

E-mail: admissions@covenant.edu

Getting in Last Year
715 applied
61% were accepted
243 enrolled (56%)
25% from top tenth of their h.s. class
3.60 average high school GPA
58% had SAT verbal scores over 600
49% had SAT math scores over 600
64% had ACT scores over 24
16% had SAT verbal scores over 700
10% had SAT math scores over 700
17% had ACT scores over 30

Graduation and After
48% graduated in 4 years
10% graduated in 5 years
3% graduated in 6 years
100 organizations recruited on campus

Financial Matters
$18,230 tuition and fees (2003–04)
$5600 room and board
84% average percent of need met
$15,903 average financial aid amount received
per undergraduate (2002–03 estimated)

Academics
Covenant awards associate, bachelor's, and master's **degrees** (master's degree in education only). Challenging opportunities include advanced placement credit, student-designed majors, double majors, independent study, and a senior project. Special programs include internships, summer session for credit, and off-campus study.

The most frequently chosen **baccalaureate** fields are social sciences and history, English, and biological/life sciences. A complete listing of majors at Covenant appears in the Majors Index beginning on page 460.

The **faculty** at Covenant has 53 full-time members, 83% with terminal degrees. The student-faculty ratio is 15:1.

Students of Covenant
The student body totals 1,266, of whom 1,198 are undergraduates. 59.2% are women and 40.8% are men. Students come from 49 states and territories and 7 other countries. 24% are from Georgia. 1.2% are international students. 6.2% are African American, 0.6% American Indian, 2.7% Asian American, and 2% Hispanic American. 79% returned for their sophomore year.

Facilities and Resources
135 **computers** are available on campus that provide access to the Internet. The **library** has 85,000 books and 475 subscriptions.

Campus Life
There are 48 active organizations on campus, including a drama/theater group, newspaper, and choral group. No national or local **fraternities** or **sororities**.

Covenant is a member of the NAIA. **Intercollegiate sports** (some offering scholarships) include basketball, cross-country running, soccer, volleyball (w).

Campus Safety
Student safety services include night security guards.

Applying
Covenant requires an essay, SAT I or ACT, a high school transcript, an interview, 2 recommendations, and a minimum high school GPA of 2.5. It recommends ACT. Application deadline: rolling admissions; 3/31 priority date for financial aid. Early and deferred admission are possible.

CREIGHTON UNIVERSITY

URBAN SETTING ■ PRIVATE ■ INDEPENDENT RELIGIOUS ■ COED
OMAHA, NEBRASKA

Web site: www.creighton.edu
Contact: Ms. Mary Chase, Director of Admissions-Scholarships, 2500 California Plaza, Omaha, NE 68178-0001
Telephone: 402-280-3105 or toll-free 800-282-5835 **Fax:** 402-280-2685
E-mail: admissions@creighton.edu

Academics

Creighton awards associate, bachelor's, master's, doctoral, and first-professional **degrees**. Challenging opportunities include advanced placement credit, accelerated degree programs, an honors program, double majors, independent study, and a senior project. Special programs include internships, summer session for credit, off-campus study, study-abroad, and Army and Air Force ROTC.

The most frequently chosen **baccalaureate** fields are health professions and related sciences, business/marketing, and biological/life sciences. A complete listing of majors at Creighton appears in the Majors Index beginning on page 460.

The **faculty** at Creighton has 622 full-time members, 92% with terminal degrees. The student-faculty ratio is 14:1.

Students of Creighton

The student body totals 6,537, of whom 3,736 are undergraduates. 60.8% are women and 39.2% are men. Students come from 44 states and territories and 52 other countries. 51% are from Nebraska. 1.5% are international students. 3% are African American, 1.2% American Indian, 6.9% Asian American, and 3.4% Hispanic American. 86% returned for their sophomore year.

Facilities and Resources

Student rooms are linked to a campus network. 520 **computers** are available on campus that provide access to online grade information and the Internet. The 3 **libraries** have 481,848 books and 1,666 subscriptions.

Campus Life

There are 190 active organizations on campus, including a drama/theater group, newspaper, radio station, television station, and choral group. 21% of eligible men and 28% of eligible women are members of national **fraternities** and national **sororities**.

Creighton is a member of the NCAA (Division I). **Intercollegiate sports** (some offering scholarships) include baseball (m), basketball, crew (w), cross-country running, golf, soccer, softball (w), tennis, volleyball (w).

Campus Safety

Student safety services include late-night transport/escort service, 24-hour emergency telephone alarm devices, 24-hour patrols by trained security personnel, student patrols, and electronically operated dormitory entrances.

Applying

Creighton requires an essay, SAT I or ACT, a high school transcript, 1 recommendation, and a minimum high school GPA of 2.75. Application deadline: 8/1; 5/15 priority date for financial aid. Deferred admission is possible.

Getting in Last Year

3,199 applied
88% were accepted
933 enrolled (33%)
38% from top tenth of their h.s. class
3.72 average high school GPA
47% had SAT verbal scores over 600
52% had SAT math scores over 600
70% had ACT scores over 24
10% had SAT verbal scores over 700
10% had SAT math scores over 700
17% had ACT scores over 30
140 class presidents
80 valedictorians

Graduation and After

58% graduated in 4 years
11% graduated in 5 years
2% graduated in 6 years
54 organizations recruited on campus

Financial Matters

$19,922 tuition and fees (2003–04)
$6826 room and board
85% average percent of need met
$17,552 average financial aid amount received per undergraduate (2002–03 estimated)

DARTMOUTH COLLEGE

SMALL-TOWN SETTING ■ PRIVATE ■ INDEPENDENT ■ COED
HANOVER, NEW HAMPSHIRE

Web site: www.dartmouth.edu
Contact: Mr. Karl M. Furstenberg, Dean of Admissions and Financial Aid,
6016 McNutt Hall, Hanover, NH 03755
Telephone: 603-646-2875 or toll-free 603-646 ext. 2875 (in-state)
E-mail: admissions.office@dartmouth.edu

Unique among Ivy League schools in offering students a quarter-system calendar, Dartmouth is considered to have one of the most flexible academic programs in the country. With a low student-to-faculty member ratio and ample opportunities for study abroad and independent research, students at Dartmouth are able to exercise an unusual degree of autonomy in pursuing their studies. Dartmouth students are drawn from a wide range of backgrounds from within the U.S. and 74 different countries. The various perspectives and aspirations represented create a diverse, pluralistic student body, and a dynamic intellectual community.

Getting in Last Year
11,855 applied
18% were accepted
1,077 enrolled (50%)
84% from top tenth of their h.s. class
3.66 average high school GPA
91% had SAT verbal scores over 600
92% had SAT math scores over 600
62% had SAT verbal scores over 700
63% had SAT math scores over 700

Graduation and After
86% graduated in 4 years
7% graduated in 5 years
1% graduated in 6 years
20% pursued further study
215 organizations recruited on campus

Financial Matters
$29,256 tuition and fees (2003–04)
$8739 room and board
100% average percent of need met
$25,549 average financial aid amount received
per undergraduate (2001–02)

Academics
Dartmouth awards bachelor's, master's, doctoral, and first-professional **degrees**. Challenging opportunities include advanced placement credit, student-designed majors, an honors program, double majors, independent study, and a senior project. Special programs include internships, summer session for credit, off-campus study, study-abroad, and Army ROTC.

The most frequently chosen **baccalaureate** fields are social sciences and history, engineering/engineering technologies, and biological/life sciences. A complete listing of majors at Dartmouth appears in the Majors Index beginning on page 460.

The **faculty** at Dartmouth has 477 full-time members, 91% with terminal degrees. The student-faculty ratio is 8:1.

Students of Dartmouth
The student body totals 5,683, of whom 4,098 are undergraduates. 49% are women and 51% are men. Students come from 52 states and territories and 64 other countries. 3% are from New Hampshire. 5.3% are international students. 6.2% are African American, 2.9% American Indian, 12% Asian American, and 6.3% Hispanic American. 97% returned for their sophomore year.

Facilities and Resources
Student rooms are linked to a campus network. 200 **computers** are available on campus that provide access to the Internet. The 11 **libraries** have 5,009,690 books and 20,834 subscriptions.

Campus Life
There are 250 active organizations on campus, including a drama/theater group, newspaper, radio station, television station, choral group, and marching band. 50% of eligible men and 48% of eligible women are members of national **fraternities**, national **sororities**, local fraternities, local sororities, and coed fraternities.

Dartmouth is a member of the NCAA (Division I). **Intercollegiate sports** include baseball (m), basketball, crew, cross-country running, equestrian sports, field hockey (w), football (m), golf, ice hockey, lacrosse, sailing, skiing (cross-country), skiing (downhill), soccer, softball (w), squash, swimming, tennis, track and field, volleyball (w).

Campus Safety
Student safety services include late-night transport/escort service, 24-hour emergency telephone alarm devices, 24-hour patrols by trained security personnel, student patrols, and electronically operated dormitory entrances.

Applying
Dartmouth requires an essay, SAT II Subject Tests, SAT I or ACT, a high school transcript, 2 recommendations, and Peer Evaluation. It recommends an interview. Application deadline: 1/1; 2/1 for financial aid. Early and deferred admission are possible.

DAVIDSON COLLEGE

SMALL-TOWN SETTING ■ PRIVATE ■ INDEPENDENT RELIGIOUS ■ COED
DAVIDSON, NORTH CAROLINA

Web site: www.davidson.edu
Contact: Dr. Nancy J. Cable, Dean of Admission and Financial Aid, Box 7156, Davidson, NC 28035-7156
Telephone: 704-894-2230 or toll-free 800-768-0380 **Fax:** 704-894-2016
E-mail: admission@davidson.edu

Academics

Davidson awards bachelor's **degrees**. Challenging opportunities include advanced placement credit, student-designed majors, an honors program, double majors, independent study, and a senior project. Special programs include off-campus study, study-abroad, and Army and Air Force ROTC.

The most frequently chosen **baccalaureate** fields are social sciences and history, English, and biological/life sciences. A complete listing of majors at Davidson appears in the Majors Index beginning on page 460.

The **faculty** at Davidson has 162 full-time members, 99% with terminal degrees. The student-faculty ratio is 11:1.

Students of Davidson

The student body is made up of 1,712 undergraduates. 49.9% are women and 50.1% are men. Students come from 46 states and territories and 34 other countries. 22% are from North Carolina. 3.1% are international students. 5.6% are African American, 0.3% American Indian, 2.2% Asian American, and 3% Hispanic American. 96% returned for their sophomore year.

Facilities and Resources

Student rooms are linked to a campus network. 142 **computers** are available on campus that provide access to the Internet. The 2 **libraries** have 422,035 books and 2,767 subscriptions.

Campus Life

There are 162 active organizations on campus, including a drama/theater group, newspaper, radio station, and choral group. 41% of eligible men and 73% of eligible women are members of national **fraternities** and women's eating houses.

Davidson is a member of the NCAA (Division I). **Intercollegiate sports** (some offering scholarships) include baseball (m), basketball, cross-country running, field hockey (w), football (m), golf (m), lacrosse (w), soccer, swimming, tennis, track and field, volleyball (w), wrestling (m).

Campus Safety

Student safety services include late-night transport/escort service, 24-hour emergency telephone alarm devices, 24-hour patrols by trained security personnel, and electronically operated dormitory entrances.

Applying

Davidson requires an essay, SAT I or ACT, a high school transcript, and 3 recommendations. It recommends SAT II Subject Tests, SAT II: Writing Test, and an interview. Application deadline: 1/2; 2/15 priority date for financial aid. Early and deferred admission are possible.

Davidson College is one of the nation's premier academic institutions, a college of the liberal arts and sciences respected for its intellectual vigor, the high quality of its faculty and students, and the achievements of its alumni. It is distinguished by its strong honor system, close interaction between professors and students, an environment that encourages both intellectual growth and community service, and a strong commitment to international education. Davidson places great value on student participation in extracurricular activities, intercollegiate athletics, and intramural sports. Nearby Charlotte, North Carolina, offers students the cultural, international, and internship opportunities of a major metropolitan center.

Getting in Last Year
3,927 applied
32% were accepted
490 enrolled (39%)
76% from top tenth of their h.s. class
87% had SAT verbal scores over 600
91% had SAT math scores over 600
95% had ACT scores over 24
38% had SAT verbal scores over 700
39% had SAT math scores over 700
47% had ACT scores over 30

Graduation and After
88% graduated in 4 years
1% graduated in 5 years
26% pursued further study
70% had job offers within 6 months
280 organizations recruited on campus

Financial Matters
$25,903 tuition and fees (2003–04)
$7371 room and board
100% average percent of need met
$17,432 average financial aid amount received per undergraduate (2002–03 estimated)

DENISON UNIVERSITY

SMALL-TOWN SETTING ■ PRIVATE ■ INDEPENDENT ■ COED
GRANVILLE, OHIO

Web site: www.denison.edu
Contact: Mr. Perry Robinson, Director of Admissions, Box H, Granville, OH 43023
Telephone: 740-587-6276 or toll-free 800-DENISON
E-mail: admissions@denison.edu

Denison University, a 4-year, highly selective, national, residential liberal arts college for men and women, located in Granville, Ohio, is known for its intellectual rigor, curricular innovation, and unique faculty-student learning partnerships. Students may choose from 49 academic majors and concentrations and 9 preprofessional programs or design their own programs of study while living on the beautiful 1,200-acre hillside campus. Founded in 1831, Denison has 27,000 alumni and an endowment of $425 million.

Getting in Last Year
3,141 applied
68% were accepted
629 enrolled (30%)
46% from top tenth of their h.s. class
3.60 average high school GPA
57% had SAT verbal scores over 600
59% had SAT math scores over 600
81% had ACT scores over 24
12% had SAT verbal scores over 700
11% had SAT math scores over 700
22% had ACT scores over 30
8 National Merit Scholars
10 class presidents
22 valedictorians

Graduation and After
73% graduated in 4 years
3% graduated in 5 years
1% graduated in 6 years
21% pursued further study (10% arts and sciences, 6% law, 4% medicine)
75% had job offers within 6 months
85 organizations recruited on campus

Financial Matters
$25,760 tuition and fees (2003–04)
$7290 room and board
99% average percent of need met
$21,560 average financial aid amount received per undergraduate (2002–03 estimated)

Academics

Denison awards bachelor's **degrees**. Challenging opportunities include advanced placement credit, student-designed majors, an honors program, double majors, independent study, and a senior project. Special programs include cooperative education, internships, off-campus study, study-abroad, and Army ROTC.

The most frequently chosen **baccalaureate** fields are social sciences and history, communications/communication technologies, and English. A complete listing of majors at Denison appears in the Majors Index beginning on page 460.

The **faculty** at Denison has 180 full-time members, 96% with terminal degrees. The student-faculty ratio is 11:1.

Students of Denison

The student body is made up of 2,232 undergraduates. 55.9% are women and 44.1% are men. Students come from 48 states and territories and 31 other countries. 45% are from Ohio. 4.3% are international students. 5% are African American, 0.1% American Indian, 2.1% Asian American, and 2.5% Hispanic American. 89% returned for their sophomore year.

Facilities and Resources

Student rooms are linked to a campus network. 460 **computers** are available on campus that provide access to the Internet. The **library** has 728,949 books and 4,445 subscriptions.

Campus Life

There are 147 active organizations on campus, including a drama/theater group, newspaper, radio station, television station, and choral group. 37% of eligible men and 44% of eligible women are members of national **fraternities** and national **sororities**.

Denison is a member of the NCAA (Division III). **Intercollegiate sports** include baseball (m), basketball, cross-country running, field hockey (w), football (m), golf (m), lacrosse, soccer, softball (w), swimming, tennis, track and field, volleyball (w).

Campus Safety

Student safety services include security lighting, escort service, late-night transport/escort service, 24-hour emergency telephone alarm devices, 24-hour patrols by trained security personnel, student patrols, and electronically operated dormitory entrances.

Applying

Denison requires an essay, SAT I or ACT, a high school transcript, and 2 recommendations. It recommends SAT II Subject Tests and an interview. Application deadline: 2/1; 2/15 priority date for financial aid. Early and deferred admission are possible.

DePauw University

SMALL-TOWN SETTING ■ PRIVATE ■ INDEPENDENT RELIGIOUS ■ COED
GREENCASTLE, INDIANA

Web site: www.depauw.edu
Contact: Director of Admission, 101 East Seminary Street, Greencastle, IN 46135-0037
Telephone: 765-658-4006 or toll-free 800-447-2495 **Fax:** 765-658-4007
E-mail: admission@depauw.edu

Founded in 1837, DePauw is nationally recognized for a distinctive liberal arts approach that links intellectual rigor with life's work through extensive internship opportunities and study abroad. The prize-winning faculty prepares graduates to creatively address the challenges of the world. The professional and volunteer achievements of the alumni provide ample evidence that uncommon success begins at DePauw University.

Academics

DePauw awards bachelor's **degrees**. Challenging opportunities include advanced placement credit, student-designed majors, an honors program, double majors, independent study, and a senior project. Special programs include internships, off-campus study, study-abroad, and Army and Air Force ROTC.

The most frequently chosen **baccalaureate** fields are social sciences and history, communications/communication technologies, and English. A complete listing of majors at DePauw appears in the Majors Index beginning on page 460.

The **faculty** at DePauw has 210 full-time members, 94% with terminal degrees. The student-faculty ratio is 10:1.

Students of DePauw

The student body is made up of 2,365 undergraduates. 54.8% are women and 45.2% are men. Students come from 41 states and territories and 19 other countries. 51% are from Indiana. 1.9% are international students. 5.8% are African American, 0.3% American Indian, 1.9% Asian American, and 2.9% Hispanic American. 93% returned for their sophomore year.

Facilities and Resources

Student rooms are linked to a campus network. 158 **computers** are available on campus that provide access to the Internet. The 4 **libraries** have 545,736 books and 2,134 subscriptions.

Campus Life

There are 90 active organizations on campus, including a drama/theater group, newspaper, radio station, television station, and choral group. 74% of eligible men and 70% of eligible women are members of national **fraternities** and national **sororities**.

DePauw is a member of the NCAA (Division III). **Intercollegiate sports** include baseball (m), basketball, cross-country running, field hockey (w), football (m), golf, soccer, softball (w), swimming, tennis, track and field, volleyball (w).

Campus Safety

Student safety services include late-night transport/escort service, 24-hour emergency telephone alarm devices, 24-hour patrols by trained security personnel, student patrols, and electronically operated dormitory entrances.

Applying

DePauw requires an essay, SAT I or ACT, a high school transcript, and 1 recommendation. It recommends an interview and a minimum high school GPA of 3.25. Application deadline: 2/1; 2/15 for financial aid. Early and deferred admission are possible.

Getting in Last Year
3,651 applied
63% were accepted
581 enrolled (25%)
57% from top tenth of their h.s. class
3.66 average high school GPA
54% had SAT verbal scores over 600
63% had SAT math scores over 600
84% had ACT scores over 24
13% had SAT verbal scores over 700
12% had SAT math scores over 700
24% had ACT scores over 30
10 National Merit Scholars
41 valedictorians

Graduation and After
71% graduated in 4 years
4% graduated in 5 years
21% pursued further study (25% law, 8% medicine, 5% arts and sciences)
90% had job offers within 6 months
40 organizations recruited on campus

Financial Matters
$24,450 tuition and fees (2003–04)
$7050 room and board
99% average percent of need met
$20,223 average financial aid amount received per undergraduate (2002–03 estimated)

DICKINSON COLLEGE

SUBURBAN SETTING ■ PRIVATE ■ INDEPENDENT ■ COED
CARLISLE, PENNSYLVANIA

Web site: www.dickinson.edu
Contact: Mr. Christopher Seth Allen, Director of Admissions, PO Box 1773, Carlisle, PA 17013-2896
Telephone: 717-245-1231 or toll-free 800-644-1773 **Fax:** 717-245-1442
E-mail: admit@dickinson.edu

Getting in Last Year
4,633 applied
52% were accepted
624 enrolled (26%)
50% from top tenth of their h.s. class
73% had SAT verbal scores over 600
74% had SAT math scores over 600
14% had SAT verbal scores over 700
18% had SAT math scores over 700

Graduation and After
76% graduated in 4 years
2% graduated in 5 years
1% graduated in 6 years
20% pursued further study (7% arts and sciences, 4% law, 2% education)
98% had job offers within 6 months
42 organizations recruited on campus

Financial Matters
$28,640 tuition and fees (2003–04)
$7210 room and board
97% average percent of need met
$22,973 average financial aid amount received per undergraduate

Academics

Dickinson awards bachelor's **degrees**. Challenging opportunities include advanced placement credit, accelerated degree programs, student-designed majors, double majors, independent study, and a senior project. Special programs include internships, summer session for credit, off-campus study, study-abroad, and Army ROTC.

The most frequently chosen **baccalaureate** fields are social sciences and history, foreign language/literature, and biological/life sciences. A complete listing of majors at Dickinson appears in the Majors Index beginning on page 460.

The **faculty** at Dickinson has 166 full-time members, 96% with terminal degrees. The student-faculty ratio is 13:1.

Students of Dickinson

The student body is made up of 2,276 undergraduates. 56.4% are women and 43.6% are men. Students come from 43 states and territories and 20 other countries. 35% are from Pennsylvania. 1.9% are international students. 2.6% are African American, 0.4% American Indian, 3% Asian American, and 2.3% Hispanic American. 90% returned for their sophomore year.

Facilities and Resources

Student rooms are linked to a campus network. 520 **computers** are available on campus that provide access to the Internet. The 7 **libraries** have 305,272 books and 6,163 subscriptions.

Campus Life

There are 120 active organizations on campus, including a drama/theater group, newspaper, radio station, and choral group. 23% of eligible men and 24% of eligible women are members of national **fraternities**, national **sororities**, local fraternities, and local sororities.

Dickinson is a member of the NCAA (Division III). **Intercollegiate sports** include baseball (m), basketball, cross-country running, field hockey (w), football (m), golf, lacrosse, soccer, softball (w), swimming, tennis, track and field, volleyball (w).

Campus Safety

Student safety services include late-night transport/escort service, 24-hour emergency telephone alarm devices, 24-hour patrols by trained security personnel, student patrols, and electronically operated dormitory entrances.

Applying

Dickinson requires an essay, a high school transcript, and 2 recommendations. It recommends SAT I and SAT II or ACT, an interview, and a minimum high school GPA of 3.0. Application deadline: 2/1; 2/1 for financial aid, with a 11/15 priority date. Deferred admission is possible.

DRAKE UNIVERSITY

SUBURBAN SETTING ■ PRIVATE ■ INDEPENDENT ■ COED
DES MOINES, IOWA

Web site: www.drake.edu
Contact: Mr. Thomas F. Willoughby, Vice President for Admission and Financial Aid, 2507 University Avenue, Des Moines, IA 50311
Telephone: 515-271-3181 or toll-free 800-44DRAKE ext. 3181 **Fax:** 515-271-2831
E-mail: admission@drake.edu

Academics

Drake awards bachelor's, master's, doctoral, and first-professional **degrees** and post-master's certificates. Challenging opportunities include advanced placement credit, accelerated degree programs, student-designed majors, an honors program, double majors, independent study, and a senior project. Special programs include cooperative education, internships, summer session for credit, off-campus study, study-abroad, and Army and Air Force ROTC.

The most frequently chosen **baccalaureate** fields are business/marketing, communications/communication technologies, and education. A complete listing of majors at Drake appears in the Majors Index beginning on page 460.

The **faculty** at Drake has 237 full-time members, 93% with terminal degrees. The student-faculty ratio is 18:1.

Students of Drake

The student body totals 5,164, of whom 3,434 are undergraduates. 59.5% are women and 40.5% are men. Students come from 40 states and territories and 53 other countries. 39% are from Iowa. 83% returned for their sophomore year.

Facilities and Resources

Student rooms are linked to a campus network. 360 **computers** are available on campus that provide access to the Internet. The 2 **libraries** have 472,110 books and 2,000 subscriptions.

Campus Life

There are 160 active organizations on campus, including a drama/theater group, newspaper, radio station, television station, choral group, and marching band. 30% of eligible men and 28% of eligible women are members of national **fraternities** and national **sororities**.

Drake is a member of the NCAA (Division I). **Intercollegiate sports** (some offering scholarships) include basketball, cheerleading, crew (w), cross-country running, football (m), golf (m), soccer, softball (w), tennis, track and field, volleyball (w).

Campus Safety

Student safety services include 24-hour desk attendants in residence halls, late-night transport/escort service, 24-hour emergency telephone alarm devices, and 24-hour patrols by trained security personnel.

Applying

Drake requires SAT I or ACT and a high school transcript, and in some cases PCAT for pharmacy transfers. It recommends an essay and an interview. Application deadline: 3/1; 3/1 priority date for financial aid. Early and deferred admission are possible.

A Drake education offers a unique mix of advantages for future success. Drake is large enough to offer more than 70 undergraduate academic programs, 160 organizations, and a community of students from around the world. Yet Drake's exceptional faculty and academic and extracurricular options are highly accessible to students beginning their first year of college. Drake's location in Des Moines, Iowa's capital, offers numerous professional internships; 70% of Drake's undergraduates have at least one. Drake is affordable; 94% of its students receive financial assistance. It is a great value, too—more than 93% of Drake's graduates obtain career positions or enter graduate school within 6 months of graduating.

Getting in Last Year
3,174 applied
83% were accepted
815 enrolled (31%)
31% from top tenth of their h.s. class
3.60 average high school GPA
46% had SAT verbal scores over 600
52% had SAT math scores over 600
73% had ACT scores over 24
7% had SAT verbal scores over 700
12% had SAT math scores over 700
16% had ACT scores over 30
6 National Merit Scholars

Graduation and After
21% pursued further study (9% arts and sciences, 4% business, 3% law)
70 organizations recruited on campus

Financial Matters
$19,420 tuition and fees (2003–04)
$5700 room and board
88% average percent of need met
$15,701 average financial aid amount received per undergraduate (2002–03 estimated)

DREW UNIVERSITY

SUBURBAN SETTING ■ PRIVATE ■ INDEPENDENT RELIGIOUS ■ COED
MADISON, NEW JERSEY

Web site: www.drew.edu
Contact: Ms. Mary Beth Carey, Dean of Admissions and Financial Assistance,
36 Madison Avenue, Madison, NJ 07940-1493
Telephone: 973-408-3739 **Fax:** 973-408-3068
E-mail: cadm@drew.edu

Getting in Last Year

2,746 applied
69% were accepted
421 enrolled (22%)
41% from top tenth of their h.s. class
57% had SAT verbal scores over 600
53% had SAT math scores over 600
18% had SAT verbal scores over 700
9% had SAT math scores over 700

Graduation and After

23% pursued further study (5% law, 2%
medicine)
38 organizations recruited on campus

Financial Matters

$27,906 tuition and fees (2003–04)
$7644 room and board
82% average percent of need met
$19,955 average financial aid amount received
per undergraduate (2002–03)

Academics

Drew awards bachelor's, master's, doctoral, and first-professional **degrees** and post-bachelor's certificates. Challenging opportunities include advanced placement credit, accelerated degree programs, student-designed majors, double majors, independent study, and a senior project. Special programs include internships, summer session for credit, off-campus study, study-abroad, and Army and Air Force ROTC.

The most frequently chosen **baccalaureate** fields are social sciences and history, visual/performing arts, and interdisciplinary studies. A complete listing of majors at Drew appears in the Majors Index beginning on page 460.

The **faculty** at Drew has 120 full-time members, 97% with terminal degrees. The student-faculty ratio is 12:1.

Students of Drew

The student body totals 2,521, of whom 1,606 are undergraduates. 60.8% are women and 39.2% are men. Students come from 40 states and territories and 8 other countries. 57% are from New Jersey. 0.7% are international students. 3.9% are African American, 0.4% American Indian, 5.6% Asian American, and 5.5% Hispanic American. 87% returned for their sophomore year.

Facilities and Resources

Student rooms are linked to a campus network. 200 **computers** are available on campus that provide access to the Internet. The **library** has 491,489 books and 2,589 subscriptions.

Campus Life

There are 80 active organizations on campus, including a drama/theater group, newspaper, radio station, television station, and choral group. No national or local **fraternities** or **sororities**.

Drew is a member of the NCAA (Division III). **Intercollegiate sports** include baseball (m), basketball, cross-country running, equestrian sports, fencing, field hockey (w), lacrosse, soccer, softball (w), swimming, tennis.

Campus Safety

Student safety services include late-night transport/escort service, 24-hour emergency telephone alarm devices, 24-hour patrols by trained security personnel, and electronically operated dormitory entrances.

Applying

Drew requires an essay, SAT I or ACT, a high school transcript, and 1 recommendation. It recommends an interview. Application deadline: 2/15; 2/15 for financial aid. Early and deferred admission are possible.

DRURY UNIVERSITY

URBAN SETTING ■ PRIVATE ■ INDEPENDENT ■ COED
SPRINGFIELD, MISSOURI

Web site: www.drury.edu
Contact: Mr. Chip Parker, Director of Admission, 900 North Benton, Bay
Hall, Springfield, MO 65802
Telephone: 417-873-7205 or toll-free 800-922-2274 **Fax:** 417-866-3873
E-mail: druryad@drury.edu

Academics

Drury awards bachelor's **degrees** (also offers evening program with significant enrollment not reflected in profile). Challenging opportunities include advanced placement
credit, accelerated degree programs, student-designed majors, an honors program,
double majors, independent study, and a senior project. Special programs include
cooperative education, internships, summer session for credit, off-campus study, study-
abroad, and Army ROTC. A complete listing of majors at Drury appears in the Majors
Index beginning on page 460.

The **faculty** at Drury has 120 full-time members, 93% with terminal degrees. The
student-faculty ratio is 11:1.

Students of Drury

The student body totals 1,933, of whom 1,541 are undergraduates. 56.2% are women
and 43.8% are men. Students come from 35 states and territories and 50 other countries.
81% are from Missouri. 4.6% are international students. 1.4% are African American,
0.5% American Indian, 1.9% Asian American, and 1% Hispanic American. 83%
returned for their sophomore year.

Facilities and Resources

Student rooms are linked to a campus network. 323 **computers** are available on campus
that provide access to digital imaging lab and the Internet. The 2 **libraries** have 177,794
books and 868 subscriptions.

Campus Life

There are 60 active organizations on campus, including a drama/theater group,
newspaper, radio station, television station, and choral group. 40% of eligible men and
40% of eligible women are members of national **fraternities** and national **sororities**.

Drury is a member of the NCAA (Division II). **Intercollegiate sports** (some offering scholarships) include basketball (m), cross-country running, golf, soccer, swimming,
tennis, volleyball (w).

Campus Safety

Student safety services include security cameras in parking areas, late-night transport/
escort service, 24-hour emergency telephone alarm devices, 24-hour patrols by trained
security personnel, student patrols, and electronically operated dormitory entrances.

Applying

Drury requires an essay, SAT I or ACT, a high school transcript, 1 recommendation,
minimum ACT score of 21, and a minimum high school GPA of 2.7. It recommends an
interview. Application deadline: 3/15; 3/15 priority date for financial aid. Deferred
admission is possible.

Getting in Last Year

1,128 applied
77% were accepted
365 enrolled (42%)
38% from top tenth of their h.s. class
3.67 average high school GPA
50% had SAT verbal scores over 600
54% had SAT math scores over 600
67% had ACT scores over 24
18% had SAT verbal scores over 700
11% had SAT math scores over 700
16% had ACT scores over 30
9 National Merit Scholars
26 valedictorians

Graduation and After

50% graduated in 4 years
14% graduated in 5 years
1% graduated in 6 years
36% pursued further study
60% had job offers within 6 months
16 organizations recruited on campus

Financial Matters

$13,214 tuition and fees (2003–04)
$4885 room and board
83% average percent of need met
$7695 average financial aid amount received
per undergraduate

DUKE UNIVERSITY

SUBURBAN SETTING ■ PRIVATE ■ INDEPENDENT RELIGIOUS ■ COED
DURHAM, NORTH CAROLINA

Web site: www.duke.edu
Contact: Mr. Christoph Guttentag, Director of Admissions, 2138 Campus
    Drive, Durham, NC 27708
Telephone: 919-684-3214 **Fax:** 919-684-8941
E-mail: askduke@admiss.duke.edu

Getting in Last Year
16,729 applied
23% were accepted
1,619 enrolled (42%)
89% from top tenth of their h.s. class
3.93 average high school GPA
91% had SAT verbal scores over 600
94% had SAT math scores over 600
96% had ACT scores over 24
51% had SAT verbal scores over 700
66% had SAT math scores over 700
61% had ACT scores over 30
197 valedictorians

Graduation and After
88% graduated in 4 years
5% graduated in 5 years
27% pursued further study (8% law, 6%
    medicine, 4% arts and sciences)
45% had job offers within 6 months
280 organizations recruited on campus

Financial Matters
$29,345 tuition and fees (2003–04)
$8210 room and board
100% average percent of need met
$26,250 average financial aid amount received
    per undergraduate

Academics

Duke awards bachelor's, master's, doctoral, and first-professional **degrees** and post-bachelor's and post-master's certificates. Challenging opportunities include advanced placement credit, accelerated degree programs, student-designed majors, an honors program, independent study, and a senior project. Special programs include internships, summer session for credit, off-campus study, study-abroad, and Army and Air Force ROTC.

The most frequently chosen **baccalaureate** fields are social sciences and history, engineering/engineering technologies, and protective services/public administration. A complete listing of majors at Duke appears in the Majors Index beginning on page 460.

The **faculty** at Duke has 958 full-time members, 97% with terminal degrees. The student-faculty ratio is 11:1.

Students of Duke

The student body totals 12,398, of whom 6,248 are undergraduates. 48.8% are women and 51.2% are men. Students come from 53 states and territories and 84 other countries. 15% are from North Carolina. 4.8% are international students. 10.4% are African American, 0.3% American Indian, 11.9% Asian American, and 6.8% Hispanic American. 96% returned for their sophomore year.

Facilities and Resources

Student rooms are linked to a campus network. 600 **computers** are available on campus that provide access to the Internet. The 12 **libraries** have 5,149,772 books and 28,274 subscriptions.

Campus Life

There are 350 active organizations on campus, including a drama/theater group, newspaper, radio station, television station, choral group, and marching band. 29% of eligible men and 42% of eligible women are members of national **fraternities** and national **sororities**.

Duke is a member of the NCAA (Division I). **Intercollegiate sports** (some offering scholarships) include baseball (m), basketball, crew (w), cross-country running, fencing, field hockey (w), football (m), golf, lacrosse, soccer, swimming, tennis, track and field, volleyball (w), wrestling (m).

Campus Safety

Student safety services include late-night transport/escort service, 24-hour emergency telephone alarm devices, 24-hour patrols by trained security personnel, and electronically operated dormitory entrances.

Applying

Duke requires an essay, SAT I or ACT, a high school transcript, and 3 recommendations, and in some cases SAT II Subject Tests and SAT II: Writing Test. It recommends an interview, audition tape for applicants with outstanding dance, dramatic, or musical talent; slides of artwork, and a minimum high school GPA of 3.0. Application deadline: 1/2; 2/1 for financial aid. Early and deferred admission are possible.

EARLHAM COLLEGE

SMALL-TOWN SETTING ■ PRIVATE ■ INDEPENDENT RELIGIOUS ■ COED
RICHMOND, INDIANA

Web site: www.earlham.edu
Contact: Mr. Jeff Rickey, Dean of Admissions and Financial Aid, 801 National
   Road West, Richmond, IN 47374
Telephone: 765-983-1600 or toll-free 800-327-5426 **Fax:** 765-983-1560
E-mail: admission@earlham.edu

Academics
Earlham awards bachelor's, master's, and first-professional **degrees**. Challenging opportunities include advanced placement credit, accelerated degree programs, student-designed majors, double majors, independent study, and a senior project. Special programs include internships, off-campus study, and study-abroad.

   The most frequently chosen **baccalaureate** fields are social sciences and history, visual/performing arts, and biological/life sciences. A complete listing of majors at Earlham appears in the Majors Index beginning on page 460.

   The **faculty** at Earlham has 96 full-time members, 84% with terminal degrees. The student-faculty ratio is 11:1.

Students of Earlham
The student body totals 1,262, of whom 1,170 are undergraduates. 56.1% are women and 43.9% are men. Students come from 46 states and territories and 34 other countries. 26% are from Indiana. 4.4% are international students. 6.4% are African American, 0.2% American Indian, 1.9% Asian American, and 2.3% Hispanic American. 84% returned for their sophomore year.

Facilities and Resources
Student rooms are linked to a campus network. 154 **computers** are available on campus that provide access to the Internet. The 2 **libraries** have 392,100 books and 1,660 subscriptions.

Campus Life
There are 70 active organizations on campus, including a drama/theater group, newspaper, radio station, and choral group. No national or local **fraternities** or **sororities**.

   Earlham is a member of the NCAA (Division III). **Intercollegiate sports** include baseball (m), basketball, cross-country running, field hockey (w), football (m), soccer, tennis, track and field, volleyball (w).

Campus Safety
Student safety services include late-night transport/escort service, 24-hour emergency telephone alarm devices, 24-hour patrols by trained security personnel, student patrols, and electronically operated dormitory entrances.

Applying
Earlham requires an essay, SAT I or ACT, a high school transcript, 2 recommendations, and a minimum high school GPA of 3.0. It recommends SAT I and an interview. Application deadline: 2/15; 3/1 priority date for financial aid. Early and deferred admission are possible.

E arlham College, founded in 1847 by the Society of Friends, is an independent liberal arts college. Earlham students live in a community in which learning is challenging, exciting, and cooperative. More than 50% of students study abroad, with another 15 to 20% studying off campus at locations in the U.S. In the classroom, Earlham introduces students to a learning style that encourages questions and discussion. Outside the classroom, students are encouraged to become involved in any of the more than 65 student organizations and to fully engage in the fun of college life. Earlham alumni are leaders in education, medicine, politics, and business.

Getting in Last Year
1,410 applied
77% were accepted
348 enrolled (32%)
30% from top tenth of their h.s. class
3.45 average high school GPA
63% had SAT verbal scores over 600
45% had SAT math scores over 600
67% had ACT scores over 24
25% had SAT verbal scores over 700
14% had SAT math scores over 700
26% had ACT scores over 30
7 National Merit Scholars
21 class presidents
8 valedictorians

Graduation and After
22% pursued further study (10% arts and sciences, 2% medicine, 1% engineering)
73% had job offers within 6 months
65 organizations recruited on campus

Financial Matters
$24,560 tuition and fees (2003–04)
$5416 room and board
95% average percent of need met
$21,215 average financial aid amount received per undergraduate

EASTERN MENNONITE UNIVERSITY

SMALL-TOWN SETTING ■ PRIVATE ■ INDEPENDENT RELIGIOUS ■ COED
HARRISONBURG, VIRGINIA

Web site: www.emu.edu
Contact: Mr. Lawrence W. Miller, Director of Admissions, 1200 Park Road,
Harrisonburg, VA 22802-2462
Telephone: 540-432-4118 or toll-free 800-368-2665 **Fax:** 540-432-4444
E-mail: admiss@emu.edu

Getting in Last Year
605 applied
82% were accepted
196 enrolled (39%)
20% from top tenth of their h.s. class
3.40 average high school GPA
32% had SAT verbal scores over 600
32% had SAT math scores over 600
49% had ACT scores over 24
5% had SAT verbal scores over 700
13% had SAT math scores over 700
9% had ACT scores over 30
8 valedictorians

Graduation and After
40% graduated in 4 years
17% graduated in 5 years
4% graduated in 6 years
4% pursued further study (1% medicine, 1%
arts and sciences, 1% dentistry)
85% had job offers within 6 months
49 organizations recruited on campus

Financial Matters
$17,350 tuition and fees (2003–04)
$5640 room and board
85% average percent of need met
$13,140 average financial aid amount received
per undergraduate (2002–03 estimated)

Academics

EMU awards associate, bachelor's, master's, and first-professional **degrees** and post-bachelor's certificates. Challenging opportunities include advanced placement credit, an honors program, double majors, independent study, and a senior project. Special programs include internships, summer session for credit, off-campus study, and study-abroad.

The most frequently chosen **baccalaureate** fields are business/marketing, health professions and related sciences, and education. A complete listing of majors at EMU appears in the Majors Index beginning on page 460.

The **faculty** at EMU has 108 full-time members, 69% with terminal degrees. The student-faculty ratio is 9:1.

Students of EMU

The student body totals 1,245, of whom 965 are undergraduates. 60.1% are women and 39.9% are men. Students come from 35 states and territories and 21 other countries. 44% are from Virginia. 4.7% are international students. 5.1% are African American, 0.1% American Indian, 1.8% Asian American, and 1.3% Hispanic American. 75% returned for their sophomore year.

Facilities and Resources

Student rooms are linked to a campus network. 110 **computers** are available on campus that provide access to the Internet. The **library** has 156,268 books and 1,287 subscriptions.

Campus Life

There are 47 active organizations on campus, including a drama/theater group, newspaper, radio station, and choral group. No national or local **fraternities** or **sororities**.

EMU is a member of the NCAA (Division III). **Intercollegiate sports** include baseball (m), basketball, cross-country running, soccer, softball (w), tennis, track and field, volleyball.

Campus Safety

Student safety services include night watchman, 24-hour emergency telephone alarm devices, and electronically operated dormitory entrances.

Applying

EMU requires SAT I or ACT, a high school transcript, 1 recommendation, statement of commitment, and a minimum high school GPA of 2.2. It recommends an interview. Application deadline: 8/1; 3/15 priority date for financial aid. Early and deferred admission are possible.

ECKERD COLLEGE

SUBURBAN SETTING ■ PRIVATE ■ INDEPENDENT RELIGIOUS ■ COED
ST. PETERSBURG, FLORIDA

Web site: www.eckerd.edu
Contact: Dr. Richard R. Hallin, Dean of Admissions, 4200 54th Avenue South, St. Petersburg, FL 33711
Telephone: 727-864-8331 or toll-free 800-456-9009 **Fax:** 727-866-2304
E-mail: admissions@eckerd.edu

Academics

Eckerd awards bachelor's **degrees**. Challenging opportunities include advanced placement credit, accelerated degree programs, student-designed majors, an honors program, double majors, independent study, and a senior project. Special programs include cooperative education, internships, summer session for credit, off-campus study, study-abroad, and Army and Air Force ROTC.

The most frequently chosen **baccalaureate** fields are business/marketing, biological/life sciences, and social sciences and history. A complete listing of majors at Eckerd appears in the Majors Index beginning on page 460.

The **faculty** at Eckerd has 102 full-time members, 94% with terminal degrees. The student-faculty ratio is 13:1.

Students of Eckerd

The student body is made up of 1,631 undergraduates. 54.6% are women and 45.4% are men. Students come from 50 states and territories and 49 other countries. 31% are from Florida. 8.5% are international students. 2.7% are African American, 0.1% American Indian, 1.6% Asian American, and 4.1% Hispanic American. 84% returned for their sophomore year.

Facilities and Resources

Student rooms are linked to a campus network. 144 **computers** are available on campus that provide access to the Internet. The **library** has 113,850 books and 3,009 subscriptions.

Campus Life

There are 50 active organizations on campus, including a drama/theater group, newspaper, radio station, television station, and choral group. No national or local **fraternities** or **sororities**.

Eckerd is a member of the NCAA (Division II). **Intercollegiate sports** (some offering scholarships) include baseball (m), basketball, cross-country running (w), golf (m), sailing, soccer, softball (w), tennis, volleyball (w).

Campus Safety

Student safety services include late-night transport/escort service, 24-hour emergency telephone alarm devices, 24-hour patrols by trained security personnel, student patrols, and electronically operated dormitory entrances.

Applying

Eckerd requires an essay, SAT I or ACT, a high school transcript, and 1 recommendation. It recommends SAT II Subject Tests, SAT II: Writing Test, an interview, and a minimum high school GPA of 3.0. Application deadline: rolling admissions; 4/1 priority date for financial aid. Early and deferred admission are possible.

Getting in Last Year

2,046 applied
77% were accepted
433 enrolled (28%)
27% from top tenth of their h.s. class
3.30 average high school GPA
35% had SAT verbal scores over 600
33% had SAT math scores over 600
51% had ACT scores over 24
7% had SAT verbal scores over 700
4% had SAT math scores over 700
14% had ACT scores over 30
4 National Merit Scholars
23 class presidents
17 valedictorians

Graduation and After

60% graduated in 4 years
4% graduated in 5 years
1% graduated in 6 years
30% pursued further study
59% had job offers within 6 months
170 organizations recruited on campus

Financial Matters

$22,774 tuition and fees (2003–04)
$5970 room and board
85% average percent of need met
$17,500 average financial aid amount received per undergraduate (2002–03 estimated)

ELIZABETHTOWN COLLEGE

SMALL-TOWN SETTING ■ PRIVATE ■ INDEPENDENT RELIGIOUS ■ COED
ELIZABETHTOWN, PENNSYLVANIA

Web site: www.etown.edu
Contact: Mr. W. Kent Barnds, Dean of Admissions and Enrollment
   Management, One Alpha Drive, Elizabethtown, PA 17022
Telephone: 717-361-1400 **Fax:** 717-361-1365
E-mail: admissions@acad.etown.edu

Elizabethtown College is exceeding expectations for personal attention, experiential learning, and combining the liberal arts with professional programs. The College is located in south-central Pennsylvania, near Hershey and Harrisburg, the state capital. Faculty members put student learning first and take pride in mentoring. Diverse opportunities, great facilities, collaborative research, internships, and the College's residential environment provide the perfect atmosphere for experiential learning. Athletes excel within nationally competitive programs. Musical ensembles and theater groups perform throughout the region, and students are leaders in more than 80 clubs and organizations. The College offers 43 majors and 50 minors and has an enrollment of 1,800 students. Elizabethtown allows graduates to distinguish themselves to employers and graduate schools.

Getting in Last Year
2,541 applied
70% were accepted
496 enrolled (28%)
28% from top tenth of their h.s. class
3.53 average high school GPA
28% had SAT verbal scores over 600
32% had SAT math scores over 600
36% had ACT scores over 24
4% had SAT verbal scores over 700
4% had SAT math scores over 700
6% had ACT scores over 30
86 class presidents
12 valedictorians

Graduation and After
62% graduated in 4 years
8% graduated in 5 years
27% pursued further study
90% had job offers within 6 months
39 organizations recruited on campus

Financial Matters
$22,500 tuition and fees (2003–04)
$6300 room and board
87% average percent of need met
$15,897 average financial aid amount received
   per undergraduate (2002–03 estimated)

Academics
E-town awards associate, bachelor's, and master's **degrees** and post-bachelor's certificates. Challenging opportunities include advanced placement credit, an honors program, double majors, independent study, and a senior project. Special programs include cooperative education, internships, summer session for credit, off-campus study, and study-abroad.

The most frequently chosen **baccalaureate** fields are business/marketing, education, and health professions and related sciences. A complete listing of majors at E-town appears in the Majors Index beginning on page 460.

The **faculty** at E-town has 126 full-time members, 78% with terminal degrees. The student-faculty ratio is 12:1.

Students of E-town
The student body totals 1,988, of whom 1,975 are undergraduates. 65.3% are women and 34.7% are men. Students come from 31 states and territories and 41 other countries. 72% are from Pennsylvania. 3.8% are international students. 1.2% are African American, 0.3% American Indian, 1.6% Asian American, and 1.1% Hispanic American. 84% returned for their sophomore year.

Facilities and Resources
Student rooms are linked to a campus network. 200 **computers** are available on campus that provide access to e-mail, file space, personal web page and the Internet. The 2 **libraries** have 143,302 books and 1,090 subscriptions.

Campus Life
There are 85 active organizations on campus, including a drama/theater group, newspaper, radio station, television station, and choral group. No national or local **fraternities** or **sororities**.

E-town is a member of the NCAA (Division III). **Intercollegiate sports** include baseball (m), basketball, cross-country running, field hockey (w), golf (m), lacrosse, soccer, softball (w), swimming, tennis, track and field, volleyball (w), wrestling (m).

Campus Safety
Student safety services include self-defense workshops, crime prevention program, late-night transport/escort service, 24-hour emergency telephone alarm devices, 24-hour patrols by trained security personnel, and student patrols.

Applying
E-town requires an essay, SAT I or ACT, a high school transcript, 2 recommendations, and a minimum high school GPA of 2.0, and in some cases an interview. It recommends an interview and a minimum high school GPA of 3.0. Application deadline: rolling admissions. Early and deferred admission are possible.

EMBRY-RIDDLE AERONAUTICAL UNIVERSITY

SMALL-TOWN SETTING ■ PRIVATE ■ INDEPENDENT ■ COED, PRIMARILY MEN
PRESCOTT, ARIZONA

Web site: www.embryriddle.edu
Contact: Mr. Bill Thompson, Director of Admissions, 3700 Willow Creek
    Road, Prescott, AZ 86301-3720
Telephone: 928-777-6692 or toll-free 800-888-3728 **Fax:** 928-777-6606
E-mail: pradmit@erau.edu

Academics
Embry-Riddle awards bachelor's and master's **degrees**. Challenging opportunities
include advanced placement credit, double majors, independent study, and a senior
project. Special programs include cooperative education, internships, summer session for
credit, study-abroad, and Army and Air Force ROTC.

The most frequently chosen **baccalaureate** fields are trade and industry, engineer-
ing/engineering technologies, and interdisciplinary studies. A complete listing of majors
at Embry-Riddle appears in the Majors Index beginning on page 460.

The **faculty** at Embry-Riddle has 89 full-time members, 60% with terminal degrees.
The student-faculty ratio is 15:1.

Students of Embry-Riddle
The student body totals 1,669, of whom 1,631 are undergraduates. 16.3% are women
and 83.7% are men. Students come from 52 states and territories and 31 other countries.
23% are from Arizona. 2% are international students. 1.7% are African American, 1.1%
American Indian, 5.7% Asian American, and 5.7% Hispanic American. 75% returned for
their sophomore year.

Facilities and Resources
Student rooms are linked to a campus network. 200 **computers** are available on campus
that provide access to the Internet. The **library** has 28,264 books and 629 subscriptions.

Campus Life
There are 61 active organizations on campus, including a newspaper, radio station, and
television station. 85% of eligible men and 93% of eligible women are members of
national **fraternities** and national **sororities**.

Embry-Riddle is a member of the NAIA. **Intercollegiate sports** (some offering
scholarships) include volleyball (w), wrestling (m).

Campus Safety
Student safety services include late-night transport/escort service, 24-hour emergency
telephone alarm devices, 24-hour patrols by trained security personnel, and student
patrols.

Applying
Embry-Riddle requires SAT I or ACT, a high school transcript, and a minimum high
school GPA of 2.0, and in some cases medical examination for flight students and a
minimum high school GPA of 3.0. It recommends an essay, an interview, and recommendations. Application deadline: 3/1; 6/30 for financial aid, with a 4/15 priority date.
Early and deferred admission are possible.

E mbry-Riddle continues to
integrate engineering,
technology, and global
education with bachelor's degrees
related to careers in the aviation
and aerospace industry.
Embry-Riddle graduates are uniquely
prepared to be leaders and global
citizens with the skill-set to
understand and function effectively
within global relationships, political
systems, cultures, and natural
environments. Students enjoy small
class sizes, classes related to current
topics in the industry, and caring
professors. Students have the
opportunity to engage in
international exchange programs,
present design projects at national
conferences, get involved in
internships, and take field trips—all
leading to exciting career options
upon graduation.

Getting in Last Year
1,250 applied
80% were accepted
304 enrolled (30%)
23% from top tenth of their h.s. class
3.00 average high school GPA
32% had SAT verbal scores over 600
44% had SAT math scores over 600
57% had ACT scores over 24
4% had SAT verbal scores over 700
7% had SAT math scores over 700
13% had ACT scores over 30

Graduation and After
26% graduated in 4 years
22% graduated in 5 years
3% graduated in 6 years
5% pursued further study
90% had job offers within 6 months
50 organizations recruited on campus

Financial Matters
$21,330 tuition and fees (2003–04)
$5808 room and board
$12,420 average financial aid amount received
    per undergraduate

EMERSON COLLEGE

URBAN SETTING ▪ PRIVATE ▪ INDEPENDENT ▪ COED
BOSTON, MASSACHUSETTS

Web site: www.emerson.edu
Contact: Ms. Sara Ramirez, Director of Undergraduate Admission, 120 Boylston Street, Boston, MA 02116-4624
Telephone: 617-824-8600 **Fax:** 617-824-8609
E-mail: admission@emerson.edu

Boston is arguably one of the country's best known college towns, and Emerson is located on Boston Common in the heart of the city's Theatre District. The campus is home to WERS-FM, the 1,200-seat Cutler Majestic Theatre, and the award-winning literary journal, *Ploughshares.* Emerson's 2,800 students come from more than 45 states and 60 other countries and participate in more than 60 student organizations and performance groups, 13 NCAA intercollegiate teams, student publications, and honor societies. The College also sponsors programs in Los Angeles, Kasteel Well (the Netherlands), summer film study in Prague, and course cross-registration with the 6-member Boston ProArts Consortium.

Getting in Last Year
4,321 applied
48% were accepted
701 enrolled (34%)
34% from top tenth of their h.s. class
3.51 average high school GPA
64% had SAT verbal scores over 600
46% had SAT math scores over 600
79% had ACT scores over 24
13% had SAT verbal scores over 700
6% had SAT math scores over 700
21% had ACT scores over 30
11 valedictorians

Graduation and After
63% graduated in 4 years
3% graduated in 5 years
6% pursued further study
82% had job offers within 6 months
110 organizations recruited on campus

Financial Matters
$22,693 tuition and fees (2003–04)
$9828 room and board
76% average percent of need met
$11,820 average financial aid amount received per undergraduate (2002–03)

Academics

Emerson awards bachelor's, master's, and doctoral **degrees**. Challenging opportunities include advanced placement credit, student-designed majors, an honors program, double majors, independent study, and a senior project. Special programs include internships, summer session for credit, off-campus study, and study-abroad.

The most frequently chosen **baccalaureate** fields are visual/performing arts, communications/communication technologies, and business/marketing. A complete listing of majors at Emerson appears in the Majors Index beginning on page 460.

The **faculty** at Emerson has 136 full-time members, 79% with terminal degrees. The student-faculty ratio is 15:1.

Students of Emerson

The student body totals 4,385, of whom 3,401 are undergraduates. 61.3% are women and 38.7% are men. Students come from 48 states and territories and 59 other countries. 35% are from Massachusetts. 3.8% are international students. 2% are African American, 0.3% American Indian, 3.8% Asian American, and 5.1% Hispanic American. 83% returned for their sophomore year.

Facilities and Resources

Student rooms are linked to a campus network. 296 **computers** are available on campus that provide access to the Internet. The 2 **libraries** have 141,715 books and 679 subscriptions.

Campus Life

There are 60 active organizations on campus, including a drama/theater group, newspaper, radio station, television station, and choral group. 4% of eligible men and 4% of eligible women are members of national **fraternities**, national **sororities**, local fraternities, and local sororities.

Emerson is a member of the NCAA (Division III). **Intercollegiate sports** (some offering scholarships) include baseball (m), basketball, cheerleading, cross-country running, lacrosse, soccer, softball (w), tennis, volleyball (w).

Campus Safety

Student safety services include late-night transport/escort service, 24-hour emergency telephone alarm devices, 24-hour patrols by trained security personnel, and electronically operated dormitory entrances.

Applying

Emerson requires an essay, SAT I or ACT, a high school transcript, and 2 recommendations, and in some cases an interview and audition, essay, portfolio, or resume for performing arts applicants. Application deadline: 1/15; 3/1 priority date for financial aid. Early and deferred admission are possible.

EMORY UNIVERSITY
SUBURBAN SETTING ■ PRIVATE ■ INDEPENDENT RELIGIOUS ■ COED
ATLANTA, GEORGIA

Web site: www.emory.edu
Contact: Mr. Daniel C. Walls, Dean of Admission, 200 Boisfeuillet Jones
   Center, Atlanta, GA 30322-1100
Telephone: 404-727-6036 or toll-free 800-727-6036
E-mail: admiss@unix.cc.emory.edu

Academics
Emory awards associate, bachelor's, master's, doctoral, and first-professional **degrees**
(enrollment figures include Emory University, Oxford College; application data for main
campus only). Challenging opportunities include advanced placement credit, accelerated
degree programs, an honors program, double majors, and a senior project. Special
programs include internships, summer session for credit, off-campus study, study-abroad,
and Air Force ROTC.

The most frequently chosen **baccalaureate** fields are social sciences and history,
business/marketing, and biological/life sciences. A complete listing of majors at Emory
appears in the Majors Index beginning on page 460.

The **faculty** at Emory has 2,512 full-time members. The student-faculty ratio is 7:1.

Students of Emory
The student body totals 11,362, of whom 6,297 are undergraduates. 56.1% are women
and 43.9% are men. Students come from 52 states and territories and 64 other countries.
20% are from Georgia. 3.6% are international students. 8.9% are African American,
0.2% American Indian, 15.6% Asian American, and 3% Hispanic American. 94%
returned for their sophomore year.

Facilities and Resources
Student rooms are linked to a campus network. 600 **computers** are available on campus
that provide access to the Internet. The 8 **libraries** have 2,500,000 books and 24,687
subscriptions.

Campus Life
There are 220 active organizations on campus, including a drama/theater group,
newspaper, radio station, television station, and choral group. 35% of eligible men and
35% of eligible women are members of national **fraternities** and national **sororities**.

Emory is a member of the NCAA (Division III). **Intercollegiate sports** include
baseball (m), basketball, cross-country running, golf (m), soccer, softball (w), swimming,
tennis, track and field, volleyball (w).

Campus Safety
Student safety services include late-night transport/escort service, 24-hour emergency
telephone alarm devices, 24-hour patrols by trained security personnel, and student
patrols.

Applying
Emory requires an essay, SAT I or ACT, a high school transcript, and 1 recommendation. It recommends SAT II Subject Tests and a minimum high school GPA of
3.0. Application deadline: 1/15; 4/1 for financial aid, with a 2/15 priority date. Early and
deferred admission are possible.

> **S**elective and innovative, with
> an emphasis on excellent
> teaching, Emory University
> seeks students with serious
> intellectual and professional
> interests. Emory is located 5 miles
> northeast of downtown Atlanta. Of
> the 11,000 students enrolled at
> Emory, more than 6,000 are
> undergraduates from every region of
> the U.S. and more than 60 other
> nations. Emory offers a broad-based
> liberal arts program that includes
> more than 70 majors. Many student
> organizations encourage widespread
> involvement in campus life. Oxford
> College of Emory University, a
> small-campus option, is located 40
> miles east of the Atlanta campus
> and enrolls 600 students in a
> 2-year program that is part of a
> 4-year program.

Getting in Last Year
10,372 applied
42% were accepted
1,606 enrolled (37%)
90% from top tenth of their h.s. class
3.80 average high school GPA
90% had SAT verbal scores over 600
95% had SAT math scores over 600
100% had ACT scores over 24
40% had SAT verbal scores over 700
51% had SAT math scores over 700
54% had ACT scores over 30
53 National Merit Scholars

Graduation and After
82% graduated in 4 years
4% graduated in 5 years
1% graduated in 6 years
65% pursued further study
250 organizations recruited on campus

Financial Matters
$27,952 tuition and fees (2003–04)
$8920 room and board
100% average percent of need met
$25,238 average financial aid amount received
   per undergraduate

ERSKINE COLLEGE

RURAL SETTING ■ PRIVATE ■ INDEPENDENT RELIGIOUS ■ COED
DUE WEST, SOUTH CAROLINA

Web site: www.erskine.edu
Contact: Mr. Bart Walker, Director of Admissions, PO Box 176, Due West, SC 29639
Telephone: 864-379-8830 or toll-free 800-241-8721 **Fax:** 864-379-8759
E-mail: admissions@erskine.edu

Getting in Last Year
806 applied
70% were accepted
176 enrolled (31%)
37% from top tenth of their h.s. class
3.59 average high school GPA
32% had SAT verbal scores over 600
33% had SAT math scores over 600
61% had ACT scores over 24
10% had SAT verbal scores over 700
6% had SAT math scores over 700
10% had ACT scores over 30
7 valedictorians

Graduation and After
64% graduated in 4 years
4% graduated in 5 years
1% graduated in 6 years
24% pursued further study
64% had job offers within 6 months

Financial Matters
$17,367 tuition and fees (2003–04)
$5799 room and board
84% average percent of need met
$16,500 average financial aid amount received per undergraduate

Academics

Erskine awards bachelor's, master's, doctoral, and first-professional **degrees**. Challenging opportunities include advanced placement credit, double majors, independent study, and a senior project. Special programs include internships, summer session for credit, off-campus study, and study-abroad.

The most frequently chosen **baccalaureate** fields are biological/life sciences, business/marketing, and education. A complete listing of majors at Erskine appears in the Majors Index beginning on page 460.

The **faculty** at Erskine has 38 full-time members, 97% with terminal degrees. The student-faculty ratio is 12:1.

Students of Erskine

The student body totals 904, of whom 589 are undergraduates. 58.2% are women and 41.8% are men. Students come from 20 states and territories and 10 other countries. 74% are from South Carolina. 1.7% are international students. 5.9% are African American, 0.2% American Indian, 0.5% Asian American, and 0.7% Hispanic American. 68% returned for their sophomore year.

Facilities and Resources

Student rooms are linked to a campus network. 65 **computers** are available on campus that provide access to the Internet. The **library** has 352,292 books and 683 subscriptions.

Campus Life

There are 49 active organizations on campus, including a drama/theater group, newspaper, radio station, and choral group. 14% of eligible men and 25% of eligible women are members of local **fraternities** and local **sororities**.

Erskine is a member of the NCAA (Division II). **Intercollegiate sports** (some offering scholarships) include baseball (m), basketball, cross-country running, soccer, softball (w), tennis.

Campus Safety

Student safety services include late-night transport/escort service, 24-hour patrols by trained security personnel, and electronically operated dormitory entrances.

Applying

Erskine requires SAT I or ACT, a high school transcript, and 1 recommendation, and in some cases an essay, SAT II Subject Tests, and an interview. It recommends an interview. Application deadline: rolling admissions; 4/1 priority date for financial aid.

EUGENE LANG COLLEGE, NEW SCHOOL UNIVERSITY

URBAN SETTING ■ PRIVATE ■ INDEPENDENT ■ COED
NEW YORK, NEW YORK

Web site: www.lang.edu
Contact: Mr. Terence Peavy, Director of Admissions, 65 West 11th Street, New York, NY 10011-8601
Telephone: 212-229-5665 or toll-free 877-528-3321 **Fax:** 212-229-5166
E-mail: lang@newschool.edu

Academics

Eugene Lang College awards bachelor's **degrees**. Challenging opportunities include advanced placement credit, accelerated degree programs, student-designed majors, independent study, and a senior project. Special programs include internships, summer session for credit, off-campus study, and study-abroad.

The most frequently chosen **baccalaureate** field is liberal arts/general studies. A complete listing of majors at Eugene Lang College appears in the Majors Index beginning on page 460.

The **faculty** at Eugene Lang College has 35 full-time members. The student-faculty ratio is 12:1.

Students of Eugene Lang College

The student body is made up of 742 undergraduates. 68.2% are women and 31.8% are men. Students come from 26 states and territories and 11 other countries. 45% are from New York. 2.8% are international students. 4.7% are African American, 3.6% Asian American, and 4.7% Hispanic American. 71% returned for their sophomore year.

Facilities and Resources

Student rooms are linked to a campus network. 934 **computers** are available on campus for student use. The 3 **libraries** have 4,137,530 books and 22,150 subscriptions.

Campus Life

There are 10 active organizations on campus, including a drama/theater group and choral group. No national or local **fraternities** or **sororities**.

This institution has no intercollegiate sports.

Campus Safety

Student safety services include 24-hour desk attendants in residence halls, 24-hour emergency telephone alarm devices, and electronically operated dormitory entrances.

Applying

Eugene Lang College requires an essay, SAT I, ACT, or 4 SAT II Subject Tests, a high school transcript, an interview, 2 recommendations, and a minimum high school GPA of 2.0. It recommends a minimum high school GPA of 3.0. Application deadline: 2/1; 3/1 priority date for financial aid. Early and deferred admission are possible.

Eugene Lang College offers students of diverse backgrounds the opportunity to help design their own program of study within one of 12 interdisciplinary liberal arts concentrations in the social sciences and the humanities. Students discuss and debate issues in small seminar courses that are never larger than 20 students. They enrich their programs with internships in a wide variety of areas, such as media and publishing, community service, and education, and they can pursue a dual degree at one of the University's 5 other divisions. The Greenwich Village location makes all the cultural treasures of the city—museums, libraries, dance, music, and theater—a distinct part of the campus.

Getting in Last Year

862 applied
65% were accepted
188 enrolled (34%)
21% from top tenth of their h.s. class
2.99 average high school GPA
65% had SAT verbal scores over 600
32% had SAT math scores over 600
59% had ACT scores over 24
17% had SAT verbal scores over 700
4% had SAT math scores over 700
14% had ACT scores over 30
5 class presidents
4 valedictorians

Graduation and After

33% graduated in 4 years
9% graduated in 5 years
6% graduated in 6 years
82% had job offers within 6 months

Financial Matters

$24,130 tuition and fees (2003–04)
$10,810 room and board
69% average percent of need met
$17,793 average financial aid amount received per undergraduate

FAIRFIELD UNIVERSITY

SUBURBAN SETTING ■ PRIVATE ■ INDEPENDENT RELIGIOUS ■ COED
FAIRFIELD, CONNECTICUT

Web site: www.fairfield.edu
Contact: Ms. Marianne Gumpper, Interim Director of Admission, 1073 North Benson Road, Fairfield, CT 06824-5195
Telephone: 203-254-4100 **Fax:** 203-254-4199
E-mail: admis@mail.fairfield.edu

Getting in Last Year
7,655 applied
49% were accepted
789 enrolled (21%)
35% from top tenth of their h.s. class
3.39 average high school GPA
46% had SAT verbal scores over 600
57% had SAT math scores over 600
5% had SAT verbal scores over 700
7% had SAT math scores over 700
6 National Merit Scholars
27 class presidents
6 valedictorians

Graduation and After
74% graduated in 4 years
4% graduated in 5 years
18% pursued further study (5% medicine, 4% arts and sciences, 4% law)
85% had job offers within 6 months
111 organizations recruited on campus

Financial Matters
$26,585 tuition and fees (2003–04)
$8920 room and board
78% average percent of need met
$17,603 average financial aid amount received per undergraduate

Academics

Fairfield awards bachelor's and master's **degrees** and post-master's certificates. Challenging opportunities include advanced placement credit, student-designed majors, an honors program, double majors, independent study, and a senior project. Special programs include internships, summer session for credit, and study-abroad.

The most frequently chosen **baccalaureate** fields are business/marketing, trade and industry, and communications/communication technologies. A complete listing of majors at Fairfield appears in the Majors Index beginning on page 460.

The **faculty** at Fairfield has 222 full-time members, 93% with terminal degrees. The student-faculty ratio is 13:1.

Students of Fairfield

The student body totals 5,053, of whom 4,020 are undergraduates. 58.2% are women and 41.8% are men. Students come from 35 states and territories and 45 other countries. 24% are from Connecticut. 1% are international students. 2.2% are African American, 0.4% American Indian, 3.3% Asian American, and 5.3% Hispanic American. 85% returned for their sophomore year.

Facilities and Resources

Student rooms are linked to a campus network. 150 **computers** are available on campus that provide access to the Internet. The **library** has 219,893 books and 1,790 subscriptions.

Campus Life

There are 100 active organizations on campus, including a drama/theater group, newspaper, radio station, television station, and choral group. No national or local **fraternities** or **sororities**.

Fairfield is a member of the NCAA (Division I). **Intercollegiate sports** (some offering scholarships) include baseball (m), basketball, crew (w), cross-country running, field hockey (w), golf, lacrosse, soccer, softball (w), swimming, tennis, volleyball (w).

Campus Safety

Student safety services include bicycle patrols, late-night transport/escort service, 24-hour emergency telephone alarm devices, 24-hour patrols by trained security personnel, and electronically operated dormitory entrances.

Applying

Fairfield requires an essay, SAT I or ACT, a high school transcript, 1 recommendation, rank in upper 20% of high school class, and a minimum high school GPA of 3.0. It recommends an interview. Application deadline: 1/15; 2/15 priority date for financial aid. Early and deferred admission are possible.

FLORIDA INSTITUTE OF TECHNOLOGY

SMALL-TOWN SETTING ■ PRIVATE ■ INDEPENDENT ■ COED
MELBOURNE, FLORIDA

Web site: www.fit.edu
Contact: Ms. Judith Marino, Director of Undergraduate Admissions, 150
  West University Boulevard, Melbourne, FL 32901-6975
Telephone: 321-674-8030 or toll-free 800-888-4348 **Fax:** 321-723-9468
E-mail: admissions@fit.edu

Academics

Florida Tech awards bachelor's, master's, and doctoral **degrees** and post-master's
certificates. Challenging opportunities include advanced placement credit, accelerated
degree programs, double majors, and a senior project. Special programs include cooperative education, internships, summer session for credit, study-abroad, and Army ROTC.

The most frequently chosen **baccalaureate** fields are engineering/engineering
technologies, trade and industry, and biological/life sciences. A complete listing of majors
at Florida Tech appears in the Majors Index beginning on page 460.

The **faculty** at Florida Tech has 218 full-time members, 89% with terminal degrees.
The student-faculty ratio is 12:1.

Students of Florida Tech

The student body totals 4,689, of whom 2,346 are undergraduates. 30.3% are women
and 69.7% are men. Students come from 50 states and territories and 88 other countries.
54% are from Florida. 20.3% are international students. 3.4% are African American,
0.3% American Indian, 2.7% Asian American, and 6.1% Hispanic American. 79%
returned for their sophomore year.

Facilities and Resources

Student rooms are linked to a campus network. 400 **computers** are available on campus
that provide access to the Internet. The **library** has 146,419 books and 6,079 subscriptions.

Campus Life

There are 110 active organizations on campus, including a drama/theater group,
newspaper, radio station, television station, choral group, and marching band. 15% of
eligible men and 16% of eligible women are members of national **fraternities**, national
sororities, and local sororities.

Florida Tech is a member of the NCAA (Division II). **Intercollegiate sports** (some
offering scholarships) include baseball (m), basketball, cheerleading, crew, cross-country
running, golf, soccer, softball (w), tennis, volleyball (w).

Campus Safety

Student safety services include self-defense education, late-night transport/escort service,
24-hour emergency telephone alarm devices, and 24-hour patrols by trained security
personnel.

Applying

Florida Tech requires SAT I or ACT, a high school transcript, and a minimum high
school GPA of 2.5, and in some cases a minimum high school GPA of 3.0. It recommends an essay, an interview, and a minimum high school GPA of 2.8. Application
deadline: rolling admissions; 3/15 priority date for financial aid. Early and deferred
admission are possible.

As part of a hands-on
education, Florida Tech
students participate in
sponsored research, multidisciplinary
design projects, internships,
work-study, and co-operative
education. These are just a few
areas to explore: parallel computing;
software engineering; courses at
Kennedy Space Center; airport
planning; DNA replication; artificial
reef structures; robotics; cognitive
behavior; high-energy particle
physics; bio-organic chemistry; naval
architecture; feeding ecology of
dolphins; alternative fuels; space
plasma; the origin of the universe;
Hubble Space Telescope projects;
aerospace structures; shark and
stingray research; lightning research;
manatee distribution in the Indian
River Lagoon; molecular biology;
bacterial cell cycles; and business
management technology.

Getting in Last Year
2,146 applied
86% were accepted
551 enrolled (30%)
27% from top tenth of their h.s. class
3.54 average high school GPA
34% had SAT verbal scores over 600
54% had SAT math scores over 600
63% had ACT scores over 24
4% had SAT verbal scores over 700
10% had SAT math scores over 700
13% had ACT scores over 30
2 National Merit Scholars
12 valedictorians

Graduation and After
35% graduated in 4 years
17% graduated in 5 years
2% graduated in 6 years
28% pursued further study (15% engineering,
  11% arts and sciences, 2% business)
98% had job offers within 6 months
100 organizations recruited on campus

Financial Matters
$22,600 tuition and fees (2003–04)
$6140 room and board
83% average percent of need met
$20,497 average financial aid amount received
  per undergraduate

FLORIDA INTERNATIONAL UNIVERSITY
URBAN SETTING ■ PUBLIC ■ STATE-SUPPORTED ■ COED
MIAMI, FLORIDA

Web site: www.fiu.edu/~wellness
Contact: Ms. Carmen Brown, Director of Admissions, University Park, PC 140, 11200 SW 8 Street, PC140, Miami, FL 33199
Telephone: 305-348-3675 **Fax:** 305-348-3648
E-mail: admiss@fiu.edu

Getting in Last Year
8,450 applied
43% were accepted
3,071 enrolled (85%)
42% from top tenth of their h.s. class
3.59 average high school GPA
34% had SAT verbal scores over 600
35% had SAT math scores over 600
75% had ACT scores over 24
4% had SAT verbal scores over 700
4% had SAT math scores over 700
4% had ACT scores over 30
2 National Merit Scholars
10 valedictorians

Graduation and After
18% graduated in 4 years
20% graduated in 5 years
8% graduated in 6 years
70% had job offers within 6 months
600 organizations recruited on campus

Financial Matters
$2889 resident tuition and fees (2003–04)
$13,917 nonresident tuition and fees (2003–04)
$8822 room and board
56% average percent of need met
$6351 average financial aid amount received per undergraduate (2001–02)

Academics
FIU awards bachelor's, master's, doctoral, and first-professional **degrees**. Challenging opportunities include advanced placement credit, accelerated degree programs, freshman honors college, an honors program, double majors, independent study, and a senior project. Special programs include cooperative education, internships, summer session for credit, off-campus study, study-abroad, and Army and Air Force ROTC.

The most frequently chosen **baccalaureate** fields are business/marketing, education, and health professions and related sciences. A complete listing of majors at FIU appears in the Majors Index beginning on page 460.

The **faculty** at FIU has 745 full-time members, 98% with terminal degrees. The student-faculty ratio is 17:1.

Students of FIU
The student body totals 33,228, of whom 27,269 are undergraduates. 57.2% are women and 42.8% are men. Students come from 52 states and territories and 115 other countries. 94% are from Florida. 5.8% are international students. 13.8% are African American, 0.2% American Indian, 3.8% Asian American, and 56.3% Hispanic American. 88% returned for their sophomore year.

Facilities and Resources
Student rooms are linked to a campus network. 600 **computers** are available on campus that provide access to the Internet. The 3 **libraries** have 2,234,911 books and 14,978 subscriptions.

Campus Life
There are 190 active organizations on campus, including a drama/theater group, newspaper, radio station, choral group, and marching band. 8% of eligible men and 9% of eligible women are members of national **fraternities** and national **sororities**.

FIU is a member of the NCAA (Division I). **Intercollegiate sports** (some offering scholarships) include baseball (m), basketball, cross-country running, football (m), golf (w), soccer, softball (w), tennis (w), track and field, volleyball (w).

Campus Safety
Student safety services include late-night transport/escort service, 24-hour emergency telephone alarm devices, 24-hour patrols by trained security personnel, and electronically operated dormitory entrances.

Applying
FIU requires SAT I or ACT, a high school transcript, and a minimum high school GPA of 3.0, and in some cases 1 recommendation. Application deadline: rolling admissions; 3/1 priority date for financial aid. Early and deferred admission are possible.

FLORIDA STATE UNIVERSITY

SUBURBAN SETTING ■ PUBLIC ■ STATE-SUPPORTED ■ COED
TALLAHASSEE, FLORIDA

Web site: www.fsu.edu
Contact: Office of Admissions, A2500 University Center, Tallahassee, FL 32306-2400
Telephone: 850-644-6200 Fax: 850-644-0197
E-mail: admissions@admin.fsu.edu

Academics

Florida State awards associate, bachelor's, master's, doctoral, and first-professional **degrees** and post-bachelor's and post-master's certificates. Challenging opportunities include advanced placement credit, accelerated degree programs, an honors program, double majors, independent study, and a senior project. Special programs include cooperative education, internships, summer session for credit, off-campus study, study-abroad, and Army, Navy and Air Force ROTC.

The most frequently chosen **baccalaureate** fields are business/marketing, social sciences and history, and education. A complete listing of majors at Florida State appears in the Majors Index beginning on page 460.

The **faculty** at Florida State has 1,086 full-time members, 92% with terminal degrees. The student-faculty ratio is 23:1.

Students of Florida State

The student body totals 36,884, of whom 29,630 are undergraduates. 56.5% are women and 43.5% are men. Students come from 51 states and territories and 120 other countries. 87% are from Florida. 0.6% are international students. 11.8% are African American, 0.4% American Indian, 3% Asian American, and 9.9% Hispanic American. 85% returned for their sophomore year.

Facilities and Resources

Student rooms are linked to a campus network. 2,707 **computers** are available on campus that provide access to course home pages, course search, online fee payment and the Internet. The 7 **libraries** have 2,488,398 books and 19,309 subscriptions.

Campus Life

There are 266 active organizations on campus, including a drama/theater group, newspaper, radio station, television station, choral group, and marching band. 15% of eligible men and 13% of eligible women are members of national **fraternities**, national **sororities**, local fraternities, and local sororities.

Florida State is a member of the NCAA (Division I). **Intercollegiate sports** (some offering scholarships) include baseball (m), basketball, cheerleading, cross-country running, football (m), golf, soccer (w), softball (w), swimming, tennis, track and field, volleyball (w).

Campus Safety

Student safety services include late-night transport/escort service, 24-hour emergency telephone alarm devices, 24-hour patrols by trained security personnel, and electronically operated dormitory entrances.

Applying

Florida State requires SAT I or ACT and a high school transcript, and in some cases audition. It recommends an essay and a minimum high school GPA of 3.0. Application deadline: 3/1; 2/15 priority date for financial aid. Early admission is possible.

Getting in Last Year

31,264 applied
42% were accepted
6,081 enrolled (47%)
55% from top tenth of their h.s. class
3.8 average high school GPA
40% had SAT verbal scores over 600
43% had SAT math scores over 600
59% had ACT scores over 24
5% had SAT verbal scores over 700
5% had SAT math scores over 700
4% had ACT scores over 30
19 National Merit Scholars

Graduation and After

38% graduated in 4 years
22% graduated in 5 years
4% graduated in 6 years
35% pursued further study
947 organizations recruited on campus

Financial Matters

$2860 resident tuition and fees (2003–04)
$13,888 nonresident tuition and fees (2003–04)
$6168 room and board
25% average percent of need met
$6529 average financial aid amount received per undergraduate (2002–03 estimated)

FORDHAM UNIVERSITY

URBAN SETTING ■ PRIVATE ■ INDEPENDENT RELIGIOUS ■ COED
NEW YORK, NEW YORK

Web site: www.fordham.edu
Contact: Ms. Karen Pellegrino, Director of Admission, Theband Hall, 441
    East Fordham Road, New York, NY 10458
Telephone: 718-817-4000 or toll-free 800-FORDHAM **Fax:** 718-367-9404
E-mail: enroll@fordham.edu

Fordham, New York City's Jesuit university, offers a distinctive educational experience, including the rigors of a 450-year Jesuit tradition in education, in the "capital of the world." Fordham has 3 residential campuses—green and gothic Rose Hill, Lincoln Center, in the cultural heart of Manhattan, and Marymount, just a train ride away in Tarrytown, New York. The distinguished faculty are committed to challenging each student to excel, and the low student-faculty ratio of 11:1 ensures individual attention. Fordham offers more than 65 majors, 130 extracurricular activities, and a successful internship program in the world's most competitive market.

Getting in Last Year
12,801 applied
54% were accepted
1,728 enrolled (25%)
32% from top tenth of their h.s. class
3.64 average high school GPA
50% had SAT verbal scores over 600
50% had SAT math scores over 600
72% had ACT scores over 24
9% had SAT verbal scores over 700
6% had SAT math scores over 700
14% had ACT scores over 30

Graduation and After
68% graduated in 4 years
4% graduated in 5 years
1% graduated in 6 years
25% pursued further study (7% arts and sciences, 6% law, 5% business)
90% had job offers within 6 months
632 organizations recruited on campus

Financial Matters
$24,720 tuition and fees (2003–04)
$9700 room and board
79% average percent of need met
$19,536 average financial aid amount received per undergraduate (2001–02)

Academics
Fordham awards bachelor's, master's, doctoral, and first-professional **degrees** and post-master's certificates (branch locations: an 85-acre campus at Rose Hill and an 8-acre campus at Lincoln Center). Challenging opportunities include advanced placement credit, accelerated degree programs, student-designed majors, an honors program, double majors, independent study, and a senior project. Special programs include internships, summer session for credit, off-campus study, study-abroad, and Army, Navy and Air Force ROTC.

The most frequently chosen **baccalaureate** fields are business/marketing, social sciences and history, and communications/communication technologies. A complete listing of majors at Fordham appears in the Majors Index beginning on page 460.

The **faculty** at Fordham has 601 full-time members, 16% with terminal degrees. The student-faculty ratio is 11:1.

Students of Fordham
The student body totals 14,731, of whom 7,403 are undergraduates. 59.7% are women and 40.3% are men. Students come from 53 states and territories and 50 other countries. 59% are from New York. 1.2% are international students. 5.5% are African American, 0.2% American Indian, 5.7% Asian American, and 10.5% Hispanic American. 90% returned for their sophomore year.

Facilities and Resources
Student rooms are linked to a campus network. 617 **computers** are available on campus that provide access to the Internet. The 4 **libraries** have 1,799,171 books and 14,094 subscriptions.

Campus Life
There are 133 active organizations on campus, including a drama/theater group, newspaper, radio station, choral group, and marching band. No national or local **fraternities** or **sororities**.

Fordham is a member of the NCAA (Division I). **Intercollegiate sports** (some offering scholarships) include baseball (m), basketball (m), crew (w), cross-country running, football (m), golf (m), soccer, softball (w), squash (m), swimming, tennis, track and field, volleyball (w), water polo (m).

Campus Safety
Student safety services include security at each campus entrance and at residence halls, late-night transport/escort service, 24-hour emergency telephone alarm devices, 24-hour patrols by trained security personnel, student patrols, and electronically operated dormitory entrances.

Applying
Fordham requires an essay, SAT I or ACT, a high school transcript, and 1 recommendation, and in some cases an interview. It recommends SAT II Subject Tests, an interview, and a minimum high school GPA of 3.0. Application deadline: 2/1; 2/1 priority date for financial aid. Early admission is possible.

FRANCISCAN UNIVERSITY OF STEUBENVILLE

SUBURBAN SETTING ■ PRIVATE ■ INDEPENDENT RELIGIOUS ■ COED
STEUBENVILLE, OHIO

Web site: www.franciscan.edu
Contact: Mrs. Margaret Weber, Director of Admissions, 1235 University
   Boulevard, Steubenville, OH 43952-1763
Telephone: 740-283-6226 or toll-free 800-783-6220 **Fax:** 740-284-5456
E-mail: admissions@franciscan.edu

Academics

Franciscan University of Steubenville awards associate, bachelor's, and master's **degrees**.
Challenging opportunities include advanced placement credit, accelerated degree
programs, an honors program, double majors, independent study, and a senior project.
Special programs include internships, summer session for credit, and study-abroad.

   The most frequently chosen **baccalaureate** fields are business/marketing, education,
and psychology. A complete listing of majors at Franciscan University of Steubenville
appears in the Majors Index beginning on page 460.

   The **faculty** at Franciscan University of Steubenville has 103 full-time members,
75% with terminal degrees. The student-faculty ratio is 16:1.

Students of Franciscan University of Steubenville

The student body totals 2,281, of whom 1,844 are undergraduates. 60.4% are women
and 39.6% are men. Students come from 52 states and territories and 24 other countries.
24% are from Ohio. 1.5% are international students. 0.4% are African American, 0.5%
American Indian, 1.8% Asian American, and 4.4% Hispanic American. 84% returned for
their sophomore year.

Facilities and Resources

126 **computers** are available on campus that provide access to the Internet. The **library**
has 231,176 books and 578 subscriptions.

Campus Life

There are 8 active organizations on campus, including a drama/theater group,
newspaper, radio station, and choral group. Franciscan University of Steubenville has
national **fraternities** and national **sororities**.

   This institution has no intercollegiate sports.

Campus Safety

Student safety services include late-night transport/escort service, 24-hour emergency
telephone alarm devices, 24-hour patrols by trained security personnel, and student
patrols.

Applying

Franciscan University of Steubenville requires an essay, SAT I or ACT, a high school
transcript, recommendations, and a minimum high school GPA of 2.4. It recommends an
interview. Application deadline: 5/1; 4/15 priority date for financial aid. Early and
deferred admission are possible.

Founded in 1946, Franciscan University of Steubenville stands tall among the preeminent Catholic universities in North America, providing a demanding curriculum integrated with a spiritually rich living environment. This exciting intellectual and faith community attracts top students from 50 states and more than 20 countries, as well as first-rate professors who hold teaching and mentoring students as a sacred trust. In the spirit of Christian humanism, they seek the truth together through a curriculum that aims to develop intellectual virtue, wisdom, and a life-long passion for knowledge. The 2,200 students choose from among 35 undergraduate and 7 graduate programs, and many round out their education in the study abroad program at a beautifully-restored medieval monastery in the Austrian Alps.

Getting in Last Year
846 applied
84% were accepted
357 enrolled (50%)
26% from top tenth of their h.s. class
3.53 average high school GPA
47% had SAT verbal scores over 600
35% had SAT math scores over 600
54% had ACT scores over 24
10% had SAT verbal scores over 700
4% had SAT math scores over 700
7% had ACT scores over 30
12 valedictorians

Graduation and After
63% graduated in 4 years
7% graduated in 5 years
1% graduated in 6 years
13% pursued further study (3% theology, 2%
   arts and sciences, 2% law)
96% had job offers within 6 months
50 organizations recruited on campus

Financial Matters
$15,050 tuition and fees (2003–04)
$5250 room and board
75% average percent of need met
$8570 average financial aid amount received
   per undergraduate (2002–03 estimated)

FRANKLIN AND MARSHALL COLLEGE

SUBURBAN SETTING ■ PRIVATE ■ INDEPENDENT ■ COED
LANCASTER, PENNSYLVANIA

Web site: www.fandm.edu
Contact: Mr. Dennis Trotter, Vice President for Enrollment Management, PO Box 3003, Lancaster, PA 17604-3003
Telephone: 717-291-3953 **Fax:** 717-291-4389
E-mail: admission@fandm.edu

Getting in Last Year

3,616 applied
58% were accepted
503 enrolled (24%)
45% from top tenth of their h.s. class
64% had SAT verbal scores over 600
70% had SAT math scores over 600
15% had SAT verbal scores over 700
21% had SAT math scores over 700

Graduation and After

80% graduated in 4 years
3% graduated in 5 years
1% graduated in 6 years
29% pursued further study (14% arts and sciences, 7% law, 5% medicine)
65% had job offers within 6 months
64 organizations recruited on campus

Financial Matters

$28,860 tuition and fees (2003–04)
$7070 room and board
97% average percent of need met
$20,915 average financial aid amount received per undergraduate

Academics

F&M awards bachelor's **degrees**. Challenging opportunities include advanced placement credit, accelerated degree programs, student-designed majors, an honors program, double majors, independent study, and a senior project. Special programs include internships, summer session for credit, off-campus study, and study-abroad.

The most frequently chosen **baccalaureate** fields are social sciences and history, business/marketing, and interdisciplinary studies. A complete listing of majors at F&M appears in the Majors Index beginning on page 460.

The **faculty** at F&M has 167 full-time members, 97% with terminal degrees. The student-faculty ratio is 11:1.

Students of F&M

The student body is made up of 1,923 undergraduates. 47.6% are women and 52.4% are men. Students come from 40 states and territories and 40 other countries. 36% are from Pennsylvania. 8.9% are international students. 2.3% are African American, 4.2% Asian American, and 2.6% Hispanic American. 90% returned for their sophomore year.

Facilities and Resources

Student rooms are linked to a campus network. 139 **computers** are available on campus that provide access to the Internet. The 2 **libraries** have 435,771 books and 2,090 subscriptions.

Campus Life

There are 120 active organizations on campus, including a drama/theater group, newspaper, radio station, television station, and choral group. F&M has national **fraternities** and national **sororities**.

F&M is a member of the NCAA (Division III). **Intercollegiate sports** include baseball (m), basketball, cheerleading, cross-country running, field hockey (w), football (m), golf, lacrosse, soccer, softball (w), squash, swimming, tennis, track and field, volleyball (w), wrestling (m).

Campus Safety

Student safety services include residence hall security, campus security connected to city police and fire company, late-night transport/escort service, 24-hour emergency telephone alarm devices, 24-hour patrols by trained security personnel, and electronically operated dormitory entrances.

Applying

F&M requires an essay, SAT II: Writing Test, SAT I and SAT II or ACT, a high school transcript, and 2 recommendations. It recommends an interview. Application deadline: 2/1; 2/1 for financial aid. Early and deferred admission are possible.

FREED-HARDEMAN UNIVERSITY

SMALL-TOWN SETTING ■ PRIVATE ■ INDEPENDENT RELIGIOUS ■ COED
HENDERSON, TENNESSEE

Web site: www.fhu.edu
Contact: Mr. Jim Brown, Director of Admissions, 158 East Main Street,
   Henderson, TN 38340
Telephone: 731-989-6651 or toll-free 800-630-3480 **Fax:** 731-989-6047
E-mail: admissions@fhu.edu

Academics

FHU awards bachelor's and master's **degrees** and post-bachelor's certificates. Challenging opportunities include advanced placement credit, accelerated degree programs, student-designed majors, an honors program, double majors, independent study, and a senior project. Special programs include cooperative education, internships, summer session for credit, off-campus study, and study-abroad.

The most frequently chosen **baccalaureate** fields are business/marketing, interdisciplinary studies, and psychology. A complete listing of majors at FHU appears in the Majors Index beginning on page 460.

The **faculty** at FHU has 97 full-time members, 76% with terminal degrees. The student-faculty ratio is 16:1.

Students of FHU

The student body totals 1,966, of whom 1,447 are undergraduates. 53.3% are women and 46.7% are men. Students come from 36 states and territories and 17 other countries. 50% are from Tennessee. 1.8% are international students. 4.3% are African American, 0.5% American Indian, 0.6% Asian American, and 0.6% Hispanic American. 74% returned for their sophomore year.

Facilities and Resources

Student rooms are linked to a campus network. 250 **computers** are available on campus that provide access to the Internet. The **library** has 154,689 books and 1,715 subscriptions.

Campus Life

There are 35 active organizations on campus, including a drama/theater group, newspaper, radio station, television station, and choral group. 48% of eligible men and 48% of eligible women are members of coed social clubs.

FHU is a member of the NAIA. **Intercollegiate sports** (some offering scholarships) include baseball (m), basketball, cheerleading, cross-country running, golf, soccer, softball (w), tennis, volleyball (w).

Campus Safety

Student safety services include late-night transport/escort service, 24-hour emergency telephone alarm devices, 24-hour patrols by trained security personnel, and electronically operated dormitory entrances.

Applying

FHU requires SAT I or ACT, a high school transcript, and a minimum high school GPA of 2.25, and in some cases an interview. It recommends an essay and recommendations. Application deadline: rolling admissions; 4/1 priority date for financial aid. Early and deferred admission are possible.

Getting in Last Year
663 applied
99% were accepted
375 enrolled (57%)
17% from top tenth of their h.s. class
3.38 average high school GPA
40% had ACT scores over 24
8% had ACT scores over 30
13 valedictorians

Graduation and After
39% graduated in 4 years
16% graduated in 5 years
2% graduated in 6 years
86 organizations recruited on campus

Financial Matters
$11,046 tuition and fees (2003–04)
$5320 room and board
74% average percent of need met
$11,220 average financial aid amount received
   per undergraduate (2002–03 estimated)

FURMAN UNIVERSITY

SUBURBAN SETTING ■ PRIVATE ■ INDEPENDENT ■ COED
GREENVILLE, SOUTH CAROLINA

Web site: www.furman.edu
Contact: Mr. David R. O'Cain, Director of Admissions, 3300 Poinsett
   Highway, Greenville, SC 29613
Telephone: 864-294-2034 **Fax:** 864-294-3127
E-mail: admissions@furman.edu

Getting in Last Year

3,773 applied
60% were accepted
687 enrolled (30%)
68% from top tenth of their h.s. class
3.80 average high school GPA
75% had SAT verbal scores over 600
75% had SAT math scores over 600
90% had ACT scores over 24
23% had SAT verbal scores over 700
19% had SAT math scores over 700
32% had ACT scores over 30
29 National Merit Scholars
40 class presidents
45 valedictorians

Graduation and After

78% graduated in 4 years
5% graduated in 5 years
32% pursued further study (9% arts and sciences, 6% education, 4% law)
74% had job offers within 6 months
89 organizations recruited on campus

Financial Matters

$22,712 tuition and fees (2003–04)
$5968 room and board
90% average percent of need met
$18,349 average financial aid amount received per undergraduate (2002–03 estimated)

Academics

Furman awards bachelor's and master's **degrees** and post-bachelor's certificates. Challenging opportunities include advanced placement credit, accelerated degree programs, student-designed majors, double majors, independent study, and a senior project. Special programs include internships, summer session for credit, study-abroad, and Army ROTC.

The most frequently chosen **baccalaureate** fields are social sciences and history, business/marketing, and parks and recreation. A complete listing of majors at Furman appears in the Majors Index beginning on page 460.

The **faculty** at Furman has 216 full-time members, 98% with terminal degrees. The student-faculty ratio is 12:1.

Students of Furman

The student body totals 3,320, of whom 2,814 are undergraduates. 57.3% are women and 42.7% are men. Students come from 45 states and territories and 27 other countries. 30% are from South Carolina. 1.2% are international students. 5.9% are African American, 0.1% American Indian, 1.7% Asian American, and 1.1% Hispanic American. 90% returned for their sophomore year.

Facilities and Resources

Student rooms are linked to a campus network. 340 **computers** are available on campus that provide access to the Internet. The 3 **libraries** have 453,211 books and 2,052 subscriptions.

Campus Life

There are 130 active organizations on campus, including a drama/theater group, newspaper, radio station, television station, choral group, and marching band. 30% of eligible men and 35% of eligible women are members of national **fraternities** and national **sororities**.

Furman is a member of the NCAA (Division I). **Intercollegiate sports** (some offering scholarships) include baseball (m), basketball, cheerleading, cross-country running, football (m), golf, soccer, softball (w), tennis, track and field, volleyball (w).

Campus Safety

Student safety services include late-night transport/escort service, 24-hour emergency telephone alarm devices, 24-hour patrols by trained security personnel, student patrols, and electronically operated dormitory entrances.

Applying

Furman requires an essay, SAT I or ACT, and a high school transcript, and in some cases SAT II Subject Tests and SAT II: Writing Test. It recommends 2 recommendations and a minimum high school GPA of 3.0. Application deadline: 1/15; 1/15 for financial aid. Early admission is possible.

George Fox University

SMALL-TOWN SETTING ■ PRIVATE ■ INDEPENDENT RELIGIOUS ■ COED
NEWBERG, OREGON

Web site: www.georgefox.edu
Contact: Mr. Dale Seipp, Director of Admissions, 414 North Meridian Street, Newberg, OR 97132
Telephone: 503-554-2240 or toll-free 800-765-4369 **Fax:** 503-554-3110
E-mail: admissions@georgefox.edu

Academics

George Fox awards bachelor's, master's, doctoral, and first-professional **degrees**. Challenging opportunities include advanced placement credit, accelerated degree programs, student-designed majors, an honors program, double majors, independent study, and a senior project. Special programs include cooperative education, internships, off-campus study, study-abroad, and Air Force ROTC.

The most frequently chosen **baccalaureate** fields are business/marketing, education, and interdisciplinary studies. A complete listing of majors at George Fox appears in the Majors Index beginning on page 460.

The **faculty** at George Fox has 134 full-time members, 66% with terminal degrees. The student-faculty ratio is 15:1.

Students of George Fox

The student body totals 3,022, of whom 1,717 are undergraduates. 58.7% are women and 41.3% are men. Students come from 25 states and territories and 16 other countries. 64% are from Oregon. 2.9% are international students. 0.8% are African American, 1.1% American Indian, 3.1% Asian American, and 3.2% Hispanic American. 83% returned for their sophomore year.

Facilities and Resources

Student rooms are linked to a campus network. 1,300 **computers** are available on campus that provide access to the Internet. The 2 **libraries** have 123,734 books and 1,323 subscriptions.

Campus Life

There are 18 active organizations on campus, including a drama/theater group, newspaper, radio station, and choral group. No national or local **fraternities** or **sororities**.

George Fox is a member of the NCAA (Division III). **Intercollegiate sports** include baseball (m), basketball, cross-country running, soccer, softball (w), tennis, track and field, volleyball (w).

Campus Safety

Student safety services include late-night transport/escort service, 24-hour emergency telephone alarm devices, 24-hour patrols by trained security personnel, student patrols, and electronically operated dormitory entrances.

Applying

George Fox requires an essay, SAT I or ACT, a high school transcript, and 2 recommendations, and in some cases an interview. It recommends an interview. Application deadline: 6/1; 2/1 priority date for financial aid. Early and deferred admission are possible.

Getting in Last Year
876 applied
93% were accepted
337 enrolled (41%)
31% from top tenth of their h.s. class
4.00 average high school GPA
36% had SAT verbal scores over 600
32% had SAT math scores over 600
63% had ACT scores over 24
6% had SAT verbal scores over 700
4% had SAT math scores over 700
18% had ACT scores over 30

Graduation and After
52% graduated in 4 years
6% graduated in 5 years
1% graduated in 6 years
18% pursued further study (78% arts and sciences, 7% business, 7% education)
64% had job offers within 6 months
200 organizations recruited on campus

Financial Matters
$19,810 tuition and fees (2003–04)
$6300 room and board
83% average percent of need met
$15,332 average financial aid amount received per undergraduate (2001–02)

Georgetown College

Suburban setting ■ Private ■ Independent Religious ■ Coed
Georgetown, Kentucky

Web site: www.georgetowncollege.edu
Contact: Mr. Johnnie Johnson, Director of Admissions, 400 East College Street, Georgetown, KY 40324
Telephone: 502-863-8009 or toll-free 800-788-9985 **Fax:** 502-868-7733
E-mail: admissions@georgetowncollege.edu

Getting in Last Year

1,065 applied
80% were accepted
368 enrolled (43%)
39% from top tenth of their h.s. class
3.52 average high school GPA
20% had SAT verbal scores over 600
17% had SAT math scores over 600
50% had ACT scores over 24
8% had SAT verbal scores over 700
2% had SAT math scores over 700
9% had ACT scores over 30
36 valedictorians

Graduation and After

43% graduated in 4 years
16% graduated in 5 years
1% graduated in 6 years
45% pursued further study
45 organizations recruited on campus

Financial Matters

$16,370 tuition and fees (2003–04)
$5190 room and board
83% average percent of need met
$14,518 average financial aid amount received per undergraduate (2002–03 estimated)

Academics

Georgetown awards bachelor's and master's **degrees** and post-master's certificates. Challenging opportunities include advanced placement credit, student-designed majors, an honors program, double majors, independent study, and a senior project. Special programs include cooperative education, internships, summer session for credit, off-campus study, study-abroad, and Army and Air Force ROTC.

The most frequently chosen **baccalaureate** fields are business/marketing, visual/performing arts, and biological/life sciences. A complete listing of majors at Georgetown appears in the Majors Index beginning on page 460.

The **faculty** at Georgetown has 93 full-time members, 89% with terminal degrees. The student-faculty ratio is 12:1.

Students of Georgetown

The student body totals 1,708, of whom 1,321 are undergraduates. 56.8% are women and 43.2% are men. Students come from 24 states and territories and 12 other countries. 82% are from Kentucky. 1.2% are international students. 3.6% are African American, 0.1% American Indian, 0.5% Asian American, and 0.5% Hispanic American. 71% returned for their sophomore year.

Facilities and Resources

Student rooms are linked to a campus network. 175 **computers** are available on campus that provide access to the Internet. The 2 **libraries** have 152,531 books and 733 subscriptions.

Campus Life

There are 97 active organizations on campus, including a drama/theater group, newspaper, radio station, and choral group. 28% of eligible men and 40% of eligible women are members of national **fraternities**, national **sororities**, and local fraternities.

Georgetown is a member of the NAIA. **Intercollegiate sports** (some offering scholarships) include baseball (m), basketball, cheerleading (w), cross-country running, football (m), golf, soccer, softball (w), tennis, track and field, volleyball (w).

Campus Safety

Student safety services include late-night transport/escort service and 24-hour patrols by trained security personnel.

Applying

Georgetown requires an essay, SAT I or ACT, a high school transcript, and a minimum high school GPA of 2.5, and in some cases an interview and recommendations. It recommends ACT. Application deadline: 7/1; 2/15 priority date for financial aid. Deferred admission is possible.

GEORGETOWN UNIVERSITY

URBAN SETTING ■ PRIVATE ■ INDEPENDENT RELIGIOUS ■ COED
WASHINGTON, DISTRICT OF COLUMBIA

Web site: www.georgetown.edu
Contact: Mr. Charles A. Deacon, Dean of Undergraduate Admissions, 37th and O Street, NW, Washington, DC 20057
Telephone: 202-687-3600 **Fax:** 202-687-6660

Academics

Georgetown awards bachelor's, master's, doctoral, and first-professional **degrees**. Challenging opportunities include advanced placement credit, student-designed majors, an honors program, double majors, independent study, and a senior project. Special programs include internships, summer session for credit, off-campus study, study-abroad, and Army, Navy and Air Force ROTC.

The most frequently chosen **baccalaureate** fields are social sciences and history, business/marketing, and English. A complete listing of majors at Georgetown appears in the Majors Index beginning on page 460.

The **faculty** at Georgetown has 694 full-time members, 92% with terminal degrees. The student-faculty ratio is 10:1.

Students of Georgetown

The student body totals 13,164, of whom 6,550 are undergraduates. 53.9% are women and 46.1% are men. Students come from 50 states and territories and 92 other countries. 3% are from District of Columbia. 5% are international students. 6.6% are African American, 0.1% American Indian, 9.7% Asian American, and 4.9% Hispanic American. 95% returned for their sophomore year.

Facilities and Resources

Student rooms are linked to a campus network. 360 **computers** are available on campus that provide access to online grade reports and the Internet. The 7 **libraries** have 2,234,338 books and 21,901 subscriptions.

Campus Life

There are 129 active organizations on campus, including a drama/theater group, newspaper, radio station, and choral group. No national or local **fraternities** or **sororities**.

Georgetown is a member of the NCAA (Division I). **Intercollegiate sports** (some offering scholarships) include baseball (m), basketball, crew, cross-country running, field hockey (w), football (m), golf (m), lacrosse, sailing, soccer, swimming, tennis, track and field, volleyball (w).

Campus Safety

Student safety services include student guards at residence halls and academic facilities, late-night transport/escort service, 24-hour emergency telephone alarm devices, 24-hour patrols by trained security personnel, and electronically operated dormitory entrances.

Applying

Georgetown requires an essay, SAT I or ACT, a high school transcript, an interview, and 2 recommendations. It recommends SAT II Subject Tests and SAT II: Writing Test. Application deadline: 1/10; 2/1 priority date for financial aid. Early and deferred admission are possible.

Getting in Last Year

15,420 applied
23% were accepted
1,528 enrolled (44%)
83% from top tenth of their h.s. class
3.87 average high school GPA
88% had SAT verbal scores over 600
91% had SAT math scores over 600
93% had ACT scores over 24
39% had SAT verbal scores over 700
43% had SAT math scores over 700
54% had ACT scores over 30
50 class presidents
286 valedictorians

Graduation and After

90% graduated in 4 years
3% graduated in 5 years
1% graduated in 6 years
26% pursued further study (10% law, 9% engineering, 9% arts and sciences)
77% had job offers within 6 months
443 organizations recruited on campus

Financial Matters

$28,209 tuition and fees (2003–04)
$10,033 room and board
100% average percent of need met
$21,650 average financial aid amount received per undergraduate (2002–03 estimated)

THE GEORGE WASHINGTON UNIVERSITY

URBAN SETTING ■ PRIVATE ■ INDEPENDENT ■ COED
WASHINGTON, DISTRICT OF COLUMBIA

Web site: www.gwu.edu
Contact: Dr. Kathryn M. Napper, Director of Admission, 2121 I Street, NW, Suite 201, Washington, DC 20052
Telephone: 202-994-6040 or toll-free 800-447-3765 **Fax:** 202-944-0325
E-mail: gwadm@gwu.edu

Getting in Last Year

18,442 applied
39% were accepted
2,266 enrolled (32%)
65% from top tenth of their h.s. class
72% had SAT verbal scores over 600
73% had SAT math scores over 600
88% had ACT scores over 24
20% had SAT verbal scores over 700
18% had SAT math scores over 700
23% had ACT scores over 30
36 National Merit Scholars

Graduation and After

69% graduated in 4 years
5% graduated in 5 years
1% graduated in 6 years
21% pursued further study (7% arts and sciences, 6% law, 4% medicine)
383 organizations recruited on campus

Financial Matters

$29,350 tuition and fees (2003–04)
$10,040 room and board
94% average percent of need met
$25,695 average financial aid amount received per undergraduate (2001–02)

Academics

GW awards associate, bachelor's, master's, doctoral, and first-professional **degrees** and post-bachelor's and post-master's certificates. Challenging opportunities include advanced placement credit, accelerated degree programs, student-designed majors, an honors program, double majors, independent study, and a senior project. Special programs include cooperative education, internships, summer session for credit, off-campus study, study-abroad, and Army, Navy and Air Force ROTC.

The most frequently chosen **baccalaureate** fields are social sciences and history, business/marketing, and psychology. A complete listing of majors at GW appears in the Majors Index beginning on page 460.

The **faculty** at GW has 787 full-time members, 90% with terminal degrees. The student-faculty ratio is 14:1.

Students of GW

The student body totals 23,417, of whom 10,436 are undergraduates. 57% are women and 43% are men. Students come from 55 states and territories and 101 other countries. 2% are from District of Columbia. 4.5% are international students. 5.3% are African American, 0.2% American Indian, 9.3% Asian American, and 4.6% Hispanic American. 93% returned for their sophomore year.

Facilities and Resources

Student rooms are linked to a campus network. 550 **computers** are available on campus for student use. The 3 **libraries** have 1,984,094 books and 15,365 subscriptions.

Campus Life

There are 208 active organizations on campus, including a drama/theater group, newspaper, radio station, television station, choral group, and marching band. 14% of eligible men and 11% of eligible women are members of national **fraternities** and national **sororities**.

GW is a member of the NCAA (Division I). **Intercollegiate sports** (some offering scholarships) include baseball (m), basketball, crew, cross-country running, golf (m), gymnastics (w), soccer, swimming, tennis, volleyball (w), water polo (m).

Campus Safety

Student safety services include late-night transport/escort service, 24-hour emergency telephone alarm devices, 24-hour patrols by trained security personnel, and electronically operated dormitory entrances.

Applying

GW requires an essay, SAT I or ACT, a high school transcript, and 2 recommendations, and in some cases SAT II Subject Tests. It recommends SAT I, SAT II: Writing Test, and an interview. Application deadline: 1/15; 1/31 priority date for financial aid. Early and deferred admission are possible.

GEORGIA INSTITUTE OF TECHNOLOGY

URBAN SETTING ■ PUBLIC ■ STATE-SUPPORTED ■ COED
ATLANTA, GEORGIA

Web site: www.gatech.edu
Contact: Ms. Ingrid Hayes, Director of Admissions (Undergraduate), 225
  North Avenue, NW, Atlanta, GA 30332-0320
Telephone: 404-894-4154 **Fax:** 404-894-9511
E-mail: admission@gatech.edu

Academics

Georgia Tech awards bachelor's, master's, and doctoral **degrees**. Challenging opportunities include advanced placement credit, accelerated degree programs, student-designed majors, an honors program, double majors, independent study, and a senior project. Special programs include cooperative education, internships, summer session for credit, off-campus study, study-abroad, and Army, Navy and Air Force ROTC.

The most frequently chosen **baccalaureate** fields are engineering/engineering technologies, business/marketing, and computer/information sciences. A complete listing of majors at Georgia Tech appears in the Majors Index beginning on page 460.

The **faculty** at Georgia Tech has 807 full-time members, 95% with terminal degrees. The student-faculty ratio is 13:1.

Students of Georgia Tech

The student body totals 16,643, of whom 11,257 are undergraduates. 27.9% are women and 72.1% are men. Students come from 52 states and territories and 90 other countries. 65% are from Georgia. 4.8% are international students. 7.3% are African American, 0.2% American Indian, 14.6% Asian American, and 2.7% Hispanic American. 90% returned for their sophomore year.

Facilities and Resources

Student rooms are linked to a campus network. 180 **computers** are available on campus that provide access to the Internet. The **library** has 2,258,892 books and 21,248 subscriptions.

Campus Life

There are 308 active organizations on campus, including a drama/theater group, newspaper, radio station, choral group, and marching band. 23% of eligible men and 25% of eligible women are members of national **fraternities**, national **sororities**, and local sororities.

Georgia Tech is a member of the NCAA (Division I). **Intercollegiate sports** (some offering scholarships) include baseball (m), basketball, cross-country running, football (m), golf (m), softball (w), swimming, tennis, track and field, volleyball (w).

Campus Safety

Student safety services include self defense education, lighted pathways and walks, video cameras, late-night transport/escort service, 24-hour emergency telephone alarm devices, 24-hour patrols by trained security personnel, student patrols, and electronically operated dormitory entrances.

Applying

Georgia Tech requires an essay, SAT I or ACT, and a high school transcript, and in some cases SAT II Subject Tests. It recommends SAT I. Application deadline: 1/15; 3/1 priority date for financial aid. Early admission is possible.

Getting in Last Year
8,573 applied
63% were accepted
2,235 enrolled (41%)
58% from top tenth of their h.s. class
3.74 average high school GPA
77% had SAT verbal scores over 600
95% had SAT math scores over 600
23% had SAT verbal scores over 700
50% had SAT math scores over 700

Graduation and After
24% graduated in 4 years
36% graduated in 5 years
9% graduated in 6 years
20% pursued further study
70% had job offers within 6 months
800 organizations recruited on campus

Financial Matters
$4076 resident tuition and fees (2003–04)
$16,002 nonresident tuition and fees (2003–04)
$6264 room and board
67% average percent of need met
$7141 average financial aid amount received per undergraduate (2002–03 estimated)

GEORGIA STATE UNIVERSITY

URBAN SETTING ■ PUBLIC ■ STATE-SUPPORTED ■ COED
ATLANTA, GEORGIA

Web site: www.gsu.edu
Contact: Mr. Rob Sheinkopf, Dean of Admissions and Acting Dean for Enrollment Services, PO Box 4009, Atlanta, GA 30302-4009
Telephone: 404-651-2365 **Fax:** 404-651-4811

Undergraduate education is a strong focus at Georgia State, with small classes and opportunities for students to work with faculty members in a research setting. There are almost 1,000 faculty members in 217 fields of study. Students can live in University housing and participate in more than 100 different student organizations. Georgia State is located in the heart of Atlanta, an exciting metropolis that offers a variety of job and internship opportunities. Students can walk to such places as the State Capitol and CNN Center or take the rapid transit system to explore all that Atlanta has to offer.

Getting in Last Year
9,654 applied
57% were accepted
3,001 enrolled (54%)
3.3 average high school GPA
18% had SAT verbal scores over 600
21% had SAT math scores over 600
25% had ACT scores over 24
2% had SAT verbal scores over 700
2% had SAT math scores over 700
2% had ACT scores over 30

Graduation and After
45% had job offers within 6 months
368 organizations recruited on campus

Financial Matters
$3920 resident tuition and fees (2003–04)
$13,544 nonresident tuition and fees (2003–04)
$4930 room only
20% average percent of need met
$6062 average financial aid amount received per undergraduate (2001–02)

Academics

Georgia State awards bachelor's, master's, doctoral, and first-professional **degrees** and post-master's certificates. Challenging opportunities include accelerated degree programs, student-designed majors, an honors program, double majors, and independent study. Special programs include cooperative education, internships, summer session for credit, off-campus study, and study-abroad.

The most frequently chosen **baccalaureate** fields are business/marketing, social sciences and history, and computer/information sciences. A complete listing of majors at Georgia State appears in the Majors Index beginning on page 460.

The **faculty** at Georgia State has 998 full-time members, 85% with terminal degrees. The student-faculty ratio is 24:1.

Students of Georgia State

The student body totals 27,502, of whom 19,681 are undergraduates. 61.1% are women and 38.9% are men. Students come from 49 states and territories and 96 other countries. 96% are from Georgia. 5.6% are international students. 29.5% are African American, 0.2% American Indian, 9.6% Asian American, and 2.8% Hispanic American. 80% returned for their sophomore year.

Facilities and Resources

Student rooms are linked to a campus network. 500 **computers** are available on campus for student use. The 2 **libraries** have 1,309,321 books and 8,929 subscriptions.

Campus Life

There are 162 active organizations on campus, including a drama/theater group, newspaper, radio station, television station, and choral group. 4% of eligible men and 3% of eligible women are members of national **fraternities**, national **sororities**, local fraternities, and local sororities.

Georgia State is a member of the NCAA (Division I). **Intercollegiate sports** (some offering scholarships) include baseball (m), basketball, cross-country running, golf, soccer (m), softball (w), tennis, track and field, volleyball (w).

Campus Safety

Student safety services include late-night transport/escort service, 24-hour emergency telephone alarm devices, 24-hour patrols by trained security personnel, and electronically operated dormitory entrances.

Applying

Georgia State requires SAT I or ACT and a high school transcript, and in some cases SAT II Subject Tests and an interview. It recommends an essay and a minimum high school GPA of 2.9. Application deadline: 4/1; 4/1 priority date for financial aid. Deferred admission is possible.

GETTYSBURG COLLEGE

SUBURBAN SETTING ■ PRIVATE ■ INDEPENDENT RELIGIOUS ■ COED
GETTYSBURG, PENNSYLVANIA

Web site: www.gettysburg.edu
Contact: Ms. Gail Sweezey, Director of Admissions, 300 North Washington Street, Gettysburg, PA 17325
Telephone: 717-337-6100 or toll-free 800-431-0803 **Fax:** 717-337-6145
E-mail: admiss@gettysburg.edu

Academics

Gettysburg College awards bachelor's **degrees**. Challenging opportunities include advanced placement credit, student-designed majors, double majors, independent study, and a senior project. Special programs include internships, off-campus study, study-abroad, and Army ROTC.

The most frequently chosen **baccalaureate** fields are social sciences and history, business/marketing, and psychology. A complete listing of majors at Gettysburg College appears in the Majors Index beginning on page 460.

The **faculty** at Gettysburg College has 186 full-time members, 92% with terminal degrees. The student-faculty ratio is 11:1.

Students of Gettysburg College

The student body is made up of 2,597 undergraduates. 52.3% are women and 47.7% are men. Students come from 40 states and territories and 32 other countries. 28% are from Pennsylvania. 2.4% are international students. 4% are African American, 1% Asian American, and 1.5% Hispanic American. 91% returned for their sophomore year.

Facilities and Resources

Student rooms are linked to a campus network. The **library** has 351,848 books and 4,778 subscriptions.

Campus Life

There are 100 active organizations on campus, including a drama/theater group, newspaper, radio station, television station, choral group, and marching band. 42% of eligible men and 38% of eligible women are members of national **fraternities** and national **sororities**.

Gettysburg College is a member of the NCAA (Division III). **Intercollegiate sports** include baseball (m), basketball, cheerleading, cross-country running, field hockey (w), football (m), golf, lacrosse, soccer, softball (w), swimming, tennis, track and field, volleyball (w), wrestling (m).

Campus Safety

Student safety services include late-night transport/escort service, 24-hour emergency telephone alarm devices, 24-hour patrols by trained security personnel, and electronically operated dormitory entrances.

Applying

Gettysburg College requires an essay, SAT I or ACT, a high school transcript, and 2 recommendations. It recommends SAT II Subject Tests, an interview, extracurricular activities, and a minimum high school GPA of 3.0. Application deadline: 2/15; 3/15 for financial aid, with a 2/15 priority date. Early and deferred admission are possible.

As the 21st century dawns, higher education faces a new world of change and challenge. Revolutionary advances in technology, unprecedented access to information, a rich diversity of perspectives, and frequent calls to social action demand more from a liberal arts education than ever before. Leading colleges must respond with innovative programs, appropriate resources, and exceptional teaching. Gettysburg College is committed to preparing students for the opportunities of this changing world. Its founding principles embrace a rigorous liberal arts education that fosters a global perspective, a spirit of collaboration, a dedication to public service, and an enriching campus life. Gettysburg believes that this approach to education instills in students a lifelong desire for learning, a drive for discovery and contribution, and a compassionate respect for others and the world.

Getting in Last Year
5,017 applied
46% were accepted
695 enrolled (30%)
62% from top tenth of their h.s. class
66% had SAT verbal scores over 600
72% had SAT math scores over 600
10% had SAT verbal scores over 700
8% had SAT math scores over 700

Graduation and After
70% graduated in 4 years
4% graduated in 5 years
42% pursued further study (15% education, 9% arts and sciences, 7% law)
81% had job offers within 6 months
170 organizations recruited on campus

Financial Matters
$28,674 tuition and fees (2003–04)
$6972 room and board
100% average percent of need met
$24,317 average financial aid amount received per undergraduate

GONZAGA UNIVERSITY

URBAN SETTING ■ PRIVATE ■ INDEPENDENT RELIGIOUS ■ COED
SPOKANE, WASHINGTON

Web site: www.gonzaga.edu
Contact: Ms. Julie McCulloh, Dean of Admission, 502 East Boone Avenue,
Spokane, WA 99258-0102
Telephone: 509-323-6591 or toll-free 800-322-2584 ext. 6572 **Fax:**
509-323-5780
E-mail: admissions@gonzaga.edu

Getting in Last Year

3,713 applied
77% were accepted
908 enrolled (32%)
38% from top tenth of their h.s. class
3.66 average high school GPA
48% had SAT verbal scores over 600
50% had SAT math scores over 600
81% had ACT scores over 24
9% had SAT verbal scores over 700
9% had SAT math scores over 700
20% had ACT scores over 30
10 National Merit Scholars
17 class presidents

Graduation and After

62% graduated in 4 years
10% graduated in 5 years
3% graduated in 6 years
64 organizations recruited on campus

Financial Matters

$20,735 tuition and fees (2003–04)
$5960 room and board
83% average percent of need met
$13,271 average financial aid amount received
per undergraduate (2002–03)

Academics

Gonzaga awards bachelor's, master's, doctoral, and first-professional **degrees** and post-master's certificates. Challenging opportunities include advanced placement credit, student-designed majors, an honors program, double majors, independent study, and a senior project. Special programs include internships, summer session for credit, off-campus study, study-abroad, and Army ROTC.

The most frequently chosen **baccalaureate** fields are business/marketing, social sciences and history, and engineering/engineering technologies. A complete listing of majors at Gonzaga appears in the Majors Index beginning on page 460.

The **faculty** at Gonzaga has 304 full-time members, 87% with terminal degrees. The student-faculty ratio is 12:1.

Students of Gonzaga

The student body totals 5,778, of whom 3,981 are undergraduates. 54.8% are women and 45.2% are men. Students come from 44 states and territories and 33 other countries. 52% are from Washington. 1.3% are international students. 1.1% are African American, 1.2% American Indian, 5.1% Asian American, and 3.3% Hispanic American. 90% returned for their sophomore year.

Facilities and Resources

Student rooms are linked to a campus network. 350 **computers** are available on campus that provide access to the Internet. The 2 **libraries** have 228,622 books and 1,435 subscriptions.

Campus Life

There are 69 active organizations on campus, including a drama/theater group, newspaper, radio station, television station, and choral group. No national or local **fraternities** or **sororities**.

Gonzaga is a member of the NCAA (Division I). **Intercollegiate sports** (some offering scholarships) include baseball (m), basketball, cheerleading, cross-country running, golf, soccer, tennis, track and field, volleyball (w).

Campus Safety

Student safety services include late-night transport/escort service, 24-hour emergency telephone alarm devices, 24-hour patrols by trained security personnel, and electronically operated dormitory entrances.

Applying

Gonzaga requires an essay, SAT I or ACT, a high school transcript, 1 recommendation, and a minimum high school GPA of 3.0. It recommends an interview. Application deadline: 2/1; 2/1 priority date for financial aid. Early and deferred admission are possible.

GORDON COLLEGE

SMALL-TOWN SETTING ■ PRIVATE ■ INDEPENDENT RELIGIOUS ■ COED
WENHAM, MASSACHUSETTS

Web site: www.gordon.edu
Contact: Nancy Mering, Director of Admissions, 255 Grapevine Road,
   Wenham, MA 01984-1899
Telephone: 978-867-4218 or toll-free 800-343-1379 **Fax:** 978-867-4657
E-mail: admissions@hope.gordon.edu

The phrase *Freedom within a framework of faith* is the essence of Gordon College. Gordon is a nationally recognized private college with a select faculty and Christian emphasis that prepares students for the 21st century. Students who are ready to grow are ready for Gordon.

Academics

Gordon awards bachelor's and master's **degrees**. Challenging opportunities include advanced placement credit, student-designed majors, an honors program, double majors, independent study, and a senior project. Special programs include cooperative education, internships, off-campus study, study-abroad, and Army and Air Force ROTC.

The most frequently chosen **baccalaureate** fields are English, social sciences and history, and business/marketing. A complete listing of majors at Gordon appears in the Majors Index beginning on page 460.

The **faculty** at Gordon has 93 full-time members, 76% with terminal degrees. The student-faculty ratio is 14:1.

Students of Gordon

The student body totals 1,683, of whom 1,640 are undergraduates. 64.6% are women and 35.4% are men. Students come from 46 states and territories and 25 other countries. 28% are from Massachusetts. 2% are international students. 1.3% are African American, 0.2% American Indian, 2.1% Asian American, and 1.5% Hispanic American. 87% returned for their sophomore year.

Facilities and Resources

Student rooms are linked to a campus network. 141 **computers** are available on campus that provide access to the Internet. The **library** has 142,688 books and 8,555 subscriptions.

Campus Life

There are 35 active organizations on campus, including a drama/theater group, newspaper, and choral group. No national or local **fraternities** or **sororities**.

Gordon is a member of the NCAA (Division III). **Intercollegiate sports** include baseball (m), basketball, cheerleading, cross-country running, field hockey (w), lacrosse, soccer, softball (w), swimming, tennis, volleyball (w).

Campus Safety

Student safety services include late-night transport/escort service, 24-hour emergency telephone alarm devices, 24-hour patrols by trained security personnel, and electronically operated dormitory entrances.

Applying

Gordon requires an essay, SAT I or ACT, a high school transcript, an interview, 2 recommendations, and pastoral recommendation, statement of Christian faith. It recommends a minimum high school GPA of 3.0. Application deadline: rolling admissions; 3/1 priority date for financial aid. Early and deferred admission are possible.

Getting in Last Year
1,080 applied
78% were accepted
427 enrolled (51%)
31% from top tenth of their h.s. class
3.62 average high school GPA
62% had SAT verbal scores over 600
60% had SAT math scores over 600
15% had SAT verbal scores over 700
10% had SAT math scores over 700
17 National Merit Scholars

Graduation and After
55% graduated in 4 years
11% graduated in 5 years
1% graduated in 6 years
20% pursued further study
73 organizations recruited on campus

Financial Matters
$20,234 tuition and fees (2003–04)
$5748 room and board
75% average percent of need met
$14,375 average financial aid amount received
   per undergraduate

GOSHEN COLLEGE

SMALL-TOWN SETTING ■ PRIVATE ■ INDEPENDENT RELIGIOUS ■ COED
GOSHEN, INDIANA

Web site: www.goshen.edu
Contact: Ms. Karen Lowe Raftus, Director of Admission, 1700 South Main
  Street, Goshen, IN 46526-4794
Telephone: 574-535-7535 or toll-free 800-348-7422 **Fax:** 574-535-7609
E-mail: admissions@goshen.edu

Getting in Last Year
608 applied
61% were accepted
182 enrolled (49%)
34% from top tenth of their h.s. class
3.25 average high school GPA
49% had SAT verbal scores over 600
44% had SAT math scores over 600
64% had ACT scores over 24
18% had SAT verbal scores over 700
10% had SAT math scores over 700
23% had ACT scores over 30
9 National Merit Scholars
6 valedictorians

Graduation and After
43% graduated in 4 years
18% graduated in 5 years
1% graduated in 6 years
**40% pursued further study (15% arts and
  sciences, 11% medicine, 5% business)**
40 organizations recruited on campus

Financial Matters
$16,650 tuition and fees (2003–04)
$5800 room and board
88% average percent of need met
**$13,629 average financial aid amount received
  per undergraduate (2002–03 estimated)**

Academics

Goshen awards bachelor's **degrees**. Challenging opportunities include advanced placement credit, accelerated degree programs, student-designed majors, freshman honors
college, an honors program, double majors, independent study, and a senior project.
Special programs include cooperative education, internships, summer session for credit,
off-campus study, and study-abroad.

The most frequently chosen **baccalaureate** fields are business/marketing, education,
and health professions and related sciences. A complete listing of majors at Goshen appears in the Majors Index beginning on page 460.

The **faculty** at Goshen has 69 full-time members, 58% with terminal degrees. The
student-faculty ratio is 10:1.

Students of Goshen

The student body is made up of 920 undergraduates. 61.7% are women and 38.3% are
men. Students come from 36 states and territories and 30 other countries. 57% are from
Indiana. 8.7% are international students. 3.5% are African American, 0.2% American
Indian, 1.1% Asian American, and 3.7% Hispanic American. 77% returned for their
sophomore year.

Facilities and Resources

Student rooms are linked to a campus network. 160 **computers** are available on campus
that provide access to online services and the Internet. The 3 **libraries** have 127,028
books and 750 subscriptions.

Campus Life

There are 26 active organizations on campus, including a drama/theater group,
newspaper, radio station, television station, and choral group. No national or local
fraternities or **sororities.**

Goshen is a member of the NAIA. **Intercollegiate sports** (some offering scholarships) include baseball (m), basketball, cross-country running, golf (m), soccer, softball
(w), tennis, track and field, volleyball (w).

Campus Safety

Student safety services include late-night transport/escort service, 24-hour emergency
telephone alarm devices, and 24-hour patrols by trained security personnel.

Applying

Goshen requires an essay, SAT I or ACT, a high school transcript, 2 recommendations,
rank in upper 50% of high school class, minimum SAT score of 1000, ACT score of 22,
and a minimum high school GPA of 2.5. It recommends an interview. Application
deadline: 8/15; 2/15 priority date for financial aid. Early and deferred admission are possible.

Goucher College

Suburban setting ■ Private ■ Independent ■ Coed
Baltimore, Maryland

Web site: www.goucher.edu
Contact: Mr. Carlton E. Surbeck III, Director of Admissions, 1021 Dulaney
Valley Road, Baltimore, MD 21204-2794
Telephone: 410-337-6100 or toll-free 800-468-2437 **Fax:** 410-337-6354
E-mail: admission@goucher.edu

Academics
Goucher awards bachelor's and master's **degrees** and post-bachelor's certificates. Challenging opportunities include advanced placement credit, student-designed majors, an honors program, double majors, independent study, and a senior project. Special programs include internships, off-campus study, and study-abroad.

The most frequently chosen **baccalaureate** fields are social sciences and history, psychology, and visual/performing arts. A complete listing of majors at Goucher appears in the Majors Index beginning on page 460.

The **faculty** at Goucher has 98 full-time members, 90% with terminal degrees. The student-faculty ratio is 10:1.

Students of Goucher
The student body totals 2,311, of whom 1,310 are undergraduates. 68.1% are women and 31.9% are men. 37% are from Maryland. 0.9% are international students. 5.5% are African American, 0.2% American Indian, 3.1% Asian American, and 2.6% Hispanic American. 80% returned for their sophomore year.

Facilities and Resources
Student rooms are linked to a campus network. 150 **computers** are available on campus that provide access to the Internet. The **library** has 303,364 books and 1,098 subscriptions.

Campus Life
There are 38 active organizations on campus, including a drama/theater group, newspaper, radio station, television station, and choral group. No national or local **fraternities** or **sororities**.

Goucher is a member of the NCAA (Division III). **Intercollegiate sports** include basketball, cross-country running, equestrian sports, field hockey (w), lacrosse, soccer, swimming, tennis, volleyball (w).

Campus Safety
Student safety services include late-night transport/escort service, 24-hour emergency telephone alarm devices, 24-hour patrols by trained security personnel, and electronically operated dormitory entrances.

Applying
Goucher requires an essay, SAT I or ACT, a high school transcript, 3 recommendations, and a minimum high school GPA of 2.0. It recommends SAT II Subject Tests, SAT II: Writing Test, an interview, and a minimum high school GPA of 3.0. Application deadline: 2/1; 2/15 priority date for financial aid. Early and deferred admission are possible.

Goucher College is a small, private, coeducational liberal arts and sciences college in Baltimore, Maryland, with an international emphasis and an academic program that partners classroom learning with real, hands-on experience. Since it was founded in 1885, Goucher has provided a truly global kind of education that puts learning in perspective against the events and developments of the entire world, encouraging students to test what they've learned against experience in service-learning, study abroad, and internship programs around the nation and around the globe. Goucher is a small college with a big view of the world—an educational community without boundaries.

Getting in Last Year
2,751 applied
65% were accepted
342 enrolled (19%)
27% from top tenth of their h.s. class
3.23 average high school GPA
61% had SAT verbal scores over 600
51% had SAT math scores over 600
81% had ACT scores over 24
14% had SAT verbal scores over 700
8% had SAT math scores over 700
22% had ACT scores over 30

Graduation and After
63% graduated in 4 years
5% graduated in 5 years
1% graduated in 6 years
84% had job offers within 6 months
17 organizations recruited on campus

Financial Matters
$24,450 tuition and fees (2003–04)
$8350 room and board
72% average percent of need met
$18,813 average financial aid amount received per undergraduate (2002–03)

GRINNELL COLLEGE

SMALL-TOWN SETTING ■ PRIVATE ■ INDEPENDENT ■ COED
GRINNELL, IOWA

Web site: www.grinnell.edu
Contact: Mr. James Sumner, Dean for Admission and Financial Aid, 1103 Park Street, Grinnell, IA 50112
Telephone: 641-269-3600 or toll-free 800-247-0113 **Fax:** 641-269-4800
E-mail: askgrin@grinnell.edu

Academics
Grinnell College awards bachelor's **degrees**. Challenging opportunities include advanced placement credit, accelerated degree programs, student-designed majors, double majors, and independent study. Special programs include internships, off-campus study, and study-abroad.

The most frequently chosen **baccalaureate** fields are social sciences and history, biological/life sciences, and foreign language/literature. A complete listing of majors at Grinnell College appears in the Majors Index beginning on page 460.

The **faculty** at Grinnell College has 139 full-time members, 98% with terminal degrees. The student-faculty ratio is 10:1.

Students of Grinnell College
The student body is made up of 1,524 undergraduates. 55% are women and 45% are men. Students come from 52 states and territories and 52 other countries. 13% are from Iowa. 10.3% are international students. 3.8% are African American, 0.9% American Indian, 4.6% Asian American, and 3.8% Hispanic American. 92% returned for their sophomore year.

Facilities and Resources
Student rooms are linked to a campus network. 208 **computers** are available on campus that provide access to e-mail and the Internet. The 3 **libraries** have 1,020,921 books and 3,470 subscriptions.

Campus Life
There are 168 active organizations on campus, including a drama/theater group, newspaper, radio station, and choral group. No national or local **fraternities** or **sororities**.

Grinnell College is a member of the NCAA (Division III). **Intercollegiate sports** include baseball (m), basketball, cross-country running, football (m), golf, soccer, softball (w), swimming, tennis, track and field, volleyball (w).

Campus Safety
Student safety services include late-night transport/escort service, 24-hour emergency telephone alarm devices, 24-hour patrols by trained security personnel, student patrols, and electronically operated dormitory entrances.

Applying
Grinnell College requires an essay, SAT I or ACT, a high school transcript, and 3 recommendations. It recommends an interview. Application deadline: 1/20; 2/1 for financial aid. Early and deferred admission are possible.

GROVE CITY COLLEGE

SMALL-TOWN SETTING ■ PRIVATE ■ INDEPENDENT RELIGIOUS ■ COED
GROVE CITY, PENNSYLVANIA

Web site: www.gcc.edu
Contact: Mr. Jeffrey C. Mincey, Director of Admissions, 100 Campus Drive,
Grove City, PA 16127-2104
Telephone: 724-458-2100 **Fax:** 724-458-3395
E-mail: admissions@gcc.edu

Academics

Grove City awards bachelor's **degrees**. Challenging opportunities include advanced
placement credit, student-designed majors, double majors, independent study, and a
senior project. Special programs include internships, summer session for credit, study-
abroad, and Army ROTC.

The most frequently chosen **baccalaureate** fields are business/marketing, biological/
life sciences, and education. A complete listing of majors at Grove City appears in the
Majors Index beginning on page 460.

The **faculty** at Grove City has 125 full-time members, 77% with terminal degrees.
The student-faculty ratio is 18:1.

Students of Grove City

The student body is made up of 2,314 undergraduates. 50.3% are women and 49.7% are
men. Students come from 44 states and territories and 13 other countries. 53% are from
Pennsylvania. 0.8% are international students. 0.2% are African American, 0.1%
American Indian, 1.3% Asian American, and 0.3% Hispanic American. 88% returned for
their sophomore year.

Facilities and Resources

Student rooms are linked to a campus network. 50 **computers** are available on campus
that provide access to the Internet. The **library** has 139,000 books and 550 subscriptions.

Campus Life

There are 123 active organizations on campus, including a drama/theater group,
newspaper, radio station, choral group, and marching band. 13% of eligible men and
16% of eligible women are members of local **fraternities** and local **sororities**.

Grove City is a member of the NCAA (Division III). **Intercollegiate sports** include
baseball (m), basketball, cheerleading (w), cross-country running, football (m), golf, soccer, softball (w), swimming, tennis, track and field, volleyball (w), water polo.

Campus Safety

Student safety services include monitored women's residence hall entrances, late-night
transport/escort service, 24-hour emergency telephone alarm devices, 24-hour patrols by
trained security personnel, student patrols, and electronically operated dormitory
entrances.

Applying

Grove City requires an essay, SAT I or ACT, a high school transcript, and 2 recommendations. It recommends an interview. Application deadline: 2/1; 4/15 for financial
aid. Early and deferred admission are possible.

> **G**rove City has professors
> who like to teach,
> students who welcome
> the idea of being stretched
> intellectually, and a spiritual vitality
> that drifts far beyond the Chapel
> walls, permeating classrooms and
> dorm life. Also, the annual cost
> including tuition, room and board,
> and a laptop computer and printer
> are less than $14,300.

Getting in Last Year

2,199 applied
41% were accepted
567 enrolled (63%)
62% from top tenth of their h.s. class
3.73 average high school GPA
72% had SAT verbal scores over 600
72% had SAT math scores over 600
88% had ACT scores over 24
18% had SAT verbal scores over 700
21% had SAT math scores over 700
32% had ACT scores over 30
18 National Merit Scholars
2 class presidents
66 valedictorians

Graduation and After

78% graduated in 4 years
8% graduated in 5 years
18% pursued further study (11% arts and
sciences, 2% education, 2% medicine)
83% had job offers within 6 months
147 organizations recruited on campus

Financial Matters

$9526 tuition and fees (2003–04)
$4852 room and board
58% average percent of need met
$4385 average financial aid amount received
per undergraduate

GUSTAVUS ADOLPHUS COLLEGE

SMALL-TOWN SETTING ■ PRIVATE ■ INDEPENDENT RELIGIOUS ■ COED
ST. PETER, MINNESOTA

Web site: www.gustavus.edu
Contact: Mr. Mark H. Anderson, Dean of Admission, 800 West College Avenue, St. Peter, MN 56082-1498
Telephone: 507-933-7676 or toll-free 800-GUSTAVU(S) **Fax:** 507-933-7474
E-mail: admission@gac.edu

Getting in Last Year
2,317 applied
77% were accepted
688 enrolled (38%)
38% from top tenth of their h.s. class
3.63 average high school GPA
58% had SAT verbal scores over 600
63% had SAT math scores over 600
71% had ACT scores over 24
17% had SAT verbal scores over 700
14% had SAT math scores over 700
14% had ACT scores over 30
12 National Merit Scholars
57 valedictorians

Graduation and After
78% graduated in 4 years
3% graduated in 5 years
36% pursued further study (13% arts and sciences, 7% business, 5% law)
92% had job offers within 6 months

Financial Matters
$21,660 tuition and fees (2003–04)
$5460 room and board
88% average percent of need met
$14,765 average financial aid amount received per undergraduate (2002–03)

Academics
Gustavus awards bachelor's **degrees**. Challenging opportunities include advanced placement credit, accelerated degree programs, student-designed majors, an honors program, double majors, independent study, and a senior project. Special programs include cooperative education, internships, summer session for credit, off-campus study, study-abroad, and Army ROTC.

The most frequently chosen **baccalaureate** fields are social sciences and history, business/marketing, and biological/life sciences. A complete listing of majors at Gustavus appears in the Majors Index beginning on page 460.

The **faculty** at Gustavus has 178 full-time members, 87% with terminal degrees. The student-faculty ratio is 13:1.

Students of Gustavus
The student body is made up of 2,574 undergraduates. 57.3% are women and 42.7% are men. Students come from 38 states and territories and 18 other countries. 81% are from Minnesota. 1.2% are international students. 0.8% are African American, 0.3% American Indian, 4% Asian American, and 1.2% Hispanic American. 89% returned for their sophomore year.

Facilities and Resources
Student rooms are linked to a campus network. 441 **computers** are available on campus that provide access to the Internet. The 3 **libraries** have 287,761 books and 1,001 subscriptions.

Campus Life
There are 110 active organizations on campus, including a drama/theater group, newspaper, radio station, and choral group. 20% of eligible men and 17% of eligible women are members of local **fraternities** and local **sororities**.

Gustavus is a member of the NCAA (Division III). **Intercollegiate sports** include baseball (m), basketball, cross-country running, football (m), golf, gymnastics (w), ice hockey, skiing (cross-country), soccer, softball (w), swimming, tennis, track and field, volleyball (w).

Campus Safety
Student safety services include late-night transport/escort service, 24-hour emergency telephone alarm devices, 24-hour patrols by trained security personnel, and electronically operated dormitory entrances.

Applying
Gustavus requires an essay, SAT I or ACT, a high school transcript, and 2 recommendations. It recommends an interview. Application deadline: 4/1; 2/15 priority date for financial aid. Early and deferred admission are possible.

Hamilton College

SMALL-TOWN SETTING ■ PRIVATE ■ INDEPENDENT ■ COED
CLINTON, NEW YORK

Web site: www.hamilton.edu
Contact: Ms. Lora Schilder, Dean of Admission and Financial Aid, 198 College Hill Road, Clinton, NY 13323
Telephone: 315-859-4421 or toll-free 800-843-2655 **Fax:** 315-859-4457
E-mail: admission@hamilton.edu

Academics

Hamilton awards bachelor's **degrees**. Challenging opportunities include advanced placement credit, accelerated degree programs, student-designed majors, double majors, independent study, and a senior project. Special programs include internships, off-campus study, study-abroad, and Army and Air Force ROTC.

The most frequently chosen **baccalaureate** fields are social sciences and history, visual/performing arts, and English. A complete listing of majors at Hamilton appears in the Majors Index beginning on page 460.

The **faculty** at Hamilton has 183 full-time members, 91% with terminal degrees. The student-faculty ratio is 9:1.

Students of Hamilton

The student body is made up of 1,797 undergraduates. 51.1% are women and 48.9% are men. Students come from 41 states and territories and 40 other countries. 37% are from New York. 4.7% are international students. 4.3% are African American, 0.4% American Indian, 5% Asian American, and 3.4% Hispanic American. 94% returned for their sophomore year.

Facilities and Resources

Student rooms are linked to a campus network. 475 **computers** are available on campus that provide access to the Internet. The 4 **libraries** have 538,377 books and 3,585 subscriptions.

Campus Life

There are 80 active organizations on campus, including a drama/theater group, newspaper, radio station, and choral group. 34% of eligible men and 20% of eligible women are members of national **fraternities** and local **sororities**.

Hamilton is a member of the NCAA (Division III). **Intercollegiate sports** include baseball (m), basketball, crew (w), cross-country running, field hockey (w), football (m), golf (m), ice hockey, lacrosse, soccer, softball (w), squash, swimming, tennis, track and field, volleyball (w).

Campus Safety

Student safety services include student safety program, late-night transport/escort service, 24-hour emergency telephone alarm devices, 24-hour patrols by trained security personnel, and electronically operated dormitory entrances.

Applying

Hamilton requires an essay, SAT I, SAT II or ACT, a high school transcript, 1 recommendation, and sample of expository prose. It recommends an interview. Application deadline: 1/1; 2/1 priority date for financial aid. Early and deferred admission are possible.

> **H**amilton is a highly selective, residential liberal arts college with an emphasis on individualized instruction and independent research. Renowned for its strong sense of community, internationally recognized faculty members, and its beautiful campus in the foothills of the Adirondack Mountains, Hamilton is a national leader in teaching effective writing and persuasive speaking.

Getting in Last Year
4,405 applied
33% were accepted
467 enrolled (32%)
68% from top tenth of their h.s. class
80% had SAT verbal scores over 600
88% had SAT math scores over 600
30% had SAT verbal scores over 700
28% had SAT math scores over 700
5 National Merit Scholars
12 valedictorians

Graduation and After
83% graduated in 4 years
4% graduated in 5 years
20% pursued further study (6% arts and sciences, 3% education, 3% law)
40 organizations recruited on campus

Financial Matters
$30,200 tuition and fees (2003–04)
$7360 room and board
99% average percent of need met
$22,980 average financial aid amount received per undergraduate

HAMLINE UNIVERSITY

URBAN SETTING ■ PRIVATE ■ INDEPENDENT RELIGIOUS ■ COED
ST. PAUL, MINNESOTA

Web site: www.hamline.edu
Contact: Mr. Steven Bjork, Director of Undergraduate Admission, 1536
Hewitt Avenue C1930, St. Paul, MN 55104-1284
Telephone: 651-523-2207 or toll-free 800-753-9753 **Fax:** 651-523-2458
E-mail: cla-admis@gw.hamline.edu

Getting in Last Year

1,815 applied
75% were accepted
455 enrolled (34%)
29% from top tenth of their h.s. class
3.51 average high school GPA
53% had SAT verbal scores over 600
42% had SAT math scores over 600
54% had ACT scores over 24
14% had SAT verbal scores over 700
8% had SAT math scores over 700
10% had ACT scores over 30
6 National Merit Scholars
14 valedictorians

Graduation and After

60% graduated in 4 years
7% graduated in 5 years
2% graduated in 6 years
25% pursued further study (9% arts and sciences, 3% education, 3% law)
81% had job offers within 6 months
24 organizations recruited on campus

Financial Matters

$20,832 tuition and fees (2003–04)
$6220 room and board
68% average percent of need met
$16,865 average financial aid amount received per undergraduate (2002–03 estimated)

Academics

Hamline awards bachelor's, master's, doctoral, and first-professional **degrees** and post-bachelor's, post-master's, and first-professional certificates. Challenging opportunities include advanced placement credit, student-designed majors, an honors program, double majors, independent study, and a senior project. Special programs include cooperative education, internships, summer session for credit, off-campus study, study-abroad, and Air Force ROTC.

The most frequently chosen **baccalaureate** fields are social sciences and history, business/marketing, and psychology. A complete listing of majors at Hamline appears in the Majors Index beginning on page 460.

The **faculty** at Hamline has 176 full-time members, 91% with terminal degrees. The student-faculty ratio is 13:1.

Students of Hamline

The student body totals 4,469, of whom 1,980 are undergraduates. 62.7% are women and 37.3% are men. Students come from 27 states and territories and 21 other countries. 29% are from Minnesota. 3.4% are international students. 3.9% are African American, 0.8% American Indian, 5.8% Asian American, and 2.2% Hispanic American. 84% returned for their sophomore year.

Facilities and Resources

Student rooms are linked to a campus network. The 2 **libraries** have 556,450 books and 3,858 subscriptions.

Campus Life

There are 85 active organizations on campus, including a drama/theater group, newspaper, radio station, and choral group. 5% of eligible women are members of local **sororities** and international dining club.

Hamline is a member of the NCAA (Division III). **Intercollegiate sports** include baseball (m), basketball, cheerleading, cross-country running, football (m), gymnastics (w), ice hockey (m), soccer, softball (w), swimming, tennis, track and field, volleyball (w).

Campus Safety

Student safety services include late-night transport/escort service, 24-hour emergency telephone alarm devices, 24-hour patrols by trained security personnel, student patrols, and electronically operated dormitory entrances.

Applying

Hamline requires an essay, SAT I or ACT, a high school transcript, and 2 recommendations. It recommends an interview and activity resume. Application deadline: rolling admissions; 5/1 priority date for financial aid. Early and deferred admission are possible.

HAMPSHIRE COLLEGE

RURAL SETTING ■ PRIVATE ■ INDEPENDENT ■ COED
AMHERST, MASSACHUSETTS

Web site: www.hampshire.edu
Contact: Ms. Karen S. Parker, Director of Admissions, 893 West Street, Amherst, MA 01002
Telephone: 413-559-5471 or toll-free 877-937-4267 (out-of-state) **Fax:** 413-559-5631
E-mail: admissions@hampshire.edu

Academics

Hampshire awards bachelor's **degrees**. Challenging opportunities include advanced placement credit, accelerated degree programs, student-designed majors, double majors, independent study, and a senior project. Special programs include internships, off-campus study, study-abroad, and Army ROTC.

The most frequently chosen **baccalaureate** fields are visual/performing arts, English, and social sciences and history. A complete listing of majors at Hampshire appears in the Majors Index beginning on page 460.

The **faculty** at Hampshire has 114 full-time members, 91% with terminal degrees. The student-faculty ratio is 11:1.

Students of Hampshire

The student body is made up of 1,332 undergraduates. 58.1% are women and 41.9% are men. Students come from 46 states and territories and 25 other countries. 14% are from Massachusetts. 3.2% are international students. 2.9% are African American, 0.8% American Indian, 4.2% Asian American, and 5% Hispanic American. 79% returned for their sophomore year.

Facilities and Resources

Student rooms are linked to a campus network. 125 **computers** are available on campus for student use. The **library** has 124,710 books and 731 subscriptions.

Campus Life

There are 80 active organizations on campus, including a drama/theater group, newspaper, radio station, television station, and choral group. No national or local **fraternities** or **sororities**.

This institution has no intercollegiate sports.

Campus Safety

Student safety services include late-night transport/escort service, 24-hour emergency telephone alarm devices, 24-hour patrols by trained security personnel, and student patrols.

Applying

Hampshire requires an essay, a high school transcript, and 2 recommendations. It recommends an interview. Application deadline: 2/1; 2/1 priority date for financial aid. Early and deferred admission are possible.

> **H**ampshire College's bold, innovative approach to the liberal arts creates an academic atmosphere that energizes students to work hard and grow tremendously, both personally and intellectually. Students have the freedom to design an individualized course of study in a graduate school–like environment, culminating in original final projects such as science or social science research, academic study, or a body of work in writing, performing, visual, or media arts. Students work closely with faculty mentors, often integrating different disciplines. Independent thinking is expected. Hampshire students and faculty members agree: if you incorporate what you love into your education, you will love your education.

Getting in Last Year
2,270 applied
55% were accepted
383 enrolled (31%)
30% from top tenth of their h.s. class
3.47 average high school GPA
78% had SAT verbal scores over 600
56% had SAT math scores over 600
83% had ACT scores over 24
28% had SAT verbal scores over 700
11% had SAT math scores over 700
23% had ACT scores over 30
7 National Merit Scholars

Graduation and After
44% graduated in 4 years
13% graduated in 5 years
6% graduated in 6 years

Financial Matters
$29,392 tuition and fees (2003–04)
$7689 room and board
100% average percent of need met
$27,015 average financial aid amount received per undergraduate (2002–03 estimated)

HANOVER COLLEGE

RURAL SETTING ■ PRIVATE ■ INDEPENDENT RELIGIOUS ■ COED
HANOVER, INDIANA

Getting in Last Year
1,364 applied
79% were accepted
292 enrolled (27%)
42% from top tenth of their h.s. class
39% had SAT verbal scores over 600
43% had SAT math scores over 600
64% had ACT scores over 24
6% had SAT verbal scores over 700
8% had SAT math scores over 700
8% had ACT scores over 30
14 valedictorians

Graduation and After
65% graduated in 4 years
2% graduated in 5 years
27% pursued further study (7% arts and sciences, 7% law, 3% medicine)
30 organizations recruited on campus

Financial Matters
$14,700 tuition and fees (2003–04)
$5900 room and board
91% average percent of need met
$12,050 average financial aid amount received per undergraduate (2002–03 estimated)

Web site: www.hanover.edu
Contact: Mr. Kenneth Moyer, Dean of Admission, PO Box 108, Hanover, IN 47243-0108
Telephone: 812-866-7021 or toll-free 800-213-2178 **Fax:** 812-866-7098
E-mail: admission@hanover.edu

Academics
Hanover awards bachelor's **degrees**. Challenging opportunities include advanced placement credit, accelerated degree programs, double majors, independent study, and a senior project. Special programs include internships, off-campus study, and study-abroad.

The most frequently chosen **baccalaureate** fields are social sciences and history, education, and business/marketing. A complete listing of majors at Hanover appears in the Majors Index beginning on page 460.

The **faculty** at Hanover has 85 full-time members, 99% with terminal degrees. The student-faculty ratio is 10:1.

Students of Hanover
The student body is made up of 997 undergraduates. 53.8% are women and 46.2% are men. Students come from 35 states and territories and 15 other countries. 71% are from Indiana. 3.5% are international students. 1.7% are African American, 0.2% American Indian, 2.7% Asian American, and 1.7% Hispanic American. 75% returned for their sophomore year.

Facilities and Resources
Student rooms are linked to a campus network. 90 **computers** are available on campus that provide access to the Internet. The **library** has 224,478 books and 1,035 subscriptions.

Campus Life
There are 41 active organizations on campus, including a drama/theater group, newspaper, television station, and choral group. 37% of eligible men and 44% of eligible women are members of national **fraternities** and national **sororities**.

Hanover is a member of the NCAA (Division III). **Intercollegiate sports** include baseball (m), basketball, cross-country running, field hockey (w), football (m), golf, soccer, softball (w), tennis, track and field, volleyball (w).

Campus Safety
Student safety services include late-night transport/escort service, 24-hour emergency telephone alarm devices, 24-hour patrols by trained security personnel, and electronically operated dormitory entrances.

Applying
Hanover requires an essay, SAT I or ACT, a high school transcript, and 1 recommendation. It recommends an interview. Application deadline: 3/1; 3/10 priority date for financial aid. Early and deferred admission are possible.

HARDING UNIVERSITY

SMALL-TOWN SETTING ■ PRIVATE ■ INDEPENDENT RELIGIOUS ■ COED
SEARCY, ARKANSAS

Web site: www.harding.edu
Contact: Mr. Glenn Dillard, Director of Enrollment Management, Box
  11255, Searcy, AR 72149-0001
Telephone: 501-279-4407 or toll-free 800-477-4407 **Fax:** 501-279-4865
E-mail: admissions@harding.edu

Academics

Harding awards bachelor's and master's **degrees**. Challenging opportunities include advanced placement credit, accelerated degree programs, student-designed majors, freshman honors college, an honors program, double majors, and a senior project. Special programs include cooperative education, internships, summer session for credit, study-abroad, and Army ROTC.

The most frequently chosen **baccalaureate** fields are business/marketing, education, and health professions and related sciences. A complete listing of majors at Harding appears in the Majors Index beginning on page 460.

The **faculty** at Harding has 204 full-time members, 66% with terminal degrees. The student-faculty ratio is 19:1.

Students of Harding

The student body totals 5,110, of whom 4,036 are undergraduates. 54.5% are women and 45.5% are men. Students come from 50 states and territories and 41 other countries. 29% are from Arkansas. 3.7% are international students. 3.9% are African American, 0.5% American Indian, 0.7% Asian American, and 1.3% Hispanic American. 78% returned for their sophomore year.

Facilities and Resources

Student rooms are linked to a campus network. 192 **computers** are available on campus that provide access to the Internet. The 2 **libraries** have 321,928 books and 1,368 subscriptions.

Campus Life

There are 52 active organizations on campus, including a drama/theater group, newspaper, radio station, television station, choral group, and marching band. 50% of eligible men and 39% of eligible women are members of local **fraternities** and local **sororities**.

Harding is a member of the NCAA (Division II). **Intercollegiate sports** (some offering scholarships) include baseball (m), basketball, cheerleading, cross-country running, football (m), golf (m), soccer, tennis, track and field, ultimate Frisbee, volleyball (w).

Campus Safety

Student safety services include 24-hour emergency telephone alarm devices and 24-hour patrols by trained security personnel.

Applying

Harding requires SAT I or ACT, a high school transcript, an interview, and 2 recommendations. Application deadline: 7/1. Early and deferred admission are possible.

L ocated in the beautiful foothills of the Ozark Mountains, Harding is one of America's more highly regarded private universities. At Harding, students build lifetime friendships and, upon graduation, are highly recruited. Harding's Christian environment and challenging academic program develop students who can compete and succeed. Whether on the main campus or in the international studies program in Chile, Italy, Greece, England, or Australia, students find Harding to be a caring and serving family. From Missouri flood relief to working with orphans in Haiti or farmers in Kenya, hundreds of Harding students serve others worldwide each year.

Getting in Last Year
1,750 applied
58% were accepted
971 enrolled (95%)
23% from top tenth of their h.s. class
3.34 average high school GPA
30% had SAT verbal scores over 600
31% had SAT math scores over 600
47% had ACT scores over 24
6% had SAT verbal scores over 700
6% had SAT math scores over 700
12% had ACT scores over 30
13 National Merit Scholars
50 valedictorians

Graduation and After
30% graduated in 4 years
26% graduated in 5 years
8% graduated in 6 years
25% pursued further study (9% education, 6% arts and sciences, 3% business)
90% had job offers within 6 months
216 organizations recruited on campus

Financial Matters
$10,120 tuition and fees (2003–04)
$4770 room and board
64% average percent of need met
$8673 average financial aid amount received per undergraduate (2002–03 estimated)

HARVARD UNIVERSITY

URBAN SETTING ■ PRIVATE ■ INDEPENDENT ■ COED
CAMBRIDGE, MASSACHUSETTS

Web site: www.harvard.edu
Contact: Office of Admissions and Financial Aid, Byerly Hall, 8 Garden
    Street, Cambridge, MA 02138
Telephone: 617-495-1551
E-mail: college@harvard.edu

Getting in Last Year
20,987 applied
10% were accepted
1,635 enrolled (78%)
90% from top tenth of their h.s. class

Graduation and After
86% graduated in 4 years
9% graduated in 5 years
2% graduated in 6 years

Financial Matters
$29,060 tuition and fees (2003–04)
$8868 room and board
100% average percent of need met
$25,299 average financial aid amount received
    per undergraduate (2002–03)

Academics
Harvard awards bachelor's, master's, doctoral, and first-professional **degrees**. Challenging opportunities include advanced placement credit, accelerated degree programs, student-designed majors, an honors program, double majors, independent study, and a senior project. Special programs include internships, summer session for credit, off-campus study, study-abroad, and Army and Air Force ROTC. A complete listing of majors at Harvard appears in the Majors Index beginning on page 460.

The **faculty** at Harvard has 760 members, 100% with terminal degrees. The student-faculty ratio is 8:1.

Students of Harvard
The student body totals 20,130, of whom 6,635 are undergraduates. 47.2% are women and 52.8% are men. Students come from 53 states and territories and 82 other countries. 7% are international students. 8% are African American, 0.7% American Indian, 17.5% Asian American, and 7.7% Hispanic American. 97% returned for their sophomore year.

Facilities and Resources
Student rooms are linked to a campus network. The 91 **libraries** have 14,000,000 books and 97,568 subscriptions.

Campus Life
There are 250 active organizations on campus, including a drama/theater group, newspaper, radio station, television station, choral group, and marching band. 99% of eligible men and 99% of eligible women are members of "House" system.

Harvard is a member of the NCAA (Division I). **Intercollegiate sports** include baseball (m), basketball, crew, cross-country running, fencing, field hockey (w), football (m), golf, ice hockey, lacrosse, sailing, skiing (cross-country), skiing (downhill), soccer, softball (w), squash, swimming, tennis, track and field, volleyball, water polo, wrestling (m).

Campus Safety
Student safety services include required and optional safety courses, late-night transport/escort service, 24-hour emergency telephone alarm devices, 24-hour patrols by trained security personnel, and electronically operated dormitory entrances.

Applying
Harvard requires an essay, SAT II Subject Tests, SAT I or ACT, a high school transcript, an interview, and 2 recommendations. Application deadline: 1/1; 2/1 priority date for financial aid. Deferred admission is possible.

HARVEY MUDD COLLEGE

SUBURBAN SETTING ■ PRIVATE ■ INDEPENDENT ■ COED
CLAREMONT, CALIFORNIA

Web site: www.hmc.edu
Contact: Mr. Deren Finks, Vice President and Dean of Admissions and
Financial Aid, 301 East 12th Street, Claremont, CA 91711
Telephone: 909-621-8011 **Fax:** 909-607-7046
E-mail: admission@hmc.edu

Academics

Harvey Mudd awards bachelor's and master's **degrees**. Challenging opportunities
include advanced placement credit, student-designed majors, double majors, and a senior
project. Special programs include internships, off-campus study, study-abroad, and Army
and Air Force ROTC.

The most frequently chosen **baccalaureate** fields are engineering/engineering
technologies, computer/information sciences, and mathematics. A complete listing of
majors at Harvey Mudd appears in the Majors Index beginning on page 460.

The **faculty** at Harvey Mudd has 83 full-time members, 100% with terminal degrees.
The student-faculty ratio is 9:1.

Students of Harvey Mudd

The student body is made up of 704 undergraduates. 32.4% are women and 67.6% are
men. Students come from 47 states and territories and 14 other countries. 43% are from
California. 3% are international students. 0.4% are African American, 0.4% American
Indian, 18.5% Asian American, and 5.1% Hispanic American. 95% returned for their
sophomore year.

Facilities and Resources

Student rooms are linked to a campus network. 360 **computers** are available on campus
that provide access to the Internet. The 2 **libraries** have 1,381,108 books and 4,321
subscriptions.

Campus Life

There are 80 active organizations on campus, including a drama/theater group,
newspaper, radio station, and choral group. No national or local **fraternities** or **sororities.**

Harvey Mudd is a member of the NCAA (Division III). **Intercollegiate sports**
include baseball (m), basketball, cross-country running, football (m), golf (m), lacrosse
(w), soccer, softball (w), swimming, tennis, track and field, volleyball (w), water polo.

Campus Safety

Student safety services include late-night transport/escort service, 24-hour emergency
telephone alarm devices, and 24-hour patrols by trained security personnel.

Applying

Harvey Mudd requires an essay, SAT I, SAT II: Writing Test, SAT II Subject Test in
Math 2C, third SAT II Subject Test (Math 1C is not accepted), a high school transcript,
and 3 recommendations. It recommends an interview. Application deadline: 1/15; 2/1 for
financial aid. Deferred admission is possible.

Getting in Last Year
1,773 applied
40% were accepted
191 enrolled (27%)
89% from top tenth of their h.s. class
4.00 average high school GPA
91% had SAT verbal scores over 600
99% had SAT math scores over 600
57% had SAT verbal scores over 700
86% had SAT math scores over 700
45 National Merit Scholars
51 valedictorians

Graduation and After
72% graduated in 4 years
11% graduated in 5 years
1% graduated in 6 years
42% pursued further study (28% arts and
sciences, 13% engineering)
80% had job offers within 6 months
70 organizations recruited on campus

Financial Matters
$28,660 tuition and fees (2003–04)
$9420 room and board
100% average percent of need met
$21,358 average financial aid amount received
per undergraduate (2002–03 estimated)

Haverford is a liberal arts college of 1,100 students located 10 miles outside of Philadelphia. Academic rigor, integrity, and concern for others form the foundation of Haverford's approach to education. Aspects such as a student-run Honor Code, a sense of Quaker heritage, and a cooperative program with Bryn Mawr College, Swarthmore College, and the University of Pennsylvania mark Haverford as unique. Students thrive in part because classes are small and extracurricular commitment is expected and because the community is passionate about learning, understanding, and making sound and thoughtful judgments.

Getting in Last Year
2,973 applied
30% were accepted
313 enrolled (36%)
84% from top tenth of their h.s. class
92% had SAT verbal scores over 600
92% had SAT math scores over 600
46% had SAT verbal scores over 700
44% had SAT math scores over 700

Graduation and After
89% graduated in 4 years
2% graduated in 5 years
1% graduated in 6 years
17% pursued further study (10% arts and sciences, 4% law, 3% medicine)
68% had job offers within 6 months
142 organizations recruited on campus

Financial Matters
$28,880 tuition and fees (2003–04)
$9020 room and board
100% average percent of need met
$23,550 average financial aid amount received per undergraduate (2002–03 estimated)

HAVERFORD COLLEGE
SUBURBAN SETTING ■ PRIVATE ■ INDEPENDENT ■ COED
HAVERFORD, PENNSYLVANIA

Web site: www.haverford.edu
Contact: Ms. Delsie Z. Phillips, Director of Admission, 370 Lancaster Avenue, Haverford, PA 19041-1392
Telephone: 610-896-1350 **Fax:** 610-896-1338
E-mail: admitme@haverford.edu

Academics
Haverford awards bachelor's **degrees**. Challenging opportunities include advanced placement credit, accelerated degree programs, student-designed majors, double majors, independent study, and a senior project. Special programs include internships, off-campus study, and study-abroad.

The most frequently chosen **baccalaureate** fields are social sciences and history, English, and biological/life sciences. A complete listing of majors at Haverford appears in the Majors Index beginning on page 460.

The **faculty** at Haverford has 108 full-time members, 100% with terminal degrees. The student-faculty ratio is 8:1.

Students of Haverford
The student body is made up of 1,163 undergraduates. 52.4% are women and 47.6% are men. Students come from 50 states and territories. 17% are from Pennsylvania. 2.2% are international students. 4.9% are African American, 0.9% American Indian, 14.4% Asian American, and 5.7% Hispanic American. 96% returned for their sophomore year.

Facilities and Resources
Student rooms are linked to a campus network. 260 **computers** are available on campus that provide access to the Internet. The 5 **libraries** have 395,799 books and 3,240 subscriptions.

Campus Life
There are 50 active organizations on campus, including a drama/theater group, newspaper, radio station, and choral group. No national or local **fraternities** or **sororities**.

Haverford is a member of the NCAA (Division III). **Intercollegiate sports** include baseball (m), basketball, cross-country running, fencing, field hockey (w), lacrosse, soccer, softball (w), squash, tennis, track and field, volleyball (w).

Campus Safety
Student safety services include late-night transport/escort service, 24-hour emergency telephone alarm devices, and 24-hour patrols by trained security personnel.

Applying
Haverford requires an essay, SAT II Subject Tests, SAT II: Writing Test, SAT I or ACT, a high school transcript, and 2 recommendations. It recommends an interview. Application deadline: 1/15; 1/31 for financial aid. Early and deferred admission are possible.

HENDRIX COLLEGE

SUBURBAN SETTING ■ PRIVATE ■ INDEPENDENT RELIGIOUS ■ COED
CONWAY, ARKANSAS

Web site: www.hendrix.edu
Contact: Ms. Karen R. Forest, Vice President for Enrollment, 1600
Washington Avenue, Conway, AR 72032
Telephone: 501-450-1362 or toll-free 800-277-9017 **Fax:** 501-450-3843
E-mail: adm@hendrix.edu

Academics

Hendrix awards bachelor's and master's **degrees**. Challenging opportunities include
advanced placement credit, student-designed majors, double majors, independent study,
and a senior project. Special programs include internships, off-campus study, study-
abroad, and Army ROTC.

The most frequently chosen **baccalaureate** fields are social sciences and history,
biological/life sciences, and psychology. A complete listing of majors at Hendrix appears
in the Majors Index beginning on page 460.

The **faculty** at Hendrix has 81 full-time members, 100% with terminal degrees. The
student-faculty ratio is 12:1.

Students of Hendrix

The student body totals 1,059, of whom 1,050 are undergraduates. 56.6% are women
and 43.4% are men. Students come from 36 states and territories and 12 other countries.
60% are from Arkansas. 1.3% are international students. 4.4% are African American,
1.2% American Indian, 2.4% Asian American, and 3% Hispanic American. 85%
returned for their sophomore year.

Facilities and Resources

Student rooms are linked to a campus network. 75 **computers** are available on campus
for student use. The **library** has 211,374 books and 819 subscriptions.

Campus Life

There are 53 active organizations on campus, including a drama/theater group,
newspaper, radio station, and choral group. No national or local **fraternities** or **sororities.**

Hendrix is a member of the NCAA (Division III). **Intercollegiate sports** include
baseball (m), basketball, cheerleading, cross-country running, golf, soccer, softball (w),
swimming, tennis, track and field, volleyball (w).

Campus Safety

Student safety services include late-night transport/escort service, 24-hour emergency
telephone alarm devices, 24-hour patrols by trained security personnel, and electronically operated dormitory entrances.

Applying

Hendrix requires an essay, SAT I or ACT, and a high school transcript, and in some cases
an interview. It recommends 1 recommendation. Application deadline: rolling admissions; 2/15 priority date for financial aid. Deferred admission is possible.

A hands-on, liberal arts,
Hendrix prepares students
for the finest professional
and graduate schools in the country.
The College typically enrolls 1,100
students who are taught by 80
professors, all of whom have PhDs
or appropriate terminal degrees in
their fields. Most students
participate in an undergraduate
research project and 25 percent
study abroad. Eighty percent of
Hendrix students live on campus,
fostering an intimate community in
which students and faculty members
interact in all aspects of campus life.
Hendrix is located in Conway, a
suburb of Little Rock in the foothills
of the Ozark Mountains.

Getting in Last Year
891 applied
86% were accepted
267 enrolled (35%)
34% from top tenth of their h.s. class
3.60 average high school GPA
67% had SAT verbal scores over 600
61% had SAT math scores over 600
77% had ACT scores over 24
21% had SAT verbal scores over 700
15% had SAT math scores over 700
27% had ACT scores over 30
7 National Merit Scholars
11 valedictorians

Graduation and After
56% graduated in 4 years
7% graduated in 5 years
1% graduated in 6 years
40% pursued further study (16% arts and
sciences, 7% medicine, 5% law)
31% had job offers within 6 months
73 organizations recruited on campus

Financial Matters
$15,630 tuition and fees (2003–04)
$5340 room and board
86% average percent of need met
$13,995 average financial aid amount received
per undergraduate

HILLSDALE COLLEGE

SMALL-TOWN SETTING ■ PRIVATE ■ INDEPENDENT ■ COED
HILLSDALE, MICHIGAN

Web site: www.hillsdale.edu
Contact: Mr. Jeffrey S. Lantis, Director of Admissions, 33 East College
Street, Hillsdale, MI 49242-1298
Telephone: 517-607-2327 ext. 2327 **Fax:** 517-607-2223
E-mail: admissions@hillsdale.edu

A t Hillsdale College, our curriculum and daily campus life are guided by a set of ideals basic to the American way of life. Hillsdale's history of independence has tangible consequences in shaping how we run our school and what we teach. Our Judeo-Christian heritage and the honored truths of Western civilization form the basis for our curriculum.

Getting in Last Year

1,150 applied
77% were accepted
360 enrolled (41%)
42% from top tenth of their h.s. class
3.63 average high school GPA
71% had SAT verbal scores over 600
62% had SAT math scores over 600
78% had ACT scores over 24
25% had SAT verbal scores over 700
14% had SAT math scores over 700
24% had ACT scores over 30
11 National Merit Scholars
40 class presidents
27 valedictorians

Graduation and After

54% graduated in 4 years
18% graduated in 5 years
1% graduated in 6 years
Graduates pursuing further study: 8% arts and
sciences, 6% business, 4% law
98% had job offers within 6 months
46 organizations recruited on campus

Financial Matters

$16,050 tuition and fees (2003–04)
$6400 room and board
80% average percent of need met
$12,714 average financial aid amount received
per undergraduate (2002–03)

Academics

Hillsdale awards bachelor's **degrees**. Challenging opportunities include advanced placement credit, accelerated degree programs, an honors program, double majors, independent study, and a senior project. Special programs include internships, summer session for credit, and study-abroad.

The most frequently chosen **baccalaureate** fields are business/marketing, social sciences and history, and biological/life sciences. A complete listing of majors at Hillsdale appears in the Majors Index beginning on page 460.

The **faculty** at Hillsdale has 96 full-time members, 90% with terminal degrees. The student-faculty ratio is 11:1.

Students of Hillsdale

The student body is made up of 1,230 undergraduates. 53.2% are women and 46.8% are men. Students come from 47 states and territories and 14 other countries. 47% are from Michigan. 87% returned for their sophomore year.

Facilities and Resources

Student rooms are linked to a campus network. 185 **computers** are available on campus that provide access to the Internet. The 4 **libraries** have 205,000 books and 1,625 subscriptions.

Campus Life

There are 45 active organizations on campus, including a drama/theater group, newspaper, and choral group. 33% of eligible men and 44% of eligible women are members of national **fraternities** and national **sororities**.

Hillsdale is a member of the NCAA (Division II). **Intercollegiate sports** (some offering scholarships) include baseball (m), basketball, cheerleading, cross-country running, equestrian sports (w), football (m), golf (m), ice hockey (m), lacrosse (m), riflery, soccer, softball (w), swimming (w), tennis (w), track and field, volleyball (w).

Campus Safety

Student safety services include late-night transport/escort service, 24-hour emergency telephone alarm devices, 24-hour patrols by trained security personnel, and electronically operated dormitory entrances.

Applying

Hillsdale requires an essay, SAT I or ACT, a high school transcript, 1 recommendation, and a minimum high school GPA of 3.15, and in some cases an interview and 2 recommendations. It recommends SAT II Subject Tests, SAT II: Writing Test, an interview, and 2 recommendations. Application deadline: rolling admissions; 2/15 priority date for financial aid. Early and deferred admission are possible.

Hiram College

RURAL SETTING ■ PRIVATE ■ INDEPENDENT RELIGIOUS ■ COED
HIRAM, OHIO

Web site: www.hiram.edu
Contact: Ms. Brenda Swihart Meyer, Director of Admission, PO Box 96,
  Hiram, OH 44234
Telephone: 330-569-5169 or toll-free 800-362-5280 **Fax:** 330-569-5944
E-mail: admission@hiram.edu

Academics

Hiram awards bachelor's **degrees**. Challenging opportunities include advanced place-ment credit, accelerated degree programs, student-designed majors, double majors, independent study, and a senior project. Special programs include internships, summer session for credit, off-campus study, and study-abroad.

The most frequently chosen **baccalaureate** fields are business/marketing, computer/ information sciences, and social sciences and history. A complete listing of majors at Hiram appears in the Majors Index beginning on page 460.

The **faculty** at Hiram has 72 full-time members, 92% with terminal degrees. The student-faculty ratio is 11:1.

Students of Hiram

The student body is made up of 1,110 undergraduates. 57.7% are women and 42.3% are men. Students come from 31 states and territories and 20 other countries. 80% are from Ohio. 2.9% are international students. 11% are African American, .3% American Indian, 1.1% Asian American, and 1.5% Hispanic American. 73% returned for their sophomore year.

Facilities and Resources

Student rooms are linked to a campus network. The **library** has 187,451 books and 3,993 subscriptions.

Campus Life

There are 60 active organizations on campus, including a drama/theater group, newspaper, radio station, and choral group. 8% of eligible men and 12% of eligible women are members of local **fraternities** and local **sororities**.

Hiram is a member of the NCAA (Division III). **Intercollegiate sports** include baseball (m), basketball, cross-country running, football (m), golf, soccer, softball (w), swimming, tennis, track and field, volleyball (w).

Campus Safety

Student safety services include late-night transport/escort service, 24-hour emergency telephone alarm devices, 24-hour patrols by trained security personnel, and electroni-cally operated dormitory entrances.

Applying

Hiram requires an essay, SAT I or ACT, a high school transcript, and 2 recommenda-tions, and in some cases an interview. It recommends an interview and 3 recommenda-tions. Application deadline: 2/1; 2/15 priority date for financial aid. Early and deferred admission are possible.

H iram's 12-3 academic calendar is unique among colleges and universities. Each 15-week semester combines a comprehensive 12-week session of 3 courses with an intensive, 3-week immersion in a single seminar either on or off campus. Hiram supplements classroom study through career-oriented internships and an extensive and distinctive study-abroad program that takes Hiram students all over the world. More than 40% of Hiram students participate, and all courses are taught by Hiram faculty members and are a regular part of the curriculum. Hiram has a new Tuition Guarantee Program, which assists families in planning for college.

Getting in Last Year

888 applied
88% were accepted
236 enrolled (30%)
24% from top tenth of their h.s. class
3.37 average high school GPA
42% had SAT verbal scores over 600
32% had SAT math scores over 600
50% had ACT scores over 24
11% had SAT verbal scores over 700
3% had SAT math scores over 700
7% had ACT scores over 30
11 valedictorians

Graduation and After

96% graduated in 4 years
4% graduated in 5 years
61% had job offers within 6 months
70 organizations recruited on campus

Financial Matters

$21,134 tuition and fees (2003–04)
$7100 room and board
89% average percent of need met
$20,675 average financial aid amount received per undergraduate (2002–03 estimated)

HOBART AND WILLIAM SMITH COLLEGES

SMALL-TOWN SETTING ▪ PRIVATE ▪ INDEPENDENT ▪ COED
GENEVA, NEW YORK

Web site: www.hws.edu
Contact: Ms. Mara O'Laughlin, Director of Admissions, 629 South Main
Street, Geneva, NY 14456-3397
Telephone: 315-781-3472 or toll-free 800-245-0100 **Fax:** 315-781-5471
E-mail: admissions@hws.edu

Hobart and William Smith Colleges are dedicated to providing a liberal arts education that is not merely informative, but also transformative, by emphasizing ideals as well as knowledge. In other words, they are committed to nurturing the whole person, not just the academic student. To achieve this goal, HWS melds an interdisciplinary curriculum with a world view of learning, the highlights of which are an extensive and vibrant study-abroad program; local, national, and global internships; and a strong community service component.

Getting in Last Year
3,277 applied
62% were accepted
516 enrolled (25%)
31% from top tenth of their h.s. class
3.30 average high school GPA
41% had SAT verbal scores over 600
46% had SAT math scores over 600
5% had SAT verbal scores over 700
5% had SAT math scores over 700
8 National Merit Scholars
16 class presidents
3 valedictorians

Graduation and After
64% graduated in 4 years
6% graduated in 5 years
1% graduated in 6 years
30% pursued further study (14% arts and
   sciences, 5% medicine, 4% law)
70% had job offers within 6 months
48 organizations recruited on campus

Financial Matters
$28,948 tuition and fees (2003–04)
$7588 room and board
90% average percent of need met
$22,903 average financial aid amount received
   per undergraduate

Academics
HWS awards bachelor's **degrees**. Challenging opportunities include advanced place-ment credit, accelerated degree programs, student-designed majors, an honors program, double majors, independent study, and a senior project. Special programs include intern-ships, off-campus study, and study-abroad.

The most frequently chosen **baccalaureate** fields are social sciences and history, English, and psychology. A complete listing of majors at HWS appears in the Majors Index beginning on page 460.

The **faculty** at HWS has 156 full-time members, 92% with terminal degrees. The student-faculty ratio is 11:1.

Students of HWS
The student body is made up of 1,873 undergraduates. 55.4% are women and 44.6% are men. Students come from 40 states and territories and 18 other countries. 46% are from New York. 2.3% are international students. 3.3% are African American, 0.3% American Indian, 1.7% Asian American, and 4% Hispanic American. 84% returned for their sophomore year.

Facilities and Resources
Student rooms are linked to a campus network. 250 **computers** are available on campus that provide access to the Internet. The 2 **libraries** have 370,770 books and 1,153 subscriptions.

Campus Life
There are 60 active organizations on campus, including a drama/theater group, newspaper, radio station, and choral group. 15% of eligible men are members of national **fraternities**.

HWS is a member of the NCAA (Division III). **Intercollegiate sports** include basketball, cheerleading, crew, cross-country running, field hockey (w), football (m), golf, ice hockey (m), lacrosse, sailing, soccer, squash, swimming (w), tennis.

Campus Safety
Student safety services include late-night transport/escort service, 24-hour emergency telephone alarm devices, 24-hour patrols by trained security personnel, and electroni-cally operated dormitory entrances.

Applying
HWS requires an essay, SAT I or ACT, a high school transcript, and 2 recommenda-tions. It recommends SAT II Subject Tests and an interview. Application deadline: 2/1; 3/15 for financial aid, with a 2/15 priority date. Early and deferred admission are pos-sible.

HOOD COLLEGE

SUBURBAN SETTING ■ PRIVATE ■ INDEPENDENT ■ COED
FREDERICK, MARYLAND

Web site: www.hood.edu
Contact: Dr. Susan Hallenbeck, Dean of Admissions, 401 Rosemont Avenue, Frederick, MD 21701
Telephone: 301-696-3400 or toll-free 800-922-1599 **Fax:** 301-696-3819
E-mail: admissions@hood.edu

Academics

Hood awards bachelor's and master's **degrees** and post-bachelor's certificates (also offers adult program with significant enrollment not reflected in profile). Challenging opportunities include advanced placement credit, accelerated degree programs, student-designed majors, an honors program, double majors, independent study, and a senior project. Special programs include internships, summer session for credit, off-campus study, study-abroad, and Army ROTC.

The most frequently chosen **baccalaureate** fields are psychology, business/marketing, and social sciences and history. A complete listing of majors at Hood appears in the Majors Index beginning on page 460.

The **faculty** at Hood has 76 full-time members, 95% with terminal degrees. The student-faculty ratio is 10:1.

Students of Hood

The student body totals 1,325, of whom 864 are undergraduates. 85.2% are women and 14.8% are men. Students come from 27 states and territories and 22 other countries. 79% are from Maryland. 6.5% are international students. 12.7% are African American, 0.2% American Indian, 1.6% Asian American, and 2.2% Hispanic American. 75% returned for their sophomore year.

Facilities and Resources

Student rooms are linked to a campus network. 277 **computers** are available on campus that provide access to the Internet. The **library** has 182,786 books and 1,057 subscriptions.

Campus Life

There are 59 active organizations on campus, including a drama/theater group, newspaper, and choral group. No national or local **fraternities** or **sororities**.

Hood is a member of the NCAA (Division III). **Intercollegiate sports** include basketball, cheerleading, field hockey (w), lacrosse (w), soccer (w), softball (w), swimming, tennis, volleyball (w).

Campus Safety

Student safety services include residence hall security, late-night transport/escort service, 24-hour emergency telephone alarm devices, 24-hour patrols by trained security personnel, and electronically operated dormitory entrances.

Applying

Hood requires an essay, SAT I or ACT, a high school transcript, and 1 recommendation. It recommends SAT II Subject Tests and an interview. Application deadline: 2/1; 2/15 priority date for financial aid. Early and deferred admission are possible.

Getting in Last Year

1,001 applied
55% were accepted
181 enrolled (33%)
21% from top tenth of their h.s. class
3.50 average high school GPA
31% had SAT verbal scores over 600
26% had SAT math scores over 600
31% had ACT scores over 24
5% had SAT verbal scores over 700
2% had SAT math scores over 700
5% had ACT scores over 30
9 valedictorians

Graduation and After

70% graduated in 4 years
4% graduated in 5 years
1% graduated in 6 years
36% pursued further study (25% arts and sciences, 4% business, 4% law)
52% had job offers within 6 months
168 organizations recruited on campus

Financial Matters

$20,275 tuition and fees (2003–04)
$7520 room and board
90% average percent of need met
$17,518 average financial aid amount received per undergraduate

Getting in Last Year

2,481 applied
83% were accepted
811 enrolled (39%)
31% from top tenth of their h.s. class
3.72 average high school GPA
49% had SAT verbal scores over 600
52% had SAT math scores over 600
67% had ACT scores over 24
13% had SAT verbal scores over 700
13% had SAT math scores over 700
17% had ACT scores over 30
14 National Merit Scholars

Graduation and After

62% graduated in 4 years
11% graduated in 5 years
2% graduated in 6 years
20% pursued further study (13% arts and
  sciences, 5% medicine, 2% law)
50 organizations recruited on campus

Financial Matters

$19,322 tuition and fees (2003–04)
$6018 room and board
87% average percent of need met
$16,860 average financial aid amount received
  per undergraduate (2002–03 estimated)

HOPE COLLEGE

SMALL-TOWN SETTING ■ PRIVATE ■ INDEPENDENT RELIGIOUS ■ COED
HOLLAND, MICHIGAN

Web site: www.hope.edu
Contact: Dr. James R. Bekkering, Vice President for Admissions, 69 East 10th
  Street, PO Box 9000, Holland, MI 49422-9000
Telephone: 616-395-7955 or toll-free 800-968-7850 **Fax:** 616-395-7130
E-mail: admissions@hope.edu

Academics

Hope awards bachelor's **degrees**. Challenging opportunities include advanced placement credit, student-designed majors, double majors, and independent study. Special
programs include internships, summer session for credit, off-campus study, and study-
abroad.

The most frequently chosen **baccalaureate** fields are business/marketing, education,
and social sciences and history. A complete listing of majors at Hope appears in the
Majors Index beginning on page 460.

The **faculty** at Hope has 203 full-time members, 76% with terminal degrees. The
student-faculty ratio is 13:1.

Students of Hope

The student body is made up of 3,068 undergraduates. 62.1% are women and 37.9% are
men. Students come from 45 states and territories and 32 other countries. 76% are from
Michigan. 1.4% are international students. 1.2% are African American, 0.2% American
Indian, 2% Asian American, and 1.9% Hispanic American. 88% returned for their
sophomore year.

Facilities and Resources

Student rooms are linked to a campus network. 300 **computers** are available on campus
that provide access to the Internet. The 2 **libraries** have 343,865 books and 2,250
subscriptions.

Campus Life

There are 67 active organizations on campus, including a drama/theater group,
newspaper, radio station, television station, and choral group. 6% of eligible men and
15% of eligible women are members of local **fraternities** and local **sororities**.

Hope is a member of the NCAA (Division III). **Intercollegiate sports** include
baseball (m), basketball, cheerleading, cross-country running, football (m), golf, soccer,
softball (w), swimming, tennis, track and field, volleyball (w).

Campus Safety

Student safety services include late-night transport/escort service, 24-hour emergency
telephone alarm devices, 24-hour patrols by trained security personnel, and electronically operated dormitory entrances.

Applying

Hope requires an essay, SAT I or ACT, and a high school transcript, and in some cases 1
recommendation. It recommends an interview. Application deadline: rolling admissions;
3/1 priority date for financial aid. Early and deferred admission are possible.

HOUGHTON COLLEGE

RURAL SETTING ■ PRIVATE ■ INDEPENDENT RELIGIOUS ■ COED
HOUGHTON, NEW YORK

Web site: www.houghton.edu
Contact: Mr. Bruce Campbell, Director of Admission, PO Box 128,
   Houghton, NY 14744
Telephone: 585-567-9353 or toll-free 800-777-2556 **Fax:** 585-567-9522
E-mail: admission@houghton.edu

Academics

Houghton awards associate, bachelor's, and master's **degrees**. Challenging opportunities include advanced placement credit, an honors program, double majors, independent study, and a senior project. Special programs include internships, summer session for credit, off-campus study, study-abroad, and Army ROTC.

The most frequently chosen **baccalaureate** fields are business/marketing, education, and English. A complete listing of majors at Houghton appears in the Majors Index beginning on page 460.

The **faculty** at Houghton has 83 full-time members, 78% with terminal degrees. The student-faculty ratio is 14:1.

Students of Houghton

The student body totals 1,467, of whom 1,458 are undergraduates. 65% are women and 35% are men. Students come from 43 states and territories and 18 other countries. 61% are from New York. 4% are international students. 2.7% are African American, 0.4% American Indian, 1.3% Asian American, and 0.6% Hispanic American. 83% returned for their sophomore year.

Facilities and Resources

Student rooms are linked to a campus network. 50 **computers** are available on campus that provide access to the Internet. The 2 **libraries** have 238,300 books and 4,102 subscriptions.

Campus Life

There are 50 active organizations on campus, including a drama/theater group, newspaper, radio station, and choral group. No national or local **fraternities** or **sororities**.

Houghton is a member of the NAIA. **Intercollegiate sports** (some offering scholarships) include basketball, cheerleading, cross-country running, field hockey (w), soccer, track and field, volleyball (w).

Campus Safety

Student safety services include phone connection to security patrols, late-night transport/escort service, 24-hour patrols by trained security personnel, and electronically operated dormitory entrances.

Applying

Houghton requires an essay, SAT I or ACT, a high school transcript, 1 recommendation, and pastoral recommendation. It recommends an interview and a minimum high school GPA of 2.5. Application deadline: rolling admissions; 3/1 priority date for financial aid. Deferred admission is possible.

Getting in Last Year

1,071 applied
85% were accepted
304 enrolled (33%)
34% from top tenth of their h.s. class
3.48 average high school GPA
48% had SAT verbal scores over 600
37% had SAT math scores over 600
64% had ACT scores over 24
13% had SAT verbal scores over 700
6% had SAT math scores over 700
9% had ACT scores over 30
3 National Merit Scholars
21 valedictorians

Graduation and After

58% graduated in 4 years
15% graduated in 5 years
1% graduated in 6 years
27% pursued further study (10% education, 8% arts and sciences, 4% medicine)
70% had job offers within 6 months
56 organizations recruited on campus

Financial Matters

$17,984 tuition and fees (2003–04)
$6000 room and board
77% average percent of need met
$15,078 average financial aid amount received per undergraduate

HUNTINGDON COLLEGE

SUBURBAN SETTING ■ PRIVATE ■ INDEPENDENT RELIGIOUS ■ COED
MONTGOMERY, ALABAMA

Web site: www.huntingdon.edu
Contact: Ms. Christy C. Mehaffey, Director of Admissions, 1500 East
   Fairview Avenue, Montgomery, AL 36106
Telephone: 334-833-4517 or toll-free 800-763-0313 **Fax:** 334-833-4347
E-mail: admiss@huntingdon.edu

Getting in Last Year
1,108 applied
59% were accepted
201 enrolled (31%)
34% from top tenth of their h.s. class
3.26 average high school GPA
39% had SAT verbal scores over 600
48% had SAT math scores over 600
50% had ACT scores over 24
4% had SAT verbal scores over 700
7% had SAT math scores over 700
3% had ACT scores over 30
19 class presidents
6 valedictorians

Graduation and After
47% graduated in 4 years
10% graduated in 5 years
1% graduated in 6 years
30% pursued further study (10% arts and
   sciences, 6% law, 4% business)
50% had job offers within 6 months
50 organizations recruited on campus

Financial Matters
$14,560 tuition and fees (2003–04)
$5940 room and board
83% average percent of need met
$10,686 average financial aid amount received
   per undergraduate (2002–03 estimated)

Academics
Huntingdon awards associate and bachelor's **degrees**. Challenging opportunities include advanced placement credit, accelerated degree programs, student-designed majors, an honors program, double majors, independent study, and a senior project. Special programs include cooperative education, internships, summer session for credit, off-campus study, study-abroad, and Army and Air Force ROTC.

The most frequently chosen **baccalaureate** fields are business/marketing, parks and recreation, and visual/performing arts. A complete listing of majors at Huntingdon appears in the Majors Index beginning on page 460.

The **faculty** at Huntingdon has 33 full-time members, 88% with terminal degrees. The student-faculty ratio is 14:1.

Students of Huntingdon
The student body is made up of 660 undergraduates. 55.2% are women and 44.8% are men. Students come from 19 states and territories. 80% are from Alabama. 3.2% are international students. 9.5% are African American, 1.1% American Indian, 0.8% Asian American, and 0.8% Hispanic American. 76% returned for their sophomore year.

Facilities and Resources
Student rooms are linked to a campus network. 75 **computers** are available on campus that provide access to personal computer given to each entering student and the Internet. The **library** has 97,436 books and 443 subscriptions.

Campus Life
There are 50 active organizations on campus, including a drama/theater group, newspaper, and choral group. 23% of eligible men and 25% of eligible women are members of national **fraternities** and national **sororities**.

Huntingdon is a member of the NCAA (Division III). **Intercollegiate sports** (some offering scholarships) include baseball (m), basketball, cheerleading, cross-country running, football (m), golf (m), soccer, softball (w), tennis (w), volleyball (w).

Campus Safety
Student safety services include electronic video surveillance, late-night transport/escort service, 24-hour emergency telephone alarm devices, 24-hour patrols by trained security personnel, and electronically operated dormitory entrances.

Applying
Huntingdon requires SAT I or ACT, a high school transcript, and a minimum high school GPA of 2.25, and in some cases an essay, an interview, and 2 recommendations. It recommends 3 recommendations. Application deadline: rolling admissions; 4/15 priority date for financial aid. Early and deferred admission are possible.

HUNTINGTON COLLEGE

SMALL-TOWN SETTING ■ PRIVATE ■ INDEPENDENT RELIGIOUS ■ COED
HUNTINGTON, INDIANA

Web site: www.huntington.edu
Contact: Mr. Jeff Berggren, Dean of Enrollment, 2303 College Avenue,
    Huntington, IN 46750-1299
Telephone: 260-356-6000 ext. 4016 or toll-free 800-642-6493 **Fax:**
    260-356-9448
E-mail: admissions@huntington.edu

Academics

Huntington awards associate, bachelor's, and master's **degrees** and post-bachelor's
certificates. Challenging opportunities include advanced placement credit, accelerated
degree programs, double majors, independent study, and a senior project. Special
programs include internships, summer session for credit, off-campus study, and study-
abroad.

The most frequently chosen **baccalaureate** fields are education, business/marketing,
and psychology. A complete listing of majors at Huntington appears in the Majors Index
beginning on page 460.

The **faculty** at Huntington has 55 full-time members, 84% with terminal degrees.
The student-faculty ratio is 18:1.

Students of Huntington

The student body totals 976, of whom 923 are undergraduates. 56.8% are women and
43.2% are men. Students come from 27 states and territories and 15 other countries.
60% are from Indiana. 2.6% are international students. 1% are African American, 0.1%
American Indian, 0.7% Asian American, and 0.7% Hispanic American. 77% returned for
their sophomore year.

Facilities and Resources

Student rooms are linked to a campus network. 190 **computers** are available on campus
that provide access to the Internet. The **library** has 91,709 books and 553 subscriptions.

Campus Life

There are 35 active organizations on campus, including a drama/theater group,
newspaper, radio station, television station, and choral group. No national or local
fraternities or **sororities**.

Huntington is a member of the NAIA. **Intercollegiate sports** (some offering
scholarships) include baseball (m), basketball, cheerleading, cross-country running, golf
(m), soccer, softball (w), tennis, track and field, volleyball (w).

Campus Safety

Student safety services include night patrols by trained security personnel, late-night
transport/escort service, and 24-hour emergency telephone alarm devices.

Applying

Huntington requires an essay, SAT I or ACT, a high school transcript, and a minimum
high school GPA of 2.3. It recommends an interview. Application deadline: 8/15; 3/1
priority date for financial aid. Deferred admission is possible.

Getting in Last Year
620 applied
92% were accepted
192 enrolled (34%)
27% from top tenth of their h.s. class
3.45 average high school GPA
33% had SAT verbal scores over 600
33% had SAT math scores over 600
48% had ACT scores over 24
8% had SAT verbal scores over 700
6% had SAT math scores over 700
9% had ACT scores over 30
3 National Merit Scholars
13 class presidents
23 valedictorians

Graduation and After
49% graduated in 4 years
11% graduated in 5 years
10% pursued further study
67 organizations recruited on campus

Financial Matters
$17,700 tuition and fees (2003–04)
$5890 room and board
96% average percent of need met
$11,823 average financial aid amount received
    per undergraduate (2002–03 estimated)

ILLINOIS COLLEGE

Small-town setting ■ Private ■ Independent Religious ■ Coed
Jacksonville, Illinois

Web site: www.ic.edu

Contact: Mr. Rick Bystry, Associate Director of Admission, 1101 West College, Jacksonville, IL 62650

Telephone: 217-245-3030 or toll-free 866-464-5265 **Fax:** 217-245-3034

E-mail: admissions@ic.edu

Founded in 1829, Illinois College is a private, liberal arts institution enrolling approximately 1,000 students. The College offers more than 45 recognized academic programs, leading to bachelor of arts and bachelor of science degrees, and is distinguished as a Phi Beta Kappa institution. Recognized as a "hidden treasure" by *Kaplan/Newsweek* and "best value" by *U.S. News & World Report,* the campus boasts new, state-of-the-art science and fitness centers. An impressive 1:14 faculty member/student ratio and average class size of 15 ensure an individualized edicational experience. Illinois College sponsors unique Break Away experiences with diverse opportunities, ranging from international adventures to internships and research projects.

Getting in Last Year
1,005 applied
72% were accepted
318 enrolled (44%)
24% from top tenth of their h.s. class
3.31 average high school GPA
48% had SAT verbal scores over 600
52% had SAT math scores over 600
49% had ACT scores over 24
10% had SAT verbal scores over 700
14% had SAT math scores over 700
5% had ACT scores over 30
12 valedictorians

Graduation and After
42% graduated in 4 years
11% graduated in 5 years
2% graduated in 6 years
27% pursued further study
95% had job offers within 6 months

Financial Matters
$13,300 tuition and fees (2003–04)
$5800 room and board
69% average percent of need met
$13,273 average financial aid amount received per undergraduate

Academics
IC awards bachelor's **degrees**. Challenging opportunities include advanced placement credit, accelerated degree programs, double majors, independent study, and a senior project. Special programs include internships, summer session for credit, and study-abroad.

The most frequently chosen **baccalaureate** fields are business/marketing, social sciences and history, and education. A complete listing of majors at IC appears in the Majors Index beginning on page 460.

The **faculty** at IC has 61 full-time members, 85% with terminal degrees. The student-faculty ratio is 14:1.

Students of IC
The student body is made up of 1,016 undergraduates. 56% are women and 44% are men. Students come from 15 states and territories and 7 other countries. 97% are from Illinois. 0.9% are international students. 2.2% are African American, 0.2% American Indian, 0.4% Asian American, and 2% Hispanic American. 75% returned for their sophomore year.

Facilities and Resources
Student rooms are linked to a campus network. 97 **computers** are available on campus that provide access to the Internet. The 2 **libraries** have 143,500 books and 620 subscriptions.

Campus Life
There are 50 active organizations on campus, including a drama/theater group, newspaper, television station, and choral group. 30% of eligible men and 30% of eligible women are members of local **fraternities** and local **sororities**.

IC is a member of the NCAA (Division III). **Intercollegiate sports** include baseball (m), cheerleading (w), cross-country running, football (m), golf, soccer, softball (w), tennis, track and field, volleyball (w), wrestling (m).

Campus Safety
Student safety services include late-night transport/escort service, 24-hour emergency telephone alarm devices, 24-hour patrols by trained security personnel, and electronically operated dormitory entrances.

Applying
IC requires SAT I or ACT, a high school transcript, and 1 recommendation, and in some cases an essay. It recommends an essay, an interview, and a minimum high school GPA of 2.5. Application deadline: 7/1; 3/1 priority date for financial aid.

ILLINOIS INSTITUTE OF TECHNOLOGY
URBAN SETTING ■ PRIVATE ■ INDEPENDENT ■ COED
CHICAGO, ILLINOIS

Web site: www.iit.edu
Contact: Mr. Brent Benner, Director of Undergraduate Admission, 10 West 33rd Street PH101, Chicago, IL 60616-3793
Telephone: 312-567-3025 or toll-free 800-448-2329 (out-of-state) **Fax:** 312-567-6939
E-mail: admission@iit.edu

Academics
IIT awards bachelor's, master's, doctoral, and first-professional **degrees** and post-bachelor's certificates. Challenging opportunities include advanced placement credit, accelerated degree programs, double majors, independent study, and a senior project. Special programs include cooperative education, internships, summer session for credit, study-abroad, and Army, Navy and Air Force ROTC.

The most frequently chosen **baccalaureate** fields are engineering/engineering technologies, computer/information sciences, and architecture. A complete listing of majors at IIT appears in the Majors Index beginning on page 460.

The **faculty** at IIT has 306 full-time members, 100% with terminal degrees. The student-faculty ratio is 12:1.

Students of IIT
The student body totals 6,167, of whom 1,941 are undergraduates. 24.6% are women and 75.4% are men. Students come from 50 states and territories and 58 other countries. 63% are from Illinois. 16.9% are international students. 5.1% are African American, 0.4% American Indian, 15.4% Asian American, and 7% Hispanic American. 81% returned for their sophomore year.

Facilities and Resources
Student rooms are linked to a campus network. 650 **computers** are available on campus that provide access to the Internet. The 6 **libraries** have 854,771 books and 773 subscriptions.

Campus Life
There are 98 active organizations on campus, including a drama/theater group, newspaper, radio station, and choral group. 13% of eligible men and 13% of eligible women are members of national **fraternities**, national **sororities**, and local sororities.

IIT is a member of the NAIA. **Intercollegiate sports** (some offering scholarships) include baseball (m), basketball, cross-country running, soccer, swimming, volleyball (w).

Campus Safety
Student safety services include late-night transport/escort service, 24-hour emergency telephone alarm devices, 24-hour patrols by trained security personnel, and electronically operated dormitory entrances.

Applying
IIT requires an essay, SAT I or ACT, a high school transcript, 1 recommendation, SAT score over 1150; ACT score over 24, and a minimum high school GPA of 3.0, and in some cases an interview. It recommends SAT II Subject Tests. Application deadline: rolling admissions; 4/15 priority date for financial aid. Deferred admission is possible.

As a member of the Association of Independent Technological Universities, Illinois Institute of Technology (IIT) is known for its excellent programs in architecture, business administration, engineering, psychology, science, premed, prepharmacy, and prelaw. A small undergraduate population of approximately 1,500 students results in small class size and a 12:1 student-faculty member ratio. Admission is competitive and the student body is diverse. Approximately 70% of students live on campus. (Freshman on-campus housing is guaranteed.) Located in the city of Chicago, IIT offers numerous opportunities to explore a variety of cultural and recreational activities. IIT offers need-based financial aid and generous scholarship programs up to full tuition and room.

Getting in Last Year
2,538 applied
59% were accepted
398 enrolled (26%)
3.6 average high school GPA
63% had SAT verbal scores over 600
84% had SAT math scores over 600
94% had ACT scores over 24
18% had SAT verbal scores over 700
41% had SAT math scores over 700
35% had ACT scores over 30
17 valedictorians

Graduation and After
28% graduated in 4 years
34% graduated in 5 years
4% graduated in 6 years
46% pursued further study (61% engineering, 23% medicine, 8% arts and sciences)
69% had job offers within 6 months
90 organizations recruited on campus

Financial Matters
$20,339 tuition and fees (2003–04)
$6282 room and board
88% average percent of need met
$19,588 average financial aid amount received per undergraduate (2002–03)

ILLINOIS WESLEYAN UNIVERSITY

SUBURBAN SETTING ■ PRIVATE ■ INDEPENDENT ■ COED
BLOOMINGTON, ILLINOIS

Web site: www.iwu.edu
Contact: Mr. Jerry Pope, Dean of Admissions, PO Box 2900, Bloomington, IL 61702-2900
Telephone: 309-556-3031 or toll-free 800-332-2498 **Fax:** 309-556-3820
E-mail: iwuadmit@titan.iwu.edu

Getting in Last Year

3,331 applied
43% were accepted
578 enrolled (40%)
52% from top tenth of their h.s. class
68% had SAT verbal scores over 600
76% had SAT math scores over 600
95% had ACT scores over 24
23% had SAT verbal scores over 700
23% had SAT math scores over 700
37% had ACT scores over 30
15 National Merit Scholars
38 valedictorians

Graduation and After

70% graduated in 4 years
3% graduated in 5 years
29% pursued further study (12% arts and sciences, 6% medicine, 5% law)
68% had job offers within 6 months
69 organizations recruited on campus

Financial Matters

$24,540 tuition and fees (2003–04)
$5840 room and board
95% average percent of need met
$16,671 average financial aid amount received per undergraduate (2002–03 estimated)

Academics

IWU awards bachelor's **degrees**. Challenging opportunities include advanced placement credit, student-designed majors, an honors program, double majors, and independent study. Special programs include cooperative education, internships, summer session for credit, off-campus study, study-abroad, and Army ROTC.

The most frequently chosen **baccalaureate** fields are business/marketing, social sciences and history, and visual/performing arts. A complete listing of majors at IWU appears in the Majors Index beginning on page 460.

The **faculty** at IWU has 159 full-time members, 92% with terminal degrees. The student-faculty ratio is 12:1.

Students of IWU

The student body is made up of 2,106 undergraduates. 56.9% are women and 43.1% are men. Students come from 36 states and territories and 20 other countries. 87% are from Illinois. 2.1% are international students. 3% are African American, 0.1% American Indian, 2.2% Asian American, and 2.3% Hispanic American. 93% returned for their sophomore year.

Facilities and Resources

Student rooms are linked to a campus network. 490 **computers** are available on campus that provide access to the Internet. The **library** has 307,861 books and 14,264 subscriptions.

Campus Life

There are 160 active organizations on campus, including a drama/theater group, newspaper, radio station, television station, and choral group. 40% of eligible men and 32% of eligible women are members of national **fraternities**, national **sororities**, and local sororities.

IWU is a member of the NCAA (Division III). **Intercollegiate sports** include baseball (m), basketball, cross-country running, football (m), golf, soccer, softball (w), swimming, tennis, track and field, volleyball (w).

Campus Safety

Student safety services include Emergency Response Team, late-night transport/escort service, 24-hour emergency telephone alarm devices, and 24-hour patrols by trained security personnel.

Applying

IWU requires an essay, SAT I or ACT, a high school transcript, and a minimum high school GPA of 2.0. It recommends an interview, 3 recommendations, and a minimum high school GPA of 3.0. Application deadline: 2/15; 3/1 for financial aid. Early and deferred admission are possible.

Iowa State University of Science and Technology

Suburban setting ■ Public ■ State-supported ■ Coed
Ames, Iowa

Web site: www.iastate.edu
Contact: Mr. Phil Caffrey, Associate Director for Freshman Admissions, 100 Alumni Hall, Ames, IA 50011-2010
Telephone: 515-294-5836 or toll-free 800-262-3810 **Fax:** 515-294-2592
E-mail: admissions@iastate.edu

Academics

Iowa State awards bachelor's, master's, doctoral, and first-professional **degrees** and post-master's certificates. Challenging opportunities include advanced placement credit, accelerated degree programs, student-designed majors, freshman honors college, an honors program, double majors, independent study, and a senior project. Special programs include cooperative education, internships, summer session for credit, off-campus study, study-abroad, and Army, Navy and Air Force ROTC.

The most frequently chosen **baccalaureate** fields are business/marketing, engineering/engineering technologies, and agriculture. A complete listing of majors at Iowa State appears in the Majors Index beginning on page 460.

The **faculty** at Iowa State has 1,415 full-time members, 92% with terminal degrees. The student-faculty ratio is 16:1.

Students of Iowa State

The student body totals 27,380, of whom 22,230 are undergraduates. 43.9% are women and 56.1% are men. Students come from 54 states and territories and 113 other countries. 81% are from Iowa. 3.9% are international students. 2.7% are African American, 0.3% American Indian, 3% Asian American, and 2.1% Hispanic American. 84% returned for their sophomore year.

Facilities and Resources

Student rooms are linked to a campus network. 2,700 **computers** are available on campus that provide access to e-mail, network services and the Internet. The 2 **libraries** have 2,348,646 books and 20,681 subscriptions.

Campus Life

There are 515 active organizations on campus, including a drama/theater group, newspaper, radio station, television station, choral group, and marching band. 16% of eligible men and 16% of eligible women are members of national **fraternities**, national **sororities**, local fraternities, and local sororities.

Iowa State is a member of the NCAA (Division I). **Intercollegiate sports** (some offering scholarships) include basketball, cross-country running, football (m), golf, gymnastics (w), soccer (w), softball (w), swimming, tennis (w), track and field, volleyball (w), wrestling (m).

Campus Safety

Student safety services include crime prevention programs, threat assessment team, motor vehicle help van, late-night transport/escort service, 24-hour emergency telephone alarm devices, 24-hour patrols by trained security personnel, student patrols, and electronically operated dormitory entrances.

Applying

Iowa State requires SAT I or ACT, a high school transcript, and rank in upper 50% of high school class. Application deadline: 8/1; 3/1 priority date for financial aid. Deferred admission is possible.

> **I**owa State has a national and international reputation for academic excellence, offering more than 100 majors in 7 undergraduate colleges. Known for technology (the first electronic digital computer and fax technology were both developed there), Iowa State was named one of the "most wired" college campuses—students have 24-hour access to more than 1,600 computer workstations, instant e-mail accounts, personal Web page space, and Internet access from every residence hall room. Out-of-class activities, leadership opportunities, and excellent job placement rates, together with a top-notch faculty and challenging in-class work, add up to an outstanding college experience.

Getting in Last Year
9,035 applied
90% were accepted
3,897 enrolled (48%)
24% from top tenth of their h.s. class
3.49 average high school GPA
48% had SAT verbal scores over 600
61% had SAT math scores over 600
59% had ACT scores over 24
14% had SAT verbal scores over 700
20% had SAT math scores over 700
12% had ACT scores over 30
69 National Merit Scholars

Graduation and After
27% graduated in 4 years
32% graduated in 5 years
6% graduated in 6 years
19% pursued further study
77.7% had job offers within 6 months
1820 organizations recruited on campus

Financial Matters
$5028 resident tuition and fees (2003–04)
$14,370 nonresident tuition and fees (2003–04)
$5740 room and board
100% average percent of need met
$6772 average financial aid amount received per undergraduate (2001–02)

ITHACA COLLEGE

SMALL-TOWN SETTING ■ PRIVATE ■ INDEPENDENT ■ COED
ITHACA, NEW YORK

Web site: www.ithaca.edu
Contact: Ms. Paula J. Mitchell, Director of Admission, 100 Job Hall, Ithaca,
  NY 14850-7020
Telephone: 607-274-3124 or toll-free 800-429-4274 **Fax:** 607-274-1900
E-mail: admission@ithaca.edu

Ithaca College is a nationally recognized coeducational and nonsectarian comprehensive college. Founded in 1892 as a music conservatory, Ithaca continues its committment to excellence and performance. Its modern, residential 750-acre campus, equipped with state-of-the-art facilities, is home to 6,500 students and 453 full-time faculty members. Its Schools of Business, Communications, Health Sciences and Human Performance, Humanities and Sciences, and Music—and its new Division of Interdisciplinary and International Studies—offer more than 100 degree programs with teacher certification options in over a dozen fields. An Ithaca education emphasizes hands-on learning, collaborative student-faculty member research, and development of the whole student.

Getting in Last Year
10,650 applied
63% were accepted
1,585 enrolled (23%)
36% from top tenth of their h.s. class
46% had SAT verbal scores over 600
49% had SAT math scores over 600
8% had SAT verbal scores over 700
7% had SAT math scores over 700
7 National Merit Scholars
32 valedictorians

Graduation and After
64% graduated in 4 years
8% graduated in 5 years
1% graduated in 6 years
33% pursued further study (26% arts and
  sciences, 4% education, 1% business)
303 organizations recruited on campus

Financial Matters
$22,264 tuition and fees (2003–04)
$9466 room and board
87% average percent of need met
$19,830 average financial aid amount received
  per undergraduate (2002–03 estimated)

Academics
Ithaca College awards bachelor's and master's **degrees**. Challenging opportunities include advanced placement credit, accelerated degree programs, student-designed majors, freshman honors college, an honors program, double majors, independent study, and a senior project. Special programs include internships, summer session for credit, off-campus study, study-abroad, and Army and Air Force ROTC.

The most frequently chosen **baccalaureate** fields are communications/communication technologies, visual/performing arts, and health professions and related sciences. A complete listing of majors at Ithaca College appears in the Majors Index beginning on page 460.

The **faculty** at Ithaca College has 453 full-time members, 90% with terminal degrees. The student-faculty ratio is 12:1.

Students of Ithaca College
The student body totals 6,496, of whom 6,260 are undergraduates. 57% are women and 43% are men. Students come from 48 states and territories and 66 other countries. 49% are from New York. 3% are international students. 2.4% are African American, 0.3% American Indian, 2.7% Asian American, and 3% Hispanic American. 88% returned for their sophomore year.

Facilities and Resources
Student rooms are linked to a campus network. 624 **computers** are available on campus that provide access to the Internet. The **library** has 246,545 books and 2,305 subscriptions.

Campus Life
There are 165 active organizations on campus, including a drama/theater group, newspaper, radio station, television station, and choral group. 1% of eligible men and 1% of eligible women are members of national **fraternities**, national **sororities**, and local fraternities.

Ithaca College is a member of the NCAA (Division III). **Intercollegiate sports** include baseball (m), basketball, crew, cross-country running, field hockey (w), football (m), gymnastics (w), lacrosse, soccer, softball (w), swimming, tennis, track and field, volleyball (w), wrestling (m).

Campus Safety
Student safety services include patrols by trained security personnel 11 p.m. to 7 a.m, late-night transport/escort service, 24-hour emergency telephone alarm devices, student patrols, and electronically operated dormitory entrances.

Applying
Ithaca College requires an essay, SAT I or ACT, a high school transcript, and 1 recommendation, and in some cases audition. It recommends an interview and a minimum high school GPA of 3.0. Application deadline: 3/1; 2/1 priority date for financial aid. Early and deferred admission are possible.

JAMES MADISON UNIVERSITY

SMALL-TOWN SETTING ■ PUBLIC ■ STATE-SUPPORTED ■ COED
HARRISONBURG, VIRGINIA

Web site: www.jmu.edu
Contact: Ms. Laika K. Tamny, Associate Director of Admissions, Office of Admission, Sonner Hall MSC 0101, Harrisonburg, VA 22807
Telephone: 540-568-5681 **Fax:** 540-568-3332
E-mail: gotojmu@jmu.edu

Academics

JMU awards bachelor's, master's, and doctoral **degrees** and post-master's certificates (also offers specialist in education degree). Challenging opportunities include advanced placement credit, accelerated degree programs, freshman honors college, an honors program, double majors, independent study, and a senior project. Special programs include internships, summer session for credit, study-abroad, and Army and Air Force ROTC.

The most frequently chosen **baccalaureate** fields are business/marketing, social sciences and history, and health professions and related sciences. A complete listing of majors at JMU appears in the Majors Index beginning on page 460.

The **faculty** at JMU has 721 full-time members, 82% with terminal degrees. The student-faculty ratio is 17:1.

Students of JMU

The student body totals 16,203, of whom 14,991 are undergraduates. 59.8% are women and 40.2% are men. Students come from 49 states and territories and 48 other countries. 70% are from Virginia. 0.9% are international students. 3.2% are African American, 0.2% American Indian, 4.9% Asian American, and 1.9% Hispanic American. 92% returned for their sophomore year.

Facilities and Resources

Student rooms are linked to a campus network. 600 **computers** are available on campus that provide access to the Internet. The 3 **libraries** have 744,041 books and 3,367 subscriptions.

Campus Life

There are 286 active organizations on campus, including a drama/theater group, newspaper, radio station, choral group, and marching band. 10% of eligible men and 16% of eligible women are members of national **fraternities** and national **sororities**.

JMU is a member of the NCAA (Division I). **Intercollegiate sports** (some offering scholarships) include archery, baseball (m), basketball, cross-country running, fencing (w), field hockey (w), football (m), golf, gymnastics, lacrosse (w), soccer, softball (w), swimming, tennis, track and field, volleyball (w), wrestling (m).

Campus Safety

Student safety services include lighted pathways, late-night transport/escort service, 24-hour emergency telephone alarm devices, 24-hour patrols by trained security personnel, student patrols, and electronically operated dormitory entrances.

Applying

JMU requires an essay, SAT I or ACT, and a high school transcript. It recommends a minimum high school GPA of 3.0. Application deadline: 1/15; 3/1 priority date for financial aid. Deferred admission is possible.

Getting in Last Year

15,056 applied
62% were accepted
3,388 enrolled (36%)
30% from top tenth of their h.s. class
35% had SAT verbal scores over 600
39% had SAT math scores over 600
3% had SAT verbal scores over 700
3% had SAT math scores over 700

Graduation and After

61% graduated in 4 years
17% graduated in 5 years
2% graduated in 6 years
64% had job offers within 6 months
131 organizations recruited on campus

Financial Matters

$5058 resident tuition and fees (2003–04)
$13,280 nonresident tuition and fees (2003–04)
$5966 room and board
52% average percent of need met
$6102 average financial aid amount received per undergraduate

JOHN BROWN UNIVERSITY

SMALL-TOWN SETTING ■ PRIVATE ■ INDEPENDENT RELIGIOUS ■ COED
SILOAM SPRINGS, ARKANSAS

Web site: www.jbu.edu

Contact: Mrs. Karen Elliott, Admissions Systems Manager, 200 West University Street, Siloam Springs, AR 72761-2121

Telephone: 501-524-7454 or toll-free 877-JBU-INFO **Fax:** 501-524-4196

E-mail: jbuinfo@acc.jbu.edu

Getting in Last Year

620 applied
82% were accepted
33% from top tenth of their h.s. class
3.51 average high school GPA
37% had SAT verbal scores over 600
35% had SAT math scores over 600
54% had ACT scores over 24
11% had SAT verbal scores over 700
9% had SAT math scores over 700
12% had ACT scores over 30
2 National Merit Scholars
17 valedictorians

Graduation and After

28% pursued further study (11% business, 9% education, 2% law)
97% had job offers within 6 months
77 organizations recruited on campus

Financial Matters

$14,356 tuition and fees (2003–04)
$5040 room and board
65% average percent of need met
$11,400 average financial aid amount received per undergraduate

Academics

JBU awards associate, bachelor's, and master's **degrees**. Challenging opportunities include advanced placement credit, freshman honors college, an honors program, double majors, independent study, and a senior project. Special programs include internships, study-abroad, and Army and Air Force ROTC.

The most frequently chosen **baccalaureate** fields are education, communications/communication technologies, and business/marketing. A complete listing of majors at JBU appears in the Majors Index beginning on page 460.

The **faculty** at JBU has 86 full-time members. The student-faculty ratio is 16:1.

Students of JBU

The student body totals 1,834, of whom 1,652 are undergraduates. Students come from 44 states and territories and 37 other countries. 36% are from Arkansas. 8.2% are international students. 1.8% are African American, 1.6% American Indian, 1.3% Asian American, and 2.1% Hispanic American. 83% returned for their sophomore year.

Facilities and Resources

Student rooms are linked to a campus network. 93 **computers** are available on campus that provide access to the Internet. The 5 **libraries** have 114,799 books and 3,775 subscriptions.

Campus Life

There are 20 active organizations on campus, including a drama/theater group, newspaper, radio station, television station, and choral group. No national or local **fraternities** or **sororities**.

JBU is a member of the NAIA. **Intercollegiate sports** (some offering scholarships) include basketball, soccer, swimming, tennis, volleyball (w).

Campus Safety

Student safety services include late-night transport/escort service, 24-hour emergency telephone alarm devices, and 24-hour patrols by trained security personnel.

Applying

JBU requires an essay, SAT I or ACT, a high school transcript, 2 recommendations, and a minimum high school GPA of 2.5. It recommends an interview. Application deadline: 3/1; 3/1 priority date for financial aid. Deferred admission is possible.

JOHN CARROLL UNIVERSITY

SUBURBAN SETTING ■ PRIVATE ■ INDEPENDENT RELIGIOUS ■ COED
UNIVERSITY HEIGHTS, OHIO

Web site: www.jcu.edu
Contact: Mr. Thomas P. Fanning, Director of Admission, 20700 North Park
   Boulevard, University Heights, OH 44118
Telephone: 216-397-4294 **Fax:** 216-397-4981
E-mail: admission@jcu.edu

Academics

John Carroll awards bachelor's and master's **degrees**. Challenging opportunities include advanced placement credit, accelerated degree programs, student-designed majors, an honors program, double majors, independent study, and a senior project. Special programs include cooperative education, internships, summer session for credit, off-campus study, study-abroad, and Army ROTC.

The most frequently chosen **baccalaureate** fields are business/marketing, social sciences and history, and communications/communication technologies. A complete listing of majors at John Carroll appears in the Majors Index beginning on page 460.

The **faculty** at John Carroll has 244 full-time members. The student-faculty ratio is 15:1.

Students of John Carroll

The student body totals 4,242, of whom 3,279 are undergraduates. Students come from 35 states and territories. 73% are from Ohio. 86% returned for their sophomore year.

Facilities and Resources

Student rooms are linked to a campus network. 210 **computers** are available on campus that provide access to the Internet. The **library** has 620,000 books and 2,198 subscriptions.

Campus Life

There are 87 active organizations on campus, including a drama/theater group, newspaper, radio station, and choral group. 13% of eligible men and 18% of eligible women are members of national **fraternities** and national **sororities**.

John Carroll is a member of the NCAA (Division III). **Intercollegiate sports** include baseball (m), basketball, cross-country running, football (m), golf, soccer, softball (w), swimming, tennis, track and field, volleyball (w), wrestling (m).

Campus Safety

Student safety services include late-night transport/escort service, 24-hour emergency telephone alarm devices, and 24-hour patrols by trained security personnel.

Applying

John Carroll requires SAT I or ACT, a high school transcript, and 1 recommendation, and in some cases an interview. It recommends an essay and an interview. Application deadline: 2/1; 3/1 priority date for financial aid. Early and deferred admission are possible.

Founded in 1886, John Carroll University, is one of 28 Catholic colleges and universities operated in the United States by the Society of Jesus. In the Jesuit tradition of leadership, faith, and service, John Carroll provides its students with a rigorous education rooted in the liberal arts and focused on questions of moral and ethical values. John Carroll offers more than 85 student organizations, community volunteer service opportunities, and academic honor societies to foster leadership activities outside the classroom.

Getting in Last Year
2,764 applied
86% were accepted
24% from top tenth of their h.s. class
3.27 average high school GPA
32% had SAT verbal scores over 600
43% had SAT math scores over 600
48% had ACT scores over 24
6% had SAT verbal scores over 700
4% had SAT math scores over 700
6% had ACT scores over 30
5 National Merit Scholars
12 valedictorians

Graduation and After
22% pursued further study (12% arts and
   sciences, 4% law, 2% business)
64% had job offers within 6 months
332 organizations recruited on campus

Financial Matters
$20,766 tuition and fees (2003–04)
$6892 room and board
$14,104 average financial aid amount received
   per undergraduate (2000–01 estimated)

THE JOHNS HOPKINS UNIVERSITY

URBAN SETTING ■ PRIVATE ■ INDEPENDENT ■ COED
BALTIMORE, MARYLAND

Web site: www.jhu.edu
Contact: Mr. John Latting, Director of Undergraduate Admissions, 140 Garland Hall, 3400 North Charles Street, Baltimore, MD 21218-2699
Telephone: 410-516-8341 **Fax:** 410-516-6025
E-mail: gotojhu@jhu.edu

Getting in Last Year
10,022 applied
30% were accepted
1,048 enrolled (34%)
76% from top tenth of their h.s. class
3.66 average high school GPA
88% had SAT verbal scores over 600
94% had SAT math scores over 600
98% had ACT scores over 24
38% had SAT verbal scores over 700
59% had SAT math scores over 700
59% had ACT scores over 30
17 National Merit Scholars

Graduation and After
80% graduated in 4 years
7% graduated in 5 years
1% graduated in 6 years
40% pursued further study
63% had job offers within 6 months

Financial Matters
$29,230 tuition and fees (2003–04)
$9142 room and board
95% average percent of need met
$25,210 average financial aid amount received per undergraduate (2002–03 estimated)

Academics

Johns Hopkins awards bachelor's, master's, doctoral, and first-professional **degrees** and post-bachelor's and post-master's certificates. Challenging opportunities include advanced placement credit, accelerated degree programs, student-designed majors, an honors program, double majors, independent study, and a senior project. Special programs include internships, summer session for credit, off-campus study, study-abroad, and Army and Air Force ROTC.

The most frequently chosen **baccalaureate** fields are social sciences and history, health professions and related sciences, and engineering/engineering technologies. A complete listing of majors at Johns Hopkins appears in the Majors Index beginning on page 460.

The **faculty** at Johns Hopkins has 455 full-time members, 96% with terminal degrees.

Students of Johns Hopkins

The student body totals 6,229, of whom 4,177 are undergraduates. 42.9% are women and 57.1% are men. Students come from 51 states and territories and 50 other countries. 20% are from Maryland. 5.6% are international students. 4.9% are African American. 0.3% American Indian, 21.1% Asian American, and 4.2% Hispanic American.

Facilities and Resources

Student rooms are linked to a campus network. 460 **computers** are available on campus that provide access to the Internet. The 7 **libraries** have 3,509,413 books and 30,023 subscriptions.

Campus Life

There are 180 active organizations on campus, including a drama/theater group, newspaper, radio station, and choral group. 23% of eligible men and 22% of eligible women are members of national **fraternities** and national **sororities**.

Johns Hopkins is a member of the NCAA (Division III). **Intercollegiate sports** (some offering scholarships) include baseball (m), basketball, crew, cross-country running, fencing, field hockey (w), football (m), lacrosse, soccer, swimming, tennis, track and field, volleyball (w), water polo (m), wrestling (m).

Campus Safety

Student safety services include late-night transport/escort service, 24-hour emergency telephone alarm devices, 24-hour patrols by trained security personnel, student patrols, and electronically operated dormitory entrances.

Applying

Johns Hopkins requires an essay, SAT II: Writing Test, SAT I and SAT II or ACT, a high school transcript, and 1 recommendation. It recommends an interview. Application deadline: 1/1; 2/15 for financial aid, with a 2/1 priority date. Early and deferred admission are possible.

JUNIATA COLLEGE

SMALL-TOWN SETTING ■ PRIVATE ■ INDEPENDENT RELIGIOUS ■ COED
HUNTINGDON, PENNSYLVANIA

Web site: www.juniata.edu
Contact: Terry Bollman, Director of Admissions, 1700 Moore Street,
Huntingdon, PA 16652
Telephone: 814-641-3424 or toll-free 877-JUNIATA **Fax:** 814-641-3100
E-mail: info@juniata.edu

Academics

Juniata awards bachelor's **degrees**. Challenging opportunities include advanced placement credit, accelerated degree programs, student-designed majors, freshman honors
college, an honors program, double majors, independent study, and a senior project.
Special programs include internships, summer session for credit, off-campus study, and
study-abroad.

The most frequently chosen **baccalaureate** fields are biological/life sciences, busi-
ness/marketing, and education. A complete listing of majors at Juniata appears in the
Majors Index beginning on page 460.

The **faculty** at Juniata has 93 full-time members, 95% with terminal degrees. The
student-faculty ratio is 13:1.

Students of Juniata

The student body is made up of 1,396 undergraduates. 55.9% are women and 44.1% are
men. Students come from 32 states and territories and 21 other countries. 75% are from
Pennsylvania. 2.6% are international students. 1.2% are African American, 0.2%
American Indian, 1% Asian American, and 0.8% Hispanic American. 86% returned for
their sophomore year.

Facilities and Resources

Student rooms are linked to a campus network. 375 **computers** are available on campus
that provide access to the Internet. The **library** has 255,000 books and 1,000 subscriptions.

Campus Life

There are 86 active organizations on campus, including a drama/theater group,
newspaper, radio station, and choral group. No national or local **fraternities** or **sororities**.

Juniata is a member of the NCAA (Division III). **Intercollegiate sports** include
baseball (m), basketball, cross-country running, field hockey (w), football (m), soccer,
softball (w), swimming (w), tennis, track and field, volleyball.

Campus Safety

Student safety services include fire safety training, adopt-an-officer program, security
website, weather/terror alerts, travel forecast, crime statistics, late-night transport/escort
service, 24-hour emergency telephone alarm devices, 24-hour patrols by trained security
personnel, and student patrols.

Applying

Juniata requires an essay, SAT I or ACT, a high school transcript, 1 recommendation,
and a minimum high school GPA of 3.0. It recommends an interview. Application
deadline: 3/15; 3/1 priority date for financial aid. Early and deferred admission are possible.

A caring and supportive
learning community, Juniata
challenges its students to
think and to question, while
discovering countless opportunities
for engaged learning. Juniata's
1,380 students benefit from
top-flight academics, state-of-the-art
technological resources, and guidance
from two dedicated faculty advisors.
From the $20 million William J. von
Liebig Center for Science to the
Entrepreneur-based Business
Program, Juniata offers
groundbreaking educational
opportunities. Juniata is a place
where students are encouraged to
design their academic program and
contribute to their community. The
campus, located in the rolling hills of
central Pennsylvania, is a friendly
environment where students develop
into successful leaders.

Getting in Last Year
1,578 applied
75% were accepted
381 enrolled (32%)
35% from top tenth of their h.s. class
3.71 average high school GPA
41% had SAT verbal scores over 600
45% had SAT math scores over 600
7% had SAT verbal scores over 700
7% had SAT math scores over 700
12 National Merit Scholars
15 valedictorians

Graduation and After
68% graduated in 4 years
6% graduated in 5 years
1% graduated in 6 years
33% pursued further study (17% arts and
sciences, 5% medicine, 2% business)
60% had job offers within 6 months
55 organizations recruited on campus

Financial Matters
$22,760 tuition and fees (2003–04)
$6290 room and board
89% average percent of need met
$17,936 average financial aid amount received
per undergraduate (2002–03 estimated)

KALAMAZOO COLLEGE

SUBURBAN SETTING ■ PRIVATE ■ INDEPENDENT RELIGIOUS ■ COED
KALAMAZOO, MICHIGAN

Web site: www.kzoo.edu
Contact: Mrs. Linda Wirgau, Records Manager, Mandelle Hall, 1200
   Academy Street, Kalamazoo, MI 49006-3295
Telephone: 269-337-7166 or toll-free 800-253-3602
E-mail: admission@kzoo.edu

Getting in Last Year
1,603 applied
70% were accepted
383 enrolled (34%)
48% from top tenth of their h.s. class
3.65 average high school GPA
83% had SAT verbal scores over 600
81% had SAT math scores over 600
93% had ACT scores over 24
32% had SAT verbal scores over 700
25% had SAT math scores over 700
26% had ACT scores over 30
9 National Merit Scholars
22 valedictorians

Graduation and After
70% graduated in 4 years
6% graduated in 5 years
1% graduated in 6 years
33% pursued further study
19 organizations recruited on campus

Financial Matters
$22,908 tuition and fees (2003–04)
$6480 room and board
$19,000 average financial aid amount received
   per undergraduate (2002–03 estimated)

Academics
K-College awards bachelor's **degrees**. Challenging opportunities include advanced placement credit, double majors, independent study, and a senior project. Special programs include cooperative education, internships, off-campus study, study-abroad, and Army ROTC.

The most frequently chosen **baccalaureate** fields are social sciences and history, psychology, and English. A complete listing of majors at K-College appears in the Majors Index beginning on page 460.

The **faculty** at K-College has 103 full-time members, 86% with terminal degrees. The student-faculty ratio is 12:1.

Students of K-College
The student body is made up of 1,280 undergraduates. 56.1% are women and 43.9% are men. Students come from 35 states and territories and 14 other countries. 74% are from Michigan. 1.9% are international students. 2.8% are African American, 0.2% American Indian, 4.4% Asian American, and 1.4% Hispanic American. 86% returned for their sophomore year.

Facilities and Resources
Student rooms are linked to a campus network. 130 **computers** are available on campus that provide access to the Internet. The 2 **libraries** have 342,939 books and 1,495 subscriptions.

Campus Life
There are 50 active organizations on campus, including a drama/theater group, newspaper, radio station, and choral group. No national or local **fraternities** or **sororities**.

K-College is a member of the NCAA (Division III). **Intercollegiate sports** include baseball (m), basketball, cross-country running, football (m), golf, soccer, softball (w), swimming, tennis, volleyball (w).

Campus Safety
Student safety services include late-night transport/escort service, 24-hour emergency telephone alarm devices, 24-hour patrols by trained security personnel, and electronically operated dormitory entrances.

Applying
K-College requires an essay, SAT I or ACT, a high school transcript, and 2 recommendations. It recommends an interview and a minimum high school GPA of 3.0. Application deadline: 2/15; 2/15 priority date for financial aid. Deferred admission is possible.

KANSAS STATE UNIVERSITY

SUBURBAN SETTING ■ PUBLIC ■ STATE-SUPPORTED ■ COED
MANHATTAN, KANSAS

Web site: www.ksu.edu
Contact: Ms. Christy Crenshaw, Associate Director of Admissions, 119
   Anderson Hall, Manhattan, KS 66506
Telephone: 785-532-6250 or toll-free 800-432-8270 (in-state) **Fax:**
   785-532-6393
E-mail: kstate@ksu.edu

Academics

KSU awards associate, bachelor's, master's, doctoral, and first-professional **degrees**.
Challenging opportunities include advanced placement credit, accelerated degree
programs, freshman honors college, an honors program, double majors, independent
study, and a senior project. Special programs include cooperative education, internships,
summer session for credit, off-campus study, study-abroad, and Army and Air Force
ROTC.

The most frequently chosen **baccalaureate** fields are business/marketing, engineer-
ing/engineering technologies, and agriculture. A complete listing of majors at KSU appears in the Majors Index beginning on page 460.

The **faculty** at KSU has 851 full-time members, 88% with terminal degrees. The
student-faculty ratio is 12:1.

Students of KSU

The student body totals 23,050, of whom 19,083 are undergraduates. 48.3% are women
and 51.7% are men. Students come from 50 states and territories and 100 other
countries. 90% are from Kansas. 1% are international students. 3% are African
American, 0.5% American Indian, 1.4% Asian American, and 2.3% Hispanic American.
79% returned for their sophomore year.

Facilities and Resources

Student rooms are linked to a campus network. 556 **computers** are available on campus
that provide access to the Internet. The 4 **libraries** have 1,573,645 books and 1,365
subscriptions.

Campus Life

There are 372 active organizations on campus, including a drama/theater group,
newspaper, radio station, choral group, and marching band. 20% of eligible men and
20% of eligible women are members of national **fraternities** and national **sororities**.

KSU is a member of the NCAA (Division I). **Intercollegiate sports** (some offering
scholarships) include baseball (m), basketball, crew (w), cross-country running, football
(m), golf, tennis (w), track and field, volleyball (w).

Campus Safety

Student safety services include late-night transport/escort service, 24-hour emergency
telephone alarm devices, 24-hour patrols by trained security personnel, and electronically operated dormitory entrances.

Applying

KSU requires SAT I or ACT, a high school transcript, and a minimum high school GPA
of 2.0. It recommends ACT. Application deadline: rolling admissions; 3/1 priority date
for financial aid.

Getting in Last Year
7,952 applied
60% were accepted
3,439 enrolled (73%)
3.47 average high school GPA
49% had ACT scores over 24
8% had ACT scores over 30

Graduation and After
22% graduated in 4 years
28% graduated in 5 years
6% graduated in 6 years
18% pursued further study
62% had job offers within 6 months
470 organizations recruited on campus

Financial Matters
$4059 resident tuition and fees (2003–04)
$11,949 nonresident tuition and fees (2003–
   04)
$5080 room and board
75% average percent of need met
$4882 average financial aid amount received
   per undergraduate (2001–02)

KENTUCKY MOUNTAIN BIBLE COLLEGE

RURAL SETTING ■ PRIVATE ■ INDEPENDENT RELIGIOUS ■ COED
VANCLEVE, KENTUCKY

Web site: www.kmbc.edu
Contact: Mr. Dana Beland, Director of Recruiting, PO Box 10, 855 Route 41, Vancleve, KY 41385
Telephone: 606-693-5000 ext. 130 or toll-free 800-879-KMBC ext. 130 (in-state), 800-879-KMBC ext. 136 (out-of-state) **Fax:** 606-693-4884
E-mail: jnelson@kmbc.edu

Getting in Last Year
33% from top tenth of their h.s. class
3.33 average high school GPA

Graduation and After
44% graduated in 4 years
6% graduated in 5 years
13% graduated in 6 years
13% pursued further study (13% theology)

Financial Matters
$4930 tuition and fees (2003–04)
$3000 room and board
30% average percent of need met
$2000 average financial aid amount received per undergraduate

Academics
KMBC awards associate and bachelor's **degrees**. A senior project is a challenging opportunity. Internships is a special program. A complete listing of majors at KMBC appears in the Majors Index beginning on page 460.

The **faculty** at KMBC has 9 full-time members, 22% with terminal degrees. The student-faculty ratio is 6:1.

Students of KMBC
The student body is made up of 82 undergraduates. Students come from 17 states and territories. 29% are from Kentucky. 12% are international students. 1.3% are African American. 64% returned for their sophomore year.

Facilities and Resources
12 **computers** are available on campus that provide access to the Internet. The **library** has 23,520 books and 175 subscriptions.

Campus Life
There are 40 active organizations on campus, including a choral group. No national or local **fraternities** or **sororities**.

This institution has no intercollegiate sports.

Campus Safety
Student safety services include student patrols.

Applying
KMBC requires an essay, ACT, a high school transcript, recommendations, and a minimum high school GPA of 2.0. It recommends an interview. Application deadline: rolling admissions; 4/1 priority date for financial aid. Deferred admission is possible.

KENYON COLLEGE

RURAL SETTING ■ PRIVATE ■ INDEPENDENT ■ COED
GAMBIER, OHIO

Web site: www.kenyon.edu
Contact: Ms. Jennifer Britz, Dean of Admissions, Ransom Hall, Gambier, OH
  43022
Telephone: 740-427-5776 or toll-free 800-848-2468 **Fax:** 740-427-5770
E-mail: admissions@kenyon.edu

Academics

Kenyon awards bachelor's **degrees**. Challenging opportunities include advanced placement credit, accelerated degree programs, student-designed majors, an honors program,
double majors, independent study, and a senior project. Special programs include internships, off-campus study, and study-abroad.

The most frequently chosen **baccalaureate** fields are English, social sciences and
history, and visual/performing arts. A complete listing of majors at Kenyon appears in
the Majors Index beginning on page 460.

The **faculty** at Kenyon has 145 full-time members, 97% with terminal degrees. The
student-faculty ratio is 10:1.

Students of Kenyon

The student body is made up of 1,612 undergraduates. 54.9% are women and 45.1% are
men. 22% are from Ohio. 2.4% are international students. 3% are African American,
0.1% American Indian, 3.2% Asian American, and 2.3% Hispanic American. 92%
returned for their sophomore year.

Facilities and Resources

Student rooms are linked to a campus network. 300 **computers** are available on campus
that provide access to commercial databases and the Internet. The 2 **libraries** have
858,000 books and 5,300 subscriptions.

Campus Life

There are 138 active organizations on campus, including a drama/theater group,
newspaper, radio station, and choral group. 19% of eligible men and 7% of eligible
women are members of national **fraternities**, local fraternities, and local **sororities**.

Kenyon is a member of the NCAA (Division III). **Intercollegiate sports** include
baseball (m), basketball, cross-country running, field hockey (w), football (m), golf (m),
lacrosse, soccer, softball (w), swimming, tennis, track and field, volleyball (w).

Campus Safety

Student safety services include late-night transport/escort service, 24-hour emergency
telephone alarm devices, 24-hour patrols by trained security personnel, and student
patrols.

Applying

Kenyon requires an essay, SAT I or ACT, a high school transcript, 1 recommendation,
and a minimum high school GPA of 2.0. It recommends an interview, 2 recommendations, and a minimum high school GPA of 3.0. Application deadline: 2/1; 2/15 priority
date for financial aid. Early and deferred admission are possible.

Getting in Last Year
3,360 applied
46% were accepted
454 enrolled (30%)
53% from top tenth of their h.s. class
3.76 average high school GPA
86% had SAT verbal scores over 600
78% had SAT math scores over 600
99% had ACT scores over 24
40% had SAT verbal scores over 700
23% had SAT math scores over 700
57% had ACT scores over 30
41 National Merit Scholars
8 class presidents
20 valedictorians

Graduation and After
79% graduated in 4 years
4% graduated in 5 years
25% pursued further study
27 organizations recruited on campus

Financial Matters
$30,330 tuition and fees (2003–04)
$5040 room and board
98% average percent of need met
$21,499 average financial aid amount received
  per undergraduate (2002–03 estimated)

KETTERING UNIVERSITY

SUBURBAN SETTING ■ PRIVATE ■ INDEPENDENT ■ COED
FLINT, MICHIGAN

Web site: www.kettering.edu
Contact: Ms. Barbara Sosin, Director of Admissions, 1700 West Third
Avenue, Flint, MI 48504-4898
Telephone: 810-762-7865 or toll-free 800-955-4464 ext. 7865 (in-state),
800-955-4464 (out-of-state) **Fax:** 810-762-9837
E-mail: admissions@kettering.edu

Getting in Last Year

2,365 applied
71% were accepted
561 enrolled (34%)
30% from top tenth of their h.s. class
3.6 average high school GPA
48% had SAT verbal scores over 600
78% had SAT math scores over 600
74% had ACT scores over 24
8% had SAT verbal scores over 700
22% had SAT math scores over 700
12% had ACT scores over 30
19 valedictorians

Graduation and After

3% graduated in 4 years
51% graduated in 5 years
10% graduated in 6 years
33% pursued further study (17% business,
  10% engineering, 4% arts and sciences)
98% had job offers within 6 months
550 organizations recruited on campus

Financial Matters

$21,554 tuition and fees (2003–04)
$4924 room and board
43% average percent of need met
$10,740 average financial aid amount received
  per undergraduate

Academics

Kettering/GMI awards bachelor's and master's **degrees**. Challenging opportunities include advanced placement credit, accelerated degree programs, double majors, independent study, and a senior project. Special programs include cooperative education, internships, and study-abroad.

The most frequently chosen **baccalaureate** fields are engineering/engineering technologies, business/marketing, and computer/information sciences. A complete listing of majors at Kettering/GMI appears in the Majors Index beginning on page 460.

The **faculty** at Kettering/GMI has 139 full-time members, 89% with terminal degrees. The student-faculty ratio is 12:1.

Students of Kettering/GMI

The student body totals 3,126, of whom 2,558 are undergraduates. 17.3% are women and 82.7% are men. Students come from 52 states and territories and 24 other countries. 63% are from Michigan. 2.3% are international students. 7.2% are African American, 0.3% American Indian, 5.1% Asian American, and 2.2% Hispanic American. 88% returned for their sophomore year.

Facilities and Resources

Student rooms are linked to a campus network. 300 **computers** are available on campus that provide access to the Internet. The 2 **libraries** have 115,000 books and 1,200 subscriptions.

Campus Life

There are 40 active organizations on campus, including a drama/theater group, newspaper, radio station, and choral group. 40% of eligible men and 33% of eligible women are members of national **fraternities** and national **sororities**.

Intercollegiate sports include cheerleading.

Campus Safety

Student safety services include late-night transport/escort service, 24-hour emergency telephone alarm devices, 24-hour patrols by trained security personnel, and electronically operated dormitory entrances.

Applying

Kettering/GMI requires SAT I or ACT and a high school transcript, and in some cases an essay. It recommends SAT II Subject Tests, an interview, and a minimum high school GPA of 3.0. Application deadline: rolling admissions; 2/14 priority date for financial aid. Deferred admission is possible.

KING COLLEGE

SUBURBAN SETTING ■ PRIVATE ■ INDEPENDENT RELIGIOUS ■ COED
BRISTOL, TENNESSEE

Web site: www.king.edu
Contact: Mr. Darren Parker, Director of Recruitment, 1350 King College
   Road, Bristol, TN 37620-2699
Telephone: 423-652-4861 or toll-free 800-362-0014 **Fax:** 423-652-4727
E-mail: admissions@king.edu

Academics

King awards bachelor's and master's **degrees**. Challenging opportunities include advanced placement credit, accelerated degree programs, an honors program, double majors, independent study, and a senior project. Special programs include internships, summer session for credit, off-campus study, study-abroad, and Army ROTC. A complete listing of majors at King appears in the Majors Index beginning on page 460.

The **faculty** at King has 55 full-time members. The student-faculty ratio is 11:1.

Students of King

The student body totals 740, of whom 687 are undergraduates. 62.3% are women and 37.7% are men. 58% are from Tennessee. 1.7% are international students. 1% are African American, 0.3% American Indian, 0.4% Asian American, and 1% Hispanic American. 77% returned for their sophomore year.

Facilities and Resources

Student rooms are linked to a campus network. 80 **computers** are available on campus that provide access to the Internet. The **library** has 80,888 books and 1,539 subscriptions.

Campus Life

There are 29 active organizations on campus, including a drama/theater group, newspaper, and choral group. No national or local **fraternities** or **sororities**.

King is a member of the NAIA. **Intercollegiate sports** (some offering scholarships) include baseball (m), basketball, golf (m), soccer, tennis, volleyball (w).

Campus Safety

Student safety services include late-night transport/escort service.

Applying

King requires an essay, SAT I or ACT, a high school transcript, minimum ACT score of 20 or SAT score of 1000, and a minimum high school GPA of 2.4. It recommends an interview. Application deadline: rolling admissions. Early and deferred admission are possible.

Getting in Last Year
627 applied
87% were accepted
98 enrolled (18%)
24% from top tenth of their h.s. class
3.50 average high school GPA
45% had SAT verbal scores over 600
34% had SAT math scores over 600
61% had ACT scores over 24
7% had SAT verbal scores over 700
10% had SAT math scores over 700
7% had ACT scores over 30

Graduation and After
39% graduated in 4 years
4% graduated in 5 years
30% pursued further study
34% had job offers within 6 months
150 organizations recruited on campus

Financial Matters
$17,040 tuition and fees (2003–04)
$5460 room and board
65% average percent of need met
$14,330 average financial aid amount received
   per undergraduate (2002–03 estimated)

KNOX COLLEGE

SMALL-TOWN SETTING ■ PRIVATE ■ INDEPENDENT ■ COED
GALESBURG, ILLINOIS

Web site: www.knox.edu
Contact: Mr. Paul Steenis, Director of Admissions, Box K-148, Galesburg, IL 61401
Telephone: 309-341-7100 or toll-free 800-678-KNOX **Fax:** 309-341-7070
E-mail: admission@knox.edu

Getting in Last Year
1,538 applied
73% were accepted
268 enrolled (24%)
29% from top tenth of their h.s. class
59% had SAT verbal scores over 600
56% had SAT math scores over 600
82% had ACT scores over 24
23% had SAT verbal scores over 700
9% had SAT math scores over 700
25% had ACT scores over 30
3 National Merit Scholars
8 valedictorians

Graduation and After
71% graduated in 4 years
7% graduated in 5 years
35% pursued further study (22% arts and sciences, 3% law, 3% medicine)
53% had job offers within 6 months
80 organizations recruited on campus

Financial Matters
$24,369 tuition and fees (2003–04)
$5925 room and board
97% average percent of need met
$20,770 average financial aid amount received per undergraduate

Academics

Knox awards bachelor's **degrees**. Challenging opportunities include advanced placement credit, student-designed majors, an honors program, double majors, independent study, and a senior project. Special programs include internships, off-campus study, and study-abroad.

The most frequently chosen **baccalaureate** fields are social sciences and history, biological/life sciences, and visual/performing arts. A complete listing of majors at Knox appears in the Majors Index beginning on page 460.

The **faculty** at Knox has 92 full-time members, 95% with terminal degrees. The student-faculty ratio is 12:1.

Students of Knox

The student body is made up of 1,127 undergraduates. 53.4% are women and 46.6% are men. Students come from 46 states and territories and 50 other countries. 56% are from Illinois. 8.7% are international students. 4.1% are African American, 0.5% American Indian, 4.8% Asian American, and 4% Hispanic American. 87% returned for their sophomore year.

Facilities and Resources

Student rooms are linked to a campus network. 171 **computers** are available on campus that provide access to software applications and the Internet. The 3 **libraries** have 185,923 books and 1,037 subscriptions.

Campus Life

There are 102 active organizations on campus, including a drama/theater group, newspaper, radio station, and choral group. 37% of eligible men and 15% of eligible women are members of national **fraternities** and national **sororities**.

Knox is a member of the NCAA. **Intercollegiate sports** include baseball (m), basketball, cross-country running, football (m), golf, soccer, softball (w), swimming, tennis, track and field, volleyball (w), wrestling (m).

Campus Safety

Student safety services include late-night transport/escort service, 24-hour emergency telephone alarm devices, and 24-hour patrols by trained security personnel.

Applying

Knox requires an essay, SAT I or ACT, a high school transcript, and 2 recommendations. It recommends an interview. Application deadline: 2/1; 3/1 priority date for financial aid. Early and deferred admission are possible.

LAFAYETTE COLLEGE

SUBURBAN SETTING ■ PRIVATE ■ INDEPENDENT RELIGIOUS ■ COED
EASTON, PENNSYLVANIA

Web site: www.lafayette.edu
Contact: Ms. Carol Rowlands, Director of Admissions, Easton, PA
18042-1798
Telephone: 610-330-5100 **Fax:** 610-330-5355
E-mail: admissions@lafayette.edu

Lafayette has achieved a unique niche in American higher education: liberal arts, sciences, and engineering programs in a most academically competitive, small-college setting. Lafayette offers small classes, interdisciplinary first-year seminars, and student-faculty collaborative research on a residential campus located in eastern Pennsylvania, close to New York and Philadelphia.

Academics

Lafayette awards bachelor's **degrees**. Challenging opportunities include advanced placement credit, accelerated degree programs, student-designed majors, and an honors program. Special programs include internships, summer session for credit, off-campus study, study-abroad, and Army ROTC.

The most frequently chosen **baccalaureate** fields are trade and industry, engineering/engineering technologies, and business/marketing. A complete listing of majors at Lafayette appears in the Majors Index beginning on page 460.

The **faculty** at Lafayette has 188 full-time members, 100% with terminal degrees. The student-faculty ratio is 11:1.

Students of Lafayette

The student body is made up of 2,285 undergraduates. 47.2% are women and 52.8% are men. Students come from 35 states and territories and 40 other countries. 29% are from Pennsylvania. 5.2% are international students. 4.5% are African American, 0.3% American Indian, 1.9% Asian American, and 3% Hispanic American. 94% returned for their sophomore year.

Facilities and Resources

Student rooms are linked to a campus network. 480 **computers** are available on campus that provide access to the Internet. The 2 **libraries** have 521,000 books and 2,750 subscriptions.

Campus Life

There are 250 active organizations on campus, including a drama/theater group, newspaper, radio station, and choral group. 26% of eligible men and 45% of eligible women are members of national **fraternities**, national **sororities**, and social dorms.

Lafayette is a member of the NCAA (Division I). **Intercollegiate sports** include baseball (m), basketball, cross-country running, fencing, field hockey (w), football (m), golf (m), lacrosse, soccer, softball (w), swimming, tennis, track and field, volleyball (w).

Campus Safety

Student safety services include late-night transport/escort service, 24-hour emergency telephone alarm devices, 24-hour patrols by trained security personnel, student patrols, and electronically operated dormitory entrances.

Applying

Lafayette requires an essay, SAT I, SAT II Subject Tests, a high school transcript, and 1 recommendation. It recommends SAT II: Writing Test and an interview. Application deadline: 1/1; 3/15 for financial aid, with a 2/1 priority date. Early and deferred admission are possible.

Getting in Last Year
5,835 applied
36% were accepted
584 enrolled (28%)
61% from top tenth of their h.s. class
3.90 average high school GPA
64% had SAT verbal scores over 600
79% had SAT math scores over 600
90% had ACT scores over 24
15% had SAT verbal scores over 700
25% had SAT math scores over 700
18% had ACT scores over 30
6 National Merit Scholars

Graduation and After
80% graduated in 4 years
5% graduated in 5 years
34% pursued further study (12% arts and sciences, 8% engineering, 6% law)
43% had job offers within 6 months
240 organizations recruited on campus

Financial Matters
$26,044 tuition and fees (2003–04)
$8069 room and board
99% average percent of need met
$22,407 average financial aid amount received per undergraduate

LAKE FOREST COLLEGE

SUBURBAN SETTING ■ PRIVATE ■ INDEPENDENT ■ COED
LAKE FOREST, ILLINOIS

Web site: www.lakeforest.edu
Contact: Mr. William G. Motzer Jr., Director of Admissions, 555 North
    Sheridan Road, Lake Forest, IL 60045-2399
Telephone: 847-735-5000 or toll-free 800-828-4751 **Fax:** 847-735-6271
E-mail: admissions@lakeforest.edu

Getting in Last Year

1,835 applied
68% were accepted
347 enrolled (28%)
24% from top tenth of their h.s. class
3.40 average high school GPA
44% had SAT verbal scores over 600
44% had SAT math scores over 600
68% had ACT scores over 24
8% had SAT verbal scores over 700
8% had SAT math scores over 700
16% had ACT scores over 30
22 class presidents
5 valedictorians

Graduation and After

61% graduated in 4 years
5% graduated in 5 years
32% pursued further study
89% had job offers within 6 months
125 organizations recruited on campus

Financial Matters

$24,406 tuition and fees (2003–04)
$5764 room and board
100% average percent of need met
$20,020 average financial aid amount received
    per undergraduate (2002–03 estimated)

Academics

Lake Forest awards bachelor's and master's **degrees**. Challenging opportunities include advanced placement credit, accelerated degree programs, student-designed majors, freshman honors college, an honors program, double majors, independent study, and a senior project. Special programs include internships, summer session for credit, off-campus study, and study-abroad.

The most frequently chosen **baccalaureate** fields are social sciences and history, business/marketing, and communications/communication technologies. A complete listing of majors at Lake Forest appears in the Majors Index beginning on page 460.

The **faculty** at Lake Forest has 87 full-time members, 97% with terminal degrees. The student-faculty ratio is 12:1.

Students of Lake Forest

The student body totals 1,348, of whom 1,336 are undergraduates. 57% are women and 43% are men. Students come from 47 states and territories and 50 other countries. 48% are from Illinois. 9.7% are international students. 4.9% are African American, 0.2% American Indian, 4% Asian American, and 3.8% Hispanic American. 81% returned for their sophomore year.

Facilities and Resources

Student rooms are linked to a campus network. 120 **computers** are available on campus that provide access to file storage and the Internet. The 2 **libraries** have 268,760 books and 886 subscriptions.

Campus Life

There are 67 active organizations on campus, including a drama/theater group, newspaper, radio station, and choral group. 18% of eligible men and 14% of eligible women are members of national **fraternities**, local fraternities, and local **sororities**.

Lake Forest is a member of the NCAA (Division III). **Intercollegiate sports** include basketball, cross-country running, football (m), ice hockey, soccer, softball (w), swimming, tennis, volleyball (w), water polo (m).

Campus Safety

Student safety services include late-night transport/escort service, 24-hour emergency telephone alarm devices, 24-hour patrols by trained security personnel, and student patrols.

Applying

Lake Forest requires an essay, SAT I or ACT, a high school transcript, 2 recommendations, and graded paper. It recommends an interview. Application deadline: 3/1; 3/1 priority date for financial aid. Early and deferred admission are possible.

LAWRENCE TECHNOLOGICAL UNIVERSITY

SUBURBAN SETTING ■ PRIVATE ■ INDEPENDENT ■ COED
SOUTHFIELD, MICHIGAN

Web site: www.ltu.edu
Contact: Ms. Jane Rohrback, Director of Admissions, 21000 West Ten Mile Road, Southfield, MI 48075
Telephone: 248-204-3180 or toll-free 800-225-5588 **Fax:** 248-204-3188
E-mail: admissions@ltu.edu

Academics

Lawrence Tech awards associate, bachelor's, and master's **degrees**. Challenging opportunities include advanced placement credit, double majors, independent study, and a senior project. Special programs include cooperative education, internships, summer session for credit, off-campus study, study-abroad, and Army and Air Force ROTC.

The most frequently chosen **baccalaureate** fields are engineering/engineering technologies, architecture, and computer/information sciences. A complete listing of majors at Lawrence Tech appears in the Majors Index beginning on page 460.

The **faculty** at Lawrence Tech has 114 full-time members, 78% with terminal degrees. The student-faculty ratio is 13:1.

Students of Lawrence Tech

The student body totals 4,241, of whom 2,958 are undergraduates. 24% are women and 76% are men. Students come from 16 states and territories and 16 other countries. 99% are from Michigan. 4.4% are international students. 10.9% are African American, 0.4% American Indian, 8.1% Asian American, and 1.4% Hispanic American. 64% returned for their sophomore year.

Facilities and Resources

Student rooms are linked to a campus network. 60 **computers** are available on campus that provide access to degree audit, black board, SCT Banner (student information) and the Internet. The 2 **libraries** have 110,250 books and 700 subscriptions.

Campus Life

There are 40 active organizations on campus, including a newspaper. 5% of eligible men and 9% of eligible women are members of national **fraternities**, national **sororities**, local fraternities, and local sororities.

This institution has no intercollegiate sports.

Campus Safety

Student safety services include late-night transport/escort service, 24-hour emergency telephone alarm devices, 24-hour patrols by trained security personnel, and electronically operated dormitory entrances.

Applying

Lawrence Tech requires ACT, SAT I or ACT, a high school transcript, and a minimum high school GPA of 2.5, and in some cases an essay, an interview, and recommendations. It recommends SAT I. Application deadline: 8/15; 4/1 priority date for financial aid. Early and deferred admission are possible.

Named a Best Value by *U.S. News and World Report's America's Best Colleges,* Lawrence Tech offers nearly 50 undergraduate and graduate degree programs in Colleges of Architecture and Design, Arts and Sciences, Engineering, and Management. Growth, opportunity, personal attention, knowledge, experience, and career direction are important priorities at Lawrence Technological University, and its commitment is to prepare students for leadership through theory and practice. A remarkable 97% of recent graduates found positions matching their academic preparation within a year of graduation. Lawrence Tech ranks first among all of Michigan's independent colleges and universities as a source of recent graduates sought by leading employers in southeastern Michigan.

Getting in Last Year
1,417 applied
76% were accepted
470 enrolled (43%)
20% from top tenth of their h.s. class
3.24 average high school GPA
27% had SAT verbal scores over 600
41% had SAT math scores over 600
48% had ACT scores over 24
7% had SAT verbal scores over 700
16% had SAT math scores over 700
5% had ACT scores over 30

Graduation and After
98% had job offers within 6 months
125 organizations recruited on campus

Financial Matters
$14,362 tuition and fees (2003–04)
$6125 room and board
73% average percent of need met
$11,137 average financial aid amount received per undergraduate (2002–03)

LAWRENCE UNIVERSITY

SMALL-TOWN SETTING ■ PRIVATE ■ INDEPENDENT ■ COED
APPLETON, WISCONSIN

Web site: www.lawrence.edu
Contact: Mr. Steven T. Syverson, Dean of Admissions and Financial Aid, PO
   Box 599, Appleton, WI 54912-0599
Telephone: 920-832-6500 or toll-free 800-227-0982 **Fax:** 920-832-6782
E-mail: excel@lawrence.edu

Getting in Last Year

2,044 applied
58% were accepted
356 enrolled (30%)
42% from top tenth of their h.s. class
3.67 average high school GPA
63% had SAT verbal scores over 600
62% had SAT math scores over 600
84% had ACT scores over 24
19% had SAT verbal scores over 700
18% had SAT math scores over 700
30% had ACT scores over 30
11 National Merit Scholars
14 valedictorians

Graduation and After

49% graduated in 4 years
16% graduated in 5 years
4% graduated in 6 years
30% pursued further study
61% had job offers within 6 months
45 organizations recruited on campus

Financial Matters

$25,089 tuition and fees (2003–04)
$5652 room and board
100% average percent of need met
$20,275 average financial aid amount received
   per undergraduate (2002–03 estimated)

Academics

Lawrence awards bachelor's **degrees**. Challenging opportunities include advanced placement credit, student-designed majors, double majors, independent study, and a senior
project. Special programs include internships, off-campus study, and study-abroad.

The most frequently chosen **baccalaureate** fields are visual/performing arts, social
sciences and history, and interdisciplinary studies. A complete listing of majors at Lawrence appears in the Majors Index beginning on page 460.

The **faculty** at Lawrence has 130 full-time members, 91% with terminal degrees.
The student-faculty ratio is 11:1.

Students of Lawrence

The student body is made up of 1,407 undergraduates. 53.4% are women and 46.6% are
men. Students come from 49 states and territories and 51 other countries. 42% are from
Wisconsin. 11.4% are international students. 2.2% are African American, 0.2%
American Indian, 2.3% Asian American, and 2.8% Hispanic American.

Facilities and Resources

Student rooms are linked to a campus network. 160 **computers** are available on campus
for student use. The **library** has 376,814 books and 1,586 subscriptions.

Campus Life

There are 130 active organizations on campus, including a drama/theater group,
newspaper, radio station, and choral group. 24% of eligible men and 11% of eligible
women are members of national **fraternities** and national **sororities**.

Lawrence is a member of the NCAA (Division III). **Intercollegiate sports** include
baseball (m), basketball, cross-country running, fencing, football (m), golf (m), ice hockey
(m), soccer, softball (w), swimming, tennis, track and field, volleyball (w), wrestling (m).

Campus Safety

Student safety services include evening patrols by trained security personnel, late-night
transport/escort service, 24-hour emergency telephone alarm devices, student patrols,
and electronically operated dormitory entrances.

Applying

Lawrence requires an essay, SAT I or ACT, a high school transcript, 2 recommendations,
and audition for music program. It recommends an interview and a minimum high
school GPA of 3.0. Application deadline: 1/15; 3/15 priority date for financial aid. Early
and deferred admission are possible.

LEBANON VALLEY COLLEGE

SMALL-TOWN SETTING ■ PRIVATE ■ INDEPENDENT RELIGIOUS ■ COED
ANNVILLE, PENNSYLVANIA

Web site: www.lvc.edu
Contact: William J. Brown Jr., Dean of Admission and Financial Aid, 101
  North College Avenue, Annville, PA 17003-1400
Telephone: 717-867-6181 or toll-free 866-LVC-4ADM **Fax:** 717-867-6026
E-mail: admission@lvc.edu

> **L**ebanon Valley College offers bachelor's degrees in 34 majors; master's degrees in business administration, music education, and science education; and a doctoral degree in physical therapy. Thirteen graduates have been named Fulbright scholars, and, since 1970, more than half of the College's graduates in the sciences have earned advanced degrees, including PhD's. More than 72 percent of students rank in the top 30 percent of their high school class and receive scholarships of up to half tuition. Lebanon Valley College was named the eleventh-safest college campus in the nation by APBnews.com.

Academics

LVC awards associate, bachelor's, master's, and doctoral **degrees** and post-bachelor's certificates (offers master of business administration degree on a part-time basis only). Challenging opportunities include advanced placement credit, student-designed majors, double majors, and independent study. Special programs include internships, summer session for credit, off-campus study, study-abroad, and Army ROTC.

The most frequently chosen **baccalaureate** fields are business/marketing, education, and social sciences and history. A complete listing of majors at LVC appears in the Majors Index beginning on page 460.

The **faculty** at LVC has 99 full-time members, 88% with terminal degrees. The student-faculty ratio is 13:1.

Students of LVC

The student body totals 1,906, of whom 1,765 are undergraduates. 58% are women and 42% are men. Students come from 21 states and territories and 8 other countries. 80% are from Pennsylvania. 0.5% are international students. 1.7% are African American, 0.1% American Indian, 1.3% Asian American, and 1% Hispanic American. 83% returned for their sophomore year.

Facilities and Resources

Student rooms are linked to a campus network. 175 **computers** are available on campus that provide access to the Internet. The **library** has 168,709 books and 11,071 subscriptions.

Campus Life

There are 74 active organizations on campus, including a drama/theater group, newspaper, radio station, choral group, and marching band. 11% of eligible men and 12% of eligible women are members of national **fraternities**, national **sororities**, local fraternities, and local sororities.

LVC is a member of the NCAA (Division III). **Intercollegiate sports** include baseball (m), basketball, cross-country running, field hockey (w), football (m), golf (m), ice hockey (m), soccer, softball (w), swimming, tennis, track and field, volleyball (w).

Campus Safety

Student safety services include dormitory entrances locked at midnight, late-night transport/escort service, 24-hour emergency telephone alarm devices, 24-hour patrols by trained security personnel, and electronically operated dormitory entrances.

Applying

LVC requires SAT I or ACT and a high school transcript, and in some cases an essay and audition for music majors. It recommends SAT I, an interview, and 2 recommendations. Application deadline: rolling admissions; 3/1 priority date for financial aid.

Getting in Last Year
2,083 applied
73% were accepted
429 enrolled (28%)
31% from top tenth of their h.s. class
27% had SAT verbal scores over 600
36% had SAT math scores over 600
2% had SAT verbal scores over 700
4% had SAT math scores over 700
10 class presidents
8 valedictorians

Graduation and After
61% graduated in 4 years
8% graduated in 5 years
1% graduated in 6 years
11% pursued further study (5% arts and sciences, 1% business, 1% dentistry)
82.6% had job offers within 6 months
130 organizations recruited on campus

Financial Matters
$22,510 tuition and fees (2003–04)
$6360 room and board
86% average percent of need met
$17,055 average financial aid amount received per undergraduate

LEHIGH UNIVERSITY

SUBURBAN SETTING ■ PRIVATE ■ INDEPENDENT ■ COED
BETHLEHEM, PENNSYLVANIA

Web site: www.lehigh.edu
Contact: Mr. J. Bruce Gardiner, Interim Dean of Admissions and Financial
    Aid, 27 Memorial Drive West, Bethlehem, PA 18015
Telephone: 610-758-3100 **Fax:** 610-758-4361
E-mail: admissions@lehigh.edu

Getting in Last Year

9,087 applied
40% were accepted
1,125 enrolled (31%)
55% from top tenth of their h.s. class
3.75 average high school GPA
71% had SAT verbal scores over 600
87% had SAT math scores over 600
12% had SAT verbal scores over 700
35% had SAT math scores over 700

Graduation and After

73% graduated in 4 years
11% graduated in 5 years
2% graduated in 6 years
32% pursued further study
257 organizations recruited on campus

Financial Matters

$27,430 tuition and fees (2003–04)
$7440 room and board
99% average percent of need met
$23,533 average financial aid amount received
    per undergraduate

Academics

Lehigh awards bachelor's, master's, and doctoral **degrees** and post-master's certificates. Challenging opportunities include advanced placement credit, accelerated degree programs, an honors program, double majors, independent study, and a senior project. Special programs include cooperative education, internships, summer session for credit, off-campus study, study-abroad, and Army ROTC.

The most frequently chosen **baccalaureate** fields are business/marketing, engineering/engineering technologies, and social sciences and history. A complete listing of majors at Lehigh appears in the Majors Index beginning on page 460.

The **faculty** at Lehigh has 430 full-time members, 99% with terminal degrees. The student-faculty ratio is 10:1.

Students of Lehigh

The student body totals 6,732, of whom 4,679 are undergraduates. 39.8% are women and 60.2% are men. Students come from 52 states and territories. 32% are from Pennsylvania. 2.8% are international students. 3.1% are African American, 0.2% American Indian, 5.9% Asian American, and 2.5% Hispanic American. 93% returned for their sophomore year.

Facilities and Resources

Student rooms are linked to a campus network. 572 **computers** are available on campus that provide access to the Internet. The 2 **libraries** have 1,176,028 books and 6,271 subscriptions.

Campus Life

There are 130 active organizations on campus, including a drama/theater group, newspaper, radio station, choral group, and marching band. 41% of eligible men and 43% of eligible women are members of national **fraternities** and national **sororities**.

Lehigh is a member of the NCAA (Division I). **Intercollegiate sports** (some offering scholarships) include baseball (m), basketball, cross-country running, field hockey (w), football (m), golf, lacrosse, riflery, soccer, softball (w), swimming, tennis, track and field, volleyball (w), wrestling (m).

Campus Safety

Student safety services include late-night transport/escort service, 24-hour emergency telephone alarm devices, 24-hour patrols by trained security personnel, student patrols, and electronically operated dormitory entrances.

Applying

Lehigh requires SAT I or ACT, a high school transcript, 1 recommendation, and graded writing sample. It recommends an essay, SAT II Subject Tests, and an interview. Application deadline: 1/1; 2/1 for financial aid. Early and deferred admission are possible.

LeTourneau University

SUBURBAN SETTING ■ PRIVATE ■ INDEPENDENT RELIGIOUS ■ COED
LONGVIEW, TEXAS

Web site: www.letu.edu
Contact: Mr. James Townsend, Director of Admissions, PO Box 7001, 2100 South Mobberly Avenue, Longview, TX 75607-7001
Telephone: 903-233-3400 or toll-free 800-759-8811 **Fax:** 903-233-3411
E-mail: admissions@letu.edu

Academics

LeTourneau awards associate, bachelor's, and master's **degrees**. Challenging opportunities include an honors program, double majors, and independent study. Special programs include cooperative education, internships, and study-abroad.

The most frequently chosen **baccalaureate** fields are engineering/engineering technologies, business/marketing, and education. A complete listing of majors at LeTourneau appears in the Majors Index beginning on page 460.

The **faculty** at LeTourneau has 66 full-time members, 67% with terminal degrees. The student-faculty ratio is 16:1.

Students of LeTourneau

The student body totals 3,597, of whom 3,175 are undergraduates. 52.9% are women and 47.1% are men. 50% are from Texas. 1% are international students. 19.1% are African American, 0.5% American Indian, 1.5% Asian American, and 6.9% Hispanic American. 66% returned for their sophomore year.

Facilities and Resources

The **library** has 84,779 books and 383 subscriptions.

Campus Life

There are 22 active organizations on campus, including a drama/theater group, newspaper, and choral group. 8% of eligible men and 3% of eligible women are members of 3 societies for men, 1 society for women.

Intercollegiate sports include cheerleading.

Campus Safety

Student safety services include late-night transport/escort service, 24-hour emergency telephone alarm devices, 24-hour patrols by trained security personnel, and electronically operated dormitory entrances.

Applying

LeTourneau requires SAT I or ACT. Application deadline: 8/1; 2/15 priority date for financial aid. Deferred admission is possible.

Getting in Last Year

849 applied
80% were accepted
340 enrolled (50%)
29% from top tenth of their h.s. class
3.52 average high school GPA
48% had SAT verbal scores over 600
46% had SAT math scores over 600
62% had ACT scores over 24
13% had SAT verbal scores over 700
12% had SAT math scores over 700
15% had ACT scores over 30

Graduation and After

32% graduated in 4 years
19% graduated in 5 years
1% graduated in 6 years

Financial Matters

$14,190 tuition and fees (2003–04)
$5820 room and board
76% average percent of need met
$12,190 average financial aid amount received per undergraduate (2002–03)

LEWIS & CLARK COLLEGE

SUBURBAN SETTING ■ PRIVATE ■ INDEPENDENT ■ COED
PORTLAND, OREGON

Web site: www.lclark.edu
Contact: Mr. Michael Sexton, Dean of Admissions, 0615 SW Palatine Hill Road, Portland, OR 97219-7899
Telephone: 503-768-7040 or toll-free 800-444-4111 **Fax:** 503-768-7055
E-mail: admissions@lclark.edu

Getting in Last Year
3,405 applied
68% were accepted
493 enrolled (21%)
41% from top tenth of their h.s. class
3.66 average high school GPA
78% had SAT verbal scores over 600
68% had SAT math scores over 600
85% had ACT scores over 24
30% had SAT verbal scores over 700
17% had SAT math scores over 700
25% had ACT scores over 30
8 National Merit Scholars
21 valedictorians

Graduation and After
63% graduated in 4 years
7% graduated in 5 years
1% graduated in 6 years
19% pursued further study (12% arts and sciences, 2% medicine, 1% business)
46 organizations recruited on campus

Financial Matters
$24,670 tuition and fees (2003–04)
$7030 room and board
79% average percent of need met
$18,654 average financial aid amount received per undergraduate

Academics

L & C awards bachelor's, master's, and first-professional **degrees** and first-professional certificates. Challenging opportunities include advanced placement credit, accelerated degree programs, student-designed majors, an honors program, double majors, independent study, and a senior project. Special programs include internships, summer session for credit, off-campus study, and study-abroad.

The most frequently chosen **baccalaureate** fields are social sciences and history, foreign language/literature, and psychology. A complete listing of majors at L & C appears in the Majors Index beginning on page 460.

The **faculty** at L & C has 195 full-time members, 94% with terminal degrees. The student-faculty ratio is 12:1.

Students of L & C

The student body totals 3,071, of whom 1,792 are undergraduates. 60.7% are women and 39.3% are men. Students come from 51 states and territories and 40 other countries. 20% are from Oregon. 4.7% are international students. 1.1% are African American, 1.5% American Indian, 5.7% Asian American, and 2.9% Hispanic American. 84% returned for their sophomore year.

Facilities and Resources

Student rooms are linked to a campus network. 158 **computers** are available on campus that provide access to the Internet. The 2 **libraries** have 227,609 books and 7,477 subscriptions.

Campus Life

There are 70 active organizations on campus, including a drama/theater group, newspaper, radio station, television station, and choral group. No national or local **fraternities** or **sororities**.

L & C is a member of the NCAA (Division III) and NAIA. **Intercollegiate sports** include baseball (m), basketball, crew, cross-country running, football (m), golf, soccer (w), softball (w), swimming, tennis, track and field, volleyball (w).

Campus Safety

Student safety services include late-night transport/escort service, 24-hour emergency telephone alarm devices, 24-hour patrols by trained security personnel, student patrols, and electronically operated dormitory entrances.

Applying

L & C requires an essay, SAT I, ACT, or academic portfolio, a high school transcript, 2 recommendations, and a minimum high school GPA of 2.0, and in some cases 4 recommendations and portfolio applicants must submit samples of graded work. It recommends an interview and a minimum high school GPA of 3.0. Application deadline: 2/1; 3/1 priority date for financial aid. Early and deferred admission are possible.

LINCOLN MEMORIAL UNIVERSITY

SMALL-TOWN SETTING ■ PRIVATE ■ INDEPENDENT ■ COED
HARROGATE, TENNESSEE

Web site: www.lmunet.edu
Contact: Mr. Conrad Daniels, Dean of Admissions and Recruitment, 6965
   Cumberland Gap Parkway, Harrogate, TN 37752-1901
Telephone: 423-869-6280 or toll-free 800-325-0900 **Fax:** 423-869-6250
E-mail: admissions@lmunet.edu

Academics

LMU awards associate, bachelor's, and master's **degrees** and post-master's certificates.
Challenging opportunities include advanced placement credit, accelerated degree
programs, student-designed majors, an honors program, double majors, and independent
study. Summer session for credit is a special program.

The most frequently chosen **baccalaureate** fields are education, business/marketing,
and health professions and related sciences. A complete listing of majors at LMU appears
in the Majors Index beginning on page 460.

The **faculty** at LMU has 86 full-time members, 55% with terminal degrees. The
student-faculty ratio is 9:1.

Students of LMU

The student body totals 2,442, of whom 1,117 are undergraduates. 72.8% are women
and 27.2% are men. Students come from 30 states and territories and 15 other countries.
67% are from Tennessee. 4.3% are international students. 3.4% are African American,
0.2% American Indian, 0.4% Asian American, and 0.2% Hispanic American. 54%
returned for their sophomore year.

Facilities and Resources

Student rooms are linked to a campus network. 150 **computers** are available on campus
that provide access to the Internet. The **library** has 145,537 books and 251 subscriptions.

Campus Life

There are 26 active organizations on campus, including a drama/theater group,
newspaper, radio station, television station, and choral group. 3% of eligible men and 6%
of eligible women are members of local **fraternities** and local **sororities**.

LMU is a member of the NCAA (Division II). **Intercollegiate sports** (some offering
scholarships) include baseball (m), basketball, cross-country running, golf, soccer, softball
(w), tennis, volleyball (w).

Campus Safety

Student safety services include 24-hour emergency telephone alarm devices and 24-hour
patrols by trained security personnel.

Applying

LMU requires SAT I or ACT, a high school transcript, and a minimum high school GPA
of 2.3, and in some cases an essay. It recommends an interview. Application deadline:
rolling admissions; 4/1 priority date for financial aid.

Getting in Last Year

577 applied
85% were accepted
279 enrolled (57%)
36% from top tenth of their h.s. class
3.40 average high school GPA
42% had ACT scores over 24
3% had ACT scores over 30

Graduation and After

39% graduated in 4 years
6% graduated in 5 years
1% graduated in 6 years

Financial Matters

$11,760 tuition and fees (2003–04)
$4640 room and board
90% average percent of need met
$9800 average financial aid amount received
   per undergraduate (2001–02 estimated)

LINFIELD COLLEGE
SMALL-TOWN SETTING ■ PRIVATE ■ INDEPENDENT RELIGIOUS ■ COED
MCMINNVILLE, OREGON

Web site: www.linfield.edu
Contact: Ms. Lisa Knodle-Bragiel, Director of Admissions, 900 SE Baker
    Street, McMinnville, OR 97128-6894
Telephone: 503-883-2213 or toll-free 800-640-2287 **Fax:** 503-883-2472
E-mail: admission@linfield.edu

Getting in Last Year
1,903 applied
78% were accepted
453 enrolled (31%)
40% from top tenth of their h.s. class
3.56 average high school GPA
29% had SAT verbal scores over 600
35% had SAT math scores over 600
51% had ACT scores over 24
5% had SAT verbal scores over 700
5% had SAT math scores over 700
5% had ACT scores over 30
23 class presidents

Graduation and After
61% graduated in 4 years
4% graduated in 5 years
2% graduated in 6 years
20% pursued further study
85% had job offers within 6 months
10 organizations recruited on campus

Financial Matters
$20,970 tuition and fees (2003–04)
$6120 room and board
90% average percent of need met
$15,709 average financial aid amount received
    per undergraduate (2002–03 estimated)

Academics
Linfield awards bachelor's **degrees**. Challenging opportunities include advanced placement credit, accelerated degree programs, student-designed majors, an honors program,
double majors, independent study, and a senior project. Special programs include
cooperative education, internships, summer session for credit, off-campus study, study-
abroad, and Army and Air Force ROTC.

The most frequently chosen **baccalaureate** fields are business/marketing, education,
and parks and recreation. A complete listing of majors at Linfield appears in the Majors
Index beginning on page 460.

The **faculty** at Linfield has 103 full-time members, 88% with terminal degrees. The
student-faculty ratio is 13:1.

Students of Linfield
The student body is made up of 1,659 undergraduates. 55.1% are women and 44.9% are
men. Students come from 30 states and territories and 19 other countries. 55% are from
Oregon. 2.1% are international students. 1.5% are African American, 1.2% American
Indian, 5.5% Asian American, and 2.3% Hispanic American. 83% returned for their
sophomore year.

Facilities and Resources
Student rooms are linked to a campus network. 189 **computers** are available on campus
that provide access to the Internet. The **library** has 163,744 books and 1,296 subscriptions.

Campus Life
There are 42 active organizations on campus, including a drama/theater group,
newspaper, radio station, and choral group. 22% of eligible men and 28% of eligible
women are members of national **fraternities**, national **sororities**, local fraternities, and
local sororities.

Linfield is a member of the NCAA (Division III). **Intercollegiate sports** include
baseball (m), basketball, cross-country running, football (m), golf, lacrosse (w), soccer,
softball (w), swimming, tennis, track and field, volleyball (w).

Campus Safety
Student safety services include late-night transport/escort service, 24-hour emergency
telephone alarm devices, 24-hour patrols by trained security personnel, and electronically operated dormitory entrances.

Applying
Linfield requires an essay, SAT I or ACT, a high school transcript, and 1 recommendation. It recommends an interview. Application deadline: 2/15; 2/1 priority date for
financial aid. Deferred admission is possible.

LIPSCOMB UNIVERSITY

URBAN SETTING ■ PRIVATE ■ INDEPENDENT RELIGIOUS ■ COED
NASHVILLE, TENNESSEE

Web site: www.lipscomb.edu
Contact: Mr. Phillip Doncan, Director of Admissions, 3901 Granny White
Pike, Nashville, TN 37204-3951
Telephone: 615-269-1000 or toll-free 877-582-4766 **Fax:** 615-269-1804
E-mail: admissions@lipscomb.edu

Academics

Lipscomb University awards bachelor's, master's, and first-professional **degrees**. Challenging opportunities include advanced placement credit, accelerated degree programs, an honors program, double majors, independent study, and a senior project. Special programs include internships, summer session for credit, study-abroad, and Army and Air Force ROTC. A complete listing of majors at Lipscomb University appears in the Majors Index beginning on page 460.

The **faculty** at Lipscomb University has 117 full-time members, 79% with terminal degrees. The student-faculty ratio is 16:1.

Students of Lipscomb University

The student body totals 2,661, of whom 2,433 are undergraduates. 55.6% are women and 44.4% are men. Students come from 46 states and territories. 62% are from Tennessee. 0.9% are international students. 4.6% are African American, 0.2% American Indian, 0.1% Asian American, and 1.2% Hispanic American. 78% returned for their sophomore year.

Facilities and Resources

Student rooms are linked to a campus network. 232 **computers** are available on campus that provide access to the Internet. The 2 **libraries** have 199,400 books and 886 subscriptions.

Campus Life

There are 60 active organizations on campus, including a drama/theater group, newspaper, radio station, and choral group. 15% of eligible men and 20% of eligible women are members of local **fraternities** and local **sororities**.

Lipscomb University is a member of the NCAA (Division I). **Intercollegiate sports** (some offering scholarships) include baseball (m), basketball, cross-country running, golf, soccer, softball (w), tennis, volleyball (w).

Campus Safety

Student safety services include late-night transport/escort service, 24-hour emergency telephone alarm devices, 24-hour patrols by trained security personnel, and electronically operated dormitory entrances.

Applying

Lipscomb University requires SAT I or ACT, a high school transcript, 2 recommendations, and a minimum high school GPA of 2.25. It recommends an essay and an interview. Application deadline: rolling admissions; 2/28 priority date for financial aid. Early admission is possible.

Founded in 1891, Lipscomb is a distinctly Christian university with a sterling academic reputation. Lipscomb University delivers a complete education characterized by a distinctive integration of Christian faith and practice with academic excellence. This complete education, which includes liberal arts studies and professional preparation, does not suggest a finished education. Rather, it reflects Lipscomb's commitment to the comprehensive development of each student—spiritually, intellectually, socially, and physically—to prepare graduates for life and eternity.

Getting in Last Year
2,344 applied
73% were accepted
596 enrolled (35%)
29% from top tenth of their h.s. class
3.35 average high school GPA
30% had SAT verbal scores over 600
28% had SAT math scores over 600
48% had ACT scores over 24
7% had SAT verbal scores over 700
7% had SAT math scores over 700
10% had ACT scores over 30
1 National Merit Scholar
23 valedictorians

Graduation and After
169 organizations recruited on campus

Financial Matters
$12,600 tuition and fees (2003–04)
$5590 room and board
$12,000 average financial aid amount received per undergraduate (2002–03 estimated)

LIST COLLEGE, JEWISH THEOLOGICAL SEMINARY OF AMERICA

URBAN SETTING ■ PRIVATE ■ INDEPENDENT RELIGIOUS ■ COED
NEW YORK, NEW YORK

Web site: www.jtsa.edu
Contact: Ms. Reena Kamins, Assistant Director of Admissions, Room 614
    Schiff, 3080 Broadway, New York, NY 10027-4649
Telephone: 212-678-8832 **Fax:** 212-678-8947
E-mail: rekamins@jtsa.edu

The Albert A. List College of Jewish Studies offers students a unique opportunity to pursue 2 bachelor's degrees simultaneously. Students earn a degree from List in one of a dozen areas of Jewish study and a second degree in the liberal arts field of their choice from Columbia University or Barnard College. This exciting 4-year program enables students to experience an intimate and supportive Jewish community as well as a diverse and dynamic campus life. Merit- and need-based aid are available for qualified students.

Getting in Last Year
135 applied
53% were accepted
52 enrolled (72%)
3.80 average high school GPA

Graduation and After
60% pursued further study

Financial Matters
$10,600 tuition and fees (2003–04)
$7270 room only
75% average percent of need met

Academics

List College awards bachelor's, master's, doctoral, and first-professional **degrees** (double bachelor's degree with Barnard College, Columbia University, joint bachelor's degree with Columbia University). Challenging opportunities include advanced placement credit, student-designed majors, freshman honors college, an honors program, double majors, and a senior project. Special programs include internships, summer session for credit, off-campus study, and study-abroad. A complete listing of majors at List College appears in the Majors Index beginning on page 460.

The **faculty** at List College has 115 members. The student-faculty ratio is 5:1.

Students of List College

The student body totals 671, of whom 191 are undergraduates. 61.8% are women and 38.2% are men. Students come from 23 states and territories and 2 other countries. 40% are from New York. 92% returned for their sophomore year.

Facilities and Resources

Student rooms are linked to a campus network. 20 **computers** are available on campus that provide access to the Internet. The **library** has 271,000 books and 720 subscriptions.

Campus Life

Active organizations on campus include a drama/theater group, newspaper, radio station, and choral group. No national or local **fraternities** or **sororities**.

This institution has no intercollegiate sports.

Campus Safety

Student safety services include late-night transport/escort service, 24-hour emergency telephone alarm devices, 24-hour patrols by trained security personnel, and electronically operated dormitory entrances.

Applying

List College requires an essay, SAT II: Writing Test, SAT I and SAT II or ACT, a high school transcript, and 2 recommendations. It recommends an interview and a minimum high school GPA of 3.0. Application deadline: 2/15; 3/1 for financial aid. Early and deferred admission are possible.

LOUISIANA COLLEGE

SMALL-TOWN SETTING ■ PRIVATE ■ INDEPENDENT RELIGIOUS ■ COED
PINEVILLE, LOUISIANA

Web site: www.lacollege.edu
Contact: Mrs. Mary Wagner, Director of Enrollment Management and
Institutional Research, 1140 College Drive, Box 560, Pineville, LA 71359
Telephone: 318-487-7259 ext. 7301 or toll-free 800-487-1906 **Fax:**
318-487-7550
E-mail: admissions@lacollege.edu

Academics

LC awards bachelor's **degrees**. Challenging opportunities include advanced placement
credit, accelerated degree programs, student-designed majors, an honors program,
double majors, independent study, and a senior project. Special programs include internships, summer session for credit, study-abroad, and Army ROTC.

The most frequently chosen **baccalaureate** fields are education, social sciences and
history, and business/marketing. A complete listing of majors at LC appears in the
Majors Index beginning on page 460.

The **faculty** at LC has 68 full-time members, 60% with terminal degrees. The student-faculty ratio is 13:1.

Students of LC

The student body is made up of 1,135 undergraduates. 57.4% are women and 42.6% are
men. Students come from 16 states and territories. 91% are from Louisiana. 0.8% are
international students. 7.1% are African American, 0.2% American Indian, 1.2% Asian
American, and 1.6% Hispanic American. 59% returned for their sophomore year.

Facilities and Resources

242 **computers** are available on campus that provide access to the Internet. The **library**
has 134,454 books and 432 subscriptions.

Campus Life

There are 40 active organizations on campus, including a drama/theater group,
newspaper, and choral group. 20% of eligible men and 35% of eligible women are
members of local **fraternities** and local **sororities**.

LC is a member of the NCAA (Division III) and NCCAA. **Intercollegiate sports**
include baseball (m), basketball, cheerleading, cross-country running, football (m), golf,
sailing, soccer, softball, swimming, tennis (w).

Campus Safety

Student safety services include late-night transport/escort service, 24-hour patrols by
trained security personnel, student patrols, and electronically operated dormitory
entrances.

Applying

LC requires SAT I or ACT, a high school transcript, and recommendations, and in some
cases 3 recommendations, class rank, and a minimum high school GPA of 2.0. It recommends an interview. Application deadline: 8/15; 3/31 priority date for financial aid. Early
admission is possible.

Getting in Last Year

727 applied
85% were accepted
266 enrolled (43%)
29% from top tenth of their h.s. class
3.48 average high school GPA
9% had SAT verbal scores over 600
25% had SAT math scores over 600
42% had ACT scores over 24
3% had SAT math scores over 700
7% had ACT scores over 30
1 National Merit Scholar
10 class presidents
18 valedictorians

Graduation and After

25% graduated in 4 years
17% graduated in 5 years
4% graduated in 6 years
48% pursued further study (12% medicine,
11% arts and sciences, 10% law)
65 organizations recruited on campus

Financial Matters

$9650 tuition and fees (2003–04)
$3610 room and board
44% average percent of need met
$10,591 average financial aid amount received
per undergraduate (2001–02)

Getting in Last Year
10,147 applied
81% were accepted
5,428 enrolled (66%)
25% from top tenth of their h.s. class
3.49 average high school GPA
54% had ACT scores over 24
7% had ACT scores over 30
50 National Merit Scholars
150 valedictorians

Graduation and After
23% graduated in 4 years
27% graduated in 5 years
8% graduated in 6 years
1087 organizations recruited on campus

Financial Matters
$3910 resident tuition and fees (2003–04)
$9210 nonresident tuition and fees (2003–04)
$5216 room and board
68% average percent of need met
$6223 average financial aid amount received
  per undergraduate (2002–03)

LOUISIANA STATE UNIVERSITY AND AGRICULTURAL AND MECHANICAL COLLEGE
URBAN SETTING ■ PUBLIC ■ STATE-SUPPORTED ■ COED
BATON ROUGE, LOUISIANA

Web site: www.lsu.edu
Contact: Mr. Cleve Brooks, Director of Admissions, 110 Thomas Boyd Hall,
  Baton Rouge, LA 70803
Telephone: 225-578-1175 **Fax:** 225-578-4433
E-mail: admissions@lsu.edu

Academics
LSU awards bachelor's, master's, doctoral, and first-professional **degrees** and post-master's certificates. Challenging opportunities include advanced placement credit, accelerated degree programs, student-designed majors, freshman honors college, an honors program, double majors, independent study, and a senior project. Special programs include cooperative education, internships, summer session for credit, off-campus study, study-abroad, and Army, Navy and Air Force ROTC.

The most frequently chosen **baccalaureate** fields are business/marketing, engineering/engineering technologies, and education. A complete listing of majors at LSU appears in the Majors Index beginning on page 460.

The **faculty** at LSU has 1,302 full-time members, 80% with terminal degrees. The student-faculty ratio is 21:1.

Students of LSU
The student body totals 31,934, of whom 26,156 are undergraduates. 52.6% are women and 47.4% are men. Students come from 49 states and territories and 93 other countries. 90% are from Louisiana. 2.1% are international students. 9.1% are African American, 0.3% American Indian, 3% Asian American, and 2.3% Hispanic American. 84% returned for their sophomore year.

Facilities and Resources
Student rooms are linked to a campus network. 7,000 **computers** are available on campus that provide access to e-mail, wireless, grades, payroll, storage and the Internet. The 8 **libraries** have 1,369,607 books and 24,304 subscriptions.

Campus Life
There are 335 active organizations on campus, including a drama/theater group, newspaper, radio station, television station, choral group, and marching band. 10% of eligible men and 15% of eligible women are members of national **fraternities** and national **sororities**.

LSU is a member of the NCAA (Division I). **Intercollegiate sports** (some offering scholarships) include baseball (m), basketball, cheerleading, cross-country running, football (m), golf, gymnastics (w), soccer (w), softball (w), swimming, tennis, track and field, volleyball (w).

Campus Safety
Student safety services include self-defense education, crime prevention programs, late-night transport/escort service, 24-hour emergency telephone alarm devices, 24-hour patrols by trained security personnel, and electronically operated dormitory entrances.

Applying
LSU requires SAT I or ACT, a high school transcript, minimum ACT score of 20 or SAT I score of 940, and a minimum high school GPA of 2.8, and in some cases an essay, SAT I and SAT II or ACT, an interview, and 3 recommendations. Application deadline: 4/15. Early admission is possible.

LOUISIANA TECH UNIVERSITY

SMALL-TOWN SETTING ■ PUBLIC ■ STATE-SUPPORTED ■ COED
RUSTON, LOUISIANA

Web site: www.latech.edu
Contact: Mrs. Jan B. Albritton, Director of Admissions, PO Box 3178,
Ruston, LA 71272
Telephone: 318-257-3036 or toll-free 800-528-3241 **Fax:** 318-257-2499
E-mail: bulldog@latech.edu

Academics

Louisiana Tech awards associate, bachelor's, master's, and doctoral **degrees** and first-professional certificates. Challenging opportunities include advanced placement credit, an honors program, double majors, independent study, and a senior project. Special programs include cooperative education, internships, summer session for credit, off-campus study, study-abroad, and Army and Navy ROTC.

The most frequently chosen **baccalaureate** fields are business/marketing, engineering/engineering technologies, and liberal arts/general studies. A complete listing of majors at Louisiana Tech appears in the Majors Index beginning on page 460.

The **faculty** at Louisiana Tech has 397 full-time members, 80% with terminal degrees. The student-faculty ratio is 23:1.

Students of Louisiana Tech

The student body totals 11,960, of whom 9,739 are undergraduates. 48.4% are women and 51.6% are men. Students come from 48 states and territories and 70 other countries. 88% are from Louisiana. 1.7% are international students. 15.4% are African American, 0.7% American Indian, 0.8% Asian American, and 1.3% Hispanic American. 74% returned for their sophomore year.

Facilities and Resources

Student rooms are linked to a campus network. 1,800 **computers** are available on campus for student use. The **library** has 3,319 books and 2,469 subscriptions.

Campus Life

There are 121 active organizations on campus, including a drama/theater group, newspaper, radio station, choral group, and marching band. 10% of eligible men and 12% of eligible women are members of national **fraternities** and national **sororities**.

Louisiana Tech is a member of the NCAA (Division I). **Intercollegiate sports** (some offering scholarships) include baseball (m), basketball, cross-country running, football (m), golf (m), softball (w), tennis (w), track and field, volleyball (w), weight lifting.

Campus Safety

Student safety services include late-night transport/escort service, 24-hour emergency telephone alarm devices, 24-hour patrols by trained security personnel, student patrols, and electronically operated dormitory entrances.

Applying

Louisiana Tech requires SAT I or ACT, a high school transcript, and a minimum high school GPA of 2.2. It recommends ACT. Application deadline: 7/31. Early admission is possible.

Getting in Last Year
3,768 applied
92% were accepted
2,107 enrolled (61%)
18% from top tenth of their h.s. class
3.30 average high school GPA
34% had ACT scores over 24
4% had ACT scores over 30
2 National Merit Scholars

Graduation and After
22% graduated in 4 years
24% graduated in 5 years
5% graduated in 6 years
32% pursued further study
921 organizations recruited on campus

Financial Matters
$3270 resident tuition and fees (2003–04)
$7065 nonresident tuition and fees (2003–04)
$3885 room and board
65% average percent of need met
$5473 average financial aid amount received
per undergraduate (2001–02)

LOYOLA COLLEGE IN MARYLAND

URBAN SETTING ■ PRIVATE ■ INDEPENDENT RELIGIOUS ■ COED
BALTIMORE, MARYLAND

Web site: www.loyola.edu
Contact: Mr. David Dukor-Jackson, Director of Undergraduate Admissions, 4501 North Charles Street, Baltimore, MD 21210
Telephone: 410-617-2015 or toll-free 800-221-9107 ext. 2252 (in-state) **Fax:** 410-617-2176

Traditional academic standards are central to Jesuit education. Loyola's curriculum is rigorous, and the faculty's expectations for students are high. The aim is to challenge students and to try to develop their skills and abilities. Hard work is required for a good education, and Loyola is interested in admitting students who have been ambitious in their course selection in high school and who have shown that they can do well in academic work.

Getting in Last Year
6,611 applied
71% were accepted
916 enrolled (20%)
32% from top tenth of their h.s. class
3.41 average high school GPA
52% had SAT verbal scores over 600
62% had SAT math scores over 600
11% had SAT verbal scores over 700
10% had SAT math scores over 700

Graduation and After
78% graduated in 4 years
3% graduated in 5 years
1% graduated in 6 years
62% had job offers within 6 months
150 organizations recruited on campus

Financial Matters
$26,610 tuition and fees (2003–04)
$8630 room and board
98% average percent of need met
$17,370 average financial aid amount received per undergraduate

Academics
Loyola awards bachelor's, master's, and doctoral **degrees** and post-master's certificates. Challenging opportunities include advanced placement credit, accelerated degree programs, an honors program, double majors, independent study, and a senior project. Special programs include internships, summer session for credit, off-campus study, study-abroad, and Army and Air Force ROTC.

The most frequently chosen **baccalaureate** fields are business/marketing, communications/communication technologies, and social sciences and history. A complete listing of majors at Loyola appears in the Majors Index beginning on page 460.

The **faculty** at Loyola has 284 full-time members, 85% with terminal degrees. The student-faculty ratio is 13:1.

Students of Loyola
The student body totals 6,033, of whom 3,413 are undergraduates. 57.6% are women and 42.4% are men. Students come from 38 states and territories and 19 other countries. 20% are from Maryland. 0.6% are international students. 4.8% are African American, 1.7% Asian American, and 1.8% Hispanic American. 92% returned for their sophomore year.

Facilities and Resources
Student rooms are linked to a campus network. 292 **computers** are available on campus that provide access to the Internet. The **library** has 293,639 books and 2,126 subscriptions.

Campus Life
Active organizations on campus include a drama/theater group, newspaper, and choral group. No national or local **fraternities** or **sororities**.

Loyola is a member of the NCAA (Division I). **Intercollegiate sports** include basketball, cheerleading, crew, cross-country running, golf (m), lacrosse, soccer, swimming, tennis, volleyball (w).

Campus Safety
Student safety services include late-night transport/escort service, 24-hour emergency telephone alarm devices, 24-hour patrols by trained security personnel, and electronically operated dormitory entrances.

Applying
Loyola requires an essay, SAT I, and a high school transcript. It recommends an interview. Application deadline: 1/15; 2/15 for financial aid. Early and deferred admission are possible.

LOYOLA MARYMOUNT UNIVERSITY

SUBURBAN SETTING ■ PRIVATE ■ INDEPENDENT RELIGIOUS ■ COED
LOS ANGELES, CALIFORNIA

Web site: www.lmu.edu
Contact: Mr. Matthew X. Fissinger, Director of Admissions, 1 LMU Drive
Suite 100, Los Angeles, CA 90045-8350
Telephone: 310-338-2750 or toll-free 800-LMU-INFO
E-mail: admissions@lmu.edu

Academics

LMU awards bachelor's, master's, and first-professional **degrees** and post-bachelor's certificates. Challenging opportunities include advanced placement credit, accelerated degree programs, student-designed majors, an honors program, double majors, and independent study. Special programs include cooperative education, internships, summer session for credit, study-abroad, and Army and Air Force ROTC.

The most frequently chosen **baccalaureate** fields are business/marketing, visual/performing arts, and biological/life sciences. A complete listing of majors at LMU appears in the Majors Index beginning on page 460.

The **faculty** at LMU has 419 full-time members, 87% with terminal degrees. The student-faculty ratio is 13:1.

Students of LMU

The student body totals 8,880, of whom 5,699 are undergraduates. 59.5% are women and 40.5% are men. Students come from 51 states and territories and 52 other countries. 77% are from California. 1.9% are international students. 6.6% are African American, 0.6% American Indian, 11.3% Asian American, and 18.2% Hispanic American. 88% returned for their sophomore year.

Facilities and Resources

Student rooms are linked to a campus network. 300 **computers** are available on campus that provide access to the Internet. The 2 **libraries** have 484,273 books and 36,650 subscriptions.

Campus Life

There are 120 active organizations on campus, including a drama/theater group, newspaper, radio station, television station, and choral group. 56% of eligible men and 48% of eligible women are members of national **fraternities** and national **sororities**.

LMU is a member of the NCAA (Division I). **Intercollegiate sports** (some offering scholarships) include baseball (m), basketball, crew, cross-country running, golf (m), soccer, softball (w), swimming (w), tennis, volleyball (w), water polo.

Campus Safety

Student safety services include late-night transport/escort service, 24-hour emergency telephone alarm devices, 24-hour patrols by trained security personnel, and electronically operated dormitory entrances.

Applying

LMU requires an essay, SAT I or ACT, a high school transcript, and 1 recommendation. It recommends an interview. Application deadline: 2/1; 2/15 priority date for financial aid. Early and deferred admission are possible.

Getting in Last Year
7,833 applied
58% were accepted
1,335 enrolled (29%)
30% from top tenth of their h.s. class
3.37 average high school GPA
36% had SAT verbal scores over 600
42% had SAT math scores over 600
72% had ACT scores over 24
4% had SAT verbal scores over 700
6% had SAT math scores over 700
8% had ACT scores over 30

Graduation and After
62% graduated in 4 years
9% graduated in 5 years
3% graduated in 6 years

Financial Matters
$23,934 tuition and fees (2003–04)
$8260 room and board
80% average percent of need met
$19,970 average financial aid amount received per undergraduate (2001–02)

LOYOLA UNIVERSITY CHICAGO
URBAN SETTING ■ PRIVATE ■ INDEPENDENT RELIGIOUS ■ COED
CHICAGO, ILLINOIS

Web site: www.luc.edu
Contact: Ms. April Hansen, Director of Admissions, 820 North Michigan Avenue, Suite 613, Chicago, IL 60611-9810
Telephone: 773-508-3080 or toll-free 800-262-2373 **Fax:** 312-915-7216
E-mail: admission@luc.edu

Chicago offers an ideal environment to enrich students' academic experience, with its world-class museums and performing arts; professional sports; culturally rich diversity; and international headquarters for media, commerce, medicine, and banking. Loyola's partnership with the city of Chicago adds an extra dimension—vast resources for internships, fieldwork, and independent exploration—rare in universities of Loyola's affiliation (Jesuit, Catholic), size (medium), and ranking (national research university). Extraordinary resources include a distinguished and dedicated faculty (97% with the PhD) teaching classes averaging 23 students. Students' living and learning experience is enhanced on Loyola's residential lakefront campus on Chicago's popular North Side.

Getting in Last Year
11,009 applied
82% were accepted
1,915 enrolled (21%)
28% from top tenth of their h.s. class
3.53 average high school GPA
44% had SAT verbal scores over 600
40% had SAT math scores over 600
63% had ACT scores over 24
8% had SAT verbal scores over 700
5% had SAT math scores over 700
10% had ACT scores over 30
34 valedictorians

Graduation and After
46% graduated in 4 years
20% graduated in 5 years
3% graduated in 6 years

Financial Matters
$21,054 tuition and fees (2003–04)
$7900 room and board
89% average percent of need met
$20,087 average financial aid amount received per undergraduate (2002–03 estimated)

Academics
Loyola awards bachelor's, master's, doctoral, and first-professional **degrees** and post-bachelor's and post-master's certificates (also offers adult part-time program with significant enrollment not reflected in profile). Challenging opportunities include advanced placement credit, accelerated degree programs, an honors program, and double majors. Special programs include internships, summer session for credit, off-campus study, study-abroad, and Army and Navy ROTC.

The most frequently chosen **baccalaureate** fields are business/marketing, social sciences and history, and psychology. A complete listing of majors at Loyola appears in the Majors Index beginning on page 460.

The **faculty** at Loyola has 524 full-time members, 98% with terminal degrees. The student-faculty ratio is 13:1.

Students of Loyola
The student body totals 13,362, of whom 7,916 are undergraduates. 66.1% are women and 33.9% are men. Students come from 50 states and territories and 60 other countries. 66% are from Illinois. 1.7% are international students. 8.2% are African American, 0.2% American Indian, 10.8% Asian American, and 10.5% Hispanic American. 84% returned for their sophomore year.

Facilities and Resources
Student rooms are linked to a campus network. 318 **computers** are available on campus that provide access to the Internet. The 5 **libraries** have 1,108,157 books and 68,886 subscriptions.

Campus Life
There are 136 active organizations on campus, including a drama/theater group, newspaper, radio station, and choral group. 8% of eligible men and 7% of eligible women are members of national **fraternities** and national **sororities**.

Loyola is a member of the NCAA (Division I). **Intercollegiate sports** (some offering scholarships) include basketball, cross-country running, golf, soccer, softball (w), track and field, volleyball.

Campus Safety
Student safety services include late-night transport/escort service, 24-hour emergency telephone alarm devices, 24-hour patrols by trained security personnel, and electronically operated dormitory entrances.

Applying
Loyola requires an essay, SAT I or ACT, and a high school transcript. It recommends an interview. Application deadline: 4/1; 3/1 priority date for financial aid. Deferred admission is possible.

LOYOLA UNIVERSITY NEW ORLEANS

URBAN SETTING ■ PRIVATE ■ INDEPENDENT RELIGIOUS ■ COED
NEW ORLEANS, LOUISIANA

Web site: www.loyno.edu

Contact: Ms. Deborah C. Stieffel, Dean of Admission and Enrollment
Management, 6363 Saint Charles Avenue, Box 18, New Orleans, LA
70118-6195

Telephone: 504-865-3240 or toll-free 800-4-LOYOLA **Fax:** 504-865-3383

E-mail: admit@loyno.edu

Academics

Loyola awards bachelor's, master's, and first-professional **degrees** and post-bachelor's
certificates. Challenging opportunities include advanced placement credit, accelerated
degree programs, student-designed majors, an honors program, double majors,
independent study, and a senior project. Special programs include internships, summer
session for credit, off-campus study, study-abroad, and Army, Navy and Air Force
ROTC.

The most frequently chosen **baccalaureate** fields are business/marketing, com-
munications/communication technologies, and social sciences and history. A complete
listing of majors at Loyola appears in the Majors Index beginning on page 460.

The **faculty** at Loyola has 293 full-time members, 88% with terminal degrees. The
student-faculty ratio is 13:1.

Students of Loyola

The student body totals 5,518, of whom 3,747 are undergraduates. 62% are women and
38% are men. Students come from 52 states and territories and 55 other countries. 45%
are from Louisiana. 3.3% are international students. 8.6% are African American, 0.5%
American Indian, 4.6% Asian American, and 10.7% Hispanic American. 82% returned
for their sophomore year.

Facilities and Resources

Student rooms are linked to a campus network. 458 **computers** are available on campus
that provide access to the Internet. The 2 **libraries** have 401,548 books and 4,948
subscriptions.

Campus Life

There are 140 active organizations on campus, including a drama/theater group,
newspaper, radio station, television station, and choral group. 17% of eligible men and
18% of eligible women are members of national **fraternities**, national **sororities**, and
local fraternities.

Loyola is a member of the NAIA. **Intercollegiate sports** include baseball (m),
basketball, cross-country running, soccer (w), track and field.

Campus Safety

Student safety services include self-defense education, bicycle patrols, closed circuit TV
monitors, door alarms, crime prevention programs, late-night transport/escort service,
24-hour emergency telephone alarm devices, 24-hour patrols by trained security personnel, and electronically operated dormitory entrances.

Applying

Loyola requires an essay, SAT I or ACT, a high school transcript, and 1 recommendation, and in some cases PAA and an interview. It recommends an interview. Application deadline: 1/15; 2/15 priority date for financial aid. Early and deferred admission
are possible.

H olding fast to its core
Jesuit values, Loyola
University New Orleans
strives to instill in its students a
sense of social responsibility, a
respect for the dignity of their
fellow man, and the ability to
discern truth in the midst of
ambiguity. A unique combination of
quality faculty members and
academic programs and facilities, an
ideal size that fosters a positive
learning environment and individual
student attention, and the
centuries-old Jesuit tradition of
educating the whole person
distinguish Loyola from other
institutions.

Getting in Last Year
3,609 applied
69% were accepted
864 enrolled (35%)
29% from top tenth of their h.s. class
3.72 average high school GPA
67% had SAT verbal scores over 600
59% had SAT math scores over 600
84% had ACT scores over 24
11% had SAT verbal scores over 700
7% had SAT math scores over 700
11% had ACT scores over 30

Graduation and After
22% pursued further study (65% arts and
   sciences, 17% law, 8% medicine)
33% had job offers within 6 months
226 organizations recruited on campus

Financial Matters
$20,106 tuition and fees (2003–04)
$7660 room and board
84% average percent of need met
$15,288 average financial aid amount received
   per undergraduate (2002–03 estimated)

LUTHER COLLEGE

SMALL-TOWN SETTING ■ PRIVATE ■ INDEPENDENT RELIGIOUS ■ COED
DECORAH, IOWA

Web site: www.luther.edu

Contact: Mr. Jon Lund, Vice President for Enrollment and Marketing, 700 College Drive, Decorah, IA 52101

Telephone: 563-387-1287 or toll-free 800-458-8437 **Fax:** 563-387-2159

E-mail: admissions@luther.edu

Getting in Last Year

1,998 applied
77% were accepted
668 enrolled (43%)
36% from top tenth of their h.s. class
3.60 average high school GPA
44% had SAT verbal scores over 600
54% had SAT math scores over 600
66% had ACT scores over 24
12% had SAT verbal scores over 700
10% had SAT math scores over 700
12% had ACT scores over 30
7 National Merit Scholars
15 class presidents
51 valedictorians

Graduation and After

69% graduated in 4 years
10% graduated in 5 years
1% graduated in 6 years
23% pursued further study (9% arts and sciences, 6% medicine, 3% law)
69% had job offers within 6 months
157 organizations recruited on campus

Financial Matters

$21,600 tuition and fees (2003–04)
$4100 room and board
85% average percent of need met
$16,554 average financial aid amount received per undergraduate (2001–02)

Academics

Luther awards bachelor's **degrees**. Challenging opportunities include advanced placement credit, student-designed majors, an honors program, double majors, independent study, and a senior project. Special programs include internships, summer session for credit, off-campus study, and study-abroad.

The most frequently chosen **baccalaureate** fields are business/marketing, biological/life sciences, and social sciences and history. A complete listing of majors at Luther appears in the Majors Index beginning on page 460.

The **faculty** at Luther has 176 full-time members, 85% with terminal degrees. The student-faculty ratio is 13:1.

Students of Luther

The student body is made up of 2,565 undergraduates. 60.1% are women and 39.9% are men. Students come from 35 states and territories and 32 other countries. 36% are from Iowa. 4.4% are international students. 0.5% are African American, 0.2% American Indian, 1.4% Asian American, and 1% Hispanic American. 85% returned for their sophomore year.

Facilities and Resources

Student rooms are linked to a campus network. 526 **computers** are available on campus that provide access to the Internet. The **library** has 336,605 books and 1,600 subscriptions.

Campus Life

There are 139 active organizations on campus, including a drama/theater group, newspaper, radio station, and choral group. 7% of eligible men and 9% of eligible women are members of national **fraternities**, local fraternities, and local **sororities**.

Luther is a member of the NCAA (Division III). **Intercollegiate sports** include baseball (m), basketball, cheerleading, cross-country running, football (m), golf, soccer, softball (w), swimming, tennis, track and field, volleyball (w), wrestling (m).

Campus Safety

Student safety services include late-night transport/escort service, 24-hour emergency telephone alarm devices, 24-hour patrols by trained security personnel, and electronically operated dormitory entrances.

Applying

Luther requires an essay, SAT I or ACT, a high school transcript, and 1 recommendation. It recommends an interview. Application deadline: 2/15 priority date for financial aid. Early and deferred admission are possible.

LYCOMING COLLEGE

SMALL-TOWN SETTING ■ PRIVATE ■ INDEPENDENT RELIGIOUS ■ COED
WILLIAMSPORT, PENNSYLVANIA

Web site: www.lycoming.edu
Contact: Mr. James Spencer, Dean of Admissions and Financial Aid, 700
  College Place, Williamsport, PA 17701
Telephone: 570-321-4026 or toll-free 800-345-3920 ext. 4026 **Fax:**
  570-321-4317
E-mail: admissions@lycoming.edu

Academics

Lycoming awards bachelor's **degrees**. Challenging opportunities include advanced
placement credit, accelerated degree programs, student-designed majors, an honors
program, double majors, independent study, and a senior project. Special programs
include internships, summer session for credit, off-campus study, study-abroad, and
Army ROTC.

The most frequently chosen **baccalaureate** fields are psychology, business/market-
ing, and social sciences and history. A complete listing of majors at Lycoming appears in
the Majors Index beginning on page 460.

The **faculty** at Lycoming has 88 full-time members, 91% with terminal degrees. The
student-faculty ratio is 13:1.

Students of Lycoming

The student body is made up of 1,417 undergraduates. 54.9% are women and 45.1% are
men. Students come from 22 states and territories and 11 other countries. 77% are from
Pennsylvania. 1% are international students. 2.1% are African American, 0.3% American
Indian, 0.8% Asian American, and 0.6% Hispanic American. 81% returned for their
sophomore year.

Facilities and Resources

Student rooms are linked to a campus network. 140 **computers** are available on campus
that provide access to the Internet. The 2 **libraries** have 170,000 books and 950
subscriptions.

Campus Life

There are 64 active organizations on campus, including a drama/theater group,
newspaper, radio station, television station, and choral group. 14% of eligible men and
17% of eligible women are members of national **fraternities**, national **sororities**, and
local sororities.

Lycoming is a member of the NCAA (Division III). **Intercollegiate sports** (some
offering scholarships) include basketball, cheerleading, cross-country running, football
(m), golf (m), lacrosse, soccer, softball (w), swimming, tennis, volleyball (w), wrestling
(m).

Campus Safety

Student safety services include late-night transport/escort service, 24-hour emergency
telephone alarm devices, 24-hour patrols by trained security personnel, student patrols,
and electronically operated dormitory entrances.

Applying

Lycoming requires an essay, SAT I or ACT, a high school transcript, and 2 recommendations. It recommends an interview and a minimum high school GPA of 2.3. Application
deadline: 4/1; 4/15 priority date for financial aid. Early and deferred admission are possible.

Scenic north-central
Pennsylvania provides an
ideal location for
Williamsport, with a population of
35,000, and Lycoming College, with
an enrollment of 1,500. Founded in
1812, Lycoming is exclusively a
4-year residential college with an
emphasis on the liberal arts and
sciences. It's the extras that make a
Lycoming education distinctive. The
College offers extensive internship
opportunities, nationally funded
student research projects, a 4-year
scholars program, and study-abroad
opportunities at 5 affiliate
international schools. Balance is a
key theme at Lycoming. While a
student-faculty ratio of 13:1 keeps
students engaged academically, 19
intercollegiate sports and more than
75 clubs and organizations provide
students with meaningful activity on
campus and in the community.

Getting in Last Year
1,449 applied
80% were accepted
366 enrolled (32%)
21% from top tenth of their h.s. class
3.20 average high school GPA
26% had SAT verbal scores over 600
27% had SAT math scores over 600
2% had SAT verbal scores over 700
1% had SAT math scores over 700
18 class presidents
20 valedictorians

Graduation and After
59% graduated in 4 years
7% graduated in 5 years
18% pursued further study (5% arts and sciences, 4% medicine, 3% law)
98% had job offers within 6 months
40 organizations recruited on campus

Financial Matters
$21,723 tuition and fees (2003–04)
$5866 room and board
81% average percent of need met
$16,676 average financial aid amount received
  per undergraduate (2002–03 estimated)

LYON COLLEGE

SMALL-TOWN SETTING ■ PRIVATE ■ INDEPENDENT RELIGIOUS ■ COED
BATESVILLE, ARKANSAS

Web site: www.lyon.edu
Contact: Mr. Denny Bardos, Vice President for Enrollment Services, PO Box
2317, Batesville, AR 72503-2317
Telephone: 870-698-4250 or toll-free 800-423-2542 **Fax:** 870-793-1791
E-mail: admissions@lyon.edu

Getting in Last Year

427 applied
72% were accepted
120 enrolled (39%)
32% from top tenth of their h.s. class
3.46 average high school GPA
37% had SAT verbal scores over 600
30% had SAT math scores over 600
59% had ACT scores over 24
11% had SAT verbal scores over 700
8% had SAT math scores over 700
15% had ACT scores over 30
9 valedictorians

Graduation and After

44% graduated in 4 years
5% graduated in 5 years
1% graduated in 6 years
16% pursued further study
56% had job offers within 6 months
1 organization recruited on campus

Financial Matters

$12,395 tuition and fees (2003–04)
$5600 room and board
87% average percent of need met
$13,006 average financial aid amount received
   per undergraduate (2002–03 estimated)

Academics

Lyon awards bachelor's **degrees**. Challenging opportunities include advanced placement credit, accelerated degree programs, student-designed majors, double majors, independent study, and a senior project. Special programs include internships, summer session for credit, and study-abroad.

The most frequently chosen **baccalaureate** fields are business/marketing, biological/ life sciences, and social sciences and history. A complete listing of majors at Lyon appears in the Majors Index beginning on page 460.

The **faculty** at Lyon has 44 full-time members, 91% with terminal degrees. The student-faculty ratio is 10:1.

Students of Lyon

The student body is made up of 490 undergraduates. 52.4% are women and 47.6% are men. Students come from 18 states and territories and 15 other countries. 86% are from Arkansas. 4.4% are international students. 3.8% are African American, 2.1% American Indian, 1.1% Asian American, and 1.9% Hispanic American. 78% returned for their sophomore year.

Facilities and Resources

Student rooms are linked to a campus network. 71 **computers** are available on campus that provide access to the Internet. The **library** has 172,738 books and 854 subscriptions.

Campus Life

There are 48 active organizations on campus, including a drama/theater group, newspaper, and choral group. 17% of eligible men and 28% of eligible women are members of national **fraternities** and national **sororities**.

Lyon is a member of the NAIA. **Intercollegiate sports** (some offering scholarships) include baseball (m), basketball, cross-country running, golf, soccer, tennis, volleyball (w).

Campus Safety

Student safety services include late-night transport/escort service and 24-hour patrols by trained security personnel.

Applying

Lyon requires an essay, SAT I or ACT, and a high school transcript. It recommends 2 recommendations and a minimum high school GPA of 2.5. Application deadline: rolling admissions; 3/15 priority date for financial aid. Early and deferred admission are possible.

MACALESTER COLLEGE

URBAN SETTING ■ PRIVATE ■ INDEPENDENT RELIGIOUS ■ COED
ST. PAUL, MINNESOTA

Web site: www.macalester.edu
Contact: Mr. Lorne T. Robinson, Dean of Admissions and Financial Aid,
1600 Grand Avenue, St. Paul, MN 55105-1899
Telephone: 651-696-6357 or toll-free 800-231-7974 **Fax:** 651-696-6724
E-mail: admissions@macalester.edu

Academics

Mac awards bachelor's **degrees**. Challenging opportunities include student-designed majors, an honors program, double majors, independent study, and a senior project. Special programs include internships, off-campus study, study-abroad, and Navy and Air Force ROTC.

The most frequently chosen **baccalaureate** fields are social sciences and history, English, and psychology. A complete listing of majors at Mac appears in the Majors Index beginning on page 460.

The **faculty** at Mac has 149 full-time members, 95% with terminal degrees. The student-faculty ratio is 11:1.

Students of Mac

The student body is made up of 1,884 undergraduates. 57.5% are women and 42.5% are men. Students come from 50 states and territories and 86 other countries. 25% are from Minnesota. 14% are international students. 2.5% are African American, 1.1% American Indian, 4.8% Asian American, and 2.9% Hispanic American. 92% returned for their sophomore year.

Facilities and Resources

Student rooms are linked to a campus network. 350 **computers** are available on campus that provide access to the Internet. The **library** has 407,321 books and 2,119 subscriptions.

Campus Life

There are 70 active organizations on campus, including a drama/theater group, newspaper, radio station, television station, and choral group. No national or local **fraternities** or **sororities**.

Mac is a member of the NCAA (Division III). **Intercollegiate sports** include baseball (m), basketball, cross-country running, football (m), golf, skiing (cross-country), soccer, softball (w), swimming, tennis, track and field, volleyball (w), water polo (w).

Campus Safety

Student safety services include late-night transport/escort service, 24-hour emergency telephone alarm devices, 24-hour patrols by trained security personnel, and electronically operated dormitory entrances.

Applying

Mac requires an essay, SAT I or ACT, a high school transcript, and 3 recommendations. It recommends an interview. Application deadline: 1/15; 2/7 priority date for financial aid. Early and deferred admission are possible.

Getting in Last Year
4,341 applied
44% were accepted
513 enrolled (27%)
68% from top tenth of their h.s. class
90% had SAT verbal scores over 600
87% had SAT math scores over 600
98% had ACT scores over 24
50% had SAT verbal scores over 700
30% had SAT math scores over 700
55% had ACT scores over 30
50 National Merit Scholars
31 valedictorians

Graduation and After
75% graduated in 4 years
6% graduated in 5 years
1% graduated in 6 years
64% had job offers within 6 months
100 organizations recruited on campus

Financial Matters
$25,070 tuition and fees (2003–04)
$6874 room and board
100% average percent of need met
$20,539 average financial aid amount received per undergraduate (2002–03 estimated)

MAHARISHI UNIVERSITY OF MANAGEMENT

SMALL-TOWN SETTING ■ PRIVATE ■ INDEPENDENT ■ COED
FAIRFIELD, IOWA

Web site: www.mum.edu
Contact: Mrs. Lois Neate, Associate Director of Admissions, Office of
  Admissions, Fairfield, IA 52557
Telephone: 641-472-1110 or toll-free 800-369-6480 **Fax:** 641-472-1179
E-mail: admissions@mum.edu

Getting in Last Year
91 applied
69% were accepted
59 enrolled (94%)
3.38 average high school GPA
48% had SAT verbal scores over 600
43% had SAT math scores over 600
59% had ACT scores over 24
11% had SAT verbal scores over 700
6% had SAT math scores over 700
12% had ACT scores over 30
1 National Merit Scholar

Graduation and After
18% graduated in 4 years
15% graduated in 5 years
4% graduated in 6 years
27% pursued further study (16% business,
  11% arts and sciences)
75% had job offers within 6 months
20 organizations recruited on campus

Financial Matters
$24,030 tuition and fees (2003–04)
$5200 room and board
95% average percent of need met
$29,462 average financial aid amount received
  per undergraduate (2002–03 estimated)

Academics
M.U.M. awards bachelor's, master's, and doctoral **degrees** and post-bachelor's
certificates. Challenging opportunities include advanced placement credit, student-
designed majors, an honors program, double majors, independent study, and a senior
project. Special programs include cooperative education, internships, and study-abroad.

The most frequently chosen **baccalaureate** fields are business/marketing, visual/
performing arts, and computer/information sciences. A complete listing of majors at
M.U.M. appears in the Majors Index beginning on page 460.

The **faculty** at M.U.M. has 45 full-time members, 62% with terminal degrees. The
student-faculty ratio is 14:1.

Students of M.U.M.
The student body totals 790, of whom 251 are undergraduates. 47.4% are women and
52.6% are men. Students come from 32 states and territories and 22 other countries.
52% are from Iowa. 30.4% are international students. 2.4% are African American, 0.4%
American Indian, 3.6% Asian American, and 1.6% Hispanic American. 74% returned for
their sophomore year.

Facilities and Resources
Student rooms are linked to a campus network. 120 **computers** are available on campus
that provide access to the Internet. The 2 **libraries** have 113,580 books and 868
subscriptions.

Campus Life
There are 10 active organizations on campus, including a drama/theater group,
newspaper, radio station, and choral group. No national or local **fraternities** or **sororities**.

Intercollegiate sports include golf.

Campus Safety
Student safety services include late-night transport/escort service, 24-hour emergency
telephone alarm devices, 24-hour patrols by trained security personnel, and electronically operated dormitory entrances.

Applying
M.U.M. requires an essay, SAT I or ACT, a high school transcript, 2 recommendations,
minimum SAT score of 950 or ACT score of 19, and a minimum high school GPA of
2.5. It recommends an interview. Application deadline: 8/1; 4/15 priority date for
financial aid. Early and deferred admission are possible.

MARIETTA COLLEGE

SMALL-TOWN SETTING ■ PRIVATE ■ INDEPENDENT ■ COED
MARIETTA, OHIO

Web site: www.marietta.edu
Contact: Ms. Marke Vickers, Director of Admission, 215 Fifth Street, Marietta, OH 45750
Telephone: 740-376-4600 or toll-free 800-331-7896 **Fax:** 740-376-8888
E-mail: admit@marietta.edu

Academics

Marietta awards associate, bachelor's, and master's **degrees**. Challenging opportunities include advanced placement credit, accelerated degree programs, student-designed majors, an honors program, double majors, independent study, and a senior project. Special programs include internships, summer session for credit, off-campus study, and study-abroad.

The most frequently chosen **baccalaureate** fields are business/marketing, social sciences and history, and education. A complete listing of majors at Marietta appears in the Majors Index beginning on page 460.

The **faculty** at Marietta has 78 full-time members, 86% with terminal degrees. The student-faculty ratio is 12:1.

Students of Marietta

The student body totals 1,341, of whom 1,222 are undergraduates. 49.1% are women and 50.9% are men. Students come from 42 states and territories and 13 other countries. 50% are from Ohio. 5.7% are international students. 2.4% are African American, 0.7% American Indian, 3.5% Asian American, and 1.1% Hispanic American. 87% returned for their sophomore year.

Facilities and Resources

Student rooms are linked to a campus network. 200 **computers** are available on campus that provide access to the Internet. The **library** has 250,000 books and 7,100 subscriptions.

Campus Life

There are 100 active organizations on campus, including a drama/theater group, newspaper, radio station, television station, and choral group. 20% of eligible men and 30% of eligible women are members of national **fraternities** and national **sororities**.

Marietta is a member of the NCAA (Division III). **Intercollegiate sports** include baseball (m), basketball, crew, cross-country running, football (m), soccer, softball (w), tennis, track and field, volleyball (w).

Campus Safety

Student safety services include late-night transport/escort service, 24-hour emergency telephone alarm devices, 24-hour patrols by trained security personnel, student patrols, and electronically operated dormitory entrances.

Applying

Marietta requires an essay, SAT I or ACT, a high school transcript, 2 recommendations, and a minimum high school GPA of 2.0. It recommends SAT II Subject Tests, an interview, and a minimum high school GPA of 3.0. Application deadline: 4/15; 3/1 priority date for financial aid. Early and deferred admission are possible.

Founded in 1788, Marietta, Ohio, has the distinction of being the first permanent settlement of America's Northwest Territory. The College traces its beginning to 1797. Both the city and the College are rich in history, with stately homes, brick-paved streets, and antique stores. In 1860, Marietta College became only the 16th college in America to be awarded a chapter of Phi Beta Kappa. Students' academic life is enriched by the McDonough Leadership Program, the most comprehensive program in leadership studies in the country, whereby students may earn a minor, be actively involved in volunteer work, and participate in internships throughout the world.

Getting in Last Year
1,912 applied
78% were accepted
378 enrolled (25%)
19% from top tenth of their h.s. class
3.30 average high school GPA
24% had SAT verbal scores over 600
21% had SAT math scores over 600
41% had ACT scores over 24
3% had SAT verbal scores over 700
3% had SAT math scores over 700
5% had ACT scores over 30

Graduation and After
39% graduated in 4 years
9% graduated in 5 years
6% graduated in 6 years
30% pursued further study (15% arts and sciences, 2% business, 6% education, 3% dentistry)
75% had job offers within 6 months
23 organizations recruited on campus

Financial Matters
$20,892 tuition and fees (2003–04)
$5946 room and board
91% average percent of need met
$17,455 average financial aid amount received per undergraduate (2001–02)

MARQUETTE UNIVERSITY
URBAN SETTING ■ PRIVATE ■ INDEPENDENT RELIGIOUS ■ COED
MILWAUKEE, WISCONSIN

Web site: www.marquette.edu
Contact: Mr. Robert Blust, Dean of Undergraduate Admissions, PO Box 1881, Milwaukee, WI 53201-1881
Telephone: 414-288-7004 or toll-free 800-222-6544 **Fax:** 414-288-3764
E-mail: admissions@marquette.edu

Marquette University, a Catholic, Jesuit university in the heart of Milwaukee, Wisconsin, is dedicated to transforming the lives of women and men by helping them become not merely leaders in their professions, but leaders in the human community. More than 7,500 graduates come to Marquette from all 50 states and more than 80 countries to create a vibrant, diverse, residential learning experience. Students learn from professors who believe that there is such a thing as a student-centered university that conducts world-class research.

Getting in Last Year
8,232 applied
83% were accepted
1,889 enrolled (28%)
30% from top tenth of their h.s. class
42% had SAT verbal scores over 600
49% had SAT math scores over 600
65% had ACT scores over 24
7% had SAT verbal scores over 700
9% had SAT math scores over 700
14% had ACT scores over 30
10 National Merit Scholars

Graduation and After
55% graduated in 4 years
19% graduated in 5 years
2% graduated in 6 years
26% pursued further study (2% education, 2% medicine, 2% business)
226 organizations recruited on campus

Financial Matters
$20,710 tuition and fees (2003–04)
$7000 room and board
89% average percent of need met
$16,400 average financial aid amount received per undergraduate (2002–03 estimated)

Academics
Marquette awards associate, bachelor's, master's, doctoral, and first-professional **degrees** and post-bachelor's and post-master's certificates. Challenging opportunities include advanced placement credit, an honors program, double majors, and a senior project. Special programs include cooperative education, internships, summer session for credit, off-campus study, study-abroad, and Army, Navy and Air Force ROTC.

The most frequently chosen **baccalaureate** fields are business/marketing, health professions and related sciences, and communications/communication technologies. A complete listing of majors at Marquette appears in the Majors Index beginning on page 460.

The **faculty** at Marquette has 578 full-time members, 87% with terminal degrees. The student-faculty ratio is 15:1.

Students of Marquette
The student body totals 11,355, of whom 7,775 are undergraduates. 55.3% are women and 44.7% are men. Students come from 54 states and territories and 80 other countries. 42% are from Wisconsin. 2% are international students. 4.7% are African American, 0.3% American Indian, 4.4% Asian American, and 3.8% Hispanic American. 89% returned for their sophomore year.

Facilities and Resources
Student rooms are linked to a campus network. 1,003 **computers** are available on campus that provide access to the Internet. The 3 **libraries** have 1,120,694 books and 5,894 subscriptions.

Campus Life
There are 180 active organizations on campus, including a drama/theater group, newspaper, radio station, television station, and choral group. 6% of eligible men and 8% of eligible women are members of national **fraternities** and national **sororities**.

Marquette is a member of the NCAA (Division I). **Intercollegiate sports** (some offering scholarships) include basketball, cheerleading, cross-country running, golf (m), soccer, tennis, track and field, volleyball (w).

Campus Safety
Student safety services include 24-hour desk attendants in residence halls, late-night transport/escort service, 24-hour emergency telephone alarm devices, 24-hour patrols by trained security personnel, and student patrols.

Applying
Marquette requires an essay, SAT I or ACT, a high school transcript, 1 recommendation, and a minimum high school GPA of 2.5. It recommends a minimum high school GPA of 3.4. Application deadline: rolling admissions. Early and deferred admission are possible.

MARYLAND INSTITUTE COLLEGE OF ART

URBAN SETTING ■ PRIVATE ■ INDEPENDENT ■ COED
BALTIMORE, MARYLAND

Web site: www.mica.edu
Contact: Mr. Hans Ever, Director of Undergraduate Admission, 1300 Mount Royal Avenue, Baltimore, MD 21217-4191
Telephone: 410-225-2222 **Fax:** 410-225-2337
E-mail: admissions@mica.edu

Academics

MICA awards bachelor's and master's **degrees** and post-bachelor's certificates. Challenging opportunities include advanced placement credit, accelerated degree programs, student-designed majors, double majors, independent study, and a senior project. Special programs include internships, summer session for credit, off-campus study, study-abroad, and Army ROTC.

The most frequently chosen **baccalaureate** fields are visual/performing arts and education. A complete listing of majors at MICA appears in the Majors Index beginning on page 460.

The **faculty** at MICA has 118 full-time members, 77% with terminal degrees. The student-faculty ratio is 10:1.

Students of MICA

The student body totals 1,476, of whom 1,290 are undergraduates. 62.4% are women and 37.6% are men. Students come from 44 states and territories and 52 other countries. 24% are from Maryland. 4.7% are international students. 4.2% are African American, 0.5% American Indian, 8.1% Asian American, and 4.7% Hispanic American. 85% returned for their sophomore year.

Facilities and Resources

Student rooms are linked to a campus network. 250 **computers** are available on campus that provide access to e-mail and the Internet. The 2 **libraries** have 53,000 books and 305 subscriptions.

Campus Life

There are 22 active organizations on campus, including a drama/theater group and choral group. No national or local **fraternities** or **sororities**.

This institution has no intercollegiate sports.

Campus Safety

Student safety services include self-defense education, 24-hour building security, safety awareness programs, campus patrols by city police, late-night transport/escort service, 24-hour emergency telephone alarm devices, 24-hour patrols by trained security personnel, student patrols, and electronically operated dormitory entrances.

Applying

MICA requires an essay, SAT I or ACT, a high school transcript, and art portfolio. It recommends an interview and 3 recommendations. Application deadline: 1/15; 3/1 priority date for financial aid. Early and deferred admission are possible.

Getting in Last Year

1,944 applied
50% were accepted
385 enrolled (40%)
24% from top tenth of their h.s. class
3.49 average high school GPA
51% had SAT verbal scores over 600
35% had SAT math scores over 600
10% had SAT verbal scores over 700
4% had SAT math scores over 700
5 National Merit Scholars

Graduation and After

63% graduated in 4 years
4% graduated in 5 years
2% graduated in 6 years
26% pursued further study (18% arts and sciences, 8% education)
30% had job offers within 6 months
40 organizations recruited on campus

Financial Matters

$23,710 tuition and fees (2003–04)
$7180 room and board

MARYVILLE COLLEGE

SUBURBAN SETTING ■ PRIVATE ■ INDEPENDENT RELIGIOUS ■ COED
MARYVILLE, TENNESSEE

Web site: www.maryvillecollege.edu
Contact: Ms. Linda L. Moore, Administrative Assistant of Admissions, 502
    East Lamar Alexander Parkway, Maryville, TN 37804-5907
Telephone: 865-981-8092 or toll-free 800-597-2687 **Fax:** 865-981-8005
E-mail: admissions@maryvillecollege.edu

Maryville provides a total learning experience for each student. Through the unique Maryville curriculum and individual attention from faculty members, staff members, and peers, students are prepared for a fulfilling life as an educated person. Classroom studies are supported by a rich array of experiental learning opportunities, including internships, study abroad, service learning, and the College's distinctive outdoor adventure program, Mountain Challenge. Affiliated with the Presbyterian Church (U.S.A.) through a voluntary covenant, Maryville is located in Tennessee near Great Smoky Mountain National Park.

Getting in Last Year
1,378 applied
81% were accepted
292 enrolled (26%)
30% from top tenth of their h.s. class
3.56 average high school GPA
39% had SAT verbal scores over 600
40% had SAT math scores over 600
55% had ACT scores over 24
4% had SAT verbal scores over 700
7% had SAT math scores over 700
8% had ACT scores over 30
9 valedictorians

Graduation and After
40% graduated in 4 years
11% graduated in 5 years
2% graduated in 6 years
30% pursued further study
73% had job offers within 6 months
19 organizations recruited on campus

Financial Matters
$19,780 tuition and fees (2003–04)
$6180 room and board
88% average percent of need met
$17,427 average financial aid amount received
    per undergraduate (2002–03 estimated)

Academics
MC awards bachelor's **degrees**. Challenging opportunities include advanced placement credit, student-designed majors, an honors program, double majors, independent study, and a senior project. Special programs include internships, summer session for credit, off-campus study, and study-abroad.

The most frequently chosen **baccalaureate** fields are business/marketing, education, and biological/life sciences. A complete listing of majors at MC appears in the Majors Index beginning on page 460.

The **faculty** at MC has 70 full-time members, 91% with terminal degrees. The student-faculty ratio is 12:1.

Students of MC
The student body is made up of 1,052 undergraduates. 55.6% are women and 44.4% are men. Students come from 29 states and territories and 19 other countries. 79% are from Tennessee. 4.4% are international students. 6.4% are African American, 0.4% American Indian, 0.8% Asian American, and 1% Hispanic American. 70% returned for their sophomore year.

Facilities and Resources
Student rooms are linked to a campus network. 79 **computers** are available on campus that provide access to the Internet. The 2 **libraries** have 103,912 books and 16,000 subscriptions.

Campus Life
There are 47 active organizations on campus, including a drama/theater group, newspaper, radio station, and choral group. No national or local **fraternities** or **sororities**.

MC is a member of the NCAA (Division III). **Intercollegiate sports** include baseball (m), basketball, cheerleading, cross-country running, equestrian sports, football (m), soccer, softball (w), tennis, volleyball (w), wrestling (m).

Campus Safety
Student safety services include late-night transport/escort service, 24-hour emergency telephone alarm devices, 24-hour patrols by trained security personnel, and electronically operated dormitory entrances.

Applying
MC requires SAT I or ACT, a high school transcript, and a minimum high school GPA of 2.5, and in some cases an essay, an interview, and recommendations. It recommends a minimum high school GPA of 3.0. Application deadline: 3/1; 3/1 priority date for financial aid. Early and deferred admission are possible.

MARYVILLE UNIVERSITY OF SAINT LOUIS

SUBURBAN SETTING ■ PRIVATE ■ INDEPENDENT ■ COED
ST. LOUIS, MISSOURI

Web site: www.maryville.edu
Contact: Ms. Lynn Jackson, Admissions Director, 13550 Conway Road, St. Louis, MO 63141-7299
Telephone: 314-529-9350 or toll-free 800-627-9855 **Fax:** 314-529-9927
E-mail: admissions@maryville.edu

Academics

Maryville awards bachelor's and master's **degrees**. Challenging opportunities include advanced placement credit, accelerated degree programs, student-designed majors, freshman honors college, an honors program, double majors, independent study, and a senior project. Special programs include cooperative education, internships, summer session for credit, off-campus study, study-abroad, and Army ROTC.

The most frequently chosen **baccalaureate** fields are business/marketing, health professions and related sciences, and psychology. A complete listing of majors at Maryville appears in the Majors Index beginning on page 460.

The **faculty** at Maryville has 88 full-time members, 90% with terminal degrees. The student-faculty ratio is 13:1.

Students of Maryville

The student body totals 3,301, of whom 2,705 are undergraduates. 75.7% are women and 24.3% are men. Students come from 17 states and territories and 20 other countries. 91% are from Missouri. 1.7% are international students. 6.3% are African American, 0.3% American Indian, 1.3% Asian American, and 1.1% Hispanic American. 74% returned for their sophomore year.

Facilities and Resources

Student rooms are linked to a campus network. 250 **computers** are available on campus that provide access to e-mail, specialized software, university catalog, schedules and the Internet. The **library** has 205,512 books and 9,004 subscriptions.

Campus Life

There are 33 active organizations on campus, including a drama/theater group, newspaper, and choral group. No national or local **fraternities** or **sororities**.

Maryville is a member of the NCAA (Division III). **Intercollegiate sports** include baseball (m), basketball, cross-country running, golf (m), soccer, softball (w), tennis, volleyball (w).

Campus Safety

Student safety services include video security system in residence halls, self-defense and education programs, late-night transport/escort service, 24-hour emergency telephone alarm devices, 24-hour patrols by trained security personnel, and electronically operated dormitory entrances.

Applying

Maryville requires SAT I or ACT, a high school transcript, and a minimum high school GPA of 2.5, and in some cases an essay, an interview, recommendations, and audition, portfolio. Application deadline: 8/15; 4/1 priority date for financial aid. Early and deferred admission are possible.

Getting in Last Year

1,154 applied
73% were accepted
335 enrolled (40%)
21% from top tenth of their h.s. class
3.51 average high school GPA
50% had ACT scores over 24
6% had ACT scores over 30
4 valedictorians

Graduation and After

46% graduated in 4 years
13% graduated in 5 years
1% graduated in 6 years
85 organizations recruited on campus

Financial Matters

$15,440 tuition and fees (2003–04)
$6650 room and board
59% average percent of need met
$8110 average financial aid amount received per undergraduate (2002–03 estimated)

MARY WASHINGTON COLLEGE

SMALL-TOWN SETTING ■ PUBLIC ■ STATE-SUPPORTED ■ COED
FREDERICKSBURG, VIRGINIA

Web site: www.mwc.edu
Contact: Dr. Martin A. Wilder, Vice President for Enrollment, 1301 College
    Avenue, Fredericksburg, VA 22401-5358
Telephone: 540-654-2000 or toll-free 800-468-5614 **Fax:** 540-654-1857
E-mail: admit@mwc.edu

Getting in Last Year

4,472 applied
60% were accepted
869 enrolled (32%)
50% from top tenth of their h.s. class
3.63 average high school GPA
63% had SAT verbal scores over 600
57% had SAT math scores over 600
11% had SAT verbal scores over 700
8% had SAT math scores over 700
1 National Merit Scholar
150 class presidents
7 valedictorians

Graduation and After

59% graduated in 4 years
7% graduated in 5 years
1% graduated in 6 years
23% pursued further study (6% arts and sci-
    ences, 3% law, 2% education)
70% had job offers within 6 months
64 organizations recruited on campus

Financial Matters

$4424 resident tuition and fees (2003–04)
$12,172 nonresident tuition and fees (2003–
    04)
$5478 room and board
56% average percent of need met
$5300 average financial aid amount received
    per undergraduate

Academics

Mary Washington awards bachelor's and master's **degrees** and post-bachelor's
certificates. Challenging opportunities include advanced placement credit, accelerated
degree programs, student-designed majors, double majors, independent study, and a
senior project. Special programs include cooperative education, internships, summer
session for credit, and study-abroad.

The most frequently chosen **baccalaureate** fields are social sciences and history,
business/marketing, and English. A complete listing of majors at Mary Washington appears in the Majors Index beginning on page 460.

The **faculty** at Mary Washington has 206 full-time members, 87% with terminal
degrees. The student-faculty ratio is 17:1.

Students of Mary Washington

The student body totals 4,792, of whom 4,220 are undergraduates. 66.6% are women
and 33.4% are men. Students come from 44 states and territories and 15 other countries.
65% are from Virginia. 0.5% are international students. 3.6% are African American,
0.4% American Indian, 4.5% Asian American, and 2.9% Hispanic American. 85%
returned for their sophomore year.

Facilities and Resources

Student rooms are linked to a campus network. 244 **computers** are available on campus
that provide access to the Internet. The **library** has 355,478 books and 2,419 subscriptions.

Campus Life

There are 96 active organizations on campus, including a drama/theater group,
newspaper, radio station, and choral group. No national or local **fraternities** or **sororities**.

Mary Washington is a member of the NCAA (Division III). **Intercollegiate sports**
include baseball (m), basketball, crew, cross-country running, equestrian sports, field
hockey (w), lacrosse, soccer, softball (w), swimming, tennis, track and field, volleyball (w).

Campus Safety

Student safety services include self-defense and safety classes, late-night transport/escort
service, 24-hour emergency telephone alarm devices, 24-hour patrols by trained security
personnel, student patrols, and electronically operated dormitory entrances.

Applying

Mary Washington requires an essay, SAT I or ACT, and a high school transcript. It
recommends SAT II Subject Tests. Application deadline: 2/1; 3/1 priority date for
financial aid. Deferred admission is possible.

MASSACHUSETTS INSTITUTE OF TECHNOLOGY
URBAN SETTING ■ PRIVATE ■ INDEPENDENT ■ COED
CAMBRIDGE, MASSACHUSETTS

Web site: web.mit.edu
Contact: Ms. Marilee Jones, Dean of Admissions, Room 3-108, 77
   Massachusetts Avenue, Cambridge, MA 02139-4307
Telephone: 617-253-4791 **Fax:** 617-258-8304

Academics
MIT awards bachelor's, master's, and doctoral **degrees**. Challenging opportunities
include advanced placement credit, accelerated degree programs, student-designed
majors, and a senior project. Special programs include cooperative education, internships, summer session for credit, off-campus study, and Army, Navy and Air Force
ROTC.

The most frequently chosen **baccalaureate** fields are engineering/engineering
technologies, computer/information sciences, and business/marketing. A complete listing of majors at MIT appears in the Majors Index beginning on page 460.

The **faculty** at MIT has 1,543 full-time members, 94% with terminal degrees. The
student-faculty ratio is 6:1.

Students of MIT
The student body totals 10,340, of whom 4,112 are undergraduates. 42.3% are women
and 57.7% are men. Students come from 55 states and territories and 79 other countries.
9% are from Massachusetts. 8% are international students. 6.1% are African American,
1.7% American Indian, 28.2% Asian American, and 11.8% Hispanic American. 98%
returned for their sophomore year.

Facilities and Resources
Student rooms are linked to a campus network. 950 **computers** are available on campus
for student use. The 11 **libraries** have 2,667,215 books and 22,358 subscriptions.

Campus Life
There are 330 active organizations on campus, including a drama/theater group,
newspaper, radio station, television station, choral group, and marching band. 40% of
eligible men and 26% of eligible women are members of national **fraternities**, national
sororities, local fraternities, and cooperative style living groups.

MIT is a member of the NCAA (Division III). **Intercollegiate sports** include
baseball (m), basketball, crew, cross-country running, fencing, field hockey (w), football
(m), golf (m), gymnastics, ice hockey (w), lacrosse, riflery, sailing, skiing (cross-country),
skiing (downhill), soccer, softball (w), squash (m), swimming, tennis, track and field, volleyball, water polo (m), wrestling (m).

Campus Safety
Student safety services include late-night transport/escort service, 24-hour emergency
telephone alarm devices, 24-hour patrols by trained security personnel, and electronically operated dormitory entrances.

Applying
MIT requires an essay, SAT II Subject Tests, SAT I or ACT, a high school transcript, and
2 recommendations. It recommends an interview. Application deadline: 1/1; 2/1 for
financial aid. Deferred admission is possible.

Getting in Last Year
10,549 applied
16% were accepted
1,019 enrolled (59%)
97% from top tenth of their h.s. class
3.90 average high school GPA
95% had SAT verbal scores over 600
100% had SAT math scores over 600
99% had ACT scores over 24
63% had SAT verbal scores over 700
89% had SAT math scores over 700
76% had ACT scores over 30
241 valedictorians

Graduation and After
81% graduated in 4 years
9% graduated in 5 years
3% graduated in 6 years
55% pursued further study (31% engineering,
   12% arts and sciences, 6% medicine)
950 organizations recruited on campus

Financial Matters
$29,600 tuition and fees (2003–04)
$8710 room and board
100% average percent of need met
$22,983 average financial aid amount received
   per undergraduate (2001–02)

THE MASTER'S COLLEGE AND SEMINARY

SUBURBAN SETTING ■ PRIVATE ■ INDEPENDENT RELIGIOUS ■ COED
SANTA CLARITA, CALIFORNIA

Web site: www.masters.edu
Contact: Mr. Yaphet Peterson, Director of Enrollment, 21726 Placerita
Canyon Road, Santa Clarita, CA 91321-1200
Telephone: 661-259-3540 ext. 3365 or toll-free 800-568-6248 **Fax:**
661-288-1037
E-mail: enrollment@masters.edu

Getting in Last Year

412 applied
54% were accepted
209 enrolled (95%)
30% from top tenth of their h.s. class
3.62 average high school GPA
40% had SAT verbal scores over 600
32% had SAT math scores over 600
60% had ACT scores over 24
6% had SAT verbal scores over 700
5% had SAT math scores over 700
12% had ACT scores over 30
7 valedictorians

Graduation and After

51% graduated in 4 years
3% graduated in 5 years
4% graduated in 6 years
Graduates pursuing further study: 10% theology, 1% law
30 organizations recruited on campus

Financial Matters

$17,200 tuition and fees (2003–04)
$6050 room and board
76% average percent of need met
$13,872 average financial aid amount received
per undergraduate (2002–03 estimated)

Academics

Master's awards bachelor's, master's, doctoral, and first-professional **degrees** and first-professional certificates. Challenging opportunities include advanced placement credit, accelerated degree programs, double majors, independent study, and a senior project. Special programs include cooperative education, internships, summer session for credit, and study-abroad.

The most frequently chosen **baccalaureate** fields are business/marketing, education, and communications/communication technologies. A complete listing of majors at Master's appears in the Majors Index beginning on page 460.

The **faculty** at Master's has 68 full-time members, 81% with terminal degrees. The student-faculty ratio is 14:1.

Students of Master's

The student body totals 1,426, of whom 1,132 are undergraduates. 51.1% are women and 48.9% are men. Students come from 42 states and territories and 24 other countries. 67% are from California. 2.9% are international students. 2.8% are African American, 0.6% American Indian, 3.4% Asian American, and 6.2% Hispanic American. 83% returned for their sophomore year.

Facilities and Resources

Student rooms are linked to a campus network. 57 **computers** are available on campus that provide access to the Internet. The 2 **libraries** have 211,895 books and 1,288 subscriptions.

Campus Life

There are 15 active organizations on campus, including a choral group. No national or local **fraternities** or **sororities**.

Master's is a member of the NAIA and NCCAA. **Intercollegiate sports** (some offering scholarships) include baseball (m), basketball, cross-country running, golf (m), soccer, softball (w), volleyball (w).

Campus Safety

Student safety services include 24-hour patrols by trained security personnel.

Applying

Master's requires an essay, SAT I or ACT, a high school transcript, an interview, 2 recommendations, and a minimum high school GPA of 2.50. Application deadline: 3/2 priority date for financial aid. Early and deferred admission are possible.

McDaniel College

SUBURBAN SETTING ■ PRIVATE ■ INDEPENDENT ■ COED
WESTMINSTER, MARYLAND

Web site: www.mcdaniel.edu
Contact: Ms. M. Martha O'Connell, Dean of Admissions, 2 College Hill,
   Westminster, MD 21157-4390
Telephone: 410-857-2230 or toll-free 800-638-5005 **Fax:** 410-857-2757
E-mail: admissions@mcdaniel.edu

Academics
McDaniel College awards bachelor's and master's **degrees**. Challenging opportunities include advanced placement credit, student-designed majors, an honors program, double majors, independent study, and a senior project. Special programs include internships, summer session for credit, off-campus study, study-abroad, and Army ROTC.

The most frequently chosen **baccalaureate** fields are social sciences and history, business/marketing, and communications/communication technologies. A complete listing of majors at McDaniel College appears in the Majors Index beginning on page 460.

The **faculty** at McDaniel College has 93 full-time members, 96% with terminal degrees. The student-faculty ratio is 13:1.

Students of McDaniel College
The student body totals 3,294, of whom 1,744 are undergraduates. 57% are women and 43% are men. Students come from 30 states and territories and 12 other countries. 74% are from Maryland. 2.3% are international students. 8.8% are African American, 0.6% American Indian, 1.2% Asian American, and 1.5% Hispanic American. 83% returned for their sophomore year.

Facilities and Resources
Student rooms are linked to a campus network. 171 **computers** are available on campus that provide access to the Internet. The **library** has 629,965 books and 3,500 subscriptions.

Campus Life
There are 128 active organizations on campus, including a drama/theater group, newspaper, radio station, television station, and choral group. 16% of eligible men and 12% of eligible women are members of national **fraternities**, national **sororities**, local fraternities, and local sororities.

McDaniel College is a member of the NCAA (Division III). **Intercollegiate sports** include baseball (m), basketball, cross-country running, field hockey (w), football (m), golf, lacrosse, soccer, softball (w), swimming, tennis, track and field, volleyball (w), wrestling (m).

Campus Safety
Student safety services include late-night transport/escort service, 24-hour emergency telephone alarm devices, 24-hour patrols by trained security personnel, and electronically operated dormitory entrances.

Applying
McDaniel College requires an essay, SAT I or ACT, a high school transcript, and a minimum high school GPA of 2.5, and in some cases an interview. It recommends SAT II Subject Tests, an interview, and recommendations. Application deadline: 2/1; 3/1 priority date for financial aid. Early and deferred admission are possible.

McDaniel students become involved, connected, and confident. First-year seminars, a January mini-mester of uncommon courses, and options for self-designed majors provide learning opportunities beyond the norm. Less than an hour's drive from Washington D.C., students take advantage of all the career and cultural possibilities of the nation's capital while honing leadership skills on campus as faculty-research assistants across all majors; as volunteers directing more than 100 student clubs or as teammates on the playing fields of 24 intercollegiate sports. A nine-hole golf course doubles as both a place to practice golf swings or snowboard downhill in winter.

Getting in Last Year
2,008 applied
83% were accepted
451 enrolled (27%)
25% from top tenth of their h.s. class
3.40 average high school GPA
28% had SAT verbal scores over 600
28% had SAT math scores over 600
5% had SAT verbal scores over 700
3% had SAT math scores over 700

Graduation and After
66% graduated in 4 years
6% graduated in 5 years
1% graduated in 6 years
43% pursued further study (13% arts and sciences, 9% education, 6% medicine)
75% had job offers within 6 months
189 organizations recruited on campus

Financial Matters
$23,160 tuition and fees (2003–04)
$5280 room and board
92% average percent of need met
$18,978 average financial aid amount received per undergraduate

McGill University

URBAN SETTING ■ PUBLIC ■ COED
MONTRÉAL, QUEBEC

Web site: www.mcgill.ca
Contact: Ms. Kim Bartlett, Director of Admissions, 845 Sherbrooke Street
    West, Montreal, QC H3A 2T5 Canada
Telephone: 514-398-4462 Fax: 514-398-4193
E-mail: admissions@mcgill.ca

Getting in Last Year
20,635 applied
48% were accepted
4,493 enrolled (45%)
90% from top tenth of their h.s. class
3.50 average high school GPA

Graduation and After
3000 organizations recruited on campus

Financial Matters
$2060 resident tuition and fees (2003–04)
$3860 nonresident tuition and fees (2003–04)
$5755 room and board

Academics

McGill awards bachelor's, master's, doctoral, and first-professional **degrees** and post-bachelor's certificates. Challenging opportunities include advanced placement credit, student-designed majors, an honors program, and double majors. Special programs include internships, summer session for credit, off-campus study, and study-abroad.

The most frequently chosen **baccalaureate** fields are social sciences and history, biological/life sciences, and business/marketing. A complete listing of majors at McGill appears in the Majors Index beginning on page 460.

The **faculty** at McGill has 1,534 full-time members, 95% with terminal degrees. The student-faculty ratio is 12:1.

Students of McGill

The student body totals 30,662, of whom 21,827 are undergraduates. 60.4% are women and 39.6% are men. Students come from 12 states and territories and 133 other countries. 71% are from Quebec.

Facilities and Resources

Student rooms are linked to a campus network. 1,500 **computers** are available on campus that provide access to the Internet. The 17 **libraries** have 4,029,960 books and 22,513 subscriptions.

Campus Life

There are 180 active organizations on campus, including a drama/theater group, newspaper, radio station, and choral group. 4% of eligible men and 2% of eligible women are members of national **fraternities**, national **sororities**, and local fraternities.

Intercollegiate sports include badminton, baseball (m), basketball, cheerleading (w), crew, cross-country running, fencing, field hockey (w), football (m), golf, ice hockey, lacrosse, rugby, sailing, skiing (cross-country), skiing (downhill), soccer, squash, swimming, tennis, track and field, ultimate Frisbee, volleyball, wrestling.

Campus Safety

Student safety services include late-night transport/escort service, 24-hour emergency telephone alarm devices, 24-hour patrols by trained security personnel, student patrols, and electronically operated dormitory entrances.

Applying

McGill requires SAT I and SAT II or ACT, a high school transcript, and a minimum high school GPA of 3.3, and in some cases recommendations and audition for music program, portfolio for architecture program. Application deadline: 1/15. Deferred admission is possible.

MCKENDREE COLLEGE

SMALL-TOWN SETTING ■ PRIVATE ■ INDEPENDENT RELIGIOUS ■ COED
LEBANON, ILLINOIS

Web site: www.mckendree.edu
Contact: Mr. Mark Campbell, Vice President for Admissions and Financial
Aid, 701 College Road, Lebanon, IL 62254
Telephone: 800-232-7228 ext. 6835 or toll-free 800-232-7228 ext. 6831 **Fax:**
618-537-6496
E-mail: inquiry@mckendree.edu

Academics

McKendree awards bachelor's and master's **degrees**. Challenging opportunities include
advanced placement credit, accelerated degree programs, student-designed majors, an
honors program, double majors, independent study, and a senior project. Special
programs include internships, summer session for credit, off-campus study, study-abroad,
and Army and Air Force ROTC.

The most frequently chosen **baccalaureate** fields are business/marketing, education,
and health professions and related sciences. A complete listing of majors at McKendree
appears in the Majors Index beginning on page 460.

The **faculty** at McKendree has 70 full-time members, 84% with terminal degrees.
The student-faculty ratio is 12:1.

Students of McKendree

The student body is made up of 2,115 undergraduates. 60.5% are women and 39.5% are
men. Students come from 23 states and territories and 15 other countries. 69% are from
Illinois. 1.2% are international students. 10.3% are African American, 0.2% American
Indian, 1% Asian American, and 1.3% Hispanic American. 79% returned for their
sophomore year.

Facilities and Resources

Student rooms are linked to a campus network. 140 **computers** are available on campus
that provide access to the Internet. The **library** has 105,000 books and 450 subscriptions.

Campus Life

There are 54 active organizations on campus, including a drama/theater group,
newspaper, choral group, and marching band. 8% of eligible men and 6% of eligible
women are members of national **fraternities**, local fraternities, and local **sororities**.

McKendree is a member of the NAIA. **Intercollegiate sports** (some offering
scholarships) include baseball (m), basketball, bowling, cheerleading, cross-country running, football (m), golf, ice hockey (m), soccer, softball (w), tennis, track and field, volleyball (w), wrestling (m).

Campus Safety

Student safety services include late-night transport/escort service, 24-hour emergency
telephone alarm devices, 24-hour patrols by trained security personnel, student patrols,
and electronically operated dormitory entrances.

Applying

McKendree requires an essay, SAT I or ACT, a high school transcript, 1 recommendation, top half of class, ACT of 20 or greater, and a minimum high school GPA of
2.5, and in some cases an essay and an interview. Application deadline: rolling admissions; 5/31 priority date for financial aid. Deferred admission is possible.

Getting in Last Year

1,182 applied
73% were accepted
310 enrolled (36%)
36% from top tenth of their h.s. class
3.70 average high school GPA
56% had ACT scores over 24
7% had ACT scores over 30
19 valedictorians

Graduation and After

40% graduated in 4 years
16% graduated in 5 years
4% graduated in 6 years
18% pursued further study (6% business, 5%
arts and sciences, 3% law)
97% had job offers within 6 months
115 organizations recruited on campus

Financial Matters

$15,200 tuition and fees (2003–04)
$5920 room and board
79% average percent of need met
$12,400 average financial aid amount received
per undergraduate

MERCER UNIVERSITY

SUBURBAN SETTING ■ PRIVATE ■ INDEPENDENT RELIGIOUS ■ COED
MACON, GEORGIA

Web site: www.mercer.edu
Contact: Mr. Allen S. London, Vice President, University Admissions, 1400 Coleman Avenue, Macon, GA 31207-0003
Telephone: 478-301-2650 or toll-free 800-840-8577 **Fax:** 478-301-2828
E-mail: admissions@mercer.edu

Mercer University is a private, coeducational institution located in Macon, Georgia, just 80 miles south of Atlanta. Founded in 1833, the University is composed of 10 schools: the College of Liberal Arts, the Eugene W. Stetson School of Business and Economics, the School of Engineering, the Tift College of Education, the Walter F. George School of Law, the School of Medicine, the Southern School of Pharmacy, the James and Carolyn McAfee School of Theology, the Georgia Baptist College of Nursing, and the College of Continuing and Professional Studies.

Getting in Last Year
3,034 applied
79% were accepted
696 enrolled (29%)
40% from top tenth of their h.s. class
3.60 average high school GPA
42% had SAT verbal scores over 600
50% had SAT math scores over 600
64% had ACT scores over 24
8% had SAT verbal scores over 700
11% had SAT math scores over 700
16% had ACT scores over 30
2 National Merit Scholars
73 class presidents
110 valedictorians

Graduation and After
32% graduated in 4 years
13% graduated in 5 years
5% graduated in 6 years
45% pursued further study
70% had job offers within 6 months
258 organizations recruited on campus

Financial Matters
$20,796 tuition and fees (2003–04)
$6720 room and board
89% average percent of need met
$21,250 average financial aid amount received per undergraduate

Academics
Mercer awards bachelor's, master's, doctoral, and first-professional **degrees** and post-bachelor's, post-master's, and first-professional certificates. Challenging opportunities include advanced placement credit, accelerated degree programs, student-designed majors, an honors program, double majors, independent study, and a senior project. Special programs include cooperative education, internships, summer session for credit, off-campus study, study-abroad, and Army ROTC.

The most frequently chosen **baccalaureate** fields are business/marketing, education, and protective services/public administration. A complete listing of majors at Mercer appears in the Majors Index beginning on page 460.

The **faculty** at Mercer has 328 full-time members, 88% with terminal degrees. The student-faculty ratio is 14:1.

Students of Mercer
The student body totals 7,200, of whom 4,580 are undergraduates. 66.7% are women and 33.3% are men. Students come from 30 states and territories and 35 other countries. 80% are from Georgia. 3% are international students. 27.9% are African American, 0.2% American Indian, 3.2% Asian American, and 1.4% Hispanic American. 79% returned for their sophomore year.

Facilities and Resources
Student rooms are linked to a campus network. 140 **computers** are available on campus that provide access to the Internet. The 4 **libraries** have 391,800 books and 5,729 subscriptions.

Campus Life
There are 120 active organizations on campus, including a drama/theater group, newspaper, and choral group. 29% of eligible men and 27% of eligible women are members of national **fraternities**, national **sororities**, and local sororities.

Mercer is a member of the NCAA (Division I). **Intercollegiate sports** (some offering scholarships) include baseball (m), basketball, cross-country running, golf, riflery, soccer, softball (w), tennis, volleyball (w).

Campus Safety
Student safety services include patrols by police officers, late-night transport/escort service, 24-hour emergency telephone alarm devices, 24-hour patrols by trained security personnel, student patrols, and electronically operated dormitory entrances.

Applying
Mercer requires SAT I or ACT, a high school transcript, and a minimum high school GPA of 3.0, and in some cases an interview, 2 recommendations, and a minimum high school GPA of 3.0. It recommends an interview, counselor's evaluation, and a minimum high school GPA of 3.0. Application deadline: 6/1; 4/1 priority date for financial aid. Early and deferred admission are possible.

MESSIAH COLLEGE

SMALL-TOWN SETTING ■ PRIVATE ■ INDEPENDENT RELIGIOUS ■ COED
GRANTHAM, PENNSYLVANIA

Web site: www.messiah.edu
Contact: Dr. William G. Strausbaugh, Dean for Enrollment Management,
One College Avenue, PO Box 3005, Grantham, PA 17027
Telephone: 717-691-6000 or toll-free 800-233-4220 **Fax:** 717-796-5374
E-mail: admiss@messiah.edu

Academics

Messiah College awards bachelor's **degrees**. Challenging opportunities include advanced placement credit, accelerated degree programs, student-designed majors, an honors program, double majors, independent study, and a senior project. Special programs include internships, summer session for credit, off-campus study, and study-abroad.

The most frequently chosen **baccalaureate** fields are education, business/marketing, and social sciences and history. A complete listing of majors at Messiah College appears in the Majors Index beginning on page 460.

The **faculty** at Messiah College has 166 full-time members, 73% with terminal degrees. The student-faculty ratio is 13:1.

Students of Messiah College

The student body is made up of 2,952 undergraduates. 62.6% are women and 37.4% are men. Students come from 41 states and territories and 35 other countries. 52% are from Pennsylvania. 2.6% are international students. 2.9% are African American, 0.1% American Indian, 1.6% Asian American, and 2.1% Hispanic American. 86% returned for their sophomore year.

Facilities and Resources

Student rooms are linked to a campus network. 463 **computers** are available on campus that provide access to the Internet. The **library** has 258,097 books and 1,327 subscriptions.

Campus Life

There are 60 active organizations on campus, including a drama/theater group, newspaper, radio station, and choral group. No national or local **fraternities** or **sororities**.

Messiah College is a member of the NCAA (Division III). **Intercollegiate sports** include baseball (m), basketball, cross-country running, field hockey (w), golf (m), lacrosse, soccer, softball (w), tennis, track and field, volleyball (w), wrestling (m).

Campus Safety

Student safety services include bicycle patrols, security lighting, self-defense classes, prevention/awareness programs, late-night transport/escort service, 24-hour emergency telephone alarm devices, 24-hour patrols by trained security personnel, student patrols, and electronically operated dormitory entrances.

Applying

Messiah College requires an essay, a high school transcript, and 2 recommendations, and in some cases SAT I or ACT. It recommends an interview and a minimum high school GPA of 3.0. Application deadline: rolling admissions; 4/1 priority date for financial aid. Early and deferred admission are possible.

M essiah College provides an education that is both rigorously academic and unapologetically Christian. The learning process is characterized by lively student-faculty interaction that actively integrates academic content and faith issues. Messiah offers a strategically located campus, impressive academic and residence life facilities, and over 50 majors and 50 minors in the applied and liberal arts and sciences. Students pursue extracurricular interests in 20 intercollegiate sports, ministries, service learning areas, music ensembles, and scores of other activities. A multifaceted internship program provides career experience for students before they graduate. After graduation, 99% of graduates report employment/voluntary service or enrollment in graduate school within 6 months.

Getting in Last Year
2,252 applied
79% were accepted
736 enrolled (41%)
41% from top tenth of their h.s. class
3.76 average high school GPA
52% had SAT verbal scores over 600
48% had SAT math scores over 600
73% had ACT scores over 24
11% had SAT verbal scores over 700
11% had SAT math scores over 700
23% had ACT scores over 30
13 National Merit Scholars
42 valedictorians

Graduation and After
65% graduated in 4 years
6% graduated in 5 years
1% graduated in 6 years
13% pursued further study (9% arts and sciences, 1% business, 1% education)
90% had job offers within 6 months
466 organizations recruited on campus

Financial Matters
$19,550 tuition and fees (2003–04)
$6340 room and board
65% average percent of need met
$12,798 average financial aid amount received per undergraduate

MIAMI UNIVERSITY

SMALL-TOWN SETTING ■ PUBLIC ■ STATE-RELATED ■ COED
OXFORD, OHIO

Web site: www.muohio.edu
Contact: Mr. Michael E. Mills, Director of Undergraduate Admissions, 301 South Campus Avenue, Oxford, OH 45056
Telephone: 513-529-2531 **Fax:** 513-529-1550
E-mail: admission@muohio.edu

Getting in Last Year
13,859 applied
71% were accepted
3,309 enrolled (34%)
40% from top tenth of their h.s. class
55% had SAT verbal scores over 600
70% had SAT math scores over 600
87% had ACT scores over 24
8% had SAT verbal scores over 700
11% had SAT math scores over 700
18% had ACT scores over 30
130 National Merit Scholars

Graduation and After
67% graduated in 4 years
14% graduated in 5 years
2% graduated in 6 years
Graduates pursuing further study: 14% arts and sciences, 7% law, 7% medicine
550 organizations recruited on campus

Financial Matters
$8353 resident tuition and fees (2003–04)
$18,123 nonresident tuition and fees (2003–04)
$6680 room and board
68% average percent of need met
$6997 average financial aid amount received per undergraduate (2002–03 estimated)

Academics

Miami University awards associate, bachelor's, master's, and doctoral **degrees** and post-master's certificates. Challenging opportunities include advanced placement credit, student-designed majors, an honors program, double majors, independent study, and a senior project. Special programs include cooperative education, internships, summer session for credit, off-campus study, study-abroad, and Army, Navy and Air Force ROTC.

The most frequently chosen **baccalaureate** fields are business/marketing, education, and social sciences and history. A complete listing of majors at Miami University appears in the Majors Index beginning on page 460.

The **faculty** at Miami University has 825 full-time members, 88% with terminal degrees. The student-faculty ratio is 18:1.

Students of Miami University

The student body totals 16,795, of whom 15,174 are undergraduates. 54.3% are women and 45.7% are men. Students come from 48 states and territories and 59 other countries. 72% are from Ohio. 0.8% are international students. 3.5% are African American, 0.5% American Indian, 2.4% Asian American, and 1.6% Hispanic American. 90% returned for their sophomore year.

Facilities and Resources

Student rooms are linked to a campus network. 1,000 **computers** are available on campus that provide access to the Internet. The 4 **libraries** have 2,697,078 books and 14,089 subscriptions.

Campus Life

There are 350 active organizations on campus, including a drama/theater group, newspaper, radio station, television station, choral group, and marching band. 24% of eligible men and 27% of eligible women are members of national **fraternities** and national **sororities**.

Miami University is a member of the NCAA (Division I). **Intercollegiate sports** (some offering scholarships) include baseball (m), basketball, cross-country running, field hockey (w), football (m), golf (m), ice hockey (m), soccer (w), softball (w), swimming, tennis (w), track and field, volleyball (w).

Campus Safety

Student safety services include late-night transport/escort service, 24-hour emergency telephone alarm devices, 24-hour patrols by trained security personnel, student patrols, and electronically operated dormitory entrances.

Applying

Miami University requires SAT I or ACT and a high school transcript. It recommends an essay and 1 recommendation. Application deadline: 1/31; 2/15 priority date for financial aid.

MICHIGAN STATE UNIVERSITY
SUBURBAN SETTING ■ PUBLIC ■ STATE-SUPPORTED ■ COED
EAST LANSING, MICHIGAN

Web site: www.msu.edu
Contact: Ms. Pamela Horne, Assistant to the Provost for Enrollment and
Director of Admissions, 250 Administration Building, East Lansing, MI
48824
Telephone: 517-355-8332 **Fax:** 517-353-1647
E-mail: admis@msu.edu

Academics
Michigan State awards bachelor's, master's, doctoral, and first-professional **degrees** and
post-master's certificates. Challenging opportunities include advanced placement credit,
accelerated degree programs, student-designed majors, freshman honors college, an
honors program, double majors, independent study, and a senior project. Special
programs include cooperative education, internships, summer session for credit, off-
campus study, study-abroad, and Army and Air Force ROTC.

The most frequently chosen **baccalaureate** fields are business/marketing, com-
munications/communication technologies, and social sciences and history. A complete
listing of majors at Michigan State appears in the Majors Index beginning on page 460.

The **faculty** at Michigan State has 2,312 full-time members, 94% with terminal
degrees. The student-faculty ratio is 18:1.

Students of Michigan State
The student body totals 44,542, of whom 34,853 are undergraduates. 53.6% are women
and 46.4% are men. Students come from 54 states and territories and 120 other
countries. 93% are from Michigan. 2.8% are international students. 8.7% are African
American, 0.7% American Indian, 5.4% Asian American, and 2.7% Hispanic American.
90% returned for their sophomore year.

Facilities and Resources
Student rooms are linked to a campus network. 2,000 **computers** are available on
campus that provide access to the Internet. The 15 **libraries** have 4,420,208 books and
29,470 subscriptions.

Campus Life
There are 500 active organizations on campus, including a drama/theater group,
newspaper, radio station, television station, choral group, and marching band. Michigan
State has national **fraternities** and national **sororities**.

Michigan State is a member of the NCAA (Division I). **Intercollegiate sports** (some
offering scholarships) include baseball (m), basketball, cheerleading, crew (w), cross-
country running, field hockey (w), football (m), golf, gymnastics, ice hockey (m), soccer
(m), softball (w), swimming, tennis, track and field, volleyball (w), wrestling (m).

Campus Safety
Student safety services include self-defense workshops, late-night transport/escort
service, 24-hour emergency telephone alarm devices, and 24-hour patrols by trained
security personnel.

Applying
Michigan State requires SAT I or ACT and a high school transcript. Application
deadline: rolling admissions; 6/30 for financial aid, with a 2/21 priority date. Deferred
admission is possible.

O
n a Big Ten campus
known and loved for its
beauty, Michigan State
University's modern facilities,
historic buildings, and park-like
setting provide a unique
environment of tradition and
innovation. A diverse and talented
student body, dynamic faculty, and
dedicated staff all create a friendly
and stimulating academic community
that balances intellectual challenge
and support for student success.
Undergraduate education comes first
at MSU, with more than 150
undergraduate programs of study,
the nationally recognized Honors
College, and other highly regarded
living-learning programs. The largest
study abroad program in the world
boasts more than 200 programs on
all 7 continents. An MSU education
attracts students who are interested
in combining high quality liberal
education with extraordinary
opportunities for hands-on
experience through internships,
undergraduate research, outreach,
and public service.

Getting in Last Year
24,973 applied
71% were accepted
7,122 enrolled (40%)
28% from top tenth of their h.s. class
3.58 average high school GPA
36% had SAT verbal scores over 600
46% had SAT math scores over 600
61% had ACT scores over 24
7% had SAT verbal scores over 700
11% had SAT math scores over 700
10% had ACT scores over 30
60 National Merit Scholars

Graduation and After
31% graduated in 4 years
29% graduated in 5 years
5% graduated in 6 years
600 organizations recruited on campus

Financial Matters
$6703 resident tuition and fees (2003–04)
$16,663 nonresident tuition and fees (2003–
04)
$5230 room and board
98% average percent of need met
$9355 average financial aid amount received
per undergraduate (2002–03 estimated)

Michigan Technological University

SMALL-TOWN SETTING ■ PUBLIC ■ STATE-SUPPORTED ■ COED
HOUGHTON, MICHIGAN

Web site: www.mtu.edu
Contact: Ms. Nancy Rehling, Director of Undergraduate Admissions, 1400 Townsend Drive, Houghton, MI 49931-1295
Telephone: 906-487-2335 or toll-free 888-MTU-1885 **Fax:** 906-487-2125
E-mail: mtu4u@mtu.edu

Getting in Last Year
3,080 applied
93% were accepted
1,187 enrolled (41%)
30% from top tenth of their h.s. class
3.54 average high school GPA
41% had SAT verbal scores over 600
62% had SAT math scores over 600
70% had ACT scores over 24
10% had SAT verbal scores over 700
14% had SAT math scores over 700
14% had ACT scores over 30
6 National Merit Scholars
70 valedictorians

Graduation and After
27% graduated in 4 years
27% graduated in 5 years
6% graduated in 6 years
20% pursued further study
85% had job offers within 6 months
253 organizations recruited on campus

Financial Matters
$7440 resident tuition and fees (2003–04)
$18,330 nonresident tuition and fees (2003–04)
$5795 room and board
81% average percent of need met
$7855 average financial aid amount received per undergraduate (2002–03 estimated)

Academics
Michigan Tech awards associate, bachelor's, master's, and doctoral **degrees**. Challenging opportunities include advanced placement credit, student-designed majors, double majors, and a senior project. Special programs include cooperative education, internships, summer session for credit, off-campus study, study-abroad, and Army and Air Force ROTC.

The most frequently chosen **baccalaureate** fields are engineering/engineering technologies, business/marketing, and computer/information sciences. A complete listing of majors at Michigan Tech appears in the Majors Index beginning on page 460.

The **faculty** at Michigan Tech has 346 full-time members, 89% with terminal degrees. The student-faculty ratio is 12:1.

Students of Michigan Tech
The student body totals 6,565, of whom 5,765 are undergraduates. 23.8% are women and 76.2% are men. Students come from 45 states and territories and 80 other countries. 79% are from Michigan. 5.8% are international students. 2.2% are African American, 0.8% American Indian, 1.2% Asian American, and 1% Hispanic American. 81% returned for their sophomore year.

Facilities and Resources
Student rooms are linked to a campus network. 1,555 **computers** are available on campus that provide access to the Internet. The **library** has 820,414 books and 10,369 subscriptions.

Campus Life
There are 145 active organizations on campus, including a drama/theater group, newspaper, radio station, and choral group. 8% of eligible men and 13% of eligible women are members of national **fraternities**, national **sororities**, local fraternities, and local sororities.

Michigan Tech is a member of the NCAA (Division II). **Intercollegiate sports** (some offering scholarships) include basketball, cross-country running, football (m), ice hockey (m), skiing (cross-country), tennis, track and field, volleyball (w).

Campus Safety
Student safety services include late-night transport/escort service, 24-hour emergency telephone alarm devices, and 24-hour patrols by trained security personnel.

Applying
Michigan Tech requires SAT I or ACT and a high school transcript. It recommends an interview. Application deadline: rolling admissions; 2/21 priority date for financial aid. Deferred admission is possible.

MIDDLEBURY COLLEGE

SMALL-TOWN SETTING ■ PRIVATE ■ INDEPENDENT ■ COED
MIDDLEBURY, VERMONT

Web site: www.middlebury.edu
Contact: Mr. John Hanson, Director of Admissions, Emma Willard House,
   Middlebury, VT 05753-6002
Telephone: 802-443-3000 **Fax:** 802-443-2056
E-mail: admissions@middlebury.edu

Academics

Middlebury awards bachelor's, master's, and doctoral **degrees**. Challenging opportunities include advanced placement credit, accelerated degree programs, student-designed majors, an honors program, double majors, and independent study. Special programs include internships, summer session for credit, off-campus study, study-abroad, and Army ROTC.

The most frequently chosen **baccalaureate** fields are social sciences and history, foreign language/literature, and English. A complete listing of majors at Middlebury appears in the Majors Index beginning on page 460.

The **faculty** at Middlebury has 218 full-time members, 94% with terminal degrees. The student-faculty ratio is 11:1.

Students of Middlebury

The student body is made up of 2,424 undergraduates. 52.8% are women and 47.2% are men. Students come from 52 states and territories and 70 other countries. 14% are from Vermont. 8.3% are international students. 2.7% are African American, 0.9% American Indian, 7.4% Asian American, and 5.3% Hispanic American.

Facilities and Resources

Student rooms are linked to a campus network. 225 **computers** are available on campus that provide access to computer help-line, e-mail, personal web pages, file servers and the Internet. The 4 **libraries** have 950,000 books and 2,694 subscriptions.

Campus Life

There are 95 active organizations on campus, including a drama/theater group, newspaper, radio station, and choral group. Middlebury has social houses, commons system.

Middlebury is a member of the NCAA (Division III). **Intercollegiate sports** include baseball (m), basketball, cheerleading, cross-country running, field hockey (w), football (m), golf, ice hockey, lacrosse, skiing (cross-country), skiing (downhill), soccer, softball (w), squash (w), swimming, tennis, track and field, volleyball (w).

Campus Safety

Student safety services include late-night transport/escort service, 24-hour patrols by trained security personnel, student patrols, and electronically operated dormitory entrances.

Applying

Middlebury requires an essay, ACT or 3 SAT II Subject Tests (including SAT II: Writing Test and 1 quantitative SAT II Test), or 3 Advanced Placement Tests (including AP English and 1 quantitative AP Test), or 3 I.B. Subsidiary Tests (including I.B. Languages and 1 quantitative I.B. Test), a high school transcript, and 3 recommendations. It recommends an interview. Application deadline: 1/1; 12/31 priority date for financial aid. Early and deferred admission are possible.

Literary study, global understanding based on language proficiency and cultural knowledge, environmental studies grounded in science, language study and pedagogy, instruction by leading faculty members and scholars, application of learning to the real world—these elements form the academic core of excellence at this 200-year-old institution. The beautiful campus has a new state-of-the-art library and technology center, a nationally recognized interdisciplinary science facility, a contemporary arts center, sophisticated computer networks, multimedia workstations for language study, and outstanding athletic facilities, including a ski area and golf course. To attend Middlebury is to have a lifetime of opportunities, made possible by one of the world's foremost liberal arts colleges.

Getting in Last Year
5,468 applied
23% were accepted
580 enrolled (46%)
77% from top tenth of their h.s. class
97% had SAT verbal scores over 600
95% had SAT math scores over 600
96% had ACT scores over 24
69% had SAT verbal scores over 700
61% had SAT math scores over 700
62% had ACT scores over 30
66 class presidents

Graduation and After
50% had job offers within 6 months
70 organizations recruited on campus

Financial Matters
$38,100 comprehensive fee (2003–04)
100% average percent of need met
$26,979 average financial aid amount received per undergraduate (2002–03 estimated)

MILLIGAN COLLEGE

SUBURBAN SETTING ■ PRIVATE ■ INDEPENDENT RELIGIOUS ■ COED
MILLIGAN COLLEGE, TENNESSEE

Web site: www.milligan.edu
Contact: Mr. David Mee, Vice President for Enrollment Management, PO
   Box 210, Milligan College, TN 37682
Telephone: 423-461-8730 or toll-free 800-262-8337 (in-state) **Fax:**
   423-461-8982
E-mail: admissions@milligan.edu

Getting in Last Year

613 applied
76% were accepted
179 enrolled (38%)
3.58 average high school GPA
31% had SAT verbal scores over 600
26% had SAT math scores over 600
54% had ACT scores over 24
4% had SAT verbal scores over 700
4% had SAT math scores over 700
9% had ACT scores over 30

Graduation and After

40% graduated in 4 years
8% graduated in 5 years
1% graduated in 6 years

Financial Matters

$15,260 tuition and fees (2003–04)
$4600 room and board
89% average percent of need met
$14,993 average financial aid amount received
   per undergraduate (2001–02)

Academics

Milligan awards bachelor's and master's **degrees**. Challenging opportunities include
advanced placement credit, double majors, independent study, and a senior project.
Special programs include cooperative education, internships, summer session for credit,
off-campus study, study-abroad, and Army ROTC.

The most frequently chosen **baccalaureate** fields are business/marketing, com-
munications/communication technologies, and health professions and related sciences. A
complete listing of majors at Milligan appears in the Majors Index beginning on page
460.

The **faculty** at Milligan has 66 full-time members, 70% with terminal degrees. The
student-faculty ratio is 11:1.

Students of Milligan

The student body totals 838, of whom 733 are undergraduates. 60.6% are women and
39.4% are men. Students come from 35 states and territories and 8 other countries. 44%
are from Tennessee. 2.3% are international students. 1.4% are African American, 0.1%
American Indian, 0.4% Asian American, and 0.4% Hispanic American. 83% returned for
their sophomore year.

Facilities and Resources

Student rooms are linked to a campus network. 119 **computers** are available on campus
that provide access to the Internet. The **library** has 125,504 books and 6,332 subscriptions.

Campus Life

There are 31 active organizations on campus, including a drama/theater group,
newspaper, radio station, and choral group. No national or local **fraternities** or **sororities**.

Milligan is a member of the NAIA. **Intercollegiate sports** (some offering scholarships) include baseball (m), basketball, cross-country running, golf (m), soccer, softball
(w), tennis, volleyball (w).

Campus Safety

Student safety services include late-night transport/escort service and 24-hour patrols by
trained security personnel.

Applying

Milligan requires an essay, SAT I or ACT, a high school transcript, 2 recommendations,
and a minimum high school GPA of 2.0, and in some cases an interview. It recommends
a minimum high school GPA of 3.0. Application deadline: 8/1; 3/1 priority date for
financial aid. Deferred admission is possible.

MILLSAPS COLLEGE

URBAN SETTING ■ PRIVATE ■ INDEPENDENT RELIGIOUS ■ COED
JACKSON, MISSISSIPPI

Web site: www.millsaps.edu
Contact: Ms. Ann Hendrick, Dean of Admissions and Financial Aid, 1701
  North State Street, Jackson, MS 39210-0001
Telephone: 601-974-1050 or toll-free 800-352-1050 **Fax:** 601-974-1059
E-mail: admissions@millsaps.edu

Academics

Millsaps awards bachelor's and master's **degrees**. Challenging opportunities include advanced placement credit, an honors program, double majors, independent study, and a senior project. Special programs include cooperative education, internships, summer session for credit, off-campus study, study-abroad, and Army ROTC.

The most frequently chosen **baccalaureate** fields are business/marketing, social sciences and history, and biological/life sciences. A complete listing of majors at Millsaps appears in the Majors Index beginning on page 460.

The **faculty** at Millsaps has 93 full-time members, 95% with terminal degrees. The student-faculty ratio is 13:1.

Students of Millsaps

The student body totals 1,200, of whom 1,123 are undergraduates. 54.1% are women and 45.9% are men. Students come from 30 states and territories and 5 other countries. 56% are from Mississippi. 0.7% are international students. 10.5% are African American, 0.6% American Indian, 3.4% Asian American, and 1.4% Hispanic American. 83% returned for their sophomore year.

Facilities and Resources

Student rooms are linked to a campus network. 117 **computers** are available on campus that provide access to the Internet. The **library** has 136,937 books and 3,434 subscriptions.

Campus Life

There are 80 active organizations on campus, including a drama/theater group, newspaper, and choral group. 55% of eligible men and 56% of eligible women are members of national **fraternities** and national **sororities**.

Millsaps is a member of the NCAA (Division III). **Intercollegiate sports** include baseball (m), basketball, cheerleading, cross-country running, football (m), golf, soccer, softball (w), tennis, volleyball (w).

Campus Safety

Student safety services include self-defense education, lighted pathways, late-night transport/escort service, 24-hour emergency telephone alarm devices, 24-hour patrols by trained security personnel, student patrols, and electronically operated dormitory entrances.

Applying

Millsaps requires an essay, SAT I or ACT, a high school transcript, recommendations, and a minimum high school GPA of 2.5. It recommends an interview. Application deadline: rolling admissions; 3/1 priority date for financial aid. Early and deferred admission are possible.

Getting in Last Year

1,045 applied
84% were accepted
259 enrolled (29%)
38% from top tenth of their h.s. class
3.51 average high school GPA
48% had SAT verbal scores over 600
38% had SAT math scores over 600
69% had ACT scores over 24
12% had SAT verbal scores over 700
10% had SAT math scores over 700
14% had ACT scores over 30

Graduation and After

70% graduated in 4 years
7% graduated in 5 years
1% graduated in 6 years
43% pursued further study
44% had job offers within 6 months
60 organizations recruited on campus

Financial Matters

$18,414 tuition and fees (2003–04)
$6768 room and board
85% average percent of need met
$16,463 average financial aid amount received
  per undergraduate

MILLS COLLEGE

<small>URBAN SETTING ■ PRIVATE ■ INDEPENDENT ■ WOMEN ONLY</small>
OAKLAND, CALIFORNIA

Web site: www.mills.edu

Contact: Myrt Whitcomb, Dean of Admission, 5000 MacArthur Boulevard,
Oakland, CA 94613-1301

Telephone: 510-430-2135 or toll-free 800-87-MILLS **Fax:** 510-430-3314

E-mail: admission@mills.edu

Why a women's college? "I came to college to study, and I wanted a college that was very pro-women— a college that would prepare me to do well and succeed," says Mills regional scholar Leah Hathaway. And Mills does. Even in their first year, bright students like Leah can tackle original hands-on research that most students don't experience until graduate school. Since half the professors at Mills are women (not the case in coeducational institutions), students have successful role models in every field. And all of Mills' undergraduate resources are committed to women. When women graduate from Mills, they *know* they can succeed. That confidence makes all the difference.

Getting in Last Year
537 applied
73% were accepted
115 enrolled (29%)
32% from top tenth of their h.s. class
3.54 average high school GPA
48% had SAT verbal scores over 600
27% had SAT math scores over 600
63% had ACT scores over 24
12% had SAT verbal scores over 700
5% had SAT math scores over 700
11% had ACT scores over 30

Graduation and After
58% graduated in 4 years
5% graduated in 5 years
2% graduated in 6 years
17 organizations recruited on campus

Financial Matters
$24,441 tuition and fees (2003–04)
$8930 room and board
86% average percent of need met
$20,357 average financial aid amount received
  per undergraduate (2002–03 estimated)

Academics

Mills awards bachelor's, master's, and doctoral **degrees** and post-bachelor's certificates. Challenging opportunities include advanced placement credit, student-designed majors, double majors, independent study, and a senior project. Special programs include internships, off-campus study, and Army ROTC.

The most frequently chosen **baccalaureate** fields are visual/performing arts, area/ethnic studies, and social sciences and history. A complete listing of majors at Mills appears in the Majors Index beginning on page 460.

The **faculty** at Mills has 96 full-time members, 85% with terminal degrees. The student-faculty ratio is 10:1.

Students of Mills

The student body totals 1,210, of whom 735 are undergraduates. Students come from 35 states and territories and 6 other countries. 76% are from California. 3.8% are international students. 10.9% are African American, 0.7% American Indian, 8.3% Asian American, and 9.8% Hispanic American. 72% returned for their sophomore year.

Facilities and Resources

Student rooms are linked to a campus network. 66 **computers** are available on campus for student use. The 2 **libraries** have 189,814 books and 2,029 subscriptions.

Campus Life

There are 30 active organizations on campus, including a drama/theater group, newspaper, and choral group. No national or local **sororities**.

Mills is a member of the NCAA (Division III). **Intercollegiate sports** include crew, cross-country running, soccer, tennis, volleyball.

Campus Safety

Student safety services include late-night transport/escort service, 24-hour emergency telephone alarm devices, 24-hour patrols by trained security personnel, and electronically operated dormitory entrances.

Applying

Mills requires SAT I or ACT, a high school transcript, 3 recommendations, and essay or graded paper. It recommends SAT II Subject Tests and an interview. Application deadline: 3/1; 2/15 priority date for financial aid. Deferred admission is possible.

MILWAUKEE SCHOOL OF ENGINEERING

URBAN SETTING ■ PRIVATE ■ INDEPENDENT ■ COED, PRIMARILY MEN
MILWAUKEE, WISCONSIN

Web site: www.msoe.edu
Contact: Mr. Paul Borens, Director, Admission, 1025 North Broadway,
Milwaukee, WI 53202-3109
Telephone: 414-277-6765 or toll-free 800-332-6763 **Fax:** 414-277-7475
E-mail: explore@msoe.edu

Academics

MSOE awards bachelor's and master's **degrees**. Challenging opportunities include advanced placement credit, accelerated degree programs, double majors, independent study, and a senior project. Special programs include internships, summer session for credit, study-abroad, and Army, Navy and Air Force ROTC.

The most frequently chosen **baccalaureate** fields are engineering/engineering technologies, business/marketing, and health professions and related sciences. A complete listing of majors at MSOE appears in the Majors Index beginning on page 460.

The **faculty** at MSOE has 127 full-time members, 62% with terminal degrees. The student-faculty ratio is 11:1.

Students of MSOE

The student body totals 2,383, of whom 2,101 are undergraduates. 16.8% are women and 83.2% are men. Students come from 31 states and territories and 24 other countries. 69% are from Wisconsin. 2.5% are international students. 3.1% are African American, 0.3% American Indian, 2.8% Asian American, and 2.3% Hispanic American. 74% returned for their sophomore year.

Facilities and Resources

Student rooms are linked to a campus network. 105 **computers** are available on campus that provide access to e-mail and the Internet. The **library** has 56,044 books and 416 subscriptions.

Campus Life

There are 61 active organizations on campus, including a drama/theater group, newspaper, and radio station. 7% of eligible men and 12% of eligible women are members of national **fraternities**, national **sororities**, local fraternities, and local sororities.

MSOE is a member of the NCAA (Division III). **Intercollegiate sports** include baseball (m), basketball, cross-country running, golf, ice hockey (m), soccer, softball (w), tennis, track and field, volleyball, wrestling (m).

Campus Safety

Student safety services include late-night transport/escort service, 24-hour emergency telephone alarm devices, 24-hour patrols by trained security personnel, and electronically operated dormitory entrances.

Applying

MSOE requires SAT I or ACT, a high school transcript, and a minimum high school GPA of 2.5, and in some cases an essay and an interview. Application deadline: rolling admissions. Deferred admission is possible.

Getting in Last Year

1,809 applied
65% were accepted
439 enrolled (37%)
3.48 average high school GPA
43% had SAT verbal scores over 600
61% had SAT math scores over 600
75% had ACT scores over 24
9% had SAT verbal scores over 700
16% had SAT math scores over 700
15% had ACT scores over 30

Graduation and After

38% graduated in 4 years
15% graduated in 5 years
3% graduated in 6 years
7% pursued further study (3% engineering,
1% business, 1% law)
98% had job offers within 6 months
166 organizations recruited on campus

Financial Matters

$23,034 tuition and fees (2003–04)
$5445 room and board
70% average percent of need met
$15,348 average financial aid amount received
per undergraduate (2001–02)

Minneapolis College of Art and Design

Urban setting ■ Private ■ Independent ■ Coed
Minneapolis, Minnesota

Getting in Last Year
407 applied
71% were accepted
117 enrolled (41%)
3.20 average high school GPA
57% had SAT verbal scores over 600
25% had SAT math scores over 600
46% had ACT scores over 24
13% had SAT verbal scores over 700
3% had ACT scores over 30
2 valedictorians

Graduation and After
28% graduated in 4 years
5% graduated in 5 years
3% graduated in 6 years
10% pursued further study (8% arts and sciences)
90% had job offers within 6 months
9 organizations recruited on campus

Financial Matters
$22,770 tuition and fees (2003–04)
$5400 room and board
55% average percent of need met
$11,794 average financial aid amount received per undergraduate

Web site: www.mcad.edu
Contact: Mr. William Mullen, Director of Admissions, 2501 Stevens Avenue South, Minneapolis, MN 55404
Telephone: 612-874-3762 or toll-free 800-874-6223
E-mail: admissions@mn.mcad.edu

Academics
MCAD awards bachelor's and master's **degrees** and post-bachelor's certificates. Challenging opportunities include advanced placement credit, independent study, and a senior project. Special programs include cooperative education, internships, summer session for credit, off-campus study, and study-abroad.

The most frequently chosen **baccalaureate** field is visual/performing arts. A complete listing of majors at MCAD appears in the Majors Index beginning on page 460.

The **faculty** at MCAD has 40 full-time members, 58% with terminal degrees. The student-faculty ratio is 15:1.

Students of MCAD
The student body totals 673, of whom 615 are undergraduates. 46.3% are women and 53.7% are men. Students come from 37 states and territories. 2.9% are African American, 1% American Indian, 2.9% Asian American, and 2.5% Hispanic American. 75% returned for their sophomore year.

Facilities and Resources
110 **computers** are available on campus that provide access to the Internet. The **library** has 47,166 books and 196 subscriptions.

Campus Life
There are 2 active organizations on campus, including a drama/theater group and radio station. No national or local **fraternities** or **sororities**.

Intercollegiate sports include cheerleading.

Campus Safety
Student safety services include late-night transport/escort service, 24-hour emergency telephone alarm devices, and 24-hour patrols by trained security personnel.

Applying
MCAD requires an essay, SAT I or ACT, a high school transcript, and 1 recommendation, and in some cases portfolio. It recommends an interview. Application deadline: rolling admissions; 3/15 priority date for financial aid. Early and deferred admission are possible.

MISSISSIPPI STATE UNIVERSITY

SMALL-TOWN SETTING ▪ PUBLIC ▪ STATE-SUPPORTED ▪ COED
MISSISSIPPI STATE, MISSISSIPPI

Web site: www.msstate.edu
Contact: Ms. Diane D. Wolfe, Director of Admissions, PO Box 6305, Mississippi State, MS 39762
Telephone: 662-325-2224 **Fax:** 662-325-7360
E-mail: admit@admissions.msstate.edu

Academics

MSU awards bachelor's, master's, doctoral, and first-professional **degrees** and post-master's certificates. Challenging opportunities include advanced placement credit, accelerated degree programs, student-designed majors, freshman honors college, an honors program, double majors, independent study, and a senior project. Special programs include cooperative education, internships, summer session for credit, off-campus study, study-abroad, and Army and Air Force ROTC.

The most frequently chosen **baccalaureate** fields are business/marketing, education, and engineering/engineering technologies. A complete listing of majors at MSU appears in the Majors Index beginning on page 460.

The **faculty** at MSU has 849 full-time members, 78% with terminal degrees. The student-faculty ratio is 16:1.

Students of MSU

The student body totals 16,173, of whom 12,839 are undergraduates. 47.4% are women and 52.6% are men. Students come from 52 states and territories and 42 other countries. 80% are from Mississippi. 1.1% are international students. 19.4% are African American, 0.4% American Indian, 1.1% Asian American, and 0.9% Hispanic American. 81% returned for their sophomore year.

Facilities and Resources

Student rooms are linked to a campus network. 2,000 **computers** are available on campus that provide access to wireless network with partial campus coverage and the Internet. The 3 **libraries** have 2,026,894 books and 17,722 subscriptions.

Campus Life

There are 283 active organizations on campus, including a drama/theater group, newspaper, radio station, television station, choral group, and marching band. 17% of eligible men and 18% of eligible women are members of national **fraternities** and national **sororities**.

MSU is a member of the NCAA (Division I). **Intercollegiate sports** (some offering scholarships) include baseball (m), basketball, cross-country running (w), football (m), golf, soccer (w), softball (w), tennis, track and field, volleyball (w).

Campus Safety

Student safety services include bicycle patrols, crime prevention program, RAD program, general law enforcement services, late-night transport/escort service, 24-hour emergency telephone alarm devices, 24-hour patrols by trained security personnel, and electronically operated dormitory entrances.

Applying

MSU requires SAT I or ACT, a high school transcript, and a minimum high school GPA of 2.0, and in some cases Placement testing and counseling for entering students with academic deficiencies and recommendations. Application deadline: 8/1; 4/1 priority date for financial aid. Early and deferred admission are possible.

Getting in Last Year

4,646 applied
75% were accepted
1,688 enrolled (48%)
21% from top tenth of their h.s. class
3.23 average high school GPA
47% had ACT scores over 24
12% had ACT scores over 30
22 National Merit Scholars

Graduation and After

23% graduated in 4 years
27% graduated in 5 years
8% graduated in 6 years
70% had job offers within 6 months
790 organizations recruited on campus

Financial Matters

$3874 resident tuition and fees (2003–04)
$8780 nonresident tuition and fees (2003–04)
$5265 room and board
72% average percent of need met
$7142 average financial aid amount received per undergraduate (2001–02)

MOREHOUSE COLLEGE
URBAN SETTING ■ PRIVATE ■ INDEPENDENT ■ MEN ONLY
ATLANTA, GEORGIA

Web site: www.morehouse.edu
Contact: Mr. Terrance Dixon, Associate Dean for Admissions and
Recruitment, 830 Westview Drive, SW, Atlanta, GA 30314
Telephone: 404-215-2632 or toll-free 800-851-1254 **Fax:** 404-524-5635
E-mail: admissions@morehouse.edu

Morehouse College seeks to develop leaders who will be qualified and committed to solving the problems of society, with special attention given to those of African Americans. Inspired by the legacy of distinguished alumni, presidents, and professors—persons who have initiated and inspired significant social changes—the College supports and encourages programs that benefit all people and that seek to eradicate discrimination and injustice. Morehouse is firmly committed to attracting and enrolling students of high caliber from a wide variety of educational and economic backgrounds and providing them with learning and leadership development opportunities.

Getting in Last Year
2,225 applied
72% were accepted
766 enrolled (48%)
22% from top tenth of their h.s. class
3.14 average high school GPA
18% had SAT verbal scores over 600
24% had SAT math scores over 600
28% had ACT scores over 24
2% had SAT verbal scores over 700
2% had SAT math scores over 700
2% had ACT scores over 30

Graduation and After
38% graduated in 4 years
12% graduated in 5 years
5% graduated in 6 years
Graduates pursuing further study: 14% arts and sciences, 5% law, 4% medicine
51% had job offers within 6 months
60 organizations recruited on campus

Financial Matters
$14,310 tuition and fees (2003–04)
$8418 room and board

Academics
Morehouse College awards bachelor's **degrees**. Challenging opportunities include advanced placement credit, an honors program, double majors, and a senior project. Special programs include cooperative education, internships, summer session for credit, off-campus study, study-abroad, and Army, Navy and Air Force ROTC.

The most frequently chosen **baccalaureate** fields are business/marketing, social sciences and history, and biological/life sciences. A complete listing of majors at Morehouse College appears in the Majors Index beginning on page 460.

The **faculty** at Morehouse College has 158 full-time members, 81% with terminal degrees. The student-faculty ratio is 15:1.

Students of Morehouse College
The student body is made up of 2,859 undergraduates. Students come from 45 states and territories and 18 other countries. 27% are from Georgia. 3.5% are international students. 93.1% are African American, 0.1% American Indian, and 0.3% Hispanic American. 85% returned for their sophomore year.

Facilities and Resources
Student rooms are linked to a campus network. 490 **computers** are available on campus that provide access to the Internet. The 2 **libraries** have 560,000 books and 1,000 subscriptions.

Campus Life
There are 34 active organizations on campus, including a drama/theater group, newspaper, choral group, and marching band. 7% of eligible undergraduates are members of national **fraternities**.

Morehouse College is a member of the NCAA (Division II). **Intercollegiate sports** (some offering scholarships) include basketball, cross-country running, football, tennis, track and field.

Campus Safety
Student safety services include late-night transport/escort service, 24-hour emergency telephone alarm devices, and 24-hour patrols by trained security personnel.

Applying
Morehouse College requires an essay, SAT I or ACT, a high school transcript, recommendations, and a minimum high school GPA of 2.8. It recommends an interview and a minimum high school GPA of 3.0. Application deadline: 2/15; 4/1 priority date for financial aid. Early and deferred admission are possible.

MOUNT HOLYOKE COLLEGE

SMALL-TOWN SETTING ■ PRIVATE ■ INDEPENDENT ■ WOMEN ONLY
SOUTH HADLEY, MASSACHUSETTS

Web site: www.mtholyoke.edu
Contact: Ms. Diane Anci, Dean of Admission, 50 College Street, South
   Hadley, MA 01075
Telephone: 413-538-2023 **Fax:** 413-538-2409
E-mail: admission@mtholyoke.edu

Academics

Mount Holyoke awards bachelor's and master's **degrees** and post-bachelor's certificates. Challenging opportunities include advanced placement credit, student-designed majors, an honors program, double majors, independent study, and a senior project. Special programs include internships, off-campus study, study-abroad, and Army and Air Force ROTC.

   The most frequently chosen **baccalaureate** fields are social sciences and history, biological/life sciences, and interdisciplinary studies. A complete listing of majors at Mount Holyoke appears in the Majors Index beginning on page 460.

   The **faculty** at Mount Holyoke has 211 full-time members, 96% with terminal degrees. The student-faculty ratio is 10:1.

Students of Mount Holyoke

The student body totals 2,152, of whom 2,148 are undergraduates. Students come from 48 states and territories and 79 other countries. 36% are from Massachusetts. 14.9% are international students. 3.8% are African American, 0.6% American Indian, 9.8% Asian American, and 4.4% Hispanic American. 92% returned for their sophomore year.

Facilities and Resources

Student rooms are linked to a campus network. 500 **computers** are available on campus that provide access to personal web pages and the Internet. The 8 **libraries** have 670,304 books and 1,537 subscriptions.

Campus Life

There are 145 active organizations on campus, including a drama/theater group, newspaper, radio station, and choral group. No national or local **sororities**.

   Mount Holyoke is a member of the NCAA (Division III). **Intercollegiate sports** (some offering scholarships) include basketball, cheerleading, crew, cross-country running, equestrian sports, field hockey, golf, lacrosse, soccer, softball, squash, swimming, tennis, track and field, volleyball.

Campus Safety

Student safety services include police officers on-campus, late-night transport/escort service, 24-hour emergency telephone alarm devices, 24-hour patrols by trained security personnel, student patrols, and electronically operated dormitory entrances.

Applying

Mount Holyoke requires an essay, a high school transcript, and 2 recommendations, and in some cases SAT II Subject Tests and SAT II: Writing Test. It recommends an interview. Application deadline: 1/15; 2/1 for financial aid. Early and deferred admission are possible.

Mount Holyoke is a highly selective, nondenominational, residential, liberal arts college for women located in South Hadley, Massachusetts. Founded in 1837 by revolutionary educator, Mary Lyon, the College is recognized worldwide for its rigorous and innovative academic program, its global community, its legacy of women leaders, and its commitment to connecting the work of the academy to the concerns of the world. Students benefit from membership in the Five College Consortium with Amherst, Hampshire, and Smith Colleges and the University of Massachusetts.

Getting in Last Year
2,845 applied
52% were accepted
508 enrolled (34%)
52% from top tenth of their h.s. class
3.65 average high school GPA
86% had SAT verbal scores over 600
74% had SAT math scores over 600
96% had ACT scores over 24
28% had SAT verbal scores over 700
14% had SAT math scores over 700
33% had ACT scores over 30
16 National Merit Scholars
29 valedictorians

Graduation and After
72% graduated in 4 years
5% graduated in 5 years
2% graduated in 6 years
18% pursued further study (9% arts and sciences, 5% law, 1% business)
58 organizations recruited on campus

Financial Matters
$29,338 tuition and fees (2003–04)
$8580 room and board
100% average percent of need met
$25,469 average financial aid amount received per undergraduate

MUHLENBERG COLLEGE
SUBURBAN SETTING ■ PRIVATE ■ INDEPENDENT RELIGIOUS ■ COED
ALLENTOWN, PENNSYLVANIA

Web site: www.muhlenberg.edu
Contact: Mr. Christopher Hooker-Haring, Dean of Admissions, 2400 Chew Street, Allentown, PA 18104-5586
Telephone: 484-664-3245 **Fax:** 484-664-3234
E-mail: adm@muhlenberg.edu

Located in a beautiful campus setting on the outskirts of a small city, Muhlenberg offers its students an active, highly participatory educational experience within the context of a friendly, very supportive community. Local internships, field study, study abroad, and a Washington semester all supplement the traditional classroom experience. Every year, large numbers of Muhlenberg students go on to law and medical school as well as into a variety of competitive entry-level career positions. They take with them an ability to analyze and think critically as well as an ability to express themselves effectively in person and in writing. These are the most prized outcomes of a Muhlenberg education.

Getting in Last Year
4,111 applied
42% were accepted
589 enrolled (34%)
39% from top tenth of their h.s. class
3.45 average high school GPA
56% had SAT verbal scores over 600
60% had SAT math scores over 600
8% had SAT verbal scores over 700
9% had SAT math scores over 700
15 class presidents
4 valedictorians

Graduation and After
72% graduated in 4 years
4% graduated in 5 years
2% graduated in 6 years
31% pursued further study (13% arts and sciences, 7% medicine, 4% law)
60% had job offers within 6 months
64 organizations recruited on campus

Financial Matters
$25,160 tuition and fees (2003–04)
$6540 room and board
96% average percent of need met
$16,023 average financial aid amount received per undergraduate (2002–03 estimated)

Academics
Muhlenberg awards bachelor's **degrees**. Challenging opportunities include advanced placement credit, accelerated degree programs, student-designed majors, an honors program, double majors, independent study, and a senior project. Special programs include internships, summer session for credit, off-campus study, study-abroad, and Army ROTC.

The most frequently chosen **baccalaureate** fields are health professions and related sciences, business/marketing, and social sciences and history. A complete listing of majors at Muhlenberg appears in the Majors Index beginning on page 460.

The **faculty** at Muhlenberg has 157 full-time members, 87% with terminal degrees. The student-faculty ratio is 12:1.

Students of Muhlenberg
The student body is made up of 2,452 undergraduates. 57.5% are women and 42.5% are men. Students come from 36 states and territories and 5 other countries. 37% are from Pennsylvania. 0.5% are international students. 2.1% are African American, 0.2% American Indian, 2.2% Asian American, and 3% Hispanic American. 92% returned for their sophomore year.

Facilities and Resources
Student rooms are linked to a campus network. 379 **computers** are available on campus that provide access to the Internet. The **library** has 270,700 books and 1,700 subscriptions.

Campus Life
There are 109 active organizations on campus, including a drama/theater group, newspaper, radio station, television station, and choral group. 23% of eligible men and 26% of eligible women are members of national **fraternities** and national **sororities**.

Muhlenberg is a member of the NCAA (Division III). **Intercollegiate sports** include baseball (m), basketball, cheerleading, cross-country running, field hockey (w), football (m), golf, lacrosse, soccer, softball (w), tennis, track and field, volleyball (w), wrestling (m).

Campus Safety
Student safety services include late-night transport/escort service, 24-hour emergency telephone alarm devices, 24-hour patrols by trained security personnel, and electronically operated dormitory entrances.

Applying
Muhlenberg requires an essay, a high school transcript, and 2 recommendations, and in some cases SAT I or ACT and an interview. It recommends an interview. Application deadline: 2/15; 2/15 for financial aid. Early and deferred admission are possible.

MURRAY STATE UNIVERSITY

SMALL-TOWN SETTING ■ PUBLIC ■ STATE-SUPPORTED ■ COED
MURRAY, KENTUCKY

Web site: www.murraystate.edu
Contact: Mrs. Stacy Bell, Admission Clerk, PO Box 9, Murray, KY
42071-0009
Telephone: 270-762-3035 or toll-free 800-272-4678 **Fax:** 270-762-3050
E-mail: admissions@murraystate.edu

Academics

Murray State awards associate, bachelor's, and master's **degrees** and post-bachelor's and post-master's certificates. Challenging opportunities include advanced placement credit, accelerated degree programs, freshman honors college, an honors program, double majors, independent study, and a senior project. Special programs include cooperative education, internships, summer session for credit, off-campus study, study-abroad, and Army ROTC.

The most frequently chosen **baccalaureate** fields are education, business/marketing, and communications/communication technologies. A complete listing of majors at Murray State appears in the Majors Index beginning on page 460.

The **faculty** at Murray State has 393 full-time members, 79% with terminal degrees. The student-faculty ratio is 16:1.

Students of Murray State

The student body totals 10,093, of whom 8,378 are undergraduates. 58.9% are women and 41.1% are men. Students come from 43 states and territories and 59 other countries. 71% are from Kentucky. 2.4% are international students. 6.3% are African American, 0.5% American Indian, 0.8% Asian American, and 0.8% Hispanic American. 74% returned for their sophomore year.

Facilities and Resources

Student rooms are linked to a campus network. 1,500 **computers** are available on campus that provide access to the Internet. The 2 **libraries** have 470,000 books and 3,000 subscriptions.

Campus Life

There are 210 active organizations on campus, including a drama/theater group, newspaper, radio station, television station, choral group, and marching band. 17% of eligible men and 10% of eligible women are members of national **fraternities**, national **sororities**, local fraternities, and local sororities.

Murray State is a member of the NCAA (Division I). **Intercollegiate sports** (some offering scholarships) include baseball (m), basketball, bowling, cheerleading, crew, cross-country running, equestrian sports, football (m), golf, riflery, soccer (w), tennis, track and field, volleyball (w).

Campus Safety

Student safety services include late-night transport/escort service, 24-hour emergency telephone alarm devices, 24-hour patrols by trained security personnel, student patrols, and electronically operated dormitory entrances.

Applying

Murray State requires ACT, a high school transcript, rank in top 50% of graduating class, and a minimum high school GPA of 3.0, and in some cases recommendations. It recommends an interview. Application deadline: rolling admissions, 8/1 for nonresidents; 4/1 priority date for financial aid. Early and deferred admission are possible.

Getting in Last Year

2,972 applied
63% were accepted
1,511 enrolled (81%)
32% from top tenth of their h.s. class
3.5 average high school GPA
39% had ACT scores over 24
3% had ACT scores over 30
85 valedictorians

Graduation and After

38% graduated in 4 years
14% graduated in 5 years
3% graduated in 6 years
320 organizations recruited on campus

Financial Matters

$3436 resident tuition and fees (2003–04)
$5492 nonresident tuition and fees (2003–04)
$4380 room and board
90% average percent of need met
$4580 average financial aid amount received per undergraduate (2001–02)

NAZARETH COLLEGE OF ROCHESTER

SUBURBAN SETTING ■ PRIVATE ■ INDEPENDENT ■ COED
ROCHESTER, NEW YORK

Web site: www.naz.edu
Contact: Mr. Thomas K. DaRin, Vice President for Enrollment Management, 4245 East Avenue, Rochester, NY 14618-3790
Telephone: 585-389-2860 or toll-free 800-462-3944 (in-state) **Fax:** 585-389-2826
E-mail: admissions@naz.edu

Getting in Last Year

1,627 applied
83% were accepted
383 enrolled (28%)
26% from top tenth of their h.s. class
3.39 average high school GPA
37% had SAT verbal scores over 600
33% had SAT math scores over 600
51% had ACT scores over 24
5% had SAT verbal scores over 700
4% had SAT math scores over 700
8% had ACT scores over 30
5 valedictorians

Graduation and After

61% graduated in 4 years
10% graduated in 5 years
1% graduated in 6 years
39% pursued further study
71% had job offers within 6 months
18 organizations recruited on campus

Financial Matters

$17,536 tuition and fees (2003–04)
$7400 room and board
80% average percent of need met
$14,497 average financial aid amount received per undergraduate

Academics

Nazareth College awards bachelor's and master's **degrees** and post-master's certificates. Challenging opportunities include advanced placement credit, an honors program, double majors, independent study, and a senior project. Special programs include cooperative education, internships, summer session for credit, off-campus study, study-abroad, and Army and Air Force ROTC.

The most frequently chosen **baccalaureate** fields are health professions and related sciences, business/marketing, and psychology. A complete listing of majors at Nazareth College appears in the Majors Index beginning on page 460.

The **faculty** at Nazareth College has 135 full-time members, 95% with terminal degrees. The student-faculty ratio is 13:1.

Students of Nazareth College

The student body totals 3,062, of whom 1,997 are undergraduates. 75.6% are women and 24.4% are men. Students come from 23 states and territories. 94% are from New York. 0.4% are international students. 4.4% are African American, 0.2% American Indian, 2% Asian American, and 1.6% Hispanic American. 83% returned for their sophomore year.

Facilities and Resources

Student rooms are linked to a campus network. 150 **computers** are available on campus that provide access to the Internet. The **library** has 162,593 books and 1,888 subscriptions.

Campus Life

There are 33 active organizations on campus, including a drama/theater group, newspaper, radio station, and choral group. No national or local **fraternities** or **sororities**.

Nazareth College is a member of the NCAA (Division III). **Intercollegiate sports** include basketball, cheerleading (w), cross-country running, equestrian sports, field hockey (w), golf, lacrosse, soccer, softball (w), swimming, tennis, track and field, volleyball.

Campus Safety

Student safety services include alarm system, security beeper, lighted pathways, late-night transport/escort service, 24-hour emergency telephone alarm devices, 24-hour patrols by trained security personnel, student patrols, and electronically operated dormitory entrances.

Applying

Nazareth College requires an essay, SAT I or ACT, a high school transcript, and 1 recommendation, and in some cases audition/portfolio review. It recommends an interview and 2 recommendations. Application deadline: 2/15; 2/15 priority date for financial aid. Early and deferred admission are possible.

NEW COLLEGE OF FLORIDA

SUBURBAN SETTING ■ PUBLIC ■ STATE-SUPPORTED ■ COED
SARASOTA, FLORIDA

Web site: www.ncf.edu
Contact: Ms. Kathleen M. Killian, Interim Dean of Admissions and Financial
Aid, 5700 North Tamiami Trail, Sarasota, FL 34243-2197
Telephone: 941-359-4269 **Fax:** 941-359-4435
E-mail: admissions@ncf.edu

Academics
New College of Florida awards bachelor's **degrees**. Challenging opportunities include accelerated degree programs, student-designed majors, an honors program, double majors, independent study, and a senior project. Special programs include internships, off-campus study, and study-abroad.

The most frequently chosen **baccalaureate** field is liberal arts/general studies. A complete listing of majors at New College of Florida appears in the Majors Index beginning on page 460.

The **faculty** at New College of Florida has 62 full-time members, 100% with terminal degrees. The student-faculty ratio is 11:1.

Students of New College of Florida
The student body is made up of 671 undergraduates. 61% are women and 39% are men. Students come from 40 states and territories and 12 other countries. 77% are from Florida. 2.4% are international students. 1.6% are African American, 0.3% American Indian, 3.3% Asian American, and 7% Hispanic American. 75% returned for their sophomore year.

Facilities and Resources
Student rooms are linked to a campus network. 41 **computers** are available on campus that provide access to the Internet. The **library** has 256,581 books and 1,925 subscriptions.

Campus Life
There are 43 active organizations on campus, including a drama/theater group, newspaper, radio station, and choral group. 25% of eligible men and 40% of eligible women are members of
This institution has no intercollegiate sports.

Campus Safety
Student safety services include late-night transport/escort service, 24-hour emergency telephone alarm devices, and 24-hour patrols by trained security personnel.

Applying
New College of Florida requires an essay, SAT I or ACT, a high school transcript, and 2 recommendations, and in some cases an interview. It recommends an interview, analytical paper, and a minimum high school GPA of 3.0. Application deadline: 3/1 priority date for financial aid. Early and deferred admission are possible.

New College offers an innovative, rigorous approach to the liberal arts and sciences. Students choose courses through discussion with their faculty sponsor, create credited courses of study through individualized research projects and tutorials, and receive written narrative evaluations instead of grades. Located on the beautiful Gulf of Mexico in Sarasota, Florida, New College is the public honors college of Florida and is designed for independent and motivated students who are eager to take responsibility for their own education. Novo Collegians are a diverse group, with active alumni ranging from a Fields Medal winner in mathematics to the first chair of the Florida Fish and Wildlife Conservation Commission.

Getting in Last Year
565 applied
61% were accepted
157 enrolled (46%)
45% from top tenth of their h.s. class
3.82 average high school GPA
92% had SAT verbal scores over 600
73% had SAT math scores over 600
94% had ACT scores over 24
42% had SAT verbal scores over 700
15% had SAT math scores over 700
28% had ACT scores over 30
7 National Merit Scholars
6 valedictorians

Graduation and After
63% graduated in 4 years
10% graduated in 5 years
2% graduated in 6 years
19% pursued further study (17% arts and sciences, 1% law)
75 organizations recruited on campus

Financial Matters
$3240 resident tuition and fees (2003–04)
$16,473 nonresident tuition and fees (2003–04)
$5658 room and board
79% average percent of need met
$8886 average financial aid amount received per undergraduate

NEW JERSEY INSTITUTE OF TECHNOLOGY
URBAN SETTING ■ PUBLIC ■ STATE-SUPPORTED ■ COED
NEWARK, NEW JERSEY

Web site: www.njit.edu
Contact: Ms. Kathy Kelly, Director of Admissions, University Heights,
   Newark, NJ 07102-1982
Telephone: 973-596-3300 or toll-free 800-925-NJIT **Fax:** 973-596-3461
E-mail: admissions@njit.edu

With nearly a century of experience in educating leaders in business and government, NJIT's Newark College of Engineering is also a pioneer in applying new technologies as learning tools. The College's curriculum emphasizes design, multidisciplinary teamwork, real-world experience, and computing as a tool in every specialty area.

Getting in Last Year
2,566 applied
68% were accepted
709 enrolled (41%)
25% from top tenth of their h.s. class
23% had SAT verbal scores over 600
54% had SAT math scores over 600
2% had SAT verbal scores over 700
12% had SAT math scores over 700

Graduation and After
15% graduated in 4 years
23% graduated in 5 years
10% graduated in 6 years
22% pursued further study
85% had job offers within 6 months
400 organizations recruited on campus

Financial Matters
$8500 resident tuition and fees (2003–04)
$13,868 nonresident tuition and fees (2003–04)
$8076 room and board
90% average percent of need met
$5400 average financial aid amount received per undergraduate (2002–03)

Academics
NJIT awards bachelor's, master's, and doctoral **degrees** and post-bachelor's certificates. Challenging opportunities include advanced placement credit, accelerated degree programs, freshman honors college, an honors program, double majors, independent study, and a senior project. Special programs include cooperative education, internships, summer session for credit, off-campus study, study-abroad, and Air Force ROTC.

The most frequently chosen **baccalaureate** fields are engineering/engineering technologies, computer/information sciences, and architecture. A complete listing of majors at NJIT appears in the Majors Index beginning on page 460.

The **faculty** at NJIT has 404 full-time members, 100% with terminal degrees. The student-faculty ratio is 13:1.

Students of NJIT
The student body totals 8,770, of whom 5,712 are undergraduates. 21% are women and 79% are men. Students come from 27 states and territories and 53 other countries. 94% are from New Jersey. 5.2% are international students. 10.2% are African American, 0.2% American Indian, 22.9% Asian American, and 12.3% Hispanic American. 85% returned for their sophomore year.

Facilities and Resources
Student rooms are linked to a campus network. 4,500 **computers** are available on campus for student use. The 2 **libraries** have 160,000 books and 1,100 subscriptions.

Campus Life
There are 70 active organizations on campus, including a drama/theater group, newspaper, and radio station. 12% of eligible men and 9% of eligible women are members of national **fraternities**, national **sororities**, local fraternities, and local sororities.

NJIT is a member of the NCAA (Division II). **Intercollegiate sports** include baseball (m), basketball, cross-country running, fencing (m), golf (m), soccer (m), softball (w), swimming (w), tennis, track and field (w), volleyball.

Campus Safety
Student safety services include bicycle patrols, sexual assault response team, late-night transport/escort service, 24-hour emergency telephone alarm devices, 24-hour patrols by trained security personnel, and electronically operated dormitory entrances.

Applying
NJIT requires SAT I or ACT and a high school transcript, and in some cases an essay, SAT II Subject Tests, and an interview. It recommends 1 recommendation. Application deadline: 4/1; 5/15 for financial aid, with a 3/15 priority date. Early and deferred admission are possible.

New Mexico Institute of Mining and Technology

Small-town setting ■ Public ■ State-supported ■ Coed
Socorro, New Mexico

Web site: www.nmt.edu
Contact: Mr. Mike Kloeppel, Director of Admissions, 801 Leroy Place, Socorro, NM 87801
Telephone: 505-835-5424 or toll-free 800-428-TECH **Fax:** 505-835-5989
E-mail: admission@admin.nmt.edu

Academics

New Mexico Tech awards associate, bachelor's, master's, and doctoral **degrees**. Challenging opportunities include advanced placement credit, accelerated degree programs, student-designed majors, double majors, independent study, and a senior project. Special programs include cooperative education, internships, and summer session for credit.

The most frequently chosen **baccalaureate** fields are engineering/engineering technologies, physical sciences, and computer/information sciences. A complete listing of majors at New Mexico Tech appears in the Majors Index beginning on page 460.

The **faculty** at New Mexico Tech has 121 full-time members, 97% with terminal degrees. The student-faculty ratio is 12:1.

Students of New Mexico Tech

The student body totals 1,798, of whom 1,365 are undergraduates. 32% are women and 68% are men. Students come from 52 states and territories and 14 other countries. 84% are from New Mexico. 2.8% are international students. 1% are African American, 3.1% American Indian, 3.2% Asian American, and 19.3% Hispanic American. 72% returned for their sophomore year.

Facilities and Resources

Student rooms are linked to a campus network. 225 **computers** are available on campus that provide access to the Internet. The 2 **libraries** have 318,429 books and 833 subscriptions.

Campus Life

There are 55 active organizations on campus, including a drama/theater group, newspaper, radio station, and choral group. No national or local **fraternities** or **sororities**.

This institution has no intercollegiate sports.

Campus Safety

Student safety services include late-night transport/escort service, 24-hour emergency telephone alarm devices, and 24-hour patrols by trained security personnel.

Applying

New Mexico Tech requires SAT I or ACT, a high school transcript, and a minimum high school GPA of 2.5, and in some cases 2 recommendations. It recommends an interview. Application deadline: 8/1; 6/1 priority date for financial aid. Deferred admission is possible.

Getting in Last Year
363 applied
98% were accepted
285 enrolled (80%)
37% from top tenth of their h.s. class
3.6 average high school GPA
66% had SAT verbal scores over 600
70% had SAT math scores over 600
69% had ACT scores over 24
12% had SAT verbal scores over 700
17% had SAT math scores over 700
17% had ACT scores over 30

Graduation and After
15% graduated in 4 years
17% graduated in 5 years
5% graduated in 6 years
75% had job offers within 6 months
22 organizations recruited on campus

Financial Matters
$3080 resident tuition and fees (2003–04)
$9601 nonresident tuition and fees (2003–04)
$4200 room and board
90% average percent of need met
$7641 average financial aid amount received per undergraduate

NEW YORK SCHOOL OF INTERIOR DESIGN
URBAN SETTING ■ PRIVATE ■ INDEPENDENT ■ COED, PRIMARILY WOMEN
NEW YORK, NEW YORK

Web site: www.nysid.edu
Contact: Ms. Briana Cristantiello, Admissions Associate, 170 East 70th Street, New York, NY 10021-5110
Telephone: 212-472-1500 ext. 204 or toll-free 800-336-9743 **Fax:** 212-472-1867
E-mail: admissions@nysid.edu

Manhattan, with its world-famous museums, showrooms, and architectural landmarks, is home to the New York School of Interior Design (NYSID). NYSID is a single-major college dedicated solely to the study of interior design. Facilities include a lighting lab, a computer-aided design (CAD) lab, and an extensive reference library. Many NYSID graduates have gone on to find work in the best design and architectural firms in New York City and around the world. The Bachelor of Fine Arts degree is a FIDER-accredited program.

Getting in Last Year
107 applied
62% were accepted
66 enrolled (100%)
3.00 average high school GPA
8% had SAT verbal scores over 600
8% had SAT math scores over 600
8% had SAT verbal scores over 700
8% had SAT math scores over 700

Graduation and After
5% graduated in 5 years
15% graduated in 6 years

Financial Matters
$18,070 tuition and fees (2003–04)
50% average percent of need met
$8500 average financial aid amount received per undergraduate (2002–03 estimated)

Academics
NYSID awards associate, bachelor's, and master's **degrees**. Challenging opportunities include advanced placement credit, independent study, and a senior project. Special programs include internships, summer session for credit, and study-abroad.

The most frequently chosen **baccalaureate** field is visual/performing arts. A complete listing of majors at NYSID appears in the Majors Index beginning on page 460.

The **faculty** at NYSID has 2 full-time members. The student-faculty ratio is 10:1.

Students of NYSID
The student body totals 777, of whom 760 are undergraduates. 91.6% are women and 8.4% are men. Students come from 16 states and territories and 30 other countries. 83% are from New York. 11.3% are international students. 1.2% are African American, 10.1% Asian American, and 5.2% Hispanic American. 50% returned for their sophomore year.

Facilities and Resources
70 **computers** are available on campus that provide access to the Internet. The **library** has 10,000 books and 88 subscriptions.

Campus Life
There is 1 active organization on campus. No national or local **fraternities** or **sororities**.

This institution has no intercollegiate sports.

Campus Safety
Student safety services include security during school hours.

Applying
NYSID requires an essay, SAT I or ACT, a high school transcript, 2 recommendations, portfolio, and a minimum high school GPA of 2.7, and in some cases an interview. It recommends an interview. Application deadline: rolling admissions; 5/1 priority date for financial aid. Deferred admission is possible.

NEW YORK UNIVERSITY
URBAN SETTING ■ PRIVATE ■ INDEPENDENT ■ COED
NEW YORK, NEW YORK

Web site: www.nyu.edu
Contact: Ms. Barbara Hall, Associate Provost for Admissions and Financial Aid, 22 Washington Square North, New York, NY 10011
Telephone: 212-998-4500 **Fax:** 212-995-4902

Academics
NYU awards associate, bachelor's, master's, doctoral, and first-professional **degrees** and post-bachelor's, post-master's, and first-professional certificates. Challenging opportunities include advanced placement credit, accelerated degree programs, student-designed majors, freshman honors college, an honors program, double majors, independent study, and a senior project. Special programs include internships, summer session for credit, off-campus study, and study-abroad.

The most frequently chosen **baccalaureate** fields are visual/performing arts, social sciences and history, and business/marketing. A complete listing of majors at NYU appears in the Majors Index beginning on page 460.

The **faculty** at NYU has 1,899 full-time members. The student-faculty ratio is 12:1.

Students of NYU
The student body totals 38,188, of whom 19,506 are undergraduates. 60.3% are women and 39.7% are men. Students come from 52 states and territories and 91 other countries. 42% are from New York. 4.1% are international students. 5.3% are African American, 0.2% American Indian, 14.2% Asian American, and 7% Hispanic American. 92% returned for their sophomore year.

Facilities and Resources
Student rooms are linked to a campus network. 1,400 **computers** are available on campus that provide access to the Internet. The 12 **libraries** have 4,172,898 books and 33,405 subscriptions.

Campus Life
There are 300 active organizations on campus, including a drama/theater group, newspaper, radio station, television station, and choral group. 4% of eligible men and 2% of eligible women are members of national **fraternities**, national **sororities**, and local sororities.

NYU is a member of the NCAA (Division III). **Intercollegiate sports** include basketball, cross-country running, fencing, golf (m), soccer, swimming, tennis, volleyball, wrestling (m).

Campus Safety
Student safety services include 24-hour security in residence halls, late-night transport/escort service, 24-hour emergency telephone alarm devices, 24-hour patrols by trained security personnel, student patrols, and electronically operated dormitory entrances.

Applying
NYU requires an essay, SAT I or ACT, a high school transcript, 2 recommendations, and a minimum high school GPA of 3.0, and in some cases SAT II Subject Tests, an interview, and audition, portfolio. It recommends SAT II Subject Tests and SAT II: Writing Test. Application deadline: 1/15; 2/15 priority date for financial aid. Deferred admission is possible.

Getting in Last Year
33,776 applied
32% were accepted
4,254 enrolled (39%)
63% from top tenth of their h.s. class
3.65 average high school GPA
81% had SAT verbal scores over 600
83% had SAT math scores over 600
98% had ACT scores over 24
29% had SAT verbal scores over 700
32% had SAT math scores over 700
52% had ACT scores over 30
133 National Merit Scholars
79 valedictorians

Graduation and After
71% graduated in 4 years
6% graduated in 5 years
1% graduated in 6 years
18% pursued further study (4% arts and sciences, 4% law, 3% education)
78% had job offers within 6 months
539 organizations recruited on campus

Financial Matters
$28,496 tuition and fees (2003–04)
$10,910 room and board
67% average percent of need met
$18,686 average financial aid amount received per undergraduate

NORTH CAROLINA STATE UNIVERSITY

SUBURBAN SETTING ■ PUBLIC ■ STATE-SUPPORTED ■ COED
RALEIGH, NORTH CAROLINA

Web site: www.ncsu.edu
Contact: Mr. Thomas H. Griffin, Director of Undergraduate Admissions, Box
7103, 112 Peele Hall, Raleigh, NC 27695
Telephone: 919-515-2434 **Fax:** 919-515-5039
E-mail: undergrad_admissions@ncsu.edu

Getting in Last Year

12,852 applied
62% were accepted
3,931 enrolled (49%)
40% from top tenth of their h.s. class
4.05 average high school GPA
42% had SAT verbal scores over 600
60% had SAT math scores over 600
68% had ACT scores over 24
6% had SAT verbal scores over 700
14% had SAT math scores over 700
21% had ACT scores over 30
43 National Merit Scholars
88 valedictorians

Graduation and After

25% graduated in 4 years
28% graduated in 5 years
7% graduated in 6 years
20% pursued further study
92% had job offers within 6 months
722 organizations recruited on campus

Financial Matters

$3970 resident tuition and fees (2003–04)
$15,818 nonresident tuition and fees (2003–04)
$5918 room and board
84% average percent of need met
$7497 average financial aid amount received per undergraduate

Academics

NC State awards associate, bachelor's, master's, doctoral, and first-professional **degrees** and first-professional certificates. Challenging opportunities include advanced placement credit, accelerated degree programs, student-designed majors, freshman honors college, an honors program, double majors, independent study, and a senior project. Special programs include cooperative education, internships, summer session for credit, off-campus study, study-abroad, and Army, Navy and Air Force ROTC.

The most frequently chosen **baccalaureate** fields are engineering/engineering technologies, business/marketing, and biological/life sciences. A complete listing of majors at NC State appears in the Majors Index beginning on page 460.

The **faculty** at NC State has 1,647 full-time members, 91% with terminal degrees. The student-faculty ratio is 15:1.

Students of NC State

The student body totals 29,854, of whom 22,971 are undergraduates. 42.3% are women and 57.7% are men. Students come from 51 states and territories and 65 other countries. 92% are from North Carolina. 1% are international students. 10.2% are African American, 0.7% American Indian, 5.4% Asian American, and 2.1% Hispanic American. 90% returned for their sophomore year.

Facilities and Resources

Student rooms are linked to a campus network. 4,600 **computers** are available on campus that provide access to the Internet. The 5 **libraries** have 986,993 books and 17,050 subscriptions.

Campus Life

There are 300 active organizations on campus, including a drama/theater group, newspaper, radio station, television station, choral group, and marching band. 11% of eligible men and 11% of eligible women are members of national **fraternities**, national **sororities**, and local sororities.

NC State is a member of the NCAA (Division I). **Intercollegiate sports** (some offering scholarships) include baseball (m), basketball, cheerleading, cross-country running, fencing, football (m), golf, gymnastics, riflery, soccer, softball (w), swimming, tennis, track and field, volleyball (w), wrestling (m).

Campus Safety

Student safety services include late-night transport/escort service, 24-hour emergency telephone alarm devices, 24-hour patrols by trained security personnel, student patrols, and electronically operated dormitory entrances.

Applying

NC State requires SAT I or ACT and a high school transcript, and in some cases an interview. It recommends an essay, SAT II Subject Tests, and a minimum high school GPA of 3.0. Application deadline: 2/1; 3/1 priority date for financial aid. Early and deferred admission are possible.

NORTH CENTRAL COLLEGE

SUBURBAN SETTING ■ PRIVATE ■ INDEPENDENT RELIGIOUS ■ COED
NAPERVILLE, ILLINOIS

Web site: www.northcentralcollege.edu
Contact: Mr. Michael Brown, Director of Freshman Admission, 30 North
  Brainard Street, PO Box 3063, Naperville, IL 60566-7063
Telephone: 630-637-5800 or toll-free 800-411-1861 **Fax:** 630-637-5819
E-mail: ncadm@noctrl.edu

Academics

North Central awards bachelor's and master's **degrees**. Challenging opportunities
include advanced placement credit, accelerated degree programs, student-designed
majors, an honors program, double majors, independent study, and a senior project.
Special programs include cooperative education, internships, summer session for credit,
off-campus study, study-abroad, and Army and Air Force ROTC.

The most frequently chosen **baccalaureate** fields are business/marketing, social sciences and history, and communications/communication technologies. A complete listing
of majors at North Central appears in the Majors Index beginning on page 460.

The **faculty** at North Central has 125 full-time members, 89% with terminal
degrees. The student-faculty ratio is 14:1.

Students of North Central

The student body totals 2,458, of whom 2,086 are undergraduates. 59.4% are women
and 40.6% are men. Students come from 26 states and territories and 18 other countries.
91% are from Illinois. 1.5% are international students. 4.6% are African American, 0.1%
American Indian, 2.5% Asian American, and 4% Hispanic American. 76% returned for
their sophomore year.

Facilities and Resources

Student rooms are linked to a campus network. 200 **computers** are available on campus
that provide access to software packages and the Internet. The **library** has 145,707 books
and 707 subscriptions.

Campus Life

There are 42 active organizations on campus, including a drama/theater group,
newspaper, radio station, and choral group. No national or local **fraternities** or **sororities**.

North Central is a member of the NCAA (Division III). **Intercollegiate sports**
include baseball (m), basketball, cheerleading (w), cross-country running, football (m),
golf, soccer, softball (w), swimming, tennis, track and field, volleyball (w), wrestling (m).

Campus Safety

Student safety services include late-night transport/escort service, 24-hour emergency
telephone alarm devices, and 24-hour patrols by trained security personnel.

Applying

North Central requires SAT I or ACT, a high school transcript, and a minimum high
school GPA of 2.0, and in some cases an interview. It recommends an essay, ACT, and 1
recommendation. Application deadline: rolling admissions. Early and deferred admission
are possible.

North Central College,
located in Naperville,
Illinois, is 29 miles west
of Chicago and nestled in a
residential historic district. The
College is committed to
undergraduate teaching and to
sustaining its strong campus life
tradition. The curriculum is grounded
in a liberal arts foundation with an
emphasis on leadership, ethics, and
values. North Central College offers
more than 50 academic areas of
concentration in business, science,
education, communication, liberal
arts and pre-professional programs.
Co-curricular opportunities include
nationally-recognized Division III
intercollegiate athletics, student
radio station, Model UN team,
community conflict resolution minor,
forensics, and community service.

Getting in Last Year
1,654 applied
71% were accepted
408 enrolled (35%)
25% from top tenth of their h.s. class
3.53 average high school GPA
45% had SAT verbal scores over 600
47% had SAT math scores over 600
59% had ACT scores over 24
12% had SAT verbal scores over 700
12% had SAT math scores over 700
9% had ACT scores over 30
12 valedictorians

Graduation and After
54% graduated in 4 years
11% graduated in 5 years
1% graduated in 6 years
10% pursued further study (6% arts and sciences, 2% business, 1% education)
80% had job offers within 6 months
46 organizations recruited on campus

Financial Matters
$19,281 tuition and fees (2003–04)
$6375 room and board
87% average percent of need met
$18,212 average financial aid amount received
  per undergraduate

NORTHWESTERN COLLEGE

SUBURBAN SETTING ■ PRIVATE ■ INDEPENDENT RELIGIOUS ■ COED
ST. PAUL, MINNESOTA

Web site: www.nwc.edu
Contact: Mr. Kenneth K. Faffler, Director of Admissions, 3003 Snelling
 Avenue North, Nazareth Hall, Room 2122, St. Paul, MN 55113-1598
Telephone: 651-631-5209 or toll-free 800-827-6827 **Fax:** 651-631-5680
E-mail: admissions@nwc.edu

Getting in Last Year
980 applied
94% were accepted
459 enrolled (50%)
27% from top tenth of their h.s. class
3.51 average high school GPA
48% had SAT verbal scores over 600
39% had SAT math scores over 600
50% had ACT scores over 24
22% had SAT verbal scores over 700
8% had SAT math scores over 700
7% had ACT scores over 30
15 valedictorians

Graduation and After
45% graduated in 4 years
10% graduated in 5 years
4% graduated in 6 years
8% pursued further study (3% arts and sciences, 2% theology, 1% education)
63% had job offers within 6 months
125 organizations recruited on campus

Financial Matters
$17,400 tuition and fees (2003–04)
$5620 room and board
77% average percent of need met
$13,037 average financial aid amount received per undergraduate (2002–03)

Academics

Northwestern awards associate and bachelor's **degrees**. Challenging opportunities include advanced placement credit, an honors program, double majors, independent study, and a senior project. Special programs include internships, summer session for credit, off-campus study, study-abroad, and Army and Air Force ROTC.

The most frequently chosen **baccalaureate** fields are business/marketing, education, and psychology. A complete listing of majors at Northwestern appears in the Majors Index beginning on page 460.

The **faculty** at Northwestern has 84 full-time members, 64% with terminal degrees. The student-faculty ratio is 16:1.

Students of Northwestern

The student body is made up of 2,592 undergraduates. 62.6% are women and 37.4% are men. Students come from 32 states and territories. 72% are from Minnesota. 0.4% are international students. 3.9% are African American, 0.3% American Indian, 2.6% Asian American, and 1.4% Hispanic American. 75% returned for their sophomore year.

Facilities and Resources

Student rooms are linked to a campus network. 165 **computers** are available on campus that provide access to the Internet. The **library** has 75,082 books and 560 subscriptions.

Campus Life

There are 25 active organizations on campus, including a drama/theater group, newspaper, radio station, and choral group. No national or local **fraternities** or **sororities**.

Northwestern is a member of the NAIA and NCCAA. **Intercollegiate sports** include baseball (m), basketball, cheerleading (w), cross-country running, football (m), golf, soccer, softball (w), tennis, track and field, volleyball (w).

Campus Safety

Student safety services include late-night transport/escort service, 24-hour patrols by trained security personnel, and electronically operated dormitory entrances.

Applying

Northwestern requires an essay, SAT I or ACT, a high school transcript, 2 recommendations, lifestyle agreement, statement of Christian faith, and a minimum high school GPA of 2.0, and in some cases an interview. It recommends a minimum high school GPA of 3.0. Application deadline: 8/1; 6/1 for financial aid, with a 3/1 priority date. Early and deferred admission are possible.

NORTHWESTERN COLLEGE

RURAL SETTING ■ PRIVATE ■ INDEPENDENT RELIGIOUS ■ COED

ORANGE CITY, IOWA

Web site: www.nwciowa.edu

Contact: Mr. Ronald K. DeJong, Director of Admissions, 101 College Lane, Orange City, IA 51041-1996

Telephone: 712-737-7130 or toll-free 800-747-4757 **Fax:** 712-707-7164

E-mail: markb@nwciowa.edu

Academics

Northwestern awards associate and bachelor's **degrees**. Challenging opportunities include advanced placement credit, accelerated degree programs, student-designed majors, freshman honors college, an honors program, double majors, independent study, and a senior project. Special programs include cooperative education, internships, summer session for credit, off-campus study, and study-abroad.

The most frequently chosen **baccalaureate** fields are business/marketing, education, and biological/life sciences. A complete listing of majors at Northwestern appears in the Majors Index beginning on page 460.

The **faculty** at Northwestern has 77 full-time members, 82% with terminal degrees. The student-faculty ratio is 14:1.

Students of Northwestern

The student body is made up of 1,285 undergraduates. 60.9% are women and 39.1% are men. Students come from 29 states and territories and 12 other countries. 59% are from Iowa. 2.7% are international students. 0.5% are African American, 0.9% Asian American, and 1% Hispanic American. 78% returned for their sophomore year.

Facilities and Resources

Student rooms are linked to a campus network. 250 **computers** are available on campus that provide access to the Internet. The 2 **libraries** have 125,000 books and 615 subscriptions.

Campus Life

There are 30 active organizations on campus, including a drama/theater group, newspaper, television station, and choral group. No national or local **fraternities** or **sororities**.

Northwestern is a member of the NAIA. **Intercollegiate sports** (some offering scholarships) include baseball (m), basketball, cross-country running, football (m), golf, soccer, softball (w), tennis, track and field, volleyball (w), wrestling (m).

Campus Safety

Student safety services include 24-hour emergency telephone alarm devices and electronically operated dormitory entrances.

Applying

Northwestern requires an essay, SAT I or ACT, a high school transcript, 1 recommendation, and a minimum high school GPA of 2.0. It recommends an interview and a minimum high school GPA of 2.5. Application deadline: rolling admissions; 4/1 priority date for financial aid. Deferred admission is possible.

Getting in Last Year

1,311 applied
83% were accepted
311 enrolled (29%)
26% from top tenth of their h.s. class
3.49 average high school GPA
55% had ACT scores over 24
8% had ACT scores over 30
19 valedictorians

Graduation and After

51% graduated in 4 years
8% graduated in 5 years
22% pursued further study
93% had job offers within 6 months
35 organizations recruited on campus

Financial Matters

$15,290 tuition and fees (2003–04)
$4350 room and board
81% average percent of need met
$11,634 average financial aid amount received per undergraduate (2002–03 estimated)

NORTHWESTERN UNIVERSITY

SUBURBAN SETTING ■ PRIVATE ■ INDEPENDENT ■ COED
EVANSTON, ILLINOIS

Web site: www.northwestern.edu
Contact: Ms. Carol Lunkenheimer, Dean of Undergraduate Admission, PO Box 3060, Evanston, IL 60204-3060
Telephone: 847-491-7271
E-mail: ug-admission@northwestern.edu

Getting in Last Year
14,137 applied
33% were accepted
1,941 enrolled (41%)
83% from top tenth of their h.s. class
90% had SAT verbal scores over 600
93% had SAT math scores over 600
95% had ACT scores over 24
50% had SAT verbal scores over 700
56% had SAT math scores over 700
70% had ACT scores over 30
100 National Merit Scholars
187 valedictorians

Graduation and After
84% graduated in 4 years
8% graduated in 5 years
1% graduated in 6 years
569 organizations recruited on campus

Financial Matters
$28,524 tuition and fees (2003–04)
$8967 room and board
100% average percent of need met
$24,508 average financial aid amount received per undergraduate

Academics

Northwestern awards bachelor's, master's, doctoral, and first-professional **degrees** and post-master's certificates. Challenging opportunities include advanced placement credit, accelerated degree programs, student-designed majors, an honors program, double majors, independent study, and a senior project. Special programs include cooperative education, internships, summer session for credit, study-abroad, and Army, Navy and Air Force ROTC.

The most frequently chosen **baccalaureate** fields are social sciences and history, communications/communication technologies, and engineering/engineering technologies. A complete listing of majors at Northwestern appears in the Majors Index beginning on page 460.

The **faculty** at Northwestern has 900 full-time members, 100% with terminal degrees. The student-faculty ratio is 7:1.

Students of Northwestern

The student body totals 16,266, of whom 8,001 are undergraduates. 52.8% are women and 47.2% are men. Students come from 51 states and territories and 51 other countries. 25% are from Illinois. 5.3% are international students. 5.4% are African American, 0.2% American Indian, 16.9% Asian American, and 5% Hispanic American. 97% returned for their sophomore year.

Facilities and Resources

Student rooms are linked to a campus network. 608 **computers** are available on campus that provide access to the Internet. The 7 **libraries** have 4,217,321 books and 39,423 subscriptions.

Campus Life

There are 415 active organizations on campus, including a drama/theater group, newspaper, radio station, television station, choral group, and marching band. 30% of eligible men and 39% of eligible women are members of national **fraternities** and national **sororities**.

Northwestern is a member of the NCAA (Division I). **Intercollegiate sports** (some offering scholarships) include baseball (m), basketball, cheerleading, cross-country running (w), fencing (w), field hockey (w), football (m), golf, lacrosse (w), soccer, softball (w), swimming, tennis, volleyball (w), wrestling (m).

Campus Safety

Student safety services include late-night transport/escort service, 24-hour emergency telephone alarm devices, 24-hour patrols by trained security personnel, and electronically operated dormitory entrances.

Applying

Northwestern requires an essay, SAT I or ACT, a high school transcript, and 1 recommendation, and in some cases SAT II Subject Tests, SAT II: Writing Test, and audition for music program. It recommends SAT II Subject Tests and SAT II: Writing Test. Application deadline: 1/1; 2/1 priority date for financial aid. Early and deferred admission are possible.

OBERLIN COLLEGE

SMALL-TOWN SETTING ■ PRIVATE ■ INDEPENDENT ■ COED
OBERLIN, OHIO

Web site: www.oberlin.edu
Contact: Ms. Debra Chermonte, Dean of Admissions and Financial Aid,
  Admissions Office, Carnegie Building, Oberlin, OH 44074-1090
Telephone: 440-775-8411 or toll-free 800-622-OBIE **Fax:** 440-775-6905
E-mail: college.admissions@oberlin.edu

Academics

Oberlin awards bachelor's and master's **degrees** and post-bachelor's certificates. Challenging opportunities include advanced placement credit, student-designed majors, an honors program, double majors, independent study, and a senior project. Special programs include internships, off-campus study, and study-abroad.

The most frequently chosen **baccalaureate** fields are visual/performing arts, social sciences and history, and English. A complete listing of majors at Oberlin appears in the Majors Index beginning on page 460.

The **faculty** at Oberlin has 272 full-time members, 94% with terminal degrees. The student-faculty ratio is 10:1.

Students of Oberlin

The student body totals 2,898, of whom 2,883 are undergraduates. 55.1% are women and 44.9% are men. Students come from 50 states and territories and 44 other countries. 10% are from Ohio. 6.2% are international students. 6.9% are African American, 0.9% American Indian, 7% Asian American, and 4.8% Hispanic American. 90% returned for their sophomore year.

Facilities and Resources

Student rooms are linked to a campus network. 340 **computers** are available on campus that provide access to the Internet. The 4 **libraries** have 1,541,260 books and 4,560 subscriptions.

Campus Life

There are 120 active organizations on campus, including a drama/theater group, newspaper, radio station, choral group, and marching band. No national or local **fraternities** or **sororities**.

Oberlin is a member of the NCAA (Division III). **Intercollegiate sports** include baseball (m), basketball, cross-country running, field hockey (w), football (m), golf, lacrosse, soccer, swimming, tennis, track and field, volleyball (w).

Campus Safety

Student safety services include crime prevention programs, late-night transport/escort service, 24-hour emergency telephone alarm devices, 24-hour patrols by trained security personnel, student patrols, and electronically operated dormitory entrances.

Applying

Oberlin requires an essay, SAT I or ACT, a high school transcript, and 2 recommendations, and in some cases an interview. It recommends SAT II Subject Tests and SAT II: Writing Test. Application deadline: 1/15; 2/1 priority date for financial aid. Early and deferred admission are possible.

From its founding, Oberlin has been a pioneering college. Oberlin was the first coeducational school in the United States and a historic leader in educating African-American students. Among primarily undergraduate institutions, Oberlin ranks first for the number of students going on to earn PhD degrees. Oberlin alumni include 3 Nobel laureates and leaders in law, scientific and scholarly research, medicine, the arts, theology, communication, business, and government. Oberlin has more students, programs, and facilities than most small colleges, including a 5-year double-degree program, combining studies at the Conservatory of Music and the College of Arts and Sciences.

Getting in Last Year
5,983 applied
36% were accepted
764 enrolled (35%)
62% from top tenth of their h.s. class
3.52 average high school GPA
86% had SAT verbal scores over 600
79% had SAT math scores over 600
93% had ACT scores over 24
43% had SAT verbal scores over 700
30% had SAT math scores over 700
38% had ACT scores over 30
33 National Merit Scholars
43 valedictorians

Graduation and After
64% graduated in 4 years
16% graduated in 5 years
2% graduated in 6 years
22% pursued further study
90% had job offers within 6 months
32 organizations recruited on campus

Financial Matters
$29,688 tuition and fees (2003–04)
$7250 room and board
100% average percent of need met
$22,576 average financial aid amount received
  per undergraduate

OCCIDENTAL COLLEGE

URBAN SETTING ■ PRIVATE ■ INDEPENDENT ■ COED
LOS ANGELES, CALIFORNIA

Web site: www.oxy.edu
Contact: Mr. Vince Cuseo, Director of Admission, 1600 Campus Road M-18, Los Angeles, CA 90041
Telephone: 323-259-2700 or toll-free 800-825-5262 **Fax:** 323-341-4875
E-mail: admission@oxy.edu

Getting in Last Year
4,513 applied
44% were accepted
441 enrolled (22%)
59% from top tenth of their h.s. class
61% had SAT verbal scores over 600
61% had SAT math scores over 600
18% had SAT verbal scores over 700
16% had SAT math scores over 700
19 class presidents
13 valedictorians

Graduation and After
73% graduated in 4 years
4% graduated in 5 years
1% graduated in 6 years
30% pursued further study (23% arts and sciences, 3% law, 3% medicine)
62 organizations recruited on campus

Financial Matters
$28,306 tuition and fees (2003–04)
$7820 room and board
94% average percent of need met
$26,883 average financial aid amount received per undergraduate (2002–03 estimated)

Academics

OXY awards bachelor's and master's **degrees**. Challenging opportunities include advanced placement credit, accelerated degree programs, student-designed majors, an honors program, double majors, independent study, and a senior project. Special programs include internships, summer session for credit, off-campus study, study-abroad, and Army, Navy and Air Force ROTC.

The most frequently chosen **baccalaureate** fields are social sciences and history, business/marketing, and visual/performing arts. A complete listing of majors at OXY appears in the Majors Index beginning on page 460.

The **faculty** at OXY has 135 full-time members, 99% with terminal degrees. The student-faculty ratio is 11:1.

Students of OXY

The student body totals 1,858, of whom 1,840 are undergraduates. 58.1% are women and 41.9% are men. Students come from 45 states and territories and 24 other countries. 68% are from California. 4.1% are international students. 6.9% are African American, 1.1% American Indian, 12.3% Asian American, and 15% Hispanic American. 91% returned for their sophomore year.

Facilities and Resources

Student rooms are linked to a campus network. 131 **computers** are available on campus that provide access to the Internet. The 3 **libraries** have 481,822 books and 1,135 subscriptions.

Campus Life

There are 104 active organizations on campus, including a drama/theater group, newspaper, radio station, and choral group. 5% of eligible men and 11% of eligible women are members of national **fraternities** and local **sororities**.

OXY is a member of the NCAA (Division III). **Intercollegiate sports** include baseball (m), basketball, cross-country running, football (m), golf, soccer, softball (w), swimming, tennis, track and field, volleyball (w), water polo.

Campus Safety

Student safety services include lighted pathways and sidewalks; whistle alert program, late-night transport/escort service, 24-hour emergency telephone alarm devices, 24-hour patrols by trained security personnel, and electronically operated dormitory entrances.

Applying

OXY requires an essay, SAT I or ACT, a high school transcript, and 2 recommendations. It recommends SAT II Subject Tests, SAT II: Writing Test, and an interview. Application deadline: 1/10; 2/1 priority date for financial aid. Early and deferred admission are possible.

OGLETHORPE UNIVERSITY

SUBURBAN SETTING ■ PRIVATE ■ INDEPENDENT ■ COED
ATLANTA, GEORGIA

Web site: www.oglethorpe.edu
Contact: Mr. David Rhodes, Vice President for Enrollment Management, 4484 Peachtree Road, NE, Atlanta, GA 30319
Telephone: 404-364-8307 or toll-free 800-428-4484 **Fax:** 404-364-8491
E-mail: admission@oglethorpe.edu

Academics

Oglethorpe awards bachelor's and master's **degrees**. Challenging opportunities include advanced placement credit, accelerated degree programs, student-designed majors, an honors program, double majors, independent study, and a senior project. Special programs include cooperative education, internships, summer session for credit, off-campus study, and study-abroad.

The most frequently chosen **baccalaureate** fields are business/marketing, social sciences and history, and communications/communication technologies. A complete listing of majors at Oglethorpe appears in the Majors Index beginning on page 460.

The **faculty** at Oglethorpe has 55 full-time members, 93% with terminal degrees. The student-faculty ratio is 11:1.

Students of Oglethorpe

The student body totals 1,029, of whom 945 are undergraduates. 65.2% are women and 34.8% are men. Students come from 36 states and territories and 21 other countries. 63% are from Georgia. 3.3% are international students. 20.2% are African American, 0.1% American Indian, 3.4% Asian American, and 3% Hispanic American. 87% returned for their sophomore year.

Facilities and Resources

Student rooms are linked to a campus network. 60 **computers** are available on campus for student use. The **library** has 150,000 books and 710 subscriptions.

Campus Life

There are 52 active organizations on campus, including a drama/theater group, newspaper, radio station, and choral group. 33% of eligible men and 28% of eligible women are members of national **fraternities** and national **sororities**.

Oglethorpe is a member of the NCAA (Division III). **Intercollegiate sports** include baseball (m), basketball, cross-country running, golf, soccer, tennis, track and field, volleyball (w).

Campus Safety

Student safety services include late-night transport/escort service, 24-hour emergency telephone alarm devices, 24-hour patrols by trained security personnel, student patrols, and electronically operated dormitory entrances.

Applying

Oglethorpe requires an essay, SAT I or ACT, a high school transcript, and 1 recommendation, and in some cases an interview. It recommends an interview and a minimum high school GPA of 2.5. Application deadline: rolling admissions; 9/1 for financial aid, with a 3/1 priority date. Deferred admission is possible.

> **I**t's not just the rigorous core curriculum, the small class discussions, and the motivating professors that make Oglethorpe different. It's the location—near the center of one of the country's most exciting, dynamic, and international cities, Atlanta. A distinctive honors program and a dynamic Rich Foundation Urban Leadership Program are gaining much recognition from city leaders as Oglethorpe helps connect students to the rich resources of Atlanta. Internships are available in every major and are very popular among the student body.

Getting in Last Year
746 applied
66% were accepted
167 enrolled (34%)
43% from top tenth of their h.s. class
3.67 average high school GPA
54% had SAT verbal scores over 600
40% had SAT math scores over 600
66% had ACT scores over 24
14% had SAT verbal scores over 700
6% had SAT math scores over 700
13% had ACT scores over 30

Graduation and After
54% graduated in 4 years
5% graduated in 5 years
34% pursued further study (14% business, 11% arts and sciences, 4% medicine)
70% had job offers within 6 months

Financial Matters
$20,370 tuition and fees (2003–04)
$6550 room and board
86% average percent of need met
$20,779 average financial aid amount received per undergraduate

OHIO NORTHERN UNIVERSITY

SMALL-TOWN SETTING ■ PRIVATE ■ INDEPENDENT RELIGIOUS ■ COED
ADA, OHIO

Web site: www.onu.edu
Contact: Mrs. Karen Condeni, Vice President of Admissions and Financial
 Aid, 525 South Main, Ada, OH 45810-1599
Telephone: 419-772-2260 or toll-free 888-408-4ONU **Fax:** 419-772-2313
E-mail: admissions-ug@onu.edu

National recognition, smaller classes, excellent facilities, and outstanding faculty members are just a few of the features that set Ohio Northern apart from other universities in the Midwest. The unique and dynamic partnership of the arts and sciences with professional programs is rich in cross-learning opportunities. But what makes ONU truly special is its students. They are scholars reflecting the values of service and leadership, which are the products of the individual attention and encouragement they receive from the faculty and staff of ONU.

Getting in Last Year
2,841 applied
80% were accepted
554 enrolled (24%)
40% from top tenth of their h.s. class
3.57 average high school GPA
37% had SAT verbal scores over 600
51% had SAT math scores over 600
63% had ACT scores over 24
6% had SAT verbal scores over 700
9% had SAT math scores over 700
10% had ACT scores over 30

Graduation and After
40% graduated in 4 years
19% graduated in 5 years
6% graduated in 6 years
26% pursued further study (29% arts and sciences, 20% engineering, 16% law)
77% had job offers within 6 months
269 organizations recruited on campus

Financial Matters
$24,645 tuition and fees (2003–04)
$6030 room and board
91% average percent of need met
$19,711 average financial aid amount received per undergraduate (2002–03 estimated)

Academics
Ohio Northern awards bachelor's, master's, and first-professional **degrees** and post-bachelor's certificates. Challenging opportunities include advanced placement credit, an honors program, double majors, independent study, and a senior project. Special programs include cooperative education, internships, summer session for credit, off-campus study, study-abroad, and Army and Air Force ROTC.

The most frequently chosen **baccalaureate** fields are engineering/engineering technologies, business/marketing, and health professions and related sciences. A complete listing of majors at Ohio Northern appears in the Majors Index beginning on page 460.

The **faculty** at Ohio Northern has 207 full-time members, 84% with terminal degrees. The student-faculty ratio is 13:1.

Students of Ohio Northern
The student body totals 3,451, of whom 2,214 are undergraduates. 47% are women and 53% are men. Students come from 37 states and territories. 87% are from Ohio. 0.6% are international students. 1.3% are African American, 0.1% American Indian, 0.6% Asian American, and 0.7% Hispanic American. 85% returned for their sophomore year.

Facilities and Resources
Student rooms are linked to a campus network. 550 **computers** are available on campus that provide access to the Internet. The 2 **libraries** have 250,231 books and 9,220 subscriptions.

Campus Life
There are 150 active organizations on campus, including a drama/theater group, newspaper, radio station, television station, choral group, and marching band. 17% of eligible men and 14% of eligible women are members of national **fraternities** and national **sororities**.

Ohio Northern is a member of the NCAA (Division III). **Intercollegiate sports** include baseball (m), basketball, cross-country running, football (m), golf, soccer, softball (w), swimming, tennis, track and field, volleyball (w), wrestling (m).

Campus Safety
Student safety services include late-night transport/escort service, 24-hour emergency telephone alarm devices, 24-hour patrols by trained security personnel, and electronically operated dormitory entrances.

Applying
Ohio Northern requires SAT I or ACT and a high school transcript, and in some cases 2 recommendations. It recommends an essay, an interview, and a minimum high school GPA of 2.5. Application deadline: 8/15; 6/1 for financial aid, with a 4/15 priority date. Early and deferred admission are possible.

THE OHIO STATE UNIVERSITY

URBAN SETTING ■ PUBLIC ■ STATE-SUPPORTED ■ COED
COLUMBUS, OHIO

Web site: www.osu.edu
Contact: Dr. Mabel G. Freeman, Assistant Vice President for Undergraduate
  Admissions and First Year Experience, Enarson Hall, 154 West 12th
  Avenue, Columbus, OH 43210
Telephone: 614-247-6281 **Fax:** 614-292-4818
E-mail: askabuckeye@osu.edu

Academics

Ohio State awards associate, bachelor's, master's, doctoral, and first-professional
degrees and post-bachelor's and post-master's certificates. Challenging opportunities
include advanced placement credit, accelerated degree programs, student-designed
majors, freshman honors college, an honors program, double majors, independent study,
and a senior project. Special programs include cooperative education, internships, summer session for credit, off-campus study, study-abroad, and Army and Air Force ROTC.

The most frequently chosen **baccalaureate** fields are business/marketing, social sciences and history, and home economics/vocational home economics. A complete listing
of majors at Ohio State appears in the Majors Index beginning on page 460.

The **faculty** at Ohio State has 2,752 full-time members, 99% with terminal degrees.
The student-faculty ratio is 14:1.

Students of Ohio State

The student body totals 50,731, of whom 37,605 are undergraduates. 47.7% are women
and 52.3% are men. Students come from 53 states and territories and 85 other countries.
89% are from Ohio. 3.9% are international students. 8.1% are African American, 0.4%
American Indian, 5.5% Asian American, and 2.3% Hispanic American. 88% returned for
their sophomore year.

Facilities and Resources

Student rooms are linked to a campus network. 1,000 **computers** are available on
campus that provide access to the Internet. The 13 **libraries** have 5,603,403 books and
43,086 subscriptions.

Campus Life

There are 750 active organizations on campus, including a drama/theater group,
newspaper, radio station, television station, choral group, and marching band. 5% of
eligible men and 6% of eligible women are members of national **fraternities**, national
sororities, local fraternities, and local sororities.

Ohio State is a member of the NCAA (Division I). **Intercollegiate sports** (some
offering scholarships) include baseball (m), basketball, cross-country running, fencing,
field hockey (w), football (m), golf, gymnastics, ice hockey, lacrosse, riflery, soccer,
softball (w), swimming, tennis, track and field, volleyball, wrestling (m).

Campus Safety

Student safety services include dorm entrances locked after 9 p.m, lighted pathways and
sidewalks, self-defense education, late-night transport/escort service, 24-hour emergency
telephone alarm devices, 24-hour patrols by trained security personnel, student patrols,
and electronically operated dormitory entrances.

Applying

Ohio State requires an essay, SAT I or ACT, and a high school transcript. Application
deadline: 2/1; 2/15 priority date for financial aid.

Getting in Last Year

20,122 applied
72% were accepted
6,390 enrolled (44%)
33% from top tenth of their h.s. class
43% had SAT verbal scores over 600
53% had SAT math scores over 600
70% had ACT scores over 24
8% had SAT verbal scores over 700
12% had SAT math scores over 700
12% had ACT scores over 30
102 National Merit Scholars
240 valedictorians

Graduation and After

29% graduated in 4 years
27% graduated in 5 years
6% graduated in 6 years
10% pursued further study

Financial Matters

$6651 resident tuition and fees (2003–04)
$16,638 nonresident tuition and fees (2003–04)
$6429 room and board
75% average percent of need met
$8211 average financial aid amount received per undergraduate (2002–03 estimated)

OHIO WESLEYAN UNIVERSITY

SMALL-TOWN SETTING ■ PRIVATE ■ INDEPENDENT RELIGIOUS ■ COED
DELAWARE, OHIO

Web site: web.owu.edu
Contact: Ms. Carol Wheatley, Director of Admission, 61 South Sandusky
  Street, Delaware, OH 43015
Telephone: 740-368-3020 or toll-free 800-922-8953 **Fax:** 740-368-3314
E-mail: owuadmit@owu.edu

Ohio Wesleyan is a selective national liberal arts university in Delaware, Ohio. Personalized honors study offers unusual opportunities to talented students while internships and research are encouraged of all students. Small classes afford personalized attention from professors. Students can choose from 81 areas of study in the arts, humanities, natural sciences, and social sciences, and can participate in more than 80 campus organizations, community service groups, and NCAA Division III athletic teams. The University's distinctive commitment to public service is reflected in annual student work trips across the U.S. and abroad, the acclaimed Sagan National Colloquium, and extensive community service opportunities.

Getting in Last Year
2,580 applied
74% were accepted
567 enrolled (30%)
32% from top tenth of their h.s. class
3.33 average high school GPA
55% had SAT verbal scores over 600
53% had SAT math scores over 600
84% had ACT scores over 24
14% had SAT verbal scores over 700
11% had SAT math scores over 700
20% had ACT scores over 30
17 National Merit Scholars
19 valedictorians

Graduation and After
58% graduated in 4 years
6% graduated in 5 years
2% graduated in 6 years
32% pursued further study (13% arts and
  sciences, 6% education, 6% medicine)
95% had job offers within 6 months
30 organizations recruited on campus

Financial Matters
$25,440 tuition and fees (2003–04)
$7110 room and board
90% average percent of need met
$22,149 average financial aid amount received
  per undergraduate

Academics
Ohio Wesleyan awards bachelor's **degrees**. Challenging opportunities include advanced placement credit, student-designed majors, freshman honors college, an honors program, double majors, independent study, and a senior project. Special programs include internships, summer session for credit, off-campus study, study-abroad, and Army ROTC.

The most frequently chosen **baccalaureate** fields are social sciences and history, business/marketing, and psychology. A complete listing of majors at Ohio Wesleyan appears in the Majors Index beginning on page 460.

The **faculty** at Ohio Wesleyan has 129 full-time members, 98% with terminal degrees. The student-faculty ratio is 13:1.

Students of Ohio Wesleyan
The student body is made up of 1,929 undergraduates. 54% are women and 46% are men. Students come from 44 states and territories and 45 other countries. 59% are from Ohio. 10% are international students. 4.8% are African American, 0.1% American Indian, 1.7% Asian American, and 1.4% Hispanic American. 78% returned for their sophomore year.

Facilities and Resources
Student rooms are linked to a campus network. 295 **computers** are available on campus that provide access to the Internet. The 4 **libraries** have 420,936 books and 1,084 subscriptions.

Campus Life
There are 85 active organizations on campus, including a drama/theater group, newspaper, radio station, and choral group. 44% of eligible men and 34% of eligible women are members of national **fraternities** and national **sororities**.

Ohio Wesleyan is a member of the NCAA (Division III). **Intercollegiate sports** include baseball (m), basketball, cross-country running, field hockey (w), football (m), golf (m), lacrosse, soccer, softball (w), swimming, tennis, track and field, volleyball (w).

Campus Safety
Student safety services include late-night transport/escort service, 24-hour emergency telephone alarm devices, 24-hour patrols by trained security personnel, and electronically operated dormitory entrances.

Applying
Ohio Wesleyan requires an essay, SAT I or ACT, a high school transcript, and 1 recommendation. It recommends SAT II Subject Tests, an interview, 2 recommendations, and a minimum high school GPA of 2.5. Application deadline: 3/1; 5/15 for financial aid, with a 3/15 priority date. Early and deferred admission are possible.

OKLAHOMA BAPTIST UNIVERSITY

SMALL-TOWN SETTING ■ PRIVATE ■ INDEPENDENT RELIGIOUS ■ COED
SHAWNEE, OKLAHOMA

Web site: www.okbu.edu
Contact: Mr. Trent Argo, Dean of Enrollment Management, Box 61174,
Shawnee, OK 74804
Telephone: 405-878-2033 or toll-free 800-654-3285 **Fax:** 405-878-2046
E-mail: admissions@mail.okbu.edu

Academics

OBU awards bachelor's and master's **degrees**. Challenging opportunities include
advanced placement credit, student-designed majors, an honors program, double majors,
independent study, and a senior project. Special programs include cooperative education,
internships, summer session for credit, off-campus study, study-abroad, and Air Force
ROTC.

The most frequently chosen **baccalaureate** fields are education, health professions
and related sciences, and business/marketing. A complete listing of majors at OBU appears in the Majors Index beginning on page 460.

The **faculty** at OBU has 119 members. The student-faculty ratio is 15:1.

Students of OBU

The student body totals 1,883, of whom 1,866 are undergraduates. 55.6% are women
and 44.4% are men. Students come from 42 states and territories and 17 other countries.
61% are from Oklahoma. 74% returned for their sophomore year.

Facilities and Resources

Student rooms are linked to a campus network. 170 **computers** are available on campus
that provide access to the Internet. The **library** has 230,000 books and 1,800 subscriptions.

Campus Life

There are 50 active organizations on campus, including a drama/theater group,
newspaper, television station, and choral group. 10% of eligible men and 10% of eligible
women are members of local **fraternities** and local **sororities**.

OBU is a member of the NAIA. **Intercollegiate sports** (some offering scholarships)
include baseball (m), basketball, cross-country running, golf, softball (w), tennis, track
and field.

Campus Safety

Student safety services include late-night transport/escort service, 24-hour emergency
telephone alarm devices, 24-hour patrols by trained security personnel, and electronically operated dormitory entrances.

Applying

OBU requires SAT I or ACT, a high school transcript, and a minimum high school GPA
of 2.5, and in some cases an essay, an interview, and recommendations. Application
deadline: rolling admissions; 3/1 priority date for financial aid. Early and deferred admission are possible.

Getting in Last Year
1,098 applied
85% were accepted
411 enrolled (44%)
45% from top tenth of their h.s. class
3.65 average high school GPA
48% had SAT verbal scores over 600
38% had SAT math scores over 600
55% had ACT scores over 24
12% had SAT verbal scores over 700
9% had SAT math scores over 700
10% had ACT scores over 30
6 National Merit Scholars
42 valedictorians

Graduation and After
35% graduated in 4 years
14% graduated in 5 years
4% graduated in 6 years
Graduates pursuing further study: 16% theology, 12% arts and sciences, 5% business
45 organizations recruited on campus

Financial Matters
$11,580 tuition and fees (2003–04)
$3640 room and board
70% average percent of need met
$11,142 average financial aid amount received
per undergraduate (2002–03 estimated)

OKLAHOMA CITY UNIVERSITY

URBAN SETTING ■ PRIVATE ■ INDEPENDENT RELIGIOUS ■ COED
OKLAHOMA CITY, OKLAHOMA

Web site: www.okcu.edu
Contact: Ms. Shery Boyles, Director of Admissions, 2501 North Blackwelder, Oklahoma City, OK 73106-1402
Telephone: 405-521-5050 or toll-free 800-633-7242 **Fax:** 405-521-5916
E-mail: uadmissions@okcu.edu

Getting in Last Year
822 applied
78% were accepted
319 enrolled (50%)
34% from top tenth of their h.s. class
3.51 average high school GPA
33% had SAT verbal scores over 600
37% had SAT math scores over 600
54% had ACT scores over 24
1% had SAT verbal scores over 700
4% had SAT math scores over 700
18% had ACT scores over 30

Graduation and After
40% graduated in 4 years
12% graduated in 5 years
1% graduated in 6 years
64 organizations recruited on campus

Financial Matters
$14,030 tuition and fees (2003–04)
$5550 room and board
82% average percent of need met
$10,680 average financial aid amount received per undergraduate (2002–03)

Academics

OCU awards bachelor's, master's, and first-professional **degrees**. Challenging opportunities include advanced placement credit, accelerated degree programs, student-designed majors, an honors program, double majors, independent study, and a senior project. Special programs include cooperative education, internships, summer session for credit, off-campus study, study-abroad, and Army and Air Force ROTC.

The most frequently chosen **baccalaureate** fields are liberal arts/general studies, visual/performing arts, and business/marketing. A complete listing of majors at OCU appears in the Majors Index beginning on page 460.

The **faculty** at OCU has 151 full-time members, 89% with terminal degrees. The student-faculty ratio is 11:1.

Students of OCU

The student body totals 3,668, of whom 1,793 are undergraduates. 61.9% are women and 38.1% are men. Students come from 48 states and territories and 67 other countries. 69% are from Oklahoma. 22.9% are international students. 6.9% are African American, 3.7% American Indian, 1.7% Asian American, and 4% Hispanic American. 73% returned for their sophomore year.

Facilities and Resources

Student rooms are linked to a campus network. 264 **computers** are available on campus that provide access to the Internet. The 2 **libraries** have 321,093 books and 5,498 subscriptions.

Campus Life

There are 42 active organizations on campus, including a drama/theater group, newspaper, television station, and choral group. 11% of eligible men and 15% of eligible women are members of national **fraternities** and national **sororities**.

OCU is a member of the NAIA. **Intercollegiate sports** (some offering scholarships) include baseball (m), basketball, cheerleading, crew, golf, soccer, softball (w).

Campus Safety

Student safety services include Operation ID, late-night transport/escort service, 24-hour emergency telephone alarm devices, 24-hour patrols by trained security personnel, and student patrols.

Applying

OCU requires SAT I or ACT, a high school transcript, and a minimum high school GPA of 3.0, and in some cases an interview and audition for music and dance programs. Application deadline: 8/20; 3/1 priority date for financial aid. Deferred admission is possible.

OKLAHOMA STATE UNIVERSITY

SMALL-TOWN SETTING ■ PUBLIC ■ STATE-SUPPORTED ■ COED
STILLWATER, OKLAHOMA

Web site: www.okstate.edu
Contact: Ms. Paulette Cundiff, Coordinator of Admissions Processing, 324
Student Union, Stillwater, OK 74078
Telephone: 405-744-6858 or toll-free 800-233-5019 (in-state), 800-852-1255
(out-of-state) **Fax:** 405-744-5285
E-mail: admit@okstate.edu

Academics

OSU awards bachelor's, master's, doctoral, and first-professional **degrees**. Challenging
opportunities include advanced placement credit, accelerated degree programs, student-
designed majors, freshman honors college, an honors program, double majors,
independent study, and a senior project. Special programs include cooperative education,
internships, summer session for credit, off-campus study, study-abroad, and Army and
Air Force ROTC.

The most frequently chosen **baccalaureate** fields are business/marketing, engineer-
ing/engineering technologies, and education. A complete listing of majors at OSU appears in the Majors Index beginning on page 460.

The **faculty** at OSU has 905 full-time members, 91% with terminal degrees. The
student-faculty ratio is 21:1.

Students of OSU

The student body totals 23,577, of whom 18,689 are undergraduates. 49% are women
and 51% are men. Students come from 50 states and territories and 122 other countries.
87% are from Oklahoma. 4.5% are international students. 3.5% are African American,
8.6% American Indian, 1.5% Asian American, and 2% Hispanic American. 80%
returned for their sophomore year.

Facilities and Resources

Student rooms are linked to a campus network. 2,000 **computers** are available on
campus that provide access to the Internet. The 5 **libraries** have 2,409,875 books and
24,806 subscriptions.

Campus Life

There are 360 active organizations on campus, including a drama/theater group,
newspaper, radio station, television station, choral group, and marching band. 18% of
eligible men and 24% of eligible women are members of national **fraternities** and
national **sororities**.

OSU is a member of the NCAA (Division I). **Intercollegiate sports** (some offering
scholarships) include baseball (m), basketball, cross-country running, equestrian sports
(w), football (m), golf, soccer (w), softball (w), tennis, track and field, wrestling (m).

Campus Safety

Student safety services include 24-hour emergency telephone alarm devices, 24-hour
patrols by trained security personnel, student patrols, and electronically operated dormitory entrances.

Applying

OSU requires SAT I or ACT, a high school transcript, class rank, and a minimum high
school GPA of 3.0, and in some cases an interview. It recommends ACT. Application
deadline: rolling admissions. Early admission is possible.

A long with academic
excellence, Oklahoma State
University (OSU)
emphasizes student success,
leadership opportunities, and career
preparation. OSU has a nationally
recognized Honors College, a library
with more than 2 million volumes,
and an extensive freshman research
scholars program. OSU is a Truman
Honor Institution and has been
recognized for its success in the
Rhodes, Marshall, and Goldwater
Scholarship competitions. Students
can choose from more than 200
majors at a comprehensive research
university that prides itself on a
friendly atmosphere and low
student-faculty member ratio. The
University has spent more than
$200 million in recent years on new
classrooms and laboratories,
computer labs, and apartment-style
housing.

Getting in Last Year
6,629 applied
89% were accepted
3,490 enrolled (59%)
25% from top tenth of their h.s. class
3.49 average high school GPA
26% had SAT verbal scores over 600
31% had SAT math scores over 600
47% had ACT scores over 24
4% had SAT verbal scores over 700
5% had SAT math scores over 700
8% had ACT scores over 30
19 National Merit Scholars
325 valedictorians

Graduation and After
25% graduated in 4 years
27% graduated in 5 years
7% graduated in 6 years
68% had job offers within 6 months
406 organizations recruited on campus

Financial Matters
$3665 resident tuition and fees (2003–04)
$9611 nonresident tuition and fees (2003–04)
$5468 room and board
82% average percent of need met
$7550 average financial aid amount received
per undergraduate (2001–02)

Oral Roberts University

Urban setting ■ Private ■ Independent Religious ■ Coed
Tulsa, Oklahoma

Getting in Last Year
1,363 applied
64% were accepted
644 enrolled (74%)
26% from top tenth of their h.s. class
3.90 average high school GPA
25% had SAT verbal scores over 600
22% had SAT math scores over 600
5% had SAT verbal scores over 700
3% had SAT math scores over 700
6 National Merit Scholars

Graduation and After
38% graduated in 4 years
13% graduated in 5 years
3% graduated in 6 years
70 organizations recruited on campus

Financial Matters
$13,970 tuition and fees (2003–04)
$5900 room and board
90% average percent of need met
$12,448 average financial aid amount received
    per undergraduate (2001–02)

Web site: www.oru.edu
Contact: Chris Miller, Director of Undergraduate Admissions, 7777 South
    Lewis Avenue, Tulsa, OK 74171
Telephone: 918-495-6518 or toll-free 800-678-8876 **Fax:** 918-495-6222
E-mail: admissions@oru.edu

Academics
ORU awards bachelor's, master's, doctoral, and first-professional **degrees**. Challenging opportunities include advanced placement credit, student-designed majors, freshman honors college, an honors program, double majors, independent study, and a senior project. Special programs include internships, summer session for credit, off-campus study, study-abroad, and Air Force ROTC.

The most frequently chosen **baccalaureate** fields are business/marketing, communications/communication technologies, and education. A complete listing of majors at ORU appears in the Majors Index beginning on page 460.

The **faculty** at ORU has 198 full-time members, 57% with terminal degrees. The student-faculty ratio is 16:1.

Students of ORU
The student body totals 4,117, of whom 3,363 are undergraduates. 61% are women and 39% are men. 36% are from Oklahoma. 3.2% are international students. 16.2% are African American, 1.8% American Indian, 2.4% Asian American, and 4.6% Hispanic American. 82% returned for their sophomore year.

Facilities and Resources
Student rooms are linked to a campus network. 253 **computers** are available on campus that provide access to the Internet. The 2 **libraries** have 216,691 books and 600 subscriptions.

Campus Life
There are 37 active organizations on campus, including a drama/theater group, newspaper, radio station, television station, and choral group. No national or local **fraternities** or **sororities**.

ORU is a member of the NCAA (Division I). **Intercollegiate sports** (some offering scholarships) include baseball (m), basketball, cross-country running, golf, soccer, tennis, track and field, volleyball (w).

Campus Safety
Student safety services include late-night transport/escort service, 24-hour emergency telephone alarm devices, and 24-hour patrols by trained security personnel.

Applying
ORU requires an essay, SAT I or ACT, a high school transcript, 1 recommendation, proof of immunization, and a minimum high school GPA of 2.0, and in some cases an interview. Application deadline: rolling admissions; 3/15 priority date for financial aid. Early and deferred admission are possible.

OUACHITA BAPTIST UNIVERSITY

SMALL-TOWN SETTING ■ PRIVATE ■ INDEPENDENT RELIGIOUS ■ COED
ARKADELPHIA, ARKANSAS

Web site: www.obu.edu
Contact: Mr. David Goodman, Director of Admissions Counseling, OBU Box 3776, Arkadelphia, AR 71998-0001
Telephone: 870-245-5110 or toll-free 800-342-5628 (in-state) **Fax:** 870-245-5500
E-mail: goodmand@obu.edu

Academics

Ouachita awards associate and bachelor's **degrees**. Challenging opportunities include advanced placement credit, accelerated degree programs, an honors program, double majors, and a senior project. Special programs include cooperative education, internships, summer session for credit, off-campus study, study-abroad, and Army ROTC.

The most frequently chosen **baccalaureate** fields are business/marketing, education, and social sciences and history. A complete listing of majors at Ouachita appears in the Majors Index beginning on page 460.

The **faculty** at Ouachita has 113 full-time members, 81% with terminal degrees. The student-faculty ratio is 13:1.

Students of Ouachita

The student body is made up of 1,530 undergraduates. 54% are women and 46% are men. Students come from 33 states and territories. 54% are from Arkansas. 3.1% are international students. 6% are African American, 0.3% American Indian, 0.3% Asian American, and 0.9% Hispanic American. 79% returned for their sophomore year.

Facilities and Resources

Student rooms are linked to a campus network. 189 **computers** are available on campus that provide access to the Internet. The 2 **libraries** have 139,278 books and 1,931 subscriptions.

Campus Life

There are 60 active organizations on campus, including a drama/theater group, newspaper, television station, choral group, and marching band. 20% of eligible men and 25% of eligible women are members of local **fraternities** and local **sororities**.

Ouachita is a member of the NCAA (Division II). **Intercollegiate sports** (some offering scholarships) include baseball (m), basketball, cross-country running (w), football (m), golf (m), soccer, softball (w), swimming, tennis, volleyball (w).

Campus Safety

Student safety services include 24-hour emergency telephone alarm devices, 24-hour patrols by trained security personnel, and electronically operated dormitory entrances.

Applying

Ouachita requires SAT I or ACT, a high school transcript, and a minimum high school GPA of 2.75. It recommends an interview. Application deadline: 8/15; 6/1 for financial aid, with a 2/15 priority date. Early and deferred admission are possible.

Getting in Last Year

879 applied
80% were accepted
343 enrolled (49%)
31% from top tenth of their h.s. class
3.48 average high school GPA
32% had SAT verbal scores over 600
29% had SAT math scores over 600
50% had ACT scores over 24
8% had SAT verbal scores over 700
7% had SAT math scores over 700
6% had ACT scores over 30
6 National Merit Scholars
10 valedictorians

Graduation and After

49% graduated in 4 years
7% graduated in 5 years
2% graduated in 6 years
25% pursued further study (5% theology, 4% medicine, 3% education)
60% had job offers within 6 months
15 organizations recruited on campus

Financial Matters

$14,100 tuition and fees (2003–04)
$4800 room and board
97% average percent of need met
$12,033 average financial aid amount received per undergraduate (2001–02)

PACIFIC LUTHERAN UNIVERSITY

SUBURBAN SETTING ■ PRIVATE ■ INDEPENDENT RELIGIOUS ■ COED
TACOMA, WASHINGTON

Web site: www.plu.edu
Contact: Office of Admissions, Tacoma, WA 98447
Telephone: 253-535-7151 or toll-free 800-274-6758 Fax: 253-536-5136
E-mail: admissions@plu.edu

Getting in Last Year

1,973 applied
80% were accepted
694 enrolled (44%)
39% from top tenth of their h.s. class
3.62 average high school GPA
38% had SAT verbal scores over 600
35% had SAT math scores over 600
61% had ACT scores over 24
8% had SAT verbal scores over 700
3% had SAT math scores over 700
13% had ACT scores over 30
5 National Merit Scholars
28 valedictorians

Graduation and After

45% graduated in 4 years
20% graduated in 5 years
3% graduated in 6 years
13% pursued further study
75% had job offers within 6 months
75 organizations recruited on campus

Financial Matters

$19,610 tuition and fees (2003–04)
$6105 room and board
88% average percent of need met
$17,229 average financial aid amount received
   per undergraduate

Academics

PLU awards bachelor's and master's **degrees** and post-bachelor's and post-master's certificates. Challenging opportunities include advanced placement credit, accelerated degree programs, student-designed majors, an honors program, double majors, independent study, and a senior project. Special programs include cooperative education, internships, summer session for credit, study-abroad, and Army ROTC.

The most frequently chosen **baccalaureate** fields are business/marketing, education, and social sciences and history. A complete listing of majors at PLU appears in the Majors Index beginning on page 460.

The **faculty** at PLU has 235 full-time members, 90% with terminal degrees. The student-faculty ratio is 13:1.

Students of PLU

The student body totals 3,462, of whom 3,185 are undergraduates. 62.9% are women and 37.1% are men. Students come from 42 states and territories and 23 other countries. 74% are from Washington. 5% are international students. 2% are African American, 0.7% American Indian, 5.4% Asian American, and 2.1% Hispanic American. 83% returned for their sophomore year.

Facilities and Resources

Student rooms are linked to a campus network. 200 **computers** are available on campus that provide access to the Internet. The **library** has 367,628 books and 1,949 subscriptions.

Campus Life

There are 45 active organizations on campus, including a drama/theater group, newspaper, radio station, television station, and choral group. PLU has Language and Culture hall.

PLU is a member of the NCAA (Division III). **Intercollegiate sports** include baseball (m), basketball, cheerleading, crew, cross-country running, football (m), golf, soccer, softball (w), swimming, tennis, track and field, volleyball (w).

Campus Safety

Student safety services include late-night transport/escort service, 24-hour emergency telephone alarm devices, 24-hour patrols by trained security personnel, and student patrols.

Applying

PLU requires an essay, SAT I or ACT, a high school transcript, 1 recommendation, and a minimum high school GPA of 2.5, and in some cases an interview. Application deadline: rolling admissions; 3/1 priority date for financial aid. Early and deferred admission are possible.

PACIFIC UNIVERSITY

SMALL-TOWN SETTING ■ PRIVATE ■ INDEPENDENT ■ COED
FOREST GROVE, OREGON

Web site: www.pacificu.edu
Contact: Mr. Ian Symmonds, Executive Director of Admissions, 2043 College
    Way, Forest Grove, OR 97116-1797
Telephone: 503-352-2218 or toll-free 877-722-8648 **Fax:** 503-352-2975
E-mail: admissions@pacificu.edu

Academics

Pacific awards bachelor's, master's, doctoral, and first-professional **degrees**. Challenging opportunities include advanced placement credit, accelerated degree programs, an honors program, double majors, independent study, and a senior project. Special programs include internships, summer session for credit, off-campus study, study-abroad, and Army and Air Force ROTC.

The most frequently chosen **baccalaureate** fields are business/marketing, education, and parks and recreation. A complete listing of majors at Pacific appears in the Majors Index beginning on page 460.

The **faculty** at Pacific has 84 full-time members, 86% with terminal degrees. The student-faculty ratio is 11:1.

Students of Pacific

The student body totals 2,420, of whom 1,203 are undergraduates. 60.8% are women and 39.2% are men. Students come from 35 states and territories and 6 other countries. 53% are from Oregon. 0.4% are international students. 0.9% are African American, 0.9% American Indian, 19.2% Asian American, and 2.9% Hispanic American. 81% returned for their sophomore year.

Facilities and Resources

Student rooms are linked to a campus network. 150 **computers** are available on campus that provide access to email, web space and the Internet. The **library** has 244,691 books and 1,180 subscriptions.

Campus Life

There are 60 active organizations on campus, including a drama/theater group, newspaper, radio station, and choral group. 10% of eligible men and 17% of eligible women are members of local **fraternities** and local **sororities**.

Pacific is a member of the NCAA (Division III). **Intercollegiate sports** include baseball (m), basketball, cross-country running, golf, soccer, softball (w), swimming (w), tennis, track and field, volleyball (w), wrestling.

Campus Safety

Student safety services include late-night transport/escort service, 24-hour emergency telephone alarm devices, and 24-hour patrols by trained security personnel.

Applying

Pacific requires an essay, SAT I or ACT, a high school transcript, 1 recommendation, and a minimum high school GPA of 3.0. It recommends an interview. Application deadline: 8/15; 2/15 priority date for financial aid. Deferred admission is possible.

Getting in Last Year

1,214 applied
84% were accepted
303 enrolled (30%)
32% from top tenth of their h.s. class
3.55 average high school GPA
32% had SAT verbal scores over 600
31% had SAT math scores over 600
51% had ACT scores over 24
1% had SAT verbal scores over 700
3% had SAT math scores over 700
6% had ACT scores over 30
13 valedictorians

Graduation and After

52% graduated in 4 years
7% graduated in 5 years
40% pursued further study (10% arts and
    sciences, 10% education, 10% medicine)
50% had job offers within 6 months
300 organizations recruited on campus

Financial Matters

$19,890 tuition and fees (2003–04)
$5540 room and board
89% average percent of need met
$17,369 average financial aid amount received
    per undergraduate

PEABODY CONSERVATORY OF MUSIC OF THE JOHNS HOPKINS UNIVERSITY

URBAN SETTING ■ PRIVATE ■ INDEPENDENT ■ COED
BALTIMORE, MARYLAND

Web site: www.peabody.jhu.edu
Contact: Mr. David Lane, Director of Admissions, Peabody Conservatory Admissions Office, One East Mount Vernon Place, Baltimore, MD 21202-2397
Telephone: 410-659-8110 or toll-free 800-368-2521 (out-of-state)

Getting in Last Year

567 applied
49% were accepted
77 enrolled (28%)
59% had SAT verbal scores over 600
52% had SAT math scores over 600
22% had SAT verbal scores over 700
22% had SAT math scores over 700

Graduation and After

63% graduated in 4 years
10% graduated in 5 years
3% graduated in 6 years
20% had job offers within 6 months
13 organizations recruited on campus

Financial Matters

$26,150 tuition and fees (2003–04)
$8950 room and board
85% average percent of need met
$15,856 average financial aid amount received per undergraduate (2002–03)

Academics

Peabody Conservatory awards bachelor's, master's, and doctoral **degrees** and post-bachelor's certificates. Challenging opportunities include advanced placement credit, accelerated degree programs, an honors program, double majors, and independent study. Special programs include internships and off-campus study.

The most frequently chosen **baccalaureate** field is visual/performing arts. A complete listing of majors at Peabody Conservatory appears in the Majors Index beginning on page 460.

The **faculty** at Peabody Conservatory has 162 members, 24% with terminal degrees. The student-faculty ratio is 4:1.

Students of Peabody Conservatory

The student body totals 639, of whom 302 are undergraduates. 47.4% are women and 52.6% are men. Students come from 38 states and territories and 9 other countries. 33% are from Maryland. 13.3% are international students. 4.3% are African American, 13.3% Asian American, and 2.3% Hispanic American. 78% returned for their sophomore year.

Facilities and Resources

Student rooms are linked to a campus network. 40 **computers** are available on campus that provide access to word processing, music processing and the Internet. The **library** has 82,816 books and 261 subscriptions.

Campus Life

There are 84 active organizations on campus, including a choral group. No national or local **fraternities** or **sororities**.

This institution has no intercollegiate sports.

Campus Safety

Student safety services include late-night transport/escort service, 24-hour emergency telephone alarm devices, 24-hour patrols by trained security personnel, and electronically operated dormitory entrances.

Applying

Peabody Conservatory requires an essay, a high school transcript, an interview, 3 recommendations, and audition, and in some cases SAT I or ACT. Application deadline: 12/15; 3/1 priority date for financial aid.

THE PENNSYLVANIA STATE UNIVERSITY
UNIVERSITY PARK CAMPUS

SMALL-TOWN SETTING ■ PUBLIC ■ STATE-RELATED ■ COED
UNIVERSITY PARK, PENNSYLVANIA

Web site: www.psu.edu
Contact: Undergraduate Admissions Office, 201 Shields Building, Box 3000, University Park, PA 16804-3000
Telephone: 814-865-5471 **Fax:** 814-863-7590
E-mail: admissions@psu.edu

Academics

Penn State awards associate, bachelor's, master's, and doctoral **degrees** and post-bachelor's certificates. Challenging opportunities include advanced placement credit, accelerated degree programs, student-designed majors, freshman honors college, an honors program, double majors, independent study, and a senior project. Special programs include cooperative education, internships, summer session for credit, study-abroad, and Army, Navy and Air Force ROTC.

The most frequently chosen **baccalaureate** fields are business/marketing, engineering/engineering technologies, and communications/communication technologies. A complete listing of majors at Penn State appears in the Majors Index beginning on page 460.

The **faculty** at Penn State has 2,191 full-time members, 77% with terminal degrees. The student-faculty ratio is 17:1.

Students of Penn State

The student body totals 41,795, of whom 35,002 are undergraduates. 46.8% are women and 53.2% are men. Students come from 54 states and territories. 75% are from Pennsylvania. 2.3% are international students. 4.2% are African American, 0.1% American Indian, 5.6% Asian American, and 3.3% Hispanic American. 91% returned for their sophomore year.

Facilities and Resources

Student rooms are linked to a campus network. 3,589 **computers** are available on campus that provide access to the Internet. The 8 **libraries** have 3,117,880 books and 36,856 subscriptions.

Campus Life

There are 400 active organizations on campus, including a drama/theater group, newspaper, radio station, television station, choral group, and marching band. 13% of eligible men and 10% of eligible women are members of national **fraternities** and national **sororities**.

Penn State is a member of the NCAA (Division I). **Intercollegiate sports** (some offering scholarships) include baseball (m), basketball, cheerleading, cross-country running, fencing, field hockey (w), football (m), golf, gymnastics, lacrosse, soccer, softball (w), swimming, tennis, track and field, volleyball, wrestling (m).

Campus Safety

Student safety services include late-night transport/escort service, 24-hour emergency telephone alarm devices, 24-hour patrols by trained security personnel, student patrols, and electronically operated dormitory entrances.

Applying

Penn State requires SAT I or ACT, a high school transcript, and a minimum high school GPA of 2.0, and in some cases an interview and 1 recommendation. It recommends an essay. Application deadline: rolling admissions. Early and deferred admission are possible.

Getting in Last Year
31,264 applied
55% were accepted
6,048 enrolled (35%)
43% from top tenth of their h.s. class
3.54 average high school GPA
44% had SAT verbal scores over 600
62% had SAT math scores over 600
8% had SAT verbal scores over 700
15% had SAT math scores over 700

Graduation and After
44% graduated in 4 years
33% graduated in 5 years
3% graduated in 6 years
70% had job offers within 6 months
970 organizations recruited on campus

Financial Matters
$9706 resident tuition and fees (2003–04)
$19,328 nonresident tuition and fees (2003–04)
$5940 room and board
72% average percent of need met
$11,831 average financial aid amount received per undergraduate (2002–03)

PEPPERDINE UNIVERSITY

SMALL-TOWN SETTING ■ PRIVATE ■ INDEPENDENT RELIGIOUS ■ COED
MALIBU, CALIFORNIA

Web site: www.pepperdine.edu
Contact: Mr. Paul A. Long, Dean of Admission and Enrollment Management,
 24255 Pacific Coast Highway, Malibu, CA 90263-4392
Telephone: 310-506-4392 **Fax:** 310-506-4861
E-mail: admission-seaver@pepperdine.edu

Getting in Last Year
5,503 applied
37% were accepted
802 enrolled (39%)
72% from top tenth of their h.s. class
3.61 average high school GPA
48% had SAT verbal scores over 600
55% had SAT math scores over 600
72% had ACT scores over 24
8% had SAT verbal scores over 700
12% had SAT math scores over 700
17% had ACT scores over 30

Graduation and After
63% pursued further study
40% had job offers within 6 months
65 organizations recruited on campus

Financial Matters
$27,520 tuition and fees (2003–04)
$8270 room and board
89% average percent of need met
$22,611 average financial aid amount received
 per undergraduate (2001–02)

Academics
Pepperdine awards bachelor's, master's, doctoral, and first-professional **degrees**. Challenging opportunities include advanced placement credit, accelerated degree programs, student-designed majors, an honors program, double majors, independent study, and a senior project. Special programs include internships, summer session for credit, study-abroad, and Army, Navy and Air Force ROTC.

The most frequently chosen **baccalaureate** fields are communications/communication technologies, business/marketing, and social sciences and history. A complete listing of majors at Pepperdine appears in the Majors Index beginning on page 460.

The **faculty** at Pepperdine has 366 full-time members, 97% with terminal degrees. The student-faculty ratio is 12:1.

Students of Pepperdine
The student body totals 7,791, of whom 3,153 are undergraduates. 56.1% are women and 43.9% are men. Students come from 51 states and territories and 70 other countries. 52% are from California. 6.7% are international students. 6.8% are African American, 1.5% American Indian, 9.4% Asian American, and 11.1% Hispanic American. 87% returned for their sophomore year.

Facilities and Resources
Student rooms are linked to a campus network. 292 **computers** are available on campus that provide access to the Internet. The 3 **libraries** have 315,078 books and 3,182 subscriptions.

Campus Life
There are 50 active organizations on campus, including a drama/theater group, newspaper, radio station, television station, and choral group. 25% of eligible men and 25% of eligible women are members of national **fraternities** and national **sororities**.

Pepperdine is a member of the NCAA (Division I). **Intercollegiate sports** (some offering scholarships) include baseball (m), basketball, cheerleading, cross-country running, golf, soccer (w), swimming (w), tennis, volleyball, water polo (m).

Campus Safety
Student safety services include front gate security, 24-hour security in residence halls, controlled access, crime prevention programs, late-night transport/escort service, 24-hour emergency telephone alarm devices, 24-hour patrols by trained security personnel, and student patrols.

Applying
Pepperdine requires an essay, SAT I or ACT, a high school transcript, and 2 recommendations. It recommends an interview. Application deadline: 1/15; 2/15 priority date for financial aid.

PITZER COLLEGE

SUBURBAN SETTING ■ PRIVATE ■ INDEPENDENT ■ COED
CLAREMONT, CALIFORNIA

Web site: www.pitzer.edu
Contact: Dr. Arnaldo Rodriguez, Vice President for Admission and Financial
Aid, 1050 North Mills Avenue, Claremont, CA 91711-6101
Telephone: 909-621-8129 or toll-free 800-748-9371 **Fax:** 909-621-8770
E-mail: admission@pitzer.edu

Academics

Pitzer awards bachelor's **degrees**. Challenging opportunities include advanced place-ment credit, student-designed majors, an honors program, double majors, independent study, and a senior project. Special programs include cooperative education, internships, off-campus study, and study-abroad.

The most frequently chosen **baccalaureate** fields are social sciences and history, psychology, and English. A complete listing of majors at Pitzer appears in the Majors Index beginning on page 460.

The **faculty** at Pitzer has 71 full-time members, 96% with terminal degrees. The student-faculty ratio is 11:1.

Students of Pitzer

The student body is made up of 942 undergraduates. 59.6% are women and 40.4% are men. Students come from 44 states and territories and 11 other countries. 53% are from California. 3% are international students. 5.4% are African American, 1.1% American Indian, 9.8% Asian American, and 13% Hispanic American. 84% returned for their sophomore year.

Facilities and Resources

Student rooms are linked to a campus network. 100 **computers** are available on campus that provide access to the Internet. The 4 **libraries** have 2,000,000 books and 6,000 subscriptions.

Campus Life

There are 75 active organizations on campus, including a drama/theater group, radio station, and choral group. No national or local **fraternities** or **sororities**.

Pitzer is a member of the NCAA (Division III). **Intercollegiate sports** include baseball (m), basketball, cross-country running, football (m), golf (m), soccer, softball (w), swimming, tennis, track and field, volleyball (w), water polo, wrestling (m).

Campus Safety

Student safety services include late-night transport/escort service, 24-hour emergency telephone alarm devices, 24-hour patrols by trained security personnel, and electroni-cally operated dormitory entrances.

Applying

Pitzer requires an essay, a high school transcript, and 3 recommendations, and in some cases SAT I or ACT. It recommends an interview. Application deadline: 1/15; 2/1 for financial aid. Early and deferred admission are possible.

Pitzer, a liberal arts and sciences college, offers students membership in a closely knit academic community and access to the resources of a midsized university through its partnership with the Claremont Colleges. Pitzer's distinctive curriculum encourages students to discover the relationship among different academic subjects (interdisciplinary learning), gives students a chance to see issues and events from different cultural perspectives (intercultural understanding), and shows students how to take responsibility for making the world a better place (social responsibility). Pitzer believes that students should have the freedom and responsibility for selecting what courses to take. Therefore, required general education courses are few.

Getting in Last Year

2,425 applied
50% were accepted
230 enrolled (19%)
40% from top tenth of their h.s. class
3.58 average high school GPA
61% had SAT verbal scores over 600
60% had SAT math scores over 600
66% had ACT scores over 24
15% had SAT verbal scores over 700
12% had SAT math scores over 700
14% had ACT scores over 30

Graduation and After

65% graduated in 4 years
5% graduated in 5 years
1% graduated in 6 years
63% had job offers within 6 months
31 organizations recruited on campus

Financial Matters

$29,794 tuition and fees (2003–04)
$7796 room and board
100% average percent of need met
$25,947 average financial aid amount received
    per undergraduate (2002–03 estimated)

Point Loma Nazarene University

Suburban setting ■ Private ■ Independent Religious ■ Coed
San Diego, California

Web site: www.ptloma.edu
Contact: Mr. Scott Shoemaker, Dean of Enrollment, 3900 Lomaland Drive, San Diego, CA 92106
Telephone: 619-849-2273 or toll-free 800-733-7770 **Fax:** 619-849-2601
E-mail: admissions@ptloma.edu

Getting in Last Year
1,672 applied
64% were accepted
555 enrolled (52%)
32% from top tenth of their h.s. class
3.72 average high school GPA
35% had SAT verbal scores over 600
39% had SAT math scores over 600
56% had ACT scores over 24
5% had SAT verbal scores over 700
4% had SAT math scores over 700
9% had ACT scores over 30
17 valedictorians

Graduation and After
37% graduated in 4 years
11% graduated in 5 years
3% graduated in 6 years
173 organizations recruited on campus

Financial Matters
$18,500 tuition and fees (2003–04)
$6380 room and board
71% average percent of need met
$11,509 average financial aid amount received per undergraduate (2001–02)

Academics
PLNU awards bachelor's and master's **degrees**. Challenging opportunities include advanced placement credit, double majors, and a senior project. Special programs include internships, summer session for credit, off-campus study, study-abroad, and Army, Navy and Air Force ROTC.

The most frequently chosen **baccalaureate** fields are business/marketing, psychology, and liberal arts/general studies. A complete listing of majors at PLNU appears in the Majors Index beginning on page 460.

The **faculty** at PLNU has 135 full-time members, 70% with terminal degrees. The student-faculty ratio is 16:1.

Students of PLNU
The student body totals 3,170, of whom 2,375 are undergraduates. 59.5% are women and 40.5% are men. Students come from 42 states and territories and 17 other countries. 78% are from California. 1.1% are international students. 2% are African American, 0.6% American Indian, 5% Asian American, and 8.2% Hispanic American. 82% returned for their sophomore year.

Facilities and Resources
Student rooms are linked to a campus network. 125 **computers** are available on campus that provide access to the Internet. The **library** has 146,016 books and 836 subscriptions.

Campus Life
There are 30 active organizations on campus, including a drama/theater group, newspaper, radio station, and choral group. PLNU has national **sororities**, local **fraternities**, and local sororities.

PLNU is a member of the NAIA. **Intercollegiate sports** (some offering scholarships) include baseball (m), basketball, cross-country running, golf (m), soccer (m), softball (w), tennis, track and field, volleyball (w).

Campus Safety
Student safety services include late-night transport/escort service, 24-hour patrols by trained security personnel, and student patrols.

Applying
PLNU requires an essay, SAT I or ACT, a high school transcript, 2 recommendations, and a minimum high school GPA of 2.8, and in some cases an interview. It recommends SAT I. Application deadline: 3/1; 3/15 priority date for financial aid. Deferred admission is possible.

POLYTECHNIC UNIVERSITY, BROOKLYN CAMPUS

URBAN SETTING ■ PRIVATE ■ INDEPENDENT ■ COED
BROOKLYN, NEW YORK

Web site: www.poly.edu
Contact: Jonathan D. Wexlar, Dean of Undergraduate Admissions, Six
  Metrotech Center, Brooklyn, NY 11201-2990
Telephone: 718-260-3100 or toll-free 800-POLYTECH **Fax:** 718-260-3446
E-mail: admitme@poly.edu

Academics

Polytechnic awards bachelor's, master's, and doctoral **degrees** and post-bachelor's certificates. Challenging opportunities include advanced placement credit, accelerated degree programs, an honors program, double majors, and a senior project. Special programs include cooperative education, internships, summer session for credit, and Air Force ROTC.

The most frequently chosen **baccalaureate** fields are engineering/engineering technologies, computer/information sciences, and mathematics. A complete listing of majors at Polytechnic appears in the Majors Index beginning on page 460.

The **faculty** at Polytechnic has 151 full-time members, 95% with terminal degrees. The student-faculty ratio is 12:1.

Students of Polytechnic

The student body totals 2,846, of whom 1,559 are undergraduates. 17.9% are women and 82.1% are men. Students come from 18 states and territories and 31 other countries. 96% are from New York. 8% are international students. 10.5% are African American, 0.3% American Indian, 37.9% Asian American, and 8% Hispanic American. 81% returned for their sophomore year.

Facilities and Resources

Student rooms are linked to a campus network. 1,330 **computers** are available on campus that provide access to the Internet. The 2 **libraries** have 148,000 books and 613 subscriptions.

Campus Life

There are 58 active organizations on campus, including a newspaper. 6% of eligible men and 3% of eligible women are members of national **fraternities**, national **sororities**, local fraternities, local sororities, and a coed fraternity.

Polytechnic is a member of the NCAA (Division III). **Intercollegiate sports** include baseball (m), basketball, cross-country running, soccer, softball (w), tennis, track and field, volleyball.

Campus Safety

Student safety services include 24-hour patrols by trained security personnel and electronically operated dormitory entrances.

Applying

Polytechnic requires an essay, SAT I or ACT, a high school transcript, and 2 recommendations. It recommends SAT II Subject Tests, SAT II: Writing Test, and an interview. Application deadline: 2/1. Deferred admission is possible.

Getting in Last Year

1,307 applied
73% were accepted
396 enrolled (41%)
3.20 average high school GPA
25% had SAT verbal scores over 600
69% had SAT math scores over 600
3% had SAT verbal scores over 700
20% had SAT math scores over 700
25 National Merit Scholars
2 valedictorians

Graduation and After

37% graduated in 4 years
14% graduated in 5 years
3% graduated in 6 years
19% pursued further study
91% had job offers within 6 months
120 organizations recruited on campus

Financial Matters

$25,772 tuition and fees (2003–04)
$8000 room and board
84% average percent of need met
$18,578 average financial aid amount received
  per undergraduate (2001–02)

POMONA COLLEGE

SUBURBAN SETTING ■ PRIVATE ■ INDEPENDENT ■ COED
CLAREMONT, CALIFORNIA

Web site: www.pomona.edu
Contact: Mr. Bruce Poch, Vice President and Dean of Admissions, 333 North College Way, Claremont, CA 91711
Telephone: 909-621-8134 **Fax:** 909-621-8952
E-mail: admissions@pomona.edu

Pomona College is located in Claremont, California, 35 miles east of Los Angeles, and is the founding member of the Claremont Colleges. Recognized as one of the nation's premier liberal arts colleges, Pomona offers a comprehensive undergraduate curriculum and enrolls students from around the nation and across class and ethnicity. With financial resources among the strongest of any national liberal arts college, Pomona offers a broad range of resources and opportunities, including an extensive study-abroad program. The community enjoys academic, cultural, and extracurricular activities usually found only at large universities, with all of the benefits and advantages of a small college.

Getting in Last Year
4,539 applied
21% were accepted
399 enrolled (41%)
84% from top tenth of their h.s. class
3.90 average high school GPA
97% had SAT verbal scores over 600
97% had SAT math scores over 600
95% had ACT scores over 24
74% had SAT verbal scores over 700
70% had SAT math scores over 700
73% had ACT scores over 30
66 National Merit Scholars
9 class presidents
47 valedictorians

Graduation and After
86% graduated in 4 years
3% graduated in 5 years
2% graduated in 6 years
33% pursued further study (12% arts and sciences, 9% law, 9% medicine)
60% had job offers within 6 months
145 organizations recruited on campus

Financial Matters
$27,150 tuition and fees (2003–04)
$9980 room and board
100% average percent of need met
$25,700 average financial aid amount received per undergraduate (2002–03)

Academics
Pomona awards bachelor's **degrees**. Challenging opportunities include advanced placement credit, student-designed majors, double majors, independent study, and a senior project. Special programs include internships, off-campus study, and study-abroad.

The most frequently chosen **baccalaureate** fields are social sciences and history, interdisciplinary studies, and English. A complete listing of majors at Pomona appears in the Majors Index beginning on page 460.

The **faculty** at Pomona has 160 full-time members, 96% with terminal degrees. The student-faculty ratio is 8:1.

Students of Pomona
The student body is made up of 1,555 undergraduates. 50.6% are women and 49.4% are men. Students come from 48 states and territories and 18 other countries. 35% are from California. 2% are international students. 5.8% are African American, 0.9% American Indian, 13.1% Asian American, and 7% Hispanic American. 97% returned for their sophomore year.

Facilities and Resources
Student rooms are linked to a campus network. 180 **computers** are available on campus that provide access to the Internet. The 4 **libraries** have 2,232,086 books and 5,968 subscriptions.

Campus Life
There are 280 active organizations on campus, including a drama/theater group, newspaper, radio station, and choral group. 6% of eligible men are members of local **fraternities** and local coed fraternities.

Pomona is a member of the NCAA (Division III). **Intercollegiate sports** include baseball (m), basketball, cross-country running, football (m), golf, soccer, softball (w), swimming, tennis, track and field, volleyball (w), water polo.

Campus Safety
Student safety services include late-night transport/escort service, 24-hour emergency telephone alarm devices, 24-hour patrols by trained security personnel, and electronically operated dormitory entrances.

Applying
Pomona requires an essay, SAT I and SAT II or ACT, 3 SAT II Subject Tests (including SAT II: Writing Test), a high school transcript, and 2 recommendations. It recommends an interview, portfolio or tapes for art and performing arts programs, and a minimum high school GPA of 3.0. Application deadline: 1/2; 2/1 for financial aid. Early and deferred admission are possible.

PRESBYTERIAN COLLEGE

SMALL-TOWN SETTING ■ PRIVATE ■ INDEPENDENT RELIGIOUS ■ COED
CLINTON, SOUTH CAROLINA

Web site: www.presby.edu
Contact: Mr. Richard Dana Paul, Vice President of Enrollment and Dean of Admissions, South Broad Street, Clinton, SC 29325
Telephone: 864-833-8229 or toll-free 800-476-7272 **Fax:** 864-833-8481
E-mail: rdpaul@presby.edu

Academics

Presbyterian College awards bachelor's **degrees**. Challenging opportunities include advanced placement credit, freshman honors college, an honors program, double majors, independent study, and a senior project. Special programs include internships, summer session for credit, off-campus study, study-abroad, and Army ROTC.

The most frequently chosen **baccalaureate** fields are social sciences and history, business/marketing, and psychology. A complete listing of majors at Presbyterian College appears in the Majors Index beginning on page 460.

The **faculty** at Presbyterian College has 79 full-time members, 95% with terminal degrees. The student-faculty ratio is 13:1.

Students of Presbyterian College

The student body is made up of 1,175 undergraduates. Students come from 28 states and territories and 10 other countries. 61% are from South Carolina. 4.8% are African American, 0.9% Asian American, and 1% Hispanic American. 85% returned for their sophomore year.

Facilities and Resources

Student rooms are linked to a campus network. 130 **computers** are available on campus that provide access to the Internet. The **library** has 149,273 books and 797 subscriptions.

Campus Life

There are 60 active organizations on campus, including a drama/theater group, newspaper, radio station, and choral group. 44% of eligible men and 43% of eligible women are members of national **fraternities** and national **sororities**.

Presbyterian College is a member of the NCAA (Division II). **Intercollegiate sports** (some offering scholarships) include baseball (m), basketball, cross-country running, football (m), golf (m), riflery, soccer, softball (w), tennis, volleyball (w).

Campus Safety

Student safety services include late-night transport/escort service, 24-hour emergency telephone alarm devices, 24-hour patrols by trained security personnel, and electronically operated dormitory entrances.

Applying

Presbyterian College requires an essay, SAT I or ACT, a high school transcript, and 1 recommendation. It recommends an interview. Application deadline: 4/1; 3/1 priority date for financial aid. Deferred admission is possible.

Presbyterian College—with 53 national and international scholarship recipients in recent years—provides an environment that nurtures the best and brightest. Students respect and live by a strong Honor Code, and nearly half volunteer for community service. Students may also participate in a comprehensive Honors Program or study abroad in locations around the world. To prepare for graduate school and the job market, students may intern or conduct research with professors. A scholarship program for outstanding students is supported by one of the largest per-student endowments in the region.

Getting in Last Year
1,103 applied
78% were accepted
35% from top tenth of their h.s. class
3.39 average high school GPA
36% had SAT verbal scores over 600
38% had SAT math scores over 600
49% had ACT scores over 24
5% had SAT verbal scores over 700
4% had SAT math scores over 700
5% had ACT scores over 30

Graduation and After
61% graduated in 4 years
10% graduated in 5 years
19% pursued further study
76% had job offers within 6 months
45 organizations recruited on campus

Financial Matters
$20,110 tuition and fees (2003–04)
$5811 room and board
88% average percent of need met
$19,081 average financial aid amount received per undergraduate (2002–03 estimated)

PRINCETON UNIVERSITY

SUBURBAN SETTING ■ PRIVATE ■ INDEPENDENT ■ COED
PRINCETON, NEW JERSEY

Web site: www.princeton.edu
Contact: Ms. Janet Rapelye, Dean of Admission, PO Box 430, Princeton, NJ 08544
Telephone: 609-258-3062 **Fax:** 609-258-6743

The 4th-oldest college in the country, Princeton was chartered in 1746. Any list of the most frequently cited strengths of Princeton would doubtless include the following: the quality of its academic programs, its relatively small size combined with the resources of one of the world's major research universities, and the emphasis it has always placed on undergraduate education. Distinctive features of Princeton also include its focus on independent work in a student's junior and senior years and the highly participatory nature of the student body.

Getting in Last Year
15,726 applied
10% were accepted
1,168 enrolled (73%)
94% from top tenth of their h.s. class
3.83 average high school GPA
96% had SAT verbal scores over 600
98% had SAT math scores over 600
71% had SAT verbal scores over 700
73% had SAT math scores over 700

Graduation and After
91% graduated in 4 years
5% graduated in 5 years
300 organizations recruited on campus

Financial Matters
$28,540 tuition and fees (2003–04)
$8109 room and board
100% average percent of need met
$24,078 average financial aid amount received per undergraduate (2002–03)

Academics

Princeton awards bachelor's, master's, and doctoral **degrees**. Challenging opportunities include advanced placement credit, accelerated degree programs, student-designed majors, an honors program, independent study, and a senior project. Special programs include cooperative education, internships, off-campus study, study-abroad, and Army and Air Force ROTC.

The most frequently chosen **baccalaureate** fields are social sciences and history, engineering/engineering technologies, and English. A complete listing of majors at Princeton appears in the Majors Index beginning on page 460.

The **faculty** at Princeton has 797 full-time members, 94% with terminal degrees. The student-faculty ratio is 5:1.

Students of Princeton

The student body totals 6,849, of whom 4,837 are undergraduates. 47.9% are women and 52.1% are men. Students come from 54 states and territories and 65 other countries. 14% are from New Jersey. 8.3% are international students. 8.2% are African American, 0.7% American Indian, 12.9% Asian American, and 6.3% Hispanic American. 98% returned for their sophomore year.

Facilities and Resources

Student rooms are linked to a campus network. 500 **computers** are available on campus that provide access to academic applications and courseware and the Internet. The 15 **libraries** have 6,340,095 books and 32,446 subscriptions.

Campus Life

There are 250 active organizations on campus, including a drama/theater group, newspaper, radio station, choral group, and marching band. Princeton has eating clubs.

Princeton is a member of the NCAA (Division I). **Intercollegiate sports** include baseball (m), basketball, crew, cross-country running, fencing, field hockey (w), football (m), golf, ice hockey, lacrosse, soccer, softball (w), squash, swimming, tennis, track and field, volleyball, water polo, wrestling (m).

Campus Safety

Student safety services include late-night transport/escort service, 24-hour emergency telephone alarm devices, 24-hour patrols by trained security personnel, student patrols, and electronically operated dormitory entrances.

Applying

Princeton requires an essay, SAT II Subject Tests, SAT I or ACT, a high school transcript, and 3 recommendations. It recommends an interview. Application deadline: 1/2; 2/1 priority date for financial aid. Early and deferred admission are possible.

Providence College

Suburban setting ■ Private ■ Independent Religious ■ Coed
Providence, Rhode Island

Web site: www.providence.edu
Contact: Mr. Christopher Lydon, Dean of Enrollment Management, River Avenue and Eaton Street, Providence, RI 02918
Telephone: 401-865-2535 or toll-free 800-721-6444 **Fax:** 401-865-2826
E-mail: pcadmiss@providence.edu

Academics

PC awards associate, bachelor's, and master's **degrees**. Challenging opportunities include advanced placement credit, student-designed majors, an honors program, double majors, independent study, and a senior project. Special programs include cooperative education, internships, summer session for credit, study-abroad, and Army ROTC.

The most frequently chosen **baccalaureate** fields are business/marketing, social sciences and history, and education. A complete listing of majors at PC appears in the Majors Index beginning on page 460.

The **faculty** at PC has 262 full-time members, 87% with terminal degrees. The student-faculty ratio is 13:1.

Students of PC

The student body totals 5,258, of whom 4,342 are undergraduates. 58.2% are women and 41.8% are men. Students come from 38 states and territories and 16 other countries. 20% are from Rhode Island. 0.9% are international students. 1.6% are African American, 0% American Indian, 1.5% Asian American, and 2.5% Hispanic American. 91% returned for their sophomore year.

Facilities and Resources

Student rooms are linked to a campus network. 160 **computers** are available on campus that provide access to the Internet. The **library** has 397,630 books and 1,759 subscriptions.

Campus Life

There are 94 active organizations on campus, including a drama/theater group, newspaper, radio station, television station, and choral group. No national or local **fraternities** or **sororities**.

PC is a member of the NCAA (Division I). **Intercollegiate sports** (some offering scholarships) include basketball, cross-country running, field hockey (w), ice hockey, lacrosse (m), soccer, softball (w), swimming, tennis (w), track and field, volleyball (w).

Campus Safety

Student safety services include late-night transport/escort service, 24-hour emergency telephone alarm devices, 24-hour patrols by trained security personnel, student patrols, and electronically operated dormitory entrances.

Applying

PC requires an essay, SAT I or ACT, a high school transcript, and 2 recommendations. It recommends SAT II Subject Tests and SAT II: Writing Test. Application deadline: 1/15; 2/1 for financial aid. Early and deferred admission are possible.

Providence College (PC) is the only liberal arts college in the U.S. that was founded and administered by the Dominican Friars, a Catholic teaching order whose heritage spans nearly 800 years. The College is not only concerned with the rigors of intellectual life but also recognizes the importance of students' experiences outside the classroom, including service to others. Scholarship, service, and the exuberant PC spirit—these are the qualities that shape the character of Providence College. The 105-acre campus of Providence College, situated in Rhode Island's capital city, is removed from the traffic and noise of the metropolitan area but still remains close to the many cultural and educational offerings of Providence, a city that is enjoying a lively urban renaissance. The city is located only an hour's drive from Boston and just a few hours' drive from New York City. Interstate bus, train, and air transportation are conveniently available.

Getting in Last Year
7,397 applied
53% were accepted
975 enrolled (25%)
42% from top tenth of their h.s. class
3.44 average high school GPA
53% had SAT verbal scores over 600
58% had SAT math scores over 600
75% had ACT scores over 24
8% had SAT verbal scores over 700
8% had SAT math scores over 700
15% had ACT scores over 30
43 National Merit Scholars
45 class presidents
22 valedictorians

Graduation and After
82% graduated in 4 years
2% graduated in 5 years
20% pursued further study
84% had job offers within 6 months
110 organizations recruited on campus

Financial Matters
$22,104 tuition and fees (2003–04)
$8500 room and board
85% average percent of need met
$14,600 average financial aid amount received per undergraduate

PURDUE UNIVERSITY

SUBURBAN SETTING ■ PUBLIC ■ STATE-SUPPORTED ■ COED
WEST LAFAYETTE, INDIANA

Web site: www.purdue.edu
Contact: Director of Admissions, 1080 Schleman Hall, West Lafayette, IN 47907-1080
Telephone: 765-494-4600 **Fax:** 765-494-0544
E-mail: admissions@purdue.edu

Getting in Last Year
22,977 applied
79% were accepted
6,371 enrolled (35%)
27% from top tenth of their h.s. class
31% had SAT verbal scores over 600
42% had SAT math scores over 600
68% had ACT scores over 24
5% had SAT verbal scores over 700
10% had SAT math scores over 700
15% had ACT scores over 30
91 National Merit Scholars
202 valedictorians

Graduation and After
28% graduated in 4 years
30% graduated in 5 years
5% graduated in 6 years
71% had job offers within 6 months
448 organizations recruited on campus

Financial Matters
$5860 resident tuition and fees (2003–04)
$17,480 nonresident tuition and fees (2003–04)
$6700 room and board
90% average percent of need met
$8796 average financial aid amount received per undergraduate

Academics

Purdue awards associate, bachelor's, master's, doctoral, and first-professional **degrees**. Challenging opportunities include advanced placement credit, freshman honors college, an honors program, double majors, independent study, and a senior project. Special programs include cooperative education, internships, summer session for credit, study-abroad, and Army, Navy and Air Force ROTC.

The most frequently chosen **baccalaureate** fields are engineering/engineering technologies, business/marketing, and education. A complete listing of majors at Purdue appears in the Majors Index beginning on page 460.

The **faculty** at Purdue has 1,918 full-time members, 99% with terminal degrees. The student-faculty ratio is 16:1.

Students of Purdue

The student body totals 38,847, of whom 30,851 are undergraduates. 41% are women and 59% are men. Students come from 51 states and territories and 96 other countries. 75% are from Indiana. 6.4% are international students. 3.4% are African American, 0.4% American Indian, 4.8% Asian American, and 2.3% Hispanic American. 89% returned for their sophomore year.

Facilities and Resources

Student rooms are linked to a campus network. 2,100 **computers** are available on campus that provide access to the Internet. The 15 **libraries** have 1,200,797 books and 18,374 subscriptions.

Campus Life

There are 601 active organizations on campus, including a drama/theater group, newspaper, radio station, television station, choral group, and marching band. 17% of eligible men and 17% of eligible women are members of national **fraternities** and national **sororities**.

Purdue is a member of the NCAA (Division I). **Intercollegiate sports** (some offering scholarships) include baseball (m), basketball, cross-country running, football (m), golf, soccer (w), softball (w), swimming, tennis, track and field, volleyball (w), wrestling (m).

Campus Safety

Student safety services include late-night transport/escort service, 24-hour emergency telephone alarm devices, 24-hour patrols by trained security personnel, student patrols, and electronically operated dormitory entrances.

Applying

Purdue requires SAT I or ACT and a high school transcript. Application deadline: 3/1; 3/1 priority date for financial aid. Early and deferred admission are possible.

QUEEN'S UNIVERSITY AT KINGSTON

URBAN SETTING ■ PUBLIC ■ COED
KINGSTON, ONTARIO

Web site: www.queensu.ca
Contact: Mr. Nicholas Snider, Manager of Student Recruitment, Richardson
   Hall, Kingston, ON K7L 3N6 Canada
Telephone: 613-533-2217 **Fax:** 613-533-6810
E-mail: admissn@post.queensu.ca

Academics

Queen's awards bachelor's, master's, doctoral, and first-professional **degrees**. Challenging opportunities include accelerated degree programs, student-designed majors, an honors program, and double majors. Special programs include cooperative education, internships, summer session for credit, and study-abroad.

The most frequently chosen **baccalaureate** fields are social sciences and history, education, and engineering/engineering technologies. A complete listing of majors at Queen's appears in the Majors Index beginning on page 460.

The **faculty** at Queen's has 984 members. The student-faculty ratio is 13:1.

Students of Queen's

The student body totals 19,296, of whom 15,190 are undergraduates. Students come from 13 states and territories and 76 other countries. 89% are from Ontario.

Facilities and Resources

Student rooms are linked to a campus network. 455 **computers** are available on campus that provide access to e-mail and the Internet. The **library** has 3,509,317 books and 16,109 subscriptions.

Campus Life

There are 235 active organizations on campus, including a drama/theater group, newspaper, radio station, choral group, and marching band. No national or local **fraternities** or **sororities**.

Intercollegiate sports include basketball, crew, cross-country running, fencing, field hockey (w), football (m), golf (m), ice hockey, lacrosse (w), rugby, skiing (cross-country), soccer, squash, swimming, tennis, track and field, volleyball, water polo, wrestling.

Campus Safety

Student safety services include late-night transport/escort service, 24-hour emergency telephone alarm devices, 24-hour patrols by trained security personnel, student patrols, and electronically operated dormitory entrances.

Applying

Queen's requires an essay, SAT I or ACT, a high school transcript, and a minimum high school GPA of 2.3, and in some cases SAT II Subject Tests and 1 recommendation. Application deadline: 2/20. Deferred admission is possible.

Getting in Last Year
31,844 applied
38% were accepted
3.50 average high school GPA
49% had SAT verbal scores over 600
66% had SAT math scores over 600
15% had SAT verbal scores over 700
25% had SAT math scores over 700

Graduation and After
96.85% had job offers within 6 months
331 organizations recruited on campus

Financial Matters
$4932 nonresident tuition and fees (2003–04)
$7966 room and board

QUINCY UNIVERSITY

SMALL-TOWN SETTING ■ PRIVATE ■ INDEPENDENT RELIGIOUS ■ COED
QUINCY, ILLINOIS

Web site: www.quincy.edu
Contact: Mr. Kevin A. Brown, Director of Admissions, 1800 College Avenue,
  Quincy, IL 62301-2699
Telephone: 217-222-8020 ext. 5215 or toll-free 800-688-4295
E-mail: admissions@quincy.edu

Quincy University (QU) is a dynamic community located in the heart of Quincy, Illinois. The liberal arts–based curriculum and extensive internship program prepare students for their chosen fields; the numerous opportunities for leadership outside the classroom help prepare students to take an active role in society. Strong scholarship opportunities enable students from all walks of life to experience the Quincy advantage. While many things make Quincy unique, most important are the people who make up the University community. QU's Franciscan heritage of complete respect for all individuals and their unique gifts is at the heart of University life.

Getting in Last Year
1,056 applied
94% were accepted
222 enrolled (22%)
11% from top tenth of their h.s. class
3.1 average high school GPA
13% had SAT verbal scores over 600
20% had SAT math scores over 600
27% had ACT scores over 24
1% had ACT scores over 30

Graduation and After
29% graduated in 4 years
15% graduated in 5 years
2% graduated in 6 years
18% pursued further study (9% arts and sciences, 3% law, 2% business)
80% had job offers within 6 months
23 organizations recruited on campus

Financial Matters
$16,850 tuition and fees (2003–04)
$6735 room and board
93% average percent of need met
$14,444 average financial aid amount received per undergraduate (2001–02)

Academics
Quincy University awards associate, bachelor's, and master's **degrees**. Challenging opportunities include advanced placement credit, accelerated degree programs, student-designed majors, an honors program, double majors, independent study, and a senior project. Special programs include internships, summer session for credit, and study-abroad.

The most frequently chosen **baccalaureate** fields are business/marketing, education, and health professions and related sciences. A complete listing of majors at Quincy University appears in the Majors Index beginning on page 460.

The **faculty** at Quincy University has 48 full-time members, 85% with terminal degrees. The student-faculty ratio is 15:1.

Students of Quincy University
The student body totals 1,269, of whom 1,130 are undergraduates. 55% are women and 45% are men. Students come from 22 states and territories and 5 other countries. 74% are from Illinois. 0.7% are international students. 5.9% are African American, 0.3% American Indian, 0.2% Asian American, and 2.7% Hispanic American. 71% returned for their sophomore year.

Facilities and Resources
Student rooms are linked to a campus network. 200 **computers** are available on campus that provide access to the Internet. The **library** has 239,368 books and 814 subscriptions.

Campus Life
There are 41 active organizations on campus, including a drama/theater group, newspaper, radio station, and choral group. 15% of eligible men and 28% of eligible women are members of national **fraternities** and national **sororities**.

Quincy University is a member of the NCAA (Division II). **Intercollegiate sports** (some offering scholarships) include baseball (m), basketball, golf, soccer, softball (w), tennis, volleyball.

Campus Safety
Student safety services include late-night transport/escort service, 24-hour emergency telephone alarm devices, 24-hour patrols by trained security personnel, student patrols, and electronically operated dormitory entrances.

Applying
Quincy University requires SAT I or ACT and a high school transcript. It recommends an interview and a minimum high school GPA of 2.0. Application deadline: rolling admissions; 4/15 priority date for financial aid. Early and deferred admission are possible.

QUINNIPIAC UNIVERSITY
SUBURBAN SETTING ■ PRIVATE ■ INDEPENDENT ■ COED
HAMDEN, CONNECTICUT

Web site: www.quinnipiac.edu

Contact: Ms. Joan Isaac Mohr, Vice President and Dean of Admissions, 275 Mount Carmel Avenue, Hamden, CT 06518-1940

Telephone: 203-582-8600 or toll-free 800-462-1944 (out-of-state) **Fax:** 203-582-8906

E-mail: admissions@quinnipiac.edu

Quinnipiac University, following a period of intense growth and a move from Quinnipiac College to University, remains focused on its mission to provide strong academic programs in a student-oriented environment on a campus with a strong sense of community. Students are enthusiastic, bright, and involved in leadership development, service learning, and technology. In 2002, Quinnipiac became the home of the "Bobcats", the new athletic nickname (replacing the "Braves"). Students compete in twenty-one Division I teams using the broad athletic fields, indoor gymnasium, and the newly expanded recreation center with a suspended indoor track. Ice hockey teams use a nearby rink, while preparations are underway for new on-campus ice hockey and basketball arenas.

Academics

Quinnipiac awards associate, bachelor's, master's, and first-professional **degrees** and post-bachelor's certificates. Challenging opportunities include advanced placement credit, student-designed majors, an honors program, double majors, independent study, and a senior project. Special programs include internships, summer session for credit, study-abroad, and Army and Air Force ROTC.

The most frequently chosen **baccalaureate** fields are health professions and related sciences, business/marketing, and communications/communication technologies. A complete listing of majors at Quinnipiac appears in the Majors Index beginning on page 460.

The **faculty** at Quinnipiac has 271 full-time members, 79% with terminal degrees. The student-faculty ratio is 15:1.

Students of Quinnipiac

The student body totals 7,121, of whom 5,470 are undergraduates. 61.5% are women and 38.5% are men. Students come from 28 states and territories and 20 other countries. 28% are from Connecticut. 1% are international students. 2.1% are African American, 0.2% American Indian, 2.1% Asian American, and 3.8% Hispanic American. 86% returned for their sophomore year.

Facilities and Resources

Student rooms are linked to a campus network. 300 **computers** are available on campus that provide access to the Internet. The 2 **libraries** have 285,000 books and 4,400 subscriptions.

Campus Life

There are 75 active organizations on campus, including a drama/theater group, newspaper, radio station, television station, and choral group. 5% of eligible men and 7% of eligible women are members of national **fraternities**, national **sororities**, and local sororities.

Quinnipiac is a member of the NCAA. **Intercollegiate sports** (some offering scholarships) include baseball (m), basketball, cross-country running, field hockey (w), golf (m), ice hockey, lacrosse, soccer, softball (w), tennis, track and field, volleyball (w).

Campus Safety

Student safety services include late-night transport/escort service, 24-hour emergency telephone alarm devices, 24-hour patrols by trained security personnel, and electronically operated dormitory entrances.

Applying

Quinnipiac requires an essay, SAT I or ACT, a high school transcript, and 1 recommendation, and in some cases a minimum high school GPA of 3.0. It recommends an interview and a minimum high school GPA of 2.5. Application deadline: 2/1; 3/1 priority date for financial aid. Early and deferred admission are possible.

Getting in Last Year
8,881 applied
62% were accepted
1,318 enrolled (24%)
21% from top tenth of their h.s. class
3.30 average high school GPA
18% had SAT verbal scores over 600
27% had SAT math scores over 600
53% had ACT scores over 24
1% had SAT verbal scores over 700
2% had SAT math scores over 700
6% had ACT scores over 30

Graduation and After
56% graduated in 4 years
10% graduated in 5 years
3% graduated in 6 years
23% pursued further study (7% business, 4% education, 4% medicine)
84% had job offers within 6 months
125 organizations recruited on campus

Financial Matters
$21,140 tuition and fees (2003–04)
$9450 room and board
67% average percent of need met
$13,160 average financial aid amount received per undergraduate

RANDOLPH-MACON WOMAN'S COLLEGE

SUBURBAN SETTING ■ PRIVATE ■ INDEPENDENT RELIGIOUS ■ WOMEN ONLY
LYNCHBURG, VIRGINIA

Web site: www.rmwc.edu
Contact: Pat LeDonne, Director of Admissions, 2500 Rivermont Avenue,
Lynchburg, VA 24503-1526
Telephone: 434-947-8100 or toll-free 800-745-7692 **Fax:** 434-947-8996
E-mail: admissions@rmwc.edu

Individualized education,
self-awareness, and
involvement—these are the
priorities at Randolph-Macon
Woman's College. Students seize
opportunities to study abroad,
participate in internships, conduct
original research with faculty
members, coordinate programs, hold
leadership positions in campus
organizations, and volunteer in the
community. The exciting and
engaging atmosphere fosters
academic excellence and helps
develop leadership potential. Since
class size is small (70% of all
classes have 15 or fewer students),
students have easy access to their
professors. Contemporary facilities
and advanced technology afford
women a competitive edge for
career prospects or advanced study.
The College provides a setting for
learning and living that prepares
women for meaningful personal and
professional lives.

Getting in Last Year
716 applied
86% were accepted
177 enrolled (29%)
37% from top tenth of their h.s. class
3.4 average high school GPA
54% had SAT verbal scores over 600
32% had SAT math scores over 600
65% had ACT scores over 24
14% had SAT verbal scores over 700
4% had SAT math scores over 700
13% had ACT scores over 30
3 class presidents
4 valedictorians

Graduation and After
59% graduated in 4 years
2% graduated in 5 years
31% pursued further study (19% arts and
   sciences, 5% education, 2% law)
60% had job offers within 6 months
12 organizations recruited on campus

Financial Matters
$20,530 tuition and fees (2003–04)
$7900 room and board
89% average percent of need met
$19,958 average financial aid amount received
   per undergraduate

Academics
R-MWC awards bachelor's **degrees**. Challenging opportunities include advanced placement credit, accelerated degree programs, student-designed majors, an honors program,
double majors, independent study, and a senior project. Special programs include internships, off-campus study, and study-abroad.

   The most frequently chosen **baccalaureate** fields are social sciences and history,
biological/life sciences, and foreign language/literature. A complete listing of majors at
R-MWC appears in the Majors Index beginning on page 460.

   The **faculty** at R-MWC has 75 full-time members, 91% with terminal degrees. The
student-faculty ratio is 9:1.

Students of R-MWC
The student body is made up of 737 undergraduates. Students come from 45 states and
territories and 46 other countries. 42% are from Virginia. 10.5% are international
students. 7.6% are African American, 0.3% American Indian, 3% Asian American, and
3.1% Hispanic American. 79% returned for their sophomore year.

Facilities and Resources
Student rooms are linked to a campus network. 154 **computers** are available on campus
that provide access to the Internet. The **library** has 197,332 books and 618 subscriptions.

Campus Life
There are 41 active organizations on campus, including a drama/theater group,
newspaper, radio station, and choral group. R-MWC has secret societies.

   R-MWC is a member of the NCAA (Division III). **Intercollegiate sports** include
basketball, equestrian sports, field hockey, soccer, softball, swimming, tennis, volleyball.

Campus Safety
Student safety services include late-night transport/escort service, 24-hour emergency
telephone alarm devices, and 24-hour patrols by trained security personnel.

Applying
R-MWC requires an essay, SAT I or ACT, a high school transcript, and 2 recommendations. It recommends an interview. Application deadline: 3/1; 3/1 priority date for
financial aid. Early and deferred admission are possible.

REED COLLEGE

SUBURBAN SETTING ■ PRIVATE ■ INDEPENDENT ■ COED
PORTLAND, OREGON

Web site: www.reed.edu
Contact: Mr. Paul Marthers, Dean of Admission, 3203 Southeast Woodstock Boulevard, Portland, OR 97202-8199
Telephone: 503-777-7511 or toll-free 800-547-4750 (out-of-state) **Fax:** 503-777-7553
E-mail: admission@reed.edu

Academics

Reed awards bachelor's and master's **degrees**. Challenging opportunities include advanced placement credit, accelerated degree programs, student-designed majors, double majors, independent study, and a senior project. Special programs include off-campus study, study-abroad, and Army ROTC.

The most frequently chosen **baccalaureate** fields are social sciences and history, English, and biological/life sciences. A complete listing of majors at Reed appears in the Majors Index beginning on page 460.

The **faculty** at Reed has 120 full-time members, 88% with terminal degrees. The student-faculty ratio is 10:1.

Students of Reed

The student body totals 1,340, of whom 1,312 are undergraduates. 54.4% are women and 45.6% are men. Students come from 49 states and territories and 38 other countries. 18% are from Oregon. 3.3% are international students. 0.9% are African American, 1.1% American Indian, 5.1% Asian American, and 4.1% Hispanic American. 87% returned for their sophomore year.

Facilities and Resources

Student rooms are linked to a campus network. 324 **computers** are available on campus that provide access to the Internet. The 2 **libraries** have 494,784 books and 1,872 subscriptions.

Campus Life

There are 41 active organizations on campus, including a drama/theater group, newspaper, radio station, and choral group. No national or local **fraternities** or **sororities**.

This institution has no intercollegiate sports.

Campus Safety

Student safety services include 24-hour emergency dispatch, late-night transport/escort service, 24-hour emergency telephone alarm devices, 24-hour patrols by trained security personnel, student patrols, and electronically operated dormitory entrances.

Applying

Reed requires an essay, SAT I or ACT, a high school transcript, and 2 recommendations. It recommends SAT II Subject Tests, SAT II: Writing Test, an interview, and a minimum high school GPA of 3.0. Application deadline: 1/15; 2/1 for financial aid, with a 1/15 priority date. Early and deferred admission are possible.

Reed's uniqueness lies in the uncompromising rigor of its academic program and the self-discipline and intellectual curiosity of its students. Ranked first among national undergraduate institutions in percentage of graduates earning PhD's and second in the number of Rhodes Scholars, Reed has long been known as a socially progressive and intellectually dynamic school. The Reed campus features Tudor Gothic brick buildings, state-of-the-art research facilities, and plentiful greenspace, while Portland offers all the advantages of a major city. Reed graduates are leaders in the fields of science and technology, entrepreneurship, social reform, and academia and carry on the school's tradition of scholarship, service, ingenuity, and responsibility.

Getting in Last Year

2,282 applied
46% were accepted
301 enrolled (29%)
60% from top tenth of their h.s. class
3.80 average high school GPA
93% had SAT verbal scores over 600
84% had SAT math scores over 600
99% had ACT scores over 24
55% had SAT verbal scores over 700
31% had SAT math scores over 700
60% had ACT scores over 30
19 National Merit Scholars
11 valedictorians

Graduation and After

46% graduated in 4 years
21% graduated in 5 years
5% graduated in 6 years
Graduates pursuing further study: 36% arts and sciences, 7% law, 5% business
24 organizations recruited on campus

Financial Matters

$29,200 tuition and fees (2003–04)
$7750 room and board
100% average percent of need met
$24,309 average financial aid amount received per undergraduate

REGIS UNIVERSITY

SUBURBAN SETTING ■ PRIVATE ■ INDEPENDENT RELIGIOUS ■ COED
DENVER, COLORADO

Web site: www.regis.edu
Contact: Mr. Vic Davolt, Director of Admissions, 3333 Regis Boulevard, Denver, CO 80221-1099
Telephone: 303-458-4905 or toll-free 800-388-2366 ext. 4900 **Fax:** 303-964-5534
E-mail: regisadm@regis.edu

The Rocky Mountain region's only Jesuit University, Regis University has been educating leaders since 1877. Rooted in the strong liberal arts tradition the Jesuits are reknowned for, Regis has kept its curriculum current with 26 structured majors and opportunities for interdisciplinary studies and student-designed majors. While the average class size is sixteen, the personal touch can lend a hand to help a struggling student or raise the bar for added challenge—either way, the student/professor relationship can be tailored to individual needs. At Regis, community is not just where students live, but an active commitment to our neighbors—living the Jesuit motto of "Men and women in the service of others."

Getting in Last Year
1,528 applied
83% were accepted
381 enrolled (30%)
24% from top tenth of their h.s. class
3.27 average high school GPA
23% had SAT verbal scores over 600
21% had SAT math scores over 600
46% had ACT scores over 24
1% had SAT verbal scores over 700
2% had SAT math scores over 700
7% had ACT scores over 30
6 valedictorians

Graduation and After
29% graduated in 4 years
13% graduated in 5 years
2% graduated in 6 years
15% pursued further study
25 organizations recruited on campus

Financial Matters
$20,900 tuition and fees (2003–04)
$7600 room and board
84% average percent of need met
$17,315 average financial aid amount received per undergraduate (2002–03 estimated)

Academics
Regis University awards bachelor's and master's **degrees**. Challenging opportunities include advanced placement credit, accelerated degree programs, student-designed majors, freshman honors college, an honors program, double majors, independent study, and a senior project. Special programs include cooperative education, internships, summer session for credit, off-campus study, study-abroad, and Army and Air Force ROTC. A complete listing of majors at Regis University appears in the Majors Index beginning on page 460.

The **faculty** at Regis University has 176 full-time members, 95% with terminal degrees. The student-faculty ratio is 14:1.

Students of Regis University
Undergraduate enrollment, 1,268. Students come from 40 states and territories and 11 other countries. 57% are from Colorado. 79% returned for their sophomore year.

Facilities and Resources
Student rooms are linked to a campus network. 300 **computers** are available on campus for student use. The **library** has 430,514 books and 7,850 subscriptions.

Campus Life
There are 30 active organizations on campus, including a drama/theater group, newspaper, radio station, and choral group. No national or local **fraternities** or **sororities**.

Regis University is a member of the NCAA (Division II). **Intercollegiate sports** (some offering scholarships) include baseball (m), basketball, golf (m), lacrosse (w), soccer, softball (w), volleyball (w).

Campus Safety
Student safety services include late-night transport/escort service, 24-hour emergency telephone alarm devices, 24-hour patrols by trained security personnel, student patrols, and electronically operated dormitory entrances.

Applying
Regis University requires an essay, SAT I or ACT, a high school transcript, 1 recommendation, and a minimum high school GPA of 2.5, and in some cases an interview and 2 recommendations. It recommends SAT II Subject Tests. Application deadline: rolling admissions; 3/5 priority date for financial aid.

RENSSELAER POLYTECHNIC INSTITUTE

SUBURBAN SETTING ■ PRIVATE ■ INDEPENDENT ■ COED
TROY, NEW YORK

Web site: www.rpi.edu
Contact: Ms. Teresa Duffy, Dean of Enrollment Management, 110 8th Street,
Troy, NY 12180-3590
Telephone: 518-276-6216 or toll-free 800-448-6562 **Fax:** 518-276-4072
E-mail: admissions@rpi.edu

Academics

Rensselaer awards bachelor's, master's, and doctoral **degrees**. Challenging opportunities include advanced placement credit, accelerated degree programs, student-designed majors, double majors, independent study, and a senior project. Special programs include cooperative education, internships, summer session for credit, off-campus study, study-abroad, and Army, Navy and Air Force ROTC.

The most frequently chosen **baccalaureate** fields are engineering/engineering technologies, computer/information sciences, and business/marketing. A complete listing of majors at Rensselaer appears in the Majors Index beginning on page 460.

The **faculty** at Rensselaer has 383 full-time members, 95% with terminal degrees. The student-faculty ratio is 15:1.

Students of Rensselaer

The student body totals 8,265, of whom 5,210 are undergraduates. 24.9% are women and 75.1% are men. Students come from 51 states and territories and 37 other countries. 46% are from New York. 4.2% are international students. 4.1% are African American, 0.4% American Indian, 12.1% Asian American, and 5% Hispanic American. 93% returned for their sophomore year.

Facilities and Resources

Student rooms are linked to a campus network. 500 **computers** are available on campus that provide access to the Internet. The 2 **libraries** have 309,171 books and 10,210 subscriptions.

Campus Life

There are 130 active organizations on campus, including a drama/theater group, newspaper, radio station, and choral group. 80% of eligible men and 80% of eligible women are members of national **fraternities**, national **sororities**, local fraternities, and local sororities.

Rensselaer is a member of the NCAA (Division III). **Intercollegiate sports** (some offering scholarships) include baseball (m), basketball, cross-country running, field hockey (w), football (m), golf (m), ice hockey, lacrosse, soccer, softball (w), swimming, tennis, track and field, volleyball (w).

Campus Safety

Student safety services include campus foot patrols at night, late-night transport/escort service, 24-hour emergency telephone alarm devices, 24-hour patrols by trained security personnel, and electronically operated dormitory entrances.

Applying

Rensselaer requires an essay, SAT I or ACT, a high school transcript, and 1 recommendation, and in some cases SAT II Subject Tests and portfolio for architecture and electronic arts programs. Application deadline: 1/1; 2/15 priority date for financial aid. Early and deferred admission are possible.

Rensselaer Polytechnic Institute, founded in 1824, is the nations first technological university, offering degrees in engineering, the sciences, information technology, architecture, management, and the humanities and social sciences. The Institute serves undergraduates, graduate students, and working professionals around the world. Rensselaer is well known for its success in the transfer of technology from the research laboratory to the world. Undergraduates can conduct research alongside world-renowned faculty members or gain valuable job experience as a co-op in industry. Among successful graduates are Ray Tomlinson '63, creator of the Internet e-mail protocol @ symbol; Dr. Claire Fraser '77, head of the Institute of Genomic Research; and Bobby Farrelly '81, *Something About Mary* and *Dumb and Dumber* movie maker.

Getting in Last Year
5,252 applied
80% were accepted
1,341 enrolled (32%)
58% from top tenth of their h.s. class
70% had SAT verbal scores over 600
90% had SAT math scores over 600
79% had ACT scores over 24
19% had SAT verbal scores over 700
44% had SAT math scores over 700
9% had ACT scores over 30
26 National Merit Scholars
63 valedictorians

Graduation and After
55% graduated in 4 years
24% graduated in 5 years
2% graduated in 6 years
21% pursued further study
80% had job offers within 6 months
347 organizations recruited on campus

Financial Matters
$28,496 tuition and fees (2003–04)
$9083 room and board
90% average percent of need met
$22,791 average financial aid amount received per undergraduate (2002–03 estimated)

RESEARCH COLLEGE OF NURSING

URBAN SETTING ■ PRIVATE ■ INDEPENDENT ■ COED, PRIMARILY WOMEN
KANSAS CITY, MISSOURI

Web site: www.researchcollege.edu
Contact: Ms. Amy Johnson, Rockhurst College Admission Office, 1100
  Rockhurst Road, Kansas City, MO 64110
Telephone: 816-501-4100 ext. 4654 or toll-free 800-842-6776 **Fax:**
  816-501-4588
E-mail: mendenhall@vax2.rockhurst.edu

Getting in Last Year
94 applied
77% were accepted
35 enrolled (49%)
24% from top tenth of their h.s. class
3.46 average high school GPA
85% had ACT scores over 24
35% had ACT scores over 30

Graduation and After
95% had job offers within 6 months

Financial Matters
$17,400 tuition and fees (2003–04)
$5450 room and board
60% average percent of need met
$18,933 average financial aid amount received
  per undergraduate

Academics
Research College of Nursing awards bachelor's and master's **degrees** (bachelor's degree offered jointly with Rockhurst College). Challenging opportunities include advanced placement credit, accelerated degree programs, an honors program, double majors, and independent study. Special programs include summer session for credit, study-abroad, and Army ROTC.

The most frequently chosen **baccalaureate** field is health professions and related sciences. A complete listing of majors at Research College of Nursing appears in the Majors Index beginning on page 460.

The **faculty** at Research College of Nursing has 25 full-time members. The student-faculty ratio is 7:1.

Students of Research College of Nursing
The student body totals 219, of whom 197 are undergraduates. 87.8% are women and 12.2% are men. Students come from 7 states and territories. 5.1% are African American, 2.3% Asian American, and 3.4% Hispanic American.

Facilities and Resources
Student rooms are linked to a campus network. 125 **computers** are available on campus that provide access to the Internet. The **library** has 150,000 books and 675 subscriptions.

Campus Life
There are 40 active organizations on campus, including a drama/theater group, newspaper, radio station, and choral group. 75% of eligible men and 75% of eligible women are members of national **fraternities**, national **sororities**, and local sororities.

Research College of Nursing is a member of the NCAA (Division II). **Intercollegiate sports** (some offering scholarships) include baseball (m), basketball, golf, soccer, tennis, volleyball (w).

Campus Safety
Student safety services include late-night transport/escort service, 24-hour emergency telephone alarm devices, 24-hour patrols by trained security personnel, and electronically operated dormitory entrances.

Applying
Research College of Nursing requires SAT I or ACT, a high school transcript, and 1 recommendation. It recommends an interview, minimum ACT score of 20, and a minimum high school GPA of 2.8. Application deadline: 6/30; 3/15 priority date for financial aid. Deferred admission is possible.

RHODE ISLAND SCHOOL OF DESIGN

URBAN SETTING ■ PRIVATE ■ INDEPENDENT ■ COED
PROVIDENCE, RHODE ISLAND

Web site: www.risd.edu
Contact: Mr. Edward Newhall, Director of Admissions, 2 College Street,
   Providence, RI 02905-2791
Telephone: 401-454-6300 or toll-free 800-364-RISD **Fax:** 401-454-6309
E-mail: admissions@risd.edu

Academics

RISD awards bachelor's, master's, and first-professional **degrees**. Challenging opportunities include advanced placement credit, independent study, and a senior project. Special programs include internships, off-campus study, and study-abroad.

   The most frequently chosen **baccalaureate** fields are visual/performing arts and architecture. A complete listing of majors at RISD appears in the Majors Index beginning on page 460.

   The **faculty** at RISD has 145 full-time members. The student-faculty ratio is 11:1.

Students of RISD

The student body totals 2,294, of whom 1,920 are undergraduates. Students come from 51 states and territories and 53 other countries. 6% are from Rhode Island. 12.3% are international students. 2.3% are African American, 0.5% American Indian, 12.5% Asian American, and 4.9% Hispanic American. 96% returned for their sophomore year.

Facilities and Resources

Student rooms are linked to a campus network. 300 **computers** are available on campus that provide access to the Internet. The 2 **libraries** have 100,961 books and 419 subscriptions.

Campus Life

There are 60 active organizations on campus, including a drama/theater group and newspaper. No national or local **fraternities** or **sororities**.

   This institution has no intercollegiate sports.

Campus Safety

Student safety services include late-night transport/escort service, 24-hour emergency telephone alarm devices, 24-hour patrols by trained security personnel, and electronically operated dormitory entrances.

Applying

RISD requires an essay, SAT I or ACT, a high school transcript, and portfolio, drawing assignments. It recommends 3 recommendations. Application deadline: 2/15; 2/15 priority date for financial aid. Early and deferred admission are possible.

Getting in Last Year
2,420 applied
35% were accepted
391 enrolled (47%)
26% from top tenth of their h.s. class
3.30 average high school GPA

Graduation and After
5% pursued further study (5% arts and sciences)
96% had job offers within 6 months
50 organizations recruited on campus

Financial Matters
$26,665 tuition and fees (2003–04)
$7370 room and board
69% average percent of need met
$15,100 average financial aid amount received per undergraduate (2002–03 estimated)

Getting in Last Year

2,326 applied
72% were accepted
457 enrolled (27%)
59% from top tenth of their h.s. class
3.45 average high school GPA
75% had SAT verbal scores over 600
68% had SAT math scores over 600
93% had ACT scores over 24
22% had SAT verbal scores over 700
16% had SAT math scores over 700
29% had ACT scores over 30
10 National Merit Scholars
11 class presidents
23 valedictorians

Graduation and After

71% graduated in 4 years
3% graduated in 5 years
33% pursued further study (15% arts and
  sciences, 6% law, 5% medicine)
67 organizations recruited on campus

Financial Matters

$22,938 tuition and fees (2003–04)
$6382 room and board
84% average percent of need met
$16,054 average financial aid amount received
  per undergraduate (2002–03 estimated)

RHODES COLLEGE

SUBURBAN SETTING ■ PRIVATE ■ INDEPENDENT RELIGIOUS ■ COED
MEMPHIS, TENNESSEE

Web site: www.rhodes.edu
Contact: Mr. David J. Wottle, Dean of Admissions and Financial Aid, 2000
  North Parkway, Memphis, TN 38112
Telephone: 901-843-3700 or toll-free 800-844-5969 (out-of-state) **Fax:**
  901-843-3631
E-mail: adminfo@rhodes.edu

Academics

Rhodes awards bachelor's and master's **degrees** (master's degree in accounting only).
Challenging opportunities include advanced placement credit, accelerated degree
programs, student-designed majors, an honors program, double majors, independent
study, and a senior project. Special programs include internships, off-campus study,
study-abroad, and Army and Air Force ROTC.

The most frequently chosen **baccalaureate** fields are social sciences and history,
biological/life sciences, and English. A complete listing of majors at Rhodes appears in
the Majors Index beginning on page 460.

The **faculty** at Rhodes has 131 full-time members, 95% with terminal degrees. The
student-faculty ratio is 11:1.

Students of Rhodes

The student body totals 1,560, of whom 1,551 are undergraduates. 57.9% are women
and 42.1% are men. Students come from 43 states and territories. 29% are from Tennessee. 0.6% are international students. 4.4% are African American, 0.3% American Indian,
3.1% Asian American, and 1.3% Hispanic American. 83% returned for their sophomore
year.

Facilities and Resources

Student rooms are linked to a campus network. 220 **computers** are available on campus
for student use. The 4 **libraries** have 270,761 books and 1,179 subscriptions.

Campus Life

There are 44 active organizations on campus, including a drama/theater group,
newspaper, and choral group. 47% of eligible men and 58% of eligible women are
members of national **fraternities** and national **sororities**.

Rhodes is a member of the NCAA (Division III). **Intercollegiate sports** include
baseball (m), basketball, cross-country running, field hockey (w), football (m), golf, soccer, softball (w), swimming, tennis, track and field, volleyball (w).

Campus Safety

Student safety services include 24-hour monitored security cameras in parking areas,
fenced campus with monitored access at night, late-night transport/escort service, 24-
hour emergency telephone alarm devices, 24-hour patrols by trained security personnel,
and student patrols.

Applying

Rhodes requires an essay, SAT I or ACT, a high school transcript, and 2 recommendations. It recommends an interview. Application deadline: 2/1; 3/1 priority date for
financial aid. Early and deferred admission are possible.

RICE UNIVERSITY
URBAN SETTING ■ PRIVATE ■ INDEPENDENT ■ COED
HOUSTON, TEXAS

Web site: www.rice.edu
Contact: Ms. Julie M. Browning, Dean for Undergraduate Enrollment, Office of Admission, PO Box 1892, MS 17, Houston, TX 77251-1892
Telephone: 713-348-RICE or toll-free 800-527-OWLS

Academics
Rice awards bachelor's, master's, and doctoral **degrees**. Challenging opportunities include advanced placement credit, accelerated degree programs, student-designed majors, an honors program, double majors, independent study, and a senior project. Special programs include internships, summer session for credit, off-campus study, study-abroad, and Army and Navy ROTC.

The most frequently chosen **baccalaureate** fields are social sciences and history, engineering/engineering technologies, and biological/life sciences. A complete listing of majors at Rice appears in the Majors Index beginning on page 460.

The **faculty** at Rice has 530 full-time members, 96% with terminal degrees. The student-faculty ratio is 5:1.

Students of Rice
The student body totals 4,959, of whom 2,921 are undergraduates. 48.1% are women and 51.9% are men. Students come from 53 states and territories and 37 other countries. 52% are from Texas. 3.2% are international students. 6.3% are African American, 0.5% American Indian, 14.8% Asian American, and 11.4% Hispanic American. 96% returned for their sophomore year.

Facilities and Resources
Student rooms are linked to a campus network. 600 **computers** are available on campus that provide access to the Internet. The **library** has 2,100,000 books and 28,000 subscriptions.

Campus Life
There are 204 active organizations on campus, including a drama/theater group, newspaper, radio station, television station, choral group, and marching band. No national or local **fraternities** or **sororities**.

Rice is a member of the NCAA (Division I). **Intercollegiate sports** (some offering scholarships) include baseball (m), basketball, cross-country running, football (m), golf (m), soccer (w), swimming (w), tennis, track and field, volleyball (w).

Campus Safety
Student safety services include late-night transport/escort service, 24-hour emergency telephone alarm devices, 24-hour patrols by trained security personnel, and electronically operated dormitory entrances.

Applying
Rice requires an essay, SAT II Subject Tests, SAT II: Writing Test, SAT I or ACT, a high school transcript, 2 recommendations, and portfolio required for architecture students; audition required for music students. It recommends an interview. Application deadline: 1/10; 3/1 priority date for financial aid. Early and deferred admission are possible.

Nobel Prize–winning scholars teaching freshmen, the lowest debt burden among graduates of highly selective schools, undergraduates conducting hands-on primary research alongside faculty members, the cultural richness and resources of the nation's fourth-largest city, and a student-faculty ratio of 5:1—Rice University has all of this and more. Along with top students, professors devoted to undergraduate teaching, and world-class facilities, Rice offers residential college life that fosters a strong sense of community. Even the price is right. Rice has long been recognized as one of the best values in higher education and recently was awarded the title of "coolest school" by *Seventeen* magazine.

Getting in Last Year
7,501 applied
24% were accepted
715 enrolled (39%)
86% from top tenth of their h.s. class
91% had SAT verbal scores over 600
93% had SAT math scores over 600
94% had ACT scores over 24
57% had SAT verbal scores over 700
64% had SAT math scores over 700
66% had ACT scores over 30
173 National Merit Scholars
9 class presidents
96 valedictorians

Graduation and After
75% graduated in 4 years
14% graduated in 5 years
3% graduated in 6 years
43% pursued further study (31% medicine, 21% arts and sciences, 19% engineering)
200 organizations recruited on campus

Financial Matters
$19,670 tuition and fees (2003–04)
$7880 room and board
100% average percent of need met
$15,498 average financial aid amount received per undergraduate (2002–03 estimated)

RIPON COLLEGE

SMALL-TOWN SETTING ■ PRIVATE ■ INDEPENDENT ■ COED
RIPON, WISCONSIN

Web site: www.ripon.edu
Contact: Mr. Scott J. Goplin, Vice President and Dean of Admission and
Financial Aid, 300 Seward Street, PO Box 248, Ripon, WI 54971
Telephone: 920-748-8185 or toll-free 800-947-4766 **Fax:** 920-748-8335
E-mail: adminfo@ripon.edu

ounded in 1851, Ripon College continues in its steadfast belief that mastery of the liberal arts and sciences is the key to a life of both professional and personal success. Ripon graduates have the abilities, the attitudes, and the values for a contributing and productive life. Each student works closely with faculty and staff members and fellow students to develop the fundamental analytical and communicative skills demanded for success, and all students and staff and faculty members work collaboratively to build a better future for themselves, their country, and the world.

Getting in Last Year
959 applied
84% were accepted
259 enrolled (32%)
28% from top tenth of their h.s. class
3.45 average high school GPA
51% had SAT verbal scores over 600
46% had SAT math scores over 600
56% had ACT scores over 24
14% had SAT verbal scores over 700
25% had SAT math scores over 700
11% had ACT scores over 30
4 valedictorians

Graduation and After
53% graduated in 4 years
8% graduated in 5 years
1% graduated in 6 years
22% pursued further study (15% arts and
    sciences, 2% business, 2% medicine)
98% had job offers within 6 months
18 organizations recruited on campus

Financial Matters
$19,940 tuition and fees (2003–04)
$5055 room and board
82% average percent of need met
$18,573 average financial aid amount received
    per undergraduate (2002–03 estimated)

Academics

Ripon awards bachelor's **degrees**. Challenging opportunities include advanced placement credit, accelerated degree programs, student-designed majors, double majors, and a senior project. Special programs include internships, off-campus study, study-abroad, and Army ROTC.

The most frequently chosen **baccalaureate** fields are social sciences and history, education, and psychology. A complete listing of majors at Ripon appears in the Majors Index beginning on page 460.

The **faculty** at Ripon has 50 full-time members, 96% with terminal degrees. The student-faculty ratio is 15:1.

Students of Ripon

The student body is made up of 998 undergraduates. 52.1% are women and 47.9% are men. Students come from 33 states and territories and 14 other countries. 69% are from Wisconsin. 1.8% are international students. 2% are African American, 0.7% American Indian, 1.8% Asian American, and 4.3% Hispanic American. 84% returned for their sophomore year.

Facilities and Resources

Student rooms are linked to a campus network. 150 **computers** are available on campus that provide access to the Internet. The **library** has 169,523 books and 985 subscriptions.

Campus Life

There are 45 active organizations on campus, including a drama/theater group, newspaper, radio station, and choral group. 55% of eligible men and 21% of eligible women are members of national **fraternities**, national **sororities**, local fraternities, and local sororities.

Ripon is a member of the NCAA (Division III). **Intercollegiate sports** include baseball (m), basketball, cheerleading (w), cross-country running, football (m), golf, soccer, softball (w), swimming, tennis, track and field, volleyball (w).

Campus Safety

Student safety services include late-night transport/escort service, 24-hour emergency telephone alarm devices, 24-hour patrols by trained security personnel, student patrols, and electronically operated dormitory entrances.

Applying

Ripon requires SAT I or ACT, a high school transcript, 1 recommendation, and a minimum high school GPA of 2.0. It recommends an essay and an interview. Application deadline: rolling admissions; 3/1 priority date for financial aid. Deferred admission is possible.

ROCHESTER INSTITUTE OF TECHNOLOGY

SUBURBAN SETTING ■ PRIVATE ■ INDEPENDENT ■ COED
ROCHESTER, NEW YORK

Web site: www.rit.edu
Contact: Dr. Daniel Shelley, Director of Undergraduate Admissions, 60 Lomb
    Memorial Drive, Rochester, NY 14623-5604
Telephone: 585-475-6631 **Fax:** 585-475-7424
E-mail: admissions@rit.edu

Academics

RIT awards associate, bachelor's, master's, and doctoral **degrees** and post-bachelor's and post-master's certificates. Challenging opportunities include advanced placement credit, accelerated degree programs, student-designed majors, an honors program, independent study, and a senior project. Special programs include cooperative education, internships, summer session for credit, off-campus study, study-abroad, and Army and Air Force ROTC.

The most frequently chosen **baccalaureate** fields are engineering/engineering technologies, visual/performing arts, and computer/information sciences. A complete listing of majors at RIT appears in the Majors Index beginning on page 460.

The **faculty** at RIT has 701 full-time members, 85% with terminal degrees. The student-faculty ratio is 13:1.

Students of RIT

The student body totals 14,685, of whom 12,381 are undergraduates. 30.8% are women and 69.2% are men. Students come from 50 states and territories and 85 other countries. 55% are from New York. 5.3% are international students. 4.8% are African American, 0.4% American Indian, 6.9% Asian American, and 3.2% Hispanic American. 88% returned for their sophomore year.

Facilities and Resources

Student rooms are linked to a campus network. 2,500 **computers** are available on campus that provide access to student account information and the Internet. The **library** has 350,000 books and 4,305 subscriptions.

Campus Life

There are 170 active organizations on campus, including a drama/theater group, newspaper, radio station, and choral group. 7% of eligible men and 5% of eligible women are members of national **fraternities**, national **sororities**, local fraternities, and local sororities.

RIT is a member of the NCAA (Division III). **Intercollegiate sports** include baseball (m), basketball, crew, cross-country running, ice hockey, lacrosse, soccer, softball (w), swimming, tennis, track and field, volleyball (w), wrestling (m).

Campus Safety

Student safety services include late-night transport/escort service, 24-hour emergency telephone alarm devices, 24-hour patrols by trained security personnel, and student patrols.

Applying

RIT requires an essay, SAT I or ACT, and a high school transcript, and in some cases portfolio. It recommends an interview, 1 recommendation, and a minimum high school GPA of 3.0. Application deadline: 3/15; 3/1 priority date for financial aid. Early and deferred admission are possible.

Respected internationally as a leader in career-oriented education, RIT has been an innovative pacesetter since 1829. RIT offers outstanding teaching, a strong foundation in the liberal arts and sciences, modern facilities, and student work experience gained through the university's cooperative education program. Innovative programs include microelectronic engineering, imaging science, film and animation, biotechnology, international business, and new media design, software engineering, and professional communicatons. RIT draws students from every state and 90 other countries.

Getting in Last Year
8,317 applied
70% were accepted
2,203 enrolled (38%)
33% from top tenth of their h.s. class
3.70 average high school GPA
46% had SAT verbal scores over 600
65% had SAT math scores over 600
76% had ACT scores over 24
8% had SAT verbal scores over 700
16% had SAT math scores over 700
19% had ACT scores over 30
17 National Merit Scholars
33 valedictorians

Graduation and After
10% pursued further study
92% had job offers within 6 months
600 organizations recruited on campus

Financial Matters
$21,384 tuition and fees (2003–04)
$7833 room and board
90% average percent of need met
$16,000 average financial aid amount received
    per undergraduate (2002–03)

ROLLINS COLLEGE

SUBURBAN SETTING ■ PRIVATE ■ INDEPENDENT ■ COED
WINTER PARK, FLORIDA

Web site: www.rollins.edu

Contact: Mr. David Erdmann, Dean of Admission and Enrollment, 1000 Holt
  Avenue, Box 2720, Winter Park, FL 32789-4499

Telephone: 407-646-2161 **Fax:** 407-646-1502

E-mail: admission@rollins.edu

Getting in Last Year
2,271 applied
66% were accepted
497 enrolled (33%)
38% from top tenth of their h.s. class
3.40 average high school GPA
39% had SAT verbal scores over 600
42% had SAT math scores over 600
58% had ACT scores over 24
6% had SAT verbal scores over 700
6% had SAT math scores over 700
8% had ACT scores over 30

Graduation and After
46% graduated in 4 years
11% graduated in 5 years
1% graduated in 6 years
24% pursued further study
60% had job offers within 6 months
122 organizations recruited on campus

Financial Matters
$26,250 tuition and fees (2003–04)
$8050 room and board
91% average percent of need met
$26,716 average financial aid amount received
  per undergraduate (2002–03 estimated)

Academics

Rollins awards bachelor's and master's **degrees**. Challenging opportunities include advanced placement credit, accelerated degree programs, student-designed majors, an honors program, double majors, independent study, and a senior project. Special programs include internships, off-campus study, and study-abroad.

The most frequently chosen **baccalaureate** fields are social sciences and history, visual/performing arts, and business/marketing. A complete listing of majors at Rollins appears in the Majors Index beginning on page 460.

The **faculty** at Rollins has 179 full-time members. The student-faculty ratio is 11:1.

Students of Rollins

The student body totals 2,565, of whom 1,733 are undergraduates. 61% are women and 39% are men. Students come from 46 states and territories and 51 other countries. 43% are from Florida. 3.6% are international students. 4% are African American, 0.6% American Indian, 3.2% Asian American, and 6.9% Hispanic American. 83% returned for their sophomore year.

Facilities and Resources

Student rooms are linked to a campus network. 200 **computers** are available on campus that provide access to the Internet. The **library** has 237,333 books and 2,259 subscriptions.

Campus Life

There are 122 active organizations on campus, including a drama/theater group, newspaper, radio station, television station, and choral group. Rollins has national **fraternities**, national **sororities**, local fraternities, and local sororities.

Rollins is a member of the NCAA (Division II). **Intercollegiate sports** (some offering scholarships) include baseball (m), basketball, cheerleading, crew, cross-country running, golf, soccer, softball (w), swimming, tennis, volleyball (w).

Campus Safety

Student safety services include late-night transport/escort service, 24-hour emergency telephone alarm devices, 24-hour patrols by trained security personnel, and electronically operated dormitory entrances.

Applying

Rollins requires an essay, SAT I or ACT, a high school transcript, and 1 recommendation. It recommends an interview. Application deadline: 2/15; 2/15 priority date for financial aid. Early and deferred admission are possible.

Rose-Hulman Institute of Technology

Suburban setting ■ Private ■ Independent ■ Coed, Primarily Men
Terre Haute, Indiana

Web site: www.rose-hulman.edu
Contact: Mr. Charles G. Howard, Dean of Admissions/Vice President, 5500 Wabash Avenue, CM 1, Terre Haute, IN 47803-3920
Telephone: 812-877-8213 or toll-free 800-248-7448 **Fax:** 812-877-8941
E-mail: admis.ofc@rose-hulman.edu

Academics

Rose-Hulman awards bachelor's and master's **degrees**. Challenging opportunities include advanced placement credit, accelerated degree programs, an honors program, double majors, independent study, and a senior project. Special programs include cooperative education, summer session for credit, off-campus study, study-abroad, and Army and Air Force ROTC.

The most frequently chosen **baccalaureate** fields are engineering/engineering technologies, computer/information sciences, and physical sciences. A complete listing of majors at Rose-Hulman appears in the Majors Index beginning on page 460.

The **faculty** at Rose-Hulman has 139 full-time members, 96% with terminal degrees. The student-faculty ratio is 13:1.

Students of Rose-Hulman

The student body totals 1,864, of whom 1,721 are undergraduates. 17.5% are women and 82.5% are men. Students come from 49 states and territories and 9 other countries. 48% are from Indiana. 0.9% are international students. 2.1% are African American, 0.1% American Indian, 2.9% Asian American, and 1.2% Hispanic American. 91% returned for their sophomore year.

Facilities and Resources

Student rooms are linked to a campus network. 150 **computers** are available on campus that provide access to the Internet. The **library** has 77,348 books and 280 subscriptions.

Campus Life

There are 40 active organizations on campus, including a drama/theater group, newspaper, radio station, and choral group. 47% of eligible men and 58% of eligible women are members of national **fraternities** and national **sororities**.

Rose-Hulman is a member of the NCAA (Division III). **Intercollegiate sports** include baseball (m), basketball, cheerleading, cross-country running, football (m), golf, riflery, soccer, softball (w), swimming, tennis, track and field, volleyball (w), wrestling (m).

Campus Safety

Student safety services include late-night transport/escort service, 24-hour emergency telephone alarm devices, 24-hour patrols by trained security personnel, and electronically operated dormitory entrances.

Applying

Rose-Hulman requires SAT I or ACT, a high school transcript, and 1 recommendation. It recommends an essay and an interview. Application deadline: 3/1; 3/1 priority date for financial aid. Deferred admission is possible.

Getting in Last Year

3,188 applied
71% were accepted
490 enrolled (22%)
62% from top tenth of their h.s. class
64% had SAT verbal scores over 600
90% had SAT math scores over 600
94% had ACT scores over 24
22% had SAT verbal scores over 700
47% had SAT math scores over 700
49% had ACT scores over 30
26 National Merit Scholars
50 valedictorians

Graduation and After

65% graduated in 4 years
14% graduated in 5 years
2% graduated in 6 years
18% pursued further study (14% engineering, 1% arts and sciences, 1% business)
95% had job offers within 6 months
185 organizations recruited on campus

Financial Matters

$24,705 tuition and fees (2003–04)
$6720 room and board
83% average percent of need met
$15,261 average financial aid amount received per undergraduate

RUTGERS, THE STATE UNIVERSITY OF NEW JERSEY, NEW BRUNSWICK/PISCATAWAY

PUBLIC ■ STATE-SUPPORTED ■ COED
NEW BRUNSWICK, NEW JERSEY

Web site: www.rutgers.edu
Contact: Ms. Diane Williams Harris, Associate Director of University
    Undergraduate Admissions, 65 Davidson Road, Piscataway, NJ 08854-8097
Telephone: 732-932-4636 **Fax:** 732-445-0237
E-mail: admissions@rutgers.edu

Getting in Last Year
26,175 applied
54% were accepted
4,717 enrolled (33%)
36% from top tenth of their h.s. class
47% had SAT verbal scores over 600
63% had SAT math scores over 600
9% had SAT verbal scores over 700
17% had SAT math scores over 700

Graduation and After
44% graduated in 4 years
22% graduated in 5 years
7% graduated in 6 years
80% had job offers within 6 months
500 organizations recruited on campus

Financial Matters
$7927 resident tuition and fees (2003–04)
$14,441 nonresident tuition and fees (2003–04)
$7711 room and board
86% average percent of need met
$9952 average financial aid amount received per undergraduate (2002–03 estimated)

Academics
Rutgers, The State University of New Jersey, New Brunswick/Piscataway awards bachelor's, master's, doctoral, and first-professional **degrees**. Challenging opportunities include advanced placement credit, accelerated degree programs, student-designed majors, an honors program, double majors, independent study, and a senior project. Special programs include cooperative education, study-abroad, and Army and Air Force ROTC.

The most frequently chosen **baccalaureate** fields are social sciences and history, psychology, and biological/life sciences. A complete listing of majors at Rutgers, The State University of New Jersey, New Brunswick/Piscataway appears in the Majors Index beginning on page 460.

The **faculty** at Rutgers, The State University of New Jersey, New Brunswick/Piscataway has 1,502 full-time members, 99% with terminal degrees. The student-faculty ratio is 15:1.

Students of Rutgers, The State University of New Jersey, New Brunswick/Piscataway
The student body totals 35,318, of whom 27,365 are undergraduates. 52.4% are women and 47.6% are men. 89% are from New Jersey. 2.3% are international students. 8.4% are African American, 0.2% American Indian, 20.5% Asian American, and 8.1% Hispanic American. 89% returned for their sophomore year.

Facilities and Resources
Student rooms are linked to a campus network. 1,450 **computers** are available on campus that provide access to online grade reports and the Internet. The 15 **libraries** have 4,737,147 books and 17,182 subscriptions.

Campus Life
Active organizations on campus include a drama/theater group, newspaper, radio station, television station, choral group, and marching band. Rutgers, The State University of New Jersey, New Brunswick/Piscataway has national **fraternities** and national **sororities**.

Rutgers, The State University of New Jersey, New Brunswick/Piscataway is a member of the NCAA (Division I). **Intercollegiate sports** include baseball (m), basketball, crew, cross-country running, fencing, football (m), golf, gymnastics (w), lacrosse, soccer, softball (w), swimming, tennis, track and field, volleyball (w), wrestling (m).

Applying
Rutgers, The State University of New Jersey, New Brunswick/Piscataway requires SAT I or ACT and a high school transcript, and in some cases SAT II: Writing Test. Application deadline: rolling admissions; 3/15 priority date for financial aid. Early admission is possible.

SAINT FRANCIS UNIVERSITY

RURAL SETTING ■ PRIVATE ■ INDEPENDENT RELIGIOUS ■ COED
LORETTO, PENNSYLVANIA

Web site: www.sfcpa.edu
Contact: Mr. Evan E. Lipp, Dean for Enrollment Management, PO Box 600,
  Loretto, PA 15940-0600
Telephone: 814-472-3000 or toll-free 800-342-5732 **Fax:** 814-472-3335
E-mail: admission@sfcpa.edu

Academics

Saint Francis awards associate, bachelor's, and master's **degrees**. Challenging opportunities include advanced placement credit, accelerated degree programs, student-designed majors, freshman honors college, an honors program, double majors, and a senior project. Special programs include internships, summer session for credit, off-campus study, study-abroad, and Army ROTC. A complete listing of majors at Saint Francis appears in the Majors Index beginning on page 460.

The **faculty** at Saint Francis has 87 full-time members, 71% with terminal degrees. The student-faculty ratio is 11:1.

Students of Saint Francis

The student body totals 1,945, of whom 1,401 are undergraduates. 60.2% are women and 39.8% are men. Students come from 29 states and territories. 77% are from Pennsylvania. 0.6% are international students. 6.4% are African American, 0.2% American Indian, 0.3% Asian American, and 0.8% Hispanic American. 70% returned for their sophomore year.

Facilities and Resources

Student rooms are linked to a campus network. 60 **computers** are available on campus for student use. The **library** has 121,940 books and 5,386 subscriptions.

Campus Life

There are 54 active organizations on campus, including a drama/theater group, newspaper, radio station, television station, and choral group. 17% of eligible men and 12% of eligible women are members of national **fraternities**, national **sororities**, and local sororities.

Saint Francis is a member of the NCAA (Division I). **Intercollegiate sports** (some offering scholarships) include basketball, cross-country running, field hockey (w), football (m), golf, lacrosse (w), soccer, softball (w), swimming, tennis, track and field, volleyball.

Campus Safety

Student safety services include late-night transport/escort service, 24-hour emergency telephone alarm devices, 24-hour patrols by trained security personnel, and electronically operated dormitory entrances.

Applying

Saint Francis requires SAT I or ACT, a high school transcript, and 1 recommendation, and in some cases an interview and 3 recommendations. It recommends an essay and an interview. Application deadline: rolling admissions. Deferred admission is possible.

Founded in 1847, Saint Francis is the oldest Franciscan university in the United States. Saint Francis has been helping students to use their minds to reach higher and go farther than they ever dreamed. They've gone on to become teachers, journalists, physical therapists, politicians, engineers, doctors, accountants, chemists, and environmentalists. Nationally ranked programs, a solid and diverse liberal arts curriculum, and a 99% placement rate are a few of the outstanding features students experience at Saint Francis. Saint Francis has consistently fostered the ability to be forward thinking, while maintaining the values on which the University is based.

Getting in Last Year
1,280 applied
87% were accepted
335 enrolled (30%)
22% from top tenth of their h.s. class
3.39 average high school GPA
12% had SAT verbal scores over 600
18% had SAT math scores over 600
47% had ACT scores over 24
1% had SAT verbal scores over 700
3% had SAT math scores over 700
1 National Merit Scholar
5 valedictorians

Graduation and After
41% graduated in 4 years
21% graduated in 5 years
1% graduated in 6 years
39% pursued further study (6% arts and sciences, 4% education, 2% law)
93% had job offers within 6 months
160 organizations recruited on campus

Financial Matters
$19,342 tuition and fees (2003–04)
$7346 room and board
82% average percent of need met
$15,810 average financial aid amount received per undergraduate (2002–03 estimated)

St. John's College

SMALL-TOWN SETTING ■ PRIVATE ■ INDEPENDENT ■ COED
SANTA FE, NEW MEXICO

Web site: www.sjcsf.edu
Contact: Mr. Larry Clendenin, Director of Admissions, 1160 Camino Cruz Blanca, Santa Fe, NM 87505
Telephone: 505-984-6060 or toll-free 800-331-5232 **Fax:** 505-984-6162
E-mail: admissions@sjcsf.edu

St. John's attracts intellectually adventurous students who want an education based on the reading and serious discussions of great books. The texts and their authors are not treated with blind reverence; their conclusions are not swallowed whole. Instead, students learn to question, doubt, analyze, interpret, reject, and most importantly, think for themselves. There are no majors, lectures, or written finals. Instead students work with original texts in discussion-based classes of 17–21 students where professors are as likely as students to be asked to defend their points of view.

Getting in Last Year
338 applied
81% were accepted
138 enrolled (50%)
20% from top tenth of their h.s. class
86% had SAT verbal scores over 600
63% had SAT math scores over 600
87% had ACT scores over 24
31% had SAT verbal scores over 700
13% had SAT math scores over 700
36% had ACT scores over 30
2 National Merit Scholars
3 class presidents
2 valedictorians

Graduation and After
53% graduated in 4 years
9% graduated in 5 years
1% graduated in 6 years
75% pursued further study
25% had job offers within 6 months
10 organizations recruited on campus

Financial Matters
$29,040 tuition and fees (2003–04)
$7320 room and board
91% average percent of need met
$20,424 average financial aid amount received per undergraduate (2002–03 estimated)

Academics
St. John's awards bachelor's and master's **degrees**. A senior project is a challenging opportunity. Special programs include summer session for credit and off-campus study.

The most frequently chosen **baccalaureate** field is liberal arts/general studies. A complete listing of majors at St. John's appears in the Majors Index beginning on page 460.

The **faculty** at St. John's has 68 full-time members, 79% with terminal degrees. The student-faculty ratio is 8:1.

Students of St. John's
The student body totals 535, of whom 434 are undergraduates. 45.6% are women and 54.4% are men. Students come from 57 states and territories and 8 other countries. 12% are from New Mexico. 1.8% are international students. 0.7% are African American, 1.8% American Indian, 2.5% Asian American, and 5.5% Hispanic American. 69% returned for their sophomore year.

Facilities and Resources
20 **computers** are available on campus for student use. The **library** has 65,000 books and 140 subscriptions.

Campus Life
There are 32 active organizations on campus, including a drama/theater group, newspaper, and choral group. No national or local **fraternities** or **sororities**.

Intercollegiate sports include fencing, soccer.

Campus Safety
Student safety services include late-night transport/escort service, 24-hour emergency telephone alarm devices, 24-hour patrols by trained security personnel, and student patrols.

Applying
St. John's requires an essay, a high school transcript, and 2 recommendations, and in some cases SAT I or ACT and an interview. It recommends an interview and 3 recommendations. Application deadline: rolling admissions; 2/15 priority date for financial aid. Early and deferred admission are possible.

St. John's College

SMALL-TOWN SETTING ■ PRIVATE ■ INDEPENDENT ■ COED
ANNAPOLIS, MARYLAND

Web site: www.sjca.edu
Contact: Mr. John Christensen, Director of Admissions, PO Box 2800, 60 College Avenue, Annapolis, MD 21404
Telephone: 410-626-2522 or toll-free 800-727-9238 **Fax:** 410-269-7916
E-mail: admissions@sjca.edu

Academics

St. John's awards bachelor's and master's **degrees**. A senior project is a challenging opportunity. Special programs include internships and off-campus study.

The most frequently chosen **baccalaureate** field is liberal arts/general studies. A complete listing of majors at St. John's appears in the Majors Index beginning on page 460.

The **faculty** at St. John's has 73 full-time members, 70% with terminal degrees. The student-faculty ratio is 8:1.

Students of St. John's

The student body totals 557, of whom 472 are undergraduates. 46.2% are women and 53.8% are men. Students come from 47 states and territories and 6 other countries. 14% are from Maryland. 1.5% are international students. 0.6% are African American, 0.6% American Indian, 1.5% Asian American, and 2.8% Hispanic American. 83% returned for their sophomore year.

Facilities and Resources

Student rooms are linked to a campus network. 16 **computers** are available on campus that provide access to the Internet. The 2 **libraries** have 93,668 books and 114 subscriptions.

Campus Life

There are 35 active organizations on campus, including a drama/theater group, newspaper, choral group, and marching band. No national or local **fraternities** or **sororities**.

This institution has no intercollegiate sports.

Campus Safety

Student safety services include late-night transport/escort service, 24-hour emergency telephone alarm devices, 24-hour patrols by trained security personnel, and electronically operated dormitory entrances.

Applying

St. John's requires an essay, a high school transcript, and 2 recommendations, and in some cases SAT I or ACT. It recommends SAT I or ACT and an interview. Application deadline: rolling admissions; 2/15 priority date for financial aid. Early and deferred admission are possible.

Great Books Program: St. John's offers an integrated liberal arts and sciences curriculum structured around seminar discussions of major works of Western civilization. These discussions are supported by tutorials in mathematics, music, language, and the physical sciences. Only original sources are read, and all classes are small discussion groups.

Getting in Last Year
531 applied
73% were accepted
138 enrolled (35%)
36% from top tenth of their h.s. class
92% had SAT verbal scores over 600
75% had SAT math scores over 600
51% had SAT verbal scores over 700
25% had SAT math scores over 700
14 National Merit Scholars

Graduation and After
58% graduated in 4 years
7% graduated in 5 years
1% graduated in 6 years
12% pursued further study (5% arts and sciences, 3% law, 1% business)
50% had job offers within 6 months
9 organizations recruited on campus

Financial Matters
$29,040 tuition and fees (2003–04)
$7320 room and board
90% average percent of need met
$22,262 average financial aid amount received per undergraduate (2002–03 estimated)

Saint John's University
COORDINATE WITH COLLEGE OF SAINT BENEDICT

RURAL SETTING ■ PRIVATE ■ INDEPENDENT RELIGIOUS ■ COED, PRIMARILY MEN
COLLEGEVILLE, MINNESOTA

Web site: www.csbsju.edu
Contact: Ms. Renee Miller, Director of Admission, PO Box 7155, Collegeville, MN 56321-7155
Telephone: 320-363-2196 or toll-free 800-544-1489 **Fax:** 320-363-2750
E-mail: admissions@csbsju.edu

Through a partnership of 2 national liberal arts colleges, the College of Saint Benedict (for women) and Saint John's University (for men) come together to offer one exceptional education. Enriched by a Catholic and Benedictine tradition, the colleges promote an integrated learning experience that combines a challenging academic program with extensive opportunities for international study, leadership, service, spiritual growth, and cultural and athletic involvement. The colleges' residential campuses, set amid the woods and lakes of central Minnesota, are excellent places for active students to become fully immersed in their college education.

Getting in Last Year
1,049 applied
89% were accepted
490 enrolled (53%)
20% from top tenth of their h.s. class
3.49 average high school GPA
45% had SAT verbal scores over 600
53% had SAT math scores over 600
64% had ACT scores over 24
5% had SAT verbal scores over 700
10% had SAT math scores over 700
14% had ACT scores over 30
1 National Merit Scholar

Graduation and After
74% graduated in 4 years
8% graduated in 5 years
1% graduated in 6 years
16% pursued further study (5% arts and sciences, 2% law, 2% medicine)
70 organizations recruited on campus

Financial Matters
$20,685 tuition and fees (2003–04)
$5788 room and board
86% average percent of need met
$17,585 average financial aid amount received per undergraduate

Academics

St. John's awards bachelor's, master's, and first-professional **degrees** (coordinate with College of Saint Benedict for women). Challenging opportunities include advanced placement credit, accelerated degree programs, student-designed majors, an honors program, double majors, independent study, and a senior project. Special programs include internships, off-campus study, study-abroad, and Army ROTC.

The most frequently chosen **baccalaureate** fields are business/marketing, social sciences and history, and English. A complete listing of majors at St. John's appears in the Majors Index beginning on page 460.

The **faculty** at St. John's has 149 full-time members, 85% with terminal degrees. The student-faculty ratio is 13:1.

Students of St. John's

The student body totals 2,067, of whom 1,940 are undergraduates. 100% are men. Students come from 34 states and territories and 25 other countries. 86% are from Minnesota. 3.5% are international students. 0.5% are African American, 0.4% American Indian, 1.9% Asian American, and 1.2% Hispanic American. 90% returned for their sophomore year.

Facilities and Resources

Student rooms are linked to a campus network. 541 **computers** are available on campus that provide access to the Internet. The 3 **libraries** have 805,376 books and 5,735 subscriptions.

Campus Life

There are 90 active organizations on campus, including a drama/theater group, newspaper, radio station, and choral group. No national or local **fraternities** or **sororities**.

St. John's is a member of the NCAA (Division III). **Intercollegiate sports** include baseball (m), basketball (m), cross-country running (m), football (m), golf (m), ice hockey (m), skiing (cross-country) (m), soccer (m), swimming (m), tennis (m), track and field (m), wrestling (m).

Campus Safety

Student safety services include well-lit pathways, 911 center on campus, closed circuit TV monitors, late-night transport/escort service, 24-hour emergency telephone alarm devices, and 24-hour patrols by trained security personnel.

Applying

St. John's requires an essay, SAT I or ACT, a high school transcript, and 1 recommendation. It recommends an interview and a minimum high school GPA of 3.0. Application deadline: 1/15; 3/15 priority date for financial aid. Early and deferred admission are possible.

SAINT JOSEPH'S UNIVERSITY

SUBURBAN SETTING ■ PRIVATE ■ INDEPENDENT RELIGIOUS ■ COED
PHILADELPHIA, PENNSYLVANIA

Web site: www.sju.edu
Contact: Ms. Susan Kassab, Director of Admissions, 5600 City Avenue,
   Philadelphia, PA 19131-1395
Telephone: 610-660-1300 or toll-free 888-BEAHAWK (in-state) **Fax:**
   610-660-1314
E-mail: admit@sju.edu

Academics

St. Joseph's awards bachelor's, master's, and doctoral **degrees** and post-bachelor's and post-master's certificates. Challenging opportunities include advanced placement credit, student-designed majors, an honors program, double majors, independent study, and a senior project. Special programs include cooperative education, internships, summer session for credit, off-campus study, study-abroad, and Army and Air Force ROTC.

The most frequently chosen **baccalaureate** fields are business/marketing, social sciences and history, and education. A complete listing of majors at St. Joseph's appears in the Majors Index beginning on page 460.

The **faculty** at St. Joseph's has 250 full-time members, 91% with terminal degrees. The student-faculty ratio is 15:1.

Students of St. Joseph's

The student body totals 7,565, of whom 4,656 are undergraduates. 53.2% are women and 46.8% are men. Students come from 35 states and territories and 29 other countries. 56% are from Pennsylvania. 1.1% are international students. 7% are African American, 0.1% American Indian, 2.7% Asian American, and 2.4% Hispanic American. 88% returned for their sophomore year.

Facilities and Resources

Student rooms are linked to a campus network. 180 **computers** are available on campus that provide access to the Internet. The 2 **libraries** have 347,877 books.

Campus Life

There are 70 active organizations on campus, including a drama/theater group, newspaper, radio station, and choral group. 11% of eligible men and 16% of eligible women are members of national **fraternities** and national **sororities**.

St. Joseph's is a member of the NCAA (Division I). **Intercollegiate sports** (some offering scholarships) include baseball (m), basketball, cross-country running, field hockey (w), golf (m), lacrosse, soccer, softball (w), tennis, track and field.

Campus Safety

Student safety services include 24-hour shuttle/escort service, bicycle patrols, late-night transport/escort service, 24-hour emergency telephone alarm devices, 24-hour patrols by trained security personnel, and electronically operated dormitory entrances.

Applying

St. Joseph's requires an essay, SAT I or ACT, a high school transcript, and 1 recommendation. It recommends SAT II Subject Tests and a minimum high school GPA of 3.0. Application deadline: 2/15 priority date for financial aid. Deferred admission is possible.

Saint Joseph's, Philadelphia's Jesuit university, is located on a beautiful 65-acre suburban campus on the western edge of the city and offers its students a vital relationship with the educational opportunities and rich cultural resources of both the suburban and metropolitan Philadelphia areas. Distinguished by its comprehensive academic opportunities, respected teaching faculty, personal size, and highly successful students and alumni, Saint Joseph's draws top students from across the country and around the world while remaining dedicated to its tradition of service to others. Included in Saint Joseph's list of offerings are several 5-year programs (student earns both a BS and MS) in education, international marketing, psychology, and writing studies.

Getting in Last Year
7,765 applied
48% were accepted
998 enrolled (27%)
3.41 average high school GPA
33% had SAT verbal scores over 600
40% had SAT math scores over 600
5% had SAT verbal scores over 700
6% had SAT math scores over 700

Graduation and After
68% graduated in 4 years
6% graduated in 5 years
1% graduated in 6 years
23% pursued further study (26% education, 25% arts and sciences, 14% law)
70% had job offers within 6 months
150 organizations recruited on campus

Financial Matters
$24,230 tuition and fees (2003–04)
$9040 room and board
80% average percent of need met
$11,300 average financial aid amount received per undergraduate (2001–02)

St. Lawrence University

SMALL-TOWN SETTING ■ PRIVATE ■ INDEPENDENT ■ COED
CANTON, NEW YORK

Web site: www.stlawu.edu
Contact: Ms. Terry Cowdrey, Dean of Admissions and Financial Aid, Payson
  Hall, Canton, NY 13617-1455
Telephone: 315-229-5261 or toll-free 800-285-1856 **Fax:** 315-229-5818
E-mail: admissions@stlawu.edu

With more than 30 majors and minors from which to choose, St. Lawrence students can sample from a variety of disciplines and specialize in those areas that are most intriguing to them. The diverse options for cocurricular activities, including 32 varsity sports, encourage students to further develop their abilities and interests outside of the classroom. The University's location provides students with a residential community while providing access to the Adirondack Mountains as well as to Ottawa and Montreal. St. Lawrence alumni successfully pursue careers and graduate study, consistently achieving placement rates higher than 95% within one year of graduation.

Getting in Last Year
3,082 applied
57% were accepted
566 enrolled (32%)
36% from top tenth of their h.s. class
3.37 average high school GPA
38% had SAT verbal scores over 600
40% had SAT math scores over 600
65% had ACT scores over 24
5% had SAT verbal scores over 700
4% had SAT math scores over 700
7% had ACT scores over 30
15 valedictorians

Graduation and After
69% graduated in 4 years
5% graduated in 5 years
20% pursued further study (7% arts and sciences, 7% education, 4% medicine)
72% had job offers within 6 months
22 organizations recruited on campus

Financial Matters
$28,190 tuition and fees (2003–04)
$7755 room and board
91% average percent of need met
$25,373 average financial aid amount received per undergraduate (2002–03 estimated)

Academics
St. Lawrence awards bachelor's and master's **degrees** and post-master's certificates. Challenging opportunities include advanced placement credit, student-designed majors, double majors, independent study, and a senior project. Special programs include internships, summer session for credit, off-campus study, study-abroad, and Army and Air Force ROTC.

The most frequently chosen **baccalaureate** fields are social sciences and history, English, and psychology. A complete listing of majors at St. Lawrence appears in the Majors Index beginning on page 460.

The **faculty** at St. Lawrence has 161 full-time members, 98% with terminal degrees. The student-faculty ratio is 12:1.

Students of St. Lawrence
The student body totals 2,277, of whom 2,148 are undergraduates. 53.2% are women and 46.8% are men. Students come from 41 states and territories and 21 other countries. 52% are from New York. 4% are international students. 2% are African American, 0.6% American Indian, 1.3% Asian American, and 2.6% Hispanic American. 86% returned for their sophomore year.

Facilities and Resources
Student rooms are linked to a campus network. 600 **computers** are available on campus that provide access to the Internet. The 2 **libraries** have 533,463 books and 2,065 subscriptions.

Campus Life
There are 100 active organizations on campus, including a drama/theater group, newspaper, radio station, television station, and choral group. 15% of eligible men and 23% of eligible women are members of national **fraternities**, national **sororities**, and local sororities.

St. Lawrence is a member of the NCAA (Division III). **Intercollegiate sports** (some offering scholarships) include baseball (m), basketball, crew, cross-country running, equestrian sports, field hockey (w), football (m), golf, ice hockey, lacrosse, skiing (cross-country), skiing (downhill), soccer, softball (w), squash, swimming, tennis, track and field, volleyball (w).

Campus Safety
Student safety services include late-night transport/escort service, 24-hour emergency telephone alarm devices, 24-hour patrols by trained security personnel, student patrols, and electronically operated dormitory entrances.

Applying
St. Lawrence requires an essay, SAT I or ACT, a high school transcript, and 2 recommendations. It recommends SAT II Subject Tests, an interview, and a minimum high school GPA of 2.0. Application deadline: 2/15; 2/15 priority date for financial aid. Deferred admission is possible.

St. Louis College of Pharmacy

Urban setting ■ Private ■ Independent ■ Coed
St. Louis, Missouri

Web site: www.stlcop.edu
Contact: Ms. Patty Kulage, Admissions and Financial Aid Coordinator, 4588 Parkview Place, St. Louis, MO 63110-1088
Telephone: 314-446-8328 or toll-free 800-278-5267 (in-state) **Fax:** 314-446-8310
E-mail: pkulage@stlcop.edu

Academics

St. Louis College of Pharmacy awards bachelor's, master's, and first-professional **degrees** (bachelor of science degree program in pharmaceutical studies cannot be applied to directly; students have the option to transfer in after their second year in the PharmD program. Bachelor's degree candidates are not eligible to take the pharmacist's licensing examination). Advanced placement credit is a challenging opportunity. Special programs include internships, summer session for credit, and Army and Air Force ROTC.

The most frequently chosen **baccalaureate** field is health professions and related sciences. A complete listing of majors at St. Louis College of Pharmacy appears in the Majors Index beginning on page 460.

The **faculty** at St. Louis College of Pharmacy has 67 full-time members, 94% with terminal degrees. The student-faculty ratio is 12:1.

Students of St. Louis College of Pharmacy

The student body totals 927, of whom 170 are undergraduates. 65.3% are women and 34.7% are men. Students come from 10 states and territories. 52% are from Missouri. 0.6% are international students. 4.7% are African American, 11.2% Asian American, and 2.4% Hispanic American. 84% returned for their sophomore year.

Facilities and Resources

Student rooms are linked to a campus network. 75 **computers** are available on campus that provide access to the Internet. The **library** has 59,012 books and 234 subscriptions.

Campus Life

There are 15 active organizations on campus, including a drama/theater group, newspaper, and choral group. 70% of eligible men and 65% of eligible women are members of national **fraternities** and national **sororities**.

St. Louis College of Pharmacy is a member of the NAIA. **Intercollegiate sports** include basketball, cross-country running, volleyball (w).

Campus Safety

Student safety services include late-night transport/escort service, 24-hour emergency telephone alarm devices, 24-hour patrols by trained security personnel, and electronically operated dormitory entrances.

Applying

St. Louis College of Pharmacy requires an essay, SAT I or ACT, a high school transcript, 2 recommendations, and a minimum high school GPA of 3.0, and in some cases an interview. Application deadline: rolling admissions; 11/15 for financial aid, with a 4/1 priority date.

Getting in Last Year

514 applied
44% were accepted
34% from top tenth of their h.s. class
3.70 average high school GPA
75% had ACT scores over 24
11% had ACT scores over 30

Graduation and After

57% graduated in 5 years
17% graduated in 6 years
6% pursued further study (2% arts and sciences, 2% business, 1% law)

Financial Matters

$16,450 tuition and fees (2003–04)
$6500 room and board
31% average percent of need met
$11,324 average financial aid amount received per undergraduate (2000–01 estimated)

SAINT LOUIS UNIVERSITY

URBAN SETTING ■ PRIVATE ■ INDEPENDENT RELIGIOUS ■ COED
ST. LOUIS, MISSOURI

Web site: www.slu.edu
Contact: Ms. Shani Lenore, Director, 221 North Grand Boulevard, St. Louis, MO 63103-2097
Telephone: 314-977-3415 or toll-free 800-758-3678 (out-of-state) **Fax:** 314-977-7136
E-mail: admitme@slu.edu

Founded in 1818 as the second Jesuit university in the nation, Saint Louis University offers more than 2,600 courses each semester with an average class size of 22. Along with its recognition as a national research university, the University's academic rigor and wide variety of programs draw students from nearly all 50 states. SLU is committed to developing the whole person intellectually, spiritually, physically, and socially.

Getting in Last Year
6,405 applied
70% were accepted
1,526 enrolled (34%)
31% from top tenth of their h.s. class
3.60 average high school GPA
48% had SAT verbal scores over 600
55% had SAT math scores over 600
74% had ACT scores over 24
9% had SAT verbal scores over 700
11% had SAT math scores over 700
18% had ACT scores over 30
45 National Merit Scholars

Graduation and After
55% graduated in 4 years
13% graduated in 5 years
2% graduated in 6 years
28% pursued further study
63% had job offers within 6 months
125 organizations recruited on campus

Financial Matters
$22,218 tuition and fees (2003–04)
$7740 room and board
62% average percent of need met
$18,526 average financial aid amount received per undergraduate

Academics
SLU awards associate, bachelor's, master's, doctoral, and first-professional **degrees** and post-bachelor's and post-master's certificates. Challenging opportunities include advanced placement credit, accelerated degree programs, student-designed majors, an honors program, double majors, independent study, and a senior project. Special programs include cooperative education, internships, summer session for credit, off-campus study, study-abroad, and Army and Air Force ROTC.

The most frequently chosen **baccalaureate** fields are business/marketing, health professions and related sciences, and communications/communication technologies. A complete listing of majors at SLU appears in the Majors Index beginning on page 460.

The **faculty** at SLU has 629 full-time members, 94% with terminal degrees. The student-faculty ratio is 12:1.

Students of SLU
The student body totals 11,217, of whom 7,091 are undergraduates. 54.7% are women and 45.3% are men. Students come from 48 states and territories and 78 other countries. 51% are from Missouri. 2.3% are international students. 7.3% are African American, 0.4% American Indian, 4.4% Asian American, and 2.2% Hispanic American. 88% returned for their sophomore year.

Facilities and Resources
Student rooms are linked to a campus network. 6,500 **computers** are available on campus that provide access to the Internet. The 3 **libraries** have 1,340,251 books and 12,881 subscriptions.

Campus Life
There are 100 active organizations on campus, including a drama/theater group, newspaper, radio station, television station, and choral group. 21% of eligible men and 18% of eligible women are members of national **fraternities** and national **sororities**.

SLU is a member of the NCAA (Division I). **Intercollegiate sports** (some offering scholarships) include baseball (m), basketball, cross-country running, field hockey (w), golf (m), softball (w), swimming, tennis.

Campus Safety
Student safety services include crime prevention program, bicycle patrols, pamphlets, posters, films, late-night transport/escort service, 24-hour emergency telephone alarm devices, 24-hour patrols by trained security personnel, student patrols, and electronically operated dormitory entrances.

Applying
SLU requires an essay, SAT I or ACT, a high school transcript, and secondary school report form. It recommends an interview, 2 recommendations, and a minimum high school GPA of 2.5. Application deadline: rolling admissions; 3/1 priority date for financial aid. Deferred admission is possible.

SAINT MARY'S COLLEGE

SUBURBAN SETTING ■ PRIVATE ■ INDEPENDENT RELIGIOUS ■ WOMEN ONLY
NOTRE DAME, INDIANA

Web site: www.saintmarys.edu
Contact: Ms. Mary Pat Nolan, Director of Admission, Notre Dame, IN
  46556
Telephone: 574-284-4587 or toll-free 800-551-7621
E-mail: admission@saintmarys.edu

Academics
Saint Mary's awards bachelor's **degrees**. Challenging opportunities include advanced placement credit, accelerated degree programs, student-designed majors, double majors, independent study, and a senior project. Special programs include cooperative education, internships, summer session for credit, off-campus study, study-abroad, and Army, Navy and Air Force ROTC.

The most frequently chosen **baccalaureate** fields are communications/communication technologies, social sciences and history, and business/marketing. A complete listing of majors at Saint Mary's appears in the Majors Index beginning on page 460.

The **faculty** at Saint Mary's has 114 full-time members, 89% with terminal degrees. The student-faculty ratio is 11:1.

Students of Saint Mary's
The student body is made up of 1,475 undergraduates. Students come from 47 states and territories and 12 other countries. 27% are from Indiana. 1% are international students. 1.2% are African American, 0.3% American Indian, 1.9% Asian American, and 4.9% Hispanic American. 85% returned for their sophomore year.

Facilities and Resources
Student rooms are linked to a campus network. 198 **computers** are available on campus that provide access to the Internet. The **library** has 210,812 books and 776 subscriptions.

Campus Life
There are 116 active organizations on campus, including a drama/theater group, newspaper, radio station, choral group, and marching band. No national or local **sororities**.

Saint Mary's is a member of the NCAA (Division III). **Intercollegiate sports** include basketball, soccer, softball, swimming, tennis, volleyball.

Campus Safety
Student safety services include late-night transport/escort service, 24-hour emergency telephone alarm devices, 24-hour patrols by trained security personnel, and electronically operated dormitory entrances.

Applying
Saint Mary's requires an essay, SAT I or ACT, a high school transcript, and 1 recommendation. It recommends an interview. Application deadline: 3/1; 3/1 priority date for financial aid. Early and deferred admission are possible.

Founded and still sponsored by the Congregation of the Sisters of the Holy Cross in 1844, Saint Mary's College has preserved the best of its rich heritage even as it pioneers new approaches to educating today's women. At Saint Mary's, students get a solid liberal arts foundation as well as great preparation for career opportunities or graduate and professional programs. Students also enjoy "the best of both worlds" through academic and social co-exchange programs with the University of Notre Dame located across the street. With 1,600 students from forty-nine states and twelve countries, Saint Mary's brings together women from a wide range of geographical areas, social backgrounds, and education experiences.

Getting in Last Year
1,014 applied
82% were accepted
402 enrolled (49%)
33% from top tenth of their h.s. class
3.65 average high school GPA
32% had SAT verbal scores over 600
31% had SAT math scores over 600
4% had SAT verbal scores over 700
3% had SAT math scores over 700
1 National Merit Scholar
8 class presidents
12 valedictorians

Graduation and After
75% graduated in 4 years
3% graduated in 5 years
1% graduated in 6 years
22% pursued further study (5% arts and sciences, 4% business, 3% education)
77% had job offers within 6 months
53 organizations recruited on campus

Financial Matters
$21,974 tuition and fees (2003–04)
$7289 room and board
86% average percent of need met
$16,507 average financial aid amount received per undergraduate (2002–03 estimated)

SAINT MARY'S COLLEGE OF CALIFORNIA

SUBURBAN SETTING ■ PRIVATE ■ INDEPENDENT RELIGIOUS ■ COED
MORAGA, CALIFORNIA

Web site: www.stmarys-ca.edu
Contact: Ms. Dorothy Jones, Dean of Admissions, PO Box 4800, Moraga, CA 94556-4800
Telephone: 925-631-4224 or toll-free 800-800-4SMC **Fax:** 925-376-7193
E-mail: smcadmit@stmarys-ca.edu

It has been said that Saint Mary's College is "a classic example of a school committed to teaching students *how* to think rather than *what* to think." It is home to some of the "happiest students in the nation," has a safe and beautiful campus, and is a "good buy." Saint Mary's intimate academic community of 2,500 undergraduates is located 20 miles east of San Francisco. Operated and owned by the Christian Brothers, the College is committed to providing students with a comprehensive liberal arts education that includes reading and discussing the Great Books.

Getting in Last Year
3,172 applied
82% were accepted
562 enrolled (22%)
3.33 average high school GPA
22% had SAT verbal scores over 600
27% had SAT math scores over 600
34% had ACT scores over 24
3% had SAT verbal scores over 700
2% had SAT math scores over 700
2% had ACT scores over 30

Graduation and After
65% graduated in 4 years
3% graduated in 5 years
1% graduated in 6 years
18% pursued further study
46% had job offers within 6 months
74 organizations recruited on campus

Financial Matters
$23,775 tuition and fees (2003–04)
$9075 room and board
76% average percent of need met
$20,460 average financial aid amount received per undergraduate

Academics

Saint Mary's awards bachelor's, master's, and doctoral **degrees**. Challenging opportunities include advanced placement credit, student-designed majors, an honors program, double majors, independent study, and a senior project. Special programs include internships, off-campus study, study-abroad, and Army and Air Force ROTC.

The most frequently chosen **baccalaureate** fields are business/marketing, communications/communication technologies, and psychology. A complete listing of majors at Saint Mary's appears in the Majors Index beginning on page 460.

The **faculty** at Saint Mary's has 208 full-time members, 90% with terminal degrees. The student-faculty ratio is 12:1.

Students of Saint Mary's

The student body totals 4,486, of whom 3,337 are undergraduates. 59.8% are women and 40.2% are men. Students come from 26 states and territories and 21 other countries. 83% are from California. 3% are international students. 6.6% are African American, 0.8% American Indian, 10.1% Asian American, and 17.7% Hispanic American. 84% returned for their sophomore year.

Facilities and Resources

Student rooms are linked to a campus network. 250 **computers** are available on campus that provide access to the Internet. The 2 **libraries** have 207,076 books and 1,070 subscriptions.

Campus Life

There are 42 active organizations on campus, including a drama/theater group, newspaper, radio station, television station, and choral group. No national or local **fraternities** or **sororities**.

Saint Mary's is a member of the NCAA (Division I). **Intercollegiate sports** (some offering scholarships) include baseball (m), basketball, cheerleading, crew (w), cross-country running, football (m), golf (m), lacrosse (w), soccer, softball (w), tennis, volleyball (w).

Campus Safety

Student safety services include late-night transport/escort service, 24-hour emergency telephone alarm devices, and 24-hour patrols by trained security personnel.

Applying

Saint Mary's requires an essay, SAT I or ACT, a high school transcript, 1 recommendation, and a minimum high school GPA of 2.0, and in some cases an interview and a minimum high school GPA of 3.0. It recommends a minimum high school GPA of 3.0. Application deadline: 2/1; 3/2 for financial aid. Deferred admission is possible.

St. Mary's College of Maryland

RURAL SETTING ■ PUBLIC ■ STATE-SUPPORTED ■ COED
ST. MARY'S CITY, MARYLAND

Web site: www.smcm.edu
Contact: Mr. Richard J. Edgar, Director of Admissions, 18952 East Fisher Road, St. Mary's City, MD 20686-3001
Telephone: 240-895-5000 or toll-free 800-492-7181 **Fax:** 240-895-5001
E-mail: admissions@smcm.edu

Academics

St. Mary's awards bachelor's **degrees**. Challenging opportunities include advanced placement credit, student-designed majors, freshman honors college, an honors program, double majors, independent study, and a senior project. Special programs include cooperative education, internships, summer session for credit, off-campus study, and study-abroad.

The most frequently chosen **baccalaureate** fields are social sciences and history, psychology, and biological/life sciences. A complete listing of majors at St. Mary's appears in the Majors Index beginning on page 460.

The **faculty** at St. Mary's has 117 full-time members, 97% with terminal degrees. The student-faculty ratio is 13:1.

Students of St. Mary's

The student body is made up of 1,922 undergraduates. 60.3% are women and 39.7% are men. Students come from 38 states and territories and 27 other countries. 83% are from Maryland. 0.7% are international students. 6.2% are African American, 0.4% American Indian, 3.6% Asian American, and 2.8% Hispanic American. 85% returned for their sophomore year.

Facilities and Resources

Student rooms are linked to a campus network. 180 **computers** are available on campus that provide access to e-mail and the Internet. The **library** has 153,827 books and 1,797 subscriptions.

Campus Life

There are 75 active organizations on campus, including a drama/theater group, newspaper, radio station, television station, and choral group. No national or local **fraternities** or **sororities**.

St. Mary's is a member of the NCAA (Division III). **Intercollegiate sports** include baseball (m), basketball, field hockey (w), lacrosse, sailing, soccer, swimming, tennis, volleyball (w).

Campus Safety

Student safety services include late-night transport/escort service, 24-hour emergency telephone alarm devices, 24-hour patrols by trained security personnel, student patrols, and electronically operated dormitory entrances.

Applying

St. Mary's requires an essay, SAT I or ACT, a high school transcript, and a minimum high school GPA of 2.0. It recommends an interview and 2 recommendations. Application deadline: 1/15; 3/1 for financial aid. Early admission is possible.

St. Mary's College of Maryland, with its distinctive identity as Maryland's "Public Honors College," is one of the finest liberal arts and sciences colleges in the country. The lively academic atmosphere and stunning beauty of the riverfront campus create a challenging and memorable college experience. Fifty percent of graduates go directly to graduate or professional school. Apartment-style residences opened in 2003 and athletic facilities will be completed in 2004.

Getting in Last Year

2,262 applied
55% were accepted
421 enrolled (34%)
47% from top tenth of their h.s. class
3.50 average high school GPA
72% had SAT verbal scores over 600
66% had SAT math scores over 600
20% had SAT verbal scores over 700
15% had SAT math scores over 700

Graduation and After

67% graduated in 4 years
7% graduated in 5 years
1% graduated in 6 years
32% pursued further study (9% arts and sciences, 8% education, 6% law)
55% had job offers within 6 months
132 organizations recruited on campus

Financial Matters

$8803 resident tuition and fees (2003–04)
$15,123 nonresident tuition and fees (2003–04)
$7105 room and board
62% average percent of need met
$6755 average financial aid amount received per undergraduate

St. Norbert College

Suburban setting ■ Private ■ Independent Religious ■ Coed
De Pere, Wisconsin

Web site: www.snc.edu
Contact: Mr. Daniel L. Meyer, Dean of Admission and Enrollment
Management, 100 Grant Street, De Pere, WI 54115-2099
Telephone: 920-403-3005 or toll-free 800-236-4878 **Fax:** 920-403-4072
E-mail: admit@snc.edu

Recognized nationally for its academic program, St. Norbert College provides students with the resources necessary to compete with the nation's best. With a faculty determined to provide the best instruction and advising possible, the College is committed to helping students achieve their educational goals. The College community, steeped in the values of the Norbertine tradition, encourages students to discover ways in which they can use their talents to enrich their lives, society, and the world. St. Norbert students contribute their talents to 27 on-campus community service organizations.

Getting in Last Year
1,658 applied
86% were accepted
529 enrolled (37%)
26% from top tenth of their h.s. class
3.43 average high school GPA
54% had ACT scores over 24
9% had ACT scores over 30
6 National Merit Scholars
13 class presidents
14 valedictorians

Graduation and After
67% graduated in 4 years
8% graduated in 5 years
1% graduated in 6 years
20% pursued further study
83.13% had job offers within 6 months
41 organizations recruited on campus

Financial Matters
$20,072 tuition and fees (2003–04)
$5738 room and board
88% average percent of need met
$14,718 average financial aid amount received per undergraduate (2002–03 estimated)

Academics

St. Norbert awards bachelor's and master's **degrees**. Challenging opportunities include advanced placement credit, student-designed majors, an honors program, double majors, independent study, and a senior project. Special programs include cooperative education, internships, summer session for credit, off-campus study, study-abroad, and Army ROTC.

The most frequently chosen **baccalaureate** fields are business/marketing, social sciences and history, and communications/communication technologies. A complete listing of majors at St. Norbert appears in the Majors Index beginning on page 460.

The **faculty** at St. Norbert has 121 full-time members, 93% with terminal degrees. The student-faculty ratio is 15:1.

Students of St. Norbert

The student body totals 2,155, of whom 2,086 are undergraduates. 56.5% are women and 43.5% are men. Students come from 26 states and territories and 15 other countries. 71% are from Wisconsin. 2.5% are international students. 0.8% are African American, 0.8% American Indian, 1.5% Asian American, and 1.6% Hispanic American. 85% returned for their sophomore year.

Facilities and Resources

Student rooms are linked to a campus network. 202 **computers** are available on campus that provide access to the Internet. The **library** has 115,553 books and 690 subscriptions.

Campus Life

There are 70 active organizations on campus, including a drama/theater group, newspaper, radio station, television station, and choral group. 15% of eligible women are members of national **fraternities**, national **sororities**, local fraternities, and local sororities.

St. Norbert is a member of the NCAA (Division III). **Intercollegiate sports** include baseball (m), basketball, cheerleading, cross-country running, football (m), golf, ice hockey (m), soccer, softball (w), swimming (w), tennis, track and field, volleyball (w).

Campus Safety

Student safety services include crime prevention programs, late-night transport/escort service, 24-hour emergency telephone alarm devices, 24-hour patrols by trained security personnel, student patrols, and electronically operated dormitory entrances.

Applying

St. Norbert requires an essay, SAT I or ACT, a high school transcript, and 1 recommendation. It recommends an interview. Application deadline: rolling admissions; 3/1 priority date for financial aid. Deferred admission is possible.

St. Olaf College

SMALL-TOWN SETTING ■ PRIVATE ■ INDEPENDENT RELIGIOUS ■ COED
NORTHFIELD, MINNESOTA

Web site: www.stolaf.edu
Contact: Mr. Jeff McLaughlin, Director of Admissions, 1520 St. Olaf Avenue, Northfield, MN 55057
Telephone: 507-646-3025 or toll-free 800-800-3025 **Fax:** 507-646-3832
E-mail: admiss@stolaf.edu

Academics

St. Olaf awards bachelor's **degrees**. Challenging opportunities include advanced placement credit, student-designed majors, double majors, independent study, and a senior project. Special programs include internships, summer session for credit, off-campus study, and study-abroad.

The most frequently chosen **baccalaureate** fields are social sciences and history, visual/performing arts, and biological/life sciences. A complete listing of majors at St. Olaf appears in the Majors Index beginning on page 460.

The **faculty** at St. Olaf has 206 full-time members, 91% with terminal degrees. The student-faculty ratio is 12:1.

Students of St. Olaf

The student body is made up of 2,994 undergraduates. 58.9% are women and 41.1% are men. Students come from 49 states and territories and 22 other countries. 55% are from Minnesota. 1% are international students. 1.2% are African American, 0.2% American Indian, 3.8% Asian American, and 1.5% Hispanic American. 92% returned for their sophomore year.

Facilities and Resources

Student rooms are linked to a campus network. 805 **computers** are available on campus that provide access to the Internet. The 4 **libraries** have 654,950 books and 1,616 subscriptions.

Campus Life

There are 114 active organizations on campus, including a drama/theater group, newspaper, radio station, and choral group. No national or local **fraternities** or **sororities**.

St. Olaf is a member of the NCAA (Division III). **Intercollegiate sports** include baseball (m), basketball, cross-country running, football (m), golf, ice hockey, skiing (cross-country), skiing (downhill), soccer, softball (w), swimming, tennis, track and field, volleyball (w), wrestling (m).

Campus Safety

Student safety services include lighted pathways and sidewalks, late-night transport/escort service, 24-hour emergency telephone alarm devices, 24-hour patrols by trained security personnel, and electronically operated dormitory entrances.

Applying

St. Olaf requires an essay, SAT I or ACT, a high school transcript, and 2 recommendations. It recommends an interview. Application deadline: rolling admissions; 2/15 priority date for financial aid. Deferred admission is possible.

Getting in Last Year

2,517 applied
75% were accepted
720 enrolled (38%)
47% from top tenth of their h.s. class
3.64 average high school GPA
70% had SAT verbal scores over 600
72% had SAT math scores over 600
85% had ACT scores over 24
26% had SAT verbal scores over 700
21% had SAT math scores over 700
28% had ACT scores over 30
39 National Merit Scholars
22 class presidents
64 valedictorians

Graduation and After

75% graduated in 4 years
6% graduated in 5 years
1% graduated in 6 years
27% pursued further study (14% arts and sciences, 4% medicine, 3% law)
65.4% had job offers within 6 months
121 organizations recruited on campus

Financial Matters

$23,650 tuition and fees (2003–04)
$4850 room and board
100% average percent of need met
$16,873 average financial aid amount received per undergraduate (2002–03 estimated)

SALEM COLLEGE

URBAN SETTING ■ PRIVATE ■ INDEPENDENT RELIGIOUS ■ WOMEN ONLY
WINSTON-SALEM, NORTH CAROLINA

Getting in Last Year
438 applied
70% were accepted
163 enrolled (53%)
35% from top tenth of their h.s. class
3.50 average high school GPA
40% had SAT verbal scores over 600
34% had SAT math scores over 600
7% had SAT verbal scores over 700
4% had SAT math scores over 700

Graduation and After
54% graduated in 4 years
4% graduated in 5 years
20% pursued further study (13% arts and
    sciences, 3% education, 1% business)
77% had job offers within 6 months

Financial Matters
$15,715 tuition and fees (2003–04)
$8870 room and board
$12,300 average financial aid amount received
    per undergraduate

Web site: www.salem.edu
Contact: Ms. Dana E. Evans, Dean of Admissions and Financial Aid, PO Box
    10548, Shober House, Winston-Salem, NC 27108
Telephone: 336-721-2621 or toll-free 800-327-2536 **Fax:** 336-724-7102
E-mail: admissions@salem.edu

Academics

Salem awards bachelor's and master's **degrees** (only students 23 or over are eligible to enroll part-time; men may attend evening program only). Challenging opportunities include advanced placement credit, student-designed majors, an honors program, double majors, independent study, and a senior project. Special programs include internships, summer session for credit, off-campus study, study-abroad, and Army ROTC.

The most frequently chosen **baccalaureate** fields are social sciences and history, communications/communication technologies, and psychology. A complete listing of majors at Salem appears in the Majors Index beginning on page 460.

The **faculty** at Salem has 52 full-time members, 90% with terminal degrees. The student-faculty ratio is 13:1.

Students of Salem

The student body totals 1,091, of whom 910 are undergraduates. Students come from 25 states and territories and 17 other countries. 58% are from North Carolina. 5.7% are international students. 19.9% are African American, 0.6% American Indian, 1.3% Asian American, and 2.6% Hispanic American. 79% returned for their sophomore year.

Facilities and Resources

Student rooms are linked to a campus network. 54 **computers** are available on campus that provide access to e-mail and the Internet. The 2 **libraries** have 128,072 books and 427 subscriptions.

Campus Life

There are 41 active organizations on campus, including a drama/theater group, newspaper, choral group, and marching band. No national or local **sororities**.

Intercollegiate sports include basketball, cross-country running, equestrian sports, field hockey, soccer, softball, swimming, tennis, volleyball.

Campus Safety

Student safety services include late-night transport/escort service, 24-hour emergency telephone alarm devices, 24-hour patrols by trained security personnel, and electronically operated dormitory entrances.

Applying

Salem requires an essay, SAT I or ACT, a high school transcript, and 2 recommendations. It recommends an interview. Application deadline: rolling admissions; 3/1 priority date for financial aid. Early and deferred admission are possible.

SAMFORD UNIVERSITY

SUBURBAN SETTING ■ PRIVATE ■ INDEPENDENT RELIGIOUS ■ COED
BIRMINGHAM, ALABAMA

Web site: www.samford.edu
Contact: Dr. Phil Kimrey, Dean of Admissions and Financial Aid, 800
Lakeshore Drive, Samford Hall, Birmingham, AL 35229-0002
Telephone: 205-726-3673 or toll-free 800-888-7218 **Fax:** 205-726-2171
E-mail: admiss@samford.edu

Academics

Samford awards associate, bachelor's, master's, doctoral, and first-professional **degrees** and post-master's certificates. Challenging opportunities include advanced placement credit, accelerated degree programs, an honors program, double majors, and a senior project. Special programs include cooperative education, internships, summer session for credit, off-campus study, study-abroad, and Army and Air Force ROTC.

The most frequently chosen **baccalaureate** fields are business/marketing, education, and social sciences and history. A complete listing of majors at Samford appears in the Majors Index beginning on page 460.

The **faculty** at Samford has 264 full-time members, 80% with terminal degrees. The student-faculty ratio is 13:1.

Students of Samford

The student body totals 4,440, of whom 2,882 are undergraduates. 64% are women and 36% are men. Students come from 41 states and territories. 46% are from Alabama. 0.4% are international students. 6.2% are African American, 0.5% American Indian, 0.3% Asian American, and 0.6% Hispanic American. 89% returned for their sophomore year.

Facilities and Resources

Student rooms are linked to a campus network. 350 **computers** are available on campus that provide access to the Internet. The 4 **libraries** have 439,760 books and 3,724 subscriptions.

Campus Life

There are 102 active organizations on campus, including a drama/theater group, newspaper, radio station, choral group, and marching band. 35% of eligible men and 48% of eligible women are members of national **fraternities** and national **sororities**.

Samford is a member of the NCAA (Division I). **Intercollegiate sports** (some offering scholarships) include baseball (m), basketball, cross-country running, football (m), golf, soccer (w), softball (w), tennis, track and field, volleyball (w).

Campus Safety

Student safety services include late-night transport/escort service, 24-hour emergency telephone alarm devices, 24-hour patrols by trained security personnel, and student patrols.

Applying

Samford requires an essay, SAT I or ACT, a high school transcript, 1 recommendation, and leadership resumé. It recommends an interview. Application deadline: 3/1 priority date for financial aid. Early and deferred admission are possible.

Samford University is the largest private accredited university in Alabama, yet, with 4,500 students, it is an ideal size. More than half the undergraduates reside on campus. Students from 39 states and territories and 25 other countries enjoy a beautiful setting characterized by Georgian-Colonial architecture. The institution takes seriously its Christian heritage and is consistently listed in rankings of Southeastern institutions. Faculty members have earned degrees from more than 160 colleges and universities, with more than 80% holding the terminal degree in their field. Excellent opportunities to "stretch" academically, socially, physically, and spiritually are provided, as are special opportunities in computer competency, international experiences, and externships.

Getting in Last Year
2,074 applied
90% were accepted
684 enrolled (37%)
36% from top tenth of their h.s. class
3.63 average high school GPA
35% had SAT verbal scores over 600
38% had SAT math scores over 600
64% had ACT scores over 24
10% had SAT verbal scores over 700
6% had SAT math scores over 700
12% had ACT scores over 30
7 National Merit Scholars
15 class presidents
27 valedictorians

Graduation and After
150 organizations recruited on campus

Financial Matters
$13,154 tuition and fees (2003–04)
$5244 room and board
72% average percent of need met
$9708 average financial aid amount received per undergraduate (2002–03)

SANTA CLARA UNIVERSITY

SUBURBAN SETTING ■ PRIVATE ■ INDEPENDENT RELIGIOUS ■ COED
SANTA CLARA, CALIFORNIA

Web site: www.scu.edu
Contact: Ms. Sandra Hayes, Dean of Undergraduate Admissions, 500 El
  Camino Real, Santa Clara, CA 95053
Telephone: 408-554-4700 **Fax:** 408-554-5255
E-mail: ugadmissions@scu.edu

Getting in Last Year
6,388 applied
66% were accepted
897 enrolled (21%)
38% from top tenth of their h.s. class
3.53 average high school GPA
43% had SAT verbal scores over 600
58% had SAT math scores over 600
75% had ACT scores over 24
6% had SAT verbal scores over 700
10% had SAT math scores over 700
13% had ACT scores over 30
14 National Merit Scholars
31 valedictorians

Graduation and After
76% graduated in 4 years
7% graduated in 5 years
2% graduated in 6 years
20% pursued further study (4% arts and sciences, 4% medicine, 3% education)
297 organizations recruited on campus

Financial Matters
$25,365 tuition and fees (2003–04)
$9336 room and board
81% average percent of need met
$14,718 average financial aid amount received per undergraduate (2001–02)

Academics

Santa Clara awards bachelor's, master's, doctoral, and first-professional **degrees** and post-bachelor's, post-master's, and first-professional certificates. Challenging opportunities include advanced placement credit, student-designed majors, an honors program, double majors, independent study, and a senior project. Special programs include cooperative education, internships, summer session for credit, study-abroad, and Army and Air Force ROTC.

The most frequently chosen **baccalaureate** fields are business/marketing, social sciences and history, and engineering/engineering technologies. A complete listing of majors at Santa Clara appears in the Majors Index beginning on page 460.

The **faculty** at Santa Clara has 416 full-time members, 92% with terminal degrees. The student-faculty ratio is 12:1.

Students of Santa Clara

The student body totals 7,794, of whom 4,298 are undergraduates. 54.8% are women and 45.2% are men. Students come from 35 states and territories and 12 other countries. 66% are from California. 2.9% are international students. 2% are African American, 0.6% American Indian, 18.7% Asian American, and 13.7% Hispanic American. 92% returned for their sophomore year.

Facilities and Resources

Student rooms are linked to a campus network. 682 **computers** are available on campus that provide access to the Internet. The 2 **libraries** have 639,691 books and 11,952 subscriptions.

Campus Life

There are 86 active organizations on campus, including a drama/theater group, newspaper, radio station, television station, and choral group. No national or local **fraternities** or **sororities**.

Santa Clara is a member of the NCAA (Division I). **Intercollegiate sports** (some offering scholarships) include baseball (m), basketball, crew, cross-country running, golf, soccer, softball (w), tennis, volleyball (w), water polo (m).

Campus Safety

Student safety services include late-night transport/escort service, 24-hour emergency telephone alarm devices, 24-hour patrols by trained security personnel, and electronically operated dormitory entrances.

Applying

Santa Clara requires an essay, SAT I or ACT, a high school transcript, and 1 recommendation. It recommends an interview. Application deadline: 1/15; 2/1 priority date for financial aid. Deferred admission is possible.

SARAH LAWRENCE COLLEGE

SUBURBAN SETTING ■ PRIVATE ■ INDEPENDENT ■ COED
BRONXVILLE, NEW YORK

Web site: www.sarahlawrence.edu
Contact: Ms. Thyra L. Briggs, Dean of Admission, 1 Mead Way, Bronxville, NY 10708-5999
Telephone: 914-395-2510 or toll-free 800-888-2858 **Fax:** 914-395-2515
E-mail: slcadmit@slc.edu

Academics

Sarah Lawrence awards bachelor's and master's **degrees**. Challenging opportunities include advanced placement credit, student-designed majors, and independent study. Special programs include internships, off-campus study, and study-abroad.

The most frequently chosen **baccalaureate** field is liberal arts/general studies. A complete listing of majors at Sarah Lawrence appears in the Majors Index beginning on page 460.

The **faculty** at Sarah Lawrence has 180 full-time members. The student-faculty ratio is 6:1.

Students of Sarah Lawrence

The student body totals 1,606, of whom 1,292 are undergraduates. 73.8% are women and 26.2% are men. Students come from 46 states and territories and 25 other countries. 19% are from New York. 2% are international students. 4.6% are African American, 0.5% American Indian, 4.6% Asian American, and 3.5% Hispanic American. 93% returned for their sophomore year.

Facilities and Resources

Student rooms are linked to a campus network. 110 **computers** are available on campus that provide access to the Internet. The 3 **libraries** have 193,581 books and 1,260 subscriptions.

Campus Life

There are 30 active organizations on campus, including a drama/theater group, newspaper, radio station, and choral group. No national or local **fraternities** or **sororities**.

Intercollegiate sports include crew, cross-country running, equestrian sports, swimming (w), tennis, volleyball (w).

Campus Safety

Student safety services include late-night transport/escort service, 24-hour emergency telephone alarm devices, 24-hour patrols by trained security personnel, student patrols, and electronically operated dormitory entrances.

Applying

Sarah Lawrence requires an essay, a high school transcript, and 3 recommendations. It recommends an interview and a minimum high school GPA of 3.0. Application deadline: 1/1; 2/1 for financial aid. Early and deferred admission are possible.

Sarah Lawrence, a private, coeducational liberal arts college founded in 1926, is a lively community of students, scholars, and artists just 30 minutes from midtown Manhattan. In its distinctive seminar/conference system, each course consists of two parts: the seminar, limited to 15 students, and the conference, a private biweekly meeting with the seminar professor. In conference, student and teacher create a project that extends the seminar material and connects it to the student's academic goals. To prepare for this rigorous work, all first-year students enroll in a First-Year Studies Seminar. This seminar teacher will be the student's don, or adviser, throughout his or her Sarah Lawrence years.

Getting in Last Year
2,672 applied
41% were accepted
326 enrolled (29%)
36% from top tenth of their h.s. class
3.60 average high school GPA
77% had SAT verbal scores over 600
47% had SAT math scores over 600
86% had ACT scores over 24
27% had SAT verbal scores over 700
7% had SAT math scores over 700
21% had ACT scores over 30
4 National Merit Scholars
4 valedictorians

Graduation and After
61% graduated in 4 years
10% graduated in 5 years
1% graduated in 6 years
30% pursued further study (10% arts and sciences, 10% law, 5% education)

Financial Matters
$30,824 tuition and fees (2003–04)
$10,394 room and board
95% average percent of need met
$25,826 average financial aid amount received per undergraduate

SCRIPPS COLLEGE

SUBURBAN SETTING ■ PRIVATE ■ INDEPENDENT ■ WOMEN ONLY
CLAREMONT, CALIFORNIA

Web site: www.scrippscollege.edu
Contact: Ms. Patricia F. Goldsmith, Dean of Admission and Financial Aid,
   1030 Columbia Avenue, Claremont, CA 91711-3948
Telephone: 909-621-8149 or toll-free 800-770-1333 **Fax:** 909-607-7508
E-mail: admission@scrippscollege.edu

Getting in Last Year

1,378 applied
54% were accepted
210 enrolled (28%)
67% from top tenth of their h.s. class
3.90 average high school GPA
87% had SAT verbal scores over 600
82% had SAT math scores over 600
90% had ACT scores over 24
35% had SAT verbal scores over 700
24% had SAT math scores over 700
39% had ACT scores over 30
20 National Merit Scholars
11 valedictorians

Graduation and After

63% graduated in 4 years
5% graduated in 5 years
36% pursued further study
300 organizations recruited on campus

Financial Matters

$27,100 tuition and fees (2003–04)
$8600 room and board
100% average percent of need met
$23,861 average financial aid amount received
   per undergraduate (2002–03)

Academics

Scripps awards bachelor's **degrees** and post-bachelor's certificates. Challenging opportunities include advanced placement credit, accelerated degree programs, student-designed majors, an honors program, double majors, independent study, and a senior project. Special programs include internships, off-campus study, study-abroad, and Army and Air Force ROTC.

The most frequently chosen **baccalaureate** fields are social sciences and history, visual/performing arts, and area/ethnic studies. A complete listing of majors at Scripps appears in the Majors Index beginning on page 460.

The **faculty** at Scripps has 61 full-time members, 97% with terminal degrees. The student-faculty ratio is 11:1.

Students of Scripps

The student body totals 834, of whom 819 are undergraduates. Students come from 45 states and territories. 44% are from California. 1.7% are international students. 3.3% are African American, 0.4% American Indian, 13.2% Asian American, and 5.4% Hispanic American. 92% returned for their sophomore year.

Facilities and Resources

Student rooms are linked to a campus network. 72 **computers** are available on campus that provide access to the Internet. The 5 **libraries** have 998,823 books and 5,733 subscriptions.

Campus Life

There are 200 active organizations on campus, including a drama/theater group, newspaper, radio station, and choral group. No national or local **sororities**.

Scripps is a member of the NCAA (Division III). **Intercollegiate sports** include basketball, cheerleading, cross-country running, golf, lacrosse, soccer, softball, swimming, tennis, track and field, volleyball, water polo.

Campus Safety

Student safety services include late-night transport/escort service, 24-hour emergency telephone alarm devices, 24-hour patrols by trained security personnel, and electronically operated dormitory entrances.

Applying

Scripps requires an essay, SAT I or ACT, a high school transcript, 3 recommendations, and graded writing sample. It recommends an interview and a minimum high school GPA of 3.0. Application deadline: 2/1; 2/1 priority date for financial aid. Deferred admission is possible.

SEATTLE PACIFIC UNIVERSITY

URBAN SETTING ■ PRIVATE ■ INDEPENDENT RELIGIOUS ■ COED
SEATTLE, WASHINGTON

Web site: www.spu.edu
Contact: Mrs. Jennifer Feddern Kenney, Director of Admissions, 3307 Third
   Avenue West, Seattle, WA 98119-1997
Telephone: 206-281-2517 or toll-free 800-366-3344 **Fax:** 206-281-2544
E-mail: admissions@spu.edu

Academics

SPU awards bachelor's, master's, and doctoral **degrees** and post-master's certificates.
Challenging opportunities include advanced placement credit, student-designed majors,
an honors program, double majors, independent study, and a senior project. Special
programs include cooperative education, internships, summer session for credit, off-
campus study, study-abroad, and Army, Navy and Air Force ROTC.

The most frequently chosen **baccalaureate** fields are business/marketing, health
professions and related sciences, and social sciences and history. A complete listing of
majors at SPU appears in the Majors Index beginning on page 460.

The **faculty** at SPU has 169 full-time members, 86% with terminal degrees. The
student-faculty ratio is 15:1.

Students of SPU

The student body totals 3,728, of whom 2,859 are undergraduates. 66.6% are women
and 33.4% are men. Students come from 39 states and territories and 34 other countries.
63% are from Washington. 1% are international students. 1.9% are African American,
0.8% American Indian, 5.9% Asian American, and 1.9% Hispanic American. 79%
returned for their sophomore year.

Facilities and Resources

Student rooms are linked to a campus network. 150 **computers** are available on campus
that provide access to the Internet. The **library** has 169,527 books and 1,336 subscriptions.

Campus Life

There are 50 active organizations on campus, including a drama/theater group,
newspaper, radio station, and choral group. No national or local **fraternities** or **sororities**.

SPU is a member of the NCAA (Division II). **Intercollegiate sports** (some offering
scholarships) include basketball, cheerleading, crew, cross-country running, gymnastics
(w), soccer, track and field, volleyball (w).

Campus Safety

Student safety services include closed circuit TV monitors, late-night transport/escort
service, 24-hour emergency telephone alarm devices, 24-hour patrols by trained security
personnel, and student patrols.

Applying

SPU requires an essay, SAT I or ACT, a high school transcript, 2 recommendations, and
a minimum high school GPA of 2.5. It recommends SAT I. Application deadline: 6/1;
4/1 priority date for financial aid. Early and deferred admission are possible.

Getting in Last Year

1,778 applied
92% were accepted
683 enrolled (42%)
29% from top tenth of their h.s. class
3.65 average high school GPA
42% had SAT verbal scores over 600
40% had SAT math scores over 600
63% had ACT scores over 24
9% had SAT verbal scores over 700
5% had SAT math scores over 700
11% had ACT scores over 30
8 National Merit Scholars
41 valedictorians

Graduation and After

40% graduated in 4 years
19% graduated in 5 years
3% graduated in 6 years
12% pursued further study
86% had job offers within 6 months
56 organizations recruited on campus

Financial Matters

$19,158 tuition and fees (2003–04)
$7017 room and board
80% average percent of need met
$16,249 average financial aid amount received
   per undergraduate (2002–03)

SEATTLE UNIVERSITY

URBAN SETTING ■ PRIVATE ■ INDEPENDENT RELIGIOUS ■ COED
SEATTLE, WASHINGTON

Web site: www.seattleu.edu
Contact: Mr. Michael K. McKeon, Dean of Admissions, 900 Broadway,
Seattle, WA 98122-4340
Telephone: 206-296-2000 or toll-free 800-542-0833 (in-state), 800-426-7123
(out-of-state) **Fax:** 206-296-5656
E-mail: admissions@seattleu.edu

Seattle University is the
Pacific Northwest's only
truly urban institution.
Seattle is used as an extension of
the classroom, complementing the
academic foundation provided on
campus. This strategic location
ensures a multitude of internship
and part-time employment
opportunities for all students.
Seattle's holistic Jesuit educational
philosophy, which emphasizes
preparation for leadership and
service, coupled with a concern for
social justice, results in graduates
who are competitive in seeking
employment or admission to
graduate programs. In addition,
within the past 15 years, campus
facilities have been enhanced by
$157 million in both new
construction and renovation.

Getting in Last Year
2,985 applied
78% were accepted
665 enrolled (29%)
33% from top tenth of their h.s. class
3.52 average high school GPA
38% had SAT verbal scores over 600
35% had SAT math scores over 600
66% had ACT scores over 24
6% had SAT verbal scores over 700
4% had SAT math scores over 700
17% had ACT scores over 30

Graduation and After
44% graduated in 4 years
15% graduated in 5 years
4% graduated in 6 years
220 organizations recruited on campus

Financial Matters
$20,070 tuition and fees (2003–04)
$6858 room and board
90% average percent of need met
$18,926 average financial aid amount received
per undergraduate (2002–03 estimated)

Academics

Seattle U awards bachelor's, master's, doctoral, and first-professional **degrees** and post-
bachelor's and post-master's certificates. Challenging opportunities include advanced
placement credit, accelerated degree programs, student-designed majors, freshman
honors college, an honors program, double majors, independent study, and a senior
project. Special programs include internships, summer session for credit, off-campus
study, study-abroad, and Army and Air Force ROTC.

The most frequently chosen **baccalaureate** fields are business/marketing, health
professions and related sciences, and social sciences and history. A complete listing of
majors at Seattle U appears in the Majors Index beginning on page 460.

The **faculty** at Seattle U has 345 full-time members, 88% with terminal degrees.
The student-faculty ratio is 14:1.

Students of Seattle U

The student body totals 6,659, of whom 3,765 are undergraduates. 61.9% are women
and 38.1% are men. Students come from 49 states and territories and 75 other countries.
65% are from Washington. 9.9% are international students. 4.7% are African American,
1.4% American Indian, 21.3% Asian American, and 7% Hispanic American. 84%
returned for their sophomore year.

Facilities and Resources

Student rooms are linked to a campus network. 401 **computers** are available on campus
that provide access to the Internet. The 2 **libraries** have 141,478 books and 2,701
subscriptions.

Campus Life

There are 78 active organizations on campus, including a drama/theater group,
newspaper, radio station, and choral group. No national or local **fraternities** or **sororities**.

Seattle U is a member of the NCAA (Division II) and NAIA. **Intercollegiate sports**
(some offering scholarships) include basketball, cross-country running, soccer, softball
(w), swimming, track and field, volleyball (w).

Campus Safety

Student safety services include bicycle patrols, late-night transport/escort service, 24-
hour emergency telephone alarm devices, 24-hour patrols by trained security personnel,
and electronically operated dormitory entrances.

Applying

Seattle U requires an essay, SAT I or ACT, a high school transcript, 2 recommendations,
and a minimum high school GPA of 2.5. Application deadline: 7/1; 2/1 priority date for
financial aid. Early and deferred admission are possible.

SIENA COLLEGE

SUBURBAN SETTING ■ PRIVATE ■ INDEPENDENT RELIGIOUS ■ COED
LOUDONVILLE, NEW YORK

Web site: www.siena.edu
Contact: Mr. Edward Jones, Director of Admissions, 515 Loudon Road,
Loudonville, NY 12211-1462
Telephone: 518-783-2423 or toll-free 888-AT-SIENA **Fax:** 518-783-2436
E-mail: admit@siena.edu

Academics

Siena awards bachelor's **degrees**. Challenging opportunities include advanced placement credit, accelerated degree programs, an honors program, double majors, independent study, and a senior project. Special programs include internships, summer session for credit, off-campus study, study-abroad, and Army and Air Force ROTC.

The most frequently chosen **baccalaureate** fields are business/marketing, social sciences and history, and psychology. A complete listing of majors at Siena appears in the Majors Index beginning on page 460.

The **faculty** at Siena has 167 full-time members, 87% with terminal degrees. The student-faculty ratio is 14:1.

Students of Siena

The student body is made up of 3,379 undergraduates. 55.8% are women and 44.2% are men. Students come from 30 states and territories and 6 other countries. 80% are from New York. 0.4% are international students. 2.2% are African American, 0.2% American Indian, 2.6% Asian American, and 3.3% Hispanic American. 91% returned for their sophomore year.

Facilities and Resources

Student rooms are linked to a campus network. 650 **computers** are available on campus that provide access to the Internet. The **library** has 314,942 books and 1,063 subscriptions.

Campus Life

There are 78 active organizations on campus, including a drama/theater group, newspaper, radio station, and choral group. No national or local **fraternities** or **sororities**.

Siena is a member of the NCAA (Division I). **Intercollegiate sports** (some offering scholarships) include baseball (m), basketball, cross-country running, field hockey (w), golf, lacrosse, soccer, softball (w), swimming (w), tennis, volleyball (w), water polo (w).

Campus Safety

Student safety services include call boxes in parking lots and on roadways, late-night transport/escort service, 24-hour emergency telephone alarm devices, 24-hour patrols by trained security personnel, and electronically operated dormitory entrances.

Applying

Siena requires an essay, SAT I or ACT, a high school transcript, and 1 recommendation, and in some cases an interview. Application deadline: 3/1; 2/1 priority date for financial aid. Early and deferred admission are possible.

> One of the Northeast's premier small, private liberal arts colleges, Siena offers a broad, time-tested liberal arts curriculum that is a journey taken with mentoring, thoughtful faculty members, friars, and friends. It is a journey that empowers students with competence, confidence, and compassion, buttressing classwork with real-world experience. The curriculum includes 25 majors in business, liberal arts, and sciences. In addition, there are more than 15 preprofessional and special academic programs. Siena's 152-acre campus is located in Loudonville, a suburb of Albany, New York, the state capital.

Getting in Last Year
4,112 applied
63% were accepted
759 enrolled (29%)
20% from top tenth of their h.s. class
3.50 average high school GPA
25% had SAT verbal scores over 600
36% had SAT math scores over 600
48% had ACT scores over 24
2% had SAT verbal scores over 700
3% had SAT math scores over 700
5% had ACT scores over 30

Graduation and After
62% graduated in 4 years
11% graduated in 5 years
1% graduated in 6 years
Graduates pursuing further study: 7% education, 7% arts and sciences, 5% business
75% had job offers within 6 months
180 organizations recruited on campus

Financial Matters
$18,095 tuition and fees (2003–04)
$7215 room and board
80% average percent of need met
$12,655 average financial aid amount received per undergraduate (2002–03)

SIMON'S ROCK COLLEGE OF BARD

RURAL SETTING ■ PRIVATE ■ INDEPENDENT ■ COED
GREAT BARRINGTON, MASSACHUSETTS

Web site: www.simons-rock.edu
Contact: Ms. Mary King Austin, Director of Admissions, 84 Alford Road, Great Barrington, MA 01230
Telephone: 413-528-7317 or toll-free 800-235-7186 **Fax:** 413-528-7334
E-mail: admit@simons-rock.edu

Simon's Rock College of Bard is a college for inspired students determined to take control of their own education after the 10th or 11th grade of traditional high school. Simon's Rock is designed to give academically qualified students the opportunity to begin college early. Of the several fine early entrance programs in the United States, it is the oldest, largest, and the only one devoted exclusively to high school age students. The admissions staff looks for students who show evidence of a lively intellect, sustained achievement, and scholarly potential. The college awards the BA in liberal arts and sciences.

Getting in Last Year
404 applied
46% were accepted
143 enrolled (78%)
75% had SAT verbal scores over 600
56% had SAT math scores over 600
82% had ACT scores over 24
25% had SAT verbal scores over 700
23% had SAT math scores over 700
27% had ACT scores over 30

Graduation and After
77% graduated in 4 years
9% graduated in 5 years
6% graduated in 6 years

Financial Matters
$28,950 tuition and fees (2003–04)
$7630 room and board
70% average percent of need met
$15,763 average financial aid amount received per undergraduate (2002–03 estimated)

Academics
Simon's Rock awards associate and bachelor's **degrees**. Challenging opportunities include student-designed majors, double majors, independent study, and a senior project. Special programs include internships, off-campus study, and study-abroad.

The most frequently chosen **baccalaureate** fields are social sciences and history, visual/performing arts, and area/ethnic studies. A complete listing of majors at Simon's Rock appears in the Majors Index beginning on page 460.

The **faculty** at Simon's Rock has 37 full-time members, 89% with terminal degrees. The student-faculty ratio is 8:1.

Students of Simon's Rock
The student body is made up of 399 undergraduates. 57.6% are women and 42.4% are men. Students come from 44 states and territories. 20% are from Massachusetts. 0.5% are international students. 3.1% are African American, 1.8% American Indian, 6.4% Asian American, and 1.3% Hispanic American. 78% returned for their sophomore year.

Facilities and Resources
Student rooms are linked to a campus network. 50 **computers** are available on campus that provide access to the Internet. The **library** has 65,370 books and 437 subscriptions.

Campus Life
There are 21 active organizations on campus, including a drama/theater group, newspaper, radio station, and choral group. No national or local **fraternities** or **sororities**.

Intercollegiate sports include basketball, soccer, water polo.

Campus Safety
Student safety services include 24-hour weekend patrols by trained security personnel, late-night transport/escort service, 24-hour emergency telephone alarm devices, and electronically operated dormitory entrances.

Applying
Simon's Rock requires an essay, SAT I, PSAT, a high school transcript, an interview, 2 recommendations, parent application, and a minimum high school GPA of 2.0. It recommends ACT and a minimum high school GPA of 3.0. Application deadline: 6/15. Early and deferred admission are possible.

SIMPSON COLLEGE

SMALL-TOWN SETTING ■ PRIVATE ■ INDEPENDENT RELIGIOUS ■ COED
INDIANOLA, IOWA

Web site: www.simpson.edu
Contact: Ms. Deborah Tierney, Vice President for Enrollment, 701 North C Street, Indianola, IA 50125
Telephone: 515-961-1624 or toll-free 800-362-2454 **Fax:** 515-961-1870
E-mail: admiss@simpson.edu

Academics

Simpson awards bachelor's **degrees** and post-bachelor's certificates. Challenging opportunities include advanced placement credit, accelerated degree programs, student-designed majors, freshman honors college, an honors program, double majors, independent study, and a senior project. Special programs include cooperative education, internships, summer session for credit, off-campus study, and study-abroad.

The most frequently chosen **baccalaureate** fields are business/marketing, education, and communications/communication technologies. A complete listing of majors at Simpson appears in the Majors Index beginning on page 460.

The **faculty** at Simpson has 84 full-time members. The student-faculty ratio is 14:1.

Students of Simpson

The student body is made up of 1,937 undergraduates. 58.8% are women and 41.2% are men. Students come from 27 states and territories and 20 other countries. 88% are from Iowa. 1.9% are international students. 0.9% are African American, 0.2% American Indian, 1.1% Asian American, and 1.2% Hispanic American. 81% returned for their sophomore year.

Facilities and Resources

Student rooms are linked to a campus network. 274 **computers** are available on campus that provide access to the Internet. The 2 **libraries** have 151,359 books and 599 subscriptions.

Campus Life

There are 81 active organizations on campus, including a drama/theater group, newspaper, radio station, and choral group. 25% of eligible men and 24% of eligible women are members of national **fraternities**, national **sororities**, and local fraternities.

Simpson is a member of the NCAA (Division III). **Intercollegiate sports** include baseball (m), basketball, cheerleading, cross-country running, football (m), golf, soccer, softball (w), swimming (w), tennis, track and field, volleyball (w), wrestling (m).

Campus Safety

Student safety services include late-night transport/escort service, 24-hour emergency telephone alarm devices, 24-hour patrols by trained security personnel, student patrols, and electronically operated dormitory entrances.

Applying

Simpson requires SAT I or ACT, a high school transcript, and 1 recommendation. It recommends rank in upper 50% of high school class. Application deadline: 8/15. Early and deferred admission are possible.

Simpson College combines the best of a liberal arts education with outstanding career preparation and extracurricular programs. Activities range from an award-winning music program to nationally recognized NCAA Division III teams. Located 12 miles from Des Moines, Simpson offers the friendliness of a small town and the advantages of a metropolitan area. Outstanding facilities have been enhanced with multimillion-dollar expansions and renovations, including the Carver Science Center, named after Simpson's most distinguished alumnus, George Washington Carver. The 4-4-1 academic calendar includes a May Term that provides students with unique learning opportunities. Simpson's beautiful 73-acre, tree-lined campus provides a setting that nurtures creativity, energy, and productivity.

Getting in Last Year

1,271 applied
86% were accepted
413 enrolled (38%)
25% from top tenth of their h.s. class
55% had ACT scores over 24
6% had ACT scores over 30
27 valedictorians

Graduation and After

54% graduated in 4 years
9% graduated in 5 years
1% graduated in 6 years
11% pursued further study
98% had job offers within 6 months
145 organizations recruited on campus

Financial Matters

$18,097 tuition and fees (2003–04)
$5561 room and board
87% average percent of need met
$17,124 average financial aid amount received per undergraduate

SKIDMORE COLLEGE
SMALL-TOWN SETTING ■ PRIVATE ■ INDEPENDENT ■ COED
SARATOGA SPRINGS, NEW YORK

Web site: www.skidmore.edu
Contact: John W. Young, Director of Admissions, 815 North Broadway,
Saratoga Springs, NY 12866-1632
Telephone: 518-580-5570 or toll-free 800-867-6007 **Fax:** 518-580-5584
E-mail: admissions@skidmore.edu

S kidmore College, located on a beautiful 850-acre campus, is a liberal arts college where creative thought matters. An interdisciplinary liberal studies curriculum challenges students to explore broadly. A rich cocurricular program provides further opportunities for personal growth and leadership. Among the largest majors are business, studio art, English, psychology, government, and biology. Students from 44 states and territories and 23 countries live and learn in Skidmore's lively intellectual climate and beautiful campus surroundings.

Getting in Last Year
5,903 applied
46% were accepted
642 enrolled (24%)
38% from top tenth of their h.s. class
3.29 average high school GPA
67% had SAT verbal scores over 600
69% had SAT math scores over 600
84% had ACT scores over 24
16% had SAT verbal scores over 700
12% had SAT math scores over 700
12% had ACT scores over 30

Graduation and After
75% graduated in 4 years
4% graduated in 5 years
13% pursued further study (5% arts and sciences, 2% education, 2% law)
89% had job offers within 6 months
155 organizations recruited on campus

Financial Matters
$29,630 tuition and fees (2003–04)
$8300 room and board
94% average percent of need met
$24,114 average financial aid amount received per undergraduate

Academics
Skidmore awards bachelor's and master's **degrees**. Challenging opportunities include advanced placement credit, accelerated degree programs, student-designed majors, an honors program, double majors, independent study, and a senior project. Special programs include internships, summer session for credit, off-campus study, study-abroad, and Army and Air Force ROTC.

The most frequently chosen **baccalaureate** fields are visual/performing arts, social sciences and history, and business/marketing. A complete listing of majors at Skidmore appears in the Majors Index beginning on page 460.

The **faculty** at Skidmore has 193 full-time members, 85% with terminal degrees. The student-faculty ratio is 11:1.

Students of Skidmore
The student body totals 2,584, of whom 2,532 are undergraduates. 59.2% are women and 40.8% are men. Students come from 44 states and territories and 25 other countries. 30% are from New York. 1% are international students. 3% are African American, 0.6% American Indian, 5% Asian American, and 4.1% Hispanic American. 90% returned for their sophomore year.

Facilities and Resources
Student rooms are linked to a campus network. 173 **computers** are available on campus that provide access to the Internet. The **library** has 372,769 books and 1,983 subscriptions.

Campus Life
There are 80 active organizations on campus, including a drama/theater group, newspaper, radio station, television station, and choral group. No national or local **fraternities** or **sororities**.

Skidmore is a member of the NCAA (Division III). **Intercollegiate sports** include baseball (m), basketball, crew, equestrian sports, field hockey (w), golf (m), ice hockey (m), lacrosse, soccer, softball (w), swimming, tennis, volleyball (w).

Campus Safety
Student safety services include well-lit campus, late-night transport/escort service, 24-hour emergency telephone alarm devices, 24-hour patrols by trained security personnel, and electronically operated dormitory entrances.

Applying
Skidmore requires an essay, SAT I or ACT, a high school transcript, and 2 recommendations. It recommends an interview. Application deadline: 1/15; 1/15 for financial aid. Early and deferred admission are possible.

SMITH COLLEGE

SMALL-TOWN SETTING ■ PRIVATE ■ INDEPENDENT ■ WOMEN ONLY
NORTHAMPTON, MASSACHUSETTS

Web site: www.smith.edu
Contact: Ms. Debra Shaver, Director of Admissions, 7 College Lane,
   Northampton, MA 01063
Telephone: 413-585-2500 or toll-free 800-383-3232 **Fax:** 413-585-2527
E-mail: admission@smith.edu

Academics

Smith awards bachelor's, master's, and doctoral **degrees** and post-bachelor's and post-master's certificates. Challenging opportunities include advanced placement credit, accelerated degree programs, student-designed majors, double majors, independent study, and a senior project. Special programs include internships, off-campus study, study-abroad, and Army and Air Force ROTC.

The most frequently chosen **baccalaureate** fields are social sciences and history, area/ethnic studies, and psychology. A complete listing of majors at Smith appears in the Majors Index beginning on page 460.

The **faculty** at Smith has 285 full-time members, 95% with terminal degrees. The student-faculty ratio is 9:1.

Students of Smith

The student body totals 3,159, of whom 2,682 are undergraduates. Students come from 53 states and territories and 62 other countries. 24% are from Massachusetts. 6.9% are international students. 5.9% are African American, 1% American Indian, 9.5% Asian American, and 6% Hispanic American. 92% returned for their sophomore year.

Facilities and Resources

Student rooms are linked to a campus network. 608 **computers** are available on campus that provide access to e-mail and the Internet. The 4 **libraries** have 1,296,828 books and 6,530 subscriptions.

Campus Life

There are 112 active organizations on campus, including a drama/theater group, newspaper, radio station, and choral group. No national or local **sororities**.

Smith is a member of the NCAA (Division III). **Intercollegiate sports** include basketball, crew, cross-country running, equestrian sports, field hockey, lacrosse, skiing (downhill), soccer, softball, squash, swimming, tennis, track and field, volleyball.

Campus Safety

Student safety services include self-defense workshops, emergency telephones, programs in crime and sexual assault prevention, late-night transport/escort service, 24-hour emergency telephone alarm devices, and 24-hour patrols by trained security personnel.

Applying

Smith requires an essay, SAT I or ACT, a high school transcript, and 3 recommendations. It recommends SAT II Subject Tests, SAT II: Writing Test, and an interview. Application deadline: 1/15; 2/1 for financial aid. Early and deferred admission are possible.

> **S**tudents choose Smith because of its outstanding academic reputation. From its founding in 1871, the College has been committed to providing women with countless opportunities for personal and intellectual growth. The open curriculum allows each student, with the assistance of a faculty adviser, to plan an individualized course of study outside the major. Superb facilities, a beautiful New England campus, and a diverse student body complement the rigorous academic schedule. Unique programs include the first engineering science major at a women's college and the guarantee that all students will receive funding for an internship related to career and academic goals.

Getting in Last Year
3,304 applied
52% were accepted
635 enrolled (37%)
59% from top tenth of their h.s. class
3.80 average high school GPA
70% had SAT verbal scores over 600
61% had SAT math scores over 600
82% had ACT scores over 24
27% had SAT verbal scores over 700
15% had SAT math scores over 700
29% had ACT scores over 30

Graduation and After
80% graduated in 4 years
6% graduated in 5 years
16% pursued further study (7% arts and sciences, 3% law, 1% education)
45 organizations recruited on campus

Financial Matters
$27,544 tuition and fees (2003–04)
$9490 room and board
100% average percent of need met
$25,647 average financial aid amount received per undergraduate (2002–03 estimated)

Getting in Last Year
811 applied
94% were accepted
420 enrolled (55%)
20% from top tenth of their h.s. class
3.32 average high school GPA
30% had SAT verbal scores over 600
46% had SAT math scores over 600
56% had ACT scores over 24
7% had SAT verbal scores over 700
8% had SAT math scores over 700
10% had ACT scores over 30

Graduation and After
7% graduated in 4 years
23% graduated in 5 years
7% graduated in 6 years
94% had job offers within 6 months
121 organizations recruited on campus

Financial Matters
$4293 resident tuition and fees (2003–04)
$9005 nonresident tuition and fees (2003–04)
$3561 room and board
76% average percent of need met
$6048 average financial aid amount received
  per undergraduate

SOUTH DAKOTA SCHOOL OF MINES AND TECHNOLOGY
SUBURBAN SETTING ■ PUBLIC ■ STATE-SUPPORTED ■ COED
RAPID CITY, SOUTH DAKOTA

Web site: www.sdsmt.edu
Contact: Mr. Joseph Mueller, Director of Admissions, 501 East Saint Joseph, Rapid City, SD 57701-3995
Telephone: 605-394-2414 ext. 1266 or toll-free 800-544-8162 ext. 2414 **Fax:** 605-394-1268
E-mail: admissions@sdsmt.edu

Academics
SDSM&T awards associate, bachelor's, master's, and doctoral **degrees**. Challenging opportunities include advanced placement credit, double majors, independent study, and a senior project. Special programs include cooperative education, internships, summer session for credit, study-abroad, and Army ROTC.

The most frequently chosen **baccalaureate** fields are engineering/engineering technologies, interdisciplinary studies, and physical sciences. A complete listing of majors at SDSM&T appears in the Majors Index beginning on page 460.

The **faculty** at SDSM&T has 104 full-time members, 84% with terminal degrees. The student-faculty ratio is 18:1.

Students of SDSM&T
The student body totals 2,454, of whom 2,112 are undergraduates. 31.3% are women and 68.7% are men. Students come from 34 states and territories and 8 other countries. 73% are from South Dakota. 0.8% are international students. 0.7% are African American, 2.8% American Indian, 1.3% Asian American, and 1.2% Hispanic American. 73% returned for their sophomore year.

Facilities and Resources
Student rooms are linked to a campus network. 210 **computers** are available on campus that provide access to the Internet. The **library** has 219,961 books and 496 subscriptions.

Campus Life
Active organizations on campus include a drama/theater group, newspaper, radio station, and choral group. SDSM&T has national **fraternities** and national **sororities**.

SDSM&T is a member of the NAIA. **Intercollegiate sports** (some offering scholarships) include basketball, cross-country running, football (m), golf, tennis (m), track and field, volleyball (w).

Campus Safety
Student safety services include late-night transport/escort service, 24-hour emergency telephone alarm devices, 24-hour patrols by trained security personnel, student patrols, and electronically operated dormitory entrances.

Applying
SDSM&T requires SAT I or ACT and a high school transcript, and in some cases ACT. It recommends a minimum high school GPA of 2.6. Application deadline: rolling admissions; 3/15 priority date for financial aid.

SOUTHERN METHODIST UNIVERSITY

SUBURBAN SETTING ■ PRIVATE ■ INDEPENDENT RELIGIOUS ■ COED
DALLAS, TEXAS

Web site: www.smu.edu
Contact: Mr. Ron W. Moss, Director of Admission and Enrollment
  Management, PO Box 750181, Dallas, TX 75275-0181
Telephone: 214-768-2058 or toll-free 800-323-0672 **Fax:** 214-768-0103
E-mail: enrol_serv@mail.smu.edu

> SMU is a vibrant, diverse academic community in the heart of a dynamic city. Ecellence is the standard and success is the goal through nearly 80 majors, access to expert faculty members in relatively small classes, and opportunities to pursue an honors curriculum, research, internships, study abroad, and community service.

Academics

SMU awards bachelor's, master's, doctoral, and first-professional **degrees** and post-bachelor's certificates. Challenging opportunities include advanced placement credit, accelerated degree programs, student-designed majors, an honors program, double majors, and independent study. Special programs include internships, summer session for credit, study-abroad, and Army and Air Force ROTC.

The most frequently chosen **baccalaureate** fields are business/marketing, communications/communication technologies, and social sciences and history. A complete listing of majors at SMU appears in the Majors Index beginning on page 460.

The **faculty** at SMU has 566 full-time members, 86% with terminal degrees. The student-faculty ratio is 11:1.

Students of SMU

The student body totals 11,161, of whom 6,299 are undergraduates. 55.3% are women and 44.7% are men. Students come from 45 states and territories and 105 other countries. 64% are from Texas. 4.6% are international students. 5.7% are African American, 0.7% American Indian, 6.1% Asian American, and 8.5% Hispanic American. 87% returned for their sophomore year.

Facilities and Resources

Student rooms are linked to a campus network. 409 **computers** are available on campus for student use. The 8 **libraries** have 2,577,345 books and 11,727 subscriptions.

Campus Life

There are 152 active organizations on campus, including a drama/theater group, newspaper, radio station, choral group, and marching band. 34% of eligible men and 47% of eligible women are members of national **fraternities** and national **sororities**.

SMU is a member of the NCAA (Division I). **Intercollegiate sports** (some offering scholarships) include basketball, crew (w), cross-country running, football (m), golf, soccer, swimming, tennis, track and field, volleyball (w).

Campus Safety

Student safety services include late-night transport/escort service, 24-hour emergency telephone alarm devices, 24-hour patrols by trained security personnel, and electronically operated dormitory entrances.

Applying

SMU requires an essay, SAT I or ACT, a high school transcript, and 1 recommendation, and in some cases SAT II Subject Tests. Application deadline: 1/15; 2/1 priority date for financial aid. Early and deferred admission are possible.

Getting in Last Year
6,293 applied
65% were accepted
1,383 enrolled (34%)
35% from top tenth of their h.s. class
3.47 average high school GPA
48% had SAT verbal scores over 600
57% had SAT math scores over 600
82% had ACT scores over 24
8% had SAT verbal scores over 700
11% had SAT math scores over 700
15% had ACT scores over 30
16 National Merit Scholars

Graduation and After
56% graduated in 4 years
13% graduated in 5 years
2% graduated in 6 years
16% pursued further study (5% arts and sciences, 4% engineering, 3% law)
80% had job offers within 6 months
210 organizations recruited on campus

Financial Matters
$23,588 tuition and fees (2003–04)
$8391 room and board
91% average percent of need met
$20,885 average financial aid amount received per undergraduate (2002–03 estimated)

SOUTHWEST BAPTIST UNIVERSITY

SMALL-TOWN SETTING ■ PRIVATE ■ INDEPENDENT RELIGIOUS ■ COED
BOLIVAR, MISSOURI

Web site: www.sbuniv.edu
Contact: Mr. Rob Harris, Director of Admissions, 1600 University Avenue,
Bolivar, MO 65613-2597
Telephone: 417-328-1809 or toll-free 800-526-5859 **Fax:** 417-328-1514
E-mail: rharris@sbuniv.edu

Getting in Last Year

768 applied
86% were accepted
470 enrolled (71%)
27% from top tenth of their h.s. class
3.36 average high school GPA
46% had ACT scores over 24
6% had ACT scores over 30
21 valedictorians

Graduation and After

52% graduated in 4 years
2% graduated in 5 years
80% had job offers within 6 months
630 organizations recruited on campus

Financial Matters

$11,609 tuition and fees (2003–04)
$3700 room and board
71% average percent of need met
$9613 average financial aid amount received
    per undergraduate (2002–03 estimated)

Academics

SBU awards associate, bachelor's, and master's **degrees** and post-master's certificates.
Challenging opportunities include advanced placement credit, accelerated degree
programs, an honors program, double majors, independent study, and a senior project.
Special programs include cooperative education, internships, summer session for credit,
study-abroad, and Army ROTC.

The most frequently chosen **baccalaureate** fields are education, psychology, and
health professions and related sciences. A complete listing of majors at SBU appears in
the Majors Index beginning on page 460.

The **faculty** at SBU has 104 full-time members, 61% with terminal degrees. The
student-faculty ratio is 21:1.

Students of SBU

The student body totals 3,563, of whom 2,746 are undergraduates. 66% are women and
34% are men. Students come from 40 states and territories and 11 other countries. 49%
are from Missouri. 0.7% are international students. 2.1% are African American, 0.7%
American Indian, 0.7% Asian American, and 0.8% Hispanic American. 70% returned for
their sophomore year.

Facilities and Resources

130 **computers** are available on campus that provide access to the Internet. The **library**
has 108,128 books and 2,518 subscriptions.

Campus Life

There are 27 active organizations on campus, including a drama/theater group,
newspaper, and choral group. No national or local **fraternities** or **sororities**.

SBU is a member of the NCAA (Division II). **Intercollegiate sports** (some offering
scholarships) include baseball (m), basketball, cheerleading, cross-country running,
football (m), golf (m), soccer, softball (w), tennis, track and field, volleyball (w).

Campus Safety

Student safety services include 24-hour emergency telephone alarm devices and 24-hour
patrols by trained security personnel.

Applying

SBU requires an essay, SAT I or ACT, and a high school transcript, and in some cases 3
recommendations. It recommends an interview. Application deadline: rolling admissions;
3/15 priority date for financial aid.

SOUTHWESTERN UNIVERSITY

SUBURBAN SETTING ■ PRIVATE ■ INDEPENDENT RELIGIOUS ■ COED
GEORGETOWN, TEXAS

Web site: www.southwestern.edu
Contact: Mr. John W. Lind, Vice President for Enrollment Management,
    1001 East University Avenue, Georgetown, TX 78626
Telephone: 512-863-1200 or toll-free 800-252-3166 **Fax:** 512-863-9601
E-mail: admission@southwestern.edu

Academics

SU awards bachelor's **degrees**. Challenging opportunities include advanced placement credit, accelerated degree programs, student-designed majors, freshman honors college, an honors program, double majors, independent study, and a senior project. Special programs include internships, summer session for credit, off-campus study, and study-abroad.

The most frequently chosen **baccalaureate** fields are social sciences and history, business/marketing, and psychology. A complete listing of majors at SU appears in the Majors Index beginning on page 460.

The **faculty** at SU has 114 full-time members, 88% with terminal degrees. The student-faculty ratio is 10:1.

Students of SU

The student body is made up of 1,265 undergraduates. 57.6% are women and 42.4% are men. Students come from 33 states and territories. 91% are from Texas. 3.3% are African American, 0.6% American Indian, 3.5% Asian American, and 14.4% Hispanic American. 86% returned for their sophomore year.

Facilities and Resources

Student rooms are linked to a campus network. 223 **computers** are available on campus that provide access to course schedule, course catalog and the Internet. The **library** has 312,982 books and 1,469 subscriptions.

Campus Life

There are 105 active organizations on campus, including a drama/theater group, newspaper, television station, and choral group. 31% of eligible men and 32% of eligible women are members of national **fraternities** and national **sororities**.

SU is a member of the NCAA (Division III). **Intercollegiate sports** include baseball (m), basketball, cross-country running, golf, soccer, swimming, tennis, volleyball (w).

Campus Safety

Student safety services include late-night transport/escort service, 24-hour emergency telephone alarm devices, 24-hour patrols by trained security personnel, student patrols, and electronically operated dormitory entrances.

Applying

SU requires an essay, SAT I or ACT, a high school transcript, and 1 recommendation, and in some cases an interview. It recommends an interview. Application deadline: 2/15; 3/1 for financial aid. Early and deferred admission are possible.

Southwestern University (SU) is a selective national liberal arts college recognized for a high-quality undergraduate academic program, professor-scholars who are dedicated to teaching, superior facilities, and a price that is significantly lower than comparable institutions. Located just north of vibrant Austin, Texas, SU offers its 1,265 students a values-centered educational experience through a broad-based curriculum, preprofessional programs, and extensive extracurricular opportunities, such as internships, study abroad, collaborative research with faculty members, and NCAA Division III competition. SU recently used an $8.5 million grant to inaugurate the Paideia Program—a distinctive academic option to help students connect their in-classroom and out-of-classroom experiences. SU's facilities are exemplary among schools of its type.

Getting in Last Year

1,765 applied
63% were accepted
343 enrolled (31%)
47% from top tenth of their h.s. class
3.5 average high school GPA
64% had SAT verbal scores over 600
64% had SAT math scores over 600
76% had ACT scores over 24
17% had SAT verbal scores over 700
12% had SAT math scores over 700
19% had ACT scores over 30
5 National Merit Scholars
52 class presidents
7 valedictorians

Graduation and After

64% graduated in 4 years
11% graduated in 5 years
23% pursued further study (8% medicine, 7% arts and sciences, 7% law)
63% had job offers within 6 months
32 organizations recruited on campus

Financial Matters

$18,870 tuition and fees (2003–04)
$6540 room and board
98% average percent of need met
$15,038 average financial aid amount received per undergraduate (2002–03 estimated)

Southwest Missouri State University

Suburban setting ■ Public ■ State-supported ■ Coed
Springfield, Missouri

Web site: www.smsu.edu
Contact: Ms. Jill Duncan, Associate Director of Admissions, 901 South
    National, Springfield, MO 65804
Telephone: 417-836-5517 or toll-free 800-492-7900 **Fax:** 417-836-6334
E-mail: smsuinfo@smsu.edu

Academics

SMSU awards bachelor's and master's **degrees** and post-bachelor's certificates. Challenging opportunities include advanced placement credit, accelerated degree programs, student-designed majors, freshman honors college, an honors program, double majors, independent study, and a senior project. Special programs include cooperative education, internships, summer session for credit, off-campus study, study-abroad, and Army ROTC.

The most frequently chosen **baccalaureate** fields are business/marketing, education, and communications/communication technologies. A complete listing of majors at SMSU appears in the Majors Index beginning on page 460.

The **faculty** at SMSU has 731 full-time members, 79% with terminal degrees. The student-faculty ratio is 18:1.

Students of SMSU

The student body totals 18,930, of whom 15,771 are undergraduates. 55.8% are women and 44.2% are men. Students come from 48 states and territories and 80 other countries. 92% are from Missouri. 1.9% are international students. 2.4% are African American, 0.9% American Indian, 1.4% Asian American, and 1.3% Hispanic American. 74% returned for their sophomore year.

Facilities and Resources

Student rooms are linked to a campus network. 1,800 **computers** are available on campus that provide access to the Internet. The 4 **libraries** have 1,699,860 books and 4,238 subscriptions.

Campus Life

There are 260 active organizations on campus, including a drama/theater group, newspaper, radio station, television station, choral group, and marching band. 4% of eligible men and 4% of eligible women are members of national **fraternities** and national **sororities**.

SMSU is a member of the NCAA (Division I). **Intercollegiate sports** (some offering scholarships) include baseball (m), basketball, cross-country running, field hockey (w), football (m), golf, soccer, softball (w), swimming, tennis, track and field, volleyball (w).

Campus Safety

Student safety services include on-campus police substation, late-night transport/escort service, 24-hour emergency telephone alarm devices, 24-hour patrols by trained security personnel, and electronically operated dormitory entrances.

Applying

SMSU requires SAT I or ACT and a high school transcript, and in some cases an essay and an interview. It recommends ACT. Application deadline: 6/20; 3/30 priority date for financial aid.

Getting in Last Year
6,316 applied
86% were accepted
2,695 enrolled (49%)
21% from top tenth of their h.s. class
3.50 average high school GPA
46% had ACT scores over 24
8% had ACT scores over 30
1 National Merit Scholar
93 valedictorians

Graduation and After
20% pursued further study (6% business, 4% arts and sciences, 4% education)
68% had job offers within 6 months
465 organizations recruited on campus

Financial Matters
$4636 resident tuition and fees (2003–04)
$8776 nonresident tuition and fees (2003–04)
$4282 room and board
63% average percent of need met
$7253 average financial aid amount received per undergraduate (2001–02)

STANFORD UNIVERSITY

SUBURBAN SETTING ■ PRIVATE ■ INDEPENDENT ■ COED
STANFORD, CALIFORNIA

Web site: www.stanford.edu
Contact: Ms. Robin G. Mamlet, Dean of Undergraduate Admissions and
Financial Aid, Old Union 232, 520 Lasuen Mall, Stanford, CA 94305
Telephone: 650-723-2091 **Fax:** 650-723-6050
E-mail: admission@stanford.edu

Academics

Stanford awards bachelor's, master's, doctoral, and first-professional **degrees**. Challenging opportunities include advanced placement credit, student-designed majors, an honors program, double majors, independent study, and a senior project. Special programs include internships, summer session for credit, off-campus study, study-abroad, and Army, Navy and Air Force ROTC.

The most frequently chosen **baccalaureate** fields are social sciences and history, engineering/engineering technologies, and interdisciplinary studies. A complete listing of majors at Stanford appears in the Majors Index beginning on page 460.

The **faculty** at Stanford has 1,714 full-time members, 99% with terminal degrees. The student-faculty ratio is 7:1.

Students of Stanford

The student body totals 17,823, of whom 7,054 are undergraduates. 50.1% are women and 49.9% are men. Students come from 52 states and territories and 62 other countries. 52% are from California. 5.8% are international students. 10.4% are African American, 1.9% American Indian, 25.2% Asian American, and 12% Hispanic American. 98% returned for their sophomore year.

Facilities and Resources

Student rooms are linked to a campus network. 1,000 **computers** are available on campus that provide access to the Internet. The 19 **libraries** have 8,000,000 books and 50,056 subscriptions.

Campus Life

There are 600 active organizations on campus, including a drama/theater group, newspaper, radio station, television station, choral group, and marching band. Stanford has national **fraternities**, national **sororities**, and eating clubs.

Stanford is a member of the NCAA (Division I) and NAIA. **Intercollegiate sports** (some offering scholarships) include baseball (m), basketball, crew, cross-country running, fencing, field hockey (w), football (m), golf, gymnastics, lacrosse (w), sailing (w), soccer, softball (w), swimming, tennis, track and field, ultimate Frisbee, volleyball, water polo, wrestling (m).

Campus Safety

Student safety services include late-night transport/escort service, 24-hour emergency telephone alarm devices, 24-hour patrols by trained security personnel, and electronically operated dormitory entrances.

Applying

Stanford requires an essay, SAT I or ACT, a high school transcript, and 2 recommendations. It recommends SAT II Subject Tests and SAT II: Writing Test. Application deadline: 12/15; 2/1 priority date for financial aid. Deferred admission is possible.

Getting in Last Year
18,628 applied
13% were accepted
1,640 enrolled (70%)
90% from top tenth of their h.s. class
3.90 average high school GPA
91% had SAT verbal scores over 600
95% had SAT math scores over 600
95% had ACT scores over 24
63% had SAT verbal scores over 700
69% had SAT math scores over 700
66% had ACT scores over 30

Graduation and After
80% graduated in 4 years
11% graduated in 5 years
3% graduated in 6 years
30% pursued further study
62% had job offers within 6 months
365 organizations recruited on campus

Financial Matters
$28,923 tuition and fees (2003–04)
$9073 room and board
100% average percent of need met
$24,648 average financial aid amount received per undergraduate (2001–02)

STATE UNIVERSITY OF NEW YORK AT BINGHAMTON

SUBURBAN SETTING ■ PUBLIC ■ STATE-SUPPORTED ■ COED
BINGHAMTON, NEW YORK

Web site: www.binghamton.edu
Contact: Ms. Cheryl S. Brown, Director of Admissions, PO Box 6001,
    Binghamton, NY 13902-6001
Telephone: 607-777-2000 **Fax:** 607-777-4445
E-mail: admit@binghamton.edu

Binghamton University is a nationally recognized university that enrolls student scholars. The most selective public research university in New York, Binghamton has earned the reputation as "the Ivy of the State University of New York system." Binghamton offers more than 80 major degree programs across 5 academic divisions. The engaging teaching faculty and the "living-learning environment" found in the residential communities where students are mentored and classes are taught where they reside, fuel the intellectual climate on Binghamton's suburban campus. Extensive Study Abroad opportunities, internships, and an array of out of classroom learning opportunities and experiences yield motivated, successful graduates. National and international recognition is a result of groundbreaking research discoveries, an NCAA Division I athletic program, and success launching students into careers, graduate, and professional studies. Binghamton University has earned annual citations as an exceptional educational value.

Getting in Last Year
19,076 applied
45% were accepted
2,291 enrolled (27%)
3.60 average high school GPA
53% had SAT verbal scores over 600
73% had SAT math scores over 600
87% had ACT scores over 24
7% had SAT verbal scores over 700
17% had SAT math scores over 700
15% had ACT scores over 30

Graduation and After
70% graduated in 4 years
8% graduated in 5 years
2% graduated in 6 years
38% pursued further study (9% medicine, 7% education, 7% law)
129 organizations recruited on campus

Financial Matters
$5687 resident tuition and fees (2003–04)
$11,637 nonresident tuition and fees (2003–04)
$7100 room and board
80% average percent of need met
$9136 average financial aid amount received per undergraduate (2002–03 estimated)

Academics
Binghamton University awards bachelor's, master's, and doctoral **degrees** and post-master's certificates. Challenging opportunities include advanced placement credit, accelerated degree programs, student-designed majors, an honors program, double majors, independent study, and a senior project. Special programs include internships, summer session for credit, off-campus study, and Air Force ROTC.

The most frequently chosen **baccalaureate** fields are social sciences and history, business/marketing, and psychology. A complete listing of majors at Binghamton University appears in the Majors Index beginning on page 460.

The **faculty** at Binghamton University has 504 full-time members, 93% with terminal degrees. The student-faculty ratio is 22:1.

Students of Binghamton University
The student body totals 13,385, of whom 10,563 are undergraduates. 51.5% are women and 48.5% are men. Students come from 39 states and territories and 56 other countries. 95% are from New York. 3.2% are international students. 5.2% are African American, 0.2% American Indian, 16.2% Asian American, and 5.6% Hispanic American. 92% returned for their sophomore year.

Facilities and Resources
Student rooms are linked to a campus network. 6,228 **computers** are available on campus that provide access to the Internet. The 2 **libraries** have 1,787,062 books and 8,630 subscriptions.

Campus Life
There are 176 active organizations on campus, including a drama/theater group, newspaper, radio station, television station, and choral group. 8% of eligible men and 8% of eligible women are members of national **fraternities**, national **sororities**, local fraternities, and local sororities.

Binghamton University is a member of the NCAA (Division I). **Intercollegiate sports** (some offering scholarships) include baseball (m), basketball, cross-country running, golf (m), lacrosse, soccer, softball (w), swimming, tennis, track and field, volleyball (w).

Campus Safety
Student safety services include safety awareness programs, well-lit campus, self-defense education, secured campus entrance 12 a.m. to 5 a.m., emergency telephones, late-night transport/escort service, 24-hour emergency telephone alarm devices, 24-hour patrols by trained security personnel, student patrols, and electronically operated dormitory entrances.

Applying
Binghamton University requires an essay, SAT I or ACT, and a high school transcript, and in some cases 1 recommendation and portfolio, audition. Application deadline: 1/15; 3/1 priority date for financial aid. Early and deferred admission are possible.

STATE UNIVERSITY OF NEW YORK COLLEGE AT GENESEO

SMALL-TOWN SETTING ■ PUBLIC ■ STATE-SUPPORTED ■ COED
GENESEO, NEW YORK

Web site: www.geneseo.edu
Contact: Kris Shay, Associate Director of Admissions, 1 College Circle,
    Geneseo, NY 14454-1401
Telephone: 585-245-5571 or toll-free 866-245-5211 **Fax:** 585-245-5550
E-mail: admissions@geneseo.edu

Academics

Geneseo College awards bachelor's and master's **degrees**. Challenging opportunities
include advanced placement credit, an honors program, double majors, independent
study, and a senior project. Special programs include internships, summer session for
credit, off-campus study, study-abroad, and Army and Air Force ROTC.

The most frequently chosen **baccalaureate** fields are education, business/marketing,
and social sciences and history. A complete listing of majors at Geneseo College appears
in the Majors Index beginning on page 460.

The **faculty** at Geneseo College has 246 full-time members, 85% with terminal
degrees. The student-faculty ratio is 19:1.

Students of Geneseo College

The student body totals 5,550, of whom 5,307 are undergraduates. 62.8% are women
and 37.2% are men. Students come from 20 states and territories and 23 other countries.
99% are from New York. 1.7% are international students. 1.9% are African American,
0.2% American Indian, 5.2% Asian American, and 2.6% Hispanic American. 92%
returned for their sophomore year.

Facilities and Resources

Student rooms are linked to a campus network. 900 **computers** are available on campus
that provide access to the Internet. The 2 **libraries** have 524,692 books and 2,048
subscriptions.

Campus Life

There are 164 active organizations on campus, including a drama/theater group,
newspaper, radio station, television station, and choral group. 10% of eligible men and
12% of eligible women are members of national **fraternities**, national **sororities**, local
fraternities, and local sororities.

Geneseo College is a member of the NCAA (Division III). **Intercollegiate sports**
include basketball, cross-country running, field hockey (w), ice hockey (m), lacrosse, soccer, softball (w), swimming, tennis (w), track and field, volleyball (w).

Campus Safety

Student safety services include late-night transport/escort service, 24-hour emergency
telephone alarm devices, 24-hour patrols by trained security personnel, student patrols,
and electronically operated dormitory entrances.

Applying

Geneseo College requires an essay, SAT I or ACT, and a high school transcript. It
recommends an interview and recommendations. Application deadline: 1/15; 2/15 priority date for financial aid. Early and deferred admission are possible.

Getting in Last Year

8,783 applied
42% were accepted
996 enrolled (27%)
48% from top tenth of their h.s. class
3.70 average high school GPA
70% had SAT verbal scores over 600
77% had SAT math scores over 600
94% had ACT scores over 24
12% had SAT verbal scores over 700
9% had SAT math scores over 700
12% had ACT scores over 30
35 valedictorians

Graduation and After

62% graduated in 4 years
14% graduated in 5 years
1% graduated in 6 years
27% pursued further study
61% had job offers within 6 months
57 organizations recruited on campus

Financial Matters

$5390 resident tuition and fees (2003–04)
$11,340 nonresident tuition and fees (2003–04)
$6750 room and board
87% average percent of need met
$8555 average financial aid amount received per undergraduate

STEPHENS COLLEGE

URBAN SETTING ■ PRIVATE ■ INDEPENDENT ■ WOMEN ONLY
COLUMBIA, MISSOURI

Web site: www.stephens.edu
Contact: Ms. Amy Shaver, Director of Enrollment Services, 1200 East
   Broadway, Box 2121, Columbia, MO 65215-0002
Telephone: 573-876-7207 or toll-free 800-876-7207 **Fax:** 573-876-7237
E-mail: apply@stephens.edu

Getting in Last Year

390 applied
79% were accepted
136 enrolled (44%)
17% from top tenth of their h.s. class
3.50 average high school GPA
34% had SAT verbal scores over 600
24% had SAT math scores over 600
52% had ACT scores over 24
2% had SAT verbal scores over 700
2% had SAT math scores over 700
4% had ACT scores over 30

Graduation and After

41% graduated in 4 years
8% graduated in 5 years
113 organizations recruited on campus

Financial Matters

$17,360 tuition and fees (2003–04)
$6900 room and board
82% average percent of need met
$16,576 average financial aid amount received
   per undergraduate

Academics

Stephens awards bachelor's and master's **degrees** and post-bachelor's certificates. Challenging opportunities include advanced placement credit, accelerated degree programs, student-designed majors, freshman honors college, an honors program, double majors, independent study, and a senior project. Special programs include cooperative education, internships, off-campus study, study-abroad, and Army and Air Force ROTC.

   The most frequently chosen **baccalaureate** fields are visual/performing arts, communications/communication technologies, and psychology. A complete listing of majors at Stephens appears in the Majors Index beginning on page 460.

   The **faculty** at Stephens has 47 full-time members. The student-faculty ratio is 10:1.

Students of Stephens

The student body totals 647, of whom 577 are undergraduates. Students come from 41 states and territories and 3 other countries. 45% are from Missouri. 0.5% are international students. 7.6% are African American, 0.7% American Indian, 1.4% Asian American, and 3.5% Hispanic American. 73% returned for their sophomore year.

Facilities and Resources

Student rooms are linked to a campus network. 64 **computers** are available on campus that provide access to the Internet. The **library** has 121,084 books and 534 subscriptions.

Campus Life

There are 45 active organizations on campus, including a drama/theater group, newspaper, radio station, television station, and choral group. 10% of eligible undergraduates are members of national **sororities**.

   Stephens is a member of the NCAA (Division III). **Intercollegiate sports** include basketball, soccer, swimming, tennis, volleyball.

Campus Safety

Student safety services include late-night transport/escort service, 24-hour emergency telephone alarm devices, 24-hour patrols by trained security personnel, student patrols, and electronically operated dormitory entrances.

Applying

Stephens requires an essay, SAT I or ACT, a high school transcript, 1 recommendation, and a minimum high school GPA of 2.5. It recommends an interview. Application deadline: 7/31; 3/15 priority date for financial aid. Early and deferred admission are possible.

STETSON UNIVERSITY
SMALL-TOWN SETTING ■ PRIVATE ■ INDEPENDENT ■ COED
DeLAND, FLORIDA

Web site: www.stetson.edu
Contact: Ms. Deborah Thompson, Vice President for Admissions, Unit 8378, Griffith Hall, DeLand, FL 32723
Telephone: 386-822-7100 or toll-free 800-688-0101 **Fax:** 386-822-8832
E-mail: admissions@stetson.edu

Academics
Stetson awards bachelor's, master's, and first-professional **degrees** and post-master's and first-professional certificates. Challenging opportunities include advanced placement credit, accelerated degree programs, student-designed majors, an honors program, double majors, independent study, and a senior project. Special programs include internships, summer session for credit, off-campus study, study-abroad, and Army ROTC.

The most frequently chosen **baccalaureate** fields are business/marketing, social sciences and history, and education. A complete listing of majors at Stetson appears in the Majors Index beginning on page 460.

The **faculty** at Stetson has 186 full-time members, 90% with terminal degrees. The student-faculty ratio is 11:1.

Students of Stetson
The student body totals 3,439, of whom 2,161 are undergraduates. 57.1% are women and 42.9% are men. Students come from 40 states and territories and 35 other countries. 80% are from Florida. 3% are international students. 3.6% are African American, 0.4% American Indian, 2.1% Asian American, and 4.8% Hispanic American. 81% returned for their sophomore year.

Facilities and Resources
Student rooms are linked to a campus network. 320 **computers** are available on campus that provide access to the Internet. The 3 **libraries** have 377,319 books and 10,079 subscriptions.

Campus Life
There are 93 active organizations on campus, including a drama/theater group, newspaper, radio station, and choral group. 33% of eligible men and 29% of eligible women are members of national **fraternities** and national **sororities**.

Stetson is a member of the NCAA (Division I). **Intercollegiate sports** (some offering scholarships) include baseball (m), basketball, crew, cross-country running, golf, soccer, softball (w), tennis, volleyball (w).

Campus Safety
Student safety services include late-night transport/escort service, 24-hour emergency telephone alarm devices, and 24-hour patrols by trained security personnel.

Applying
Stetson requires an essay, SAT I or ACT, a high school transcript, and recommendations. It recommends an interview. Application deadline: 3/1; 4/15 priority date for financial aid. Early admission is possible.

Getting in Last Year
1,992 applied
76% were accepted
529 enrolled (35%)
32% from top tenth of their h.s. class
3.54 average high school GPA
36% had SAT verbal scores over 600
33% had SAT math scores over 600
56% had ACT scores over 24
7% had SAT verbal scores over 700
4% had SAT math scores over 700
7% had ACT scores over 30
17 valedictorians

Graduation and After
56% graduated in 4 years
10% graduated in 5 years
2% graduated in 6 years
35% pursued further study (11% arts and sciences, 9% business, 5% law)
50 organizations recruited on campus

Financial Matters
$22,380 tuition and fees (2003–04)
$6855 room and board
84% average percent of need met
$18,791 average financial aid amount received per undergraduate (2002–03 estimated)

STEVENS INSTITUTE OF TECHNOLOGY

URBAN SETTING ■ PRIVATE ■ INDEPENDENT ■ COED
HOBOKEN, NEW JERSEY

Web site: www.stevens.edu
Contact: Mr. Daniel Gallagher, Dean of University Admissions, Castle Point on Hudson, Hoboken, NJ 07030
Telephone: 201-216-5197 or toll-free 800-458-5323 **Fax:** 201-216-8348
E-mail: admissions@stevens-tech.edu

Stevens ranks in the top 5% among the nation's technological universities as it continues to educate leaders and innovators. Each undergraduate program—business, engineering, the sciences, computer science, and the humanities—follows a broad-based course curriculum taught by distinguished faculty members. The 9:1 student-faculty ratio enables personal attention and growth. All students combine their classroom and laboratory experience with cooperative education, summer internships, and/or research opportunities to enhance their prestigious Stevens education. Located in Hoboken, one of America's most desirable towns, Stevens is just minutes from New York City and all of the educational, cultural, and extracurricular opportunities it offers.

Getting in Last Year
1,999 applied
51% were accepted
395 enrolled (38%)
3.80 average high school GPA
56% had SAT verbal scores over 600
88% had SAT math scores over 600
12% had SAT verbal scores over 700
34% had SAT math scores over 700
7 valedictorians

Graduation and After
18% pursued further study
90% had job offers within 6 months
350 organizations recruited on campus

Financial Matters
$26,960 tuition and fees (2003–04)
$8500 room and board
85% average percent of need met
$18,336 average financial aid amount received per undergraduate

Academics

Stevens awards bachelor's, master's, and doctoral **degrees** and post-bachelor's certificates. Challenging opportunities include advanced placement credit, accelerated degree programs, an honors program, double majors, independent study, and a senior project. Special programs include cooperative education, internships, summer session for credit, off-campus study, study-abroad, and Army and Air Force ROTC.

The most frequently chosen **baccalaureate** fields are engineering/engineering technologies, computer/information sciences, and business/marketing. A complete listing of majors at Stevens appears in the Majors Index beginning on page 460.

The **faculty** at Stevens has 171 full-time members, 94% with terminal degrees. The student-faculty ratio is 9:1.

Students of Stevens

The student body totals 4,548, of whom 1,707 are undergraduates. 24.9% are women and 75.1% are men. Students come from 34 states and territories and 29 other countries. 65% are from New Jersey. 5% are international students. 4% are African American, 0.2% American Indian, 19.8% Asian American, and 8.5% Hispanic American. 90% returned for their sophomore year.

Facilities and Resources

Student rooms are linked to a campus network. 1,700 **computers** are available on campus that provide access to online grade and account information and the Internet. The **library** has 59,489 books and 162 subscriptions.

Campus Life

There are 70 active organizations on campus, including a drama/theater group, newspaper, radio station, television station, and choral group. Stevens has national **fraternities**, national **sororities**, and local sororities.

Stevens is a member of the NCAA (Division III). **Intercollegiate sports** include baseball (m), basketball, cross-country running, equestrian sports (w), fencing, field hockey (w), lacrosse, soccer, swimming, tennis, track and field, volleyball, wrestling (m).

Campus Safety

Student safety services include late-night transport/escort service, 24-hour emergency telephone alarm devices, 24-hour patrols by trained security personnel, and electronically operated dormitory entrances.

Applying

Stevens requires SAT I or ACT, a high school transcript, and an interview, and in some cases SAT II Subject Tests, SAT II: Writing Test, and SAT I and SAT II or ACT. It recommends an essay, SAT II Subject Tests, SAT II: Writing Test, and recommendations. Application deadline: 2/15; 2/15 priority date for financial aid. Early and deferred admission are possible.

STONEHILL COLLEGE

SUBURBAN SETTING ■ PRIVATE ■ INDEPENDENT RELIGIOUS ■ COED
EASTON, MASSACHUSETTS

Web site: www.stonehill.edu
Contact: Mr. Brian P. Murphy, Dean of Admissions and Enrollment, 320
   Washington Street, Easton, MA 02357-5610
Telephone: 508-565-1373 **Fax:** 508-565-1545
E-mail: admissions@stonehill.edu

Academics

Stonehill awards bachelor's and master's **degrees**. Challenging opportunities include advanced placement credit, student-designed majors, an honors program, double majors, independent study, and a senior project. Special programs include internships, summer session for credit, off-campus study, study-abroad, and Army ROTC.

   The most frequently chosen **baccalaureate** fields are business/marketing, social sciences and history, and education. A complete listing of majors at Stonehill appears in the Majors Index beginning on page 460.

   The **faculty** at Stonehill has 130 full-time members, 82% with terminal degrees. The student-faculty ratio is 14:1.

Students of Stonehill

The student body totals 2,582, of whom 2,567 are undergraduates. 58.7% are women and 41.3% are men. Students come from 29 states and territories and 16 other countries. 62% are from Massachusetts. 0.8% are international students. 2.9% are African American, 0.2% American Indian, 2.9% Asian American, and 2.5% Hispanic American. 89% returned for their sophomore year.

Facilities and Resources

Student rooms are linked to a campus network. 287 **computers** are available on campus that provide access to online schedules, assignments, grades and student accounts and the Internet. The 2 **libraries** have 194,587 books and 1,612 subscriptions.

Campus Life

There are 66 active organizations on campus, including a drama/theater group, newspaper, radio station, and choral group. No national or local **fraternities** or **sororities**.

   Stonehill is a member of the NCAA (Division II). **Intercollegiate sports** (some offering scholarships) include baseball (m), basketball, cross-country running, equestrian sports (w), field hockey (w), football (m), ice hockey (m), lacrosse (w), soccer, softball (w), tennis, track and field, volleyball (w).

Campus Safety

Student safety services include late-night transport/escort service, 24-hour emergency telephone alarm devices, and 24-hour patrols by trained security personnel.

Applying

Stonehill requires an essay, SAT I or ACT, a high school transcript, and 2 recommendations, and in some cases an interview. It recommends campus visit. Application deadline: 1/15; 2/1 priority date for financial aid. Early and deferred admission are possible.

Getting in Last Year

4,808 applied
49% were accepted
568 enrolled (24%)
49% from top tenth of their h.s. class
3.53 average high school GPA
48% had SAT verbal scores over 600
54% had SAT math scores over 600
75% had ACT scores over 24
5% had SAT verbal scores over 700
5% had SAT math scores over 700
6% had ACT scores over 30
7 class presidents
3 valedictorians

Graduation and After

81% graduated in 4 years
3% graduated in 5 years
1% graduated in 6 years
16% pursued further study
76% had job offers within 6 months
68 organizations recruited on campus

Financial Matters

$21,302 tuition and fees (2003–04)
$9450 room and board
82% average percent of need met
$15,639 average financial aid amount received
   per undergraduate

SUSQUEHANNA UNIVERSITY
SUBURBAN SETTING ■ PRIVATE ■ INDEPENDENT RELIGIOUS ■ COED
SELINSGROVE, PENNSYLVANIA

Web site: www.susqu.edu
Contact: Mr. Chris Markle, Director of Admissions, 514 University Avenue,
 Selinsgrove, PA 17870-1040
Telephone: 570-372-4260 or toll-free 800-326-9672 **Fax:** 570-372-2722
E-mail: suadmiss@susqu.edu

Susquehanna University is a national liberal arts college on a beautiful 220-acre campus in Selinsgrove, Pennsylvania. Strong professional programs in areas such as music and business enhance distinctive liberal arts programs, including biology and writing. Faculty members are excellent teachers highly engaged in student learning and many involve students in their research. A vibrant campus enables students to customize their experience with internships, volunteer service, and leadership opportunities. New, award-winning facilities include a high-technology academic center, athletic complex, and music and art center. Students gain worldwide connections through a fully-wired campus and array of off-campus programs.

Getting in Last Year
2,373 applied
70% were accepted
499 enrolled (30%)
30% from top tenth of their h.s. class
33% had SAT verbal scores over 600
42% had SAT math scores over 600
3% had SAT verbal scores over 700
3% had SAT math scores over 700
2 National Merit Scholars
13 class presidents
13 valedictorians

Graduation and After
76% graduated in 4 years
2% graduated in 5 years
15% pursued further study (7% arts and sciences, 2% law, 1% dentistry)
78% had job offers within 6 months
48 organizations recruited on campus

Financial Matters
$23,480 tuition and fees (2003–04)
$6510 room and board
83% average percent of need met
$16,624 average financial aid amount received per undergraduate (2002–03 estimated)

Academics
Susquehanna awards bachelor's **degrees** (also offers associate degree through evening program to local students). Challenging opportunities include advanced placement credit, accelerated degree programs, student-designed majors, an honors program, double majors, independent study, and a senior project. Special programs include internships, summer session for credit, off-campus study, study-abroad, and Army ROTC.

The most frequently chosen **baccalaureate** fields are business/marketing, communications/communication technologies, and education. A complete listing of majors at Susquehanna appears in the Majors Index beginning on page 460.

The **faculty** at Susquehanna has 118 full-time members, 90% with terminal degrees. The student-faculty ratio is 13:1.

Students of Susquehanna
The student body is made up of 2,009 undergraduates. 56.8% are women and 43.2% are men. Students come from 24 states and territories and 11 other countries. 60% are from Pennsylvania. 0.6% are international students. 2.1% are African American, 0.3% American Indian, 1.8% Asian American, and 1.9% Hispanic American. 88% returned for their sophomore year.

Facilities and Resources
Student rooms are linked to a campus network. 295 **computers** are available on campus that provide access to e-mail, class listings and assignments, online voting booth and the Internet. The **library** has 279,149 books and 11,078 subscriptions.

Campus Life
There are 100 active organizations on campus, including a drama/theater group, newspaper, radio station, and choral group. 25% of eligible men and 25% of eligible women are members of national **fraternities** and national **sororities**.

Susquehanna is a member of the NCAA (Division III). **Intercollegiate sports** include baseball (m), basketball, cross-country running, field hockey (w), football (m), golf (m), lacrosse, soccer, softball (w), swimming, tennis, track and field, volleyball (w).

Campus Safety
Student safety services include late-night transport/escort service, 24-hour patrols by trained security personnel, and electronically operated dormitory entrances.

Applying
Susquehanna requires an essay, a high school transcript, 1 recommendation, and a minimum high school GPA of 2.5, and in some cases SAT I or ACT and writing portfolio, auditions for music programs. It recommends SAT II Subject Tests, SAT II: Writing Test, an interview, and a minimum high school GPA of 3.0. Application deadline: 3/1; 5/1 for financial aid, with a 3/1 priority date. Early and deferred admission are possible.

SWARTHMORE COLLEGE

SUBURBAN SETTING ■ PRIVATE ■ INDEPENDENT ■ COED
SWARTHMORE, PENNSYLVANIA

Web site: www.swarthmore.edu
Contact: Office of Admissions, 500 College Avenue, Swarthmore, PA
    19081-1397
Telephone: 610-328-8300 or toll-free 800-667-3110 **Fax:** 610-328-8580
E-mail: admissions@swarthmore.edu

Academics

Swarthmore awards bachelor's **degrees**. Challenging opportunities include advanced placement credit, student-designed majors, an honors program, double majors, independent study, and a senior project. Special programs include internships, off-campus study, study-abroad, and Army and Air Force ROTC.

The most frequently chosen **baccalaureate** fields are social sciences and history, biological/life sciences, and English. A complete listing of majors at Swarthmore appears in the Majors Index beginning on page 460.

The **faculty** at Swarthmore has 168 full-time members, 99% with terminal degrees. The student-faculty ratio is 8:1.

Students of Swarthmore

The student body is made up of 1,500 undergraduates. 52.9% are women and 47.1% are men. Students come from 53 states and territories and 42 other countries. 16% are from Pennsylvania. 5.3% are international students. 7.2% are African American, 0.9% American Indian, 15.5% Asian American, and 8.4% Hispanic American. 97% returned for their sophomore year.

Facilities and Resources

Student rooms are linked to a campus network. 168 **computers** are available on campus that provide access to the Internet. The 4 **libraries** have 567,875 books and 4,949 subscriptions.

Campus Life

There are 100 active organizations on campus, including a drama/theater group, newspaper, radio station, and choral group. 6% of eligible men are members of national **fraternities** and local fraternities.

Swarthmore is a member of the NCAA (Division III). **Intercollegiate sports** include badminton (w), baseball (m), basketball, cross-country running, field hockey (w), golf (m), lacrosse, soccer, softball (w), swimming, tennis, track and field, volleyball (w).

Campus Safety

Student safety services include late-night transport/escort service, 24-hour emergency telephone alarm devices, 24-hour patrols by trained security personnel, and student patrols.

Applying

Swarthmore requires an essay, SAT I and SAT II or ACT, a high school transcript, and 2 recommendations, and in some cases SAT II Subject Tests in mathematics. It recommends an interview. Application deadline: 1/1; 2/15 priority date for financial aid. Early and deferred admission are possible.

Swarthmore is a highly selective college of liberal arts and engineering, located 11 miles southwest of Philadelphia. Founded as a coeducational institution in 1864, it is nonsectarian but reflects many traditions and values of its Quaker founders and attracts students who are engaged in the community as well as the classroom. Swarthmore's Honors Program provides an option to study in small seminars during the junior and senior years. A small school by deliberate policy, its enrollment is about 1,400, with a student-faculty ratio of 8:1. The student body represents students from 50 states, 3 territories, and 61 other countries.

Getting in Last Year
3,908 applied
24% were accepted
368 enrolled (40%)
92% from top tenth of their h.s. class
93% had SAT verbal scores over 600
92% had SAT math scores over 600
67% had SAT verbal scores over 700
65% had SAT math scores over 700
33 National Merit Scholars
49 valedictorians

Graduation and After
83% graduated in 4 years
7% graduated in 5 years
2% graduated in 6 years
29% pursued further study (18% arts and sciences, 5% law, 5% medicine)
70 organizations recruited on campus

Financial Matters
$28,802 tuition and fees (2003–04)
$8914 room and board
100% average percent of need met
$26,088 average financial aid amount received per undergraduate

SWEET BRIAR COLLEGE

RURAL SETTING ■ PRIVATE ■ INDEPENDENT ■ WOMEN ONLY
SWEET BRIAR, VIRGINIA

Web site: www.sbc.edu

Contact: Mr. Ken Huus, Director of Admissions, PO Box B, Sweet Briar, VA 24595

Telephone: 434-381-6142 or toll-free 800-381-6142 **Fax:** 434-381-6152

E-mail: admissions@sbc.edu

Deeply committed to the education of women since its founding in 1901, Sweet Briar College is consistently ranked as one of the leading national liberal arts and sciences colleges in the country. Sweet Briar women are intellectually adventurous, willing to explore new fields, and challenge boundaries. Their strong preparation allows the College's graduates to obtain significant research grants, gain admission to premiere graduate programs, and secure leading positions in the corporate world as scientists, writers, lawyers, dancers, educators, and businesswomen. Sweet Briar students are taken seriously, and professors take an interest in their intellectual development and personal growth.

Academics

Sweet Briar awards bachelor's **degrees**. Challenging opportunities include advanced placement credit, accelerated degree programs, student-designed majors, an honors program, double majors, independent study, and a senior project. Special programs include internships, summer session for credit, off-campus study, and study-abroad.

The most frequently chosen **baccalaureate** fields are social sciences and history, visual/performing arts, and psychology. A complete listing of majors at Sweet Briar appears in the Majors Index beginning on page 460.

The **faculty** at Sweet Briar has 72 full-time members, 96% with terminal degrees. The student-faculty ratio is 7:1.

Students of Sweet Briar

The student body is made up of 709 undergraduates. Students come from 44 states and territories. 49% are from Virginia. 2.7% are international students. 3.4% are African American, 1% American Indian, 2.1% Asian American, and 2.1% Hispanic American. 79% returned for their sophomore year.

Facilities and Resources

Student rooms are linked to a campus network. 117 **computers** are available on campus that provide access to the Internet. The 4 **libraries** have 177,110 books and 996 subscriptions.

Campus Life

There are 43 active organizations on campus, including a drama/theater group, newspaper, radio station, television station, and choral group. No national or local **sororities**.

Sweet Briar is a member of the NCAA (Division III). **Intercollegiate sports** include field hockey, lacrosse, soccer, swimming, tennis, volleyball.

Campus Safety

Student safety services include front gate security, late-night transport/escort service, 24-hour emergency telephone alarm devices, 24-hour patrols by trained security personnel, and electronically operated dormitory entrances.

Applying

Sweet Briar requires an essay, SAT I or ACT, a high school transcript, and 2 recommendations, and in some cases an interview and portfolio with courses taken, list of texts covered, essay about homeschooling, campus visit, interview for homeschooled applicants. It recommends SAT II Subject Tests. Application deadline: 2/1; 3/1 priority date for financial aid. Early and deferred admission are possible.

Getting in Last Year
404 applied
88% were accepted
133 enrolled (37%)
23% from top tenth of their h.s. class
3.39 average high school GPA
36% had SAT verbal scores over 600
20% had SAT math scores over 600
56% had ACT scores over 24
10% had SAT verbal scores over 700
2% had SAT math scores over 700
9% had ACT scores over 30
1 National Merit Scholar
3 valedictorians

Graduation and After
64% graduated in 4 years
3% graduated in 5 years
25% pursued further study (3% arts and sciences, 2% education, 2% law)
55% had job offers within 6 months
40 organizations recruited on campus

Financial Matters
$19,900 tuition and fees (2003–04)
$8040 room and board
92% average percent of need met
$16,690 average financial aid amount received per undergraduate (2001–02)

Syracuse University

URBAN SETTING ■ PRIVATE ■ INDEPENDENT ■ COED
SYRACUSE, NEW YORK

Web site: www.syracuse.edu
Contact: Office of Admissions, 201 Tolley Administration Building, Syracuse, NY 13244-1100
Telephone: 315-443-3611
E-mail: orange@syr.edu

Academics

SU awards bachelor's, master's, doctoral, and first-professional **degrees** and post-master's certificates. Challenging opportunities include advanced placement credit, accelerated degree programs, student-designed majors, an honors program, double majors, independent study, and a senior project. Special programs include cooperative education, internships, summer session for credit, off-campus study, study-abroad, and Army and Air Force ROTC.

The most frequently chosen **baccalaureate** fields are visual/performing arts, business/marketing, and social sciences and history. A complete listing of majors at SU appears in the Majors Index beginning on page 460.

The **faculty** at SU has 864 full-time members, 87% with terminal degrees. The student-faculty ratio is 12:1.

Students of SU

The student body totals 15,598, of whom 10,840 are undergraduates. 55.9% are women and 44.1% are men. Students come from 51 states and territories and 63 other countries. 40% are from New York. 2.7% are international students. 6.1% are African American, 0.3% American Indian, 5.7% Asian American, and 4.2% Hispanic American. 91% returned for their sophomore year.

Facilities and Resources

Student rooms are linked to a campus network. 1,200 **computers** are available on campus that provide access to online services, networked client and server computing and the Internet. The 7 **libraries** have 3,115,566 books and 14,462 subscriptions.

Campus Life

There are 250 active organizations on campus, including a drama/theater group, newspaper, radio station, television station, choral group, and marching band. 12% of eligible men and 16% of eligible women are members of national **fraternities**, national **sororities**, and local fraternities.

SU is a member of the NCAA (Division I). **Intercollegiate sports** (some offering scholarships) include basketball, cheerleading, crew, cross-country running, field hockey (w), football (m), lacrosse, soccer, softball (w), swimming, tennis (w), track and field, volleyball (w).

Campus Safety

Student safety services include crime prevention and neighborhood outreach programs, late-night transport/escort service, 24-hour emergency telephone alarm devices, 24-hour patrols by trained security personnel, and electronically operated dormitory entrances.

Applying

SU requires an essay, SAT I or ACT, a high school transcript, and 2 recommendations, and in some cases audition for drama and music programs, portfolio for art and architecture programs. It recommends an interview. Application deadline: 1/1; 2/1 priority date for financial aid. Early and deferred admission are possible.

As a leading student-centered research university, Syracuse University is committed to giving students the very best education available. Faculty members encourage interaction through small classes and integrate research into teaching. A continued commitment to the liberal arts complements professional teaching in all colleges. Students' individual needs are met through the University's enhanced system of orientation and advising, expanded use of introductory courses, and an increased selection of interdisciplinary majors and minors. Syracuse students augment their course work with internships, study-abroad opportunities, and a wide variety of extracurricular activities.

Getting in Last Year
14,144 applied
62% were accepted
2,650 enrolled (30%)
44% from top tenth of their h.s. class
3.60 average high school GPA
55% had SAT verbal scores over 600
63% had SAT math scores over 600
9% had SAT verbal scores over 700
14% had SAT math scores over 700

Graduation and After
65% graduated in 4 years
11% graduated in 5 years
1% graduated in 6 years
20% pursued further study (25% business, 20% arts and sciences, 15% education)
74% had job offers within 6 months
170 organizations recruited on campus

Financial Matters
$24,830 tuition and fees (2003–04)
$9590 room and board
80% average percent of need met
$18,000 average financial aid amount received per undergraduate (2002–03 estimated)

TAYLOR UNIVERSITY

RURAL SETTING ■ PRIVATE ■ INDEPENDENT RELIGIOUS ■ COED
UPLAND, INDIANA

Web site: www.tayloru.edu
Contact: Mr. Stephen R. Mortland, Director of Admissions, 236 West Reade
Avenue, Upland, IN 46989-1001
Telephone: 765-998-5134 or toll-free 800-882-3456 **Fax:** 765-998-4925
E-mail: admissions_u@tayloru.edu

Getting in Last Year
1,312 applied
84% were accepted
470 enrolled (43%)
33% from top tenth of their h.s. class
3.57 average high school GPA
53% had SAT verbal scores over 600
44% had SAT math scores over 600
31% had ACT scores over 24
10% had SAT verbal scores over 700
10% had SAT math scores over 700
2% had ACT scores over 30
9 National Merit Scholars
36 valedictorians

Graduation and After
67% graduated in 4 years
8% graduated in 5 years
1% graduated in 6 years
13% pursued further study (3% theology, 2% medicine, 2% education)
48% had job offers within 6 months
12 organizations recruited on campus

Financial Matters
$18,528 tuition and fees (2003–04)
$5292 room and board
81% average percent of need met
$13,351 average financial aid amount received per undergraduate

Academics

Taylor awards associate, bachelor's, and master's **degrees**. Challenging opportunities include advanced placement credit, student-designed majors, an honors program, double majors, independent study, and a senior project. Special programs include cooperative education, internships, summer session for credit, off-campus study, and study-abroad.

The most frequently chosen **baccalaureate** fields are business/marketing, education, and psychology. A complete listing of majors at Taylor appears in the Majors Index beginning on page 460.

The **faculty** at Taylor has 119 full-time members, 75% with terminal degrees. The student-faculty ratio is 14:1.

Students of Taylor

The student body totals 1,843, of whom 1,834 are undergraduates. 53.2% are women and 46.8% are men. Students come from 47 states and territories. 33% are from Indiana. 0.9% are international students. 1.2% are African American, 0.4% American Indian, 1.9% Asian American, and 1.3% Hispanic American. 87% returned for their sophomore year.

Facilities and Resources

Student rooms are linked to a campus network. 228 **computers** are available on campus that provide access to the Internet. The **library** has 193,343 books and 902 subscriptions.

Campus Life

There are 200 active organizations on campus, including a drama/theater group, newspaper, radio station, television station, and choral group. No national or local **fraternities** or **sororities**.

Taylor is a member of the NAIA and NCCAA. **Intercollegiate sports** (some offering scholarships) include baseball (m), basketball, cross-country running, football (m), golf (m), soccer, softball (w), tennis, track and field, volleyball (w).

Campus Safety

Student safety services include late-night transport/escort service, 24-hour patrols by trained security personnel, and student patrols.

Applying

Taylor requires an essay, SAT I or ACT, a high school transcript, an interview, and 2 recommendations. It recommends a minimum high school GPA of 2.8. Application deadline: 1/15; 3/10 for financial aid. Deferred admission is possible.

Texas A&M University

SUBURBAN SETTING ■ PUBLIC ■ STATE-SUPPORTED ■ COED
COLLEGE STATION, TEXAS

Web site: www.tamu.edu
Contact: Dr. Frank Ashley, Director of Admissions, 217 John J. Koldus
Building, College Station, TX 77843-1265
Telephone: 979-845-3741 Fax: 979-845-8737
E-mail: admissions@tamu.edu

Academics

Texas A&M awards bachelor's, master's, doctoral, and first-professional **degrees** and post-bachelor's certificates. Challenging opportunities include advanced placement credit, accelerated degree programs, an honors program, double majors, independent study, and a senior project. Special programs include cooperative education, internships, summer session for credit, off-campus study, study-abroad, and Army, Navy and Air Force ROTC.

The most frequently chosen **baccalaureate** fields are business/marketing, engineering/engineering technologies, and agriculture. A complete listing of majors at Texas A&M appears in the Majors Index beginning on page 460.

The **faculty** at Texas A&M has 1,917 full-time members, 91% with terminal degrees. The student-faculty ratio is 21:1.

Students of Texas A&M

The student body totals 44,813, of whom 36,066 are undergraduates. 49.1% are women and 50.9% are men. Students come from 52 states and territories and 111 other countries. 97% are from Texas. 1.4% are international students. 2.4% are African American, 0.5% American Indian, 3.1% Asian American, and 9.3% Hispanic American. 89% returned for their sophomore year.

Facilities and Resources

Student rooms are linked to a campus network. 1,500 **computers** are available on campus that provide access to the Internet. The 5 **libraries** have 4,425,478 books and 30,459 subscriptions.

Campus Life

There are 700 active organizations on campus, including a drama/theater group, newspaper, radio station, television station, choral group, and marching band. 4% of eligible men and 7% of eligible women are members of national **fraternities**, national **sororities**, local fraternities, and local sororities.

Texas A&M is a member of the NCAA (Division I). **Intercollegiate sports** (some offering scholarships) include archery (w), baseball (m), basketball, cross-country running, equestrian sports (w), football (m), golf, soccer (w), softball (w), swimming, tennis, track and field, volleyball (w).

Campus Safety

Student safety services include student escorts, late-night transport/escort service, 24-hour emergency telephone alarm devices, 24-hour patrols by trained security personnel, and electronically operated dormitory entrances.

Applying

Texas A&M requires an essay, SAT I or ACT, and a high school transcript. Application deadline: 2/1.

Getting in Last Year

17,250 applied
67% were accepted
6,726 enrolled (58%)
53% from top tenth of their h.s. class
43% had SAT verbal scores over 600
58% had SAT math scores over 600
67% had ACT scores over 24
8% had SAT verbal scores over 700
17% had SAT math scores over 700
18% had ACT scores over 30
156 National Merit Scholars
242 valedictorians

Graduation and After

32% graduated in 4 years
37% graduated in 5 years
7% graduated in 6 years
17% pursued further study
915 organizations recruited on campus

Financial Matters

$5051 resident tuition and fees (2003–04)
$12,131 nonresident tuition and fees (2003–04)
$6030 room and board
82% average percent of need met
$6664 average financial aid amount received per undergraduate (2002–03 estimated)

TEXAS CHRISTIAN UNIVERSITY
SUBURBAN SETTING ■ PRIVATE ■ INDEPENDENT RELIGIOUS ■ COED
FORT WORTH, TEXAS

Web site: www.tcu.edu
Contact: Mr. Tom Oliver, Director of Freshman Admissions, TCU Box
    297013, Fort Worth, TX 76129-0002
Telephone: 817-257-7490 or toll-free 800-828-3764 **Fax:** 817-257-7268
E-mail: frogmail@tcu.edu

TCU's mission—*to educate individuals to think and act as ethical leaders and responsible citizens in the global community*—influences every area of this person-centered, private university. TCU ranks seventh in the nation in percentage of students who study abroad. Our degree programs offer internships as part of the education. The Freshman Commitment provides the opportunities students need to succeed, from writing enhancement to Internet connections in every residence room. A Division I-A teaching and research university, TCU provides the personal attention crucial to every student's success. The final grade? TCU students earn more than degrees that will improve their lives. They learn to change their world.

Getting in Last Year
7,654 applied
65% were accepted
1,596 enrolled (32%)
33% from top tenth of their h.s. class

Graduation and After
64% graduated in 6 years
275 organizations recruited on campus

Financial Matters
$17,630 tuition and fees (2003–04)
$5780 room and board
94% average percent of need met
$12,614 average financial aid amount received
    per undergraduate

Academics
TCU awards bachelor's, master's, doctoral, and first-professional **degrees** and post-bachelor's and first-professional certificates. Challenging opportunities include advanced placement credit, an honors program, double majors, independent study, and a senior project. Special programs include internships, summer session for credit, study-abroad, and Army and Air Force ROTC.

The most frequently chosen **baccalaureate** fields are business/marketing, communications/communication technologies, and social sciences and history. A complete listing of majors at TCU appears in the Majors Index beginning on page 460.

The **faculty** at TCU has 420 full-time members, 91% with terminal degrees. The student-faculty ratio is 15:1.

Students of TCU
The student body totals 8,275, of whom 6,933 are undergraduates. 59.3% are women and 40.7% are men. Students come from 50 states and territories and 75 other countries. 78% are from Texas. 3.9% are international students. 5.3% are African American, 0.5% American Indian, 2.1% Asian American, and 6.3% Hispanic American. 81% returned for their sophomore year.

Facilities and Resources
Student rooms are linked to a campus network. 4,225 **computers** are available on campus that provide access to the Internet. The **library** has 1,299,875 books and 4,629 subscriptions.

Campus Life
There are 195 active organizations on campus, including a drama/theater group, newspaper, radio station, television station, choral group, and marching band. TCU has national **fraternities**, national **sororities**, local fraternities, local sororities, and local coed music fraternities.

TCU is a member of the NCAA (Division I). **Intercollegiate sports** (some offering scholarships) include baseball (m), basketball, cross-country running, football (m), golf, riflery (w), soccer, swimming, tennis, track and field, volleyball (w).

Campus Safety
Student safety services include emergency call boxes, video camera surveillance in parking lots, late-night transport/escort service, 24-hour emergency telephone alarm devices, 24-hour patrols by trained security personnel, student patrols, and electronically operated dormitory entrances.

Applying
TCU requires an essay, SAT I or ACT, a high school transcript, 2 recommendations, and a minimum high school GPA of 2.0. It recommends an interview and a minimum high school GPA of 3.0. Application deadline: 2/15; 5/1 priority date for financial aid. Deferred admission is possible.

TEXAS TECH UNIVERSITY

URBAN SETTING ■ PUBLIC ■ STATE-SUPPORTED ■ COED
LUBBOCK, TEXAS

Web site: www.ttu.edu
Contact: Ms. Marlene Hernandez, Associate Director, Admissions and School
   Relations, Box 45005, Lubbock, TX 79409-5005
Telephone: 806-742-1480 **Fax:** 806-742-0980
E-mail: admissions@ttu.edu

Academics

Texas Tech awards bachelor's, master's, doctoral, and first-professional **degrees**. Challenging opportunities include advanced placement credit, accelerated degree programs, student-designed majors, freshman honors college, an honors program, double majors, independent study, and a senior project. Special programs include cooperative education, internships, summer session for credit, off-campus study, study-abroad, and Army and Air Force ROTC.

The most frequently chosen **baccalaureate** fields are business/marketing, home economics/vocational home economics, and engineering/engineering technologies. A complete listing of majors at Texas Tech appears in the Majors Index beginning on page 460.

The **faculty** at Texas Tech has 978 full-time members, 93% with terminal degrees. The student-faculty ratio is 21:1.

Students of Texas Tech

The student body totals 28,549, of whom 23,595 are undergraduates. 45.4% are women and 54.6% are men. Students come from 49 states and territories and 87 other countries. 95% are from Texas. 0.9% are international students. 3.1% are African American, 0.6% American Indian, 2.2% Asian American, and 10.9% Hispanic American. 82% returned for their sophomore year.

Facilities and Resources

Student rooms are linked to a campus network. 3,000 **computers** are available on campus that provide access to online degree plans, accounts, transcripts, schedules and the Internet. The 4 **libraries** have 2,234,274 books and 18,082 subscriptions.

Campus Life

There are 388 active organizations on campus, including a drama/theater group, newspaper, radio station, television station, choral group, and marching band. 12% of eligible men and 19% of eligible women are members of national **fraternities**, national **sororities**, local fraternities, and local sororities.

Texas Tech is a member of the NCAA (Division I). **Intercollegiate sports** (some offering scholarships) include baseball (m), basketball, cross-country running, football (m), golf, soccer (w), softball (w), tennis, track and field, volleyball (w).

Campus Safety

Student safety services include late-night transport/escort service, 24-hour emergency telephone alarm devices, 24-hour patrols by trained security personnel, and electronically operated dormitory entrances.

Applying

Texas Tech requires SAT I or ACT, a high school transcript, and a minimum high school GPA of 2.0, and in some cases an essay. Application deadline: rolling admissions; 5/1 priority date for financial aid. Early and deferred admission are possible.

Texas Tech University is a residential, state-assisted university with more than 28,500 students. The university offers more than 150 areas of study through its 10 academic colleges. These colleges consist of: Agricultural Sciences and Natural Resources, Architecture, Arts and Sciences, Business Administration, Education, Engineering, Human Sciences, Mass Communications (effective Fall 2004), Visual and Performing Arts, and the Honors College. Texas Tech prides itself in offering students options to enhance their undergraduate degree. Undergraduate research programs are one of the many areas that allow Texas Tech to provide a small college atmosphere in a large research university environment.

Getting in Last Year
13,755 applied
67% were accepted
4,445 enrolled (48%)
21% from top tenth of their h.s. class
26% had SAT verbal scores over 600
37% had SAT math scores over 600
50% had ACT scores over 24
3% had SAT verbal scores over 700
5% had SAT math scores over 700
6% had ACT scores over 30
19 National Merit Scholars
116 valedictorians

Graduation and After
24% graduated in 4 years
24% graduated in 5 years
6% graduated in 6 years
80% had job offers within 6 months
730 organizations recruited on campus

Financial Matters
$4745 resident tuition and fees (2003–04)
$11,825 nonresident tuition and fees (2003–04)
$6023 room and board
52% average percent of need met
$5710 average financial aid amount received per undergraduate (2001–02)

THOMAS AQUINAS COLLEGE

RURAL SETTING ■ PRIVATE ■ INDEPENDENT RELIGIOUS ■ COED
SANTA PAULA, CALIFORNIA

Web site: www.thomasaquinas.edu
Contact: Mr. Thomas J. Susanka Jr., Director of Admissions, 10000 North
Ojai Road, Santa Paula, CA 93060-9980
Telephone: 805-525-4417 ext. 361 or toll-free 800-634-9797 **Fax:**
805-525-9342
E-mail: admissions@thomasaquinas.edu

Getting in Last Year
184 applied
78% were accepted
101 enrolled (70%)
42% from top tenth of their h.s. class
3.71 average high school GPA
88% had SAT verbal scores over 600
61% had SAT math scores over 600
93% had ACT scores over 24
32% had SAT verbal scores over 700
10% had SAT math scores over 700
41% had ACT scores over 30
4 valedictorians

Graduation and After
62% graduated in 4 years
12% graduated in 5 years
1% graduated in 6 years
62% had job offers within 6 months
4 organizations recruited on campus

Financial Matters
$16,800 tuition and fees (2003–04)
$5200 room and board
100% average percent of need met
$14,936 average financial aid amount received
per undergraduate

Academics
TAC awards bachelor's **degrees**. A senior project is a challenging opportunity.
The most frequently chosen **baccalaureate** field is liberal arts/general studies. A
complete listing of majors at TAC appears in the Majors Index beginning on page 460.
The **faculty** at TAC has 30 full-time members, 73% with terminal degrees. The stu-
dent-faculty ratio is 11:1.

Students of TAC
The student body is made up of 332 undergraduates. 53.9% are women and 46.1% are
men. Students come from 42 states and territories and 7 other countries. 47% are from
California. 7.8% are international students. 0.3% are African American, 0.9% American
Indian, 3.9% Asian American, and 5.1% Hispanic American. 86% returned for their
sophomore year.

Facilities and Resources
15 **computers** are available on campus that provide access to e-mail. The **library** has
51,000 books and 80 subscriptions.

Campus Life
There are 5 active organizations on campus, including a drama/theater group and choral
group. No national or local **fraternities** or **sororities**.
Intercollegiate sports include cheerleading.

Campus Safety
Student safety services include daily security daytime patrol, 24-hour emergency
telephone alarm devices, and student patrols.

Applying
TAC requires an essay, SAT I or ACT, a high school transcript, and 3 recommendations,
and in some cases an interview. It recommends a minimum high school GPA of 2.0. Application deadline: rolling admissions. Early and deferred admission are possible.

TRANSYLVANIA UNIVERSITY

URBAN SETTING ■ PRIVATE ■ INDEPENDENT RELIGIOUS ■ COED
LEXINGTON, KENTUCKY

Web site: www.transy.edu
Contact: Ms. Sarah Coen, Director of Admissions, 300 North Broadway,
   Lexington, KY 40508-1797
Telephone: 859-233-8242 or toll-free 800-872-6798 **Fax:** 859-233-8797
E-mail: admissions@transy.edu

Academics

Transylvania awards bachelor's **degrees**. Challenging opportunities include advanced placement credit, student-designed majors, double majors, and independent study. Special programs include internships, summer session for credit, off-campus study, study-abroad, and Army and Air Force ROTC.

The most frequently chosen **baccalaureate** fields are business/marketing, social sciences and history, and psychology. A complete listing of majors at Transylvania appears in the Majors Index beginning on page 460.

The **faculty** at Transylvania has 79 full-time members, 89% with terminal degrees. The student-faculty ratio is 13:1.

Students of Transylvania

The student body is made up of 1,134 undergraduates. 57% are women and 43% are men. Students come from 32 states and territories and 3 other countries. 80% are from Kentucky. 0.3% are international students. 2.6% are African American, 0.4% American Indian, 2.1% Asian American, and 1.2% Hispanic American. 84% returned for their sophomore year.

Facilities and Resources

Student rooms are linked to a campus network. 250 **computers** are available on campus that provide access to the Internet. The **library** has 93,019 books and 500 subscriptions.

Campus Life

There are 51 active organizations on campus, including a drama/theater group, newspaper, radio station, and choral group. 60% of eligible men and 60% of eligible women are members of national **fraternities** and national **sororities**.

Transylvania is a member of the NCAA (Division III). **Intercollegiate sports** include baseball (m), basketball, cross-country running, field hockey (w), golf, soccer, softball (w), swimming, tennis, volleyball (w).

Campus Safety

Student safety services include late-night transport/escort service, 24-hour emergency telephone alarm devices, and 24-hour patrols by trained security personnel.

Applying

Transylvania requires an essay, SAT I or ACT, a high school transcript, 2 recommendations, and a minimum high school GPA of 2.75, and in some cases an interview. It recommends an interview. Application deadline: 2/1; 3/1 priority date for financial aid. Early and deferred admission are possible.

Founded in 1780 as the nation's 16th college, Transylvania is known for its ongoing legacy of academic excellence. It is consistently ranked among the nation's best liberal arts colleges and is considered an exceptional value in education. Students benefit from an innovative teacher-recognition program, the first in the nation to attract and reward outstanding teaching on a substantial scale. Small classes and individual attention from faculty members prepare students well for highly selective graduate and professional schools, especially in law and medicine. Transylvania's location in a historic district near downtown Lexington, Kentucky, provides opportunities for internships, jobs, and cultural activities.

Getting in Last Year

1,098 applied
88% were accepted
300 enrolled (31%)
50% from top tenth of their h.s. class
3.50 average high school GPA
49% had SAT verbal scores over 600
51% had SAT math scores over 600
74% had ACT scores over 24
15% had SAT verbal scores over 700
10% had SAT math scores over 700
18% had ACT scores over 30
7 National Merit Scholars
24 valedictorians

Graduation and After

60% graduated in 4 years
3% graduated in 5 years
32% pursued further study (15% arts and sciences, 5% medicine, 4% business)
55% had job offers within 6 months
86 organizations recruited on campus

Financial Matters

$17,660 tuition and fees (2003–04)
$6120 room and board
88% average percent of need met
$14,175 average financial aid amount received per undergraduate (2002–03 estimated)

TRINITY COLLEGE

URBAN SETTING ■ PRIVATE ■ INDEPENDENT ■ COED
HARTFORD, CONNECTICUT

Web site: www.trincoll.edu
Contact: Mr. Larry Dow, Dean of Admissions and Financial Aid, 300 Summit Street, Hartford, CT 06106-3100
Telephone: 860-297-2180 **Fax:** 860-297-2287
E-mail: admissions.office@trincoll.edu

ounded in 1823, Trinity College in Hartford is one of the oldest and finest liberal arts colleges in the nation. Its rigorous curriculum includes the traditional liberal arts disciplines as well as outstanding science, engineering, and interdisciplinary programs. As a residential college in the heart of the city, Trinity offers unique opportunities for combining challenging, personalized classroom instruction with applied, experiential learning in the urban environment. Two thirds of the students take part in internships, and more than half study abroad at global learning sites and participate in community service. Whether they choose to study further or go on to rewarding careers, Trinity graduates have learned to make a difference in the world.

Getting in Last Year
5,510 applied
36% were accepted
550 enrolled (28%)
51% from top tenth of their h.s. class
73% had SAT verbal scores over 600
83% had SAT math scores over 600
87% had ACT scores over 24
26% had SAT verbal scores over 700
30% had SAT math scores over 700
17% had ACT scores over 30

Graduation and After
77% graduated in 4 years
6% graduated in 5 years
1% graduated in 6 years
68% had job offers within 6 months

Financial Matters
$30,230 tuition and fees (2003–04)
$7810 room and board
100% average percent of need met
$22,161 average financial aid amount received per undergraduate (2002–03)

Academics

Trinity College awards bachelor's and master's **degrees**. Challenging opportunities include advanced placement credit, accelerated degree programs, student-designed majors, an honors program, double majors, independent study, and a senior project. Special programs include internships, summer session for credit, off-campus study, study-abroad, and Army ROTC.

The most frequently chosen **baccalaureate** fields are social sciences and history, area/ethnic studies, and English. A complete listing of majors at Trinity College appears in the Majors Index beginning on page 460.

The **faculty** at Trinity College has 187 full-time members, 90% with terminal degrees. The student-faculty ratio is 10:1.

Students of Trinity College

The student body totals 2,371, of whom 2,188 are undergraduates. 50.8% are women and 49.2% are men. Students come from 44 states and territories and 28 other countries. 22% are from Connecticut. 1.7% are international students. 4.5% are African American, 0.2% American Indian, 5.7% Asian American, and 5% Hispanic American. 91% returned for their sophomore year.

Facilities and Resources

Student rooms are linked to a campus network. 315 **computers** are available on campus that provide access to e-mail, web pages and the Internet. The 3 **libraries** have 988,536 books and 2,434 subscriptions.

Campus Life

There are 112 active organizations on campus, including a drama/theater group, newspaper, radio station, television station, and choral group. 20% of eligible men and 16% of eligible women are members of coed fraternities.

Trinity College is a member of the NCAA (Division III). **Intercollegiate sports** include baseball (m), basketball, crew, cross-country running, field hockey (w), football (m), golf (m), ice hockey, lacrosse, soccer, softball (w), squash, swimming, tennis, track and field, volleyball (w), wrestling (m).

Campus Safety

Student safety services include late-night transport/escort service, 24-hour emergency telephone alarm devices, 24-hour patrols by trained security personnel, and electronically operated dormitory entrances.

Applying

Trinity College requires an essay, ACT or SAT I and SAT II Writing Test or SAT II Writing Test and two additional SAT II subject tests, a high school transcript, and 3 recommendations. It recommends an interview. Application deadline: 1/15; 3/1 for financial aid, with a 2/1 priority date. Early and deferred admission are possible.

TRINITY UNIVERSITY
Urban setting ■ Private ■ Independent Religious ■ Coed
San Antonio, Texas

Web site: www.trinity.edu
Contact: Mr. Christopher Ellertson, Dean of Admissions and Financial Aid,
One Trinity Place, San Antonio, TX 78212-7200
Telephone: 210-999-7207 or toll-free 800-TRINITY **Fax:** 210-999-8164
E-mail: admissions@trinity.edu

Academics
Trinity awards bachelor's and master's **degrees**. Challenging opportunities include advanced placement credit, accelerated degree programs, an honors program, double majors, independent study, and a senior project. Special programs include internships, summer session for credit, study-abroad, and Air Force ROTC.

The most frequently chosen **baccalaureate** fields are social sciences and history, business/marketing, and foreign language/literature. A complete listing of majors at Trinity appears in the Majors Index beginning on page 460.

The **faculty** at Trinity has 228 full-time members, 99% with terminal degrees. The student-faculty ratio is 10:1.

Students of Trinity
The student body totals 2,633, of whom 2,407 are undergraduates. 52.5% are women and 47.5% are men. Students come from 51 states and territories and 18 other countries. 1.3% are international students. 1.9% are African American, 0.5% American Indian, 6.1% Asian American, and 10.6% Hispanic American. 86% returned for their sophomore year.

Facilities and Resources
Student rooms are linked to a campus network. 100 **computers** are available on campus that provide access to the Internet. The **library** has 898,527 books and 2,311 subscriptions.

Campus Life
Active organizations on campus include a drama/theater group, newspaper, radio station, television station, and choral group. 26% of eligible men and 28% of eligible women are members of local **fraternities** and local **sororities**.

Trinity is a member of the NCAA (Division III). **Intercollegiate sports** include baseball (m), basketball, cross-country running, football (m), golf, soccer, softball (w), swimming, tennis, track and field, volleyball (w).

Campus Safety
Student safety services include late-night transport/escort service, 24-hour emergency telephone alarm devices, 24-hour patrols by trained security personnel, and electronically operated dormitory entrances.

Applying
Trinity requires an essay, a high school transcript, and 2 recommendations. It recommends SAT I or ACT and an interview. Application deadline: 2/1; 2/1 priority date for financial aid. Deferred admission is possible.

Trinity University is a highly selective liberal arts and sciences institution that also offers several professional programs that are nationally cited as models in their fields. Trinity offers its students a unique undergraduate experience. Class sizes are small, research labs and other facilities equal to those of moderate-sized Ph.D.-granting institutions are devoted exclusively to undergraduates, and contact with professors is frequent and personal. (Trinity employs no graduate assistants and few part-time faculty members.) The 117-acre campus is known for its beauty and for its skyline view of downtown San Antonio, one of America's most interesting multicultural cities.

Getting in Last Year
3,675 applied
64% were accepted
633 enrolled (27%)
51% from top tenth of their h.s. class
3.50 average high school GPA
79% had SAT verbal scores over 600
84% had SAT math scores over 600
99% had ACT scores over 24
21% had SAT verbal scores over 700
22% had SAT math scores over 700
40% had ACT scores over 30

Graduation and After
63% graduated in 4 years
11% graduated in 5 years
1% graduated in 6 years
31% pursued further study (8% arts and sciences, 5% education, 4% dentistry)
43% had job offers within 6 months
28 organizations recruited on campus

Financial Matters
$19,176 tuition and fees (2003–04)
$7290 room and board
86% average percent of need met
$14,518 average financial aid amount received per undergraduate (2002–03 estimated)

TRUMAN STATE UNIVERSITY

SMALL-TOWN SETTING ■ PUBLIC ■ STATE-SUPPORTED ■ COED
KIRKSVILLE, MISSOURI

Web site: www.truman.edu

Contact: Mr. Brad Chambers, Co-Director of Admissions, 205 McClain Hall, Kirksville, MO 63501-4221

Telephone: 660-785-4114 or toll-free 800-892-7792 (in-state) **Fax:** 660-785-7456

E-mail: admissions@truman.edu

Getting in Last Year

4,334 applied
84% were accepted
1,317 enrolled (36%)
50% from top tenth of their h.s. class
3.77 average high school GPA
59% had SAT verbal scores over 600
58% had SAT math scores over 600
87% had ACT scores over 24
18% had SAT verbal scores over 700
12% had SAT math scores over 700
32% had ACT scores over 30
16 National Merit Scholars
144 valedictorians

Graduation and After

42% graduated in 4 years
21% graduated in 5 years
1% graduated in 6 years
41% pursued further study
56% had job offers within 6 months
294 organizations recruited on campus

Financial Matters

$4656 resident tuition and fees (2003–04)
$8456 nonresident tuition and fees (2003–04)
$5072 room and board
83% average percent of need met
$5774 average financial aid amount received per undergraduate (2002–03)

Academics

Truman awards bachelor's and master's **degrees**. Challenging opportunities include advanced placement credit, accelerated degree programs, an honors program, double majors, and a senior project. Special programs include internships, summer session for credit, off-campus study, study-abroad, and Army ROTC.

The most frequently chosen **baccalaureate** fields are business/marketing, English, and biological/life sciences. A complete listing of majors at Truman appears in the Majors Index beginning on page 460.

The **faculty** at Truman has 354 full-time members, 86% with terminal degrees. The student-faculty ratio is 15:1.

Students of Truman

The student body totals 5,833, of whom 5,479 are undergraduates. 58.7% are women and 41.3% are men. Students come from 37 states and territories and 48 other countries. 76% are from Missouri. 4.7% are international students. 3.8% are African American, 0.5% American Indian, 2% Asian American, and 1.8% Hispanic American. 85% returned for their sophomore year.

Facilities and Resources

Student rooms are linked to a campus network. 840 **computers** are available on campus that provide access to the Internet. The **library** has 481,424 books and 3,197 subscriptions.

Campus Life

There are 210 active organizations on campus, including a drama/theater group, newspaper, radio station, television station, choral group, and marching band. 30% of eligible men and 20% of eligible women are members of national **fraternities**, national **sororities**, and local sororities.

Truman is a member of the NCAA (Division II). **Intercollegiate sports** (some offering scholarships) include baseball (m), basketball, cross-country running, football (m), golf, soccer, softball (w), swimming, tennis, track and field, volleyball (w), wrestling (m).

Campus Safety

Student safety services include patrols by commissioned officers, late-night transport/escort service, 24-hour emergency telephone alarm devices, 24-hour patrols by trained security personnel, and student patrols.

Applying

Truman requires an essay, SAT I or ACT, and a high school transcript. It recommends ACT, an interview, and a minimum high school GPA of 3.0. Application deadline: 3/1; 4/1 priority date for financial aid. Early and deferred admission are possible.

TUFTS UNIVERSITY

SUBURBAN SETTING ■ PRIVATE ■ INDEPENDENT ■ COED
MEDFORD, MASSACHUSETTS

Web site: www.tufts.edu
Contact: Mr. Lee A. Coffin, Dean of Undergraduate Admissions, Bendetson
   Hall, Medford, MA 02155
Telephone: 617-627-3170 **Fax:** 617-627-3860
E-mail: admissions.inquiry@ase.tufts.edu

Academics

Tufts awards bachelor's, master's, doctoral, and first-professional **degrees** and post-master's certificates. Challenging opportunities include advanced placement credit, student-designed majors, an honors program, double majors, independent study, and a senior project. Special programs include internships, summer session for credit, off-campus study, study-abroad, and Army, Navy and Air Force ROTC.

The most frequently chosen **baccalaureate** fields are social sciences and history, engineering/engineering technologies, and psychology. A complete listing of majors at Tufts appears in the Majors Index beginning on page 460.

The **faculty** at Tufts has 583 full-time members. The student-faculty ratio is 9:1.

Students of Tufts

The student body totals 9,509, of whom 4,892 are undergraduates. 54.2% are women and 45.8% are men. Students come from 51 states and territories and 67 other countries. 25% are from Massachusetts. 6.4% are international students. 7.4% are African American, 0.4% American Indian, 13.5% Asian American, and 7.7% Hispanic American. 96% returned for their sophomore year.

Facilities and Resources

Student rooms are linked to a campus network. 254 **computers** are available on campus that provide access to the Internet. The 2 **libraries** have 1,613,000 books and 5,204 subscriptions.

Campus Life

There are 160 active organizations on campus, including a drama/theater group, newspaper, radio station, television station, choral group, and marching band. 15% of eligible men and 4% of eligible women are members of national **fraternities** and national **sororities**.

Tufts is a member of the NCAA (Division III). **Intercollegiate sports** include baseball (m), basketball, crew, cross-country running, fencing (w), field hockey (w), football (m), golf (m), ice hockey (m), lacrosse, sailing, soccer, softball (w), squash, swimming, tennis, track and field, volleyball (w).

Campus Safety

Student safety services include security lighting, call boxes to campus police, late-night transport/escort service, 24-hour emergency telephone alarm devices, 24-hour patrols by trained security personnel, and electronically operated dormitory entrances.

Applying

Tufts requires an essay, SAT I and SAT II or ACT, a high school transcript, and 1 recommendation, and in some cases SAT II: Writing Test. It recommends an interview. Application deadline: 1/1; 2/15 for financial aid, with a 2/15 priority date. Early and deferred admission are possible.

Getting in Last Year
14,528 applied
26% were accepted
1,282 enrolled (33%)
70% from top tenth of their h.s. class
82% had SAT verbal scores over 600
88% had SAT math scores over 600
92% had ACT scores over 24
31% had SAT verbal scores over 700
44% had SAT math scores over 700
45% had ACT scores over 30

Graduation and After
82% graduated in 4 years
7% graduated in 5 years
1% graduated in 6 years
30% pursued further study (11% law, 9% medicine, 8% business)
211 organizations recruited on campus

Financial Matters
$29,593 tuition and fees (2003–04)
$8640 room and board
100% average percent of need met
$24,084 average financial aid amount received per undergraduate

TULANE UNIVERSITY
URBAN SETTING ■ PRIVATE ■ INDEPENDENT ■ COED
NEW ORLEANS, LOUISIANA

Web site: www.tulane.edu
Contact: Mr. Richard Whiteside, Vice President of Enrollment Management, Office of Admissions, 210 Gibson Hall, New Orleans, LA 70118
Telephone: 504-865-5731 or toll-free 800-873-9283 **Fax:** 504-862-8715
E-mail: undergrad.admission@tulane.edu

Among national universities, Tulane is known for its emphasis on undergraduate teaching and its accomplishments in research. The same senior faculty members who do research regularly teach freshmen and sophomores. With approximately 6,000 students in 6 divisions, Tulane gives each student the personal attention and teaching excellence typically associated with smaller colleges, while providing the state-of-the-art facilities and interdisciplinary resources usually found only at major universities. Tulane students play active roles in more than 300 campus organizations and have numerous internship opportunities in the exciting city of New Orleans. Close student-teacher relationships pay off—graduates frequently win prestigious fellowships, and many go on to earn advanced degrees in their chosen field of study.

Getting in Last Year
13,931 applied
56% were accepted
1,678 enrolled (22%)
65% from top tenth of their h.s. class
84% had SAT verbal scores over 600
79% had SAT math scores over 600
32% had SAT verbal scores over 700
25% had SAT math scores over 700

Graduation and After
62% graduated in 4 years
10% graduated in 5 years
2% graduated in 6 years
55% pursued further study (30% arts and sciences, 15% law, 10% medicine)
557 organizations recruited on campus

Financial Matters
$32,120 tuition and fees (2003–04)
$7641 room and board
94% average percent of need met
$22,948 average financial aid amount received per undergraduate

Academics
Tulane awards associate, bachelor's, master's, doctoral, and first-professional **degrees** and post-bachelor's certificates. Challenging opportunities include advanced placement credit, accelerated degree programs, student-designed majors, freshman honors college, an honors program, double majors, independent study, and a senior project. Special programs include cooperative education, internships, summer session for credit, off-campus study, study-abroad, and Army, Navy and Air Force ROTC.

The most frequently chosen **baccalaureate** fields are business/marketing, social sciences and history, and engineering/engineering technologies. A complete listing of majors at Tulane appears in the Majors Index beginning on page 460.

The **faculty** at Tulane has 1,049 full-time members, 99% with terminal degrees. The student-faculty ratio is 10:1.

Students of Tulane
The student body totals 12,443, of whom 7,862 are undergraduates. 52.6% are women and 47.4% are men. 2.7% are international students. 8.3% are African American, 0.5% American Indian, 4.1% Asian American, and 3.5% Hispanic American. 86% returned for their sophomore year.

Facilities and Resources
Student rooms are linked to a campus network. 900 **computers** are available on campus that provide access to wireless access to the Internet and the Internet. The 9 **libraries** have 2,285,029 books and 15,308 subscriptions.

Campus Life
There are 250 active organizations on campus, including a drama/theater group, newspaper, radio station, television station, choral group, and marching band. Tulane has national **fraternities** and national **sororities**.

Tulane is a member of the NCAA (Division I). **Intercollegiate sports** (some offering scholarships) include baseball (m), basketball, cross-country running, football (m), golf, soccer (w), swimming (w), tennis, track and field (w), volleyball (w).

Campus Safety
Student safety services include on and off-campus shuttle service, crime prevention programs, lighted pathways, late-night transport/escort service, 24-hour emergency telephone alarm devices, 24-hour patrols by trained security personnel, student patrols, and electronically operated dormitory entrances.

Applying
Tulane requires an essay, SAT I or ACT, a high school transcript, and 1 recommendation, and in some cases SAT II Subject Tests. It recommends SAT II Subject Tests. Application deadline: 1/15; 2/1 for financial aid, with a 1/15 priority date. Early and deferred admission are possible.

UNION COLLEGE

SUBURBAN SETTING ▪ PRIVATE ▪ INDEPENDENT ▪ COED
SCHENECTADY, NEW YORK

Web site: www.union.edu
Contact: Ms. Dianne Crozier, Director of Admissions, Grant Hall,
    Schenectady, NY 12308
Telephone: 518-388-6112 or toll-free 888-843-6688 (in-state) **Fax:**
    518-388-6986
E-mail: admissions@union.edu

Academics

Union College awards bachelor's **degrees**. Challenging opportunities include advanced placement credit, accelerated degree programs, student-designed majors, an honors program, double majors, independent study, and a senior project. Special programs include cooperative education, internships, summer session for credit, off-campus study, study-abroad, and Army, Navy and Air Force ROTC.

The most frequently chosen **baccalaureate** fields are social sciences and history, engineering/engineering technologies, and biological/life sciences. A complete listing of majors at Union College appears in the Majors Index beginning on page 460.

The **faculty** at Union College has 192 full-time members, 94% with terminal degrees. The student-faculty ratio is 11:1.

Students of Union College

The student body is made up of 2,174 undergraduates. 46.9% are women and 53.1% are men. Students come from 37 states and territories and 17 other countries. 45% are from New York. 1.9% are international students. 3.5% are African American, 5.4% Asian American, and 4.3% Hispanic American. 93% returned for their sophomore year.

Facilities and Resources

Student rooms are linked to a campus network. 435 **computers** are available on campus that provide access to the Internet. The **library** has 301,101 books and 1,988 subscriptions.

Campus Life

There are 95 active organizations on campus, including a drama/theater group, newspaper, radio station, and choral group. 36% of eligible men and 37% of eligible women are members of national **fraternities**, national **sororities**, local fraternities, local sororities, and theme houses.

Union College is a member of the NCAA (Division III). **Intercollegiate sports** include baseball (m), basketball, crew, cross-country running, field hockey (w), football (m), ice hockey, lacrosse, soccer, softball (w), swimming, tennis, track and field, volleyball (w).

Campus Safety

Student safety services include awareness programs, bicycle patrol, shuttle service, late-night transport/escort service, 24-hour emergency telephone alarm devices, 24-hour patrols by trained security personnel, and electronically operated dormitory entrances.

Applying

Union College requires an essay, SAT I or ACT, 3 SAT II Subject Tests (including SAT II: Writing Test), a high school transcript, and 2 recommendations, and in some cases SAT II Subject Tests. It recommends an interview. Application deadline: 1/15; 2/1 for financial aid, with a 2/1 priority date. Early and deferred admission are possible.

Union College, one of the oldest nondenominational colleges in America, is located in the small city of Schenectady, about 3 hours north of New York City. Its distinctive curriculum combines the traditional liberal arts with engineering study. Three basic tenets undergird a Union education: commitments to lifelong learning, the liberal arts, and a close working relationship between students and faculty members. People from many different backgrounds come to Union, attracted by these values and the opportunities they imply: small classes, excellent access to superb facilities, a caring and committed faculty, and an academic program of depth and diversity.

Getting in Last Year
4,159 applied
44% were accepted
559 enrolled (31%)
58% from top tenth of their h.s. class
3.49 average high school GPA
60% had SAT verbal scores over 600
72% had SAT math scores over 600
12% had SAT verbal scores over 700
22% had SAT math scores over 700

Graduation and After
77% graduated in 4 years
6% graduated in 5 years
1% graduated in 6 years
31% pursued further study (7% arts and sciences, 6% law, 6% medicine)
67% had job offers within 6 months
46 organizations recruited on campus

Financial Matters
$28,928 tuition and fees (2003–04)
$7077 room and board
100% average percent of need met
$22,601 average financial aid amount received per undergraduate

UNION COLLEGE

SUBURBAN SETTING ■ PRIVATE ■ INDEPENDENT RELIGIOUS ■ COED
LINCOLN, NEBRASKA

Web site: www.ucollege.edu
Contact: Huda McClelland, Director of Admissions, 3800 South 48th Street,
  Lincoln, NE 68506
Telephone: 402-486-2504 or toll-free 800-228-4600 (out-of-state) **Fax:**
  402-486-2895
E-mail: ucenrol@ucollege.edu

Getting in Last Year
549 applied
49% were accepted
165 enrolled (62%)
8% from top tenth of their h.s. class
3.27 average high school GPA
32% had ACT scores over 24
3% had ACT scores over 30

Graduation and After
44% graduated in 6 years
Graduates pursuing further study: 4% education, 4% medicine, 2% arts and sciences
89% had job offers within 6 months
96 organizations recruited on campus

Financial Matters
$12,878 tuition and fees (2003–04)
$3630 room and board
44% average percent of need met
$8376 average financial aid amount received per undergraduate (2002–03 estimated)

Academics
Union awards associate and bachelor's **degrees**. Challenging opportunities include advanced placement credit, accelerated degree programs, student-designed majors, an honors program, double majors, independent study, and a senior project. Special programs include cooperative education, internships, summer session for credit, off-campus study, and study-abroad.

The most frequently chosen **baccalaureate** fields are health professions and related sciences, business/marketing, and education. A complete listing of majors at Union appears in the Majors Index beginning on page 460.

The **faculty** at Union has 52 full-time members, 48% with terminal degrees. The student-faculty ratio is 14:1.

Students of Union
The student body is made up of 903 undergraduates. 59.1% are women and 40.9% are men. Students come from 41 states and territories and 34 other countries. 23% are from Nebraska. 12.3% are international students. 2.1% are African American, 0.7% American Indian, 0.6% Asian American, and 4.3% Hispanic American. 67% returned for their sophomore year.

Facilities and Resources
Student rooms are linked to a campus network. 520 **computers** are available on campus that provide access to the Internet. The **library** has 147,813 books and 1,357 subscriptions.

Campus Life
Active organizations on campus include a drama/theater group, newspaper, and choral group. No national or local **fraternities** or **sororities**.

Intercollegiate sports include basketball, volleyball (w).

Campus Safety
Student safety services include late-night transport/escort service, 24-hour emergency telephone alarm devices, and student patrols.

Applying
Union requires ACT, a high school transcript, 3 recommendations, and a minimum high school GPA of 2.5, and in some cases an interview. It recommends an essay. Application deadline: rolling admissions; 5/1 priority date for financial aid.

UNION UNIVERSITY

SMALL-TOWN SETTING ■ PRIVATE ■ INDEPENDENT RELIGIOUS ■ COED
JACKSON, TENNESSEE

Web site: www.uu.edu
Contact: Mr. Robbie Graves, Director of Enrollment Services, 1050 Union
    University Drive, Jackson, TN 38305-3697
Telephone: 731-661-5008 or toll-free 800-33-UNION **Fax:** 731-661-5017
E-mail: info@uu.edu

Academics

Union awards associate, bachelor's, master's, and doctoral **degrees** and post-master's
certificates. Challenging opportunities include advanced placement credit, accelerated
degree programs, an honors program, double majors, independent study, and a senior
project. Special programs include cooperative education, internships, summer session for
credit, off-campus study, and study-abroad.

The most frequently chosen **baccalaureate** fields are business/marketing, health
professions and related sciences, and education. A complete listing of majors at Union
appears in the Majors Index beginning on page 460.

The **faculty** at Union has 146 full-time members, 79% with terminal degrees. The
student-faculty ratio is 12:1.

Students of Union

The student body totals 2,774, of whom 2,022 are undergraduates. 60.7% are women
and 39.3% are men. Students come from 43 states and territories and 36 other countries.
68% are from Tennessee. 2.1% are international students. 7.9% are African American,
0% American Indian, 0.7% Asian American, and 0.6% Hispanic American. 67%
returned for their sophomore year.

Facilities and Resources

Student rooms are linked to a campus network. 236 **computers** are available on campus
that provide access to the Internet. The 2 **libraries** have 135,877 books and 4,655
subscriptions.

Campus Life

There are 52 active organizations on campus, including a drama/theater group,
newspaper, and choral group. 7% of eligible men and 12% of eligible women are
members of national **fraternities** and national **sororities**.

Union is a member of the NAIA and NCCAA. **Intercollegiate sports** (some offering scholarships) include baseball (m), basketball, cheerleading (w), cross-country running, soccer (m), softball (w), track and field, volleyball (w).

Campus Safety

Student safety services include late-night transport/escort service, 24-hour emergency
telephone alarm devices, 24-hour patrols by trained security personnel, and student
patrols.

Applying

Union requires SAT I or ACT, a high school transcript, and a minimum high school
GPA of 2.5, and in some cases recommendations. It recommends an essay and an
interview. Application deadline: rolling admissions; 1/30 priority date for financial aid.
Early and deferred admission are possible.

C onscious of the changing
global atmosphere
awaiting the next
generation of students, Union
University is preparing leaders and
change agents for the coming
century. High-quality classroom
teaching is a University trademark,
as students are challenged to
become influential players in their
chosen field of study. Union's vision
and goals of excellence in liberal
arts education are shaped by an
enduring faith in God and an
unfaltering commitment to Christian
values. Union is a place where
students grow both in faith and
vision, fulfilling their dreams and
changing the world.

Getting in Last Year
1,461 applied
61% were accepted
450 enrolled (50%)
37% from top tenth of their h.s. class
3.54 average high school GPA
33% had SAT verbal scores over 600
36% had SAT math scores over 600
54% had ACT scores over 24
9% had SAT verbal scores over 700
16% had SAT math scores over 700
14% had ACT scores over 30
6 National Merit Scholars
44 valedictorians

Graduation and After
38% graduated in 4 years
13% graduated in 5 years
1% graduated in 6 years
40% pursued further study (13% education,
  13% theology, 4% arts and sciences)
83% had job offers within 6 months
85 organizations recruited on campus

Financial Matters
$14,250 tuition and fees (2003–04)
$4640 room and board
$10,492 average financial aid amount received
  per undergraduate

UNITED STATES AIR FORCE ACADEMY

SUBURBAN SETTING ■ PUBLIC ■ FEDERALLY SUPPORTED ■ COED, PRIMARILY MEN
USAF ACADEMY, COLORADO

Web site: www.usafa.edu/rr
Contact: Mr. Rolland Stoneman, Associate Director of Admissions/Selections,
HQ USAFA/RR 2304 Cadet Drive, Suite 200, USAF Academy, CO
80840-5025
Telephone: 719-333-2520 or toll-free 800-443-9266 **Fax:** 719-333-3012
E-mail: rr_webmail@usafa.af.mil

The Air Force Academy challenge requires a well-rounded academic, physical, and leadership background. Cadets must accept discipline, be competitive, and have a desire to serve others with a sense of duty and integrity. Applicants should prepare early to meet the admissions requirements, competition, and demands they will face at the Academy.

Getting in Last Year
10,780 applied
12% were accepted
1,214 enrolled (94%)
57% from top tenth of their h.s. class
3.80 average high school GPA
70% had SAT verbal scores over 600
84% had SAT math scores over 600
16% had SAT verbal scores over 700
28% had SAT math scores over 700

Graduation and After
97% graduated in 4 years
1% graduated in 5 years
1% graduated in 6 years
7% pursued further study (3% arts and sciences, 2% medicine, 2% engineering)
100% had job offers within 6 months
1 organization recruited on campus

Academics

USAFA awards bachelor's **degrees**. Challenging opportunities include advanced placement credit, student-designed majors, double majors, independent study, and a senior project. Special programs include internships, summer session for credit, off-campus study, and study-abroad.

The most frequently chosen **baccalaureate** fields are engineering/engineering technologies, business/marketing, and social sciences and history. A complete listing of majors at USAFA appears in the Majors Index beginning on page 460.

The **faculty** at USAFA has 531 full-time members, 57% with terminal degrees. The student-faculty ratio is 8:1.

Students of USAFA

The student body is made up of 4,157 undergraduates. 17% are women and 83% are men. Students come from 54 states and territories and 21 other countries. 5% are from Colorado. 1.1% are international students. 5.1% are African American, 1% American Indian, 5.4% Asian American, and 6.1% Hispanic American. 82% returned for their sophomore year.

Facilities and Resources

Student rooms are linked to a campus network. The 3 **libraries** have 445,379 books and 1,693 subscriptions.

Campus Life

There are 100 active organizations on campus, including a drama/theater group, newspaper, radio station, choral group, and marching band. No national or local **fraternities** or **sororities**.

USAFA is a member of the NCAA (Division I). **Intercollegiate sports** include baseball (m), basketball, cheerleading, cross-country running, fencing, football (m), golf (m), gymnastics, ice hockey (m), lacrosse (m), riflery, soccer, swimming, tennis, track and field, volleyball (w), water polo (m), wrestling (m).

Campus Safety

Student safety services include self-defense education, well-lit campus, late-night transport/escort service, 24-hour emergency telephone alarm devices, and 24-hour patrols by trained security personnel.

Applying

USAFA requires an essay, SAT I or ACT, a high school transcript, an interview, authorized nomination, and a minimum high school GPA of 2.0. It recommends SAT I or ACT. Application deadline: 1/31.

UNITED STATES COAST GUARD ACADEMY

SUBURBAN SETTING ■ PUBLIC ■ FEDERALLY SUPPORTED ■ COED
NEW LONDON, CONNECTICUT

Web site: www.cga.edu
Contact: Capt. Susan D. Bibeau, Director of Admissions, 31 Mohegan
    Avenue, New London, CT 06320-4195
Telephone: 860-444-8500 or toll-free 800-883-8724 **Fax:** 860-701-6700
E-mail: admissions@cga.uscg.mil

Academics

USCGA awards bachelor's **degrees**. Challenging opportunities include an honors
program, double majors, independent study, and a senior project. Special programs
include cooperative education, internships, summer session for credit, and off-campus
study.

The most frequently chosen **baccalaureate** fields are engineering/engineering
technologies, business/marketing, and social sciences and history. A complete listing of
majors at USCGA appears in the Majors Index beginning on page 460.

The student-faculty ratio is 10:1.

Students of USCGA

The student body is made up of 1,016 undergraduates. 29.6% are women and 70.4% are
men. Students come from 49 states and territories and 12 other countries. 7% are from
Connecticut. 1.5% are international students. 4.2% are African American, 0.5%
American Indian, 5.3% Asian American, and 5.2% Hispanic American. 81% returned for
their sophomore year.

Facilities and Resources

Student rooms are linked to a campus network.

Campus Life

Active organizations on campus include a drama/theater group, choral group, and
marching band. No national or local **fraternities** or **sororities**.

USCGA is a member of the NCAA (Division III). **Intercollegiate sports** include
baseball (m), basketball, crew, cross-country running, football (m), riflery, sailing, soccer,
softball (w), swimming, tennis (m), track and field, volleyball (w), wrestling (m).

Campus Safety

Student safety services include 24-hour patrols by trained security personnel and student
patrols.

Applying

USCGA requires an essay, SAT I or ACT, a high school transcript, 3 recommendations,
and medical exam, physical fitness exam. It recommends an interview. Application
deadline: 1/31.

Getting in Last Year
6,028 applied
7% were accepted
309 enrolled (72%)
58% from top tenth of their h.s. class
64% had SAT verbal scores over 600
83% had SAT math scores over 600
97% had ACT scores over 24
15% had SAT verbal scores over 700
18% had SAT math scores over 700
21% had ACT scores over 30
31 class presidents
16 valedictorians

Graduation and After
55% graduated in 4 years
2% graduated in 5 years

UNITED STATES MERCHANT MARINE ACADEMY

SUBURBAN SETTING ■ PUBLIC ■ FEDERALLY SUPPORTED ■ COED
KINGS POINT, NEW YORK

Web site: www.usmma.edu
Contact: Capt. James M. Skinner, Director of Admissions, 300 Steamboat
    Road, Kings Point, NY 11024-1699
Telephone: 516-773-5391 or toll-free 866-546-4778 **Fax:** 516-773-5390
E-mail: admissions@usmma.edu

The United States Merchant Marine Academy is a 4-year federal service academy dedicated to educating and training young men and women as officers in America's merchant marine and U.S. Naval Reserve and as future leaders of the maritime and transportation industries. The Academy, in Kings Point, Long Island, offers accredited programs in marine transportation and engineering leading to a BS degree, a U.S. merchant marine officer's license, and a Naval Reserve commission. Students spend 3 trimesters at sea aboard U.S. merchant ships as part of their training.

Getting in Last Year
1,919 applied
16% were accepted
303 enrolled (100%)
26% from top tenth of their h.s. class
3.60 average high school GPA
64% had SAT verbal scores over 600
61% had SAT math scores over 600
22% had SAT verbal scores over 700
8% had SAT math scores over 700
17 class presidents
7 valedictorians

Graduation and After
61% graduated in 4 years
19% graduated in 5 years
2% pursued further study (1% business, 1% engineering)
90% had job offers within 6 months
70 organizations recruited on campus

Academics

United States Merchant Marine Academy awards bachelor's **degrees**. Challenging opportunities include an honors program and a senior project. Internships is a special program.

The most frequently chosen **baccalaureate** field is engineering/engineering technologies. A complete listing of majors at United States Merchant Marine Academy appears in the Majors Index beginning on page 460.

The **faculty** at United States Merchant Marine Academy has 85 full-time members. The student-faculty ratio is 11:1.

Students of United States Merchant Marine Academy

The student body is made up of 971 undergraduates. 12.8% are women and 87.2% are men. Students come from 49 states and territories and 3 other countries. 14% are from New York. 92% returned for their sophomore year.

Facilities and Resources

Student rooms are linked to a campus network. 1,200 **computers** are available on campus that provide access to engineering and economics software and the Internet. The **library** has 185,000 books and 950 subscriptions.

Campus Life

There are 45 active organizations on campus, including a drama/theater group, newspaper, choral group, and marching band. No national or local **fraternities** or **sororities**.

United States Merchant Marine Academy is a member of the NCAA (Division III). **Intercollegiate sports** include baseball (m), basketball, crew, cross-country running, football (m), golf, lacrosse (m), sailing, soccer (m), softball (w), swimming, tennis, track and field, volleyball (w), wrestling (m).

Campus Safety

Student safety services include 24-hour patrols by trained security personnel.

Applying

United States Merchant Marine Academy requires an essay, SAT I or ACT, a high school transcript, and 3 recommendations. It recommends an interview. Application deadline: 3/1.

UNITED STATES MILITARY ACADEMY

SMALL-TOWN SETTING ■ PUBLIC ■ FEDERALLY SUPPORTED ■ COED, PRIMARILY MEN
WEST POINT, NEW YORK

Web site: www.usma.edu
Contact: Col. Michael C. Jones, Director of Admissions, Building 606, West
Point, NY 10996
Telephone: 845-938-4041
E-mail: 8dad@sunams.usma.army.mil

Academics

West Point awards bachelor's **degrees**. Challenging opportunities include advanced placement credit and double majors. Special programs include summer session for credit and off-campus study.

The most frequently chosen **baccalaureate** fields are engineering/engineering technologies, social sciences and history, and physical sciences. A complete listing of majors at West Point appears in the Majors Index beginning on page 460.

The **faculty** at West Point has 598 full-time members, 51% with terminal degrees. The student-faculty ratio is 7:1.

Students of West Point

The student body is made up of 4,242 undergraduates. 15.5% are women and 84.5% are men. Students come from 53 states and territories and 25 other countries. 8% are from New York. 0.8% are international students. 7.6% are African American, 0.7% American Indian, 6.5% Asian American, and 6.7% Hispanic American. 92% returned for their sophomore year.

Facilities and Resources

Student rooms are linked to a campus network. 5,500 **computers** are available on campus that provide access to the Internet. The 2 **libraries** have 457,340 books and 2,220 subscriptions.

Campus Life

There are 120 active organizations on campus, including a drama/theater group, radio station, and choral group. No national or local **fraternities** or **sororities**.

West Point is a member of the NCAA (Division I). **Intercollegiate sports** include baseball (m), basketball, cross-country running, football (m), golf (m), gymnastics (m), ice hockey (m), lacrosse (m), soccer, softball (w), swimming, tennis, track and field, volleyball (w), wrestling (m).

Campus Safety

Student safety services include late-night transport/escort service, 24-hour emergency telephone alarm devices, 24-hour patrols by trained security personnel, and student patrols.

Applying

West Point requires an essay, SAT I or ACT, a high school transcript, 4 recommendations, and medical examination, authorized nomination. It recommends an interview. Application deadline: 3/21.

> **W**est Point is about leadership. For more than 200 years, West Point has developed many of the nation's finest leaders. If you want to lead, then choose West Point. The academy offers a highly respected academic program, extensive military leadership training, and memorable life experiences. West Point builds a foundation for career success as an Army officer. West Point is tough, but it is worth the challenge. One cadet may have said it best: "The person I have become is so much better than the person who first came here."

Getting in Last Year
12,688 applied
10% were accepted
1,314 enrolled (100%)
50% from top tenth of their h.s. class
69% had SAT verbal scores over 600
82% had SAT math scores over 600
97% had ACT scores over 24
18% had SAT verbal scores over 700
25% had SAT math scores over 700
34% had ACT scores over 30
192 National Merit Scholars
234 class presidents
100 valedictorians

Graduation and After
80% graduated in 4 years
2% graduated in 5 years
1% graduated in 6 years
2% pursued further study (2% medicine)
100% had job offers within 6 months

UNITED STATES NAVAL ACADEMY

SMALL-TOWN SETTING ■ PUBLIC ■ FEDERALLY SUPPORTED ■ COED, PRIMARILY MEN
ANNAPOLIS, MARYLAND

Web site: www.usna.edu
Contact: Col. David A. Vetter, Dean of Admissions, 117 Decatur Road,
    Annapolis, MD 21402-5000
Telephone: 410-293-4361 **Fax:** 410-293-4348
E-mail: webmail@gwmail.usna.edu

Getting in Last Year

14,101 applied
10% were accepted
1,178 enrolled (80%)
57% from top tenth of their h.s. class
75% had SAT verbal scores over 600
86% had SAT math scores over 600
24% had SAT verbal scores over 700
35% had SAT math scores over 700
135 class presidents

Graduation and After

86% graduated in 4 years
2% pursued further study (1% medicine)
100% had job offers within 6 months
2 organizations recruited on campus

Academics

Naval Academy awards bachelor's **degrees**. Challenging opportunities include advanced placement credit, an honors program, double majors, and independent study. Summer session for credit is a special program.

The most frequently chosen **baccalaureate** fields are social sciences and history, engineering/engineering technologies, and physical sciences. A complete listing of majors at Naval Academy appears in the Majors Index beginning on page 460.

The **faculty** at Naval Academy has 560 full-time members, 60% with terminal degrees. The student-faculty ratio is 7:1.

Students of Naval Academy

The student body is made up of 4,335 undergraduates. 15.5% are women and 84.5% are men. Students come from 54 states and territories and 20 other countries. 4% are from Maryland. 0.9% are international students. 6.7% are African American, 1.8% American Indian, 4.5% Asian American, and 8.6% Hispanic American. 96% returned for their sophomore year.

Facilities and Resources

Student rooms are linked to a campus network. 6,100 **computers** are available on campus that provide access to the Internet. The 2 **libraries** have 800,000 books and 1,892 subscriptions.

Campus Life

There are 75 active organizations on campus, including a drama/theater group, radio station, choral group, and marching band. No national or local **fraternities** or **sororities**.

Naval Academy is a member of the NCAA (Division I). **Intercollegiate sports** include baseball (m), basketball, cheerleading, crew, cross-country running, football (m), golf (m), gymnastics (m), lacrosse (m), riflery, sailing, soccer, squash (m), swimming, tennis (m), track and field, volleyball (w), water polo (m), wrestling (m).

Campus Safety

Student safety services include front gate security, 24-hour emergency telephone alarm devices, 24-hour patrols by trained security personnel, and student patrols.

Applying

Naval Academy requires an essay, SAT I or ACT, a high school transcript, an interview, 2 recommendations, authorized nomination, and a minimum high school GPA of 2.0. Application deadline: 1/31.

University at Buffalo, The State University of New York

Suburban setting ■ Public ■ State-supported ■ Coed
Buffalo, New York

Web site: www.buffalo.edu
Contact: Ms. Patricia Armstrong, Director of Admissions, Capen Hall, Room 15, North Campus, Buffalo, NY 14260-1660
Telephone: 716-645-6900 or toll-free 888-UB-ADMIT **Fax:** 716-645-6411
E-mail: ub-admissions@buffalo.edu

Academics

UB awards associate, bachelor's, master's, doctoral, and first-professional **degrees** and post-master's and first-professional certificates. Challenging opportunities include advanced placement credit, accelerated degree programs, student-designed majors, freshman honors college, an honors program, double majors, independent study, and a senior project. Special programs include internships, summer session for credit, off-campus study, study-abroad, and Army ROTC.

The most frequently chosen **baccalaureate** fields are business/marketing, engineering/engineering technologies, and social sciences and history. A complete listing of majors at UB appears in the Majors Index beginning on page 460.

The **faculty** at UB has 1,124 full-time members. The student-faculty ratio is 15:1.

Students of UB

The student body totals 27,255, of whom 17,818 are undergraduates. 45.2% are women and 54.8% are men. Students come from 42 states and territories and 78 other countries. 98% are from New York. 5.9% are international students. 7.2% are African American, 0.3% American Indian, 8.8% Asian American, and 3.5% Hispanic American. 85% returned for their sophomore year.

Facilities and Resources

Student rooms are linked to a campus network. 2,391 **computers** are available on campus that provide access to the Internet. The 8 **libraries** have 2,000,000 books and 32,179 subscriptions.

Campus Life

Active organizations on campus include a drama/theater group, newspaper, radio station, television station, choral group, and marching band. 2% of eligible men and 4% of eligible women are members of national **fraternities**, national **sororities**, local fraternities, and local sororities.

UB is a member of the NCAA (Division I). **Intercollegiate sports** (some offering scholarships) include baseball (m), basketball, crew (w), cross-country running, football (m), soccer, softball (w), swimming, tennis, track and field, volleyball (w), wrestling (m).

Campus Safety

Student safety services include self-defense and awareness programs, late-night transport/escort service, 24-hour emergency telephone alarm devices, 24-hour patrols by trained security personnel, student patrols, and electronically operated dormitory entrances.

Applying

UB requires SAT I or ACT and a high school transcript, and in some cases recommendations and portfolio, audition. Application deadline: rolling admissions; 3/1 priority date for financial aid. Early admission is possible.

The University at Buffalo (UB) is New York's premier public research university—an academic community in which undergraduates work side by side with faculty members who are on the cutting edge of their fields. UB offers the most comprehensive scholarship programs in the State University of New York System and more undergraduate degree programs than any other public university in New York and New England. In a true community of scholars, students are encouraged to explore the possibilities among extensive programs in architecture, arts and letters, engineering, health sciences, informatics, management, medicine and biomedical sciences, natural sciences and mathematics, nursing, pharmacy, and social sciences.

Getting in Last Year
17,448 applied
62% were accepted
3,593 enrolled (33%)
21% from top tenth of their h.s. class
3.10 average high school GPA
28% had SAT verbal scores over 600
42% had SAT math scores over 600
74% had ACT scores over 24
4% had SAT verbal scores over 700
6% had SAT math scores over 700
14% had ACT scores over 30
4 National Merit Scholars
24 valedictorians

Graduation and After
33% graduated in 4 years
19% graduated in 5 years
5% graduated in 6 years
36% pursued further study (35% arts and sciences)
78% had job offers within 6 months
210 organizations recruited on campus

Financial Matters
$5851 resident tuition and fees (2003–04)
$11,801 nonresident tuition and fees (2003–04)
$6816 room and board
71% average percent of need met
$7520 average financial aid amount received per undergraduate

THE UNIVERSITY OF ALABAMA

SUBURBAN SETTING ■ PUBLIC ■ STATE-SUPPORTED ■ COED
TUSCALOOSA, ALABAMA

Web site: www.ua.edu
Contact: Ms. Mary K. Spiegel, Director of Admissions, Box 870132, 203 Student Services Center, Tuscaloosa, AL 35487-0132
Telephone: 205-348-5666 or toll-free 800-933-BAMA **Fax:** 205-348-9046
E-mail: admissions@ua.edu

Getting in Last Year

8,298 applied
87% were accepted
3,077 enrolled (43%)
24% from top tenth of their h.s. class
3.33 average high school GPA
30% had SAT verbal scores over 600
29% had SAT math scores over 600
46% had ACT scores over 24
8% had SAT verbal scores over 700
6% had SAT math scores over 700
6% had ACT scores over 30
34 National Merit Scholars

Graduation and After

33% graduated in 4 years
22% graduated in 5 years
7% graduated in 6 years
27% pursued further study
55% had job offers within 6 months
632 organizations recruited on campus

Financial Matters

$4134 resident tuition and fees (2003–04)
$11,294 nonresident tuition and fees (2003–04)
$4906 room and board
72% average percent of need met
$7622 average financial aid amount received per undergraduate (2001–02)

Academics

Alabama awards bachelor's, master's, doctoral, and first-professional **degrees** and post-bachelor's and post-master's certificates. Challenging opportunities include advanced placement credit, accelerated degree programs, student-designed majors, freshman honors college, an honors program, double majors, independent study, and a senior project. Special programs include cooperative education, internships, summer session for credit, off-campus study, study-abroad, and Army and Air Force ROTC.

The most frequently chosen **baccalaureate** fields are business/marketing, communications/communication technologies, and home economics/vocational home economics. A complete listing of majors at Alabama appears in the Majors Index beginning on page 460.

The **faculty** at Alabama has 896 full-time members, 92% with terminal degrees. The student-faculty ratio is 19:1.

Students of Alabama

The student body totals 20,291, of whom 15,889 are undergraduates. 53.5% are women and 46.5% are men. Students come from 52 states and territories and 92 other countries. 80% are from Alabama. 1.1% are international students. 13.8% are African American, 0.6% American Indian, 1% Asian American, and 1.1% Hispanic American. 84% returned for their sophomore year.

Facilities and Resources

Student rooms are linked to a campus network. 2,000 **computers** are available on campus that provide access to the Internet. The 9 **libraries** have 2,261,000 books and 16,590 subscriptions.

Campus Life

There are 318 active organizations on campus, including a drama/theater group, newspaper, radio station, television station, choral group, and marching band. 16% of eligible men and 25% of eligible women are members of national **fraternities**, national **sororities**, local fraternities, and local sororities.

Alabama is a member of the NCAA (Division I). **Intercollegiate sports** (some offering scholarships) include baseball (m), basketball, cross-country running, football (m), golf, gymnastics (w), soccer (w), softball (w), swimming, tennis, track and field, volleyball (w).

Campus Safety

Student safety services include crime prevention programs, community police protection, late-night transport/escort service, 24-hour emergency telephone alarm devices, 24-hour patrols by trained security personnel, student patrols, and electronically operated dormitory entrances.

Applying

Alabama requires SAT I or ACT, a high school transcript, and a minimum high school GPA of 2.0, and in some cases an interview. Application deadline: 8/1; 3/1 priority date for financial aid. Early and deferred admission are possible.

THE UNIVERSITY OF ALABAMA IN HUNTSVILLE

SUBURBAN SETTING ■ PUBLIC ■ STATE-SUPPORTED ■ COED
HUNTSVILLE, ALABAMA

Web site: www.uah.edu
Contact: Ms. Ginger Reed, Senior Associate Director of Admissions, 301
  Sparkman Drive, Huntsville, AL 35899
Telephone: 256-824-6070 or toll-free 800-UAH-CALL **Fax:** 256-824-6073
E-mail: admitme@email.uah.edu

Academics

UAH awards bachelor's, master's, and doctoral **degrees** and post-bachelor's and post-master's certificates. Challenging opportunities include advanced placement credit, accelerated degree programs, an honors program, double majors, independent study, and a senior project. Special programs include cooperative education, internships, summer session for credit, off-campus study, and Army ROTC.

The most frequently chosen **baccalaureate** fields are business/marketing, engineering/engineering technologies, and health professions and related sciences. A complete listing of majors at UAH appears in the Majors Index beginning on page 460.

The **faculty** at UAH has 277 full-time members, 87% with terminal degrees. The student-faculty ratio is 16:1.

Students of UAH

The student body totals 7,051, of whom 5,481 are undergraduates. 49.4% are women and 50.6% are men. Students come from 45 states and territories and 55 other countries. 86% are from Alabama. 3% are international students. 14.2% are African American, 1.7% American Indian, 3.8% Asian American, and 2.2% Hispanic American. 76% returned for their sophomore year.

Facilities and Resources

Student rooms are linked to a campus network. 960 **computers** are available on campus that provide access to the Internet. The **library** has 277,878 books and 1,120 subscriptions.

Campus Life

There are 111 active organizations on campus, including a drama/theater group, newspaper, and choral group. 7% of eligible men and 6% of eligible women are members of national **fraternities** and national **sororities**.

UAH is a member of the NCAA (Division II). **Intercollegiate sports** (some offering scholarships) include baseball (m), basketball, cross-country running, ice hockey (m), soccer, softball (w), tennis, track and field, volleyball (w).

Campus Safety

Student safety services include late-night transport/escort service, 24-hour emergency telephone alarm devices, 24-hour patrols by trained security personnel, and electronically operated dormitory entrances.

Applying

UAH requires SAT I or ACT and a high school transcript. Application deadline: 8/15; 7/31 for financial aid, with a 4/1 priority date. Early and deferred admission are possible.

The University of Alabama in Huntsville (UAH) is strategically located in the 2nd-largest research park in America. UAH is a partner with more than 100 high-tech industries as well as major federal laboratories, such as NASA's Marshall Space Flight Center and the U.S. Army. Huntsville is an international university: 7,000 students hail from 93 countries. Students have many opportunities to work with some of the top scientists and companies in the country through internships, research, and co-operative education positions. Some of their research has flown aboard the space shuttle, while others have helped solve human problems and improve business management. UAH offers a high-quality education at a reasonable public school cost.

Getting in Last Year
1,785 applied
88% were accepted
798 enrolled (51%)
31% from top tenth of their h.s. class
3.40 average high school GPA
38% had SAT verbal scores over 600
37% had SAT math scores over 600
60% had ACT scores over 24
8% had SAT verbal scores over 700
7% had SAT math scores over 700
9% had ACT scores over 30
6 National Merit Scholars
15 valedictorians

Graduation and After
9% graduated in 4 years
22% graduated in 5 years
12% graduated in 6 years
350 organizations recruited on campus

Financial Matters
$4126 resident tuition and fees (2003–04)
$8702 nonresident tuition and fees (2003–04)
$5000 room and board
54% average percent of need met
$5702 average financial aid amount received
  per undergraduate (2002–03 estimated)

THE UNIVERSITY OF ARIZONA

URBAN SETTING ■ PUBLIC ■ STATE-SUPPORTED ■ COED
TUCSON, ARIZONA

Web site: www.arizona.edu
Contact: Ms. Lori Goldman, Director of Admissions, PO Box 210011, Tucson, AZ 85721-0040
Telephone: 520-621-3237 **Fax:** 520-621-9799
E-mail: appinfo@arizona.edu

Getting in Last Year
20,924 applied
85% were accepted
5,958 enrolled (33%)
34% from top tenth of their h.s. class
3.40 average high school GPA
31% had SAT verbal scores over 600
36% had SAT math scores over 600
49% had ACT scores over 24
5% had SAT verbal scores over 700
6% had SAT math scores over 700
7% had ACT scores over 30
58 National Merit Scholars

Graduation and After
29% graduated in 4 years
20% graduated in 5 years
5% graduated in 6 years
92% had job offers within 6 months
251 organizations recruited on campus

Financial Matters
$3603 resident tuition and fees (2003–04)
$12,373 nonresident tuition and fees (2003–04)
$6810 room and board
$9993 average financial aid amount received per undergraduate (2002–03)

Academics

UA awards bachelor's, master's, doctoral, and first-professional **degrees** and post-bachelor's certificates. Challenging opportunities include advanced placement credit, freshman honors college, an honors program, double majors, independent study, and a senior project. Special programs include internships, summer session for credit, study-abroad, and Army, Navy and Air Force ROTC.

The most frequently chosen **baccalaureate** fields are business/marketing, social sciences and history, and communications/communication technologies. A complete listing of majors at UA appears in the Majors Index beginning on page 460.

The **faculty** at UA has 1,362 members. The student-faculty ratio is 20:1.

Students of UA

The student body totals 37,083, of whom 28,482 are undergraduates. 53.1% are women and 46.9% are men. Students come from 56 states and territories and 135 other countries. 72% are from Arizona. 3.4% are international students. 3% are African American, 1.9% American Indian, 5.7% Asian American, and 14.9% Hispanic American. 77% returned for their sophomore year.

Facilities and Resources

Student rooms are linked to a campus network. 1,950 **computers** are available on campus that provide access to the Internet. The 6 **libraries** have 4,359,195 books and 23,790 subscriptions.

Campus Life

There are 280 active organizations on campus, including a drama/theater group, newspaper, radio station, television station, choral group, and marching band. 15% of eligible men and 15% of eligible women are members of national **fraternities**, national **sororities**, local fraternities, and local sororities.

UA is a member of the NCAA (Division I). **Intercollegiate sports** (some offering scholarships) include baseball (m), basketball, cheerleading, cross-country running, football (m), golf, gymnastics (w), soccer (w), softball (w), swimming, tennis, track and field, volleyball (w).

Campus Safety

Student safety services include emergency telephones, late-night transport/escort service, 24-hour patrols by trained security personnel, and student patrols.

Applying

UA requires SAT I or ACT and a high school transcript, and in some cases an interview, recommendations, and a minimum high school GPA of 3.0. Application deadline: 4/1; 3/1 priority date for financial aid. Early admission is possible.

UNIVERSITY OF ARKANSAS

SUBURBAN SETTING ■ PUBLIC ■ STATE-SUPPORTED ■ COED
FAYETTEVILLE, ARKANSAS

Web site: www.uark.edu
Contact: Mr. Clark Adams, Assistant Director of Admissions, 200 Silas H. Hunt Hall, Fayetteville, AR 72701-1201
Telephone: 479-575-7724 or toll-free 800-377-5346 (in-state), 800-377-8632 (out-of-state) **Fax:** 479-575-7515
E-mail: uofa@uark.edu

Academics

Arkansas awards bachelor's, master's, doctoral, and first-professional **degrees** and post-bachelor's and post-master's certificates. Challenging opportunities include advanced placement credit, accelerated degree programs, freshman honors college, an honors program, double majors, independent study, and a senior project. Special programs include cooperative education, internships, summer session for credit, study-abroad, and Army and Air Force ROTC.

The most frequently chosen **baccalaureate** fields are business/marketing, engineering/engineering technologies, and education. A complete listing of majors at Arkansas appears in the Majors Index beginning on page 460.

The **faculty** at Arkansas has 792 full-time members, 92% with terminal degrees. The student-faculty ratio is 17:1.

Students of Arkansas

The student body totals 16,405, of whom 13,083 are undergraduates. 49.2% are women and 50.8% are men. Students come from 50 states and territories and 107 other countries. 88% are from Arkansas. 2.3% are international students. 5.8% are African American, 1.9% American Indian, 2.7% Asian American, and 1.7% Hispanic American. 83% returned for their sophomore year.

Facilities and Resources

Student rooms are linked to a campus network. 1,275 **computers** are available on campus that provide access to the Internet. The 6 **libraries** have 851,714 books and 14,168 subscriptions.

Campus Life

There are 273 active organizations on campus, including a drama/theater group, newspaper, radio station, television station, choral group, and marching band. 15% of eligible men and 20% of eligible women are members of national **fraternities** and national **sororities**.

Arkansas is a member of the NCAA (Division I). **Intercollegiate sports** (some offering scholarships) include baseball (m), basketball, cross-country running, football (m), golf, gymnastics (w), soccer (w), softball (w), swimming (w), tennis, track and field, volleyball (w).

Campus Safety

Student safety services include RAD (Rape Aggression Defense program), late-night transport/escort service, 24-hour emergency telephone alarm devices, 24-hour patrols by trained security personnel, student patrols, and electronically operated dormitory entrances.

Applying

Arkansas requires SAT I or ACT and a high school transcript. It recommends a minimum high school GPA of 3.0. Application deadline: 8/15. Early and deferred admission are possible.

Getting in Last Year
5,491 applied
85% were accepted
2,357 enrolled (51%)
36% from top tenth of their h.s. class
3.60 average high school GPA
45% had SAT verbal scores over 600
49% had SAT math scores over 600
64% had ACT scores over 24
11% had SAT verbal scores over 700
13% had SAT math scores over 700
19% had ACT scores over 30
45 National Merit Scholars
160 valedictorians

Graduation and After
23% graduated in 4 years
19% graduated in 5 years
6% graduated in 6 years
25% pursued further study (20% arts and sciences, 15% business, 15% education)
34% had job offers within 6 months
200 organizations recruited on campus

Financial Matters
$4768 resident tuition and fees (2003–04)
$11,518 nonresident tuition and fees (2003–04)
$5087 room and board
75% average percent of need met
$8052 average financial aid amount received per undergraduate (2002–03 estimated)

UNIVERSITY OF CALIFORNIA, BERKELEY

URBAN SETTING ■ PUBLIC ■ STATE-SUPPORTED ■ COED
BERKELEY, CALIFORNIA

Web site: www.berkeley.edu
Contact: Pre-Admission Advising, Office of Undergraduate Admission and Relations With Schools, Berkeley, CA 94720-1500
Telephone: 510-642-3175 **Fax:** 510-642-7333
E-mail: ouars@uclink.berkeley.edu

Getting in Last Year
36,976 applied
24% were accepted
3,653 enrolled (41%)
98% from top tenth of their h.s. class
3.94 average high school GPA
67% had SAT verbal scores over 600
80% had SAT math scores over 600
28% had SAT verbal scores over 700
45% had SAT math scores over 700

Graduation and After
52% graduated in 4 years
30% graduated in 5 years
4% graduated in 6 years
600 organizations recruited on campus

Financial Matters
$5250 resident tuition and fees (2003–04)
$19,460 nonresident tuition and fees (2003–04)
$11,212 room and board
90% average percent of need met
$11,952 average financial aid amount received per undergraduate (2002–03 estimated)

Academics

Cal awards bachelor's, master's, doctoral, and first-professional **degrees**. Challenging opportunities include advanced placement credit, accelerated degree programs, student-designed majors, an honors program, double majors, independent study, and a senior project. Special programs include internships, summer session for credit, off-campus study, study-abroad, and Army, Navy and Air Force ROTC.

The most frequently chosen **baccalaureate** fields are social sciences and history, engineering/engineering technologies, and biological/life sciences. A complete listing of majors at Cal appears in the Majors Index beginning on page 460.

The **faculty** at Cal has 1,462 full-time members, 98% with terminal degrees. The student-faculty ratio is 16:1.

Students of Cal

The student body totals 33,076, of whom 23,206 are undergraduates. 54% are women and 46% are men. Students come from 53 states and territories and 100 other countries. 89% are from California. 3% are international students. 3.7% are African American, 0.6% American Indian, 41.6% Asian American, and 9.9% Hispanic American. 95% returned for their sophomore year.

Facilities and Resources

Student rooms are linked to a campus network. 600 **computers** are available on campus that provide access to the Internet. The 31 **libraries** have 13,915,488 books and 181,071 subscriptions.

Campus Life

There are 400 active organizations on campus, including a drama/theater group, newspaper, radio station, television station, choral group, and marching band. 11% of eligible men and 10% of eligible women are members of national **fraternities**, national **sororities**, local fraternities, and local sororities.

Cal is a member of the NCAA (Division I). **Intercollegiate sports** (some offering scholarships) include baseball (m), basketball, cheerleading, crew, cross-country running, field hockey (w), football (m), golf, gymnastics, lacrosse (w), rugby (m), soccer, softball (w), swimming, tennis, track and field, volleyball (w), water polo.

Campus Safety

Student safety services include Office of Emergency Preparedness, late-night transport/escort service, 24-hour emergency telephone alarm devices, 24-hour patrols by trained security personnel, and electronically operated dormitory entrances.

Applying

Cal requires an essay, SAT II Subject Tests, SAT II: Writing Test, SAT I or ACT, and a high school transcript. Application deadline: 11/30; 3/2 priority date for financial aid.

UNIVERSITY OF CALIFORNIA, DAVIS

SUBURBAN SETTING ■ PUBLIC ■ STATE-SUPPORTED ■ COED
DAVIS, CALIFORNIA

Web site: www.ucdavis.edu
Contact: Dr. Gary Tudor, Director of Undergraduate Admissions,
Undergraduate Admission and Outreach Services, 175 Mrak Hall, Davis,
CA 95616
Telephone: 530-752-2971 **Fax:** 530-752-1280
E-mail: thinkucd@ucdavis.edu

Academics

UC Davis awards bachelor's, master's, doctoral, and first-professional **degrees** and post-bachelor's certificates. Challenging opportunities include advanced placement credit, student-designed majors, freshman honors college, an honors program, double majors, independent study, and a senior project. Special programs include internships, summer session for credit, study-abroad, and Army and Air Force ROTC.

The most frequently chosen **baccalaureate** fields are social sciences and history, biological/life sciences, and engineering/engineering technologies. A complete listing of majors at UC Davis appears in the Majors Index beginning on page 460.

The **faculty** at UC Davis has 1,620 full-time members, 98% with terminal degrees. The student-faculty ratio is 20:1.

Students of UC Davis

The student body totals 30,229, of whom 23,472 are undergraduates. 55.9% are women and 44.1% are men. Students come from 49 states and territories and 113 other countries. 96% are from California. 1.8% are international students. 2.5% are African American, 0.7% American Indian, 37% Asian American, and 10.4% Hispanic American. 99% returned for their sophomore year.

Facilities and Resources

Student rooms are linked to a campus network. 600 **computers** are available on campus that provide access to software packages and the Internet. The 6 **libraries** have 2,879,533 books and 45,665 subscriptions.

Campus Life

There are 320 active organizations on campus, including a drama/theater group, newspaper, radio station, choral group, and marching band. 9% of eligible men and 9% of eligible women are members of national **fraternities**, national **sororities**, and state fraternities and sororities.

UC Davis is a member of the NCAA (Division II). **Intercollegiate sports** include baseball (m), basketball, cross-country running, football (m), golf (m), gymnastics (w), soccer, softball (w), swimming, tennis, track and field, volleyball (w), water polo (m), wrestling (m).

Campus Safety

Student safety services include rape prevention programs, late-night transport/escort service, 24-hour emergency telephone alarm devices, 24-hour patrols by trained security personnel, student patrols, and electronically operated dormitory entrances.

Applying

UC Davis requires an essay, SAT II: Writing Test, SAT I and SAT II or ACT, and a high school transcript. Application deadline: 11/30.

Getting in Last Year
32,506 applied
60% were accepted
4,786 enrolled (25%)
3.72 average high school GPA
41% had SAT verbal scores over 600
63% had SAT math scores over 600
57% had ACT scores over 24
8% had SAT verbal scores over 700
16% had SAT math scores over 700
10% had ACT scores over 30
92 National Merit Scholars

Graduation and After
28% graduated in 4 years
37% graduated in 5 years
10% graduated in 6 years
38% pursued further study (15% arts and sciences, 9% education, 7% medicine)
91% had job offers within 6 months

Financial Matters
$5853 resident tuition and fees (2003–04)
$20,063 nonresident tuition and fees (2003–04)
$9143 room and board
77% average percent of need met
$8623 average financial aid amount received per undergraduate (2002–03 estimated)

UNIVERSITY OF CALIFORNIA, IRVINE

SUBURBAN SETTING ■ PUBLIC ■ STATE-SUPPORTED ■ COED
IRVINE, CALIFORNIA

Web site: www.uci.edu
Contact: Marguerit Bonous-Hammarth, Director of Admissions and Relations with Schools, 204 Administration, Irvine, CA 92697-1075
Telephone: 949-824-6703

Getting in Last Year
34,417 applied
54% were accepted
4,043 enrolled (22%)
95% from top tenth of their h.s. class
3.61 average high school GPA
39% had SAT verbal scores over 600
65% had SAT math scores over 600
7% had SAT verbal scores over 700
19% had SAT math scores over 700

Graduation and After
241 organizations recruited on campus

Financial Matters
$6165 resident tuition and fees (2003–04)
$20,375 nonresident tuition and fees (2003–04)
$8055 room and board
81% average percent of need met
$10,021 average financial aid amount received per undergraduate (2002–03 estimated)

Academics
UCI awards bachelor's, master's, doctoral, and first-professional **degrees** and post-bachelor's certificates. Challenging opportunities include advanced placement credit, an honors program, double majors, independent study, and a senior project. Special programs include cooperative education, internships, summer session for credit, off-campus study, study-abroad, and Army and Air Force ROTC.

The most frequently chosen **baccalaureate** fields are social sciences and history, biological/life sciences, and psychology. A complete listing of majors at UCI appears in the Majors Index beginning on page 460.

The **faculty** at UCI has 845 full-time members, 98% with terminal degrees. The student-faculty ratio is 18:1.

Students of UCI
The student body totals 24,874, of whom 19,967 are undergraduates. 50.5% are women and 49.5% are men. Students come from 45 states and territories and 38 other countries. 98% are from California. 2.6% are international students. 2.2% are African American, 0.4% American Indian, 50.4% Asian American, and 11.5% Hispanic American.

Facilities and Resources
Student rooms are linked to a campus network. 500 **computers** are available on campus that provide access to the Internet. The 2 **libraries** have 2,560,259 books and 28,416 subscriptions.

Campus Life
There are 275 active organizations on campus, including a drama/theater group, newspaper, radio station, and choral group. 8% of eligible men and 8% of eligible women are members of national **fraternities**, national **sororities**, local fraternities, and local sororities.

UCI is a member of the NCAA (Division I). **Intercollegiate sports** (some offering scholarships) include baseball (m), basketball, crew, cross-country running, golf, sailing, soccer, swimming, tennis, track and field, volleyball, water polo.

Campus Safety
Student safety services include late-night transport/escort service, 24-hour emergency telephone alarm devices, and 24-hour patrols by trained security personnel.

Applying
UCI requires an essay, SAT II: Writing Test, SAT I and SAT II or ACT, a high school transcript, and a minimum high school GPA of 2.0. Application deadline: 11/30; 3/2 priority date for financial aid.

UNIVERSITY OF CALIFORNIA, LOS ANGELES

URBAN SETTING ■ PUBLIC ■ STATE-SUPPORTED ■ COED
LOS ANGELES, CALIFORNIA

Web site: www.ucla.edu
Contact: Mr. Vu T. Tran, Director of Undergraduate Admissions, 405 Hilgard
  Avenue, Box 951436, Los Angeles, CA 90095-1436
Telephone: 310-825-3101
E-mail: ugadm@saonet.ucla.edu

Academics

UCLA awards bachelor's, master's, doctoral, and first-professional **degrees**. Challenging opportunities include advanced placement credit, student-designed majors, freshman honors college, an honors program, double majors, independent study, and a senior project. Special programs include internships, summer session for credit, off-campus study, study-abroad, and Army, Navy and Air Force ROTC.

The most frequently chosen **baccalaureate** fields are social sciences and history, psychology, and biological/life sciences. A complete listing of majors at UCLA appears in the Majors Index beginning on page 460.

The **faculty** at UCLA has 1,871 full-time members, 98% with terminal degrees. The student-faculty ratio is 18:1.

Students of UCLA

The student body totals 38,598, of whom 25,715 are undergraduates. 56.4% are women and 43.6% are men. Students come from 49 states and territories and 66 other countries. 96% are from California. 3.4% are international students. 3.5% are African American, 0.4% American Indian, 37.6% Asian American, and 15.4% Hispanic American. 96% returned for their sophomore year.

Facilities and Resources

Student rooms are linked to a campus network. The 14 **libraries** have 7,616,016 books and 94,801 subscriptions.

Campus Life

Active organizations on campus include a drama/theater group, newspaper, radio station, choral group, and marching band. 11% of eligible men and 9% of eligible women are members of national **fraternities**, national **sororities**, local fraternities, and local sororities.

UCLA is a member of the NCAA (Division I). **Intercollegiate sports** (some offering scholarships) include baseball (m), basketball, cross-country running, football (m), golf, gymnastics (w), soccer, softball (w), swimming (w), tennis, track and field, volleyball, water polo.

Campus Safety

Student safety services include late-night transport/escort service, 24-hour emergency telephone alarm devices, and student patrols.

Applying

UCLA requires an essay, SAT II Subject Tests, SAT II: Writing Test, SAT I or ACT, SAT II Subject Test in math, third SAT II Subject Test, and a high school transcript. Application deadline: 11/30; 3/2 priority date for financial aid.

Getting in Last Year

44,994 applied
24% were accepted
4,268 enrolled (40%)
97% from top tenth of their h.s. class
64% had SAT verbal scores over 600
76% had SAT math scores over 600
72% had ACT scores over 24
21% had SAT verbal scores over 700
39% had SAT math scores over 700
24% had ACT scores over 30
304 National Merit Scholars

Graduation and After

53% graduated in 4 years
31% graduated in 5 years
3% graduated in 6 years
425 organizations recruited on campus

Financial Matters

$5820 resident tuition and fees (2003–04)
$20,030 nonresident tuition and fees (2003–04)
$10,452 room and board
82% average percent of need met
$10,634 average financial aid amount received per undergraduate (2002–03 estimated)

UNIVERSITY OF CALIFORNIA, RIVERSIDE

URBAN SETTING ■ PUBLIC ■ STATE-SUPPORTED ■ COED
RIVERSIDE, CALIFORNIA

Web site: www.ucr.edu
Contact: LaRae Lundgren, Director of Undergraduate Admission, 1138
   Hinderaker Hall, 900 University Avenue, Riverside, CA 92521
Telephone: 909-787-3411 **Fax:** 909-787-6344
E-mail: discover@pop.ucr.edu

Getting in Last Year

20,060 applied
79% were accepted
3,889 enrolled (25%)
94% from top tenth of their h.s. class
3.42 average high school GPA
16% had SAT verbal scores over 600
33% had SAT math scores over 600
2% had SAT verbal scores over 700
6% had SAT math scores over 700

Graduation and After

37% graduated in 4 years
23% graduated in 5 years
5% graduated in 6 years
35% pursued further study
54% had job offers within 6 months
276 organizations recruited on campus

Financial Matters

$5950 resident tuition and fees (2003–04)
$19,681 nonresident tuition and fees (2003–04)
$9350 room and board
82% average percent of need met
$9274 average financial aid amount received per undergraduate (2001–02)

Academics

UCR awards bachelor's, master's, and doctoral **degrees**. Challenging opportunities include advanced placement credit, accelerated degree programs, student-designed majors, freshman honors college, an honors program, double majors, independent study, and a senior project. Special programs include cooperative education, internships, summer session for credit, off-campus study, study-abroad, and Army and Air Force ROTC.

The most frequently chosen **baccalaureate** fields are business/marketing, social sciences and history, and biological/life sciences. A complete listing of majors at UCR appears in the Majors Index beginning on page 460.

The **faculty** at UCR has 659 full-time members, 98% with terminal degrees. The student-faculty ratio is 19:1.

Students of UCR

The student body totals 17,302, of whom 15,282 are undergraduates. 54.3% are women and 45.7% are men. Students come from 40 states and territories and 21 other countries. 99% are from California. 1.7% are international students. 6.4% are African American, 0.4% American Indian, 40.6% Asian American, and 23.5% Hispanic American. 85% returned for their sophomore year.

Facilities and Resources

Student rooms are linked to a campus network. 600 **computers** are available on campus that provide access to the Internet. The 7 **libraries** have 2,081,146 books and 21,323 subscriptions.

Campus Life

There are 280 active organizations on campus, including a drama/theater group, newspaper, radio station, and choral group. UCR has national **fraternities**, national **sororities**, local fraternities, local sororities, and coed fraternities.

UCR is a member of the NCAA (Division I). **Intercollegiate sports** (some offering scholarships) include baseball (m), basketball, cross-country running, softball (w), tennis, track and field, volleyball (w).

Campus Safety

Student safety services include late-night transport/escort service, 24-hour emergency telephone alarm devices, 24-hour patrols by trained security personnel, student patrols, and electronically operated dormitory entrances.

Applying

UCR requires an essay, SAT II Subject Tests, SAT II: Writing Test, SAT I or ACT, a high school transcript, and a minimum high school GPA of 2.82. Application deadline: 11/30; 3/2 priority date for financial aid. Early admission is possible.

University of California, San Diego

Suburban setting ■ Public ■ State-supported ■ Coed
La Jolla, California

Web site: www.ucsd.edu
Contact: Mr. Nathan Evans, Associate Director of Admissions and Relations with Schools, 9500 Gilman Drive, 0021, La Jolla, CA 92093-0021
Telephone: 858-534-4831
E-mail: admissionsinfo@ucsd.edu

Academics

UCSD awards bachelor's, master's, doctoral, and first-professional **degrees**. Challenging opportunities include advanced placement credit, accelerated degree programs, student-designed majors, freshman honors college, an honors program, double majors, independent study, and a senior project. Special programs include cooperative education, internships, summer session for credit, off-campus study, study-abroad, and Army and Navy ROTC.

The most frequently chosen **baccalaureate** fields are social sciences and history, biological/life sciences, and engineering/engineering technologies. A complete listing of majors at UCSD appears in the Majors Index beginning on page 460.

The **faculty** at UCSD has 917 full-time members, 98% with terminal degrees. The student-faculty ratio is 19:1.

Students of UCSD

The student body totals 24,707, of whom 19,872 are undergraduates. 52.1% are women and 47.9% are men. 97% are from California. 3.2% are international students. 1.2% are African American, 0.4% American Indian, 36.9% Asian American, and 10.2% Hispanic American. 93% returned for their sophomore year.

Facilities and Resources

Student rooms are linked to a campus network. 1,020 **computers** are available on campus that provide access to e-mail and the Internet. The 8 **libraries** have 2,938,357 books and 19,517 subscriptions.

Campus Life

There are 450 active organizations on campus, including a drama/theater group, newspaper, radio station, television station, and choral group. 10% of eligible men and 10% of eligible women are members of national **fraternities** and national **sororities**.

UCSD is a member of the NCAA (Division II). **Intercollegiate sports** include baseball (m), basketball, cheerleading, crew, cross-country running, fencing, golf (m), soccer, softball (w), swimming, tennis, track and field, volleyball, water polo.

Campus Safety

Student safety services include crime prevention programs, late-night transport/escort service, 24-hour emergency telephone alarm devices, 24-hour patrols by trained security personnel, and student patrols.

Applying

UCSD requires an essay, SAT I or ACT, 3 SAT II Subject Tests (including SAT II: Writing Test), a high school transcript, and a minimum high school GPA of 2.8, and in some cases a minimum high school GPA of 3.4. Application deadline: 11/30; 3/2 priority date for financial aid.

Getting in Last Year

43,438 applied
42% were accepted
3,799 enrolled (21%)
99% from top tenth of their h.s. class
3.95 average high school GPA
56% had SAT verbal scores over 600
77% had SAT math scores over 600
73% had ACT scores over 24
13% had SAT verbal scores over 700
30% had SAT math scores over 700
18% had ACT scores over 30
49 National Merit Scholars

Graduation and After

53% graduated in 4 years
25% graduated in 5 years
35% pursued further study
85% had job offers within 6 months
4300 organizations recruited on campus

Financial Matters

$5507 resident tuition and fees (2003–04)
$19,237 nonresident tuition and fees (2003–04)
$8620 room and board
85% average percent of need met
$10,405 average financial aid amount received per undergraduate (2002–03 estimated)

University of California, Santa Barbara

Suburban setting ■ Public ■ State-supported ■ Coed
Santa Barbara, California

Web site: www.ucsb.edu
Contact: Ms. Christine Van Gieson, Director of Admissions/Outreach Services, 1234 Cheadle Hall, Santa Barbara, CA 93106-2014
Telephone: 805-893-2485 Fax: 805-893-2676
E-mail: appinfo@sa.ucsb.edu

Getting in Last Year

37,599 applied
50% were accepted
3,993 enrolled (21%)
3.72 average high school GPA
45% had SAT verbal scores over 600
57% had SAT math scores over 600
75% had ACT scores over 24
8% had SAT verbal scores over 700
12% had SAT math scores over 700
14% had ACT scores over 30

Graduation and After

45% graduated in 4 years
24% graduated in 5 years
5% graduated in 6 years
24% pursued further study (9% arts and sciences, 9% education, 5% law)
91% had job offers within 6 months

Financial Matters

$5639 resident tuition and fees (2003–04)
$19,370 nonresident tuition and fees (2003–04)
$9236 room and board
87% average percent of need met
$8851 average financial aid amount received per undergraduate (2001–02)

Academics

UCSB awards bachelor's, master's, and doctoral **degrees** and first-professional certificates. Challenging opportunities include advanced placement credit, accelerated degree programs, student-designed majors, an honors program, double majors, independent study, and a senior project. Special programs include cooperative education, internships, summer session for credit, off-campus study, study-abroad, and Army ROTC.

The most frequently chosen **baccalaureate** fields are social sciences and history, business/marketing, and interdisciplinary studies. A complete listing of majors at UCSB appears in the Majors Index beginning on page 460.

The **faculty** at UCSB has 862 full-time members. The student-faculty ratio is 19:1.

Students of UCSB

The student body totals 20,847, of whom 17,844 are undergraduates. 54.8% are women and 45.2% are men. Students come from 51 states and territories and 110 other countries. 95% are from California. 1.4% are international students. 2.5% are African American, 0.7% American Indian, 15.4% Asian American, and 16.1% Hispanic American. 91% returned for their sophomore year.

Facilities and Resources

3,000 **computers** are available on campus for student use. The **library** has 2,674,331 books and 18,898 subscriptions.

Campus Life

There are 241 active organizations on campus, including a drama/theater group, newspaper, radio station, and choral group. 8% of eligible men and 10% of eligible women are members of national **fraternities**, national **sororities**, local fraternities, and local sororities.

UCSB is a member of the NCAA (Division I). **Intercollegiate sports** (some offering scholarships) include baseball (m), basketball, cross-country running, golf (m), gymnastics, soccer, softball (w), swimming, tennis, track and field, volleyball, water polo.

Campus Safety

Student safety services include late-night transport/escort service and 24-hour emergency telephone alarm devices.

Applying

UCSB requires an essay, SAT II Subject Tests, SAT II: Writing Test, SAT I or ACT, and a high school transcript, and in some cases an interview. Application deadline: 11/30; 3/2 priority date for financial aid.

UNIVERSITY OF CALIFORNIA, SANTA CRUZ

SMALL-TOWN SETTING ■ PUBLIC ■ STATE-SUPPORTED ■ COED
SANTA CRUZ, CALIFORNIA

Web site: www.ucsc.edu
Contact: Mr. Kevin M. Browne, Executive Director of Admissions and University Registrar, Admissions Office, Cook House, Santa Cruz, CA 95064
Telephone: 831-459-5779 **Fax:** 831-459-4452
E-mail: admissions@ucsc.edu

Academics

UCSC awards bachelor's, master's, and doctoral **degrees** and post-bachelor's certificates. Challenging opportunities include advanced placement credit, student-designed majors, freshman honors college, an honors program, double majors, independent study, and a senior project. Special programs include cooperative education, internships, summer session for credit, off-campus study, study-abroad, and Army, Navy and Air Force ROTC.

The most frequently chosen **baccalaureate** fields are social sciences and history, visual/performing arts, and psychology. A complete listing of majors at UCSC appears in the Majors Index beginning on page 460.

The **faculty** at UCSC has 516 full-time members, 98% with terminal degrees. The student-faculty ratio is 19:1.

Students of UCSC

The student body totals 14,997, of whom 13,660 are undergraduates. 54.8% are women and 45.2% are men. 95% are from California. 0.9% are international students. 2.4% are African American, 0.9% American Indian, 17.4% Asian American, and 14.3% Hispanic American. 87% returned for their sophomore year.

Facilities and Resources

Student rooms are linked to a campus network. 200 **computers** are available on campus that provide access to the Internet. The 10 **libraries** have 1,470,000 books and 9,190 subscriptions.

Campus Life

There are 100 active organizations on campus, including a drama/theater group, newspaper, radio station, and choral group. 1% of eligible men and 1% of eligible women are members of national **fraternities**, national **sororities**, local fraternities, and local sororities.

UCSC is a member of the NCAA (Division III). **Intercollegiate sports** include basketball, soccer (m), swimming, tennis, volleyball, water polo.

Campus Safety

Student safety services include evening main gate security, campus police force and fire station, late-night transport/escort service, 24-hour emergency telephone alarm devices, 24-hour patrols by trained security personnel, and electronically operated dormitory entrances.

Applying

UCSC requires an essay, SAT I and SAT II or ACT, SAT I or ACT composite score and three SAT II subject tests required including SAT II Writing, Math Level 1 or 2, and one test from each of the following areas: english literature, foreign language, science or social studies, and a high school transcript. Application deadline: 11/30; 3/2 priority date for financial aid.

Getting in Last Year
21,525 applied
80% were accepted
3,434 enrolled (20%)
90% from top tenth of their h.s. class
3.48 average high school GPA
40% had SAT verbal scores over 600
42% had SAT math scores over 600
53% had ACT scores over 24
8% had SAT verbal scores over 700
6% had SAT math scores over 700
7% had ACT scores over 30

Graduation and After
42% graduated in 4 years
18% graduated in 5 years
5% graduated in 6 years
237 organizations recruited on campus

Financial Matters
$4629 resident tuition and fees (2003–04)
$22,738 nonresident tuition and fees (2003–04)
$10,314 room and board
90% average percent of need met
$11,124 average financial aid amount received per undergraduate (2002–03 estimated)

UNIVERSITY OF CENTRAL ARKANSAS

SMALL-TOWN SETTING ■ PUBLIC ■ STATE-SUPPORTED ■ COED
CONWAY, ARKANSAS

Web site: www.uca.edu
Contact: Ms. Penny Hatfield, Director of Admissions, 201 Donaghey Avenue,
Conway, AR 72035
Telephone: 501-450-5145 or toll-free 800-243-8245 (in-state) **Fax:**
501-450-5228
E-mail: admissons@uca.edu

Getting in Last Year
5,655 applied
70% were accepted
2,428 enrolled (61%)
21% from top tenth of their h.s. class
3.66 average high school GPA
51% had ACT scores over 24
7% had ACT scores over 30

Graduation and After
15% graduated in 4 years
18% graduated in 5 years
8% graduated in 6 years
60 organizations recruited on campus

Financial Matters
$4505 resident tuition and fees (2003–04)
$7817 nonresident tuition and fees (2003–04)
$3786 room and board

Academics
UCA awards associate, bachelor's, master's, and doctoral **degrees**. Challenging opportunities include advanced placement credit, accelerated degree programs, freshman honors college, an honors program, double majors, independent study, and a senior project. Special programs include cooperative education, internships, summer session for credit, study-abroad, and Army ROTC.

The most frequently chosen **baccalaureate** fields are business/marketing, health professions and related sciences, and social sciences and history. A complete listing of majors at UCA appears in the Majors Index beginning on page 460.

The **faculty** at UCA has 453 full-time members. The student-faculty ratio is 18:1.

Students of UCA
The student body totals 9,516, of whom 8,580 are undergraduates. 59.9% are women and 40.1% are men. Students come from 39 states and territories and 58 other countries. 95% are from Arkansas. 2% are international students. 16.8% are African American, 0.9% American Indian, 1.2% Asian American, and 1.2% Hispanic American. 70% returned for their sophomore year.

Facilities and Resources
Student rooms are linked to a campus network. 1,500 **computers** are available on campus that provide access to the Internet. The **library** has 587,714 books and 1,824 subscriptions.

Campus Life
There are 32 active organizations on campus, including a drama/theater group, newspaper, radio station, television station, choral group, and marching band. 10% of eligible men and 10% of eligible women are members of national **fraternities** and national **sororities**.

UCA is a member of the NCAA (Division II). **Intercollegiate sports** (some offering scholarships) include baseball (m), basketball, cheerleading, cross-country running (w), football, golf, soccer, softball (w), tennis (w), track and field (w), volleyball (w).

Campus Safety
Student safety services include security personnel at entrances during evening hours, late-night transport/escort service, 24-hour emergency telephone alarm devices, 24-hour patrols by trained security personnel, student patrols, and electronically operated dormitory entrances.

Applying
UCA requires SAT I or ACT and a high school transcript, and in some cases a minimum high school GPA of 2.75. Application deadline: rolling admissions; 2/15 priority date for financial aid. Early and deferred admission are possible.

UNIVERSITY OF CENTRAL FLORIDA

SUBURBAN SETTING ■ PUBLIC ■ STATE-SUPPORTED ■ COED
ORLANDO, FLORIDA

Web site: www.ucf.edu
Contact: Undergraduate Admissions Office, PO Box 160111, Orlando, FL
32816
Telephone: 407-823-2000 **Fax:** 407-823-5625
E-mail: admission@mail.ucf.edu

Academics

UCF awards associate, bachelor's, master's, and doctoral **degrees** and post-bachelor's
certificates. Challenging opportunities include advanced placement credit, accelerated
degree programs, student-designed majors, freshman honors college, an honors
program, double majors, independent study, and a senior project. Special programs
include cooperative education, internships, summer session for credit, off-campus study,
study-abroad, and Army and Air Force ROTC.

The most frequently chosen **baccalaureate** fields are business/marketing, education,
and psychology. A complete listing of majors at UCF appears in the Majors Index beginning on page 460.

The **faculty** at UCF has 1,152 full-time members, 78% with terminal degrees. The
student-faculty ratio is 25:1.

Students of UCF

The student body totals 41,102, of whom 34,170 are undergraduates. 54.9% are women
and 45.1% are men. Students come from 52 states and territories and 131 other
countries. 97% are from Florida. 1.2% are international students. 8.3% are African
American, 0.6% American Indian, 4.9% Asian American, and 11.8% Hispanic American.
83% returned for their sophomore year.

Facilities and Resources

Student rooms are linked to a campus network. 2,420 **computers** are available on
campus that provide access to the Internet. The **library** has 1,152,653 books and 9,866
subscriptions.

Campus Life

There are 329 active organizations on campus, including a drama/theater group,
newspaper, radio station, choral group, and marching band. 13% of eligible men and
12% of eligible women are members of national **fraternities** and national **sororities**.

UCF is a member of the NCAA (Division I). **Intercollegiate sports** (some offering
scholarships) include baseball (m), basketball, cheerleading, crew (w), cross-country running, football (m), golf, soccer, tennis, track and field (w), volleyball (w).

Campus Safety

Student safety services include late-night transport/escort service, 24-hour emergency
telephone alarm devices, 24-hour patrols by trained security personnel, and electronically operated dormitory entrances.

Applying

UCF requires SAT I or ACT, a high school transcript, and a minimum high school GPA
of 2.0. It recommends an essay. Application deadline: 5/1; 6/30 for financial aid, with a
3/1 priority date. Early admission is possible.

Getting in Last Year
20,533 applied
60% were accepted
5,965 enrolled (49%)
35% from top tenth of their h.s. class
3.80 average high school GPA
32% had SAT verbal scores over 600
38% had SAT math scores over 600
62% had ACT scores over 24
4% had SAT verbal scores over 700
5% had SAT math scores over 700
5% had ACT scores over 30
34 National Merit Scholars
55 valedictorians

Graduation and After
28% graduated in 4 years
21% graduated in 5 years
5% graduated in 6 years
21% pursued further study
95% had job offers within 6 months
3200 organizations recruited on campus

Financial Matters
$3013 resident tuition and fees (2003–04)
$14,041 nonresident tuition and fees (2003–04)
$7026 room and board
77% average percent of need met
$7109 average financial aid amount received
per undergraduate (2002–03 estimated)

UNIVERSITY OF CHICAGO

URBAN SETTING ■ PRIVATE ■ INDEPENDENT ■ COED
CHICAGO, ILLINOIS

Web site: www.uchicago.edu
Contact: Mr. Theodore O'Neill, Dean of Admissions, 1116 East 59th Street, Chicago, IL 60637-1513
Telephone: 773-702-8650 **Fax:** 773-702-4199

Getting in Last Year

8,162 applied
42% were accepted
1,081 enrolled (32%)
78% from top tenth of their h.s. class
89% had ACT scores over 24
56% had ACT scores over 30
183 National Merit Scholars

Graduation and After

Graduates pursuing further study: 17% arts and sciences, 8% law, 8% medicine

Financial Matters

$29,238 tuition and fees (2003–04)
$9165 room and board

Academics

Chicago awards bachelor's, master's, doctoral, and first-professional **degrees**. Challenging opportunities include advanced placement credit, accelerated degree programs, student-designed majors, double majors, independent study, and a senior project. Special programs include internships, summer session for credit, off-campus study, study-abroad, and Army and Air Force ROTC.

The most frequently chosen **baccalaureate** fields are social sciences and history, biological/life sciences, and English. A complete listing of majors at Chicago appears in the Majors Index beginning on page 460.

The **faculty** at Chicago has 1,595 full-time members. The student-faculty ratio is 4:1.

Students of Chicago

The student body totals 12,576, of whom 4,075 are undergraduates. 50.5% are women and 49.5% are men. Students come from 52 states and territories and 49 other countries. 22% are from Illinois. 7% are international students. 4.2% are African American, 0.2% American Indian, 16.3% Asian American, and 7.2% Hispanic American. 95% returned for their sophomore year.

Facilities and Resources

Student rooms are linked to a campus network. 1,000 **computers** are available on campus for student use. The 9 **libraries** have 5,800,000 books and 47,000 subscriptions.

Campus Life

There are 300 active organizations on campus, including a drama/theater group, newspaper, radio station, and choral group. 12% of eligible men and 5% of eligible women are members of national **fraternities** and national **sororities**.

Chicago is a member of the NCAA (Division III). **Intercollegiate sports** include baseball (m), basketball, cross-country running, football (m), soccer, softball (w), swimming, tennis, track and field, volleyball (w), wrestling (m).

Campus Safety

Student safety services include late-night transport/escort service, 24-hour emergency telephone alarm devices, 24-hour patrols by trained security personnel, and electronically operated dormitory entrances.

Applying

Chicago requires an essay, SAT I or ACT, a high school transcript, and 3 recommendations. It recommends an interview. Application deadline: 1/1; 2/1 priority date for financial aid. Early and deferred admission are possible.

UNIVERSITY OF COLORADO AT BOULDER

SUBURBAN SETTING ■ PUBLIC ■ STATE-SUPPORTED ■ COED
BOULDER, COLORADO

Web site: www.colorado.edu
Contact: Mr. Kevin MacLennan, Associate Director, 552 UCB, Boulder, CO
80309-0030
Telephone: 303-492-1394 **Fax:** 303-492-7115

Academics

CU-Boulder awards bachelor's, master's, doctoral, and first-professional **degrees**. Challenging opportunities include advanced placement credit, accelerated degree programs, student-designed majors, freshman honors college, an honors program, double majors, independent study, and a senior project. Special programs include cooperative education, internships, summer session for credit, off-campus study, study-abroad, and Army, Navy and Air Force ROTC.

The most frequently chosen **baccalaureate** fields are social sciences and history, business/marketing, and communications/communication technologies. A complete listing of majors at CU-Boulder appears in the Majors Index beginning on page 460.

The **faculty** at CU-Boulder has 1,176 full-time members, 90% with terminal degrees. The student-faculty ratio is 17:1.

Students of CU-Boulder

The student body totals 32,041, of whom 26,186 are undergraduates. 47.5% are women and 52.5% are men. Students come from 53 states and territories and 100 other countries. 67% are from Colorado. 1.3% are international students. 1.6% are African American, 0.7% American Indian, 5.8% Asian American, and 5.7% Hispanic American. 83% returned for their sophomore year.

Facilities and Resources

Student rooms are linked to a campus network. 1,525 **computers** are available on campus that provide access to standard and academic software, student government voting and the Internet. The 6 **libraries** have 2,179,492 books and 25,607 subscriptions.

Campus Life

There are 200 active organizations on campus, including a drama/theater group, newspaper, radio station, television station, choral group, and marching band. 9% of eligible men and 14% of eligible women are members of national **fraternities**, national **sororities**, and local sororities.

CU-Boulder is a member of the NCAA (Division I). **Intercollegiate sports** (some offering scholarships) include basketball, cross-country running, football (m), golf, skiing (cross-country), skiing (downhill), soccer (w), tennis, track and field, volleyball (w).

Campus Safety

Student safety services include University police department, late-night transport/escort service, 24-hour emergency telephone alarm devices, 24-hour patrols by trained security personnel, and student patrols.

Applying

CU-Boulder requires SAT I or ACT, a high school transcript, and a minimum high school GPA of 2.0, and in some cases audition for music program. It recommends an essay, recommendations, and a minimum high school GPA of 3.0. Application deadline: 1/15; 4/1 priority date for financial aid. Deferred admission is possible.

Getting in Last Year

20,920 applied
80% were accepted
5,630 enrolled (34%)
24% from top tenth of their h.s. class
3.52 average high school GPA
41% had SAT verbal scores over 600
51% had SAT math scores over 600
69% had ACT scores over 24
6% had SAT verbal scores over 700
9% had SAT math scores over 700
11% had ACT scores over 30
7 National Merit Scholars
155 valedictorians

Graduation and After

37% graduated in 4 years
26% graduated in 5 years
5% graduated in 6 years
Graduates pursuing further study: 9% business, 8% arts and sciences, 8% education
79% had job offers within 6 months
466 organizations recruited on campus

Financial Matters

$4020 resident tuition and fees (2003–04)
$20,336 nonresident tuition and fees (2003–04)
$6754 room and board
75% average percent of need met
$9434 average financial aid amount received per undergraduate (2001–02)

University of Dallas

Suburban setting ■ Private ■ Independent Religious ■ Coed
Irving, Texas

Web site: www.udallas.edu
Contact: Sr. Mary Brian Poole, SSND, Assistant Dean of Admission, 1845
    East Northgate Drive, Irving, TX 75062-4799
Telephone: 972-721-5266 or toll-free 800-628-6999 **Fax:** 972-721-5017
E-mail: ugadmis@mailadmin.udallas.edu

Getting in Last Year
1,080 applied
89% were accepted
299 enrolled (31%)
42% from top tenth of their h.s. class
53% had SAT verbal scores over 600
47% had SAT math scores over 600
69% had ACT scores over 24
18% had SAT verbal scores over 700
7% had SAT math scores over 700
15% had ACT scores over 30
13 National Merit Scholars
9 valedictorians

Graduation and After
52% graduated in 4 years
6% graduated in 5 years
2% graduated in 6 years
40% pursued further study (14% arts and
    sciences, 7% business, 4% medicine)
40% had job offers within 6 months
40 organizations recruited on campus

Financial Matters
$18,104 tuition and fees (2003–04)
$6494 room and board
77% average percent of need met
$14,409 average financial aid amount received
    per undergraduate (2001–02)

Academics

UD awards bachelor's, master's, and doctoral **degrees**. Challenging opportunities include advanced placement credit, accelerated degree programs, student-designed majors, double majors, independent study, and a senior project. Special programs include internships, summer session for credit, off-campus study, study-abroad, and Army and Air Force ROTC.

The most frequently chosen **baccalaureate** fields are social sciences and history, biological/life sciences, and English. A complete listing of majors at UD appears in the Majors Index beginning on page 460.

The **faculty** at UD has 125 full-time members, 92% with terminal degrees. The student-faculty ratio is 12:1.

Students of UD

The student body totals 3,157, of whom 1,250 are undergraduates. 55.6% are women and 44.4% are men. Students come from 46 states and territories and 19 other countries. 63% are from Texas. 2.2% are international students. 1.6% are African American, 0.3% American Indian, 7% Asian American, and 15.4% Hispanic American. 73% returned for their sophomore year.

Facilities and Resources

Student rooms are linked to a campus network. 105 **computers** are available on campus that provide access to the Internet. The **library** has 232,472 books and 767 subscriptions.

Campus Life

There are 42 active organizations on campus, including a drama/theater group, newspaper, radio station, and choral group. No national or local **fraternities** or **sororities**.

UD is a member of the NCAA (Division III). **Intercollegiate sports** include baseball (m), basketball, cross-country running, golf, lacrosse (w), soccer, softball (w), tennis, track and field, volleyball (w).

Campus Safety

Student safety services include late-night transport/escort service, 24-hour emergency telephone alarm devices, 24-hour patrols by trained security personnel, and electronically operated dormitory entrances.

Applying

UD requires an essay, SAT I or ACT, a high school transcript, and 1 recommendation, and in some cases an interview. It recommends an interview. Application deadline: 8/1; 3/1 priority date for financial aid. Early and deferred admission are possible.

UNIVERSITY OF DAYTON

SUBURBAN SETTING ■ PRIVATE ■ INDEPENDENT RELIGIOUS ■ COED
DAYTON, OHIO

Web site: www.udayton.edu
Contact: Mr. Robert F. Durkle, Director of Admission, 300 College Park,
   Dayton, OH 45469-1300
Telephone: 937-229-4411 or toll-free 800-837-7433 **Fax:** 937-229-4729
E-mail: admission@udayton.edu

Academics

UD awards bachelor's, master's, doctoral, and first-professional **degrees** and post-master's certificates. Challenging opportunities include advanced placement credit, accelerated degree programs, an honors program, double majors, independent study, and a senior project. Special programs include cooperative education, internships, summer session for credit, off-campus study, study-abroad, and Army and Air Force ROTC.

The most frequently chosen **baccalaureate** fields are business/marketing, engineering/engineering technologies, and education. A complete listing of majors at UD appears in the Majors Index beginning on page 460.

The **faculty** at UD has 401 full-time members, 94% with terminal degrees. The student-faculty ratio is 15:1.

Students of UD

The student body totals 10,284, of whom 7,103 are undergraduates. 49.8% are women and 50.2% are men. Students come from 48 states and territories and 29 other countries. 66% are from Ohio. 0.6% are international students. 4.5% are African American, 0.2% American Indian, 1.3% Asian American, and 2.4% Hispanic American. 86% returned for their sophomore year.

Facilities and Resources

Student rooms are linked to a campus network. 1,000 **computers** are available on campus that provide access to the Internet. The 2 **libraries** have 849,244 books and 7,318 subscriptions.

Campus Life

There are 200 active organizations on campus, including a drama/theater group, newspaper, radio station, television station, choral group, and marching band. 15% of eligible men and 18% of eligible women are members of national **fraternities**, national **sororities**, local fraternities, and local sororities.

UD is a member of the NCAA (Division I). **Intercollegiate sports** (some offering scholarships) include baseball (m), basketball, crew (w), cross-country running, football (m), golf, soccer, softball (w), tennis, track and field (w), volleyball (w).

Campus Safety

Student safety services include late-night transport/escort service, 24-hour emergency telephone alarm devices, 24-hour patrols by trained security personnel, student patrols, and electronically operated dormitory entrances.

Applying

UD requires SAT I or ACT, a high school transcript, and 1 recommendation, and in some cases audition required for music, music therapy, music education programs. It recommends an essay and an interview. Application deadline: rolling admissions; 3/31 priority date for financial aid. Deferred admission is possible.

The University of Dayton is Ohio's largest private university and a national leader in Catholic higher education. Personal attention, close-knit community, excellent academic programs, and first-rate opportunties are hallmarks of the UD experience enjoyed by 90,000 alumni around the world, including four-time Super Bowl winner Chuck Noll, ESPN anchor Dan Patrick, and the late humorist Erma Bombeck. University of Dayton students are encouraged to look critically at the world's problems and to become part of the solution—from joining service projects in Cameroon and India to boosting literacy and building housing in their own backyard. Academic challenge and friendliness characterize the campus atmosphere, with students from throughout the United States and many parts of the world. The University of Dayton is a place where the mind and heart serve the human community.

Getting in Last Year
7,052 applied
97% were accepted
1,858 enrolled (27%)
19% from top tenth of their h.s. class
34% had SAT verbal scores over 600
45% had SAT math scores over 600
62% had ACT scores over 24
6% had SAT verbal scores over 700
10% had SAT math scores over 700
14% had ACT scores over 30
15 National Merit Scholars
35 valedictorians

Graduation and After
55% graduated in 4 years
19% graduated in 5 years
83% had job offers within 6 months
387 organizations recruited on campus

Financial Matters
$18,960 tuition and fees (2003–04)
$5890 room and board
81% average percent of need met
$13,258 average financial aid amount received
   per undergraduate (2002–03)

UNIVERSITY OF DELAWARE

SMALL-TOWN SETTING ■ PUBLIC ■ STATE-RELATED ■ COED
NEWARK, DELAWARE

Web site: www.udel.edu
Contact: Mr. Lou Hirsh, Director of Admissions, 116 Hullihen Hall, Newark, DE 19716
Telephone: 302-831-8123 **Fax:** 302-831-6905
E-mail: admissions@udel.edu

Getting in Last Year

22,020 applied
42% were accepted
3,384 enrolled (37%)
35% from top tenth of their h.s. class
3.5 average high school GPA
42% had SAT verbal scores over 600
54% had SAT math scores over 600
71% had ACT scores over 24
6% had SAT verbal scores over 700
9% had SAT math scores over 700
11% had ACT scores over 30

Graduation and After

57% graduated in 4 years
14% graduated in 5 years
2% graduated in 6 years
18% pursued further study (10% arts and sciences, 4% law, 3% business)
78% had job offers within 6 months
510 organizations recruited on campus

Financial Matters

$6498 resident tuition and fees (2003–04)
$16,028 nonresident tuition and fees (2003–04)
$6118 room and board
79% average percent of need met
$9750 average financial aid amount received per undergraduate

Academics

Delaware awards associate, bachelor's, master's, and doctoral **degrees** (enrollment data for undergraduate students does not include non-degree-seeking students). Challenging opportunities include advanced placement credit, accelerated degree programs, student-designed majors, an honors program, double majors, independent study, and a senior project. Special programs include cooperative education, internships, summer session for credit, study-abroad, and Army and Air Force ROTC.

The most frequently chosen **baccalaureate** fields are business/marketing, social sciences and history, and education. A complete listing of majors at Delaware appears in the Majors Index beginning on page 460.

The **faculty** at Delaware has 1,111 full-time members, 83% with terminal degrees. The student-faculty ratio is 13:1.

Students of Delaware

The student body totals 19,109, of whom 15,808 are undergraduates. 62.9% are women and 37.1% are men. Students come from 52 states and territories and 100 other countries. 42% are from Delaware. 1.1% are international students. 5.6% are African American, 0.3% American Indian, 3.3% Asian American, and 3.1% Hispanic American. 90% returned for their sophomore year.

Facilities and Resources

Student rooms are linked to a campus network. 900 **computers** are available on campus that provide access to the Internet. The 5 **libraries** have 2,540,162 books and 13,541 subscriptions.

Campus Life

There are 200 active organizations on campus, including a drama/theater group, newspaper, radio station, television station, choral group, and marching band. 15% of eligible men and 15% of eligible women are members of national **fraternities**, national **sororities**, local fraternities, and local sororities.

Delaware is a member of the NCAA (Division I). **Intercollegiate sports** (some offering scholarships) include baseball (m), basketball, cheerleading, crew (w), cross-country running, field hockey (w), football (m), golf (m), lacrosse, soccer, softball (w), swimming, tennis, track and field, volleyball (w).

Campus Safety

Student safety services include late-night transport/escort service, 24-hour emergency telephone alarm devices, 24-hour patrols by trained security personnel, student patrols, and electronically operated dormitory entrances.

Applying

Delaware requires an essay, SAT I or ACT, a high school transcript, and 1 recommendation. It recommends SAT II Subject Tests and SAT II: Writing Test. Application deadline: 2/15; 2/1 priority date for financial aid. Deferred admission is possible.

UNIVERSITY OF DENVER

SUBURBAN SETTING ■ PRIVATE ■ INDEPENDENT ■ COED
DENVER, COLORADO

Web site: www.du.edu
Contact: Cezar Mesquita, Director of Admission Counselors, University Park, Denver, CO 80208
Telephone: 303-871-3312 or toll-free 800-525-9495 (out-of-state) **Fax:** 303-871-3301
E-mail: admission@du.edu

Academics

DU awards bachelor's, master's, doctoral, and first-professional **degrees**. Challenging opportunities include advanced placement credit, accelerated degree programs, student-designed majors, freshman honors college, an honors program, double majors, independent study, and a senior project. Special programs include cooperative education, internships, summer session for credit, study-abroad, and Army and Air Force ROTC.

The most frequently chosen **baccalaureate** fields are business/marketing, communications/communication technologies, and social sciences and history. A complete listing of majors at DU appears in the Majors Index beginning on page 460.

The **faculty** at DU has 440 full-time members, 93% with terminal degrees. The student-faculty ratio is 9:1.

Students of DU

The student body totals 9,521, of whom 4,456 are undergraduates. 55.7% are women and 44.3% are men. Students come from 52 states and territories and 54 other countries. 50% are from Colorado. 85% returned for their sophomore year.

Facilities and Resources

Student rooms are linked to a campus network. 130 **computers** are available on campus that provide access to online grade reports and the Internet. The **library** has 1,212,392 books and 6,283 subscriptions.

Campus Life

There are 82 active organizations on campus, including a drama/theater group, newspaper, and choral group. 23% of eligible men and 22% of eligible women are members of national **fraternities** and national **sororities**.

DU is a member of the NCAA (Division I). **Intercollegiate sports** (some offering scholarships) include basketball, golf, gymnastics (w), ice hockey (m), lacrosse, skiing (cross-country), skiing (downhill), soccer, swimming, tennis, volleyball (w).

Campus Safety

Student safety services include 24-hour locked residence hall entrances, late-night transport/escort service, 24-hour emergency telephone alarm devices, 24-hour patrols by trained security personnel, and electronically operated dormitory entrances.

Applying

DU requires an essay, SAT I or ACT, a high school transcript, and 2 recommendations, and in some cases a minimum high school GPA of 2.0. It recommends an interview and a minimum high school GPA of 2.7. Application deadline: 1/15; 2/15 priority date for financial aid. Early and deferred admission are possible.

Getting in Last Year

4,334 applied
79% were accepted
1,031 enrolled (30%)
13% from top tenth of their h.s. class
3.49 average high school GPA
37% had SAT verbal scores over 600
40% had SAT math scores over 600
63% had ACT scores over 24
6% had SAT verbal scores over 700
6% had SAT math scores over 700
12% had ACT scores over 30

Graduation and After

54% graduated in 4 years
13% graduated in 5 years
2% graduated in 6 years
24% pursued further study
66.6% had job offers within 6 months
196 organizations recruited on campus

Financial Matters

$24,873 tuition and fees (2003–04)
$7275 room and board
72% average percent of need met
$17,271 average financial aid amount received per undergraduate (2002–03)

UNIVERSITY OF EVANSVILLE

SUBURBAN SETTING ■ PRIVATE ■ INDEPENDENT RELIGIOUS ■ COED
EVANSVILLE, INDIANA

Web site: www.evansville.edu
Contact: Dr. Tom Bear, Dean of Admission, 1800 Lincoln Avenue, Evansville, IN 47722-0002
Telephone: 812-479-2468 or toll-free 800-423-8633 **Fax:** 812-474-4076
E-mail: admission@evansville.edu

Getting in Last Year

2,292 applied
86% were accepted
663 enrolled (34%)
41% from top tenth of their h.s. class
3.54 average high school GPA
41% had SAT verbal scores over 600
39% had SAT math scores over 600
55% had ACT scores over 24
9% had SAT verbal scores over 700
7% had SAT math scores over 700
9% had ACT scores over 30
9 National Merit Scholars
101 valedictorians

Graduation and After

46% graduated in 4 years
15% graduated in 5 years
1% graduated in 6 years
27% pursued further study
86% had job offers within 6 months
95 organizations recruited on campus

Financial Matters

$19,230 tuition and fees (2003–04)
$5510 room and board
91% average percent of need met
$17,375 average financial aid amount received per undergraduate

Academics

UE awards associate, bachelor's, and master's **degrees**. Challenging opportunities include advanced placement credit, accelerated degree programs, student-designed majors, freshman honors college, an honors program, double majors, independent study, and a senior project. Special programs include cooperative education, internships, summer session for credit, and study-abroad.

The most frequently chosen **baccalaureate** fields are business/marketing, visual/performing arts, and liberal arts/general studies. A complete listing of majors at UE appears in the Majors Index beginning on page 460.

The **faculty** at UE has 168 full-time members, 85% with terminal degrees. The student-faculty ratio is 13:1.

Students of UE

The student body totals 2,650, of whom 2,566 are undergraduates. 62.2% are women and 37.8% are men. Students come from 44 states and territories and 38 other countries. 66% are from Indiana. 5.6% are international students. 2.2% are African American, 0.3% American Indian, 0.9% Asian American, and 0.9% Hispanic American. 80% returned for their sophomore year.

Facilities and Resources

Student rooms are linked to a campus network. 375 **computers** are available on campus that provide access to the Internet. The 2 **libraries** have 275,980 books and 1,320 subscriptions.

Campus Life

There are 134 active organizations on campus, including a drama/theater group, newspaper, radio station, and choral group. 30% of eligible men and 20% of eligible women are members of national **fraternities** and national **sororities**.

UE is a member of the NCAA (Division I). **Intercollegiate sports** (some offering scholarships) include baseball (m), basketball, cross-country running, golf (m), soccer, softball (w), swimming, tennis, volleyball (w).

Campus Safety

Student safety services include late-night transport/escort service, 24-hour emergency telephone alarm devices, 24-hour patrols by trained security personnel, and electronically operated dormitory entrances.

Applying

UE requires an essay, SAT I or ACT, a high school transcript, 1 recommendation, and a minimum high school GPA of 2.0, and in some cases an interview. It recommends an interview and a minimum high school GPA of 3.0. Application deadline: rolling admissions; 3/1 priority date for financial aid. Early and deferred admission are possible.

UNIVERSITY OF FLORIDA

SUBURBAN SETTING ■ PUBLIC ■ STATE-SUPPORTED ■ COED
GAINESVILLE, FLORIDA

Web site: www.ufl.edu
Contact: Office of Admissions, 201 Criser Hall, PO Box 114000, Gainesville,
  FL 32611-4000
Telephone: 352-392-1365
E-mail: freshmen@ufl.edu

Academics

UF awards bachelor's, master's, doctoral, and first-professional **degrees**. Challenging opportunities include advanced placement credit, accelerated degree programs, student-designed majors, an honors program, double majors, independent study, and a senior project. Special programs include cooperative education, internships, summer session for credit, off-campus study, study-abroad, and Army, Navy and Air Force ROTC.

The most frequently chosen **baccalaureate** fields are business/marketing, social sciences and history, and engineering/engineering technologies. A complete listing of majors at UF appears in the Majors Index beginning on page 460.

The **faculty** at UF has 1,679 full-time members, 92% with terminal degrees. The student-faculty ratio is 22:1.

Students of UF

The student body totals 47,858, of whom 33,982 are undergraduates. 53.4% are women and 46.6% are men. Students come from 52 states and territories and 114 other countries. 96% are from Florida. 0.9% are international students. 8.6% are African American, 0.5% American Indian, 6.9% Asian American, and 12% Hispanic American. 93% returned for their sophomore year.

Facilities and Resources

Student rooms are linked to a campus network. 472 **computers** are available on campus that provide access to the Internet. The 9 **libraries** have 5,024,637 books and 28,103 subscriptions.

Campus Life

There are 525 active organizations on campus, including a drama/theater group, newspaper, radio station, television station, choral group, and marching band. 15% of eligible men and 15% of eligible women are members of national **fraternities**, national **sororities**, local fraternities, and local sororities.

UF is a member of the NCAA (Division I). **Intercollegiate sports** (some offering scholarships) include baseball (m), basketball, cheerleading, cross-country running, football (m), golf, gymnastics (w), soccer (w), softball (w), swimming, tennis, track and field, volleyball (w).

Campus Safety

Student safety services include crime and rape prevention programs, late-night transport/escort service, 24-hour emergency telephone alarm devices, 24-hour patrols by trained security personnel, student patrols, and electronically operated dormitory entrances.

Applying

UF requires SAT I or ACT and a high school transcript. Application deadline: 1/12; 3/15 priority date for financial aid. Early admission is possible.

Getting in Last Year

22,973 applied
52% were accepted
6,596 enrolled (55%)
79% from top tenth of their h.s. class
3.8 average high school GPA
59% had SAT verbal scores over 600
69% had SAT math scores over 600
80% had ACT scores over 24
14% had SAT verbal scores over 700
19% had SAT math scores over 700
21% had ACT scores over 30
130 National Merit Scholars

Graduation and After

50% graduated in 4 years
21% graduated in 5 years
5% graduated in 6 years
1250 organizations recruited on campus

Financial Matters

$2780 resident tuition and fees (2003–04)
$13,808 nonresident tuition and fees (2003–04)
$5800 room and board
85% average percent of need met
$9380 average financial aid amount received per undergraduate (2002–03)

UNIVERSITY OF GEORGIA

SUBURBAN SETTING ■ PUBLIC ■ STATE-SUPPORTED ■ COED
ATHENS, GEORGIA

Web site: www.uga.edu
Contact: Mr. J. Robert Spatig, Associate Director of Admissions, Athens, GA 30602
Telephone: 706-542-3000 **Fax:** 706-542-1466
E-mail: undergrad@admissions.uga.edu

Located in the quintessential college town of Athens, the University of Georgia (UGA) is ranked among the top public research universities nationally and recognized widely as an outstanding value because of its competitive costs, exceptional undergraduate instruction and research opportunities, and enviable student satisfaction record. Through its programs and practices, UGA seeks to foster the understanding of and respect for cultural differences necessary for an enlightened and educated citizenry. UGA's Honors Program, one of the oldest and most respected in the nation, provides an enhanced liberal arts foundation for superior undergraduates, along with faculty-guided individual research and progress into graduate-level work.

Getting in Last Year
11,813 applied
75% were accepted
5,177 enrolled (58%)
43% from top tenth of their h.s. class
3.61 average high school GPA
52% had SAT verbal scores over 600
56% had SAT math scores over 600
70% had ACT scores over 24
10% had SAT verbal scores over 700
10% had SAT math scores over 700
11% had ACT scores over 30
59 National Merit Scholars

Graduation and After
46% graduated in 4 years
16% graduated in 5 years
4% graduated in 6 years
Graduates pursuing further study: 39% arts and sciences, 31% education, 15% business
56% had job offers within 6 months
892 organizations recruited on campus

Financial Matters
$4078 resident tuition and fees (2003–04)
$14,854 nonresident tuition and fees (2003–04)
$5756 room and board
73% average percent of need met
$7323 average financial aid amount received per undergraduate

Academics
UGA awards associate, bachelor's, master's, doctoral, and first-professional **degrees**. Challenging opportunities include advanced placement credit, accelerated degree programs, student-designed majors, an honors program, double majors, independent study, and a senior project. Special programs include cooperative education, internships, summer session for credit, off-campus study, study-abroad, and Army and Air Force ROTC.

The most frequently chosen **baccalaureate** fields are business/marketing, education, and social sciences and history. A complete listing of majors at UGA appears in the Majors Index beginning on page 460.

The **faculty** at UGA has 1,689 full-time members, 94% with terminal degrees. The student-faculty ratio is 14:1.

Students of UGA
The student body totals 33,878, of whom 25,415 are undergraduates. 57% are women and 43% are men. Students come from 54 states and territories and 105 other countries. 89% are from Georgia. 0.7% are international students. 4.8% are African American, 0.1% American Indian, 4.2% Asian American, and 1.7% Hispanic American. 93% returned for their sophomore year.

Facilities and Resources
Student rooms are linked to a campus network. 2,500 **computers** are available on campus that provide access to e-mail, web pages and the Internet. The 3 **libraries** have 3,789,228 books and 46,431 subscriptions.

Campus Life
There are 430 active organizations on campus, including a drama/theater group, newspaper, radio station, television station, choral group, and marching band. 16% of eligible men and 21% of eligible women are members of national **fraternities**, national **sororities**, local fraternities, and local sororities.

UGA is a member of the NCAA (Division I). **Intercollegiate sports** (some offering scholarships) include baseball (m), basketball, cheerleading, cross-country running, equestrian sports, football (m), golf, gymnastics (w), soccer (w), swimming, tennis, track and field, volleyball (w).

Campus Safety
Student safety services include late-night transport/escort service, 24-hour emergency telephone alarm devices, 24-hour patrols by trained security personnel, and electronically operated dormitory entrances.

Applying
UGA requires SAT I or ACT and a high school transcript, and in some cases SAT II: Writing Test and SAT I and SAT II or ACT. It recommends an essay and a minimum high school GPA of 2.0. Application deadline: 2/1; 3/1 priority date for financial aid. Early and deferred admission are possible.

UNIVERSITY OF IDAHO
SMALL-TOWN SETTING ■ PUBLIC ■ STATE-SUPPORTED ■ COED
MOSCOW, IDAHO

Web site: www.uidaho.edu
Contact: Mr. Dan Davenport, Director of Admissions, PO Box 444264, Moscow, ID 83844-4264
Telephone: 208-885-6326 or toll-free 888-884-3246 (out-of-state) **Fax:** 208-885-9119
E-mail: admappl@uidaho.edu

Academics
Idaho awards bachelor's, master's, doctoral, and first-professional **degrees** and post-master's certificates. Challenging opportunities include advanced placement credit, accelerated degree programs, student-designed majors, an honors program, double majors, independent study, and a senior project. Special programs include cooperative education, internships, summer session for credit, off-campus study, study-abroad, and Army, Navy and Air Force ROTC.

The most frequently chosen **baccalaureate** fields are business/marketing, education, and engineering/engineering technologies. A complete listing of majors at Idaho appears in the Majors Index beginning on page 460.

The **faculty** at Idaho has 545 full-time members, 80% with terminal degrees. The student-faculty ratio is 20:1.

Students of Idaho
The student body totals 12,894, of whom 9,607 are undergraduates. 45.3% are women and 54.7% are men. 78% are from Idaho. 2.4% are international students. 0.9% are African American, 1.3% American Indian, 2.1% Asian American, and 3.5% Hispanic American. 82% returned for their sophomore year.

Facilities and Resources
Student rooms are linked to a campus network. 670 **computers** are available on campus that provide access to student evaluations of teaching and the Internet. The 2 **libraries** have 1,355,911 books and 14,230 subscriptions.

Campus Life
There are 132 active organizations on campus, including a drama/theater group, newspaper, radio station, television station, choral group, and marching band. 16% of eligible men and 13% of eligible women are members of national **fraternities** and national **sororities**.

Idaho is a member of the NCAA (Division I). **Intercollegiate sports** (some offering scholarships) include basketball, cross-country running, football (m), golf, soccer (w), tennis, track and field, volleyball (w).

Campus Safety
Student safety services include late-night transport/escort service and electronically operated dormitory entrances.

Applying
Idaho requires SAT I or ACT, a high school transcript, and a minimum high school GPA of 2.2, and in some cases an essay. It recommends SAT I. Application deadline: 8/1; 2/15 priority date for financial aid. Deferred admission is possible.

Getting in Last Year
3,973 applied
81% were accepted
1,650 enrolled (52%)
20% from top tenth of their h.s. class
3.40 average high school GPA
30% had SAT verbal scores over 600
34% had SAT math scores over 600
46% had ACT scores over 24
5% had SAT verbal scores over 700
5% had SAT math scores over 700
8% had ACT scores over 30
8 National Merit Scholars
31 class presidents
71 valedictorians

Graduation and After
19% graduated in 4 years
28% graduated in 5 years
8% graduated in 6 years
93% had job offers within 6 months
250 organizations recruited on campus

Financial Matters
$3348 resident tuition and fees (2003–04)
$10,740 nonresident tuition and fees (2003–04)
$4868 room and board
79% average percent of need met
$8951 average financial aid amount received per undergraduate (2002–03)

UNIVERSITY OF ILLINOIS AT CHICAGO

URBAN SETTING ■ PUBLIC ■ STATE-SUPPORTED ■ COED
CHICAGO, ILLINOIS

Web site: www.uic.edu/grad
Contact: Mr. Thomas E. Glenn, Executive Director of Admissions, Box 5220,
Chicago, IL 60680-5220
Telephone: 312-996-4350 **Fax:** 312-413-7628
E-mail: uic.admit@uic.edu

Getting in Last Year
12,250 applied
61% were accepted
2,942 enrolled (40%)
23% from top tenth of their h.s. class
45% had ACT scores over 24
6% had ACT scores over 30

Graduation and After
Graduates pursuing further study: 10% arts
and sciences, 5% business, 3% law
92% had job offers within 6 months
917 organizations recruited on campus

Financial Matters
$6798 resident tuition and fees (2003–04)
$16,494 nonresident tuition and fees (2003–
04)
$6620 room and board
86% average percent of need met
$11,900 average financial aid amount received
per undergraduate (2001–02)

Academics

UIC awards bachelor's, master's, doctoral, and first-professional **degrees** and first-professional certificates. Challenging opportunities include advanced placement credit, accelerated degree programs, student-designed majors, an honors program, double majors, independent study, and a senior project. Special programs include cooperative education, internships, summer session for credit, off-campus study, study-abroad, and Army, Navy and Air Force ROTC.

The most frequently chosen **baccalaureate** fields are business/marketing, engineering/engineering technologies, and psychology. A complete listing of majors at UIC appears in the Majors Index beginning on page 460.

The **faculty** at UIC has 1,193 full-time members, 85% with terminal degrees. The student-faculty ratio is 16:1.

Students of UIC

The student body totals 25,763, of whom 16,012 are undergraduates. 54.8% are women and 45.2% are men. Students come from 52 states and territories and 48 other countries. 98% are from Illinois. 1.2% are international students. 8.9% are African American, 0.2% American Indian, 25.3% Asian American, and 15.8% Hispanic American. 78% returned for their sophomore year.

Facilities and Resources

Student rooms are linked to a campus network. 1,100 **computers** are available on campus for student use. The 8 **libraries** have 2,216,589 books and 21,571 subscriptions.

Campus Life

There are 233 active organizations on campus, including a drama/theater group, newspaper, radio station, and choral group. 4% of eligible men and 3% of eligible women are members of national **fraternities**, national **sororities**, local fraternities, and local sororities.

UIC is a member of the NCAA (Division I). **Intercollegiate sports** (some offering scholarships) include baseball (m), basketball, cross-country running, gymnastics, soccer (m), softball (w), swimming, tennis, track and field, volleyball (w).

Campus Safety

Student safety services include housing ID stickers, guest escort policy, 24-hour closed circuit videos for exits and entrances, security screen for first floor, late-night transport/escort service, 24-hour emergency telephone alarm devices, 24-hour patrols by trained security personnel, student patrols, and electronically operated dormitory entrances.

Applying

UIC requires SAT I or ACT and a high school transcript, and in some cases an essay and an interview. Application deadline: 1/15; 3/1 priority date for financial aid.

UNIVERSITY OF ILLINOIS AT URBANA–CHAMPAIGN

SMALL-TOWN SETTING ■ PUBLIC ■ STATE-SUPPORTED ■ COED
CHAMPAIGN, ILLINOIS

Web site: www.uiuc.edu
Contact: Mr. Abel Montoya, Acting Associate Director, 901 West Illinois, Urbana, IL 61801
Telephone: 217-333-0302
E-mail: admissions@oar.uiuc.edu

Academics

Illinois awards bachelor's, master's, doctoral, and first-professional **degrees** and post-master's certificates. Challenging opportunities include advanced placement credit, accelerated degree programs, student-designed majors, an honors program, double majors, and a senior project. Special programs include cooperative education, internships, summer session for credit, off-campus study, study-abroad, and Army and Air Force ROTC.

The most frequently chosen **baccalaureate** fields are business/marketing, social sciences and history, and engineering/engineering technologies. A complete listing of majors at Illinois appears in the Majors Index beginning on page 460.

The **faculty** at Illinois has 2,174 full-time members, 90% with terminal degrees. The student-faculty ratio is 12:1.

Students of Illinois

The student body totals 40,458, of whom 29,226 are undergraduates. 47.1% are women and 52.9% are men. Students come from 52 states and territories and 70 other countries. 88% are from Illinois. 3.2% are international students. 7.6% are African American, 0.3% American Indian, 12.8% Asian American, and 6.4% Hispanic American. 93% returned for their sophomore year.

Facilities and Resources

Student rooms are linked to a campus network. 3,500 **computers** are available on campus that provide access to the Internet. The 43 **libraries** have 9,861,988 books and 90,707 subscriptions.

Campus Life

There are 1,000 active organizations on campus, including a drama/theater group, newspaper, radio station, television station, choral group, and marching band. 22% of eligible men and 22% of eligible women are members of national **fraternities**, national **sororities**, local fraternities, and local sororities.

Illinois is a member of the NCAA (Division I). **Intercollegiate sports** (some offering scholarships) include baseball (m), basketball, cheerleading, cross-country running, football (m), golf, gymnastics, soccer (w), swimming (w), tennis, track and field, volleyball (w), wrestling (m).

Campus Safety

Student safety services include safety training classes, ID cards with safety numbers, late-night transport/escort service, 24-hour emergency telephone alarm devices, 24-hour patrols by trained security personnel, student patrols, and electronically operated dormitory entrances.

Applying

Illinois requires an essay, SAT I or ACT, and a high school transcript, and in some cases audition, statement of professional interest. Application deadline: 1/1; 3/15 priority date for financial aid. Deferred admission is possible.

The University of Illinois at Urbana-Champaign is the state's premier public university, attracting the most impressive students from across Illinois, the nation, and the world. Founded in 1867 as a land-grant institution, the University now offers more than 4,000 courses in 150 undergraduate programs. The 28,000 undergraduate students often participate in study-abroad programs, research opportunities, living/learning communities, and more than 900 student organizations. One undergraduate student describes her college selection process, "I based my decision on opportunity, diversity, flexibility, quality, and value. In the end, I chose the University of Illinois at Urbana–Champaign. It's a great school."

Getting in Last Year

22,269 applied
63% were accepted
6,811 enrolled (49%)
57% from top tenth of their h.s. class
58% had SAT verbal scores over 600
79% had SAT math scores over 600
86% had ACT scores over 24
14% had SAT verbal scores over 700
37% had SAT math scores over 700
34% had ACT scores over 30

Graduation and After

57% graduated in 4 years
21% graduated in 5 years
2% graduated in 6 years
56% pursued further study (10% law, 9% medicine, 5% business)
88.5% had job offers within 6 months
582 organizations recruited on campus

Financial Matters

$8452 resident tuition and fees (2003–04)
$19,492 nonresident tuition and fees (2003–04)
$6620 room and board
87% average percent of need met
$9263 average financial aid amount received per undergraduate (2002–03 estimated)

Getting in Last Year

13,337 applied
82% were accepted
4,083 enrolled (37%)
21% from top tenth of their h.s. class
3.54 average high school GPA
47% had SAT verbal scores over 600
53% had SAT math scores over 600
64% had ACT scores over 24
11% had SAT verbal scores over 700
14% had SAT math scores over 700
10% had ACT scores over 30
23 National Merit Scholars
169 valedictorians

Graduation and After

38% graduated in 4 years
24% graduated in 5 years
3% graduated in 6 years
320 organizations recruited on campus

Financial Matters

$4993 resident tuition and fees (2003–04)
$15,285 nonresident tuition and fees (2003–04)
$5930 room and board
88% average percent of need met
$6806 average financial aid amount received per undergraduate (2001–02)

THE UNIVERSITY OF IOWA

SMALL-TOWN SETTING ■ PUBLIC ■ STATE-SUPPORTED ■ COED
IOWA CITY, IOWA

Web site: www.uiowa.edu
Contact: Mr. Michael Barron, Director of Admissions, 107 Calvin Hall, Iowa City, IA 52242
Telephone: 319-335-3847 or toll-free 800-553-4692 Fax: 319-335-1535
E-mail: admissions@uiowa.edu

Academics

Iowa awards bachelor's, master's, doctoral, and first-professional **degrees**. Challenging opportunities include advanced placement credit, accelerated degree programs, student-designed majors, an honors program, double majors, independent study, and a senior project. Special programs include cooperative education, internships, summer session for credit, off-campus study, study-abroad, and Army and Air Force ROTC.

The most frequently chosen **baccalaureate** fields are business/marketing, social sciences and history, and communications/communication technologies. A complete listing of majors at Iowa appears in the Majors Index beginning on page 460.

The **faculty** at Iowa has 1,623 full-time members, 96% with terminal degrees. The student-faculty ratio is 15:1.

Students of Iowa

The student body totals 29,744, of whom 20,233 are undergraduates. 54.4% are women and 45.6% are men. Students come from 52 states and territories and 65 other countries. 67% are from Iowa. 1.2% are international students. 2.2% are African American, 0.4% American Indian, 3.5% Asian American, and 2.5% Hispanic American. 81% returned for their sophomore year.

Facilities and Resources

Student rooms are linked to a campus network. 1,200 **computers** are available on campus that provide access to online degree process, grades, financial aid summary, bills and the Internet. The 13 **libraries** have 4,027,546 books and 44,644 subscriptions.

Campus Life

There are 408 active organizations on campus, including a drama/theater group, newspaper, radio station, choral group, and marching band. 9% of eligible men and 13% of eligible women are members of national **fraternities** and national **sororities**.

Iowa is a member of the NCAA (Division I). **Intercollegiate sports** (some offering scholarships) include baseball (m), basketball, cheerleading, crew (w), cross-country running, field hockey (w), football (m), golf, gymnastics, soccer (w), softball (w), swimming, tennis, track and field, volleyball (w), wrestling (m).

Campus Safety

Student safety services include late-night transport/escort service, 24-hour emergency telephone alarm devices, 24-hour patrols by trained security personnel, and electronically operated dormitory entrances.

Applying

Iowa requires SAT I or ACT, a high school transcript, and rank in top 50% for residents, rank in top 30% for nonresidents. Application deadline: 4/1. Early and deferred admission are possible.

UNIVERSITY OF KANSAS
SUBURBAN SETTING ■ PUBLIC ■ STATE-SUPPORTED ■ COED
LAWRENCE, KANSAS

Web site: www.ku.edu
Contact: Ms. Lisa Pinamonti, Director of Admissions and Scholarships, KU Visitor Center, 1502 Iowa Street, Lawrence, KS 66045-7576
Telephone: 785-864-3911 or toll-free 888-686-7323 (in-state) **Fax:** 785-864-5006
E-mail: adm@ku.edu

Academics
KU awards bachelor's, master's, doctoral, and first-professional **degrees** and post-master's certificates (University of Kansas is a single institution with academic programs and facilities at two primary locations: Lawrence and Kansas City. Undergraduate, graduate, and professional education are the principal missions of the Lawrence campus, with medicine and related professional education the focus of the Kansas City campus). Challenging opportunities include advanced placement credit, accelerated degree programs, an honors program, double majors, independent study, and a senior project. Special programs include cooperative education, internships, summer session for credit, study-abroad, and Army, Navy and Air Force ROTC.

The most frequently chosen **baccalaureate** fields are business/marketing, social sciences and history, and English. A complete listing of majors at KU appears in the Majors Index beginning on page 460.

The **faculty** at KU has 1,194 full-time members, 92% with terminal degrees. The student-faculty ratio is 19:1.

Students of KU
The student body totals 28,580, of whom 20,866 are undergraduates. 51.9% are women and 48.1% are men. Students come from 53 states and territories and 111 other countries. 76% are from Kansas. 3.1% are international students. 3.2% are African American, 1.2% American Indian, 3.9% Asian American, and 3.2% Hispanic American. 82% returned for their sophomore year.

Facilities and Resources
Student rooms are linked to a campus network. 1,100 **computers** are available on campus that provide access to the Internet. The 12 **libraries** have 4,623,079 books and 33,874 subscriptions.

Campus Life
There are 400 active organizations on campus, including a drama/theater group, newspaper, radio station, television station, choral group, and marching band. 14% of eligible men and 20% of eligible women are members of national **fraternities** and national **sororities**.

KU is a member of the NCAA (Division I). **Intercollegiate sports** (some offering scholarships) include baseball (m), basketball, crew (w), cross-country running, football (m), golf, soccer (w), softball (w), swimming (w), tennis (w), track and field, volleyball (w).

Campus Safety
Student safety services include University police department; security guards are included, late-night transport/escort service, 24-hour emergency telephone alarm devices, 24-hour patrols by trained security personnel, and electronically operated dormitory entrances.

Applying
KU requires SAT I or ACT, a high school transcript, Kansas Board of Regents admissions criteria with GPA of 2.0/2.5; top third of high school class; minimum ACT score of 24 or minimum SAT score of 1090, and a minimum high school GPA of 2.0, and in some cases a minimum high school GPA of 2.5. Application deadline: 4/1; 3/1 priority date for financial aid. Deferred admission is possible.

Getting in Last Year
9,573 applied
67% were accepted
4,066 enrolled (63%)
28% from top tenth of their h.s. class
3.43 average high school GPA
54% had ACT scores over 24
10% had ACT scores over 30
46 National Merit Scholars

Graduation and After
26% graduated in 4 years
25% graduated in 5 years
5% graduated in 6 years
28% pursued further study
45% had job offers within 6 months
500 organizations recruited on campus

Financial Matters
$4101 resident tuition and fees (2003–04)
$11,577 nonresident tuition and fees (2003–04)
$4822 room and board
76% average percent of need met
$6173 average financial aid amount received per undergraduate (2001–02)

UNIVERSITY OF KENTUCKY

URBAN SETTING ■ PUBLIC ■ STATE-SUPPORTED ■ COED
LEXINGTON, KENTUCKY

Web site: www.uky.edu
Contact: Ms. Michelle Nordin, Associate Director of Admissions, 100 W.D.
   Funkhouser Building, Lexington, KY 40506-0054
Telephone: 859-257-2000 or toll-free 800-432-0967 (in-state)
E-mail: admissio@uky.edu

Getting in Last Year
9,418 applied
81% were accepted
3,688 enrolled (49%)
28% from top tenth of their h.s. class
3.56 average high school GPA
34% had SAT verbal scores over 600
39% had SAT math scores over 600
54% had ACT scores over 24
6% had SAT verbal scores over 700
7% had SAT math scores over 700
9% had ACT scores over 30
47 National Merit Scholars
145 valedictorians

Graduation and After
27% graduated in 4 years
27% graduated in 5 years
7% graduated in 6 years
574 organizations recruited on campus

Financial Matters
$4547 resident tuition and fees (2003–04)
$11,227 nonresident tuition and fees (2003–04)
$4285 room and board
86% average percent of need met
$8106 average financial aid amount received per undergraduate (2001–02)

Academics

UK awards bachelor's, master's, doctoral, and first-professional **degrees** and post-master's certificates. Challenging opportunities include advanced placement credit, accelerated degree programs, student-designed majors, an honors program, double majors, and independent study. Special programs include cooperative education, internships, summer session for credit, off-campus study, study-abroad, and Army and Air Force ROTC.

The most frequently chosen **baccalaureate** fields are business/marketing, communications/communication technologies, and social sciences and history. A complete listing of majors at UK appears in the Majors Index beginning on page 460.

The **faculty** at UK has 1,209 full-time members, 97% with terminal degrees. The student-faculty ratio is 16:1.

Students of UK

The student body totals 25,397, of whom 18,108 are undergraduates. 51.8% are women and 48.2% are men. Students come from 53 states and territories and 123 other countries. 86% are from Kentucky. 1.1% are international students. 5.4% are African American, 0.1% American Indian, 1.6% Asian American, and 1% Hispanic American. 77% returned for their sophomore year.

Facilities and Resources

Student rooms are linked to a campus network. 1,400 **computers** are available on campus that provide access to various software packages and the Internet. The 16 **libraries** have 2,860,457 books and 29,850 subscriptions.

Campus Life

There are 305 active organizations on campus, including a drama/theater group, newspaper, radio station, choral group, and marching band. 12% of eligible men and 18% of eligible women are members of national **fraternities** and national **sororities**.

UK is a member of the NCAA (Division I). **Intercollegiate sports** (some offering scholarships) include baseball (m), basketball, cross-country running, football (m), golf, gymnastics (w), riflery, soccer, softball (w), swimming, tennis, track and field, volleyball (w).

Campus Safety

Student safety services include late-night transport/escort service, 24-hour emergency telephone alarm devices, 24-hour patrols by trained security personnel, and electronically operated dormitory entrances.

Applying

UK requires SAT I or ACT, a high school transcript, and a minimum high school GPA of 2.0. Application deadline: 2/15; 2/15 priority date for financial aid. Early admission is possible.

UNIVERSITY OF MARYLAND, BALTIMORE COUNTY

Suburban setting ■ Public ■ State-supported ■ Coed
Baltimore, Maryland

Web site: www.umbc.edu
Contact: Ms. Yvette Mozie-Ross, Director of Admissions, 1000 Hilltop Circle,
Baltimore, MD 21250
Telephone: 410-455-3799 or toll-free 800-UMBC-4U2 (in-state),
800-862-2402 (out-of-state) Fax: 410-455-1094
E-mail: admissions@umbc.edu

Academics

UMBC awards bachelor's, master's, and doctoral **degrees** and post-bachelor's
certificates. Challenging opportunities include advanced placement credit, student-
designed majors, freshman honors college, an honors program, double majors,
independent study, and a senior project. Special programs include cooperative education,
internships, summer session for credit, off-campus study, study-abroad, and Army and
Air Force ROTC.

The most frequently chosen **baccalaureate** fields are computer/information sciences,
social sciences and history, and visual/performing arts. A complete listing of majors at
UMBC appears in the Majors Index beginning on page 460.

The **faculty** at UMBC has 464 full-time members, 85% with terminal degrees. The
student-faculty ratio is 18:1.

Students of UMBC

The student body totals 11,872, of whom 9,646 are undergraduates. 47.5% are women
and 52.5% are men. Students come from 45 states and territories and 108 other
countries. 92% are from Maryland. 4.8% are international students. 15% are African
American, 0.4% American Indian, 19.5% Asian American, and 3% Hispanic American.
82% returned for their sophomore year.

Facilities and Resources

Student rooms are linked to a campus network. 673 **computers** are available on campus
that provide access to student account and grade information and the Internet. The 2
libraries have 749,618 books and 4,282 subscriptions.

Campus Life

There are 180 active organizations on campus, including a drama/theater group,
newspaper, radio station, television station, choral group, and marching band. 3% of
eligible men and 3% of eligible women are members of national **fraternities** and
national **sororities**.

UMBC is a member of the NCAA (Division I). **Intercollegiate sports** (some offering scholarships) include baseball (m), basketball, cross-country running, lacrosse, soccer,
softball (w), swimming, tennis, track and field, volleyball (w).

Campus Safety

Student safety services include late-night transport/escort service, 24-hour emergency
telephone alarm devices, and 24-hour patrols by trained security personnel.

Applying

UMBC requires an essay, SAT I or ACT, and a high school transcript. It recommends
SAT I, 2 recommendations, and a minimum high school GPA of 3. Application deadline:
2/1; 3/1 priority date for financial aid. Early and deferred admission are possible.

Getting in Last Year

5,501 applied
58% were accepted
1,505 enrolled (48%)
33% from top tenth of their h.s. class
3.53 average high school GPA
47% had SAT verbal scores over 600
65% had SAT math scores over 600
64% had ACT scores over 24
9% had SAT verbal scores over 700
17% had SAT math scores over 700
12% had ACT scores over 30
1 National Merit Scholar

Graduation and After

28% graduated in 4 years
20% graduated in 5 years
6% graduated in 6 years
35% pursued further study (25% arts and
sciences, 2% business, 2% law)
69% had job offers within 6 months
402 organizations recruited on campus

Financial Matters

$7388 resident tuition and fees (2003–04)
$14,240 nonresident tuition and fees (2003–
04)
$7007 room and board
61% average percent of need met
$6212 average financial aid amount received
per undergraduate (2001–02)

UNIVERSITY OF MARYLAND, COLLEGE PARK

SUBURBAN SETTING ■ PUBLIC ■ STATE-SUPPORTED ■ COED
COLLEGE PARK, MARYLAND

Getting in Last Year
25,028 applied
43% were accepted
4,063 enrolled (38%)
56% from top tenth of their h.s. class
3.88 average high school GPA
64% had SAT verbal scores over 600
77% had SAT math scores over 600
15% had SAT verbal scores over 700
26% had SAT math scores over 700
112 National Merit Scholars

Graduation and After
41% graduated in 4 years
23% graduated in 5 years
5% graduated in 6 years
42% pursued further study
75% had job offers within 6 months
650 organizations recruited on campus

Financial Matters
$6758 resident tuition and fees (2003–04)
$17,432 nonresident tuition and fees (2003–04)
$7608 room and board
72% average percent of need met
$8051 average financial aid amount received per undergraduate (2001–02)

Web site: www.maryland.edu
Contact: Ms. Barbara Gill, Director of Undergraduate Admissions, Mitchell Building, College Park, MD 20742-5235
Telephone: 301-314-8385 or toll-free 800-422-5867 **Fax:** 301-314-9693
E-mail: um-admit@uga.umd.edu

Academics

University of Maryland, College Park awards bachelor's, master's, doctoral, and first-professional **degrees** and post-bachelor's and post-master's certificates. Challenging opportunities include advanced placement credit, accelerated degree programs, student-designed majors, an honors program, double majors, independent study, and a senior project. Special programs include cooperative education, internships, summer session for credit, off-campus study, study-abroad, and Army, Navy and Air Force ROTC.

The most frequently chosen **baccalaureate** fields are social sciences and history, business/marketing, and communications/communication technologies. A complete listing of majors at University of Maryland, College Park appears in the Majors Index beginning on page 460.

The **faculty** at University of Maryland, College Park has 1,575 full-time members, 94% with terminal degrees. The student-faculty ratio is 13:1.

Students of University of Maryland, College Park

The student body totals 35,262, of whom 25,379 are undergraduates. 49.3% are women and 50.7% are men. Students come from 54 states and territories and 159 other countries. 76% are from Maryland. 2.3% are international students. 12.3% are African American, 0.3% American Indian, 13.8% Asian American, and 5.6% Hispanic American. 93% returned for their sophomore year.

Facilities and Resources

Student rooms are linked to a campus network. 791 **computers** are available on campus that provide access to student account information, financial aid summary and the Internet. The 7 **libraries** have 2,956,648 books and 33,858 subscriptions.

Campus Life

There are 515 active organizations on campus, including a drama/theater group, newspaper, radio station, television station, choral group, and marching band. 9% of eligible men and 9% of eligible women are members of national **fraternities** and national **sororities**.

University of Maryland, College Park is a member of the NCAA (Division I). **Intercollegiate sports** (some offering scholarships) include baseball (m), basketball (m), cheerleading (w), cross-country running, field hockey (w), football (m), golf, gymnastics (w), lacrosse, soccer, softball (w), swimming, tennis, track and field, volleyball (w), water polo (w), wrestling (m).

Campus Safety

Student safety services include campus police, video camera surveillance, late-night transport/escort service, 24-hour emergency telephone alarm devices, 24-hour patrols by trained security personnel, student patrols, and electronically operated dormitory entrances.

Applying

University of Maryland, College Park requires an essay, SAT I or ACT, a high school transcript, and 1 recommendation, and in some cases resume of activities, auditions. It recommends 2 recommendations. Application deadline: 1/20; 2/15 priority date for financial aid. Early admission is possible.

UNIVERSITY OF MIAMI

SUBURBAN SETTING ■ PRIVATE ■ INDEPENDENT ■ COED
CORAL GABLES, FLORIDA

Web site: www.miami.edu
Contact: Mr. Edward M. Gillis, Associate Dean of Enrollment and Director
of Admission, PO Box 248025, Ashe Building Room 132, 1252 Memorial
Drive, Coral Gables, FL 33146-4616
Telephone: 305-284-4323 **Fax:** 305-284-2507
E-mail: admission@miami.edu

Academics

UM awards bachelor's, master's, doctoral, and first-professional **degrees** and post-
bachelor's and post-master's certificates. Challenging opportunities include advanced
placement credit, accelerated degree programs, student-designed majors, an honors
program, double majors, independent study, and a senior project. Special programs
include internships, summer session for credit, study-abroad, and Army and Air Force
ROTC.

The most frequently chosen **baccalaureate** fields are business/marketing, visual/
performing arts, and biological/life sciences. A complete listing of majors at UM appears
in the Majors Index beginning on page 460.

The **faculty** at UM has 853 full-time members, 88% with terminal degrees. The student-faculty ratio is 13:1.

Students of UM

The student body totals 15,235, of whom 9,996 are undergraduates. 58.1% are women
and 41.9% are men. Students come from 53 states and territories and 99 other countries.
55% are from Florida. 6.7% are international students. 9.5% are African American,
0.3% American Indian, 5.5% Asian American, and 24% Hispanic American. 87%
returned for their sophomore year.

Facilities and Resources

Student rooms are linked to a campus network. 1,800 **computers** are available on
campus that provide access to online student account and grade information and the
Internet. The 8 **libraries** have 1,415,781 books and 16,305 subscriptions.

Campus Life

There are 175 active organizations on campus, including a drama/theater group,
newspaper, radio station, television station, choral group, and marching band. 13% of
eligible men and 12% of eligible women are members of national **fraternities** and
national **sororities**.

UM is a member of the NCAA (Division I). **Intercollegiate sports** (some offering
scholarships) include baseball (m), basketball, cheerleading, crew (w), cross-country running, football (m), golf (w), soccer (w), swimming (w), tennis, track and field, volleyball
(w).

Campus Safety

Student safety services include crime prevention and safety workshops, residential college crime watch, late-night transport/escort service, 24-hour emergency telephone
alarm devices, 24-hour patrols by trained security personnel, student patrols, and
electronically operated dormitory entrances.

Applying

UM requires an essay, SAT I or ACT, a high school transcript, 1 recommendation, and
counselor evaluation form, and in some cases SAT II Subject Tests and an interview. It
recommends a minimum high school GPA of 3.0. Application deadline: 2/1; 2/15 priority date for financial aid. Early and deferred admission are possible.

Getting in Last Year

16,851 applied
44% were accepted
2,078 enrolled (28%)
60% from top tenth of their h.s. class
54% had SAT verbal scores over 600
64% had SAT math scores over 600
91% had ACT scores over 24
13% had SAT verbal scores over 700
18% had SAT math scores over 700
28% had ACT scores over 30
74 valedictorians

Graduation and After

53% graduated in 4 years
12% graduated in 5 years
2% graduated in 6 years
29% pursued further study (7% law, 6%
medicine, 3% business)
153 organizations recruited on campus

Financial Matters

$26,722 tuition and fees (2003–04)
$8323 room and board
82% average percent of need met
$22,940 average financial aid amount received
per undergraduate

UNIVERSITY OF MICHIGAN

SUBURBAN SETTING ■ PUBLIC ■ STATE-SUPPORTED ■ COED
ANN ARBOR, MICHIGAN

Web site: www.umich.edu
Contact: Mr. Ted Spencer, Director of Undergraduate Admissions, 1220
    Student Activities Building, 515 East Jefferson, Ann Arbor, MI 48109-1316
Telephone: 734-764-7433 **Fax:** 734-936-0740
E-mail: ugadmiss@umich.edu

The University of Michigan, Ann Arbor, is one of the nation's top-ranked public universities and is consistently rated among the top 25 academic institutions in the country. Nearly every one of the University's 19 academic schools and colleges is rated among the top in its field. Students and faculty members come from 129 different countries and all 50 states. The academic and personal growth achieved by students is unique and diverse, and Michigan graduates are prepared to face the challenges of the future. Extensive resources, dedicated faculty members, exceptional students, and a friendly campus and lively town—this is the Wolverine spirit, the Michigan tradition.

Getting in Last Year
25,943 applied
53% were accepted
5,551 enrolled (40%)
70% had SAT verbal scores over 600
84% had SAT math scores over 600
90% had ACT scores over 24
20% had SAT verbal scores over 700
39% had SAT math scores over 700
34% had ACT scores over 30

Graduation and After
64% graduated in 4 years
18% graduated in 5 years
3% graduated in 6 years
34% pursued further study
76% had job offers within 6 months
1481 organizations recruited on campus

Financial Matters
$7975 resident tuition and fees (2003–04)
$24,777 nonresident tuition and fees (2003–04)
$6704 room and board
90% average percent of need met
$11,375 average financial aid amount received per undergraduate (2002–03)

Academics

Michigan awards bachelor's, master's, doctoral, and first-professional **degrees** and post-bachelor's and post-master's certificates. Challenging opportunities include advanced placement credit, accelerated degree programs, student-designed majors, an honors program, double majors, independent study, and a senior project. Special programs include cooperative education, internships, summer session for credit, off-campus study, study-abroad, and Army and Air Force ROTC.

The most frequently chosen **baccalaureate** fields are social sciences and history, engineering/engineering technologies, and psychology. A complete listing of majors at Michigan appears in the Majors Index beginning on page 460.

The **faculty** at Michigan has 2,225 full-time members, 91% with terminal degrees. The student-faculty ratio is 15:1.

Students of Michigan

The student body totals 39,031, of whom 24,517 are undergraduates. 51.2% are women and 48.8% are men. Students come from 54 states and territories and 87 other countries. 68% are from Michigan. 4.6% are international students. 8% are African American, 0.8% American Indian, 12.6% Asian American, and 4.8% Hispanic American. 96% returned for their sophomore year.

Facilities and Resources

Student rooms are linked to a campus network. 2,600 **computers** are available on campus that provide access to the Internet. The 21 **libraries** have 7,484,343 books and 69,849 subscriptions.

Campus Life

There are 900 active organizations on campus, including a drama/theater group, newspaper, radio station, television station, choral group, and marching band. 16% of eligible men and 15% of eligible women are members of national **fraternities**, national **sororities**, local fraternities, and local sororities.

Michigan is a member of the NCAA (Division I). **Intercollegiate sports** (some offering scholarships) include baseball (m), basketball, cheerleading (w), crew (w), cross-country running, field hockey (w), football (m), golf, gymnastics, ice hockey (m), soccer (w), softball (w), swimming, tennis, track and field, volleyball (w), water polo (w), wrestling (m).

Campus Safety

Student safety services include bicycle patrols, late-night transport/escort service, 24-hour emergency telephone alarm devices, 24-hour patrols by trained security personnel, student patrols, and electronically operated dormitory entrances.

Applying

Michigan requires an essay, SAT I or ACT, and a high school transcript, and in some cases SAT II Subject Tests, SAT II: Writing Test, an interview, and recommendations. Application deadline: 2/1; 4/30 for financial aid, with a 2/15 priority date. Deferred admission is possible.

University of Minnesota, Morris

SMALL-TOWN SETTING ■ PUBLIC ■ STATE-SUPPORTED ■ COED
MORRIS, MINNESOTA

Web site: www.mrs.umn.edu
Contact: Dr. James Mootz, Associate Vice Chancellor for Enrollment, 600
East 4th Street, Morris, MN 56267-2199
Telephone: 320-539-6035 or toll-free 800-992-8863 **Fax:** 320-589-1673
E-mail: admissions@mrs.umn.edu

Academics

UMM awards bachelor's **degrees**. Challenging opportunities include advanced placement credit, accelerated degree programs, student-designed majors, freshman honors
college, an honors program, double majors, and a senior project. Special programs
include internships, summer session for credit, off-campus study, and study-abroad.

The most frequently chosen **baccalaureate** fields are psychology, education, and
biological/life sciences. A complete listing of majors at UMM appears in the Majors
Index beginning on page 460.

The **faculty** at UMM has 132 members, 94% with terminal degrees. The student-
faculty ratio is 14:1.

Students of UMM

The student body is made up of 1,861 undergraduates. 60.1% are women and 39.9% are
men. Students come from 31 states and territories and 18 other countries. 83% are from
Minnesota. 1.1% are international students. 2.8% are African American, 7.2% American
Indian, 3.1% Asian American, and 1.5% Hispanic American. 83% returned for their
sophomore year.

Facilities and Resources

Student rooms are linked to a campus network. 133 **computers** are available on campus
that provide access to the Internet. The 2 **libraries** have 191,469 books and 9,042
subscriptions.

Campus Life

There are 91 active organizations on campus, including a drama/theater group,
newspaper, radio station, television station, and choral group. No national or local
fraternities or **sororities**.

UMM is a member of the NCAA (Division III). **Intercollegiate sports** include
baseball (m), basketball, cross-country running (w), football (m), golf, soccer (w), softball
(w), swimming (w), tennis, track and field, volleyball (w).

Campus Safety

Student safety services include late-night transport/escort service, 24-hour emergency
telephone alarm devices, 24-hour patrols by trained security personnel, and electronically operated dormitory entrances.

Applying

UMM requires an essay, SAT I or ACT, and a high school transcript, and in some cases
an interview. It recommends a minimum high school GPA of 3.0. Application deadline:
3/15; 3/1 priority date for financial aid. Early and deferred admission are possible.

Getting in Last Year

1,117 applied
83% were accepted
412 enrolled (45%)
40% from top tenth of their h.s. class
59% had SAT verbal scores over 600
46% had SAT math scores over 600
60% had ACT scores over 24
14% had SAT verbal scores over 700
6% had SAT math scores over 700
12% had ACT scores over 30
27 class presidents
31 valedictorians

Graduation and After

43% graduated in 4 years
17% graduated in 5 years
8% graduated in 6 years
30% pursued further study (13% arts and
sciences, 3% law, 2% education)
80% had job offers within 6 months
80 organizations recruited on campus

Financial Matters

$8096 resident tuition and fees (2003–04)
$8096 nonresident tuition and fees (2003–04)
$4800 room and board
81% average percent of need met
$9754 average financial aid amount received
per undergraduate (2002–03 estimated)

UNIVERSITY OF MINNESOTA, TWIN CITIES CAMPUS

URBAN SETTING ■ PUBLIC ■ STATE-SUPPORTED ■ COED
MINNEAPOLIS, MINNESOTA

Web site: www.umn.edu/tc
Contact: Ms. Patricia Jones Whyte, Associate Director of Admissions, 240 Williamson Hall, Minneapolis, MN 55455-0115
Telephone: 612-625-2008 or toll-free 800-752-1000 **Fax:** 612-626-1693
E-mail: admissions@tc.umn.edu

On this beautiful Big Ten campus in the heart of the Twin Cities of Minneapolis and St. Paul, the hallmarks are quality and opportunity. The quality of a U of M–Twin Cities education is a matter of record. So are the opportunities—more than 145 undergraduate majors, many nationally ranked; an Undergraduate Research Opportunities Program that is a national model; one of the largest study-abroad programs in the country; more than 500 student organizations; one of the country's biggest higher education library systems; and extraordinary opportunities for internships, employment, and personal enrichment in the culturally rich and thriving Twin Cities area.

Getting in Last Year
17,164 applied
76% were accepted
5,186 enrolled (40%)
33% from top tenth of their h.s. class
56% had SAT verbal scores over 600
61% had SAT math scores over 600
66% had ACT scores over 24
12% had SAT verbal scores over 700
18% had SAT math scores over 700
13% had ACT scores over 30
314 valedictorians

Graduation and After
28% graduated in 4 years
21% graduated in 5 years
6% graduated in 6 years

Financial Matters
$7116 resident tuition and fees (2003–04)
$18,746 nonresident tuition and fees (2003–04)
$6044 room and board
79% average percent of need met
$8496 average financial aid amount received per undergraduate (2002–03 estimated)

Academics
U of M-Twin Cities Campus awards bachelor's, master's, doctoral, and first-professional **degrees** and post-bachelor's and post-master's certificates. Challenging opportunities include advanced placement credit, accelerated degree programs, student-designed majors, freshman honors college, an honors program, double majors, independent study, and a senior project. Special programs include cooperative education, internships, summer session for credit, off-campus study, study-abroad, and Army, Navy and Air Force ROTC.

The most frequently chosen **baccalaureate** fields are social sciences and history, business/marketing, and engineering/engineering technologies. A complete listing of majors at U of M-Twin Cities Campus appears in the Majors Index beginning on page 460.

The **faculty** at U of M-Twin Cities Campus has 2,711 full-time members, 96% with terminal degrees. The student-faculty ratio is 22:1.

Students of U of M-Twin Cities Campus
The student body totals 49,474, of whom 32,474 are undergraduates. 52.8% are women and 47.2% are men. Students come from 55 states and territories and 85 other countries. 74% are from Minnesota. 2% are international students. 4.4% are African American, 0.6% American Indian, 9% Asian American, and 2% Hispanic American. 86% returned for their sophomore year.

Facilities and Resources
Student rooms are linked to a campus network. The 18 **libraries** have 5,700,000 books and 45,000 subscriptions.

Campus Life
There are 350 active organizations on campus, including a drama/theater group, newspaper, radio station, television station, choral group, and marching band. 3% of eligible men and 3% of eligible women are members of national **fraternities**, national **sororities**, and local sororities.

U of M-Twin Cities Campus is a member of the NCAA (Division I). **Intercollegiate sports** (some offering scholarships) include baseball (m), basketball, cross-country running, football (m), golf, gymnastics, ice hockey, soccer (w), softball (w), swimming, tennis, track and field, volleyball (w), wrestling (m).

Campus Safety
Student safety services include safety/security orientation, security lighting, late-night transport/escort service, 24-hour emergency telephone alarm devices, 24-hour patrols by trained security personnel, student patrols, and electronically operated dormitory entrances.

Applying
U of M-Twin Cities Campus requires SAT I or ACT and a high school transcript. It recommends a minimum high school GPA of 2.0. Application deadline: rolling admissions; 1/15 priority date for financial aid. Early and deferred admission are possible.

University of Mississippi

Small-town setting ■ Public ■ State-supported ■ Coed
University, Mississippi

Web site: www.olemiss.edu
Contact: Mr. Beckett Howorth, Director of Admissions, 145 Martindale Student Services Center, University, MS 38677
Telephone: 662-915-7226 or toll-free 800-653-6477 (in-state) **Fax:** 662-915-5869
E-mail: admissions@olemiss.edu

Academics

Ole Miss awards bachelor's, master's, doctoral, and first-professional **degrees**. Challenging opportunities include advanced placement credit, accelerated degree programs, freshman honors college, an honors program, double majors, independent study, and a senior project. Special programs include internships, summer session for credit, study-abroad, and Army and Air Force ROTC. A complete listing of majors at Ole Miss appears in the Majors Index beginning on page 460.

The student-faculty ratio is 19:1.

Students of Ole Miss

The student body totals 13,804, of whom 11,250 are undergraduates. 52.7% are women and 47.3% are men. Students come from 47 states and territories and 63 other countries. 68% are from Mississippi. 1% are international students. 12.8% are African American, 0.4% American Indian, 1.1% Asian American, and 0.5% Hispanic American. 77% returned for their sophomore year.

Facilities and Resources

Student rooms are linked to a campus network. 3,500 **computers** are available on campus for student use. The 4 **libraries** have 951,259 books and 8,495 subscriptions.

Campus Life

There are 200 active organizations on campus, including a drama/theater group, newspaper, radio station, television station, choral group, and marching band. 28% of eligible men and 35% of eligible women are members of national **fraternities** and national **sororities**.

Ole Miss is a member of the NCAA (Division I). **Intercollegiate sports** (some offering scholarships) include baseball (m), basketball, cross-country running, football (m), golf, riflery (w), soccer (w), softball (w), tennis, track and field, volleyball (w).

Campus Safety

Student safety services include crime prevention programs, late-night transport/escort service, 24-hour emergency telephone alarm devices, 24-hour patrols by trained security personnel, and electronically operated dormitory entrances.

Applying

Ole Miss requires a high school transcript and a minimum high school GPA of 2.0. It recommends SAT I or ACT. Application deadline: 7/20; 3/15 priority date for financial aid. Early admission is possible.

Getting in Last Year
6,601 applied
80% were accepted
2,380 enrolled (45%)
37% from top tenth of their h.s. class
3.34 average high school GPA
46% had ACT scores over 24
11% had ACT scores over 30
27 National Merit Scholars

Graduation and After
29% graduated in 4 years
15% graduated in 5 years
4% graduated in 6 years
245 organizations recruited on campus

Financial Matters
$3916 resident tuition and fees (2003–04)
$8826 nonresident tuition and fees (2003–04)
$5300 room and board
76% average percent of need met
$7374 average financial aid amount received per undergraduate (2001–02)

UNIVERSITY OF MISSOURI–COLUMBIA

SMALL-TOWN SETTING ■ PUBLIC ■ STATE-SUPPORTED ■ COED
COLUMBIA, MISSOURI

Web site: www.missouri.edu

Contact: Ms. Georgeanne Porter, Director of Admissions, 230 Jesse Hall, Columbia, MO 65211

Telephone: 573-882-7786 or toll-free 800-225-6075 (in-state) **Fax:** 573-882-7887

E-mail: mu4u@missouri.edu

Getting in Last Year
10,449 applied
89% were accepted
4,669 enrolled (50%)
29% from top tenth of their h.s. class
68% had ACT scores over 24
16% had ACT scores over 30
25 National Merit Scholars

Graduation and After
37% graduated in 4 years
26% graduated in 5 years
4% graduated in 6 years
1400 organizations recruited on campus

Financial Matters
$6558 resident tuition and fees (2003–04)
$16,005 nonresident tuition and fees (2003–04)
$5770 room and board
87% average percent of need met
$7544 average financial aid amount received per undergraduate (2002–03 estimated)

Academics

MU awards bachelor's, master's, doctoral, and first-professional **degrees** and post-master's certificates. Challenging opportunities include advanced placement credit, accelerated degree programs, student-designed majors, freshman honors college, an honors program, double majors, independent study, and a senior project. Special programs include cooperative education, internships, summer session for credit, off-campus study, study-abroad, and Army, Navy and Air Force ROTC.

The most frequently chosen **baccalaureate** fields are business/marketing, communications/communication technologies, and social sciences and history. A complete listing of majors at MU appears in the Majors Index beginning on page 460.

The **faculty** at MU has 1,487 full-time members, 94% with terminal degrees. The student-faculty ratio is 18:1.

Students of MU

The student body totals 26,805, of whom 20,441 are undergraduates. 51.6% are women and 48.4% are men. Students come from 51 states and territories and 85 other countries. 88% are from Missouri. 1.4% are international students. 5.6% are African American, 0.6% American Indian, 2.7% Asian American, and 1.5% Hispanic American. 84% returned for their sophomore year.

Facilities and Resources

Student rooms are linked to a campus network. 1,176 **computers** are available on campus that provide access to telephone registration and the Internet. The 12 **libraries** have 3,111,319 books and 16,073 subscriptions.

Campus Life

There are 442 active organizations on campus, including a drama/theater group, newspaper, radio station, television station, choral group, and marching band. 20% of eligible men and 25% of eligible women are members of national **fraternities** and national **sororities**.

MU is a member of the NCAA (Division I). **Intercollegiate sports** (some offering scholarships) include baseball (m), basketball, cross-country running, football (m), golf, gymnastics (w), soccer (w), softball (w), swimming, tennis (w), track and field, volleyball (w), wrestling (m).

Campus Safety

Student safety services include late-night transport/escort service, 24-hour emergency telephone alarm devices, 24-hour patrols by trained security personnel, and electronically operated dormitory entrances.

Applying

MU requires SAT I or ACT, a high school transcript, and specific high school curriculum. Application deadline: rolling admissions; 3/1 priority date for financial aid. Deferred admission is possible.

University of Missouri–Kansas City

Urban setting ■ Public ■ State-supported ■ Coed
Kansas City, Missouri

Web site: www.umkc.edu
Contact: Ms. Jennifer DeHaemers, Director of Admissions, Office of Admissions, 5100 Rockhill Road, Kansas City, MO 64110-2499
Telephone: 816-235-1111 or toll-free 800-775-8652 (out-of-state) **Fax:** 816-235-5544
E-mail: admit@umkc.edu

Academics
UMKC awards bachelor's, master's, doctoral, and first-professional **degrees** and post-master's and first-professional certificates. Challenging opportunities include advanced placement credit, accelerated degree programs, student-designed majors, an honors program, and a senior project. Special programs include cooperative education, internships, summer session for credit, off-campus study, study-abroad, and Army ROTC.

The most frequently chosen **baccalaureate** fields are liberal arts/general studies, business/marketing, and education. A complete listing of majors at UMKC appears in the Majors Index beginning on page 460.

The **faculty** at UMKC has 524 full-time members, 85% with terminal degrees. The student-faculty ratio is 9:1.

Students of UMKC
The student body totals 14,226, of whom 9,167 are undergraduates. 60.2% are women and 39.8% are men. Students come from 42 states and territories and 105 other countries. 77% are from Missouri. 4.5% are international students. 13.6% are African American, 1% American Indian, 5.3% Asian American, and 4.1% Hispanic American. 72% returned for their sophomore year.

Facilities and Resources
Student rooms are linked to a campus network. 400 **computers** are available on campus that provide access to the Internet. The 4 **libraries** have 1,241,084 books and 6,951 subscriptions.

Campus Life
There are 75 active organizations on campus, including a drama/theater group, newspaper, and choral group. 20% of eligible men and 17% of eligible women are members of national **fraternities**, national **sororities**, and local sororities.

UMKC is a member of the NCAA (Division I). **Intercollegiate sports** (some offering scholarships) include basketball, cheerleading (w), cross-country running, golf, riflery, soccer (m), softball (w), tennis, track and field, volleyball (w).

Campus Safety
Student safety services include late-night transport/escort service, 24-hour emergency telephone alarm devices, 24-hour patrols by trained security personnel, and electronically operated dormitory entrances.

Applying
UMKC requires ACT and a high school transcript. Application deadline: rolling admissions; 3/1 priority date for financial aid. Deferred admission is possible.

Getting in Last Year
1,884 applied
93% were accepted
785 enrolled (45%)
34% from top tenth of their h.s. class
52% had ACT scores over 24
12% had ACT scores over 30

Graduation and After
11% graduated in 4 years
24% graduated in 5 years
42% graduated in 6 years
85% had job offers within 6 months
320 organizations recruited on campus

Financial Matters
$6146 resident tuition and fees (2003–04)
$14,964 nonresident tuition and fees (2003–04)
$7270 room and board
64% average percent of need met
$11,547 average financial aid amount received per undergraduate

UNIVERSITY OF MISSOURI–ROLLA

SMALL-TOWN SETTING ■ PUBLIC ■ STATE-SUPPORTED ■ COED
ROLLA, MISSOURI

Web site: www.umr.edu

Contact: Ms. Lynn Stichnote, Director of Admissions, 106 Parker Hall, Rolla, MO 65409

Telephone: 573-341-4164 or toll-free 800-522-0938 **Fax:** 573-341-4082

E-mail: umrolla@umr.edu

Getting in Last Year

1,942 applied
90% were accepted
878 enrolled (50%)
40% from top tenth of their h.s. class
3.50 average high school GPA
85% had ACT scores over 24
32% had ACT scores over 30
44 National Merit Scholars
37 valedictorians

Graduation and After

15% graduated in 4 years
36% graduated in 5 years
9% graduated in 6 years
17% pursued further study
82% had job offers within 6 months
480 organizations recruited on campus

Financial Matters

$6839 resident tuition and fees (2003–04)
$16,286 nonresident tuition and fees (2003–04)
$5453 room and board
87% average percent of need met
$8203 average financial aid amount received per undergraduate (2001–02)

Academics

UMR awards bachelor's, master's, and doctoral **degrees** and post-bachelor's certificates. Challenging opportunities include advanced placement credit, accelerated degree programs, freshman honors college, an honors program, double majors, independent study, and a senior project. Special programs include cooperative education, internships, summer session for credit, off-campus study, study-abroad, and Army and Air Force ROTC.

The most frequently chosen **baccalaureate** fields are engineering/engineering technologies, computer/information sciences, and physical sciences. A complete listing of majors at UMR appears in the Majors Index beginning on page 460.

The **faculty** at UMR has 304 full-time members, 91% with terminal degrees. The student-faculty ratio is 14:1.

Students of UMR

The student body totals 5,459, of whom 4,089 are undergraduates. 23.5% are women and 76.5% are men. Students come from 45 states and territories and 34 other countries. 79% are from Missouri. 2.5% are international students. 4.6% are African American, 0.6% American Indian, 2.8% Asian American, and 2% Hispanic American. 83% returned for their sophomore year.

Facilities and Resources

Student rooms are linked to a campus network. 800 **computers** are available on campus that provide access to the Internet. The **library** has 255,768 books and 1,495 subscriptions.

Campus Life

There are 197 active organizations on campus, including a drama/theater group, newspaper, radio station, choral group, and marching band. 27% of eligible men and 24% of eligible women are members of national **fraternities**, national **sororities**, and local sororities.

UMR is a member of the NCAA (Division II). **Intercollegiate sports** (some offering scholarships) include baseball (m), basketball, cheerleading, cross-country running, football (m), soccer, softball (w), swimming (m), track and field.

Campus Safety

Student safety services include crime prevention programs, late-night transport/escort service, 24-hour emergency telephone alarm devices, 24-hour patrols by trained security personnel, student patrols, and electronically operated dormitory entrances.

Applying

UMR requires SAT I or ACT and a high school transcript. Application deadline: 7/1; 3/1 priority date for financial aid. Early and deferred admission are possible.

University of Nebraska–Lincoln

Urban setting ■ Public ■ State-supported ■ Coed
Lincoln, Nebraska

Web site: www.unl.edu
Contact: Pat McBride, Director, New Student Enrollment, 313 North 13th
Street, Ross Van Brunt Building, Lincoln, NE 68588-0256
Telephone: 402-472-8141 or toll-free 800-742-8800 **Fax:** 402-472-0670
E-mail: nuhusker@unl.edu

Academics

UNL awards associate, bachelor's, master's, doctoral, and first-professional **degrees** and post-master's certificates. Challenging opportunities include advanced placement credit, accelerated degree programs, student-designed majors, an honors program, double majors, and independent study. Special programs include cooperative education, internships, summer session for credit, off-campus study, study-abroad, and Army, Navy and Air Force ROTC.

The most frequently chosen **baccalaureate** fields are business/marketing, engineering/engineering technologies, and communications/communication technologies. A complete listing of majors at UNL appears in the Majors Index beginning on page 460.

The **faculty** at UNL has 1,010 full-time members, 96% with terminal degrees. The student-faculty ratio is 17:1.

Students of UNL

The student body totals 22,559, of whom 17,851 are undergraduates. 47.5% are women and 52.5% are men. Students come from 51 states and territories and 80 other countries. 88% are from Nebraska. 2.6% are international students. 2.2% are African American, 0.5% American Indian, 2.5% Asian American, and 2% Hispanic American. 80% returned for their sophomore year.

Facilities and Resources

Student rooms are linked to a campus network. 600 **computers** are available on campus that provide access to the Internet. The 11 **libraries** have 1,184,824 books and 21,309 subscriptions.

Campus Life

There are 335 active organizations on campus, including a drama/theater group, newspaper, radio station, choral group, and marching band. 14% of eligible men and 18% of eligible women are members of national **fraternities**, national **sororities**, local fraternities, and local sororities.

UNL is a member of the NCAA (Division I). **Intercollegiate sports** (some offering scholarships) include baseball (m), basketball, bowling, cheerleading, cross-country running, football (m), golf, gymnastics, riflery (w), soccer (w), softball (w), swimming (w), tennis, track and field, volleyball (w), wrestling (m).

Campus Safety

Student safety services include late-night transport/escort service, 24-hour emergency telephone alarm devices, 24-hour patrols by trained security personnel, student patrols, and electronically operated dormitory entrances.

Applying

UNL requires SAT I or ACT and a high school transcript, and in some cases rank in upper 50% of high school class. Application deadline: 6/30.

> The University of Nebraska–Lincoln is one of today's most dynamic universities. Over the past decade, the University has developed a national reputation for undergraduate education grounded in technology, research, innovation, and student engagement. Undergraduates have the opportunity to work with world-renowned researchers, dedicated professors, and accomplished peers. The University's residential campus embodies the traditional collegiate atmosphere, while providing immediate access to downtown Lincoln, the state capital of Nebraska. Nebraska's student body, a confluence of attitudes—rural and urban, artful and scientific—represents every state in the nation and many countries around the world.

Getting in Last Year

7,375 applied
76% were accepted
3,679 enrolled (66%)
25% from top tenth of their h.s. class
45% had SAT verbal scores over 600
51% had SAT math scores over 600
55% had ACT scores over 24
14% had SAT verbal scores over 700
16% had SAT math scores over 700
13% had ACT scores over 30
52 National Merit Scholars

Graduation and After

21% graduated in 4 years
31% graduated in 5 years
7% graduated in 6 years
300 organizations recruited on campus

Financial Matters

$4711 resident tuition and fees (2003–04)
$12,293 nonresident tuition and fees (2003–04)
$5204 room and board
84% average percent of need met
$6334 average financial aid amount received per undergraduate (2002–03 estimated)

THE UNIVERSITY OF NORTH CAROLINA AT ASHEVILLE

SUBURBAN SETTING ■ PUBLIC ■ STATE-SUPPORTED ■ COED
ASHEVILLE, NORTH CAROLINA

Web site: www.unca.edu

Contact: Mr. Scot Schaeffer, Director of Admissions and Financial Aid, 117 Lipinsky Hall, CPO 2210, One University Heights, Asheville, NC 28804-8510

Telephone: 828-251-6481 or toll-free 800-531-9842 **Fax:** 828-251-6482

E-mail: admissions@unca.edu

Getting in Last Year

2,293 applied
73% were accepted
599 enrolled (36%)
21% from top tenth of their h.s. class
3.70 average high school GPA
38% had SAT verbal scores over 600
38% had SAT math scores over 600
58% had ACT scores over 24
5% had SAT verbal scores over 700
3% had SAT math scores over 700
9% had ACT scores over 30
7 valedictorians

Graduation and After

29% graduated in 4 years
18% graduated in 5 years
4% graduated in 6 years
21% pursued further study
73% had job offers within 6 months
137 organizations recruited on campus

Financial Matters

$3101 resident tuition and fees (2003–04)
$11,926 nonresident tuition and fees (2003–04)
$4978 room and board
83% average percent of need met
$7758 average financial aid amount received per undergraduate (2002–03)

Academics

UNC Asheville awards bachelor's and master's **degrees** and post-bachelor's certificates. Challenging opportunities include advanced placement credit, student-designed majors, an honors program, double majors, independent study, and a senior project. Special programs include internships, summer session for credit, off-campus study, and study-abroad.

The most frequently chosen **baccalaureate** fields are social sciences and history, psychology, and business/marketing. A complete listing of majors at UNC Asheville appears in the Majors Index beginning on page 460.

The **faculty** at UNC Asheville has 177 full-time members, 88% with terminal degrees. The student-faculty ratio is 13:1.

Students of UNC Asheville

The student body totals 3,446, of whom 3,410 are undergraduates. 57.4% are women and 42.6% are men. Students come from 40 states and territories and 24 other countries. 87% are from North Carolina. 1.1% are international students. 2.4% are African American, 0.4% American Indian, 1.5% Asian American, and 1.7% Hispanic American. 78% returned for their sophomore year.

Facilities and Resources

Student rooms are linked to a campus network. 350 **computers** are available on campus that provide access to online grade reports and the Internet. The **library** has 254,179 books and 2,014 subscriptions.

Campus Life

There are 66 active organizations on campus, including a drama/theater group, newspaper, radio station, and choral group. 4% of eligible men and 3% of eligible women are members of national **fraternities** and national **sororities**.

UNC Asheville is a member of the NCAA (Division I). **Intercollegiate sports** (some offering scholarships) include baseball (m), basketball, cheerleading, cross-country running, soccer, tennis, track and field, volleyball (w).

Campus Safety

Student safety services include dorm entrances secured at night, late-night transport/escort service, 24-hour emergency telephone alarm devices, and 24-hour patrols by trained security personnel.

Applying

UNC Asheville requires SAT I or ACT and a high school transcript, and in some cases an interview. It recommends an essay and a minimum high school GPA of 3.0. Application deadline: 3/12; 3/1 priority date for financial aid. Deferred admission is possible.

THE UNIVERSITY OF NORTH CAROLINA AT CHAPEL HILL

SUBURBAN SETTING ■ PUBLIC ■ STATE-SUPPORTED ■ COED
CHAPEL HILL, NORTH CAROLINA

Web site: www.unc.edu
Contact: Mr. Jerome A. Lucido, Vice Provost and Director of Undergraduate Admissions, Campus Box # 2200, Jackson Hall, Chapel Hill, NC 27599-2200
Telephone: 919-966-3621 **Fax:** 919-962-3045
E-mail: uadm@email.unc.edu

Academics

UNC Chapel Hill awards bachelor's, master's, doctoral, and first-professional **degrees** and post-master's certificates. Challenging opportunities include advanced placement credit, student-designed majors, freshman honors college, an honors program, double majors, and independent study. Special programs include internships, summer session for credit, off-campus study, study-abroad, and Army, Navy and Air Force ROTC.

The most frequently chosen **baccalaureate** fields are communications/communication technologies, social sciences and history, and business/marketing. A complete listing of majors at UNC Chapel Hill appears in the Majors Index beginning on page 460.

The **faculty** at UNC Chapel Hill has 1,296 full-time members, 84% with terminal degrees. The student-faculty ratio is 14:1.

Students of UNC Chapel Hill

The student body totals 26,359, of whom 16,144 are undergraduates. 58.8% are women and 41.2% are men. Students come from 54 states and territories and 105 other countries. 82% are from North Carolina. 1.2% are international students. 11.1% are African American, 0.8% American Indian, 5.9% Asian American, and 2.3% Hispanic American. 95% returned for their sophomore year.

Facilities and Resources

Student rooms are linked to a campus network. 600 **computers** are available on campus that provide access to online grade reports and the Internet. The 15 **libraries** have 2,573,328 books and 42,635 subscriptions.

Campus Life

There are 565 active organizations on campus, including a drama/theater group, newspaper, radio station, television station, choral group, and marching band. UNC Chapel Hill has national **fraternities**, national **sororities**, local fraternities, and local sororities.

UNC Chapel Hill is a member of the NCAA (Division I). **Intercollegiate sports** (some offering scholarships) include baseball (m), basketball, crew (w), cross-country running, fencing, field hockey (w), football (m), golf, gymnastics (w), lacrosse, soccer, softball (w), swimming, tennis, track and field, volleyball (w), wrestling (m).

Campus Safety

Student safety services include crime prevention programs, late-night transport/escort service, 24-hour emergency telephone alarm devices, 24-hour patrols by trained security personnel, student patrols, and electronically operated dormitory entrances.

Applying

UNC Chapel Hill requires an essay, SAT I or ACT, a high school transcript, 1 recommendation, and counselor's statement. Application deadline: 1/15; 3/1 priority date for financial aid. Deferred admission is possible.

Getting in Last Year

17,591 applied
37% were accepted
3,516 enrolled (55%)
70% from top tenth of their h.s. class
72% had SAT verbal scores over 600
78% had SAT math scores over 600
83% had ACT scores over 24
21% had SAT verbal scores over 700
26% had SAT math scores over 700
26% had ACT scores over 30
136 National Merit Scholars
183 valedictorians

Graduation and After

67% graduated in 4 years
12% graduated in 5 years
2% graduated in 6 years
26% pursued further study
55.8% had job offers within 6 months
703 organizations recruited on campus

Financial Matters

$4072 resident tuition and fees (2003–04)
$15,920 nonresident tuition and fees (2003–04)
$6045 room and board
100% average percent of need met
$8983 average financial aid amount received per undergraduate (2002–03)

UNIVERSITY OF NOTRE DAME

SUBURBAN SETTING ■ PRIVATE ■ INDEPENDENT RELIGIOUS ■ COED
NOTRE DAME, INDIANA

Getting in Last Year
12,095 applied
29% were accepted
1,996 enrolled (57%)
83% from top tenth of their h.s. class
84% had SAT verbal scores over 600
90% had SAT math scores over 600
97% had ACT scores over 24
39% had SAT verbal scores over 700
51% had SAT math scores over 700
78% had ACT scores over 30
65 National Merit Scholars
180 class presidents
226 valedictorians

Graduation and After
37% pursued further study (8% arts and sciences, 8% medicine, 8% law)
69% had job offers within 6 months
718 organizations recruited on campus

Financial Matters
$27,612 tuition and fees (2003–04)
$6930 room and board
100% average percent of need met
$23,432 average financial aid amount received per undergraduate (2002–03 estimated)

Web site: www.nd.edu
Contact: Mr. Daniel J. Saracino, Assistant Provost for Admissions, 220 Main Building, Notre Dame, IN 46556-5612
Telephone: 574-631-7505 **Fax:** 574-631-8865
E-mail: admissio.1@nd.edu

Academics

Notre Dame awards bachelor's, master's, doctoral, and first-professional **degrees**. Challenging opportunities include advanced placement credit, accelerated degree programs, student-designed majors, an honors program, double majors, independent study, and a senior project. Special programs include cooperative education, internships, summer session for credit, off-campus study, study-abroad, and Army, Navy and Air Force ROTC.

The most frequently chosen **baccalaureate** fields are business/marketing, social sciences and history, and engineering/engineering technologies. A complete listing of majors at Notre Dame appears in the Majors Index beginning on page 460.

Students of Notre Dame

The student body totals 11,415, of whom 8,311 are undergraduates. 46.6% are women and 53.4% are men. Students come from 54 states and territories and 65 other countries. 13% are from Indiana. 3.6% are international students. 3.6% are African American, 0.6% American Indian, 4.9% Asian American, and 7.8% Hispanic American.

Facilities and Resources

Student rooms are linked to a campus network. 880 **computers** are available on campus that provide access to the Internet. The 10 **libraries** have 2,673,446 books and 19,232 subscriptions.

Campus Life

There are 263 active organizations on campus, including a drama/theater group, newspaper, radio station, choral group, and marching band. No national or local **fraternities** or **sororities**.

Notre Dame is a member of the NCAA (Division I). **Intercollegiate sports** (some offering scholarships) include baseball (m), basketball, crew (w), cross-country running, fencing, football (m), golf, ice hockey (m), lacrosse, soccer, softball (w), swimming, tennis, track and field, volleyball (w).

Campus Safety

Student safety services include crime prevention and personal safety workshops, full time trained police investigators, sprinkler fire suppression in all residence hal, late-night transport/escort service, 24-hour emergency telephone alarm devices, 24-hour patrols by trained security personnel, student patrols, and electronically operated dormitory entrances.

Applying

Notre Dame requires an essay, SAT I or ACT, a high school transcript, and 1 recommendation. Application deadline: 1/9; 2/15 for financial aid. Deferred admission is possible.

UNIVERSITY OF OKLAHOMA
SUBURBAN SETTING ■ PUBLIC ■ STATE-SUPPORTED ■ COED
NORMAN, OKLAHOMA

Web site: www.ou.edu
Contact: Ms. Karen Renfroe, Executive Director of Recruitment Services, 1000 Asp Avenue, Norman, OK 73019
Telephone: 405-325-2151 or toll-free 800-234-6868 **Fax:** 405-325-7124
E-mail: admrec@ou.edu

Academics
OU awards bachelor's, master's, doctoral, and first-professional **degrees** and post-master's certificates. Challenging opportunities include advanced placement credit, accelerated degree programs, student-designed majors, freshman honors college, an honors program, double majors, independent study, and a senior project. Special programs include cooperative education, internships, summer session for credit, off-campus study, study-abroad, and Army and Air Force ROTC.

The most frequently chosen **baccalaureate** fields are business/marketing, communications/communication technologies, and social sciences and history. A complete listing of majors at OU appears in the Majors Index beginning on page 460.

The **faculty** at OU has 971 full-time members, 88% with terminal degrees. The student-faculty ratio is 21:1.

Students of OU
The student body totals 24,483, of whom 20,254 are undergraduates. 49.3% are women and 50.7% are men. Students come from 50 states and territories and 85 other countries. 81% are from Oklahoma. 2.6% are international students. 5.8% are African American, 7.5% American Indian, 5.3% Asian American, and 3.9% Hispanic American. 83% returned for their sophomore year.

Facilities and Resources
Student rooms are linked to a campus network. 2,187 **computers** are available on campus that provide access to the Internet. The 9 **libraries** have 3,951,370 books and 26,696 subscriptions.

Campus Life
There are 300 active organizations on campus, including a drama/theater group, newspaper, radio station, television station, choral group, and marching band. 17% of eligible men and 25% of eligible women are members of national **fraternities**, national **sororities**, local sororities, and international social clubs.

OU is a member of the NCAA (Division I). **Intercollegiate sports** (some offering scholarships) include baseball (m), basketball, cross-country running, football (m), golf, gymnastics, soccer (w), softball (w), tennis, track and field, volleyball (w), wrestling (m).

Campus Safety
Student safety services include crime prevention programs, police bicycle patrols, self-defense classes, late-night transport/escort service, 24-hour emergency telephone alarm devices, 24-hour patrols by trained security personnel, student patrols, and electronically operated dormitory entrances.

Applying
OU requires SAT I or ACT, a high school transcript, and a minimum high school GPA of 3.0, and in some cases an essay. Application deadline: 6/1.

The University of Oklahoma is becoming a passenger for public higher education in the United States. Many of the brightest and best select OU, including students from all 50 states and more than 100 foreign countries. OU one of the top two public universities in the nation in the number of National Merit Scholars enrolled per capita. OU students are taught and mentored by a world-renowned faculty and have numerous opportunities to hear from some of the world's most influential policy makers. Diversity and a commitment to a sense of family and community are hallmarks of Oklahoma's flagship university.

Getting in Last Year
8,140 applied
82% were accepted
3,808 enrolled (57%)
36% from top tenth of their h.s. class
3.59 average high school GPA
76% had ACT scores over 24
17% had ACT scores over 30
170 National Merit Scholars
302 valedictorians

Graduation and After
19% graduated in 4 years
25% graduated in 5 years
10% graduated in 6 years
381 organizations recruited on campus

Financial Matters
$3741 resident tuition and fees (2003–04)
$10,254 nonresident tuition and fees (2003–04)
$5485 room and board
88% average percent of need met
$7635 average financial aid amount received per undergraduate (2001–02)

UNIVERSITY OF PENNSYLVANIA

URBAN SETTING ■ PRIVATE ■ INDEPENDENT ■ COED
PHILADELPHIA, PENNSYLVANIA

Web site: www.upenn.edu
Contact: Mr. Willis J. Stetson Jr., Dean of Admissions, 1 College Hall, Levy
Park, Philadelphia, PA 19104
Telephone: 215-898-7507

Getting in Last Year

18,831 applied
20% were accepted
2,419 enrolled (63%)
93% from top tenth of their h.s. class
3.84 average high school GPA
93% had SAT verbal scores over 600
96% had SAT math scores over 600
97% had ACT scores over 24
51% had SAT verbal scores over 700
65% had SAT math scores over 700
63% had ACT scores over 30
80 National Merit Scholars
77 class presidents
250 valedictorians

Graduation and After

79% graduated in 4 years
11% graduated in 5 years
2% graduated in 6 years
23% pursued further study (7% law, 5% arts
and sciences, 4% medicine)
60% had job offers within 6 months
450 organizations recruited on campus

Financial Matters

$29,318 tuition and fees (2003–04)
$8642 room and board
100% average percent of need met
$23,875 average financial aid amount received
per undergraduate (2001–02)

Academics

Penn awards associate, bachelor's, master's, doctoral, and first-professional **degrees** and
post-bachelor's, post-master's, and first-professional certificates (also offers evening
program with significant enrollment not reflected in profile). Challenging opportunities
include advanced placement credit, accelerated degree programs, student-designed
majors, an honors program, double majors, independent study, and a senior project.
Special programs include internships, summer session for credit, off-campus study,
study-abroad, and Army, Navy and Air Force ROTC.

The most frequently chosen **baccalaureate** fields are social sciences and history,
business/marketing, and engineering/engineering technologies. A complete listing of
majors at Penn appears in the Majors Index beginning on page 460.

The **faculty** at Penn has 1,382 full-time members, 100% with terminal degrees. The
student-faculty ratio is 6:1.

Students of Penn

The student body totals 19,428, of whom 9,836 are undergraduates. 50.4% are women
and 49.6% are men. Students come from 54 states and territories and 109 other
countries. 19% are from Pennsylvania. 11.8% are international students. 5.9% are
African American, 0.3% American Indian, 16.4% Asian American, and 5.4% Hispanic
American. 97% returned for their sophomore year.

Facilities and Resources

Student rooms are linked to a campus network. 1,575 **computers** are available on
campus that provide access to the Internet. The 14 **libraries** have 5,152,960 books and
40,840 subscriptions.

Campus Life

There are 384 active organizations on campus, including a drama/theater group,
newspaper, radio station, television station, choral group, and marching band. 23% of
eligible men and 16% of eligible women are members of national **fraternities** and
national **sororities**.

Penn is a member of the NCAA (Division I). **Intercollegiate sports** include baseball
(m), basketball, crew, cross-country running, fencing, field hockey (w), football (m), golf,
gymnastics (w), lacrosse, soccer, softball (w), squash, swimming, tennis, track and field,
volleyball (w), wrestling (m).

Campus Safety

Student safety services include late-night transport/escort service, 24-hour emergency
telephone alarm devices, 24-hour patrols by trained security personnel, student patrols,
and electronically operated dormitory entrances.

Applying

Penn requires an essay, SAT II: Writing Test, SAT I and SAT II or ACT, a high school
transcript, and 2 recommendations. Application deadline: 1/1; 2/15 priority date for
financial aid. Early and deferred admission are possible.

UNIVERSITY OF PITTSBURGH

URBAN SETTING ■ PUBLIC ■ STATE-RELATED ■ COED
PITTSBURGH, PENNSYLVANIA

Web site: www.pitt.edu
Contact: Dr. Betsy A. Porter, Director of Office of Admissions and Financial Aid, 4227 Fifth Avenue, First Floor, Alumni Hall, Pittsburgh, PA 15213
Telephone: 412-624-7488 **Fax:** 412-648-8815
E-mail: oafa@pitt.edu

Academics

Pitt awards bachelor's, master's, doctoral, and first-professional **degrees** and post-bachelor's and post-master's certificates. Challenging opportunities include advanced placement credit, student-designed majors, freshman honors college, an honors program, double majors, independent study, and a senior project. Special programs include cooperative education, internships, summer session for credit, off-campus study, study-abroad, and Army, Navy and Air Force ROTC.

The most frequently chosen **baccalaureate** fields are business/marketing, social sciences and history, and English. A complete listing of majors at Pitt appears in the Majors Index beginning on page 460.

The **faculty** at Pitt has 1,439 full-time members, 92% with terminal degrees. The student-faculty ratio is 17:1.

Students of Pitt

The student body totals 26,795, of whom 17,413 are undergraduates. 52.4% are women and 47.6% are men. Students come from 53 states and territories. 86% are from Pennsylvania. 0.8% are international students. 9.4% are African American, 0.2% American Indian, 3.9% Asian American, and 1% Hispanic American. 88% returned for their sophomore year.

Facilities and Resources

Student rooms are linked to a campus network. 600 **computers** are available on campus that provide access to online class listings and the Internet. The 27 **libraries** have 3,551,548 books and 22,058 subscriptions.

Campus Life

There are 300 active organizations on campus, including a drama/theater group, newspaper, radio station, television station, choral group, and marching band. Pitt has national **fraternities** and national **sororities**.

Pitt is a member of the NCAA (Division I). **Intercollegiate sports** (some offering scholarships) include baseball (m), basketball, cross-country running, football (m), gymnastics (w), soccer, softball (w), swimming, tennis (w), track and field, volleyball (w), wrestling (m).

Campus Safety

Student safety services include on-call van transportation, late-night transport/escort service, 24-hour emergency telephone alarm devices, 24-hour patrols by trained security personnel, and electronically operated dormitory entrances.

Applying

Pitt requires SAT I or ACT and a high school transcript. It recommends an essay, SAT I, an interview, and recommendations. Application deadline: rolling admissions; 3/1 priority date for financial aid. Early and deferred admission are possible.

Getting in Last Year

17,332 applied
49% were accepted
2,964 enrolled (35%)
48% had SAT verbal scores over 600
56% had SAT math scores over 600
75% had ACT scores over 24
10% had SAT verbal scores over 700
12% had SAT math scores over 700
17% had ACT scores over 30
76 valedictorians

Graduation and After

35% graduated in 4 years
21% graduated in 5 years
4% graduated in 6 years
40% pursued further study (8% education, 6% arts and sciences, 5% business)

Financial Matters

$9274 resident tuition and fees (2003–04)
$18,586 nonresident tuition and fees (2003–04)
$6800 room and board
86% average percent of need met
$10,798 average financial aid amount received per undergraduate (2002–03 estimated)

UNIVERSITY OF PORTLAND

URBAN SETTING ■ PRIVATE ■ INDEPENDENT RELIGIOUS ■ COED
PORTLAND, OREGON

Web site: www.up.edu

Contact: Mr. James C. Lyons, Dean of Admissions, 5000 North Willamette Boulevard, Portland, OR 97203

Telephone: 503-943-7147 or toll-free 888-627-5601 (out-of-state) **Fax:** 503-943-7315

E-mail: admissio@up.edu

Getting in Last Year

2,964 applied
72% were accepted
674 enrolled (32%)
41% from top tenth of their h.s. class
3.62 average high school GPA
47% had SAT verbal scores over 600
47% had SAT math scores over 600
8% had SAT verbal scores over 700
8% had SAT math scores over 700

Graduation and After

56% graduated in 4 years
9% graduated in 5 years
1% graduated in 6 years
163 organizations recruited on campus

Financial Matters

$22,140 tuition and fees (2003–04)
$6670 room and board
83% average percent of need met
$19,304 average financial aid amount received per undergraduate

Academics

U of P awards bachelor's and master's **degrees** and post-master's certificates. Challenging opportunities include advanced placement credit, an honors program, double majors, independent study, and a senior project. Special programs include internships, summer session for credit, off-campus study, study-abroad, and Army and Air Force ROTC.

The most frequently chosen **baccalaureate** fields are business/marketing, health professions and related sciences, and engineering/engineering technologies. A complete listing of majors at U of P appears in the Majors Index beginning on page 460.

The **faculty** at U of P has 175 full-time members, 90% with terminal degrees. The student-faculty ratio is 13:1.

Students of U of P

The student body totals 3,263, of whom 2,739 are undergraduates. 59.6% are women and 40.4% are men. Students come from 42 states and territories and 19 other countries. 44% are from Oregon. 2.1% are international students. 1.7% are African American, 0.4% American Indian, 9.7% Asian American, and 3.2% Hispanic American. 84% returned for their sophomore year.

Facilities and Resources

Student rooms are linked to a campus network. 200 **computers** are available on campus that provide access to the Internet. The 2 **libraries** have 350,000 books and 1,400 subscriptions.

Campus Life

There are 40 active organizations on campus, including a drama/theater group, newspaper, radio station, and choral group. No national or local **fraternities** or **sororities**.

U of P is a member of the NCAA (Division I). **Intercollegiate sports** (some offering scholarships) include baseball (m), basketball, cross-country running, golf, soccer, tennis, track and field, volleyball (w).

Campus Safety

Student safety services include late-night transport/escort service, 24-hour patrols by trained security personnel, student patrols, and electronically operated dormitory entrances.

Applying

U of P requires an essay, SAT I or ACT, a high school transcript, and 1 recommendation. Application deadline: 6/1; 3/1 priority date for financial aid. Deferred admission is possible.

UNIVERSITY OF PUGET SOUND

SUBURBAN SETTING ■ PRIVATE ■ INDEPENDENT ■ COED
TACOMA, WASHINGTON

Web site: www.ups.edu
Contact: Dr. George H. Mills Jr., Vice President for Enrollment, 1500 North Warner Street, Tacoma, WA 98416-1062
Telephone: 253-879-3211 or toll-free 800-396-7191 **Fax:** 253-879-3993
E-mail: admission@ups.edu

Academics

Puget Sound awards bachelor's, master's, and first-professional **degrees** and post-master's certificates. Challenging opportunities include advanced placement credit, student-designed majors, an honors program, double majors, independent study, and a senior project. Special programs include cooperative education, internships, summer session for credit, study-abroad, and Army ROTC.

The most frequently chosen **baccalaureate** fields are social sciences and history, business/marketing, and biological/life sciences. A complete listing of majors at Puget Sound appears in the Majors Index beginning on page 460.

The **faculty** at Puget Sound has 214 full-time members, 86% with terminal degrees. The student-faculty ratio is 11:1.

Students of Puget Sound

The student body totals 2,760, of whom 2,516 are undergraduates. 58.9% are women and 41.1% are men. Students come from 46 states and territories and 14 other countries. 29% are from Washington. 0.9% are international students. 2.2% are African American, 1.2% American Indian, 9.4% Asian American, and 3.1% Hispanic American. 85% returned for their sophomore year.

Facilities and Resources

Student rooms are linked to a campus network. 304 **computers** are available on campus that provide access to financial aid, admission, student employment and the Internet. The **library** has 343,787 books and 5,609 subscriptions.

Campus Life

There are 65 active organizations on campus, including a drama/theater group, newspaper, radio station, and choral group. 18% of eligible men and 21% of eligible women are members of national **fraternities**, national **sororities**, and theme houses.

Puget Sound is a member of the NCAA (Division III). **Intercollegiate sports** include baseball (m), basketball, cheerleading, crew, cross-country running, football (m), golf, lacrosse (w), skiing (downhill), soccer, softball (w), swimming, tennis, track and field, volleyball (w).

Campus Safety

Student safety services include 24-hour locked residence hall entrances, late-night transport/escort service, 24-hour emergency telephone alarm devices, 24-hour patrols by trained security personnel, student patrols, and electronically operated dormitory entrances.

Applying

Puget Sound requires an essay, SAT I or ACT, a high school transcript, and 2 recommendations. It recommends an interview and a minimum high school GPA of 3.0. Application deadline: 5/1; 2/1 for financial aid. Early and deferred admission are possible.

Getting in Last Year

4,237 applied
71% were accepted
641 enrolled (21%)
39% from top tenth of their h.s. class
3.53 average high school GPA
66% had SAT verbal scores over 600
60% had SAT math scores over 600
81% had ACT scores over 24
19% had SAT verbal scores over 700
14% had SAT math scores over 700
17% had ACT scores over 30
47 National Merit Scholars
41 valedictorians

Graduation and After

67% graduated in 4 years
9% graduated in 5 years
1% graduated in 6 years
34% pursued further study (13% arts and sciences, 10% education, 4% law)
70% had job offers within 6 months
150 organizations recruited on campus

Financial Matters

$25,360 tuition and fees (2003–04)
$6400 room and board
88% average percent of need met
$18,963 average financial aid amount received per undergraduate (2002–03 estimated)

UNIVERSITY OF REDLANDS

SMALL-TOWN SETTING ■ PRIVATE ■ INDEPENDENT ■ COED
REDLANDS, CALIFORNIA

Web site: www.redlands.edu
Contact: Mr. Paul Driscoll, Dean of Admissions, PO Box 3080, Redlands, CA 92373-0999
Telephone: 909-335-4074 or toll-free 800-455-5064 **Fax:** 909-335-4089
E-mail: admissions@redlands.edu

A t the University of Redlands, students explore connections, blurring the barriers often artificially imposed between academic disciplines, between the classroom and the real world, and between their own views and the way others see things. Academics are combined with a community-based residential life and a range of opportunities to gain firsthand experience through internships, international study, and original faculty-directed research. Students take ownership of their education with the active support of professors who are truly committed to student participation in the learning process; they coax, challenge, captivate, support, nourish, and actively engage students in an exchange of stimulating and provocative ideas.

Academics

Redlands awards bachelor's and master's **degrees** and post-bachelor's and post-master's certificates. Challenging opportunities include advanced placement credit, student-designed majors, freshman honors college, an honors program, double majors, independent study, and a senior project. Special programs include internships, off-campus study, and study-abroad.

The most frequently chosen **baccalaureate** fields are liberal arts/general studies, social sciences and history, and business/marketing. A complete listing of majors at Redlands appears in the Majors Index beginning on page 460.

The **faculty** at Redlands has 156 full-time members, 86% with terminal degrees. The student-faculty ratio is 12:1.

Students of Redlands

The student body totals 2,311, of whom 2,223 are undergraduates. 58.8% are women and 41.2% are men. Students come from 42 states and territories and 10 other countries. 73% are from California. 0.9% are international students. 2.2% are African American, 0.7% American Indian, 5.4% Asian American, and 11.9% Hispanic American. 86% returned for their sophomore year.

Facilities and Resources

Student rooms are linked to a campus network. 563 **computers** are available on campus that provide access to the Internet. The **library** has 251,053 books and 7,786 subscriptions.

Campus Life

There are 105 active organizations on campus, including a drama/theater group, newspaper, and choral group. 10% of eligible men and 13% of eligible women are members of local **fraternities** and local **sororities**.

Redlands is a member of the NCAA (Division III). **Intercollegiate sports** include baseball (m), basketball, cross-country running, football (m), golf (m), lacrosse (w), soccer, softball (w), swimming, tennis, track and field, volleyball (w), water polo.

Campus Safety

Student safety services include safety whistles, late-night transport/escort service, 24-hour emergency telephone alarm devices, 24-hour patrols by trained security personnel, student patrols, and electronically operated dormitory entrances.

Applying

Redlands requires an essay, SAT I or ACT, a high school transcript, and 2 recommendations. It recommends an interview. Application deadline: 12/15; 2/15 priority date for financial aid. Deferred admission is possible.

Getting in Last Year
2,669 applied
71% were accepted
574 enrolled (30%)
22% from top tenth of their h.s. class
3.52 average high school GPA
39% had SAT verbal scores over 600
38% had SAT math scores over 600
56% had ACT scores over 24
5% had SAT verbal scores over 700
6% had SAT math scores over 700
8% had ACT scores over 30
4 National Merit Scholars

Graduation and After
57% graduated in 4 years
4% graduated in 5 years
1% graduated in 6 years
50% had job offers within 6 months
5 organizations recruited on campus

Financial Matters
$24,096 tuition and fees (2003–04)
$8478 room and board
91% average percent of need met
$22,020 average financial aid amount received per undergraduate (2002–03 estimated)

UNIVERSITY OF RHODE ISLAND

SMALL-TOWN SETTING ■ PUBLIC ■ STATE-SUPPORTED ■ COED
KINGSTON, RHODE ISLAND

Web site: www.uri.edu
Contact: Ms. Catherine Zeiser, Assistant Dean of Admissions, 8 Ranger Road,
   Suite 1, Kingston, RI 02881-2020
Telephone: 401-874-7100 **Fax:** 401-874-5523
E-mail: uriadmit@etal.uri.edu

Academics

Rhode Island awards bachelor's, master's, doctoral, and first-professional **degrees** and
post-bachelor's certificates. Challenging opportunities include advanced placement
credit, accelerated degree programs, student-designed majors, an honors program,
double majors, independent study, and a senior project. Special programs include
cooperative education, internships, summer session for credit, off-campus study, study-
abroad, and Army ROTC.

The most frequently chosen **baccalaureate** fields are business/marketing, com-
munications/communication technologies, and personal/miscellaneous services. A
complete listing of majors at Rhode Island appears in the Majors Index beginning on
page 460.

The **faculty** at Rhode Island has 651 full-time members, 90% with terminal degrees.
The student-faculty ratio is 19:1.

Students of Rhode Island

The student body totals 14,791, of whom 11,298 are undergraduates. 56.5% are women
and 43.5% are men. Students come from 38 states and territories and 47 other countries.
61% are from Rhode Island. 0.3% are international students. 4.4% are African
American, 0.4% American Indian, 2.9% Asian American, and 4.2% Hispanic American.
80% returned for their sophomore year.

Facilities and Resources

552 **computers** are available on campus for student use. The 2 **libraries** have 1,205,138
books and 7,926 subscriptions.

Campus Life

There are 85 active organizations on campus, including a drama/theater group,
newspaper, radio station, television station, choral group, and marching band. 10% of
eligible men and 13% of eligible women are members of national **fraternities**, national
sororities, and local sororities.

Rhode Island is a member of the NCAA (Division I). **Intercollegiate sports** (some
offering scholarships) include baseball (m), basketball, crew (w), cross-country running,
field hockey (w), football (m), golf (m), gymnastics (w), soccer, softball (w), swimming,
tennis, track and field, volleyball (w).

Campus Safety

Student safety services include late-night transport/escort service, 24-hour emergency
telephone alarm devices, 24-hour patrols by trained security personnel, student patrols,
and electronically operated dormitory entrances.

Applying

Rhode Island requires SAT I or ACT and a high school transcript, and in some cases a
minimum high school GPA of 3.0. It recommends an interview, recommendations, and a
minimum high school GPA of 3.0. Application deadline: 2/1; 3/1 priority date for
financial aid. Early admission is possible.

O utstanding freshman
candidates with strong
academic credentials are
eligible to be considered for a
Centennial Scholarship, ranging up to
full tuition. These scholarships are
based on the student's total
academic profile, including rank in
class and standardized test scores.
They are renewable each semester if
the student maintains continuous
full-time enrollment and a minimum
3.0 average. Eligibility requires a
completed admissions application
received by the December 15 early
action deadline. Applications and
information received after that date
are not considered. If a student's
residency changes from out-of-state
to in-state, the Centennial award is
reduced because of the change in
tuition charged.

Getting in Last Year
12,963 applied
70% were accepted
2,590 enrolled (29%)
19% from top tenth of their h.s. class
25% had SAT verbal scores over 600
32% had SAT math scores over 600
3% had SAT verbal scores over 700
4% had SAT math scores over 700

Graduation and After
33% graduated in 4 years
19% graduated in 5 years
6% graduated in 6 years
155 organizations recruited on campus

Financial Matters
$6202 resident tuition and fees (2003–04)
$16,334 nonresident tuition and fees (2003–
   04)
$7518 room and board
68% average percent of need met
$8965 average financial aid amount received
   per undergraduate (2002–03 estimated)

SUBURBAN SETTING ■ PRIVATE ■ INDEPENDENT ■ COED
UNIVERSITY OF RICHMOND, VIRGINIA

Web site: www.richmond.edu
Contact: Ms. Pamela Spence, Dean of Admission, 28 Westhampton Way, University of Richmond, VA 23173
Telephone: 804-289-8640 or toll-free 800-700-1662 **Fax:** 804-287-6003
E-mail: admissions@richmond.edu

Getting in Last Year
6,079 applied
42% were accepted
835 enrolled (33%)
60% from top tenth of their h.s. class
3.53 average high school GPA
80% had SAT verbal scores over 600
87% had SAT math scores over 600
92% had ACT scores over 24
21% had SAT verbal scores over 700
28% had SAT math scores over 700
33% had ACT scores over 30
93 National Merit Scholars
54 class presidents
43 valedictorians

Graduation and After
76% graduated in 4 years
8% graduated in 5 years
1% graduated in 6 years
169 organizations recruited on campus

Financial Matters
$24,940 tuition and fees (2003–04)
$5160 room and board
96% average percent of need met
$19,220 average financial aid amount received per undergraduate

Academics
University of Richmond awards associate, bachelor's, master's, and first-professional **degrees** and post-bachelor's certificates. Challenging opportunities include advanced placement credit, accelerated degree programs, student-designed majors, an honors program, double majors, independent study, and a senior project. Special programs include cooperative education, internships, summer session for credit, off-campus study, study-abroad, and Army ROTC.

The most frequently chosen **baccalaureate** fields are business/marketing, social sciences and history, and English. A complete listing of majors at University of Richmond appears in the Majors Index beginning on page 460.

The **faculty** at University of Richmond has 290 full-time members, 89% with terminal degrees. The student-faculty ratio is 9:1.

Students of University of Richmond
The student body totals 3,626, of whom 2,926 are undergraduates. 51.3% are women and 48.7% are men. Students come from 48 states and territories and 75 other countries. 16% are from Virginia. 3.9% are international students. 4.6% are African American, 0.1% American Indian, 3.9% Asian American, and 1.5% Hispanic American. 92% returned for their sophomore year.

Facilities and Resources
Student rooms are linked to a campus network. 500 **computers** are available on campus that provide access to the Internet. The 5 **libraries** have 1,049,365 books and 703,111 subscriptions.

Campus Life
There are 225 active organizations on campus, including a drama/theater group, newspaper, radio station, and choral group. 39% of eligible men and 49% of eligible women are members of national **fraternities** and national **sororities**.

University of Richmond is a member of the NCAA (Division I). **Intercollegiate sports** (some offering scholarships) include baseball (m), basketball, cheerleading, cross-country running, field hockey (w), football (m), golf, lacrosse (w), soccer, swimming (w), tennis, track and field.

Campus Safety
Student safety services include campus police, late-night transport/escort service, 24-hour emergency telephone alarm devices, 24-hour patrols by trained security personnel, and electronically operated dormitory entrances.

Applying
University of Richmond requires an essay, SAT II: Writing Test, SAT I and SAT II or ACT, SAT II Subject Test in math, a high school transcript, 1 recommendation, signed character statement, and a minimum high school GPA of 2.0. Application deadline: 1/15; 2/25 for financial aid. Early and deferred admission are possible.

UNIVERSITY OF ROCHESTER

SUBURBAN SETTING ■ PRIVATE ■ INDEPENDENT ■ COED
ROCHESTER, NEW YORK

Web site: www.rochester.edu
Contact: Mr. Gregory MacDonald, Director of Admissions, PO Box 270251,
W. Allen Wallis Hall, 300 Wilson Boulevard, Rochester, NY 14627-0251
Telephone: 585-275-3221 or toll-free 888-822-2256 **Fax:** 585-461-4595
E-mail: admit@admissions.rochester.edu

Academics

University of Rochester awards bachelor's, master's, doctoral, and first-professional
degrees and post-bachelor's and post-master's certificates. Challenging opportunities
include advanced placement credit, student-designed majors, double majors, and
independent study. Special programs include internships, summer session for credit, off-
campus study, study-abroad, and Army and Air Force ROTC.

The most frequently chosen **baccalaureate** fields are social sciences and history,
biological/life sciences, and psychology. A complete listing of majors at University of
Rochester appears in the Majors Index beginning on page 460.

The **faculty** at University of Rochester has 513 full-time members, 91% with
terminal degrees. The student-faculty ratio is 9:1.

Students of University of Rochester

The student body totals 8,543, of whom 4,581 are undergraduates. 47.1% are women
and 52.9% are men. Students come from 52 states and territories and 36 other countries.
50% are from New York. 3.4% are international students. 4.7% are African American,
0.4% American Indian, 11.7% Asian American, and 4% Hispanic American. 94%
returned for their sophomore year.

Facilities and Resources

Student rooms are linked to a campus network. 260 **computers** are available on campus
for student use. The 6 **libraries** have 2,992,204 books and 11,254 subscriptions.

Campus Life

There are 200 active organizations on campus, including a drama/theater group,
newspaper, radio station, and choral group. 25% of eligible men and 20% of eligible
women are members of national **fraternities** and national **sororities**.

– University of Rochester is a member of the NCAA (Division III). **Intercollegiate
sports** include baseball (m), basketball, cross-country running, field hockey (w), football
(m), golf (m), lacrosse (w), soccer, softball (w), squash (m), swimming, tennis, track and
field, volleyball (w).

Campus Safety

Student safety services include late-night transport/escort service, 24-hour emergency
telephone alarm devices, 24-hour patrols by trained security personnel, and electronically operated dormitory entrances.

Applying

University of Rochester requires an essay, SAT I or ACT, a high school transcript, and 1
recommendation, and in some cases audition, portfolio. It recommends an interview and
2 recommendations. Application deadline: 1/20; 2/1 priority date for financial aid. Early
and deferred admission are possible.

Founded in 1850, the
University of Rochester is
one of the leading private
universities in the country. The
University of Rochester balances the
choices and intellectual excitement of
a major research university with the
intimacy and opportunities for
personal involvement of a small
liberal arts college. Programs are
available in 6 divisions, including the
College (Arts and Sciences and
Engineering), Nursing, Education,
Business, Medicine, and the Eastman
School of Music. Special
undergraduate opportunities include
the Take Five program (fifth-year
tuition free), an 8-year bachelor's/
medical degree, and seminar-style
Quest courses for first-year
students.

Getting in Last Year
10,486 applied
49% were accepted
1,091 enrolled (21%)
71% from top tenth of their h.s. class
3.70 average high school GPA
73% had SAT verbal scores over 600
84% had SAT math scores over 600
91% had ACT scores over 24
22% had SAT verbal scores over 700
35% had SAT math scores over 700
35% had ACT scores over 30
16 National Merit Scholars
43 valedictorians

Graduation and After
71% graduated in 4 years
8% graduated in 5 years
1% graduated in 6 years
37% pursued further study (19% arts and
sciences, 5% law, 2% engineering)
57% had job offers within 6 months
127 organizations recruited on campus

Financial Matters
$27,573 tuition and fees (2003–04)
$8770 room and board
100% average percent of need met
$22,854 average financial aid amount received
per undergraduate

UNIVERSITY OF ST. THOMAS

URBAN SETTING ■ PRIVATE ■ INDEPENDENT RELIGIOUS ■ COED
ST. PAUL, MINNESOTA

Web site: www.stthomas.edu
Contact: Ms. Marla Friederichs, Associate Vice President of Enrollment Management, 2115 Summit Avenue, Mail #32F-1, St. Paul, MN 55105-1096
Telephone: 651-962-6150 or toll-free 800-328-6819 ext. 26150 **Fax:** 651-962-6160
E-mail: admissions@stthomas.edu

The University of St. Thomas, founded in 1885, is a Catholic, independent, liberal arts university with more than 11,000 undergraduate and graduate students—the largest independent college or university in Minnesota has campuses in a quiet St. Paul neighborhood and in thriving downtown Minneapolis. St. Thomas offers more than 80 majors, including business administration, computer science, journalism, biology, engineering, and pre-professional programs. St. Thomas ranked 5th (and highest among schools) in a newspaper-sponsored survey on "Which Minnesota nonprofit organizations have the most respected reputations?" St. Thomas emphasizes value-centered, career-oriented education.

Academics

St. Thomas awards bachelor's, master's, doctoral, and first-professional **degrees** and post-bachelor's and post-master's certificates. Challenging opportunities include advanced placement credit, student-designed majors, an honors program, double majors, independent study, and a senior project. Special programs include internships, summer session for credit, off-campus study, study-abroad, and Army, Navy and Air Force ROTC.

The most frequently chosen **baccalaureate** fields are business/marketing, communications/communication technologies, and social sciences and history. A complete listing of majors at St. Thomas appears in the Majors Index beginning on page 460.

The **faculty** at St. Thomas has 399 full-time members, 87% with terminal degrees. The student-faculty ratio is 14:1.

Students of St. Thomas

The student body totals 11,037, of whom 5,236 are undergraduates. 50.6% are women and 49.4% are men. Students come from 44 states and territories and 36 other countries. 82% are from Minnesota. 1.1% are international students. 1.9% are African American, 0.6% American Indian, 5.3% Asian American, and 1.9% Hispanic American. 85% returned for their sophomore year.

Facilities and Resources

Student rooms are linked to a campus network. 1,249 **computers** are available on campus that provide access to the Internet. The 3 **libraries** have 440,023 books and 4,168 subscriptions.

Campus Life

There are 94 active organizations on campus, including a drama/theater group, newspaper, and choral group. No national or local **fraternities** or **sororities**.

St. Thomas is a member of the NCAA (Division III). **Intercollegiate sports** include baseball (m), basketball, cross-country running, football (m), golf, ice hockey, soccer, softball (w), swimming, tennis, track and field, volleyball (w).

Campus Safety

Student safety services include late-night transport/escort service, 24-hour emergency telephone alarm devices, 24-hour patrols by trained security personnel, and electronically operated dormitory entrances.

Applying

St. Thomas requires an essay, SAT I or ACT, and a high school transcript. It recommends ACT, an interview, and recommendations. Application deadline: rolling admissions; 4/1 priority date for financial aid. Deferred admission is possible.

Getting in Last Year
2,979 applied
87% were accepted
1,039 enrolled (40%)
28% from top tenth of their h.s. class
3.56 average high school GPA
38% had SAT verbal scores over 600
43% had SAT math scores over 600
63% had ACT scores over 24
10% had SAT verbal scores over 700
9% had SAT math scores over 700
9% had ACT scores over 30
11 National Merit Scholars
34 valedictorians

Graduation and After
62% graduated in 4 years
12% graduated in 5 years
2% graduated in 6 years
15% pursued further study (4% law, 3% education, 3% veterinary medicine)
80% had job offers within 6 months
122 organizations recruited on campus

Financial Matters
$19,343 tuition and fees (2003–04)
$6484 room and board
85% average percent of need met
$15,313 average financial aid amount received per undergraduate (2002–03 estimated)

University of St. Thomas

Urban setting ■ Private ■ Independent Religious ■ Coed
Houston, Texas

Web site: www.stthom.edu
Contact: Mr. Eduardo Prieto, Dean of Admissions, 3800 Montrose Boulevard,
Houston, TX 77006-4696
Telephone: 713-525-3500 or toll-free 800-856-8565 Fax: 713-525-3558
E-mail: admissions@stthom.edu

Academics
St. Thomas awards bachelor's, master's, doctoral, and first-professional **degrees**. Challenging opportunities include advanced placement credit, accelerated degree programs, an honors program, double majors, independent study, and a senior project. Special programs include cooperative education, internships, summer session for credit, off-campus study, study-abroad, and Army ROTC.

The most frequently chosen **baccalaureate** fields are business/marketing, liberal arts/general studies, and social sciences and history. A complete listing of majors at St. Thomas appears in the Majors Index beginning on page 460.

The **faculty** at St. Thomas has 114 full-time members, 89% with terminal degrees. The student-faculty ratio is 14:1.

Students of St. Thomas
The student body totals 4,875, of whom 1,907 are undergraduates. 64.7% are women and 35.3% are men. Students come from 27 states and territories and 32 other countries. 97% are from Texas. 3.3% are international students. 5.7% are African American, 0.7% American Indian, 13.8% Asian American, and 26.8% Hispanic American. 68% returned for their sophomore year.

Facilities and Resources
Student rooms are linked to a campus network. 153 **computers** are available on campus that provide access to the Internet. The 2 **libraries** have 206,410 books and 10,000 subscriptions.

Campus Life
There are 58 active organizations on campus, including a drama/theater group, newspaper, and choral group. No national or local **fraternities** or **sororities**.

This institution has no intercollegiate sports.

Campus Safety
Student safety services include late-night transport/escort service, 24-hour emergency telephone alarm devices, 24-hour patrols by trained security personnel, and electronically operated dormitory entrances.

Applying
St. Thomas requires an essay, SAT I or ACT, a high school transcript, and a minimum high school GPA of 2.25. Application deadline: rolling admissions; 3/1 priority date for financial aid. Deferred admission is possible.

Getting in Last Year
808 applied
89% were accepted
302 enrolled (42%)
26% from top tenth of their h.s. class
3.54 average high school GPA
39% had SAT verbal scores over 600
38% had SAT math scores over 600
56% had ACT scores over 24
6% had SAT verbal scores over 700
5% had SAT math scores over 700
7% had ACT scores over 30

Graduation and After
24% graduated in 4 years
17% graduated in 5 years
6% graduated in 6 years
9 organizations recruited on campus

Financial Matters
$15,112 tuition and fees (2003–04)
$6840 room and board
72% average percent of need met
$11,832 average financial aid amount received per undergraduate (2002–03 estimated)

UNIVERSITY OF SAN DIEGO

URBAN SETTING ■ PRIVATE ■ INDEPENDENT RELIGIOUS ■ COED
SAN DIEGO, CALIFORNIA

Web site: www.sandiego.edu
Contact: Mr. Stephen Pultz, Director of Admission, 5998 Alcala Park, San Diego, CA 92110
Telephone: 619-260-4506 or toll-free 800-248-4873 **Fax:** 619-260-6836
E-mail: admissions@sandiego.edu

The University of San Diego is located in the heart of San Diego—one of America's finest and most livable cities. The 180-acre campus sits on a mesa overlooking Mission Bay and the Pacific Ocean. As an independent Roman Catholic University, USD holds a rare position in America higher education. The University is operated by a Board of Trustees and is committed to cultural diversity, intellectual honesty, and to open-minded inquiry. Moreover, students are encouraged to exemplify the core beliefs of the university-belief in the existence of God, the dignity of individual human beings, and service to the community.

Getting in Last Year
7,273 applied
51% were accepted
1,064 enrolled (29%)
45% from top tenth of their h.s. class
3.80 average high school GPA
42% had SAT verbal scores over 600
52% had SAT math scores over 600
70% had ACT scores over 24
3% had SAT verbal scores over 700
9% had SAT math scores over 700
9% had ACT scores over 30
34 valedictorians

Graduation and After
57% graduated in 4 years
14% graduated in 5 years
1% graduated in 6 years
40% pursued further study
96% had job offers within 6 months
105 organizations recruited on campus

Financial Matters
$23,518 tuition and fees (2003–04)
$9630 room and board
100% average percent of need met
$21,804 average financial aid amount received per undergraduate (2002–03)

Academics
USD awards bachelor's, master's, doctoral, and first-professional **degrees** and post-bachelor's, post-master's, and first-professional certificates. Challenging opportunities include advanced placement credit, an honors program, double majors, independent study, and a senior project. Special programs include internships, summer session for credit, study-abroad, and Army, Navy and Air Force ROTC.

The most frequently chosen **baccalaureate** fields are business/marketing, social sciences and history, and communications/communication technologies. A complete listing of majors at USD appears in the Majors Index beginning on page 460.

The **faculty** at USD has 349 full-time members, 97% with terminal degrees. The student-faculty ratio is 14:1.

Students of USD
The student body totals 7,262, of whom 4,803 are undergraduates. 61.8% are women and 38.2% are men. Students come from 50 states and territories and 63 other countries. 62% are from California. 2.4% are international students. 2% are African American, 1.2% American Indian, 7.1% Asian American, and 15.7% Hispanic American. 85% returned for their sophomore year.

Facilities and Resources
Student rooms are linked to a campus network. 260 **computers** are available on campus that provide access to the Internet. The 2 **libraries** have 500,000 books and 4,986 subscriptions.

Campus Life
There are 75 active organizations on campus, including a drama/theater group, newspaper, television station, and choral group. 25% of eligible men and 25% of eligible women are members of national **fraternities** and national **sororities**.

USD is a member of the NCAA (Division I). **Intercollegiate sports** (some offering scholarships) include baseball (m), basketball, crew, cross-country running, football (m), golf (m), soccer, softball (w), swimming (w), tennis, volleyball (w).

Campus Safety
Student safety services include late-night transport/escort service, 24-hour emergency telephone alarm devices, 24-hour patrols by trained security personnel, student patrols, and electronically operated dormitory entrances.

Applying
USD requires an essay, SAT I or ACT, a high school transcript, and 1 recommendation. It recommends SAT II: Writing Test. Application deadline: 1/5; 2/20 priority date for financial aid. Early admission is possible.

THE UNIVERSITY OF SCRANTON

URBAN SETTING ■ PRIVATE ■ INDEPENDENT RELIGIOUS ■ COED
SCRANTON, PENNSYLVANIA

Web site: www.scranton.edu
Contact: Mr. Joseph Roback, Director of Admissions, 800 Linden Street,
   Scranton, PA 18510
Telephone: 570-941-7540 or toll-free 888-SCRANTON **Fax:** 570-941-4370
E-mail: admissions@uofs.edu

Academics

Scranton awards associate, bachelor's, master's, and doctoral **degrees** and post-bachelor's and post-master's certificates. Challenging opportunities include advanced placement credit, student-designed majors, freshman honors college, an honors program, double majors, independent study, and a senior project. Special programs include internships, summer session for credit, off-campus study, study-abroad, and Army and Air Force ROTC.

The most frequently chosen **baccalaureate** fields are business/marketing, education, and communications/communication technologies. A complete listing of majors at Scranton appears in the Majors Index beginning on page 460.

The **faculty** at Scranton has 247 full-time members, 85% with terminal degrees. The student-faculty ratio is 13:1.

Students of Scranton

The student body totals 4,679, of whom 4,073 are undergraduates. 57.2% are women and 42.8% are men. Students come from 30 states and territories and 12 other countries. 51% are from Pennsylvania. 0.5% are international students. 1.3% are African American, 0.1% American Indian, 2.3% Asian American, and 3.2% Hispanic American. 89% returned for their sophomore year.

Facilities and Resources

Student rooms are linked to a campus network. 837 **computers** are available on campus that provide access to the Internet. The 2 **libraries** have 443,144 books and 1,750 subscriptions.

Campus Life

There are 80 active organizations on campus, including a drama/theater group, newspaper, radio station, and choral group. No national or local **fraternities** or **sororities**.

Scranton is a member of the NCAA (Division III). **Intercollegiate sports** include baseball (m), basketball, cross-country running, field hockey (w), golf (m), ice hockey (m), lacrosse (m), soccer, softball (w), swimming, tennis, volleyball (w), wrestling (m).

Campus Safety

Student safety services include late-night transport/escort service, 24-hour emergency telephone alarm devices, 24-hour patrols by trained security personnel, student patrols, and electronically operated dormitory entrances.

Applying

Scranton requires SAT I or ACT and a high school transcript, and in some cases an interview and 2 recommendations. It recommends an essay. Application deadline: 3/1; 2/15 priority date for financial aid. Early and deferred admission are possible.

The University of Scranton is known for its outstanding academic programs, well-equipped campus, state-of-the-art technology, strong sense of community, and, most of all, the remarkable success of its graduates. In 2001, for example, medical schools accepted 90% of Scranton's pre-law graduates, and in 2002, medical schools accepted 100% of pre-med graduates. In addition, 111 Scranton graduates have won Fulbrights and other prestigious international fellowships. Scranton graduates tend to become leaders in whatever fields they choose. They have benefited from something few schools can offer: a Jesuit education that provides the rock-solid confidence to make it in the real world from day one.

Getting in Last Year
5,669 applied
75% were accepted
980 enrolled (23%)
23% from top tenth of their h.s. class
3.35 average high school GPA
27% had SAT verbal scores over 600
32% had SAT math scores over 600
3% had SAT verbal scores over 700
4% had SAT math scores over 700
22 National Merit Scholars
17 class presidents
16 valedictorians

Graduation and After
67% graduated in 4 years
9% graduated in 5 years
1% graduated in 6 years
Graduates pursuing further study: 16% arts and sciences, 5% medicine, 4% law
87 organizations recruited on campus

Financial Matters
$21,408 tuition and fees (2003–04)
$9335 room and board
74% average percent of need met
$14,346 average financial aid amount received per undergraduate (2002–03 estimated)

UNIVERSITY OF SOUTH CAROLINA
URBAN SETTING ■ PUBLIC ■ STATE-SUPPORTED ■ COED
COLUMBIA, SOUTH CAROLINA

Web site: www.sc.edu
Contact: Ms. Terry L. Davis, Director of Undergraduate Admissions, Columbia, SC 29208
Telephone: 803-777-7700 or toll-free 800-868-5872 (in-state) **Fax:** 803-777-0101
E-mail: admissions-ugrad@sc.edu

The University of South Carolina offers a wealth of resources. It has 16 schools and colleges, including the Honors College, Graduate School, School of Medicine and School of Law, and it offers more than 70 majors and 350 degree programs. There are nearly 300 student organizations, and students are encouraged to join at least one as soon as they arrive at Carolina. New students are quickly made to feel at home both academically and socially through a course called University 101, a program that was recently cited number one in the country for "programs that really work" by *U.S. News & World Report.* In fact, USC academic programs, including the top-ranked undergraduate international program, are consistently recognized nationally for excellence.

Getting in Last Year
12,817 applied
64% were accepted
3,491 enrolled (42%)
26% from top tenth of their h.s. class
3.77 average high school GPA
35% had SAT verbal scores over 600
39% had SAT math scores over 600
57% had ACT scores over 24
7% had SAT verbal scores over 700
7% had SAT math scores over 700
11% had ACT scores over 30
31 National Merit Scholars
65 valedictorians

Graduation and After
36% graduated in 4 years
21% graduated in 5 years
3% graduated in 6 years
80% had job offers within 6 months
19016 organizations recruited on campus

Financial Matters
$5748 resident tuition and fees (2003–04)
$15,086 nonresident tuition and fees (2003–04)
$5327 room and board
91% average percent of need met
$8263 average financial aid amount received per undergraduate (2001–02)

Academics
Carolina awards associate, bachelor's, master's, doctoral, and first-professional **degrees** and post-bachelor's and post-master's certificates. Challenging opportunities include advanced placement credit, accelerated degree programs, student-designed majors, freshman honors college, an honors program, double majors, independent study, and a senior project. Special programs include cooperative education, internships, summer session for credit, study-abroad, and Army and Air Force ROTC.

The most frequently chosen **baccalaureate** fields are business/marketing, social sciences and history, and communications/communication technologies. A complete listing of majors at Carolina appears in the Majors Index beginning on page 460.

The **faculty** at Carolina has 1,099 full-time members, 87% with terminal degrees. The student-faculty ratio is 17:1.

Students of Carolina
The student body totals 25,288, of whom 17,133 are undergraduates. 55% are women and 45% are men. Students come from 54 states and territories and 72 other countries. 88% are from South Carolina. 1.4% are international students. 15.4% are African American, 0.3% American Indian, 2.8% Asian American, and 1.5% Hispanic American. 84% returned for their sophomore year.

Facilities and Resources
Student rooms are linked to a campus network. 11,000 **computers** are available on campus that provide access to the Internet. The 8 **libraries** have 3,333,764 books and 21,836 subscriptions.

Campus Life
There are 270 active organizations on campus, including a drama/theater group, newspaper, radio station, choral group, and marching band. 17% of eligible men and 17% of eligible women are members of national **fraternities** and national **sororities**.

Carolina is a member of the NCAA (Division I). **Intercollegiate sports** (some offering scholarships) include baseball (m), basketball, cross-country running (w), equestrian sports (w), football (m), golf, soccer, softball (w), swimming, tennis, track and field, volleyball (w).

Campus Safety
Student safety services include Division of Law Enforcement and Safety, late-night transport/escort service, 24-hour emergency telephone alarm devices, 24-hour patrols by trained security personnel, student patrols, and electronically operated dormitory entrances.

Applying
Carolina requires SAT I or ACT, a high school transcript, and a minimum high school GPA of 2.0. Application deadline: 2/15; 4/1 priority date for financial aid.

University of Southern California

URBAN SETTING ■ PRIVATE ■ INDEPENDENT ■ COED
LOS ANGELES, CALIFORNIA

Web site: www.usc.edu
Contact: Ms. Laurel Baker-Tew, Director of Admission, University Park
  Campus, Los Angeles, CA 90089
Telephone: 213-740-1111 **Fax:** 213-740-6364
E-mail: admitusc@usc.edu

Academics

USC awards bachelor's, master's, doctoral, and first-professional **degrees** and post-bachelor's, post-master's, and first-professional certificates. Challenging opportunities include advanced placement credit, accelerated degree programs, student-designed majors, freshman honors college, an honors program, double majors, independent study, and a senior project. Special programs include cooperative education, internships, summer session for credit, off-campus study, study-abroad, and Army, Navy and Air Force ROTC.

The most frequently chosen **baccalaureate** fields are business/marketing, social sciences and history, and visual/performing arts. A complete listing of majors at USC appears in the Majors Index beginning on page 460.

The **faculty** at USC has 1,450 full-time members, 86% with terminal degrees. The student-faculty ratio is 10:1.

Students of USC

The student body totals 31,606, of whom 16,381 are undergraduates. 50.5% are women and 49.5% are men. Students come from 52 states and territories and 148 other countries. 67% are from California. 8.1% are international students. 6.7% are African American, 0.8% American Indian, 21.4% Asian American, and 12.8% Hispanic American. 94% returned for their sophomore year.

Facilities and Resources

Student rooms are linked to a campus network. 2,500 **computers** are available on campus that provide access to online degree progress, grades, financial aid summary and the Internet. The 21 **libraries** have 3,526,134 books and 28,561 subscriptions.

Campus Life

There are 450 active organizations on campus, including a drama/theater group, newspaper, radio station, television station, choral group, and marching band. 16% of eligible men and 17% of eligible women are members of national **fraternities**, national **sororities**, local fraternities, and local sororities.

USC is a member of the NCAA (Division I). **Intercollegiate sports** (some offering scholarships) include baseball (m), basketball, crew (w), cross-country running, football (m), golf, soccer (w), swimming, tennis, track and field, volleyball, water polo.

Campus Safety

Student safety services include late-night transport/escort service, 24-hour emergency telephone alarm devices, 24-hour patrols by trained security personnel, student patrols, and electronically operated dormitory entrances.

Applying

USC requires an essay, SAT I or ACT, and a high school transcript, and in some cases SAT II Subject Tests and recommendations. It recommends an interview and recommendations. Application deadline: 1/10; 1/22 priority date for financial aid.

One of the country's leading private research universities, USC provides outstanding teachers, excellent facilities, and a wide array of academic offerings, including interdisciplinary programs and undergraduate research opportunities. With a student-faculty member ratio of 10:1 and small classes, students work with world-acclaimed professors in every discipline as participants, not spectators. USC offers bachelor's degrees in 79 majors and more than 100 minors, spanning 17 professional schools in addition to the College of Letters, Arts and Sciences.

Getting in Last Year
29,278 applied
30% were accepted
2,976 enrolled (34%)
3.99 average high school GPA
80% had SAT verbal scores over 600
91% had SAT math scores over 600
97% had ACT scores over 24
28% had SAT verbal scores over 700
42% had SAT math scores over 700
43% had ACT scores over 30
154 National Merit Scholars

Graduation and After
61% graduated in 4 years
16% graduated in 5 years
4% graduated in 6 years
600 organizations recruited on campus

Financial Matters
$28,692 tuition and fees (2003–04)
$8632 room and board
99% average percent of need met
$23,961 average financial aid amount received
  per undergraduate (2000–01)

The University of Texas at Austin

Urban setting ■ Public ■ State-supported ■ Coed

Austin, Texas

Web site: www.utexas.edu

Contact: Freshman Admissions Center, PO Box 8058, Austin, TX 78713-8058

Telephone: 512-475-7440 **Fax:** 512-475-7475

Getting in Last Year

24,519 applied
47% were accepted
6,544 enrolled (57%)
69% from top tenth of their h.s. class
55% had SAT verbal scores over 600
67% had SAT math scores over 600
72% had ACT scores over 24
15% had SAT verbal scores over 700
24% had SAT math scores over 700
19% had ACT scores over 30
259 National Merit Scholars

Graduation and After

36% graduated in 4 years
27% graduated in 5 years
7% graduated in 6 years

Financial Matters

$4548 resident tuition and fees (2003–04)
$11,668 nonresident tuition and fees (2003–04)
$6082 room and board
94% average percent of need met
$7470 average financial aid amount received per undergraduate (2001–02)

Academics

UT Austin awards bachelor's, master's, doctoral, and first-professional **degrees**. Challenging opportunities include advanced placement credit, accelerated degree programs, student-designed majors, an honors program, double majors, independent study, and a senior project. Special programs include cooperative education, internships, summer session for credit, study-abroad, and Army, Navy and Air Force ROTC.

The most frequently chosen **baccalaureate** fields are social sciences and history, communications/communication technologies, and business/marketing. A complete listing of majors at UT Austin appears in the Majors Index beginning on page 460.

The **faculty** at UT Austin has 2,432 full-time members. The student-faculty ratio is 19:1.

Students of UT Austin

The student body totals 51,426, of whom 38,383 are undergraduates. 51.3% are women and 48.7% are men. Students come from 53 states and territories and 94 other countries. 95% are from Texas. 3.5% are international students. 3.7% are African American, 0.4% American Indian, 17.1% Asian American, and 14.4% Hispanic American. 92% returned for their sophomore year.

Facilities and Resources

Student rooms are linked to a campus network. 4,000 **computers** are available on campus that provide access to e-mail and the Internet. The 17 **libraries** have 4,346,398 books and 49,771 subscriptions.

Campus Life

There are 900 active organizations on campus, including a drama/theater group, newspaper, radio station, television station, choral group, and marching band. 9% of eligible men and 14% of eligible women are members of national **fraternities** and national **sororities**.

UT Austin is a member of the NCAA (Division I). **Intercollegiate sports** (some offering scholarships) include baseball (m), basketball, cheerleading, crew (w), cross-country running, football (m), golf, soccer (w), softball (w), swimming, tennis, track and field, volleyball (w).

Campus Safety

Student safety services include late-night transport/escort service, 24-hour emergency telephone alarm devices, 24-hour patrols by trained security personnel, student patrols, and electronically operated dormitory entrances.

Applying

UT Austin requires SAT I or ACT and a high school transcript, and in some cases an essay. Application deadline: 2/1. Deferred admission is possible.

THE UNIVERSITY OF TEXAS AT DALLAS

SUBURBAN SETTING ■ PUBLIC ■ STATE-SUPPORTED ■ COED
RICHARDSON, TEXAS

Web site: www.utdallas.edu
Contact: Mr. Barry Samsula, Director of Enrollment Services, PO Box
   830688 Mail Station MC11, Richardson, TX 75083-0688
Telephone: 972-883-2270 or toll-free 800-889-2443 **Fax:** 972-883-2599
E-mail: admissions-status@utdallas.edu

Academics

U.T. Dallas awards bachelor's, master's, and doctoral **degrees**. Challenging opportunities include advanced placement credit, accelerated degree programs, student-designed majors, freshman honors college, an honors program, double majors, independent study, and a senior project. Special programs include cooperative education, internships, summer session for credit, study-abroad, and Army and Air Force ROTC.

The most frequently chosen **baccalaureate** fields are business/marketing, computer/information sciences, and interdisciplinary studies. A complete listing of majors at U.T. Dallas appears in the Majors Index beginning on page 460.

The **faculty** at U.T. Dallas has 416 full-time members, 99% with terminal degrees. The student-faculty ratio is 20:1.

Students of U.T. Dallas

The student body totals 13,718, of whom 8,688 are undergraduates. 48.6% are women and 51.4% are men. Students come from 46 states and territories and 129 other countries. 98% are from Texas. 5.2% are international students. 7.3% are African American, 0.7% American Indian, 19.8% Asian American, and 9.6% Hispanic American. 84% returned for their sophomore year.

Facilities and Resources

Student rooms are linked to a campus network. 630 **computers** are available on campus that provide access to the Internet. The 3 **libraries** have 754,491 books and 3,078 subscriptions.

Campus Life

There are 115 active organizations on campus, including a drama/theater group, newspaper, and radio station. 6% of eligible men and 3% of eligible women are members of national **fraternities**, national **sororities**, and local sororities.

U.T. Dallas is a member of the NCAA (Division III). **Intercollegiate sports** include baseball (m), basketball, cross-country running, golf, soccer, softball (w), tennis.

Campus Safety

Student safety services include late-night transport/escort service, 24-hour emergency telephone alarm devices, and 24-hour patrols by trained security personnel.

Applying

U.T. Dallas requires an essay, SAT I or ACT, and a high school transcript, and in some cases TASP and an interview. It recommends SAT II: Writing Test and 3 recommendations. Application deadline: 7/1; 3/12 priority date for financial aid. Deferred admission is possible.

Getting in Last Year
5,048 applied
50% were accepted
1,060 enrolled (42%)
41% from top tenth of their h.s. class
3.44 average high school GPA
55% had SAT verbal scores over 600
66% had SAT math scores over 600
74% had ACT scores over 24
14% had SAT verbal scores over 700
21% had SAT math scores over 700
22% had ACT scores over 30
21 valedictorians

Graduation and After
32% graduated in 4 years
20% graduated in 5 years
5% graduated in 6 years
15% pursued further study
76% had job offers within 6 months
232 organizations recruited on campus

Financial Matters
$5493 resident tuition and fees (2003–04)
$12,573 nonresident tuition and fees (2003–04)
$6122 room and board
69% average percent of need met
$9376 average financial aid amount received per undergraduate (2002–03 estimated)

University of the Pacific

Suburban setting ■ Private ■ Independent ■ Coed
Stockton, California

Web site: www.pacific.edu
Contact: Mr. Marc McGee, Director of Admissions, 3601 Pacific Avenue,
Stockton, CA 95211
Telephone: 209-946-2211 or toll-free 800-959-2867 Fax: 209-946-2413
E-mail: admissions@pacific.edu

Getting in Last Year

4,501 applied
70% were accepted
818 enrolled (26%)
37% from top tenth of their h.s. class
3.45 average high school GPA
35% had SAT verbal scores over 600
50% had SAT math scores over 600
58% had ACT scores over 24
3% had SAT verbal scores over 700
12% had SAT math scores over 700
5% had ACT scores over 30

Graduation and After

45% graduated in 4 years
18% graduated in 5 years
4% graduated in 6 years
80 organizations recruited on campus

Financial Matters

$23,600 tuition and fees (2003–04)
$7490 room and board
$22,096 average financial aid amount received
per undergraduate

Academics

UOP awards bachelor's, master's, doctoral, and first-professional **degrees**. Challenging opportunities include advanced placement credit, accelerated degree programs, student-designed majors, an honors program, double majors, independent study, and a senior project. Special programs include cooperative education, internships, summer session for credit, and study-abroad.

The most frequently chosen **baccalaureate** fields are business/marketing, biological/life sciences, and social sciences and history. A complete listing of majors at UOP appears in the Majors Index beginning on page 460.

The **faculty** at UOP has 389 full-time members, 92% with terminal degrees. The student-faculty ratio is 13:1.

Students of UOP

The student body totals 6,121, of whom 3,357 are undergraduates. 57.7% are women and 42.3% are men. Students come from 41 states and territories and 16 other countries. 87% are from California. 2.6% are international students. 3% are African American, 0.7% American Indian, 27.3% Asian American, and 10.5% Hispanic American. 85% returned for their sophomore year.

Facilities and Resources

Student rooms are linked to a campus network. 274 **computers** are available on campus that provide access to the Internet. The 2 **libraries** have 268,365 books and 1,361 subscriptions.

Campus Life

There are 100 active organizations on campus, including a drama/theater group, newspaper, radio station, and choral group. 18% of eligible men and 22% of eligible women are members of national **fraternities**, national **sororities**, and local fraternities.

UOP is a member of the NCAA (Division I). **Intercollegiate sports** (some offering scholarships) include baseball (m), basketball, cross-country running (w), field hockey (w), golf (m), soccer (w), softball (w), swimming, tennis, volleyball, water polo.

Campus Safety

Student safety services include late-night transport/escort service, 24-hour emergency telephone alarm devices, 24-hour patrols by trained security personnel, and electronically operated dormitory entrances.

Applying

UOP requires an essay, SAT I or ACT, a high school transcript, 1 recommendation, and a minimum high school GPA of 2.5, and in some cases audition for music program. It recommends an interview and a minimum high school GPA of 3.0. Application deadline: 1/15; 2/15 priority date for financial aid.

UNIVERSITY OF THE SCIENCES IN PHILADELPHIA

URBAN SETTING ■ PRIVATE ■ INDEPENDENT ■ COED
PHILADELPHIA, PENNSYLVANIA

Web site: www.usip.edu
Contact: Mr. Louis L. Hegyes, Director of Admission, 600 South 43rd Street,
 Philadelphia, PA 19104-4495
Telephone: 215-596-8810 or toll-free 888-996-8747 (in-state) **Fax:**
 215-596-8821
E-mail: admit@usip.edu

Academics

USP awards bachelor's, master's, doctoral, and first-professional **degrees**. Challenging
opportunities include advanced placement credit, an honors program, double majors,
and a senior project. Special programs include cooperative education, internships, summer session for credit, off-campus study, and Army and Air Force ROTC.

The most frequently chosen **baccalaureate** fields are health professions and related
sciences, biological/life sciences, and business/marketing. A complete listing of majors at
USP appears in the Majors Index beginning on page 460.

The **faculty** at USP has 138 full-time members, 77% with terminal degrees. The
student-faculty ratio is 14:1.

Students of USP

The student body totals 2,687, of whom 2,323 are undergraduates. 67.3% are women
and 32.7% are men. Students come from 30 states and territories and 16 other countries.
52% are from Pennsylvania. 2.3% are international students. 6% are African American,
0.3% American Indian, 33.7% Asian American, and 2% Hispanic American. 87%
returned for their sophomore year.

Facilities and Resources

Student rooms are linked to a campus network. 105 **computers** are available on campus
that provide access to the Internet. The **library** has 84,848 books and 6,500 subscriptions.

Campus Life

There are 65 active organizations on campus, including a drama/theater group,
newspaper, and choral group. USP has national **fraternities**, national **sororities**, local
fraternities, and local sororities.

USP is a member of the NCAA (Division II) and NAIA. **Intercollegiate sports**
(some offering scholarships) include baseball (m), basketball, cross-country running, golf,
riflery, softball (w), tennis, volleyball (w).

Campus Safety

Student safety services include late-night transport/escort service, 24-hour emergency
telephone alarm devices, 24-hour patrols by trained security personnel, and electronically operated dormitory entrances.

Applying

USP requires SAT I or ACT and a high school transcript. It recommends SAT I and a
minimum high school GPA of 3.0. Application deadline: rolling admissions; 3/15 priority
date for financial aid. Deferred admission is possible.

Getting in Last Year

2,966 applied
68% were accepted
532 enrolled (26%)
26% from top tenth of their h.s. class
3.40 average high school GPA
20% had SAT verbal scores over 600
39% had SAT math scores over 600
1% had SAT verbal scores over 700
5% had SAT math scores over 700

Graduation and After

13% graduated in 4 years
19% graduated in 5 years
38% graduated in 6 years
95% had job offers within 6 months
113 organizations recruited on campus

Financial Matters

$20,958 tuition and fees (2003–04)
$8352 room and board

UNIVERSITY OF THE SOUTH

SMALL-TOWN SETTING ■ PRIVATE ■ INDEPENDENT RELIGIOUS ■ COED
SEWANEE, TENNESSEE

Web site: www.sewanee.edu
Contact: Mr. David Lesesne, Dean of Admission, 735 University Avenue, Sewanee, TN 37383-1000
Telephone: 931-598-1238 or toll-free 800-522-2234 **Fax:** 931-598-3248
E-mail: collegeadmission@sewanee.edu

S ewanee: The University of the South is considered one of the nation's top liberal arts and sciences colleges. More than 70 percent of Sewanee graduates pursue post-graduate study, which is twice the national average. This level of achievement is forged in the relationships that develop between the inquiring students and the talented faculty members. Sewanee is located atop the Cumberland Plateau between Nashville and Chattanooga, Tennessee. Sewanee's physical environment, which includes a beautiful 10,000-acre campus and dramatic gothic architecture, provides an unparalled place in which to study. Whether a student is interested in arts or science, Sewanee provides a challenging, but nurturing environment that helps each student achieve their very best.

Academics

Sewanee awards bachelor's, master's, doctoral, and first-professional **degrees** and post-bachelor's, post-master's, and first-professional certificates. Challenging opportunities include advanced placement credit, student-designed majors, double majors, independent study, and a senior project. Special programs include internships, summer session for credit, and study-abroad.

The most frequently chosen **baccalaureate** fields are social sciences and history, English, and visual/performing arts. A complete listing of majors at Sewanee appears in the Majors Index beginning on page 460.

The **faculty** at Sewanee has 133 full-time members, 95% with terminal degrees. The student-faculty ratio is 10:1.

Students of Sewanee

The student body totals 1,485, of whom 1,374 are undergraduates. 53.8% are women and 46.2% are men. Students come from 76 states and territories. 24% are from Tennessee. 1.3% are international students. 4.3% are African American, 0.2% American Indian, 1.3% Asian American, and 1.8% Hispanic American. 84% returned for their sophomore year.

Facilities and Resources

Student rooms are linked to a campus network. 92 **computers** are available on campus for student use. The **library** has 648,459 books and 3,444 subscriptions.

Campus Life

There are 110 active organizations on campus, including a drama/theater group, newspaper, radio station, and choral group. 65% of eligible men and 55% of eligible women are members of national **fraternities** and local **sororities**.

Sewanee is a member of the NCAA (Division III). **Intercollegiate sports** include baseball (m), basketball, cross-country running, field hockey (w), football (m), golf, soccer, swimming, tennis, track and field, volleyball (w).

Campus Safety

Student safety services include security lighting, late-night transport/escort service, 24-hour emergency telephone alarm devices, and 24-hour patrols by trained security personnel.

Applying

Sewanee requires an essay, SAT I or ACT, a high school transcript, and 2 recommendations. It recommends SAT II Subject Tests and an interview. Application deadline: 2/1; 3/1 priority date for financial aid. Early and deferred admission are possible.

Getting in Last Year
1,825 applied
72% were accepted
427 enrolled (32%)
45% from top tenth of their h.s. class
3.41 average high school GPA
63% had SAT verbal scores over 600
64% had SAT math scores over 600
83% had ACT scores over 24
16% had SAT verbal scores over 700
10% had SAT math scores over 700
23% had ACT scores over 30
13 National Merit Scholars

Graduation and After
78% graduated in 4 years
4% graduated in 5 years
1% graduated in 6 years
38% pursued further study (14% arts and sciences, 6% law, 4% business)
74% had job offers within 6 months
17 organizations recruited on campus

Financial Matters
$24,135 tuition and fees (2003–04)
$6720 room and board
100% average percent of need met
$21,067 average financial aid amount received per undergraduate (2001–02)

University of Tulsa

Urban setting ■ Private ■ Independent Religious ■ Coed
Tulsa, Oklahoma

Web site: www.utulsa.edu
Contact: Mr. John C. Corso, Associate Vice President for Administration/
Dean of Admission, 600 South College Avenue, Tulsa, OK 74104
Telephone: 918-631-2307 or toll-free 800-331-3050 **Fax:** 918-631-5003
E-mail: admission@utulsa.edu

Academics

TU awards bachelor's, master's, doctoral, and first-professional **degrees** and post-bachelor's and first-professional certificates. Challenging opportunities include advanced placement credit, accelerated degree programs, student-designed majors, an honors program, double majors, independent study, and a senior project. Special programs include internships, summer session for credit, study-abroad, and Air Force ROTC.

The most frequently chosen **baccalaureate** fields are business/marketing, engineering/engineering technologies, and visual/performing arts. A complete listing of majors at TU appears in the Majors Index beginning on page 460.

The **faculty** at TU has 304 full-time members, 96% with terminal degrees. The student-faculty ratio is 11:1.

Students of TU

The student body totals 4,072, of whom 2,672 are undergraduates. 50% are women and 50% are men. Students come from 37 states and territories and 48 other countries. 72% are from Oklahoma. 10.3% are international students. 7.5% are African American, 5.1% American Indian, 2.2% Asian American, and 3.4% Hispanic American. 78% returned for their sophomore year.

Facilities and Resources

Student rooms are linked to a campus network. 900 **computers** are available on campus that provide access to the Internet. The 2 **libraries** have 940,105 books and 6,317 subscriptions.

Campus Life

There are 272 active organizations on campus, including a drama/theater group, newspaper, radio station, television station, choral group, and marching band. 21% of eligible men and 23% of eligible women are members of national **fraternities** and national **sororities**.

TU is a member of the NCAA (Division I). **Intercollegiate sports** (some offering scholarships) include basketball, crew (w), cross-country running, football (m), golf, soccer, softball (w), tennis, track and field, volleyball (w).

Campus Safety

Student safety services include late-night transport/escort service, 24-hour emergency telephone alarm devices, 24-hour patrols by trained security personnel, and electronically operated dormitory entrances.

Applying

TU requires SAT I or ACT, a high school transcript, and 1 recommendation. It recommends an essay, an interview, and a minimum high school GPA of 3.0. Application deadline: rolling admissions; 4/1 priority date for financial aid. Early and deferred admission are possible.

Getting in Last Year
2,292 applied
76% were accepted
590 enrolled (34%)
60% from top tenth of their h.s. class
3.70 average high school GPA
54% had SAT verbal scores over 600
51% had SAT math scores over 600
67% had ACT scores over 24
22% had SAT verbal scores over 700
18% had SAT math scores over 700
23% had ACT scores over 30
49 National Merit Scholars
41 valedictorians

Graduation and After
37% graduated in 4 years
16% graduated in 5 years
1% graduated in 6 years
27% pursued further study (6% arts and sciences, 6% medicine, 5% business)
84% had job offers within 6 months
220 organizations recruited on campus

Financial Matters
$15,736 tuition and fees (2003–04)
$5610 room and board
91% average percent of need met
$13,737 average financial aid amount received per undergraduate

UNIVERSITY OF UTAH

URBAN SETTING ■ PUBLIC ■ STATE-SUPPORTED ■ COED
SALT LAKE CITY, UTAH

Web site: www.utah.edu
Contact: Ms. Suzanne Espinoza, Director of High School Services, 250 South Student Services Building, 201 South, 460 E Room 205, Salt Lake City, UT 84112
Telephone: 801-581-8761 or toll-free 800-444-8638 **Fax:** 801-585-7864
E-mail: admissions@sa.utah.edu

Getting in Last Year
5,842 applied
86% were accepted
2,653 enrolled (53%)
25% from top tenth of their h.s. class
3.48 average high school GPA
48% had ACT scores over 24
8% had ACT scores over 30

Graduation and After
18% graduated in 4 years
21% graduated in 5 years
14% graduated in 6 years
80% had job offers within 6 months
471 organizations recruited on campus

Financial Matters
$3647 resident tuition and fees (2003–04)
$11,293 nonresident tuition and fees (2003–04)
$5036 room and board
59% average percent of need met
$7286 average financial aid amount received per undergraduate

Academics
U of U awards bachelor's, master's, doctoral, and first-professional **degrees** and post-bachelor's and post-master's certificates. Challenging opportunities include advanced placement credit, accelerated degree programs, student-designed majors, an honors program, double majors, independent study, and a senior project. Special programs include cooperative education, internships, summer session for credit, off-campus study, study-abroad, and Army, Navy and Air Force ROTC.

The most frequently chosen **baccalaureate** fields are social sciences and history, business/marketing, and communications/communication technologies. A complete listing of majors at U of U appears in the Majors Index beginning on page 460.

The **faculty** at U of U has 1,104 full-time members, 90% with terminal degrees. The student-faculty ratio is 16:1.

Students of U of U
The student body totals 28,437, of whom 22,421 are undergraduates. 45.4% are women and 54.6% are men. Students come from 55 states and territories and 106 other countries. 93% are from Utah. 2.6% are international students. 0.6% are African American, 0.7% American Indian, 4.2% Asian American, and 3.8% Hispanic American. 79% returned for their sophomore year.

Facilities and Resources
Student rooms are linked to a campus network. 5,000 **computers** are available on campus that provide access to online classes and the Internet. The 4 **libraries** have 2,991,692 books and 33,517 subscriptions.

Campus Life
There are 170 active organizations on campus, including a drama/theater group, newspaper, radio station, television station, choral group, and marching band. 5% of eligible men and 5% of eligible women are members of national **fraternities**, national **sororities**, local fraternities, and local sororities.

U of U is a member of the NCAA (Division I). **Intercollegiate sports** (some offering scholarships) include baseball (m), basketball, cheerleading, cross-country running, football (m), golf (m), gymnastics (w), skiing (cross-country), skiing (downhill), soccer (w), softball (w), swimming, tennis, track and field, volleyball (w).

Campus Safety
Student safety services include late-night transport/escort service, 24-hour emergency telephone alarm devices, 24-hour patrols by trained security personnel, student patrols, and electronically operated dormitory entrances.

Applying
U of U requires SAT I or ACT, a high school transcript, and a minimum high school GPA of 2.0. It recommends ACT and a minimum high school GPA of 3.0. Application deadline: 4/1; 3/15 priority date for financial aid. Early and deferred admission are possible.

UNIVERSITY OF VIRGINIA

SUBURBAN SETTING ■ PUBLIC ■ STATE-SUPPORTED ■ COED
CHARLOTTESVILLE, VIRGINIA

Web site: www.virginia.edu
Contact: Mr. John A. Blackburn, Dean of Admission, PO Box 400160,
    Charlottesville, VA 22904-4160
Telephone: 434-982-3200 **Fax:** 434-924-3587
E-mail: undergradadmission@virginia.edu

Academics

UVA awards bachelor's, master's, doctoral, and first-professional **degrees** and post-master's certificates. Challenging opportunities include advanced placement credit, accelerated degree programs, student-designed majors, an honors program, double majors, independent study, and a senior project. Special programs include cooperative education, internships, summer session for credit, study-abroad, and Army, Navy and Air Force ROTC.

The most frequently chosen **baccalaureate** fields are social sciences and history, engineering/engineering technologies, and business/marketing. A complete listing of majors at UVA appears in the Majors Index beginning on page 460.

The **faculty** at UVA has 1,142 full-time members, 92% with terminal degrees. The student-faculty ratio is 16:1.

Students of UVA

The student body totals 23,077, of whom 13,829 are undergraduates. 53.4% are women and 46.6% are men. Students come from 52 states and territories and 110 other countries. 72% are from Virginia. 4.2% are international students. 8.8% are African American, 0.3% American Indian, 10.9% Asian American, and 2.9% Hispanic American. 97% returned for their sophomore year.

Facilities and Resources

Student rooms are linked to a campus network. 1,645 **computers** are available on campus that provide access to the Internet. The 15 **libraries** have 3,398,441 books and 55,843 subscriptions.

Campus Life

There are 300 active organizations on campus, including a drama/theater group, newspaper, radio station, television station, choral group, and marching band. 30% of eligible men and 30% of eligible women are members of national **fraternities**, national **sororities**, and local fraternities.

UVA is a member of the NCAA (Division I). **Intercollegiate sports** (some offering scholarships) include baseball (m), basketball, crew (w), cross-country running, field hockey (w), football (m), golf, lacrosse, soccer, softball (w), swimming, tennis, track and field, volleyball (w), wrestling (m).

Campus Safety

Student safety services include late-night transport/escort service, 24-hour emergency telephone alarm devices, 24-hour patrols by trained security personnel, and electronically operated dormitory entrances.

Applying

UVA requires an essay, SAT II Subject Tests, SAT II: Writing Test, SAT I or ACT, SAT II Math and one other subject test, a high school transcript, and 1 recommendation. Application deadline: 1/2; 3/1 priority date for financial aid. Deferred admission is possible.

Getting in Last Year

14,627 applied
39% were accepted
3,101 enrolled (54%)
85% from top tenth of their h.s. class
4.00 average high school GPA
80% had SAT verbal scores over 600
84% had SAT math scores over 600
85% had ACT scores over 24
32% had SAT verbal scores over 700
39% had SAT math scores over 700
43% had ACT scores over 30
193 valedictorians

Graduation and After

83% graduated in 4 years
8% graduated in 5 years
1% graduated in 6 years
32% pursued further study
450 organizations recruited on campus

Financial Matters

$6149 resident tuition and fees (2003–04)
$22,119 nonresident tuition and fees (2003–04)
$5591 room and board
92% average percent of need met
$12,408 average financial aid amount received per undergraduate

UNIVERSITY OF WASHINGTON

URBAN SETTING ■ PUBLIC ■ STATE-SUPPORTED ■ COED
SEATTLE, WASHINGTON

Web site: www.washington.edu
Contact: Mr. Wilbur W. Washburn, IV, Assistant Vice President for
    Enrollment Services, Box 355852, Seattle, WA 98195-5852
Telephone: 206-543-9686

Getting in Last Year
15,950 applied
68% were accepted
4,771 enrolled (44%)
48% from top tenth of their h.s. class
3.67 average high school GPA
44% had SAT verbal scores over 600
58% had SAT math scores over 600
68% had ACT scores over 24
10% had SAT verbal scores over 700
15% had SAT math scores over 700
16% had ACT scores over 30

Graduation and After
40% graduated in 4 years
450 organizations recruited on campus

Financial Matters
$4968 resident tuition and fees (2003–04)
$16,124 nonresident tuition and fees (2003–04)
$6726 room and board
88% average percent of need met
$9784 average financial aid amount received per undergraduate (2002–03 estimated)

Academics

UW awards bachelor's, master's, doctoral, and first-professional **degrees**. Challenging opportunities include advanced placement credit, accelerated degree programs, student-designed majors, an honors program, double majors, independent study, and a senior project. Special programs include cooperative education, internships, summer session for credit, study-abroad, and Army, Navy and Air Force ROTC.

The most frequently chosen **baccalaureate** fields are social sciences and history, business/marketing, and biological/life sciences. A complete listing of majors at UW appears in the Majors Index beginning on page 460.

The **faculty** at UW has 2,764 full-time members, 94% with terminal degrees. The student-faculty ratio is 11:1.

Students of UW

The student body totals 39,246, of whom 28,362 are undergraduates. 51.7% are women and 48.3% are men. Students come from 52 states and territories and 59 other countries. 87% are from Washington. 3.3% are international students. 2.7% are African American, 1.1% American Indian, 24.3% Asian American, and 3.5% Hispanic American. 91% returned for their sophomore year.

Facilities and Resources

Student rooms are linked to a campus network. 285 **computers** are available on campus that provide access to the Internet. The 22 **libraries** have 5,820,229 books and 50,245 subscriptions.

Campus Life

There are 300 active organizations on campus, including a drama/theater group, newspaper, radio station, television station, choral group, and marching band. 12% of eligible men and 11% of eligible women are members of national **fraternities** and national **sororities**.

UW is a member of the NCAA (Division I). **Intercollegiate sports** (some offering scholarships) include baseball (m), basketball, crew, cross-country running, football (m), golf, gymnastics (w), soccer, softball (w), swimming, tennis, track and field, volleyball (w).

Campus Safety

Student safety services include late-night transport/escort service, 24-hour emergency telephone alarm devices, 24-hour patrols by trained security personnel, and electronically operated dormitory entrances.

Applying

UW requires an essay, SAT I or ACT, a high school transcript, and a minimum high school GPA of 2.0. Application deadline: 1/15; 2/28 priority date for financial aid. Early admission is possible.

UNIVERSITY OF WISCONSIN–MADISON

URBAN SETTING ■ PUBLIC ■ STATE-SUPPORTED ■ COED
MADISON, WISCONSIN

Web site: www.wisc.edu
Contact: Mr. Keith White, Associate Director of Admission, 716 Langdon
   Street, Madison, WI 53706-1481
Telephone: 608-262-3961 **Fax:** 608-262-7706
E-mail: on.wisconsin@admissions.wisc.edu

Academics

Wisconsin awards bachelor's, master's, doctoral, and first-professional **degrees** and post-bachelor's and post-master's certificates. Challenging opportunities include advanced placement credit, student-designed majors, freshman honors college, an honors program, double majors, independent study, and a senior project. Special programs include cooperative education, internships, summer session for credit, study-abroad, and Army ROTC. A complete listing of majors at Wisconsin appears in the Majors Index beginning on page 460.

The **faculty** at Wisconsin has 2,225 full-time members, 100% with terminal degrees. The student-faculty ratio is 14:1.

Students of Wisconsin

The student body totals 41,588, of whom 28,583 are undergraduates. Students come from 54 states and territories and 131 other countries. 62% are from Wisconsin. 96% returned for their sophomore year.

Facilities and Resources

Student rooms are linked to a campus network. 2,800 **computers** are available on campus that provide access to the Internet. The 41 **libraries** have 6,100,000 books and 66,000 subscriptions.

Campus Life

There are 690 active organizations on campus, including a drama/theater group, newspaper, radio station, choral group, and marching band. 20% of eligible men and 20% of eligible women are members of national **fraternities**, national **sororities**, and eating clubs.

Wisconsin is a member of the NCAA (Division I). **Intercollegiate sports** (some offering scholarships) include basketball, cheerleading, crew, cross-country running, football (m), golf, ice hockey, lacrosse (w), soccer, softball (w), swimming, tennis, track and field, volleyball (w), wrestling (m).

Campus Safety

Student safety services include free cab rides throughout the city, late-night transport/escort service, 24-hour emergency telephone alarm devices, 24-hour patrols by trained security personnel, and electronically operated dormitory entrances.

Applying

Wisconsin requires an essay, SAT I or ACT, and a high school transcript, and in some cases SAT II Subject Tests. It recommends SAT II Subject Tests and an interview. Application deadline: 2/1. Early and deferred admission are possible.

Getting in Last Year

21,335 applied
61% were accepted
57% from top tenth of their h.s. class
3.88 average high school GPA
71% had SAT verbal scores over 600
79% had SAT math scores over 600
87% had ACT scores over 24
26% had SAT verbal scores over 700
25% had SAT math scores over 700
39% had ACT scores over 30
193 National Merit Scholars
625 valedictorians

Graduation and After

36% graduated in 4 years
69% pursued further study

Financial Matters

$5140 resident tuition and fees (2003–04)
$19,150 nonresident tuition and fees (2003–04)
$6130 room and board
$8722 average financial aid amount received per undergraduate (2001–02)

UNIVERSITY OF WYOMING

SMALL-TOWN SETTING ■ PUBLIC ■ STATE-SUPPORTED ■ COED
LARAMIE, WYOMING

Web site: www.uwyo.edu
Contact: Ms. Sara Axelson, Associate Vice President Enrollment and Director of Admissions, Box 3435, Laramie, WY 82071
Telephone: 307-766-5160 or toll-free 800-342-5996 **Fax:** 307-766-4042
E-mail: why-wyo@uwyo.edu

Getting in Last Year

2,948 applied
95% were accepted
1,416 enrolled (51%)
19% from top tenth of their h.s. class
3.41 average high school GPA
24% had SAT verbal scores over 600
30% had SAT math scores over 600
45% had ACT scores over 24
3% had SAT verbal scores over 700
5% had SAT math scores over 700
6% had ACT scores over 30

Graduation and After

25% graduated in 4 years
24% graduated in 5 years
5% graduated in 6 years
102 organizations recruited on campus

Financial Matters

$3090 resident tuition and fees (2003–04)
$8940 nonresident tuition and fees (2003–04)
$5546 room and board
75% average percent of need met
$7467 average financial aid amount received per undergraduate (2001–02)

Academics

UW awards bachelor's, master's, doctoral, and first-professional **degrees** and post-master's certificates. Challenging opportunities include advanced placement credit, accelerated degree programs, student-designed majors, an honors program, double majors, independent study, and a senior project. Special programs include internships, summer session for credit, off-campus study, study-abroad, and Army and Air Force ROTC.

The most frequently chosen **baccalaureate** fields are business/marketing, education, and engineering/engineering technologies. A complete listing of majors at UW appears in the Majors Index beginning on page 460.

The **faculty** at UW has 623 full-time members, 86% with terminal degrees. The student-faculty ratio is 16:1.

Students of UW

The student body totals 13,130, of whom 9,385 are undergraduates. 53.3% are women and 46.7% are men. Students come from 52 states and territories and 48 other countries. 73% are from Wyoming. 1% are international students. 1% are African American, 1% American Indian, 1% Asian American, and 3.6% Hispanic American. 75% returned for their sophomore year.

Facilities and Resources

Student rooms are linked to a campus network. 1,300 **computers** are available on campus that provide access to the Internet. The 7 **libraries** have 1,297,778 books and 13,256 subscriptions.

Campus Life

There are 180 active organizations on campus, including a drama/theater group, newspaper, radio station, television station, choral group, and marching band. 8% of eligible men and 5% of eligible women are members of national **fraternities** and national **sororities**.

UW is a member of the NCAA (Division I). **Intercollegiate sports** (some offering scholarships) include basketball, cheerleading, cross-country running, football (m), golf, soccer (w), swimming, tennis (w), track and field, volleyball (w), wrestling (m).

Campus Safety

Student safety services include late-night transport/escort service, 24-hour emergency telephone alarm devices, 24-hour patrols by trained security personnel, student patrols, and electronically operated dormitory entrances.

Applying

UW requires a high school transcript and a minimum high school GPA of 2.75, and in some cases SAT I or ACT and a minimum high school GPA of 3.0. It recommends an interview. Application deadline: 8/10; 2/1 priority date for financial aid. Deferred admission is possible.

URSINUS COLLEGE

SUBURBAN SETTING ■ PRIVATE ■ INDEPENDENT ■ COED
COLLEGEVILLE, PENNSYLVANIA

Web site: www.ursinus.edu
Contact: Mr. Paul M. Cramer, Director of Admissions, Box 1000, Main
  Street, Collegeville, PA 19426
Telephone: 610-409-3200 Fax: 610-409-3662
E-mail: admissions@ursinus.edu

Academics

Ursinus awards bachelor's **degrees**. Challenging opportunities include advanced placement credit, student-designed majors, an honors program, double majors, independent
study, and a senior project. Special programs include internships, off-campus study, and
study-abroad.

The most frequently chosen **baccalaureate** fields are social sciences and history,
area/ethnic studies, and psychology. A complete listing of majors at Ursinus appears in
the Majors Index beginning on page 460.

The **faculty** at Ursinus has 110 full-time members, 90% with terminal degrees. The
student-faculty ratio is 11:1.

Students of Ursinus

The student body is made up of 1,485 undergraduates. 53.6% are women and 46.4% are
men. Students come from 28 states and territories and 14 other countries. 63% are from
Pennsylvania. 1.5% are international students. 8% are African American, 0.3% American
Indian, 3.9% Asian American, and 2.7% Hispanic American. 88% returned for their
sophomore year.

Facilities and Resources

Student rooms are linked to a campus network. 350 **computers** are available on campus
that provide access to laptop computers and the Internet. The 3 **libraries** have 200,000
books and 900 subscriptions.

Campus Life

There are 105 active organizations on campus, including a drama/theater group,
newspaper, radio station, television station, and choral group. 26% of eligible men and
38% of eligible women are members of national **fraternities**, national **sororities**, local
fraternities, and local sororities.

Ursinus is a member of the NCAA (Division III). **Intercollegiate sports** include
baseball (m), basketball, cross-country running, field hockey (w), football (m), golf,
gymnastics (w), lacrosse, soccer, softball (w), swimming, tennis, track and field, volleyball
(w), wrestling (m).

Campus Safety

Student safety services include student EMT Corps for first aid/emergency first
response, late-night transport/escort service, 24-hour emergency telephone alarm
devices, and 24-hour patrols by trained security personnel.

Applying

Ursinus requires an essay, a high school transcript, 2 recommendations, and a graded
paper, and in some cases SAT I or ACT. It recommends SAT II Subject Tests and an
interview. Application deadline: 2/15; 2/15 priority date for financial aid. Early and
deferred admission are possible.

Getting in Last Year

1,775 applied
74% were accepted
454 enrolled (34%)
44% from top tenth of their h.s. class
3.50 average high school GPA
52% had SAT verbal scores over 600
57% had SAT math scores over 600
12% had SAT verbal scores over 700
12% had SAT math scores over 700
4 National Merit Scholars
8 class presidents
17 valedictorians

Graduation and After

75% graduated in 4 years
3% graduated in 5 years
32% pursued further study
60% had job offers within 6 months
50 organizations recruited on campus

Financial Matters

$27,500 tuition and fees (2003–04)
$6900 room and board
90% average percent of need met
$21,981 average financial aid amount received
  per undergraduate (2002–03 estimated)

VALPARAISO UNIVERSITY

SMALL-TOWN SETTING ■ PRIVATE ■ INDEPENDENT RELIGIOUS ■ COED
VALPARAISO, INDIANA

Web site: www.valpo.edu
Contact: Ms. Joyce Lantz, Director of Admissions, Kretzmann Hall, 1700 Chapel Drive, Valparaiso, IN 46383-6493
Telephone: 219-464-5011 or toll-free 888-GO-VALPO **Fax:** 219-464-6898
E-mail: undergrad.admissions@valpo.edu

Valparaiso University is home to 3,600 students seeking academic excellence in the Colleges of Arts & Sciences, Business Administration, Engineering, Nursing, and Christ College—The Honors College. Nestled in a residential community of 26,000, the University offers more than 60 areas of study in the liberal arts within a Christian atmosphere. Located one hour east of Chicago, "Valpo" is consistently ranked by *U.S. News & World Report* as a top regional university and best value. A low student-faculty ratio strengthens mentoring relationships. The required interdisciplinary freshman curriculum, Valpo Core, fosters a sense of true community. Students who apply before November ! are considered for Early Action.

Getting in Last Year
3,576 applied
82% were accepted
795 enrolled (27%)
36% from top tenth of their h.s. class
41% had SAT verbal scores over 600
45% had SAT math scores over 600
71% had ACT scores over 24
10% had SAT verbal scores over 700
12% had SAT math scores over 700
18% had ACT scores over 30
10 National Merit Scholars
42 valedictorians

Graduation and After
60% graduated in 4 years
12% graduated in 5 years
1% graduated in 6 years
27% pursued further study (3% law, 2% medicine, 2% theology)
71% had job offers within 6 months
81 organizations recruited on campus

Financial Matters
$20,632 tuition and fees (2003–04)
$5480 room and board
94% average percent of need met
$16,448 average financial aid amount received per undergraduate (2002–03 estimated)

Academics
Valpo awards associate, bachelor's, master's, and first-professional **degrees** and post-bachelor's and post-master's certificates. Challenging opportunities include advanced placement credit, accelerated degree programs, student-designed majors, freshman honors college, an honors program, double majors, independent study, and a senior project. Special programs include cooperative education, internships, summer session for credit, off-campus study, study-abroad, and Air Force ROTC.

The most frequently chosen **baccalaureate** fields are engineering/engineering technologies, business/marketing, and social sciences and history. A complete listing of majors at Valpo appears in the Majors Index beginning on page 460.

The **faculty** at Valpo has 232 full-time members, 88% with terminal degrees. The student-faculty ratio is 13:1.

Students of Valpo
The student body totals 3,850, of whom 3,026 are undergraduates. 53.5% are women and 46.5% are men. Students come from 47 states and territories and 41 other countries. 33% are from Indiana. 1.7% are international students. 3.2% are African American, 0.2% American Indian, 2% Asian American, and 3% Hispanic American. 86% returned for their sophomore year.

Facilities and Resources
Student rooms are linked to a campus network. 585 **computers** are available on campus that provide access to the Internet. The 2 **libraries** have 521,907 books and 5,282 subscriptions.

Campus Life
There are 100 active organizations on campus, including a drama/theater group, newspaper, radio station, and choral group. 30% of eligible men and 20% of eligible women are members of national **fraternities** and local **sororities**.

Valpo is a member of the NCAA (Division I). **Intercollegiate sports** (some offering scholarships) include baseball (m), basketball, cross-country running, football (m), soccer, softball (w), swimming, tennis, volleyball (w).

Campus Safety
Student safety services include late-night transport/escort service, 24-hour emergency telephone alarm devices, 24-hour patrols by trained security personnel, and electronically operated dormitory entrances.

Applying
Valpo requires an essay, SAT I or ACT, and a high school transcript, and in some cases an interview. It recommends 2 recommendations. Application deadline: 8/15; 3/1 priority date for financial aid. Deferred admission is possible.

VANDERBILT UNIVERSITY

URBAN SETTING ■ PRIVATE ■ INDEPENDENT ■ COED
NASHVILLE, TENNESSEE

Web site: www.vanderbilt.edu
Contact: Mr. Bill Shain, Dean of Undergraduate Admissions, 2305 West End
   Avenue, Nashville, TN 37203
Telephone: 615-322-2561 or toll-free 800-288-0432 **Fax:** 615-343-7765
E-mail: admissions@vanderbilt.edu

Academics

Vanderbilt awards bachelor's, master's, doctoral, and first-professional **degrees**. Challenging opportunities include advanced placement credit, accelerated degree programs, student-designed majors, an honors program, double majors, independent study, and a senior project. Special programs include cooperative education, internships, summer session for credit, off-campus study, study-abroad, and Army, Navy and Air Force ROTC.

The most frequently chosen **baccalaureate** fields are social sciences and history, engineering/engineering technologies, and psychology. A complete listing of majors at Vanderbilt appears in the Majors Index beginning on page 460.

The **faculty** at Vanderbilt has 713 full-time members, 97% with terminal degrees. The student-faculty ratio is 9:1.

Students of Vanderbilt

The student body totals 11,092, of whom 6,283 are undergraduates. 51.9% are women and 48.1% are men. Students come from 54 states and territories and 36 other countries. 2.2% are international students. 6.6% are African American, 0.2% American Indian, 5.7% Asian American, and 4.2% Hispanic American. 94% returned for their sophomore year.

Facilities and Resources

Student rooms are linked to a campus network. 400 **computers** are available on campus that provide access to productivity and educational software. The 8 **libraries** have 1,812,869 books and 26,885 subscriptions.

Campus Life

There are 264 active organizations on campus, including a drama/theater group, newspaper, radio station, choral group, and marching band. 34% of eligible men and 48% of eligible women are members of national **fraternities** and national **sororities**.

Vanderbilt is a member of the NCAA (Division I). **Intercollegiate sports** (some offering scholarships) include baseball (m), basketball, cross-country running, football (m), golf, lacrosse (w), soccer, tennis, track and field (w).

Campus Safety

Student safety services include late-night transport/escort service, 24-hour emergency telephone alarm devices, 24-hour patrols by trained security personnel, student patrols, and electronically operated dormitory entrances.

Applying

Vanderbilt requires an essay, SAT I or ACT, a high school transcript, and 2 recommendations. It recommends SAT II Subject Tests and SAT II: Writing Test. Application deadline: 1/2; 2/1 priority date for financial aid. Early and deferred admission are possible.

Getting in Last Year

10,960 applied
40% were accepted
1,546 enrolled (35%)
77% from top tenth of their h.s. class
84% had SAT verbal scores over 600
89% had SAT math scores over 600
95% had ACT scores over 24
31% had SAT verbal scores over 700
39% had SAT math scores over 700
56% had ACT scores over 30
85 National Merit Scholars
30 class presidents
101 valedictorians

Graduation and After

75% graduated in 4 years
7% graduated in 5 years
1% graduated in 6 years
32% pursued further study (20% arts and sciences, 7% law, 4% medicine)
63% had job offers within 6 months
250 organizations recruited on campus

Financial Matters

$28,440 tuition and fees (2003–04)
$9457 room and board
99% average percent of need met
$27,981 average financial aid amount received per undergraduate (2002–03 estimated)

VASSAR COLLEGE

SUBURBAN SETTING ■ PRIVATE ■ INDEPENDENT ■ COED
POUGHKEEPSIE, NEW YORK

Web site: www.vassar.edu
Contact: Dr. David M. Borus, Dean of Admission and Financial Aid, 124
  Raymond Avenue, Poughkeepsie, NY 12604
Telephone: 845-437-7300 or toll-free 800-827-7270 **Fax:** 914-437-7063
E-mail: admissions@vassar.edu

Getting in Last Year

6,207 applied
29% were accepted
632 enrolled (35%)
65% from top tenth of their h.s. class
3.60 average high school GPA
96% had SAT verbal scores over 600
92% had SAT math scores over 600
50% had SAT verbal scores over 700
37% had SAT math scores over 700
28 class presidents
20 valedictorians

Graduation and After

82% graduated in 4 years
6% graduated in 5 years
1% graduated in 6 years
20% pursued further study
62.1% had job offers within 6 months
20 organizations recruited on campus

Financial Matters

$29,540 tuition and fees (2003–04)
$7490 room and board
100% average percent of need met
$24,305 average financial aid amount received
  per undergraduate

Academics

Vassar awards bachelor's and master's **degrees**. Challenging opportunities include advanced placement credit, student-designed majors, double majors, independent study, and a senior project. Special programs include cooperative education, internships, off-campus study, and study-abroad.

The most frequently chosen **baccalaureate** fields are social sciences and history, visual/performing arts, and English. A complete listing of majors at Vassar appears in the Majors Index beginning on page 460.

The **faculty** at Vassar has 254 full-time members, 94% with terminal degrees. The student-faculty ratio is 9:1.

Students of Vassar

The student body is made up of 2,444 undergraduates. 59.6% are women and 40.4% are men. Students come from 53 states and territories and 49 other countries. 28% are from New York. 4.3% are international students. 4.8% are African American, 0.4% American Indian, 8.7% Asian American, and 4.8% Hispanic American. 95% returned for their sophomore year.

Facilities and Resources

Student rooms are linked to a campus network. 300 **computers** are available on campus that provide access to Ethernet and the Internet. The 2 **libraries** have 830,235 books and 5,028 subscriptions.

Campus Life

There are 85 active organizations on campus, including a drama/theater group, newspaper, radio station, television station, and choral group. No national or local **fraternities** or **sororities**.

Vassar is a member of the NCAA (Division III). **Intercollegiate sports** include baseball (m), basketball, crew, cross-country running, fencing, field hockey (w), lacrosse, soccer, squash, swimming, tennis, volleyball.

Campus Safety

Student safety services include late-night transport/escort service, 24-hour emergency telephone alarm devices, 24-hour patrols by trained security personnel, student patrols, and electronically operated dormitory entrances.

Applying

Vassar requires an essay, SAT I and SAT II or ACT, a high school transcript, and 2 recommendations. Application deadline: 1/1; 2/1 for financial aid. Deferred admission is possible.

Villanova University

SUBURBAN SETTING ■ PRIVATE ■ INDEPENDENT RELIGIOUS ■ COED
VILLANOVA, PENNSYLVANIA

Web site: www.villanova.edu
Contact: Mr. Michael M. Gaynor, Director of University Admission, 800 Lancaster Avenue, Villanova, PA 19085-1672
Telephone: 610-519-4000 or toll-free 610-519-4000 **Fax:** 610-519-6450
E-mail: gotovu@villanova.edu

Academics

Villanova awards associate, bachelor's, master's, doctoral, and first-professional **degrees**. Challenging opportunities include advanced placement credit, accelerated degree programs, an honors program, double majors, independent study, and a senior project. Special programs include internships, summer session for credit, off-campus study, study-abroad, and Army, Navy and Air Force ROTC.

The most frequently chosen **baccalaureate** fields are business/marketing, engineering/engineering technologies, and social sciences and history. A complete listing of majors at Villanova appears in the Majors Index beginning on page 460.

The **faculty** at Villanova has 549 full-time members, 91% with terminal degrees. The student-faculty ratio is 13:1.

Students of Villanova

The student body totals 10,619, of whom 7,267 are undergraduates. 50.9% are women and 49.1% are men. Students come from 49 states and territories and 28 other countries. 34% are from Pennsylvania. 2.4% are international students. 2.9% are African American, 0.2% American Indian, 4.8% Asian American, and 5.1% Hispanic American. 94% returned for their sophomore year.

Facilities and Resources

Student rooms are linked to a campus network. 800 **computers** are available on campus that provide access to the Internet. The 3 **libraries** have 1,010,560 books and 5,338 subscriptions.

Campus Life

There are 100 active organizations on campus, including a drama/theater group, newspaper, radio station, television station, choral group, and marching band. 18% of eligible men and 34% of eligible women are members of national **fraternities** and national **sororities**.

Villanova is a member of the NCAA (Division I). **Intercollegiate sports** (some offering scholarships) include baseball (m), basketball, cheerleading, crew (w), cross-country running, field hockey (w), football (m), golf (m), lacrosse, soccer, softball (w), swimming, tennis, track and field, volleyball (w), water polo (w).

Campus Safety

Student safety services include late-night transport/escort service, 24-hour emergency telephone alarm devices, 24-hour patrols by trained security personnel, student patrols, and electronically operated dormitory entrances.

Applying

Villanova requires an essay, SAT I or ACT, a high school transcript, and activities resume. Application deadline: 1/7; 2/14 priority date for financial aid. Early and deferred admission are possible.

Vision and education go hand in hand at Villanova. The University invests in students' futures by updating its facilities and resources. Three of its newest initiatives include the construction of the $20-million Center for Engineering Education and Research, the completion of $35 million in expansion and enhancement of the Mendel Science Center, and $20 million in renovation of the College of Commerce and Finance's Bartley Hall. Overall in the last 10 years, Villanova has dedicated more than $200 million to these initiatives and more, including 4 new apartment-style buildings, the new Student Health Center, and improvements to the computing infrastructure.

Getting in Last Year
10,896 applied
53% were accepted
1,566 enrolled (27%)
41% from top tenth of their h.s. class
3.63 average high school GPA
61% had SAT verbal scores over 600
77% had SAT math scores over 600
10% had SAT verbal scores over 700
17% had SAT math scores over 700
16 valedictorians

Graduation and After
80% graduated in 4 years
5% graduated in 5 years
28% pursued further study (7% arts and sciences, 6% law, 3% business)
78% had job offers within 6 months
375 organizations recruited on campus

Financial Matters
$26,223 tuition and fees (2003–04)
$8827 room and board
76% average percent of need met
$18,217 average financial aid amount received per undergraduate

VIRGINIA MILITARY INSTITUTE

SMALL-TOWN SETTING ■ PUBLIC ■ STATE-SUPPORTED ■ COED, PRIMARILY MEN
LEXINGTON, VIRGINIA

Web site: www.vmi.edu
Contact: Lt. Col. Tom Mortenson, Associate Director of Admissions, 309
   Letcher Avenue, Lexington, VA 24450
Telephone: 540-464-7211 or toll-free 800-767-4207 **Fax:** 540-464-7746
E-mail: admissions@vmi.edu

VMI offers a challenging curricular and cocurricular undergraduate experience, with the mission of producing educated and honorable men and women who will be leaders in all walks of life. Its 1,250 cadets pursue BA or BS degrees in 14 disciplines in the general fields of engineering, science, and liberal arts. VMI combines a full college curriculum within a framework of military discipline that emphasizes the qualities of honor, integrity, and responsibility. Undergirding all aspects of cadet life is the VMI Honor Code, to which all cadets subscribe.

Getting in Last Year
1,711 applied
50% were accepted
359 enrolled (42%)
3.35 average high school GPA
33% had SAT verbal scores over 600
37% had SAT math scores over 600
58% had ACT scores over 24
6% had SAT verbal scores over 700
3% had SAT math scores over 700
4% had ACT scores over 30

Graduation and After
47% graduated in 4 years
14% graduated in 5 years
4% graduated in 6 years
Graduates pursuing further study: 9% arts and sciences, 7% engineering, 1% dentistry
98% had job offers within 6 months
40 organizations recruited on campus

Financial Matters
$6181 resident tuition and fees (2003–04)
$18,893 nonresident tuition and fees (2003–04)
$5266 room and board
92% average percent of need met
$12,369 average financial aid amount received per undergraduate (2002–03 estimated)

Academics
VMI awards bachelor's **degrees**. Challenging opportunities include advanced placement credit, accelerated degree programs, an honors program, double majors, independent study, and a senior project. Special programs include internships, summer session for credit, study-abroad, and Army, Navy and Air Force ROTC. A complete listing of majors at VMI appears in the Majors Index beginning on page 460.

   The **faculty** at VMI has 145 members, 96% with terminal degrees. The student-faculty ratio is 12:1.

Students of VMI
The student body is made up of 1,299 undergraduates. 5.9% are women and 94.1% are men. Students come from 45 states and territories and 17 other countries. 51% are from Virginia. 3% are international students. 5.9% are African American, 0.5% American Indian, 3.2% Asian American, and 3.2% Hispanic American. 86% returned for their sophomore year.

Facilities and Resources
Student rooms are linked to a campus network. 200 **computers** are available on campus that provide access to the Internet. The 2 **libraries** have 162,053 books and 785 subscriptions.

Campus Life
There are 47 active organizations on campus, including a drama/theater group, newspaper, choral group, and marching band. No national or local **fraternities** or **sororities**.

   VMI is a member of the NCAA (Division I). **Intercollegiate sports** (some offering scholarships) include baseball (m), basketball (m), cross-country running, football (m), golf (m), lacrosse (m), riflery, soccer (m), swimming, tennis (m), track and field, wrestling (m).

Campus Safety
Student safety services include 24-hour emergency telephone alarm devices, 24-hour patrols by trained security personnel, and student patrols.

Applying
VMI requires SAT I or ACT and a high school transcript. It recommends an essay, an interview, and 2 recommendations. Application deadline: 2/15; 3/1 priority date for financial aid. Early admission is possible.

VIRGINIA POLYTECHNIC INSTITUTE AND STATE UNIVERSITY

SMALL-TOWN SETTING ■ PUBLIC ■ STATE-SUPPORTED ■ COED
BLACKSBURG, VIRGINIA

Web site: www.vt.edu
Contact: Ms. Mildred Johnson, Associate Director for Freshmen Admissions, 201 Burruss Hall, Blacksburg, VA 24061
Telephone: 540-231-6267 **Fax:** 540-231-3242
E-mail: vtadmiss@vt.edu

Academics

Virginia Tech awards associate, bachelor's, master's, doctoral, and first-professional **degrees**. Challenging opportunities include advanced placement credit, accelerated degree programs, an honors program, double majors, independent study, and a senior project. Special programs include cooperative education, internships, summer session for credit, study-abroad, and Army, Navy and Air Force ROTC.

The most frequently chosen **baccalaureate** fields are business/marketing, engineering/engineering technologies, and home economics/vocational home economics. A complete listing of majors at Virginia Tech appears in the Majors Index beginning on page 460.

The **faculty** at Virginia Tech has 1,259 full-time members. The student-faculty ratio is 16:1.

Students of Virginia Tech

The student body is made up of 21,343 undergraduates. 41.1% are women and 58.9% are men. Students come from 52 states and territories and 104 other countries. 73% are from Virginia. 2.8% are international students. 5.8% are African American, 0.3% American Indian, 6.9% Asian American, and 2% Hispanic American. 90% returned for their sophomore year.

Facilities and Resources

Student rooms are linked to a campus network. 8,000 **computers** are available on campus that provide access to the Internet. The 5 **libraries** have 2,098,074 books and 17,562 subscriptions.

Campus Life

There are 524 active organizations on campus, including a drama/theater group, newspaper, radio station, television station, choral group, and marching band. 13% of eligible men and 15% of eligible women are members of national **fraternities**, national **sororities**, and local fraternities.

Virginia Tech is a member of the NCAA (Division I). **Intercollegiate sports** (some offering scholarships) include baseball (m), basketball, cross-country running, football (m), golf (m), lacrosse (w), soccer, softball (w), swimming, tennis, track and field, ultimate Frisbee, volleyball (w), wrestling (m).

Campus Safety

Student safety services include late-night transport/escort service, 24-hour emergency telephone alarm devices, 24-hour patrols by trained security personnel, student patrols, and electronically operated dormitory entrances.

Applying

Virginia Tech requires SAT I or ACT, a high school transcript, and a minimum high school GPA of 2.0. It recommends a minimum high school GPA of 3.3. Application deadline: 1/15; 3/11 priority date for financial aid. Early and deferred admission are possible.

Students wishing to learn in a high-technology environment choose Virginia Tech, the largest university in Virginia and the commonwealth's top research university. A leading magazine ranked Virginia Tech 28th among the top national public universities. Tech has also been named one of the most wired colleges in America for its innovative use of technology in the classroom (from English to engineering) and student computer access. Virginia Tech even prefers that students apply online! Undergraduate research opportunities and cutting-edge facilities make Virginia Tech the high-tech choice.

Getting in Last Year
18,028 applied
69% were accepted
5,874 enrolled (47%)
40% from top tenth of their h.s. class
3.6 average high school GPA
39% had SAT verbal scores over 600
52% had SAT math scores over 600
5% had SAT verbal scores over 700
11% had SAT math scores over 700

Graduation and After
42% graduated in 4 years
38% graduated in 5 years
7% graduated in 6 years
13% pursued further study
79% had job offers within 6 months
340 organizations recruited on campus

Financial Matters
$5095 resident tuition and fees (2003–04)
$14,979 nonresident tuition and fees (2003–04)
$4146 room and board
64% average percent of need met
$7044 average financial aid amount received per undergraduate (2002–03 estimated)

WABASH COLLEGE
SMALL-TOWN SETTING ■ PRIVATE ■ INDEPENDENT ■ MEN ONLY
CRAWFORDSVILLE, INDIANA

Web site: www.wabash.edu
Contact: Mr. Steve Klein, Director of Admissions, PO Box 362,
   Crawfordsville, IN 47933-0352
Telephone: 765-361-6225 or toll-free 800-345-5385 **Fax:** 765-361-6437
E-mail: admissions@wabash.edu

As a college for men, Wabash helps students achieve their full potential—intellectually, athletically, emotionally, and artistically. Wabash prepares students for leadership in an ever-changing world. The College helps them learn to think clearly and openly and to explore a variety of interests. Independence and responsibility are emphasized and defined by the Gentlemen's Rule, which calls on students to conduct themselves as gentlemen at all times. With the guidance of professors who are accessible, a support staff that cares, and a nationwide network of alumni willing to offer assistance and encouragement, Wabash men frequently surpass even their own expectations.

Getting in Last Year
1,299 applied
50% were accepted
239 enrolled (37%)
38% from top tenth of their h.s. class
3.61 average high school GPA
39% had SAT verbal scores over 600
56% had SAT math scores over 600
9% had SAT verbal scores over 700
14% had SAT math scores over 700
7 National Merit Scholars
12 class presidents
6 valedictorians

Graduation and After
70% graduated in 4 years
3% graduated in 5 years
2% graduated in 6 years
37% pursued further study (16% arts and
   sciences, 10% law, 9% medicine)
60% had job offers within 6 months
55 organizations recruited on campus

Financial Matters
$21,215 tuition and fees (2003–04)
$6717 room and board
100% average percent of need met
$18,585 average financial aid amount received
   per undergraduate (2001–02)

Academics
Wabash awards bachelor's **degrees**. Challenging opportunities include advanced placement credit, accelerated degree programs, double majors, independent study, and a senior project. Special programs include cooperative education, internships, off-campus study, study-abroad, and Army ROTC.

The most frequently chosen **baccalaureate** fields are social sciences and history, English, and psychology. A complete listing of majors at Wabash appears in the Majors Index beginning on page 460.

The **faculty** at Wabash has 86 full-time members, 93% with terminal degrees. The student-faculty ratio is 10:1.

Students of Wabash
The student body is made up of 863 undergraduates. Students come from 34 states and territories and 14 other countries. 73% are from Indiana. 3.7% are international students. 7.6% are African American, 0.2% American Indian, 3.2% Asian American, and 5% Hispanic American. 87% returned for their sophomore year.

Facilities and Resources
Student rooms are linked to a campus network. 160 **computers** are available on campus that provide access to the Internet. The **library** has 420,906 books and 1,634 subscriptions.

Campus Life
There are 45 active organizations on campus, including a drama/theater group, newspaper, radio station, and choral group. 62% of eligible undergraduates are members of national **fraternities** and language houses.

Wabash is a member of the NCAA (Division III). **Intercollegiate sports** include baseball, basketball, cross-country running, football, golf, soccer, swimming, tennis, track and field, wrestling.

Campus Safety
Student safety services include late-night transport/escort service, 24-hour emergency telephone alarm devices, and 24-hour patrols by trained security personnel.

Applying
Wabash requires an essay, SAT I or ACT, a high school transcript, 1 recommendation, and a minimum high school GPA of 2.0. It recommends an interview and a minimum high school GPA of 3.0. Application deadline: 3/15; 3/1 for financial aid, with a 2/15 priority date. Early and deferred admission are possible.

WAKE FOREST UNIVERSITY

SUBURBAN SETTING ■ PRIVATE ■ INDEPENDENT ■ COED
WINSTON-SALEM, NORTH CAROLINA

Web site: www.wfu.edu
Contact: Ms. Martha Allman, Director of Admissions, PO Box 7305,
   Winston-Salem, NC 27109
Telephone: 336-758-5201
E-mail: admissions@wfu.edu

Academics

Wake Forest awards bachelor's, master's, doctoral, and first-professional **degrees**. Challenging opportunities include advanced placement credit, accelerated degree programs, an honors program, double majors, independent study, and a senior project. Special programs include internships, summer session for credit, off-campus study, study-abroad, and Army ROTC.

The most frequently chosen **baccalaureate** fields are social sciences and history, business/marketing, and communications/communication technologies. A complete listing of majors at Wake Forest appears in the Majors Index beginning on page 460.

The **faculty** at Wake Forest has 445 full-time members, 91% with terminal degrees. The student-faculty ratio is 10:1.

Students of Wake Forest

The student body totals 6,451, of whom 4,031 are undergraduates. 51.2% are women and 48.8% are men. Students come from 50 states and territories and 26 other countries. 26% are from North Carolina. 0.9% are international students. 6.7% are African American, 0.2% American Indian, 3.4% Asian American, and 1.8% Hispanic American. 93% returned for their sophomore year.

Facilities and Resources

Student rooms are linked to a campus network. 150 **computers** are available on campus that provide access to personal computer and the Internet. The 4 **libraries** have 923,123 books and 16,448 subscriptions.

Campus Life

There are 135 active organizations on campus, including a drama/theater group, newspaper, radio station, television station, choral group, and marching band. 36% of eligible men and 51% of eligible women are members of national **fraternities** and national **sororities**.

Wake Forest is a member of the NCAA (Division I). **Intercollegiate sports** (some offering scholarships) include baseball (m), basketball, cross-country running, field hockey (w), football (m), golf, soccer, tennis, track and field, volleyball (w).

Campus Safety

Student safety services include late-night transport/escort service, 24-hour emergency telephone alarm devices, 24-hour patrols by trained security personnel, and electronically operated dormitory entrances.

Applying

Wake Forest requires an essay, SAT I, a high school transcript, and 1 recommendation. It recommends SAT II Subject Tests. Application deadline: 1/15; 3/1 priority date for financial aid. Early and deferred admission are possible.

Getting in Last Year
5,752 applied
45% were accepted
1,004 enrolled (39%)
65% from top tenth of their h.s. class
83% had SAT verbal scores over 600
87% had SAT math scores over 600
24% had SAT verbal scores over 700
31% had SAT math scores over 700
4 National Merit Scholars
29 class presidents
93 valedictorians

Graduation and After
77% graduated in 4 years
10% graduated in 5 years
1% graduated in 6 years
29% pursued further study
60.4% had job offers within 6 months
548 organizations recruited on campus

Financial Matters
$26,490 tuition and fees (2003–04)
$8260 room and board
90% average percent of need met
$19,394 average financial aid amount received
   per undergraduate (2001–02)

Wartburg College

SMALL-TOWN SETTING ■ PRIVATE ■ INDEPENDENT RELIGIOUS ■ COED
WAVERLY, IOWA

Web site: www.wartburg.edu
Contact: Mr. Doug Bowman, Dean of Admissions/Financial Aid, 100
    Wartburg Boulevard, PO Box 1003, Waverly, IA 50677-0903
Telephone: 319-352-8264 or toll-free 800-772-2085 **Fax:** 319-352-8579
E-mail: admissions@wartburg.edu

Getting in Last Year

1,841 applied
83% were accepted
504 enrolled (33%)
33% from top tenth of their h.s. class
3.46 average high school GPA
38% had SAT verbal scores over 600
53% had SAT math scores over 600
50% had ACT scores over 24
5% had SAT verbal scores over 700
5% had SAT math scores over 700
8% had ACT scores over 30
42 valedictorians

Graduation and After

67% graduated in 4 years
4% graduated in 5 years
1% graduated in 6 years
Graduates pursuing further study: 6% arts and
    sciences, 3% medicine, 1% education
67% had job offers within 6 months
70 organizations recruited on campus

Financial Matters

$18,550 tuition and fees (2003–04)
$5180 room and board
95% average percent of need met
$17,031 average financial aid amount received
    per undergraduate

Academics

Wartburg awards bachelor's **degrees**. Challenging opportunities include advanced placement credit, accelerated degree programs, student-designed majors, double majors, independent study, and a senior project. Special programs include internships, summer session for credit, off-campus study, and study-abroad.

The most frequently chosen **baccalaureate** fields are education, business/marketing, and communications/communication technologies. A complete listing of majors at Wartburg appears in the Majors Index beginning on page 460.

The **faculty** at Wartburg has 103 full-time members, 81% with terminal degrees. The student-faculty ratio is 14:1.

Students of Wartburg

The student body is made up of 1,775 undergraduates. 54.9% are women and 45.1% are men. Students come from 23 states and territories and 32 other countries. 81% are from Iowa. 4.3% are international students. 3.7% are African American, 0.1% American Indian, 1.1% Asian American, and 0.7% Hispanic American. 77% returned for their sophomore year.

Facilities and Resources

Student rooms are linked to a campus network. 250 **computers** are available on campus that provide access to the Internet. The **library** has 171,852 books and 826 subscriptions.

Campus Life

There are 96 active organizations on campus, including a drama/theater group, newspaper, radio station, television station, and choral group. No national or local **fraternities** or **sororities**.

Wartburg is a member of the NCAA (Division III). **Intercollegiate sports** include baseball (m), basketball, cheerleading (w), cross-country running, football (m), golf, soccer, softball (w), tennis, track and field, volleyball (w), wrestling (m).

Campus Safety

Student safety services include late-night transport/escort service, 24-hour emergency telephone alarm devices, 24-hour patrols by trained security personnel, and electronically operated dormitory entrances.

Applying

Wartburg requires SAT I or ACT, a high school transcript, and a minimum high school GPA of 2.0, and in some cases an interview. It recommends recommendations and secondary school report. Application deadline: 3/1 priority date for financial aid. Deferred admission is possible.

WASHINGTON & JEFFERSON COLLEGE

SMALL-TOWN SETTING ■ PRIVATE ■ INDEPENDENT ■ COED
WASHINGTON, PENNSYLVANIA

Web site: www.washjeff.edu
Contact: Mr. Alton E. Newell, Dean of Enrollment, 60 South Lincoln Street, Washington, PA 15301
Telephone: 724-223-6025 or toll-free 888-WANDJAY **Fax:** 724-223-6534
E-mail: admission@washjeff.edu

Academics

W & J awards associate and bachelor's **degrees**. Challenging opportunities include advanced placement credit, accelerated degree programs, student-designed majors, an honors program, double majors, independent study, and a senior project. Special programs include internships, summer session for credit, study-abroad, and Army and Air Force ROTC.

The most frequently chosen **baccalaureate** fields are business/marketing, social sciences and history, and English. A complete listing of majors at W & J appears in the Majors Index beginning on page 460.

The **faculty** at W & J has 95 full-time members, 87% with terminal degrees. The student-faculty ratio is 11:1.

Students of W & J

The student body is made up of 1,233 undergraduates. 48.3% are women and 51.7% are men. Students come from 28 states and territories and 4 other countries. 80% are from Pennsylvania. 0.2% are international students. 2.4% are African American, 0.2% American Indian, 1.5% Asian American, and 1% Hispanic American. 84% returned for their sophomore year.

Facilities and Resources

Student rooms are linked to a campus network. 237 **computers** are available on campus that provide access to the Internet. The **library** has 184,858 books and 8,124 subscriptions.

Campus Life

There are 88 active organizations on campus, including a drama/theater group, newspaper, radio station, and choral group. 47% of eligible men and 44% of eligible women are members of national **fraternities** and national **sororities**.

W & J is a member of the NCAA (Division III). **Intercollegiate sports** include baseball (m), basketball, cross-country running, field hockey (w), football (m), golf, lacrosse (m), soccer, softball (w), swimming, tennis, track and field, volleyball (w), water polo, wrestling (m).

Campus Safety

Student safety services include late-night transport/escort service, 24-hour emergency telephone alarm devices, 24-hour patrols by trained security personnel, and electronically operated dormitory entrances.

Applying

W & J requires an essay, SAT I or ACT, and a high school transcript. It recommends an interview and 1 recommendation. Application deadline: 3/1; 2/15 priority date for financial aid. Early and deferred admission are possible.

Getting in Last Year

3,135 applied
40% were accepted
347 enrolled (28%)
31% from top tenth of their h.s. class
3.13 average high school GPA
32% had SAT verbal scores over 600
40% had SAT math scores over 600
53% had ACT scores over 24
4% had SAT verbal scores over 700
6% had SAT math scores over 700
8% had ACT scores over 30

Graduation and After

69% graduated in 4 years
6% graduated in 5 years
33% pursued further study (10% law, 6% medicine, 5% arts and sciences)
63% had job offers within 6 months
33 organizations recruited on campus

Financial Matters

$23,260 tuition and fees (2003–04)
$6310 room and board
72% average percent of need met
$15,658 average financial aid amount received per undergraduate

WASHINGTON AND LEE UNIVERSITY

SMALL-TOWN SETTING ■ PRIVATE ■ INDEPENDENT ■ COED
LEXINGTON, VIRGINIA

Web site: www.wlu.edu
Contact: Mr. William M. Hartog, Dean of Admissions and Financial Aid,
Lexington, VA 24450-0303
Telephone: 540-458-8710 **Fax:** 540-458-8062
E-mail: admissions@wlu.edu

Getting in Last Year
3,185 applied
31% were accepted
453 enrolled (45%)
78% from top tenth of their h.s. class
92% had SAT verbal scores over 600
96% had SAT math scores over 600
100% had ACT scores over 24
44% had SAT verbal scores over 700
46% had SAT math scores over 700
47% had ACT scores over 30
31 National Merit Scholars
47 valedictorians

Graduation and After
85% graduated in 4 years
2% graduated in 5 years
22% pursued further study (7% arts and sciences, 7% engineering, 5% law)
65% had job offers within 6 months
60 organizations recruited on campus

Financial Matters
$23,295 tuition and fees (2003–04)
$6368 room and board
99% average percent of need met
$16,928 average financial aid amount received per undergraduate (2001–02)

Academics

W & L awards bachelor's, master's, and first-professional **degrees**. Challenging opportunities include advanced placement credit, accelerated degree programs, student-designed majors, an honors program, double majors, independent study, and a senior project. Special programs include internships, off-campus study, study-abroad, and Army ROTC.

The most frequently chosen **baccalaureate** fields are social sciences and history, business/marketing, and foreign language/literature. A complete listing of majors at W & L appears in the Majors Index beginning on page 460.

The **faculty** at W & L has 202 full-time members, 91% with terminal degrees. The student-faculty ratio is 11:1.

Students of W & L

The student body totals 2,137, of whom 1,740 are undergraduates. 47.9% are women and 52.1% are men. Students come from 47 states and territories and 37 other countries. 15% are from Virginia. 4.3% are international students. 4% are African American, 0.1% American Indian, 2.3% Asian American, and 0.9% Hispanic American. 95% returned for their sophomore year.

Facilities and Resources

Student rooms are linked to a campus network. 291 **computers** are available on campus that provide access to e-mail and the Internet. The 5 **libraries** have 1,037,413 books and 7,811 subscriptions.

Campus Life

There are 127 active organizations on campus, including a drama/theater group, newspaper, radio station, television station, and choral group. 75% of eligible men and 70% of eligible women are members of national **fraternities** and national **sororities**.

W & L is a member of the NCAA (Division III). **Intercollegiate sports** (some offering scholarships) include baseball (m), basketball, cross-country running, equestrian sports, field hockey (w), football (m), golf (m), lacrosse, soccer, swimming, tennis, track and field, volleyball (w), wrestling (m).

Campus Safety

Student safety services include late-night transport/escort service, 24-hour emergency telephone alarm devices, 24-hour patrols by trained security personnel, and electronically operated dormitory entrances.

Applying

W & L requires an essay, SAT I or ACT, 3 unrelated SAT II Subject Tests (including SAT II: Writing Test), a high school transcript, and 3 recommendations. It recommends an interview. Application deadline: 1/15; 2/1 priority date for financial aid. Deferred admission is possible.

WASHINGTON COLLEGE
SMALL-TOWN SETTING ■ PRIVATE ■ INDEPENDENT ■ COED
CHESTERTOWN, MARYLAND

Web site: www.washcoll.edu
Contact: Mr. Kevin Coveney, Vice President for Admissions, 300 Washington Avenue, Chestertown, MD 21620-1197
Telephone: 410-778-7700 or toll-free 800-422-1782
E-mail: admissions_office@washcoll.edu

Academics
WC awards bachelor's and master's **degrees**. Challenging opportunities include advanced placement credit, student-designed majors, double majors, independent study, and a senior project. Special programs include cooperative education, internships, off-campus study, and study-abroad.

The most frequently chosen **baccalaureate** fields are business/marketing, liberal arts/general studies, and psychology. A complete listing of majors at WC appears in the Majors Index beginning on page 460.

The **faculty** at WC has 86 full-time members, 88% with terminal degrees. The student-faculty ratio is 12:1.

Students of WC
The student body totals 1,481, of whom 1,398 are undergraduates. 62.9% are women and 37.1% are men. Students come from 36 states and territories and 40 other countries. 56% are from Maryland. 3.6% are international students. 3.6% are African American, 0.2% American Indian, 1.4% Asian American, and 0.8% Hispanic American. 88% returned for their sophomore year.

Facilities and Resources
Student rooms are linked to a campus network. 150 **computers** are available on campus that provide access to e-mail and the Internet. The **library** has 243,030 books and 4,667 subscriptions.

Campus Life
There are 50 active organizations on campus, including a drama/theater group, newspaper, and choral group. 25% of eligible men and 25% of eligible women are members of national **fraternities** and national **sororities**.

WC is a member of the NCAA (Division III). **Intercollegiate sports** include baseball (m), basketball, crew, field hockey (w), lacrosse, soccer, softball (w), swimming, tennis, volleyball (w).

Campus Safety
Student safety services include late-night transport/escort service, 24-hour emergency telephone alarm devices, 24-hour patrols by trained security personnel, student patrols, and electronically operated dormitory entrances.

Applying
WC requires an essay, SAT I or ACT, a high school transcript, and 1 recommendation, and in some cases an interview. It recommends an interview. Application deadline: 3/15; 2/15 priority date for financial aid. Early and deferred admission are possible.

Washington College (WC) has initiated a $40,000 scholarship program expressly for National Honor Society (NHS) members. Washington College NHS Scholarships are $10,000 annual awards renewable through the completion of 8 semesters (full-time enrollment and cumulative GPA of 3.0–4.0 required). To be eligible for WC/NHS Scholarship consideration, a student must apply for freshman admission no later than February 1 of the senior year, be admitted to Washington College, and be a member of NHS prior to March 1 of the senior year. For more information, students can contact the Admission Office or visit the WC Web site at http://www.washcoll.edu.

Getting in Last Year
2,114 applied
61% were accepted
359 enrolled (28%)
36% from top tenth of their h.s. class
3.44 average high school GPA
44% had SAT verbal scores over 600
33% had SAT math scores over 600
49% had ACT scores over 24
7% had SAT verbal scores over 700
4% had SAT math scores over 700
3% had ACT scores over 30

Graduation and After
63% graduated in 4 years
2% graduated in 5 years
1% graduated in 6 years
39% pursued further study
90% had job offers within 6 months
30 organizations recruited on campus

Financial Matters
$24,300 tuition and fees (2003–04)
$5740 room and board
88% average percent of need met
$19,395 average financial aid amount received per undergraduate

WASHINGTON UNIVERSITY IN ST. LOUIS

SUBURBAN SETTING ■ PRIVATE ■ INDEPENDENT ■ COED
ST. LOUIS, MISSOURI

Web site: www.wustl.edu
Contact: Ms. Nanette Tarbouni, Director of Admissions, Campus Box 1089,
One Brookings Drive, St. Louis, MO 63130-4899
Telephone: 314-935-6000 or toll-free 800-638-0700 **Fax:** 314-935-4290
E-mail: admissions@wustl.edu

Learning across disciplines is
a way of life at
Washington University in
St. Louis. Students enrolled in one of
the undergraduate schools—
Architecture, Art, Arts and Sciences,
Business, and Engineering and
Applied Science—are able to enroll
in courses offered by any of the
others. The University also offers
the benefit of graduate programs in
law, medicine (including occupational
therapy and physical therapy), and
social work. Students are challenged
in the classroom and in labs and
studios, where they work
side-by-side with their professors on
research and other special projects.

Getting in Last Year
20,378 applied
20% were accepted
1,367 enrolled (34%)
94% had SAT verbal scores over 600
98% had SAT math scores over 600
99% had ACT scores over 24
47% had SAT verbal scores over 700
60% had SAT math scores over 700
70% had ACT scores over 30

Graduation and After
79% graduated in 4 years
9% graduated in 5 years
1% graduated in 6 years
33% pursued further study (16% arts and
sciences, 12% law, 6% medicine)
60% had job offers within 6 months
360 organizations recruited on campus

Financial Matters
$29,053 tuition and fees (2003–04)
$9240 room and board
100% average percent of need met
$24,461 average financial aid amount received
per undergraduate

Academics

Washington awards bachelor's, master's, doctoral, and first-professional **degrees** and post-bachelor's certificates. Challenging opportunities include advanced placement credit, accelerated degree programs, student-designed majors, double majors, and independent study. Special programs include cooperative education, internships, summer session for credit, off-campus study, study-abroad, and Army and Air Force ROTC.

The most frequently chosen **baccalaureate** fields are social sciences and history, business/marketing, and engineering/engineering technologies. A complete listing of majors at Washington appears in the Majors Index beginning on page 460.

The **faculty** at Washington has 837 full-time members, 99% with terminal degrees. The student-faculty ratio is 7:1.

Students of Washington

The student body totals 13,020, of whom 7,188 are undergraduates. 53.4% are women and 46.6% are men. Students come from 53 states and territories and 88 other countries. 11% are from Missouri. 4.2% are international students. 8.7% are African American, 0.2% American Indian, 8.8% Asian American, and 3.4% Hispanic American. 97% returned for their sophomore year.

Facilities and Resources

Student rooms are linked to a campus network. 2,500 **computers** are available on campus that provide access to e-mail and the Internet. The 14 **libraries** have 1,565,626 books and 18,316 subscriptions.

Campus Life

There are 200 active organizations on campus, including a drama/theater group, newspaper, radio station, television station, and choral group. 28% of eligible men and 24% of eligible women are members of national **fraternities** and national **sororities**.

Washington is a member of the NCAA (Division III). **Intercollegiate sports** include baseball (m), basketball, cross-country running, football (m), soccer, softball (w), swimming, track and field, volleyball (w).

Campus Safety

Student safety services include late-night transport/escort service, 24-hour emergency telephone alarm devices, 24-hour patrols by trained security personnel, student patrols, and electronically operated dormitory entrances.

Applying

Washington requires an essay, SAT I or ACT, a high school transcript, and 2 recommendations. It recommends portfolio for art and architecture programs and a minimum high school GPA of 3.0. Application deadline: 1/15; 2/15 for financial aid. Early and deferred admission are possible.

WEBB INSTITUTE

SUBURBAN SETTING ■ PRIVATE ■ INDEPENDENT ■ COED
GLEN COVE, NEW YORK

Web site: www.webb-institute.edu
Contact: Mr. William G. Murray, Executive Director of Student
  Administrative Services, Crescent Beach Road, Glen Cove, NY 11542-1398
Telephone: 516-671-2213 **Fax:** 516-674-9838
E-mail: admissions@webb-institute.edu

Academics

Webb awards bachelor's **degrees**. Challenging opportunities include double majors, independent study, and a senior project. Special programs include cooperative education, internships, and off-campus study.

The most frequently chosen **baccalaureate** field is engineering/engineering technologies. A complete listing of majors at Webb appears in the Majors Index beginning on page 460.

The **faculty** at Webb has 8 full-time members, 50% with terminal degrees. The student-faculty ratio is 7:1.

Students of Webb

The student body is made up of 72 undergraduates. 20.8% are women and 79.2% are men. Students come from 20 states and territories. 32% are from New York. 1.4% are African American and 2.8% Asian American. 95% returned for their sophomore year.

Facilities and Resources

Student rooms are linked to a campus network. 75 **computers** are available on campus that provide access to the Internet. The **library** has 43,104 books and 262 subscriptions.

Campus Life

Active organizations on campus include a drama/theater group, newspaper, and choral group. 100% of eligible women are members of The Webb Women.

Intercollegiate sports include basketball, cross-country running, sailing, soccer, tennis, volleyball.

Campus Safety

Student safety services include 24-hour emergency telephone alarm devices, 24-hour patrols by trained security personnel, and electronically operated dormitory entrances.

Applying

Webb requires SAT I, SAT II: Writing Test, SAT II Subject Tests in math and either physics or chemistry, a high school transcript, an interview, 2 recommendations, proof of U.S. citizenship, and a minimum high school GPA of 3.5. Application deadline: 2/15; 7/1 priority date for financial aid.

Getting in Last Year
106 applied
31% were accepted
26 enrolled (79%)
65% from top tenth of their h.s. class
3.90 average high school GPA
88% had SAT verbal scores over 600
100% had SAT math scores over 600
38% had SAT verbal scores over 700
85% had SAT math scores over 700
4 National Merit Scholars
2 valedictorians

Graduation and After
70% graduated in 4 years
4% graduated in 6 years
31% pursued further study (31% engineering)
100% had job offers within 6 months
11 organizations recruited on campus

Financial Matters
$0 tuition and fees (2003–04)
$6950 room and board
20% average percent of need met
$800 average financial aid amount received per
  undergraduate (2001–02)

WELLESLEY COLLEGE

SUBURBAN SETTING ■ PRIVATE ■ INDEPENDENT ■ WOMEN ONLY
WELLESLEY, MASSACHUSETTS

Web site: www.wellesley.edu
Contact: Ms. Jennifer Desjarlais, Director of Admission, 106 Central Street,
Green Hall 240, Wellesley, MA 02481-8203
Telephone: 781-283-2270 **Fax:** 781-283-3678
E-mail: admission@wellesley.edu

W ellesley College is a liberal arts institution for exceptional women. The College provides an individualized education, with an average class size of 20 students in more than 1,000 courses offered. Wellesley uses technology as a vital component of classroom teaching and offers cross-registration and a double-degree program with MIT. Located just 12 miles from Boston and its 250,000 college students, Wellesley is a multicultural community in which students learn as much from each other as from their classes. Women who attend Wellesley learn the skills necessary to successfully pursue any interest; Wellesley graduates are leaders in the laboratory, the classroom, the courtroom, the boardroom, and their communities—anywhere they choose.

Getting in Last Year
3,434 applied
41% were accepted
591 enrolled (42%)
62% from top tenth of their h.s. class
88% had SAT verbal scores over 600
87% had SAT math scores over 600
94% had ACT scores over 24
45% had SAT verbal scores over 700
41% had SAT math scores over 700
55% had ACT scores over 30

Graduation and After
86% graduated in 4 years
4% graduated in 5 years
1% graduated in 6 years
28% pursued further study
179 organizations recruited on campus

Financial Matters
$27,724 tuition and fees (2003–04)
$8612 room and board
100% average percent of need met
$22,614 average financial aid amount received per undergraduate (2002–03 estimated)

Academics

Wellesley awards bachelor's **degrees** (double bachelor's degree with Massachusetts Institute of Technology). Challenging opportunities include advanced placement credit, student-designed majors, double majors, independent study, and a senior project. Special programs include internships, summer session for credit, off-campus study, study-abroad, and Army and Air Force ROTC.

The most frequently chosen **baccalaureate** fields are social sciences and history, area/ethnic studies, and foreign language/literature. A complete listing of majors at Wellesley appears in the Majors Index beginning on page 460.

The **faculty** at Wellesley has 221 full-time members, 99% with terminal degrees. The student-faculty ratio is 9:1.

Students of Wellesley

The student body is made up of 2,312 undergraduates. Students come from 52 states and territories and 79 other countries. 17% are from Massachusetts. 7.8% are international students. 5.6% are African American, 0.4% American Indian, 25.5% Asian American, and 5.3% Hispanic American. 95% returned for their sophomore year.

Facilities and Resources

Student rooms are linked to a campus network. 200 **computers** are available on campus that provide access to electronic bulletin boards and the Internet. The 4 **libraries** have 765,530 books and 4,945 subscriptions.

Campus Life

There are 160 active organizations on campus, including a drama/theater group, newspaper, radio station, and choral group. No national or local **sororities**.

Wellesley is a member of the NCAA (Division III). **Intercollegiate sports** include basketball, crew, cross-country running, fencing, field hockey, golf, lacrosse, soccer, softball, squash, swimming, tennis, volleyball.

Campus Safety

Student safety services include late-night transport/escort service, 24-hour emergency telephone alarm devices, 24-hour patrols by trained security personnel, and electronically operated dormitory entrances.

Applying

Wellesley requires an essay, SAT II Subject Tests, SAT I and SAT II or ACT, a high school transcript, and 3 recommendations, and in some cases an interview. It recommends an interview. Application deadline: 1/15; 1/15 priority date for financial aid. Early and deferred admission are possible.

WELLS COLLEGE

RURAL SETTING ■ PRIVATE ■ INDEPENDENT ■ WOMEN ONLY
AURORA, NEW YORK

Web site: www.wells.edu
Contact: Ms. Susan Raith Sloan, Director of Admissions, 170 Main Street, Aurora, NY 13026
Telephone: 315-364-3264 or toll-free 800-952-9355 **Fax:** 315-364-3227
E-mail: admissions@wells.edu

Academics

Wells awards bachelor's **degrees.** Challenging opportunities include advanced placement credit, accelerated degree programs, student-designed majors, double majors, independent study, and a senior project. Special programs include internships, off-campus study, study-abroad, and Air Force ROTC.

The most frequently chosen **baccalaureate** fields are social sciences and history, psychology, and biological/life sciences. A complete listing of majors at Wells appears in the Majors Index beginning on page 460.

The **faculty** at Wells has 48 full-time members, 94% with terminal degrees. The student-faculty ratio is 8:1.

Students of Wells

The student body is made up of 420 undergraduates. Students come from 35 states and territories and 6 other countries. 69% are from New York. 2% are international students. 5.6% are African American, 0.3% American Indian, 3.5% Asian American, and 3.3% Hispanic American. 78% returned for their sophomore year.

Facilities and Resources

Student rooms are linked to a campus network. 89 **computers** are available on campus that provide access to the Internet. The **library** has 250,893 books and 407 subscriptions.

Campus Life

There are 35 active organizations on campus, including a drama/theater group, newspaper, and choral group. No national or local **sororities.**

Wells is a member of the NCAA (Division III). **Intercollegiate sports** include field hockey, lacrosse, soccer, softball, swimming, tennis.

Campus Safety

Student safety services include late-night transport/escort service, 24-hour emergency telephone alarm devices, 24-hour patrols by trained security personnel, and electronically operated dormitory entrances.

Applying

Wells requires an essay, SAT I or ACT, a high school transcript, and 2 recommendations. It recommends an interview. Application deadline: 3/1; 2/15 priority date for financial aid. Early and deferred admission are possible.

Wells College believes that the 21st century needs women with the ability, self confidence, and vision to contribute to an everchanging world. Wells offers an outstanding classroom experience and innovative liberal arts curriculum that prepares students for leadership in a variety of fields, including business, government, the arts, sciences, medicine, and education. By directly connecting the liberal arts curriculum to experience and career development through internships; off-campus study; study-abroad opportunities; research with professors; and community service; each student has ideal preparation for graduate and professional school, as well as for their future in the 21st century.

Getting in Last Year
410 applied
84% were accepted
100 enrolled (29%)
19% from top tenth of their h.s. class
3.50 average high school GPA
43% had SAT verbal scores over 600
27% had SAT math scores over 600
54% had ACT scores over 24
4% had SAT verbal scores over 700
1% had SAT math scores over 700
11% had ACT scores over 30

Graduation and After
66% graduated in 4 years
3% graduated in 5 years
17% pursued further study (17% arts and sciences, 1% law)
39% had job offers within 6 months
3 organizations recruited on campus

Financial Matters
$14,292 tuition and fees (2003–04)
$6830 room and board
91% average percent of need met
$15,475 average financial aid amount received per undergraduate

WESLEYAN COLLEGE
SUBURBAN SETTING ■ PRIVATE ■ INDEPENDENT RELIGIOUS ■ WOMEN ONLY
MACON, GEORGIA

Web site: www.wesleyancollege.edu
Contact: Ms. Rachel Powell, Director of Recruitment, 4760 Forsyth Road, Macon, GA 31210-4462
Telephone: 478-757-5206 or toll-free 800-447-6610 **Fax:** 478-757-4030
E-mail: admissions@wesleyancollege.edu

The world's first degree-granting college for women, Wesleyan College was founded in 1836. Today, the Macon, Georgia, college is one of the nation's most diverse and affordable liberal arts colleges, drawing students from across the U.S. and 24 countries. Students value the academic rigor and close ties to the faculty members, and credit both with preparing them to enter graduate studies at Yale, Stanford, Emory, Duke, and other top universities. Internships sites have included The Centers for Disease Control, The Carter Center, the GBI, and Mercer Medical Center. Beyond the academic, Wesleyan offers a thriving residence life program, NCAA Division III athletics, and volunteer opportunities through its Center for Community Engagement and Service.

Getting in Last Year
323 applied
77% were accepted
92 enrolled (37%)
39% from top tenth of their h.s. class
3.60 average high school GPA
33% had SAT verbal scores over 600
24% had SAT math scores over 600
38% had ACT scores over 24
5% had SAT verbal scores over 700
6% had SAT math scores over 700
1 National Merit Scholar
3 class presidents

Graduation and After
40% graduated in 4 years
3% graduated in 5 years
1% graduated in 6 years
22% pursued further study (14% arts and sciences, 14% education, 14% medicine)

Financial Matters
$10,420 tuition and fees (2003–04)
$7450 room and board
87% average percent of need met
$11,409 average financial aid amount received per undergraduate (2002–03 estimated)

Academics
Wesleyan awards bachelor's and master's **degrees**. Challenging opportunities include advanced placement credit, student-designed majors, an honors program, double majors, independent study, and a senior project. Special programs include cooperative education, internships, summer session for credit, off-campus study, and study-abroad.

The most frequently chosen **baccalaureate** fields are psychology, business/marketing, and biological/life sciences. A complete listing of majors at Wesleyan appears in the Majors Index beginning on page 460.

The **faculty** at Wesleyan has 47 full-time members, 91% with terminal degrees. The student-faculty ratio is 11:1.

Students of Wesleyan
The student body totals 744, of whom 661 are undergraduates. Students come from 27 states and territories and 31 other countries. 79% are from Georgia. 19% are international students. 29.3% are African American, 1.8% Asian American, and 1.8% Hispanic American. 78% returned for their sophomore year.

Facilities and Resources
Student rooms are linked to a campus network. 100 **computers** are available on campus that provide access to the Internet. The **library** has 140,923 books and 506 subscriptions.

Campus Life
There are 40 active organizations on campus, including a drama/theater group, newspaper, and choral group. No national or local **sororities**.

Wesleyan is a member of the NCAA (Division III). **Intercollegiate sports** include basketball, equestrian sports, soccer, softball, tennis, volleyball.

Campus Safety
Student safety services include late-night transport/escort service, 24-hour emergency telephone alarm devices, 24-hour patrols by trained security personnel, and electronically operated dormitory entrances.

Applying
Wesleyan requires an essay, SAT I or ACT, a high school transcript, and 1 recommendation. It recommends an interview and 2 recommendations. Application deadline: 3/1. Early and deferred admission are possible.

WESLEYAN UNIVERSITY
SMALL-TOWN SETTING ■ PRIVATE ■ INDEPENDENT ■ COED
MIDDLETOWN, CONNECTICUT

Web site: www.wesleyan.edu
Contact: Ms. Nancy Hargrave Meislahn, Dean of Admission and Financial Aid, Stewart M Reid House, 70 Wyllys Avenue, Middletown, CT 06459-0265
Telephone: 860-685-3000 **Fax:** 860-685-3001
E-mail: admissions@wesleyan.edu

Academics
Wesleyan awards bachelor's, master's, and doctoral **degrees** and post-master's certificates. Challenging opportunities include advanced placement credit, accelerated degree programs, student-designed majors, an honors program, double majors, independent study, and a senior project. Special programs include internships, summer session for credit, off-campus study, study-abroad, and Air Force ROTC. A complete listing of majors at Wesleyan appears in the Majors Index beginning on page 460.

The **faculty** at Wesleyan has 329 full-time members, 93% with terminal degrees. The student-faculty ratio is 9:1.

Students of Wesleyan
The student body totals 3,221, of whom 2,730 are undergraduates. 52.7% are women and 47.3% are men. Students come from 50 states and territories and 47 other countries. 10% are from Connecticut. 6.3% are international students. 7.7% are African American, 0.3% American Indian, 8.2% Asian American, and 6.4% Hispanic American. 95% returned for their sophomore year.

Facilities and Resources
Student rooms are linked to a campus network. 250 **computers** are available on campus that provide access to electronic portfolio and the Internet. The 4 **libraries** have 1,224,750 books and 4,281 subscriptions.

Campus Life
There are 231 active organizations on campus, including a drama/theater group, newspaper, radio station, and choral group. 4% of eligible men and 3% of eligible women are members of national **fraternities**, national **sororities**, local fraternities, and eating clubs.

Wesleyan is a member of the NCAA (Division III). **Intercollegiate sports** include baseball (m), basketball, crew, cross-country running, field hockey (w), football (m), golf, ice hockey, lacrosse, soccer, softball (w), squash, swimming, tennis, track and field, volleyball (w), wrestling (m).

Campus Safety
Student safety services include late-night transport/escort service, 24-hour emergency telephone alarm devices, 24-hour patrols by trained security personnel, student patrols, and electronically operated dormitory entrances.

Applying
Wesleyan requires an essay, SAT I and SAT II or ACT, a high school transcript, and 3 recommendations. It recommends an interview. Application deadline: 1/1; 2/1 for financial aid. Early and deferred admission are possible.

Wesleyan University is among the largest colleges of liberal arts and sciences, offering a wide range of programs, courses, and resources. Students at Wesleyan make their mark in the wider world through their creativity, intellectual independence, and drive to improve the world. About 30% of the undergraduates are students of color, while 12-14% are the first in their families to attend college. Wesleyan is committed to need-based financial aid and meeting the full demonstrated financial need of all students.

Getting in Last Year
6,955 applied
27% were accepted
715 enrolled (39%)
73% from top tenth of their h.s. class
87% had SAT verbal scores over 600
92% had SAT math scores over 600
97% had ACT scores over 24
51% had SAT verbal scores over 700
44% had SAT math scores over 700
62% had ACT scores over 30

Graduation and After
84% graduated in 4 years
7% graduated in 5 years
1% graduated in 6 years
70% had job offers within 6 months
98 organizations recruited on campus

Financial Matters
$29,998 tuition and fees (2003–04)
$8226 room and board
100% average percent of need met
$24,553 average financial aid amount received per undergraduate (2002–03)

Western Baptist College

Suburban Setting ■ Private ■ Independent Religious ■ Coed
Salem, Oregon

Getting in Last Year
550 applied
84% were accepted
167 enrolled (36%)
23% from top tenth of their h.s. class
3.51 average high school GPA
31% had SAT verbal scores over 600
26% had SAT math scores over 600
34% had ACT scores over 24
3% had SAT verbal scores over 700
3% had SAT math scores over 700
7% had ACT scores over 30

Graduation and After
35% graduated in 4 years
11% graduated in 5 years
80% had job offers within 6 months
50 organizations recruited on campus

Financial Matters
$16,075 tuition and fees (2003–04)
$5725 room and board
68% average percent of need met
$12,087 average financial aid amount received per undergraduate (2002–03 estimated)

Web site: www.wbc.edu
Contact: Mr. Marty Ziesemer, Director of Admissions, 5000 Deer Park Drive, SE, Salem, OR 97301-9392
Telephone: 503-375-7115 or toll-free 800-845-3005 (out-of-state)
E-mail: admissions@wbc.edu

Academics
Western awards associate and bachelor's **degrees**. Challenging opportunities include advanced placement credit, accelerated degree programs, freshman honors college, an honors program, double majors, independent study, and a senior project. Special programs include internships, summer session for credit, off-campus study, study-abroad, and Army and Air Force ROTC.

The most frequently chosen **baccalaureate** fields are business/marketing, home economics/vocational home economics, and education. A complete listing of majors at Western appears in the Majors Index beginning on page 460.

The **faculty** at Western has 34 full-time members, 41% with terminal degrees. The student-faculty ratio is 15:1.

Students of Western
The student body is made up of 737 undergraduates. 59% are women and 41% are men. Students come from 30 states and territories and 5 other countries. 69% are from Oregon. 0.7% are international students. 0.6% are African American, 1.5% American Indian, 1.4% Asian American, and 2.8% Hispanic American. 76% returned for their sophomore year.

Facilities and Resources
Student rooms are linked to a campus network. 34 **computers** are available on campus that provide access to the Internet. The **library** has 85,000 books and 600 subscriptions.

Campus Life
There are 6 active organizations on campus, including a drama/theater group, newspaper, and choral group. 75% of eligible men and 75% of eligible women are members of fellowship groups.

Western is a member of the NAIA and NCCAA. **Intercollegiate sports** (some offering scholarships) include baseball (m), basketball, cross-country running, golf (m), soccer, softball (w), volleyball (w).

Campus Safety
Student safety services include late-night transport/escort service, 24-hour emergency telephone alarm devices, and student patrols.

Applying
Western requires an essay, SAT I or ACT, a high school transcript, 3 recommendations, and a minimum high school GPA of 2.5. Application deadline: 8/1; 2/15 priority date for financial aid. Early admission is possible.

Westminster Choir College of Rider University

Small-town setting ■ Private ■ Independent ■ Coed
Princeton, New Jersey

Web site: westminster.rider.edu
Contact: Elizabeth S. Rush, Assistant Director of Admissions, 101 Walnut
    Lane, Princeton, NJ 08540-3899
Telephone: 609-921-7144 ext. 8221 or toll-free 800-96-CHOIR **Fax:**
    609-921-2538
E-mail: wccadmission@rider.edu

Academics

Westminster awards bachelor's and master's **degrees**. Challenging opportunities include advanced placement credit, an honors program, double majors, independent study, and a senior project. Special programs include internships, summer session for credit, and off-campus study.

The most frequently chosen **baccalaureate** field is visual/performing arts. A complete listing of majors at Westminster appears in the Majors Index beginning on page 460.

The **faculty** at Westminster has 35 full-time members. The student-faculty ratio is 7:1.

Students of Westminster

The student body totals 455, of whom 340 are undergraduates. 61.8% are women and 38.2% are men. Students come from 40 states and territories. 36% are from New Jersey. 3.7% are international students. 8.7% are African American, 2.8% Asian American, and 5% Hispanic American. 84% returned for their sophomore year.

Facilities and Resources

60 **computers** are available on campus for student use. The **library** has 55,000 books and 160 subscriptions.

Campus Life

Active organizations on campus include a drama/theater group, newspaper, radio station, and choral group. No national or local **fraternities** or **sororities**.

This institution has no intercollegiate sports.

Campus Safety

Student safety services include late-night transport/escort service, 24-hour emergency telephone alarm devices, and 24-hour patrols by trained security personnel.

Applying

Westminster requires an essay, SAT I or ACT, a high school transcript, 2 recommendations, and audition, music examination. It recommends an interview and a minimum high school GPA of 2.5. Application deadline: rolling admissions; 3/1 priority date for financial aid. Deferred admission is possible.

Getting in Last Year
178 applied
83% were accepted
97 enrolled (66%)
3.41 average high school GPA
33% had SAT verbal scores over 600
35% had SAT math scores over 600
6% had SAT verbal scores over 700
8% had SAT math scores over 700
1 class president

Graduation and After
42% graduated in 4 years
15% graduated in 5 years
3% graduated in 6 years

Financial Matters
$20,830 tuition and fees (2003–04)
$8370 room and board
75% average percent of need met
$15,424 average financial aid amount received
    per undergraduate (2002–03 estimated)

WESTMINSTER COLLEGE

SUBURBAN SETTING ■ PRIVATE ■ INDEPENDENT ■ COED
SALT LAKE CITY, UTAH

Web site: www.westminstercollege.edu
Contact: Ms. Mary Hyland, Director of Admissions, 1840 South 1300 East, Salt Lake City, UT 84105-3697
Telephone: 801-832-2200 or toll-free 800-748-4753 **Fax:** 801-832-3101
E-mail: admispub@westminstercollege.edu

The only independent, private college in the state of Utah, Westminster serves the entire Rocky Mountain region and northwestern United States. The beautiful campus and setting reflect the College's combination of traditional private education and western pioneering spirit. Westminster is recognized nationally for excellent programs in business, education, arts and sciences, and nursing. The College has been continually ranked among the top tier of colleges and universities in the western United States and is consistently named a "Top Ten Value" in higher education. Student involvement, technology, and broad-based education, combined with close interaction with outstanding faculty members, are at the heart of a Westminster education.

Getting in Last Year
865 applied
82% were accepted
374 enrolled (52%)
33% from top tenth of their h.s. class
3.48 average high school GPA
47% had ACT scores over 24
9% had ACT scores over 30
2 National Merit Scholars

Graduation and After
42% graduated in 4 years
12% graduated in 5 years
4% graduated in 6 years
38% pursued further study (13% business, 2% arts and sciences, 2% education)
113 organizations recruited on campus

Financial Matters
$16,994 tuition and fees (2003–04)
$5300 room and board
87% average percent of need met
$13,573 average financial aid amount received per undergraduate (2002–03 estimated)

Academics
Westminster College awards bachelor's and master's **degrees** and post-bachelor's certificates. Challenging opportunities include advanced placement credit, accelerated degree programs, student-designed majors, an honors program, independent study, and a senior project. Special programs include cooperative education, internships, summer session for credit, and Army, Navy and Air Force ROTC.

The most frequently chosen **baccalaureate** fields are business/marketing, health professions and related sciences, and education. A complete listing of majors at Westminster College appears in the Majors Index beginning on page 460.

The **faculty** at Westminster College has 118 full-time members, 74% with terminal degrees. The student-faculty ratio is 11:1.

Students of Westminster College
The student body totals 2,498, of whom 2,017 are undergraduates. 58.1% are women and 41.9% are men. Students come from 34 states and territories and 28 other countries. 92% are from Utah. 1.9% are international students. 0.4% are African American, 0.8% American Indian, 3.1% Asian American, and 3.9% Hispanic American. 77% returned for their sophomore year.

Facilities and Resources
Student rooms are linked to a campus network. 409 **computers** are available on campus that provide access to the Internet. The 2 **libraries** have 119,212 books and 437 subscriptions.

Campus Life
There are 41 active organizations on campus, including a drama/theater group, newspaper, and choral group. No national or local **fraternities** or **sororities**.

Westminster College is a member of the NAIA. **Intercollegiate sports** include basketball, cheerleading, golf, soccer (m), volleyball (w).

Campus Safety
Student safety services include late-night transport/escort service, 24-hour emergency telephone alarm devices, 24-hour patrols by trained security personnel, student patrols, and electronically operated dormitory entrances.

Applying
Westminster College requires SAT I or ACT, a high school transcript, and a minimum high school GPA of 2.5. It recommends an essay, an interview, 1 recommendation, and a minimum high school GPA of 3.0. Application deadline: rolling admissions. Early and deferred admission are possible.

WESTMONT COLLEGE

SUBURBAN SETTING ■ PRIVATE ■ INDEPENDENT RELIGIOUS ■ COED
SANTA BARBARA, CALIFORNIA

Web site: www.westmont.edu
Contact: Mrs. Joyce Luy, Director of Admissions, 955 La Paz Road, Santa
    Barbara, CA 93108
Telephone: 805-565-6200 ext. 6005 or toll-free 800-777-9011 **Fax:**
    805-565-6234
E-mail: admissions@westmont.edu

> **A**Westmont education is rigorous, wide-ranging, faith-based, service-oriented, and relevant for life. As a member of the Westmont community, students grow deeper in wisdom, integrity, and their beliefs and understanding of the world. A national Christian college in the classic liberal arts tradition (which includes disciplines in neuroscience, engineering, and medicine), Westmont helps students become the person God means them to be. Westmost is located in Santa Barbara, California. Encounter Westmont, where character and wisdom meet.

Academics

Westmont awards bachelor's **degrees** and post-bachelor's certificates. Challenging opportunities include advanced placement credit, accelerated degree programs, student-designed majors, an honors program, double majors, independent study, and a senior project. Special programs include cooperative education, internships, summer session for credit, off-campus study, study-abroad, and Army and Air Force ROTC.

The most frequently chosen **baccalaureate** fields are social sciences and history, communications/communication technologies, and English. A complete listing of majors at Westmont appears in the Majors Index beginning on page 460.

The **faculty** at Westmont has 83 full-time members, 88% with terminal degrees. The student-faculty ratio is 13:1.

Students of Westmont

The student body is made up of 1,343 undergraduates. 65.3% are women and 34.7% are men. Students come from 41 states and territories. 66% are from California. 0.8% are international students. 1.1% are African American, 1.2% American Indian, 5.7% Asian American, and 6.7% Hispanic American. 89% returned for their sophomore year.

Facilities and Resources

Student rooms are linked to a campus network. 100 **computers** are available on campus that provide access to the Internet. The **library** has 165,512 books and 3,211 subscriptions.

Campus Life

Active organizations on campus include a drama/theater group, newspaper, radio station, and choral group. No national or local **fraternities** or **sororities**.

Westmont is a member of the NAIA. **Intercollegiate sports** (some offering scholarships) include baseball (m), basketball, cross-country running, soccer, tennis, track and field, volleyball (w).

Campus Safety

Student safety services include late-night transport/escort service, 24-hour emergency telephone alarm devices, 24-hour patrols by trained security personnel, and electronically operated dormitory entrances.

Applying

Westmont requires an essay, SAT I or ACT, a high school transcript, and 3 recommendations, and in some cases an interview. It recommends SAT II: Writing Test, an interview, and a minimum high school GPA of 3.0. Application deadline: 2/15; 3/1 priority date for financial aid.

Getting in Last Year
1,404 applied
85% were accepted
355 enrolled (30%)
40% from top tenth of their h.s. class
3.65 average high school GPA
57% had SAT verbal scores over 600
62% had SAT math scores over 600
78% had ACT scores over 24
12% had SAT verbal scores over 700
21% had SAT math scores over 700
15% had ACT scores over 30
8 National Merit Scholars
81 class presidents
37 valedictorians

Graduation and After
62% graduated in 4 years
8% graduated in 5 years
1% graduated in 6 years
69% pursued further study
66 organizations recruited on campus

Financial Matters
$24,890 tuition and fees (2003–04)
$8390 room and board
68% average percent of need met
$16,571 average financial aid amount received
    per undergraduate

WHEATON COLLEGE

SMALL-TOWN SETTING ■ PRIVATE ■ INDEPENDENT ■ COED
NORTON, MASSACHUSETTS

Getting in Last Year
3,465 applied
43% were accepted
445 enrolled (30%)
43% from top tenth of their h.s. class
3.45 average high school GPA
63% had SAT verbal scores over 600
56% had SAT math scores over 600
91% had ACT scores over 24
11% had SAT verbal scores over 700
6% had SAT math scores over 700
13% had ACT scores over 30

Graduation and After
68% graduated in 4 years
5% graduated in 5 years
2% graduated in 6 years
Graduates pursuing further study: 17% arts
  and sciences, 7% education, 5% law
60% had job offers within 6 months
25 organizations recruited on campus

Financial Matters
$28,900 tuition and fees (2003–04)
$7430 room and board
92% average percent of need met
$21,159 average financial aid amount received
  per undergraduate

Web site: www.wheatoncollege.edu
Contact: Ms. Lynne M. Stack, Director of Admission, 26 East Main Street,
  Norton, MA 02766
Telephone: 508-286-8251 or toll-free 800-394-6003 **Fax:** 508-286-8271
E-mail: admission@wheatoncollege.edu

Academics
Wheaton awards bachelor's **degrees**. Challenging opportunities include advanced placement credit, accelerated degree programs, student-designed majors, an honors program,
double majors, independent study, and a senior project. Special programs include internships, off-campus study, study-abroad, and Army ROTC.

The most frequently chosen **baccalaureate** fields are social sciences and history,
psychology, and visual/performing arts. A complete listing of majors at Wheaton appears
in the Majors Index beginning on page 460.

The **faculty** at Wheaton has 121 full-time members, 98% with terminal degrees.
The student-faculty ratio is 11:1.

Students of Wheaton
The student body is made up of 1,565 undergraduates. 63.6% are women and 36.4% are
men. Students come from 43 states and territories and 26 other countries. 33% are from
Massachusetts. 1.7% are international students. 2.9% are African American, 0.4%
American Indian, 2.4% Asian American, and 3.9% Hispanic American. 89% returned for
their sophomore year.

Facilities and Resources
Student rooms are linked to a campus network. 157 **computers** are available on campus
that provide access to the Internet. The 2 **libraries** have 381,749 books and 2,046
subscriptions.

Campus Life
There are 65 active organizations on campus, including a drama/theater group,
newspaper, radio station, and choral group. No national or local **fraternities** or **sororities**.

Wheaton is a member of the NCAA (Division III). **Intercollegiate sports** include
baseball (m), basketball, cross-country running, field hockey (w), lacrosse, soccer, softball
(w), swimming, tennis, track and field, volleyball (w).

Campus Safety
Student safety services include late-night transport/escort service, 24-hour emergency
telephone alarm devices, 24-hour patrols by trained security personnel, student patrols,
and electronically operated dormitory entrances.

Applying
Wheaton requires an essay, a high school transcript, and 2 recommendations. It recommends an interview. Application deadline: 1/15; 2/1 for financial aid. Early and deferred
admission are possible.

WHEATON COLLEGE

SUBURBAN SETTING ■ PRIVATE ■ INDEPENDENT RELIGIOUS ■ COED
WHEATON, ILLINOIS

Web site: www.wheaton.edu

Contact: Ms. Shawn Leftwich, Director of Admissions, 501 College Avenue,
Wheaton, IL 60187

Telephone: 630-752-5011 or toll-free 800-222-2419 (out-of-state) **Fax:**
630-752-5285

E-mail: admissions@wheaton.edu

Academics

Wheaton awards bachelor's, master's, and doctoral **degrees** and post-bachelor's
certificates. Challenging opportunities include advanced placement credit, student-
designed majors, double majors, independent study, and a senior project. Special
programs include internships, summer session for credit, off-campus study, study-abroad,
and Army and Air Force ROTC.

The most frequently chosen **baccalaureate** fields are social sciences and history,
business/marketing, and English. A complete listing of majors at Wheaton appears in the
Majors Index beginning on page 460.

The **faculty** at Wheaton has 190 full-time members, 93% with terminal degrees.
The student-faculty ratio is 11:1.

Students of Wheaton

The student body totals 2,944, of whom 2,430 are undergraduates. 50.8% are women
and 49.2% are men. Students come from 51 states and territories and 16 other countries.
31% are from Illinois. 1.1% are international students. 2.2% are African American, 0.3%
American Indian, 7% Asian American, and 2.2% Hispanic American. 93% returned for
their sophomore year.

Facilities and Resources

Student rooms are linked to a campus network. 238 **computers** are available on campus
that provide access to the Internet. The 2 **libraries** have 429,892 books and 2,751
subscriptions.

Campus Life

There are 60 active organizations on campus, including a drama/theater group,
newspaper, radio station, television station, and choral group. No national or local
fraternities or **sororities**.

Wheaton is a member of the NCAA (Division III). **Intercollegiate sports** include
baseball (m), basketball, cross-country running, football (m), golf, soccer, softball (w),
swimming, tennis, track and field, volleyball (w), water polo (w), wrestling (m).

Campus Safety

Student safety services include late-night transport/escort service, 24-hour emergency
telephone alarm devices, 24-hour patrols by trained security personnel, student patrols,
and electronically operated dormitory entrances.

Applying

Wheaton requires an essay, SAT I or ACT, a high school transcript, and 2 recommendations. It recommends SAT II: Writing Test, SAT II Subject Test in French, German,
Latin, Spanish or Hebrew, and an interview. Application deadline: 1/15; 2/15 priority
date for financial aid. Deferred admission is possible.

Getting in Last Year

2,170 applied
53% were accepted
576 enrolled (50%)
61% from top tenth of their h.s. class
3.71 average high school GPA
85% had SAT verbal scores over 600
82% had SAT math scores over 600
92% had ACT scores over 24
37% had SAT verbal scores over 700
29% had SAT math scores over 700
45% had ACT scores over 30
49 National Merit Scholars

Graduation and After

76% graduated in 4 years
9% graduated in 5 years
1% graduated in 6 years
22% pursued further study (7% arts and sciences, 5% veterinary medicine, 5%
medicine)
202 organizations recruited on campus

Financial Matters

$18,500 tuition and fees (2003–04)
$6100 room and board
86% average percent of need met
$16,040 average financial aid amount received
per undergraduate

WHITMAN COLLEGE
SMALL-TOWN SETTING ■ PRIVATE ■ INDEPENDENT ■ COED
WALLA WALLA, WASHINGTON

Web site: www.whitman.edu
Contact: Mr. Tony Cabasco, Acting Dean of Admission and Financial Aid,
345 Boyer Avenue, Walla Walla, WA 99362-2083
Telephone: 509-527-5176 or toll-free 877-462-9448 **Fax:** 509-527-4967
E-mail: admission@whitman.edu

Getting in Last Year
2,143 applied
56% were accepted
362 enrolled (30%)
59% from top tenth of their h.s. class
3.76 average high school GPA
85% had SAT verbal scores over 600
82% had SAT math scores over 600
88% had ACT scores over 24
40% had SAT verbal scores over 700
28% had SAT math scores over 700
45% had ACT scores over 30
24 National Merit Scholars
66 valedictorians

Graduation and After
74% graduated in 4 years
11% graduated in 5 years
11% graduated in 6 years
50 organizations recruited on campus

Financial Matters
$25,626 tuition and fees (2003–04)
$6900 room and board
89% average percent of need met
$17,750 average financial aid amount received
per undergraduate

Academics
Whitman awards bachelor's **degrees**. Challenging opportunities include advanced placement credit, student-designed majors, an honors program, double majors, independent study, and a senior project. Special programs include internships, off-campus study, and study-abroad.

The most frequently chosen **baccalaureate** fields are social sciences and history, biological/life sciences, and psychology. A complete listing of majors at Whitman appears in the Majors Index beginning on page 460.

The **faculty** at Whitman has 116 full-time members, 93% with terminal degrees. The student-faculty ratio is 10:1.

Students of Whitman
The student body is made up of 1,454 undergraduates. 55.6% are women and 44.4% are men. Students come from 27 states and territories and 24 other countries. 49% are from Washington. 2.5% are international students. 2% are African American, 0.8% American Indian, 7.6% Asian American, and 3.5% Hispanic American. 95% returned for their sophomore year.

Facilities and Resources
Student rooms are linked to a campus network. 250 **computers** are available on campus that provide access to course registration information and the Internet. The 2 **libraries** have 350,699 books and 2,175 subscriptions.

Campus Life
There are 60 active organizations on campus, including a drama/theater group, newspaper, radio station, and choral group. 36% of eligible men and 34% of eligible women are members of national **fraternities** and national **sororities**.

Whitman is a member of the NCAA (Division III). **Intercollegiate sports** (some offering scholarships) include baseball (m), basketball, cheerleading, cross-country running, golf, skiing (cross-country), skiing (downhill), soccer, swimming, tennis, volleyball (w).

Campus Safety
Student safety services include late-night transport/escort service, 24-hour emergency telephone alarm devices, 24-hour patrols by trained security personnel, student patrols, and electronically operated dormitory entrances.

Applying
Whitman requires an essay, SAT I or ACT, a high school transcript, and 1 recommendation. It recommends SAT II: Writing Test and an interview. Application deadline: 1/15; 11/15 priority date for financial aid. Deferred admission is possible.

WHITWORTH COLLEGE

SUBURBAN SETTING ■ PRIVATE ■ INDEPENDENT RELIGIOUS ■ COED
SPOKANE, WASHINGTON

Web site: www.whitworth.edu
Contact: Ms. Marianne Hansen, Director of Admission, 300 West, Hawthorne Road, Spokane, WA 99251
Telephone: 800-533-4668 or toll-free 800-533-4668 (out-of-state) **Fax:** 509-777-3758
E-mail: admission@whitworth.edu

Academics

Whitworth awards bachelor's and master's **degrees**. Challenging opportunities include advanced placement credit, student-designed majors, double majors, independent study, and a senior project. Special programs include cooperative education, internships, summer session for credit, off-campus study, study-abroad, and Army ROTC. A complete listing of majors at Whitworth appears in the Majors Index beginning on page 460.

The student-faculty ratio is 13:1.

Students of Whitworth

The student body totals 2,298, of whom 2,071 are undergraduates. 59.2% are women and 40.8% are men. Students come from 31 states and territories and 25 other countries. 62% are from Washington. 2.8% are international students. 1.7% are African American, 1.1% American Indian, 4.5% Asian American, and 2% Hispanic American. 87% returned for their sophomore year.

Facilities and Resources

Student rooms are linked to a campus network. 200 **computers** are available on campus that provide access to the Internet. The 3 **libraries** have 17,982 books and 773 subscriptions.

Campus Life

There are 80 active organizations on campus, including a drama/theater group, newspaper, radio station, and choral group. No national or local **fraternities** or **sororities**.

Whitworth is a member of the NCAA (Division III). **Intercollegiate sports** include baseball (m), basketball, cross-country running, football (m), golf, soccer, swimming, tennis, track and field, volleyball (w).

Campus Safety

Student safety services include late-night transport/escort service, 24-hour emergency telephone alarm devices, and 24-hour patrols by trained security personnel.

Applying

Whitworth requires an essay, SAT I or ACT, a high school transcript, and recommendations, and in some cases an interview. Application deadline: 3/1; 3/1 priority date for financial aid. Early and deferred admission are possible.

Getting in Last Year

1,890 applied
75% were accepted
42% from top tenth of their h.s. class
3.59 average high school GPA
40% had SAT verbal scores over 600
40% had SAT math scores over 600
7% had SAT verbal scores over 700
5% had SAT math scores over 700
40 valedictorians

Graduation and After

56% graduated in 4 years
13% graduated in 5 years
3% graduated in 6 years
20% pursued further study
110 organizations recruited on campus

Financial Matters

$20,078 tuition and fees (2003–04)
$6350 room and board
84% average percent of need met
$17,443 average financial aid amount received per undergraduate

WILLAMETTE UNIVERSITY

URBAN SETTING ■ PRIVATE ■ INDEPENDENT RELIGIOUS ■ COED
SALEM, OREGON

Web site: www.willamette.edu
Contact: Dr. Robin Brown, Vice President for Enrollment, 900 State Street,
  Salem, OR 97301-3931
Telephone: 503-370-6303 or toll-free 877-542-2787 **Fax:** 503-375-5363
E-mail: libarts@willamette.edu

Getting in Last Year

2,164 applied
74% were accepted
541 enrolled (34%)
49% from top tenth of their h.s. class
3.74 average high school GPA
64% had SAT verbal scores over 600
65% had SAT math scores over 600
86% had ACT scores over 24
17% had SAT verbal scores over 700
14% had SAT math scores over 700
21% had ACT scores over 30
12 National Merit Scholars
13 class presidents
65 valedictorians

Graduation and After

76% graduated in 4 years
8% graduated in 5 years
25% pursued further study
150 organizations recruited on campus

Financial Matters

$25,462 tuition and fees (2003–04)
$6600 room and board
93% average percent of need met
$21,886 average financial aid amount received
  per undergraduate (2002–03 estimated)

Academics

Willamette awards bachelor's, master's, and first-professional **degrees** and post-bachelor's and first-professional certificates. Challenging opportunities include advanced placement credit, accelerated degree programs, student-designed majors, double majors, independent study, and a senior project. Special programs include cooperative education, internships, off-campus study, study-abroad, and Air Force ROTC.

The most frequently chosen **baccalaureate** fields are social sciences and history, English, and foreign language/literature. A complete listing of majors at Willamette appears in the Majors Index beginning on page 460.

The **faculty** at Willamette has 186 full-time members, 91% with terminal degrees. The student-faculty ratio is 11:1.

Students of Willamette

The student body totals 2,590, of whom 1,945 are undergraduates. 55.1% are women and 44.9% are men. Students come from 36 states and territories and 12 other countries. 41% are from Oregon. 0.7% are international students. 2.2% are African American, 1% American Indian, 7.3% Asian American, and 4.6% Hispanic American. 87% returned for their sophomore year.

Facilities and Resources

Student rooms are linked to a campus network. 400 **computers** are available on campus for student use. The 2 **libraries** have 317,000 books and 1,400 subscriptions.

Campus Life

There are 100 active organizations on campus, including a drama/theater group, newspaper, radio station, and choral group. 25% of eligible men and 25% of eligible women are members of national **fraternities** and national **sororities**.

Willamette is a member of the NCAA (Division III). **Intercollegiate sports** include baseball (m), basketball, crew, cross-country running, football (m), golf, soccer, softball (w), swimming, tennis, track and field, volleyball (w).

Campus Safety

Student safety services include late-night transport/escort service, 24-hour emergency telephone alarm devices, 24-hour patrols by trained security personnel, student patrols, and electronically operated dormitory entrances.

Applying

Willamette requires an essay, SAT I or ACT, a high school transcript, 1 recommendation, and a minimum high school GPA of 2.0, and in some cases an interview. It recommends an interview. Application deadline: 2/1; 2/1 priority date for financial aid. Early and deferred admission are possible.

WILLIAM JEWELL COLLEGE

SMALL-TOWN SETTING ■ PRIVATE ■ INDEPENDENT RELIGIOUS ■ COED
LIBERTY, MISSOURI

Web site: www.jewell.edu
Contact: Mr. Chad Jolly, Dean of Enrollment Development, 500 College Hill, Liberty, MO 64068
Telephone: 816-781-7700 or toll-free 800-753-7009 **Fax:** 816-415-5027
E-mail: admission@william.jewell.edu

Academics

William Jewell awards bachelor's **degrees** (also offers evening program with significant enrollment not reflected in profile). Challenging opportunities include advanced placement credit, student-designed majors, an honors program, double majors, independent study, and a senior project. Special programs include cooperative education, internships, summer session for credit, and study-abroad.

The most frequently chosen **baccalaureate** fields are business/marketing, psychology, and communications/communication technologies. A complete listing of majors at William Jewell appears in the Majors Index beginning on page 460.

The **faculty** at William Jewell has 75 full-time members, 84% with terminal degrees. The student-faculty ratio is 13:1.

Students of William Jewell

The student body is made up of 1,274 undergraduates. 58.8% are women and 41.2% are men. Students come from 32 states and territories and 12 other countries. 78% are from Missouri. 1% are international students. 3.2% are African American, 0.3% American Indian, 0.5% Asian American, and 1.4% Hispanic American. 86% returned for their sophomore year.

Facilities and Resources

Student rooms are linked to a campus network. 160 **computers** are available on campus that provide access to the Internet. The **library** has 260,119 books and 868 subscriptions.

Campus Life

There are 47 active organizations on campus, including a drama/theater group, newspaper, radio station, and choral group. 32% of eligible men and 34% of eligible women are members of national **fraternities** and national **sororities**.

William Jewell is a member of the NAIA. **Intercollegiate sports** (some offering scholarships) include baseball (m), basketball, cheerleading, cross-country running, football (m), golf, soccer, softball (w), tennis, track and field, volleyball (w).

Campus Safety

Student safety services include late-night transport/escort service, 24-hour emergency telephone alarm devices, 24-hour patrols by trained security personnel, and electronically operated dormitory entrances.

Applying

William Jewell requires SAT I or ACT, a high school transcript, and a minimum high school GPA of 2.0. It recommends an essay, an interview, 2 recommendations, and a minimum high school GPA of 2.5. Application deadline: 8/25; 3/1 priority date for financial aid. Deferred admission is possible.

Getting in Last Year

907 applied
95% were accepted
358 enrolled (41%)
31% from top tenth of their h.s. class
3.66 average high school GPA
45% had SAT verbal scores over 600
46% had SAT math scores over 600
56% had ACT scores over 24
7% had SAT verbal scores over 700
10% had SAT math scores over 700
13% had ACT scores over 30
18 valedictorians

Graduation and After

48% graduated in 4 years
8% graduated in 5 years
1% graduated in 6 years
24% pursued further study (5% arts and sciences, 4% business, 4% education)
74% had job offers within 6 months
111 organizations recruited on campus

Financial Matters

$16,500 tuition and fees (2003–04)
$4820 room and board
$11,899 average financial aid amount received per undergraduate (2002–03 estimated)

WILLIAMS COLLEGE

SMALL-TOWN SETTING ■ PRIVATE ■ INDEPENDENT ■ COED
WILLIAMSTOWN, MASSACHUSETTS

Web site: www.williams.edu
Contact: Mr. Richard L. Nesbitt, Director of Admission, PO Box 487, Williamstown, MA 01267
Telephone: 413-597-2211 **Fax:** 413-597-4052
E-mail: admission@williams.edu

Williams is a tightly knit residential community with a focus on the direct educational partnership between students and faculty members. The College emphasizes the continuities between academic and extracurricular life while maintaining a firm commitment to excellence in teaching, artistic endeavor, and scholarly research. Williams admits both domestic and international students without regard to financial need and provides financial assistance to meet 100% of demonstrated need. The College places a high priority on fostering a multicultural community—to promote an enriched exchange of ideas and to prepare its graduates for a world of increasing diversification.

Getting in Last Year
5,341 applied
21% were accepted
533 enrolled (47%)
92% had SAT verbal scores over 600
93% had SAT math scores over 600
60% had SAT verbal scores over 700
60% had SAT math scores over 700

Graduation and After
92% graduated in 4 years
3% graduated in 5 years
1% graduated in 6 years
19% pursued further study
65% had job offers within 6 months
100 organizations recruited on campus

Financial Matters
$28,090 tuition and fees (2003–04)
$7660 room and board
100% average percent of need met
$24,390 average financial aid amount received per undergraduate (2002–03 estimated)

Academics

Williams awards bachelor's and master's **degrees**. Challenging opportunities include advanced placement credit, accelerated degree programs, student-designed majors, an honors program, double majors, independent study, and a senior project. Special programs include internships, off-campus study, and study-abroad.

The most frequently chosen **baccalaureate** fields are social sciences and history, psychology, and English. A complete listing of majors at Williams appears in the Majors Index beginning on page 460.

The **faculty** at Williams has 243 full-time members, 98% with terminal degrees. The student-faculty ratio is 8:1.

Students of Williams

The student body totals 2,102, of whom 2,045 are undergraduates. 50.2% are women and 49.8% are men. Students come from 51 states and territories and 32 other countries. 20% are from Massachusetts. 5.6% are international students. 8.9% are African American, 0.2% American Indian, 8.7% Asian American, and 7.6% Hispanic American. 97% returned for their sophomore year.

Facilities and Resources

Student rooms are linked to a campus network. 150 **computers** are available on campus for student use. The 10 **libraries** have 888,504 books and 1,904 subscriptions.

Campus Life

There are 110 active organizations on campus, including a drama/theater group, newspaper, radio station, choral group, and marching band. No national or local **fraternities** or **sororities**.

Williams is a member of the NCAA (Division III). **Intercollegiate sports** include baseball (m), basketball, crew, cross-country running, field hockey (w), football (m), golf (m), ice hockey, lacrosse, skiing (cross-country), skiing (downhill), soccer, softball (w), squash, swimming, tennis, track and field, volleyball (w), wrestling (m).

Campus Safety

Student safety services include late-night transport/escort service, 24-hour emergency telephone alarm devices, 24-hour patrols by trained security personnel, student patrols, and electronically operated dormitory entrances.

Applying

Williams requires an essay, SAT I and SAT II or ACT, a high school transcript, and 2 recommendations. Application deadline: 1/1; 2/1 for financial aid. Early and deferred admission are possible.

WISCONSIN LUTHERAN COLLEGE

SUBURBAN SETTING ■ PRIVATE ■ INDEPENDENT RELIGIOUS ■ COED
MILWAUKEE, WISCONSIN

Web site: www.wlc.edu
Contact: Mr. Craig Swiontek, Director of Admissions, 8800 West Bluemound
   Road, Milwaukee, WI 53226-9942
Telephone: 414-443-8811 or toll-free 888-WIS LUTH **Fax:** 414-443-8514
E-mail: admissions@wlc.edu

Academics

Wisconsin Lutheran awards bachelor's **degrees**. Challenging opportunities include advanced placement credit, student-designed majors, double majors, independent study, and a senior project. Special programs include internships, summer session for credit, study-abroad, and Army, Navy and Air Force ROTC.

The most frequently chosen **baccalaureate** fields are communications/communication technologies, biological/life sciences, and visual/performing arts. A complete listing of majors at Wisconsin Lutheran appears in the Majors Index beginning on page 460.

The **faculty** at Wisconsin Lutheran has 47 full-time members, 64% with terminal degrees. The student-faculty ratio is 11:1.

Students of Wisconsin Lutheran

The student body is made up of 706 undergraduates. 59.8% are women and 40.2% are men. Students come from 28 states and territories and 6 other countries. 81% are from Wisconsin. 1.5% are international students. 1.5% are African American, 0.6% Asian American, and 1% Hispanic American. 80% returned for their sophomore year.

Facilities and Resources

Student rooms are linked to a campus network. 200 **computers** are available on campus that provide access to the Internet. The **library** has 71,731 books and 614 subscriptions.

Campus Life

There are 31 active organizations on campus, including a drama/theater group, newspaper, and choral group. No national or local **fraternities** or **sororities**.

Wisconsin Lutheran is a member of the NCAA (Division III). **Intercollegiate sports** include baseball (m), basketball, cross-country running, football (m), golf, soccer, softball (w), tennis (w), track and field, volleyball (w).

Campus Safety

Student safety services include closed circuit TV monitors, late-night transport/escort service, 24-hour emergency telephone alarm devices, 24-hour patrols by trained security personnel, and electronically operated dormitory entrances.

Applying

Wisconsin Lutheran requires SAT I or ACT, a high school transcript, 1 recommendation, minimum ACT score of 21, and a minimum high school GPA of 2.70, and in some cases an interview. Application deadline: 3/1 priority date for financial aid.

Getting in Last Year
531 applied
84% were accepted
207 enrolled (47%)
23% from top tenth of their h.s. class
3.48 average high school GPA
59% had ACT scores over 24
5% had ACT scores over 30
10 valedictorians

Graduation and After
47% graduated in 4 years
19% graduated in 5 years
8% graduated in 6 years
63% had job offers within 6 months
10 organizations recruited on campus

Financial Matters
$15,850 tuition and fees (2003–04)
$5325 room and board
86% average percent of need met
$13,342 average financial aid amount received
   per undergraduate

WITTENBERG UNIVERSITY

SUBURBAN SETTING ■ PRIVATE ■ INDEPENDENT RELIGIOUS ■ COED
SPRINGFIELD, OHIO

Web site: www.wittenberg.edu
Contact: Mr. Kenneth G. Benne, Dean of Admissions and Financial Aid, PO
  Box 720, Springfield, OH 45501-0720
Telephone: 937-327-6314 ext. 6366 or toll-free 800-677-7558 ext. 6314 **Fax:**
  937-327-6379
E-mail: admission@wittenberg.edu

Getting in Last Year

2,524 applied
85% were accepted
652 enrolled (30%)
29% from top tenth of their h.s. class
3.50 average high school GPA
36% had SAT verbal scores over 600
41% had SAT math scores over 600
70% had ACT scores over 24
6% had SAT verbal scores over 700
6% had SAT math scores over 700
17% had ACT scores over 30
6 National Merit Scholars
42 class presidents
43 valedictorians

Graduation and After

63% graduated in 4 years
6% graduated in 5 years
1% graduated in 6 years
24% pursued further study (5% business, 5%
  medicine, 2% arts and sciences)
97% had job offers within 6 months
100 organizations recruited on campus

Financial Matters

$25,098 tuition and fees (2003–04)
$6368 room and board
91% average percent of need met
$21,286 average financial aid amount received
  per undergraduate (2002–03 estimated)

Academics

Wittenberg University awards bachelor's and master's **degrees.** Challenging opportunities include advanced placement credit, accelerated degree programs, student-designed majors, freshman honors college, an honors program, double majors, independent study, and a senior project. Special programs include cooperative education, internships, summer session for credit, off-campus study, study-abroad, and Army and Air Force ROTC. A complete listing of majors at Wittenberg University appears in the Majors Index beginning on page 460.

The **faculty** at Wittenberg University has 138 full-time members, 86% with terminal degrees. The student-faculty ratio is 14:1.

Students of Wittenberg University

The student body totals 2,346, of whom 2,320 are undergraduates. 56.5% are women and 43.5% are men. Students come from 46 states and territories and 32 other countries. 57% are from Ohio. 2.5% are international students. 7% are African American, 1% Asian American, and 0.8% Hispanic American. 85% returned for their sophomore year.

Facilities and Resources

Student rooms are linked to a campus network. 750 **computers** are available on campus that provide access to the Internet. The 3 **libraries** have 350,000 books and 1,300 subscriptions.

Campus Life

There are 100 active organizations on campus, including a drama/theater group, newspaper, radio station, and choral group. 15% of eligible men and 35% of eligible women are members of national **fraternities** and national **sororities.**

Wittenberg University is a member of the NCAA (Division III). **Intercollegiate sports** include baseball (m), basketball, bowling (w), cheerleading, cross-country running, field hockey (w), football (m), golf (m), lacrosse, soccer, softball (w), swimming, tennis, track and field, volleyball (w).

Campus Safety

Student safety services include crime prevention programs, late-night transport/escort service, 24-hour emergency telephone alarm devices, 24-hour patrols by trained security personnel, student patrols, and electronically operated dormitory entrances.

Applying

Wittenberg University requires an essay, SAT I or ACT, a high school transcript, and 1 recommendation, and in some cases an interview. It recommends SAT II Subject Tests and an interview. Application deadline: 3/15 for financial aid, with a 2/15 priority date. Early and deferred admission are possible.

WOFFORD COLLEGE

URBAN SETTING ■ PRIVATE ■ INDEPENDENT RELIGIOUS ■ COED
SPARTANBURG, SOUTH CAROLINA

Web site: www.wofford.edu
Contact: Mr. Brand Stille, Director of Admissions, 429 North Church Street,
  Spartanburg, SC 29303-3663
Telephone: 864-597-4130 **Fax:** 864-597-4147
E-mail: admissions@wofford.edu

Academics

Wofford awards bachelor's **degrees**. Challenging opportunities include advanced placement credit, accelerated degree programs, student-designed majors, double majors,
independent study, and a senior project. Special programs include internships, summer
session for credit, off-campus study, study-abroad, and Army ROTC.

The most frequently chosen **baccalaureate** fields are business/marketing, social sciences and history, and biological/life sciences. A complete listing of majors at Wofford
appears in the Majors Index beginning on page 460.

The **faculty** at Wofford has 82 full-time members, 91% with terminal degrees. The
student-faculty ratio is 12:1.

Students of Wofford

The student body is made up of 1,132 undergraduates. 51.2% are women and 48.8% are
men. Students come from 31 states and territories and 6 other countries. 65% are from
South Carolina. 0.5% are international students. 7.7% are African American, 0.1%
American Indian, 1.9% Asian American, and 1.1% Hispanic American. 93% returned for
their sophomore year.

Facilities and Resources

Student rooms are linked to a campus network. 43 **computers** are available on campus
that provide access to the Internet. The **library** has 209,084 books and 551 subscriptions.

Campus Life

There are 68 active organizations on campus, including a drama/theater group,
newspaper, and choral group. 54% of eligible men and 64% of eligible women are
members of national **fraternities** and national **sororities**.

Wofford is a member of the NCAA (Division I). **Intercollegiate sports** (some offering scholarships) include baseball (m), basketball, cross-country running, football (m),
golf, riflery, soccer, tennis, track and field, volleyball (w).

Campus Safety

Student safety services include late-night transport/escort service, 24-hour emergency
telephone alarm devices, 24-hour patrols by trained security personnel, and electronically operated dormitory entrances.

Applying

Wofford requires an essay, SAT I or ACT, and a high school transcript. It recommends
SAT II: Writing Test, an interview, and 2 recommendations. Application deadline: 2/1;
3/15 priority date for financial aid. Early and deferred admission are possible.

Getting in Last Year

1,317 applied
80% were accepted
330 enrolled (31%)
54% from top tenth of their h.s. class
62% had SAT verbal scores over 600
68% had SAT math scores over 600
64% had ACT scores over 24
13% had SAT verbal scores over 700
17% had SAT math scores over 700
5% had ACT scores over 30
7 National Merit Scholars
8 class presidents
18 valedictorians

Graduation and After

71% graduated in 4 years
5% graduated in 5 years
31% pursued further study (9% arts and sciences, 5% medicine, 4% business)
57% had job offers within 6 months

Financial Matters

$20,610 tuition and fees (2003–04)
$6100 room and board
89% average percent of need met
$15,796 average financial aid amount received
  per undergraduate (2002–03 estimated)

WORCESTER POLYTECHNIC INSTITUTE

SUBURBAN SETTING ■ PRIVATE ■ INDEPENDENT ■ COED
WORCESTER, MASSACHUSETTS

Getting in Last Year
3,576 applied
71% were accepted
633 enrolled (25%)
51% from top tenth of their h.s. class
3.60 average high school GPA
61% had SAT verbal scores over 600
87% had SAT math scores over 600
15% had SAT verbal scores over 700
32% had SAT math scores over 700
14 National Merit Scholars
50 valedictorians

Graduation and After
61% graduated in 4 years
14% graduated in 5 years
2% graduated in 6 years
150 organizations recruited on campus

Financial Matters
$28,620 tuition and fees (2003–04)
$8984 room and board
91% average percent of need met
$19,334 average financial aid amount received
    per undergraduate (2002–03 estimated)

Web site: www.wpi.edu
Contact: Ms. Kristin Tichenor, Director of Admissions, 100 Institute Road,
    Worcester, MA 01609-2280
Telephone: 508-831-5286 **Fax:** 508-831-5875
E-mail: admissions@wpi.edu

Academics

WPI awards bachelor's, master's, and doctoral **degrees** and post-bachelor's and post-master's certificates. Challenging opportunities include advanced placement credit, accelerated degree programs, student-designed majors, double majors, independent study, and a senior project. Special programs include cooperative education, summer session for credit, off-campus study, study-abroad, and Army, Navy and Air Force ROTC.

The most frequently chosen **baccalaureate** fields are education, computer/information sciences, and biological/life sciences. A complete listing of majors at WPI appears in the Majors Index beginning on page 460.

The **faculty** at WPI has 240 full-time members, 98% with terminal degrees. The student-faculty ratio is 13:1.

Students of WPI

The student body totals 3,789, of whom 2,785 are undergraduates. 23.7% are women and 76.3% are men. Students come from 45 states and territories and 70 other countries. 50% are from Massachusetts. 3.9% are international students. 1.3% are African American, 0.4% American Indian, 7% Asian American, and 3.4% Hispanic American. 92% returned for their sophomore year.

Facilities and Resources

Student rooms are linked to a campus network. 1,000 **computers** are available on campus that provide access to the Internet. The **library** has 146,372 books and 982 subscriptions.

Campus Life

There are 100 active organizations on campus, including a drama/theater group, newspaper, radio station, and choral group. WPI has national **fraternities** and national **sororities**.

WPI is a member of the NCAA (Division III). **Intercollegiate sports** include baseball (m), basketball, cross-country running, field hockey (w), football (m), golf (m), soccer, softball (w), swimming, tennis, track and field, volleyball (w), wrestling (m).

Campus Safety

Student safety services include late-night transport/escort service, 24-hour emergency telephone alarm devices, 24-hour patrols by trained security personnel, and student patrols.

Applying

WPI requires an essay, SAT I and SAT II or ACT, a high school transcript, and 2 recommendations, and in some cases an interview. Application deadline: 2/1; 3/1 priority date for financial aid. Early and deferred admission are possible.

XAVIER UNIVERSITY

SUBURBAN SETTING ■ PRIVATE ■ INDEPENDENT RELIGIOUS ■ COED
CINCINNATI, OHIO

Web site: www.xavier.edu
Contact: Mr. Marc Camille, Dean of Admission, 3800 Victory Parkway,
    Cincinnati, OH 45207-5311
Telephone: 513-745-3301 or toll-free 800-344-4698 **Fax:** 513-745-4319
E-mail: xuadmit@xavier.edu

Academics

Xavier awards associate, bachelor's, master's, and doctoral **degrees** and post-bachelor's
and post-master's certificates. Challenging opportunities include advanced placement
credit, an honors program, double majors, independent study, and a senior project.
Special programs include cooperative education, internships, summer session for credit,
off-campus study, study-abroad, and Army and Air Force ROTC.

    The most frequently chosen **baccalaureate** fields are business/marketing, liberal
arts/general studies, and communications/communication technologies. A complete listing of majors at Xavier appears in the Majors Index beginning on page 460.

    The **faculty** at Xavier has 278 full-time members, 85% with terminal degrees. The
student-faculty ratio is 13:1.

Students of Xavier

The student body totals 6,626, of whom 3,915 are undergraduates. 56.4% are women
and 43.6% are men. Students come from 46 states and territories and 53 other countries.
66% are from Ohio. 2.6% are international students. 9.8% are African American, 0.2%
American Indian, 1.8% Asian American, and 1.6% Hispanic American. 89% returned for
their sophomore year.

Facilities and Resources

Student rooms are linked to a campus network. 200 **computers** are available on campus
that provide access to the Internet. The 2 **libraries** have 191,923 books and 1,633
subscriptions.

Campus Life

There are 100 active organizations on campus, including a drama/theater group,
newspaper, radio station, television station, and choral group. No national or local
fraternities or **sororities**.

    Xavier is a member of the NCAA (Division I). **Intercollegiate sports** (some offering
scholarships) include baseball (m), basketball, cheerleading, cross-country running, golf,
riflery, soccer, swimming, tennis, volleyball (w).

Campus Safety

Student safety services include campus-wide shuttle service, late-night transport/escort
service, 24-hour emergency telephone alarm devices, and 24-hour patrols by trained
security personnel.

Applying

Xavier requires an essay, SAT I or ACT, a high school transcript, and 1 recommendation.
It recommends an interview. Application deadline: 2/1; 2/15 priority date for financial
aid. Early and deferred admission are possible.

Getting in Last Year

4,364 applied
78% were accepted
786 enrolled (23%)
29% from top tenth of their h.s. class
3.54 average high school GPA
44% had SAT verbal scores over 600
44% had SAT math scores over 600
71% had ACT scores over 24
8% had SAT verbal scores over 700
8% had SAT math scores over 700
18% had ACT scores over 30
12 National Merit Scholars
18 valedictorians

Graduation and After

68% graduated in 4 years
10% graduated in 5 years
1% graduated in 6 years
23% pursued further study (9% arts and sci-
    ences, 5% medicine, 3% education)
73.3% had job offers within 6 months
123 organizations recruited on campus

Financial Matters

$19,150 tuition and fees (2003–04)
$8000 room and board
77% average percent of need met
$12,947 average financial aid amount received
    per undergraduate (2002–03 estimated)

YALE UNIVERSITY

URBAN SETTING ■ PRIVATE ■ INDEPENDENT ■ COED
NEW HAVEN, CONNECTICUT

Web site: www.yale.edu
Contact: Admissions Director, PO Box 208234, New Haven, CT 06520-8324
Telephone: 203-432-9300 **Fax:** 203-432-9392
E-mail: undergraduate.admissions@yale.edu

Getting in Last Year
17,735 applied
11% were accepted
1,352 enrolled (67%)
95% from top tenth of their h.s. class

Graduation and After
31% pursued further study (11% arts and sciences, 7% law, 7% medicine)
62% had job offers within 6 months

Financial Matters
$28,400 tuition and fees (2003–04)
$8600 room and board
100% average percent of need met
$25,501 average financial aid amount received per undergraduate (2002–03 estimated)

Academics

Yale awards bachelor's, master's, doctoral, and first-professional **degrees** and post-master's certificates. Challenging opportunities include advanced placement credit, accelerated degree programs, student-designed majors, an honors program, double majors, independent study, and a senior project. Special programs include summer session for credit, study-abroad, and Army and Air Force ROTC.

The most frequently chosen **baccalaureate** fields are social sciences and history, biological/life sciences, and English. A complete listing of majors at Yale appears in the Majors Index beginning on page 460.

The **faculty** at Yale has 1,004 full-time members, 90% with terminal degrees. The student-faculty ratio is 7:1.

Students of Yale

The student body totals 11,471, of whom 5,354 are undergraduates. 49.9% are women and 50.1% are men. Students come from 50 states and territories and 70 other countries. 8% are from Connecticut. 8.8% are international students. 7.6% are African American, 0.6% American Indian, 13.4% Asian American, and 6.1% Hispanic American. 98% returned for their sophomore year.

Facilities and Resources

Student rooms are linked to a campus network. 350 **computers** are available on campus for student use. The 21 **libraries** have 10,800,000 books and 63,656 subscriptions.

Campus Life

There are 300 active organizations on campus, including a drama/theater group, newspaper, radio station, choral group, and marching band. Yale has national **fraternities** and national **sororities**.

Yale is a member of the NCAA (Division I). **Intercollegiate sports** (some offering scholarships) include baseball (m), basketball, cheerleading, crew, cross-country running, fencing, field hockey (w), football (m), golf, gymnastics (w), ice hockey, lacrosse, soccer, softball (w), squash, swimming, tennis, track and field, volleyball (w).

Campus Safety

Student safety services include late-night transport/escort service, 24-hour emergency telephone alarm devices, 24-hour patrols by trained security personnel, and electronically operated dormitory entrances.

Applying

Yale requires an essay, SAT I and SAT II or ACT, a high school transcript, and 3 recommendations. It recommends an interview. Application deadline: 12/31; 3/1 priority date for financial aid. Early and deferred admission are possible.

APPENDIXES

Ten Largest Colleges 454

Ten Smallest Colleges 454

Colleges Accepting Fewer than
Half of Their Applicants. 454

Single-Sex Colleges 455

Predominantly African-American
Colleges 455

Colleges with Religious Affiliation 455

Public Colleges 457

Ten Largest Colleges

The University of Texas at Austin	51,426
The Ohio State University	50,731
University of Minnesota, Twin Cities Campus	49,474
University of Florida	47,858
Texas A&M University	44,813
Michigan State University	44,542
The Pennsylvania State University University Park Campus	41,795
University of Wisconsin–Madison	41,588
University of Central Florida	41,102
University of Illinois at Urbana–Champaign	40,458

Ten Smallest Colleges

Webb Institute	72
Kentucky Mountain Bible College	82
Research College of Nursing	219
College of the Atlantic	262
Thomas Aquinas College	332
Simon's Rock College of Bard	399
Cleveland Institute of Music	413
Wells College	420
Christendom College	433
Westminster Choir College of Rider University	455

Colleges Accepting Fewer than Half of Their Applicants

Amherst College
Bard College
Barnard College
Bates College
Bentley College
Berea College
Boston College
Bowdoin College
Brandeis University
Brown University
Bryan College
Bucknell University
California Institute of Technology
California Polytechnic State University, San Luis Obispo
Carleton College
Claremont McKenna College
Cleveland Institute of Music
Colby College
Colgate University
The College of New Jersey
College of the Holy Cross
The College of William and Mary
Columbia College (NY)
Columbia University, The Fu Foundation School of Engineering and Applied Science
Connecticut College
Cooper Union for the Advancement of Science and Art
Cornell University
Dartmouth College
Davidson College
Duke University
Emerson College
Emory University
Fairfield University

Florida International University
Florida State University
Georgetown University
The George Washington University
Gettysburg College
Grove City College
Hamilton College (NY)
Harvard University
Harvey Mudd College
Haverford College
Illinois Wesleyan University
The Johns Hopkins University
Kenyon College
Lafayette College
Lehigh University
Macalester College
Maryland Institute College of Art
Massachusetts Institute of Technology
McGill University
Middlebury College
Muhlenberg College
New York University
Northwestern University
Oberlin College
Occidental College
Peabody Conservatory of Music of The Johns Hopkins University
Pepperdine University (Malibu, CA)
Pomona College
Princeton University
Queen's University at Kingston
Reed College
Rhode Island School of Design
Rice University
Saint Joseph's University
St. Louis College of Pharmacy
Sarah Lawrence College
Simon's Rock College of Bard
Skidmore College
Stanford University
State University of New York at Binghamton
State University of New York College at Geneseo
Stonehill College
Swarthmore College
Trinity College
Tufts University
Union College
Union College
United States Air Force Academy
United States Coast Guard Academy
United States Merchant Marine Academy
United States Military Academy
United States Naval Academy
University of California, Berkeley
University of California, Los Angeles
University of California, San Diego
University of California, Santa Barbara
University of Chicago
University of Delaware
University of Maryland, College Park
University of Miami

The University of North Carolina at Chapel Hill
University of Notre Dame
University of Pennsylvania
University of Pittsburgh
University of Richmond
University of Rochester
University of Southern California
The University of Texas at Austin
The University of Texas at Dallas
University of Virginia
Vanderbilt University
Vassar College
Virginia Military Institute
Wabash College
Wake Forest University
Washington & Jefferson College
Washington and Lee University
Washington University in St. Louis
Webb Institute
Wellesley College
Wesleyan University
Wheaton College
Williams College
Yale University

Single-Sex Colleges: Men Only
Morehouse College
Wabash College

Single-Sex Colleges: Women Only
Agnes Scott College
Barnard College
Bryn Mawr College
Converse College
Mills College
Mount Holyoke College
Randolph-Macon Woman's College
Saint Mary's College
Salem College
Scripps College
Smith College
Stephens College
Sweet Briar College
Wellesley College
Wells College
Wesleyan College

Predominantly African-American Colleges
Morehouse College

Colleges with Religious Affiliation

Adventist
Union College

Baptist
Baylor University
Belmont University
Bethel University
Cedarville University
Georgetown College
Kalamazoo College
Linfield College

Louisiana College
Mercer University
Oklahoma Baptist University
Ouachita Baptist University
Samford University
Southwest Baptist University
Union University
William Jewell College

Brethren
Elizabethtown College
Huntington College
Juniata College

Christian (Unspecified)
Milligan College

Christian Church (Disciples of Christ)
Chapman University
Hiram College
Texas Christian University
Transylvania University

Church of the Nazarene
Point Loma Nazarene University

Churches of Christ
Abilene Christian University
Freed-Hardeman University
Harding University
Lipscomb University
Pepperdine University (Malibu, CA)

Episcopal
University of the South

Friends
Earlham College
George Fox University

Interdenominational
Berry College
Biola University
Bryan College
Colorado Christian University
Illinois College
John Brown University
Kentucky Mountain Bible College
Messiah College
Oral Roberts University
Taylor University

Jewish
List College, Jewish Theological Seminary of America

Latter-day Saints (Mormon)
Brigham Young University

Lutheran
Augustana College (IL)
Augustana College (SD)
Concordia College (MN)
Gettysburg College
Gustavus Adolphus College
Luther College
Muhlenberg College

Pacific Lutheran University
St. Olaf College
Susquehanna University
Valparaiso University
Wartburg College
Wisconsin Lutheran College
Wittenberg University

Mennonite
Eastern Mennonite University
Goshen College

Methodist
Albion College
Albright College
American University
Baker University
Baldwin-Wallace College
Birmingham-Southern College
Centenary College of Louisiana
Cornell College
DePauw University
Drew University
Duke University
Emory University
Hamline University
Hendrix College
Huntingdon College
Lebanon Valley College
Lycoming College
McKendree College
Millsaps College
North Central College
Ohio Northern University
Ohio Wesleyan University
Oklahoma City University
Randolph-Macon Woman's College
Seattle Pacific University
Simpson College
Southern Methodist University
Southwestern University
University of Evansville
Wesleyan College
Willamette University
Wofford College

Moravian
Salem College

Nondenominational
Asbury College
Azusa Pacific University
Gordon College (MA)
LeTourneau University
The Master's College and Seminary
Northwestern College
Westmont College
Wheaton College

Presbyterian
Agnes Scott College
Alma College
Austin College

Centre College
Coe College
The College of Wooster
Covenant College
Davidson College
Eckerd College
Erskine College
Grove City College
Hanover College
King College
Lafayette College
Lyon College
Macalester College
Maryville College
Presbyterian College
Rhodes College
Trinity University
University of Tulsa
Whitworth College

Reformed Churches
Calvin College
Central College
Hope College
Northwestern College (IA)

Roman Catholic
Bellarmine University
Benedictine University
Boston College
Canisius College
Carroll College (MT)
Christendom College
Christian Brothers University
College of Saint Benedict
The College of St. Scholastica
College of the Holy Cross
Creighton University
Fairfield University
Fordham University
Franciscan University of Steubenville
Georgetown University
Gonzaga University
John Carroll University
Loyola College in Maryland
Loyola Marymount University
Loyola University Chicago
Loyola University New Orleans
Marquette University
Providence College
Quincy University
Regis University
Saint Francis University
Saint John's University (MN)
Saint Joseph's University
Saint Louis University
Saint Mary's College
Saint Mary's College of California
St. Norbert College
Santa Clara University
Seattle University
Siena College

Stonehill College
Thomas Aquinas College
University of Dallas
University of Dayton
University of Notre Dame
University of Portland
University of St. Thomas
University of St. Thomas (TX)
University of San Diego
The University of Scranton
Villanova University
Xavier University

Wesleyan
Houghton College

Public Colleges

Auburn University
California Polytechnic State University, San Luis Obispo
Clemson University
College of Charleston
The College of New Jersey
The College of William and Mary
Colorado School of Mines
Colorado State University
Florida International University
Florida State University
Georgia Institute of Technology
Georgia State University
Iowa State University of Science and Technology
James Madison University
Kansas State University
Louisiana State University and Agricultural and Mechanical
    College
Louisiana Tech University
Mary Washington College
McGill University
Miami University
Michigan State University
Michigan Technological University
Mississippi State University
Murray State University
New College of Florida
New Jersey Institute of Technology
New Mexico Institute of Mining and Technology
North Carolina State University
The Ohio State University
Oklahoma State University
The Pennsylvania State University University Park Campus
Purdue University
Queen's University at Kingston
Rutgers, The State University of New Jersey, New Brunswick/
    Piscataway
St. Mary's College of Maryland
South Dakota School of Mines and Technology
Southwest Missouri State University
State University of New York at Binghamton
State University of New York College at Geneseo
Texas A&M University

Texas Tech University
Truman State University
United States Air Force Academy
United States Coast Guard Academy
United States Merchant Marine Academy
United States Military Academy
United States Naval Academy
University at Buffalo, The State University of New York
The University of Alabama
The University of Alabama in Huntsville
The University of Arizona
University of Arkansas
University of California, Berkeley
University of California, Davis
University of California, Irvine
University of California, Los Angeles
University of California, Riverside
University of California, San Diego
University of California, Santa Barbara
University of California, Santa Cruz
University of Central Arkansas
University of Central Florida
University of Colorado at Boulder
University of Delaware
University of Florida
University of Georgia
University of Idaho
University of Illinois at Chicago
University of Illinois at Urbana–Champaign
The University of Iowa
University of Kansas
University of Kentucky
University of Maryland, Baltimore County
University of Maryland, College Park
University of Michigan
University of Minnesota, Morris
University of Minnesota, Twin Cities Campus
University of Mississippi
University of Missouri–Columbia
University of Missouri–Kansas City
University of Missouri–Rolla
University of Nebraska–Lincoln
The University of North Carolina at Asheville
The University of North Carolina at Chapel Hill
University of Oklahoma
University of Pittsburgh
University of Rhode Island
University of South Carolina
The University of Texas at Austin
The University of Texas at Dallas
University of Utah
University of Virginia
University of Washington
University of Wisconsin–Madison
University of Wyoming
Virginia Military Institute
Virginia Polytechnic Institute and State University

INDEXES

Majors by College 460

Geographic Index of Colleges 521

MAJORS BY COLLEGE

Abilene Christian University
Accounting; agribusiness; animal sciences; architecture related; area studies; art; art teacher education; biblical studies; biochemistry; biology teacher education; biology/biological sciences; business administration and management; chemistry; clinical laboratory science/medical technology; clinical/medical laboratory science and allied professions related; commercial and advertising art; communication and journalism related; computer hardware engineering; computer science; dietetics; digital communication and media/multimedia; dramatic/theatre arts; elementary education; engineering; engineering physics; engineering science; English; English/language arts teacher education; environmental science; family and consumer sciences/human sciences; finance; fine arts related; fine/studio arts; health and physical education; history; history teacher education; human development and family studies; industrial and organizational psychology; interdisciplinary studies; interior design; international/global studies; journalism; liberal arts and sciences/liberal studies; marketing/marketing management; mathematics; mathematics teacher education; medical laboratory technology; middle school education; missionary studies and missiology; multi-/interdisciplinary studies related; music; music teacher education; nursing (registered nurse training); ophthalmic laboratory technology; pastoral studies/counseling; physical education teaching and coaching; physics; piano and organ; political science and government; pre-dentistry studies; pre-law studies; pre-medical studies; pre-pharmacy studies; pre-veterinary studies; psychology; reading teacher education; science teacher education; secondary education; social sciences related; social studies teacher education; social work; sociology; Spanish; Spanish language teacher education; special education; speech and rhetoric; speech-language pathology; sport and fitness administration; theology and religious vocations related; voice and opera.

Agnes Scott College
Anthropology; art; astrophysics; biochemistry; biology/biological sciences; chemistry; classics and languages, literatures and linguistics; creative writing; dramatic/theatre arts; economics; English; French; German; history; interdisciplinary studies; international relations and affairs; literature; mathematics; music; philosophy; physics; political science and government; psychology; religious studies; sociology; Spanish; women's studies.

Albany College of Pharmacy of Union University
Biomedical sciences; health professions related; pharmacy; pharmacy, pharmaceutical sciences, and administration related.

Albertson College of Idaho
Accounting; anthropology; art; biology/biological sciences; business administration and management; chemistry; computer science; creative writing; dramatic/theatre arts; economics; English; history; international business/trade/commerce; international economics; kinesiology and exercise science; mathematics; music; philosophy; physical education teaching and coaching; physics; political science and government; pre-medical studies; psychology; religious studies; sociology; Spanish; sport and fitness administration.

Albion College
American studies; anthropology; art; biology/biological sciences; business administration and management; chemistry; computer science; dramatic/theatre arts; economics; education; elementary education; English; environmental studies; French; geology/earth science; German; history; human services; international relations and affairs; mass communication/media; mathematics; modern languages; music; philosophy; physical education teaching and coaching; physics; political science and government; pre-law studies; pre-medical studies; pre-veterinary studies; psychology; public policy analysis; religious studies; secondary education; sociology; Spanish; women's studies.

Albright College
Accounting; American studies; apparel and textiles; art; art teacher education; biochemistry; biology/biological sciences; business administration and management; chemistry; communication/speech communication and rhetoric; computer science; criminology; dramatic/theatre arts; economics; elementary education; English; environmental studies; finance; forestry; French; history; industrial and organizational psychology; information science/studies; interdisciplinary studies; international business/trade/commerce; kindergarten/preschool education; Latin American studies; marketing/marketing management; mathematics; music; natural resources management and policy; optical sciences; philosophy; physics; physiological psychology/psychobiology; political science and government; pre-dentistry studies; pre-law studies; pre-medical studies; pre-veterinary studies; psychology; religious studies; secondary education; sociology; Spanish; special education; women's studies.

Alfred University
Accounting; applied art; art; art teacher education; athletic training; biological and physical sciences; biology/biological sciences; biomedical technology; business administration and management; business teacher education; ceramic arts and ceramics; ceramic sciences and engineering; chemistry; clinical/medical laboratory technology; communication and journalism related; computer and information sciences; criminal justice/law enforcement administration; dramatic/theatre arts; economics; electrical, electronics and communications engineering; elementary education; English; environmental studies; fine/studio arts; French;

general studies; geology/earth science; German; gerontology; health/health care administration; history; interdisciplinary studies; literature; materials science; mathematics; mathematics and computer science; mechanical engineering; modern languages; philosophy; physics; political science and government; psychology; public administration; science teacher education; secondary education; sociology; Spanish.

Allegheny College
Applied economics; art; art history, criticism and conservation; biochemistry; biology/biological sciences; business/managerial economics; chemistry; communication/speech communication and rhetoric; computer science; computer software engineering; creative writing; dramatic/theatre arts; economics; education; English; environmental science; environmental studies; fine arts related; fine/studio arts; French; geology/earth science; German; health/medical preparatory programs related; history; international relations and affairs; international/global studies; journalism; mass communication/media; mathematics; multi-/interdisciplinary studies related; music; music performance; neuroscience; philosophy; physics; political science and government; pre-dentistry studies; pre-law studies; pre-medical studies; pre-nursing studies; pre-pharmacy studies; pre-veterinary studies; psychology; religious studies; Spanish; technical and business writing; women's studies.

Alma College
Accounting; anthropology; art; art teacher education; biochemistry; biological and physical sciences; biology teacher education; biology/biological sciences; business administration and management; chemistry; chemistry teacher education; communication and media related; computer science; computer teacher education; dance; design and visual communications; dramatic/theatre arts; early childhood education; economics; education; elementary education; English; English/language arts teacher education; fine/studio arts; French; French language teacher education; German; German language teacher education; gerontology; graphic design; health science; health teacher education; history; history teacher education; humanities; international business/trade/commerce; kindergarten/preschool education; kinesiology and exercise science; liberal arts and sciences/liberal studies; marketing/marketing management; mathematics; mathematics teacher education; medical illustration; modern languages; music; music performance; music teacher education; philosophy; physical education teaching and coaching; physics; physics teacher education; political science and government; pre-dentistry studies; pre-law studies; pre-medical studies; pre-theology/pre-ministerial studies; pre-veterinary studies; psychology; psychology teacher education; public health; religious studies; science teacher education; secondary education; social science teacher

education; social sciences; social studies teacher education; sociology; Spanish; Spanish language teacher education.

American University

African studies; American studies; anthropology; applied mathematics; art; art history, criticism and conservation; Asian studies; audio engineering; biochemistry; biology/biological sciences; broadcast journalism; business administration and management; business/managerial economics; chemistry; cinematography and film/video production; commercial and advertising art; computer science; criminal justice/safety; development economics and international development; dramatic/theatre arts; economics; elementary education; entrepreneurship; environmental studies; European studies; finance; fine/studio arts; French; German; health science; history; human resources management; information science/studies; interdisciplinary studies; intermedia/multimedia; international business/trade/commerce; international economics; international finance; international marketing; international relations and affairs; Islamic studies; Jewish/Judaic studies; journalism; Latin American studies; legal studies; literature; management information systems; marine biology and biological oceanography; marketing/marketing management; mathematics; music; Near and Middle Eastern studies; peace studies and conflict resolution; philosophy; physics; political science and government; pre-dentistry studies; pre-law studies; pre-medical studies; pre-pharmacy studies; pre-veterinary studies; psychology; public relations/image management; Russian; Russian studies; secondary education; sociology; Spanish; sport and fitness administration; statistics; women's studies.

Amherst College

African-American/Black studies; American studies; ancient/classical Greek; anthropology; art; Asian studies; astronomy; biology/biological sciences; chemistry; classics and languages, literatures and linguistics; computer science; dance; dramatic/theatre arts; economics; English; European studies; fine/studio arts; French; geology/earth science; German; history; interdisciplinary studies; Latin; legal studies; mathematics; music; neuroscience; philosophy; physics; political science and government; psychology; religious studies; Russian; sociology; Spanish; women's studies.

Asbury College

Accounting; ancient/classical Greek; applied mathematics; art teacher education; biblical studies; biochemistry; biology/biological sciences; business/commerce; chemistry; classics and languages, literatures and linguistics; elementary education; English; fine/studio arts; French; health and physical education; health/medical preparatory programs related; history; journalism; Latin; mathematics; middle school education; missionary studies and missiology; music; music teacher education; parks, recreation and leisure facilities management; philosophy; physical education teaching and coaching; physical sciences; psychology; radio and television broadcasting technology; religious education; social sciences; social work; sociology; Spanish; speech and rhetoric; sport and fitness administration.

Auburn University

Accounting; adult and continuing education; aerospace, aeronautical and astronautical engineering; agricultural economics; agricultural teacher education; agricultural/biological engineering and bioengineering; agriculture; agronomy and crop science; airline pilot and flight crew; animal sciences; anthropology; apparel and textiles; applied mathematics; aquaculture; architectural engineering; architecture; art; audiology and speech-language pathology; aviation/airway management; biochemistry; biology/biological sciences; biomedical sciences; botany/plant biology; broadcast journalism; business administration and management; business teacher education; business/managerial economics; chemical engineering; chemistry; child development; civil engineering; clinical laboratory science/medical technology; clinical/medical laboratory technology; commercial and advertising art; communication and journalism related; computer and information sciences; computer engineering; computer engineering related; computer hardware engineering; computer software engineering; criminology; dairy science; dramatic/theatre arts; early childhood education; economics; electrical, electronics and communications engineering; elementary education; engineering; English; English as a second/foreign language (teaching); environmental design/architecture; environmental science; environmental studies; family and consumer sciences/human sciences; finance; fine/studio arts; food science; foods, nutrition, and wellness; foreign languages and literatures; forest sciences and biology; French; French language teacher education; geography; geological/geophysical engineering; geology/earth science; German; German language teacher education; health teacher education; health/health care administration; history; history teacher education; horticultural science; hospitality administration related; hotel/motel administration; housing and human environments; human development and family studies; human resources management; industrial design; industrial engineering; interior architecture; international business/trade/commerce; journalism; kindergarten/preschool education; landscape architecture; logistics and materials management; management information systems; marine biology and biological oceanography; marketing/marketing management; mass communication/media; materials engineering; mathematics; mechanical engineering; medical laboratory technology; medical microbiology and bacteriology; microbiology; molecular biology; music teacher education; nursing (registered nurse training); nutrition sciences; operations management; ornamental horticulture; parks, recreation and leisure; philosophy; physical education teaching and coaching; physics; physics teacher education; plant pathology/phytopathology; plant sciences; plant sciences related; political science and government; poultry science; pre-dentistry studies; pre-law studies; pre-medical studies; pre-pharmacy studies; pre-veterinary studies; psychology; public administration; public relations/image management; radio and television; science teacher education; secondary education; secondary school administration/principalship; social work; sociology; Spanish; Spanish language teacher education; special education;

special education (vision impaired); special education related; speech and rhetoric; speech therapy; textile sciences and engineering; trade and industrial teacher education; wildlife and wildlands science and management; zoology/animal biology.

Augustana College (IL)

Accounting; anthropology; art; art history, criticism and conservation; art teacher education; Asian studies; biology/biological sciences; business administration and management; chemistry; Chinese; classics and languages, literatures and linguistics; computer science; creative writing; dramatic/theatre arts; economics; education; elementary education; engineering related; English; environmental studies; finance; fine/studio arts; French; geography; geology/earth science; German; history; Japanese; jazz/jazz studies; Latin; liberal arts and sciences/liberal studies; literature; marketing/marketing management; mass communication/media; mathematics; mathematics and computer science; music; music performance; music teacher education; occupational therapy; philosophy; physical education teaching and coaching; physics; piano and organ; political science and government; pre-dentistry studies; pre-law studies; pre-medical studies; pre-veterinary studies; psychology; public administration; religious studies; religious/sacred music; Scandinavian languages; science teacher education; secondary education; sociology; Spanish; speech and rhetoric; speech therapy; speech-language pathology; Swedish; violin, viola, guitar and other stringed instruments; voice and opera; wind/percussion instruments; women's studies.

Augustana College (SD)

Accounting; art; art teacher education; athletic training; audiology and speech-language pathology; biology/biological sciences; business administration and management; business/corporate communications; chemistry; clinical laboratory science/medical technology; communication/speech communication and rhetoric; computer science; dramatic/theatre arts; economics; education (K-12); elementary education; engineering physics; English; foreign languages and literatures; French; German; health/health care administration; history; international relations and affairs; journalism; kinesiology and exercise science; liberal arts and sciences/liberal studies; management information systems; mathematics; music; music teacher education; nursing (registered nurse training); philosophy; physical education teaching and coaching; physics; political science and government; pre-dentistry studies; pre-law studies; pre-medical studies; pre-veterinary studies; psychology; religious studies; secondary education; social studies teacher education; social work; sociology; Spanish; special education; special education (hearing impaired); speech/theater education; sport and fitness administration.

Austin College

American studies; art; biology/biological sciences; business administration and management; chemistry; classics and classical languages related; classics and languages, literatures and linguistics; communication/speech communication and rhetoric; computer science; economics; English; French; German; history; international economics; international relations and affairs; Latin; Latin American studies; mathematics; multi-/interdisciplinary studies related; music; philosophy; physical education teaching and coaching; physics; political science and government; psychology; religious studies; sociology; Spanish.

Azusa Pacific University

Accounting; applied art; art; athletic training; biblical studies; biochemistry; biology/biological sciences; business administration and management; chemistry; communication/speech communication and rhetoric; computer science; cultural studies; divinity/ministry; English; health science; history; international relations and affairs; liberal arts and sciences/liberal studies; management information systems; marketing/marketing management; mathematics; music; natural sciences; nursing (registered nurse training); philosophy; physical education teaching and coaching; physics; political science and government; pre-engineering; pre-law studies; psychology; religious studies; social sciences; social work; sociology; Spanish; theology; web page, digital/multimedia and information resources design.

Baker University

Accounting; art history, criticism and conservation; art teacher education; biology/biological sciences; business administration and management; chemistry; computer science; dramatic/theatre arts; economics; elementary education; engineering; English; fine/studio arts; French; German; history; information science/studies; international business/trade/commerce; mass communication/media; mathematics; molecular biochemistry; music; music teacher education; nursing (registered nurse training); philosophy; physical education teaching and coaching; physics; political science and government; psychology; religious studies; sociology; Spanish; speech and rhetoric; web/multimedia management and webmaster; wildlife biology.

Baldwin-Wallace College

Art history, criticism and conservation; art teacher education; athletic training; biology/biological sciences; broadcast journalism; business administration and management; business teacher education; chemistry; clinical/medical laboratory technology; communication disorders; communication/speech communication and rhetoric; computer science; computer software and media applications related; computer systems analysis; computer systems networking and telecommunications; criminal justice/law enforcement administration; dance; dramatic/theatre arts and stagecraft related; early childhood education; economics; education; educational leadership and administration; elementary education; engineering; English; exercise physiology; family and consumer economics related; fine/studio arts; French; geology/earth science; German; health and physical education; health professions related; health teacher education; history; human services; information science/studies; international/global studies; liberal arts and sciences and humanities related; mass communication/media; mathematics; middle school education;

multi-/interdisciplinary studies related; music; music history, literature, and theory; music performance; music teacher education; music theory and composition; music therapy; neuroscience; philosophy; physical education teaching and coaching; physics; physics teacher education; piano and organ; political science and government; pre-dentistry studies; pre-law studies; pre-medical studies; pre-veterinary studies; psychology; religious studies; science teacher education; secondary education; sociology; Spanish; special education (specific learning disabilities); sport and fitness administration; visual and performing arts related.

Bard College

Acting; African studies; American government and politics; American history; American studies; ancient/classical Greek; anthropology; archeology; area studies; art; art history, criticism and conservation; Asian history; Asian studies; biochemistry; biological and physical sciences; biology/biological sciences; chemistry; Chinese; cinematography and film/video production; classics and languages, literatures and linguistics; comparative literature; computer science; creative writing; cultural studies; dance; dramatic/theatre arts; drawing; ecology; economics; English; environmental biology; environmental studies; European history; European studies; European studies (Central and Eastern); film/cinema studies; fine/studio arts; French; German; Hebrew; history; history and philosophy of science and technology; history of philosophy; history related; humanities; interdisciplinary studies; international economics; international relations and affairs; Italian; jazz/jazz studies; Jewish/Judaic studies; Latin; Latin American studies; literature; mathematics; medieval and renaissance studies; modern Greek; modern languages; molecular biology; music; music history, literature, and theory; music performance; music theory and composition; natural sciences; painting; philosophy; photography; physical sciences; physics; playwriting and screenwriting; political science and government; pre-dentistry studies; pre-law studies; pre-medical studies; pre-veterinary studies; psychology; religious studies; romance languages; Russian; Russian studies; sculpture; social sciences; sociology; Spanish; theatre literature, history and criticism; visual and performing arts; voice and opera; western civilization.

Barnard College

African studies; American studies; ancient studies; ancient/classical Greek; anthropology; applied mathematics; architectural history and criticism; architecture; area studies related; art history, criticism and conservation; Asian studies; astronomy; astrophysics; biochemistry; biology/biological sciences; biophysics; biopsychology; chemical physics; chemistry; classics and languages, literatures and linguistics; comparative literature; computer and information sciences; dance; dramatic/theatre arts; economics; economics related; English; environmental biology; environmental science; environmental studies; European studies; film/cinema studies; French; French studies; geography; geology/earth science; German; German studies; history; Italian; jazz/jazz studies; Latin; Latin American studies; linguistics; mathematics; mathematics and statistics related;

medieval and renaissance studies; modern Greek; multi-/interdisciplinary studies related; music; Near and Middle Eastern studies; philosophy; physics; political science and government; psychology; religious studies; Russian; Russian studies; Slavic studies; sociology; Spanish; Spanish and Iberian studies; statistics; urban studies/affairs; visual and performing arts; women's studies.

Bates College

African-American/Black studies; American studies; anthropology; art; Asian studies (East); biochemistry; biology/biological sciences; chemistry; Chinese; classical, ancient Mediterranean and Near Eastern studies and archaeology; dramatic/theatre arts; economics; engineering; English; environmental studies; French; geology/earth science; German; history; Japanese; mathematics; multi-/interdisciplinary studies related; music; neuroscience; philosophy; physics; political science and government; psychology; religious studies; Russian; sociology; Spanish; speech and rhetoric; women's studies.

Baylor University

Accounting; acting; airline pilot and flight crew; American studies; ancient Near Eastern and biblical languages; ancient/classical Greek; anthropology; applied mathematics; archeology; architecture; art; art history, criticism and conservation; art teacher education; Asian studies; athletic training; biochemistry; bioinformatics; biology teacher education; biology/biological sciences; business administration and management; business statistics; business teacher education; business, management, and marketing related; business/commerce; business/managerial economics; chemistry; chemistry teacher education; classics and languages, literatures and linguistics; clinical laboratory science/medical technology; communication disorders; communication/speech communication and rhetoric; computer science; computer teacher education; drama and dance teacher education; dramatic/theatre arts; economics; education; education (specific subject areas) related; electrical, electronics and communications engineering; elementary education; engineering; English; English composition; English/language arts teacher education; entrepreneurship; environmental studies; family and consumer sciences/human sciences; fashion merchandising; fashion/apparel design; finance; financial planning and services; fine/studio arts; foreign language teacher education; forensic science and technology; forestry; French; French language teacher education; geological and earth sciences/geosciences related; geology/earth science; geophysics and seismology; German; German language teacher education; health and physical education; health occupations teacher education; health teacher education; health/medical preparatory programs related; history; history teacher education; human development and family studies; human nutrition; human resources management; humanities; insurance; interior design; international business/trade/commerce; international relations and affairs; journalism; kindergarten/preschool education; Latin; Latin American studies; Latin teacher education; linguistics; management information systems; marketing/marketing management; mathematics;

mathematics teacher education; mechanical engineering; multi-/interdisciplinary studies related; museum studies; music; music history, literature, and theory; music pedagogy; music performance; music teacher education; music theory and composition; neuroscience; nursing (registered nurse training); operations management; philosophy; physical education teaching and coaching; physics; physics teacher education; political science and government; pre-dentistry studies; pre-law studies; pre-medical studies; pre-nursing studies; psychology; public administration; radio and television; reading teacher education; real estate; religious studies; religious/sacred music; Russian; sales, distribution and marketing; science teacher education; secondary education; Slavic studies; social science teacher education; social studies teacher education; social work; sociology; Spanish; Spanish language teacher education; special education; special education (speech or language impaired); speech teacher education; sport and fitness administration; theatre design and technology; urban studies/affairs.

Bellarmine University

Accounting; actuarial science; art; arts management; biology/biological sciences; business administration and management; business/managerial economics; cardiopulmonary technology; chemistry; clinical laboratory science/medical technology; clinical/medical laboratory science and allied professions related; communication/speech communication and rhetoric; community organization and advocacy; computer and information sciences; computer engineering; computer science; criminal justice/safety; cytotechnology; economics; education; elementary education; English; French; German; health services/allied health/health sciences; history; human resources management; international business/trade/commerce; international relations and affairs; liberal arts and sciences/liberal studies; mathematics; middle school education; music; music management and merchandising; musical instrument fabrication and repair; nursing (registered nurse training); painting; pastoral studies/counseling; philosophy; political science and government; pre-dentistry studies; pre-law studies; pre-medical studies; pre-pharmacy studies; pre-veterinary studies; psychology; respiratory care therapy; sculpture; secondary education; sociology; Spanish; special education; theology; voice and opera.

Belmont University

Accounting; administrative assistant and secretarial science; advertising; ancient Near Eastern and biblical languages; applied mathematics; art; art teacher education; behavioral sciences; biblical studies; bilingual and multilingual education; biochemistry; biological and physical sciences; biology/biological sciences; broadcast journalism; business administration and management; business teacher education; business/managerial economics; chemistry; clinical laboratory science/medical technology; computer management; computer programming; computer science; consumer merchandising/retailing management; counselor education/school counseling and guidance; developmental and child psychology; divinity/ministry; dramatic/theatre arts; economics; education; education

(K-12); elementary education; engineering science; English; finance; fine/studio arts; health and physical education; health teacher education; health/health care administration; history; hospitality administration; hotel/motel administration; information science/studies; international business/trade/commerce; journalism; kindergarten/preschool education; marketing/marketing management; mass communication/media; mathematics; modern Greek; music; music history, literature, and theory; music management and merchandising; music teacher education; nursing (registered nurse training); parks, recreation and leisure; pastoral studies/counseling; pharmacology; philosophy; physical education teaching and coaching; physics; piano and organ; political science and government; psychology; radio and television; reading teacher education; religious/sacred music; social work; sociology; Spanish; special education; speech and rhetoric; voice and opera; western civilization.

Beloit College

Anthropology; art history, criticism and conservation; art teacher education; Asian studies; biochemistry; biology/biological sciences; business administration and management; business/managerial economics; cell biology and histology; chemistry; classics and languages, literatures and linguistics; comparative literature; computer science; creative writing; dramatic/theatre arts; economics; education; elementary education; engineering; English; environmental biology; environmental studies; European studies; fine/studio arts; French; geology/earth science; German; history; interdisciplinary studies; international relations and affairs; Latin American studies; literature; mass communication/media; mathematics; modern languages; molecular biology; museum studies; music; music teacher education; philosophy; physics; political science and government; pre-dentistry studies; pre-law studies; pre-medical studies; psychology; religious studies; romance languages; Russian; Russian studies; science teacher education; secondary education; sociobiology; sociology; Spanish; women's studies.

Benedictine University

Accounting; arts management; biochemistry; biology/biological sciences; business administration and management; business, management, and marketing related; business/commerce; business/managerial economics; chemistry; clinical laboratory science/medical technology; communication/speech communication and rhetoric; computer science; economics; education; elementary education; engineering science; English; environmental studies; finance; fine/studio arts; health science; health/health care administration; history; information science/studies; international business/trade/commerce; international relations and affairs; marketing/marketing management; mathematics; molecular biology; music; music teacher education; nuclear medical technology; nursing science; nutrition sciences; organizational behavior; philosophy; physics; political science and government; pre-dentistry studies; pre-law studies; pre-medical studies; pre-veterinary studies; psychology; publishing; science teacher education; secondary education; social sciences; sociology; Spanish; special education.

Bennington College

Anthropology; architecture; art; biochemistry; biological and physical sciences; biology/biological sciences; ceramic arts and ceramics; chemistry; Chinese; comparative literature; computer science; creative writing; dance; design and applied arts related; developmental and child psychology; dramatic/theatre arts; drawing; ecology; English; environmental biology; environmental studies; European studies; film/cinema studies; fine/studio arts; French; German; history; history of philosophy; humanities; interdisciplinary studies; international relations and affairs; Italian studies; Japanese; jazz/jazz studies; kindergarten/preschool education; liberal arts and sciences/liberal studies; literature; mathematics; modern languages; music; music history, literature, and theory; natural sciences; philosophy; photography; physics; pre-medical studies; pre-veterinary studies; printmaking; psychology; sculpture; social sciences; sociology; Spanish; violin, viola, guitar and other stringed instruments; visual and performing arts; voice and opera.

Bentley College

Accounting; business administration and management; business/commerce; business/corporate communications; business/managerial economics; computer and information sciences; economics; English; finance; history; interdisciplinary studies; international economics; liberal arts and sciences/liberal studies; marketing/marketing management; mathematics; philosophy; public policy analysis.

Berea College

Agricultural business and management; agriculture; art; art history, criticism and conservation; art teacher education; biology teacher education; biology/biological sciences; business administration and management; chemistry; child development; classics and languages, literatures and linguistics; developmental and child psychology; dietetics; dramatic/theatre arts; economics; education; elementary education; English; English/language arts teacher education; family and consumer economics related; family and consumer sciences/home economics teacher education; fine/studio arts; foreign language teacher education; French; French language teacher education; German; German language teacher education; history; industrial arts; industrial technology; kindergarten/preschool education; mass communication/media; mathematics; mathematics teacher education; middle school education; music; music teacher education; nursing (registered nurse training); philosophy; physical education teaching and coaching; physics; political science and government; pre-dentistry studies; pre-medical studies; pre-veterinary studies; psychology; religious studies; secondary education; sociology; Spanish; Spanish language teacher education; women's studies.

Berry College

Accounting; animal sciences; anthropology; art; biochemistry; biology/biological sciences; business administration and management; chemistry; communication and journalism related; computer science; early childhood education; economics; engineering technology; English; environmental science; finance; French; German; history; international relations and affairs; marketing/marketing management; mathematics; middle school education; multi-/interdisciplinary studies related; music; music management and merchandising; music teacher education; nursing (registered nurse training); philosophy and religious studies related; physical education teaching and coaching; physics; political science and government; psychology; social sciences; sociology; Spanish.

Bethel University

Area, ethnic, cultural, and gender studies related; art; art teacher education; athletic training; biblical studies; biology teacher education; biology/biological sciences; business administration and management; chemistry; chemistry teacher education; communication/speech communication and rhetoric; community health services counseling; computer and information sciences; dramatic/theatre arts; early childhood education; economics; elementary education; engineering science; English; English as a second/foreign language (teaching); English composition; English/language arts teacher education; environmental science; French; French language teacher education; health and physical education; health teacher education; history; international relations and affairs; kinesiology and exercise science; liberal arts and sciences/liberal studies; library science related; mass communication/media; mathematics; mathematics teacher education; molecular biology; multi-/interdisciplinary studies related; music; music performance; music teacher education; nursing (registered nurse training); philosophy; physical education teaching and coaching; physics; physics teacher education; political science and government; psychology; religious/sacred music; science teacher education; social sciences; social studies teacher education; social work; Spanish; Spanish language teacher education; youth ministry.

Biola University

Adult and continuing education; anthropology; art; biblical studies; bilingual and multilingual education; biochemistry; biology/biological sciences; business administration and management; clinical psychology; commercial and advertising art; communication disorders; computer and information sciences; divinity/ministry; drawing; education; education (K–12); elementary education; English; fine/studio arts; history; humanities; kinesiology and exercise science; mathematics; missionary studies and missiology; music; nursing (registered nurse training); pastoral studies/counseling; philosophy; physical education teaching and coaching; physical sciences; pre-law studies; psychology; radio and television; religious education; religious studies; secondary education; social sciences; sociology; Spanish; theology.

Birmingham-Southern College

Accounting; art; art history, criticism and conservation; art teacher education; Asian studies; biology/biological sciences; business administration and management; chemistry; computer science; dance; dramatic/theatre arts; drawing; economics; education; elementary

education; English; fine/studio arts; French; German; history; human resources management; interdisciplinary studies; international business/trade/commerce; kindergarten/preschool education; mathematics; music; music history, literature, and theory; music teacher education; painting; philosophy; physics; piano and organ; political science and government; pre-dentistry studies; pre-law studies; pre-medical studies; printmaking; psychology; religious studies; sculpture; secondary education; sociology; Spanish; voice and opera.

Boston College

Accounting; art history, criticism and conservation; biochemistry; biology/biological sciences; business administration and management; chemistry; classics and languages, literatures and linguistics; computer science; dramatic/theatre arts; economics; elementary education; English; environmental studies; finance; fine/studio arts; French; geology/earth science; geophysics and seismology; German; Hispanic-American, Puerto Rican, and Mexican-American/Chicano studies; history; human development and family studies; human resources management; interdisciplinary studies; Italian; kindergarten/preschool education; management information systems; marketing/marketing management; mass communication/media; mathematics; music; nursing (registered nurse training); operations research; philosophy; physics; political science and government; pre-medical studies; psychology; Russian; Russian studies; secondary education; Slavic languages; sociology; special education; theology.

Boston University

Accounting; acting; aerospace, aeronautical and astronautical engineering; American studies; ancient/classical Greek; animal physiology; anthropology; archeology; area studies related; art history, criticism and conservation; art teacher education; Asian studies (East); astronomy; astrophysics; athletic training; bilingual and multilingual education; biochemistry; biological and biomedical sciences related; biology/biological sciences; biomedical/medical engineering; business administration and management; chemistry; chemistry teacher education; cinematography and film/video production; classics and languages, literatures and linguistics; clinical laboratory science/medical technology; commercial and advertising art; communication disorders; communication/speech communication and rhetoric; computer engineering; computer science; dental laboratory technology; drama and dance teacher education; drawing; ecology; economics; education; education (specific levels and methods) related; electrical, electronics and communications engineering; elementary education; engineering; engineering related; English; English/language arts teacher education; environmental studies; ethnic, cultural minority, and gender studies related; finance; foreign language teacher education; foreign languages and literatures; French; geography; geology/earth science; German; health science; history; hospitality administration; hotel/motel administration; industrial engineering; information science/studies; interdisciplinary studies; international business/trade/commerce; international finance; international relations and affairs; Italian; journalism; journalism related;

kindergarten/preschool education; kinesiology and exercise science; Latin; Latin American studies; legal assistant/paralegal; linguistics; management information systems; marine biology and biological oceanography; marketing research; marketing/marketing management; mass communication/media; mathematics; mathematics and computer science; mathematics teacher education; mechanical engineering; modern Greek; molecular biology; music history, literature, and theory; music performance; music teacher education; music theory and composition; neuroscience; nutrition sciences; occupational therapy; operations management; organizational behavior; painting; parks, recreation and leisure; philosophy; physical education teaching and coaching; physical therapy; physics; piano and organ; political science and government; pre-dentistry studies; psychology; public relations/image management; radio and television; rehabilitation therapy; religious studies; Russian; Russian studies; science teacher education; sculpture; social sciences related; social studies teacher education; sociology; Spanish; special education; special education (hearing impaired); speech; theater education; theatre design and technology; theatre literature, history and criticism; urban studies/affairs; voice and opera.

Bowdoin College

African studies; African-American/Black studies; anthropology; archeology; art; art history, criticism and conservation; Asian studies; biochemistry; biology/biological sciences; chemical physics; chemistry; classics and languages, literatures and linguistics; computer science; dramatic/theatre arts and stagecraft related; economics; English; environmental studies; European studies (Central and Eastern); fine/studio arts; French; geochemistry; geology/earth science; geophysics and seismology; German; history; interdisciplinary studies; Latin American studies; mathematics; mathematics and computer science; mathematics related; music; neuroscience; philosophy; physics; political science and government; pre-medical studies; psychology; religious studies; romance languages; Russian; sociology; Spanish; women's studies.

Bradley University

Accounting; actuarial science; advertising; art; art history, criticism and conservation; biochemistry; biology/biological sciences; broadcast journalism; business administration and management; business/managerial economics; chemistry; civil engineering; civil engineering related; clinical laboratory science/medical technology; communication and journalism related; communication/speech communication and rhetoric; computer and information sciences; construction engineering; criminal justice/law enforcement administration; dramatic/theatre arts; ecology; economics; education (specific subject areas) related; electrical, electronic and communications engineering technology; electrical, electronics and communications engineering; elementary education; engineering physics; English; environmental/environmental health engineering; family resource management; finance; fine/studio arts; French; geology/earth science; German; health professions related; health science; history; industrial engineering; industrial technology;

information science/studies; insurance; international business/trade/commerce; international relations and affairs; journalism; kindergarten/preschool education; liberal arts and sciences/liberal studies; management information systems; marketing/marketing management; mathematics; mathematics and statistics related; mechanical engineering; molecular biology; music; music performance; music teacher education; music theory and composition; nursing (registered nurse training); philosophy; physical therapy; physics; political science and government; psychology; public relations/image management; radio and television; religious studies; social work; sociology; Spanish; special education (emotionally disturbed); special education (mentally retarded); special education (specific learning disabilities); speech and rhetoric.

Brandeis University

African studies; African-American/Black studies; American studies; ancient/classical Greek; anthropology; area, ethnic, cultural, and gender studies related; art; biochemistry; biological and biomedical sciences related; biology/biological sciences; biophysics; cell biology and anatomical sciences related; chemistry; classics and classical languages related; comparative literature; computer science; dramatic/theatre arts; economics; engineering physics; English; European studies; fine/studio arts; French; German; history; Islamic studies; Jewish/Judaic studies; Latin; Latin American studies; linguistics; mathematics; multi-/interdisciplinary studies related; music; Near and Middle Eastern studies; neuroscience; philosophy; physics; political science and government; psychology; Russian; Russian studies; sociology; Spanish.

Brigham Young University

Accounting; accounting related; acting; advertising; agribusiness; agricultural business and management; agricultural economics; American studies; ancient/classical Greek; animation, interactive technology, video graphics and special effects; anthropology; applied economics; art; art history, criticism and conservation; art teacher education; Asian studies; astronomy; athletic training; ballet; biochemistry; bioinformatics; biological and physical sciences; biology/biological sciences; biomedical sciences; biophysics; biostatistics; biotechnology; botany/plant biology; broadcast journalism; business administration and management; business family and consumer sciences/human sciences; business statistics; cartography; ceramic arts and ceramics; chemical engineering; chemistry; chemistry teacher education; child care and support services management; child care provision; child development; Chinese; cinematography and film/video production; civil engineering; classics and languages, literatures and linguistics; clinical laboratory science/medical technology; communication and journalism related; comparative literature; computer engineering; computer science; conservation biology; crafts, folk art and artisanry; dance; dance related; design and visual communications; dietetics; directing and theatrical production; drama and dance teacher education; dramatic/theatre arts; dramatic/theatre arts and stagecraft related; drawing; early childhood education; ecology, evolution, systematics and population biology

related; economics; education (specific levels and methods) related; education (specific subject areas) related; education related; electrical, electronics and communications engineering; elementary education; engineering technology; English; English as a second/foreign language (teaching); English composition; English/language arts teacher education; entrepreneurship; environmental science; European studies (Central and Eastern); family and consumer economics related; family and consumer sciences/human sciences; family and consumer sciences/human sciences business services related; family resource management; family systems; film/cinema studies; film/video and photographic arts related; financial planning and services; fine/studio arts; food science; food technology and processing; foreign language teacher education; French; French language teacher education; geography; geography related; geological and earth sciences/geosciences related; geology/earth science; German; German language teacher education; graphic design; health and physical education; health and physical education related; Hebrew; history; history teacher education; home furnishings and equipment installation; human development and family studies; human resources development; human resources management; humanities; illustration; industrial design; information technology; interior design; international finance; international marketing; international relations and affairs; Italian; Japanese; jazz/jazz studies; journalism; kinesiology and exercise science; Korean; language interpretation and translation; Latin; Latin American studies; Latin teacher education; liberal arts and sciences and humanities related; liberal arts and sciences/liberal studies; linguistic and comparative language studies related; linguistics; logistics and materials management; management information systems; manufacturing engineering; marketing/marketing management; mass communication/media; mathematics; mathematics teacher education; mechanical engineering; merchandising, sales, and marketing operations related (general); microbiology; molecular biology; music; music history, literature, and theory; music pedagogy; music performance; music teacher education; music theory and composition; neuroscience; Norwegian; nursing (registered nurse training); nutrition sciences; organizational communication; painting; parks, recreation and leisure; parks, recreation, and leisure related; philosophy; photography; physical education teaching and coaching; physics; physics related; physics teacher education; physiology; piano and organ; plant genetics; playwriting and screenwriting; political science and government; Portuguese; pre-nursing studies; printmaking; psychology; psychology teacher education; public policy analysis; public relations, advertising, and applied communication related; radio, television, and digital communication related; range science and management; retailing; Russian; science teacher education; sculpture; social psychology; social science teacher education; social work; sociology; soil sciences related; Spanish; Spanish language teacher education; special education; speech and rhetoric; speech teacher education; statistics; statistics related; Swedish; technology/industrial arts teacher education; theatre design and technology; therapeutic recreation;

veterinary/animal health technology; violin, viola, guitar and other stringed instruments; visual and performing arts related; voice and opera; wildlife and wildlands science and management; work and family studies; zoology/animal biology.

Brown University

African-American/Black studies; American studies; anthropology; applied mathematics; archeology; architectural history and criticism; art; art history, criticism and conservation; Asian studies (East); Asian studies (South); behavioral sciences; biochemistry; biology/biological sciences; biomedical sciences; biomedical/medical engineering; biophysics; chemical engineering; chemistry; civil engineering; classics and languages, literatures and linguistics; cognitive psychology and psycholinguistics; comparative literature; computer engineering; computer science; creative writing; development economics and international development; dramatic/theatre arts; economics; education; electrical, electronics and communications engineering; engineering; engineering physics; English; environmental science; environmental studies; film/cinema studies; fine/studio arts; French; French studies; geochemistry; geology/earth science; geophysics and seismology; German; German studies; Hispanic-American, Puerto Rican, and Mexican-American/Chicano studies; history; international relations and affairs; Italian; Italian studies; Jewish/Judaic studies; Latin American studies; linguistics; literature; marine biology and biological oceanography; materials engineering; mathematics; mathematics and computer science; mechanical engineering; medieval and renaissance studies; molecular biology; music; music related; musicology and ethnomusicology; Near and Middle Eastern studies; neuroscience; organizational behavior; philosophy; physics; political science and government; psychology; religious studies; Russian studies; sociology; Spanish; urban studies/affairs; visual and performing arts; women's studies.

Bryan College

Biblical studies; biology/biological sciences; business administration and management; computer science; education; elementary education; English; history; kindergarten/preschool education; liberal arts and sciences/liberal studies; literature; mass communication/media; mathematics; middle school education; music; music management and merchandising; music teacher education; physical education teaching and coaching; piano and organ; pre-medical studies; psychology; religious education; religious/sacred music; science teacher education; secondary education; voice and opera; wind/percussion instruments.

Bryn Mawr College

Ancient/classical Greek; anthropology; archeology; art; art history, criticism and conservation; Asian studies (East); astronomy; biology/biological sciences; chemistry; classics and languages, literatures and linguistics; comparative literature; economics; English; French; geology/earth science; German; history; Italian; Latin; mathematics; music; philosophy; physics; political science and government; psychology; religious studies; romance languages; Russian; sociology; Spanish; urban studies/affairs.

Bucknell University

Accounting; anthropology; area studies; art; art history, criticism and conservation; Asian studies (East); biology/biological sciences; biomedical/ medical engineering; biopsychology; business administration and management; chemical engineering; chemistry; civil engineering; classics and languages, literatures and linguistics; computer and information sciences; computer engineering; dramatic/theatre arts; economics; education; educational statistics and research methods; electrical, electronics and communications engineering; elementary education; English; environmental studies; fine/studio arts; French; geography; geological and earth sciences/geosciences related; geology/earth science; German; history; humanities; interdisciplinary studies; international relations and affairs; kindergarten/preschool education; Latin American studies; mathematics; mechanical engineering; multi-/interdisciplinary studies related; music; music history, literature, and theory; music performance; music teacher education; music theory and composition; philosophy; physics; political science and government; psychology; religious studies; Russian; secondary education; sociology; Spanish; women's studies.

Butler University

Accounting; actuarial science; anthropology; arts management; audiology and speech-language pathology; biology/biological sciences; business administration and management; business/managerial economics; chemistry; computer science; criminal justice/safety; dance; dramatic/theatre arts; economics; elementary education; English; finance; French; German; history; information science/studies; international business/trade/commerce; international relations and affairs; journalism; Latin; liberal arts and sciences/liberal studies; marketing/ marketing management; mathematics; medicinal and pharmaceutical chemistry; modern Greek; music; music history, literature, and theory; music management and merchandising; music teacher education; pharmacy; philosophy; physician assistant; physics; piano and organ; political science and government; psychology; public relations/image management; religious studies; science, technology and society; secondary education; sociology; Spanish; speech and rhetoric; telecommunications; violin, viola, guitar and other stringed instruments; voice and opera; wind/percussion instruments.

California Institute of Technology

Aerospace, aeronautical and astronautical engineering; applied mathematics; astronomy; biochemistry; biology/biological sciences; business/managerial economics; chemical engineering; chemical physics; chemistry; civil engineering; computer engineering; computer science; economics; electrical, electronics and communications engineering; engineering; engineering physics; environmental/environmental health engineering; general studies; geochemistry; geology/earth science; geophysics and seismology; history; inorganic chemistry; literature; mathematics; mechanical engineering; organic chemistry; physical sciences; physics; planetary astronomy and science; science, technology and society; social sciences.

California Polytechnic State University, San Luis Obispo

Aerospace, aeronautical and astronautical engineering; agricultural business and management; agricultural/biological engineering and bioengineering; agriculture; agronomy and crop science; animal sciences; applied art; architectural engineering; architecture; art; biochemistry; biology/biological sciences; business administration and management; chemistry; city/urban, community and regional planning; civil engineering; commercial and advertising art; computer engineering; computer science; dairy science; developmental and child psychology; economics; electrical, electronics and communications engineering; engineering science; English; environmental biology; environmental/environmental health engineering; farm and ranch management; food science; foods, nutrition, and wellness; forestry; graphic and printing equipment operation/ production; history; horticultural science; human resources management; industrial engineering; industrial technology; journalism; kindergarten/preschool education; landscape architecture; liberal arts and sciences/liberal studies; management information systems; materials engineering; mathematics; mechanical engineering; mechanical engineering/mechanical technology; medical microbiology and bacteriology; music; ornamental horticulture; parks, recreation and leisure; philosophy; physical education teaching and coaching; physical sciences; physics; political science and government; pre-medical studies; psychology; social sciences; speech and rhetoric; statistics; trade and industrial teacher education.

Calvin College

Accounting; American history; art; art history, criticism and conservation; art teacher education; athletic training; audiology and speech-language pathology; biblical studies; bilingual and multilingual education; biochemistry; biological and physical sciences; biology/ biological sciences; biotechnology; business administration and management; business/ corporate communications; chemical engineering; chemistry; civil engineering; classics and languages, literatures and linguistics; communication/speech communication and rhetoric; computer science; conducting; digital communication and media/multimedia; dramatic/theatre arts; economics; electrical, electronics and communications engineering; elementary education; engineering; English; English as a second/foreign language (teaching); environmental studies; European history; film/ cinema studies; fine/studio arts; French; geography; geology/earth science; German; Germanic languages related; history; interdisciplinary studies; international relations and affairs; kinesiology and exercise science; Latin; management information systems; mass communication/media; mathematics; mechanical engineering; modern Greek; music; music history, literature, and theory; music performance; music teacher education; music theory and composition; natural sciences; nursing (registered nurse training); occupational therapy; parks, recreation and leisure; philosophy; physical education teaching and coaching; physical sciences; physics; piano and organ; political science and government; pre-

dentistry studies; pre-law studies; pre-medical studies; pre-veterinary studies; psychology; public administration; religious studies; religious/sacred music; science teacher education; secondary education; social sciences; social work; sociology; Spanish; special education; speech and rhetoric; theology; voice and opera.

Canisius College

Accounting; accounting technology and bookkeeping; anthropology; art history, criticism and conservation; athletic training; biochemistry; bioinformatics; biological and physical sciences; business administration and management; business administration, management and operations related; chemistry; communication and media related; computer science; criminal justice/law enforcement administration; digital communication and media/multimedia; early childhood education; economics; engineering related; English; entrepreneurship; environmental science; European studies; finance; forest sciences and biology; French; general studies; Germanic languages; history; information technology; international business/trade/commerce; international relations and affairs; marketing related; mathematics and statistics related; philosophy; physical education teaching and coaching; physics; political science and government; psychology; religious studies; science teacher education; secondary education; sociology; Spanish; special education (early childhood); urban studies/affairs.

Carleton College

African studies; American studies; ancient/classical Greek; anthropology; art history, criticism and conservation; Asian studies; biology/ biological sciences; chemistry; classics and languages, literatures and linguistics; computer science; economics; English; fine/studio arts; French; French studies; geology/earth science; German; history; interdisciplinary studies; international relations and affairs; Latin; Latin American studies; mathematics; music; philosophy; physics; political science and government; psychology; religious studies; romance languages; Russian; Russian studies; sociology; Spanish; women's studies.

Carnegie Mellon University

Applied mathematics; architecture; art; biochemistry; biology/biological sciences; biomedical/medical engineering; biophysics; business administration and management; business/managerial economics; ceramic arts and ceramics; chemical engineering; chemistry; civil engineering; cognitive psychology and psycholinguistics; commercial and advertising art; computer and information sciences; computer engineering; computer science; creative writing; dramatic/theatre arts; economics; electrical, electronics and communications engineering; engineering; engineering related; English; environmental/environmental health engineering; European studies; fine/studio arts; French; German; history; humanities; industrial design; information science/studies; interdisciplinary studies; Japanese; liberal arts and sciences/liberal studies; literature; mass communication/media; materials engineering; materials science; mathematics; mechanical engineering; modern languages; music; music performance; music theory and composition; philosophy; physics;

political science and government; polymer chemistry; psychology; Russian; sculpture; social sciences; Spanish; statistics; technical and business writing; western civilization.

Carroll College (MT)

Accounting; acting; art; biology teacher education; biology/biological sciences; business administration and management; business/managerial economics; chemistry; civil engineering; clinical laboratory science/medical technology; communication/speech communication and rhetoric; computer science; dramatic/theatre arts; education; elementary education; engineering; English; English as a second/foreign language (teaching); English/language arts teacher education; environmental studies; finance; French; general studies; health information/medical records administration; history; history teacher education; international relations and affairs; Latin; mathematics; mathematics teacher education; nursing (registered nurse training); philosophy; physical education teaching and coaching; political science and government; pre-dentistry studies; pre-law studies; pre-medical studies; pre-pharmacy studies; pre-veterinary studies; psychology; public administration; public relations/image management; religious education; religious studies; secondary education; social science teacher education; social sciences; social work; sociology; Spanish; Spanish language teacher education; sport and fitness administration; technical and business writing; theatre design and technology; theology; visual and performing arts.

Case Western Reserve University

Accounting; aerospace, aeronautical and astronautical engineering; American studies; anthropology; applied mathematics; art history, criticism and conservation; art teacher education; Asian studies; astronomy; biochemistry; biology/biological sciences; biomedical/medical engineering; business administration and management; chemical engineering; chemistry; civil engineering; classics and languages, literatures and linguistics; communication disorders; comparative literature; computer engineering; computer science; dietetics; dramatic/theatre arts; economics; electrical, electronics and communications engineering; engineering; engineering physics; engineering science; English; environmental studies; evolutionary biology; French; French studies; geology/earth science; German; German studies; gerontology; history; history and philosophy of science and technology; human nutrition; international relations and affairs; international/global studies; Japanese studies; materials engineering; materials science; mathematics; mechanical engineering; music; music teacher education; natural sciences; nursing (registered nurse training); nutrition sciences; philosophy; physics; political science and government; polymer/plastics engineering; psychology; religious studies; sociology; Spanish; statistics; systems engineering; women's studies.

Cedarville University

Accounting; American studies; athletic training; biblical studies; biological and physical sciences; biology teacher education; biology/biological sciences; broadcast journalism; business

administration and management; chemistry; clinical laboratory science/medical technology; communication/speech communication and rhetoric; computer engineering; computer science; criminal justice/law enforcement administration; dramatic/theatre arts; early childhood education; early childhood education; electrical, electronics and communications engineering; English; English/language arts teacher education; environmental biology; finance; graphic design; health and physical education; health teacher education; history; information science/studies; international business/trade/commerce; international relations and affairs; kinesiology and exercise science; marketing/marketing management; mathematics; mathematics teacher education; mechanical engineering; missionary studies and missiology; music; music pedagogy; music performance; music teacher education; music theory and composition; nursing (registered nurse training); pastoral studies/counseling; philosophy; physical education teaching and coaching; physics teacher education; piano and organ; political science and government; pre-dentistry studies; pre-law studies; pre-medical studies; pre-veterinary studies; psychology; public administration; religious education; religious/sacred music; science teacher education; secondary education; social studies teacher education; social work; sociology; Spanish; Spanish language teacher education; special education; speech and rhetoric; sport and fitness administration; technical and business writing; theology; voice and opera; youth ministry.

Centenary College of Louisiana

Accounting; art; art teacher education; audiology and speech-language pathology; biochemistry; biology teacher education; biology/biological sciences; biophysics; business administration and management; business teacher education; business/managerial economics; chemistry; chemistry teacher education; communication and journalism related; communication and media related; dance; drama and dance teacher education; dramatic/theatre arts; economics; education (K-12); education related; elementary education; English; English/language arts teacher education; environmental studies; film/cinema studies; fine/studio arts; foreign languages and literatures; French; French language teacher education; geology/earth science; German; German language teacher education; health science; health teacher education; history; interdisciplinary studies; kinesiology and exercise science; Latin; Latin teacher education; liberal arts and sciences/liberal studies; mathematics; mathematics teacher education; museum studies; music; music performance; music teacher education; music theory and composition; neuroscience; occupational therapy; philosophy; physical education teaching and coaching; physical therapy; physics; physics teacher education; piano and organ; political science and government; pre-dentistry studies; pre-law studies; pre-medical studies; pre-veterinary studies; psychology; religious studies; religious/sacred music; science teacher education; secondary education; social studies teacher education; sociology; Spanish; Spanish language teacher education; visual and performing arts; voice and opera.

Central College

Accounting; art; biology/biological sciences; business administration and management; chemistry; communication/speech communication and rhetoric; computer science; dramatic/theatre arts; economics; elementary education; English; environmental studies; European studies (Western); French; general studies; German; history; information science/studies; interdisciplinary studies; international business/trade/commerce; kinesiology and exercise science; Latin American studies; linguistics; mathematics; mathematics and computer science; music; music teacher education; philosophy; physics; political science and government; psychology; religious studies; secondary education; social sciences; sociology; Spanish.

Centre College

Anthropology; art; art history, criticism and conservation; biochemistry; biology/biological sciences; chemistry; classics and languages, literatures and linguistics; computer science; dramatic/theatre arts; economics; elementary education; English; French; German; history; international relations and affairs; mathematics; molecular biology; music; philosophy; physics; physiological psychology/psychobiology; political science and government; psychology; religious studies; secondary education; sociology; Spanish.

Chapman University

Accounting; advertising; American government and politics; American history; art; art history, criticism and conservation; athletic training; biology/biological sciences; biopsychology; broadcast journalism; business administration and management; business/managerial economics; chemistry; chemistry teacher education; cinematography and film/video production; communication/speech communication and rhetoric; computer and information sciences; computer science; creative writing; dance; dance related; dramatic/theatre arts; English; English/language arts teacher education; environmental science; European history; exercise physiology; film/cinema studies; fine/studio arts; French; graphic design; health and physical education; health science; history; international business/trade/commerce; legal studies; legal studies; liberal arts and sciences/liberal studies; literature; mathematics; molecular biology; music; music performance; music teacher education; music theory and composition; music therapy; nutrition sciences; organizational behavior; peace studies and conflict resolution; philosophy; political science and government; psychology; religious studies; social work; sociology; Spanish; theatre design and technology; voice and opera; wind/percussion instruments.

Christendom College

Classics and languages, literatures and linguistics; French; history; liberal arts and sciences/liberal studies; literature; philosophy; political science and government; theology.

Christian Brothers University

Accounting; biology teacher education; biology/biological sciences; business administration and management; business/commerce; business/

managerial economics; chemical engineering; chemistry; chemistry teacher education; civil engineering; computer engineering; computer science; economics; education; educational psychology; electrical, electronics and communications engineering; elementary education; engineering physics; English; English/language arts teacher education; environmental/environmental health engineering; finance; history; history teacher education; management information systems; marketing/marketing management; mathematics; mathematics teacher education; mechanical engineering; natural sciences; physics; physics teacher education; pre-dentistry studies; pre-law studies; pre-medical studies; pre-pharmacy studies; pre-theology/pre-ministerial studies; psychology; religious studies; technical and business writing.

Claremont McKenna College

Accounting; African-American/Black studies; American government and politics; American studies; anthropology; Arabic; archeology; area studies related; area, ethnic, cultural, and gender studies related; art; art history, criticism and conservation; Asian studies; Asian-American studies; biochemistry; biology/biological sciences; biophysics; chemistry; Chinese; Chinese studies; classics and languages, literatures and linguistics; computer and information sciences; computer science; dance; dramatic/theatre arts; East Asian languages related; economics; economics related; engineering; engineering related; engineering science; engineering/industrial management; English; environmental studies; ethnic, cultural minority, and gender studies related; European studies; European studies (Western); film/cinema studies; fine/studio arts; French; French studies; German; German studies; Germanic languages; Hispanic-American, Puerto Rican, and Mexican-American/Chicano studies; history; international business/trade/commerce; international economics; international relations and affairs; Italian; Japanese; Japanese studies; Korean studies; Latin; Latin American studies; legal studies; literature; mathematics; modern Greek; modern languages; music; music related; Near and Middle Eastern studies; Pacific area/Pacific rim studies; philosophy; philosophy and religious studies related; philosophy related; physics; physiological psychology/psychobiology; political science and government; political science and government related; pre-dentistry studies; pre-law studies; pre-medical studies; psychology; religious studies; religious studies related; Russian; Russian studies; sociology; South Asian languages; Spanish; visual and performing arts; visual and performing arts related; women's studies.

Clarkson University

Accounting; aerospace, aeronautical and astronautical engineering; applied mathematics; biochemistry; biology/biological sciences; biophysics; biotechnology; business administration and management; cell biology and histology; chemical engineering; chemistry; civil engineering; communication/speech communication and rhetoric; computer and information sciences; computer engineering; computer science; computer software engineering; construction engineering; digital communication and media/multimedia; ecology; electrical, electronics and communications engineering; engineering;

environmental health; environmental studies; environmental/environmental health engineering; finance; history; human resources management; humanities; industrial and organizational psychology; information resources management; interdisciplinary studies; international business/trade/commerce; liberal arts and sciences/liberal studies; logistics and materials management; management information systems; manufacturing engineering; marketing/marketing management; materials engineering; materials science; mathematics; mechanical engineering; molecular biology; non-profit management; occupational health and industrial hygiene; operations management; physics; political science and government; pre-dentistry studies; pre-law studies; pre-medical studies; pre-veterinary studies; psychology; social sciences; sociology; statistics; structural engineering; technical and business writing; toxicology.

Clark University

Art; art history, criticism and conservation; Asian studies; biochemistry; biology/biological sciences; business administration and management; chemistry; classics and languages, literatures and linguistics; commercial and advertising art; comparative literature; computer science; cultural studies; development economics and international development; dramatic/theatre arts; ecology; economics; education; elementary education; engineering; English; environmental studies; film/cinema studies; fine/studio arts; French; geography; geology/earth science; history; interdisciplinary studies; international relations and affairs; Jewish/Judaic studies; literature; mass communication/media; mathematics; middle school education; modern languages; molecular biology; music; natural resources management and policy; neuroscience; peace studies and conflict resolution; philosophy; physics; political science and government; pre-dentistry studies; pre-law studies; pre-medical studies; pre-veterinary studies; psychology; secondary education; sociology; Spanish.

Clemson University

Accounting; agricultural business and management; agricultural economics; agricultural teacher education; agricultural/biological engineering and bioengineering; animal genetics; animal sciences; aquaculture; architecture; art; biochemistry; biology/biological sciences; biomedical/medical engineering; business administration and management; business, management, and marketing related; ceramic sciences and engineering; chemical engineering; chemistry; chemistry related; civil engineering; clinical laboratory science/medical technology; communication and journalism related; computer and information sciences; computer engineering; computer programming; counselor education/school counseling and guidance; economics; electrical, electronics and communications engineering; elementary education; engineering mechanics; English; entomology; environmental/environmental health engineering; finance; food science; foreign languages and literatures; foreign languages related; forest/forest resources management; geology/earth science; health professions related; history; horticultural science; industrial design; industrial engineering; information science/studies; kindergarten/preschool education;

landscape architecture; marketing/marketing management; materials engineering; mathematics; mathematics teacher education; mechanical engineering; microbiology; middle school education; nursing (registered nurse training); operations management; parks, recreation and leisure facilities management; philosophy; physics; plant pathology/phytopathology; political science and government; polymer chemistry; pre-medical studies; pre-pharmacy studies; pre-veterinary studies; psychology; reading teacher education; science teacher education; science technologies related; secondary education; sociology; special education; speech and rhetoric; technology/industrial arts teacher education; trade and industrial teacher education; visual and performing arts related.

Cleveland Institute of Music

Audio engineering; music; music teacher education; piano and organ; violin, viola, guitar and other stringed instruments; voice and opera; wind/percussion instruments.

Coe College

Accounting; acting; African-American/Black studies; American studies; architecture; area, ethnic, cultural, and gender studies related; art; art teacher education; Asian studies; athletic training; biochemistry; biological and physical sciences; biology/biological sciences; business administration and management; ceramic arts and ceramics; chemistry; classics and languages, literatures and linguistics; computer science; creative writing; directing and theatrical production; dramatic/theatre arts; economics; education; elementary education; English; environmental studies; fine/studio arts; French; French studies; German; German studies; health and physical education related; history; interdisciplinary studies; liberal arts and sciences/liberal studies; literature; mathematics; molecular biology; music; music performance; music teacher education; music theory and composition; nursing (registered nurse training); painting; philosophy; photography; physical education teaching and coaching; physical sciences; physics; political science and government; pre-dentistry studies; pre-law studies; pre-medical studies; pre-veterinary studies; psychology; public relations/image management; religious studies; science teacher education; secondary education; sociology; Spanish; Spanish and Iberian studies; speech and rhetoric; theatre design and technology.

Colby College

African-American/Black studies; American studies; anthropology; area studies related; art; art history, criticism and conservation; Asian studies (East); biochemistry; biology/biological sciences; cell biology and histology; chemistry; classics and languages, literatures and linguistics; computer science; creative writing; dramatic/theatre arts; economics; English; environmental science; environmental studies; fine/studio arts; foreign languages related; French; geology/earth science; German; history; international relations and affairs; Latin American studies; mathematics; molecular biology; multi-/interdisciplinary studies related; music; neuroscience; philosophy; physics; political science and government; psychology; religious studies; Russian studies; science, technology and society; sociology; Spanish; women's studies.

Colgate University

African studies; African-American/Black studies; American Indian/Native American studies; anthropology; art; art history, criticism and conservation; Asian studies; Asian studies (East); astronomy; astrophysics; biochemistry; biology/biological sciences; chemistry; Chinese; classics and languages, literatures and linguistics; computer science; dramatic/theatre arts; economics; education; English; environmental biology; environmental studies; French; geography; geology/earth science; German; history; humanities; international relations and affairs; Japanese; Latin; Latin American studies; mathematics; modern Greek; molecular biology; music; natural sciences; neuroscience; peace studies and conflict resolution; philosophy; physical sciences; physics; political science and government; psychology; religious studies; romance languages; Russian; Russian studies; social sciences; sociology; Spanish; women's studies.

College of Charleston

Accounting; anthropology; art history, criticism and conservation; arts management; biochemistry; biology/biological sciences; business administration and management; chemistry; classics and languages, literatures and linguistics; communication/speech communication and rhetoric; computer and information sciences; dramatic/theatre arts; early childhood education; economics; elementary education; English; fine/studio arts; French; geology/earth science; German; historic preservation and conservation; history; information science/studies; international business/trade/commerce; marine biology and biological oceanography; mathematics; middle school education; music; philosophy; physical education teaching and coaching; physics; political science and government; pre-dentistry studies; pre-medical studies; psychology; religious studies; secondary education; sociology; Spanish; special education; urban studies/affairs.

The College of New Jersey

Accounting; art; art history, criticism and conservation; art teacher education; biology teacher education; biology/biological sciences; biomedical/medical engineering; business administration and management; business/managerial economics; chemistry; chemistry teacher education; commercial and advertising art; computer and information sciences; computer engineering; criminal justice/law enforcement administration; economics; education; electrical, electronics and communications engineering; elementary education; engineering science; English; English/language arts teacher education; finance; fine/studio arts; history; history teacher education; intermedia/multimedia; international business/trade/commerce; international relations and affairs; kindergarten/preschool education; mathematics; mathematics teacher education; mechanical engineering; music; music teacher education; nursing (registered nurse training); philosophy; physical education teaching and coaching; physics; physics teacher education; political science and government; pre-law studies; pre-medical studies; psychology; secondary education; sociology; Spanish; Spanish language teacher education; special education; special education (hearing

impaired); speech and rhetoric; statistics; technology/industrial arts teacher education; women's studies.

College of Saint Benedict

Accounting; art; art history, criticism and conservation; art teacher education; biochemistry; biological and physical sciences; biology/biological sciences; business administration and management; chemistry; classics and languages, literatures and linguistics; computer science; dietetics; dramatic/theatre arts; economics; education; elementary education; English; environmental studies; fine/studio arts; foods, nutrition, and wellness; forestry; French; German; history; humanities; liberal arts and sciences/liberal studies; mathematics; mathematics and computer science; mathematics and statistics related; music; music teacher education; natural sciences; nursing (registered nurse training); occupational therapy; peace studies and conflict resolution; philosophy; physical therapy; physics; political science and government; pre-dentistry studies; pre-law studies; pre-medical studies; pre-pharmacy studies; pre-theology/pre-ministerial studies; pre-veterinary studies; psychology; religious education; secondary education; social sciences; social work; sociology; Spanish; speech and rhetoric; theology.

The College of St. Scholastica

Accounting; applied economics; biochemistry; biology teacher education; biology/biological sciences; business administration and management; business, management, and marketing related; chemistry; chemistry teacher education; communication/speech communication and rhetoric; computer and information sciences; education (K-12); elementary education; English; English/language arts teacher education; health information/medical records administration; health science; health services/allied health/health sciences; history; history teacher education; humanities; international business/trade/commerce; international/global studies; kinesiology and exercise science; liberal arts and sciences/liberal studies; management science; mathematics; mathematics teacher education; music history, literature, and theory; music management and merchandising; music pedagogy; music performance; music teacher education; natural sciences; nursing (registered nurse training); organizational behavior; organizational communication; physical sciences related; psychology; religious studies; school librarian/school library media; science teacher education; social science teacher education; social sciences; social work.

College of the Atlantic

Art; biological and physical sciences; biology/biological sciences; botany/plant biology; ceramic arts and ceramics; computer graphics; drawing; ecology; economics; education; elementary education; English; environmental biology; environmental design/architecture; environmental education; environmental studies; evolutionary biology; human ecology; interdisciplinary studies; landscape architecture; legal studies; liberal arts and sciences/liberal studies; literature; marine biology and biological oceanography; maritime science; middle school education; museum studies; music; natural sci-

ences; philosophy; pre-veterinary studies; psychology; public policy analysis; science teacher education; secondary education; wildlife biology; zoology/animal biology.

College of the Holy Cross

Accounting; African studies; African-American/Black studies; American Sign Language (ASL); anthropology; art history, criticism and conservation; Asian studies; biology/biological sciences; chemistry; cinematography and film/video production; classics and languages, literatures and linguistics; dramatic/theatre arts; economics; English; environmental studies; fine/studio arts; French; German; German studies; gerontology; history; history related; Italian; Latin American studies; literature; mathematics; music; Near and Middle Eastern studies; peace studies and conflict resolution; philosophy; physics; political science and government; pre-dentistry studies; pre-medical studies; psychology; religious studies; Russian; Russian studies; sociology; Spanish; women's studies.

The College of William and Mary

African-American/Black studies; American studies; anthropology; art; art history, criticism and conservation; Asian studies (East); biology/biological sciences; biopsychology; business administration and management; chemistry; classics and languages, literatures and linguistics; computer and information sciences; cultural studies; dramatic/theatre arts; economics; English; environmental studies; European studies; French; geology/earth science; German; history; interdisciplinary studies; international relations and affairs; Latin; Latin American studies; linguistics; mathematics; medieval and renaissance studies; modern Greek; modern languages; multi-/interdisciplinary studies related; music; philosophy; physical education teaching and coaching; physics; political science and government; psychology; public policy analysis; religious studies; Russian studies; sociology; Spanish; women's studies.

The College of Wooster

African-American/Black studies; archeology; area, ethnic, cultural, and gender studies related; art history, criticism and conservation; biochemistry; biology/biological sciences; business/managerial economics; chemistry; classics and languages, literatures and linguistics; communication/speech communication and rhetoric; comparative literature; computer science; dramatic/theatre arts; economics; English; fine/studio arts; French; geology/earth science; German; German studies; history; interdisciplinary studies; international relations and affairs; Latin; mass communication/media; mathematics; molecular biology; multi-/interdisciplinary studies related; music; music history, literature, and theory; music performance; music teacher education; music theory and composition; music therapy; philosophy; physics; physics related; political science and government; psychology; religious studies; Russian studies; sociology; Spanish; urban studies/affairs; women's studies.

Colorado Christian University

Accounting; art; biblical studies; biological and physical sciences; biology/biological sciences;

business administration and management; communication/speech communication and rhetoric; computer and information sciences; dramatic/theatre arts; English; fine/studio arts; health and physical education; history; international/global studies; liberal arts and sciences/liberal studies; management information systems; management science; mathematics; music; music performance; music related; music teacher education; political science and government; psychology; social sciences; youth ministry.

The Colorado College

Anthropology; art history, criticism and conservation; Asian studies; biochemistry; biology/biological sciences; chemistry; classics and languages, literatures and linguistics; comparative literature; creative writing; dance; dramatic/theatre arts; econometrics and quantitative economics; economics; economics related; English; environmental science; ethnic, cultural minority, and gender studies related; film/cinema studies; fine/studio arts; French; French studies; geology/earth science; German; Hispanic-American, Puerto Rican, and Mexican-American/Chicano studies; history; history related; international economics; Italian; liberal arts and sciences and humanities related; mathematics; mathematics and computer science; multi-/interdisciplinary studies related; music; neuroscience; philosophy; physics; political science and government; psychology; religious studies; romance languages related; Russian; Russian studies; social sciences related; sociology; Spanish; women's studies.

Colorado School of Mines

Chemical engineering; chemistry; civil engineering; computer science; economics; electrical, electronics and communications engineering; engineering; engineering physics; engineering science; environmental/environmental health engineering; geological/geophysical engineering; mathematics; mechanical engineering; metallurgical engineering; mining and mineral engineering; petroleum engineering.

Colorado State University

Accounting; agribusiness; agricultural and extension education; agricultural and horticultural plant breeding; agricultural economics; agricultural teacher education; agriculture; agronomy and crop science; American studies; animal sciences; anthropology; apparel and textiles; applied horticulture; applied mathematics; art; art history, criticism and conservation; art teacher education; Asian studies; Asian-American studies; athletic training; biochemistry; biology teacher education; biology/biological sciences; botany/plant biology; business administration and management; business teacher education; ceramic arts and ceramics; chemical engineering; chemistry; chemistry teacher education; civil engineering; commercial and advertising art; computer and information sciences; computer engineering; computer science; creative writing; criminal justice/safety; crop production; dance; dietetics; dramatic/theatre arts; drawing; economics; electrical, electronics and communications engineering; engineering physics; engineering science; English; English/language arts teacher

education; entomology; environmental health; environmental/environmental health engineering; equestrian studies; family and consumer sciences/home economics teacher education; family and consumer sciences/human sciences; farm and ranch management; fiber, textile and weaving arts; finance; fine/studio arts; fishing and fisheries sciences and management; foods, nutrition, and wellness; foreign languages and literatures; forest sciences and biology; French; French language teacher education; geology/earth science; German; German language teacher education; history; horticultural science; hotel/motel administration; human development and family studies; humanities; information science/studies; interior design; journalism; kinesiology and exercise science; landscape architecture; landscaping and groundskeeping; Latin American studies; liberal arts and sciences/liberal studies; marketing/marketing management; mathematics; mathematics teacher education; mechanical engineering; medical microbiology and bacteriology; metal and jewelry arts; music; music performance; music teacher education; music therapy; natural resources management and policy; painting; parks, recreation and leisure facilities management; philosophy; photography; physical sciences; physics; physics teacher education; plant sciences; political science and government; pre-dentistry studies; pre-law studies; pre-medical studies; pre-veterinary studies; printmaking; psychology; public relations/image management; radio and television; range science and management; real estate; sales and marketing/marketing and distribution teacher education; science teacher education; sculpture; social sciences; social studies teacher education; social work; sociology; soil science and agronomy; Spanish; Spanish language teacher education; speech and rhetoric; turf and turfgrass management; wildlife and wildlands science and management; zoology/animal biology.

Columbia College (NY)

African-American/Black studies; American studies; ancient studies; ancient/classical Greek; anthropology; archeology; architecture; architecture related; art history, criticism and conservation; Asian studies (East); Asian-American studies; astronomy; astrophysics; atomic/molecular physics; biochemistry; biology/biological sciences; biophysics; biopsychology; chemistry; classical, ancient Mediterranean and Near Eastern studies and archaeology; classics and languages, literatures and linguistics; comparative literature; computer science; creative writing; dance; dramatic/theatre arts; East Asian languages; economics; education (K–12); English; environmental biology; environmental studies; film/cinema studies; French; French studies; geochemistry; geology/earth science; German; German studies; Hispanic-American, Puerto Rican, and Mexican-American/Chicano studies; history; Italian; Italian studies; Latin American studies; linguistics; mathematics; medieval and renaissance studies; modern Greek; music; Near and Middle Eastern studies; philosophy; physics; political science and government; psychology; religious studies; Russian; Russian studies; Slavic languages; sociology; Spanish; statistics; urban studies/affairs; visual and performing arts; women's studies.

Columbia University, The Fu Foundation School of Engineering and Applied Science

Applied mathematics; biomedical/medical engineering; chemical engineering; civil engineering; computer engineering; computer science; electrical, electronics and communications engineering; engineering mechanics; engineering physics; engineering/industrial management; environmental/environmental health engineering; industrial engineering; materials science; mechanical engineering; operations research.

Concordia College (MN)

Accounting; advertising; art; art history, criticism and conservation; art teacher education; biology teacher education; biology/biological sciences; broadcast journalism; business administration and management; business teacher education; business/commerce; chemistry; chemistry teacher education; child development; classics and classical languages related; clinical laboratory science/medical technology; communication/speech communication and rhetoric; computer science; creative writing; dietetics; dramatic/theatre arts; economics; education; elementary education; English; English/language arts teacher education; environmental studies; fine/studio arts; foods, nutrition, and wellness; French; French language teacher education; German; German language teacher education; health and physical education; health teacher education; health/health care administration; history; humanities; international business/trade/commerce; international/global studies; journalism; kindergarten/preschool education; kinesiology and exercise science; Latin; mass communication/media; mathematics; mathematics teacher education; music; music performance; music teacher education; music theory and composition; nursing (registered nurse training); occupational therapy; ophthalmic and optometric support services and allied professions related; philosophy; physical education teaching and coaching; physical therapy; physics; physics teacher education; piano and organ; political science and government; pre-dentistry studies; pre-law studies; pre-medical studies; pre-theology/pre-ministerial studies; pre-veterinary studies; psychology; public relations/image management; radio and television; religious studies; Russian studies; Scandinavian languages; science teacher education; secondary education; social studies teacher education; social work; sociology; Spanish; Spanish language teacher education; speech and rhetoric; voice and opera.

Connecticut College

African studies; American studies; anthropology; architecture; art; art history, criticism and conservation; Asian studies (East); astrophysics; biochemistry; biology/biological sciences; botany/plant biology; cell and molecular biology; cell biology and anatomical sciences related; chemistry; chemistry related; Chinese; classics and languages, literatures and linguistics; computer and information sciences; dance; dramatic/theatre arts; early childhood education; ecology; economics; education (multiple levels); elementary education; engineering physics; English; environmental studies; ethnic, cultural minority, and gender studies related; European studies (Central and Eastern); film/cinema studies; French; German; German studies; Hispanic-American, Puerto Rican, and Mexican-American/Chicano studies; history; human ecology; interdisciplinary studies; international relations and affairs; Italian; Italian studies; Japanese; kindergarten/preschool education; Latin American studies; mathematics; medieval and renaissance studies; middle school education; museum studies; music; music pedagogy; music related; music teacher education; neurobiology and neurophysiology; neuroscience; philosophy; physics; physics teacher education; political science and government; psychology; religious studies; Russian; secondary education; Slavic studies; sociology; Spanish; urban studies/affairs; women's studies; zoology/animal biology.

Converse College

Accounting; applied art; art; art history, criticism and conservation; art teacher education; art therapy; biochemistry; biology/biological sciences; business administration and management; chemistry; computer science; dramatic/theatre arts; economics; education; elementary education; English; fine/studio arts; French; history; interior design; international business/trade/commerce; kindergarten/preschool education; marketing/marketing management; mathematics; modern languages; music; music history, literature, and theory; music teacher education; piano and organ; political science and government; pre-dentistry studies; pre-law studies; pre-medical studies; pre-veterinary studies; psychology; religious studies; secondary education; sign language interpretation and translation; sociology; Spanish; special education; violin, viola, guitar and other stringed instruments; voice and opera.

Cooper Union for the Advancement of Science and Art

Architecture; chemical engineering; civil engineering; electrical, electronics and communications engineering; engineering; fine/studio arts; mechanical engineering; visual and performing arts.

Cornell College

Architecture; art; art history, criticism and conservation; biochemistry; biology/biological sciences; chemistry; classics and languages, literatures and linguistics; computer science; cultural studies; dramatic/theatre arts; economics; elementary education; English; environmental studies; ethnic, cultural minority, and gender studies related; French; geology/earth science; German; health and physical education related; history; interdisciplinary studies; international business/trade/commerce; international relations and affairs; Latin; Latin American studies; liberal arts and sciences/liberal studies; mathematics; medieval and renaissance studies; modern Greek; modern languages; multi-/interdisciplinary studies related; music; music teacher education; philosophy; physical education teaching and coaching; physics; political science and government; psychology; religious studies; Russian; secondary education; sociology; Spanish; speech and rhetoric; women's studies.

Cornell University

Accounting; acting; aerospace, aeronautical and astronautical engineering; African-American/Black studies; agricultural and extension education; agricultural and horticultural plant breeding; agricultural animal breeding; agricultural business and management; agricultural economics; agricultural teacher education; agricultural/biological engineering and bioengineering; agriculture; agronomy and crop science; American government and politics; American history; American Indian/Native American studies; American literature; American studies; analysis and functional analysis; analytical chemistry; animal genetics; animal nutrition; animal physiology; animal sciences; animal sciences related; anthropology; apparel and textiles; applied art; applied economics; applied mathematics; archeology; architectural history and criticism; architecture; architecture related; art; art history, criticism and conservation; Asian history; Asian studies; Asian studies (East); astronomy; astrophysics; atmospheric sciences and meteorology; biochemistry; biochemistry/biophysics and molecular biology; biological and biomedical sciences related; biology/biological sciences; biomathematics and bioinformatics related; biomedical/medical engineering; biometry/biometrics; biophysics; biopsychology; botany/plant biology; business administration and management; business family and consumer sciences/human sciences; business/commerce; cell biology and histology; chemical engineering; chemistry; chemistry related; Chinese; city/urban, community and regional planning; civil engineering; classics and languages, literatures and linguistics; cognitive science; communication/speech communication and rhetoric; community organization and advocacy; comparative literature; computer and information sciences; computer science; consumer economics; counselor education/school counseling and guidance; creative writing; crop production; dairy science; dance; demography and population; design and visual communications; developmental and child psychology; dramatic/theatre arts; East Asian languages; ecology; economics; education; educational leadership and administration; educational psychology; educational statistics and research methods; electrical, electronics and communications engineering; engineering; engineering physics; English; English as a second/foreign language (teaching); English literature (British and Commonwealth); English/language arts teacher education; entomology; environmental design/architecture; environmental studies; environmental toxicology; environmental/environmental health engineering; epidemiology; European history; evolutionary biology; family and consumer sciences/home economics teacher education; family and consumer sciences/human sciences; family resource management; farm and ranch management; fashion/apparel design; fiber, textile and weaving arts; film/cinema studies; finance; fine/studio arts; food science; food technology and processing; foods, nutrition, and wellness; foodservice systems administration; foreign language teacher education; French; gay/lesbian studies; genetics; geochemistry; geography related; geological and earth sciences/geosciences related; geological/geophysical engineering; geology/earth science; geophysics and seismology; geotechnical engineering; German; German studies; Hispanic-American, Puerto Rican, and Mexican-American/Chicano studies; historic preservation and conservation; history; history and philosophy of science and technology; history related; horticultural science; hospitality administration; hospitality administration related; hotel/motel administration; housing and human environments; human development and family studies; human ecology; human nutrition; humanities; hydrology and water resources science; immunology; industrial engineering; information science/studies; inorganic chemistry; interdisciplinary studies; international agriculture; international relations and affairs; Italian; labor and industrial relations; landscape architecture; Latin American studies; liberal arts and sciences/liberal studies; linguistics; management science; marketing/marketing management; materials engineering; materials science; mathematics; mathematics teacher education; mechanical engineering; medical microbiology and bacteriology; medieval and renaissance studies; meteorology; microbiology; molecular biology; multi-/interdisciplinary studies related; music; music history, literature, and theory; music theory and composition; musicology and ethnomusicology; mycology; natural resource economics; natural resources/conservation; Near and Middle Eastern studies; neuroscience; nuclear engineering; nutrition sciences; operations research; organic chemistry; ornamental horticulture; painting; peace studies and conflict resolution; personality psychology; philosophy; photography; physical and theoretical chemistry; physical sciences; physics; physics related; physics teacher education; physiology; planetary astronomy and science; plant genetics; plant pathology/phytopathology; plant sciences; political science and government; political science and government related; pre-law studies; pre-medical studies; pre-veterinary studies; psychology; public administration; public administration and social service professions related; public policy analysis; religious studies; romance languages; Russian studies; science, technology and society; sculpture; Semitic languages; Slavic languages; Slavic studies; social psychology; social sciences related; sociobiology; sociology; soil science and agronomy; soil sciences related; Spanish; statistics; structural engineering; surveying engineering; systems engineering; textile science; theatre literature, history and criticism; toxicology; transportation and highway engineering; urban studies/affairs; visual and performing arts; women's studies; zoology/animal biology.

Covenant College

Art; biblical studies; biology/biological sciences; business administration and management; chemistry; computer science; economics; elementary education; English; foreign languages and literatures; health science; history; interdisciplinary studies; mathematics; middle school education; music; natural sciences; nursing (registered nurse training); philosophy; physics; pre-engineering; pre-law studies; pre-medical studies; pre-nursing studies; psychology; sociology.

Creighton University

Accounting; American Indian/Native American studies; American studies; ancient/classical

Greek; applied mathematics; art; athletic training; atmospheric sciences and meteorology; biology/biological sciences; chemistry; classical, ancient Mediterranean and Near Eastern studies and archaeology; communication/speech communication and rhetoric; computer programming; computer science; dramatic/theatre arts; economics; elementary education; emergency medical technology (EMT paramedic); English; environmental studies; finance; French; German; graphic design; health/health care administration; history; international business/trade/commerce; international relations and affairs; journalism; kinesiology and exercise science; Latin; management information systems; marketing/marketing management; mathematics; music; nursing (registered nurse training); organizational communication; philosophy; physics; political science and government; pre-law studies; psychology; social work; sociology; Spanish; speech and rhetoric; theology.

Dartmouth College

African studies; African-American/Black studies; American Indian/Native American studies; ancient/classical Greek; animal genetics; anthropology; Arabic; archeology; art history, criticism and conservation; Asian studies; astronomy; biochemistry; biology/biological sciences; chemistry; chemistry related; Chinese; classics and languages, literatures and linguistics; cognitive psychology and psycholinguistics; comparative literature; computer science; creative writing; dramatic/theatre arts; East Asian languages related; ecology; economics; engineering; engineering physics; English; environmental studies; evolutionary biology; film/cinema studies; fine/studio arts; French; geography; geology/earth science; German; Hebrew; Hispanic-American, Puerto Rican, and Mexican-American/Chicano studies; history; Italian; Japanese; Latin; Latin American studies; linguistics; mathematics; molecular biology; multi-/interdisciplinary studies related; music; Near and Middle Eastern studies; philosophy; physics; political science and government; psychology; religious studies; romance languages; Russian; Russian studies; sociology; Spanish; women's studies.

Davidson College

Anthropology; art; biology/biological sciences; chemistry; classics and languages, literatures and linguistics; dramatic/theatre arts; economics; English; French; German; history; mathematics; multi-/interdisciplinary studies related; music; philosophy; physics; political science and government; psychology; religious studies; sociology; Spanish.

Denison University

African-American/Black studies; anthropology; area studies; art; art history, criticism and conservation; Asian studies (East); biochemistry; biology/biological sciences; chemistry; classics and languages, literatures and linguistics; computer science; creative writing; dance; dramatic/theatre arts; economics; English; environmental studies; film/cinema studies; fine/studio arts; French; geology/earth science; German; history; international relations and affairs; Latin American studies; mass communication/media; mathematics; music; organizational behavior; philosophy; physical

education teaching and coaching; physics; political science and government; psychology; religious studies; sociology; Spanish; speech and rhetoric; women's studies.

DePauw University

African-American/Black studies; ancient/classical Greek; anthropology; art history, criticism and conservation; Asian studies (East); athletic training; biochemistry; biology/biological sciences; chemistry; classics and languages, literatures and linguistics; computer science; dramatic/theatre arts; economics; elementary education; English; English composition; environmental studies; fine/studio arts; French; geology/earth science; German; history; interdisciplinary studies; kinesiology and exercise science; Latin; mass communication/media; mathematics; multi-/interdisciplinary studies related; music; music management and merchandising; music performance; music teacher education; music theory and composition; peace studies and conflict resolution; philosophy; physical education teaching and coaching; physics; political science and government; psychology; religious studies; romance languages; Russian studies; sociology; Spanish; women's studies.

Dickinson College

American studies; anthropology; archeology; Asian studies (East); biochemistry; biology/biological sciences; chemistry; classics and languages, literatures and linguistics; computer science; dance; dramatic/theatre arts; economics; engineering; English; environmental science; environmental studies; fine/studio arts; French; geology/earth science; German; history; international business/trade/commerce; international relations and affairs; Italian; Jewish/Judaic studies; mathematics; medieval and renaissance studies; multi-/interdisciplinary studies related; music; music related; philosophy; physics; political science and government; pre-dentistry studies; pre-law studies; pre-medical studies; psychology; public policy analysis; religious studies; Russian; Russian studies; sociology; Spanish; theatre design and technology; women's studies.

Drake University

Accounting; accounting and finance; acting; actuarial science; advertising; anthropology; Army R.O.T.C./military science; art; art history, criticism and conservation; astronomy; biology/biological sciences; broadcast journalism; business administration and management; business teacher education; business/commerce; chemistry; commercial and advertising art; computer science; directing and theatrical production; dramatic/theatre arts; dramatic/theatre arts and stagecraft related; drawing; economics; elementary education; English; environmental science; environmental studies; finance; fine/studio arts; graphic design; history; human resources management and services related; information science/studies; international business/trade/commerce; international relations and affairs; jazz/jazz studies; journalism; marketing/marketing management; mass communication/media; mathematics; music; music management and merchandising; music performance; music teacher education; painting; pharmacy; pharmacy administration/

pharmaceutics; philosophy; physics; piano and organ; political science and government; pre-dentistry studies; pre-law studies; pre-medical studies; pre-veterinary studies; printmaking; psychology; public relations/image management; radio and television; radio, television, and digital communication related; religious studies; religious/sacred music; science teacher education; sculpture; secondary education; sociology; speech and rhetoric; voice and opera.

Drew University

Anthropology; art; behavioral sciences; biochemistry; biology/biological sciences; chemistry; classics and languages, literatures and linguistics; computer science; dramatic/theatre arts; economics; English; French; German; history; mathematics; mathematics and computer science; music; neuroscience; philosophy; physics; political science and government; psychology; religious studies; Russian; sociology; Spanish; women's studies.

Drury University

Accounting; advertising; American government and politics; architecture; art; art history, criticism and conservation; arts management; behavioral sciences; biology/biological sciences; broadcast journalism; business administration and management; chemistry; computer and information sciences; computer science; creative writing; criminology; design and visual communications; dramatic/theatre arts; economics; education; elementary education; English; environmental studies; fine/studio arts; French; German; history; international business/trade/commerce; journalism; kinesiology and exercise science; mass communication/media; mathematics; music; music performance; music theory and composition; philosophy; physics; political science and government; pre-dentistry studies; pre-law studies; pre-medical studies; pre-veterinary studies; psychology; public relations/image management; religious studies; secondary education; Spanish.

Duke University

African-American/Black studies; anatomy; ancient/classical Greek; anthropology; art; art history, criticism and conservation; Asian studies; biology/biological sciences; biomedical/medical engineering; Canadian studies; chemistry; civil engineering; classics and languages, literatures and linguistics; computer science; design and visual communications; dramatic/theatre arts; economics; electrical, electronics and communications engineering; English; environmental studies; French; geology/earth science; German; history; international relations and affairs; Italian; Latin; linguistics; literature; materials science; mathematics; mechanical engineering; medieval and renaissance studies; music; philosophy; physics; political science and government; psychology; public policy analysis; religious studies; Russian; Slavic languages; sociology; Spanish; women's studies.

Earlham College

African-American/Black studies; art; biology/biological sciences; business administration and management; chemistry; classics and languages, literatures and linguistics; computer science; dramatic/theatre arts; economics; education;

English; environmental studies; French; geology/earth science; German; history; interdisciplinary studies; international relations and affairs; Japanese studies; Latin American studies; mathematics; music; peace studies and conflict resolution; philosophy; physics; political science and government; pre-law studies; pre-medical studies; psychology; religious studies; sociology; Spanish; women's studies.

Eastern Mennonite University

Accounting; art; art teacher education; biblical studies; biochemistry; biology teacher education; biology/biological sciences; business administration and management; chemistry; chemistry teacher education; clinical laboratory science/medical technology; communication/speech communication and rhetoric; computer science; computer systems analysis; development economics and international development; dramatic/theatre arts; economics; elementary education; English; English/language arts teacher education; environmental science; French; French language teacher education; general studies; German; German language teacher education; health teacher education; history; international agriculture; international business/trade/commerce; kindergarten/preschool education; liberal arts and sciences/liberal studies; mathematics; mathematics teacher education; middle school education; multi-/interdisciplinary studies related; music; music teacher education; nursing (registered nurse training); peace studies and conflict resolution; philosophy and religious studies related; physical education teaching and coaching; pre-dentistry studies; pre-medical studies; pre-veterinary studies; psychology; secondary education; social science teacher education; social sciences; social work; sociology; Spanish; Spanish language teacher education; special education (emotionally disturbed); special education (mentally retarded); special education (specific learning disabilities); sport and fitness administration; theology.

Eckerd College

American studies; anthropology; art; biology/biological sciences; business administration and management; chemistry; Chinese; clinical laboratory science/medical technology; communication/speech communication and rhetoric; comparative literature; computer science; creative writing; dramatic/theatre arts; East Asian languages; economics; English; environmental studies; foreign languages and literatures; French; German; history; human development and family studies; human resources management; humanities; interdisciplinary studies; international business/trade/commerce; international relations and affairs; literature; marine biology and biological oceanography; mathematics; modern languages; music; philosophy; physics; political science and government; psychology; religious studies; Russian; sociology; Spanish; women's studies.

Elizabethtown College

Accounting; anthropology; art; biochemistry; biology/biological sciences; biotechnology; business administration and management; chemistry; communication/speech communication and rhetoric; computer engineering; computer science; criminal justice/safety; direct-

ing and theatrical production; economics; education; elementary education; engineering; engineering physics; English; environmental studies; French; German; history; industrial engineering; international business/trade/commerce; kindergarten/preschool education; mathematics; modern languages; music; music teacher education; music therapy; occupational therapy; peace studies and conflict resolution; philosophy; physics; political science and government; pre-dentistry studies; pre-law studies; pre-medical studies; pre-veterinary studies; psychology; religious studies; science teacher education; secondary education; social sciences; social work; sociology; Spanish; theatre design and technology; theatre/theatre arts management.

Embry-Riddle Aeronautical University

Aeronautics/aviation/aerospace science and technology; aerospace, aeronautical and astronautical engineering; airline pilot and flight crew; computer engineering; computer software engineering; electrical, electronics and communications engineering; engineering; international relations and affairs; physics related; science, technology and society.

Emerson College

Acting; advertising; audiology and speech-language pathology; broadcast journalism; cinematography and film/video production; communication disorders; communication/speech communication and rhetoric; creative writing; drama and dance teacher education; dramatic/theatre arts; film/cinema studies; interdisciplinary studies; intermedia/multimedia; journalism; marketing/marketing management; mass communication/media; playwriting and screenwriting; political communication; public relations/image management; publishing; radio and television; radio and television broadcasting technology; radio, television, and digital communication related; special education (speech or language impaired); speech and rhetoric; speech therapy; speech-language pathology; theatre design and technology; visual and performing arts.

Emory University

Accounting; African studies; African-American/Black studies; anthropology; art history, criticism and conservation; Asian studies; biology/biological sciences; biomedical sciences; business administration and management; business/managerial economics; chemistry; Chinese; classics and languages, literatures and linguistics; comparative literature; computer science; creative writing; dance; dramatic/theatre arts; economics; education; elementary education; English; European studies (Central and Eastern); film/cinema studies; finance; French; German; history; human ecology; international relations and affairs; Italian; Japanese; Jewish/Judaic studies; Latin; Latin American studies; liberal arts and sciences/liberal studies; literature; marketing/marketing management; mathematics; medieval and renaissance studies; modern Greek; music; neuroscience; nursing (registered nurse training); philosophy; physics; political science and government; psychology; religious studies; Russian; secondary education; sociology; Spanish; women's studies.

Erskine College

American studies; art; athletic training; behavioral sciences; biblical studies; biological and physical sciences; biology/biological sciences; business administration and management; chemistry; clinical laboratory science/medical technology; elementary education; English; French; health science; history; kindergarten/preschool education; mathematics; music; music teacher education; natural sciences; philosophy; physical education teaching and coaching; physics; psychology; religious education; religious studies; religious/sacred music; social studies teacher education; Spanish; special education; sport and fitness administration.

Eugene Lang College, New School University

Anthropology; creative writing; dramatic/theatre arts; economics; education; English; history; humanities; interdisciplinary studies; international relations and affairs; liberal arts and sciences/liberal studies; literature; music history, literature, and theory; philosophy; political science and government; psychology; religious studies; social sciences; sociology; urban studies/affairs; women's studies.

Fairfield University

Accounting; American studies; art; biology/biological sciences; business administration and management; chemistry; clinical psychology; computer science; computer software engineering; economics; electrical, electronics and communications engineering; engineering related; English; finance; French; German; history; information science/studies; international relations and affairs; management information systems; marketing/marketing management; mass communication/media; mathematics; mechanical engineering; modern languages; music history, literature, and theory; nursing (registered nurse training); philosophy; physics; political science and government; psychology; religious studies; secondary education; sociology; Spanish.

Florida Institute of Technology

Accounting; aeronautics/aviation/aerospace science and technology; aerospace, aeronautical and astronautical engineering; air transportation related; analytical chemistry; applied mathematics; aquatic biology/limnology; astrophysics; aviation/airway management; biochemistry; biological and physical sciences; biology teacher education; biology/biological sciences; biomedical sciences; business administration and management; business administration, management and operations related; chemical engineering; chemistry; chemistry related; chemistry teacher education; civil engineering; communication/speech communication and rhetoric; computer engineering; computer science; computer software engineering; computer teacher education; ecology; electrical, electronics and communications engineering; environmental science; forensic psychology; humanities; hydrology and water resources science; information science/studies; interdisciplinary studies; management information systems; marine biology and biological oceanography; mathematics teacher education; mechanical engineering; meteorology; molecular biology; multi-/

interdisciplinary studies related; ocean engineering; oceanography (chemical and physical); physics; physics related; physics teacher education; psychology; science teacher education.

Florida International University

Accounting; applied mathematics; architecture related; art history, criticism and conservation; art teacher education; Asian studies; biology/biological sciences; biomedical/medical engineering; broadcast journalism; business administration and management; chemical engineering; chemistry; civil engineering; communication/speech communication and rhetoric; computer and information sciences; computer engineering; computer science; construction engineering technology; criminal justice/safety; dance; dietetics; dramatic/theatre arts; economics; electrical, electronics and communications engineering; elementary education; English; English/language arts teacher education; environmental control technologies related; environmental design/architecture; environmental studies; family and consumer sciences/home economics teacher education; finance; fine/studio arts; foreign language teacher education; French; geography; geology/earth science; German; health information/medical records administration; health science; health services/allied health/health sciences; health teacher education; health/health care administration; history; hospitality administration; human resources management; humanities; information technology; insurance; interior design; international business/trade/commerce; international relations and affairs; Italian; kinesiology and exercise science; liberal arts and sciences/liberal studies; logistics and materials management; management information systems; marine biology and biological oceanography; marketing/marketing management; mathematics; mathematics teacher education; mechanical engineering; music; music teacher education; nursing (registered nurse training); occupational therapy; orthotics/prosthetics; parks, recreation and leisure facilities management; philosophy; physical education teaching and coaching; physics; political science and government; Portuguese; psychology; public administration; real estate; religious studies; science teacher education; social science teacher education; social work; sociology; Spanish; special education (emotionally disturbed); special education (mentally retarded); special education (specific learning disabilities); statistics; systems engineering; tourism and travel services management; trade and industrial teacher education; urban studies/affairs; women's studies.

Florida State University

Accounting; acting; actuarial science; advertising; African-American/Black studies; American studies; anthropology; apparel and textile marketing management; apparel and textiles; applied economics; applied mathematics; art; art history, criticism and conservation; art teacher education; Asian studies; athletic training; atmospheric sciences and meteorology; audiology and speech-language pathology; bilingual and multilingual education; bilingual, multilingual, and multicultural education related; biochemistry; biology/biological sciences; biomathematics and bioinformatics related; biomedical/medical engineering; busi-

ness administration and management; business/commerce; Caribbean studies; cell and molecular biology; chemical engineering; chemistry; chemistry related; child development; cinematography and film/video production; civil engineering; classics and languages, literatures and linguistics; commercial and advertising art; communication and media related; communication/speech communication and rhetoric; community health services counseling; computer and information sciences; computer engineering; computer programming; computer science; computer software and media applications related; computer software engineering; creative writing; criminal justice/safety; criminology; dance; dietetics; dramatic/theatre arts; early childhood education; ecology; economics; electrical, electronics and communications engineering; elementary education; English; English/language arts teacher education; entrepreneurial and small business related; environmental biology; environmental studies; environmental/environmental health engineering; European studies (Central and Eastern); evolutionary biology; family and consumer economics related; family and consumer sciences/home economics teacher education; family and consumer sciences/human sciences; fashion merchandising; fashion/apparel design; film/cinema studies; finance; fine/studio arts; foods, nutrition, and wellness; foreign language teacher education; French; geography; geology/earth science; German; gerontology; graphic design; health teacher education; history; hospitality administration; hospitality administration related; housing and human environments; human development and family studies; human resources management; humanities; industrial engineering; information science/studies; insurance; interior design; international business/trade/commerce; international relations and affairs; Italian; jazz/jazz studies; kindergarten/preschool education; kinesiology and exercise science; Latin; Latin American studies; liberal arts and sciences/liberal studies; literature; management information systems; marine biology and biological oceanography; marketing/marketing management; mass communication/media; materials engineering; mathematics; mathematics teacher education; mechanical engineering; meteorology; middle school education; modern Greek; multicultural education; music; music history, literature, and theory; music pedagogy; music performance; music teacher education; music theory and composition; music therapy; neurobiology and neurophysiology; nursing (registered nurse training); nutrition sciences; parks, recreation and leisure facilities management; philosophy; physical education teaching and coaching; physical sciences; physical sciences related; physics; piano and organ; plant physiology; political science and government; pre-dentistry studies; pre-law studies; pre-medical studies; pre-pharmacy studies; pre-theology/pre-ministerial studies; pre-veterinary studies; psychology; public relations/image management; radio and television; radio, television, and digital communication related; real estate; religious studies; Russian; Russian studies; sales, distribution and marketing; science teacher education; secondary education; social science teacher education; social sciences; social work; sociology; Spanish; special education (emotionally disturbed); special education (mentally

retarded); special education (specific learning disabilities); special education (vision impaired); sport and fitness administration; statistics; technical and business writing; textile science; theatre design and technology; violin, viola, guitar and other stringed instruments; vocational rehabilitation counseling; voice and opera; wind/percussion instruments; women's studies; zoology/animal biology.

Fordham University

Accounting; accounting and computer science; African studies; African-American/Black studies; American studies; anthropology; art; art history, criticism and conservation; bilingual and multilingual education; biological and physical sciences; biology/biological sciences; broadcast journalism; business administration and management; business/managerial economics; chemistry; classics and languages, literatures and linguistics; commercial and advertising art; comparative literature; computer and information sciences; computer management; computer science; creative writing; criminal justice/law enforcement administration; dance; dramatic/theatre arts; economics; education; elementary education; English; entrepreneurship; European studies (Central and Eastern); film/cinema studies; finance; fine/studio arts; French; French studies; German; German studies; health/medical preparatory programs related; Hispanic-American, Puerto Rican, and Mexican-American/Chicano studies; history; human resources management; information science/studies; interdisciplinary studies; international business/trade/commerce; international economics; international relations and affairs; Italian; Italian studies; journalism; Latin; Latin American studies; liberal arts and sciences/liberal studies; literature; management information systems and services related; marketing/marketing management; mass communication/media; mathematics; medieval and renaissance studies; modern Greek; modern languages; music; music history, literature, and theory; natural sciences; Near and Middle Eastern studies; peace studies and conflict resolution; philosophy; photography; physical sciences; physics; playwriting and screenwriting; political science and government; pre-dentistry studies; pre-law studies; pre-medical studies; pre-pharmacy studies; pre-veterinary studies; psychology; public administration; radio and television; religious studies; romance languages; Russian; Russian studies; secondary education; social sciences; social work; sociology; Spanish; Spanish and Iberian studies; theology; urban studies/affairs; women's studies.

Franciscan University of Steubenville

Accounting; anthropology; biology/biological sciences; business administration and management; chemistry; child development; classics and languages, literatures and linguistics; communication/speech communication and rhetoric; computer and information sciences; computer science; economics; elementary education; engineering science; English; French; general studies; German; history; humanities; legal studies; legal studies; mathematics; nursing (registered nurse training); philosophy; political science and government; psychiatric/mental health services technology; psychology; religious education; social work; sociology; Spanish; theology.

Franklin and Marshall College

Accounting and finance; African studies; American studies; ancient/classical Greek; animal behavior and ethology; anthropology; art history, criticism and conservation; astronomy; astrophysics; biochemistry; biology/biological sciences; business administration and management; chemistry; classics and languages, literatures and linguistics; creative writing; dramatic/theatre arts; economics; English; environmental science; environmental studies; fine/studio arts; French; geology/earth science; German; German studies; history; Latin; mathematics; multi-/interdisciplinary studies related; music; neuroscience; philosophy; physics; political science and government; psychology; religious studies; sociology; Spanish.

Freed-Hardeman University

Accounting; agricultural business and management; apparel and textiles; art; art teacher education; behavioral sciences; biblical studies; biochemistry; biological and physical sciences; biology teacher education; biology/biological sciences; biophysics; business administration and management; business/managerial economics; chemistry; child development; commercial and advertising art; computer and information sciences; computer science; dramatic/theatre arts; education; elementary education; English; English/language arts teacher education; family and consumer sciences/human sciences; fashion merchandising; finance; health and physical education; health services administration; health teacher education; history; human resources management; humanities; information science/studies; interdisciplinary studies; liberal arts and sciences/liberal studies; marketing/marketing management; mathematics; mathematics teacher education; missionary studies and missiology; music; music teacher education; philosophy; physical education teaching and coaching; physical sciences; psychology; public relations/image management; radio and television; science teacher education; secondary education; social sciences; social work; special education.

Furman University

Accounting; art; art history, criticism and conservation; Asian studies; biochemistry; biology/biological sciences; business administration and management; chemistry; communication/speech communication and rhetoric; computer science; dramatic/theatre arts; economics; education; elementary education; English; environmental science; fine/studio arts; French; geology/earth science; German; history; kindergarten/preschool education; kinesiology and exercise science; Latin; mathematics; modern Greek; music; music teacher education; philosophy; physics; piano and organ; political science and government; pre-dentistry studies; pre-law studies; pre-medical studies; pre-veterinary studies; psychology; religious studies; religious/sacred music; secondary education; sociology; Spanish; special education; urban studies/affairs; voice and opera.

George Fox University

Art; athletic training; biblical studies; biology teacher education; biology/biological sciences;

business administration and management; business/managerial economics; chemistry; chemistry teacher education; clinical psychology; cognitive psychology and psycholinguistics; communication/speech communication and rhetoric; computer and information sciences; education (multiple levels); elementary education; engineering; English; English/language arts teacher education; family and consumer sciences/home economics teacher education; family and consumer sciences/human sciences; family resource management; fashion merchandising; health teacher education; history; human resources management; interdisciplinary studies; international relations and affairs; management information systems; mathematics; mathematics teacher education; missionary studies and missiology; music; music teacher education; pastoral studies/counseling; physical education teaching and coaching; psychology; public relations/image management; radio and television; religious education; religious studies; social studies teacher education; social work; sociology; Spanish; sport and fitness administration.

Georgetown College

Accounting; American studies; art; biology/biological sciences; business administration and management; chemistry; computer and information sciences; computer science; dramatic/theatre arts; ecology; economics; education; elementary education; English; environmental studies; European studies; finance; fine/studio arts; French; German; history; information science/studies; international business/trade/commerce; kindergarten/preschool education; management information systems; marketing/marketing management; mass communication/media; mathematics; middle school education; multi-/interdisciplinary studies related; music; music teacher education; parks, recreation and leisure; philosophy; physics; piano and organ; political science and government; pre-dentistry studies; pre-law studies; pre-medical studies; psychology; religious studies; secondary education; sociology; Spanish; speech and rhetoric; voice and opera.

Georgetown University

Accounting; American studies; Arabic; art; biochemistry; biology/biological sciences; business administration and management; chemistry; Chinese; classics and languages, literatures and linguistics; comparative literature; computer science; economics; English; finance; French; German; history; interdisciplinary studies; international business/trade/commerce; international economics; international relations and affairs; Italian; Japanese; liberal arts and sciences/liberal studies; linguistics; marketing/marketing management; mathematics; nursing (registered nurse training); philosophy; physics; political science and government; Portuguese; psychology; religious studies; Russian; science, technology and society; social sciences related; sociology; Spanish; women's studies.

The George Washington University

Accounting; American studies; anthropology; applied mathematics; archeology; art; art his-

tory, criticism and conservation; Asian studies; Asian studies (East); audiology and speech-language pathology; biology/biological sciences; business administration and management; business/managerial economics; chemistry; Chinese; civil engineering; classics and languages, literatures and linguistics; clinical laboratory science/medical technology; clinical/medical laboratory technology; computer and information sciences; computer engineering; computer science; criminal justice/law enforcement administration; dance; dramatic/theatre arts; economics; electrical, electronics and communications engineering; emergency medical technology (EMT paramedic); engineering; English; environmental studies; environmental/environmental health engineering; European studies; finance; fine/studio arts; French; geography; geology/earth science; German; history; human resources management; human services; humanities; industrial radiologic technology; interdisciplinary studies; international business/trade/commerce; international relations and affairs; Jewish/Judaic studies; journalism; kinesiology and exercise science; Latin American studies; liberal arts and sciences/liberal studies; marketing/marketing management; mass communication/media; mathematics; mechanical engineering; medical laboratory technology; music; Near and Middle Eastern studies; nuclear medical technology; philosophy; physician assistant; physics; political science and government; pre-dentistry studies; pre-law studies; pre-medical studies; psychology; public policy analysis; radio and television; radiologic technology/science; religious studies; Russian; Russian studies; sociology; Spanish; speech and rhetoric; statistics; systems engineering.

Georgia Institute of Technology

Aerospace, aeronautical and astronautical engineering; applied mathematics related; architecture; architecture related; atmospheric sciences and meteorology; biology/biological sciences; biomedical/medical engineering; business administration and management; business/managerial economics; chemical engineering; chemistry; chemistry related; civil engineering; computer and information sciences; computer engineering; electrical, electronics and communications engineering; geological and earth sciences/geosciences related; history and philosophy of science and technology; industrial and organizational psychology; industrial design; industrial engineering; international economics; international relations and affairs; management science; materials engineering; mathematics; mechanical engineering; metallurgical engineering; modern languages; multi-/interdisciplinary studies related; nuclear engineering; operations management; physics; polymer chemistry; public policy analysis; science, technology and society; textile sciences and engineering.

Georgia State University

Accounting; actuarial science; African-American/Black studies; anthropology; art teacher education; biology/biological sciences; business administration and management; business/managerial economics; chemistry; classics and languages, literatures and linguistics; clinical laboratory science/medical technology; computer and information sciences; criminal justice/safety; dietetics; dramatic/theatre arts; drawing; economics; English; film/cinema studies; finance; French; geography; geology/earth science; German; health information/medical records administration; history; hotel/motel administration; human resources management; insurance; interdisciplinary studies; journalism; kindergarten/preschool education; liberal arts and sciences/liberal studies; marketing/marketing management; mathematics; middle school education; music performance; nursing (registered nurse training); operations research; parks, recreation and leisure facilities management; philosophy; physical education teaching and coaching; physical therapy; physics; political science and government; psychology; real estate; religious studies; respiratory care therapy; social work; sociology; Spanish; speech and rhetoric; urban studies/affairs.

Gettysburg College

Accounting; African-American/Black studies; American history; American studies; ancient/classical Greek; anthropology; area studies; area studies related; area, ethnic, cultural, and gender studies related; art; art history, criticism and conservation; Asian history; Asian studies (East); Asian studies (South); biochemistry; biological and physical sciences; biology/biological sciences; broadcast journalism; business administration and management; business administration, management and operations related; chemistry; classics and languages, literatures and linguistics; computer science; creative writing; dramatic/theatre arts; economics; education; elementary education; engineering related; English; English composition; environmental science; environmental studies; European history; fine/studio arts; French; German; health science; Hispanic-American, Puerto Rican, and Mexican-American/Chicano studies; history; interdisciplinary studies; international business/trade/commerce; international economics; international relations and affairs; Italian; Japanese; Japanese studies; journalism; Latin; Latin American studies; liberal arts and sciences/liberal studies; literature; marine biology and biological oceanography; mathematics; middle school education; modern languages; molecular biology; music; music teacher education; non-profit management; peace studies and conflict resolution; philosophy; physical education teaching and coaching; physics; political science and government; pre-dentistry studies; pre-law studies; pre-medical studies; pre-nursing studies; pre-pharmacy studies; pre-veterinary studies; psychology; religious studies; romance languages; science teacher education; secondary education; social sciences; social sciences related; sociology; Spanish; visual and performing arts; western civilization; women's studies.

Gonzaga University

Accounting; art; Asian studies; biochemistry; biology/biological sciences; broadcast journalism; business administration and management; business/managerial economics; chemistry; civil engineering; computer engineering; computer science; criminal justice/law enforcement administration; dramatic/theatre arts; economics; electrical, electronics and communications engineering; elementary education; engineering; English; finance; French; German; history; information science/studies; international busi-

ness/trade/commerce; international relations and affairs; Italian; journalism; kinesiology and exercise science; liberal arts and sciences/liberal studies; literature; marketing/marketing management; mass communication/media; mathematics; mechanical engineering; music; music teacher education; nursing (registered nurse training); philosophy; physical education teaching and coaching; physics; political science and government; psychology; public relations/image management; religious studies; secondary education; sociology; Spanish; special education; speech and rhetoric; sport and fitness administration.

Gordon College (MA)

Accounting; art; biology/biological sciences; business administration and management; chemistry; Christian studies; communication/speech communication and rhetoric; computer science; economics; elementary education; English; foreign languages and literatures; French; German; history; international relations and affairs; kinesiology and exercise science; mathematics; middle school education; music; music performance; music teacher education; parks, recreation and leisure; philosophy; physics; political science and government; psychology; social work; sociology; Spanish; special education; youth ministry.

Goshen College

Accounting; art; art teacher education; art therapy; biblical studies; bilingual and multilingual education; biology/biological sciences; broadcast journalism; business administration and management; business teacher education; chemistry; child development; computer science; dramatic/theatre arts; economics; education; elementary education; English; English as a second/foreign language (teaching); environmental studies; family and community services; German; Hispanic-American, Puerto Rican, and Mexican-American/Chicano studies; history; information science/studies; journalism; kindergarten/preschool education; liberal arts and sciences/liberal studies; mass communication/media; mathematics; music; music teacher education; natural sciences; nursing (registered nurse training); peace studies and conflict resolution; physical education teaching and coaching; physical sciences; physics; political science and government; pre-dentistry studies; pre-law studies; pre-medical studies; pre-veterinary studies; psychology; religious studies; science teacher education; secondary education; sign language interpretation and translation; social work; sociology; Spanish.

Goucher College

American studies; art; biology/biological sciences; chemistry; computer science; dance; dramatic/theatre arts; economics; education; elementary education; English; French; historic preservation and conservation; history; interdisciplinary studies; international relations and affairs; management science; mass communication/media; mathematics; music; philosophy; physics; political science and government; psychology; religious studies; Russian; sociology; Spanish; special education; women's studies.

Grinnell College

African-American/Black studies; American studies; anthropology; archeology; art; Asian studies (East); biochemistry; biological and physical sciences; biology/biological sciences; chemistry; Chinese; classics and languages, literatures and linguistics; computer science; dramatic/theatre arts; economics; education; elementary education; English; environmental biology; environmental studies; European studies (Central and Eastern); European studies (Western); French; German; history; interdisciplinary studies; international/global studies; Latin American studies; linguistics; mathematics; music; philosophy; physics; political science and government; pre-medical studies; psychology; religious studies; Russian; science, technology and society; secondary education; sociology; Spanish; women's studies.

Grove City College

Accounting; biochemistry; biology/biological sciences; business administration and management; business/corporate communications; business/managerial economics; chemistry; computer and information sciences; computer management; divinity/ministry; economics; electrical and electronic engineering technologies related; electrical, electronics and communications engineering; elementary education; English; entrepreneurship; finance; French; history; international business/trade/commerce; kindergarten/preschool education; literature; marketing/marketing management; mass communication/media; mathematics; mechanical engineering; mechanical engineering technologies related; modern languages; molecular biology; music; music management and merchandising; music performance; music teacher education; philosophy; physics; political science and government; pre-dentistry studies; pre-law studies; pre-medical studies; pre-veterinary studies; psychology; religious studies; science teacher education; secondary education; sociology; Spanish.

Gustavus Adolphus College

Accounting; anthropology; art; art history, criticism and conservation; art teacher education; athletic training; biochemistry; biology teacher education; biology/biological sciences; business administration and management; business/managerial economics; chemistry; chemistry teacher education; classics and languages, literatures and linguistics; computer science; criminal justice/law enforcement administration; dance; dramatic/theatre arts; economics; education; elementary education; English; environmental studies; French; geography; geology/earth science; German; health and physical education related; health teacher education; history; interdisciplinary studies; international business/trade/commerce; Japanese; Japanese studies; Latin American studies; mass communication/media; mathematics; mathematics teacher education; music; music teacher education; nursing (registered nurse training); philosophy; physical education teaching and coaching; physical therapy; physics; physics teacher education; political science and government; pre-dentistry studies; pre-law studies; pre-medical studies; pre-veterinary studies; psychology; religious studies; religious/sacred music; Russian; Russian studies;

Scandinavian languages; Scandinavian studies; secondary education; social sciences; social studies teacher education; sociology; Spanish; speech and rhetoric.

Hamilton College (NY)
African studies; American studies; anthropology; archeology; art; art history, criticism and conservation; Asian studies; Asian studies (East); biochemistry; biology/biological sciences; chemistry; classics and languages, literatures and linguistics; comparative literature; computer science; creative writing; dance; dramatic/theatre arts; economics; English; fine/studio arts; French; geology/earth science; German; history; history related; international relations and affairs; Latin; literature; mass communication/media; mathematics; medieval and renaissance studies; modern Greek; modern languages; molecular biology; music; neuroscience; philosophy; physics; physiological psychology/psychobiology; political science and government; psychology; public policy analysis; religious studies; Russian studies; sociology; Spanish; women's studies.

Hamline University
Anthropology; art; art history, criticism and conservation; Asian studies; Asian studies (East); athletic training; biochemistry; biology/biological sciences; business administration and management; chemistry; criminal justice/law enforcement administration; dramatic/theatre arts; economics; education; education (K-12); elementary education; English; environmental studies; European studies; European studies (Central and Eastern); fine/studio arts; French; German; health and physical education; health teacher education; history; international business/trade/commerce; international economics; international relations and affairs; Jewish/Judaic studies; kinesiology and exercise science; Latin American studies; legal assistant/paralegal; legal studies; mass communication/media; mathematics; music; music teacher education; occupational therapy; peace studies and conflict resolution; philosophy; physical education teaching and coaching; physical therapy; physics; political science and government; pre-dentistry studies; pre-law studies; pre-medical studies; pre-veterinary studies; psychology; public administration; religious studies; Russian studies; science teacher education; secondary education; social sciences; sociology; Spanish; speech/theater education; urban studies/affairs; women's studies.

Hampshire College
Acting; African studies; African-American/Black studies; agricultural economics; agriculture; American history; American Indian/Native American studies; American literature; American studies; anatomy; animal behavior and ethology; animal genetics; animal physiology; animal sciences; animation, interactive technology, video graphics and special effects; anthropology; applied mathematics; aquaculture; archeology; architectural history and criticism; architecture; area studies related; art; art history, criticism and conservation; artificial intelligence and robotics; Asian studies; Asian studies (East); Asian studies (South); Asian studies (Southeast); Asian-American studies; astronomy; astrophysics; behavioral sciences;

biochemistry; biological and physical sciences; biology/biological sciences; biophysics; botany/plant biology; business/managerial economics; Canadian studies; cell biology and histology; chemistry; child development; cinematography and film/video production; city/urban, community and regional planning; classics and languages, literatures and linguistics; cognitive psychology and psycholinguistics; cognitive science; community organization and advocacy; comparative literature; computer and information sciences; computer graphics; computer programming; computer science; creative writing; cultural studies; dance; design and applied arts related; developmental and child psychology; digital communication and media/multimedia; directing and theatrical production; dramatic/theatre arts; dramatic/theatre arts and stagecraft related; drawing; ecology; economics; education; elementary education; English; English literature (British and Commonwealth); environmental biology; environmental design/architecture; environmental health; environmental science; environmental studies; ethnic, cultural minority, and gender studies related; European history; European studies; European studies (Central and Eastern); European studies (Western); evolutionary biology; family and consumer economics related; film/cinema studies; film/video and photographic arts related; fine/studio arts; foods, nutrition, and wellness; forest sciences and biology; genetics; geochemistry; geography; geology/earth science; geophysics and seismology; health science; Hispanic-American, Puerto Rican, and Mexican-American/Chicano studies; history; history and philosophy of science and technology; history of philosophy; history related; human development and family studies; humanities; interdisciplinary studies; intermedia/multimedia; international business/trade/commerce; international economics; international relations and affairs; international/global studies; Islamic studies; jazz/jazz studies; Jewish/Judaic studies; journalism; kindergarten/preschool education; kinesiology and exercise science; labor and industrial relations; Latin American studies; legal studies; legal studies; liberal arts and sciences/liberal studies; linguistics; literature; marine biology and biological oceanography; mass communication/media; mathematics; medical microbiology and bacteriology; medieval and renaissance studies; molecular biology; multi-/interdisciplinary studies related; music; music history, literature, and theory; music theory and composition; musicology and ethnomusicology; natural sciences; Near and Middle Eastern studies; neuroscience; oceanography (chemical and physical); painting; peace studies and conflict resolution; philosophy; photography; physical sciences; physics; physiological psychology/psychobiology; plant genetics; political science and government; pre-law studies; pre-medical studies; pre-veterinary studies; psychology; public health; public policy analysis; radio and television; religious studies; Russian studies; science, technology and society; sculpture; secondary education; social and philosophical foundations of education; social sciences; sociobiology; sociology; soil chemistry and physics; soil microbiology; solar energy technology; statistics; telecommunications; theatre design and technology; theatre literature, history and

criticism; theatre/theatre arts management; Tibetan studies; urban studies/affairs; women's studies.

Hanover College
Anthropology; art; art history, criticism and conservation; biology/biological sciences; business administration and management; chemistry; classics and languages, literatures and linguistics; computer science; dramatic/theatre arts; economics; English; French; geology/earth science; German; history; international/global studies; Latin American studies; mass communication/media; mathematics; medieval and renaissance studies; music; philosophy; physical education teaching and coaching; physics; political science and government; psychology; sociology; Spanish; theology.

Harding University
Accounting; advertising; American studies; art teacher education; art therapy; athletic training; biochemistry; biology teacher education; biology/biological sciences; broadcast journalism; business administration and management; business/corporate communications; chemistry; Christian studies; clinical laboratory science/medical technology; communication and media related; communication disorders; communication/speech communication and rhetoric; computer and information sciences; computer engineering; computer science; corrections and criminal justice related; counselor education/school counseling and guidance; criminal justice/safety; design and applied arts related; dietetics; digital communication and media/multimedia; divinity/ministry; dramatic/theatre arts; early childhood education; economics; education (multiple levels); educational leadership and administration; elementary education; English; English/language arts teacher education; family and consumer sciences/home economics teacher education; family and consumer sciences/human sciences; fashion merchandising; fine/studio arts; French; general studies; graphic design; health teacher education; health/health care administration; history; human development and family studies related; human resources management; humanities; information technology; interior design; international business/trade/commerce; international relations and affairs; international/global studies; kindergarten/preschool education; kinesiology and exercise science; legal studies; marketing/marketing management; marriage and family therapy/counseling; mathematics; mathematics teacher education; middle school education; missionary studies and missiology; music; music teacher education; nursing (registered nurse training); painting; pastoral counseling and specialized ministries related; pastoral studies/counseling; physical education teaching and coaching; physics; political science and government; pre-dentistry studies; pre-medical studies; pre-veterinary studies; psychology; public administration; public relations/image management; reading teacher education; religious education; religious studies; sales, distribution and marketing; science teacher education; secondary education; social sciences; social studies teacher education; social work; Spanish; special education (early childhood); special education (specific learning disabilities); special education related; speech teacher educa-

tion; speech-language pathology; sport and fitness administration; theology; youth ministry.

Harvard University

African languages; African studies; African-American/Black studies; American studies; ancient Near Eastern and biblical languages; animal genetics; anthropology; applied mathematics; Arabic; archeology; architectural engineering; art; art history, criticism and conservation; artificial intelligence and robotics; Asian studies; Asian studies (East); Asian studies (South); Asian studies (Southeast); astronomy; astrophysics; atmospheric sciences and meteorology; behavioral sciences; biblical studies; biochemistry; biological and physical sciences; biology/biological sciences; biology/biotechnology laboratory technician; biomedical sciences; biomedical/medical engineering; biometry/biometrics; biophysics; cell biology and histology; chemical engineering; chemistry; Chinese; city/urban, community and regional planning; civil engineering; classics and languages, literatures and linguistics; cognitive psychology and psycholinguistics; cognitive science; comparative literature; computer and information sciences; computer engineering; computer engineering technology; computer graphics; computer programming; computer science; creative writing; cultural studies; dramatic/theatre arts; ecology; economics; electrical, electronics and communications engineering; engineering; engineering physics; engineering science; English; entomology; environmental biology; environmental design/architecture; environmental studies; environmental/environmental health engineering; European studies; European studies (Central and Eastern); evolutionary biology; film/cinema studies; fine/studio arts; fluid/thermal sciences; folklore; French; geochemistry; geological/geophysical engineering; geology/earth science; geophysics and seismology; German; Hebrew; Hispanic-American, Puerto Rican, and Mexican-American/Chicano studies; history; history and philosophy of science and technology; history of philosophy; human development and family studies; humanities; information science/studies; interdisciplinary studies; international economics; international relations and affairs; Islamic studies; Italian; Japanese; Jewish/Judaic studies; Latin; Latin American studies; liberal arts and sciences/liberal studies; linguistics; literature; marine biology and biological oceanography; materials engineering; materials science; mathematics; mathematics and computer science; mechanical engineering; medical microbiology and bacteriology; medieval and renaissance studies; metallurgical engineering; modern Greek; modern languages; molecular biology; music; music history, literature, and theory; natural resources/conservation; Near and Middle Eastern studies; neuroscience; nuclear physics; philosophy; physical sciences; physics; physiological psychology/psychobiology; political science and government; polymer chemistry; Portuguese; pre-dentistry studies; pre-law studies; pre-medical studies; pre-veterinary studies; psychology; public policy analysis; religious studies; romance languages; Russian; Russian studies; Scandinavian languages; Slavic languages; social sciences; sociobiology; sociology; Spanish; statistics; systems engineering; urban studies/affairs; western civilization; women's studies.

Harvey Mudd College

Biology/biological sciences; chemistry; computer science; engineering; mathematics; physics.

Haverford College

African studies; anthropology; archeology; art; art history, criticism and conservation; Asian studies (East); astronomy; biochemistry; biology/biological sciences; biophysics; chemistry; classics and languages, literatures and linguistics; comparative literature; computer science; econometrics and quantitative economics; economics; education; English; French; geology/earth science; German; history; Italian; Latin; Latin American studies; mathematics; modern Greek; music; neuroscience; peace studies and conflict resolution; philosophy; physics; political science and government; pre-law studies; pre-medical studies; pre-veterinary studies; psychology; religious studies; romance languages; Russian; sociology; Spanish; urban studies/affairs; women's studies.

Hendrix College

Accounting; anthropology; art; biology/biological sciences; business/managerial economics; chemistry; computer science; dramatic/theatre arts; economics; elementary education; English; French; German; history; interdisciplinary studies; international relations and affairs; mathematics; music; philosophy; physical education teaching and coaching; physics; political science and government; psychology; religious studies; sociology; Spanish.

Hillsdale College

Accounting; American studies; art; biology/biological sciences; business administration and management; chemistry; Christian studies; classics and languages, literatures and linguistics; comparative literature; computer science; drafting and design technology; dramatic/theatre arts; early childhood education; economics; education; education (K-12); elementary education; English; European studies; finance; French; German; history; interdisciplinary studies; international relations and affairs; kindergarten/preschool education; marketing/marketing management; mathematics; mathematics related; music; philosophy; physical education teaching and coaching; physics; political science and government; pre-dentistry studies; pre-medical studies; pre-veterinary studies; psychology; religious studies; secondary education; sociology; Spanish; speech and rhetoric.

Hiram College

Art; art history, criticism and conservation; biology/biological sciences; business administration and management; chemistry; classics and languages, literatures and linguistics; computer science; dramatic/theatre arts; economics; elementary education; English; environmental studies; fine/studio arts; French; German; health science; history; international business/trade/commerce; international economics; mass communication/media; mathematics; music; philosophy; physics; physiological psychology/psychobiology; political science and government; pre-dentistry studies; pre-law studies; pre-medical studies; pre-veterinary studies;

psychology; religious studies; secondary education; sociology; Spanish.

Hobart and William Smith Colleges

African studies; African-American/Black studies; American studies; ancient/classical Greek; anthropology; architecture; art; art history, criticism and conservation; Asian studies; biochemistry; biology/biological sciences; chemistry; Chinese; classics and languages, literatures and linguistics; comparative literature; computer science; dance; dramatic/theatre arts; economics; English; environmental studies; European studies; fine/studio arts; French; gay/lesbian studies; geology/earth science; history; interdisciplinary studies; international relations and affairs; Japanese; Latin; Latin American studies; liberal arts and sciences/liberal studies; mass communication/media; mathematics; medieval and renaissance studies; modern languages; music; philosophy; physics; political science and government; pre-dentistry studies; pre-law studies; pre-medical studies; pre-veterinary studies; psychology; public policy analysis; religious studies; Russian; Russian studies; sociology; Spanish; urban studies/affairs; women's studies.

Hood College

Art; biochemistry; biology/biological sciences; business administration and management; chemistry; communication and media related; computer and information sciences; economics; engineering; English; environmental studies; French; German; history; kindergarten/preschool education; Latin American studies; legal studies; mathematics; multi-/interdisciplinary studies related; music; philosophy; political science and government; psychology; religious studies; romance languages related; social work; sociology; Spanish; special education.

Hope College

Accounting; art history, criticism and conservation; art teacher education; athletic training; biology teacher education; biology/biological sciences; business administration and management; business/managerial economics; chemistry; chemistry teacher education; classics and languages, literatures and linguistics; communication/speech communication and rhetoric; computer science; dance; drama and dance teacher education; dramatic/theatre arts; economics; education (specific subject areas) related; elementary education; engineering; engineering physics; English; English/language arts teacher education; environmental studies; fine/studio arts; French; French language teacher education; geology/earth science; geophysics and seismology; German; German language teacher education; history; history teacher education; humanities; interdisciplinary studies; international/global studies; jazz/jazz studies; kinesiology and exercise science; Latin teacher education; mathematics; mathematics teacher education; multi-/interdisciplinary studies related; music; music performance; music teacher education; music theory and composition; nursing (registered nurse training); philosophy; physical education teaching and coaching; physics; physics teacher education; political science and government; psychology;

religious studies; science teacher education; secondary education; social studies teacher education; social work; sociology; Spanish; Spanish language teacher education; special education (emotionally disturbed); special education (specific learning disabilities).

Houghton College

Accounting; art; art teacher education; biblical studies; biological and physical sciences; biology/biological sciences; business administration and management; chemistry; clinical laboratory science/medical technology; computer science; creative writing; cultural studies; elementary education; English; French; health and physical education; history; humanities; international relations and affairs; liberal arts and sciences/liberal studies; literature; mathematics; music; music teacher education; music theory and composition; parks, recreation and leisure; pastoral studies/counseling; philosophy; physical education teaching and coaching; physics; piano and organ; political science and government; pre-dentistry studies; pre-law studies; pre-medical studies; pre-veterinary studies; psychology; religious education; religious studies; secondary education; sociology; Spanish; theology; violin, viola, guitar and other stringed instruments; voice and opera; wind/percussion instruments.

Huntingdon College

Accounting; American studies; applied art; art; art teacher education; athletic training; biology/biological sciences; business administration and management; business/managerial economics; cell biology and anatomical sciences related; chemistry; chemistry teacher education; computer and information sciences; computer graphics; computer science; counseling psychology; creative writing; dramatic/theatre arts; education; English; English/language arts teacher education; European studies; experimental psychology; history; history teacher education; interdisciplinary studies; international business/trade/commerce; international relations and affairs; kinesiology and exercise science; liberal arts and sciences/liberal studies; marketing/marketing management; mathematics; mathematics teacher education; multi-/interdisciplinary studies related; music; music teacher education; parks, recreation and leisure; physical education teaching and coaching; physical therapy; piano and organ; political science and government; public administration; religious education; religious studies; secondary education; Spanish; speech and rhetoric; sport and fitness administration; visual and performing arts related; voice and opera.

Huntington College

Accounting; art; art teacher education; biblical studies; biological and physical sciences; biology/biological sciences; broadcast journalism; business administration and management; business teacher education; business/managerial economics; chemistry; commercial and advertising art; communication/speech communication and rhetoric; computer science; digital communication and media/multimedia; divinity/ministry; dramatic/theatre arts; economics; education; elementary education; English; history; journalism; kinesiology and exercise science; mass communication/media; mathematics; music; music teacher education; natural

resources management and policy; parks, recreation and leisure; philosophy; physical education teaching and coaching; piano and organ; pre-dentistry studies; pre-law studies; pre-medical studies; pre-veterinary studies; psychology; public relations/image management; religious studies; science teacher education; secondary education; sociology; special education; theology; voice and opera.

Illinois College

Accounting; art; biology/biological sciences; business administration and management; business/managerial economics; chemistry; clinical laboratory science/medical technology; computer science; cytotechnology; dramatic/theatre arts; early childhood education; economics; education; education (K-12); elementary education; English; environmental studies; finance; French; German; history; information science/studies; interdisciplinary studies; international relations and affairs; liberal arts and sciences/liberal studies; management information systems; mass communication/media; mathematics; music; occupational therapy; philosophy; physical education teaching and coaching; physics; political science and government; pre-dentistry studies; pre-law studies; pre-medical studies; pre-veterinary studies; psychology; religious studies; secondary education; sociology; Spanish; speech and rhetoric.

Illinois Institute of Technology

Aerospace, aeronautical and astronautical engineering; applied mathematics; architectural engineering; architecture; biochemistry/biophysics and molecular biology; biology/biological sciences; biomedical/medical engineering; biophysics; business/commerce; chemical engineering; chemistry; civil engineering; communication and journalism related; computer engineering; computer science; design and visual communications; electrical, electronics and communications engineering; engineering/industrial management; environmental/environmental health engineering; industrial technology; information science/studies; information technology; manufacturing technology; materials engineering; mechanical engineering; metallurgical engineering; multi-/interdisciplinary studies related; physics; political science and government; psychology; technical and business writing.

Illinois Wesleyan University

Accounting; American studies; area studies related; art; arts management; Asian studies; biology teacher education; biology/biological sciences; business administration and management; chemistry; chemistry teacher education; classics and languages, literatures and linguistics; computer science; dramatic/theatre arts; economics; education; elementary education; English; English/language arts teacher education; environmental studies; European studies (Western); French; French language teacher education; German; history; history teacher education; insurance; interdisciplinary studies; international business/trade/commerce; international/global studies; Latin American studies; mathematics; mathematics teacher education; music; music teacher education; nursing (registered nurse training); philosophy; physics; physics teacher education; piano and organ;

political science and government; psychology; religious studies; science teacher education; secondary education; sociology; Spanish; Spanish language teacher education; violin, viola, guitar and other stringed instruments; visual and performing arts related; voice and opera; wind/percussion instruments; women's studies.

Iowa State University of Science and Technology

Accounting; advertising; aerospace, aeronautical and astronautical engineering; agricultural business and management; agricultural mechanization; agricultural teacher education; agricultural/biological engineering and bioengineering; agriculture; agronomy and crop science; animal sciences; anthropology; apparel and textiles; applied horticulture; architecture; art; atmospheric sciences and meteorology; biochemistry; biology/biological sciences; biophysics; botany/plant biology; business administration and management; business, management, and marketing related; chemical engineering; chemistry; city/urban, community and regional planning; civil engineering; commercial and advertising art; computer and information sciences; computer engineering; dairy science; design and visual communications; dietetics; dramatic/theatre arts; early childhood education; ecology; economics; education; electrical, electronics and communications engineering; elementary education; engineering; engineering related; engineering science; English; entomology; entrepreneurship; environmental studies; family and community services; family and consumer economics related; family and consumer sciences/home economics teacher education; family and consumer sciences/human sciences; family resource management; farm and ranch management; fashion/apparel design; finance; fish/game management; food services technology; foods, nutrition, and wellness; forestry; French; genetics; geology/earth science; German; graphic design; health and physical education; health teacher education; history; horticultural science; hotel/motel administration; housing and human environments; industrial engineering; interdisciplinary studies; interior design; international agriculture; international business/trade/commerce; international relations and affairs; journalism; landscape architecture; liberal arts and sciences/liberal studies; linguistics; logistics and materials management; management information systems; marketing/marketing management; mass communication/media; materials engineering; mathematics; mechanical engineering; medical illustration; microbiology; multi-/interdisciplinary studies related; music; music teacher education; natural resources management and policy; operations management; ornamental horticulture; philosophy; physics; plant protection and integrated pest management; political science and government; pre-dentistry studies; pre-law studies; pre-medical studies; pre-veterinary studies; psychology; public administration; religious studies; Russian studies; secondary education; sociology; Spanish; special products marketing; speech and rhetoric; statistics; technical and business writing; trade and industrial teacher education; visual and performing arts; women's studies; zoology/animal biology.

Ithaca College

Accounting; acting; anthropology; applied economics; applied mathematics; art; art history, criticism and conservation; art teacher education; arts management; athletic training; audiology and speech-language pathology; biochemistry; biology teacher education; biology/biological sciences; broadcast journalism; business administration and management; business/commerce; business/managerial economics; chemistry; chemistry teacher education; cinematography and film/video production; communication and journalism related; computer and information sciences; computer science; creative writing; dance; dramatic/theatre arts; economics; education (K-12); education (multiple levels); educational/instructional media design; English; English/language arts teacher education; environmental studies; film/cinema studies; finance; fine/studio arts; foods, nutrition, and wellness; French; French language teacher education; German; German language teacher education; gerontology; health and physical education; health and physical education related; health teacher education; health/health care administration; health/medical preparatory programs related; history; history teacher education; hospital and health care facilities administration; industrial and organizational psychology; interdisciplinary studies; international business/trade/commerce; jazz/jazz studies; journalism; kinesiology and exercise science; labor and industrial relations; liberal arts and sciences/liberal studies; marketing research; marketing/marketing management; mass communication/media; mathematics; mathematics and computer science; mathematics teacher education; middle school education; multi-/interdisciplinary studies related; music; music performance; music teacher education; music theory and composition; occupational therapy; parks, recreation and leisure; philosophy; photography; physical education teaching and coaching; physical therapy; physics; physics teacher education; piano and organ; political science and government; pre-law studies; pre-medical studies; psychology; public health education and promotion; public relations/image management; radio and television; rehabilitation therapy; science teacher education; secondary education; social sciences; social studies teacher education; sociology; Spanish; Spanish language teacher education; special education (speech or language impaired); speech and rhetoric; sport and fitness administration; telecommunications; theatre design and technology; therapeutic recreation; visual and performing arts; voice and opera.

James Madison University

Accounting; anthropology; art; art history, criticism and conservation; biology/biological sciences; business administration and management; business teacher education; business/managerial economics; chemistry; communication/speech communication and rhetoric; community health services counseling; computer and information sciences; dramatic/theatre arts; economics; English; finance; foods, nutrition, and wellness; foreign languages and literatures; geography; geology/earth science; health and physical education; history; hospitality administration; information science/studies; international business/trade/commerce; international relations and affairs; liberal arts and

sciences/liberal studies; marketing/marketing management; mathematics; music performance; nursing (registered nurse training); philosophy and religious studies related; physics; political science and government; psychology; public administration; science, technology and society; social sciences; social work; sociology; speech-language pathology; technical and business writing.

John Brown University

Accounting; art; athletic training; biblical studies; biochemistry; biology/biological sciences; broadcast journalism; business administration and management; business teacher education; chemistry; clinical laboratory science/medical technology; commercial and advertising art; computer graphics; construction engineering; construction management; divinity/ministry; education; electrical, electronics and communications engineering; elementary education; engineering; engineering technology; engineering/industrial management; English; English as a second/foreign language (teaching); environmental science; environmental studies; health teacher education; health/health care administration; history; interdisciplinary studies; international business/trade/commerce; international relations and affairs; journalism; kindergarten/preschool education; kinesiology and exercise science; liberal arts and sciences/liberal studies; mass communication/media; mathematics; mechanical engineering; middle school education; missionary studies and missiology; music; music teacher education; parks, recreation and leisure facilities management; pastoral studies/counseling; physical education teaching and coaching; piano and organ; pre-law studies; pre-medical studies; pre-veterinary studies; psychology; public relations/image management; radio and television; religious education; religious studies; secondary education; social sciences; special education; theology; voice and opera.

John Carroll University

Accounting; art history, criticism and conservation; Asian studies; Asian studies (East); biological and physical sciences; biology/biological sciences; business administration and management; chemistry; classics and languages, literatures and linguistics; computer science; economics; education; education (K-12); elementary education; engineering physics; English; environmental studies; finance; French; German; gerontology; history; humanities; interdisciplinary studies; international economics; international relations and affairs; kindergarten/preschool education; Latin; literature; marketing/marketing management; mass communication/media; mathematics; modern Greek; neuroscience; philosophy; physical education teaching and coaching; physics; political science and government; pre-dentistry studies; pre-law studies; pre-medical studies; pre-veterinary studies; psychology; public administration; religious education; religious studies; secondary education; sociology; Spanish; special education.

The Johns Hopkins University

American studies; anthropology; applied mathematics; art history, criticism and conservation; Asian studies (East); behavioral sciences;

biological and physical sciences; biology/biological sciences; biomedical/medical engineering; biophysics; business/commerce; chemical engineering; chemistry; civil engineering; classics and languages, literatures and linguistics; cognitive psychology and psycholinguistics; computer and information sciences; computer engineering; creative writing; economics; electrical, electronics and communications engineering; electroneurodiagnostic/electroencephalographic technology; engineering; engineering mechanics; English; environmental studies; environmental/environmental health engineering; film/cinema studies; French; geography; geology/earth science; German; history; history and philosophy of science and technology; industrial engineering; interdisciplinary studies; international relations and affairs; Italian; Latin American studies; liberal arts and sciences and humanities related; liberal arts and sciences/liberal studies; literature; materials engineering; materials science; mathematics; mechanical engineering; music; music performance; music teacher education; music theory and composition; natural sciences; Near and Middle Eastern studies; neuroscience; nursing (registered nurse training); philosophy; physics; physiological psychology/psychobiology; political science and government; psychology; public administration; public health; social sciences; sociology; Spanish.

Juniata College

Accounting; anthropology; art history, criticism and conservation; biochemistry; biological and physical sciences; biology teacher education; biology/biological sciences; botany/plant biology; business administration and management; business/commerce; cell biology and histology; chemistry; chemistry teacher education; communication and journalism related; communication/speech communication and rhetoric; computer and information sciences; criminal justice/safety; criminology; early childhood education; ecology; economics; education; education (multiple levels); education (specific subject areas) related; elementary education; engineering; engineering physics; English; English/language arts teacher education; environmental science; environmental studies; finance; fine/studio arts; foreign language teacher education; foreign languages and literatures; French; French language teacher education; geology/earth science; German; German language teacher education; health communication; health/medical preparatory programs related; history; human resources management; humanities; information resources management; information technology; interdisciplinary studies; international business/trade/commerce; international relations and affairs; international/global studies; kindergarten/preschool education; liberal arts and sciences/liberal studies; marine biology and biological oceanography; marketing/marketing management; mathematics; mathematics teacher education; medical microbiology and bacteriology; microbiology; molecular biology; museum studies; natural sciences; peace studies and conflict resolution; philosophy; philosophy and religious studies related; physical sciences; physics; physics teacher education; political science and government; pre-dentistry studies; pre-law studies; pre-medical studies; pre-pharmacy studies; pre-theology/pre-ministerial studies; pre-veterinary studies; professional studies; psychology; public administration; religious studies; Russian; science teacher education; secondary education; social sciences; social studies teacher education; social work; sociology; Spanish; Spanish language teacher education; special education; special education (early childhood); special education related; zoology/animal biology.

Kalamazoo College

Anthropology; art; art history, criticism and conservation; biology/biological sciences; business/managerial economics; chemistry; classics and languages, literatures and linguistics; computer science; dramatic/theatre arts; English; French; German; health science; history; interdisciplinary studies; mathematics; music; philosophy; physics; political science and government; psychology; religious studies; sociology; Spanish.

Kansas State University

Accounting; aeronautics/aviation/aerospace science and technology; agricultural and food products processing; agricultural business and management; agricultural economics; agricultural mechanization; agricultural/biological engineering and bioengineering; agronomy and crop science; aircraft powerplant technology; airframe mechanics and aircraft maintenance technology; airline pilot and flight crew; animal sciences; anthropology; apparel and textiles; architectural engineering; architecture; art; athletic training; biochemistry; biology/biological sciences; business administration and management; chemical engineering; chemistry; child development; civil engineering; civil engineering technology; clinical laboratory science/medical technology; communication disorders; communication/speech communication and rhetoric; computer and information sciences; computer engineering; computer engineering technology; computer programming; computer systems analysis; dietetics; dramatic/theatre arts; economics; electrical, electronic and communications engineering technology; electrical, electronics and communications engineering; elementary education; English; environmental engineering technology; finance; food science; foods, nutrition, and wellness; foreign languages and literatures; geography; geology/earth science; health science; history; horticultural science; hotel/motel administration; human development and family studies; human ecology; humanities; industrial engineering; industrial technology; information science/studies; interdisciplinary studies; interior architecture; interior design; journalism; kinesiology and exercise science; landscape architecture; marketing/marketing management; mathematics; mechanical engineering; mechanical engineering/mechanical technology; music; music teacher education; nuclear engineering; parks, recreation and leisure facilities management; philosophy; physical sciences; physics; political science and government; pre-dentistry studies; pre-medical studies; pre-veterinary studies; psychology; secondary education; social sciences; social work; sociology; statistics; survey technology; wildlife biology; women's studies.

Kentucky Mountain Bible College

Mass communication/media; missionary studies and missiology; pre-theology/pre-ministerial studies; religious education; religious studies.

Kenyon College

African studies; African-American/Black studies; American studies; ancient/classical Greek; anthropology; art; art history, criticism and conservation; Asian studies; biochemistry; biology/biological sciences; chemistry; classics and languages, literatures and linguistics; creative writing; dance; dramatic/theatre arts; economics; English; environmental studies; ethnic, cultural minority, and gender studies related; fine/studio arts; foreign languages and literatures; French; German; history; humanities; interdisciplinary studies; international relations and affairs; international/global studies; Latin; legal studies; literature; mathematics; modern Greek; modern languages; molecular biology; multi-/interdisciplinary studies related; music; natural sciences; neuroscience; philosophy; physics; political science and government; pre-dentistry studies; pre-law studies; pre-medical studies; pre-veterinary studies; psychology; public policy analysis; religious studies; romance languages; sociology; Spanish; statistics; women's studies.

Kettering University

Accounting; accounting and finance; applied mathematics; biomedical/medical engineering; business administration and management; chemistry; computer engineering; computer science; computer/information technology services administration related; electrical, electronics and communications engineering; engineering/industrial management; finance; industrial engineering; information science/studies; management information systems; marketing/marketing management; mechanical engineering; operations management; physics; polymer/plastics engineering; statistics.

King College

Accounting; American studies; behavioral sciences; biblical studies; biochemistry; biological and physical sciences; biological specializations related; biology teacher education; biology/biological sciences; biophysics; business administration and management; chemistry; chemistry teacher education; clinical laboratory science/medical technology; communication/speech communication and rhetoric; creative writing; economics; education; elementary education; English; English/language arts teacher education; fine/studio arts; French; French language teacher education; health professions related; history; history teacher education; information science/studies; international business/trade/commerce; kindergarten/preschool education; mathematics; mathematics and computer science; mathematics teacher education; middle school education; modern languages; music; nursing (registered nurse training); physics; physics teacher education; political science and government; pre-law studies; pre-medical studies; pre-pharmacy studies; pre-veterinary studies; psychology; religious studies; secondary education; Spanish; Spanish language teacher education; speech/theater education.

Knox College

African-American/Black studies; agriculture; American studies; anthropology; art; art history, criticism and conservation; biochemistry; biology/biological sciences; chemistry; classics and languages, literatures and linguistics; computer and information sciences; creative writing; dramatic/theatre arts; economics; education; English; environmental studies; foreign languages and literatures; French; German; history; international relations and affairs; mathematics; multi-/interdisciplinary studies related; music; philosophy; physics; political science and government; psychology; Russian; Russian studies; sociology; Spanish; women's studies.

Lafayette College

American studies; anthropology; art; art history, criticism and conservation; biochemistry; biology/biological sciences; business/managerial economics; chemical engineering; chemistry; civil engineering; computer science; economics; electrical, electronics and communications engineering; engineering; English; environmental/environmental health engineering; fine/studio arts; French; geology/earth science; German; history; international relations and affairs; mathematics; mechanical engineering; music; music history, literature, and theory; philosophy; physics; political science and government; psychology; religious studies; Russian studies; sociology; Spanish.

Lake Forest College

American studies; anthropology; art history, criticism and conservation; Asian studies; biology/biological sciences; business/managerial economics; chemistry; communication/speech communication and rhetoric; computer science; economics; education; elementary education; English; environmental studies; finance; fine/studio arts; French; history; international relations and affairs; Latin American studies; mathematics; music; philosophy; physics; political science and government; pre-dentistry studies; pre-law studies; pre-medical studies; pre-veterinary studies; psychology; secondary education; sociology; Spanish.

Lawrence Technological University

Architecture; business administration and management; chemical technology; chemistry; chemistry related; civil engineering; communications technology; computer engineering; computer science; construction engineering technology; construction management; electrical and electronic engineering technologies related; electrical, electronic and communications engineering technology; electrical, electronics and communications engineering; engineering technology; engineering/industrial management; environmental design/architecture; general studies; humanities; illustration; industrial technology; information technology; interior architecture; manufacturing technology; mathematics; mathematics and computer science; mechanical engineering; mechanical engineering/mechanical technology; physics; physics related; psychology.

Lawrence University

Ancient/classical Greek; anthropology; archeology; art history, criticism and conservation; art teacher education; Asian studies (East); biochemistry; biology/biological sciences; chemistry; Chinese; classics and classical languages related; classics and languages, literatures and linguistics; cognitive psychology and psycholinguistics; cognitive science; computer science; dramatic/theatre arts; ecology; economics; English; environmental studies; ethnic, cultural minority, and gender studies related; fine/studio arts; French; geology/earth science; German; history; international economics; international relations and affairs; Japanese; Latin; linguistics; mathematics; mathematics and computer science; music; music pedagogy; music performance; music teacher education; music theory and composition; neuroscience; philosophy; physics; piano and organ; political science and government; pre-dentistry studies; pre-law studies; pre-medical studies; pre-veterinary studies; psychology; religious studies; Russian; Russian studies; secondary education; Slavic studies; social psychology; Spanish; violin, viola, guitar and other stringed instruments; voice and opera; wind/percussion instruments.

Lebanon Valley College

Accounting; actuarial science; American studies; art history, criticism and conservation; biochemistry; biology teacher education; biology/biological sciences; business administration and management; chemistry; chemistry teacher education; clinical/medical laboratory science and allied professions related; computer science; digital communication and media/multimedia; economics; elementary education; English; English/language arts teacher education; fine/studio arts; French; French language teacher education; general studies; German; German language teacher education; health professions related; health services/allied health/health sciences; health/health care administration; history; liberal arts and sciences/liberal studies; mathematics; mathematics teacher education; multi-/interdisciplinary studies related; music management and merchandising; music performance; music related; music teacher education; philosophy; physics; physics teacher education; physiological psychology/psychobiology; political science and government; pre-law studies; pre-medical studies; pre-veterinary studies; psychology; recording arts technology; religious studies; science teacher education; secondary education; social studies teacher education; sociology; Spanish; Spanish language teacher education.

Lehigh University

Accounting; American studies; ancient/classical Greek; anthropology; architecture; astrophysics; bilingual and multilingual education; biochemistry; biological and biomedical sciences related; biological and physical sciences; biology/biological sciences; biomedical/medical engineering; business administration and management; business/commerce; business/managerial economics; chemical engineering; chemistry; chemistry related; civil engineering; classics and languages, literatures and linguistics; communication and journalism related; computer and information sciences and support services related; computer engineering; computer science; design and applied arts related; ecology; education; electrical, electronics and communications engineering; engineer-

ing mechanics; engineering physics; engineering related; environmental studies; finance; fine arts related; French; geological and earth sciences/geosciences related; German; health/medical preparatory programs related; history; humanities; industrial engineering; information science/studies; international relations and affairs; Japanese; journalism; Latin; management information systems; marketing/marketing management; materials engineering; mathematics; mechanical engineering; molecular biology; multi-/interdisciplinary studies related; music; philosophy; physical and theoretical chemistry; physics; political science and government; pre-medical studies; psychology; religious studies; Russian; Russian studies; science technologies related; social sciences; social sciences related; sociology; Spanish; statistics; urban studies/affairs; visual and performing arts.

LeTourneau University

Accounting; airframe mechanics and aircraft maintenance technology; airline pilot and flight crew; avionics maintenance technology; biblical studies; biology/biological sciences; biomedical/medical engineering; business administration and management; chemistry; computer engineering; computer engineering technology; computer science; drafting and design technology; electrical, electronic and communications engineering technology; electrical, electronics and communications engineering; elementary education; engineering; engineering technology; English; finance; history; information science/studies; interdisciplinary studies; international business/trade/commerce; management information systems; marketing/marketing management; mathematics; mechanical engineering; mechanical engineering/mechanical technology; missionary studies and missiology; natural sciences; physical education teaching and coaching; pre-dentistry studies; pre-law studies; pre-medical studies; pre-veterinary studies; psychology; religious studies; secondary education; sport and fitness administration; welding technology.

Lewis & Clark College

Anthropology; art; Asian studies (East); biochemistry; biology/biological sciences; chemistry; communication/speech communication and rhetoric; computer science; dramatic/theatre arts; economics; English; environmental studies; foreign languages and literatures; French; German; Hispanic-American, Puerto Rican, and Mexican-American/Chicano studies; history; international relations and affairs; mathematics; modern languages; music; philosophy; physics; political science and government; pre-engineering; psychology; religious studies; sociology; Spanish.

Lincoln Memorial University

Accounting; art; athletic training; biology teacher education; biology/biological sciences; business administration and management; business teacher education; business/managerial economics; chemistry; chemistry teacher education; clinical laboratory science/medical technology; computer and information sciences; criminal justice/law enforcement administration; economics; education; elementary education; English; environmental studies; finance; fish/game management; health and physical

education; health teacher education; history; history teacher education; humanities; kindergarten/preschool education; kinesiology and exercise science; liberal arts and sciences/liberal studies; marketing/marketing management; mass communication/media; mathematics; mathematics teacher education; nursing (registered nurse training); physical education teaching and coaching; pre-law studies; pre-medical studies; pre-veterinary studies; psychology; science teacher education; secondary education; social science teacher education; social work; veterinary sciences; veterinary technology; wildlife and wildlands science and management.

Linfield College

Accounting; anthropology; area, ethnic, cultural, and gender studies related; art; athletic training; biology/biological sciences; business/commerce; chemistry; communication/speech communication and rhetoric; computer science; creative writing; dramatic/theatre arts; economics; elementary education; English; environmental studies; finance; French; German; health and physical education; history; international business/trade/commerce; Japanese; kinesiology and exercise science; mathematics; music; philosophy; physical sciences; physics; political science and government; psychology; religious studies; sociology; Spanish.

Lipscomb University

Accounting; American government and politics; American studies; ancient Near Eastern and biblical languages; art; athletic training; biblical studies; biochemistry; biology teacher education; biology/biological sciences; business administration and management; business/managerial economics; chemistry; commercial and advertising art; computer science; dietetics; divinity/ministry; education; elementary education; engineering; engineering science; English; environmental studies; family and consumer economics related; family and consumer sciences/human sciences; fashion merchandising; finance; fine/studio arts; French; French language teacher education; German; health teacher education; history; information science/studies; kinesiology and exercise science; liberal arts and sciences/liberal studies; marketing/marketing management; mass communication/media; mathematics; middle school education; music; music teacher education; nursing (registered nurse training); philosophy; physical education teaching and coaching; physics; piano and organ; political science and government; pre-dentistry studies; pre-law studies; pre-medical studies; pre-veterinary studies; psychology; public administration; public relations/image management; secondary education; social work; Spanish; special products marketing; speech and rhetoric; theology; urban studies/affairs; violin, viola, guitar and other stringed instruments; voice and opera; wind/percussion instruments.

List College, Jewish Theological Seminary of America

Ancient Near Eastern and biblical languages; biblical studies; Hebrew; history; Jewish/Judaic studies; literature; museum studies; music; philosophy; religious education; religious studies; talmudic studies.

Louisiana College

Accounting; adult and continuing education; advertising; art; art teacher education; athletic training; biology/biological sciences; broadcast journalism; business administration and management; business teacher education; chemistry; clinical laboratory science/medical technology; commercial and advertising art; criminal justice/law enforcement administration; criminal justice/police science; dramatic/theatre arts; economics; elementary education; English; family and consumer economics related; finance; fine/studio arts; French; health teacher education; history; interdisciplinary studies; journalism; kindergarten/preschool education; kinesiology and exercise science; liberal arts and sciences/liberal studies; marketing/marketing management; mass communication/media; mathematics; modern languages; music; music teacher education; nursing (registered nurse training); philosophy; physical education teaching and coaching; physics; piano and organ; pre-law studies; psychology; public administration; religious education; religious studies; religious/sacred music; science teacher education; secondary education; social work; sociology; Spanish; special education; speech and rhetoric; theology; voice and opera.

Louisiana State University and Agricultural and Mechanical College

Accounting; agricultural business and management; animal sciences; anthropology; architecture; audiology and speech-language pathology; biochemistry; biology/biological sciences; biomedical/medical engineering; biotechnology; business administration and management; business/managerial economics; chemical engineering; chemistry; civil engineering; computer engineering; computer science; construction management; dramatic/theatre arts; early childhood education; economics; education (specific subject areas) related; electrical, electronics and communications engineering; elementary education; English; environmental science; environmental/environmental health engineering; family and consumer sciences/human sciences; fashion merchandising; finance; fine/studio arts; food science; forest/forest resources management; French; general studies; geography; geology/earth science; German; history; industrial engineering; interior architecture; international business/trade/commerce; international/global studies; landscape architecture; Latin; liberal arts and sciences/liberal studies; management science; marketing/marketing management; mass communication/media; mathematics; mechanical engineering; microbiology; music; music performance; music teacher education; nutrition sciences; petroleum engineering; philosophy; physical education teaching and coaching; physics; plant sciences; political science and government; psychology; Russian studies; secondary education; sociology; Spanish; speech and rhetoric; wildlife and wildlands science and management; women's studies.

Louisiana Tech University

Accounting; aeronautics/aviation/aerospace science and technology; agricultural business and management; agricultural teacher education;

animal sciences; architecture; art; art teacher education; audiology and speech-language pathology; aviation/airway management; biology teacher education; biology/biological sciences; biomedical/medical engineering; business administration and management; business teacher education; business/managerial economics; chemical engineering; chemistry; chemistry teacher education; child development; civil engineering; clinical laboratory science/medical technology; commercial and advertising art; computer science; construction engineering technology; consumer economics; dietetics; early childhood education; education (specific subject areas) related; electrical, electronic and communications engineering technology; electrical, electronics and communications engineering; elementary education; English; English/language arts teacher education; environmental studies; family and consumer sciences/home economics teacher education; finance; forestry; French; French language teacher education; general studies; geography; geology/earth science; health and physical education; health information/medical records administration; health information/medical records technology; history; human resources management; industrial engineering; interior architecture; journalism; kindergarten/preschool education; management information systems; management science; marketing/marketing management; mathematics; mathematics teacher education; mechanical engineering; middle school education; music; music performance; music teacher education; natural resources/conservation; nursing (registered nurse training); operations management; photography; physical education teaching and coaching; physics; physics teacher education; plant sciences; political science and government; psychology; social studies teacher education; sociology; Spanish; special education; special education (speech or language impaired); speech and rhetoric; speech teacher education.

Loyola College in Maryland

Accounting; applied mathematics; art; biology/biological sciences; business/commerce; chemistry; classics and languages, literatures and linguistics; communication/speech communication and rhetoric; computer and information sciences; creative writing; economics; education; electrical, electronics and communications engineering; elementary education; engineering; English; finance; French; German; history; interdisciplinary studies; international business/trade/commerce; mathematics; philosophy; physics; political science and government; psychology; religious studies; sociology; Spanish; special education; speech-language pathology.

Loyola Marymount University

Accounting; African-American/Black studies; art history, criticism and conservation; Asian-American studies; biochemistry; biology/biological sciences; business administration and management; chemistry; cinematography and film/video production; civil engineering; classics and languages, literatures and linguistics; computer engineering; computer science; conducting; dance; dramatic/theatre arts; economics; electrical, electronics and communications engineering; engineering physics; English; European studies; fine/studio arts;

French; Hispanic-American, Puerto Rican, and Mexican-American/Chicano studies; history; humanities; international economics; Latin; liberal arts and sciences/liberal studies; mass communication/media; mathematics; mechanical engineering; modern Greek; music; music history, literature, and theory; music theory and composition; musicology and ethnomusicology; natural sciences; philosophy; physics; playwriting and screenwriting; political science and government; psychology; sociology; Spanish; theology; urban studies/affairs; voice and opera.

Loyola University Chicago

Accounting; ancient/classical Greek; anthropology; art; art history, criticism and conservation; biochemistry; biology/biological sciences; business administration and management; business/managerial economics; ceramic arts and ceramics; chemistry; classics and languages, literatures and linguistics; communication and journalism related; communication/speech communication and rhetoric; computer science; criminal justice/safety; dramatic/theatre arts; economics; elementary education; English; environmental studies; finance; fine arts related; foods, nutrition, and wellness; French; German; history; human resources management; humanities; information science/studies; international relations and affairs; Italian; journalism; kindergarten/preschool education; Latin; management information systems; marketing/marketing management; mathematics; mathematics and computer science; metal and jewelry arts; music; natural sciences; nursing (registered nurse training); operations management; philosophy; photography; physics; political science and government; pre-dentistry studies; pre-law studies; pre-medical studies; pre-theology/pre-ministerial studies; pre-veterinary studies; psychology; psychology related; social psychology; social work; sociology; Spanish; special education; statistics; theology.

Loyola University New Orleans

Accounting; art; behavioral sciences; biology/biological sciences; business administration and management; business/managerial economics; chemistry; classics and languages, literatures and linguistics; commercial and advertising art; communication/speech communication and rhetoric; computer and information sciences; creative writing; criminal justice/safety; dramatic/theatre arts; economics; education; elementary education; English; finance; forensic science and technology; French; general studies; German; history; humanities; information science/studies; international business/trade/commerce; jazz/jazz studies; marketing/marketing management; mathematics; music; music management and merchandising; music performance; music teacher education; music theory and composition; nursing (registered nurse training); philosophy; physics; piano and organ; political science and government; psychology; religious education; religious studies; religious/sacred music; Russian; social sciences; sociology; Spanish; visual and performing arts.

Luther College

Accounting; African-American/Black studies; ancient Near Eastern and biblical languages;

ancient/classical Greek; anthropology; art; arts management; biology/biological sciences; business administration and management; chemistry; classics and languages, literatures and linguistics; communication and journalism related; computer management; computer science; dance; economics; elementary education; English; French; German; health and physical education; health teacher education; history; interdisciplinary studies; international relations and affairs; Latin; management information systems; mathematics; music; nursing (registered nurse training); philosophy; physical education teaching and coaching; physics; physiological psychology/psychobiology; political science and government; psychology; religious studies; Scandinavian studies; social work; sociology; Spanish; sport and fitness administration; statistics; theatre/theatre arts management.

Lycoming College

Accounting; actuarial science; American studies; anthropology; archeology; art; art history, criticism and conservation; art teacher education; astronomy; biology/biological sciences; business administration and management; chemistry; clinical laboratory science/medical technology; commercial and advertising art; computer science; creative writing; criminal justice/law enforcement administration; dramatic/theatre arts; economics; education; elementary education; English; finance; fine/studio arts; French; German; history; interdisciplinary studies; international business/trade/commerce; international relations and affairs; literature; marketing/marketing management; mass communication/media; mathematics; music; music teacher education; philosophy; physics; political science and government; pre-dentistry studies; pre-law studies; pre-medical studies; pre-veterinary studies; psychology; religious studies; secondary education; sociology; Spanish; special education related.

Lyon College

Accounting; art; biology/biological sciences; business administration and management; chemistry; computer science; dramatic/theatre arts; economics; English; environmental studies; history; mathematics; music; philosophy and religious studies related; political science and government; psychology; Spanish.

Macalester College

Anthropology; art history, criticism and conservation; Asian studies; biology/biological sciences; chemistry; classics and languages, literatures and linguistics; communication/speech communication and rhetoric; computer science; dramatic/theatre arts; economics; English; environmental studies; fine/studio arts; French; geography; geology/earth science; history; humanities; interdisciplinary studies; international relations and affairs; Latin; Latin American studies; linguistics; mathematics; modern Greek; music; neuroscience; philosophy; physics; political science and government; psychology; religious studies; Russian; Russian studies; sociology; Spanish; urban studies/affairs; women's studies.

Maharishi University of Management

Ayurvedic medicine; business administration and management; cinematography and film/video production; computer science; elementary education; English; environmental studies; fine/studio arts; mathematics; secondary education.

Marietta College

Accounting; art; athletic training; biochemistry; biology/biological sciences; business administration and management; business/corporate communications; chemistry; commercial and advertising art; communication/speech communication and rhetoric; computer science; dramatic/theatre arts; economics; education; elementary education; English; environmental science; environmental studies; fine/studio arts; geology/earth science; graphic design; history; human resources management; information science/studies; international business/trade/commerce; journalism; liberal arts and sciences/liberal studies; marketing/marketing management; mathematics; music; petroleum engineering; philosophy; physics; political science and government; psychology; public relations, advertising, and applied communication related; radio and television; secondary education; Spanish; speech and rhetoric.

Marquette University

Accounting; advertising; African-American/Black studies; anthropology; athletic training; audiology and speech-language pathology; biochemistry; biology/biological sciences; biomedical sciences; biomedical/medical engineering; broadcast journalism; business administration and management; business/managerial economics; chemistry; civil engineering; classics and languages, literatures and linguistics; clinical/medical laboratory technology; communication and journalism related; communication/speech communication and rhetoric; computational mathematics; computer engineering; computer science; creative writing; criminology; dental hygiene; dramatic/theatre arts; economics; education; education (specific subject areas) related; electrical, electronics and communications engineering; elementary education; engineering; engineering related; English; English/language arts teacher education; environmental/environmental health engineering; finance; foreign language teacher education; foreign languages related; French; German; history; history of philosophy; history related; human resources management; industrial engineering; information science/studies; intercultural/multicultural and diversity studies; interdisciplinary studies; international business/trade/commerce; international relations and affairs; international/global studies; journalism; kinesiology and exercise science; management information systems; marketing/marketing management; mass communication/media; mathematics; mathematics teacher education; mechanical engineering; middle school education; molecular biology; multi-/interdisciplinary studies related; nursing (registered nurse training); philosophy; physical therapy; physician assistant; physics; political science and government; pre-dentistry studies; pre-law studies; pre-medical studies; psychology; public relations/image management; religious studies; science teacher education; secondary education; social science teacher education; social studies teacher education; social work; sociology; Spanish; speech and rhetoric; statistics; women's studies.

Maryland Institute College of Art

Art; art teacher education; ceramic arts and ceramics; drawing; fiber, textile and weaving arts; film/video and photographic arts related; fine/studio arts; graphic design; illustration; interior design; intermedia/multimedia; painting; photography; printmaking; sculpture; visual and performing arts.

Maryville College

American Sign Language (ASL); art teacher education; atomic/molecular physics; biochemistry; biology teacher education; biology/biological sciences; business administration and management; chemistry; chemistry teacher education; computer and information sciences related; computer science; developmental and child psychology; dramatic/theatre arts; economics; education; engineering; English; English as a second/foreign language (teaching); English/language arts teacher education; environmental studies; fine/studio arts; health and physical education; health teacher education; history; history teacher education; international business/trade/commerce; international relations and affairs; mathematics; mathematics and computer science; mathematics teacher education; multi-/interdisciplinary studies related; music performance; music teacher education; nursing (registered nurse training); parks, recreation and leisure; physical education teaching and coaching; physics teacher education; piano and organ; political science and government; psychology; religious studies; sign language interpretation and translation; social studies teacher education; sociology; Spanish; Spanish language teacher education; technical and business writing; voice and opera; wind/percussion instruments.

Maryville University of Saint Louis

Accounting; accounting related; actuarial science; applied mathematics; art teacher education; biological and physical sciences; biology teacher education; biology/biological sciences; business administration and management; business/commerce; chemistry; chemistry teacher education; clinical laboratory science/medical technology; computer science; criminology; e-commerce; elementary education; English; English/language arts teacher education; environmental science; environmental studies; fine/studio arts; graphic design; health science; health/health care administration; health/medical preparatory programs related; history; history teacher education; industrial and organizational psychology; interdisciplinary studies; interior design; kindergarten/preschool education; legal assistant/paralegal; liberal arts and sciences/liberal studies; management information systems; marketing/marketing management; mass communication/media; mathematics; mathematics teacher education; middle school education; music therapy; nursing (registered nurse training); psychology; public health; public health related; secondary education; social psychology; sociology.

Mary Washington College

American studies; art; art history, criticism and conservation; biology/biological sciences; business administration and management; chemistry; classics and languages, literatures and linguistics; computer science; dramatic/theatre arts; economics; elementary education; English; environmental studies; fine/studio arts; French; geography; geology/earth science; German; historic preservation and conservation; history; interdisciplinary studies; international relations and affairs; Latin; liberal arts and sciences/ liberal studies; mathematics; modern languages; music; music teacher education; philosophy; physics; political science and government; pre-dentistry studies; pre-law studies; pre-medical studies; pre-veterinary studies; psychology; religious studies; secondary education; sociology; Spanish.

Massachusetts Institute of Technology

Aerospace, aeronautical and astronautical engineering; anthropology; architecture; biology/biological sciences; business administration and management; business/commerce; chemical engineering; chemistry; city/urban, community and regional planning; civil engineering; cognitive psychology and psycholinguistics; computer science; creative writing; economics; electrical, electronics and communications engineering; English; environmental/environmental health engineering; foreign languages and literatures; history; liberal arts and sciences/liberal studies; linguistics; mass communication/media; materials engineering; mathematics; mathematics and computer science; mechanical engineering; music; nuclear engineering; ocean engineering; philosophy; physics; political science and government; science, technology and society.

The Master's College and Seminary

Accounting; actuarial science; American government and politics; ancient Near Eastern and biblical languages; applied mathematics; biblical studies; biological and physical sciences; biology/biological sciences; business administration and management; computer and information sciences; divinity/ministry; education; elementary education; English; environmental biology; family and consumer sciences/human sciences; finance; foods, nutrition, and wellness; health and physical education; history; liberal arts and sciences/liberal studies; management information systems; mass communication/ media; mathematics; middle school education; music; music management and merchandising; music teacher education; natural sciences; pastoral studies/counseling; physical education teaching and coaching; physical sciences; piano and organ; political science and government; pre-law studies; pre-medical studies; public relations/image management; radio and television; religious education; religious studies; religious/ sacred music; science teacher education; secondary education; speech and rhetoric; theology; voice and opera.

McDaniel College

Art; art history, criticism and conservation; biochemistry; biology/biological sciences; business administration and management; chemistry; communication/speech communication and rhetoric; computer and information sciences; dramatic/theatre arts; economics; English; French; German; history; kinesiology

and exercise science; mathematics; multi-/ interdisciplinary studies related; music; philosophy; physics; political science and government; psychology; religious studies; social work; sociology; Spanish.

McGill University

Accounting; African studies; agribusiness; agricultural business and management; agricultural economics; agricultural/biological engineering and bioengineering; animal genetics; animal physiology; animal sciences; animal sciences related; anthropology; applied mathematics; architecture; area studies related; art history, criticism and conservation; Asian studies (East); atmospheric sciences and meteorology; biochemistry; biology teacher education; biology/biological sciences; botany/ plant biology; botany/plant biology related; business administration and management; business teacher education; business/managerial economics; Canadian studies; chemical engineering; chemistry; chemistry related; chemistry teacher education; classics and languages, literatures and linguistics; computer and information sciences; computer and information sciences related; computer engineering; computer science; dietetics; dramatic/theatre arts; ecology; economics; education; electrical, electronics and communications engineering; elementary education; engineering related; English; English as a second/foreign language (teaching); English language and literature related; English/ language arts teacher education; entrepreneurship; environmental biology; environmental studies; European studies (Central and Eastern); finance; food science; foods, nutrition, and wellness; foreign languages and literatures; French; French language teacher education; geography; geology/earth science; geophysics and seismology; German; history; history teacher education; human resources management; humanities; information science/studies; international agriculture; international business/ trade/commerce; Italian; jazz/jazz studies; Jewish/Judaic studies; kinesiology and exercise science; labor and industrial relations; Latin American studies; linguistics; management science; marine biology and biological oceanography; marketing research; mathematics; mathematics and computer science; mathematics teacher education; mechanical engineering; medical microbiology and bacteriology; metallurgical engineering; mining and mineral engineering; molecular biology; music; music history, literature, and theory; music performance; music related; music teacher education; music theory and composition; natural resources management; natural resources management and policy; natural resources/conservation; Near and Middle Eastern studies; nursing (registered nurse training); nutrition sciences; occupational therapy; organizational behavior; philosophy; philosophy and religious studies related; physical education teaching and coaching; physical therapy; physics; physics teacher education; physiological psychology/psychobiology; piano and organ; plant sciences; political science and government; psychology; religious education; religious studies; Russian; Russian studies; sales, distribution and marketing; science teacher education; secondary education; social science teacher education; social studies teacher education;

social work; sociology; soil science and agronomy; Spanish; special education; statistics; urban studies/affairs; voice and opera; wildlife and wildlands science and management; wildlife biology; women's studies; zoology/animal biology; zoology/animal biology related.

McKendree College

Accounting; art; art teacher education; athletic training; biology teacher education; biology/ biological sciences; business administration and management; business teacher education; chemistry; clinical laboratory science/medical technology; computer science; criminal justice/ law enforcement administration; economics; education (K-12); elementary education; English; English/language arts teacher education; finance; history; history teacher education; information science/studies; international relations and affairs; marketing/marketing management; mass communication/media; mathematics; mathematics teacher education; middle school education; music; music teacher education; nursing (registered nurse training); occupational therapy; organizational communication; philosophy; physical education teaching and coaching; political science and government; pre-dentistry studies; pre-law studies; pre-medical studies; pre-veterinary studies; psychology; public relations/image management; religious studies; sales, distribution and marketing; secondary education; social science teacher education; social sciences; social work; sociology; speech and rhetoric; speech/theater education.

Mercer University

African-American/Black studies; art; biochemistry; biology/biological sciences; business administration, management and operations related; business/commerce; chemistry; Christian studies; classics and languages, literatures and linguistics; communication and journalism related; community organization and advocacy; computer science; criminal justice/ safety; dramatic/theatre arts; economics; education related; elementary education; engineering; English; environmental science; environmental studies; French; German; health/medical preparatory programs related; history; human services; information science/studies; international relations and affairs; journalism; Latin; liberal arts and sciences/liberal studies; mass communication/media; mathematics; middle school education; multi-/interdisciplinary studies related; music; music performance; music related; music teacher education; nursing (registered nurse training); philosophy; physics; political science and government; pre-dentistry studies; pre-medical studies; psychology; regional studies; sociology; Spanish.

Messiah College

Accounting; art history, criticism and conservation; art teacher education; athletic training; biblical studies; biochemistry; biology teacher education; biology/biological sciences; business administration and management; business, management, and marketing related; business/ managerial economics; chemistry; chemistry teacher education; civil engineering; clinical nutrition; communication/speech communication and rhetoric; computer science; dramatic/ theatre arts; e-commerce; early childhood education; economics; elementary education; engineering; English; English/language arts teacher education; entrepreneurship; environmental science; family and community services; fine/studio arts; French; French language teacher education; German; German language teacher education; history; human resources management; humanities; information science/studies; international business/trade/commerce; journalism; kinesiology and exercise science; marketing/marketing management; mathematics; mathematics teacher education; music; music teacher education; nursing (registered nurse training); parks, recreation and leisure; philosophy; physical education teaching and coaching; physics; political science and government; psychology; radio and television; religious education; religious studies; social studies teacher education; social work; sociology; Spanish; Spanish language teacher education; therapeutic recreation.

Miami University

Accounting; aerospace, aeronautical and astronautical engineering; African-American/Black studies; American studies; ancient/classical Greek; anthropology; architecture; art; art history, criticism and conservation; art teacher education; athletic training; audiology and speech-language pathology; biochemistry; biology teacher education; biology/biological sciences; botany/plant biology; business administration and management; business/commerce; business/managerial economics; chemistry; child development; city/urban, community and regional planning; classics and languages, literatures and linguistics; clinical laboratory science/medical technology; computer and information sciences; computer systems analysis; creative writing; dietetics; dramatic/theatre arts; economics; electrical, electronics and communications engineering; elementary education; engineering physics; engineering technology; engineering technology; engineering/industrial management; English; English/language arts teacher education; environmental design/architecture; family and consumer economics related; family and consumer sciences/home economics teacher education; family and consumer sciences/human sciences; finance; fine/studio arts; French; geography; geology/earth science; German; health and physical education; health teacher education; history; human development and family studies; human resources management; industrial engineering; interdisciplinary studies; interior design; international relations and affairs; journalism; kindergarten/preschool education; kinesiology and exercise science; Latin; linguistics; management information systems; management science; marketing/marketing management; mass communication/media; mathematics; mechanical engineering; medical microbiology and bacteriology; middle school education; multi-/interdisciplinary studies related; music; music performance; music teacher education; nursing (registered nurse training); operations management; operations research; organizational behavior; philosophy; physical education teaching and coaching; physics; political science and government; predentistry studies; pre-law studies; pre-medical studies; pre-veterinary studies; psychology; public administration; purchasing, procurement/acquisitions and contracts management;

religious studies; Russian; science teacher education; secondary education; social studies teacher education; social work; sociology; Spanish; special education; speech and rhetoric; speech-language pathology; sport and fitness administration; statistics; systems science and theory; technical and business writing; wood science and wood products/pulp and paper technology; zoology/animal biology.

Michigan State University

Accounting; advertising; agricultural business and management; agricultural communication/journalism; agricultural economics; agricultural/biological engineering and bioengineering; agriculture and agriculture operations related; American studies; ancient studies; animal sciences; anthropology; apparel and textiles; applied economics; applied mathematics; art; art history, criticism and conservation; art teacher education; astrophysics; audiology and speech-language pathology; biochemistry; biochemistry/biophysics and molecular biology; biological and physical sciences; biology/biological sciences; biomedical/medical engineering; botany/plant biology; business administration and management; chemical engineering; chemical physics; chemistry; chemistry teacher education; child development; city/urban, community and regional planning; civil engineering; clinical laboratory science/medical technology; communication/speech communication and rhetoric; computational mathematics; computer and information sciences; computer engineering; construction management; criminal justice/law enforcement administration; criminal justice/safety; dietetics; dramatic/theatre arts; East Asian languages related; economics; education; electrical, electronics and communications engineering; elementary education; engineering; English; entomology; environmental biology; environmental science; environmental studies; family and consumer sciences; family and consumer sciences/home economics teacher education; family and consumer sciences/human sciences; fashion/apparel design; finance; food science; forestry; French; geography; geology/earth science; geophysics and seismology; German; history; horticultural science; hospitality administration; hotel/motel administration; human resources management; humanities; interior design; international relations and affairs; international/global studies; jazz/jazz studies; journalism; kinesiology and exercise science; landscape architecture; logistics and materials management; marketing/marketing management; mass communication/media; materials science; mathematics; mechanical engineering; merchandising; microbiology; music; music pedagogy; music performance; music teacher education; music theory and composition; music therapy; natural resource economics; nursing (registered nurse training); nutrition sciences; operations management; parks, recreation and leisure facilities management; philosophy; physical and theoretical chemistry; physical education teaching and coaching; physical sciences; physics; physiology; plant pathology/phytopathology; political science and government; pre-law studies; pre-medical studies; pre-veterinary studies; psychology; public administration; radio and television; religious studies; Russian; science, technology and society; social science teacher education; social

sciences; social work; sociology; soil science and agronomy; Spanish; special education; special education (hearing impaired); special education (specific learning disabilities); statistics; technical and business writing; telecommunications; veterinary technology; veterinary/animal health technology; zoology/animal biology.

Michigan Technological University

Accounting; applied mathematics; biochemistry; biology/biological sciences; biology/biotechnology laboratory technician; business administration and management; business/managerial economics; chemical engineering; chemistry; civil engineering; civil engineering technology; clinical laboratory science/medical technology; communication/speech communication and rhetoric; computer engineering; computer programming; computer science; computer software engineering; construction engineering; ecology; electrical, electronic and communications engineering technology; electrical, electronics and communications engineering; electromechanical technology; engineering; engineering mechanics; engineering physics; English; environmental/environmental health engineering; finance; forestry; forestry technology; general studies; geological/geophysical engineering; geology/earth science; geophysics and seismology; humanities; industrial engineering; information science/studies; management information systems; marketing/marketing management; materials engineering; mathematics; mechanical engineering; mechanical engineering/mechanical technology; medical microbiology and bacteriology; metallurgical engineering; operations management; physical sciences; physics; pre-dentistry studies; pre-medical studies; preveterinary studies; science teacher education; secondary education; social sciences; statistics; survey technology; technical and business writing.

Middlebury College

American literature; American studies; Arabic; art history, criticism and conservation; Asian studies (East); biochemistry; biology/biological sciences; chemistry; Chinese; cinematography and film/video production; classics and languages, literatures and linguistics; computer science; dance; dramatic/theatre arts; economics; education; English; environmental studies; European studies; European studies (Central and Eastern); fine/studio arts; French; geography; geology/earth science; German; history; international relations and affairs; Italian; Japanese; Latin American studies; liberal arts and sciences/liberal studies; literature; mathematics; modern languages; molecular biology; music; neuroscience; philosophy; physics; political science and government; pre-law studies; psychology; religious studies; Russian; Russian studies; sociology; Spanish; women's studies.

Milligan College

Accounting; biblical studies; biology/biological sciences; business administration and management; chemistry; communication and media related; computer and information sciences; computer science; early childhood education; education; English; English language and literature related; fine/studio arts; health and physical education; health science; history; humanities; mathematics; music; music related; music teacher education; nursing (registered nurse training); pastoral studies/counseling; psychology; public administration and social service professions related; sociology.

Millsaps College

Accounting; anthropology; art; biology/biological sciences; business administration and management; chemistry; classics and languages, literatures and linguistics; computer science; dramatic/theatre arts; economics; education; English; European studies; French; geology/earth science; German; history; mathematics; music; philosophy; physics; political science and government; psychology; religious studies; sociology; Spanish.

Mills College

American studies; anthropology; art; art history, criticism and conservation; biochemistry; biology/biological sciences; business/managerial economics; chemistry; comparative literature; computer science; creative writing; cultural studies; dance; developmental and child psychology; economics; engineering; English; environmental science; environmental studies; fine/studio arts; French; French studies; Hispanic-American, Puerto Rican, and Mexican-American/Chicano studies; history; interdisciplinary studies; intermedia/multimedia; international relations and affairs; liberal arts and sciences/liberal studies; mathematics; music; philosophy; physiological psychology/psychobiology; political science and government; psychology; public policy analysis; sociology; Spanish; women's studies.

Milwaukee School of Engineering

Architectural engineering; biomedical/medical engineering; business administration and management; business/commerce; communication and journalism related; computer engineering; computer software engineering; construction management; electrical, electronic and communications engineering technology; electrical, electronics and communications engineering; industrial engineering; international business/trade/commerce; management information systems; mechanical engineering; mechanical engineering/mechanical technology; nursing (registered nurse training).

Minneapolis College of Art and Design

Advertising; cinematography and film/video production; commercial and advertising art; drawing; fine/studio arts; interdisciplinary studies; intermedia/multimedia; painting; photography; printmaking; sculpture.

Mississippi State University

Accounting; aerospace, aeronautical and astronautical engineering; agribusiness; agricultural economics; agricultural teacher education; agricultural/biological engineering and bioengineering; agriculture; agronomy and crop science; animal sciences; anthropology; architecture; biochemistry; biological and physical sciences; biology/biological sciences;

biomedical/medical engineering; business administration and management; business teacher education; business/managerial economics; chemical engineering; chemistry; civil engineering; clinical laboratory science/medical technology; communication/speech communication and rhetoric; computer and information sciences; computer engineering; computer software engineering; construction management; economics; educational psychology; electrical, electronics and communications engineering; elementary education; English; family and consumer sciences/human sciences; finance; food science; foreign languages and literatures; forestry; geology/earth science; history; horticultural science; industrial engineering; industrial technology; insurance; landscape architecture; landscaping and groundskeeping; liberal arts and sciences/liberal studies; management information systems; marine biology and biological oceanography; marketing/marketing management; mathematics; mechanical engineering; medical microbiology and bacteriology; multi-/interdisciplinary studies related; music teacher education; philosophy; physical education teaching and coaching; physics; plant protection and integrated pest management; political science and government; poultry science; psychology; real estate; secondary education; social work; sociology; special education; technical teacher education; technology/industrial arts teacher education; visual and performing arts; wildlife and wildlands science and management; wood science and wood products/pulp and paper technology.

Morehouse College

Accounting; adult and continuing education; African-American/Black studies; art; biology/biological sciences; business administration and management; chemistry; computer and information sciences; dramatic/theatre arts; economics; elementary education; engineering; English; finance; French; German; history; interdisciplinary studies; international relations and affairs; marketing/marketing management; mathematics; middle school education; music; philosophy; physical education teaching and coaching; physics; political science and government; psychology; religious studies; secondary education; sociology; Spanish; urban studies/affairs.

Mount Holyoke College

African-American/Black studies; American studies; anthropology; art history, criticism and conservation; Asian studies; astronomy; biochemistry; biology/biological sciences; chemistry; classics and languages, literatures and linguistics; computer science; dance; dramatic/theatre arts; economics; education; English; environmental studies; European studies; film/cinema studies; fine/studio arts; French; geography; geology/earth science; German; history; interdisciplinary studies; international relations and affairs; Italian; Jewish/Judaic studies; Latin; Latin American studies; mathematics; medieval and renaissance studies; modern Greek; music; philosophy; physics; political science and government; psychology; religious studies; romance languages; Russian; Russian studies; social sciences; sociology; Spanish; statistics; women's studies.

Muhlenberg College

Accounting; American studies; anthropology; art; art history, criticism and conservation; biochemistry; biology/biological sciences; business administration and management; chemistry; computer science; dance; dramatic/theatre arts; economics; elementary education; English; environmental science; fine/studio arts; French; German; history; human resources management; international economics; international relations and affairs; mathematics; music; natural sciences; philosophy; physical sciences; physics; political science and government; pre-dentistry studies; pre-law studies; pre-medical studies; pre-veterinary studies; psychology; religious studies; Russian studies; secondary education; social sciences; sociology; Spanish.

Murray State University

Accounting; administrative assistant and secretarial science; agricultural business and management; agricultural teacher education; agriculture; apparel and textiles; art teacher education; audiology and speech-language pathology; biology teacher education; biology/biological sciences; business administration and management; business teacher education; business/commerce; chemical engineering; chemical technology; chemistry; chemistry teacher education; child care provision; civil engineering technology; clinical laboratory science/medical technology; computer and information sciences; computer engineering technology; criminal justice/safety; drafting and design technology; dramatic/theatre arts; early childhood education; economics; electrical, electronic and communications engineering technology; electromechanical technology; elementary education; engineering physics; engineering technology; English; English as a second/foreign language (teaching); English/language arts teacher education; environmental engineering technology; equestrian studies; executive assistant/executive secretary; family and consumer economics related; family and consumer sciences/home economics teacher education; finance; fine/studio arts; fishing and fisheries sciences and management; foods, nutrition, and wellness; foodservice systems administration; foreign language teacher education; French; French language teacher education; general studies; geography; geology/earth science; German; German language teacher education; graphic and printing equipment operation/production; health teacher education; history; history teacher education; horticultural science; human development and family studies; industrial technology; information science/studies; international business/trade/commerce; international relations and affairs; journalism; kinesiology and exercise science; liberal arts and sciences/liberal studies; library science; management information systems; manufacturing technology; marketing/marketing management; mass communication/media; mathematics; mathematics teacher education; mechanical drafting and CAD/CADD; mechanical engineering; mechanical engineering/mechanical technology; middle school education; music; music teacher education; nursing (registered nurse training); occupational safety and health technology; office management; parks, recreation and leisure facilities management; perioperative/operating room and surgical nursing; philosophy; physical education teaching and coaching; physics; physics teacher education; political science and government; psychology; public administration; public relations, advertising, and applied communication related; public relations/image management; radio and television; reading teacher education; science teacher education; secondary education; social science teacher education; social studies teacher education; social work; sociology; Spanish; Spanish language teacher education; special education; speech and rhetoric; speech teacher education; speech therapy; technical and business writing; technology/industrial arts teacher education; telecommunications; trade and industrial teacher education; veterinary/animal health technology; water quality and wastewater treatment management and recycling technology; wildlife and wildlands science and management.

Nazareth College of Rochester

Accounting; American studies; anthropology; art; art history, criticism and conservation; art teacher education; art therapy; audiology and speech-language pathology; biochemistry; biology teacher education; biology/biological sciences; business administration and management; business teacher education; ceramic arts and ceramics; chemistry; chemistry teacher education; commercial and advertising art; creative writing; dramatic/theatre arts; drawing; economics; education; elementary education; English; English/language arts teacher education; environmental science; environmental studies; fine/studio arts; foreign language teacher education; French; German; gerontology; history; history teacher education; human resources management; information science/studies; information technology; interdisciplinary studies; international relations and affairs; Italian; literature; management information systems; marketing/marketing management; mathematics; mathematics teacher education; modern languages; music; music history, literature, and theory; music teacher education; music therapy; nursing (registered nurse training); philosophy; photography; physical therapy; political science and government; pre-dentistry studies; pre-law studies; pre-medical studies; pre-veterinary studies; psychology; religious studies; science teacher education; secondary education; social sciences; social studies teacher education; social work; sociology; Spanish; special education; women's studies.

New College of Florida

Anthropology; art history, criticism and conservation; biology/biological sciences; chemistry; classics and classical languages related; comparative literature; economics; English; environmental studies; fine/studio arts; foreign languages and literatures; French; French studies; general studies; German; Germanic languages; history; humanities; international/global studies; liberal arts and sciences/liberal studies; literature; marine biology and biological oceanography; mathematics; medieval and renaissance studies; music; music history, literature, and theory; natural sciences; neurobiology and neurophysiology; philosophy; physics; political science and government; psychology; public policy analysis; religious studies; Russian; social sciences; sociology; Spanish; urban studies/affairs.

New Jersey Institute of Technology

Actuarial science; applied mathematics; architecture; biology/biological sciences; biomedical/medical engineering; business administration and management; chemical engineering; chemistry; civil engineering; computer and information sciences; computer and information sciences and support services related; computer engineering; electrical, electronics and communications engineering; engineering; engineering technologies related; engineering technology; environmental/environmental health engineering; geological/geophysical engineering; history; industrial engineering; information science/studies; manufacturing engineering; mechanical engineering; natural resources/conservation; nursing (registered nurse training); nursing science; physics related; science, technology and society; technical and business writing.

New Mexico Institute of Mining and Technology

Applied mathematics; astrophysics; atmospheric sciences and meteorology; behavioral sciences; biological and physical sciences; biology/biological sciences; business administration and management; chemical engineering; chemistry; civil engineering; clinical laboratory science/medical technology; computer programming; computer science; electrical, electronics and communications engineering; engineering; engineering mechanics; environmental biology; environmental studies; environmental/environmental health engineering; experimental psychology; geochemistry; geology/earth science; geophysics and seismology; information technology; interdisciplinary studies; liberal arts and sciences/liberal studies; materials engineering; mathematics; mechanical engineering; metallurgical engineering; mining and mineral engineering; petroleum engineering; physics; pre-dentistry studies; pre-medical studies; pre-veterinary studies; psychology; technical and business writing.

New York School of Interior Design

Interior design.

New York University

Accounting; actuarial science; African-American/Black studies; anthropology; archeology; area, ethnic, cultural, and gender studies related; art; art history, criticism and conservation; Asian studies (East); biochemistry; biology teacher education; biology/biological sciences; business administration and management; business, management, and marketing related; business/managerial economics; chemistry; chemistry teacher education; cinematography and film/video production; city/urban, community and regional planning; classics and languages, literatures and linguistics; communication/speech communication and rhetoric; comparative literature; computer and information sciences; computer programming; computer science; dance; dental hygiene; diagnostic medical sonography and ultrasound technology; digital communication and media/multimedia; dramatic/theatre arts; economics; education; elementary education; engineering

related; English; English/language arts teacher education; European studies; film/cinema studies; finance; fine/studio arts; foods, nutrition, and wellness; foreign language teacher education; French; French language teacher education; general studies; German; graphic communications; health information/medical records technology; health/health care administration; Hebrew; history; hospitality administration; hotel/motel administration; human services; humanities; information science/studies; interdisciplinary studies; international business/trade/commerce; international relations and affairs; Italian; Jewish/Judaic studies; journalism; kindergarten/preschool education; Latin; Latin American studies; liberal arts and sciences/liberal studies; linguistics; management information systems; marketing/marketing management; mass communication/media; mathematics; mathematics and statistics related; mathematics teacher education; medieval and renaissance studies; middle school education; modern Greek; music; music management and merchandising; music performance; music teacher education; music theory and composition; Near and Middle Eastern studies; neuroscience; nursing (registered nurse training); operations research; philosophy; photography; physical therapist assistant; physics; physics teacher education; piano and organ; playwriting and screenwriting; political science and government; Portuguese; pre-dentistry studies; pre-medical studies; psychology; radio and television; real estate; religious studies; romance languages; Russian; secondary education; social sciences; social studies teacher education; social work; sociology; Spanish; special education; special education (speech or language impaired); sport and fitness administration; statistics; theatre literature, history and criticism; tourism and travel services management; urban studies/affairs; voice and opera.

North Carolina State University

Accounting; aerospace, aeronautical and astronautical engineering; agribusiness; agricultural and extension education; agricultural and food products processing; agricultural business and management; agricultural economics; agricultural teacher education; agricultural/biological engineering and bioengineering; agriculture; agronomy and crop science; American government and politics; animal sciences; anthropology; apparel and textile manufacturing; apparel and textile marketing management; applied mathematics; architecture; arts management; biochemistry; biology teacher education; biology/biological sciences; biomedical/medical engineering; botany/plant biology; business administration and management; chemical engineering; chemistry; chemistry teacher education; civil engineering; communication/speech communication and rhetoric; computer engineering; computer science; construction engineering; construction management; creative writing; criminology; design and applied arts related; design and visual communications; ecology; economics; education; electrical, electronics and communications engineering; engineering; English; English/language arts teacher education; environmental design/architecture; environmental science; environmental studies; environmental/environmental health engineering; film/cinema studies; finance; fishing and fisheries sciences and management; food science; foreign language teacher education; forest/forest resources management; French; French language teacher education; geology/earth science; graphic design; health occupations teacher education; history; history teacher education; horticultural science; human resources management; hydrology and water resources science; industrial design; industrial engineering; information technology; landscape architecture; landscaping and groundskeeping; liberal arts and sciences/liberal studies; marketing/marketing management; mass communication/media; materials engineering; materials science; mathematics; mathematics teacher education; mechanical engineering; meteorology; microbiology; middle school education; natural resources management and policy; natural resources/conservation; nuclear engineering; oceanography (chemical and physical); paleontology; parks, recreation and leisure facilities management; parks, recreation, and leisure related; philosophy; physics; physics related; physics teacher education; plant protection and integrated pest management; political science and government; political science and government related; poultry science; psychology; psychology related; public policy analysis; public relations/image management; religious studies; sales and marketing/marketing and distribution teacher education; science teacher education; science, technology and society; secondary education; social studies teacher education; social work; sociology; soil science and agronomy; Spanish; Spanish language teacher education; sport and fitness administration; statistics; technology/industrial arts teacher education; textile science; textile sciences and engineering; tourism and travel services management; turf and turfgrass management; wildlife and wildlands science and management; wood science and wood products/pulp and paper technology; zoology/animal biology.

North Central College

Accounting; actuarial science; American history; applied mathematics; art; art teacher education; athletic training; biochemistry; biology/biological sciences; broadcast journalism; business administration and management; chemistry; computer science; dramatic/theatre arts; economics; education; elementary education; English; finance; French; German; history; humanities; international business/trade/commerce; Japanese; jazz/jazz studies; liberal arts and sciences/liberal studies; literature; management information systems; marketing/marketing management; mass communication/media; mathematics; music; natural sciences; philosophy; physical education teaching and coaching; physics; political science and government; pre-dentistry studies; pre-law studies; pre-medical studies; pre-veterinary studies; psychology; religious studies; science teacher education; secondary education; social sciences; sociology; Spanish; speech and rhetoric.

Northwestern College

Accounting; art teacher education; biblical studies; biology/biological sciences; business administration and management; communication/speech communication and rhetoric; creative writing; criminal justice/safety; dramatic/theatre arts; early childhood education; elementary education; English; English as a second/foreign language (teaching); English/language arts teacher education; finance; fine/studio arts; graphic design; history; international business/trade/commerce; journalism; kindergarten/preschool education; kinesiology and exercise science; liberal arts and sciences/liberal studies; management information systems; marketing/marketing management; mathematics; mathematics teacher education; missionary studies and missiology; music; music performance; music teacher education; music theory and composition; physical education teaching and coaching; piano and organ; pre-theology/pre-ministerial studies; psychology; public relations/image management; radio and television; religious education; social sciences; social studies teacher education; Spanish; technical and business writing; theological and ministerial studies related; voice and opera; youth ministry.

Northwestern College (IA)

Accounting; actuarial science; administrative assistant and secretarial science; agribusiness; art; art teacher education; biology teacher education; biology/biological sciences; business administration and management; business teacher education; chemistry; clinical laboratory science/medical technology; computer science; dramatic/theatre arts; economics; education (K-12); elementary education; English; environmental science; history; humanities; kinesiology and exercise science; mass communication/media; mathematics; music; music teacher education; philosophy; physical education teaching and coaching; political science and government; psychology; religious education; religious studies; secondary education; social work; sociology; Spanish; speech and rhetoric; speech/theater education.

Northwestern University

African studies; African-American/Black studies; American studies; anthropology; applied mathematics; area studies related; art; art history, criticism and conservation; Asian studies; astronomy; audiology and hearing sciences; audiology and speech-language pathology; biochemistry; biological and physical sciences; biology/biological sciences; biomedical/medical engineering; Caribbean studies; cell biology and histology; chemical engineering; chemistry; civil engineering; classics and languages, literatures and linguistics; cognitive psychology and psycholinguistics; communication and media related; communication disorders; communication/speech communication and rhetoric; community organization and advocacy; community psychology; comparative literature; computer and information sciences; computer engineering; computer science; counseling psychology; dance; dramatic/theatre arts; East Asian languages related; ecology; economics; education; electrical, electronics and communications engineering; engineering; engineering related; engineering science; English; environmental science; environmental studies; environmental/environmental health engineering; film/cinema studies; French; general studies; geography; geology/earth science; German; history; humanities; industrial engineering; information science/studies; interdisciplinary studies; international relations and affairs; Italian; jazz/jazz studies; journalism; legal studies; liberal arts and sciences/liberal studies; linguistics; manufacturing engineering; materials engineering; materials science; mathematics; mathematics teacher education; mechanical engineering; molecular biology; multi-/interdisciplinary studies related; music; music history, literature, and theory; music performance; music related; music teacher education; music theory and composition; musicology and ethnomusicology; neuroscience; organizational behavior; philosophy; physics; piano and organ; political science and government; pre-medical studies; psychology; public policy analysis; radio and television; religious studies; science, technology and society; secondary education; Slavic languages; Slavic studies; social and philosophical foundations of education; social sciences related; sociology; South Asian languages; Spanish; special education (specific learning disabilities); speech and rhetoric; speech therapy; speech-language pathology; statistics; theatre literature, history and criticism; urban studies/affairs; violin, viola, guitar and other stringed instruments; visual and performing arts; voice and opera; wind/percussion instruments; women's studies.

Oberlin College

African-American/Black studies; anthropology; archeology; art; art history, criticism and conservation; Asian studies (East); biochemistry; biology/biological sciences; chemistry; classics and languages, literatures and linguistics; comparative literature; computer science; creative writing; dance; dramatic/theatre arts; ecology; economics; English; environmental studies; fine/studio arts; French; geology/earth science; German; history; interdisciplinary studies; jazz/jazz studies; Jewish/Judaic studies; Latin; Latin American studies; legal studies; mathematics; modern Greek; music; music history, literature, and theory; music teacher education; music theory and composition; Near and Middle Eastern studies; neuroscience; philosophy; physics; physiological psychology/psychobiology; piano and organ; political science and government; psychology; religious studies; romance languages; Russian; Russian studies; sociology; Spanish; violin, viola, guitar and other stringed instruments; voice and opera; wind/percussion instruments; women's studies.

Occidental College

American studies; anthropology; art history, criticism and conservation; Asian studies; biochemistry; biology/biological sciences; business/managerial economics; chemistry; cognitive psychology and psycholinguistics; comparative literature; dramatic/theatre arts; economics; environmental studies; fine/studio arts; French; geology/earth science; geophysics and seismology; history; international relations and affairs; kinesiology and exercise science; mathematics; music; philosophy; physics; physiological psychology/psychobiology; political science and government; psychology; public policy analysis; religious studies; sociology; Spanish; women's studies.

Oglethorpe University

Accounting; American studies; art; biology/biological sciences; business administration and management; business/managerial economics; chemistry; computer science; economics; education; elementary education; English; history;

interdisciplinary studies; international relations and affairs; kindergarten/preschool education; mass communication/media; mathematics; middle school education; philosophy; physics; political science and government; pre-dentistry studies; pre-law studies; pre-medical studies; pre-veterinary studies; psychology; secondary education; social work; sociology; urban studies/affairs.

Ohio Northern University

Accounting; art; art teacher education; athletic training; biochemistry; biology teacher education; biology/biological sciences; business administration and management; business/commerce; ceramic arts and ceramics; chemistry; chemistry related; chemistry teacher education; civil engineering; civil engineering related; clinical laboratory science/medical technology; commercial and advertising art; communication and journalism related; communication/speech communication and rhetoric; computer engineering; computer engineering related; computer science; creative writing; criminal justice/law enforcement administration; criminal justice/police science; criminal justice/safety; design and visual communications; dramatic/theatre arts; early childhood education; education; education (multiple levels); education related; electrical, electronics and communications engineering; elementary education; engineering; engineering related; English; English/language arts teacher education; environmental studies; fine/studio arts; foreign language teacher education; French; French language teacher education; general studies; German language teacher education; Germanic languages related; graphic design; health and physical education; health and physical education related; health teacher education; history; history teacher education; industrial arts; industrial technology; international business/trade/commerce; international relations and affairs; journalism; kindergarten/preschool education; kinesiology and exercise science; management science; management sciences and quantitative methods related; mass communication/media; mathematics; mathematics related; mathematics teacher education; mechanical engineering; medicinal and pharmaceutical chemistry; middle school education; molecular biology; music; music management and merchandising; music performance; music related; music teacher education; organizational communication; painting; pharmacy; pharmacy, pharmaceutical sciences, and administration related; philosophy; philosophy related; physical education teaching and coaching; physics; physics related; physics teacher education; political science and government; pre-dentistry studies; pre-law studies; pre-medical studies; pre-theology/pre-ministerial studies; pre-veterinary studies; printmaking; psychology; psychology related; public relations/image management; radio and television; religious studies; religious studies related; science teacher education; sculpture; secondary education; social studies teacher education; sociology; Spanish; Spanish language teacher education; sport and fitness administration; statistics; statistics related; technical and business writing; theatre/theatre arts management; visual and performing arts; visual and performing arts related.

The Ohio State University

Accounting; actuarial science; aerospace, aeronautical and astronautical engineering; African studies; African-American/Black studies; agricultural and food products processing; agricultural business and management; agricultural economics; agricultural teacher education; agricultural/biological engineering and bioengineering; agronomy and crop science; animal genetics; animal sciences; anthropology; apparel and textiles; Arabic; architecture; art; art history, criticism and conservation; art teacher education; Asian studies (East); Asian-American studies; astronomy; athletic training; audiology and speech-language pathology; aviation/airway management; avionics maintenance technology; biochemistry; biology/biological sciences; biotechnology; botany/plant biology; business administration and management; business family and consumer sciences/human sciences; business/managerial economics; ceramic arts and ceramics; ceramic sciences and engineering; chemical engineering; chemistry; Chinese; city/urban, community and regional planning; civil engineering; classics and languages, literatures and linguistics; clinical laboratory science/medical technology; clothing/textiles; commercial and advertising art; communication and journalism related; communication/speech communication and rhetoric; comparative literature; computer and information sciences; computer engineering; computer science; creative writing; criminal justice/safety; criminology; cultural studies; dance; dental hygiene; design and visual communications; development economics and international development; dietetics; drama and dance teacher education; dramatic/theatre arts; drawing; economics; electrical, electronics and communications engineering; engineering physics; English; entomology; environmental education; environmental studies; European studies (Western); family resource management; finance; fine/studio arts; fishing and fisheries sciences and management; folklore; food science; foods, nutrition, and wellness; forestry; French; geography; geology/earth science; German; health information/medical records administration; health professions related; Hebrew; history; history related; horticultural science; hospitality administration; human development and family studies; human resources management; humanities; industrial design; industrial engineering; information science/studies; insurance; interior design; international business/trade/commerce; international relations and affairs; Islamic studies; Italian; Japanese; jazz/jazz studies; Jewish/Judaic studies; journalism; kinesiology and exercise science; landscape architecture; Latin American studies; linguistics; logistics and materials management; management information systems; marketing/marketing management; materials engineering; materials science; mathematics; mathematics and statistics related; mechanical engineering; medical microbiology and bacteriology; medical radiologic technology; metallurgical engineering; modern Greek; music; music history, literature, and theory; music performance; music teacher education; music theory and composition; natural resources management; natural resources management and policy; Near and Middle Eastern studies; nursing (registered nurse training); nursing science; occupational therapy; operations management; painting;

peace studies and conflict resolution; pharmacy; philosophy; physical education teaching and coaching; physical therapy; physics; piano and organ; plant pathology/phytopathology; plant sciences; political science and government; Portuguese; printmaking; psychology; radiologic technology/science; real estate; religious studies; respiratory care therapy; Russian; Russian studies; sculpture; social sciences; social work; sociology; soil conservation; Spanish; special education; survey technology; systems engineering; technical teacher education; technology/industrial arts teacher education; turf and turfgrass management; voice and opera; wildlife and wildlands science and management; women's studies; zoology/animal biology.

Ohio Wesleyan University

Accounting; African-American/Black studies; animal genetics; anthropology; art history, criticism and conservation; art teacher education; art therapy; Asian studies (East); astronomy; biology teacher education; biology/biological sciences; botany/plant biology; broadcast journalism; business administration and management; business/managerial economics; chemistry; chemistry teacher education; classics and languages, literatures and linguistics; computer science; creative writing; cultural studies; drama and dance teacher education; dramatic/theatre arts; early childhood education; economics; education; education (K-12); education (multiple levels); elementary education; engineering related; engineering science; English; environmental studies; fine/studio arts; foreign language teacher education; French; French language teacher education; general studies; genetics; geography; geology/earth science; German; German language teacher education; health teacher education; history; history teacher education; humanities; international business/trade/commerce; international relations and affairs; journalism; kindergarten/preschool education; Latin teacher education; literature; mathematics; mathematics teacher education; medical microbiology and bacteriology; medieval and renaissance studies; middle school education; multi-/interdisciplinary studies related; music; music performance; music teacher education; neuroscience; philosophy; physical education teaching and coaching; physics; physics teacher education; political science and government; pre-dentistry studies; pre-law studies; pre-medical studies; pre-theology/pre-ministerial studies; pre-veterinary studies; psychology; psychology teacher education; public administration; religious studies; secondary education; social studies teacher education; sociology; Spanish; Spanish language teacher education; statistics; urban studies/affairs; women's studies; zoology/animal biology.

Oklahoma Baptist University

Accounting; advertising; ancient Near Eastern and biblical languages; applied art; art; art teacher education; athletic training; biblical studies; biological and physical sciences; biology teacher education; biology/biological sciences; broadcast journalism; business administration and management; chemistry; chemistry teacher education; child development; child guidance; computer and information sciences; computer management; computer programming (specific applications); computer science; computer systems analysis; developmental and child psychology; divinity/ministry; drama and dance teacher education; dramatic/theatre arts; education; elementary education; English; English composition; English/language arts teacher education; finance; fine/studio arts; French; French language teacher education; German; German language teacher education; health and physical education; history; history teacher education; human resources management; humanities; information science/studies; interdisciplinary studies; international business/trade/commerce; international marketing; journalism; kindergarten/preschool education; kinesiology and exercise science; management information systems; marketing/marketing management; marriage and family therapy/counseling; mass communication/media; mathematics; mathematics teacher education; missionary studies and missiology; museum studies; music; music teacher education; music theory and composition; natural sciences; nursing (registered nurse training); parks, recreation and leisure; pastoral studies/counseling; philosophy; physical education teaching and coaching; physical sciences; physics; piano and organ; political science and government; pre-dentistry studies; pre-law studies; pre-medical studies; pre-pharmacy studies; pre-veterinary studies; psychology; public relations/image management; radio and television; religious education; religious studies; religious/sacred music; science teacher education; secondary education; social science teacher education; social sciences; social studies teacher education; social work; sociology; Spanish; Spanish language teacher education; special education; special education (emotionally disturbed); special education (mentally retarded); special education (specific learning disabilities); speech and rhetoric; speech teacher education; telecommunications; theology; voice and opera; wind/percussion instruments.

Oklahoma City University

Accounting; advertising; American studies; art; art history, criticism and conservation; art teacher education; arts management; biochemistry; biological and physical sciences; biology/biological sciences; biophysics; broadcast journalism; business administration and management; business/commerce; business/managerial economics; chemistry; cinematography and film/video production; commercial and advertising art; computer science; corrections; criminal justice/law enforcement administration; criminal justice/police science; dance; dramatic/theatre arts; education; elementary education; English; finance; fine/studio arts; French; German; history; humanities; international business/trade/commerce; journalism; kindergarten/preschool education; kinesiology and exercise science; liberal arts and sciences/liberal studies; management information systems; marketing/marketing management; mass communication/media; mathematics; Montessori teacher education; music; music management and merchandising; music teacher education; music theory and composition; nursing (registered nurse training); philosophy; physical education teaching and coaching; physics; piano and organ; political science and government; pre-dentistry studies; pre-law studies; pre-medical studies; pre-nursing studies; pre-pharmacy studies; pre-veterinary studies; psychology; public relations/

image management; radio and television; religious education; religious studies; religious/sacred music; science teacher education; secondary education; sociology; Spanish; speech and rhetoric; speech/theater education; theatre design and technology; violin, viola, guitar and other stringed instruments; voice and opera; wind/percussion instruments.

Oklahoma State University

Accounting; advertising; aerospace, aeronautical and astronautical engineering; agricultural business and management; agricultural communication/journalism; agricultural economics; agricultural teacher education; agriculture; airline pilot and flight crew; American studies; animal sciences; apparel and textiles; architectural engineering; architecture; art; athletic training; aviation/airway management; avionics maintenance technology; biochemistry; biochemistry, biophysics and molecular biology related; biology/biological sciences; biomedical/medical engineering; botany/plant biology; broadcast journalism; business/commerce; business/managerial economics; cell biology and histology; chemical engineering; chemistry; child development; civil engineering; clinical laboratory science/medical technology; clothing/textiles; commercial and advertising art; communication and journalism related; communication disorders; computer and information sciences; computer engineering; computer management; computer science; construction engineering technology; construction management; construction management; construction/heavy equipment/earthmoving equipment operation; creative writing; dietetics; dramatic/theatre arts; economics; education; education (specific subject areas) related; electrical, electronic and communications engineering technology; electrical, electronics and communications engineering; elementary education; engineering; engineering technology; engineering technology; English; entomology; environmental studies; family and community services; family and consumer economics related; family and consumer sciences/human sciences; fashion merchandising; fashion/apparel design; finance; fine/studio arts; fire protection and safety technology; foods, nutrition, and wellness; forestry; French; geography; geology/earth science; German; graphic design; health and physical education; health science; history; horticultural science; hotel/motel administration; human development and family studies; human resources management; industrial arts; industrial engineering; industrial technology; information science/studies; interior design; international business/trade/commerce; journalism; landscape architecture; landscaping and groundskeeping; liberal arts and sciences/liberal studies; management information systems; management science; marketing/marketing management; mathematics; mechanical engineering; mechanical engineering/mechanical technology; medical microbiology and bacteriology; music; music management and merchandising; music pedagogy; music related; music teacher education; philosophy; physical education teaching and coaching; physics; physics related; plant sciences; political science and government; pre-dentistry studies; pre-law studies; pre-medical studies; pre-nursing studies; pre-pharmacy studies; pre-veterinary studies; psychology; restaurant/food services manage-

ment; Russian; secondary education; sociology; Spanish; speech and rhetoric; statistics; technical and business writing; trade and industrial teacher education; wildlife and wildlands science and management; zoology/animal biology; zoology/animal biology related.

Oral Roberts University

Accounting; art teacher education; biblical studies; biochemistry; biology/biological sciences; biomedical technology; biomedical/medical engineering; business administration and management; chemistry; commercial and advertising art; communication/speech communication and rhetoric; computer engineering; computer science; dramatic/theatre arts; education; education (multiple levels); educational leadership and administration; electrical, electronics and communications engineering; elementary education; engineering mechanics; English as a second/foreign language (teaching); English literature (British and Commonwealth); English/language arts teacher education; finance; fine/studio arts; French; French language teacher education; German; German language teacher education; history; international relations and affairs; journalism; kindergarten/preschool education; kinesiology and exercise science; liberal arts and sciences/liberal studies; management information systems; management science; marketing/marketing management; mathematics; mathematics teacher education; mechanical engineering; missionary studies and missiology; music; music performance; music teacher education; music theory and composition; nursing (registered nurse training); pastoral studies/counseling; philosophy; physical education teaching and coaching; physics; political science and government; pre-dentistry studies; pre-medical studies; psychology; public relations/image management; radio and television; religious studies; religious/sacred music; science teacher education; social studies teacher education; social work; Spanish; Spanish language teacher education; special education; theology.

Ouachita Baptist University

Accounting; art teacher education; athletic training; biblical studies; biology/biological sciences; business administration and management; business teacher education; chemistry; communication disorders sciences and services related; computer science; dietetics; dramatic/theatre arts; early childhood education; education; English; fine/studio arts; French; graphic design; health and physical education; history; mass communication/media; mathematics; middle school education; missionary studies and missiology; music; music history, literature, and theory; music performance; music teacher education; music theory and composition; pastoral counseling and specialized ministries related; pastoral studies/counseling; philosophy; physical education teaching and coaching; physics; piano and organ; political science and government; pre-dentistry studies; pre-medical studies; pre-nursing studies; pre-pharmacy studies; pre-veterinary studies; psychology; religious/sacred music; Russian; science teacher education; secondary education; social sciences; social studies teacher education; sociology; Spanish; speech and rhetoric; theology; voice and opera; youth ministry.

Pacific Lutheran University

Accounting; anthropology; art; art history, criticism and conservation; art teacher education; biochemistry; biology/biological sciences; broadcast journalism; business administration and management; chemistry; Chinese; classics and languages, literatures and linguistics; computer engineering; computer science; dramatic/theatre arts; economics; education; electrical, electronics and communications engineering; elementary education; engineering physics; engineering science; English; environmental studies; finance; fine/studio arts; French; geology/earth science; German; history; international business/trade/commerce; international relations and affairs; journalism; kindergarten/preschool education; literature; management information systems; marketing/marketing management; mass communication/media; mathematics; modern languages; music; music teacher education; nursing (registered nurse training); philosophy; physical education teaching and coaching; physics; piano and organ; political science and government; psychology; radio and television; reading teacher education; religious studies; religious/sacred music; Scandinavian languages; science teacher education; secondary education; social work; sociology; Spanish; special education; therapeutic recreation; voice and opera; women's studies.

Pacific University

Accounting; art; art teacher education; athletic training; biology/biological sciences; broadcast journalism; business administration and management; chemistry; Chinese; computer science; creative writing; dramatic/theatre arts; economics; education; elementary education; English; environmental studies; finance; French; German; health science; history; humanities; international relations and affairs; Japanese; journalism; kindergarten/preschool education; kinesiology and exercise science; liberal arts and sciences/liberal studies; literature; marketing/marketing management; mass communication/media; mathematics; modern languages; music; music teacher education; philosophy; physics; political science and government; pre-dentistry studies; pre-medical studies; psychology; radio and television; secondary education; social work; sociology; Spanish; telecommunications.

Peabody Conservatory of Music of The Johns Hopkins University

Audio engineering; jazz/jazz studies; music; music teacher education; piano and organ; violin, viola, guitar and other stringed instruments; voice and opera; wind/percussion instruments.

The Pennsylvania State University University Park Campus

Accounting; acting; actuarial science; adult and continuing education administration; advertising; aerospace, aeronautical and astronautical engineering; African-American/Black studies; agribusiness; agricultural and extension education; agricultural business and management related; agricultural mechanization; agricultural/biological engineering and bioengineering; agriculture; American studies; animal sciences; animal sciences related; anthropology; applied

economics; archeology; architectural engineering; architecture; art; art history, criticism and conservation; art teacher education; Asian studies (East); astronomy; atmospheric sciences and meteorology; biochemistry; biological and biomedical sciences related; biological and physical sciences; biology/biological sciences; biology/biotechnology laboratory technician; biomedical/medical engineering; business/commerce; business/managerial economics; chemical engineering; chemistry; civil engineering; classics and languages, literatures and linguistics; communication and journalism related; communication disorders; communication/speech communication and rhetoric; comparative literature; computer and information sciences; computer engineering; criminal justice/law enforcement administration; cultural studies; dietitian assistant; economics; electrical, electronics and communications engineering; elementary education; engineering science; English; environmental/environmental health engineering; film/cinema studies; finance; food science; forest sciences and biology; forestry technology; French; geography; geological and earth sciences/geosciences related; geology/earth science; German; graphic design; health/health care administration; history; horticultural science; hospitality administration related; human development and family studies; human nutrition; industrial engineering; information science/studies; international business/trade/commerce; international relations and affairs; Italian; Japanese; Jewish/Judaic studies; journalism; kinesiology and exercise science; labor and industrial relations; landscape architecture; landscaping and groundskeeping; Latin American studies; liberal arts and sciences/liberal studies; logistics and materials management; management information systems; management sciences and quantitative methods related; marketing/marketing management; materials science; mathematics; mechanical engineering; medical microbiology and bacteriology; medieval and renaissance studies; mining and mineral engineering; music; music performance; music teacher education; natural resources and conservation related; natural resources/conservation; nuclear engineering; nursing (registered nurse training); organizational behavior; parks, recreation and leisure facilities management; petroleum engineering; philosophy; physics; political science and government; pre-medical studies; psychology; rehabilitation and therapeutic professions related; religious studies; Russian; secondary education; sociology; soil science and agronomy; Spanish; special education; statistics; telecommunications; theatre design and technology; turf and turfgrass management; visual and performing arts; women's studies.

Pepperdine University (Malibu, CA)

Accounting; advertising; art; athletic training; biology/biological sciences; business administration and management; chemistry; communication/speech communication and rhetoric; computer science; dramatic/theatre arts; economics; education; elementary education; English; foods, nutrition, and wellness; French; German; history; humanities; interdisciplinary studies; international business/trade/commerce; international relations and affairs; journalism; liberal arts and sciences/liberal studies;

mathematics; music; music teacher education; natural sciences; philosophy; physical education teaching and coaching; political science and government; pre-dentistry studies; pre-law studies; pre-medical studies; psychology; public relations/image management; religious education; religious studies; secondary education; sociology; Spanish; speech and rhetoric; telecommunications.

Pitzer College

African-American/Black studies; American history; American studies; anthropology; art; art history, criticism and conservation; Asian studies; Asian-American studies; biochemistry; biology/biological sciences; chemistry; classics and languages, literatures and linguistics; creative writing; dance; dramatic/theatre arts; economics; engineering; English; environmental science; environmental studies; European history; European studies; film/cinema studies; fine/studio arts; French; German; Hispanic-American, Puerto Rican, and Mexican-American/Chicano studies; history; interdisciplinary studies; international relations and affairs; Latin American studies; linguistics; literature; mathematics; neuroscience; philosophy; physics; political science and government; pre-medical studies; psychology; religious studies; romance languages; Russian; science, technology and society; sociology; Spanish; women's studies.

Point Loma Nazarene University

Accounting; art; athletic training; biochemistry; biology/biological sciences; broadcast journalism; business administration and management; business/corporate communications; chemistry; child development; communication and media related; communication/speech communication and rhetoric; computer science; development economics and international development; dramatic/theatre arts; engineering physics; English; family and consumer sciences/human sciences; family systems; foods, nutrition, and wellness; graphic communications; health and physical education; history; industrial and organizational psychology; journalism; kinesiology and exercise science; liberal arts and sciences/liberal studies; management information systems; mathematics; music; music performance; music teacher education; music theory and composition; nursing (registered nurse training); philosophy; philosophy and religious studies related; physics; political science and government; psychology; religious/sacred music; romance languages; social sciences; social work; sociology; Spanish; theological and ministerial studies related.

Polytechnic University, Brooklyn Campus

Chemical engineering; chemistry; civil engineering; computer engineering; computer science; construction management; electrical, electronics and communications engineering; journalism; liberal arts and sciences/liberal studies; management information systems; mathematics; mechanical engineering; molecular biochemistry; physics.

Pomona College

African-American/Black studies; American studies; anthropology; art; art history, criticism and conservation; Asian studies; Asian studies (East); astronomy; biochemistry; biology/biological sciences; cell biology and histology; chemistry; Chinese; classics and languages, literatures and linguistics; computer science; dance; dramatic/theatre arts; ecology; economics; English; environmental studies; film/cinema studies; fine/studio arts; French; geochemistry; geology/earth science; German; Hispanic-American, Puerto Rican, and Mexican-American/Chicano studies; history; humanities; interdisciplinary studies; international relations and affairs; Japanese; liberal arts and sciences/liberal studies; linguistics; mathematics; medical microbiology and bacteriology; modern languages; molecular biology; music; neuroscience; philosophy; physics; political science and government; pre-medical studies; psychology; public policy analysis; religious studies; romance languages; Russian; sociology; Spanish; women's studies.

Presbyterian College

Accounting; art; biology/biological sciences; business administration and management; chemistry; computer science; dramatic/theatre arts; economics; education; elementary education; English; French; German; history; kindergarten/preschool education; mathematics; modern languages; music; music teacher education; philosophy; physics; political science and government; pre-dentistry studies; pre-law studies; pre-medical studies; pre-veterinary studies; psychology; religious studies; social sciences; sociology; Spanish; special education.

Princeton University

Anthropology; architecture; art history, criticism and conservation; Asian studies (East); astrophysics; chemical engineering; chemistry; civil engineering; classics and languages, literatures and linguistics; comparative literature; computer engineering; ecology; economics; electrical, electronics and communications engineering; English; French; geological and earth sciences/geosciences related; German; history; mathematics; mechanical engineering; molecular biology; multi-/interdisciplinary studies related; music; Near and Middle Eastern studies; operations research; philosophy; physics; political science and government; psychology; public policy analysis; religious studies; Slavic languages; sociology; Spanish.

Providence College

Accounting; American studies; art history, criticism and conservation; biology/biological sciences; business administration and management; business/managerial economics; chemistry; community organization and advocacy; computer science; economics; English; finance; fine/studio arts; fire science; French; health/health care administration; history; humanities; Italian; labor and industrial relations; liberal arts and sciences/liberal studies; marketing/marketing management; mathematics; music; pastoral studies/counseling; philosophy; political science and government; psychology; secondary education; social sciences; social work; sociology; Spanish; special education; systems science and theory; theology; visual and performing arts.

Purdue University

Accounting; aeronautical/aerospace engineering technology; aeronautics/aviation/aerospace science and technology; aerospace, aeronautical and astronautical engineering; African-American/Black studies; agricultural economics; agricultural mechanization; agricultural teacher education; agricultural/biological engineering and bioengineering; agriculture; agronomy and crop science; animal sciences; apparel and textiles; architectural engineering technology; art; audiology and speech-language pathology; biochemistry; biological and physical sciences; biology/biological sciences; botany/plant biology; business administration and management; chemical engineering; chemistry; civil engineering; clinical laboratory science/medical technology; communication/speech communication and rhetoric; computer and information sciences; computer and information sciences and support services related; computer engineering; construction engineering; design and visual communications; dramatic/theatre arts; early childhood education; economics; education; electrical, electronic and communications engineering technology; electrical, electronics and communications engineering; elementary education; engineering related; English; entomology; family and consumer sciences/human sciences; food science; foods, nutrition, and wellness; foreign languages and literatures; forestry; geology/earth science; health professions related; history; horticultural science; hospitality administration related; hotel/motel administration; human development and family studies; humanities; industrial engineering; interdisciplinary studies; kindergarten/preschool education; landscape architecture; management information systems and services related; materials engineering; mathematics; mechanical drafting and CAD/CADD; mechanical engineering; mechanical engineering technologies related; multi-/interdisciplinary studies related; natural resources/conservation; nuclear engineering; nursing (registered nurse training); operations management; pharmacy; philosophy; physical education teaching and coaching; physics; political science and government; psychology; robotics technology; social sciences; sociology; statistics; survey technology; technology/industrial arts teacher education; trade and industrial teacher education; veterinary/animal health technology; wildlife and wildlands science and management.

Queen's University at Kingston

Art history, criticism and conservation; art teacher education; artificial intelligence and robotics; astrophysics; atomic/molecular physics; biochemistry; biology/biological sciences; business administration and management; Canadian studies; chemical engineering; chemistry; civil engineering; classics and languages, literatures and linguistics; cognitive psychology and psycholinguistics; computer and information sciences; computer and information sciences related; computer engineering; computer engineering related; computer hardware engineering; computer science; computer software engineering; dramatic/theatre arts; economics; education; electrical, electronics and communications engineering; elementary education; engineering; engineering physics; engineering science; English; environmental science; environmental studies; film/cinema studies; fine/studio arts; French; geography; geological/geophysical engineering; geology/earth science; German; health and

physical education; health science; health teacher education; Hispanic-American, Puerto Rican, and Mexican-American/Chicano studies; history; interdisciplinary studies; Italian; Jewish/Judaic studies; Latin; Latin American studies; linguistics; mathematics; mechanical engineering; medieval and renaissance studies; mining and mineral engineering; modern Greek; music; music teacher education; nursing (registered nurse training); philosophy; physical education teaching and coaching; physics; political science and government; psychology; religious studies; science teacher education; secondary education; sociology; Spanish; statistics; violin, viola, guitar and other stringed instruments; women's studies.

Quincy University

Accounting; airline pilot and flight crew; arts management; aviation/airway management; biology/biological sciences; business administration and management; chemistry; clinical laboratory science/medical technology; communication/speech communication and rhetoric; computer and information sciences; computer science; criminal justice/safety; elementary education; English; finance; graphic design; history; humanities; information science/studies; journalism; marketing/marketing management; music; music teacher education; nursing (registered nurse training); philosophy; physical education teaching and coaching; political science and government; pre-dentistry studies; pre-medical studies; pre-veterinary studies; psychology; public administration and social service professions related; public relations/image management; radio and television; social work; special education; sport and fitness administration; theological and ministerial studies related; theology; visual and performing arts.

Quinnipiac University

Accounting; actuarial science; advertising; applied mathematics; athletic training; biochemistry; biological and physical sciences; biology/biological sciences; broadcast journalism; business administration and management; business/managerial economics; chemistry; child development; cinematography and film/video production; communication and journalism related; computer science; criminal justice/safety; developmental and child psychology; economics; education; English; film/cinema studies; finance; gerontology; history; human resources management; human services; information science/studies; international business/trade/commerce; international relations and affairs; journalism; legal assistant/paralegal; legal studies; liberal arts and sciences/liberal studies; literature; marketing/marketing management; mass communication/media; mathematics; medical laboratory technology; medical microbiology and bacteriology; nursing (registered nurse training); occupational therapy; physical therapy; physician assistant; physiological psychology/psychobiology; political science and government; pre-dentistry studies; pre-law studies; pre-medical studies; pre-veterinary studies; psychology; public relations/image management; radiologic technology/science; respiratory care therapy; sales, distribution and marketing; social sciences; sociology; Spanish; special products marketing;

veterinary technology; web page, digital/multi-media and information resources design; zool-ogy/animal biology.

Randolph-Macon Woman's College

American studies; ancient/classical Greek; art; art history, criticism and conservation; biology/biological sciences; chemistry; classics and languages, literatures and linguistics; communication/speech communication and rhetoric; creative writing; dance; dramatic/theatre arts; economics; elementary education; engineering physics; English; environmental studies; fine/studio arts; French; German; health professions related; history; international relations and affairs; Latin; liberal arts and sciences/liberal studies; mathematics; museum studies; music history, literature, and theory; music performance; music theory and composition; philosophy; physics; political science and government; psychology; religious studies; Russian studies; sociology; Spanish.

Reed College

American studies; anthropology; art; biochemistry; biology/biological sciences; chemistry; Chinese; classics and languages, literatures and linguistics; dance; dramatic/theatre arts; economics; English; fine/studio arts; French; German; history; international relations and affairs; linguistics; literature; mathematics; music; philosophy; physics; political science and government; psychology; religious studies; Russian; sociology; Spanish.

Regis University

Accounting; biochemistry; biology/biological sciences; business administration and management; chemistry; communication/speech communication and rhetoric; computer science; criminal justice/law enforcement administration; economics; education; elementary education; English; environmental studies; French; health information/medical records administration; history; human ecology; humanities; liberal arts and sciences/liberal studies; mathematics; neuroscience; nursing (registered nurse training); philosophy; political science and government; pre-dentistry studies; pre-law studies; pre-medical studies; pre-veterinary studies; psychology; religious studies; sociology; Spanish; visual and performing arts.

Rensselaer Polytechnic Institute

Aerospace, aeronautical and astronautical engineering; Air Force R.O.T.C./air science; applied mathematics; architecture; architecture related; Army R.O.T.C./military science; biochemistry; bioinformatics; biological and biomedical sciences related; biological and physical sciences; biology/biological sciences; biomedical/medical engineering; biophysics; business administration and management; chemical engineering; chemistry; civil engineering; communication/speech communication and rhetoric; computer and information sciences; computer engineering; computer science; economics; electrical, electronics and communications engineering; engineering; engineering physics; engineering science; entrepreneurship; environmental/environmental health engineering; finance; geology/earth science; hydrology and water resources

science; industrial engineering; information technology; interdisciplinary studies; management information systems; management information systems and services related; manufacturing engineering; marketing/marketing management; materials engineering; mathematics; mechanical engineering; Navy/Marine Corps R.O.T.C./naval science; nuclear engineering; philosophy; physical sciences; physics; pre-dentistry studies; pre-law studies; pre-medical studies; psychology; science, technology and society; social sciences; systems engineering; visual and performing arts related.

Research College of Nursing

Nursing (registered nurse training).

Rhode Island School of Design

Architecture; ceramic arts and ceramics; fashion/apparel design; fiber, textile and weaving arts; film/cinema studies; fine arts related; furniture design and manufacturing; graphic design; illustration; industrial design; interior architecture; interior design; metal and jewelry arts; painting; photography; printmaking; sculpture.

Rhodes College

Anthropology; art; art history, criticism and conservation; biochemistry; biology/biological sciences; business administration and management; chemistry; classics and languages, literatures and linguistics; computer science; dramatic/theatre arts; economics; English; fine/studio arts; French; German; history; interdisciplinary studies; international business/trade/commerce; international economics; international relations and affairs; Latin; mathematics; modern Greek; music; philosophy; physics; political science and government; psychology; religious studies; Russian studies; sociology; Spanish; urban studies/affairs.

Rice University

Ancient/classical Greek; anthropology; applied mathematics; architecture; art; art history, criticism and conservation; Asian studies; astronomy; astrophysics; biochemistry; biology/biological sciences; biomedical/medical engineering; business administration and management; chemical engineering; chemistry; civil engineering; classics and languages, literatures and linguistics; computer and information sciences; computer engineering; ecology; economics; electrical, electronics and communications engineering; English; environmental/environmental health engineering; evolutionary biology; fine/studio arts; French; geology/earth science; geophysics and seismology; German; history; kinesiology and exercise science; Latin; Latin American studies; linguistics; materials engineering; materials science; mathematics; mechanical engineering; multi-/interdisciplinary studies related; music; music history, literature, and theory; music performance; music theory and composition; neuroscience; philosophy; physical and theoretical chemistry; physics; political science and government; psychology; public policy analysis; religious studies; Russian; Russian studies; sociology; Spanish; statistics; visual and performing arts related; women's studies.

Ripon College

Anthropology; art; biochemistry; biology/biological sciences; business administration and management; chemistry; communication/speech communication and rhetoric; computer science; dramatic/theatre arts; early childhood education; economics; education; elementary education; English; environmental studies; French; German; history; interdisciplinary studies; Latin American studies; mathematics; music; music teacher education; philosophy; physical education teaching and coaching; physical sciences; physiological psychology/psychobiology; political science and government; pre-dentistry studies; pre-law studies; pre-medical studies; pre-veterinary studies; psychology; religious studies; romance languages; secondary education; sociology; Spanish.

Rochester Institute of Technology

Accounting; advertising; aerospace, aeronautical and astronautical engineering; American Sign Language (ASL); animation, interactive technology, video graphics and special effects; applied art; applied mathematics; art; biochemistry; bioinformatics; biological and biomedical sciences related; biology/biological sciences; biomedical/medical engineering; biopsychology; biotechnology; business administration and management; ceramic arts and ceramics; chemistry; cinematography and film/video production; civil engineering technology; clinical laboratory science/medical technology; commercial photography; communication and media related; computer and information sciences; computer and information systems security; computer engineering; computer engineering technology; computer graphics; computer hardware engineering; computer programming (specific applications); computer science; computer software engineering; computer systems analysis; computer systems networking and telecommunications; crafts, folk art and artisanry; criminal justice/law enforcement administration; criminal justice/safety; data modeling/warehousing and database administration; design and visual communications; diagnostic medical sonography and ultrasound technology; dietetics; economics; electrical, electronic and communications engineering technology; electrical, electronics and communications engineering; electromechanical technology; engineering; engineering related; engineering science; engineering technology; engineering technology; engineering-related technologies; environmental science; finance; fine/studio arts; foodservice systems administration; furniture design and manufacturing; general studies; genetics; graphic communications; graphic design; hazardous materials management and waste technology; hospitality administration; hospitality/recreation marketing; hotel/motel administration; human nutrition; illustration; industrial design; industrial engineering; industrial safety technology; information technology; interdisciplinary studies; interior design; international business/trade/commerce; international relations and affairs; management information systems; manufacturing technology; marketing research; marketing/marketing management; mathematics; mathematics and computer science; mechanical engineering;

mechanical engineering/mechanical technology; medical illustration; metal and jewelry arts; natural resources management and policy; nuclear medical technology; occupational safety and health technology; ophthalmic laboratory technology; photographic and film/video technology; photography; photojournalism; physician assistant; physics; polymer chemistry; pre-dentistry studies; pre-law studies; pre-medical studies; pre-veterinary studies; psychology; public policy analysis; public relations, advertising, and applied communication related; public relations/image management; publishing; resort management; restaurant/food services management; sculpture; sign language interpretation and translation; social work; special products marketing; statistics; system administration; system, networking, and LAN/wan management; systems engineering; telecommunications; telecommunications technology; tourism and travel services management; tourism/travel marketing; web page, digital/multimedia and information resources design; web/multimedia management and webmaster.

Rollins College

Anthropology; art history, criticism and conservation; biochemistry; biology/biological sciences; chemistry; classics and languages, literatures and linguistics; computer science; dramatic/theatre arts; economics; education; English; environmental studies; European studies; fine/studio arts; French; history; interdisciplinary studies; international business/trade/commerce; international relations and affairs; Latin American studies; mathematics; music; philosophy; physics; political science and government; pre-dentistry studies; pre-law studies; pre-medical studies; psychology; religious studies; sociology; Spanish.

Rose-Hulman Institute of Technology

Biology/biological sciences; biomedical/medical engineering; chemical engineering; chemistry; civil engineering; computer engineering; computer science; computer software engineering; economics; electrical, electronics and communications engineering; engineering physics; engineering related; mathematics; mechanical engineering; physics.

Rutgers, The State University of New Jersey, New Brunswick/Piscataway

Accounting; African studies; agricultural/biological engineering and bioengineering; agriculture; American studies; ancient/classical Greek; animal genetics; animal physiology; animal sciences; animal/livestock husbandry and production; anthropology; art; art history, criticism and conservation; Asian studies (East); astrophysics; atmospheric sciences and meteorology; biochemistry; biology/biological sciences; biomedical sciences; biomedical/medical engineering; biometry/biometrics; biotechnology; business administration and management; cell biology and anatomical sciences related; cell biology and histology; ceramic arts and ceramics; ceramic sciences and engineering; chemical engineering; chemistry; Chinese; civil engineering; classics and languages, literatures and linguistics; clinical

laboratory science/medical technology; commercial and advertising art; communication/speech communication and rhetoric; comparative literature; computer engineering; computer science; criminal justice/law enforcement administration; cultural studies; dance; dramatic/theatre arts; drawing; ecology; economics; electrical, electronics and communications engineering; engineering science; English; environmental design/architecture; environmental studies; equestrian studies; European studies (Central and Eastern); evolutionary biology; film/cinema studies; finance; food science; foreign languages and literatures; French; geography; geology/earth science; German; Hispanic-American, Puerto Rican, and Mexican-American/Chicano studies; history; human ecology; industrial engineering; information science/studies; interdisciplinary studies; Italian; jazz/jazz studies; Jewish/Judaic studies; journalism; kinesiology and exercise science; labor and industrial relations; Latin; Latin American studies; liberal arts and sciences/liberal studies; linguistics; management science; management sciences and quantitative methods related; marine biology and biological oceanography; marketing/marketing management; mass communication/media; mathematics; mechanical engineering; medical microbiology and bacteriology; medieval and renaissance studies; molecular biology; music; music teacher education; natural resources management; natural resources/conservation; Near and Middle Eastern studies; nursing (registered nurse training); nutrition sciences; painting; pharmacy; philosophy; photography; physics; plant sciences; political science and government; Portuguese; pre-dentistry studies; pre-law studies; pre-medical studies; printmaking; psychology; public health; religious studies; Russian; Russian studies; sculpture; social sciences related; social work; sociology; Spanish; statistics; turf and turfgrass management; urban studies/affairs; veterinary sciences; visual and performing arts; women's studies.

Saint Francis University

Accounting; American studies; anthropology; biology/biological sciences; business administration and management; chemistry; clinical laboratory science/medical technology; computer programming; computer science; criminal justice/law enforcement administration; culinary arts; data processing and data processing technology; drafting and design technology; economics; education; elementary education; emergency medical technology (EMT paramedic); English; environmental studies; finance; French; history; human resources management; international business/trade/commerce; international relations and affairs; journalism; labor and industrial relations; literature; management information systems; marine biology and biological oceanography; marketing/marketing management; mass communication/media; mathematics; modern languages; nursing (registered nurse training); occupational therapy; pastoral studies/counseling; philosophy; physical therapy; physician assistant; political science and government; pre-dentistry studies; pre-law studies; pre-medical studies; pre-veterinary studies; psychology; public administration; public relations/image management; real estate; religious studies; sci-

ence teacher education; secondary education; social work; sociology; Spanish.

St. John's College

Ancient/classical Greek; classics and languages, literatures and linguistics; English; ethics; foreign languages and literatures; French; general studies; history; history of philosophy; humanities; liberal arts and sciences and humanities related; liberal arts and sciences/liberal studies; literature; mathematics; philosophy; philosophy and religious studies related; philosophy related; physical sciences; physics; pre-medical studies; religious studies; western civilization.

St. John's College (MD)

Interdisciplinary studies; liberal arts and sciences/liberal studies; western civilization.

Saint John's University (MN)

Accounting; art; art history, criticism and conservation; art teacher education; biochemistry; biology/biological sciences; business administration and management; chemistry; classics and languages, literatures and linguistics; computer science; dietetics; dramatic/theatre arts; economics; education; elementary education; English; environmental studies; fine/studio arts; foods, nutrition, and wellness; forestry; French; German; history; humanities; mathematics; mathematics and computer science; music; music teacher education; natural sciences; nursing (registered nurse training); occupational therapy; peace studies and conflict resolution; philosophy; physical therapy; physics; political science and government; pre-dentistry studies; pre-law studies; pre-medical studies; pre-pharmacy studies; pre-theology/pre-ministerial studies; pre-veterinary studies; psychology; religious education; secondary education; social sciences; social work; sociology; Spanish; speech and rhetoric; theology.

Saint Joseph's University

Accounting; biochemistry; biology/biological sciences; business administration and management; chemistry; communication/speech communication and rhetoric; computer and information sciences; computer science; criminal justice/law enforcement administration; criminology; economics; education; elementary education; English; environmental science; finance; French; French studies; German; health professions related; health/health care administration; history; hospital and health care facilities administration; human services; information science/studies; interdisciplinary studies; international relations and affairs; legal professions and studies related; liberal arts and sciences/liberal studies; management information systems; management science; marketing related; marketing/marketing management; mathematics; philosophy; physics; political science and government; psychology; public administration; purchasing, procurement/acquisitions and contracts management; religious studies; secondary education; social sciences; sociology; Spanish; special education related; theology; visual and performing arts.

St. Lawrence University

African studies; anthropology; art; art history, criticism and conservation; Asian studies;

biochemistry; biology/biological sciences; biophysics; Canadian studies; chemistry; computer science; creative writing; dramatic/theatre arts; economics; English; environmental studies; foreign languages and literatures; French; geology/earth science; geophysics and seismology; German; history; mathematics; modern languages; music; neuroscience; philosophy; physics; political science and government; psychology; religious studies; sociology; Spanish.

St. Louis College of Pharmacy
Pharmacy.

Saint Louis University
Accounting; aeronautical/aerospace engineering technology; aerospace, aeronautical and astronautical engineering; airline pilot and flight crew; American studies; applied mathematics; art history, criticism and conservation; atmospheric sciences and meteorology; aviation/airway management; biology/biological sciences; biomedical/medical engineering; business administration and management; chemistry; city/urban, community and regional planning; classics and classical languages related; clinical laboratory science/medical technology; clinical/medical laboratory science and allied professions related; communication and journalism related; communication/speech communication and rhetoric; computer and information sciences; computer and information sciences and support services related; corrections; criminal justice/law enforcement administration; criminal justice/police science; dramatic/theatre arts; economics; education; education (multiple levels); electrical, electronics and communications engineering; engineering/industrial management; English; environmental science; finance; fine/studio arts; foods, nutrition, and wellness; foreign languages and literatures; French; geology/earth science; geophysics and seismology; German; health information/medical records administration; health/health care administration; history; human resources management; humanities; international business/trade/commerce; international relations and affairs; kinesiology and exercise science; management information systems; management science; marketing/marketing management; mathematics; mechanical engineering; modern Greek; music; nuclear medical technology; nursing (registered nurse training); occupational therapy; organizational behavior; philosophy; physical therapy; physician assistant; physics; political science and government; psychology; Russian; social sciences; social work; sociology; Spanish; theology; urban studies/affairs; women's studies.

Saint Mary's College
Applied mathematics related; art; art teacher education; biology/biological sciences; business administration and management; business teacher education; chemistry; clinical laboratory science/medical technology; communication/speech communication and rhetoric; creative writing; cytotechnology; dramatic/theatre arts; economics; education; elementary education; English literature (British and Commonwealth); finance; French; history; humanities; interdisciplinary studies; international business/trade/commerce; management information systems; marketing/marketing management;

mathematics; mathematics and computer science; music; music teacher education; nursing (registered nurse training); philosophy; political science and government; psychology; religious studies; social work; sociology; Spanish.

Saint Mary's College of California
Accounting; accounting related; American studies; anthropology; archeology; area, ethnic, cultural, and gender studies related; art; art history, criticism and conservation; biochemistry; biological and biomedical sciences related; biology/biological sciences; business administration and management; business/commerce; chemistry; chemistry related; communication and journalism related; communication/speech communication and rhetoric; dance; dramatic/theatre arts; economics; engineering; English; English language and literature related; European studies; finance and financial management services related; foreign languages related; French; German; health and physical education; health and physical education related; health professions related; historic preservation and conservation; history; industrial and organizational psychology; interdisciplinary studies; international business/trade/commerce; international relations and affairs; Italian; kinesiology and exercise science; Latin; Latin American studies; liberal arts and sciences and humanities related; liberal arts and sciences/liberal studies; literature; mathematics; mathematics and computer science; mathematics and statistics related; modern Greek; modern languages; multi-/interdisciplinary studies related; music; nursing (registered nurse training); philosophy; physics; physiological psychology/psychobiology; political science and government; political science and government related; psychology; psychology related; religious studies; social sciences; social sciences related; sociology; Spanish; sport and fitness administration; theatre literature, history and criticism; theology; visual and performing arts related; women's studies.

St. Mary's College of Maryland
Anthropology; art; biochemistry; biological and physical sciences; biology/biological sciences; chemistry; computer and information sciences; dramatic/theatre arts; economics; English; foreign languages and literatures; history; mathematics; modern languages; multi-/interdisciplinary studies related; music; philosophy; physics; political science and government; psychology; psychology related; public policy analysis; religious studies; sociology.

St. Norbert College
Accounting; art; biological and physical sciences; biology/biological sciences; business/commerce; chemistry; commercial and advertising art; communication/speech communication and rhetoric; computer programming (specific applications); economics; education (K-12); elementary education; English; French; geology/earth science; German; history; humanities; interdisciplinary studies; international business/trade/commerce; international relations and affairs; management information systems; mathematics; mathematics and computer science; music; music teacher education; philosophy; physics; political science

and government; pre-dentistry studies; pre-law studies; pre-medical studies; pre-veterinary studies; psychology; religious studies; sociology; Spanish.

St. Olaf College
American studies; ancient studies; ancient/classical Greek; art; art history, criticism and conservation; Asian studies; biology/biological sciences; chemistry; classics and languages, literatures and linguistics; computer science; cultural studies; dance; dramatic/theatre arts; economics; English; environmental studies; ethnic, cultural minority, and gender studies related; French; German; Hispanic-American, Puerto Rican, and Mexican-American/Chicano studies; history; human development and family studies; kinesiology and exercise science; Latin; Latin American studies; liberal arts and sciences/liberal studies; mathematics; multi-/interdisciplinary studies related; music; music performance; music related; music teacher education; music theory and composition; nursing (registered nurse training); philosophy; physics; political science and government; psychology; religious studies; Russian; Russian studies; Scandinavian languages; social studies teacher education; social work; sociology; Spanish; visual and performing arts; women's studies.

Salem College
Accounting; American studies; art history, criticism and conservation; arts management; biology/biological sciences; business administration and management; chemistry; clinical laboratory science/medical technology; economics; education; English; fine/studio arts; French; German; history; interdisciplinary studies; interior design; international business/trade/commerce; international relations and affairs; mass communication/media; mathematics; music; music performance; philosophy; physician assistant; psychology; religious studies; sociology; Spanish.

Samford University
Accounting; art; Asian studies; athletic training; biochemistry; biology teacher education; biology/biological sciences; business administration and management; cartography; chemistry; classical, ancient Mediterranean and Near Eastern studies and archaeology; classics and languages, literatures and linguistics; commercial and advertising art; community organization and advocacy; computer science; counseling psychology; criminal justice/law enforcement administration; dramatic/theatre arts; engineering physics; engineering related; English; English/language arts teacher education; environmental science; environmental studies; foreign languages and literatures; French; general studies; geography; German; health and physical education; history; history teacher education; human development and family studies; human nutrition; human resources management; interior design; international business/trade/commerce; international relations and affairs; journalism; kinesiology and exercise science; Latin; Latin American studies; marine biology and biological oceanography; mathematics; music performance; music teacher education; music theory and composition; nursing (registered nurse training); philosophy; philosophy and religious studies related; physi-

cal education teaching and coaching; physics; piano and organ; political science and government; pre-medical studies; psychology; public administration; religious studies; religious/sacred music; science teacher education; science, technology and society; social science teacher education; social sciences; sociology; Spanish; speech and rhetoric; speech teacher education; visual and performing arts related; voice and opera.

Santa Clara University

Accounting; ancient/classical Greek; anthropology; art; art history, criticism and conservation; biological and physical sciences; biology/biological sciences; business/managerial economics; chemistry; civil engineering; classics and languages, literatures and linguistics; communication/speech communication and rhetoric; computer engineering; computer science; dramatic/theatre arts; economics; electrical, electronics and communications engineering; engineering; engineering physics; English; environmental science; environmental studies; finance; French; history; interdisciplinary studies; Italian; Latin; liberal arts and sciences/liberal studies; management information systems; marketing/marketing management; mathematics; mechanical engineering; music; philosophy; physics; political science and government; psychology; religious studies; sociology; Spanish.

Sarah Lawrence College

Acting; African studies; African-American/Black studies; American history; American literature; American studies; animal genetics; anthropology; archeology; architectural history and criticism; art; art history, criticism and conservation; Asian history; Asian studies; Asian studies (East); Asian studies (South); astronomy; biological and physical sciences; biology/biological sciences; chemistry; Chinese studies; cinematography and film/video production; classics and languages, literatures and linguistics; comparative literature; computer science; creative writing; dance; dance related; developmental and child psychology; directing and theatrical production; dramatic/theatre arts; drawing; early childhood education; ecology; economics; education; elementary education; English; English language and literature related; English literature (British and Commonwealth); environmental studies; European history; European studies; European studies (Central and Eastern); film/cinema studies; fine/studio arts; foreign languages and literatures; French; gay/lesbian studies; geology/earth science; German; history and philosophy of science and technology; history related; human development and family studies; human/medical genetics; humanities; interdisciplinary studies; international relations and affairs; Italian; Japanese; jazz/jazz studies; kindergarten/preschool education; Latin; Latin American studies; liberal arts and sciences and humanities related; liberal arts and sciences/liberal studies; literature; marine biology and biological oceanography; mathematics; Middle/Near Eastern and Semitic languages related; modern languages; molecular biology; music; music history, literature, and theory; music performance; music theory and composition; natural sciences; Near and Middle Eastern studies; organic chemistry; painting; philosophy; philosophy and

religious studies related; photography; physics; piano and organ; playwriting and screenwriting; political science and government; pre-dentistry studies; pre-law studies; pre-medical studies; pre-veterinary studies; printmaking; psychology; public policy analysis; religious studies; religious studies related; romance languages; Russian; sculpture; social sciences; social sciences related; sociology; Spanish; urban studies/affairs; violin, viola, guitar and other stringed instruments; visual and performing arts; visual and performing arts related; voice and opera; western civilization; wind/percussion instruments; women's studies.

Scripps College

African-American/Black studies; American studies; anthropology; art; art history, criticism and conservation; Asian studies; Asian studies (East); Asian-American studies; biochemistry; biology/biological sciences; chemistry; Chinese; classics and languages, literatures and linguistics; computer science; dance; dramatic/theatre arts; economics; English; environmental science; environmental studies; European studies; film/video and photographic arts related; fine/studio arts; foreign languages and literatures; French; geology/earth science; German; Hispanic-American, Puerto Rican, and Mexican-American/Chicano studies; history; international relations and affairs; Italian; Japanese; Jewish/Judaic studies; Latin; Latin American studies; legal studies; linguistics; mathematics; modern languages; molecular biology; multi-/interdisciplinary studies related; music; neuroscience; organizational behavior; philosophy; physics; physiological psychology/psychobiology; political science and government; pre-medical studies; psychology; religious studies; Russian; science, technology and society; sociology; Spanish; visual and performing arts related; women's studies.

Seattle Pacific University

Accounting; apparel and textiles; art; art teacher education; biochemistry; biology teacher education; biology/biological sciences; business administration and management; chemistry; classics and languages, literatures and linguistics; communication/speech communication and rhetoric; computer science; computer systems analysis; computer/information technology services administration related; dramatic/theatre arts; economics; electrical, electronics and communications engineering; engineering science; English; English/language arts teacher education; European studies; family and consumer economics related; family and consumer sciences/home economics teacher education; foods, nutrition, and wellness; French; general studies; German; history; kinesiology and exercise science; Latin; Latin American studies; liberal arts and sciences/liberal studies; mathematics; mathematics and statistics related; mathematics teacher education; music; music teacher education; nursing (registered nurse training); philosophy; physical education teaching and coaching; physics; political science and government; pre-dentistry studies; pre-law studies; pre-medical studies; psychology; religious education; Russian; science teacher education; social science teacher education; sociology; Spanish; special education; theology.

Seattle University

Accounting; applied mathematics; art; art history, criticism and conservation; Asian studies (East); biochemistry; biological and physical sciences; biology/biological sciences; business administration and management; business/managerial economics; chemistry; civil engineering; clinical laboratory science/medical technology; computer science; creative writing; criminal justice/law enforcement administration; diagnostic medical sonography and ultrasound technology; dramatic/theatre arts; economics; electrical, electronics and communications engineering; English; environmental studies; environmental/environmental health engineering; European studies (Western); finance; fine/studio arts; forensic science and technology; French; German; history; humanities; industrial engineering; insurance; international business/trade/commerce; international economics; international relations and affairs; journalism; liberal arts and sciences/liberal studies; management information systems; marketing/marketing management; mass communication/media; mathematics; mechanical engineering; nursing (registered nurse training); operations management; philosophy; photography; physics; political science and government; psychology; public administration; public relations/image management; religious studies; social work; sociology; Spanish.

Siena College

Accounting; American studies; biology/biological sciences; chemistry; classics and languages, literatures and linguistics; computer and information sciences; ecology; economics; English; finance; fine/studio arts; French; history; marketing/marketing management; mathematics; philosophy; physics; political science and government; pre-dentistry studies; pre-law studies; pre-medical studies; psychology; religious studies; secondary education; social work; sociology; Spanish.

Simon's Rock College of Bard

Acting; African-American/Black studies; agricultural business and management; American literature; American native/native American education; American studies; anthropology; applied mathematics; art history, criticism and conservation; Asian studies; biology/biological sciences; ceramic arts and ceramics; chemistry; Chinese; Chinese studies; cognitive psychology and psycholinguistics; computer and information sciences; computer graphics; computer science; creative writing; cultural studies; dance; developmental and child psychology; dramatic/theatre arts; drawing; ecology; economics related; English composition; environmental studies; ethnic, cultural minority, and gender studies related; European studies; fine/studio arts; foreign languages and literatures; French; French studies; geography; geology/earth science; German; German studies; interdisciplinary studies; jazz/jazz studies; Latin; Latin American studies; liberal arts and sciences/liberal studies; literature; mathematics; metal and jewelry arts; music; music theory and composition; natural sciences; painting; philosophy; photography; physics; playwriting and screenwriting; political science and government; pre-law studies; pre-medical studies; printmaking; psychology; religious studies;

sculpture; sociology; Spanish; Spanish and Iberian studies; theatre design and technology; theatre literature, history and criticism; Ukraine studies; visual and performing arts; visual and performing arts related; women's studies.

Simpson College

Accounting; advertising; art; art teacher education; athletic training; biochemistry; biological and physical sciences; biology/biological sciences; business administration and management; business/corporate communications; chemistry; clinical laboratory science/medical technology; commercial and advertising art; computer management; computer science; criminal justice/law enforcement administration; dramatic/theatre arts; economics; education; elementary education; English; environmental biology; French; German; history; information science/studies; international business/trade/commerce; international relations and affairs; kindergarten/preschool education; mass communication/media; mathematics; music; music performance; music teacher education; philosophy; physical education teaching and coaching; physical therapy; political science and government; pre-dentistry studies; pre-law studies; pre-medical studies; pre-veterinary studies; psychology; religious studies; secondary education; social sciences; sociology; Spanish; speech and rhetoric; sport and fitness administration.

Skidmore College

Anthropology; area, ethnic, cultural, and gender studies related; art history, criticism and conservation; Asian studies; biochemistry; biological and biomedical sciences related; biology/biological sciences; business, management, and marketing related; business/commerce; chemistry; classics and languages, literatures and linguistics; computer and information sciences; dance; dramatic/theatre arts; economics; elementary education; English language and literature related; environmental science; environmental studies; fine arts related; French; geology/earth science; German; history; kinesiology and exercise science; liberal arts and sciences/liberal studies; literature; mathematics; music history, literature, and theory; neuroscience; philosophy; physics; political science and government; psychology; psychology related; religious studies; social sciences related; social work; sociology; Spanish; women's studies.

Smith College

African-American/Black studies; American studies; ancient/classical Greek; anthropology; architecture; art; art history, criticism and conservation; Asian studies (East); astronomy; biochemistry; biology/biological sciences; chemistry; classics and languages, literatures and linguistics; comparative literature; computer science; dance; dramatic/theatre arts; East Asian languages; economics; education; engineering science; English; fine/studio arts; French; French studies; geology/earth science; German; German studies; history; interdisciplinary studies; Italian; Latin; Latin American studies; mathematics; medieval and renaissance studies; music; Near and Middle Eastern studies; neuroscience; philosophy; physics; political science and government; Portuguese; pre-law studies;

pre-medical studies; psychology; religious studies; Russian; Russian studies; sociology; Spanish; women's studies.

South Dakota School of Mines and Technology

Chemical engineering; chemistry; civil engineering; computer engineering; computer science; electrical, electronics and communications engineering; environmental/environmental health engineering; general studies; geological/geophysical engineering; geology/earth science; industrial engineering; interdisciplinary studies; mathematics; mechanical engineering; metallurgical engineering; mining and mineral engineering; physics.

Southern Methodist University

Accounting; advertising; African-American/Black studies; anthropology; applied economics; art history, criticism and conservation; biochemistry; biology/biological sciences; broadcast journalism; business administration and management; chemistry; computer engineering; computer science; creative writing; dance; dramatic/theatre arts; econometrics and quantitative economics; economics; electrical, electronics and communications engineering; English; environmental studies; environmental/ environmental health engineering; European studies; film/cinema studies; finance; fine/studio arts; foreign languages and literatures; French; geology/earth science; geophysics and seismology; German; Hispanic-American, Puerto Rican, and Mexican-American/Chicano studies; history; humanities; international relations and affairs; journalism; Latin American studies; management information systems; management science; marketing/marketing management; mathematics; mechanical engineering; medieval and renaissance studies; music; music performance; music teacher education; music theory and composition; music therapy; organizational behavior; philosophy; physics; piano and organ; political science and government; psychology; public policy analysis; public relations/image management; radio and television; real estate; religious studies; Russian; Russian studies; social sciences; sociology; Spanish; statistics.

Southwest Baptist University

Accounting; administrative assistant and secretarial science; art; art teacher education; athletic training; biblical studies; biology/ biological sciences; business administration and management; business teacher education; business/commerce; chemistry; chemistry teacher education; clinical laboratory science/medical technology; commercial and advertising art; communication/speech communication and rhetoric; computer science; criminal justice/law enforcement administration; dramatic/theatre arts; education (K-12); education (specific subject areas) related; elementary education; emergency medical technology (EMT paramedic); English; English/language arts teacher education; general studies; history; history teacher education; human services; information science/studies; mathematics; mathematics teacher education; middle school education; music; music teacher education; nursing (registered nurse training); occupational safety and health technology; parks, recreation

and leisure; pastoral studies/counseling; physical education teaching and coaching; political science and government; psychology; religious studies; science teacher education; secondary education; social science teacher education; social sciences; social studies teacher education; sociology; Spanish; Spanish language teacher education; speech teacher education; speech/ theater education; sport and fitness administration; theological and ministerial studies related; youth ministry.

Southwestern University

Accounting; American studies; animal sciences; art; art history, criticism and conservation; art teacher education; biology/biological sciences; business administration and management; chemistry; computer science; dramatic/theatre arts; economics; English; experimental psychology; fine/studio arts; French; German; history; international relations and affairs; literature; mass communication/media; mathematics; modern languages; music; music history, literature, and theory; music teacher education; philosophy; physical education teaching and coaching; physics; piano and organ; political science and government; psychology; religious studies; religious/sacred music; social sciences; sociology; Spanish; women's studies.

Southwest Missouri State University

Accounting; agribusiness; agricultural teacher education; agriculture; agronomy and crop science; ancient studies; animal sciences; anthropology; apparel and textiles; art; art teacher education; athletic training; audiology and speech-language pathology; biology teacher education; biology/biological sciences; business administration and management; business teacher education; business/commerce; cartography; cell and molecular biology; chemistry; chemistry teacher education; city/ urban, community and regional planning; clinical laboratory science/medical technology; communication/speech communication and rhetoric; computer science; criminal justice/ safety; dance; design and visual communications; dietetics; dramatic/theatre arts; early childhood education; economics; education (specific subject areas) related; elementary education; engineering physics; English; English/language arts teacher education; family and consumer sciences/home economics teacher education; finance; fine/studio arts; French; French language teacher education; geography; geology/earth science; German; German language teacher education; gerontology; history; history teacher education; horticultural science; hospitality administration; housing and human environments; human development and family studies; insurance; journalism; Latin; management information systems; marketing/ marketing management; mass communication/ media; mathematics; mathematics teacher education; medical radiologic technology; middle school education; molecular biology; music; music performance; music teacher education; music theory and composition; nursing (registered nurse training); parks, recreation and leisure; philosophy; physical education teaching and coaching; physical science technologies related; physics; physics teacher education; political science and government; psychology;

public administration; radiologic technology/ science; religious studies; respiratory care therapy; science teacher education; social work; sociology; Spanish; Spanish language teacher education; special education; technical and business writing; visual and performing arts; wildlife and wildlands science and management.

Stanford University

Aerospace, aeronautical and astronautical engineering; African studies; American Indian/ Native American studies; American studies; anthropology; archeology; art; Asian studies; Asian studies (East); biology/biological sciences; chemical engineering; chemistry; Chinese; civil engineering; classics and languages, literatures and linguistics; communication/speech communication and rhetoric; comparative literature; computer science; dramatic/theatre arts; economics; electrical, electronics and communications engineering; engineering; English; environmental studies; environmental/environmental health engineering; French; geology/ earth science; geophysics and seismology; German; Hispanic-American, Puerto Rican, and Mexican-American/Chicano studies; history; industrial engineering; interdisciplinary studies; international relations and affairs; Italian; Japanese; linguistics; materials engineering; materials science; mathematics; mathematics and computer science; mechanical engineering; music; petroleum engineering; philosophy; physics; political science and government; psychology; public policy analysis; religious studies; science, technology and society; Slavic languages; sociology; Spanish; systems science and theory; urban studies/affairs; women's studies.

State University of New York at Binghamton

Accounting; African studies; African-American/ Black studies; anthropology; Arabic; art; art history, criticism and conservation; Asian-American studies; biochemistry; biology/ biological sciences; biomedical/medical engineering; chemistry; classics and languages, literatures and linguistics; comparative literature; computer engineering; computer science; dramatic/theatre arts; drawing; economics; electrical, electronics and communications engineering; English; environmental studies; film/cinema studies; fine/studio arts; French; geography; geology/earth science; German; Hebrew; history; industrial engineering; information science/studies; interdisciplinary studies; Italian; Jewish/Judaic studies; Latin American studies; linguistics; literature; management science; mathematics; mechanical engineering; medieval and renaissance studies; music; music performance; nursing (registered nurse training); philosophy; physics; physiological psychology/psychobiology; political science and government; pre-law studies; psychology; sociology; Spanish.

State University of New York College at Geneseo

Accounting; African-American/Black studies; American studies; anthropology; art; art history, criticism and conservation; audiology and speech-language pathology; biochemistry; biology/biological sciences; biophysics; business administration and management; chemistry;

communication/speech communication and rhetoric; comparative literature; computer science; dramatic/theatre arts; economics; education; elementary education; English; fine/studio arts; French; geochemistry; geography; geology/ earth science; geophysics and seismology; history; international relations and affairs; kindergarten/preschool education; mathematics; music; natural sciences; philosophy; physics; political science and government; pre-dentistry studies; pre-law studies; pre-medical studies; pre-veterinary studies; psychology; sociology; Spanish; special education; speech therapy; visual and performing arts related.

Stephens College

Accounting; advertising; biology/biological sciences; biomedical sciences; broadcast journalism; business administration and management; child development; creative writing; dance; dramatic/theatre arts; early childhood education; elementary education; English; environmental studies; equestrian studies; fashion merchandising; fashion/apparel design; horse husbandry/equine science and management; interdisciplinary studies; international relations and affairs; kindergarten/preschool education; liberal arts and sciences/liberal studies; marketing/marketing management; mass communication/media; modern languages; natural sciences; occupational therapy; philosophy; political science and government; pre-law studies; pre-medical studies; pre-veterinary studies; psychology; public relations/image management; radio and television.

Stetson University

Accounting; American studies; aquatic biology/ limnology; art; biochemistry; biology/biological sciences; business administration and management; business/managerial economics; chemistry; clinical laboratory science/medical technology; communication/speech communication and rhetoric; computer science; dramatic/theatre arts; e-commerce; economics; education; elementary education; English; environmental studies; finance; French; geography; German; health services/allied health/health sciences; history; humanities; international business/trade/commerce; international relations and affairs; kinesiology and exercise science; Latin American studies; management science; marketing/marketing management; mathematics; molecular biology; music; music performance; music teacher education; music theory and composition; philosophy; physics; piano and organ; political science and government; pre-dentistry studies; pre-law studies; pre-medical studies; pre-veterinary studies; psychology; religious studies; Russian studies; secondary education; social science teacher education; social sciences; sociology; Spanish; sport and fitness administration; violin, viola, guitar and other stringed instruments; visual and performing arts related; voice and opera; web page, digital/multimedia and information resources design.

Stevens Institute of Technology

Biochemistry; biomedical/medical engineering; business administration and management; chemical engineering; chemistry; civil engineering; computational mathematics; computer engineering; computer science; electrical,

electronics and communications engineering; engineering physics; engineering/industrial management; English; environmental/environmental health engineering; history; history and philosophy of science and technology; humanities; mathematics; mechanical engineering; Near and Middle Eastern studies; philosophy; physics; pre-dentistry studies; pre-law studies; pre-medical studies; statistics; systems engineering.

Stonehill College

Accounting; American studies; biochemistry; biology/biological sciences; business administration and management; chemistry; communication/speech communication and rhetoric; computer engineering; computer science; criminal justice/safety; criminology; economics; elementary education; English; finance; fine/ studio arts; foreign languages and literatures; health/health care administration; history; international relations and affairs; kindergarten/ preschool education; marketing/marketing management; mathematics; multi-/ interdisciplinary studies related; philosophy; political science and government; psychology; public administration; religious studies; sociology; speech and rhetoric.

Susquehanna University

Accounting; art; art history, criticism and conservation; biochemistry; biology/biological sciences; broadcast journalism; business administration and management; business/ managerial economics; chemistry; communication/speech communication and rhetoric; computer science; creative writing; dramatic/ theatre arts; ecology; economics; elementary education; English; finance; French; geology/ earth science; German; graphic design; history; human resources management; information science/studies; international relations and affairs; journalism; kindergarten/preschool education; marketing/marketing management; mass communication/media; mathematics; music; music teacher education; philosophy; physics; piano and organ; political science and government; pre-dentistry studies; pre-law studies; pre-medical studies; pre-veterinary studies; psychology; public relations/image management; radio and television; religious studies; religious/sacred music; secondary education; sociology; Spanish; speech and rhetoric; violin, viola, guitar and other stringed instruments; voice and opera; wind/percussion instruments.

Swarthmore College

Ancient/classical Greek; area studies related; art history, criticism and conservation; Asian studies; astronomy; astrophysics; biochemistry; biological and biomedical sciences related; biology/biological sciences; chemical physics; chemistry; Chinese; classics and languages, literatures and linguistics; comparative literature; computer and information sciences; dance; dramatic/theatre arts; economics; education related; engineering; English; fine/studio arts; French; German; German studies; history; Latin; linguistics; mathematics; mathematics and computer science; medieval and renaissance studies; music; philosophy; physics; physiological psychology/psychobiology; political science and government; psychology; religious studies; Russian; social sciences related; Spanish; visual and performing arts related.

Sweet Briar College
Anthropology; art history, criticism and conservation; biochemistry, biophysics and molecular biology related; biology/biological sciences; business, management, and marketing related; business/commerce; chemistry; classics and languages, literatures and linguistics; communication/speech communication and rhetoric; computer science; creative writing; dance; dramatic/theatre arts; economics; engineering science; English; environmental science; environmental studies; fine/studio arts; foreign languages and literatures; French; German; history; international relations and affairs; Italian; liberal arts and sciences/liberal studies; mathematics; music; philosophy; physics; political science and government; psychology; religious studies; sociology; Spanish; theoretical and mathematical physics.

Syracuse University
Accounting; acting; advertising; aerospace, aeronautical and astronautical engineering; African-American/Black studies; American studies; anthropology; apparel and textiles; applied art; architecture; area, ethnic, cultural, and gender studies related; art; art history, criticism and conservation; art teacher education; Asian studies (South); audiology and speech-language pathology; biochemistry; biology teacher education; biology/biological sciences; biomedical/medical engineering; broadcast journalism; business administration and management; ceramic arts and ceramics; chemical engineering; chemistry; chemistry teacher education; child development; cinematography and film/video production; civil engineering; classics and languages, literatures and linguistics; clothing/textiles; commercial and advertising art; communication and journalism related; communication disorders sciences and services related; communication/speech communication and rhetoric; computer and information sciences; computer engineering; computer graphics; consumer merchandising/retailing management; consumer services and advocacy; design and visual communications; dietetics; dramatic/theatre arts; economics; education (K-12); education (specific subject areas) related; education related; electrical, electronics and communications engineering; engineering physics; engineering related; English; English literature (British and Commonwealth); English/language arts teacher education; entrepreneurship; environmental/environmental health engineering; family and community services; family and consumer sciences/home economics teacher education; family systems; fashion/apparel design; fiber, textile and weaving arts; finance; fine arts related; fine/studio arts; foods, nutrition, and wellness; foreign languages and literatures; French; geography; geology/earth science; German; health science; history; hospitality administration; housing and human environments; human development and family studies; humanities; illustration; industrial design; information science/studies; interdisciplinary studies; interior architecture; interior design; international relations and affairs; Italian; journalism; kindergarten/preschool education; kinesiology and exercise science; Latin American studies; liberal arts and sciences/liberal studies; linguistics; literature; logistics and materials management; marketing/marketing manage-

ment; mathematics; mathematics teacher education; mechanical engineering; medieval and renaissance studies; metal and jewelry arts; modern languages; music; music management and merchandising; music performance; music teacher education; music theory and composition; painting; philosophy; philosophy and religious studies related; photography; physical education teaching and coaching; physics; physics teacher education; piano and organ; political science and government; pre-dentistry studies; pre-law studies; pre-medical studies; pre-veterinary studies; printmaking; psychology; public administration; public relations/image management; radio and television; religious studies; restaurant/food services management; retailing; Russian; Russian studies; sales, distribution and marketing; sculpture; social studies teacher education; social work; sociology; Spanish; special education; speech and rhetoric; telecommunications; theatre design and technology; transportation and materials moving related; violin, viola, guitar and other stringed instruments; voice and opera; wind/percussion instruments; women's studies.

Taylor University
Accounting; ancient Near Eastern and biblical languages; art; art teacher education; athletic training; biblical studies; biology teacher education; biology/biological sciences; business administration and management; chemistry; clinical laboratory science/medical technology; commercial and advertising art; communication/speech communication and rhetoric; computer engineering; computer graphics; computer programming; computer science; creative writing; dramatic/theatre arts; economics; education; elementary education; engineering physics; English; environmental biology; environmental studies; finance; French; history; history teacher education; human resources management; information science/studies; international business/trade/commerce; international economics; international relations and affairs; kindergarten/preschool education; literature; management information systems; marketing/marketing management; mass communication/media; mathematics; middle school education; music; music management and merchandising; music performance; music teacher education; natural sciences; parks, recreation and leisure; philosophy; physical education teaching and coaching; physics; piano and organ; political science and government; pre-dentistry studies; pre-law studies; pre-medical studies; pre-veterinary studies; psychology; religious education; religious studies; religious/sacred music; science teacher education; secondary education; social science teacher education; social sciences; social work; sociology; Spanish; Spanish language teacher education; speech teacher education; sport and fitness administration; theology; voice and opera.

Texas A&M University
Accounting; aerospace, aeronautical and astronautical engineering; agribusiness; agricultural and food products processing; agricultural animal breeding; agricultural business and management; agricultural economics; agricultural production; agricultural/biological engineering and bioengineering; agricultural/farm supplies retailing and wholesaling; agriculture; agronomy and crop science;

American studies; animal sciences; animal/livestock husbandry and production; anthropology; applied horticulture; applied mathematics; aquaculture; architecture; atmospheric sciences and meteorology; biochemistry; biology/biological sciences; biomedical sciences; biomedical/medical engineering; botany/plant biology; business administration and management; cartography; cell and molecular biology; chemical engineering; chemistry; civil engineering; community health services counseling; computer engineering; computer science; construction engineering technology; curriculum and instruction; dairy science; digital communication and media/multimedia; dramatic/theatre arts; ecology; economics; electrical, electronic and communications engineering technology; electrical, electronics and communications engineering; engineering technology; English; entomology; environmental design/architecture; environmental science; environmental studies; farm and ranch management; finance; fishing and fisheries sciences and management; food science; foods, nutrition, and wellness; forest/forest resources management; forestry; French; geography; geological and earth sciences/geosciences related; geology/earth science; geophysics and seismology; German; health and physical education; history; horticultural science; industrial engineering; interdisciplinary studies; international/global studies; journalism; landscape architecture; management science; manufacturing technology; marketing/marketing management; mathematics; mechanical engineering; mechanical engineering/mechanical technology; microbiology; molecular genetics; multi-/interdisciplinary studies related; museum studies; music; natural resources/conservation; nuclear engineering; ocean engineering; ornamental horticulture; parks, recreation and leisure; parks, recreation and leisure facilities management; petroleum engineering; philosophy; physics; plant protection and integrated pest management; political science and government; poultry science; pre-veterinary studies; psychology; public relations, advertising, and applied communication related; range science and management; Russian; sales, distribution and marketing; sociology; Spanish; speech and rhetoric; tourism and travel services management; urban forestry; wildlife and wildlands science and management; zoology/animal biology.

Texas Christian University
Accounting; advertising; anthropology; art history, criticism and conservation; art teacher education; astronomy and astrophysics related; ballet; bilingual and multilingual education; biochemistry; biology/biological sciences; broadcast journalism; chemistry; communication/speech communication and rhetoric; computer and information sciences; computer and information sciences related; counselor education/school counseling and guidance; criminal justice/safety; dietetics; dietetics and clinical nutrition services related; dramatic/theatre arts; e-commerce; early childhood education; economics; educational leadership and administration; elementary education; engineering; English; English/language arts teacher education; environmental science; fashion merchandising; finance; fine/studio arts; French; general studies; geology/earth science;

health and physical education; health and physical education related; health science; history; interior design; international business/trade/commerce; international economics; international finance; international marketing; international relations and affairs; journalism; Latin American studies; liberal arts and sciences/liberal studies; management science; marketing/marketing management; mass communication/media; mathematics; mathematics teacher education; military studies; movement therapy and movement education; music; music performance; music teacher education; music theory and composition; neuroscience; nursing (registered nurse training); painting; philosophy; photography; physical education teaching and coaching; physics; piano and organ; political science and government; printmaking; psychology; radio and television; real estate; religious studies; science teacher education; sculpture; secondary education; social studies teacher education; social work; sociology; Spanish; special education; special education (gifted and talented); special education (hearing impaired); speech-language pathology; technical teacher education; theatre literature, history and criticism.

Texas Tech University

Accounting; acting; advertising; agricultural business and management; agricultural economics; agricultural production; agriculture; agronomy and crop science; animal sciences; animal/livestock husbandry and production; anthropology; apparel and textiles; applied horticulture; architectural engineering technology; architecture; art; art history, criticism and conservation; audiology and hearing sciences; biochemistry; biological and physical sciences; biology/biological sciences; business administration and management; business administration, management and operations related; cell biology and histology; chemical engineering; chemistry; child development; civil engineering; classics and languages, literatures and linguistics; commercial and advertising art; community health services counseling; computer and information sciences; computer engineering; dance; dietetics; dramatic/theatre arts; economics; electrical, electronic and communications engineering technology; electrical, electronics and communications engineering; engineering; engineering physics; engineering technology; engineering technology; English; environmental/environmental health engineering; family and consumer sciences/human sciences; family systems; fashion merchandising; fashion/apparel design; finance; fine/studio arts; fishing and fisheries sciences and management; food science; foods, nutrition, and wellness; French; general studies; geography; geology/earth science; geophysics and seismology; German; health and physical education; history; horticultural science; hotel/motel administration; human development and family studies; industrial engineering; interdisciplinary studies; interior architecture; international business/trade/commerce; journalism; kinesiology and exercise science; landscape architecture; Latin American studies; liberal arts and sciences/liberal studies; management information systems; marketing/marketing management; mathematics; mechanical engineering; mechanical engineering/mechanical technology; medical microbiology and bacteriology; molecular biol-

ogy; music; music performance; music theory and composition; natural resources/conservation; parks, recreation and leisure; petroleum engineering; philosophy; physics; plant protection and integrated pest management; political science and government; psychology; public relations/image management; radio and television; radio and television broadcasting technology; range science and management; Russian studies; social work; sociology; Spanish; speech and rhetoric; textile sciences and engineering; theatre design and technology; wildlife and wildlands science and management; zoology/animal biology.

Thomas Aquinas College

Interdisciplinary studies; liberal arts and sciences/liberal studies; multi-/interdisciplinary studies related; western civilization.

Transylvania University

Accounting; anthropology; art; art teacher education; biology/biological sciences; business administration and management; chemistry; computer science; dramatic/theatre arts; economics; elementary education; English; fine/studio arts; French; history; kinesiology and exercise science; mathematics; middle school education; music performance; music teacher education; philosophy; physical education teaching and coaching; physics; political science and government; psychology; religious studies; social sciences related; sociology; Spanish.

Trinity College

American studies; anthropology; art; art history, criticism and conservation; biochemistry; biology/biological sciences; biomedical/medical engineering; chemistry; classics and languages, literatures and linguistics; comparative literature; computer engineering; computer science; creative writing; dance; dramatic/theatre arts; economics; education; electrical, electronics and communications engineering; engineering; English; environmental science; fine/studio arts; French; German; history; interdisciplinary studies; international relations and affairs; Italian; Jewish/Judaic studies; mathematics; mechanical engineering; modern languages; music; neuroscience; philosophy; physics; political science and government; psychology; public policy analysis; religious studies; Russian; sociology; Spanish; women's studies.

Trinity University

Accounting; acting; anthropology; art; art history, criticism and conservation; Asian studies; biochemistry; biology/biological sciences; business administration and management; chemistry; Chinese; classics and languages, literatures and linguistics; communication/speech communication and rhetoric; computer and information sciences; dramatic/theatre arts; economics; engineering science; English; European studies; finance; French; geology/earth science; German; history; humanities; international business/trade/commerce; Latin American studies; management science; marketing/marketing management; mathematics; music; music performance; music theory and composition; philosophy; physics; political science and government; pre-dentistry studies; pre-law studies; pre-medical studies; pre-veterinary studies; psychology; religious studies;

Russian; sociology; Spanish; speech and rhetoric; theatre design and technology; urban studies/affairs; voice and opera.

Truman State University

Accounting; agricultural business and management; agricultural economics; agriculture; agronomy and crop science; animal sciences; applied art; art; art history, criticism and conservation; biology/biological sciences; business administration and management; chemistry; classics and languages, literatures and linguistics; commercial and advertising art; communication disorders; communication/speech communication and rhetoric; computer science; criminal justice/law enforcement administration; criminal justice/police science; design and visual communications; dramatic/theatre arts; economics; economics related; English; equestrian studies; finance; fine/studio arts; French; German; health science; history; horticultural science; journalism; kinesiology and exercise science; mass communication/media; mathematics; music; music performance; nursing (registered nurse training); philosophy; physics; piano and organ; political science and government; pre-dentistry studies; pre-law studies; pre-medical studies; pre-pharmacy studies; pre-veterinary studies; psychology; public health; religious studies; Russian; sociology; Spanish; speech and rhetoric; voice and opera.

Tufts University

African-American/Black studies; American studies; anthropology; archeology; architectural engineering; art history, criticism and conservation; Asian studies; Asian studies (Southeast); astronomy; behavioral sciences; biology/biological sciences; chemical engineering; chemistry; child development; Chinese; civil engineering; classics and languages, literatures and linguistics; community health and preventive medicine; computer engineering; computer science; developmental and child psychology; dramatic/theatre arts; ecology; economics; electrical, electronics and communications engineering; elementary education; engineering; engineering physics; engineering related; engineering science; English; environmental studies; environmental/environmental health engineering; experimental psychology; French; geological/geophysical engineering; geology/earth science; German; history; industrial engineering; international relations and affairs; Jewish/Judaic studies; kindergarten/preschool education; Latin; mathematics; mechanical engineering; mental health/rehabilitation; modern Greek; music; philosophy; physics; political science and government; psychology; public health; romance languages; Russian; Russian studies; secondary education; sociobiology; sociology; Spanish; special education; urban studies/affairs; women's studies.

Tulane University

Accounting; African studies; American studies; anatomy; anthropology; architecture; art; art history, criticism and conservation; Asian studies; biochemistry; biology/biological sciences; biomedical/medical engineering; biostatistics; business administration and management; business/commerce; cell biology and anatomical sciences related; cell biology and histology; chemical engineering; chemistry; civil engineering; classics and classical languages related; classics and languages, literatures and linguistics; cognitive psychology and psycholinguistics; communication and journalism related; communication/speech communication and rhetoric; computer and information sciences; computer engineering; computer science; corrections; criminal justice/safety; dramatic/theatre arts; ecology; economics; electrical, electronics and communications engineering; engineering science; English; environmental biology; environmental studies; environmental/environmental health engineering; evolutionary biology; finance; fine/studio arts; foreign languages and literatures; French; geology/earth science; German; Hispanic-American, Puerto Rican, and Mexican-American/Chicano studies; history; information science/studies; international relations and affairs; Italian; Jewish/Judaic studies; kinesiology and exercise science; Latin; Latin American studies; legal assistant/paralegal; legal professions and studies related; liberal arts and sciences and humanities related; liberal arts and sciences/liberal studies; linguistics; marketing/marketing management; mass communication/media; mathematics; mathematics and statistics related; mechanical engineering; medieval and renaissance studies; modern Greek; molecular biology; multi-/interdisciplinary studies related; music; neuroscience; nutrition sciences; philosophy; physics; political science and government; Portuguese; psychology; religious studies; Russian; Russian studies; sociology; Spanish; sport and fitness administration; statistics; women's studies.

Union College

Accounting; art; art teacher education; biochemistry; biology teacher education; biology/biological sciences; business administration and management; business teacher education; chemistry; chemistry teacher education; clinical laboratory science/medical technology; commercial and advertising art; computer science; computer teacher education; education; elementary education; engineering; English; English/language arts teacher education; entrepreneurship; fine/studio arts; French; German; graphic design; health science; health/medical preparatory programs related; history; history teacher education; information science/studies; international relations and affairs; journalism; kinesiology and exercise science; mathematics; mathematics teacher education; music; music performance; music teacher education; nursing (registered nurse training); pastoral studies/counseling; physical education teaching and coaching; physician assistant; physics; physics teacher education; psychology; public relations/image management; religious education; religious studies; secondary education; social science teacher education; social sciences; social work; Spanish; sport and fitness administration; theology.

Union College

American studies; anthropology; biochemistry; biological and physical sciences; biology/biological sciences; chemistry; classics and languages, literatures and linguistics; computer and information sciences; economics; electrical, electronics and communications engineering; English; fine/studio arts; foreign languages and literatures; geology/earth science; history; humanities; liberal arts and sciences/liberal

studies; mathematics; mechanical engineering; neuroscience; philosophy; physics; political science and government; psychology; social sciences; sociology.

Union University

Accounting; advertising; ancient Near Eastern and biblical languages; art; art teacher education; athletic training; biblical studies; biological and physical sciences; biology/biological sciences; broadcast journalism; business administration and management; business teacher education; business/managerial economics; chemistry; clinical laboratory science/medical technology; computer science; dramatic/theatre arts; economics; education; elementary education; English; English as a second/foreign language (teaching); family and community services; finance; foreign languages and literatures; French; history; information science/studies; journalism; kindergarten/preschool education; kinesiology and exercise science; marketing/marketing management; mass communication/media; mathematics; music; music management and merchandising; music performance; music teacher education; nursing (registered nurse training); parks, recreation and leisure facilities management; philosophy; philosophy and religious studies related; physical education teaching and coaching; physics; piano and organ; political science and government; pre-dentistry studies; pre-law studies; pre-medical studies; pre-pharmacy studies; psychology; public relations/image management; radio and television; religious studies; religious/sacred music; science teacher education; secondary education; social work; sociology; Spanish; special education; speech and rhetoric; sport and fitness administration; theology and religious vocations related; voice and opera.

United States Air Force Academy

Aerospace, aeronautical and astronautical engineering; area studies; atmospheric sciences and meteorology; behavioral sciences; biochemistry; biological and physical sciences; biology/biological sciences; business administration and management; chemistry; civil engineering; computer science; economics; electrical, electronics and communications engineering; engineering; engineering mechanics; engineering science; English; environmental/environmental health engineering; geography; history; humanities; interdisciplinary studies; legal studies; materials science; mathematics; mechanical engineering; military studies; operations research; physics; political science and government; social sciences.

United States Coast Guard Academy

Civil engineering; electrical, electronics and communications engineering; management science; marine science/merchant marine officer; mechanical engineering; naval architecture and marine engineering; operations research; political science and government.

United States Merchant Marine Academy

Engineering-related technologies; engineering/industrial management; marine science/

merchant marine officer; marine transportation related; maritime science; naval architecture and marine engineering; nuclear engineering technology; transportation and materials moving related.

United States Military Academy

Aerospace, aeronautical and astronautical engineering; American studies; applied mathematics; Arabic; Army R.O.T.C./military science; Asian studies (East); behavioral sciences; biological and physical sciences; biology/biological sciences; business administration and management; chemical engineering; chemistry; Chinese; civil engineering; computer engineering; computer science; economics; electrical, electronics and communications engineering; engineering; engineering physics; engineering/industrial management; environmental studies; environmental/environmental health engineering; European studies; European studies (Central and Eastern); French; geography; German; history; humanities; information science/studies; interdisciplinary studies; Latin American studies; literature; mathematics; mechanical engineering; modern languages; Near and Middle Eastern studies; nuclear engineering; operations research; philosophy; physics; political science and government; Portuguese; pre-law studies; pre-medical studies; psychology; public policy analysis; Russian; Spanish; systems engineering.

United States Naval Academy

Aerospace, aeronautical and astronautical engineering; chemistry; computer and information sciences; computer science; econometrics and quantitative economics; economics; electrical, electronics and communications engineering; English; history; mathematics; mechanical engineering; naval architecture and marine engineering; ocean engineering; oceanography (chemical and physical); physical sciences; physics; political science and government; systems engineering.

University at Buffalo, The State University of New York

Adult health nursing; aerospace, aeronautical and astronautical engineering; African-American/Black studies; American studies; anthropology; architecture; art; art history, criticism and conservation; Asian studies; audiology and speech-language pathology; biochemical technology; biochemistry; bioinformatics; biology/biological sciences; biophysics; biotechnology; business administration and management; chemical engineering; chemistry; civil engineering; classics and languages, literatures and linguistics; clinical laboratory science/medical technology; communication/speech communication and rhetoric; computer engineering; computer science; critical care nursing; dance; dramatic/theatre arts; dramatic/theatre arts and stagecraft related; economics; economics related; electrical, electronics and communications engineering; engineering physics; English; environmental design/architecture; environmental/environmental health engineering; family practice nursing/nurse practitioner; film/cinema studies; fine/studio arts; French; geography; geology/earth science; German; history; industrial engineering; Italian; kinesiology and exercise science; linguistics; mass communication/media; maternal/child health and neonatal nursing; mathematics; mathematics related; mechanical engineering; medicinal and pharmaceutical chemistry; multi-/interdisciplinary studies related; music; music performance; nuclear medical technology; nurse anesthetist; nursing (registered nurse training); nursing related; nutrition sciences; occupational therapy; pediatric nursing; pharmacology; pharmacy administration/pharmaceutics; pharmacy, pharmaceutical sciences, and administration related; philosophy; physics; physics related; political science and government; psychiatric/mental health nursing; psychology; social work; sociology; Spanish; structural engineering; theoretical and mathematical physics; women's studies.

The University of Alabama

Accounting; advertising; aerospace, aeronautical and astronautical engineering; American studies; anthropology; apparel and textiles; art history, criticism and conservation; athletic training; audiology and speech-language pathology; biological and physical sciences; biology/biological sciences; business administration and management; business/managerial economics; chemical engineering; chemistry; civil engineering; classics and languages, literatures and linguistics; computer and information sciences; consumer economics; criminal justice/safety; dance; dramatic/theatre arts; electrical, electronics and communications engineering; elementary education; English; family and consumer sciences/human sciences; family and consumer sciences/human sciences related; finance; fine/studio arts; foods, nutrition, and wellness; French; geography; geology/earth science; German; health professions related; history; hospital and health care facilities administration; hotel/motel administration; human development and family studies; industrial engineering; interdisciplinary studies; interior design; international relations and affairs; journalism; kindergarten/preschool education; Latin American studies; management information systems; management science; marine biology and biological oceanography; marketing/marketing management; mathematics; mechanical engineering; medical microbiology and bacteriology; metallurgical engineering; music; music teacher education; nursing (registered nurse training); philosophy; physical education teaching and coaching; physics; political science and government; psychology; public relations/image management; radio and television; religious studies; Russian; secondary education; social work; sociology; Spanish; special education; speech and rhetoric.

The University of Alabama in Huntsville

Accounting; art; biology/biological sciences; business administration and management; chemical engineering; chemistry; civil engineering; computer and information sciences; computer engineering; electrical, electronics and communications engineering; elementary education; engineering related; English; finance; foreign languages and literatures; history; industrial engineering; management information systems; marketing/marketing management; mathematics; mechanical engineering; music; nursing (registered nurse training);

philosophy; physics; political science and government; psychology; sociology; speech and rhetoric.

The University of Arizona

Accounting; aerospace, aeronautical and astronautical engineering; agricultural economics; agricultural teacher education; agricultural/biological engineering and bioengineering; agriculture; animal physiology; animal sciences; anthropology; architecture; art history, criticism and conservation; art teacher education; Asian studies (East); astronomy; atmospheric sciences and meteorology; biochemistry; biology teacher education; biology/biological sciences; business/commerce; business/managerial economics; cell biology and histology; chemical engineering; chemistry; chemistry teacher education; city/urban, community and regional planning; civil engineering; classics and languages, literatures and linguistics; clinical laboratory science/medical technology; communication disorders; communication/speech communication and rhetoric; computer and information sciences; computer engineering; consumer economics; creative writing; criminal justice/law enforcement administration; dance; drama and dance teacher education; dramatic/theatre arts; ecology; economics; education (specific subject areas) related; electrical, electronics and communications engineering; elementary education; engineering; engineering physics; engineering related; English; English/language arts teacher education; entrepreneurship; environmental studies; evolutionary biology; family and consumer sciences/home economics teacher education; finance; fine/studio arts; foreign language teacher education; French; French language teacher education; geography; geological/geophysical engineering; geology/earth science; German; German language teacher education; health teacher education; health/health care administration; Hispanic-American, Puerto Rican, and Mexican-American/Chicano studies; history; history teacher education; human development and family studies; human resources management; humanities; industrial engineering; Italian; Jewish/Judaic studies; journalism; kindergarten/preschool education; landscape architecture; Latin American studies; liberal arts and sciences/liberal studies; linguistics; management information systems; marketing/marketing management; materials science; mathematics; mathematics teacher education; mechanical engineering; medical microbiology and bacteriology; mining and mineral engineering; molecular biophysics; multi-/interdisciplinary studies related; music; music performance; music related; music teacher education; Near and Middle Eastern studies; nuclear engineering; nursing (registered nurse training); nutrition sciences; operations management; optical sciences; philosophy; physical education teaching and coaching; physics; physics teacher education; plant sciences; political science and government; pre-veterinary studies; psychology; public administration; radio and television; religious studies; Russian; science teacher education; science technologies related; secondary education; social science teacher education; social studies teacher education; sociology; soil science and agronomy; Spanish; Spanish language teacher education; special education; speech teacher education; systems engineering;

theatre design and technology; visual and performing arts; water resources engineering; wildlife and wildlands science and management; women's studies.

University of Arkansas

Accounting; adult and continuing education; agribusiness; agricultural economics; agricultural production; agricultural teacher education; agricultural/biological engineering and bioengineering; agronomy and crop science; American Sign Language related; American studies; animal sciences; anthropology; apparel and textiles; architecture; art; audiology and speech-language pathology; biology/biological sciences; botany/plant biology; business administration and management; business/commerce; business/managerial economics; cell biology and anatomical sciences related; chemical engineering; chemistry; civil engineering; classics and languages, literatures and linguistics; communication/speech communication and rhetoric; community health services counseling; comparative literature; computer and information sciences; computer engineering; computer systems analysis; counselor education/school counseling and guidance; creative writing; criminal justice/safety; curriculum and instruction; data processing and data processing technology; dramatic/theatre arts; economics; educational assessment, testing, and measurement; educational evaluation and research; educational leadership and administration; educational statistics and research methods; educational/instructional media design; electrical, electronics and communications engineering; elementary education; engineering; engineering related; English; entomology; environmental science; environmental/environmental health engineering; family and consumer sciences/home economics teacher education; family and consumer sciences/human sciences; finance; food science; foods, nutrition, and wellness; French; geography; geological and earth sciences/geosciences related; geology/earth science; German; gerontology; health and physical education; health professions related; higher education/higher education administration; history; horticultural science; housing and human environments; human development and family studies; industrial engineering; international business/trade/commerce; international relations and affairs; journalism; kinesiology and exercise science; landscape architecture; logistics and materials management; management science; marketing/marketing management; mathematics; mathematics teacher education; mechanical engineering; middle school education; multi-/interdisciplinary studies related; music performance; music teacher education; Near and Middle Eastern studies; nursing (registered nurse training); ornamental horticulture; parks, recreation and leisure; parks, recreation and leisure facilities management; philosophy; physical education teaching and coaching; physics; physics related; plant pathology/phytopathology; plant protection and integrated pest management; plant sciences; political science and government; poultry science; pre-medical studies; psychology; public administration; public policy analysis; secondary education; social work; sociology; Spanish; special education; special education related; statistics; technology/industrial arts teacher education; trade and industrial teacher education; transportation and highway engineering; vocational rehabilitation counseling.

University of California, Berkeley

African-American/Black studies; American Indian/Native American studies; American studies; ancient/classical Greek; anthropology; applied mathematics; architecture; art; art history, criticism and conservation; Asian studies; Asian studies (Southeast); Asian-American studies; astrophysics; biology/biological sciences; biomedical/medical engineering; botany/plant biology; business administration and management; cell and molecular biology; Celtic languages; chemical engineering; chemistry; chemistry related; Chinese; civil engineering; classical, ancient Mediterranean and Near Eastern studies and archaeology; classics and languages, literatures and linguistics; cognitive science; comparative literature; computer science; dance; dramatic/theatre arts; Dutch/Flemish; economics; electrical, electronics and communications engineering; engineering physics; engineering science; English; environmental science; environmental studies; environmental/environmental health engineering; ethnic, cultural minority, and gender studies related; film/cinema studies; foreign languages related; forestry; French; geography; geological/geophysical engineering; geology/earth science; German; Hispanic-American, Puerto Rican, and Mexican-American/Chicano studies; history; Italian; Japanese; landscape architecture; Latin; Latin American studies; legal studies; linguistics; manufacturing engineering; mass communication/media; materials science; mathematics; mechanical engineering; microbiology; multi-/interdisciplinary studies related; music; natural resources management and policy; natural resources/conservation; Near and Middle Eastern studies; nuclear engineering; nutrition sciences; operations research; peace studies and conflict resolution; philosophy; physical sciences; physics; political science and government; psychology; public health related; religious studies; Scandinavian languages; Slavic languages; social sciences related; social work; sociology; Spanish; speech and rhetoric; statistics; urban studies/affairs; women's studies.

University of California, Davis

Aerospace, aeronautical and astronautical engineering; African studies; African-American/Black studies; agricultural business and management; agricultural economics; agricultural teacher education; agricultural/biological engineering and bioengineering; American Indian/Native American studies; American studies; animal genetics; animal physiology; animal sciences; anthropology; apparel and textiles; art; art history, criticism and conservation; Asian studies (East); atmospheric sciences and meteorology; biochemistry; biology/biological sciences; biomedical/medical engineering; botany/plant biology; cell biology and histology; chemical engineering; chemistry; Chinese; civil engineering; comparative literature; computer engineering; design and visual communications; dramatic/theatre arts; economics; electrical, electronics and communications engineering; engineering; English; entomology; environmental biology; food science; foods, nutrition, and wellness; French; geology/earth science; German; Hispanic-American, Puerto Rican, and

Mexican-American/Chicano studies; history; horticultural science; human development and family studies; international agriculture; international relations and affairs; Italian; Japanese; landscape architecture; linguistics; materials engineering; mathematics; mechanical engineering; medical microbiology and bacteriology; music; natural resources/conservation; philosophy; physical education teaching and coaching; physics; political science and government; poultry science; psychology; range science and management; religious studies; Russian; sociology; Spanish; speech and rhetoric; statistics; women's studies; zoology/animal biology.

University of California, Irvine

Aerospace, aeronautical and astronautical engineering; African-American/Black studies; anthropology; area, ethnic, cultural, and gender studies related; art; art history, criticism and conservation; Asian studies (East); Asian-American studies; biology/biological sciences; biomedical/medical engineering; chemical engineering; chemistry; Chinese; civil engineering; classical, ancient Mediterranean and Near Eastern studies and archaeology; classics and languages, literatures and linguistics; comparative literature; computer and information sciences; computer and information sciences and support services related; computer engineering; computer science; criminology; cultural studies; dance; dramatic/theatre arts; ecology; economics; electrical, electronics and communications engineering; English; environmental design/architecture; environmental/environmental health engineering; European studies; film/cinema studies; fine/studio arts; French; geology/earth science; German; German studies; Hispanic-American, Puerto Rican, and Mexican-American/Chicano studies; history; human ecology; humanities; international/global studies; Japanese; journalism; linguistics; literature; materials engineering; mathematics; mechanical engineering; microbiology; molecular biochemistry; multi-/interdisciplinary studies related; music; music performance; neuroscience; philosophy; physics; political science and government; psychology; Russian; social psychology; social sciences; sociology; Spanish; women's studies.

University of California, Los Angeles

Aerospace, aeronautical and astronautical engineering; African languages; African studies; African-American/Black studies; agricultural/biological engineering and bioengineering; American Indian/Native American studies; American literature; American studies; ancient/classical Greek; anthropology; applied mathematics; Arabic; archeology; architecture; area studies related; art; art history, criticism and conservation; Asian studies; Asian studies (East); Asian studies (Southeast); Asian-American studies; astronomy; astrophysics; atmospheric sciences and meteorology; biochemistry; biology/biological sciences; biomathematics and bioinformatics related; biomedical/medical engineering; biophysics; biostatistics; biotechnology; botany/plant biology; business administration and management; business/managerial economics; cell and molecular biology; chemical engineering; chemistry; Chinese;

city/urban, community and regional planning; civil engineering; classical, ancient Mediterranean and Near Eastern studies and archaeology; classics and classical languages related; classics and languages, literatures and linguistics; cognitive science; communication/speech communication and rhetoric; community health and preventive medicine; comparative literature; computational mathematics; computer engineering; computer science; dance; design and applied arts related; development economics and international development; dramatic/theatre arts; East Asian languages; ecology; economics; education; educational leadership and administration; electrical, electronics and communications engineering; engineering; English; English as a second/foreign language (teaching); English language and literature related; environmental health; environmental science; epidemiology; European studies; film/cinema studies; fine arts related; foreign languages related; French; geochemistry; geography; geography related; geological and earth sciences/geosciences related; geological/geophysical engineering; geology/earth science; geophysics and seismology; German; Germanic languages related; health services administration; Hebrew; Hispanic-American, Puerto Rican, and Mexican-American/Chicano studies; history; human/medical genetics; information science/studies; international economics; Islamic studies; Italian; Japanese; Jewish/Judaic studies; kinesiology and exercise science; Korean; Latin; Latin American studies; liberal arts and sciences and humanities related; liberal arts and sciences/liberal studies; library science related; linguistic and comparative language studies related; linguistics; manufacturing engineering; marine biology and biological oceanography; materials engineering; materials science; mathematics; mathematics related; mechanical engineering; medical microbiology and bacteriology; microbiological sciences and immunology related; Middle/Near Eastern and Semitic languages related; modern Greek; molecular biochemistry; molecular biology; molecular pharmacology; molecular physiology; molecular toxicology; multi-/interdisciplinary studies related; music; music history, literature, and theory; musicology and ethnomusicology; Near and Middle Eastern studies; neurobiology and neurophysiology; neuroscience; nursing (registered nurse training); nursing related; pathology/experimental pathology; philosophy; physics; physiological psychology/psychobiology; physiology; plant sciences; political science and government; Portuguese; psychology; public administration; public health related; public policy analysis; religious studies; Russian; Russian studies; Scandinavian languages; Slavic languages; social work; sociology; Spanish; special education; statistics; visual and performing arts related; women's studies.

University of California, Riverside

African-American/Black studies; American Indian/Native American studies; anthropology; art history, criticism and conservation; Asian studies; Asian-American studies; biochemistry; biology/biological sciences; biomedical sciences; botany/plant biology; business administration and management; business/managerial economics; chemical engineering; chemistry; Chinese; classics and languages, literatures and linguistics;

comparative literature; computer science; creative writing; cultural studies; dance; dramatic/theatre arts; economics; electrical, electronics and communications engineering; English; entomology; environmental studies; environmental/environmental health engineering; fine/studio arts; French; geology/earth science; geophysics and seismology; German; Hispanic-American, Puerto Rican, and Mexican-American/Chicano studies; history; human development and family studies; humanities; Latin American studies; liberal arts and sciences/liberal studies; linguistics; mathematics; mechanical engineering; music; neuroscience; philosophy; physical sciences; physics; physiological psychology/psychobiology; political science and government; pre-law studies; psychology; public administration; religious studies; Russian; Russian studies; social sciences; sociology; Spanish; statistics; women's studies.

University of California, San Diego

Aerospace, aeronautical and astronautical engineering; animal physiology; anthropology; applied mathematics; archeology; art; art history, criticism and conservation; atomic/molecular physics; biochemistry; biology/biological sciences; biomedical/medical engineering; biophysics; biotechnology; cell biology and histology; chemical engineering; chemistry; chemistry teacher education; Chinese; classics and languages, literatures and linguistics; cognitive psychology and psycholinguistics; computer engineering; computer science; creative writing; cultural studies; dance; dramatic/theatre arts; ecology; econometrics and quantitative economics; economics; electrical, electronics and communications engineering; engineering; engineering physics; engineering science; English; environmental studies; film/cinema studies; fine/studio arts; foreign languages and literatures; French; geology/earth science; German; history; human ecology; interdisciplinary studies; intermedia/multimedia; Italian; Japanese; Jewish/Judaic studies; Latin American studies; linguistics; literature; management science; mass communication/media; mathematics; mathematics teacher education; mechanical engineering; medical microbiology and bacteriology; medicinal and pharmaceutical chemistry; molecular biology; music; music history, literature, and theory; natural resources management and policy; philosophy; physics; physics teacher education; political science and government; psychology; religious studies; Russian; Russian studies; sociology; Spanish; structural engineering; systems engineering; urban studies/affairs; women's studies.

University of California, Santa Barbara

African-American/Black studies; animal physiology; anthropology; aquatic biology/limnology; art history, criticism and conservation; Asian studies; Asian-American studies; biochemistry; biology/biological sciences; biopsychology; business/managerial economics; cell biology and histology; chemical engineering; chemistry; Chinese; classics and languages, literatures and linguistics; communication/speech communication and rhetoric; comparative literature;

computer engineering; computer science; dance; dramatic/theatre arts; ecology; economics; electrical, electronic and communications engineering technology; electrical, electronics and communications engineering; English; environmental studies; film/cinema studies; fine/studio arts; French; geography; geology/earth science; geophysics and seismology; German; Hispanic-American, Puerto Rican, and Mexican-American/Chicano studies; history; interdisciplinary studies; Islamic studies; Italian; Japanese; Latin American studies; linguistics; marine biology and biological oceanography; mathematics; mechanical engineering; medical microbiology and bacteriology; medieval and renaissance studies; molecular biology; multi-/interdisciplinary studies related; music; Near and Middle Eastern studies; pharmacology; philosophy; physics; political science and government; Portuguese; pre-law studies; psychology; public/applied history and archival administration; religious studies; Slavic languages; sociology; Spanish; statistics; women's studies; zoology/animal biology.

University of California, Santa Cruz

American studies; ancient/classical Greek; anthropology; applied mathematics; art; art history, criticism and conservation; Asian studies; Asian studies (East); Asian studies (South); Asian studies (Southeast); astrophysics; biochemistry; biology/biological sciences; botany/plant biology; business/managerial economics; cell biology and histology; chemistry; Chinese; cinematography and film/video production; classics and languages, literatures and linguistics; cognitive psychology and psycholinguistics; comparative literature; computer engineering; computer science; creative writing; dance; developmental and child psychology; dramatic/theatre arts; drawing; ecology; economics; electrical, electronics and communications engineering; English language and literature related; environmental studies; European history; family and community services; film/cinema studies; foreign languages and literatures; French; geology/earth science; geophysics and seismology; German; Hispanic-American, Puerto Rican, and Mexican-American/Chicano studies; history; information science/studies; international economics; Italian; Italian studies; Japanese; Latin; Latin American studies; legal studies; linguistics; literature; marine biology and biological oceanography; mathematics; mathematics teacher education; molecular biology; music; peace studies and conflict resolution; philosophy; photography; physics; physiological psychology/psychobiology; plant sciences; political science and government; printmaking; psychology; religious studies; Russian studies; sculpture; social psychology; sociology; Spanish; theatre design and technology; women's studies.

University of Central Arkansas

Accounting; art; athletic training; audiology and speech-language pathology; biological and physical sciences; biology/biological sciences; business administration and management; business teacher education; business/commerce; chemistry; child care and support services management; clinical laboratory science/medical technology; computer and information sci-

ences; economics; elementary and middle school administration/principalship; elementary education; English; English composition; English/language arts teacher education; environmental studies; family and consumer sciences/home economics teacher education; family and consumer sciences/human sciences; finance; French; general studies; geography; history; insurance; journalism; kinesiology and exercise science; management information systems; marketing/marketing management; mathematics; mathematics teacher education; medical radiologic technology; middle school education; music; music performance; nuclear medical technology; nursing (registered nurse training); occupational therapy; philosophy; physical education teaching and coaching; physical sciences; physical therapist assistant; physical therapy; physics; political science and government; psychology; public administration; reading teacher education; religious studies; science teacher education; social studies teacher education; sociology; Spanish; special education; speech and rhetoric.

University of Central Florida

Accounting; actuarial science; advertising; aerospace, aeronautical and astronautical engineering; anthropology; art; art teacher education; audiology and speech-language pathology; biology/biological sciences; business administration and management; business teacher education; business/commerce; business/managerial economics; chemistry; cinematography and film/video production; civil engineering; clinical laboratory science/medical technology; computer and information sciences; computer engineering; computer technology/computer systems technology; criminal justice/safety; dramatic/theatre arts; early childhood education; economics; electrical, electronic and communications engineering technology; electrical, electronics and communications engineering; elementary education; engineering technology; English; English/language arts teacher education; environmental/environmental health engineering; finance; fine/studio arts; foreign language teacher education; foreign languages and literatures; forensic science and technology; French; health information/medical records administration; health science; health services/allied health/health sciences; health/health care administration; history; hospitality administration; humanities; industrial engineering; information technology; intermedia/multimedia; journalism; legal assistant/paralegal; liberal arts and sciences/liberal studies; management information systems; marketing/marketing management; mass communication/media; mathematics; mathematics teacher education; mechanical engineering; mechanical engineering technologies related; medical microbiology and bacteriology; medical radiologic technology; music teacher education; nursing (registered nurse training); philosophy; photography; physical education teaching and coaching; physics; political science and government; psychology; public administration; radio and television; respiratory care therapy; science teacher education; social science teacher education; social sciences; social work; sociology; Spanish; special education; speech and rhetoric; statistics; trade and industrial teacher education.

University of Chicago

African studies; African-American/Black studies; American studies; ancient Near Eastern and biblical languages; ancient/classical Greek; anthropology; applied mathematics; Arabic; art; art history, criticism and conservation; Asian studies; Asian studies (East); Asian studies (South); Asian studies (Southeast); behavioral sciences; biochemistry; biology/biological sciences; chemistry; Chinese; classics and languages, literatures and linguistics; computer science; creative writing; economics; English; environmental studies; European studies (Central and Eastern); film/cinema studies; fine/studio arts; French; geography; geophysics and seismology; German; history; history and philosophy of science and technology; humanities; interdisciplinary studies; Italian; Japanese; Jewish/Judaic studies; Latin; Latin American studies; liberal arts and sciences/liberal studies; linguistics; mathematics; medieval and renaissance studies; modern languages; music; music history, literature, and theory; Near and Middle Eastern studies; philosophy; physics; political science and government; psychology; public policy analysis; religious studies; romance languages; Russian; Russian studies; Slavic languages; social sciences; sociology; Spanish; statistics.

University of Colorado at Boulder

Accounting; advertising; aerospace, aeronautical and astronautical engineering; anthropology; applied mathematics; architectural engineering; Asian studies; astronomy; biochemistry; broadcast journalism; business/commerce; cell and molecular biology; chemical engineering; chemistry; Chinese; civil engineering; classics and languages, literatures and linguistics; communication disorders; communication/speech communication and rhetoric; computer engineering; computer science; cultural studies; dance; dramatic/theatre arts; ecology, evolution, systematics and population biology related; economics; electrical, electronics and communications engineering; engineering physics; English; environmental design/architecture; environmental studies; environmental/environmental health engineering; film/cinema studies; finance; fine/studio arts; French; geography; geology/earth science; Germanic languages; history; humanities; international/global studies; Italian; Japanese; journalism; kinesiology and exercise science; linguistics; management information systems; marketing/marketing management; mathematics; mechanical engineering; multi-/interdisciplinary studies related; music; music performance; music teacher education; philosophy; physics; political science and government; psychology; religious studies; Russian studies; sociology; Spanish; women's studies.

University of Dallas

Art; art history, criticism and conservation; art teacher education; biochemistry; biology/biological sciences; ceramic arts and ceramics; chemistry; classics and languages, literatures and linguistics; computer science; dramatic/theatre arts; economics; economics related; education; elementary education; English; fine/studio arts; French; German; history; mathematics; painting; philosophy; physics; political science and

government; pre-dentistry studies; pre-law studies; pre-medical studies; pre-theology/pre-ministerial studies; printmaking; psychology; sculpture; secondary education; Spanish; theology.

University of Dayton

Accounting; American studies; applied art; applied mathematics related; art; art history, criticism and conservation; art teacher education; biochemistry; biology/biological sciences; broadcast journalism; business administration and management; business/managerial economics; chemical engineering; chemistry; civil engineering; commercial and advertising art; computer engineering; computer engineering technology; computer science; criminal justice/law enforcement administration; dietetics; dramatic/theatre arts; economics; education; electrical, electronic and communications engineering technology; electrical, electronics and communications engineering; elementary education; English; environmental biology; environmental studies; finance; fine/studio arts; foods, nutrition, and wellness; French; general studies; geology/earth science; German; health teacher education; history; industrial technology; information science/studies; international business/trade/commerce; international relations and affairs; journalism; kindergarten/preschool education; kinesiology and exercise science; management information systems; marketing/marketing management; mass communication/media; mathematics; mechanical engineering; mechanical engineering/mechanical technology; music; music teacher education; music therapy; philosophy; photography; physical education teaching and coaching; physical sciences; physics; political science and government; pre-dentistry studies; pre-law studies; pre-medical studies; psychology; public relations/image management; radio and television; religious education; religious studies; science teacher education; secondary education; sociology; Spanish; special education; sport and fitness administration.

University of Delaware

Accounting; African-American/Black studies; agribusiness; agricultural business and management; agricultural economics; agricultural teacher education; agricultural/biological engineering and bioengineering; agriculture; agronomy and crop science; animal sciences; anthropology; applied art; art; art history, criticism and conservation; Asian studies (East); astronomy; astrophysics; athletic training; bilingual and multilingual education; biochemistry; biology teacher education; biology/biological sciences; biology/biotechnology laboratory technician; biotechnology; botany/plant biology; business administration and management; business/managerial economics; chemical engineering; chemistry; chemistry teacher education; child development; civil engineering; classics and languages, literatures and linguistics; clinical laboratory science/medical technology; commercial and advertising art; communication/speech communication and rhetoric; community organization and advocacy; comparative literature; computer and information sciences; computer engineering; computer science; consumer economics; criminal justice/law enforcement administration; developmental and child psychology; dietetics; ecology;

economics; education; electrical, electronics and communications engineering; elementary education; engineering; English; English as a second/foreign language (teaching); English/language arts teacher education; entomology; environmental engineering technology; environmental studies; environmental/environmental health engineering; family and community services; family and consumer economics related; fashion merchandising; fashion/apparel design; film/cinema studies; finance; food science; foods, nutrition, and wellness; foreign language teacher education; foreign languages and literatures; French; geography; geology/earth science; geophysics and seismology; German; health and physical education; health teacher education; historic preservation and conservation; history; history teacher education; horticultural science; hospitality and recreation marketing; hotel/motel administration; human development and family studies; international relations and affairs; Italian; journalism; kindergarten/preschool education; kinesiology and exercise science; Latin; Latin American studies; liberal arts and sciences/liberal studies; linguistics; marketing/marketing management; mass communication/media; mathematics; mathematics teacher education; mechanical engineering; middle school education; music; music teacher education; music theory and composition; natural resources management and policy; neuroscience; nursing (registered nurse training); nursing science; nutrition sciences; operations management; ornamental horticulture; paleontology; parks, recreation and leisure facilities management; philosophy; physical education teaching and coaching; physics; physics teacher education; piano and organ; plant protection and integrated pest management; political science and government; pre-veterinary studies; psychology; public relations/image management; Russian; science teacher education; secondary education; sociology; soil conservation; soil science and agronomy; Spanish; special education; technical and business writing; theatre design and technology; voice and opera; wildlife and wildlands science and management; women's studies.

University of Denver

Accounting; animal sciences; anthropology; art; art history, criticism and conservation; art teacher education; Asian-American studies; biochemistry; biological and physical sciences; biology/biological sciences; biopsychology; business administration and management; business, management, and marketing related; business/commerce; business/managerial economics; chemistry; commercial and advertising art; communication/speech communication and rhetoric; computer and information sciences; computer engineering; computer systems analysis; construction management; creative writing; criminology; dramatic/theatre arts; economics; electrical, electronics and communications engineering; engineering; English; environmental studies; finance; fine/studio arts; French; geography; German; history; hospitality administration; hotel/motel administration; international business/trade/commerce; international relations and affairs; Italian; journalism; Latin American studies; management information systems; marketing/marketing management; mathematics; mechanical engineering;

molecular biology; multi-/interdisciplinary studies related; music; music performance; musicology and ethnomusicology; operations research; philosophy; physics; political science and government; psychology; public administration; real estate; religious studies; Russian; social sciences; social sciences related; sociology; Spanish; statistics; women's studies.

University of Evansville

Accounting; anthropology; archeology; art; art history, criticism and conservation; art teacher education; arts management; athletic training; biblical studies; biochemistry; biology/biological sciences; business administration and management; business/managerial economics; ceramic arts and ceramics; chemistry; civil engineering; classics and languages, literatures and linguistics; clinical laboratory science/medical technology; commercial and advertising art; computer engineering; computer science; creative writing; criminal justice/law enforcement administration; dramatic/theatre arts; drawing; economics; electrical, electronics and communications engineering; elementary education; engineering/industrial management; English; environmental studies; finance; French; German; gerontology; health/health care administration; history; international business/trade/commerce; international relations and affairs; kinesiology and exercise science; legal studies; liberal arts and sciences/liberal studies; literature; marketing/marketing management; mass communication/media; mathematics; mechanical engineering; music; music management and merchandising; music teacher education; music therapy; nursing (registered nurse training); philosophy; physical education teaching and coaching; physical therapist assistant; physical therapy; physics; physiological psychology/psychobiology; political science and government; pre-dentistry studies; pre-law studies; pre-medical studies; pre-veterinary studies; psychology; religious studies; science teacher education; sculpture; secondary education; sociology; Spanish; special education.

University of Florida

Accounting; advertising; aerospace, aeronautical and astronautical engineering; agricultural and food products processing; agricultural economics; agricultural teacher education; agricultural/biological engineering and bioengineering; agronomy and crop science; American studies; animal sciences; anthropology; architecture; art history, criticism and conservation; art teacher education; Asian studies; astronomy; audiology and speech-language pathology; botany/plant biology; business administration and management; chemical engineering; chemistry; civil engineering; classics and languages, literatures and linguistics; community health services counseling; computer and information sciences; computer engineering; construction engineering technology; criminology; dairy science; dance; dramatic/theatre arts; East Asian languages related; economics; electrical, electronics and communications engineering; elementary education; engineering science; English; entomology; environmental science; environmental/environmental health engineering; family and community services; finance; fine/studio arts; fire science; food science; forestry; French; geography; geology/earth science; German; graphic design; health services/

allied health/health sciences; health teacher education; history; horticultural science; industrial engineering; insurance; interior design; intermedia/multimedia; Jewish/Judaic studies; journalism; kinesiology and exercise science; landscape architecture; linguistics; management science; marketing/marketing management; materials engineering; mathematics; mechanical engineering; medical microbiology and bacteriology; middle school education; multi-/interdisciplinary studies related; music; music teacher education; nuclear engineering; nursing (registered nurse training); parks, recreation and leisure facilities management; philosophy; physics; plant pathology/phytopathology; plant sciences; political science and government; Portuguese; poultry science; psychology; public relations/image management; radio and television; real estate; religious studies; Russian; sociology; soil science and agronomy; Spanish; special education; statistics; survey technology; systems engineering; zoology/animal biology.

University of Georgia

Accounting; advertising; African-American/Black studies; agricultural business and management; agricultural economics; agricultural teacher education; agricultural/biological engineering and bioengineering; agronomy and crop science; ancient/classical Greek; animal genetics; animal sciences; anthropology; apparel and textiles; applied horticulture; art; art history, criticism and conservation; art teacher education; astronomy; biochemistry; biological and physical sciences; biology/biological sciences; biotechnology; botany/plant biology; broadcast journalism; business administration and management; business teacher education; business/commerce; business/managerial economics; cell biology and histology; chemistry; classics and languages, literatures and linguistics; cognitive psychology and psycholinguistics; communication disorders; comparative literature; computer and information sciences; consumer economics; criminal justice/safety; dairy science; dietetics; drama and dance teacher education; dramatic/theatre arts; ecology; economics; educational psychology; English; English/language arts teacher education; entomology; environmental health; family and consumer sciences/home economics teacher education; fashion merchandising; film/cinema studies; finance; fine/studio arts; fishing and fisheries sciences and management; food science; foods, nutrition, and wellness; foreign language teacher education; foreign languages and literatures; forest sciences and biology; forestry; French; geography; geology/earth science; German; health teacher education; history; housing and human environments; human development and family studies; insurance; international business/trade/commerce; Italian; Japanese; journalism; kindergarten/preschool education; landscape architecture; landscaping and groundskeeping; Latin; liberal arts and sciences/liberal studies; linguistics; management information systems; marketing/marketing management; mass communication/media; mathematics; mathematics teacher education; medical microbiology and bacteriology; middle school education; music; music performance; music teacher education; music theory and composition; music therapy; pharmacy; philosophy; physical education teaching and

coaching; plant protection and integrated pest management; political science and government; poultry science; psychology; public relations/image management; radio and television broadcasting technology; reading teacher education; real estate; religious studies; Russian; sales and marketing/marketing and distribution teacher education; science teacher education; Slavic languages; social science teacher education; social work; sociology; Spanish; special education; speech and rhetoric; sport and fitness administration; statistics; technology/industrial arts teacher education; turf and turfgrass management; wildlife and wildlands science and management; women's studies.

University of Idaho

Accounting; administrative assistant and secretarial science; agricultural business and management; agricultural economics; agricultural mechanization; agricultural teacher education; agricultural/biological engineering and bioengineering; agriculture; American studies; animal sciences; anthropology; apparel and textiles; applied mathematics; architecture; art; art teacher education; athletic training; biology/biological sciences; biomedical/medical engineering; botany/plant biology; business teacher education; cartography; chemical engineering; chemistry; child development; civil engineering; classics and languages, literatures and linguistics; clinical laboratory science/medical technology; communication/speech communication and rhetoric; computer engineering; computer science; criminal justice/safety; dance; dramatic/theatre arts; economics; electrical, electronics and communications engineering; elementary education; engineering; English; entomology; environmental studies; family and consumer sciences/home economics teacher education; finance; fine/studio arts; fish/game management; food science; foods, nutrition, and wellness; foreign languages and literatures; forestry; French; general studies; geography; geological/geophysical engineering; geology/earth science; German; history; horticultural science; human resources management; industrial engineering; industrial technology; interior architecture; interior design; international relations and affairs; journalism; landscape architecture; Latin; Latin American studies; liberal arts and sciences/liberal studies; management information systems; marketing/marketing management; mathematics; mechanical engineering; medical microbiology and bacteriology; metallurgical engineering; military technologies; mining and mineral engineering; molecular biology; multi-/interdisciplinary studies related; music history, literature, and theory; music management and merchandising; music performance; music teacher education; music theory and composition; natural resources management and policy; operations management; parks, recreation and leisure; philosophy; photography; physical education teaching and coaching; physics; plant sciences; political science and government; pre-medical studies; psychology; public relations/image management; radio and television; range science and management; secondary education; sociology; soil science and agronomy; Spanish; special education; technical teacher education; technology/industrial arts teacher education; trade and industrial teacher education; voice and opera; wildlife and wildlands science and management;

wood science and wood products/pulp and paper technology; zoology/animal biology.

University of Illinois at Chicago

Accounting; African-American/Black studies; anthropology; architecture; art history, criticism and conservation; art teacher education; biochemistry; biology teacher education; biology/biological sciences; biomedical/medical engineering; business administration and management; chemical engineering; chemistry; chemistry teacher education; cinematography and film/video production; civil engineering; classics and languages, literatures and linguistics; clinical laboratory science/medical technology; commercial and advertising art; computer and information sciences; computer engineering; criminal justice/safety; dietetics; dramatic/theatre arts; economics; electrical, electronics and communications engineering; elementary education; engineering physics; engineering/industrial management; English; English/language arts teacher education; entrepreneurship; finance; fine/studio arts; foreign language teacher education; French; French language teacher education; geology/earth science; German; German language teacher education; graphic design; health information/medical records administration; history; history teacher education; industrial design; industrial engineering; Italian; kinesiology and exercise science; Latin American studies; management information systems; marketing/marketing management; mathematics; mathematics and computer science; mathematics teacher education; mechanical engineering; music; nursing (registered nurse training); philosophy; photography; physics; physics teacher education; Polish; political science and government; pre-dentistry studies; pre-law studies; psychology; Russian; science teacher education; secondary education; Slavic languages; social science teacher education; social work; sociology; Spanish; Spanish language teacher education; speech and rhetoric; statistics.

University of Illinois at Urbana–Champaign

Accounting; actuarial science; advertising; aerospace, aeronautical and astronautical engineering; agribusiness; agricultural communication/journalism; agricultural economics; agricultural mechanization; agricultural/biological engineering and bioengineering; agriculture; agronomy and crop science; animal sciences; anthropology; architecture related; area studies related; art history, criticism and conservation; art teacher education; Asian studies (East); astronomy; audiology and speech-language pathology; biochemistry; biological and biomedical sciences related; biology/biological sciences; biomedical/medical engineering; biophysics; botany/plant biology; broadcast journalism; business teacher education; business/commerce; cell and molecular biology; cell biology and histology; chemical engineering; chemistry; city/urban, community and regional planning; civil engineering; classics and languages, literatures and linguistics; communication and journalism related; community health and preventive medicine; comparative literature; computer engineering; computer science; computer teacher education; crafts, folk

art and artisanry; dance; dramatic/theatre arts; ecology; economics; economics related; electrical, electronics and communications engineering; elementary education; engineering; engineering mechanics; engineering physics; English; English composition; English/language arts teacher education; entomology; environmental science; fashion merchandising; finance; food science; foreign language teacher education; forestry; French; French language teacher education; geography; geology/earth science; German; German language teacher education; graphic design; history; horticultural science; human development and family studies; humanities; industrial and organizational psychology; industrial design; industrial engineering; Italian; journalism; kindergarten/preschool education; kinesiology and exercise science; landscape architecture; Latin American studies; Latin teacher education; liberal arts and sciences/liberal studies; linguistics; marketing related; mass communication/media; materials science; mathematics; mathematics and computer science; mechanical engineering; microbiology; music; music history, literature, and theory; music performance; music teacher education; music theory and composition; nuclear engineering; ornamental horticulture; painting; parks, recreation and leisure; philosophy; photography; physics; physiology; political science and government; Portuguese; pre-veterinary studies; psychology; public health related; religious studies; restaurant, culinary, and catering management; Russian; Russian studies; sales, distribution and marketing; sculpture; social studies teacher education; sociology; Spanish; Spanish language teacher education; special education; speech and rhetoric; statistics; voice and opera.

The University of Iowa

Accounting; actuarial science; African studies; African-American/Black studies; Air Force R.O.T.C./air science; American history; American Indian/Native American studies; American studies; anthropology; Army R.O.T.C./military science; art; art history, criticism and conservation; art teacher education; arts management; Asian studies; astronomy; athletic training; audiology and speech-language pathology; biochemistry; biology/biological sciences; biomedical/medical engineering; broadcast journalism; business administration and management; business/managerial economics; ceramic arts and ceramics; chemical engineering; chemistry; chemistry teacher education; Chinese; cinematography and film/video production; civil engineering; classics and languages, literatures and linguistics; clinical laboratory science/medical technology; comparative literature; computer engineering; computer science; creative writing; dance; drama and dance teacher education; dramatic/theatre arts; drawing; economics; education; electrical, electronics and communications engineering; elementary education; engineering; engineering/industrial management; English; environmental studies; environmental/environmental health engineering; European studies (Central and Eastern); film/cinema studies; finance; fine/studio arts; French; French language teacher education; geography; geology/earth science; German; German language teacher education; health teacher education; history; history teacher education; human resources management; industrial engineering;

information science/studies; interdisciplinary studies; international business/trade/commerce; international relations and affairs; Italian; Japanese; jazz/jazz studies; journalism; kinesiology and exercise science; labor and industrial relations; Latin; Latin American studies; linguistics; literature; management information systems; management science; marketing/marketing management; mass communication/media; materials engineering; mathematics; mathematics teacher education; mechanical engineering; medical microbiology and bacteriology; medieval and renaissance studies; metal and jewelry arts; modern Greek; museum studies; music; music history, literature, and theory; music teacher education; music therapy; nuclear medical technology; nursing (registered nurse training); painting; parks, recreation and leisure; pharmacy; philosophy; photography; physics; piano and organ; political science and government; Portuguese; pre-dentistry studies; pre-law studies; pre-medical studies; pre-pharmacy studies; pre-veterinary studies; printmaking; psychology; public relations/image management; radio and television; religious studies; Russian; sales, distribution and marketing; science teacher education; sculpture; secondary education; social sciences; social studies teacher education; social work; sociology; Spanish; Spanish language teacher education; speech and rhetoric; speech teacher education; speech therapy; sport and fitness administration; statistics; therapeutic recreation; violin, viola, guitar and other stringed instruments; voice and opera; wind/percussion instruments; women's studies.

University of Kansas

Accounting; advertising; aerospace, aeronautical and astronautical engineering; African studies; African-American/Black studies; American studies; ancient studies; anthropology; architectural engineering; architectural history and criticism; architecture; art history, criticism and conservation; art teacher education; astronomy; athletic training; atmospheric sciences and meteorology; behavioral sciences; biochemistry/biophysics and molecular biology; biological and biomedical sciences related; biology/biological sciences; broadcast journalism; business/commerce; ceramic arts and ceramics; chemical engineering; chemistry; civil engineering; classics and languages, literatures and linguistics; clinical laboratory science/medical technology; cognitive psychology and psycholinguistics; communication disorders; community health services counseling; computer and information sciences; computer engineering; cytotechnology; dance; design and visual communications; dramatic/theatre arts; East Asian languages; economics; electrical, electronics and communications engineering; elementary education; engineering physics; English; environmental studies; European studies; fiber, textile and weaving arts; fine/studio arts; French; geography; geology/earth science; Germanic languages; graphic design; health and physical education; health information/medical records administration; history; humanities; illustration; industrial design; interior design; international relations and affairs; journalism; Latin American studies; liberal arts and sciences/liberal studies; linguistics; mathematics; mechanical engineering; metal and jewelry arts; microbiology; middle school education;

molecular biology; music; music history, literature, and theory; music teacher education; music theory and composition; music therapy; nursing (registered nurse training); nursing science; occupational therapy; painting; petroleum engineering; pharmacy; philosophy; physical education teaching and coaching; physics; piano and organ; political science and government; printmaking; psychology; radio and television; religious studies; respiratory care therapy; Russian studies; sculpture; secondary education; Slavic languages; social work; sociology; Spanish; speech and rhetoric; theatre design and technology; violin, viola, guitar and other stringed instruments; voice and opera; wind/percussion instruments; women's studies.

University of Kentucky

Accounting; advertising; agricultural economics; agricultural/biological engineering and bioengineering; agriculture and agriculture operations related; agronomy and crop science; animal sciences; anthropology; apparel and textiles; architecture; art history, criticism and conservation; art teacher education; arts management; audiology and speech-language pathology; biology/biological sciences; business/commerce; business/managerial economics; cell biology and anatomical sciences related; chemical engineering; chemistry; civil engineering; classics and languages, literatures and linguistics; clinical laboratory science/medical technology; communication/speech communication and rhetoric; computer and information sciences; dramatic/theatre arts; economics; education (specific subject areas) related; electrical, electronics and communications engineering; elementary education; English; family and consumer sciences/human sciences; finance; fine/studio arts; food science; foods, nutrition, and wellness; forest sciences and biology; French; geography; geology/earth science; German; health teacher education; health/health care administration; history; hospitality administration; interdisciplinary studies; interior design; journalism; kindergarten/preschool education; landscape architecture; Latin American studies; linguistics; management science; marketing/marketing management; materials engineering; mathematics; mechanical engineering; middle school education; mining and mineral engineering; multi-/interdisciplinary studies related; music history, literature, and theory; music performance; music teacher education; natural resources/conservation; nursing (registered nurse training); nursing related; philosophy; physical education teaching and coaching; physical therapy; physics; political science and government; psychology; radio and television; Russian; science teacher education; social sciences; social work; sociology; Spanish; special education.

University of Maryland, Baltimore County

African-American/Black studies; American studies; ancient studies; anthropology; applied mathematics; art; art history, criticism and conservation; biochemistry/biophysics and molecular biology; bioinformatics; biology/biological sciences; chemical engineering; chemistry; classics and languages, literatures and linguistics; computer engineering; computer science; dance; dramatic/theatre arts; econom-ics; emergency medical technology (EMT paramedic); engineering science; English; environmental science; environmental studies; film/cinema studies; French; geography; German; health science; health/health care administration; history; information science/studies; interdisciplinary studies; linguistics; mathematics; mechanical engineering; modern languages; music; philosophy; photography; physics; political science and government; pre-dentistry studies; pre-law studies; pre-medical studies; pre-veterinary studies; psychology; Russian; social work; sociology; Spanish; statistics; visual and performing arts.

University of Maryland, College Park

Accounting; aerospace, aeronautical and astronautical engineering; African-American/Black studies; agricultural economics; agricultural/biological engineering and bioengineering; agriculture; agriculture and agriculture operations related; agronomy and crop science; American studies; animal sciences; anthropology; architecture; art history, criticism and conservation; art teacher education; astronomy; biochemistry; biology/biological sciences; business administration and management; business, management, and marketing related; business/commerce; chemical engineering; chemistry; Chinese; civil engineering; classics and languages, literatures and linguistics; communication/speech communication and rhetoric; computer and information sciences; computer engineering; criminology; dance; dietetics; dramatic/theatre arts; ecology; economics; education; electrical, electronics and communications engineering; elementary education; engineering; engineering related; English; English/language arts teacher education; family and community services; finance; food science; foods, nutrition, and wellness; foreign language teacher education; foreign languages and literatures; French; geography; geology/earth science; German; health teacher education; history; horticultural science; human resources management; information science/studies; Italian; Japanese; Jewish/Judaic studies; journalism; kindergarten/preschool education; landscape architecture; Latin; linguistics; management science; marketing/marketing management; materials engineering; mathematics; mathematics teacher education; mechanical engineering; medical microbiology and bacteriology; music; music performance; music teacher education; natural resources/conservation; nuclear engineering; philosophy; physical education teaching and coaching; physical sciences; physics; plant sciences; political science and government; psychology; Russian; Russian studies; science teacher education; secondary education; social studies teacher education; sociology; Spanish; special education; speech-language pathology; visual and performing arts; women's studies.

University of Miami

Accounting; advertising; aerospace, aeronautical and astronautical engineering; African-American/Black studies; American studies; anthropology; architectural engineering; architecture; art; art history, criticism and conservation; athletic training; atmospheric sciences and meteorology; biochemistry; biology/biological sciences; biomedical/medical engineering; biophysics; broadcast journalism; business administration and management; business administration, management and operations related; business/managerial economics; ceramic arts and ceramics; chemistry; chemistry related; cinematography and film/video production; civil engineering; commercial and advertising art; communication and journalism related; communication/speech communication and rhetoric; computer and information sciences; computer engineering; computer science; computer systems analysis; conducting; creative writing; criminology; dance; dramatic/theatre arts; education; electrical, electronics and communications engineering; elementary education; engineering science; English; English literature (British and Commonwealth); entrepreneurial and small business related; entrepreneurship; environmental studies; environmental/environmental health engineering; family and community services; film/cinema studies; finance; fine/studio arts; French; general studies; geography; geological and earth sciences/geosciences related; geology/earth science; German; health and medical administrative services related; health professions related; health/medical preparatory programs related; history; human resources management; industrial engineering; information science/studies; international business/trade/commerce; international relations and affairs; Italian; Jewish/Judaic studies; journalism; kinesiology and exercise science; Latin American studies; liberal arts and sciences/liberal studies; marine biology and biological oceanography; marketing/marketing management; mass communication/media; mathematics; mathematics and statistics related; mechanical engineering; medical microbiology and bacteriology; music; music management and merchandising; music performance; music related; music teacher education; music theory and composition; music therapy; musicology and ethnomusicology; natural resources and conservation related; natural resources management and policy; neurobiology and neurophysiology; neuroscience; nursing (registered nurse training); oceanography (chemical and physical); painting; philosophy; photography; physics; physics related; physiological psychology/psychobiology; piano and organ; political science and government; pre-pharmacy studies; printmaking; psychology; public relations/image management; radio and television; religious studies; sculpture; secondary education; sociology; Spanish; special education; visual and performing arts; voice and opera; wildlife and wildlands science and management; women's studies.

University of Michigan

Accounting; aerospace, aeronautical and astronautical engineering; African studies; African-American/Black studies; American studies; anthropology; applied art; applied mathematics; Arabic; archeology; architecture; art history, criticism and conservation; art teacher education; Asian studies; Asian studies (South); Asian studies (Southeast); astronomy; athletic training; atmospheric sciences and meteorology; biblical studies; biochemistry; biology/biological sciences; biomedical sciences; biometry/biometrics; biophysics; botany/plant biology; business administration and management; cell biology and histology; ceramic arts and ceramics; chemical engineering; chemistry; Chinese; civil engineering; classics and languages, literatures and linguistics; clinical laboratory science/medical technology; commercial and advertising art; comparative literature; computer engineering; computer science; creative writing; dance; dental hygiene; design and visual communications; dramatic/theatre arts; drawing; ecology; economics; education; electrical, electronics and communications engineering; elementary education; engineering; engineering physics; engineering science; English; environmental studies; environmental/environmental health engineering; European studies; fiber, textile and weaving arts; film/cinema studies; foods, nutrition, and wellness; French; general studies; geography; geology/earth science; German; Hebrew; Hispanic-American, Puerto Rican, and Mexican-American/Chicano studies; history; humanities; industrial design; industrial engineering; interdisciplinary studies; interior design; intermedia/multimedia; international relations and affairs; Islamic studies; Italian; Japanese; jazz/jazz studies; Jewish/Judaic studies; journalism; kinesiology and exercise science; landscape architecture; Latin; Latin American studies; liberal arts and sciences/liberal studies; linguistics; literature; mass communication/media; materials engineering; materials science; mathematics; mechanical engineering; medical microbiology and bacteriology; medieval and renaissance studies; metal and jewelry arts; metallurgical engineering; modern Greek; molecular biology; music; music history, literature, and theory; music teacher education; music theory and composition; natural resources management and policy; naval architecture and marine engineering; Near and Middle Eastern studies; nuclear engineering; nursing (registered nurse training); oceanography (chemical and physical); painting; parks, recreation and leisure; pharmacy; philosophy; photography; physical education teaching and coaching; physics; piano and organ; playwriting and screenwriting; political science and government; printmaking; psychology; radiologic technology/science; religious studies; romance languages; Russian; Russian studies; Scandinavian studies; sculpture; secondary education; social sciences; sociology; Spanish; speech and rhetoric; sport and fitness administration; statistics; theatre design and technology; violin, viola, guitar and other stringed instruments; visual and performing arts; voice and opera; wildlife biology; wind/percussion instruments; women's studies; zoology/animal biology.

University of Minnesota, Morris

Anthropology; art history, criticism and conservation; biology/biological sciences; business administration and management; chemistry; computer science; dramatic/theatre arts; economics; education; education (K-12); elementary education; English; European studies; fine/studio arts; French; geology/earth science; German; history; human services; Latin American studies; liberal arts and sciences/liberal studies; management science; mathematics; music; philosophy; physical therapy; physics; political science and government; pre-dentistry studies; pre-law studies; pre-medical studies; pre-pharmacy studies; pre-veterinary studies; psychology; secondary education; social sciences; sociology; Spanish; speech and rhetoric; speech/theater education; statistics; women's studies.

University of Minnesota, Twin Cities Campus

Accounting; actuarial science; aerospace, aeronautical and astronautical engineering; African studies; African-American/Black studies; agricultural business and management; agricultural teacher education; agricultural/biological engineering and bioengineering; agriculture; agronomy and crop science; American Indian/Native American studies; American studies; animal genetics; animal physiology; animal sciences; anthropology; architecture; art; art history, criticism and conservation; art teacher education; Asian studies (East); Asian studies (South); astronomy; astrophysics; audiology and speech-language pathology; biochemistry; biology/biological sciences; botany/plant biology; business teacher education; cell biology and histology; chemical engineering; chemistry; Chinese; civil engineering; clinical laboratory science/medical technology; clothing/textiles; commercial and advertising art; comparative literature; computer science; construction management; dance; dental hygiene; developmental and child psychology; dramatic/theatre arts; ecology; economics; education; electrical, electronics and communications engineering; elementary education; emergency medical technology (EMT paramedic); English; English/language arts teacher education; environmental studies; European studies; family and community services; family and consumer sciences/home economics teacher education; film/cinema studies; finance; fish/game management; foods, nutrition, and wellness; foreign language teacher education; forest/forest resources management; forestry; French; funeral service and mortuary science; geography; geological/geophysical engineering; geology/earth science; geophysics and seismology; German; health and physical education related; Hebrew; Hispanic-American, Puerto Rican, and Mexican-American/Chicano studies; history; industrial engineering; insurance; interior design; international business/trade/commerce; international relations and affairs; Italian; Japanese; Jewish/Judaic studies; journalism; kindergarten/preschool education; landscape architecture; Latin; Latin American studies; linguistics; management information systems; marketing/marketing management; mass communication/media; materials engineering; materials science; mathematics; mathematics teacher education; mechanical engineering; medical microbiology and bacteriology; modern Greek; music; music teacher education; music therapy; natural resources management and policy; Near and Middle Eastern studies; neuroscience; nursing (registered nurse training); occupational therapy; parks, recreation and leisure facilities management; philosophy; physical education teaching and coaching; physical therapy; physics; plant sciences; political science and government; Portuguese; pre-dentistry studies; pre-law studies; pre-medical studies; pre-veterinary studies; psychology; public health; religious studies; Russian; Russian studies; Scandinavian languages; science teacher education; social science teacher education; sociology; soil science and agronomy; Spanish; urban studies/affairs; ences; sociology; Spanish; speech and rhetoric; speech/theater education; statistics; women's studies.

women's studies; wood science and wood products/pulp and paper technology.

University of Mississippi

Accounting; advertising; American studies; anthropology; art; art history, criticism and conservation; audiology and speech-language pathology; biology/biological sciences; biomedical sciences; business administration and management; business/commerce; business/managerial economics; chemical engineering; chemistry; civil engineering; classics and languages, literatures and linguistics; clinical laboratory science/medical technology; computer and information sciences; court reporting; dramatic/theatre arts; economics; electrical, electronics and communications engineering; elementary education; engineering; English; English/language arts teacher education; family and consumer sciences/human sciences; finance; forensic science and technology; French; geological/geophysical engineering; geology/earth science; German; history; insurance; international business/trade/commerce; international relations and affairs; journalism; kinesiology and exercise science; liberal arts and sciences/liberal studies; linguistics; management information systems; marketing/marketing management; mathematics; mathematics teacher education; mechanical engineering; music; parks, recreation and leisure; pharmacy; philosophy; physics; political science and government; psychology; public administration; radio and television; real estate; science teacher education; secondary education; social studies teacher education; social work; sociology; Spanish; special education.

University of Missouri–Columbia

Accounting; advertising; agricultural business and management; agricultural communication/journalism; agricultural economics; agricultural mechanization; agricultural teacher education; agriculture; animal sciences; anthropology; apparel and textiles; archeology; art; art history, criticism and conservation; art teacher education; Asian studies (East); Asian studies (South); atmospheric sciences and meteorology; behavioral sciences; biochemistry; biology teacher education; biology/biological sciences; broadcast journalism; business administration and management; business teacher education; business/managerial economics; chemical engineering; chemistry; chemistry teacher education; civil engineering; classics and languages, literatures and linguistics; communication disorders sciences and services related; communication/speech communication and rhetoric; computer and information sciences; computer engineering; computer science; diagnostic medical sonography and ultrasound technology; dietetics; dramatic/theatre arts; early childhood education; economics; education; education related; electrical, electronics and communications engineering; elementary education; English; environmental studies; European studies; European studies (Central and Eastern); family and consumer economics related; finance; fish/game management; fishing and fisheries sciences and management; food science; foods, nutrition, and wellness; forestry; French; general studies; geography; geology/earth science; German; health/medical preparatory programs related; history; hotel/motel administration; housing and human environments; human development and family studies; human nutrition; industrial engineering; interdisciplinary studies; interior architecture; international agriculture; international business/trade/commerce; international economics; journalism; kindergarten/preschool education; Latin; Latin American studies; linguistics; management information systems; marketing/marketing management; mass communication/media; mathematics; mathematics teacher education; mechanical engineering; medical radiologic technology; microbiology; middle school education; modern Greek; music; music teacher education; natural resources/conservation; nuclear medical technology; nursing (registered nurse training); nutrition sciences; occupational therapy; parks, recreation and leisure; peace studies and conflict resolution; philosophy; photojournalism; physics; physics teacher education; plant sciences; political science and government; psychology; publishing; radio and television; radiologic technology/science; real estate; religious studies; respiratory care therapy; restaurant/food services management; Russian; Russian studies; science teacher education; secondary education; social studies teacher education; social work; sociology; Spanish; special education related; statistics; technical teacher education; tourism and travel services marketing; wildlife and wildlands science and management.

University of Missouri–Kansas City

Accounting; American studies; art; art history, criticism and conservation; biology/biological sciences; business administration and management; chemistry; city/urban, community and regional planning; civil engineering; clinical/medical laboratory technology; computer science; criminal justice/law enforcement administration; dance; dental hygiene; dramatic/theatre arts; economics; education; electrical, electronics and communications engineering; elementary education; English; fine/studio arts; French; geography; geology/earth science; German; health and physical education; history; information technology; interdisciplinary studies; Jewish/Judaic studies; kindergarten/preschool education; liberal arts and sciences/liberal studies; mass communication/media; mathematics; mechanical engineering; music; music teacher education; music therapy; nursing (registered nurse training); pharmacy; philosophy; physical education teaching and coaching; physics; piano and organ; political science and government; psychology; secondary education; sociology; Spanish; statistics; urban education and leadership; urban studies/affairs; violin, viola, guitar and other stringed instruments; voice and opera; wind/percussion instruments.

University of Missouri–Rolla

Aerospace, aeronautical and astronautical engineering; agricultural/biological engineering and bioengineering; applied mathematics; architectural engineering; biology/biological sciences; business administration and management; business/commerce; ceramic sciences and engineering; chemical engineering; chemistry; civil engineering; computer and information sciences and support services related; computer engineering; computer science; economics;

electrical, electronics and communications engineering; engineering/industrial management; English; environmental/environmental health engineering; geological/geophysical engineering; geology/earth science; geophysics and seismology; history; industrial engineering; information science/studies; manufacturing engineering; materials engineering; mechanical engineering; metallurgical engineering; mining and mineral engineering; nuclear engineering; petroleum engineering; philosophy; physics; pre-dentistry studies; pre-law studies; pre-medical studies; psychology; secondary education; systems engineering.

University of Nebraska–Lincoln

Accounting; actuarial science; advertising; agricultural business and management; agricultural communication/journalism; agricultural economics; agricultural mechanization; agricultural teacher education; agricultural/biological engineering and bioengineering; agriculture; agronomy and crop science; ancient/classical Greek; animal sciences; anthropology; apparel and textiles; architectural engineering; architecture; art history, criticism and conservation; art teacher education; athletic training; atmospheric sciences and meteorology; biochemistry; biology teacher education; biology/biological sciences; biomedical/medical engineering; broadcast journalism; business administration and management; business teacher education; business/managerial economics; chemical engineering; chemistry; chemistry teacher education; civil engineering; classics and languages, literatures and linguistics; communication/speech communication and rhetoric; community health services counseling; computer and information sciences; computer engineering; computer teacher education; construction engineering technology; dance; dramatic/theatre arts; economics; education (multiple levels); education (specific subject areas) related; electrical, electronic and communications engineering technology; electrical, electronics and communications engineering; elementary education; engineering related; English; English as a second/foreign language (teaching); English/language arts teacher education; environmental studies; European studies (Western); family and consumer economics related; film/cinema studies; finance; fine/studio arts; fire protection and safety technology; food science; foods, nutrition, and wellness; foreign language teacher education; French; French language teacher education; geography; geology/earth science; German; German language teacher education; health teacher education; history; history teacher education; horticultural science; housing and human environments; industrial engineering; industrial production technologies related; industrial technology; interior architecture; international business/trade/commerce; international relations and affairs; journalism related; kinesiology and exercise science; landscaping and groundskeeping; Latin; Latin American studies; law and legal studies related; legal professions and studies related; liberal arts and sciences and humanities related; liberal arts and sciences/liberal studies; management science; marketing/marketing management; mathematics; mathematics teacher education; mechanical engineering; medieval and renaissance studies; middle school education; music; music teacher

education; natural resources management and policy; natural resources/conservation; office management; philosophy; physical education teaching and coaching; physics; physics teacher education; plant protection and integrated pest management; political science and government; pre-dentistry studies; pre-medical studies; pre-pharmacy studies; pre-veterinary studies; psychology; range science and management; reading teacher education; Russian; sales and marketing/marketing and distribution teacher education; science teacher education; social science teacher education; sociology; soil science and agronomy; Spanish; Spanish language teacher education; special education (hearing impaired); special education related; speech-language pathology; technology/industrial arts teacher education; trade and industrial teacher education; veterinary/animal health technology; women's studies.

The University of North Carolina at Asheville

Accounting; art; atmospheric sciences and meteorology; biology/biological sciences; business administration and management; chemistry; classics and languages, literatures and linguistics; computer science; dramatic/theatre arts; economics; English; environmental studies; fine/studio arts; French; German; history; journalism related; liberal arts and sciences/liberal studies; mathematics; music; music related; operations management; philosophy; physics; political science and government; psychology; sociology; Spanish.

The University of North Carolina at Chapel Hill

Accounting; African-American/Black studies; American studies; anthropology; applied mathematics; area, ethnic, cultural, and gender studies related; art history, criticism and conservation; Asian studies; biology/biological sciences; biostatistics; business administration and management; chemistry; classics and languages, literatures and linguistics; clinical laboratory science/medical technology; communication/speech communication and rhetoric; comparative literature; computer science; dental hygiene; dramatic/theatre arts; early childhood education; economics; elementary education; English; English/language arts teacher education; environmental health; environmental science; environmental studies; fine/studio arts; foods, nutrition, and wellness; French language teacher education; geography; geology/earth science; German; German language teacher education; health and physical education; health teacher education; health/health care administration; history; human resources management; information science/studies; Latin American studies; liberal arts and sciences/liberal studies; linguistics; mass communication/media; mathematics; mathematics teacher education; medical radiologic technology; middle school education; music; music performance; music teacher education; nursing (registered nurse training); parks, recreation and leisure facilities management; peace studies and conflict resolution; philosophy; physical sciences related; physics; political science and government; psychology; public health education and promotion; public policy analysis; religious studies; romance languages; Russian; Russian studies; social studies teacher education; sociology; Spanish language teacher education; speech teacher education; women's studies.

University of Notre Dame

Accounting; aerospace, aeronautical and astronautical engineering; American studies; ancient/classical Greek; anthropology; Arabic; architecture; art history, criticism and conservation; biochemistry; biology/biological sciences; business administration, management and operations related; business/commerce; chemical engineering; chemistry; chemistry related; Chinese; civil engineering; classics and languages, literatures and linguistics; computer and information sciences; computer and information sciences and support services related; computer engineering; design and visual communications; dramatic/theatre arts; economics; electrical, electronics and communications engineering; English; environmental/environmental health engineering; finance; fine/studio arts; French; geology/earth science; German; history; Italian; Japanese; Latin; liberal arts and sciences/liberal studies; management information systems; marketing/marketing management; mathematics; mechanical engineering; medieval and renaissance studies; music; philosophy; philosophy and religious studies related; physics; physics related; political science and government; pre-medical studies; psychology; Russian; science teacher education; sociology; Spanish; theology.

University of Oklahoma

Accounting; advertising; aeronautics/aviation/aerospace science and technology; aerospace, aeronautical and astronautical engineering; African-American/Black studies; American Indian/Native American studies; anthropology; architecture; architecture related; area studies; area studies related; art; art history, criticism and conservation; astronomy; astrophysics; atmospheric sciences and meteorology; biomedical/medical engineering; botany/plant biology; broadcast journalism; business administration and management; business/managerial economics; chemical engineering; chemistry; cinematography and film/video production; civil engineering; classics and languages, literatures and linguistics; clinical/medical laboratory technology; communication and journalism related; communication/speech communication and rhetoric; computer and information sciences; computer engineering; criminology; dance; design and visual communications; dramatic/theatre arts; early childhood education; economics; education (specific subject areas) related; electrical, electronics and communications engineering; elementary education; engineering; engineering physics; English; English language and literature related; English/language arts teacher education; entrepreneurship; environmental design/architecture; environmental science; environmental/environmental health engineering; finance; fine/studio arts; foreign language teacher education; French; geography; geological and earth sciences/geosciences related; geology/earth science; geophysics and seismology; German; health and physical education; history; human resources management and services related; industrial engineering; interior design; international business/trade/commerce; journal-

ism; liberal arts and sciences/liberal studies; library science; linguistics; management information systems; marketing/marketing management; mathematics; mathematics teacher education; mechanical engineering; medical laboratory technology; microbiology; multi-/interdisciplinary studies related; music; music performance; music theory and composition; petroleum engineering; philosophy; photography; physics; piano and organ; political science and government; professional studies; psychology; public administration; public relations/image management; religious studies; Russian; science teacher education; social studies teacher education; social work; sociology; Spanish; special education; violin, viola, guitar and other stringed instruments; visual and performing arts related; voice and opera; wind/percussion instruments; women's studies; zoology/animal biology.

University of Pennsylvania

Accounting; actuarial science; African studies; African-American/Black studies; American studies; anthropology; architecture; art history, criticism and conservation; Asian studies (East); Asian studies (South); biochemistry; bioinformatics; biology/biological sciences; biomedical sciences; biomedical/medical engineering; biophysics; business administration and management; business administration, management and operations related; chemical engineering; chemistry; civil engineering; classics and languages, literatures and linguistics; cognitive science; communication/speech communication and rhetoric; community health services counseling; comparative literature; computer engineering; computer graphics; computer systems networking and telecommunications; dramatic/theatre arts; e-commerce; economics; electrical, electronics and communications engineering; elementary education; engineering related; English; English language and literature related; environmental design/architecture; environmental studies; environmental/environmental health engineering; finance; fine/studio arts; French; geology/earth science; German; health professions related; health/health care administration; history; history and philosophy of science and technology; human resources management; insurance; international business/trade/commerce; international relations and affairs; international/global studies; Italian; Jewish/Judaic studies; Latin American studies; legal professions and studies related; liberal arts and sciences/liberal studies; linguistics; management information systems; management sciences and quantitative methods related; marketing/marketing management; materials engineering; materials science; mathematics; mechanical engineering; music; natural sciences; neuroscience; nursing (registered nurse training); nursing related; operations management; philosophy; philosophy related; physics; political science and government; psychology; public policy analysis; real estate; religious studies; romance languages related; Russian; sales, distribution and marketing; sociology; Spanish; statistics; systems engineering; transportation management; urban studies/affairs; visual and performing arts; women's studies.

University of Pittsburgh

Accounting; African-American/Black studies; anthropology; applied mathematics; art history, criticism and conservation; audiology and speech-language pathology; biological and physical sciences; biology/biological sciences; biomedical/medical engineering; business/commerce; chemical engineering; chemistry; child development; Chinese; civil engineering; classics and languages, literatures and linguistics; clinical laboratory science/medical technology; communication/speech communication and rhetoric; computer and information sciences and support services related; computer engineering; computer science; corrections; creative writing; dental hygiene; dietetics; dramatic/theatre arts; ecology; economics; educational psychology; electrical, electronics and communications engineering; engineering; engineering physics; English; English literature (British and Commonwealth); ethnic, cultural minority, and gender studies related; film/cinema studies; finance; fine/studio arts; French; geological and earth sciences/geosciences related; geology/earth science; German; health information/medical records administration; health professions related; history; history and philosophy of science and technology; humanities; industrial engineering; information science/studies; interdisciplinary studies; Italian; Japanese; legal studies; liberal arts and sciences/liberal studies; linguistics; marketing/marketing management; materials engineering; mathematics; mathematics and statistics related; mechanical engineering; medical microbiology and bacteriology; metallurgical engineering; molecular biology; music; neuroscience; nursing (registered nurse training); occupational therapy; pharmacy; philosophy; physical education teaching and coaching; physical sciences; physics; political science and government; psychology; public administration; rehabilitation and therapeutic professions related; religious studies; Russian; Slavic languages; social sciences; social work; sociology; Spanish; speech and rhetoric; statistics; urban studies/affairs.

University of Portland

Accounting; arts management; biology/biological sciences; business administration and management; chemistry; civil engineering; computer engineering; computer science; criminal justice/safety; dramatic/theatre arts; education; electrical, electronics and communications engineering; elementary education; engineering; engineering science; engineering/industrial management; English; environmental studies; finance; history; interdisciplinary studies; international business/trade/commerce; journalism; marketing/marketing management; mass communication/media; mathematics; mechanical engineering; music; music teacher education; nursing (registered nurse training); philosophy; physics; political science and government; pre-dentistry studies; pre-law studies; pre-medical studies; psychology; secondary education; social work; sociology; Spanish; theology.

University of Puget Sound

Art; Asian studies; biology/biological sciences; business/commerce; chemistry; classics and languages, literatures and linguistics; communication/speech communication and rhetoric; computer programming (specific applications); computer science; creative writing; dramatic/theatre arts; economics; English; French; geology/earth science; German; history; interdisciplinary studies; international business/trade/commerce; international economics; international relations and affairs; kinesiology and exercise science; mathematics; music; music management and merchandising; music performance; music teacher education; natural sciences; philosophy; physics; political science and government; pre-dentistry studies; pre-law studies; pre-medical studies; pre-veterinary studies; psychology; religious studies; science, technology and society; sociology; Spanish.

University of Redlands

Accounting; anthropology; art history, criticism and conservation; Asian studies; audiology and speech-language pathology; biology/biological sciences; business administration and management; business/commerce; chemistry; computer science; creative writing; economics; education; elementary education; English; environmental studies; fine/studio arts; French; German; history; interdisciplinary studies; international relations and affairs; liberal arts and sciences/liberal studies; literature; management information systems; mathematics; music; music history, literature, and theory; music performance; music teacher education; music theory and composition; philosophy; physics; piano and organ; political science and government; psychology; religious studies; secondary education; sociology; Spanish; speech therapy; voice and opera.

University of Rhode Island

Accounting; animal sciences; anthropology; apparel and accessories marketing; apparel and textiles; applied economics; art; art history, criticism and conservation; biology/biological sciences; biomedical/medical engineering; business administration and management; chemical engineering; chemistry; civil engineering; classics and languages, literatures and linguistics; clinical laboratory science/medical technology; communication disorders; communication/speech communication and rhetoric; comparative literature; computer and information sciences; computer engineering; consumer economics; dental hygiene; dietetics; econometrics and quantitative economics; economics; electrical, electronics and communications engineering; elementary education; English; environmental studies; finance; fishing and fisheries sciences and management; foods, nutrition, and wellness; French; geology/earth science; German; health/health care administration; history; human development and family studies; human services; industrial engineering; interdisciplinary studies; international business/trade/commerce; Italian; journalism; landscape architecture; Latin American studies; liberal arts and sciences/liberal studies; management information systems; marine biology and biological oceanography; marketing/marketing management; mathematics; mechanical engineering; medical microbiology and bacteriology; music; music performance; music teacher education; music theory and composition; natural resources management and policy; natural resources/conservation; nursing (registered nurse training); ocean engineering;

pharmacy; philosophy; physical education teaching and coaching; physics; political science and government; psychology; public policy analysis; secondary education; sociology; Spanish; turf and turfgrass management; wildlife and wildlands science and management; women's studies; zoology/animal biology.

University of Richmond

Accounting; American studies; art; art history, criticism and conservation; art teacher education; biology/biological sciences; business administration and management; business/managerial economics; chemistry; classics and languages, literatures and linguistics; computer science; criminal justice/law enforcement administration; dramatic/theatre arts; economics; education; elementary education; English; environmental studies; European studies; European studies (Central and Eastern); finance; fine/studio arts; French; German; health teacher education; history; human resources management; interdisciplinary studies; international business/trade/commerce; international economics; international relations and affairs; journalism; Latin; Latin American studies; legal administrative assistant/secretary; management information systems; marketing/marketing management; mathematics; middle school education; modern Greek; molecular biology; music; music history, literature, and theory; philosophy; physical education teaching and coaching; physics; political science and government; psychology; religious studies; secondary education; sociology; Spanish; speech and rhetoric; urban studies/affairs; women's studies.

University of Rochester

African-American/Black studies; American Sign Language (ASL); anthropology; applied mathematics; art history, criticism and conservation; biological and physical sciences; biology/biological sciences; biomedical/medical engineering; chemical engineering; chemistry; classics and languages, literatures and linguistics; cognitive science; comparative literature; computer science; economics; electrical, electronics and communications engineering; engineering science; English; environmental science; environmental studies; film/cinema studies; fine/studio arts; French; geological/geophysical engineering; geology/earth science; German; history; Japanese; jazz/jazz studies; linguistics; mathematics; mathematics and statistics related; mechanical engineering; music; music teacher education; music theory and composition; nursing (registered nurse training); optical sciences; philosophy; physics; physics related; political science and government; psychology; religious studies; Russian; Russian studies; social sciences related; Spanish; statistics; women's studies.

University of St. Thomas

Accounting; actuarial science; ancient/classical Greek; art history, criticism and conservation; Asian studies (East); biochemistry; biology teacher education; biology/biological sciences; broadcast journalism; business administration and management; business administration, management and operations related; business/corporate communications; chemistry; chemistry teacher education; classics and classi-

cal languages related; classics and languages, literatures and linguistics; clinical/medical social work; communication/speech communication and rhetoric; computer and information sciences; creative writing; criminology; drama and dance teacher education; dramatic/theatre arts; econometrics and quantitative economics; economics; education (K-12); education (specific subject areas) related; electrical, electronics and communications engineering; elementary education; English; English/language arts teacher education; entrepreneurship; finance; foreign language teacher education; foreign languages related; French; geography; geology/earth science; German; health and physical education; health science; health teacher education; history; human resources management; interdisciplinary studies; international business/trade/commerce; international economics; international relations and affairs; Japanese; journalism; journalism related; Latin; marketing/marketing management; mathematics; mathematics teacher education; mechanical engineering; middle school education; multi-/interdisciplinary studies related; music; music teacher education; operations management; peace studies and conflict resolution; philosophy; physical education teaching and coaching; physics; physics teacher education; political science and government; psychology; psychology related; public administration; public health education and promotion; real estate; religious studies; Russian; Russian studies; science teacher education; social sciences; social studies teacher education; social work; sociology; Spanish; speech/theater education; women's studies.

University of St. Thomas (TX)

Accounting; biology/biological sciences; business administration and management; chemistry; communication/speech communication and rhetoric; dramatic/theatre arts; economics; education; elementary education; English; environmental studies; finance; fine/studio arts; French; general studies; history; international relations and affairs; liberal arts and sciences/liberal studies; management information systems; marketing related; mathematics; music; music teacher education; pastoral studies/counseling; philosophy; political science and government; pre-dentistry studies; pre-law studies; pre-medical studies; pre-pharmacy studies; pre-veterinary studies; psychology; secondary education; Spanish; theology; theology and religious vocations related.

University of San Diego

Accounting; anthropology; art; biology/biological sciences; business administration and management; business/managerial economics; chemistry; computer science; economics; education; electrical, electronics and communications engineering; English; French; Hispanic-American, Puerto Rican, and Mexican-American/Chicano studies; history; humanities; industrial engineering; international relations and affairs; liberal arts and sciences/liberal studies; marine science/merchant marine officer; mass communication/media; mathematics; mechanical engineering; music; oceanography (chemical and physical); philosophy; physics; political science and government; pre-medical studies; psychology; religious studies; sociology; Spanish; urban studies/affairs.

The University of Scranton

Accounting; ancient/classical Greek; biology/biological sciences; biophysics; business administration and management; business administration, management and operations related; chemistry; chemistry related; clinical laboratory science/medical technology; communication/speech communication and rhetoric; computer engineering; computer science; criminal justice/safety; dramatic/theatre arts; economics; electrical, electronics and communications engineering; elementary education; English; entomology; entrepreneurship; environmental studies; finance; foreign languages and literatures; French; German; gerontology; health/health care administration; history; human resources management; human services; information science/studies; information technology; international business/trade/commerce; international relations and affairs; Italian; Japanese; kindergarten/preschool education; kinesiology and exercise science; Latin; management science; marketing/marketing management; mathematics; mathematics and statistics related; neuroscience; nursing (registered nurse training); occupational therapy; operations management; philosophy; physical therapy; physics; political science and government; Portuguese; psychology; religious studies; Russian; secondary education; Slavic languages; sociology; Spanish; special education.

University of South Carolina

Accounting; advertising; African-American/Black studies; anthropology; art history, criticism and conservation; art teacher education; biology/biological sciences; broadcast journalism; business administration and management; business/managerial economics; chemical engineering; chemistry; civil engineering; classics and languages, literatures and linguistics; computer and information sciences; computer engineering; criminal justice/law enforcement administration; dramatic/theatre arts; economics; electrical, electronics and communications engineering; English; European studies; experimental psychology; finance; fine/studio arts; French; general retailing/wholesaling; geography; geology/earth science; geophysics and seismology; German; history; hospitality administration; insurance; international relations and affairs; Italian; kinesiology and exercise science; Latin American studies; liberal arts and sciences/liberal studies; management science; marine biology and biological oceanography; marketing/marketing management; mathematics; mechanical engineering; music; music teacher education; nursing (registered nurse training); office management; philosophy; physical education teaching and coaching; physics; political science and government; public relations/image management; real estate; religious studies; sociology; Spanish; sport and fitness administration; statistics; women's studies.

University of Southern California

Accounting; acting; aerospace, aeronautical and astronautical engineering; African-American/Black studies; American literature; American studies; anthropology; anthropology related;

architecture; art; art history, criticism and conservation; Asian studies (East); Asian-American studies; astronomy; biochemistry; biology/biological sciences; biomedical/medical engineering; biophysics; broadcast journalism; business administration and management; business administration, management and operations related; business, management, and marketing related; chemical engineering; chemistry; cinematography and film/video production; city/urban, community and regional planning; civil engineering; civil engineering related; classics and languages, literatures and linguistics; communication/speech communication and rhetoric; comparative literature; computer and information sciences; computer engineering; computer engineering related; computer science; construction engineering; creative writing; cultural studies; dental hygiene; directing and theatrical production; dramatic/theatre arts; East Asian languages; economics; education; electrical, electronics and communications engineering; engineering; English; English literature (British and Commonwealth); environmental studies; environmental/environmental health engineering; film/cinema studies; fine/studio arts; French; general studies; geography; geology/earth science; German; gerontology; health science; Hispanic-American, Puerto Rican, and Mexican-American/Chicano studies; history; interdisciplinary studies; international business/trade/commerce; international relations and affairs; Italian; jazz/jazz studies; Jewish/Judaic studies; journalism; kinesiology and exercise science; landscape architecture; linguistics; marine biology and biological oceanography; mass communication/media; materials science; mathematics; mechanical engineering; music; music management and merchandising; music performance; music related; music teacher education; music theory and composition; occupational therapy; petroleum engineering; philosophy; philosophy related; physical sciences; physics; physiological psychology/psychobiology; piano and organ; playwriting and screenwriting; political science and government; polymer/plastics engineering; Portuguese; psychology; public administration; public health education and promotion; public relations/image management; radio and television; religious studies; Russian; Slavic languages; sociology; Spanish; structural engineering; systems engineering; theatre design and technology; theatre/theatre arts management; urban studies/affairs; violin, viola, guitar and other stringed instruments; voice and opera; water resources engineering; wind/percussion instruments; women's studies.

The University of Texas at Austin

Accounting; advertising; aerospace, aeronautical and astronautical engineering; American studies; ancient studies; ancient/classical Greek; anthropology; apparel and textiles; Arabic; archeology; architectural engineering; architecture; art; art history, criticism and conservation; Asian studies; astronomy; athletic training; biochemistry; biology/biological sciences; biomedical/medical engineering; botany/plant biology; business administration and management; business administration, management and operations related; business/commerce; chemical engineering; chemistry; civil

engineering; classics and languages, literatures and linguistics; clinical laboratory science/medical technology; communication disorders; communication/speech communication and rhetoric; computer and information sciences; Czech; dance; design and visual communications; dramatic/theatre arts; East Asian languages; ecology; economics; electrical, electronics and communications engineering; English; ethnic, cultural minority, and gender studies related; family and consumer sciences/human sciences; finance; fine/studio arts; foods, nutrition, and wellness; foreign languages and literatures; French; geography; geological and earth sciences/geosciences related; geology/earth science; geophysics and seismology; German; health and physical education; health services/allied health/health sciences; Hebrew; history; human development and family studies; humanities; hydrology and water resources science; interior design; Iranian/Persian languages; Islamic studies; Italian; Jewish/Judaic studies; journalism; Latin; Latin American studies; liberal arts and sciences/liberal studies; linguistics; management information systems; marketing/marketing management; mathematics; mechanical engineering; microbiology; molecular biology; multi-/interdisciplinary studies related; music; music history, literature, and theory; music performance; music theory and composition; Near and Middle Eastern studies; nursing (registered nurse training); petroleum engineering; philosophy; physics; political science and government; Portuguese; psychology; public relations/image management; radio and television; religious studies; Russian; Russian studies; Scandinavian languages; Semitic languages; social work; sociology; Spanish; sport and fitness administration; Turkish; urban studies/affairs; visual and performing arts; zoology/animal biology.

The University of Texas at Dallas

Accounting; American studies; applied mathematics; audiology and speech-language pathology; biochemistry; biology/biological sciences; business/commerce; chemistry; cognitive psychology and psycholinguistics; computer and information sciences; computer engineering; computer science; criminology; economics; electrical, electronics and communications engineering; ethnic, cultural minority, and gender studies related; geography; geology/earth science; history; humanities; interdisciplinary studies; international business/trade/commerce; literature; management information systems; marketing/marketing management; mathematics; molecular biology; neuroscience; organizational behavior; physics; political science and government; psychology; public administration; sociology; statistics; visual and performing arts.

University of the Pacific

Art; art history, criticism and conservation; audiology and speech-language pathology; biochemistry; biology/biological sciences; biomedical/medical engineering; business administration and management; chemistry; chemistry related; civil engineering; classics and languages, literatures and linguistics; commercial and advertising art; communication/speech communication and rhetoric; computer engineering; computer science; dramatic/theatre arts; economics; education; electrical, electronics and communications engineering; engineering physics; engineering/industrial management; English; environmental studies; fine/studio arts; French; geology/earth science; German; history; information science/studies; interdisciplinary studies; international relations and affairs; Japanese; kinesiology and exercise science; mathematics; mechanical engineering; music; music history, literature, and theory; music management and merchandising; music teacher education; music theory and composition; music therapy; pharmacy; philosophy; physical sciences; physics; piano and organ; political science and government; psychology; religious studies; social sciences; sociology; Spanish; special education; voice and opera.

University of the Sciences in Philadelphia

Biochemistry; bioinformatics; biology/biological sciences; chemistry; clinical laboratory science/medical technology; computer science; environmental science; health services/allied health/health sciences; health/medical psychology; marketing/marketing management; medical pharmacology and pharmaceutical sciences; medicinal and pharmaceutical chemistry; microbiology; pharmacology and toxicology; pharmacy, pharmaceutical sciences, and administration related; psychology.

University of the South

American studies; anthropology; applied art; art; art history, criticism and conservation; Asian studies; biology/biological sciences; chemistry; classics and languages, literatures and linguistics; comparative literature; computer science; dramatic/theatre arts; drawing; economics; English; environmental studies; European studies; fine/studio arts; forestry; French; geology/earth science; German; history; international relations and affairs; Latin; literature; mathematics; medieval and renaissance studies; modern Greek; music; music history, literature, and theory; natural resources management and policy; philosophy; physics; political science and government; psychology; religious studies; Russian; Russian studies; social sciences; Spanish.

University of Tulsa

Accounting; anthropology; applied mathematics; art history, criticism and conservation; arts management; athletic training; audiology and speech-language pathology; biochemistry; biology/biological sciences; business administration and management; chemical engineering; chemistry; communication/speech communication and rhetoric; computer science; dramatic/theatre arts; economics; education; electrical, electronics and communications engineering; elementary education; engineering physics; English; environmental studies; film/cinema studies; finance; fine/studio arts; French; geology/earth science; geophysics and seismology; German; history; information science/studies; international business/trade/commerce; kinesiology and exercise science; legal professions and studies related; liberal arts and sciences/liberal studies; management information systems; marketing/marketing management; mathematics; mechanical engineering; music; music related; music teacher education; nursing (registered nurse training); petroleum engineering; philosophy; physics; piano and organ;

political science and government; psychology; religious studies; sociology; Spanish; sport and fitness administration; voice and opera.

University of Utah

Accounting; anthropology; Arabic; architecture; architecture related; art; art history, criticism and conservation; Asian studies; atmospheric sciences and meteorology; audiology and speech-language pathology; ballet; behavioral sciences; biology teacher education; biology/biological sciences; biomedical sciences; biomedical/medical engineering; broadcast journalism; business administration and management; business, management, and marketing related; business/commerce; cell biology and histology; chemical engineering; chemistry; child development; Chinese; civil engineering; classics and languages, literatures and linguistics; clinical laboratory science/medical technology; clinical/medical laboratory technology; communication/speech communication and rhetoric; computer engineering; computer science; dance; developmental and child psychology; drama and dance teacher education; dramatic/theatre arts; economics; education; electrical, electronics and communications engineering; elementary education; engineering; English; environmental health; environmental studies; environmental/environmental health engineering; family and community services; family and consumer economics related; family and consumer sciences/home economics teacher education; family and consumer sciences/human sciences; family resource management; film/cinema studies; finance; food science; foreign languages and literatures; French; French language teacher education; geography; geological and earth sciences/geosciences related; geological/geophysical engineering; geology/earth science; geophysics and seismology; German; German language teacher education; health and physical education; health professions related; health services/allied health/health sciences; health teacher education; history; history teacher education; human development and family studies; humanities; international/global studies; Japanese; journalism; kindergarten/preschool education; kinesiology and exercise science; liberal arts and sciences and humanities related; liberal arts and sciences/liberal studies; linguistics; management information systems; marketing related; marketing/marketing management; mass communication/media; materials engineering; materials science; mathematics; mathematics teacher education; mechanical engineering; metallurgical engineering; meteorology; mining and mineral engineering; modern Greek; music; music teacher education; Near and Middle Eastern studies; nursing (registered nurse training); occupational therapy; parks, recreation and leisure; parks, recreation and leisure facilities management; pharmacy; pharmacy, pharmaceutical sciences, and administration related; philosophy; physical education teaching and coaching; physical sciences; physical sciences related; physical therapy; physics; physics teacher education; political science and government; pre-pharmacy studies; psychology; public relations/image management; radio and television; Russian; science teacher education; secondary education; social science teacher education; social sciences; social studies teacher education; social work;

sociology; Spanish; Spanish language teacher education; special education; speech and rhetoric; urban studies/affairs; visual and performing arts; women's studies.

University of Virginia

Aerospace, aeronautical and astronautical engineering; African-American/Black studies; anthropology; applied mathematics; architectural history and criticism; architecture; area studies related; art; astronomy; audiology and speech-language pathology; biology/biological sciences; biomedical/medical engineering; business/commerce; chemical engineering; chemistry; city/urban, community and regional planning; civil engineering; classics and languages, literatures and linguistics; comparative literature; computer and information sciences; computer engineering; cultural studies; dramatic/theatre arts; economics; electrical, electronics and communications engineering; engineering; English; environmental science; French; German; history; international relations and affairs; Italian; liberal arts and sciences/liberal studies; mathematics; mechanical engineering; multi-/interdisciplinary studies related; music; nursing (registered nurse training); philosophy; physical education teaching and coaching; physics; political science and government; psychology; religious studies; Slavic languages; sociology; Spanish; systems engineering.

University of Washington

Accounting; aerospace, aeronautical and astronautical engineering; African-American/Black studies; Air Force R.O.T.C./air science; American Indian/Native American studies; ancient/classical Greek; anthropology; applied mathematics; architecture; Army R.O.T.C./military science; art; art history, criticism and conservation; Asian studies; Asian studies (East); Asian studies (South); Asian studies (Southeast); astronomy; atmospheric sciences and meteorology; audiology and speech-language pathology; bilingual and multilingual education; biochemistry; biology teacher education; biology/biological sciences; biostatistics; botany/plant biology; business administration and management; business/commerce; Canadian studies; cell biology and histology; ceramic arts and ceramics; ceramic sciences and engineering; chemical engineering; chemistry; Chinese; city/urban, community and regional planning; civil engineering; classics and languages, literatures and linguistics; clinical laboratory science/medical technology; commercial and advertising art; communication/speech communication and rhetoric; comparative literature; computer and information sciences; computer engineering; computer science; construction management; creative writing; criminal justice/law enforcement administration; cultural studies; dance; data processing and data processing technology; dental hygiene; dramatic/theatre arts; economics; education (multiple levels); electrical, electronics and communications engineering; elementary education; engineering; English; English as a second/foreign language (teaching); environmental health; environmental studies; European studies; fiber, textile and weaving arts; fishing and fisheries sciences and management; forest engineering; forest sciences and biology; forest/forest resources management; forestry; French; general studies;

geography; geology/earth science; geophysics and seismology; German; Hispanic-American, Puerto Rican, and Mexican-American/Chicano studies; history; history and philosophy of science and technology; humanities; industrial design; industrial engineering; information science/studies; interdisciplinary studies; interior architecture; international business/trade/commerce; international relations and affairs; Italian; Japanese; Jewish/Judaic studies; landscape architecture; Latin; Latin American studies; liberal arts and sciences/liberal studies; linguistics; management information systems; management science; materials engineering; maternal/child health and neonatal nursing; mathematics; mechanical engineering; medical microbiology and bacteriology; metal and jewelry arts; metallurgical engineering; molecular biology; music; music history, literature, and theory; music performance; music teacher education; music theory and composition; musical instrument fabrication and repair; musicology and ethnomusicology; natural resources management and policy; Navy/Marine Corps R.O.T.C./naval science; Near and Middle Eastern studies; nursing (registered nurse training) occupational therapy; oceanography (chemical and physical); orthotics/prosthetics; painting; pharmacy; philosophy; photography; physical therapy; physician assistant; physics; piano and organ; political science and government; printmaking; psychology; public administration; public health; public health/community nursing; religious studies; romance languages; Russian; Russian studies; Scandinavian languages; Scandinavian studies; science teacher education; sculpture; secondary education; Slavic languages; social sciences; social work; sociology; Spanish; speech and rhetoric; statistics; technical and business writing; violin, viola, guitar and other stringed instruments; voice and opera; wildlife and wildlands science and management; women's studies; wood science and wood products/pulp and paper technology; zoology/animal biology.

University of Wisconsin–Madison

Accounting; actuarial science; advertising; African languages; African studies; African-American/Black studies; agricultural business and management; agricultural economics; agricultural teacher education; agricultural/biological engineering and bioengineering; agriculture; agronomy and crop science; American studies; animal genetics; animal sciences; anthropology; applied art; applied mathematics; art; art history, criticism and conservation; art teacher education; Asian studies; Asian studies (Southeast); astronomy; biochemistry; biology/biological sciences; biomedical/medical engineering; botany/plant biology; broadcast journalism; business administration and management; cartography; cell biology and histology; chemical engineering; chemistry; child development; Chinese; civil engineering; classics and languages, literatures and linguistics; clinical laboratory science/medical technology; clothing/textiles; comparative literature; computer engineering; computer science; construction management; consumer services and advocacy; dairy science; developmental and child psychology; dietetics; dramatic/theatre arts; economics; electrical, electronics and communications engineering;

elementary education; engineering; engineering mechanics; engineering physics; English; entomology; environmental/environmental health engineering; experimental psychology; family and consumer economics related; family and consumer sciences/home economics teacher education; family and consumer sciences/human sciences; farm and ranch management; fashion merchandising; finance; food science; foods, nutrition, and wellness; forestry; French; geography; geology/earth science; geophysics and seismology; German; Hebrew; Hispanic-American, Puerto Rican, and Mexican-American/Chicano studies; history; history and philosophy of science and technology; horticultural science; hydrology and water resources science; industrial engineering; insurance; interior design; international relations and affairs; Italian; Japanese; journalism; kindergarten/preschool education; labor and industrial relations; landscape architecture; Latin; Latin American studies; linguistics; mass communication/media; mathematics; mechanical engineering; medical microbiology and bacteriology; metallurgical engineering; mining and mineral engineering; modern Greek; molecular biology; music; music teacher education; natural resources management and policy; nuclear engineering; nursing (registered nurse training); occupational therapy; parks, recreation and leisure; pharmacology; pharmacy; philosophy; physical education teaching and coaching; physician assistant; physics; political science and government; Portuguese; poultry science; psychology; public relations/image management; radio and television; real estate; Russian; Scandinavian languages; science teacher education; secondary education; Slavic languages; social sciences; social work; sociology; Spanish; special education; speech therapy; statistics; survey technology; toxicology; urban studies/affairs; wildlife and wildlands science and management; women's studies; zoology/animal biology.

University of Wyoming

Accounting; agribusiness; agricultural communication/journalism; agricultural teacher education; agriculture and agriculture operations related; American studies; animal sciences related; anthropology; applied mathematics related; architectural engineering; art; astronomy and astrophysics related; audiology and speech-language pathology; biology/biological sciences; botany/plant biology; business administration and management; business/managerial economics; chemical engineering; chemistry; civil engineering; communication/speech communication and rhetoric; computer engineering; computer science; criminal justice/safety; dental hygiene; dramatic/theatre arts; electrical, electronics and communications engineering; elementary education; English; environmental studies; family and consumer sciences/human sciences; finance; French; geography; geological and earth sciences/geosciences related; geology/earth science; German; health services/allied health/health sciences; health teacher education; history; humanities; international relations and affairs; journalism; kinesiology and exercise science; management information systems; management science; marketing/marketing management; mathematics; mechanical engineering; microbiology; molecular biology; multi-/

interdisciplinary studies related; music; music performance; music teacher education; music theory and composition; natural resources/conservation; nursing (registered nurse training); parks, recreation and leisure facilities management; philosophy; physical education teaching and coaching; physics; political science and government; psychology; range science and management; Russian; secondary education; social sciences; social work; sociology; Spanish; special education; special education related; statistics; technology/industrial arts teacher education; trade and industrial teacher education; women's studies; zoology/animal biology.

Ursinus College

American studies; anthropology; art; Asian studies (East); biological and physical sciences; biology/biological sciences; business administration and management; chemistry; civil engineering; classics; classics and languages, literatures and linguistics; computer science; economics; electrical, electronics and communications engineering; English; environmental studies; fine arts related; French; German; health and physical education; history; international relations and affairs; mass communication/media; mathematics; mechanical engineering; metallurgical engineering; multi-/interdisciplinary studies related; neuroscience; philosophy; philosophy and religious studies related; physics; political science and government; psychology; social sciences related; sociology; Spanish.

Valparaiso University

Accounting; actuarial science; American studies; art; art history, criticism and conservation; art teacher education; Asian studies (East); astronomy; athletic training; atmospheric sciences and meteorology; biochemistry; biological and physical sciences; biology teacher education; biology/biological sciences; chemistry; chemistry teacher education; civil engineering; classics and languages, literatures and linguistics; communication and journalism related; communication/speech communication and rhetoric; computer engineering; computer science; criminology; drama and dance teacher education; dramatic/theatre arts; economics; economics related; electrical, electronics and communications engineering; elementary education; English; English/language arts teacher education; environmental science; finance; fine/studio arts; foreign language teacher education; French; French language teacher education; geography; geography teacher education; geology/earth science; German; German language teacher education; health and physical education; history; history teacher education; humanities; international business/trade/commerce; international economics; international relations and affairs; journalism; kinesiology and exercise science; management science; management sciences and quantitative methods related; marketing/marketing management; mass communication/media; mathematics; mathematics teacher education; mechanical engineering; middle school education; multi-/interdisciplinary studies related; music; music management and merchandising; music performance; music teacher education; music theory and composition; nursing (registered nurse training); organizational communication; philosophy; physical education teaching and coaching; physics; physics teacher education; piano and organ; political science and government; psychology; psychology teacher education; public relations/image management; radio and television; religious/sacred music; science teacher education; secondary education; social science teacher education; social sciences; social work; sociology; Spanish; Spanish language teacher education; sport and fitness administration; theology; voice and opera.

Vanderbilt University
African studies; African-American/Black studies; American studies; anthropology; art; Asian studies (East); astronomy; biology/biological sciences; biomedical/medical engineering; chemical engineering; chemistry; civil engineering; classics and languages, literatures and linguistics; cognitive psychology and psycholinguistics; computer engineering; computer science; dramatic/theatre arts; ecology; economics; education; electrical, electronics and communications engineering; elementary education; engineering; engineering science; English; European studies; French; geology/earth science; German; history; human development and family studies; human resources management; interdisciplinary studies; kindergarten/preschool education; Latin American studies; mass communication/media; mathematics; mechanical engineering; molecular biology; music; philosophy; physics; piano and organ; political science and government; Portuguese; psychology; religious studies; Russian; secondary education; sociology; Spanish; special education; urban studies/affairs; violin, viola, guitar and other stringed instruments; voice and opera; wind/percussion instruments.

Vassar College
African studies; American studies; ancient/classical Greek; anthropology; art history, criticism and conservation; Asian studies; astronomy; biochemistry; biology/biological sciences; chemistry; classics and languages, literatures and linguistics; cognitive psychology and psycholinguistics; computer and information sciences; dramatic/theatre arts; economics; English; environmental science; environmental studies; film/cinema studies; fine/studio arts; French; geography; geology/earth science; German; interdisciplinary studies; international relations and affairs; Italian; Jewish/Judaic studies; Latin; Latin American studies; liberal arts and sciences and humanities related; mathematics; medieval and renaissance studies; multi-/interdisciplinary studies related; music; philosophy; physics; physiological psychology/psychobiology; political science and government; psychology; religious studies; Russian; science, technology and society; sociology; Spanish; urban studies/affairs; visual and performing arts; women's studies.

Villanova University
Accounting; art history, criticism and conservation; astronomy; astrophysics; biology/biological sciences; business administration and management; business/managerial economics; chemical engineering; chemistry; civil engineering; classics and languages, literatures and linguistics; computer engineering; computer science; criminal justice/law enforcement administration; economics; education; electrical,

electronics and communications engineering; elementary education; English; finance; French; geography; German; history; human services; information science/studies; international business/trade/commerce; Italian; liberal arts and sciences/liberal studies; management information systems; marketing/marketing management; mass communication/media; mathematics; mechanical engineering; natural sciences; nursing (registered nurse training); philosophy; physics; political science and government; psychology; religious studies; secondary education; sociology; Spanish.

Virginia Military Institute
Biology/biological sciences; chemistry; civil engineering; computer science; economics; electrical, electronics and communications engineering; English; history; international relations and affairs; mathematics; mechanical engineering; modern languages; physics; psychology.

Virginia Polytechnic Institute and State University
Accounting; aerospace, aeronautical and astronautical engineering; agricultural economics; agricultural mechanization; agricultural teacher education; agronomy and crop science; animal sciences; architecture; art; biochemistry; biology/biological sciences; business administration and management; business teacher education; business/commerce; chemical engineering; chemistry; civil engineering; clothing/textiles; communication/speech communication and rhetoric; computer engineering; computer science; construction engineering technology; consumer/homemaking education; dairy science; dietetics; dramatic/theatre arts; economics; electrical, electronics and communications engineering; engineering; engineering science; English; environmental studies; finance; food science; foods, nutrition, and wellness; forestry; French; geography; geology/earth science; German; health teacher education; history; horticultural science; human resources management; human services; industrial design; industrial engineering; information science/studies; interdisciplinary studies; international relations and affairs; kindergarten/preschool education; landscape architecture; management information systems; marketing/marketing management; materials engineering; mathematics; mechanical engineering; mining and mineral engineering; music; ocean engineering; philosophy; physics; political science and government; poultry science; psychology; sales and marketing/marketing and distribution teacher education; sociology; Spanish; statistics; technology/industrial arts teacher education; tourism and travel services management; trade and industrial teacher education; urban studies/affairs.

Wabash College
Art; biology/biological sciences; chemistry; classics and languages, literatures and linguistics; dramatic/theatre arts; economics; English; French; German; history; Latin; mathematics; modern Greek; music; philosophy; physics; political science and government; pre-law studies; pre-medical studies; pre-veterinary studies; psychology; religious studies; Spanish; speech and rhetoric.

Wake Forest University
Accounting; ancient/classical Greek; anthropology; art history, criticism and conservation; biology/biological sciences; business/commerce; chemistry; classics and languages, literatures and linguistics; clinical laboratory science/medical technology; communication/speech communication and rhetoric; computer and information sciences; dramatic/theatre arts; econometrics and quantitative economics; economics; education (multiple levels); engineering; English; finance; fine/studio arts; French; German; history; kinesiology and exercise science; Latin; management information systems; management science; mathematics; music; philosophy; physician assistant; physics; political science and government; psychology; religious studies; Russian; sociology; Spanish.

Wartburg College
Accounting; art; art teacher education; arts management; biochemistry; biology/biological sciences; broadcast journalism; business administration and management; chemistry; clinical laboratory science/medical technology; commercial and advertising art; computer science; economics; elementary education; engineering; English; English composition; finance; French; German; history; history teacher education; information science/studies; international business/trade/commerce; international relations and affairs; journalism; kindergarten/preschool education; marketing/marketing management; mass communication/media; mathematics; mathematics teacher education; music; music performance; music teacher education; music theory and composition; music therapy; occupational therapy; philosophy; physical education teaching and coaching; physics; political science and government; psychology; public relations/image management; religious studies; religious/sacred music; secondary education; social science teacher education; social work; sociology; Spanish; speech/theater education; sport and fitness administration.

Washington & Jefferson College
Accounting; art; art teacher education; biochemistry; biology/biological sciences; business administration and management; chemistry; chemistry related; child development; dramatic/theatre arts; economics; English; French; German; history; information technology; international business/trade/commerce; mathematics; music; philosophy; physics; political science and government; psychology; sociology; Spanish.

Washington and Lee University
Accounting; anthropology; archeology; art history, criticism and conservation; Asian studies (East); biochemistry; biology/biological sciences; business administration and management; chemical engineering; chemistry; classics; computer science; dramatic/theatre arts; economics; engineering physics; English; fine/studio arts; foreign languages and literatures; French; geological and earth sciences/geosciences related; geology/earth science; German; history; interdisciplinary studies; journalism; mathematics; medieval and renaissance studies; multi-/interdisciplinary studies related; music;

neuroscience; philosophy; physics; political science and government; psychology; public policy analysis; religious studies; Russian studies; sociology; Spanish.

Washington College

American studies; anthropology; art; biology/biological sciences; business administration and management; chemistry; computer science; dramatic/theatre arts; ecology; economics; English; environmental studies; foreign languages and literatures; French; German; history; humanities; international relations and affairs; Latin American studies; liberal arts and sciences/liberal studies; mathematics; multi-/interdisciplinary studies related; music; philosophy; physics; physiological psychology/psychobiology; political science and government; pre-dentistry studies; pre-law studies; pre-medical studies; pre-veterinary studies; psychology; sociology; Spanish.

Washington University in St. Louis

Accounting; advertising; aerospace, aeronautical and astronautical engineering; African studies; African-American/Black studies; American literature; American studies; ancient/classical Greek; anthropology; applied art; applied mathematics; Arabic; archeology; architectural engineering technology; architectural technology; architecture; architecture related; area studies related; area, ethnic, cultural, and gender studies related; art; art history, criticism and conservation; art teacher education; Asian studies; Asian studies (East); biochemistry; biological and biomedical sciences related; biological and physical sciences; biology teacher education; biology/biological sciences; biomedical/medical engineering; biophysics; biopsychology; business administration and management; business administration, management and operations related; business/commerce; business/managerial economics; ceramic arts and ceramics; chemical engineering; chemistry; chemistry related; chemistry teacher education; Chinese; civil engineering; civil engineering technology; classics and languages, literatures and linguistics; cognitive psychology and psycholinguistics; commercial and advertising art; communication and journalism related; communication/speech communication and rhetoric; comparative literature; computer and information sciences; computer and information sciences and support services related; computer engineering; computer and information sciences related; computer science; computer/information technology services administration related; creative writing; cultural studies; dance; design and visual communications; drama and dance teacher education; dramatic/theatre arts; drawing; East Asian languages related; economics; education; education (K-12); education (specific levels and methods) related; electrical, electronics and communications engineering; elementary education; engineering; engineering physics; engineering science; English; English language and literature related; English literature (British and Commonwealth); English/language arts teacher education; entrepreneurship; environmental studies; ethnic, cultural minority, and gender studies related; European studies; fashion/apparel design; film/cinema studies; finance; fine/studio arts; French; French language teacher educa-

tion; geology/earth science; German; German language teacher education; Germanic languages; graphic design; health professions related; Hebrew; history; history teacher education; human resources management; humanities; illustration; industrial and organizational psychology; information science/studies; interdisciplinary studies; international business/trade/commerce; international economics; international finance; international relations and affairs; Islamic studies; Italian; Japanese; Jewish/Judaic studies; Latin; Latin American studies; liberal arts and sciences/liberal studies; literature; marketing related; marketing/marketing management; mathematics; mathematics and computer science; mathematics teacher education; mechanical engineering; medieval and renaissance studies; merchandising, sales, and marketing operations related (general); middle school education; modern languages; multi-/interdisciplinary studies related; music; music history, literature, and theory; music theory and composition; natural resources/conservation; natural sciences; Near and Middle Eastern studies; neuroscience; operations management; painting; philosophy; philosophy and religious studies related; photography; physical sciences; physics; physics teacher education; political science and government; pre-dentistry studies; pre-medical studies; pre-pharmacy studies; pre-veterinary studies; printmaking; psychology; religious studies; romance languages; Russian; Russian studies; science teacher education; science, technology and society; sculpture; secondary education; social and philosophical foundations of education; social science teacher education; social sciences; social sciences related; social studies teacher education; Spanish; Spanish language teacher education; statistics; systems engineering; systems science and theory; theatre literature, history and criticism; urban studies/affairs; voice and opera; women's studies.

Webb Institute

Naval architecture and marine engineering.

Wellesley College

African studies; African-American/Black studies; American studies; ancient/classical Greek; anthropology; archeology; architecture; art history, criticism and conservation; Asian studies (East); astronomy; astrophysics; biochemistry; biology/biological sciences; chemistry; Chinese; classics and languages, literatures and linguistics; cognitive psychology and psycholinguistics; comparative literature; computer science; dramatic/theatre arts; economics; English; environmental studies; ethnic, cultural minority, and gender studies related; film/cinema studies; fine/studio arts; French; geology/earth science; German; history; international relations and affairs; Islamic studies; Italian; Italian studies; Japanese; Jewish/Judaic studies; Latin; Latin American studies; linguistics; mathematics; medieval and renaissance studies; music; neuroscience; peace studies and conflict resolution; philosophy; physics; political science and government; psychology; religious studies; Russian; Russian studies; sociology; Spanish; women's studies.

Wells College

African-American/Black studies; American studies; anthropology; art; art history, criticism and

conservation; biochemistry; biology/biological sciences; business administration and management; chemistry; computer science; creative writing; dance; dramatic/theatre arts; economics; education; elementary education; engineering; English; environmental studies; fine/studio arts; French; history; international relations and affairs; mathematics; molecular biology; music; philosophy; physics; political science and government; pre-dentistry studies; pre-law studies; pre-medical studies; pre-veterinary studies; psychology; public policy analysis; religious studies; secondary education; sociology; Spanish; women's studies.

Wesleyan College

Advertising; American studies; art history, criticism and conservation; biology/biological sciences; business administration and management; chemistry; communication/speech communication and rhetoric; computer and information sciences; early childhood education; economics; education; English; fine/studio arts; French; history; humanities; interdisciplinary studies; international business/trade/commerce; international relations and affairs; mathematics; middle school education; music; philosophy; physical sciences; physics; political science and government; psychology; religious studies; social sciences; Spanish.

Wesleyan University

African-American/Black studies; American studies; anthropology; art history, criticism and conservation; Asian studies (East); astronomy; biochemistry; biology/biological sciences; chemistry; classics and languages, literatures and linguistics; computer science; dance; dramatic/theatre arts; economics; English; environmental studies; European studies (Central and Eastern); film/cinema studies; fine/studio arts; French; geology/earth science; German; history; humanities; interdisciplinary studies; Italian; Latin American studies; liberal arts and sciences/liberal studies; mathematics; medieval and renaissance studies; molecular biology; music; neuroscience; philosophy; physics; political science and government; psychology; religious studies; romance languages; Russian; Russian studies; science, technology and society; social sciences; sociology; Spanish; women's studies.

Western Baptist College

Accounting; biblical studies; biology teacher education; business administration and management; business teacher education; business, management, and marketing related; communication/speech communication and rhetoric; community organization and advocacy; computer science; divinity/ministry; education; elementary education; English; English/language arts teacher education; family psychology; finance; health science; health services/allied health/health sciences; humanities; industrial and organizational psychology; interdisciplinary studies; journalism; liberal arts and sciences/liberal studies; management information systems; mathematics; mathematics teacher education; missionary studies and missiology; music; music performance; music teacher education; pastoral studies/counseling; physical education teaching and coaching; pre-law studies; pre-theology/pre-ministerial studies; psychology; religious education; religious studies; religious/sacred music; secondary education; social science teacher education; social sciences; social studies teacher education; sport and fitness administration; theology; voice and opera; youth ministry.

Westminster Choir College of Rider University

Conducting; liberal arts and sciences/liberal studies; music; music pedagogy; music related; music teacher education; music theory and composition; piano and organ; religious/sacred music; voice and opera.

Westminster College (UT)

Accounting; airline pilot and flight crew; art; aviation/airway management; biology teacher education; biology/biological sciences; business administration and management; business/commerce; business/managerial economics; chemistry; communication/speech communication and rhetoric; computer science; elementary education; English; finance; history; human resources management; international business/trade/commerce; kindergarten/preschool education; management information systems and services related; marketing/marketing management; mathematics; nursing (registered nurse training); philosophy; physics; political science and government; psychology; social science teacher education; social sciences; sociology; special education.

Westmont College

Anthropology; art; art teacher education; biology/biological sciences; business/commerce; business/managerial economics; chemistry; communication/speech communication and rhetoric; computer science; dance; dramatic/theatre arts; economics; education; elementary education; engineering physics; English; English/language arts teacher education; French; history; kinesiology and exercise science; liberal arts and sciences/liberal studies; mathematics; mathematics teacher education; modern languages; music; neuroscience; philosophy; physical education teaching and coaching; physics; political science and government; pre-dentistry studies; pre-law studies; pre-medical studies; pre-pharmacy studies; pre-theology/pre-ministerial studies; pre-veterinary studies; psychology; religious studies; secondary education; social science teacher education; social sciences; sociology; Spanish.

Wheaton College

American studies; anthropology; art; art history, criticism and conservation; Asian studies; astronomy; biochemistry; biology/biological sciences; chemistry; classics and languages, literatures and linguistics; computer science; dramatic/theatre arts; economics; English; environmental studies; fine/studio arts; French; German; Hispanic-American, Puerto Rican, and Mexican-American/Chicano studies; history; interdisciplinary studies; international relations and affairs; literature; mathematics; music; philosophy; physics; physiological psychology/psychobiology; political science and government; pre-medical studies; psychology; religious studies; Russian; Russian studies; sociology; women's studies.

Wheaton College

Anthropology; archeology; art; biblical studies; biology/biological sciences; business/managerial

economics; chemistry; communication/speech communication and rhetoric; computer science; economics; elementary education; engineering related; English; environmental studies; French; geology/earth science; German; health/medical preparatory programs related; history; international relations and affairs; kinesiology and exercise science; mathematics; multi-/interdisciplinary studies related; music; music history, literature, and theory; music management and merchandising; music performance; music related; music teacher education; music theory and composition; philosophy; physics; political science and government; psychology; religious education; religious studies; science teacher education; social studies teacher education; sociology; Spanish.

Whitman College

Anthropology; art; art history, criticism and conservation; Asian studies; astronomy; biochemistry; biology/biological sciences; biophysics; chemistry; classics and languages, literatures and linguistics; dramatic/theatre arts; economics; English; environmental studies; film/cinema studies; French; geology/earth science; German; history; mathematics; molecular biology; music; philosophy; physics; political science and government; psychology; religious studies; sociology; Spanish.

Whitworth College

Accounting; American studies; art; art history, criticism and conservation; art teacher education; arts management; athletic training; biology/biological sciences; business administration and management; chemistry; computer science; dramatic/theatre arts; economics; elementary education; English; fine/studio arts; French; history; international business/trade/commerce; international relations and affairs; journalism; mass communication/media; mathematics; music; music teacher education; nursing (registered nurse training); peace studies and conflict resolution; philosophy; physical education teaching and coaching; physics; piano and organ; political science and government; pre-dentistry studies; pre-law studies; pre-medical studies; pre-veterinary studies; psychology; religious studies; secondary education; sociology; Spanish; special education; speech and rhetoric; voice and opera.

Willamette University

Anthropology; art; art history, criticism and conservation; biology/biological sciences; chemistry; classics and languages, literatures and linguistics; comparative literature; computer science; dramatic/theatre arts; economics; English; environmental science; fine/studio arts; French; German; history; humanities; international/global studies; Japanese studies; kinesiology and exercise science; Latin American studies; mathematics; music; music pedagogy; music performance; music theory and composition; philosophy; physics; piano and organ; political science and government; psychology; religious studies; sociology; Spanish; speech and rhetoric; violin, viola, guitar and other stringed instruments; voice and opera.

William Jewell College

Accounting; art; biochemistry; biology/biological sciences; business administration and

management; cell biology and histology; chemistry; clinical laboratory science/medical technology; computer science; drama and dance teacher education; dramatic/theatre arts; economics; education; elementary education; English; French; history; information science/studies; interdisciplinary studies; international business/trade/commerce; international relations and affairs; mathematics; molecular biology; music; music performance; music teacher education; music theory and composition; nursing (registered nurse training); philosophy; physics; political science and government; pre-dentistry studies; pre-law studies; pre-medical studies; pre-veterinary studies; psychology; religious studies; religious/sacred music; secondary education; Spanish; speech and rhetoric; speech teacher education.

Williams College

American studies; anthropology; art history, criticism and conservation; Asian studies; astronomy; astrophysics; biology/biological sciences; chemistry; Chinese; classics and languages, literatures and linguistics; computer science; dramatic/theatre arts; economics; English; fine/studio arts; French; geology/earth science; German; history; Japanese; literature; mathematics; music; philosophy; physics; political science and government; psychology; religious studies; Russian; sociology; Spanish.

Wisconsin Lutheran College

Art; biochemistry; biology/biological sciences; business/managerial economics; chemistry; communication and journalism related; communication/speech communication and rhetoric; dramatic/theatre arts; elementary education; English; history; interdisciplinary studies; mathematics; multi-/interdisciplinary studies related; music; political science and government; psychology; social sciences; Spanish; theology.

Wittenberg University

American studies; art; art history, criticism and conservation; art teacher education; Asian studies; Asian studies (East); behavioral sciences; biochemistry; biological and physical sciences; biology/biological sciences; botany/plant biology; business administration and management; business/managerial economics; cartography; cell biology and histology; ceramic arts and ceramics; chemistry; commercial and advertising art; communication/speech communication and rhetoric; comparative literature; computer graphics; computer science; creative writing; developmental and child psychology; dramatic/theatre arts; drawing; economics; education; elementary education; English; environmental biology; environmental studies; finance; fine/studio arts; French; geography; geology/earth science; German; history; humanities; interdisciplinary studies; international business/trade/commerce; international relations and affairs; liberal arts and sciences/liberal studies; literature; marine biology and biological oceanography; marketing/marketing management; mathematics; medical microbiology and bacteriology; middle school education; modern languages; music; music teacher education; natural sciences; philosophy; physical sciences; physics; physiological psychology/psychobiology; piano and organ; political science and government; pre-dentistry studies; pre-law studies; pre-medical studies; pre-veterinary studies; psychology; religious studies; Russian studies; science teacher education; sculpture; secondary education; social sciences; sociology; Spanish; special education; technical and business writing; theology; urban studies/affairs; voice and opera.

Wofford College

Accounting; art history, criticism and conservation; biology/biological sciences; business/managerial economics; chemistry; computer science; creative writing; dramatic/theatre arts; economics; English; finance; French; German; history; humanities; international business/trade/commerce; international relations and affairs; mathematics; neuroscience; philosophy; physics; political science and government; pre-dentistry studies; pre-law studies; pre-medical studies; pre-veterinary studies; psychology; religious studies; sociology; Spanish.

Worcester Polytechnic Institute

Actuarial science; aerospace, aeronautical and astronautical engineering; animal genetics; applied mathematics; biochemistry; biology/biological sciences; biology/biotechnology laboratory technician; biomedical sciences; biomedical/medical engineering; business administration and management; cell biology and histology; chemical engineering; chemistry; civil engineering; computer and information sciences; computer engineering; computer science; economics; electrical, electronics and communications engineering; engineering mechanics; engineering physics; engineering

related; engineering/industrial management; environmental studies; environmental/environmental health engineering; fluid/thermal sciences; history; history and philosophy of science and technology; humanities; industrial engineering; information science/studies; interdisciplinary studies; management information systems; materials engineering; materials science; mathematics; mechanical engineering; medical microbiology and bacteriology; medicinal and pharmaceutical chemistry; molecular biology; music; nuclear engineering; philosophy; physical sciences related; physics; science, technology and society; social sciences; technical and business writing.

Xavier University

Accounting; advertising; art; athletic training; biological and physical sciences; biology teacher education; biology/biological sciences; business administration and management; business/commerce; business/managerial economics; chemical engineering; chemistry; chemistry teacher education; classics and languages, literatures and linguistics; clinical laboratory science/medical technology; computer science; corrections; criminal justice/safety; economics; education; education (specific levels and methods) related; elementary education; English; finance; fine/studio arts; French; German; history; human resources management; international relations and affairs; liberal arts and sciences/liberal studies; management information systems; marketing/marketing management; mathematics; middle school education; music; music teacher education; nursing science; occupational therapy; philosophy; physics; physics teacher education; political science and government;

psychology; public relations/image management; radio and television; science teacher education; social work; sociology; Spanish; special education; sport and fitness administration; theology.

Yale University

African studies; African-American/Black studies; American studies; ancient/classical Greek; anthropology; applied mathematics; archeology; architecture; art; art history, criticism and conservation; Asian studies (East); astronomy; astrophysics; biology/biological sciences; biomedical/medical engineering; cell biology and anatomical sciences related; chemical engineering; chemistry; Chinese; classics and languages, literatures and linguistics; cognitive psychology and psycholinguistics; computer and information sciences; cultural studies; dramatic/theatre arts; ecology; economics; electrical, electronics and communications engineering; engineering physics; engineering science; English; environmental studies; environmental/environmental health engineering; ethnic, cultural minority, and gender studies related; evolutionary biology; film/cinema studies; foreign languages related; French; geological and earth sciences/geosciences related; German; history; humanities; Italian; Japanese; Jewish/Judaic studies; Latin; Latin American studies; linguistics; literature; mathematics; mathematics and computer science; mechanical engineering; molecular biology; multi-/interdisciplinary studies related; music; philosophy; physics; political science and government; Portuguese; psychology; religious studies; Russian; Russian studies; sociology; South Asian languages; Spanish; systems science and theory; women's studies.

GEOGRAPHIC INDEX OF COLLEGES

Alabama
Auburn University 31
Birmingham-Southern College 52
Huntingdon College 165
Samford University 300
The University of Alabama 347
The University of Alabama in
   Huntsville 348

Arizona
Embry-Riddle Aeronautical
   University 122
The University of Arizona 349

Arkansas
Harding University 154
Hendrix College 158
John Brown University 173
Lyon College 205
Ouachita Baptist University 256
University of Arkansas 350
University of Central Arkansas 359

California
Azusa Pacific University 35
Biola University 51
California Institute of Technology 64
California Polytechnic State
   University, San Luis Obispo 65
Chapman University 76
Claremont McKenna College 79
Harvey Mudd College 156
Loyola Marymount University 200
The Master's College and
   Seminary 215
Mills College 227
Occidental College 247
Pepperdine University 261
Pitzer College 262
Point Loma Nazarene University 263
Pomona College 265
Saint Mary's College of California 295
Santa Clara University 301
Scripps College 303
Stanford University 316
Thomas Aquinas College 331
University of California, Berkeley 351
University of California, Davis 352
University of California, Irvine 353
University of California, Los
   Angeles 354
University of California, Riverside 355
University of California, San
   Diego 356
University of California, Santa
   Barbara 357

University of California, Santa
   Cruz 358
University of Redlands 395
University of San Diego 401
University of Southern California 404
University of the Pacific 407
Westmont College 438

Colorado
Colorado Christian University 95
The Colorado College 96
Colorado School of Mines 97
Colorado State University 98
Regis University 275
United States Air Force Academy 341
University of Colorado at Boulder 362
University of Denver 366

Connecticut
Connecticut College 102
Fairfield University 127
Quinnipiac University 272
Trinity College 333
United States Coast Guard
   Academy 342
Wesleyan University 434
Yale University 451

Delaware
University of Delaware 365

District of Columbia
American University 28
Georgetown University 138
The George Washington
   University 139

Florida
Eckerd College 120
Florida Institute of Technology 128
Florida International University 129
Florida State University 130
New College of Florida 236
Rollins College 283
Stetson University 320
University of Central Florida 360
University of Florida 368
University of Miami 378

Georgia
Agnes Scott College 20
Berry College 49
Covenant College 107
Emory University 124
Georgia Institute of Technology 140
Georgia State University 141
Mercer University 219

Morehouse College 231
Oglethorpe University 248
University of Georgia 369
Wesleyan College 433

Idaho
Albertson College of Idaho 22
University of Idaho 370

Illinois
Augustana College 32
Benedictine University 45
Bradley University 56
Illinois College 167
Illinois Institute of Technology 168
Illinois Wesleyan University 169
Knox College 183
Lake Forest College 185
Loyola University Chicago 201
McKendree College 218
North Central College 242
Northwestern University 245
Quincy University 271
University of Chicago 361
University of Illinois at Chicago 371
University of Illinois at Urbana–
   Champaign 372
Wheaton College 440

Indiana
Butler University 63
DePauw University 112
Earlham College 118
Goshen College 145
Hanover College 153
Huntington College 166
Purdue University 269
Rose-Hulman Institute of
   Technology 284
Saint Mary's College 294
Taylor University 327
University of Evansville 367
University of Notre Dame 389
Valparaiso University 417
Wabash College 423

Iowa
Central College 74
Coe College 84
Cornell College 105
Drake University 114
Grinnell College 147
Iowa State University of Science
   and Technology 170
Luther College 203
Maharishi University of
   Management 207

Northwestern College 244
Simpson College 308
The University of Iowa 373
Wartburg College 425

Kansas
Baker University 36
Kansas State University 178
University of Kansas 374

Kentucky
Asbury College 30
Bellarmine University 42
Berea College 48
Centre College 75
Georgetown College 137
Kentucky Mountain Bible College 179
Murray State University 234
Transylvania University 332
University of Kentucky 375

Louisiana
Centenary College of Louisiana 73
Louisiana College 196
Louisiana State University and
    Agricultural and Mechanical
    College 197
Louisiana Tech University 198
Loyola University New Orleans 202
Tulane University 337

Maine
Bates College 40
Bowdoin College 55
Colby College 85
College of the Atlantic 91

Maryland
Goucher College 146
Hood College 162
The Johns Hopkins University 175
Loyola College in Maryland 199
Maryland Institute College of Art 210
McDaniel College 216
Peabody Conservatory of Music of
    The Johns Hopkins University 259
St. John's College 288
St. Mary's College of Maryland 296
United States Naval Academy 345
University of Maryland, Baltimore
    County 376
University of Maryland, College
    Park 377
Washington College 428

Massachusetts
Amherst College 29
Bentley College 47
Boston College 53
Boston University 54
Brandeis University 57
Clark University 81
College of the Holy Cross 92

Emerson College 123
Gordon College 144
Hampshire College 152
Harvard University 155
Massachusetts Institute of
    Technology 214
Mount Holyoke College 232
Simon's Rock College of Bard 307
Smith College 310
Stonehill College 322
Tufts University 336
Wellesley College 431
Wheaton College 439
Williams College 445
Worcester Polytechnic Institute 449

Michigan
Albion College 23
Alma College 27
Calvin College 66
Hillsdale College 159
Hope College 163
Kalamazoo College 177
Kettering University 181
Lawrence Technological University 186
Michigan State University 222
Michigan Technological University 223
University of Michigan 379

Minnesota
Bethel University 50
Carleton College 68
College of Saint Benedict 89
The College of St. Scholastica 90
Concordia College 101
Gustavus Adolphus College 149
Hamline University 151
Macalester College 206
Minneapolis College of Art and
    Design 229
Northwestern College 243
Saint John's University 289
St. Olaf College 298
University of Minnesota, Morris 380
University of Minnesota, Twin
    Cities Campus 381
University of St. Thomas 399

Mississippi
Millsaps College 226
Mississippi State University 230
University of Mississippi 382

Missouri
Drury University 116
Maryville University of Saint Louis 212
Research College of Nursing 277
St. Louis College of Pharmacy 292
Saint Louis University 293
Southwest Baptist University 313
Southwest Missouri State
    University 315
Stephens College 319

Truman State University 335
University of Missouri–Columbia 383
University of Missouri–Kansas City 384
University of Missouri–Rolla 385
Washington University in St.
    Louis 429
William Jewell College 444

Montana
Carroll College 70

Nebraska
Creighton University 108
Union College 339
University of Nebraska–Lincoln 386

New Hampshire
Dartmouth College 109

New Jersey
The College of New Jersey 88
Drew University 115
New Jersey Institute of Technology 237
Princeton University 267
Rutgers, The State University of
    New Jersey, New Brunswick/
    Piscataway 285
Stevens Institute of Technology 321
Westminster Choir College of
    Rider University 436

New Mexico
New Mexico Institute of Mining
    and Technology 238
St. John's College 287

New York
Albany College of Pharmacy of
    Union University 21
Alfred University 25
Bard College 38
Barnard College 39
Canisius College 67
Clarkson University 80
Colgate University 86
Columbia College 99
Columbia University, The Fu
    Foundation School of
    Engineering and Applied
    Science 100
Cooper Union for the
    Advancement of Science and
    Art 104
Cornell University 106
Eugene Lang College, New School
    University 126
Fordham University 131
Hamilton College 150
Hobart and William Smith
    Colleges 161
Houghton College 164
Ithaca College 171

List College, Jewish Theological
   Seminary of America 195
Nazareth College of Rochester 235
New York School of Interior
   Design 239
New York University 240
Polytechnic University, Brooklyn
   Campus 264
Rensselaer Polytechnic Institute 276
Rochester Institute of Technology 282
St. Lawrence University 291
Sarah Lawrence College 302
Siena College 306
Skidmore College 309
State University of New York at
   Binghamton 317
State University of New York
   College at Geneseo 318
Syracuse University 326
Union College 338
United States Merchant Marine
   Academy 343
United States Military Academy 344
University at Buffalo, The State
   University of New York 346
University of Rochester 398
Vassar College 419
Webb Institute 430
Wells College 432

North Carolina
Davidson College 110
Duke University 117
North Carolina State University 241
Salem College 299
The University of North Carolina
   at Asheville 387
The University of North Carolina
   at Chapel Hill 388
Wake Forest University 424

Ohio
Baldwin-Wallace College 37
Case Western Reserve University 71
Cedarville University 72
Cleveland Institute of Music 83
The College of Wooster 94
Denison University 111
Franciscan University of
   Steubenville 132
Hiram College 160
John Carroll University 174
Kenyon College 180
Marietta College 208
Miami University 221
Oberlin College 246
Ohio Northern University 249
The Ohio State University 250
Ohio Wesleyan University 251
University of Dayton 364
Wittenberg University 447
Xavier University 450

Oklahoma
Oklahoma Baptist University 252
Oklahoma City University 253
Oklahoma State University 254
Oral Roberts University 255
University of Oklahoma 390
University of Tulsa 410

Ontario Canada
Queen's University at Kingston 270

Oregon
George Fox University 136
Lewis & Clark College 191
Linfield College 193
Pacific University 258
Reed College 274
University of Portland 393
Western Baptist College 435
Willamette University 443

Pennsylvania
Albright College 24
Allegheny College 26
Bryn Mawr College 61
Bucknell University 62
Carnegie Mellon University 69
Dickinson College 113
Elizabethtown College 121
Franklin and Marshall College 133
Gettysburg College 142
Grove City College 148
Haverford College 157
Juniata College 176
Lafayette College 184
Lebanon Valley College 188
Lehigh University 189
Lycoming College 204
Messiah College 220
Muhlenberg College 233
The Pennsylvania State University
   University Park Campus 260
Saint Francis University 286
Saint Joseph's University 290
Susquehanna University 323
Swarthmore College 324
University of Pennsylvania 391
University of Pittsburgh 392
The University of Scranton 402
University of the Sciences in
   Philadelphia 408
Ursinus College 416
Villanova University 420
Washington & Jefferson College 426

Quebec Canada
McGill University 217

Rhode Island
Brown University 59
Providence College 268
Rhode Island School of Design 278
University of Rhode Island 396

South Carolina
Clemson University 82
College of Charleston 87
Converse College 103
Erskine College 125
Furman University 135
Presbyterian College 266
University of South Carolina 403
Wofford College 448

South Dakota
Augustana College 33
South Dakota School of Mines and
   Technology 311

Tennessee
Belmont University 43
Bryan College 60
Christian Brothers University 78
Freed-Hardeman University 134
King College 182
Lincoln Memorial University 192
Lipscomb University 194
Maryville College 211
Milligan College 225
Rhodes College 279
Union University 340
University of the South 409
Vanderbilt University 418

Texas
Abilene Christian University 19
Austin College 34
Baylor University 41
LeTourneau University 190
Rice University 280
Southern Methodist University 312
Southwestern University 314
Texas A&M University 328
Texas Christian University 329
Texas Tech University 330
Trinity University 334
University of Dallas 363
University of St. Thomas 400
The University of Texas at Austin 405
The University of Texas at Dallas 406

Utah
Brigham Young University 58
University of Utah 411
Westminster College 437

Vermont
Bennington College 46
Middlebury College 224

Virginia
Christendom College 77
The College of William and Mary 93
Eastern Mennonite University 119
James Madison University 172
Mary Washington College 213

Geographic Index of Colleges

Randolph-Macon Woman's
 College   273
Sweet Briar College   325
University of Richmond   397
University of Virginia   412
Virginia Military Institute   421
Virginia Polytechnic Institute and
 State University   422
Washington and Lee University   427

Washington
Gonzaga University   143

Pacific Lutheran University   257
Seattle Pacific University   304
Seattle University   305
University of Puget Sound   394
University of Washington   413
Whitman College   441
Whitworth College   442

Wisconsin
Beloit College   44
Lawrence University   187
Marquette University   209

Milwaukee School of Engineering   228
Ripon College   281
St. Norbert College   297
University of Wisconsin–Madison   414
Wisconsin Lutheran College   446

Wyoming
University of Wyoming   415